T0189556

Lecture Notes in Computer Science   10201

Commenced Publication in 1973
Founding and Former Series Editors:
Gerhard Goos, Juris Hartmanis, and Jan van Leeuwen

Advanced Research in Computing and Software Science
Subline of Lecture Notes in Computer Science

More information about this series at http://www.springer.com/series/7407

Hongseok Yang (Ed.)

Programming Languages and Systems

26th European Symposium on Programming, ESOP 2017
Held as Part of the European Joint Conferences
on Theory and Practice of Software, ETAPS 2017
Uppsala, Sweden, April 22–29, 2017
Proceedings

 Springer

Editor
Hongseok Yang
Department of Computer Science
University of Oxford
Oxford
UK

ISSN 0302-9743   ISSN 1611-3349   (electronic)
Lecture Notes in Computer Science
ISBN 978-3-662-54433-4   ISBN 978-3-662-54434-1   (eBook)
DOI 10.1007/978-3-662-54434-1

Library of Congress Control Number: 2017933868

LNCS Sublibrary: SL1 – Theoretical Computer Science and General Issues

Printed on acid-free paper

This Springer imprint is published by Springer Nature
The registered company is Springer-Verlag GmbH Germany
The registered company address is: Heidelberger Platz 3, 14197 Berlin, Germany

ETAPS Foreword

Welcome to the proceedings of ETAPS 2017, which was held in Uppsala! It was the first time ever that ETAPS took place in Scandinavia.

ETAPS 2017 was the 20th instance of the European Joint Conferences on Theory and Practice of Software. ETAPS is an annual federated conference established in 1998, and consists of five conferences: ESOP, FASE, FoSSaCS, TACAS, and POST. Each conference has its own Program Committee (PC) and its own Steering Committee. The conferences cover various aspects of software systems, ranging from theoretical computer science to foundations to programming language developments, analysis tools, formal approaches to software engineering, and security. Organizing these conferences in a coherent, highly synchronized conference program enables participation in an exciting event, offering the possibility to meet many researchers working in different directions in the field and to easily attend talks of different conferences. Before and after the main conference, numerous satellite workshops take place and attract many researchers from all over the globe.

ETAPS 2017 received 531 submissions in total, 159 of which were accepted, yielding an overall acceptance rate of 30%. I thank all authors for their interest in ETAPS, all reviewers for their peer reviewing efforts, the PC members for their contributions, and in particular the PC (co-)chairs for their hard work in running this entire intensive process. Last but not least, my congratulations to all authors of the accepted papers!

ETAPS 2017 was enriched by the unifying invited speakers Kim G. Larsen (Aalborg University, Denmark) and Michael Ernst (University of Washington, USA), as well as the conference-specific invited speakers (FoSSaCS) Joel Ouaknine (MPI-SWS, Germany, and University of Oxford, UK) and (TACAS) Dino Distefano (Facebook and Queen Mary University of London, UK). In addition, ETAPS 2017 featured a public lecture by Serge Abiteboul (Inria and ENS Cachan, France). Invited tutorials were offered by Véronique Cortier (CNRS research director at Loria, Nancy, France) on security and Ken McMillan (Microsoft Research Redmond, USA) on compositional testing. My sincere thanks to all these speakers for their inspiring and interesting talks!

ETAPS 2017 took place in Uppsala, Sweden, and was organized by the Department of Information Technology of Uppsala University. It was further supported by the following associations and societies: ETAPS e.V., EATCS (European Association for Theoretical Computer Science), EAPLS (European Association for Programming Languages and Systems), and EASST (European Association of Software Science and Technology). Facebook, Microsoft, Amazon, and the city of Uppsala financially supported ETAPS 2017. The local organization team consisted of Parosh Aziz Abdulla (general chair), Wang Yi, Björn Victor, Konstantinos Sagonas, Mohamed Faouzi Atig, Andreina Francisco, Kaj Lampka, Tjark Weber, Yunyun Zhu, and Philipp Rümmer.

The overall planning for ETAPS is the main responsibility of the Steering Committee, and in particular of its executive board. The ETAPS Steering Committee consists of an executive board, and representatives of the individual ETAPS conferences, as well as representatives of EATCS, EAPLS, and EASST. The executive board consists of Gilles Barthe (Madrid), Holger Hermanns (Saarbrücken), Joost-Pieter Katoen (chair, Aachen and Twente), Gerald Lüttgen (Bamberg), Vladimiro Sassone (Southampton), Tarmo Uustalu (Tallinn), and Lenore Zuck (Chicago). Other members of the Steering Committee are: Parosh Abdulla (Uppsala), Amal Ahmed (Boston), Christel Baier (Dresden), David Basin (Zurich), Lujo Bauer (Pittsburgh), Dirk Beyer (Munich), Giuseppe Castagna (Paris), Tom Crick (Cardiff), Javier Esparza (Munich), Jan Friso Groote (Eindhoven), Jurriaan Hage (Utrecht), Reiko Heckel (Leicester), Marieke Huisman (Twente), Panagotios Katsaros (Thessaloniki), Ralf Küsters (Trier), Ugo del Lago (Bologna), Kim G. Larsen (Aalborg), Axel Legay (Rennes), Matteo Maffei (Saarbrücken), Tiziana Margaria (Limerick), Andrzej Murawski (Warwick), Catuscia Palamidessi (Palaiseau), Julia Rubin (Vancouver), Alessandra Russo (London), Mark Ryan (Birmingham), Don Sannella (Edinburgh), Andy Schürr (Darmstadt), Gabriele Taentzer (Marburg), Igor Walukiewicz (Bordeaux), and Hongseok Yang (Oxford).

I would like to take this opportunity to thank all speakers, attendees, organizers of the satellite workshops, and Springer for their support. Finally, a big thanks to Parosh and his local organization team for all their enormous efforts enabling a fantastic ETAPS in Uppsala!

January 2017   Joost-Pieter Katoen

Preface

This volume contains the papers presented at the 26th European Symposium on Programming (ESOP 2017) held at Uppsala, Sweden, April 22–29, 2017. ESOP is one of the European Joint Conferences on Theory and Practice of Software (ETAPS). It is devoted to fundamental issues in the specification, design, analysis, and implementation of programming languages and systems.

The 36 papers in this volume are selected out of 112 submissions based on originality and quality. Each submission was reviewed by three to six Program Committee members and external reviewers, and its authors were given a chance to respond to these reviews through the rebuttal mechanism. All submissions, reviews, and author responses were considered during the extensive online discussions, which identified 64 submissions to be discussed further at the physical Program Committee meeting, which was held at Oxford during December 15–16, 2016. At the meeting, the Program Committee members compared the 64 submissions and made the final selection of 36 papers. For most of the other unselected 28 submissions, the Program Committee members added summaries of discussions at the meeting to their reviews, so as to help the authors understand decisions. The overall quality of the submissions was very high, and many good papers had to be rejected because of the strict limit on the number of papers to be presented at the conference.

The papers in the volume cover traditional as well as emerging topics in programming languages. Their topics are: semantic foundation and type system for probabilistic programming; techniques for verifying concurrent or higher-order programs; programming language for arrays or Web data; program analysis and verification of non-standard program properties; foundation and application of interactive theorem proving; graph rewriting; separation logic; session type; type theory; and implicit computational complexity.

I want to thank the authors who submitted papers for consideration, and the members of the Program Committee, who tried hard to come up with useful feedback and to reach fair decisions on the submissions. Without the help of the external reviewers, the Program Committee would not have been able to evaluate all the submissions. I am grateful to the past ESOP PC chairs and particularly to Giuseppe Castagna, who helped me to handle many organizational matters. I would like to thank the ETAPS 2017 general chair, Parosh Aziz Abdulla, and his support staff for their assistance, and the ETAPS Steering Committee and particularly its chair, Joost-Pieter Katoen, for their amazing work in organizing this big joint conference. EasyChair was used to handle the submissions, to carry out the online discussions, and to prepare these proceedings. Finally, I want to thank Microsoft Research for sponsoring the physical Program Committee meeting, and Junghun Yoo, Jayne Bullock, and Oxford CS staff for helping me to organize this meeting.

January 2017   Hongseok Yang

Preface

Organization

Program Committee

Robert Atkey	University of Strathclyde, UK
Gavin Bierman	Oracle Labs
Xinyu Feng	University of Science and Technology of China
Alexey Gotsman	IMDEA Software Institute
Martin Hofmann	LMU Munich, Germany
Neelakantan Krishnaswami	The University of Birmingham, UK
Bruno C.D.S. Oliveira	The University of Hong Kong, SAR China
Scott Owens	University of Kent, UK
David Pichardie	ENS Rennes/IRISA/Inria, France
Ruzica Piskac	Yale University, USA
Ganesan Ramalingam	Microsoft Research
Xavier Rival	Inria/ENS Paris, France
Sukyoung Ryu	KAIST, South Korea
Tom Schrijvers	KU Leuven, Belgium
Chung-chieh Shan	Indiana University, USA
Alexandra Silva	University College London, UK
Sam Staton	University of Oxford, UK
Alexander J. Summers	ETH Zurich, Switzerland
Tachio Terauchi	Japan Advanced Institute of Science and Technology, Japan
Viktor Vafeiadis	MPI-SWS
Dimitrios Vytiniotis	Microsoft Research
Stephanie Weirich	University of Pennsylvania, USA
Hongseok Yang	University of Oxford, UK
Nobuko Yoshida	Imperial College London, UK

Additional Reviewers

Abe, Tatsuya	Bengtson, Jesper
Abel, Andreas	Beringer, Lennart
Arthan, Rob	Bernardi, Giovanni
Assaf, Mounir	Besson, Frédéric
Azevedo de Amorim, Arthur	Bi, Xuan
Bae, Sora	Biernacka, Malgorzata
Baelde, David	Breitner, Joachim
Balzer, Stephanie	Brutschy, Lucas
Barth, Stephan	Caires, Luis
Ben-Amram, Amir	Cerone, Andrea

Chakraborty, Soham
Cheng, Tie
Cichon, Gordon
Cogumbreiro, Tiago
Crafa, Silvia
Cruz-Filipe, Luís
Danos, Vincent
Dardha, Ornela
Dhodapkar, Rahul
Dinsdale-Young, Thomas
Dohrau, Jérôme
Doko, Marko
Dragoi, Cezara
Drossopoulou, Sophia
Dunfield, Jana
Eilers, Marco
Ferrara, Pietro
Filliatre, Jean-Christophe
Foner, Kenny
Francalanza, Adrian
Franco, Juliana
Fu, Ming
Gabbay, Murdoch
Gaboardi, Marco
Garcia, Ron
Gehr, Timon
Geuvers, Herman
Giacobazzi, Roberto
Golan-Gueta, Guy
Gorogiannis, Nikos
Hallahan, William
Hammer, Matthew
Hayman, Jonathan
Hecking-Harbusch, Jesko
Hoffmann, Jan
Huisman, Marieke
Hüttel, Hans
Jacobs, Bart
Jagadeesan, Radha
Jost, Steffen
Kanade, Aditya
Karachalias, George
Keuchel, Steven
Khyzha, Artem
Kiefer, Stefan
Kiselyov, Oleg

Kobayashi, Naoki
Koutavas, Vasileios
Kozen, Dexter
Krishna, Siddharth
Lahav, Ori
Lange, Julien
Lange, Martin
Laporte, Vincent
Leino, Rustan
Li, Huang
Li, Huisong
Liang, Hongjin
Lindley, Sam
Mainland, Geoffrey
Mardare, Radu
Mardirosian, Klara
Mcbride, Conor
McClurg, Jedidiah
Meyer, Mark
Miné, Antoine
Morgan, Carroll
Morris, J. Garrett
Moser, Georg
Mulligan, Dominic
Munch-Maccagnoni, Guillaume
Muranushi, Takayuki
Nestmann, Uwe
Nigam, Vivek
Nordvall Forsberg, Fredrik
Oh, Hakjoo
Palsberg, Jens
Panda, Aurojit
Park, Jihyeok
Paykin, Jennifer
Pereira, Mário
Petri, Gustavo
Phillips, Iain
Piróg, Maciej
Plump, Detlef
Protzenko, Jonathan
Pérez, Jorge A.
Raad, Azalea
Raclet, Jean-Baptiste
Rot, Jurriaan
Sands, David
Santolucito, Mark

Scalas, Alceste
Schmitt, Alan
Schmitz, Sylvain
Schwerhoff, Malte
Schwoon, Stefan
Schöpp, Ulrich
Sergey, Ilya
Sewell, Thomas
Shi, Zhiyuan
Spector-Zabusky, Antal
Spoto, Fausto
Strub, Pierre-Yves
T. Vasconcelos, Vasco
Tauber, Tomas
Thiemann, Peter
Tiu, Alwen

Tsankov, Petar
Unno, Hiroshi
Urban, Caterina
Uustalu, Tarmo
van Bakel, Steffen
Vandenbroucke, Alexander
Wang, Yanlin
Wood, Tim
Xi, Hongwei
Xie, Ningning
Yang, Yanpeng
Yi, Kwangkeun
Zdancewic, Steve
Zhai, Ennan
Zhang, Haoyuan
Zimmermann, Martin

Contents

Contents xix

Disjoint Polymorphism

João Alpuim$^{(\boxtimes)}$, Bruno C.d.S. Oliveira, and Zhiyuan Shi

The University of Hong Kong, Pokfulam, Hong Kong
{alpuim,bruno,zyshi}@cs.hku.hk

Abstract. The combination of *intersection types*, a *merge operator* and *parametric polymorphism* enables important applications for programming. However, such combination makes it hard to achieve the desirable property of a *coherent semantics*: all valid reductions for the same expression should have the same value. Recent work proposed *disjoint intersections types* as a means to ensure coherence in a simply typed setting. However, the addition of parametric polymorphism was not studied. This paper presents F_i: a calculus with *disjoint intersection types*, a variant of *parametric polymorphism* and a *merge operator*. F_i is both type-safe and coherent. The key difficult occurs in an intersection type, it is not statically known whether the instantiated type will be disjoint to other components of the intersection. To address this problem we propose *disjoint polymorphism*: a constrained form of parametric polymorphism, which allows disjointness constraints for type variables. With disjoint polymorphism the calculus remains very flexible in terms of programs that can be written, while retaining coherence.

1 Introduction

Intersection types [20,43] are a popular language feature for modern languages, such as Microsoft's TypeScript [4], Redhat's Ceylon [1], Facebook's Flow [3] and Scala [37]. In those languages a typical use of intersection types, which has been known for a long time [19], is to model the subtyping aspects of OO-style multiple inheritance. For example, the following Scala declaration:

```
class A extends B with C
```

says that the class A implements *both* B *and* C. The fact that A implements two interfaces/traits is captured by an intersection type between B and C (denoted in Scala by B with C). Unlike a language like Java, where implements (which plays a similar role to with) would be a mere keyword, in Scala intersection types are first class. For example, it is possible to define functions such as:

```
def narrow(x : B with C) : B = x
```

taking an argument with an intersection type B with C.

The existence of first-class intersections has led to the discovery of other interesting applications of intersection types. For example, TypeScript's documentation motivates intersection types[1] as follows:

---

[1] https://www.typescriptlang.org/docs/handbook/advanced-types.html

© Springer-Verlag GmbH Germany 2017
H. Yang (Ed.): ESOP 2017, LNCS 10201, pp. 1–28, 2017.
DOI: 10.1007/978-3-662-54434-1_1

You will mostly see intersection types used for mixins and other concepts that don't fit in the classic object-oriented mold. (There are a lot of these in JavaScript!)

Two points are worth emphasizing. Firstly, intersection types are being used to model concepts that are not like the classical (class-based) object-oriented programming. Indeed, being a prototype-based language, JavaScript has a much more dynamic notion of object composition compared to class-based languages: objects are composed at run-time, and their types are not necessarily statically known. Secondly, the use of intersection types in TypeScript is inspired by common programming patterns in the (dynamically typed) JavaScript. This hints that intersection types are useful to capture certain programming patterns that are out-of-reach for more conventional type systems without intersection types.

Central to TypeScript's use of intersection types for modelling such a dynamic form of mixins is the function:

```
function extend<T, U>(first: T, second: U) : T & U {...}
```

The name *extend* is given as an analogy to the *extends* keyword commonly used in OO languages like Java. The function takes two objects (`first` and `second`) and produces an object with the intersection of the types of the original objects. The implementation of *extend* relies on low-level (and type-unsafe) features of JavaScript. When a method is invoked on the new object resulting from the application of `extend`, the new object tries to use the `first` object to answer the method call and, if the method invocation fails, it then uses the `second` object to answer the method call.

The *extend* function is essentially an encoding of the *merge operator*. The merge operator is used on some calculi [17,24,38,47,48] as an introduction form for intersection types. Similar encodings to those in TypeScript have been proposed for Scala to enable applications where the merge operator also plays a fundamental role [39,46]. Unfortunately, the merge operator is not directly supported by TypeScript, Scala, Ceylon or Flow. There are two possible reasons for such lack of support. One reason is simply that the merge operator is not well-known: many calculi with intersection types in the literature do not have explicit introduction forms for intersection types. The other reason is that, while powerful, the merge operator is known to introduce *(in)coherence* problems [24,47]. If care is not taken, certain programs using the merge operator do not have a unique semantics, which significantly complicates reasoning about programs.

Solutions to the problem of coherence in the presence of a merge operator exist for simply typed calculi [17,38,47,48], but no prior work addresses polymorphism. Most recently, we proposed using *disjoint intersection types* [38] to guarantee coherence in λ_i: a simply typed calculus with intersection types and a merge operator. The key idea is to allow only disjoint types in intersections. If two types are disjoint then there is no ambiguity in selecting a value of the appropriate type from an intersection, guaranteeing coherence.

Combining parametric polymorphism with disjoint intersection types, while retaining enough flexibility for practical applications, is non-trivial. The key issue is that when a type variable occurs in an intersection type it is not statically known whether the instantiated types will be disjoint to other components of the intersection. A naive way to add polymorphism is to forbid type variables in intersections, since they may be instantiated with a type which is not disjoint to other types in an intersection. Unfortunately this is too conservative and prevents many useful programs, including the extend function, which uses an intersection of two type variables T and U.

This paper presents F_i: a core calculus with *disjoint intersection types*, a variant of *parametric polymorphism* and a *merge operator*. The key innovation in the calculus is *disjoint polymorphism*: a constrained form of parametric polymorphism, which allows programmers to specify disjointness constraints for type variables. With disjoint polymorphism the calculus remains very flexible in terms of programs that can be written with intersection types, while retaining coherence. In F_i the extend function is implemented as follows:

```
let extend T (U * T) (first : T, second : U) : T & U = first ,, second
```

From the typing point of view, the difference between extend in TypeScript and F_i is that the type variable U now has a *disjointness constraint*. The notation U * T means that the type variable U can be instantiated to any types that is disjoint to the type T. Unlike TypeScript, the definition of extend is trivial, type-safe and guarantees coherence by using the built-in merge operator (, ,).

The applicability of F_i is illustrated with examples using extend ported from TypeScript, and various operations on polymorphic extensible records [29,31, 34]. The operations on polymorphic extensible records show that F_i can encode various operations of row types [52]. However, in contrast to various existing proposals for row types and extensible records, F_i supports general intersections and not just record operations.

F_i and the proofs of coherence and type-safety are formalized in the Coq theorem prover [2]. The proofs are complete except for a minor (and trivially true) variable renaming lemma used to prove the soundness between two subtyping relations used in the formalization. The problem arizes from the combination of the locally nameless representation of binding [7] and existential quantification, which prevents a Coq proof for that lemma.

In summary, the contributions of this paper are:

- **Disjoint Polymorphism:** A novel form of universal quantification where type variables can have disjointness constraints. Disjoint polymorphism enables a flexible combination of intersection types, the merge operator and parametric polymorphism.
- **Coq Formalization of F_i and Proof of Coherence:** An elaboration semantics of System F_i into System F is given. Type-soundness and coherence are proved in Coq. The proofs for these properties and all other lemmata found in this paper are available at: https://github.com/jalpuim/disjoint-polymorphism.
- **Applications:** We show how F_i provides basic support for dynamic mixins and various operations on polymorphic extensible records.

2   Overview

This section introduces F_i and its support for intersection types, parametric poly-morphism and the merge operator. It then discusses the issue of coherence and shows how the notion of disjoint intersection types and disjoint quantification achieves a coherent semantics. This section uses some syntactic sugar, as well as standard programming language features, to illustrate the various concepts in F_i. Although the minimal core language that we formalize in Sect. 4 does not present all such features and syntactic sugar, these are trivial to add.

2.1   Intersection Types and the Merge Operator

Intersection Types. The intersection of type A and B (denoted by A & B in F_i) contains exactly those values which can be used as both values of type A and of type B. For instance, consider the following program in F_i:

```
let x : Int & Bool = ... in -- definition omitted
let succ (y : Int) : Int = y+1 in
let not (y : Bool) : Bool = if y then False else True in (succ x, not x)
```

If a value x has type Int & Bool then x can be used anywhere where either a value of type Int or a value of type Bool is expected. This means that, in the program above the functions succ and not – simple functions on integers and booleans, respectively – both accept x as an argument.

Merge Operator. The previous program deliberately omitted the introduction of values of an intersection type. There are many variants of intersection types in the literature. Our work follows a particular formulation, where intersection types are introduced by a *merge operator* [17,24,38,47,48]. As Dunfield [24] has argued a merge operator adds considerable expressiveness to a calculus. The merge operator allows two values to be merged in a single intersection type. For example, an implementation of x in F_i is 1,,True. Following Dunfield's notation the merge of v_1 and v_2 is denoted by $v_1,,v_2$.

2.2   Coherence and Disjointness

Coherence is a desirable property for a semantics. A semantics is coherent if any *valid program* has exactly one meaning [47] (that is, the semantics is not ambiguous). Unfortunately the implicit nature of elimination for intersection types built with a merge operator can lead to incoherence. This is due to intersections with overlapping types, as in Int&Int. The result of the program ((1,,2) : Int) can be either 1 or 2, depending on the implementation of the language.

Disjoint Intersection Types. One option to restore coherence is to reject pro-grams which may have multiple meanings. The λ_i calculus [38] – a simply-typed calculus with intersection types and a merge operator – solves this problem by using the concept of disjoint intersections. The incoherence problem with the expression 1,,2 happens because there are two overlapping integers in the merge. Generally speaking, if both terms can be assigned some type C then both of them can be chosen as the meaning of the merge, which in its turn leads to multiple meanings of a term. Thus a natural option is to forbid such overlapping values of the same type in a merge. In λ_i intersections such as `Int&Int` are forbidden, since the types in the intersection overlap (i.e. they are not disjoint). However an intersection such as `Char&Int` is ok because the set of characters and integers are disjoint to each other.

2.3   Parametric Polymorphism

Unfortunately, combining parametric polymorphism with disjoint intersection types is non-trivial. Consider the following program (uppercase Latin letters denote type variables):

let `merge3 A (x : A) : A & Int = x,,3` **in**

The `merge3` function takes an argument `x` of some type (`A`) and merges `x` with 3. Thus the return type of the program is `A & Int`. `merge3` is unproblematic for many possible instantiations of `A`. However, if `merge3` instantiates `A` with a type that overlaps (i.e. is not disjoint) with `Int`, then incoherence may happen. For example:

`merge3 Int 2`

can evaluate to both 2 or 3.

Forbidding Type Variables in Intersections. A naive way to ensure that only programs with disjoint types are accepted is simply to forbid type variables in intersections. That is, an intersection type such as `Char&Int` would be accepted, but an intersection such as `A & Int` (where `A` is some type variable) would be rejected. The reasoning behind this design is that type variables can be instantiated to any types, including those already in the intersection. Thus forbidding type variables in the intersection will prevent invalid intersections arising from instantiations with overlapping types. Such design does guarantee coherence and would prevent **merge3** from type-checking. Unfortunately the big drawback is that the design is too conservative and many other (useful) programs would be rejected. In particular, the **extend** function from Sect. 1 would also be rejected.

Other Approaches. Another option to mitigate the issues of incoherence, without the use of disjoint intersection types, is to allow for a biased choice: multiple values of the same type may exist in an intersection, but an implementation gives preference to one of them. The encodings of merge operators in TypeScript and Scala [39,46] use such an approach. A first problem with this approach, which has already been pointed out by Dunfield [24], is that the choice of the corresponding value is tied up to a particular choice in the implementation. In other words incoherence still exists at the semantic level, but the implementation makes it predictable which overlapping value will be chosen. From the theoretical point-of-view it would be much better to have a clear, coherent semantics, which is independent from concrete implementations. Another problem is that the inter-action between biased choice and polymorphism can lead to counter-intuitive programs, since instantiation of type-variables affects the type-directed lookup of a value in an intersection.

2.4 Disjoint Polymorphism

To avoid being overly conservative, while still retaining coherence in the presence of parametric polymorphism and intersection types, F_i uses *disjoint polymorphism*. Inspired by bounded quantification [14], where a type variable is constrained by a type bound, disjoint polymorphism allows type variables to be constrained so that they are disjoint to some given types.

With disjoint quantification a variant of the program merge3, which is accepted by F_i, is written as:

```
let merge3 ( A * Int ) (x : A) : A & Int = x,,3 in
```

In this variant the type A can be instantiated to any types disjoint to Int. Such restriction is expressed by the notation A * Int, where the left-side of * denotes the type variable being declared (A), and the right-side denotes the disjointness constraint (Int). For example,

```
merge3 Bool True
```

is accepted. However, instantiating A with Int fails to type-check.

Multiple Constraints. Disjoint quantification allows multiple constraints. For example, the following variant of merge3 has an additional boolean in the merge:

```
let merge3b ( A * Int & Bool ) (x : A) : A & Int & Bool = x,,3,,True in
```

Here the type variable A needs to be disjoint to both Int and Bool. In F_i such constraint is specified using an intersection type Int & Bool. In general, multiple constraints are specified with an intersection of all required constraints.

Type Variable Constraints. Disjoint quantification also allows type variables to be disjoint to previously defined type variables. For example, the following program is accepted by F_i:

```
let fst A ( B * A ) (x: A & B) : A = x in ...
```

The program has two type variables A and B. A is unconstrained and can be instantiated with any type. However, the type variable B can only be instantiated with types that are disjoint to A. The constraint on B ensures that the intersection type A & B is disjoint for all valid instantiations of A and B. In other words, only coherent uses of fst will be accepted. For example, the following use of fst:

```
fst Int Char (1,,'c')
```

is accepted since `Int` and `Char` are disjoint, thus satisfying the constraint on the second type parameter of `fst`. Furthermore, problematic uses of `fst`, such as:

`fst Int Int (1,,2)`

are rejected because `Int` is not disjoint with `Int`, thus failing to satisfy the disjointness constraint on the second type parameter of `fst`.

Empty Constraint. The type variable A in the `fst` function has no constraint. In F_i this actually means that A should be associated with the empty constraint, which raises the question: which type should be used to represent such empty constraint? Or, in other words, which type is disjoint to every other type? It is obvious that this type should be one of the bounds of the subtyping lattice: either $\bot$ or $\top$. The essential intuition here is that the more specific a type in the subtyping relation is, the less types exist that are disjoint to it. For example, `Int` is disjoint to all types except the n-ary intersections that contain `Int`, and $\bot$; while `Int&Char` is disjoint to all types that do not contain `Int` or `Char`, and $\bot$. This reasoning that $\top$ should be treated as the empty constraint. Indeed, in F_i, a single type variable A is only syntactic sugar for $A * \top$.

3   Applications

F_i is illustrated with two applications. The first application shows how to mimic some of TypeScript's examples of dynamic mixins in F_i. The second application shows how F_i enables a powerful form of polymorphic extensible records.

3.1   Dynamic Mixins

TypeScript is a language that adds static type checking to JavaScript. Amongst numerous static typing constructs, *TypeScript supports a form of intersection types, without a merge operator.* However, it is possible to define a function `extend` that mimics the merge operator:

```
function extend<T, U>(first: T, second: U): T & U {
  let result = <T & U>{};
  for (let id in first) {
    (<any>result)[id] = (<any>first)[id];
  }
  for (let id in second) {
    if (!result.hasOwnProperty(id)) {
      (<any>result)[id] = (<any>second)[id];
    }
  }
  return result;
}
class Person { constructor(public name : string, public male : boolean) {
    } }
interface Loggable { log() : void; }
class ConsoleLogger implements Loggable { log() {...} }
var jim = extend(new Person("Jim",true), new ConsoleLogger());
```

```
var n = jim.name;
jim.log();
```

In this example, taken from TypeScript's documentation[2], an `extend` function is defined for mixin composition. Two classes `Person` and `ConsoleLogger` are also defined. Two instances of those classes are then composed in a variable `jim` with the type of the intersection of both using `extend`. It is type-safe to access both the properties from `Person` and `ConsoleLogger` in the object `jim`.

TypeScript's implementation of `extend` relies on a biased choice. The function starts by creating a variable `result` with the type of the intersection. It then iterates through `first`'s properties and copies them to `result`. Next, it iterates through `second`'s properties but it only copies the properties that `result` does not possess yet (i.e. the ones present in `first`). This means that the implementation is left-biased, as the properties of left type of the intersection are chosen in favor of the ones in the right. However, in TypeScript this may be a cause of severe problems since that, at the time of writing, intersections at type-level are right-biased! For example, the following code is well-typed:

```
class Dog { constructor(public name : string, public male : string) { } }
var fool : Dog & Person = extend(new Dog("Pluto","yes"),new
    Person("Arnold",true));
boolean b = fool.male;      /* Undetected type-error here! */
```

There are a few problems here. Firstly both `Dog` and `Person` contain a `name` field, and the use of `extend` will favour the `name` field in the first object. This could be surprising for someone unfamiliar with the semantics of `extend` and, more importantly, it could easily allow unintended name clashes to go undetected. Secondly, note how `fool.male` is statically bound to a variable of type `boolean` but, at run-time, it will contain a value of type `String`! Thus the example shows some run-time type errors can still occur when using `extend`.

Other problematic issues regarding the semantics of intersection types can include the order of the types in an intersection, or even intersections including repeated types. This motivates the need to define a clear meaning for the practical application of intersection types.

Dynamic Mixins in F_i. In F_i, the merge operator is built-in. Thus `extend` is simply defined as follows:

let `extend T (U * T) (first : T, second : U) : T & U = first ,, second` **in**

The disjointness constraint on `U` ensures that no conflicts (such as duplicated fields of the same type) exists when merging the two objects. In practice this approach is quite similar to trait-based OO approaches [50]. If conflicts exist when two objects are composed, then they have to be resolved manually (by dropping fields from some object, for example). Moreover if no existing implementation can be directly reused, a new one must be provided via record extension, analogously to standard method overriding in OO languages.

---

[2] We have added the field `male` to the class `Person`.

For the previous TypeScript examples, assuming a straightforward translation from objects to (polymorphic) records, then the composition of **person** and **consoleLogger** is well-typed in F_i:

```
type Person = {name : String} & {male : Bool};
type Loggable = {log : T → T};

let person (n : String) (s : Bool) : Person = {name = n} ,, {male = s} in
let consoleLogger : Loggable = {log = ...} in
let jim = extend Person Loggable (person "Jim" true)  consoleLogger in
let n = jim.name in
jim.log T
```

However, the intersection **Dog & Person** is not accepted. This is due to both types sharing a field with the same name (**name**) and the same type (**String**). Note that the name clash between **male** fields (which have different types) does not impose any problem in this example: F_i allows and keeps duplicated fields whose types are disjoint. This feature of F_i is further illustrated next.

3.2 Extensible Records

F_i can encode polymorphic extensible records. Describing and implementing records within programming languages is certainly not novel and has been extensively studied in the past, including systems with row types [52,53]; predicates [28–30]; flags [45]; conditional constraints [42]; cases [10]; amongst others. However, while most systems have non-trivial built-in constructs to model various aspects of records, F_i specializes the more general notion of intersection types to encode complex records.

Records and Record Operations in F_i. Systems with records usually rely on 3 basic operations: selection, restriction and extension/concatenation. Selection and concatenation (via the merge operator) are built-in in the semantics of F_i. Merges in F_i can be viewed as a generalization of record concatenation. In F_i, following well-known encodings of multi-field records in systems with intersection types and a merge operator [47,48], there are only three rather simple constructs for records: (1) single field record types; (2) single field records; (3) field accessors. Multi-field records in F_i are encoded with intersections and merges of single field records. An example is already illustrated in Sect. 3.1. The record type **Person** is the intersection of two single field record types. The record **person "Jim" true** is built with a merge of two single field records. Finally, **jim.name** and **jim.log** illustrates the use of field accessors. Note how, through the use of subtyping, accessors will accept any intersection type that contains the single record with the corresponding field. This resembles systems with record subtyping [15,41].

Restriction via Subtyping. In contrast to most record systems, restriction is not directly embedded in F_i. Instead, F_i uses subtyping for restriction:

```
let remove (x : {age : Int} & {name : String}) : {name : String} = x in
   ...
```

The function **remove** drops the field **age** from the record x.

Polymorphic Extensible Records. Records in F_i can have polymorphic fields, and disjointness enables encoding various operations expressible in systems with polymorphic records. For example, the following variant of remove

```
let remove A (B * {l : A}) (x : { l : A } & B) : B = x in ...
```

takes a value x which contains a record of type l : A, as well as some extra information of type B. The disjointness constraint on B ensures that values of type B do not contain a record with type l : A. This example shows that one can use disjoint quantification to express negative field information, which is very close to the system described by Harper and Pierce [29]. Note, however, that F_i requires explicitly stating the type of field in the constraint, whereas systems with a *lacks* (field) predicate only require the name of the field. The generality of disjoint intersection types, which allows one to encode record types, is exactly what forces us to add this extra type in the constraint. However, there is a slight gain with F_i's approach: remove allows B to contain fields with label l, as long as the field types are *disjoint* to A. Such fine-grained constraint is not possible to express only with a lacks predicate.

Expressibility. As noted by Leijen [34], systems can typically be categorized into two distinct groups in what concerns extension: strict and free. The former does not allow field overriding when extending a record (i.e. one can only extend a record with a field that is not present in it); while the latter does account for field overriding. Our system can be seen as hybrid of these two kinds of systems.

With *lightweight extensible records* [31] – a system with strict extension – an example of a function that uses record types is the following:

```
let avg₁ (R\x, R\y) => (r : {R | x:Int, y:Int}) = (r.x+r.y)/2
```

The type signature says that any record r, containing fields x and y and some more information R (which lacks both fields x and y), can be accepted returning an integer. Note how the bounded polymorphism is essential to ensure that R does not contain x nor y.

On the other hand, in Leijen's [34] system with free extension the more general program would be accepted:

```
let avg₂ R (r : {x:Int, y:Int | R}) = (r.x+r.y)/2
```

In this case, if R contains either field x or field y, they would be shadowed by the labels present in the type signature. In other words, in a record with multiple x fields, the most recent (i.e. left-most) is used in any function which accesses x.

In F_i the following program can written instead:

```
let avg₃ (R*{x:Int}&{y:Int}) (r : {x:Int}&{y:Int}&R) = (r.x+r.y)/2
```

Since F_i accepts duplicated fields as long as the types of the overlapping fields are disjoint, more inputs are accepted by this function than in the first system. However, since Leijen's system accepts duplicated fields even when types are overlapping, avg_3 accepts less types than avg_2. Another major difference between F_i and the two other mentioned systems, is the ability to combine records with arbitrary types. Our system does not account for well-formedness of record types as the other two systems do (i.e. using a special *row* kind), since our encoding of records piggybacks on the more general notion of disjoint intersection types.

4   The F_i Calculus

This section presents the syntax, subtyping, and typing of F_i: a calculus with intersection types, parametric polymorphism, records and a merge operator. This calculus is an extension of the λ_i calculus [38], which is itself inspired by Dunfield's calculus [24]. F_i extends λ_i with (disjoint) polymorphism.

4.1   Syntax

The syntax of F_i (with the differences to λ_i highlighted in gray) is:

Types $A, B ::= \top \mid \texttt{Int} \mid A \rightarrow B \mid A\&B \mid \alpha \mid \forall(\alpha * A).B \mid \{l : A\}$

Terms $e \quad ::= \top \mid i \mid x \mid \lambda x.e \mid e_1\ e_2 \mid e_1,,e_2 \mid \Lambda(\alpha * A).e \mid e\ A \mid \{l = e\} \mid e.l$

Contexts $\Gamma \quad ::= \cdot \mid \Gamma, \alpha * A \mid \Gamma, x : A$

Types. Metavariables A, B range over types. Types include all constructs in λ_i: a top type $\top$; the type of integers $\texttt{Int}$; function types $A \rightarrow B$; and intersection types A&B. The main novelty are two standard constructs of System F used to support polymorphism: type variables α and disjoint (universal) quantification $\forall(\alpha*A).B$. Unlike traditional universal quantification, the disjoint quantification includes a disjointness constraint associated to a type variable α. Finally, F_i also includes singleton record types, which consist of a label l and an associated type A. We will use $[\alpha := A]\ B$ to denote the capture-avoiding substitution of A for α inside B and $\text{ftv}(\cdot)$ for sets of free type variables.

Terms. Metavariables e range over terms. Terms include all constructs in λ_i: a canonical top value $\top$; integer literals i; variables x, lambda abstractions $(\lambda x.e)$; applications $(e_1\ e_2)$; and the *merge* of terms e_1 and e_2 denoted as $e1,,e2$. Terms are extended with two standard constructs in System F: abstraction of type variables over terms $\Lambda(\alpha*A).e$; and application of terms to types $e\ A$. The former also includes an extra disjointness constraint tied to the type variable α, due to disjoint quantification. Singleton records consists of a label l and an associated term e. Finally, the accessor for a label l in term e is denoted as $e.l$.

Contexts. Typing contexts Γ track bound type variables α with disjointness constraints A; and variables x with their type A. We will use $[\alpha := A]\ \Gamma$ to denote the capture-avoiding substitution of A for α in the co-domain of Γ where the domain is a type variable (i.e. all disjointness constraints). Throughout this paper, we will assume that all contexts are well-formed. Importantly, besides usual well-formedness conditions, in well-formed contexts type variables must not appear free within its own disjointness constraint.

$$\boxed{\text{A ordinary}}$$

$$\text{Int ordinary} \qquad \text{A} \to \text{B ordinary} \qquad \alpha \text{ ordinary} \qquad \forall(\alpha * \text{B}).\,\text{A ordinary}$$

$$\{l : \text{A}\} \text{ ordinary}$$

$$\boxed{\text{A} <: \text{B} \hookrightarrow \text{E}}$$

$$\frac{}{\text{A} <: \top \hookrightarrow \lambda x.\,()} \; \text{ST} \qquad \frac{\text{A}_1 <: \text{A}_2 \hookrightarrow \text{E}_1 \qquad \text{A}_1 <: \text{A}_3 \hookrightarrow \text{E}_2}{\text{A}_1 <: \text{A}_2 \& \text{A}_3 \hookrightarrow \lambda x.\,(\text{E}_1\, x, \text{E}_2\, x)} \; \text{S\&R}$$

$$\frac{}{\text{Int} <: \text{Int} \hookrightarrow \lambda x.\,x} \; \text{SZ} \qquad \frac{\text{A}_1 <: \text{A}_3 \hookrightarrow \text{E} \qquad \text{A}_3 \text{ ordinary}}{\text{A}_1 \& \text{A}_2 <: \text{A}_3 \hookrightarrow \lambda x.\,[\![\text{A}_3]\!]_{(\text{E}\,(\text{proj}_1\, x))}} \; \text{S\&L}_1$$

$$\frac{\text{A} <: \text{B} \hookrightarrow \text{E}}{\{l : \text{A}\} <: \{l : \text{B}\} \hookrightarrow \text{E}} \; \text{SREC} \qquad \frac{\text{A}_2 <: \text{A}_3 \hookrightarrow \text{E} \qquad \text{A}_3 \text{ ordinary}}{\text{A}_1 \& \text{A}_2 <: \text{A}_3 \hookrightarrow \lambda x.\,[\![\text{A}_3]\!]_{(\text{E}\,(\text{proj}_2\, x))}} \; \text{S\&L}_2$$

$$\frac{}{\alpha <: \alpha \hookrightarrow \lambda x.\,x} \; \text{S}\alpha \qquad \frac{\text{B}_1 <: \text{A}_1 \hookrightarrow \text{E}_1 \qquad \text{A}_2 <: \text{B}_2 \hookrightarrow \text{E}_2}{\text{A}_1 \to \text{A}_2 <: \text{B}_1 \to \text{B}_2 \hookrightarrow \lambda f.\lambda x.\,\text{E}_2\,(f\,(\text{E}_1\, x))} \; \text{S}{\to}$$

$$\frac{\text{B}_1 <: \text{B}_2 \hookrightarrow \text{E}_1 \qquad \text{A}_2 <: \text{A}_1 \hookrightarrow \text{E}_2}{\forall(\alpha * \text{A}_1).\,\text{B}_1 <: \forall(\alpha * \text{A}_2).\,\text{B}_2 \hookrightarrow \lambda f.\Lambda\alpha.\,\text{E}_1\,(f\,\alpha)} \; \text{S}\forall$$

Fig. 1. Subtyping rules of F_i.

Syntactic Sugar. In F_i we may quantify a type variable and omit its constraint. This means that its constraint is $\top$. For example, the function type $\forall\alpha.\alpha \to \alpha$ is syntactic sugar for $\forall(\alpha * \top).\,\alpha \to \alpha$. This is discussed in more detail in Sect. 6.

4.2 Subtyping

The subtyping rules of the form $\text{A} <: \text{B}$ are shown in Fig. 1. At the moment, the reader is advised to ignore the gray-shaded parts, which will be explained later. Some rules are ported from λ_i: ST, SZ, S$\to$, S&R, S&L$_1$ and S&L$_2$.

Polymorphism and Records. The subtyping rules introduced by F_i refer to polymorphic constructs and records. Sα defines subtyping as a reflexive relation on type variables. In S$\forall$ a universal quantifier ($\forall$) is covariant in its body, and contravariant in its disjointness constraints. The SREC rule says that records are covariant within their fields' types. The subtyping relation uses an auxiliary unary **ordinary** relation, which identifies types that are not intersections. The **ordinary** conditions on two of the intersection rules are necessary to produce unique coercions [38]. The ordinary relation needs to be extended with respect to λ_i. As shown at the top of Fig. 1, the new types it contains are type variables, universal quantifiers and record types.

Properties of Subtyping. The subtyping relation is reflexive and transitive.

Lemma 1 (Subtyping reflexivity). *For any type* A, A <: A.

Proof. By structural induction on A.   □

Lemma 2 (Subtyping transitivity). *If* A <: B *and* B <: C, *then* A <: C.

Proof. By double induction on both derivations.   □

4.3 Typing

Well-Formedness. The well-formedness rules are shown in the top part of Fig. 2. The new rules over λ_i are WFα and WF$\forall$. Their definition is quite straightforward, but note that the constraint in the latter must be well-formed.

Typing Rules. Our typing rules are formulated as a bi-directional type-system. Just as in λ_i, this ensures the type-system is not only syntax-directed, but also that there is no type ambiguity: that is, inferred types are unique. The typing rules are shown in the bottom part of Fig. 2. Again, the reader is advised to ignore the gray-shaded parts, as these will be explained later. The typing judgements are of the form: $\Gamma \vdash e \Leftarrow A$ and $\Gamma \vdash e \Rightarrow A$. They read: "in the typing context Γ, the term e can be checked or inferred to type A", respectively. The rules ported from λ_i are the check rules for ⊤ (T-Top), integers (T-Int), variables (T-Var), application (T-App), merge operator (T-Merge), annotations (T-Ann); and infer rules for lambda abstractions (T-Lam), and the subsumption rule (T-Sub).

Disjoint Quantification. The new rules, inspired by System F, are the infer rules for type application T-TApp, and for type abstraction T-BLam. Type abstraction is introduced by the big lambda $\Lambda(\alpha * A). e$, eliminated by the usual type application $e \ A$ (T-TApp). The disjointness constraint is added to the context in T-BLam. During a type application, the type system makes sure that the type argument satisfies the disjointness constraint. Type application performs an extra check ensuring that the type to be instantiated is compatible (i.e. disjoint) with the constraint associated with the abstracted variable. This is important, as it will retain the desired coherence of our type-system; and it will be further explained in Sect. 5. For ease of discussion, also in T-BLam, we require the type variable introduced by the quantifier to be fresh. For programs with type variable shadowing, this requirement can be met straightforwardly by variable renaming.

Records. Finally, T-Rec and T-ProjR deal with record types. The former infers a type for a record with label l if it can infer a type for the inner expression; the latter says if one can infer a record type $\{l : A\}$ from an expression e, then it is safe to access the field l, and inferring type A.

$$\boxed{\Gamma \vdash A}$$

$$\frac{}{\Gamma \vdash \text{Int}} \text{ WFZ} \qquad \frac{\alpha * A \in \Gamma}{\Gamma \vdash \alpha} \text{ WF}\alpha \qquad \frac{\Gamma \vdash A}{\Gamma \vdash \{l : A\}} \text{ WFR} \qquad \frac{\Gamma \vdash A \quad \Gamma \vdash B}{\Gamma \vdash A \to B} \text{ WF}\to$$

$$\frac{}{\Gamma \vdash \top} \text{ WF}\top \qquad \frac{\Gamma \vdash A \quad \Gamma, \alpha * A \vdash B}{\Gamma \vdash \forall(\alpha * A).\, B} \text{ WF}\forall \qquad \frac{\Gamma \vdash A \quad \Gamma \vdash B \quad \Gamma \vdash A * B}{\Gamma \vdash A\&B} \text{ WF\&}$$

$$\boxed{\Gamma \vdash e \Rightarrow A \hookrightarrow E} \qquad e \text{ synthesizes type } A$$

$$\frac{}{\Gamma \vdash \top \Rightarrow \top \hookrightarrow ()} \text{ T-Top} \qquad\qquad \frac{}{\Gamma \vdash i \Rightarrow \text{Int} \hookrightarrow i} \text{ T-Int}$$

$$\frac{x{:}A \in \Gamma}{\Gamma \vdash x \Rightarrow A \hookrightarrow x} \text{ T-Var} \qquad\qquad \frac{\Gamma \vdash e \Leftarrow A \hookrightarrow E}{\Gamma \vdash e : A \Rightarrow A \hookrightarrow E} \text{ T-Ann}$$

$$\frac{\Gamma \vdash e_1 \Rightarrow A_1 \to A_2 \hookrightarrow E_1 \quad \Gamma \vdash e_2 \Leftarrow A_1 \hookrightarrow E_2}{\Gamma \vdash e_1\, e_2 \Rightarrow A_2 \hookrightarrow E_1\, E_2} \text{ T-App}$$

$$\frac{\Gamma \vdash e \Rightarrow \forall(\alpha * B).\, C \hookrightarrow E \quad \Gamma \vdash A \quad \boxed{\Gamma \vdash A * B}}{\Gamma \vdash e\, A \Rightarrow [\alpha := A]\, C \hookrightarrow E\, |A|} \text{ T-TApp}$$

$$\frac{\Gamma \vdash e_1 \Rightarrow A \hookrightarrow E_1 \quad \Gamma \vdash e_2 \Rightarrow B \hookrightarrow E_2 \quad \Gamma \vdash A * B}{\Gamma \vdash e_1,, e_2 \Rightarrow A\&B \hookrightarrow (E_1, E_2)} \text{ T-Merge}$$

$$\frac{\Gamma \vdash e \Rightarrow A \hookrightarrow E}{\Gamma \vdash \{l = e\} \Rightarrow \{l : A\} \hookrightarrow E} \text{ T-Rec} \qquad \frac{\Gamma \vdash e \Rightarrow \{l : A\} \hookrightarrow E}{\Gamma \vdash e.l \Rightarrow A \hookrightarrow E} \text{ T-ProjR}$$

$$\frac{\Gamma \vdash A \quad \Gamma, \alpha * A \vdash e \Rightarrow B \hookrightarrow E \quad \alpha \notin \text{ftv}(\Gamma)}{\Gamma \vdash \Lambda(\alpha * A).\, e \Rightarrow \forall(\alpha * A).\, B \hookrightarrow \Lambda\alpha.\, E} \text{ T-BLam}$$

$$\boxed{\Gamma \vdash e \Leftarrow A \hookrightarrow E} \qquad e \text{ checks against given type } A$$

$$\frac{\Gamma \vdash A \quad \Gamma, x{:}A \vdash e \Leftarrow B \hookrightarrow E}{\Gamma \vdash \lambda x.\, e \Leftarrow A \to B \hookrightarrow \lambda x.\, E} \text{ T-Lam}$$

$$\frac{\Gamma \vdash e \Rightarrow A \hookrightarrow E \quad A <: B \hookrightarrow E_{sub} \quad \Gamma \vdash B}{\Gamma \vdash e \Leftarrow B \hookrightarrow E_{sub}\, E} \text{ T-Sub}$$

Fig. 2. Well-formedness and type system of F_i.

5   Disjointness

Section 4 presented a type system with disjoint intersection types and disjoint quantification. In order to prove both type-safety and coherence (in Sect. 6), it is necessary to first introduce a notion of disjointness, considering polymorphism and disjointness quantification. This section presents an algorithmic set of rules for determining whether two types are disjoint. After, it will show a few important properties regarding substitution, which will turn out to be crucial to ensure both type-safety and coherence. Finally, it will discuss the bounds of disjoint quantification and what implications they have on F_i.

5.1   Algorithmic Rules for Disjointness

The rules for the disjointness judgement are shown in Fig. 3, which consists of two judgements.

$$\boxed{\Gamma \vdash A * B}$$

$$\frac{}{\Gamma \vdash \top * A}\ \text{DT} \qquad \frac{}{\Gamma \vdash A * \top}\ \text{DTSym} \qquad \frac{\alpha * A \in \Gamma \quad A <: B}{\Gamma \vdash \alpha * B}\ \text{D}\alpha$$

$$\frac{\alpha * A \in \Gamma \quad A <: B}{\Gamma \vdash B * \alpha}\ \text{D}\alpha\text{Sym} \qquad \frac{\Gamma, \alpha * A_1 \& A_2 \vdash B * C}{\Gamma \vdash \forall(\alpha * A_1).B * \forall(\alpha * A_2).C}\ \text{D}\forall$$

$$\frac{\Gamma \vdash A * B}{\Gamma \vdash \{l : A\} * \{l : B\}}\ \text{DRec}_{=} \qquad \frac{l_1 \neq l_2}{\Gamma \vdash \{l_1 : A\} * \{l_2 : B\}}\ \text{DRec}_{\neq}$$

$$\frac{\Gamma \vdash A_2 * B_2}{\Gamma \vdash A_1 \rightarrow A_2 * B_1 \rightarrow B_2}\ \text{D}\rightarrow \qquad \frac{\Gamma \vdash A_1 * B \quad \Gamma \vdash A_2 * B}{\Gamma \vdash A_1 \& A_2 * B}\ \text{D\&L}$$

$$\frac{\Gamma \vdash A * B_1 \quad \Gamma \vdash A * B_2}{\Gamma \vdash A * B_1 \& B_2}\ \text{D\&R} \qquad \frac{A *_{ax} B}{\Gamma \vdash A * B}\ \text{DAx}$$

$$\boxed{A *_{ax} B}$$

$$\frac{B *_{ax} A}{A *_{ax} B}\ \text{DAxSym} \qquad \frac{}{\text{Int} *_{ax} A_1 \rightarrow A_2}\ \text{DAx}(\mathbb{Z}\rightarrow) \qquad \frac{}{\text{Int} *_{ax} \{l : A\}}\ \text{DAx}(\mathbb{Z}\text{Rec})$$

$$\frac{}{\text{Int} *_{ax} \forall(\alpha * B_1).B_2}\ \text{DAx}(\mathbb{Z}\forall) \qquad \frac{}{A_1 \rightarrow A_2 *_{ax} \forall(\alpha * B_1).B_2}\ \text{DAx}(\rightarrow\forall)$$

$$\frac{}{A_1 \rightarrow A_2 *_{ax} \{l : B\}}\ \text{DAx}(\rightarrow\text{Rec}) \qquad \frac{}{\forall(\alpha * A_1).A_2 *_{ax} \{l : B\}}\ \text{DAx}(\forall\text{Rec})$$

Fig. 3. Algorithmic disjointness.

Main Judgement. The judgement $\Gamma \vdash A * B$ says two types A and B are disjoint in a context Γ. The rules are inspired in the disjointness algorithm described by λ_i. DT and $DTSym$ say that any type is disjoint to T. This is a major difference to λ_i, where the notion of disjointness explicitly forbids the presence of T types in intersections. We will further discuss this difference in Sect. 6.

Type variables are dealt with two rules: $D\alpha$ is the base rule; and $D\alpha Sym$ is its twin symmetrical rule. Both rules state that a type variable is disjoint to some type B, if Γ contains any subtype of the corresponding disjointness constraint. This rule is a specialization of the more general lemma:

Lemma 3 (Covariance of disjointness). *If* $\Gamma \vdash A * B$ *and* $B <: C$, *then* $\Gamma \vdash A * C$.

Proof. By double induction, first on the disjointness derivation and then on the subtyping derivation. The first induction case for $D\alpha$ does not need the second induction as it is a straightforward application of subtyping transitivity.   □

The lemma states that if a type A is disjoint to B under Γ, then it is also disjoint to any supertype of B. Note how these two variable rules would allow one to prove $\alpha * \alpha$, for any variable α. However, under the assumption that contexts are well-formed, such derivation is not possible as α cannot occur free in A.

The rule for disjoint quantification $D\forall$ is the most interesting. To illustrate this rule, consider the following two types:

$$(\forall(\alpha * \text{Int}).\,\text{Int}\&\alpha) \qquad (\forall(\alpha * \text{Char}).\,\text{Char}\&\alpha)$$

When are these two types disjoint? In the first type α cannot be instantiated with **Int** and in the second case α cannot be instantiated with **Char**. Therefore for both bodies to be disjoint, α cannot be instantiated with either **Int** or **Char**. The rule for disjoint quantification adds a constraint composed of the intersection of both constraints into Γ and checks for disjointness in the bodies under that environment. The reader might notice how this intersection does not necessarily need to be well-formed, in the sense that the types that compose it might not be disjoint. This is not problematic because the intersections present as constraints in the environment do not contribute directly to the (coherent) coercions generated by the type-system. In other words, intersections play two different roles in F_i, as:

1. **Types**: restricted (i.e. disjoint) intersections are required to ensure coherence.
2. **Constraints**: arbitrary intersections are sufficient to serve as constraints under polymorphic instantiation.

The rules $DRec_=$ and $DRec_{\neq}$ define disjointness between two single label records. If the labels coincide, then the records are disjoint whenever their fields' types are also disjoint; otherwise they are always disjoint. Finally, the remaining rules are identical to the original rules.

Axioms. Axiom rules take care of two types with different language constructs. These rules capture the set of rules is that $A *_{ax} B$ holds for all two types of different constructs unless any of them is an intersection type, a type variable, or $\top$. Note that disjointness with type variables is already captured by $D\alpha$ and $D\alpha Sym$, and disjointness with the $\top$ type is captured by $D\top$ and $D\top Sym$.

5.2 Well-Formed Types

In F_i it is important to show that the type-system only produces well-formed types. This is crucial to ensure coherence, as shown in Sect. 6. However, in the presence of both polymorphism and disjoint intersection types, extra effort is needed to show that all types in F_i are well-formed. To achieve this, not only we need to show that a weaker version of the general substitution lemma holds, but also that disjointness between two types is preserved after substitution. To motivate the former (i.e. why general substitution does not hold in F_i), consider the type $\forall(\alpha * \text{Int}).(\alpha \& \text{Int})$. The type variable α cannot be substituted by any type: substituting with Int will lead to the ill-formed type $\text{Int}\&\text{Int}$. To motivate the latter, consider the judgement $\alpha * \text{Int} \vdash \alpha * \text{Int}$. After the substitution of Int for α on the two types, the sentence $\alpha * \text{Int} \vdash \text{Int} * \text{Int}$ is no longer true, since Int is clearly not disjoint with itself. Generally speaking, a careless substitution can violate the constraints in the context. However, if appropriate disjointness pre-conditions are met, then disjointness can be preserved. More formally, the following lemma holds:

Lemma 4 (Disjointness is stable under substitution). *If* $(\alpha * D) \in \Gamma$ *and* $\Gamma \vdash C * D$ *and* $\Gamma \vdash A * B$ *and well-formed context* $[\alpha := C] \; \Gamma$, *then* $[\alpha := C] \; \Gamma \vdash [\alpha := C] \; A * [\alpha := C] \; B$.

Proof. By induction on the disjointness derivation of C and D. Special attention is needed for the variable case, where it is necessary to prove stability of substitution for the subtyping relation. It is also needed to show that, if C and D do not contain any variable x, then it is safe to make a substitution in the co-domain of the environment.   □

We can now prove a weaker version of the general substitution lemma:

Lemma 5 (Types are stable under substitution). *If* $\Gamma \vdash A$ *and* $\Gamma \vdash B$ *and* $(\alpha * C) \in \Gamma$ *and* $\Gamma \vdash B * C$ *and well-formed context* $[\alpha := B] \; \Gamma$, *then* $[\alpha := B] \; \Gamma \vdash [\alpha := B] \; A$.

Proof. By induction on the well-formedness derivation of A. The intersection case requires the use of Lemma 4. Also, the variable case required proving that if α does not occur free in A, and it is safe to substitute it in the co-domain of Γ, then it is safe to perform the substitution.   □

Now we can finally show that all types produced by the type-system are well-formed and, more specifically, justify that the disjointness premise on T-TApp is sufficient for that purpose. More formally, we have that:

Lemma 6 (Well-formed typing). *We have that:*

- *If* $\Gamma \vdash e \Leftarrow A$, *then* $\Gamma \vdash A$.
- *If* $\Gamma \vdash e \Rightarrow A$, *then* $\Gamma \vdash A$.

Proof. By induction on the derivation and applying Lemma 5 in the case of T-TAPP. □

Even though the meta-theory is consistent, we can still ask: what are the bounds of disjoint quantification? In other words, which type(s) can be used to allow unrestricted instantiation, and which one(s) will completely restrict instantiation? As the reader might expect, the answer is tightly related to subtyping.

5.3 Bounds of Disjoint Quantification

Substitution raises the question of what range of types can be instantiated for a given variable α, under a given context Γ. To answer this question, we ask the reader to recall the rule $D\alpha$, copied below:

$$\frac{\alpha * A \in \Gamma \quad A <: B}{\Gamma \vdash \alpha * B} D\alpha$$

Given that the cardinality of F_i's types is infinite, for the sake of this example we will restrict the type universe to a finite number of primitive types (i.e. Int and String), disjoint intersections of these types, $\top$ and $\bot$. Now we may ask: how many suitable types are there to instantiate α with, depending on A? The rule above tells us that the more super-types A has, the more types α has to be disjoint with. In other words, the choices for instantiating α are inversely proportional to the number of super-types of A. It is easy to see that the number of super-types of A is directly proportional to the number of intersections in A. For example, taking A as Int leads B to be either $\top$ or Int; whereas A as Int&String leaves B as either $\top$, Int or String. Thus, the choices of α are inversely proportional to the number of intersections in A. Following the same logic, choosing $\top$ (i.e. the 0-ary intersection) as constraint leaves α with the most options for instantiation; whereas $\bot$ (i.e. the infinite intersection) will deliver the least options. Consequently, we may conclude that $\top$ is the empty constraint: a variable associated to it can be instantiated to any well-formed type. It is a subtle but very important property, since F_i is a generalization of System F. Any type variable quantified in System F, can be quantified equivalently in F_i by assigning it a $\top$ disjointness constraint (as seen in Sect. 2.4).

6 Semantics, Coherence and Type-Safety

This section discusses the elaboration semantics of F_i and proves type-safety and coherence. It will first show how the semantics is described by an elaboration to System F. Then, it will discuss the necessary extensions to retain coherence, namely in the coercions of top-like types; coercive subtyping, and bidirectional type-system's elaboration.

6.1   Target Language

The dynamic semantics of the call-by-value F_i is defined by means of a type-directed translation to an extension of System F with pairs. The syntax and typing of our target language is unsurprising:

Types $T ::= \alpha \mid \text{Int} \mid T_1 \to T_2 \mid \forall \alpha.\, T \mid () \mid (T_1, T_2)$

Terms $E ::= x \mid i \mid \lambda x.\, E \mid E_1\, E_2 \mid \Lambda \alpha.\, E \mid E\, T \mid () \mid (E_1, E_2) \mid \text{proj}_1 E \mid \text{proj}_2 E$

Contexts $G ::= \cdot \mid G, \alpha \mid G, x{:}T$

The highlighted part shows its difference with the standard System F. The interested reader can find the formalization of the full target language syntax and typing rules in our Coq development.

Type and Context Translation. Figure 4 defines the type translation function $|\cdot|$ from F_i types A to target language types T. The notation $|\cdot|$ is also overloaded for context translation from F_i contexts Γ to target language contexts G.

$$\boxed{|A| = T} \qquad\qquad \boxed{|\Gamma| = G}$$

$$|\alpha| = \alpha \qquad\qquad |\cdot| = \cdot$$
$$|\top| = () \qquad\qquad |\Gamma, \alpha * A| = |\Gamma|, \alpha$$
$$|A_1 \to A_2| = |A_1| \to |A_2| \qquad |\Gamma, \alpha{:}A| = |\Gamma|, \alpha{:}|A|$$
$$|\forall(\alpha * A).\, B| = \forall \alpha.\, |B|$$
$$|A_1 \& A_2| = (|A_1|, |A_2|)$$
$$|\{l : A\}| = |A|$$

Fig. 4. Type and context translation.

6.2   Coercive Subtyping and Coherence

Coercive Subtyping. The judgement $A_1 <: A_2 \hookrightarrow E$ present in Fig. 1, extends the subtyping relation with a coercion on the right hand side of $\hookrightarrow$. A coercion E is just a term in the target language and is ensured to have type $|A_1| \to |A_2|$ (by Lemma 7). For example, $\text{Int} \& \alpha <: \alpha \hookrightarrow \lambda x.\text{proj}_2 x$, generates a target coercion function with type: $(\text{Int}, \alpha) \to \alpha$.

Rules ST, Sα, SZ, S$\to$, S&L$_1$, S&L$_2$, and S&R are taken directly from λ_i. In rule Sα, the coercion is simply the identity function. Rule S$\forall$ elaborates disjoint quantification, reusing only the coercion of subtyping between the bodies of both types. Rule SREC elaborates records by simply reusing the coercion generated between the inner types. Finally, all rules produce type-correct coercions:

Lemma 7 (Subtyping rules produce type-correct coercions). *If* $A_1 <: A_2 \hookrightarrow E$, *then* $\cdot \vdash E : |A_1| \to |A_2|$.

Proof. By a straightforward induction on the derivation.   □

Unique Coercions. In order to prove the type-system coherent, the subtyping relation also needs to be shown coherent. In F_i the following lemma holds:

Lemma 8 (Unique subtype contributor). *If* $A_1 \& A_2 <: B$, *where* $A_1 \& A_2$ *and* B *are well-formed types, and* B *is not top-like, then it is not possible that the following holds at the same time:*

1. $A_1 <: B$
2. $A_2 <: B$

Proof. By double induction: the first on the disjointness derivation (which follows from $A_1 \& A_2$ being well-formed); the second on type B. The variable cases $D\alpha$ and $D\alpha Sym$ needed to show that, for any two well-formed and disjoint types A and B, and B is not toplike, then A cannot be a subtype of B.   □

Using this lemma, we can show that the coercion of a subtyping relation $A <: B$ is uniquely determined. This fact is captured by the following lemma:

Lemma 9 (Unique coercion). *If* $A <: B \hookrightarrow E_1$ *and* $A <: B \hookrightarrow E_2$, *where* A *and* B *are well-formed types, then* $E_1 \equiv E_2$.

Proof. By induction on the first derivation and case analysis on the second.   □

6.3   Top-Like Types and Their Coercions

Lemma 8, which is fundamental in the proof of coherence of subtyping, holds under the condition that B is not a *top-like type*. Top-like types in F_i include $\top$ as well as other syntactically different types that behave as $\top$ (such as $\top \& \top$). It is easy to see that the unique subtyping contributor lemma is invalidated if no restriction on top-like types exists. Since every type is a subtype of $\top$ then, without the restriction, the lemma would never hold.

Rules. F_i's definition of top-like types extends that from λ_i. The rules that compose this unary relation, denoted as $\rceil . \lceil$, are presented at the top of Fig. 5. The new rules are TLREC and TL∀. Both rules say that their constructs are top-like whenever their enclosing expressions are also top-like.

Coercions for Top-Like Types. Coercions for top-like types require special treatment for retaining coherence. Although Lemma 8 does not hold for top-like types, we can still ensure that that any coercions for top-like types are unique, *even if multiple derivations exist*. The meta-function $[\![A]\!]$, shown at the bottom of Fig. 5, defines coercions for top-like types. With respect to λ_i the record and ∀ cases are now defined, and there is also a change in the & case (covering types such as $\top \& \top$). With this definition, although two derivations exist for type $Char \& Int <: \top$, they both generate the coercion $\lambda x.()$.

$$\boxed{\rceil A \lceil}$$

$$\frac{}{\rceil \top \lceil} \; \text{TLT} \qquad \frac{\rceil A \lceil \quad \rceil B \lceil}{\rceil A \& B \lceil} \; \text{TL\&} \qquad \frac{\rceil B \lceil}{\rceil A \to B \lceil} \; \text{TL} \to \qquad \frac{\rceil A \lceil}{\rceil \{l : A\} \lceil} \; \text{TLREC}$$

$$\frac{\rceil A \lceil}{\rceil \forall (\alpha * B). A \lceil} \; \text{TL}\forall$$

$$\boxed{[\![A]\!]_c = T} \qquad\qquad\qquad \boxed{[\![A]\!] = T}$$

$$[\![A]\!]_c = \begin{cases} \rceil A \lceil & [\![A]\!] \\ \text{otherwise} & C \end{cases}$$

$$[\![\top]\!] = ()$$
$$[\![A_1 \to A_2]\!] = \lambda x. [\![A_2]\!]$$
$$[\![A_1 \& A_2]\!] = ([\![A_1]\!], [\![A_2]\!])$$
$$[\![\{l : A\}]\!] = [\![A]\!]$$
$$[\![\forall (\alpha * B). A]\!] = \Lambda \alpha. [\![A]\!]$$

Fig. 5. Top-like types and their coercions.

Allowing Overlapping Top-Like Types in Intersections. In F_i $\top \& \top$ is a well-formed disjoint intersection type. This may look odd at first, since all other types cannot appear more than once in an intersection. Indeed, in λ_i, $\top \& \top$ is not well-formed. However, $\top$-types are special in that they have a *unique* canonical top value, which is translated to the unit value () in the target language. In other words a merge of two $\top$-types will always return the same value regardless of which component of the merge is chosen. This is different from merges of non $\top$-types, which do not have this property. Thus, one may say that $\top$-types are *coherent* with every other type. This property makes $\top$-types perfect candidates for the empty constraint, but such can only be achieved by allowing $\top$ in intersections. This explains the more liberal treatment of top types F_i when compared to λ_i.

6.4 Elaboration of the Type-System and Coherence

In order to prove the coherence result, we refer to the bidirectional type-system introduced in Sect. 4. The bidirectional type-system is elaborating, producing a term in the target language while performing the typing derivation.

Key Idea of the Translation. This translation turns merges into usual pairs, similar to Dunfield's elaboration approach [24]. It also translates the form of disjoint quantification and disjoint type application into regular (polymorphic) quantification and type application. For example, $\Lambda(\alpha * \text{Int}). \lambda x. (x, , 1)$ in F_i will be translated into System F's $\Lambda \alpha. \lambda x. (x, 1)$.

The Translation Judgement. The translation judgement $\Gamma \vdash e : A \hookrightarrow E$ extends the typing judgement with an elaborated term on the right hand side of $\hookrightarrow$.

The translation ensures that E has type $|A|$. The two rules for type abstraction (T-BLAM) and type application (T-TAPP) generate the expected corresponding coercions in System F. The coercions generated for T-REC and T-PROJR simply erase the labels and translate the corresponding underlying term. All the remaining rules are ported from λ_i.

Type-Safety. The type-directed translation is type-safe. This property is captured by the following two theorems.

Theorem 1 (Type preservation). *We have that:*

- *If* $\Gamma \vdash e \Rightarrow A \hookrightarrow E$, *then* $|\Gamma| \vdash E : |A|$.
- *If* $\Gamma \vdash e \Leftarrow A \hookrightarrow E$, *then* $|\Gamma| \vdash E : |A|$.

Proof. By structural induction on the term and the respective inference rule. $\square$

Theorem 2 (Type safety). *If* e *is a well-typed* F_i *term, then* e *evaluates to some System* F *value* v.

Proof. Since we define the dynamic semantics of F_i in terms of the composition of the type-directed translation and the dynamic semantics of System F, type safety follows immediately. $\square$

Uniqueness of Type-Inference. An important property of the bidirectional type-checking is that, given an expression e, if it is possible to infer a type for it, then e has a unique type.

Theorem 3 (Uniqueness of type-inference). *If* $\Gamma \vdash e \Rightarrow A_1 \hookrightarrow E_1$ *and* $\Gamma \vdash e \Rightarrow A_2 \hookrightarrow E_2$, *then* $A_1 = A_2$.

Proof. By structural induction on the term and the respective inference rule. $\square$

Coherency of Elaboration. Combining the previous results, we are finally able to show the central theorem:

Theorem 4 (Unique elaboration). *We have that:*

- *If* $\Gamma \vdash e \Rightarrow A \hookrightarrow E_1$ *and* $\Gamma \vdash e \Rightarrow A \hookrightarrow E_2$, *then* $E_1 \equiv E_2$.
- *If* $\Gamma \vdash e \Leftarrow A \hookrightarrow E_1$ *and* $\Gamma \vdash e \Leftarrow A \hookrightarrow E_2$, *then* $E_1 \equiv E_2$.

("$\equiv$" means syntactical equality, up to α-equality.)

Proof. By induction on the first derivation. The most important case is the subsumption rule:

$$\frac{\Gamma \vdash e \Rightarrow A \hookrightarrow E \qquad A <: B \hookrightarrow E_{sub} \qquad \Gamma \vdash B}{\Gamma \vdash e \Leftarrow B \hookrightarrow E_{sub}\ E} \text{ T-SUB}$$

We need to show that E_{sub} is unique (by Lemma 9), and thus to show that A is well-formed (by Lemma 6). Note that this is the place where stability of substitutions (used by Lemma 6) plays a crucial role in guaranteeing coherence. We also need to show that A is unique (by Theorem 3). Uniqueness of A is needed to apply the induction hypothesis. $\square$

7 Related Work

Intersection Types, Polymorphism and the Merge Operator. To our knowledge no previous work presents a *coherent* calculus which includes parametric polymorphism, intersection types and a *merge* operator. Only Pierce's $F_\wedge$ [40] supports intersection types, polymorphism and, as an extension, the merge operator (called glue in $F_\wedge$). However, with such extension, $F_\wedge$ is incoherent. Various simply typed systems with intersections types and a merge operator have been studied in the past. The merge operator was first introduced by Reynold's in the Forsythe [48] language. The merge operator in Forsythe is coherent [47], but it has various restrictions to ensure coherence. For example Forsythe merges cannot contain more than one function. Many of those restrictions are lifted in F_i. Castagna et al. [17] studied a coherent calculus with a special merge operator that works on functions only. The goal was to model *function overloading*. Unlike Reynold's operator, multiple functions are allowed in merges, but non-functional types are forbidden. More recently, Dunfield [24] formalised a system with intersection types and a merge operator with a type-directed translation to the simply-typed lambda calculus with pairs. Although Dunfield's calculus is incoherent, it was the inspiration for the λ_i calculus [38], which F_i extends.

λ_i solves the coherence problem for a calculus similar to Dunfield's, by requiring that intersection types can only be composed of *disjoint* types. λ_i uses a specification for disjointness, which says that two types are disjoint if they do not share a common supertype. F_i does not use such specification as its adaptation to polymorphic types would require using unification, making the specification arguably more complex than the algorithmic rules (and defeating the purpose of having a specification). F_i's notion of disjointness is based on λ_i's more general notion of disjointness concerning $\top$ types, called $\top$-disjointness. $\top$-disjointness states that two types A and B are disjoint if two conditions are satisfied:

1. $(\text{not } \rceil A \lceil)$ and $(\text{not } \rceil B \lceil)$
2. $\forall C. \text{ if } A <: C \text{ and } B <: C \text{ then } \rceil C \lceil$

A significant difference between the F_i and λ_i, is that $\top$-disjointness does not allow $\top$ in intersections, while F_i allows this. In other words, condition (1) is not imposed by F_i. As a consequence, the set of well-formed *top-like* types is a superset of λ_i's. This is covered in greater detail in Sect. 6.3.

Intersection Types and Polymorphism, Without the Merge Operator. Recently, Castagna *et al.* [18] studied a coherent calculus that has polymorphism and set-theoretic type connectives (such as intersections, unions, and negations). Their calculus is based on a semantic subtyping relation due to their interpretation of intersection types. The difference to F_i, is that their intersections are used between function types, allowing overloading (i.e. branching) of types. For example, they can express a function whose domain is defined on any type, but executes different code depending on that type:

$$\lambda^{(\texttt{Int}\to\texttt{Bool})\wedge(\alpha\backslash\texttt{Int}\to\alpha\backslash\texttt{Int})}x.(x \in \texttt{Int})?(x \bmod 2) = 0 : x$$

In our system we cannot express some of these intersections, namely the ones that do not have disjoint co-domains. However, F_i accepts other kinds of intersections which are not possible to express in their calculus. For example merges with type (Int → Bool)&(Int → Int) are accepted in F_i. Similarly to Castagna et al. previous work [17], their work is focused on combining intersections with functions (but without a merge operator), whereas F_i is concerned with merges between arbitrary types. Nevertheless, both systems need to express negative information about type variables. That is, which types a given variable cannot be instantiated to. In their calculus, difference takes this role (i.e. $\alpha\backslash$Int); whereas in F_i, one can express it using disjoint quantification (i.e. $\forall(\alpha * \text{Int})$. . . .).

Going in the direction of higher kinds, Compagnoni and Pierce [19] added intersection types to System F_ω and used a new calculus, $F_\wedge^\omega$, to model multiple inheritance. In their system, types include the construct of intersection of types of the same kind K. Davies and Pfenning [22] studied the interactions between intersection types and effects in call-by-value languages. They proposed a "value restriction" for intersection types, similar to value restriction on parametric polymorphism. None of these calculi has a merge operator.

Recently, some form of intersection types has been adopted in object-oriented languages such as Scala [37], TypeScript [4], Flow [3], Ceylon [1], and Grace [9]. There is also a foundational calculus for Scala that incorporates intersection types [49]. The most significant difference between F_i and those languages/calculi is that they have no explicit introduction construct like our merge operator. The lack of a native merge operator leads to several ad-hoc solutions for defining a merge operator in those languages, as discussed in Sects. 1 and 3.1.

Extensible Records. The encoding of multi-field records using intersection types and the merge operator first appeared in Forsythe [48]. Castagna et al. [17] propose an alternative encoding for records. Similarly to F_i's treatment of elaborating records is Cardelli's work [13] on translating a calculus with extensible records ($F_{<:\rho}$) to a simpler calculus without records primitives ($F_{<:}$). However, he does not encode multi-field records as intersections/merges hence his translation is more heavyweight. Crary [21] used intersection types and existential types to address the problem arising from interpreting method dispatch as self-application, but he did not use intersection types to encode multi-field records.

Wand [52] started the work on extensible records and proposed row types [53] for records, together with a *concatenation* operator, which is used in many calculi with extensible records [29,35,42,44,51,53]. Cardelli and Mitchell [15] defined three primitive operations on records that are also standard in type-systems with record types: *selection, restriction,* and *extension.* Several calculi are based on these three primitive operators (especially extension) [10,28,31,33,34,45]. The merge operator in F_i generalizes the concatenation operator for records, as its components may contain any types (and not just records). Systems with concatenation typically use a set of constraints/filters (such as lacks and contains) which are useful to combine several, possibly polymorphic, records [34]. In F_i, constraints on labels are encoded using disjoint quantification and intersections. Although systems with records can model structurally typed OO languages, it is harder to encode nominal objects. One advantage of the generality of intersections and merges is that it is easier to have nominal objects. Unlike systems with records, which have been extensively studied, there is much less work on intersection type systems with a merge operator. An interesting avenue for future work is to see whether some known compilation and type-inference techniques for extensible records can be adapted to disjoint intersections and merges.

Traits and Mixins. Traits [23,26,36] and mixins [5,6,8,11,25,27] have become very popular in object-oriented languages. They enable restricted forms of multiple inheritance. One of the main differences between traits and mixins are the way in which ambiguity of names is dealt with. Traits reject programs which compose classes with conflicting method implementations, whereas mixins assume a resolution strategy, which is usually language dependent. Our example demonstrated in Sect. 3 suggests that disjointness in F_i enables a model with a philosophy similar to traits: merging multiple values of overlapping types is forbidden. However while our simple encodings of objects work for very dynamic forms of prototype inheritance, the work on type systems for mixins/traits usually builds on more conventional class-based OO models.

Constrained Types. The notion of disjoint quantification is inspired on *bounded polymorphism* [12,16]. Such form of polymorphism typically uses types as subtyping bounds, whereas disjoint quantification uses types as *disjoint* (i.e. coherent) bounds. Another line of work are *qualified types* [32], which uses predicates on types to express constraints. However, qualified types are only applicable to the class of Hindley-Milner languages and such predicates are only defined over monotypes. F_i falls outside this class of languages, plus its constraints can be expressed using any arbitrary type (and not just monotypes).

8   Conclusion and Future Work

This paper described F_i: a System F-based language that combines intersection types, parametric polymorphism and a merge operator. The language is proved to be type-safe and coherent. To ensure coherence the type system accepts only disjoint intersections. To provide flexibility in the presence of parametric polymorphism, universal quantification is extended with disjointness constraints. We believe that disjoint intersection types and disjoint quantification are intuitive, and at the same time flexible enough to enable practical applications.

For the future, we intend to create a prototype-based statically typed source language based on F_i. We are also interested in extending our work to systems with union types and a $\bot$ type. Union types are also widely used in languages such as Ceylon or Flow, but preserving coherence in the presence of union types is challenging. The naive addition of $\bot$ seems to be problematic. The proofs for F_i rely on the invariant that a type variable α can never be disjoint to another type that contains α. The addition of $\bot$ breaks this invariant, allowing us to derive, for example, $\Gamma \vdash \alpha * \alpha$. Finally, we could study a similar system with implicit polymorphism. Such system would require some changes in the subtyping and disjointness relations. For instance, subtyping should allow $\forall \alpha. \alpha \to \alpha <: \text{Int} \to \text{Int}$. Consequently, the disjointness relation would have to be modified, since valid statements in F_i such as $\Gamma \vdash \forall \alpha. \alpha \to \alpha * \text{Int} \to \text{Int}$ would no longer hold under the more powerful subtyping relation.

Acknowledgments. We would like to thank the ESOP reviewers for their helpful comments. This work has been sponsored by the Hong Kong Research Grant Council Early Career Scheme project number 27200514.

References

1. Ceylon. https://ceylon-lang.org/
2. The Coq Proof Assistant. https://coq.inria.fr/
3. Flow. https://flowtype.org/
4. TypeScript. https://www.typescriptlang.org/
5. Ancona, D., Lagorio, G., Zucca, E.: Jam-designing a Java extension with mixins. ACM Trans. Program. Lang. Syst. **25**(5), 641–712 (2003)
6. Ancona, D., Zucca, E.: An algebraic approach to mixins and modularity. In: Hanus, M., Rodríguez-Artalejo, M. (eds.) ALP 1996. LNCS, vol. 1139, pp. 179–193. Springer, Heidelberg (1996). doi:10.1007/3-540-61735-3_12
7. Aydemir, B.E., Charguéraud, A., Pierce, B.C., Pollack, R., Weirich, S.: Engineering formal metatheory. In: POPL 2008 (2008)
8. Bettini, L., Bono, V., Likavec, S.: A core calculus of higher-order mixins and classes. In: SAC 2004 (2004)
9. Black, A.P., Bruce, K.B., Homer, M., Noble, J.: Grace: the absence of (inessential) difficulty. In: Onward! 2012 (2012)
10. Blume, M., Acar, U.A., Chae, W.: Extensible programming with first-class cases. In: ICFP 2006 (2006)
11. Bracha, G., Cook, W.: Mixin-based inheritance. In: OOPSLA/ECOOP 1990 (1990)
12. Canning, P., Cook, W., Hill, W., Olthoff, W., Mitchell, J.C.: F-bounded polymorphism for object-oriented programming. In: FPCA 1989 (1989)
13. Cardelli, L.: Extensible records in a pure calculus of subtyping. In: Theoretical Aspects of Object-oriented Programming. MIT Press, Cambridge (1994)
14. Cardelli, L., Martini, S., Mitchell, J.C., Scedrov, A.: An extension of system F with subtyping. Inf. Comput. **109**(1–2), 4–56 (1994)
15. Cardelli, L., Mitchell, J.C.: Operations on records. In: Main, M., Melton, A., Mislove, M., Schmidt, D. (eds.) MFPS 1989. LNCS, vol. 442, pp. 22–52. Springer, Heidelberg (1990). doi:10.1007/BFb0040253
16. Cardelli, L., Wegner, P.: On understanding types, data abstraction, and polymorphism. ACM Comput. Surv. **17**(4), 471–522 (1985)
17. Castagna, G., Ghelli, G., Longo, G.: A calculus for overloaded functions with subtyping. Inf. Comput. **117**(1), 115–135 (1995)
18. Castagna, G., Nguyen, K., Xu, Z., Im, H., Lenglet, S., Padovani, L.: Polymorphic functions with set-theoretic types: part 1: syntax, semantics, and evaluation. In: POPL 2014 (2014)
19. Compagnoni, A.B., Pierce, B.C.: Higher-order intersection types and multiple inheritance. Math. Struct. Comput. Sci. **6**(5), 469–501 (1996)

20. Coppo, M., Dezani-Ciancaglini, M., Venneri, B.: Functional characters of solvable terms. Math. Logic Q. **27**(2–6), 45–58 (1981)
21. Crary, K.: Simple, efficient object encoding using intersection types. Technical report, CMU-CS-99-100, Cornell University (1998)
22. Davies, R., Pfenning, F.: Intersection types and computational effects. In: ICFP 2000 (2000)
23. Ducasse, S., Nierstrasz, O., Schärli, N., Wuyts, R., Black, A.P.: Traits: a mechanism for fine-grained reuse. ACM Trans. Program. Lang. Syst. **28**(2), 331–388 (2006)
24. Dunfield, J.: Elaborating intersection and union types. In: ICFP 2012 (2012)
25. Findler, R.B., Flatt, M.: Modular object-oriented programming with units and mixins. In: ICFP 1998 (1998)
26. Fisher, K.: A typed calculus of traits. In: FOOL 2011 (2004)
27. Flatt, M., Krishnamurthi, S., Felleisen, M.: Classes and mixins. In: POPL 1998 (1998)
28. Gaster, B.R., Jones, M.P.: A polymorphic type system for extensible records and variants. Technical report, NOTTCS-TR-96-3, University of Nottingham (1996)
29. Harper, R., Pierce, B.: A record calculus based on symmetric concatenation. In: POPL 1991 (1991)
30. Harper, R.W., Pierce, B.C.: Extensible records without subsumption. Technical report, CMU-C5-90-102 (1990)
31. Jones, M., Jones, S.P.: Lightweight extensible records for Haskell. Technical report, UU-CS-1999-28, Haskell Workshop (1999)
32. Jones, M.P.: Qualified Types: Theory and Practice. Cambridge University Press, Cambridge (1994)
33. Leijen, D.: First-class labels for extensible rows. Technical report, UU-CS-2004-051, Utrecht University (2004)
34. Leijen, D.: Extensible records with scoped labels. In: Trends in Functional Programming (2005)
35. Makholm, H., Wells, J.B.: Type inference, principal typings, and let-polymorphism for first-class mixin modules. In: ICFP 2005 (2005)
36. Odersky, M., Zenger, M.: Scalable component abstractions. In: OOPSLA 2005 (2005)
37. Odersky, M., et al.: An overview of the Scala programming language. Technical report, IC/2004/64, EPFL Lausanne, Switzerland (2004)
38. Oliveira, B.C.S., Shi, Z., Alpuim, J.: Disjoint intersection types. In: ICFP 2016 (2016)
39. Oliveira, B.C.S., Storm, T., Loh, A., Cook, W.R.: Feature-oriented programming with object algebras. In: Castagna, G. (ed.) ECOOP 2013. LNCS, vol. 7920, pp. 27–51. Springer, Heidelberg (2013). doi:10.1007/978-3-642-39038-8_2
40. Pierce, B.C.: Programming with intersection types and bounded polymorphism. Ph.D. thesis, Carnegie Mellon University (1991)
41. Pierce, B.C., Turner, D.N.: Simple type-theoretic foundations for object-oriented programming. J. Funct. Program. **4**(2), 207–247 (1994)
42. Pottier, F.: A constraint-based presentation and generalization of rows. In: LICS 2003 (2003)
43. Pottinger, G.: A type assignment for the strongly normalizable λ-terms. In: To H. B. Curry: Essays on Combinatory Logic, Lambda Calculus and Formalism (1980)
44. Rémy, D.: Typing record concatenation for free. In: POPL 1992 (1992)
45. Rémy, D.: Type inference for records in natural extension of ML. In: Theoretical Aspects of Object-Oriented Programming. MIT Press, Cambridge (1994)

46. Rendel, T., Brachthäuser, J.I., Ostermann, K.: From object algebras to attribute grammars. In: OOPSLA 2014 (2014)
47. Reynolds, J.C.: The coherence of languages with intersection types. In: Ito, T., Meyer, A.R. (eds.) TACS 1991. LNCS, vol. 526, pp. 675–700. Springer, Heidelberg (1991). doi:10.1007/3-540-54415-1_70
48. Reynolds, J.C.: Design of the programming language Forsythe. In: Algol-like languages, Birkhäuser Boston (1997)
49. Rompf, T., Amin, N.: Type soundness for dependent object types. In: OOPSLA 2016 (2016)
50. Schärli, N., Ducasse, S., Nierstrasz, O., Black, A.P.: Traits: composable units of behaviour. In: Cardelli, L. (ed.) ECOOP 2003. LNCS, vol. 2743, pp. 248–274. Springer, Heidelberg (2003). doi:10.1007/978-3-540-45070-2_12
51. Sulzmann, M.: Designing record systems. Technical report, YALEU/DCS/RR-1128, Yale University (1997)
52. Wand, M.: Complete type inference for simple objects. In: LICS 1987 (1987)
53. Wand, M.: Type inference for record concatenation and multiple inheritance. In: LICS 1989 (1989)

Generalizing Inference Systems by Coaxioms

Davide Ancona$^{(\boxtimes)}$, Francesco Dagnino, and Elena Zucca

DIBRIS, Universitá di Genova, Genoa, Italy
{davide.ancona,elena.zucca}@unige.it, fra.dagn@gmail.com

Abstract. We introduce a generalized notion of inference system to support structural recursion on non well-founded datatypes. Besides axioms and inference rules with the usual meaning, a generalized inference system allows *coaxioms*, which are, intuitively, axioms which can only be applied "at infinite depth" in a proof tree. This notion nicely subsumes standard inference systems and their inductive and coinductive interpretation, while providing more flexibility. Indeed, the classical results on the existence and constructive characterization of least and greatest fixed points can be extended to our generalized framework, interpreting recursive definitions as fixed points which are not necessarily the least, nor the greatest one. This allows formal reasoning in cases where the inductive and coinductive interpretation do not provide the intended meaning, or are mixed together.

1 Introduction

Recently several approaches [5,10,11,18,19,25,32] have been proposed to program with coinductive (coalgebraic) datatypes to support corecursion, that is, the ability of defining predicates or functions by structural recursion on non-well-founded datatypes. Such solutions are generally characterized by a strong dichotomy between inductive and coinductive definitions, the former being based on the notion of least fixed point, and the latter on that of greatest fixed point. Moreover, some proposals provide language abstractions to allow the programmer to interpret corecursive definitions not in the standard coinductive way. As a consequence, formal reasoning about programs that exploit such abstractions cannot be based on usual proof principles.

In this paper, we introduce a framework for interpreting recursive definitions as fixed points which are not necessarily the least, nor the greatest one. This allows formal reasoning in cases where the inductive and coinductive interpretation do not provide the intended meaning, or are mixed together.

To introduce the idea, let us consider the following recursive definitions of functions on lists of integers, with the meaning suggested by the name.

Special thanks go to all anonymous reviewers, who helped us improve this paper, and to Bart Jacobs for an enlightening discussion with him on the use of coaxioms for modeling divergence with big-step semantics.

H. Yang (Ed.): ESOP 2017, LNCS 10201, pp. 29–55, 2017.
DOI: 10.1007/978-3-662-54434-1_2

```
let rec allPos = function [] -> true | x::l -> x >0 &&
allPos l
let rec member y =
   function [] -> false | x::l -> x==y||member y l
let rec elems = function
   [] -> [] |
   x::l -> let xs = elems l in if member x xs then xs else
   x::xs
let rec maxElem = function [x] -> x | x::l -> max x
(maxElem l)
```

These definitions are written above in a widely-known programming language
syntax (OCaml) for concreteness, but this is not relevant here: for such first-order
functions, in most programming languages we can write analogous recursive definitions, and they are usually interpreted *inductively*. This means that, turning,
more abstractly, such recursive definitions into meta-rules of an inference system, they are interpreted as the set of judgments which have a finite proof tree.
For instance, the meta-rules for the judgment $allPos(l, b)$ are as follows:

$$\frac{}{allPos(\Lambda, T)} \qquad \frac{}{allPos(x{:}l, F)}x \leq 0 \qquad \frac{allPos(l, b)}{allPos(x{:}l, b)}x > 0$$

where Λ and : denote the empty list, and the list constructor, respectively, and
T and F denote the boolean values. This interpretation works perfectly well on
finite lists. However, with the inductive interpretation the above functions may
happen to be undefined on infinite lists. For instance, the judgment $allPos(l, b)$
obviously has no finite proof tree if l is an infinite list of positives.

Indeed, to support structural recursion on non-well-founded structures, such
as infinite lists or graphs, we typically have to use *coinduction*. The coinductive
interpretation of an inference system is the set of judgments which have a (finite
or infinite) proof tree.

In some cases, the coinductive interpretation actually yields the intended
meaning. For instance, taking a slightly different version of `allPos` as a unary
predicate $allPos(l)$, as it would be expressed in a logic program:

$$\frac{}{allPos(\Lambda)} \qquad \frac{allPos(l)}{allPos(x : l)}x > 0$$

it is easy to see that with the coinductive interpretation we obtain the intended
meaning on infinite lists as well, since we get an infinite proof tree if and only
if all the elements in the list are positive. Indeed, this interpretation has been
fruitfully used in coinductive logic programming (coLP) [3, 31–33].

However, considering instead the previous relation $allPos(l, b)$, the coinductive interpretation fails to be a function, since for infinite lists of positives both
the judgment $allPos(l, T)$ and $allPos(l, F)$ can be proved. Moreover, if we consider the predicate corresponding to the boolean function `member`:

$$\frac{}{member(x, x : l)} \qquad \frac{member(x, l)}{member(x, y : l)}x \neq y$$

then the correct interpretation is the inductive one. Indeed, the coinductive interpretation contains all judgments $member(x, l)$ where l is an infinite list. Finally, for the predicates corresponding to the other example functions, which do not return a boolean, neither the inductive nor the coinductive interpretation yields the intended semantics. In particular, the coinductive interpretation contains too many elements. For instance, taking l the infinite list of 1s, by coinductively interpreting *elems* and *maxElem* we get, together with the correct judgments, also wrong ones, as will be formally shown in the following section.

All these examples suggest the idea that we should be able to "filter out" in some way the (infinite) proof trees corresponding to the coinductive interpretation, keeping only some of them. We make this possible by introducing *coaxioms*. A coaxiom is, intuitively, an axiom which can only be applied "at infinite depth" in a proof tree. An inference system interpreted inductively corresponds to a generalized inference system with no coaxioms, while an inference system interpreted coinductively corresponds to a generalized inference system where there is a coaxiom for each judgment.

From the model-theoretic point of view, coaxioms allow the programmer to choose the desired fixed point for a recursive definition, by selecting also fixed points which are neither the least, nor the greatest one. For instance, in the inference system for $allPos(l, b)$, the intended meaning is the set of judgments $allPos(l, b)$ where b is true if and only if the (finite or infinite) list l contains only positives. This set *is a fixed point* which lies between the least, which is undefined on infinite lists of positives, and the greatest, which returns both boolean values, hence is undetermined, on such lists.

Coaxioms are partly inspired by an extension of coLP and coinductive SLD resolution (coSLD) [31–33] with `finally` clauses [5], to allow more flexible interpretations of corecursive definitions of predicates, and by a related proposal in the context of object-oriented programming [10, 11]. In this paper we take a more abstract and general approach and provide a framework for interpreting corecursive definitions in a flexible way and to formally reason on their correctness.

The rest of the paper is organized as follows: in Sect. 2 we introduce the notion of generalized inference system with coaxioms, and show how to express the previous examples and others. In Sect. 3 we formally define the fixed point semantics of inference systems with coaxioms in the more general setting of complete lattices. In Sect. 4 we discuss the equivalent semantics based on the proof-theoretic approach, and in Sect. 5 we illustrate the related proof techniques on some of the examples. In Sect. 6 we show some more involved examples and discuss some subtleties, Sect. 7 surveys related work, and finally in Sect. 8 we summarize our contribution and discuss further work. A prototype meta-interpreter[1] has been developed to test the examples provided in Sects. 2 and 6.

---

[1] Available at http://www.disi.unige.it/person/AnconaD/Software/esop17artifact.zip.

2   Inference Systems with Coaxioms

We recall some standard notions about inference systems [1, 23].

Assume in the following a set $\mathcal{U}$ called the *universe*, whose elements are called *judgments*.

An *inference system* $\mathcal{I}$ consists of a set of *inference rules*, which are pairs $\dfrac{Pr}{c}$, with $Pr \subseteq \mathcal{U}$ the set of *premises*, $c \in \mathcal{U}$ the *consequence*.

The intuitive interpretation of a rule is that if the premises Pr hold then the consequence c should hold as well. In particular, an *axiom* is (the consequence of) a rule with empty set of premises, which necessarily holds.

The *(one step) inference* operator $F_{\mathcal{I}} : \wp(\mathcal{U}) \rightarrow \wp(\mathcal{U})$ associated with an inference system $\mathcal{I}$ is defined by:

$$F_{\mathcal{I}}(S) = \{c \mid Pr \subseteq S, \frac{Pr}{c} \in \mathcal{I}\}$$

That is, $F_{\mathcal{I}}(S)$ is the set of judgments that can be inferred (in one step) from the judgments in S using the inference rules. Note that this set always includes axioms.

A set S is *closed* if $F_{\mathcal{I}}(S) \subseteq S$, and *consistent* if $S \subseteq F_{\mathcal{I}}(S)$. That is, no new judgments can be inferred from a closed set, and all judgments in a consistent set can be inferred from the set itself.

The *inductive interpretation* of $\mathcal{I}$, denoted $Ind(\mathcal{I})$, is the smallest closed set, that is, the intersection of all closed sets, and the *coinductive interpretation* of $\mathcal{I}$, denoted $CoInd(\mathcal{I})$, is the largest consistent set, that is, the union of all consistent sets. Both interpretations are well-defined and can be equivalently expressed as the least (respectively, greatest) fixed point of the inference operator. Moreover, under continuity hypotheses on $F_{\mathcal{I}}$, they can be computed as follows:

$$Ind(\mathcal{I}) = \bigcup \{F_{\mathcal{I}}^n(\emptyset) \mid n \geq 0\}$$
$$CoInd(\mathcal{I}) = \bigcap \{F_{\mathcal{I}}^n(\mathcal{U}) \mid n \geq 0\}$$

The inductive and coinductive interpretation can also be characterized in terms of proof trees. That is, defining a proof tree as a tree whose nodes are (labeled with) judgments in $\mathcal{U}$, and there is a node c with set of children Pr only if there exists a rule $\dfrac{Pr}{c}$, it can be shown [23] that $Ind(\mathcal{I})$ and $CoInd(\mathcal{I})$ are the sets of judgments which are the root of a finite[2] and an arbitrary (finite or infinite) proof tree, respectively.

We introduce now our generalization.

An *inference system with coaxioms* is a pair $(\mathcal{I}, \gamma)$ consisting of an inference system $\mathcal{I}$ and a set of *coaxioms* γ, with $\gamma \subseteq \mathcal{U}$. A coaxiom c will be written $\dfrac{\bullet}{c}$, very much like an axiom, and analogously to an axiom it can be used as an initial assumption to derive other judgments. However, coaxioms will be used in a special way, explained in the following.

---

[2] Under the common assumption that the set of premises of all the rules are finite, otherwise we should say a finite depth tree.

To illustrate the notion, we will consider an introductory example which computes the judgment $n \xrightarrow{*} \mathcal{N}$ meaning that $\mathcal{N}$ is the set of nodes reachable from a node n of a given graph. Let us represent a graph by its set of nodes V and a function adj which returns all the adjacent nodes. As usual, sets of rules can be expressed by a *metarule* with side conditions, and the same can be done for sets of coaxioms.

$$\frac{n_1 \xrightarrow{*} \mathcal{N}_1 \ \ldots \ n_k \xrightarrow{*} \mathcal{N}_k}{n \xrightarrow{*} \{n\} \cup \mathcal{N}_1 \cup \ldots \cup \mathcal{N}_k} \, adj(n) = \{n_1, \ldots, n_k\} \qquad \frac{\bullet}{n \xrightarrow{*} \emptyset} n \in V$$

For instance, in the case of a graph with nodes a, b, c, with an arc from a into b and conversely, and c isolated, we would get the following metarules and coaxioms:

$$\frac{b \xrightarrow{*} \mathcal{N}}{a \xrightarrow{*} \{a\} \cup \mathcal{N}} \qquad \frac{a \xrightarrow{*} \mathcal{N}}{b \xrightarrow{*} \{b\} \cup \mathcal{N}} \qquad \frac{}{c \xrightarrow{*} \{c\}} \qquad \frac{\bullet}{a \xrightarrow{*} \emptyset} \qquad \frac{\bullet}{b \xrightarrow{*} \emptyset} \qquad \frac{\bullet}{c \xrightarrow{*} \emptyset}$$

If we interpret the metarules inductively (excluding the coaxioms), then we get only the judgment $c \xrightarrow{*} \{c\}$. In other words, a visit computing $n \xrightarrow{*} \mathcal{N}$, like other judgments on graphs, should mark already encountered nodes to avoid non termination, since the graph structure is not well-founded. On the other hand, if we interpret the metarules coinductively (excluding again the coaxioms), then we get the correct judgments $a \xrightarrow{*} \{a, b\}$ and $b \xrightarrow{*} \{a, b\}$, but we also get the wrong judgments $a \xrightarrow{*} \{a, b, c\}$ and $b \xrightarrow{*} \{a, b, c\}$.

We define a different interpretation, called *interpretation generated by the coaxioms* and denoted $Gen(\mathcal{I}, \gamma)$, which takes into account the coaxioms in the following way.

1. First, we take the smallest closed superset of the set of coaxioms. In other words, we consider the inference system $\mathcal{I}_{\sqcup \gamma}$ obtained enriching $\mathcal{I}$ by judgments in γ considered as axioms, and we take its inductive interpretation $Ind(\mathcal{I}_{\sqcup \gamma})$.
2. Then, we take the largest consistent subset of $Ind(\mathcal{I}_{\sqcup \gamma})$. In other words, we take the coinductive interpretation of the inference system obtained from $\mathcal{I}$ by keeping only rules with consequence in $Ind(\mathcal{I}_{\sqcup \gamma})$, that is, we define
$$Gen(\mathcal{I}, \gamma) = CoInd(\mathcal{I}_{\sqcap Ind(\mathcal{I}_{\sqcup \gamma})})$$

where $\mathcal{I}_{\sqcap S}$, with $\mathcal{I}$ inference system and $S \subseteq \mathcal{U}$, denotes the inference system obtained from $\mathcal{I}$ by keeping only rules with consequence in S.

In the example, in the first phase we obtain the following judgments (each line corresponds to an iteration of the inference operator):

$a \xrightarrow{*} \emptyset, b \xrightarrow{*} \emptyset, c \xrightarrow{*} \emptyset, c \xrightarrow{*} \{c\}$
$a \xrightarrow{*} \emptyset, b \xrightarrow{*} \emptyset, c \xrightarrow{*} \emptyset, c \xrightarrow{*} \{c\}, a \xrightarrow{*} \{a\}, b \xrightarrow{*} \{b\}$
$a \xrightarrow{*} \emptyset, b \xrightarrow{*} \emptyset, c \xrightarrow{*} \emptyset, c \xrightarrow{*} \{c\}, a \xrightarrow{*} \{a\}, b \xrightarrow{*} \{b\}, a \xrightarrow{*} \{a, b\}, b \xrightarrow{*} \{a, b\}$

The last set is closed, hence it is $Ind(\mathcal{I}_{\sqcup \gamma})$.

In the second phase, each iteration of the inference operator removes judgments which cannot be inferred from the previous step, that is, we get:

$c\xrightarrow{*}\{c\}$, $a\xrightarrow{*}\{a\}$, $b\xrightarrow{*}\{b\}$, $a\xrightarrow{*}\{a,b\}$, $b\xrightarrow{*}\{a,b\}$
$c\xrightarrow{*}\{c\}$, $a\xrightarrow{*}\{a,b\}$, $b\xrightarrow{*}\{a,b\}$

This last set is consistent, hence it is $Gen(\mathcal{I},\gamma)$, and it is indeed the expected result.

Note that the inductive and coinductive interpretation can be obtained as special cases of the interpretation generated by coaxioms of an inference system, notably:

– the inductive interpretation when the set of coaxioms is empty
– the coinductive interpretation when the set of coaxioms is the universe.

In terms of proof trees, judgments in $Gen(\mathcal{I},\gamma)$ are those which have an arbitrary (finite or infinite) proof tree t in the inference system $\mathcal{I}$, whose nodes all have a finite proof tree in $\mathcal{I}_{\sqcup\gamma}$. Note that for nodes in t which are roots of a finite subtree this always holds (a finite proof tree in $\mathcal{I}$ is a finite proof tree in $\mathcal{I}_{\sqcup\gamma}$ as well), hence the condition is only significant for nodes which are roots of an infinite path in the proof tree.

For instance, in the example, the judgment $a\xrightarrow{*}\{a,b\}$ has an infinite proof tree in $\mathcal{I}$ where each node has a finite proof tree in $\mathcal{I}_{\sqcup\gamma}$, as shown below.

$$
\cfrac{\cfrac{\displaystyle\cdots}{a\xrightarrow{*}\{a,b\}}}{\cfrac{b\xrightarrow{*}\{a,b\}}{a\xrightarrow{*}\{a,b\}}}
\qquad
\cfrac{\cfrac{}{a\xrightarrow{*}\emptyset}}{\cfrac{b\xrightarrow{*}\{b\}}{a\xrightarrow{*}\{a,b\}}}
\qquad
\cfrac{\cfrac{}{b\xrightarrow{*}\emptyset}}{\cfrac{a\xrightarrow{*}\{a\}}{b\xrightarrow{*}\{a,b\}}}
$$

Moreover, there is another important property which will be proved in Sect. 4: if a judgment belongs to $Gen(\mathcal{I},\gamma)$, then, for all $n \geq 0$, it has a proof tree in the inference system $\mathcal{I}_{\sqcup\gamma}$ where coaxioms can only be used at depth greater than n.

For instance, in the example, it is easy to see that, for any n, we can obtain a finite proof tree for the judgment $a\xrightarrow{*}\{a,b\}$ in $\mathcal{I}_{\sqcup\gamma}$ where coaxioms are used at depth greater than n, as shown below.

$$
\cfrac{\cfrac{}{a\xrightarrow{*}\emptyset}}{\cfrac{b\xrightarrow{*}\{b\}}{a\xrightarrow{*}\{a,b\}}}
\qquad
\cfrac{\cfrac{}{b\xrightarrow{*}\emptyset}}{\cfrac{a\xrightarrow{*}\{a\}}{\cfrac{b\xrightarrow{*}\{a,b\}}{a\xrightarrow{*}\{a,b\}}}}
\qquad
\cfrac{\cfrac{\cfrac{}{a\xrightarrow{*}\emptyset}}{\cfrac{b\xrightarrow{*}\{b\}}{a\xrightarrow{*}\{a,b\}}}}{\cfrac{b\xrightarrow{*}\{a,b\}}{a\xrightarrow{*}\{a,b\}}}
\qquad \cdots
$$

This last property motivates the name "coaxioms". Indeed, dually to axioms, which can be used in the proof tree at every depth, including 0, coaxioms can only be used "at an infinite depth" in the proof tree. Therefore, coaxioms filter out undesired infinite proof trees; in other words, they bound from above the greatest fixed point corresponding to the semantics of the generalized inference system.

As a second example, we consider the definition of the *first* sets in a grammar. Let us represent a context-free grammar by its set of terminals T, its set of non-terminals N, and all the productions $A ::= \beta_1 \mid \ldots \mid \beta_n$ with left-hand side A, for each non-terminal A. Recall that, for each $\alpha \in (T \cup N)^+$, we can define the set $first(\alpha) = \{\sigma \mid \sigma \in T, \alpha \rightarrow^* \sigma \beta\}$. Informally, $first(\alpha)$ is the set of the initial terminal symbols of the strings which can be derived from a string α in 0 or more steps.

The following inference system with coaxioms defines the judgment $first(\alpha, \mathcal{F})$, with $\mathcal{F} \subseteq T$.

$$\frac{}{first(\sigma\alpha, \{\sigma\})}\sigma \in T \qquad \frac{first(A, \mathcal{F}) \quad A \in N}{first(A\alpha, \mathcal{F}) \quad A \not\rightarrow^* \epsilon} \qquad \frac{first(A, \mathcal{F}) \quad first(\alpha, \mathcal{F}') \quad A \in N}{first(A\alpha, \mathcal{F} \cup \mathcal{F}') \quad A \rightarrow^* \epsilon}$$

$$\frac{}{first(\epsilon, \emptyset)} \qquad \frac{first(\beta_1, \mathcal{F}_1) \quad \ldots \quad first(\beta_n, \mathcal{F}_n)}{first(A, \mathcal{F}_1 \cup \ldots \cup \mathcal{F}_n)} A ::= \beta_1 \mid \ldots \mid \beta_n \qquad \frac{\bullet}{first(A, \emptyset)} A \in N$$

The rules of the inference system correspond to the natural recursive definition of $first$. Note, in particular, that in a string of shape $A\alpha$, if the non-terminal A is *nullable*, that is, we can derive from it the empty string, then the $first$ set for $A\alpha$ should also include the $first$ set for α.

As in the previous example on graphs, the problem with this recursive definition is that, since the non-terminals in a grammar can mutually refer to each other, the function defined by the inductive interpretation can be undefined. That is, a naive top-down implementation might not terminate. For this reason, $first$ sets are typically computed by an imperative bottom-up algorithm, or the top-down implementation is corrected by marking already encountered non-terminals, analogously to what is done for visiting graphs. Again as in the previous example, the coinductive interpretation may fail to be a function, whereas, with the coaxioms, we get the expected result.

We express now as inference systems with coaxioms the recursive definitions of functions shown at the beginning of Sect. 1. Let $\mathbb{Z}$ denote the set of integers, and $\mathbb{L}$ the set of (finite and infinite) lists of integers.

The first example is the function which checks whether all the elements of a list are positive, expressed by judgments of shape $allPos(l, b)$ with $l \in \mathbb{L}$ and $b \in \{T, F\}$.

$$\frac{}{allPos(\Lambda, T)} \qquad \frac{}{allPos(x{:}l, F)}x \leq 0 \qquad \frac{allPos(l, b)}{allPos(x{:}l, b)}x > 0 \qquad \frac{\bullet}{allPos(l, T)}$$

With the coaxioms, we obtain the expected function also on infinite lists of positives: indeed, we only consider the infinite trees where the nodes have a finite proof tree in the inference system enriched by the coaxioms. In this way, the infinite tree where $b = F$ is filtered out.

The function which checks whether an element belongs to a list, expressed by judgments of shape $member(x, l, b)$ with $x \in \mathbb{Z}$, $l \in \mathbb{L}$ and $b \in \{T, F\}$, is a very similar example, with the difference that the coaxioms map every list into false rather than true.

$$\frac{}{member(x, \Lambda, F)} \qquad \frac{}{member(x, x{:}l, T)} \qquad \frac{member(x, l, b)}{member(x, y : l, b)}x \neq y \qquad \frac{\bullet}{member(x, l, F)}$$

Analogously to the previous example, with the coaxioms we obtain the expected result also on infinite lists which do not contain the element.

The function which returns the set of the elements contained in a list is expressed by judgments of shape $elems(l, xs)$, with $l \in \mathbb{L}$ and $xs \in \wp(\mathbb{Z})$.

$$\frac{}{elems(\Lambda, \emptyset)} \quad \frac{elems(l, xs)}{elems(x{:}l, \{x\} \cup xs)} \quad \frac{\bullet}{elems(l, \emptyset)}$$

In this case, the inductive interpretation gives the expected result only on finite lists, and the coinductive interpretation fails to be a function on infinite lists. For instance, for l the infinite list of 1s, any judgment $elems(l, xs)$ with $1 \in xs$ can be derived. Indeed, for any such judgment we can construct an infinite proof tree which is a chain of applications of the last metarule. With the coaxioms, we only consider the infinite trees where the node $elems(l, xs)$ has a finite proof tree in the inference system enriched by the coaxioms. This is only true for $xs = \{1\}$.

Note that coaxioms are needed to get the expected result not only on regular lists. Considering for example the infinite list $1 : 2 : 1 : 1 : 2 : 1 : 1 : 1 : 2 : \ldots$, it is easy to see that the same reasoning holds.

Finally, the function which returns the greatest element contained in a (non-empty) list is expressed by judgments of shape $max(l, x)$, with $l \in \mathbb{L}$ and $x \in \mathbb{Z}$.

$$\frac{}{max(x{:}\Lambda, x)} \quad \frac{max(l, y)}{max(x{:}l, z)} z = \max(x, y) \quad \frac{\bullet}{max(x{:}l, x)}$$

Analogously to the previous example, the coinductive interpretation fails to be a function (for instance, for l the infinite list of 1s, any judgment $max(l, x)$ with $x \geq 1$ can be derived), and the coaxioms "filter out" the wrong results.

3   Bounded Fixed Points

In this section, after recalling basic definitions, we define the *bounded fixed point generated by an element*, justifying its existence by the Knaster-Tarski theorem [34]. Then, we show that the interpretation generated by coaxioms of an inference system corresponds to a bounded fixed point in the powerset lattice. Finally, we provide a constructive characterization of bounded fixed points, again justified by a classical result (Kleene theorem). We refer to [22] for an history of these theorems with a number of good references.

In the following we assume a complete lattice $(L, \leq)$ with top and bottom elements $\top$ and $\bot$, and meet and join operations $\sqcap$ and $\sqcup$. Moreover, we use $\sqcap$ and $\bigsqcup$ to denote meet (greatest lower bound) and join (least upper bound) of a set, respectively.

Basic Definitions. Let $F : L \to L$, and $x \in L$. Then, x is a pre-fixed point of F iff $F(x) \leq x$; x is a post-fixed point of F iff $x \leq F(x)$; and x is a fixed point of F iff $x = F(x)$. Pre-fixed points will be also called *closed*, and post-fixed points will be also called *consistent* points. A function $F : L \to L$ is *monotone* if, for all $x, y \in L$, $x \leq y \Rightarrow F(x) \leq F(y)$.

In this general setting, the role of the universe is played by the top $\top$ of L, that of the inference system by a monotone function F, and that of the co-axioms by a distinguished element $\gamma \in L$, called *generator*.

Definition of Bounded Fixed-Point. In the following we assume a monotone function $F : L \to L$. The *bounded fixed point* generated by an element γ is the greatest fixed point of the monotone function obtained by restricting F to the down-set of the least pre-fixed point above γ. The construction is detailed and justified below. First of all we introduce two notations.

Definition 1. *Let $x \in L$. Then:*

- *The closure of x w.r.t. F is the element $\nabla_F(x)$ of L defined by*
  $\nabla_F(x) = \bigsqcap\{y \in L \mid x \leq y, F(y) \leq y\}$.
- *The kernel of x w.r.t. F is the element $\Delta_F(x)$ of L defined by*
  $\Delta_F(x) = \bigsqcup\{y \in L \mid y \leq x, y \leq F(y)\}$.

We can also see Δ_F and ∇_F as endofunctions on L, which are instances of well-known notions in lattice theory: closure and kernel operators.

From this definition immediately follows the *bounded coinduction principle*. Indeed, given $\beta \in L$, we have:

(CoInd) If $x \leq F(x)$ (x post-fixed), and $x \leq \beta$, then $x \leq \Delta_F(\beta)$.

The standard coinduction principle can be obtained as a specific instance of the more general principle above, by taking $\beta = \top$; for this particular case the hypothesis $x \leq \beta$ can be omitted, since it trivially holds. We will show in detail how to use this proof principle in Sect. 5.

The closure of an arbitrary element γ turns out to be *the best closed approximation of* γ, that is, the least pre-fixed point of F above γ, as shown below.

Proposition 1. *Let $\gamma \subset L$. Then, $z = \nabla_F(\gamma)$ is the least pre-fixed point of F above γ.*

Proof. Set $S = \{x \in L \mid \gamma \leq x, F(x) \leq x\}$. We have to prove that $z \in S$, which then implies, by definition, that it is its least element. Since γ is a lower bound for all $x \in S$, by definition of meet we get $\gamma \leq z$. We can show that z is a pre-fixed point of F by the following steps:

- for all $x \in S$, $F(x) \leq x$ (def. of S) and $z \leq x$ (def. of $\bigsqcap$);
- for all $x \in S$, $F(x) \leq x$ (def. of S) and $F(z) \leq F(x)$ (F is monotone);
- for all $x \in S$, $F(z) \leq x$ (transitivity);
- $F(z) \leq z$ (def. of $\bigsqcap$).

$\square$

Note that if $\gamma = \bot$ we have that $\nabla_F(\bot)$ is the least pre-fixed point of F, that, thanks to the Knaster-Tarski theorem, is the least fixed point of F.

The kernel of a pre-fixed point β turns out to be *the greatest (post-)fixed-point of F below β*, as shown below.

Proposition 2. *Let $\beta \in L$. If β is a pre-fixed point of F and $z = \Delta_F(\beta)$, then $F(z) = z$.*

Proof. If β is an element of a complete lattice, then $L_\beta = \{x \in L \mid x \le \beta\}$ is also a complete lattice, with top element β. If β is a pre-fixed point of F, then F is a monotone endofunction on L_β. Therefore, by the Knaster-Tarski theorem $F(z) = z$.

We can now define bounded fixed points generated by an element.

Definition 2 (Bounded fixed point). *Let $\gamma \in L$. The* bounded fixed point *of F generated by γ, denoted $Gen(F, \gamma)$, is the greatest fixed point of F below the closure of γ, that is, $Gen(F, \gamma) = \Delta_F(\nabla_F(\gamma))$.*

The bounded fixed point is well-defined since, thanks to Proposition 2, there exists the greatest fixed point below β, provided that the bound is a pre-fixed point. Since in general γ might not be pre-fixed, we need to construct a pre-fixed point from γ. Note that the first step of this construction *cannot* be expressed as the least fixed point of F on the complete lattice $\{x \in L \mid x \ge \gamma\}$, since in general F may fail to be an endofunction (e.g., if F is the function which maps any element to $\bot < \gamma$). Indeed, $\nabla_F(\gamma)$ is *not* a fixed point in general, but only a pre-fixed point: we need the two steps to obtain a fixed point.

Note also that the definition of bounded fixed point is asymmetric, that is, we take the greatest fixed point bounded from above by a least (pre-)fixed point, rather than the other way round. This is motivated by the intuition, explained in the previous section, that we essentially need a greatest fixed point, since we want to deal with non-well-founded structures, but we want to "constrain" in some way such greatest fixed point. Investigating the symmetric construction is a matter of further work (see the Conclusion).

An important fact is that bounded fixed points are a generalization of both least and greatest fixed points, since they can be obtained by taking particular generators, as stated in the following proposition.

Proposition 3.

1. $Gen(F, \top)$ *is the greatest fixed point of F*
2. $Gen(F, \bot)$ *is the least fixed point of F.*

Proof. 1. Note that $\nabla_F(\top) = \top$, since the only pre-fixed point above $\top$ is $\top$ itself, therefore we get $Gen(F, \top) = \Delta_F(\top)$, that is, the greatest fixed point of F, by Proposition 2.
2. As already noted $\nabla_F(\bot)$ is the least fixed point of F, in particular $\nabla_F(\bot)$ is post-fixed, therefore we get $Gen(F, \bot) = \Delta_F(\nabla_F(\bot)) = \nabla_F(\bot)$, namely it is the least fixed point of F.

$\square$

Coaxioms as Generators. In Sect. 2 we have described two steps to construct $Gen(\mathcal{I}, \gamma)$, the interpretation generated by coaxioms γ of an inference system $\mathcal{I}$.

1. First, we consider the inference system $\mathcal{I}_{\sqcup\gamma}$ obtained enriching $\mathcal{I}$ by judgments in γ considered as axioms, and we take its inductive interpretation $Ind(\mathcal{I}_{\sqcup\gamma})$.
2. Then, we take the coinductive interpretation of the inference system obtained from $\mathcal{I}$ by keeping only rules with consequence in $Ind(\mathcal{I}_{\sqcup\gamma})$, that is, we define
$$Gen(\mathcal{I}, \gamma) = CoInd(\mathcal{I}_{\cap Ind(\mathcal{I}_{\sqcup\gamma})})$$

The definition of bounded fixed point is the formulation of these two steps in the general setting of complete lattices. Indeed, the inference operator $F_{\mathcal{I}}$ is a monotone function on the complete lattice $\wp(\mathcal{U})$ obtained by taking set inclusion as order, and specifying the coaxioms γ corresponds to fixing an arbitrary element of L as generator. To show the correspondence in a precise way, we give an alternative and equivalent characterization of closure.

Proposition 4. *Let $\gamma \in L$ and consider the function $F_{\sqcup\gamma} : L \to L$ defined by $F_{\sqcup\gamma}(x) = F(x) \sqcup \gamma$, that is clearly monotone. Then, $\nabla_{F_{\sqcup\gamma}}(\bot) = \nabla_F(\gamma)$.*

Proof. To prove the statement it is enough to show that $y \in L$ is a pre-fixed point of $F_{\sqcup\gamma}$ iff y is a pre-fixed point of F and $y \geq \gamma$. This trivially follows from the definition of $F_{\sqcup\gamma}$ and $\sqcup$, indeed $F(y) \sqcup \gamma = F_{\sqcup\gamma}(y) \leq y$ is equivalent to $F(y) \leq y$ and $\gamma \leq y$. $\qquad \square$

By this alternative characterization we can formally state the correspondence with the two steps for defining $Gen(\mathcal{I}, \gamma)$.

Theorem 1. *Let $\mathcal{I}$ be an inference system and $\gamma, \beta \in \wp(\mathcal{U})$, with β closed w.r.t. $F_{\mathcal{I}}$, then the following facts hold:*

1. $(F_{\mathcal{I}})_{\sqcup\gamma} = F_{(\mathcal{I}_{\sqcup\gamma})}$ *(so we can safely omit brackets)*
2. $\nabla_{F_{\mathcal{I}}}(\gamma) = Ind(\mathcal{I}_{\sqcup\gamma})$
3. $\Delta_{F_{\mathcal{I}}}(\beta) = CoInd(\mathcal{I}_{\cap\beta})$.

Proof. 1. We have to show that, for $S \subseteq \mathcal{U}$, $(F_{\mathcal{I}})_{\sqcup\gamma}(S) = F_{(\mathcal{I}_{\sqcup\gamma})}(S)$. If $c \in (F_{\mathcal{I}})_{\sqcup\gamma}(S)$, then either $c \in \gamma$ or $c \in F_{\mathcal{I}}(S)$; in the former case there exists $\dfrac{-}{c} \in \mathcal{I}_{\sqcup\gamma}$ by definition, in the latter there exists $\dfrac{Pr}{c} \in \mathcal{I}$ such that $Pr \subseteq S$, and this implies $\dfrac{Pr}{c} \in \mathcal{I}_{\sqcup\gamma}$. Therefore in both cases $c \in F_{(\mathcal{I}_{\sqcup\gamma})}(S)$.

Conversely, if $c \in F_{(\mathcal{I}_{\sqcup\gamma})}(S)$, then there exists $\dfrac{Pr}{c} \in \mathcal{I}_{\sqcup\gamma}$ such that $Pr \subseteq S$. By definition of $\mathcal{I}_{\sqcup\gamma}$, either $\dfrac{Pr}{c} \in \mathcal{I}$ or $c \in \gamma$ and $Pr = \emptyset$, therefore in the former case $c \in F_{\mathcal{I}}(S)$ and in the latter $c \in \gamma$, thus in both cases $c \in (F_{\mathcal{I}})_{\sqcup\gamma}(S)$.

2. By Proposition 4 we get that $\nabla_{F_{\mathcal{I}}}(\gamma) = \nabla_{F_{\mathcal{I}_{\sqcup\gamma}}}(\emptyset)$, that is, the least fixed point of $F_{\mathcal{I}_{\sqcup\gamma}}$, thanks to statement (1) of this proposition and Proposition 2. Therefore, it corresponds to the *inductive interpretation* of the inference system $\mathcal{I}_{\sqcup\gamma}$, $Ind(\mathcal{I}_{\sqcup\gamma})$.

3. Let $X = CoInd(\mathcal{I}_{\sqcap\beta})$, we have to show the two inclusions. First note that X is a post-fixed point w.r.t. $F_{\mathcal{I}}$, indeed $X \subseteq F_{\mathcal{I}_{\sqcap\beta}}(X)$, by definition of the coinductive interpretation, and $F_{\mathcal{I}_{\sqcap\beta}}(X) \subseteq F_{\mathcal{I}}(X)$, since each $c \in F_{\mathcal{I}_{\sqcap\beta}}(X)$ is the consequence of a rule $\dfrac{Pr}{c} \in \mathcal{I}_{\sqcap\beta}$ and by construction of $\mathcal{I}_{\sqcap\beta}$, this rule is also a rule of $\mathcal{I}$, therefore $c \in F_{\mathcal{I}}(X)$. In addition $c \in \beta$ again by definition of $\mathcal{I}_{\sqcap\beta}$, thus $X \subseteq \beta$, therefore by (CoIND) we get $X \subseteq \Delta_{F_{\mathcal{I}}}(\beta)$.

On the other hand $\Delta_{F_{\mathcal{I}}}(\beta)$ is a post-fixed point of $F_{\mathcal{I}_{\sqcap\beta}}$. To show this fact first we note that for each $S \subseteq \beta$ we have $F_{\mathcal{I}}(S) \subseteq F_{\mathcal{I}_{\sqcap\beta}}(S)$, indeed if $c \in F_{\mathcal{I}}(S)$ then there exists a rule $\dfrac{Pr}{c} \in \mathcal{I}$ such that $Pr \subseteq S$, moreover we have that $F_{\mathcal{I}}(S) \subseteq F_{\mathcal{I}}(\beta) \subseteq \beta$ since β is closed, so $\dfrac{Pr}{c} \in \mathcal{I}_{\sqcap\beta}$ that implies that $c \in F_{\mathcal{I}_{\sqcap\beta}}$. Then, since $\Delta_{F_{\mathcal{I}}}(\beta)$ is a post-fixed point of $F_{\mathcal{I}}$ below β, we get that $\Delta_{F_{\mathcal{I}}}(\beta) \subseteq F_{\mathcal{I}}(\Delta_{F_{\mathcal{I}}}(\beta)) \subseteq F_{\mathcal{I}_{\sqcap\beta}}(\Delta_{F_{\mathcal{I}}}(\beta))$, so it is a post-fixed point. Therefore by the coinduction principle we get the other inclusion.

Thanks to Theorem 1, we can conclude that, given an inference system with coaxioms $(\mathcal{I}, \gamma)$:

$$Gen(\mathcal{I}, \gamma) = CoInd(\mathcal{I}_{\sqcap Ind(\mathcal{I}_{\sqcup\gamma})}) = \Delta_{F_{\mathcal{I}}}(\nabla_{F_{\mathcal{I}}}(\gamma)) = Gen(F_{\mathcal{I}}, \gamma)$$

That is, the interpretation generated by coaxioms γ of the inference system $\mathcal{I}$ is exactly the bounded fixed point of $F_{\mathcal{I}}$ generated by γ.

Constructive Characterization of Bounded Fixed Point. The Kleene's theorem states that, under continuity hypotheses on F, we can characterize its greatest fixed point as the greatest lower bound of the descending chain obtained by repeatedly applying F to $\top$. By considering this theorem for the sublattice obtained as down-set of the bound, we can obtain a constructive characterization of the bounded fixed point generated by an element.

We recall some basic definitions. A *descending chain* in L is a set $C = \{x_i \mid i \in \mathbb{N}\} \subseteq L$ such that, for each $i \in \mathbb{N}$, $x_i \geq x_{i+1}$. A function $F \colon L \to L$ *preserves meet of descending chains* if and only if, for all descending chains C in L, we have $F(\sqcap C) = \sqcap F(C)$ where $F(C) = \{F(x_i) \mid x_i \in C\}$.

Given a function $F \colon L \to L$ and an element $\beta \in L$, set $C_{F,\beta} = \{F^n(\beta) \mid n \in \mathbb{N}\}$.

Proposition 5. *Let $F \colon L \to L$ be a function that preserves meet of descending chains, and $\beta \in L$ a pre-fixed point of F. Then:*

1. $C_{F,\beta}$ *is a descending chain in L*
2. $\Delta_F(\beta) = \sqcap C_{F,\beta}$, *that is, $\sqcap C_{F,\beta}$ is the greatest fixed point of F below β.*

Proof. 1. Since F preserves meet of descending chains, it is monotone, therefore, since β is pre-fixed, we get the thesis.

2. If β is an element of a complete lattice, then $L_\beta = \{x \in L \mid x \le \beta\}$ is also a complete lattice, with top element β. If β is a closed point of F, then F is a monotone endofunction on L_β and it still preserves meet of descending chains. Therefore applying Kleene's theorem to L_β we get the thesis.

$\square$

Note that for this constructive characterization we need an additional hypothesis on F. Under this assumption, the result of Proposition 5 immediately applies to our construction, as stated in the following corollary.

Corollary 1. *Let $F : L \to L$ be a function that preserves meet of descending chains, and $\gamma \in L$. Set $\beta = \nabla_F(\gamma)$. Then $Gen(F, \gamma) = \bigsqcap C_{F,\beta}$.*

Proof. By definition $Gen(F, \gamma) = \Delta_F(\beta)$. Since β is pre-fixed by Proposition 1 and F preserves meet of descending chains, by Proposition 5 we get the thesis. $\square$

The characterization introduced above is important, but requires stronger assumptions on the function F. We now state a weaker result that is often enough for proving soundness, as will be illustrated in Sect. 5.

Proposition 6. *Let $F : L \to L$ be monotone and $\beta \in L$ a pre-fixed point, then*

$$\Delta_F(\beta) = \Delta_F\left(\bigsqcap C_{F,\beta}\right)$$

hence, in particular, $\Delta_F(\beta) \le \bigsqcap C_{F,\beta}$.

Proof. Set $z = \bigsqcap C_{F,\beta}$. First of all we note that z is pre-fixed, indeed $F(z) \le \bigsqcap F^{n+1}(\beta) = \beta \sqcap \bigsqcap F^{n+1}(\beta) = z$. We prove separately the two inequalities.

- $\Delta_F(z) \le \Delta_F(\beta)$. By Proposition 2 $\Delta_F(z)$ is a fixed point, so in particular it is a post-fixed point, below z, by definition of $\bigsqcap$ we get $z \le \beta$, so by transitivity $\Delta_F(z) \le \beta$. By (COIND) we get $\Delta_F(z) \le \Delta_F(\beta)$.
- $\Delta_F(\beta) \le \Delta_F(z)$. By Proposition 2 $\Delta_F(\beta)$ is a fixed point, so in particular a post-fixed point, below β. We prove by arithmetic induction that $\Delta_F(\beta) \le F^n(\beta)$ for all $n \in \mathbb{N}$.
  Base $\Delta_F(\beta) \le F^0(\beta) = \beta$ already proved.
  Induction Let us assume $\Delta_F(\beta) \le F^n(\beta)$, so by monotonicity of F we get $F(\Delta_F(\beta)) \le F^{n+1}(\beta)$. Since $\Delta_F(\beta)$ is a post-fixed point, we have that $\Delta_F(\beta) \le F(\Delta_F(\beta))$, therefore by transitivity we get $\Delta_F(\beta) \le F^{n+1}(\beta)$.
  By definition of $\bigsqcap$ we get $\Delta_F(\beta) \le \bigsqcap C_{F,\beta} = z$, so by (COIND) we get $\Delta_F(\beta) \le \Delta_F(z)$.

Finally by anti-symmetry we get the equality. $\square$

Another way to read the lemma above is that, given a bound β, we obtain the same greatest fixed point if we take as bound $\bigsqcap C_{F,\beta}$. Indeed from Proposition 6 and point 1 of Proposition 5 we can say more: given a bound β which is pre-fixed, we obtain the same greatest fixed point below β if we take as bound any element $F^n(\beta)$ of the descending chain.

4   Proof Trees

In this section we formally define several proof-theoretic characterizations of inference systems with coaxioms, and prove their equivalence[3] with the model-theoretic characterization given in the previous section.

First of all we recall the standard definition of proof trees and proof-theoretic characterization of inference systems.

Definition 3. *Given an inference system $\mathcal{I}$, a* proof tree *in $\mathcal{I}$ is a tree whose nodes are (labeled with) judgments in $\mathcal{U}$, and there is a node c with set of children Pr only if there exists a rule $\dfrac{Pr}{c}$. If a proof tree t in $\mathcal{I}$ has root j, then we say that t is a proof tree for j, or that j has proof tree t, in $\mathcal{I}$.*

Theorem 2. *Given an inference system $\mathcal{I}$, and a judgment $j \in \mathcal{U}$,*

1. *$j \in CoInd(\mathcal{I})$ iff j has a proof tree in $\mathcal{I}$*
2. *$j \in Ind(\mathcal{I})$ iff j has a finite proof tree in $\mathcal{I}$.*

See [15, 23].

The first proof-theoretic characterization is based on the following theorem, which slightly generalizes the standard correspondence between proof trees in $\mathcal{I}$ and the coinductive interpretation of $\mathcal{I}$.

Theorem 3. *Given an inference system $\mathcal{I}$, and $\beta \subseteq \mathcal{U}$ a closed set of judgments, we have that, for all $j \in \mathcal{U}$, $j \in \Delta_{F_\mathcal{I}}(\beta)$ iff there exists a proof tree t for j in $\mathcal{I}$ such that each node of t is in β.*

Proof. By Theorem 1, $\Delta_{F_\mathcal{I}}(\beta) = \Delta_{F_{\mathcal{I}_{\sqcap\beta}}}(\mathcal{U}) = CoInd(\mathcal{I}_{\sqcap\beta})$. Thanks to Theorem 2 (1), we get that $j \in CoInd(\mathcal{I}_{\sqcap\beta})$ iff there exists a proof tree t for j in $\mathcal{I}_{\sqcap\beta}$. By Definition 3, each node of t is (labeled by) a consequence c of a rule in $\mathcal{I}_{\sqcap\beta}$, that is, $c \in \beta$ by definition of $\mathcal{I}_{\sqcap\beta}$, and this implies the thesis. ☐

As a particular case, we get our first proof-theoretic characterization

Corollary 2. *Given an inference system with coaxioms $(\mathcal{I}, \gamma)$ and a judgment $j \in \mathcal{U}$, we have that $j \in Gen(\mathcal{I}, \gamma)$ iff there exists a proof tree t for j in $\mathcal{I}$ such that each node of t has a finite proof tree in $\mathcal{I}_{\sqcup\gamma}$.*

Proof. By Theorem 1, $Gen(\mathcal{I}, \gamma) = \Delta_{F_\mathcal{I}}(\beta)$, with $\beta = \nabla_{F_\mathcal{I}}(\gamma)$. Thanks to Theorem 3, we get that, for all $j \in \mathcal{U}$, $j \in Gen(\mathcal{I}, \gamma)$ iff there exists a proof tree t for j in $\mathcal{I}$ such that each node of t is in β. Again by Theorem 1 we get that $\beta = Ind(\mathcal{I}_{\sqcup\gamma})$, so by Theorem 2 (2) we get that a node j' of t is in β iff there exists a finite proof tree for j' in $\mathcal{I}_{\sqcup\gamma}$. ☐

For the second proof-theoretic characterization, we need to define *approximated proof trees*.

In the definition below, let us denote by j_t the root of tree t.

---

[3] For the last, under the hypotheses of Proposition 5.

Definition 4. *Given an inference system with coaxioms $(\mathcal{I}, \gamma)$, the sets $\mathcal{T}_n$ of approximated proof trees of level n in $(\mathcal{I}, \gamma)$, for $n \in \mathbb{N}$, are inductively defined as follows:*

$$t \in \mathcal{T}_0 \quad \text{if } t \text{ finite proof tree in } \mathcal{I}_{\sqcup\gamma}$$

$$\frac{\mathcal{T}}{c} \in \mathcal{T}_n \text{ if } \frac{Pr}{c} \in \mathcal{I}, \ Pr = \{j_t \mid t \in \mathcal{T}\}, \text{ and } \mathcal{T} \subseteq \mathcal{T}_{n-1}$$

In other words, an approximated proof tree of level n in $(\mathcal{I}, \gamma)$ is a finite proof tree in $(\mathcal{I}, \gamma)$ where coaxioms can only be used at depth $\geq n$.

The following lemma states that approximated proof trees of level n correspond to the n-th element of the descending chain $C_{F_{\mathcal{I}}, \beta} = \{F_{\mathcal{I}}^n(\beta) \mid n \in \mathbb{N}\}$, with $\beta = \nabla_{F_{\mathcal{I}}}(\gamma) = Ind(\mathcal{I}_{\sqcup\gamma})$.

Lemma 1. *Given an inference system with coaxioms $(\mathcal{I}, \gamma)$, and a judgment $j \in \mathcal{U}$, we have that, for all $n \in \mathbb{N}$, $j \in F_{\mathcal{I}}^n(\nabla_{F_{\mathcal{I}}}(\gamma))$ iff j has an approximated proof tree of level n in $(\mathcal{I}, \gamma)$.*

Proof. Let β be $\nabla_{F_{\mathcal{I}}}(\gamma)$. We prove the thesis by induction on n.

Base If $n = 0$, then, by Theorem 1, $\beta = \nabla_{F_{\mathcal{I}}}(\gamma)$ corresponds to the inductive interpretation of $\mathcal{I}_{\sqcup\gamma}$, therefore the equivalence holds by Theorem 2 (2).

Induction We assume the equivalence for n and prove it for $n + 1$. We prove separately the two implications.

$\Rightarrow$ If $c \in F_{\mathcal{I}}^{n+1}(\beta)$, then there exists $\dfrac{Pr}{c} \in \mathcal{I}$ such that $Pr \subseteq F_{\mathcal{I}}^n(\beta)$. Hence, by inductive hypothesis, each judgment in Pr has an approximated proof tree of level n, that is, $Pr = \{j_t \mid t \in \mathcal{T}\}$, with $\mathcal{T} \subseteq \mathcal{T}_n$. Hence, $t = \dfrac{\mathcal{T}}{c}$ is a proof tree for c, and by definition, $t \in \mathcal{T}_{n+1}$.

$\Leftarrow$ If $t \in \mathcal{T}_{n+1}$ is an approximated proof tree for $c \in \mathcal{U}$, then, by definition, there exists $\dfrac{Pr}{c} \in \mathcal{I}$ such that $t = \dfrac{\mathcal{T}}{c}$, $Pr = \{j_t \mid t \in \mathcal{T}\}$, and $\mathcal{T} \subseteq \mathcal{T}_n$. By inductive hypothesis we have $Pr \subseteq F_{\mathcal{I}}^n(\beta)$, and, by definition of $F_{\mathcal{I}}$, this implies $c \in F_{\mathcal{I}}^{n+1}(\beta)$ as needed.

$\square$

Corollary 3. *Given an inference system with coaxioms $(\mathcal{I}, \gamma)$, and a judgment $j \in \mathcal{U}$, the following are equivalent:*

1. *$j \in Gen(\mathcal{I}, \gamma)$*
2. *there exists a proof tree t for j in $\mathcal{I}$ such that each node has an approximated proof tree of level n in $(\mathcal{I}, \gamma)$, for all $n \in \mathbb{N}$.*

Proof. By Theorem 1, Proposition 6, and Theorem 3, we get that, for all $j \in \mathcal{U}$, $j \in Gen(\mathcal{I}, \gamma)$ iff there exists a proof tree t for j in $\mathcal{I}$ such that each node j' of t is in $\bigcap C_{F_{\mathcal{I}}, \beta}$ with $\beta = \nabla_{F_{\mathcal{I}}}(\gamma)$. By Lemma 1, $j' \in \bigcap C_{F_{\mathcal{I}}, \beta}$ iff has an approximated proof tree of level n, for all $n \in \mathbb{N}$. $\square$

If the hypotheses of Proposition 5 are satisfied, then we get a simpler equivalent proof-theoretic characterization.

Corollary 4. *Given an inference system with coaxioms* $(\mathcal{I}, \gamma)$*, and a judgment* $j \in \mathcal{U}$*, if* $F_{\mathcal{I}}$ *preserves meet of descending chains, then the following are equivalent:*

1. $j \in Gen(\mathcal{I}, \gamma)$
2. j *has an approximated proof tree of level* n *in* $(\mathcal{I}, \gamma)$*, for all* $n \in \mathbb{N}$*.*

Proof. Let β be $\nabla_{F_{\mathcal{I}}}(\gamma)$. By Theorem 1 and Proposition 5, we get that $Gen(\mathcal{I}, \gamma) = \bigcap C_{F_{\mathcal{I}}, \beta}$, therefore the thesis follows immediately from Lemma 1. $\square$

5   Reasoning with Coaxioms

In this section we discuss proof techniques for inference systems with coaxioms.

Assume that $G = Gen(\mathcal{I}, \gamma)$ is the interpretation generated by coaxioms for some $(\mathcal{I}, \gamma)$, and that S (for "specification") is the intended set of judgments, called *valid* in the following.

Typically, we are interested in proving $S \subseteq G$ (*completeness*, that is, each valid judgment can be derived) and/or $G \subseteq S$ (*soundness*, that is, each derivable judgment is valid). Proving both properties amounts to say that the inference system with coaxioms actually defines the intended set of judgments.

In the following, set $\beta = \nabla_{F_{\mathcal{I}}}(\gamma) = Ind(\mathcal{I}_{\sqcup\gamma})$.

Completeness Proofs. To show completeness, we can use the bounded coinduction principle. Indeed, since $G = \Delta_{F_{\mathcal{I}}}(\beta)$, if $S \le \beta$ and S is a post-fixed point of $F_{\mathcal{I}}$, by (COIND) we get that $S \le G$. That is, using the notations of inference systems, to prove completeness it is enough to show that:

– $S \subseteq Ind(\mathcal{I}_{\sqcup\gamma})$
– $S \subseteq F_{\mathcal{I}}(S)$

We illustrate the technique on the inference system with coaxioms $(\mathcal{I}, \gamma)$ which defines the judgment $allPos(l, b)$ (page 7). Set S^{allPos} the set of pairs (l, b) where b is T if all the elements in l are positive, F otherwise. Completeness means that the judgment $allPos(l, b)$ can be proved, for all $(l, b) \in S^{allPos}$. By the bounded coinduction principle, it is enough to show that

– $S^{allPos} \subseteq Ind(\mathcal{I}_{\sqcup\gamma})$
– $S^{allPos} \subseteq F_{\mathcal{I}}(S^{allPos})$

To prove the first condition, we have to show that, for each $(l, b) \in S^{allPos}$, $allPos(l, b)$ has a *finite* proof tree in $\mathcal{I}_{\sqcup\gamma}$. This can be easily shown, indeed:

– If l contains a (first) non-positive element, hence $l = x_1 : \ldots : x_n : x : l'$ with $x_i > 0$ for $i \in [1..n]$, $x \le 0$, and $b = F$ then we can reason by arithmetic induction on n. Indeed, for $n = 0$, (l, b) is the consequence of the second rule with no premises, and for $n > 0$ it is the consequence of the third rule where we can apply the inductive hypothesis to the premise.

- If l contains only positive elements, hence $b = T$, then (l, b) is a coaxiom, hence it is the consequence of a rule with no premises in $\mathcal{I}_{\sqcup\gamma}$.

To prove the second condition, we have to show that, for each $(l, b) \in S^{allPos}$, $allPos(l, b)$ is the consequence of a rule with premises in S^{allPos}. This can be easily shown, indeed:

- If $l = \Lambda$, hence $b = T$, then $allPos(\Lambda, T)$ is the consequence of the first rule with no premises.
- If $l = x : l'$ with $x \leq 0$, hence $b = F$, then $allPos(l, F)$ is the consequence of the second rule with no premises.
- If $l = x : l'$ with $x > 0$, and $b = T$, hence $(l', T) \in S^{allPos}$, then $allPos(l, T)$ is the consequence of the third rule with premise (l', T), and analogously if $b = F$.

Soundness Proofs. To show soundness, it is convenient to use the alternative characterization in terms of approximated proof trees given in Sect. 4, as detailed below. First of all, from Proposition 6, $G \subseteq \bigcap\{F_{\mathcal{I}}^n(\beta) \mid n \geq 0\}$. Hence, to prove $G \subseteq S$, it is enough to show that $\bigcap\{F_{\mathcal{I}}^n(\beta) \mid n \geq 0\} \subseteq S$. Moreover, by Lemma 1, for all $n \in \mathbb{N}$, judgments in $F_{\mathcal{I}}^n(\beta)$ are those which have an approximated proof tree of level n. Hence, to prove set inclusion, we can show that all judgments which have an approximated proof tree of level n for each n are in S or equivalently, by contraposition, that judgments which are not in S, that is, non-valid judgments, fail to have an approximated proof tree of level n for some n.

We illustrate the technique again on the example of $allPos$. We have to show that, for each $(l, b) \notin S^{allPos}$, there exists $n \geq 0$ such that (l, b) cannot be proved by using coaxioms at level greater than n. By cases:

- If l contains a (first) non-positive element, hence $l = x_1 : \ldots : x_n : x : l'$ with $x_i > 0$ for $i \in [1..n]$, $x \leq 0$, then, assuming that coaxioms can only be used at a level greater than $n + 1$, (l, b) can only be derived by instantiating n times the third rule, and once the second rule, hence b cannot be T.
- If l contains only positive elements, then it is immediate to see that there is no finite proof tree for (l, F).

6 Taming Coaxioms: Advanced Examples

Mutual Recursion. Circular definitions involving inductive and coinductive judgments have no semantics in standard inference systems, because all judgments have to be interpreted either inductively, or coinductively. The same problem arises in the context of coinductive logic programming [32], where a logic program has a well-defined semantics only if inductive and coinductive predicates can be stratified: each stratum defines only inductive or coinductive predicates (possibly defined in a mutually recursive way), and cannot depend on predicates defined in upper strata. Hence, it is possible to define the semantics of a logic program only if there are no mutually recursive definitions involving both inductive and coinductive predicates.

We have already seen that an inductive inference system corresponds to a generalized inference system with no coaxioms, while a coinductive one corresponds to a generalized one where coaxioms consist of all judgments in $\mathcal{U}$; however, between these two extremes, coaxioms offer many other possibilities thus allowing a finer control on the semantics of the defined judgments.

There exist cases where two or more related judgments need to be defined recursively, but for some of them the correct interpretation is inductive, while for others is coinductive [5,31,32]. In such cases, coaxioms may be employed to provide the correct definition in terms of a single inference system with no stratification, although special care is required to get from the inference system the intended meaning of judgments. To see this, let us consider the judgment $path0(t)$, where t is an infinite tree[4] over $\{0,1\}$, which holds iff there exists a path starting from the root of t and containing just 0s; trees are represented as infinite terms of shape $tree(n,l)$, where $n \in \{0,1\}$ is the root of the tree, and l is the infinite list of its direct subtrees. For instance, if t_1 and t_2 are the trees defined by the syntactic equations

$$t_1 = tree(0,l_1) \qquad l_1 = t_2{:}t_1{:}l_1 \qquad t_2 = tree(0,l_2) \qquad l_2 = tree(1,l_1){:}l_2$$

then we expect $path0(t_1)$ to hold, but not $path0(t_2)$.

To define $path0$, we introduce an auxiliary judgment $is\_in0(l)$ testing whether an infinite list l of trees contains a tree t such that $path0(t)$ holds. Intuitively, we expect $path0$ and is_in0 to be interpreted coinductively and inductively, respectively; this reflects the fact that $path0$ checks a property universally quantified over an infinite sequence (a *safety* property in the terminology of concurrent systems): all the elements of the path must equal 0; on the contrary, is_in0 checks a property existentially quantified over an infinite sequence (a *liveness* property in the terminology of concurrent systems): the list must contain a tree t with a specific property (that is, $path0(t)$ must hold). Driven by this intuition, one could be tempted to define the following inference system with coaxioms for all judgments of shape $path0(t)$, and no coaxioms for judgments of shape $is\_in0(l)$:

$$\frac{is\_in0(l)}{path0(tree(0,l))} \qquad \frac{\bullet}{path0(t)} \qquad \frac{path0(t)}{is\_in0(t{:}l)} \qquad \frac{is\_in0(l)}{is\_in0(t{:}l)}$$

Unfortunately, because of the mutual recursion between is_in0 and $path0$, the inference system above does not capture the intended behavior: $is\_in0(l)$ is derivable for every infinite list of trees l, even when l does not contain a tree t with an infinite path starting from its root and containing just 0s.

To overcome this problem, we replace the judgment is_in0 with the more general one is_in, such that $is\_in(t,l)$ holds iff the infinite list l contains the tree t. Consequently, we can define the following generalized inference system:

$$\frac{is\_in(t,l) \quad path0(t)}{path0(tree(0,l))} \qquad \frac{\bullet}{path0(t)} \qquad \frac{}{is\_in(t,t{:}l)} \qquad \frac{is\_in(t,l)}{is\_in(t,t'{:}l)}$$

---

[4] For the purpose of this example, we only consider trees with infinite depth and branching.

Now the semantics of the system corresponds to the intended one, and we do not need to stratify the definitions into two separate inference systems.

Following the characterization in terms of proof trees and the proof techniques provided in Sects. 4 and 5, we can sketch a proof of correctness. Let S be the set where elements have either shape $path0(t)$, where t represents a tree with an infinite path of just 0s starting from its root, or $is\_in(t, l)$, where l represents an infinite list containing the tree t; then a judgment belongs to S iff it can be derived in the generalized inference system defined above.

Completeness: We first show that the set S is a post-fixed point, that is, it is consistent w.r.t. the inference rules, coaxioms excluded. Indeed, if t has an infinite path of 0s, then it has necessarily shape $tree(0, l)$, where l must contain a tree t' with an infinite path of 0s. Hence, the inference rule for $path0$ can be applied with premises $is\_in(t', l) \in S$, and $path0(t') \in S$. If an infinite list contains a tree t, then it has necessarily shape $t':l$ where, either $t = t'$, and hence the axiom for is_in can be applied, or $t \neq t'$ and t is contained in l, and hence the inference rule for is_in can be applied with premise $is\_in(t, l) \in S$.

We then show that S is bounded by the closure of the coaxioms. For the elements of shape $path0(t)$ it suffices to directly apply the corresponding coaxiom; for the elements of shape $is\_in(t, l)$ we can show that there exists a finite proof tree built possibly also with the coaxioms by induction on the first position (where the head of the list corresponds to 0) in the list where t occurs. If the position is 0 (base case), then $l = t:l'$, and the axiom can be applied; if the position is $n > 0$ (inductive step), then $l = t':l'$ and t occurs in l' at position $n - 1$, therefore, by inductive hypothesis, there exists a finite proof tree for $is\_in(t, l')$, therefore we can build a finite proof tree for $is\_in(t, l)$ by applying the inference rule for is_in.

Soundness: We first observe that the only finite proof trees that can be derived for $is\_in(t, l)$ are obtained by application of the axiom for is_in, hence $is\_in(t, l)$ holds iff there exists a finite proof tree for $is\_in(t, l)$ built with the inference rules for is_in. Then, we can prove that, if $is\_in(t, l)$ holds, then t is contained in l by induction on the inference rules for is_in. For the axiom (base case) the claim trivially holds, while for the other inference rule we have that if t belongs to l, then trivially t belongs to $t':l$.

For the elements of shape $path0(t)$ we first observe that by the coaxioms they all trivially belong to the closure of the coaxioms. Then, any proof tree for $path0(t)$ must be infinite, because there are no axioms but only one inference rule for $path0$ where $path0$ is referred in the premises; furthermore, such a rule is applicable only if the root of the tree is 0. We have already proved that if $is\_in(t, l)$ is derivable, then t belongs to l, therefore we can conclude that if $path0(t)$ is derivable, then t contains an infinite path starting from its root, and containing just 0s.

A Numerical Example. It is well known that real numbers in the closed interval [0,1] can be represented by infinite sequences $(d_i)_{i \in \mathbb{N}+}$ of decimal[5] digits,

---

[5] Of course the example can be generalized to any base $B \geq 2$.

where $\mathbb{N}^+$ denotes the set of all positive natural numbers. Indeed, $(d_i)_{i\in\mathbb{N}^+}$ represents the real number which is the limit of the series $\sum_{i=1}^{\infty} 10^{-i}d_i$ in the standard complete metric space of real numbers (such a limit always exists by completeness, because the associated sequence of partial sums is always a Cauchy sequence). Such a representation is not unique for all rational numbers in $[0,1]$ (except for the bounds 0 and 1) that can be represented by a finite sequence of digits followed by an infinite sequence of 0s; for instance, 0.42 can be represented either by the sequence $42\bar{0}$, or by the sequence $41\bar{9}$, where $\bar{d}$ denotes the infinite sequence containing just the digit d.

For brevity, for $r = (d_i)_{i\in\mathbb{N}^+}$, $[\![r]\!]$ denotes $\sum_{i=1}^{\infty} 10^{-i}d_i$ (that is, the real number represented by r). We want to define the judgment $add(r_1, r_2, r, c)$ which holds iff $[\![r_1]\!] + [\![r_2]\!] = [\![r]\!] + c$ with c an integer number; that is, $add(r_1, r_2, r, c)$ holds iff the addition of the two real numbers represented by the sequences r_1 and r_2 yields the real number represented by the sequence r with carry c. We will soon discover that, to get a complete definition for add, c is required to range over a proper superset of the set $\{0, 1\}$, differently from what one could initially expect.

We can define the judgment add with the following generalized inference system, where $\div$ and mod denote the integer division, and the remainder operator, respectively.

$$\frac{add(r_1, r_2, r, c)}{add(d_1{:}r_1, d_2{:}r_2, (s \bmod 10){:}r, s \div 10)} \, s = d_1 + d_2 + c$$

$$\frac{\bullet}{add(r_1, r_2, r, c)}$$

A real number in $[0,1]$ is represented by an infinite list of decimal digits, which, therefore, can always be decomposed as $d{:}r$, where d is the first digit (corresponding to the exponent -1), and r is the rest of the list of digits. Here, r_1, r_2, and r range over the set of infinite lists of decimal digits, while the carry must range over $\{-1, 0, 1, 2\}$ to support a complete definition. As clearly emerges from the proof of completeness provided below, besides the obvious values 0 and 1, the values -1 and 2 have to be considered for the carry to ensure a complete definition of add because both $add(\bar{0}, \bar{0}, \bar{9}, -1)$ and $add(\bar{9}, \bar{9}, \bar{0}, 2)$ hold, and, hence, should be derivable; these two judgments allow the derivation of an infinite number of other valid judgments, as, for instance, $add(1\bar{0}, 1\bar{0}, 1\bar{9}, 0)$ and $add(1\bar{9}, 1\bar{9}, 4\bar{0}, 0)$, respectively.

Also in this case we can sketch a proof of correctness: for all infinite sequences of decimal digits r_1, r_2 and r, and all $c \in \{-1, 0, 1, 2\}$, $add(r_1, r_2, r, c)$ is derivable iff $[\![r_1]\!] + [\![r_2]\!] = [\![r]\!] + c$.

Completeness: By the coaxioms we trivially have that each element $add(r_1, r_2, r, c)$ such that $[\![r_1]\!] + [\![r_2]\!] = [\![r]\!] + c$ with $c \in \{-1, 0, 1, 2\}$ belongs to the closure of the coaxioms.

To show that the unique inference rule of the system is consistent with the set of all correct judgments, let us assume that $[\![r'_1]\!] + [\![r'_2]\!] = [\![r']\!] + c'$ with $r'_1 = d_1{:}r_1$, $r'_2 = d_2{:}r_2$, $r' = d{:}r$ and $c' \in \{-1, 0, 1, 2\}$. Let us set $s = 10c' + d$, and $c = s - d_1 - d_2$, then $s \bmod 10 = d$ and $s \div 10 = c'$, and we get the desired conclusion of the inference rule, and the side condition holds; it remains to show that $[\![r_1]\!] + [\![r_2]\!] = [\![r]\!] + c$ with $c \in \{-1, 0, 1, 2\}$.

We first observe that by the properties of limits w.r.t. the usual arithmetic operations, and by definition of $[\![-]\!]$, for all infinite sequence r of decimal digits, if $r = d{:}r'$, then $[\![r]\!] = 10^{-1}(d + [\![r']\!])$; then, from the hypotheses we get the equality $d_1 + [\![r_1]\!] + d_2 + [\![r_2]\!] = d + [\![r]\!] + 10c'$, and, therefore, $[\![r_1]\!] + [\![r_2]\!] = [\![r]\!] + c$; finally, since $c = [\![r_1]\!] + [\![r_2]\!] - [\![r]\!]$, and $0 \leq [\![r_1]\!], [\![r_2]\!], [\![r]\!] \leq 1$, we get $c \in \{-1, 0, 1, 2\}$.

Soundness: Let $r_1' = d_1{:}r_1$, $r_2' = d_2{:}r_2$, and $r' = d{:}r$ be infinite sequences of decimal digits, and $c' \in \{-1, 0, 1, 2\}$; we observe that the judgment $add(r_1', r_2', r', c')$ can be derived from the unique inference rule only with the premise $add(r_1, r_2, r, c)$ where c must equal $10c' + d - d_1 - d_2$ and must range over $\{-1, 0, 1, 2\}$.

To prove soundness we show that if $[\![r_1']\!] + [\![r_2']\!] \neq [\![r']\!] + c'$, then $add(r_1', r_2', r', c')$ cannot be derived in the inference system. Let us set $\delta' = |[\![r']\!] + c' - [\![r_1']\!] - [\![r_2']\!]|$; obviously, under the hypothesis $[\![r_1']\!] + [\![r_2']\!] \neq [\![r']\!] + c'$, we get $\delta' > 0$. In particular, the following fact holds: if $\delta' > 4 \cdot 10^{-1}$, then $10c' + d - d_1 - d_2 \notin \{-1, 0, 1, 2\}$. Indeed, by the identity $[\![r]\!] = 10^{-1}(d + [\![r']\!])$ already used for the proof of completeness, we have that $\delta' = 10^{-1}|[\![r]\!] + c - [\![r_1]\!] - [\![r_2]\!]|$, with $c = 10c' + d - d_1 - d_2$; $10^{-1}([\![r]\!] + c - [\![r_1]\!] - [\![r_2]\!]) \geq 4 \cdot 10^{-1}$ implies $c \geq 3$ ($[\![r_1]\!], [\![r_2]\!], [\![r]\!] \in [0, 1]$), and, hence, $c = 10c' + d - d_1 - d_2 \notin \{-1, 0, 1, 2\}$. By duality, $10^{-1}([\![r]\!] + c - [\![r_1]\!] - [\![r_2]\!]) \leq -4 \cdot 10^{-1}$ implies $c \leq -2$, hence $c = 10c' + d - d_1 - d_2 \notin \{-1, 0, 1, 2\}$.

By virtue of this fact, and thanks to the hypotheses, we can prove by arithmetic induction over n that for all $n \geq 1$, if $\delta' \geq 4 \cdot 10^{-n}$, then there exists a finite proof tree for $add(r_1', r_2', r', c')$ where the coaxioms are applied at most at depth $n - 1$. The base case is directly derived from the previously proven fact. For the inductive step we observe that if the inference rule is applicable for deriving the conclusion $add(r_1', r_2', r', c')$, then we can apply the inductive hypothesis for the premise $add(r_1, r_2, r, c)$ since we have already shown that $\delta' = 10^{-1}\delta$, therefore $\delta \geq 4 \cdot 10^{-(n-1)}$.

We can now conclude by observing that if $[\![r_1']\!] + [\![r_2']\!] \neq [\![r']\!] + c'$, then there exists n such that $\delta' \geq 4 \cdot 10^{-n}$, therefore, by the previous result, we deduce that it is not possible to build a finite tree for $add(r_1', r_2', r', c')$ where the coaxioms are applied at arbitrary depth k (in particular, k is bounded by $n - 1$); therefore $add(r_1', r_2', r', c')$ cannot be derived in the inference system.

From the proof of soundness we can also deduce that if we let c range over $\mathbb{Z}$, then the inference system becomes unsound; for instance, $add(\bar{0}, \bar{0}, \bar{0}, 1)$ would be derivable, but $[\![\bar{0}]\!] + [\![\bar{0}]\!] \neq [\![\bar{0}]\!] + 1$:

$$\vdots$$
$$\frac{add(\bar{0}, \bar{0}, \bar{0}, 10^1)}{add(\bar{0}, \bar{0}, \bar{0}, 10^0)}$$

Big-Step Operational Semantics with Divergence. It is well-known that divergence cannot be captured by the big-step operational semantics of a programming language when semantic rules are interpreted inductively (that is, in the standard way) [4,6,23]. When rules are interpreted coinductively some partial result can be obtained under suitable hypotheses, but a practical way to capture divergence with a big-step operational semantics is to introduce two different forms of judgment [14,23]: one corresponds to the standard big-step evaluation relation, and is defined inductively, while the other one captures divergence, and is defined coinductively in terms of the inductive judgment, thus requiring stratification. Other approaches consist in considering coinductive trace-based big-step semantics [27], and flag-based big-step semantics [29].

Syntax of terms and values

$$e ::= v \mid x \mid e\ e \qquad v ::= \lambda x.e \qquad v_\infty ::= v \mid \infty$$

Semantic rules

$$(\text{coax})\ \frac{\bullet}{e \Rightarrow \infty} \qquad (\text{val})\ \frac{}{v \Rightarrow v} \qquad (\text{app})\ \frac{e_1 \Rightarrow \lambda x.e \quad e_2 \Rightarrow v \quad e[x \leftarrow v] \Rightarrow v_\infty}{e_1\ e_2 \Rightarrow v_\infty}$$

$$(\text{l-inf})\ \frac{e_1 \Rightarrow \infty}{e_1\ e_2 \Rightarrow \infty} \qquad (\text{r-inf})\ \frac{e_1 \Rightarrow v \quad e_2 \Rightarrow \infty}{e_1\ e_2 \Rightarrow \infty}$$

Fig. 1. Call-by-value big-step semantics of λ-calculus with divergence

With coaxioms a unique judgment can be defined in a more direct and compact way. We show[6] how this is possible for the standard call-by-value operational semantics of the λ-calculus in big-step style. Figure 1 defines syntax, values, and semantic rules. The meta-variable v ranges over standard values, that is, lambda abstractions, while v_∞ includes also divergence, represented by ∞. The evaluation judgment has the general shape $e \Rightarrow v_\infty$, meaning that either e evaluates to a value v (when $v_\infty \neq \infty$) or diverges (when $v_\infty = \infty$).

For what concerns the semantic rules, only a coaxiom is needed, stating that every expression may diverge. This ensures that ∞ can be the only allowed outcome for the evaluation of an expression which diverges; this can only happen when the corresponding derivation tree is infinite. Rule (val) is standard. Rule (app) deals with the evaluation of application when both expressions e_1 and e_2 do not diverge; the meta-variable v is required for the judgment $e_2 \Rightarrow v$ to guarantee convergence of e_2, while v_∞ is used for the result of the whole application, since the evaluation of the body of the lambda abstraction could diverge. As usual, $e[x \leftarrow v]$ denotes capture-avoiding substitution modulo α-renaming. Rules (l-inf) and (r-inf) cover the cases when either e_1 or e_2 diverges when trying to evaluate application, assuming that a left-to-right evaluation strategy has been imposed.

We show that the only judgment derivable for $e_\Delta = (\lambda x.x\ x)\lambda x.x\ x$ is $e_\Delta \Rightarrow \infty$. To this aim, we first disregard the coaxiom and exhibit an infinite derivation tree for the judgment $e_\Delta \Rightarrow v_\infty$, derivable for all v_∞:

---

[6] This example was inspired by Bart Jacobs.

$$(\text{app}) \ \dfrac{(\text{val}) \ \dfrac{}{\lambda x.x \ x \Rightarrow \lambda x.x \ x} \qquad (\text{val}) \ \dfrac{}{\lambda x.x \ x \Rightarrow \lambda x.x \ x} \qquad (\text{app}) \ \dfrac{\vdots}{(x \ x)[x \leftarrow \lambda x.x \ x] \Rightarrow v_\infty}}{(x \ x)[x \leftarrow \lambda x.x \ x] = e_\Delta \Rightarrow v_\infty}$$

In this particular case the derivation tree is also regular, but of course there are examples of divergent computations whose derivation tree is not regular. The vertical dots indicate that the derivation continues with the same repeated pattern. The derivation corresponds to the coinductive interpretation of the standard big-step semantics rules [4,23], which may exhibit non-deterministic behavior as happens for this example; however, here the coaxiom plays a crucial role by filtering out all undesired values, and, thus, leaving only the value ∞ representing divergence; indeed, by employing also the coaxiom, finite derivation trees can be built for $e_\Delta \Rightarrow v_\infty$ only when $v_\infty = \infty$. By Corollary 3 we can get an infinite sequence of approximating derivation trees of arbitrarily increasing level:

$$(\text{coax}) \ \dfrac{}{e_\Delta \Rightarrow \infty}$$

$$(\text{app}) \ \dfrac{(\text{val}) \ \dfrac{}{\lambda x.x \ x \Rightarrow \lambda x.x \ x} \qquad (\text{val}) \ \dfrac{}{\lambda x.x \ x \Rightarrow \lambda x.x \ x} \qquad (\text{coax}) \ \dfrac{}{(x \ x)[x \leftarrow \lambda x.x \ x] \Rightarrow \infty}}{(x \ x)[x \leftarrow \lambda x.x \ x] = e_\Delta \Rightarrow \infty}$$

$\vdots$

As a consequence, in the inference system with the coaxiom a valid infinite derivation tree can be built for $e_\Delta \Rightarrow v_\infty$ only when $v_\infty = \infty$.

7   Related Work

Inference systems [1] are widely adopted to formally define operational semantics, language translations, type systems, subtyping relations, and other relevant judgments. Although inference systems have been introduced for dealing with inductive recursive definitions, in the last two decades several authors have focused on their coinductive interpretation.

Cousot and Cousot [14] define divergence by the coinductive interpretation of an inference system which extends the big-step operational semantics. The same approach is followed by other authors [16,23,30]. Leroy and Grall [23] analyze two kinds of coinductive big-step operational semantics for the call-by-value λ-calculus, and study their relationships with the small-step and denotational semantics, and their suitability for compiler correctness proofs. Coinductive big-step semantics is used as well to reason on cyclic objects stored in memory [24,26], and to prove type soundness in Java-like languages [4,6]. Coinductive inference systems are also considered in the context of type analysis and subtyping for object-oriented languages [7,9].

More recently, several solutions have been proposed to extend existing programming languages to support corecursion, and are, therefore, more focused on operational aspects, and their corresponding implementation issues; contributions can be found for all main computational paradigms: logic [5,21,25], functional [18,19], and object-oriented programming [10,11].

For the logic paradigm, the starting point is *coinductive logic programming* (coLP) [32], an extension of logic programming which provides both a declarative and a sound but not complete operational semantics for coinductive predicates, the former based on the notion of complete Herbrand base (finite and infinite terms) and greatest fixed point. However, only the standard coinductive interpretation is supported, and mixing between inductive and coinductive predicates is only partially supported through stratification. Structural resolution [21] is an extension of the operational semantics for coLP not limited to regular derivations. Other proposals [5,25] provide more flexible operational semantics. The notion of `finally` clause [5] has inspired our notion of coaxiom: `finally` clauses are user-defined facts that are resolved when an infinite, but regular, derivation is detected, in replacement of the standard coinductive semantics. Despite the existing strong correlation with this paper, the semantics of `finally` clauses does not always coincide with a fixed point of the one step inference operator. Similar considerations apply also to the work on COFJ [10,11], where `with` clauses play a role similar to that of `finally` clauses for coLP. A first attempt to provide a denotational model for this language, overtaken by the present work, has been provided in [8].

CoCaml [18,19] is an extension of OCaml where the semantics of recursive functions can be parametric in an equation solver which can be either predefined, or explicitly provided by the programmer to support corecursion. The intuition suggests that choosing a solver corresponds to choose a specific partial order, in such a way that the desired function is a fixed point in the corresponding CPO. Among the several proposed solvers, the pre-defined *iterator solver* has an expressive power similar to that of the `finally` and `with` clauses mentioned above.

As already mentioned, the spirit of our work is very different from that on CoCaml, since we do not aim to extend a practical language with corecursion, but, rather, to provide a very general framework which smoothly extends the well-known notion of inference system, and that could be used in many useful contexts, as shown in Sect. 6. On the other hand, definitions of higher order functions cannot be directly supported by inference systems. The foundation of CoCaml [20] is based on the theory of recursion in the framework of coalgebras. Our approach, instead, relies on the standard complete lattice of powersets, with set inclusion as partial order. In this way, a single and simple model based on classical results works uniformly for any possible recursive definition expressed in terms of a generalized inference system.

Recursive and well-founded coalgebras [12] are a framework for generalized structural recursion.

Completely iterative algebras [2] and corecursive and anti-founded algebras [12] are frameworks for generalized structural corecursion; iterative algebras correspond to the rational case as opposed to the coinductive one.

In *guarded recursion* [13,28] a judgment can be proved by also using recursively the judgment itself, provided that such recursive call is *guarded* by introduction rules. The goal, similar to ours, is to obtain a unique fixed point, however, there is no counterpart of the guard notion in the general framework of inference systems.

8   Conclusion

We have presented a generalized notion of inference system by introducing coaxioms, to support flexible definitions of judgments by structural recursion on non-well-founded datatypes.

Consequently, we have generalized the meta-theory of inference systems by providing two equivalent semantics, one based on fixed points in a complete lattice, and the other on the notion of proof tree. In the former case, the semantics of an inference system is the greatest fixed point of its corresponding one step inference operator, below the least pre-fixed point containing the coaxioms; in the latter case, the standard notion of proof tree for the coinductive case is generalized by requiring coaxioms to be applicable "at an infinite depth".

We have provided proof techniques for proving soundness and completeness results and shown their application to a range of different examples.

A compelling direction for further developments is exploring mechanization in proof assistants and other proof techniques [17] for coaxioms.

A necessarily not complete prototype meta-interpreter has been implemented in SWI-Prolog[7] to test the examples provided in Sects. 2 and 6. SWI-Prolog offers a natural support to regular terms (a.k.a. cyclic terms) through unification, but examples involving non-regular terms (or derivations) cannot terminate.

Extending the notion of coaxiom in the setting of object-oriented and functional programming is more challenging, because of the gap between the underlying theories.

We plan to investigate the dual notion studied here: one could consider the least fixed point above the greatest post-fixed point contained in the coaxioms, instead of the greatest fixed point below the least pre-fixed point containing the coaxioms. In particular, it would be interesting studying inference systems for which the two different semantics coincide.

References

1. Aczel, P.: An introduction to inductive definitions. In: Handbook of Mathematical Logic. North Holland (1977)
2. Adámek, J., Milius, S., Velebil, J.: Iterative algebras at work. Math. Struct. Comput. Sci. **16**(6), 1085–1131 (2006)
3. Ancona, D.: Regular corecursion in Prolog. In: SAC 2012 - ACM Symposium on Applied Computing, pp. 1897–1902 (2012)
4. Ancona, D.: Soundness of object-oriented languages with coinductive big-step semantics. In: Noble, J. (ed.) ECOOP 2012. LNCS, vol. 7313, pp. 459–483. Springer, Heidelberg (2012)
5. Ancona, D.: Regular corecursion in Prolog. Comput. Lang. Syst. Struct. **39**(4), 142–162 (2013)

---

[7] Available at http://www.disi.unige.it/person/AnconaD/Software/esop17artifact.zip.

6. Ancona, D.: How to prove type soundness of Java-like languages without forgoing big-step semantics. In: FTfJP 2014 - Formal Techniques for Java-like Programs, pp. 1:1–1:6. ACM Press (2014)
7. Ancona, D., Corradi, A.: Sound and complete subtyping between coinductive types for object-oriented languages. In: Jones, R. (ed.) ECOOP 2014. LNCS, vol. 8586, pp. 282–307. Springer, Heidelberg (2014)
8. Ancona, D., Dagnino, F., Zucca, E.: Towards a model of corecursion with default. In: FTfJP 2016 - Formal Techniques for Java-like Programs (2016)
9. Ancona, D., Lagorio, G.: Coinductive type systems for object-oriented languages. In: Drossopoulou, S. (ed.) ECOOP 2009. LNCS, vol. 5653, pp. 2–26. Springer, Heidelberg (2009)
10. Ancona, D., Zucca, E.: Corecursive featherweight Java. In: FTfJP 2012 - Formal Techniques for Java-like Programs (2012)
11. Ancona, D., Zucca, E.: Safe corecursion in coFJ. In: FTfJP 2013 - Formal Techniques for Java-like Programs (2012)
12. Capretta, V., Uustalu, T., Vene, V.: Corecursive algebras: a study of general structured corecursion. In: Oliveira, M.V.M., Woodcock, J. (eds.) SBMF 2009. LNCS, vol. 5902, pp. 84–100. Springer, Heidelberg (2009). doi:10.1007/978-3-642-10452-7_7
13. Coquand, T.: Infinite objects in type theory. In: Barendregt, H., Nipkow, T. (eds.) TYPES 1993. LNCS, vol. 806, pp. 62–78. Springer, Heidelberg (1994)
14. Cousot, P., Cousot, R.: Inductive definitions, semantics and abstract interpretations. In: ACM Symposium on Principles of Programming Languages, pp. 83–94. ACM Press (1992)
15. Grall, H.: Proving fixed point. In: FICS 2010 - Fixed Points in Computer Science (2010)
16. Hughes, J., Moran, A.: Making choices lazily. In: FPCA 1995 - Functional Programming Languages and Computer Architecture, pp. 108–119. ACM Press (1995)
17. Hur, C., Neis, G., Dreyer, D., Vafeiadis, V.: The power of parameterization in coinductive proof. In: ACM Symposium on Principles of Programming Languages, pp. 193–206 (2013)
18. Jeannin, J., Kozen, D., Silva, A.: CoCaml: programming with coinductive types. Technical report, Computing and Information Science, Cornell University, December 2012
19. Jeannin, J.-B., Kozen, D., Silva, A.: Language constructs for non-well-founded computation. In: Felleisen, M., Gardner, P. (eds.) ESOP 2013. LNCS, vol. 7792, pp. 61–80. Springer, Heidelberg (2013)
20. Jeannin, J., Kozen, D., Silva, A.: Well-founded coalgebras, revisited. Math. Struct. Comput. Sci. FirstView, 1–21 (2016)
21. Johann, P., Komendantskaya, E., Komendantskiy, V.: Structural resolution for logic programming. In: Technical Communications of (ICLP 2015) (2015)
22. Lassez, J., Nguyen, V.L., Sonenberg, L.: Fixed point theorems and semantics: a folk tale. Inf. Process. Lett. **14**(3), 112–116 (1982)
23. Leroy, X., Grall, H.: Coinductive big-step operational semantics. Inf. Comput. **207**(2), 284–304 (2009)
24. Leroy, X., Rouaix, F.: Security properties of typed applets. In: MacQueen, D.B., Cardelli, L. (eds.) ACM Symposium on Principles of Programming Languages, pp. 391–403. ACM Press (1998)
25. Mantadelis, T., Rocha, R., Moura, P.: Tabling, rational terms, and coinduction finally together!. Theory Pract. Log. Program. **14**(4–5), 429–443 (2014)

26. Milner, R., Tofte, M.: Co-induction in relational semantics. Theor. Comput. Sci. **87**(1), 209–220 (1991)
27. Nakata, K., Uustalu, T.: Trace-based coinductive operational semantics for while. In: Berghofer, S., Nipkow, T., Urban, C., Wenzel, M. (eds.) TPHOLs 2009. LNCS, vol. 5674, pp. 375–390. Springer, Heidelberg (2009)
28. Pavlovic, D.: Guarded induction on final coalgebras. Electron. Notes Theor. Comput. Sci. **11**, 140–157 (1998)
29. Poulsen, C.B., Mosses, P.D.: Flag-based big-step semantics. J. Log. Algebr. Methods Program. (2016). http://www.sciencedirect.com/science/article/pii/S2352220816300311
30. Schmidt, D.A.: Trace-based abstract interpretation of operational semantics. Lisp Symb. Comput. **10**(3), 237–271 (1998)
31. Simon, L.: Extending logic programming with coinduction. Ph.D. thesis, University of Texas at Dallas (2006)
32. Simon, L., Bansal, A., Mallya, A., Gupta, G.: Co-logic programming: extending logic programming with coinduction. In: ICALP 2007 - International Colloquium on Automata, Languages and Programming, pp. 472–483 (2007)
33. Simon, L., Mallya, A., Bansal, A., Gupta, G.: Coinductive logic programming. In: Etalle, S., Truszczyński, M. (eds.) ICLP 2006. LNCS, vol. 4079, pp. 330–345. Springer, Heidelberg (2006)
34. Tarski, A.: A lattice-theoretical fixpoint theorem and its applications. Pac. J. Math. **5**(2), 285–309 (1955)

Observed Communication Semantics
for Classical Processes

Robert Atkey[(✉)]

MSP Group, University of Strathclyde, Glasgow, UK
robert.atkey@strath.ac.uk

Abstract. Classical Linear Logic (CLL) has long inspired readings of
its proofs as communicating processes. Wadler's CP calculus is one of
these readings. Wadler gave CP an operational semantics by selecting
a subset of the cut-elimination rules of CLL to use as reduction rules.
This semantics has an appealing close connection to the logic, but does
not resolve the status of the other cut-elimination rules, and does not
admit an obvious notion of observational equivalence. We propose a new
operational semantics for CP based on the idea of observing communication. We use this semantics to define an intuitively reasonable notion
of observational equivalence. To reason about observational equivalence,
we use the standard relational denotational semantics of CLL. We show
that this denotational semantics is adequate for our operational semantics. This allows us to deduce that, for instance, all the cut-elimination
rules of CLL are observational equivalences.

1 Introduction

Right from Girard's introduction of Classical Linear Logic (CLL) [16], it has
appeared to offer the tantalising hope of a "Curry-Howard for Concurrency":
a logical basis for concurrent computation, analogous to the standard Curry-
Howard correspondence between intuitionistic logic and sequential computation
in typed λ-calculi [10,18]. To realise this hope, Abramsky proposed a programme
of "Processes as Proofs" [2] in the early nineties. Abramsky [1] and Bellin and
Scott [7] interpreted CLL proofs as terms in process calculi, matching (CUT)-
reduction to process reduction. However, these correspondences interpret CLL
proofs in an extremely restricted set of processes – those which never deadlock and
never exhibit racy or nondeterministic behaviour – and so their correspondences
could reasonably be criticised as not really capturing concurrency. Ehrhard and
Laurent [14] attempted to remedy this problem by demonstrating a correspondence between a finitary π-calculus and Differential Linear Logic. However, their
work was forcefully criticised by Mazza [23], who points out that there are crucial
differences in how both systems model nondeterminism, and further states:

> [...] all further investigations have failed to bring any deep logical insight
> into concurrency theory, in the sense that no concurrent primitive has
> found a convincing counterpart in linear logic, or anything even remotely

© Springer-Verlag GmbH Germany 2017
H. Yang (Ed.): ESOP 2017, LNCS 10201, pp. 56–82, 2017.
DOI: 10.1007/978-3-662-54434-1_3

resembling the perfect correspondence between functional languages and intuitionistic logic. In our opinion, we must simply accept that linear logic is not the right framework for carrying out Abramsky's "proofs as processes" program (which, in fact, more than 20 years after its inception has yet to see a satisfactory completion).

Despite the apparent failure of Abramsky's programme for concurrency, there has recently been interest in using Linear Logic as a basis for calculi of *structured communication*, also known as *session types*. Session types were originally proposed by Honda [17] in the context of the π-calculus as a way to ensure that processes conform to a protocol. The linear logic-based study of session types was initiated by Caires and Pfenning [9], who presented an assignment of π-calculus terms to sequent calculus proofs of Intuitionistic Linear Logic (ILL) that interprets the connectives of ILL as session types in the sense of Honda. The fundamental ideas of Caires and Pfenning were later adapted by Wadler to CLL [35,36], yielding a more symmetric system of "Classical Processes" (CP).

Wadler presents CP as a calculus with an associated reduction relation, and shows that there is a type preserving translation into Gay and Vasconcelos' functional language with session-typed communication [15]. This translation was later shown to also preserve reduction semantics, and to be reversible, by Lindley and Morris [20], establishing that CP can be seen as a foundational calculus for session-typed communication.

In this paper, we take a more direct approach to CP. We treat CP as a programming language in its own right by endowing it with an operational semantics, a notion of observational equivalence, and a denotational semantics. We do this for several reasons: *(i)* if CLL is intended as a logical foundation for programming with structured communication, there ought to be a way of interpreting CP processes as executable artefacts with observable outputs, which, as we argue below, Wadler's reduction semantics does not; *(ii)* establishing a theory of observational equivalence for CP resolves the status of the (CUT)-elimination rules on non-principal cuts by reading them as observational equivalences; and *(iii)* we can use the rich theory of denotational semantics for CLL (see, e.g., Melliès [25]) to reason about observational equivalence in CP. We further envisage that the introduction of denotational semantics into the theory of CP and session types will lead to further development of CP as a foundational calculus for session-typed communication.

1.1 Problems with Wadler's Reduction Semantics for CP

Our starting point is in asking the following question:

What is the observable output of a CP process?

The semantics proposed by Wadler [36] defines a reduction relation between CP processes, derived from the CUT-elimination rules for principal cuts. For example, processes that transmit and receive a choice interact via the following rule:

$$\nu x.(x[i].P \mid x.\text{case}(Q_0, Q_1)) \implies \nu x.(P \mid Q_i)$$

Here, a shared communication channel is established by the $\nu x.(- \mid -)$ construct, which is the syntax for the (CUT) rule. The $x[i].P$ emits a bit i along channel x and continues as P, while $x.\text{case}(Q_0, Q_1)$ receives a bit along x and proceeds as Q_0 or Q_1 according to the value of that bit.

A problem arises with CP processes that have free channels that are not connected to any other process. Since CP uses π-calculus notation, there is a relatively rigid left-to-right sequentialisation of actions. This means that the presence of attempts to communicate along unconnected channels can block other communication. An example is the following process, where communication along the unconnected x' channel blocks the communication across x:

$$\nu x.(x'[0].x[1].P \mid x.\text{case}(Q_0, Q_1))$$

This arrangement corresponds to (CUT)-elimination for a "non-principal" cut, i.e. the formula being cut in is not the last one introduced on both sides. In these cases, (CUT)-elimination commutes the offending rule past the (CUT) rule:

$$x'[0].\nu x.(x[1].P \mid x.\text{case}(Q_0, Q_1))$$

The rules that perform these rearrangements that do not correspond to any actual communication are referred to as "commuting conversions". They serve to bubble "stuck" communication to the outermost part of a process term.

With the reduction rules as proposed, we have two answers to our question. If a CP process P has no free channels, then we can always apply reduction rules corresponding to actual interaction, but we will never see the results of any of these interactions. Since CP is strongly normalising (a property it inherits from CLL [3]), all closed processes have the same termination behaviour, so this does not distinguish them. (CP, as presented by Wadler, does not admit completely closed processes unless we also include the (MIX$_0$) rule, as we do here.)

Alternatively, if a CP process P has free channels, then we can use the commuting conversion rules to move the stuck prefixes to the outermost layer. We could then either proceed to eliminate all (CUT)s deeper in the process term, or we could halt immediately, in the style of weak reduction in the λ-calculus.

This approach is appealing because it corresponds to the similar approach to defining the result of λ-calculus/proof-term reduction in sequential programming. We could also define a natural equivalence between CP processes in terms of barbed bisimulations [26], using the topmost action as the barb. However, in a multi-output calculus like CP, we run into ambiguity. The process:

$$\nu x.(y[0].x[1].P \mid z[0].x.\text{case}(Q_0, Q_1))$$

can be converted in two steps to:

$$y[0].z[0].\nu x.(x[1] \mid x.\text{case}(Q_0, Q_1)) \quad \text{or} \quad z[0].y[0].\nu x.(x[1] \mid x.\text{case}(Q_0, Q_1))$$

Intuitively, these processes are equivalent. Processes connected to distinct channels in CP are always independent so it is not possible for any observer to correlate communication over the channels y and z and to determine the difference between these processes. We could treat all CP processes quotiented by these permutations, but that would presuppose these equivalences, rather than having them induced by the actual behaviour of CP processes. (Bellin and Scott do such an identification in [7], pg. 14, rule (1).) If we were to define observational equivalence of CP processes via barbed bisimulation of CP processes up to permutations, then we would be effectively building the consequences of linearity into the definition of equivalence, rather than deducing them.

Another approach to resolving the non-determinism problem is to restrict processes to having one free channel that is designated as "the" output channel. With only one channel there can be no ambiguity over the results of the ordering of commuting conversions. This is the path taken in Caires and Pfenning's [9] ILL-based formalism. Pérez *et al.* [27] define a notion of observational equivalence for Caires and Pfenning's system based on a Labelled Transition System (LTS) over processes with one free channel. CLL, and hence CP, do not have a notion of distinguished output channel. Indeed, it is not immediately obvious why a process dealing with multiple communication partners ought to designate a particular partner as "the one" as Caires and Pfenning's system does.

1.2   A Solution: Observed Communication Semantics

We appear to have a tension between two problems. CP processes need partners to communicate with, but if we connect two CP processes with the (CUT) rule we cannot observe what they communicate! If we leave a CP process's channels free, then we need reduction rules that do not correspond to operationally justified communication steps, and we admit spurious non-determinism unless we make ad-hoc restrictions on the number of free channels.

Our solution is based on the idea that the observed behaviour of a collection of processes is the data exchanged between them, not their stuck states. In sequential calculi, stuck computations are interpreted as values, but this viewpoint does not remain valid in the world of message-passing communicating processes.

We propose a new operational semantics for CP on the idea of "visible" applications of the (CUT) rule that allow an external observer to see the data transferred. We define a big-step evaluation semantics that assigns observations to "configurations" of CP processes. For example, the configuration:

$$\vdash_c x[1].x[] \mid_x x.\mathrm{case}(x().0, x().0) :: \cdot \mid x : 1 \oplus 1$$

consists of a pair of CP processes $x[1].x[]$ and $x.\mathrm{case}(x().0, x().0)$ that will communicate over the public channel x, indicated by the $\mid_x$ notation. The split typing context on the right hand side indicates that there are no unconnected channels, $\cdot$, and one observable channel $x : 1 \oplus 1$.

Our semantics assigns the observation to $(1, *)$ to this configuration:

$$(x[1].x[] \mid_x x.\mathrm{case}(x().0, x().0)) \Downarrow (1, *)$$

This observation indicates that "1" was transferred, followed by "end-of-session".

Observations in our operational semantics are only defined for configurations with no free channels. Hence we do not have the problem of processes getting stuck for lack of communication partners, and the rules of our operational semantics (Fig. 3) are only concerned with interactions and duplication and discarding of servers. There is no need for non-operational steps.

Our operational semantics enables us to define observational equivalence between CP processes in the standard way: if two processes yield the same observed communications in all contexts, then they are observationally equivalent (Definition 1). We will see that the (CUT)-elimination rules of CLL, seen as equations between CP terms are observational equivalences in our sense (Sect. 5).

Proving observational equivalences using our definition directly is difficult, for the usual reason that the definition quantifies over all possible contexts. Therefore, we define a denotational semantics for CP processes and configurations, based on the standard relational semantics for CLL (Sect. 3). This denotational semantics affords us a compositional method for assigning sets of potential observable communication behaviours to CP processes and configurations. In Sect. 4 we show that, on closed configurations, the operational and denotational semantics agree, using a proof based on ⊥⊥-closed Kripke logical relations. Coupled with the compositionality of the denotational semantics, adequacy yields a sound technique for proving observational equivalences.

1.3 Contributions

This paper makes three contributions to logically-based session types:

1. In Sect. 2, we define a communication observing semantics for Wadler's CP calculus. This semantics assigns observations to "configurations" of processes that are communicating over channels. The data communicated over these channels constitutes the observations an external observer can make on a network of processes. Our semantics enables a definition of observational equivalence for CP processes that takes into account the restrictions imposed by CP's typing discipline.
2. In Sect. 4, we show that the standard "folklore" relational semantics of CLL proofs (spelt out in Sect. 3) is adequate for the operational semantics via a logical relations argument. Adequacy means that we can use the relational semantics, which is relatively straightforward to calculate with, to reason about observational equivalence. An additional conceptual contribution is the reading of the relational semantics of CLL in terms of observed communication between concurrent processes.
3. We use the denotational semantics to show that all of the standard CUT-elimination rules of CLL are observational equivalences in our operational semantics, in Sect. 5. This means that the CUT-elimination rules can be seen as a sound equational theory for reasoning about observational equivalence. We also show that permutations of communications along independent channels are observational equivalences.

In Sect. 7, we assess the progress made in this paper and point to areas for future work.

2   Observed Communication Semantics for CP

2.1   Classical Processes

Wadler's CP is a term language for sequent calculus proofs in Girard's Classical Linear Logic (CLL), with a syntax inspired by the π-calculus [31].

Formulas. The formulas of CLL are built by the following grammar:

$$A, B ::= 1 \mid \bot \mid A \otimes B \mid A \,\bindnasrepma\, B \mid A \oplus B \mid A \,\&\, B \mid\, !A \mid\, ?A$$

The connectives of CLL are collected into several groupings, depending on their proof-theoretic behaviour. As we shall see, these groupings will also have relevance in terms of their observed communication behaviour.

The connectives 1, $\bot$, $\otimes$ and $\bindnasrepma$ are referred as the *multiplicatives*, and $\oplus$ and $\&$ are the *additives*. Multiplicatives correspond to matters of communication topology, while the additives will correspond to actual data transfer. The ! and ? connectives are referred to as the *exponential* connectives, because they allow for unrestricted duplication of the multiplicative structure. Another grouping of the connectives distinguishes between the *positive* connectives 1, $\otimes$, $\oplus$, and ! that describe output, and the *negative* connectives $\bot$, $\bindnasrepma$, $\&$ and ? that describe input. Positive and negative are linked via *duality*: each A has a dual $A^\perp$:

$$
\begin{aligned}
1^\perp &= \bot & \bot^\perp &= 1 \\
(A \otimes B)^\perp &= A^\perp \,\bindnasrepma\, B^\perp & (A \,\bindnasrepma\, B)^\perp &= A^\perp \otimes B^\perp \\
(A \oplus B)^\perp &= A^\perp \,\&\, B^\perp & (A \,\&\, B)^\perp &= A^\perp \oplus B^\perp \\
(!A)^\perp &= ?A^\perp & (?A)^\perp &= !A^\perp
\end{aligned}
$$

The key to the structure of the CP calculus is that CLL formulas are types assigned to communication channels. Duality is how we transform the type of one end of a channel to the type of the other end. Hence the swapping of positive and negative connectives: we are swapping descriptions of input and output.

Example. The additive connective $\oplus$ indicates the transmission of a choice between two alternative sessions. Using the multiplicative unit 1 to represent the empty session, we can build a session type/formula representing transmission of a single bit, and its dual representing the receiving of a single bit:

$$Bit = 1 \oplus 1 \qquad\qquad Bit^\perp = \bot \,\&\, \bot$$

With these, we can build the type of a server that accept arbitrarily many requests to receive two bits and return a single bit:

$$Server = !(Bit^\perp \,\bindnasrepma\, Bit^\perp \,\bindnasrepma\, Bit \otimes 1)$$

We read this type as making the following requirements on a process: the outer ! indicates that it must allow for arbitrarily many uses; it then must receive two

Structural

$$\frac{}{\vdash x \leftrightarrow y :: x : A, y : A^\perp} \text{ (Ax)} \qquad \frac{\vdash P :: \Gamma, x : A \qquad \vdash Q :: \Delta, x : A^\perp}{\vdash \nu x.(P|Q) :: \Gamma, \Delta} \text{ (Cut)}$$

$$\frac{}{\vdash 0 ::} \text{ (Mix}_0)$$

Multiplicative

$$\frac{}{\vdash x[] :: x : 1} \text{ (1)} \qquad \frac{\vdash P :: \Gamma}{\vdash x().P :: \Gamma, x : \perp} \text{ ($\perp$)} \qquad \frac{\vdash P :: \Gamma, y : A \qquad \vdash Q :: \Delta, x : B}{\vdash x[y].(P|Q) :: \Gamma, \Delta, x : A \otimes B} \text{ ($\otimes$)}$$

$$\frac{\vdash P :: \Gamma, y : A, x : B}{\vdash x(y).P :: \Gamma, x : A \,\invamp\, B} \text{ ($\invamp$)}$$

Additive

$$\frac{\vdash P :: \Gamma, x : A_i}{\vdash x[i].P :: \Gamma, x : A_0 \oplus A_1} \text{ ($\oplus_i$)} \qquad \frac{\vdash P :: \Gamma, x : A_0 \qquad \vdash Q :: \Gamma, x : A_1}{\vdash x.\text{case}(P,Q) :: \Gamma, x : A_0 \,\&\, A_1} \text{ (\&)}$$

Exponential

$$\frac{\vdash P :: ?\Gamma, y : A}{\vdash !x(y).P :: ?\Gamma, x : !A} \text{ (!)} \qquad \frac{\vdash P :: \Gamma, y : A}{\vdash ?x[y].P :: \Gamma, x : ?A} \text{ (?)}$$

$$\frac{\vdash P :: \Gamma, x_1 : ?A, x_2 : ?A}{\vdash P\{x_1/x_2\} :: \Gamma, x_1 : ?A} \text{ (C)} \qquad \frac{\vdash P :: \Gamma}{\vdash P :: \Gamma, x : ?A} \text{ (W)}$$

Fig. 1. Classical processes

bits, transmit a bit, and then signal the end of the session. We obtain the type of a compatible client by taking the dual of this type:

$$Client = Server^\perp = ?(Bit \otimes Bit \otimes Bit^\perp \,\invamp\, \perp)$$

We read this as requirements that are dual to those on the server: the ? indicates that it can use the server as many times as necessary, whereupon it must transmit two bits, receive a bit and receive an end of session signal.

Processes. Processes in CP communicate along multiple named and typed channels, which we gather into contexts $\Gamma = x_1 : A_1, \ldots, x_n : A_n$ where the channel names x_i are all distinct, and we do not care about order.

The syntax of processes in CP is given by the grammar:

$$P, Q ::= x \leftrightarrow x' \mid \nu x.(P|Q) \mid 0 \mid x[] \mid x().P \mid x[x'].(P|Q) \mid$$
$$x(x').P \mid x[i].P \mid x.\text{case}(P,Q) \mid ?x[x'].P \mid !x(x').P \qquad \text{where } i \in \{0,1\}$$

The rules defining CP are given in Fig. 1. They define a judgement $\vdash P :: \Gamma$, indicating that P is well-typed with respect to type assignment Γ. We differ from Wadler by writing P to the right of the $\vdash$; it is not an assumption.

The rules are divided into four groups. The first group are the *structural* rules: (Ax) introduces a process linking two channels, note the use of duality to type the two ends of the link; (Cut) establishes communication between two processes via a hidden channel x, again note the use of duality; and (Mix$_0$) is the nil process which performs no communication over no channels.

The second group contains the *multiplicative* rules. Following Wadler's notation, square brackets $[\cdots]$ indicate output and round brackets $(\cdots)$ indicate input. Thus (1) introduces a process that outputs an end-of-session signal and dually ($\perp$) introduces a process that inputs such. Likewise, ($\otimes$) introduces a process that outputs a fresh channel name for a forked-off process P to communicate on, and dually ($\mathfrak{P}$) inputs a channel name for it to communicate on in the future. Neither of these pairs communicates any unexpected information. By duality, if a $\otimes$ process is going to send a channel and fork a process, then it is communicating with a $\mathfrak{P}$ process that is ready to receive a channel and communicate with that process. In our semantics in Sect. 2.3, multiplicative connectives affect the structure of observations, but not their information content.

Processes that communicate information are introduced by the *additive* rules in the third group. The process introduced by ($\oplus_i$) transmits a bit i along the channel x, and continues using x according to the type A_i. Dually, (&) introduces processes that receive a bit, and proceed with either P or Q given its value.

The final group covers the *exponential* rules. The rule (!) introduces an infinitely replicable server process that can communicate according to the type A on demand. To ensure that this process is infinitely replicable, all of the channels it uses must also be connected to infinitely replicable servers, i.e., channels of type $?A_i$. We indicate the requirement that all the channels in Γ be of ?'d typed by the notation $?\Gamma$. Processes introduced by the (?) rule query a server process to obtain a new channel for communication. The exponentials are given their power by the structural rules (C) and (W). Contraction, by rule (C) allows a process to use the same server twice. Weakening, by the rule (W) allows a process to discard a channel connected to a server.

Example. As a programming language, CP is very low-level. We make use of the following syntactic sugar (from [4]) for transmitting and receiving bits along channels of type *Bit* and *Bit*$^{\perp}$:

$$x[\mathbf{0}].P \qquad\qquad \stackrel{\text{def}}{=} x[y].(y[0].y[]\mid P)$$
$$x[\mathbf{1}].P \qquad\qquad \stackrel{\text{def}}{=} x[y].(y[1].y[]\mid P)$$
$$\text{case } x.\{\mathbf{0}\mapsto P; \mathbf{1}\mapsto Q\} \stackrel{\text{def}}{=} x.\text{case}(x().P, x().Q)$$

Using these abbreviations, we can write an implementation of our *Server* type that computes the logical AND of a pair of bits:

$$\vdash\ !x(y).y(p).y(q).\text{case } p.\{$$
$$\mathbf{0}\mapsto \text{case } q.\{\mathbf{0}\mapsto y[\mathbf{0}].y[]; \mathbf{1}\mapsto y[\mathbf{0}].y[]\};$$
$$\mathbf{1}\mapsto \text{case } q.\{\mathbf{0}\mapsto y[\mathbf{0}].y[]; \mathbf{1}\mapsto y[\mathbf{1}].y[]\}\}:: x : Server$$

This process creates an infinitely replicable server via (!), receives two channels via ($\mathfrak{P}$), receives two bits along them, and in each case transmits the appropriate returned value and signals end of session. A dual client process is written so:

$$\vdash ?x[y].y[\mathbf{1}].y[\mathbf{1}].\text{case } y.\{\mathbf{0} \mapsto y().0; \mathbf{1} \mapsto y().0\} :: x : \textit{Client}$$

This process contacts a server, sends the bit $\mathbf{1}$ twice, and then, no matter the outcome, receives the end of session signal and halts.

2.2 Configurations

The well-typed process judgement $\vdash P :: \Gamma$ relates processes P to unconnected channels Γ. When processes communicate via the (CUT) rule, that communication is invisible to external observers: the common channel x is removed from the context. In order to make communication visible, we introduce configurations of processes. A configuration $\vdash_c C :: \Gamma \mid \Theta$ has unconnected channels Γ and connected but observable channels Θ. Observable channel contexts $\Theta = x_1 : A_1, \ldots, x_n : A_n$ are similar to normal channel contexts Γ, except that we identify contexts whose type assignments are the same up to duality. Thus, as observable channel contexts, $x : A \otimes B, y : C \oplus D$ is equivalent to $x : A \mathfrak{P} B, y : C \& D$. We make this identification because the CLL connectives encode two things: (i) the form of the communication and (ii) its direction (i.e., whether it is positive or negative). When observing communication, we are not interested in the direction, only the content. Hence identification up to duality.

Configurations are defined using the rules in Fig. 2. The rule (CFGPROC) treats processes as configurations with unconnected channels and no publicly observable channels. The (CFGCUT) rule is similar to the (CUT) rule in that it puts two configurations together to communicate, but here the common channel is moved to the observable channel context instead of being hidden. The remainder of the rules, (CFG0), (CFGW), and (CFGC) are the analogues of the structural rules of CP, lifted to configurations. The rule (CFGC) is required to contract channel names appearing in two separate processes in a configuration, and (CFGW) is required for weakening even when there are no processes in a configuration. There are no contraction or weakening rules for observable contexts Θ. Such contexts record connected channels, which cannot be discarded or duplicated.

$$\frac{\vdash P :: \Gamma}{\vdash_c P :: \Gamma \mid \cdot} \text{(CFGPROC)} \qquad \qquad \frac{}{\vdash_c \underline{0} :: \cdot \mid \cdot} \text{(CFG0)}$$

$$\frac{\vdash_c C_1 :: \Gamma_1, x : A \mid \Theta_1 \qquad \vdash_c C_2 : \Gamma_2, x : A^{\perp} \mid \Theta_2}{\vdash_c C_1 \mid_x C_2 :: \Gamma_1, \Gamma_2 \mid \Theta_1, \Theta_2, x : A} \text{(CFGCUT)}$$

$$\frac{\vdash_c C :: \Gamma \mid \Theta}{\vdash_c C :: \Gamma, x : ?A \mid \Theta} \text{(CFGW)} \qquad \frac{\vdash_c C :: \Gamma, x_1 : ?A, x_2 : ?A \mid \Theta}{\vdash_c C\{x_1/x_2\} :: \Gamma, x_1 : ?A \mid \Theta} \text{(CFGC)}$$

Fig. 2. Configurations of classical processes

We define a structural congruence $C_1 \equiv C_2$ on configurations, generated by commutativity and associativity (where permitted by the typing) for $|_x$, with $\underline{0}$ as the unit. Structural congruence preserves typing.

A configuration with no unconnected channels, $\vdash_c C :: \cdot \mid \Theta$, is called a *closed* configuration of type Θ. Closed configurations will be our notion of complete systems: the observed communication semantics we define below in Sect. 2.4 is only defined for closed configurations.

Example. Continuing our example from above, we can connect the server process *ServerP* to the client process *ClientP* in a configuration with a visible communication channel x, using the (CFGCUT) rule:

$$\vdash_c ServerP \mid_x ClientP :: \cdot \mid x : Server$$

Note that this configuration also has typing $\vdash_c ServerP \mid_x ClientP :: \cdot \mid x : Client$ due to the conflation of dual types in observation contexts.

2.3   Observations

Our observed communication semantics assigns observations to closed configurations. The range of possible observations is defined in terms of the types of the channels named in Θ. As stated above, observations only track the data flowing across a communication channel, not the direction. Therefore, the positive and negative connective pairs each have the same sets of possible observations:

$$
\begin{aligned}
[\![1]\!] &= [\![\bot]\!] &&= \{*\} \\
[\![A \otimes B]\!] &= [\![A \,\mathbin{⅋}\, B]\!] &&= [\![A]\!] \times [\![B]\!] \\
[\![A_0 \oplus A_1]\!] &= [\![A_0 \,\&\, A_1]\!] &&= \Sigma_{i \in \{0,1\}}.\, [\![A_i]\!] \\
[\![!A]\!] &= [\![?A]\!] &&= \mathcal{M}_f([\![A]\!])
\end{aligned}
$$

where $\mathcal{M}_f(X)$ denotes finite multisets with elements from X. We will use the $\emptyset$ for empty multiset, $\uplus$ for multiset union, and $\{a_1, \ldots, a_n\}$ for multiset literals.

The sets of possible observations for a given observation context $\Theta = x_1 : A_1, \ldots, x_n : A_n$ are defined as the cartesian product of the possible observations for each channel: $[\![\Theta]\!] = [\![x_1 : A_1, \ldots, x_n : A_n]\!] = [\![A_1]\!] \times \cdots \times [\![A_n]\!]$.

2.4   Observed Communication Semantics

Observable evaluation is defined by the rules in Fig. 3. These rules relate closed configurations $\vdash_c C :: \cdot \mid \Theta$ with observations $\theta \in [\![\Theta]\!]$. To derive $C \Downarrow \theta$ is to say that execution of C completes with observed communication θ. For convenience, in Fig. 3, even though observations θ are tuples with "anonymous" fields, we refer to the individual fields by the corresponding channel name. The rules in Fig. 3 makes use of the shorthand notation $C[-]$ to indicate that the matched processes involved in each rule may appear anywhere in a configuration.

The first rule, (STOP), is the base case of evaluation, yielding the trivial observation () for the empty configuration. The next three rules, (LINK), (COMM),

$$\frac{}{\underline{0} \Downarrow ()} \text{ (Stop)} \qquad \frac{C[C'\{x/y\}] \Downarrow \theta[x \mapsto a]}{C[x \leftrightarrow y \mid_y C'] \Downarrow \theta[x \mapsto a, y \mapsto a]} \text{ (Link)}$$

$$\frac{C[P \mid_x Q] \Downarrow \theta[x \mapsto a]}{C[\nu x.(P|Q)] \Downarrow \theta} \text{ (Comm)} \qquad \frac{C[\underline{0}] \Downarrow \theta}{C[0] \Downarrow \theta} \text{ (0)} \qquad \frac{C[P] \Downarrow \theta}{C[x[] \mid_x x().P] \Downarrow \theta[x \mapsto *]} \text{ (1⊥)}$$

$$\frac{C[P \mid_y (Q \mid_x R)] \Downarrow \theta[x \mapsto a, y \mapsto b]}{C[x[y].(P|Q) \mid_x x(y).R] \Downarrow \theta[x \mapsto (a,b)]} \text{ (⊗⅋)}$$

$$\frac{C[P \mid_x Q_i] \Downarrow \theta[x \mapsto a]}{C[x[i].P \mid_x x.\text{case}(Q_0, Q_1)] \Downarrow \theta[x \mapsto (i,a)]} \text{ (⊕\&)}$$

$$\frac{C[P \mid_y Q] \Downarrow \theta[y \mapsto a]}{C[!x(y).P \mid_x ?x[y].Q] \Downarrow \theta[x \mapsto \{a\}]} \text{ (!?)} \qquad \frac{C[C'] \Downarrow \theta}{C[!x(y).P \mid_x C'] \Downarrow \theta[x \mapsto \emptyset]} \text{ (!W)}$$

$$\frac{C[!x_1(y).P \mid_{x_1} (!x_2(y).P \mid_{x_2} C')] \Downarrow \theta[x_1 \mapsto \alpha, x_2 \mapsto \beta]}{C[!x_1(y).P \mid_{x_1} C'\{x_1/x_2\}] \Downarrow \theta[x_1 \mapsto \alpha \uplus \beta]} \text{ (!C)} \qquad \frac{C' \Downarrow \theta \qquad C \equiv C'}{C \Downarrow \theta} \text{ (≡)}$$

Fig. 3. Observed communication semantics

and (0) describe the behaviour of the processes introduced by the (Ax), (Cut) and (Mix₀) rules respectively. (Link) evaluates links via substitution of channel names; and the observed communication across the link is shared between the two channels. (Comm) evaluates two processes communicating over a private channel by evaluating them over a public channel and then hiding it. (0) evaluates the empty process 0 by turning it into the empty configuration $\underline{0}$.

The rules (1⊥), (⊗⅋), (⊕\&) and (!?) describe how processes introduced by dual pairs of rules interact across public channels, and the observed communication that results. For (1⊥), the trivial message $*$ is sent. For (⊗⅋), communication that occured across two independent channels is grouped into one channel. For (⊕\&), a single bit, i is transmitted, which is paired with the rest of the communication. For (!?), an observation arising from a single use of a server is turned into a multiset observation with a single element.

The rules (!W) and (!C) describe how server processes are discarded or duplicated when they have no clients or multiple clients respectively. In terms of observed communication, these correspond to multiset union ($\uplus$) and the empty multiset ($\emptyset$), respectively. Finally, the ($\equiv$) rule states that configuration semantics is unaffected by permutation of processes (we have elided the matching reordering within θ, following our convention of using channel names to identify parts of an observation).

Example. Our operational semantics assigns the following observation to the configuration we built at the end of Sect. 2.2:

$$(ServerP \mid_x ClientP) \Downarrow (\{((1, *), (1, *), (1, *), *)\})$$

We observe the two 1-bits sent by the client, the 1-bit returned by the server, and the final $*$ indicating end of session. The additional $*$s accompanying each bit are an artifact of our encoding of bits as the formula $1 \oplus 1$.

2.5 Observational Equivalence

Observational equivalence between a pair of processes is defined as having the same set of observations in all typed contexts. By its definition in terms of typed contexts $CP[-]$, our definition of observational equivalence takes into account the (in)abilities of typed processes to interact with each other. In particular, the inability of CP processes to distinguish permutations of actions on distinct channels yields a family of observational equivalences (Fig. 8).

Our definition of observational equivalence is defined in terms of typed contexts $CP[-]$, which consist of configurations and processes with a single (typed) hole. Compared to the configuration contexts $C[-]$ in Fig. 3, configuration-process contexts allow the hole to appear within a process.

Definition 1. *Two processes* $\vdash P_1, P_2 :: \Gamma$ *are observationally equivalent, written* $P_1 \simeq P_2$, *if for all configuration-process contexts* $CP[-]$ *where* $\vdash_c CP[P_1] :: \cdot \mid \Theta$ *and* $\vdash_c CP[P_2] :: \cdot \mid \Theta$, *and all* $\theta \in [\![\Theta]\!]$, $CP[P_1] \Downarrow \theta \Leftrightarrow CP[P_2] \Downarrow \theta$.

Reasoning about observational equivalence is difficult, due to the quantification over all contexts. In the next two sections, we present a denotational semantics of CP which is sound for reasoning about observational equivalence.

3 Denotational Semantics of CP

The observed communication semantics of the previous section assigns observations to closed configurations. To reason about open configurations and processes, and hence observational equivalence, we require a semantics that assigns observations to processes and open configurations. We do this via a denotational semantics that interprets processes and open configurations as relations between the possible observations on each of their channels. Since CP processes are a syntax for CLL proofs, our denotations of processes will be identical to the relational semantics of proofs in CLL (see, for example, Barr [6]). We extend this semantics to configurations by interpreting them as relations between observations on their unconnected channels and observations on their connected channels. Compared to other denotational semantics for process calculi (e.g. [30,32]), this semantics is notable in its non-use of traces, synchronisation trees, or other temporally ordered formalism to record the I/O behaviour of processes. This is due to the linearity constraints imposed by the typing rules inherited from CLL, which enforce the invariant that distinct channels are completely independent. A trace-based semantics would impose an ordering on actions performed by processes which is not observable by a CP context. This "temporal-obliviousness" speaks to the point that CP is about structured communication determined by types, not about concurrency. We return to this in Sect. 5 when we discuss the observational equivalences between processes that permute independent actions.

In Sect. 4, we will see that on closed configurations the operational semantics and the denotational semantics agree.

3.1   Semantics of Formulas

The semantics of formulas does not take into account whether data is being transmitted or received; the relational semantics of CLL is sometimes referred to as "degenerate" in this sense. We discuss this further in Sect. 3.4. For now, we use the same interpretation of formulas as we did for observation contexts in Sect. 2.3:

$$
\begin{aligned}
[\![1]\!] &= [\![\bot]\!] &&= \{*\} \\
[\![A \otimes B]\!] &= [\![A \,\rotatebox[origin=c]{180}{\&}\, B]\!] &&= [\![A]\!] \times [\![B]\!] \\
[\![A_0 \oplus A_1]\!] &= [\![A_0 \,\&\, A_1]\!] &&= \Sigma_{i \in \{0,1\}}. [\![A_i]\!] \\
[\![!A]\!] &= [\![?A]\!] &&= \mathcal{M}_f([\![A]\!])
\end{aligned}
$$

The sets of possible observations for a given context $\Gamma = x_1 : A_1, \ldots, x_n : A_n$ are again defined as the cartesian product of the sets for each of the A_i:

$$
[\![\Gamma]\!] = [\![x_1 : A_1, \ldots, x_n : A_n]\!] = [\![A_1]\!] \times \cdots \times [\![A_n]\!]
$$

3.2   Semantics of Processes

The basic idea of the semantics of processes is that if $(a_1, \ldots, a_n) \in [\![\vdash P :: \Gamma]\!]$, then $(a_1, \ldots, a_n)$ is a possible observed behaviour of P along its unconnected channels. So, to every $\vdash P :: \Gamma$, we assign a subset of the interpretation of Γ:

$$
[\![\vdash P :: \Gamma]\!] \subseteq [\![\Gamma]\!]
$$

by induction on the derivation of $\vdash P :: \Gamma$. The (Ax) rule is interpreted by the diagonal relation, indicating that whatever is observed at one end of the linked channels is observed at the other:

$$
[\![\vdash x \leftrightarrow y :: x : A, y : A^\perp]\!] = \{(a, a) \mid a \in [\![A]\!]\}
$$

The (Cut) rule is interpreted by taking observations from both processes that share a common observation along the shared channel:

$$
[\![\vdash \nu x.(P|Q) :: \Gamma, \Delta]\!] = \{(\gamma, \delta) \mid (\gamma, a) \in [\![\vdash P :: \Gamma, x : A]\!], \\
(\delta, a) \in [\![\vdash Q :: \Delta, x : A^\perp]\!]\}
$$

The (Mix$_0$) rule is interpreted as the only possible observation in an empty context:

$$
[\![\vdash 0 :: \,]\!] = \{*\}
$$

The multiplicative units observe trivial data:

$$
\begin{aligned}
[\![\vdash x[] :: x : 1]\!] &= \{(*)\} \\
[\![\vdash x().P :: \Gamma, x : \bot]\!] &= \{(\gamma, *) \mid \gamma \in [\![\vdash P :: \Gamma]\!]\}
\end{aligned}
$$

For the multiplicative binary connectives, the ($\otimes$) rule is interpreted by combining the interpretations of its two subprocesses into a single observation; while the ($\wp$) rule is interpreted by pairing the observations on two channels into one.

$$[\![\vdash x[y].(P|Q) :: \Gamma, \Delta, x : A \otimes B]\!] = \{(\gamma, \delta, (a, b)) \mid (\gamma, a) \in [\![\vdash P :: \Gamma, y : A]\!],$$
$$(\delta, b) \in [\![\vdash Q :: \Delta, x : B]\!]\}$$
$$[\![\vdash x(y).P :: \Gamma, x : A \wp B]\!] = \{(\gamma, (a, b)) \mid (\gamma, a, b) \in [\![\vdash P :: \Gamma, y : A, x : B]\!]\}$$

For the additive connectives, sending bits via the ($\oplus_i$) rules is interpreted by prepending that bit on to the observation on that channel; and receiving a bit via (&) is interpreted by taking the union of possible observations:

$$[\![\vdash x[i].P :: \Gamma, x : A_0 \oplus A_1]\!] = \{(\gamma, (i, a)) \mid (\gamma, a) \in [\![\vdash P :: \Gamma, x : A_i]\!]\}$$
$$[\![\vdash x.\mathrm{case}(P_0, P_1) :: \Gamma, x : A_0 \mathbin{\&} A_1]\!]$$
$$= \bigcup_{i \in \{0,1\}} \{(\gamma, (i, a)) \mid (\gamma, a) \in [\![\vdash P_i :: \Gamma, x : A_i]\!]\}$$

For the exponential connectives, a "server" process introduced by the (!) rule is interpreted as the multiset of k-many observations of its underlying process, taking the union of their auxillary observations on the context $?\Gamma$. A "client" process introduced by (?) makes a singleton multiset's worth of observations:

$$[\![\vdash !x(y).P :: ?\Gamma, x : !A]\!] = \{((\biguplus_{j=1}^{k} \alpha_j^1, \dots, \biguplus_{j=1}^{k} \alpha_j^n, \{a_1, \dots, a_k \}) \mid$$
$$\forall i \in \{1, \dots, k\}.$$
$$(\alpha_i^1, \dots, \alpha_i^n, a_i) \in [\![\vdash P :: ?\Gamma, y : A]\!]\}$$
$$[\![\vdash ?x[y].P :: \Gamma, x : ?A]\!] = \{(\gamma, \{a\}) \mid (\gamma, a) \in [\![\vdash P :: \Gamma, y : A]\!]\}$$

The exponential structural rules dictate how singleton observations from client processes are combined, or channels are discarded. Contraction (C) is interpreted via multiset union, and weakening (W) is interpreted by the empty multiset:

$$[\![\vdash P\{x_1/x_2\} :: \Gamma, x_1 : ?A]\!] = \{(\gamma, \alpha_1 \uplus \alpha_2) \mid$$
$$(\gamma, \alpha_1, \alpha_2) \in [\![\vdash P :: \Gamma, x_1 : ?A, x_2 : ?A]\!]\}$$
$$[\![\vdash P :: \Gamma, x : ?A]\!] = \{(\gamma, \emptyset) \mid \gamma \in [\![\vdash P :: \Gamma]\!]\}$$

When these rules are put into communication with servers generated by (!) they will dictate the multiplicity of uses of the server process.

Example. We compute the denotation of the process *ServerP* from our running example to be the set of arbitrarily sized multisets of possible interactions with the underlying process:

$$[ServerP] = \{\{a_1, \dots, a_k \} \mid \forall i.a_i \in S\}$$

where the underlying process's denotation includes all possible 2^2 possibilities for inputs and relates them to the corresponding output (their logical AND):

$$S = \{((b_1, *), (b_2, *), (b_1 \wedge b_2, *), *) \mid b_1 \in \{0, 1\}, b_2 \in \{0, 1\}\}$$

The client's denotation is a singleton multiset (recording the fact that it uses the server only once). Dually to the server's denotation, the first two bits are determined but the last one is completely undetermined because we cannot know what the response from the server will be.

$$[\![ClientP]\!] = \{ \{\!\!\{ ((1, *), (1, *), (b, *), *) \}\!\!\} \mid b \in \{0, 1\} \}$$

3.3 Semantics of Configurations

The denotational semantics of configurations extends the semantics of processes to include the connected channels. Configurations $\vdash_c C :: \Gamma \mid \Theta$ are assigned subsets of $[\![\Gamma]\!] \times [\![\Theta]\!]$. The idea is that, if $((a_1, \dots, a_n), (b_1, \dots, b_n)) \in [\![\vdash_c C :: \Gamma \mid \Theta]\!]$, then $(a_1, \dots, a_n)$ and $(b_1, \dots, b_n)$ are a possible observed behaviour of C along its unconnected and connected channels respectively. We assign denotations to each configuration by structural recursion on their derivations:

$$[\![\Vdash_c \underline{0} :: \cdot \mid \cdot]\!] = \{(*, *)\}$$
$$[\![\Vdash_c P :: \Gamma \mid \cdot]\!] = \{(\gamma, *) \mid \gamma \in [\![\vdash P :: \Gamma]\!]\}$$
$$[\![\Vdash_c C_1 \mid_x C_2 :: \Gamma_1, \Gamma_2 \mid \Theta_1, \Theta_2, x : A]\!] =$$
$$\{((\gamma_1, \gamma_2), (\theta_1, \theta_2, a)) \mid ((\gamma_1, a), \theta_1) \in [\![\Vdash_c C_1 :: \Gamma_1, x : A \mid \Theta_1]\!],$$
$$((\gamma_2, a), \theta_2) \in [\![\Vdash_c C_2 :: \Gamma_2, x : A^\perp \mid \Theta_2]\!]\}$$
$$[\![\Vdash_c C :: \Gamma, x : ?A \mid \Theta]\!] = \{((\gamma, \emptyset), \theta) \mid (\gamma, \theta) \in [\![\Vdash_c C :: \Gamma \mid \Theta]\!]\}$$
$$[\![\Vdash_c C\{x_1/x_2\} :: \Gamma, x_1 : ?A \mid \Theta]\!] =$$
$$\{((\gamma, a_1 \uplus a_2), \theta) \mid ((\gamma, a_1, a_2), \theta) \in [\![\Vdash_c C :: \Gamma, x_1 : ?A, x_2 : ?A \mid \Theta]\!]\}$$

The interpretation of (CFG0), (CFGC), and (CFGW) are similar to the analogous rules for processes. The interpretation of (CFGCUT) is also similar, except that the observation on the shared channel is retained. The interpretation of (CFGPROC) lifts interpretations of processes up to configurations with no connected channels.

Example. Using the above rules, we compute the denotation of our example configuration linking our server to its client:

$$[\![\Vdash_c ServerP \mid_x ClientP :: \cdot \mid x :: Server]\!] = \{\{\!\!\{ ((1, *), (1, *), (1, *), *) \}\!\!\}\}$$

The denotation is the set with the single observation we computed in Sect. 2.4 for this configuration. In Sect. 4, we will see that this is no accident.

3.4 More Precise Semantics?

As we noted in Sect. 3.1, the relational semantics of CLL assigns the same interpretation to the positive and negative variants of each connective. Thus, the semantics of formulas do not model the direction of data flow for inputs and outputs. The logical relations we will define in Sect. 4 will refine the semantics of formulas to identify subsets of the observations possible for each formula that are actually feasible in terms of the input/output behaviour of connectives, but it is also possible to perform such a refinement purely at the level of the denotational semantics. Girard's motivating semantics for CLL was *coherence spaces* [16], which can be seen as a refined version of the relational semantics where particular distinguished subsets, *cliques*, are identified as the possible denotations of processes. The defining property of coherence spaces is that for every clique α in a coherence space and every clique β in its dual, the intersection $\alpha \cap \beta$ has at most one element. The coherence space semantics can be extended to configurations by stipulating that subsets X assigned to configurations must satisfy the property that if (γ_1, θ_1) and (γ_2, θ_2) are both in X, then whenever γ_1 and γ_2 are coherent (i.e., $\{\gamma_1, \gamma_2\}$ is a clique), then $\theta_1 = \theta_2$. The semantics for configurations in Sect. 3.3 satisfies this property, and the adequacy proof in the next section goes through unchanged.

Operationally, this means that CP processes can only interact in at most one way. Therefore, using a coherence space semantics would consistute a semantic proof of determinacy for CP with our semantics. It might be possible to go further and use Loader's *totality spaces* [22], which stipulate that cliques in dual spaces have exactly one element in their intersection, to also prove termination. However, the construction of exponentials in totality spaces is not clear.

4 Adequacy

We now present our main result: on closed configurations, the operational and denotational semantics agree. Consequently, we can use the denotational semantics to reason about observational equivalences between CP processes (Sect. 5).

Theorem 1. *If $\vdash_c C :: \cdot \mid \Theta$, then $C \Downarrow \theta$ iff $\theta \in [\![\vdash_c C :: \cdot \mid \Theta]\!]$.*

The forwards direction of this theorem states that if an observation can be generated by the evaluation rules, then it is also within the set of possible observations predicted by the denotational semantics. This is straightfoward to prove by induction on the derivation of $C \Downarrow \theta$. The backwards direction, which states that the denotational semantics predicts evaluation, is more complex and occupies the rest of this section.

4.1 Agreeability via $\bot\bot$-Closed Logical Relations

We adapt the standard technique for proving adequacy for sequential languages [28] and use a logical relation to relate open configurations with denotations. For each channel name x and CLL formula A, we use ternary relations that relate observable contexts, denotations, and configurations, which we call *agreeability relations*:

$$X \subseteq \Sigma\Theta{:}\mathsf{ObsCtxt}.\ \mathcal{P}([\![A]\!] \times [\![\Theta]\!]) \times \mathrm{Cfg}(x : A \mid \Theta) \tag{1}$$

where $\mathsf{ObsCtxt}$ is the set of observable contexts, $\mathcal{P}$ is the power set, and $\mathrm{Cfg}(x : A \mid \Theta)$ is the set of well-typed configurations $\vdash_c C :: x : A \mid \Theta$. We are interested in special agreeability relations: those that are closed under double negation.

Negation. Given an agreeability relation X for a channel $x : A$, its negation $X^\perp$ is an agreeability relation for $x : A^\perp$. Intuitively, if X identifies a set of configurations and denotations with some property, then $X^\perp$ is the set of configurations and denotations that "interact well" with the ones in X. For our purposes, "interact well" means that the communication we observe when the two configurations interact is predicted by their associated denotations.

Definition 2 (Negation). *Let X be a relation for $x : A$ as in* (1). *Its negation $X^\perp$ is a relation for $x : A^\perp$, defined as:*

$$X^\perp = \{(\Theta', \alpha', C') \mid \forall (\Theta, \alpha, C) \in X, \theta, \theta', a.$$
$$(a, \theta) \in \alpha \wedge (a, \theta') \in \alpha' \Rightarrow (C \mid_x C') \Downarrow (\theta, \theta', a)\}$$

We are interested in agreeability relations that are $\perp\perp$-closed: $X^{\perp\perp} = X$. These are related denotations and configurations that "interact well with anything that interacts well with them". This kind of double-negation closure was used by Girard [16] to construct the Phase Space semantics of CLL and to show weak normalisation. Ehrhard notes that double-negation closure is a common feature of many models of CLL [13]. Double-negation, $(\cdot)^{\perp\perp}$, has the following properties, which mean that it is a closure operator [12]:

Lemma 1. *1. $X \subseteq X^{\perp\perp}$;*
2. If $X \subseteq Y$, then $Y^\perp \subseteq X^\perp$;
3. $X^{\perp\perp\perp} = X^\perp$.

By (3), $X^{\perp\perp}$ is automatically $\perp\perp$-closed for any agreeability relation X.

Duplicable and Discardable. We generalise the duplicable and discardable capability of !'d processes (the (!C) and (!W) rules) to arbitrary configurations with one free channel of !'d type:

Definition 3 (Duplicable and Discardable). *A configuration $\vdash_c C :: x : !A \mid z_1 : !B_1, \ldots, z_n : !B_n$ is*

1. duplicable if, for all $\vdash_c C' :: \Gamma, x : ?A^\perp, x' : ?A^\perp \mid \Theta$,

$$D[(C' \mid_x C) \mid_{x'} C\{x'/x, z'_1/z_1, \ldots, z'_n/z_n\}] \Downarrow$$
$$\theta \begin{bmatrix} x \mapsto \alpha, & z_1 \mapsto \alpha_1, \ldots, z_n \mapsto \alpha_n, \\ x' \mapsto \alpha', z'_1 \mapsto \alpha'_1, \ldots, z'_n \mapsto \alpha'_n \end{bmatrix}$$

implies

$$D[C'\{x/x'\} \mid_x C] \Downarrow \theta[x \mapsto \alpha \uplus \alpha', z_1 \mapsto \alpha_1 \uplus \alpha'_1, \ldots, z_n \mapsto \alpha_n \uplus \alpha'_n]$$

2. discardable if, for all $\vdash_c C' :: \Gamma \mid \Theta$, $D[C'] \Downarrow \theta$ implies that $D[C' \mid_x C] \Downarrow \theta[x \mapsto \emptyset, z_1 \mapsto \emptyset, \ldots, z_n \mapsto \emptyset]$.

The definition of *duplicability* uses the (CFGC) rule to ensure that the second configuration is well-typed. Likewise, *discardability* uses the (CFGW) rule. The next lemma states that configurations built from duplicable and discardable

$$\llbracket x : 1 \rrbracket \qquad = \{(\cdot, \{*\}, C) \mid C \equiv x[]\}^{\perp\perp}$$

$$\llbracket x : \perp \rrbracket \qquad = \llbracket x : 1 \rrbracket^{\perp}$$

$$\llbracket x : A \otimes B \rrbracket \quad = \{((\Theta', \Theta), \alpha, C) \mid C \equiv (\cdots (x[x'].(P'|P) \mid_{y'_1} D'_1) \cdots \mid_{y_n} D_n),$$
$$\alpha = \{((a, b), \theta', \theta) \mid (a, \theta') \in \beta', (b, \theta) \in \beta\},$$
$$(\Theta', \beta', (\cdots (P' \mid_{y'_1} D'_1) \cdots \mid_{y'_n} D'_n)) \in \llbracket x' : A \rrbracket,$$
$$(\Theta, \beta, (\cdots (P \mid_{y_1} D_1) \cdots \mid_{y_n} D_n)) \in \llbracket x : B \rrbracket\}^{\perp\perp}$$

$$\llbracket x : A \,\invamp\, B \rrbracket \quad = \llbracket x : A^{\perp} \otimes B^{\perp} \rrbracket^{\perp}$$

$$\llbracket x : A_0 \oplus A_1 \rrbracket = \{(\Theta, \alpha, C) \mid C \equiv (\cdots (x[i].P \mid_{y_1} D_1) \cdots \mid_{y_n} D_n),$$
$$\alpha = \{((i, a), \theta) \mid (a, \theta) \in \beta\},$$
$$(\Theta, \beta, (\cdots (P \mid_{y_1} D_1) \cdots \mid_{y_n} D_n)) \in \llbracket x : A_i \rrbracket\}^{\perp\perp}$$

$$\llbracket x : A_0 \,\&\, A_1 \rrbracket = \llbracket x : A_0^{\perp} \oplus A_1^{\perp} \rrbracket^{\perp}$$

$$\llbracket x : !A \rrbracket \qquad = \{(?\Theta, \alpha, C) \mid C \equiv (\cdots (!x(x').P \mid_{y_1} D_1) \cdots \mid_{y_n} D_n),$$
$$\alpha = \{(\langle a_1, \ldots, a_k \rangle, \biguplus_{i=1}^{k} \theta_i) \mid (a_i, \theta_i) \in \beta\},$$
$$(?\Theta, \beta, (\cdots (P \mid_{y_1} D_1) \cdots \mid_{y_n} D_n)) \in \llbracket x' : A \rrbracket,$$
$$C \text{ duplicable and discardable}\}^{\perp\perp}$$

$$\llbracket x : ?A \rrbracket \qquad = \llbracket x : !A^{\perp} \rrbracket^{\perp}$$

Fig. 4. $\perp\perp$-closed agreeability relations relating denotations and configurations

parts are themselves duplicable and discardable. We will use this in the proof of Lemma 4, below, when showing that processes of the form $!x(y).P$ agree with their denotations after they have been closed by connecting their free channels to duplicable and discardable configurations.

Lemma 2. *Let* $\vdash P :: x_1 : ?A_1, \ldots x_n : ?A_n, x' : A$ *be a process, and let* $\langle \vdash_c C_i :: x_i : !A_i \mid ?\Theta_i \rangle_{1 \leq i \leq n}$ *be duplicable and discardable configurations. Then the configuration*

$$\vdash_c (\cdots (!x(x').P \mid_{x_1} C_1) \cdots \mid_{x_n} C_n) :: x : !A \mid ?\Theta_1, x_1 : ?A_1, \cdots, ?\Theta_n, x_n : ?A_n$$

is duplicable and discardable.

Interpretation of Process Types. Figure 4 defines a $\perp\perp$-closed agreeability relation on $x : A$ for each CLL proposition A by structural recursion. We only need definitions for the positive cases, relying on negation for the negative cases. We ensure that all the positive cases are $\perp\perp$-closed by explicitly doing so. The negative cases are the negations of the positive cases, and hence are automatically $\perp\perp$-closed by Lemma 1.

The general method for each definition in Fig. 4 is to define what the "ideal" configuration inhabitant and denotation of each type looks like, and then use $\perp\perp$-closure to close that relation under all possible interactions. In the case of $x : 1$, there is one possible process, $x[]$, and denotation, $*$. For the $x : A \otimes B$ case, ideal inhabitants are composed of two inhabitants of the types A and B (processes P, P' plus their associated support processes D_i and D'_i). In the $x : A_0 \oplus A_1$ case, ideal inhabitants are processes that are inhabitants of A_i after outputting some i. For the exponentials, $x : !A$, the ideal inhabitant is one whose auxillary resources are all duplicable and discardable (indicated by the

$?\Theta$). In each case, the associated denotations are determined by the denotational semantics defined in Sect. 3.

Agreeable Processes. The definition of $[\![x : A]\!]$ defines what it means for configurations with one free channel to agree with a denotation. We use this definition to define what it means for a process to agree with its denotation by connecting it to configurations and denotations that are related and stating that the communications predicted by the denotations is matched by evaluation:

Definition 4. *A process* $\vdash P :: x_1 : A_1, \ldots, x_n : A_n$ *is* agreeable *if for all*

$$(\Theta_1, \alpha_1, C_1) \in [\![x_1 : A_1]\!]^{\perp}, \ldots, (\Theta_n, \alpha_n, C_n) \in [\![x_n : A_n]\!]^{\perp},$$

if $(a_1, \ldots, a_n) \in [\![\vdash P :: x_1 : A_1, \ldots, x_n : A_n]\!]$ *and* $(a_1, \theta_1) \in \alpha_1, \ldots, (a_n, \theta_n) \in \alpha_n$, *then*

$$(\cdots (P \mid_{x_1} C_1) \cdots \mid_{x_n} C_n) \Downarrow (\theta_1, a_1, \ldots, \theta_n, a_n)$$

Closing an agreeable process so that it has one free channel yields an inhabitant of the semantic type of the free channel:

Lemma 3. *If the process* $\vdash P :: x_1 : A_1, \ldots, x_n : A_n, x : A$ *is agreeable, then for all* $(\Theta_1, \beta_1, C_1) \in [\![x_1 : A_1]\!]^{\perp}, \ldots, (\Theta_n, \beta_n, C_n) \in [\![x_n : A_n]\!]^{\perp}$, *it is the case that*

$$((\Theta_1, x_1 : A_1, \ldots, \Theta_n, x_n : A_n), \alpha, (\cdots (P \mid_{x_1} C_1) \cdots \mid_{x_n} C_n)) \in [\![x : A]\!]$$

where
$$\alpha = \{(a, \theta_1, a_1, \ldots, \theta_n, a_n) \mid (a_1, \ldots, a_n, a) \in [\![P]\!], (a_1, \theta_1) \in \beta_1, \ldots, (a_n, \theta_n) \in \beta_n\}$$

For all processes, when connected to well-typed configurations, their denotational semantics predicts their behaviour:

Lemma 4. *All processes* $\vdash P :: \Gamma$ *are agreeable.*

Proof. (Sketch) By induction on the derivation of $\vdash P :: \Gamma$. The structural rules ((Ax), (Cut), (Mix$_0$)) all involve relatively straightforward unfoldings of the definitions. The rest of the rules follow one of two patterns, depending on whether they are introducing a negative or positive connective. For the negative connectives, $\perp, \invamp, \&, ?$, and for the contraction and weakening rules, we are using (cfgCut) to connect the configuration composed of P and configurations for the other free channels with a triple (Θ, α, C) that is a semantic inhabitant of the negation of a negative type. To proceed, we use the fact that the positive types are all defined via double-negation closure to deduce the following:

$$\forall (\Theta', \alpha', C').$$
$$(\forall (\Theta'', \alpha'', C'') \in \text{``ideal''}. \ (\Theta', \alpha', C') \perp (\Theta'', \alpha'', C'')) \Rightarrow$$
$$(\Theta, \alpha, C) \perp (\Theta', \alpha', C')$$

where "ideal" indicates the defining property of the negation of the formula being introduce, as defined in Fig. 4, and $-\perp-$ indicates the property that the denotational semantics correctly predicts the operational semantics when CUT-ing two configurations. Thus we can reason *as if* the triple (Θ, α, C) is an "ideal" inhabitant of the negation of the introduced type.

For the positive connectives, $1, \otimes, \oplus, !$, the situation is slightly simpler. By point (3) of Lemma 1, we deduce that, if (Θ, α, C) is the interacting process of the negation of the introduced type, then:

$$\forall (\Theta', \alpha', C') \in \text{"ideal"}. \ (\Theta', \alpha', C') \bot (\Theta, \alpha, C)$$

Therefore, our job is to prove that the newly introduced process conforms to the "ideal" specification introduced in Fig. 4. This is mostly straightforward, save for the (!) case, where we need an auxillary induction over the context $?\Gamma$ to deduce that all the configurations connected to these channels are themselves duplicable and discardable.

Agreeable Configurations. We now extend the definition of agreeability from processes to configurations. After we show that all configurations are agreeable, the special case of this definition for closed processes will give us the backwards direction of Theorem 1 (Corollary 1).

Definition 5. *A configuration* $\vdash_c C :: x_1 : A_1, \ldots, x_n : A_n \mid \Theta$ *is agreeable if for all* $(\Theta_1, \alpha_1, C_1) \in [\![x_1 : A_1]\!]^\bot, \ldots, (\Theta_n, \alpha_n, C_n) \in [\![x_n : A_n]\!]^\bot$, *and* $(a_1, \ldots, a_n, \theta) \in [\![\vdash_c C :: x_1 : A_1, \ldots, x_n : A_n \mid \Theta]\!]$ *and* $(a_1, \theta_1) \in \alpha_1, \ldots,$ *and* $(a_n, \theta_n) \in \alpha_n$, *then* $(\cdots (C \mid_{x_1} C_1) \cdots \mid_{x_n} C_n) \Downarrow (\theta, \theta_1, a_1, \ldots, \theta_n, a_n)$.

Lemma 5. *All configurations* $\vdash_c C :: \Gamma \mid \Theta$ *are agreeable.*

Proof. By induction on the derivation of $\vdash_c C :: \Gamma \mid \Theta$. Lemma 4 is used to handle the (CFGPROC) case, and all the other cases are similar to the corresponding case in the proof of Lemma 4.

When Γ is empty, Lemma 5 yields the backwards direction of Theorem 1:

Corollary 1. *If* $\vdash_c C :: \cdot \mid \Theta$ *and* $\theta \in [\![\vdash_c C :: \cdot \mid \Theta]\!]$, *then* $C \Downarrow \theta$.

5   Observational Equivalences

Theorem 1 enables us to predict the behaviour of processes without having to first embed them in a closing configuration. In particular, we can use it as a method for proving observational equivalences:

Corollary 2. *If* $\vdash P_1, P_2 :: \Gamma$ *and* $[\![P_1]\!] = [\![P_2]\!]$, *then* $P_1 \simeq P_2$.

Proof. For any closing configuration context $CP[-]$ and observation θ, we have:

$$\begin{aligned}
CP[P_1] \Downarrow \theta &\Leftrightarrow \theta \in [\![CP[P_1]]\!] \text{ by Theorem 1} \\
&\Leftrightarrow \theta \in [\![CP[P_2]]\!] \text{ since } [\![P_1]\!] = [\![P_2]\!] \\
&\Leftrightarrow CP[P_2] \Downarrow \theta \quad \text{by Theorem 1}
\end{aligned}$$

$$\frac{\vdash P :: \Gamma, x : A}{\vdash \nu x.(P|x \leftrightarrow y) \simeq P\{y/x\} :: \Gamma, y : A}$$

$$\frac{\vdash P :: \Gamma, x : A \qquad \vdash Q :: \Delta, x : A^{\perp}, y : B \qquad \vdash R :: \Sigma, y : B^{\perp}}{\vdash \nu x.(P|\nu y.(Q|R)) \simeq \nu y.(\nu x.(P|Q)|R) :: \Gamma, \Delta, \Sigma}$$

$$\frac{\vdash P :: \Gamma, x : A \qquad \vdash Q :: \Delta, x : A^{\perp}}{\vdash \nu x.(P|Q) \simeq \nu x.(Q|P) :: \Gamma, \Delta}$$

Fig. 5. Observational equivalences arising from permutation of cuts

$$\frac{\vdash P :: \Gamma}{\vdash \nu x.(x[]|x().P) \simeq P :: \Gamma}$$

$$\frac{\vdash P :: \Gamma, y : A \qquad \vdash Q :: \Delta, x : B \qquad \vdash R :: \Sigma, y : A^{\perp}, x : B^{\perp}}{\vdash \nu x.(x[y].(P|Q)|R) \simeq \nu y.(P|\nu x.(Q|R)) :: \Gamma, \Delta, \Sigma}$$

$$\frac{\vdash P :: \Gamma, x : A_i \qquad \vdash Q_0 :: \Delta, x : A_0^{\perp} \qquad \vdash Q_1 :: \Delta, x : A_1^{\perp}}{\vdash \nu x.(x[i].P \mid x.\mathrm{case}(Q_0, Q_1)) \simeq \nu x.(P|Q_i) :: \Gamma, \Delta}$$

$$\frac{\vdash P :: ?\Gamma, y : A \qquad \vdash A :: \Delta, y : A^{\perp}}{\vdash \nu x.(!x(y).P|?x[y].Q) \simeq \nu y.(P|Q) :: ?\Gamma, \Delta}$$

$$\frac{\vdash P :: ?\Gamma, y : A \qquad \vdash Q :: \Delta, x : ?A, x' : ?A}{\vdash \nu x.(!x(y).P|Q\{x/x'\}) \simeq \nu x.(!x(y).P|\nu x'.(!x'(y).P|Q)) :: ?\Gamma, \Delta}$$

$$\frac{\vdash P :: ?\Gamma, y : A \qquad \vdash Q :: \Delta}{\vdash \nu x.(!x(y).P|Q) \simeq Q :: \Delta}$$

Fig. 6. Observational equivalences arising from elimination of principal cuts

We now use this corollary to show that the cut elimination rules of CLL and permutation rules yield observational equivalences for our operational semantics. Since we have used the standard relational semantics of CLL, which is known to be equationally sound for cut-elimination [25], all these statements are immediate. The force of Corollary 2 is that these rules also translate to observational equivalences for our independently defined operational semantics.

CUT-*Elimination Rules.* Figure 5 shows the rules arising from the interaction of (CUT) with itself and the (AX) rule: (CUT) is associative and commutative, and has (AX) as an identity element. These rules amount to the observation that one can construct a category from CLL proofs (see Melliès [25], Sect. 2).

Figure 6 shows the rules arising from elimination of "principal cuts": (CUT) rule applications that are on a formula and its dual that are introduced by the two immediate premises. Oriented left-to-right, and restricted to top-level (i.e., not

$$\frac{\vdash P :: \Gamma, y : A, z : C \qquad \vdash Q :: \Delta, x : B \qquad \vdash R :: \Sigma, z : C^{\perp}}{\vdash \nu z.(x[y].(P|Q)|R) \simeq x[y].(\nu z.(P|R)|Q) :: \Gamma, \Delta, \Sigma, x : A \otimes B}$$

$$\frac{\vdash P :: \Gamma, y : A \qquad \vdash Q :: \Delta, x : B, z : C \qquad \vdash R :: \Sigma, z : C^{\perp}}{\vdash \nu z.(x[y].(P|Q)|R) \simeq x[y].(P|\nu z.(Q|R)) :: \Gamma, \Delta, \Sigma, x : A \otimes B}$$

$$\frac{\vdash P :: \Gamma, y : A, x : B, z : C \qquad \vdash Q :: \Delta, z : C^{\perp}}{\vdash \nu z.(x(y).P \mid Q) \simeq x(y).\nu z.(P|Q) :: \Gamma, \Delta, x : A \,\mathstrut^{\mkern-3mu\gamma\mkern-3mu} B}$$

$$\frac{\vdash P :: \Gamma, x : A_i, z : C \qquad \vdash Q :: \Delta, z : C^{\perp}}{\vdash \nu z.(x[i].P|Q) \simeq x[i].\nu z.(P|Q) :: \Gamma, \Delta, x : A_0 \oplus A_1}$$

$$\frac{\vdash P :: \Gamma, x : A, z : C \qquad \vdash Q :: \Gamma, x : B, z : C \qquad \vdash R :: \Delta, z : C^{\perp}}{\vdash \nu z.(x.\mathrm{case}(P,Q)|R) \simeq x.\mathrm{case}(\nu z.(P|R), \nu z.(Q|R)) :: \Gamma, \Delta, x : A \,\&\, B}$$

$$\frac{\vdash P :: ?\Gamma, y : A, z : ?C \qquad \vdash Q :: ?\Delta, z : !C^{\perp}}{\vdash \nu z.(!x(y).P|Q) \simeq !x(y).\nu z.(P|Q) :: ?\Gamma, ?\Delta, x : !A}$$

$$\frac{\vdash P :: \Gamma, y : A, z : C \qquad \vdash Q :: \Delta, z : C^{\perp}}{\vdash \nu z.(?x[y].P|Q) \simeq ?x[y].\nu z.(P|Q) :: \Gamma, \Delta, x : ?A}$$

$$\frac{\vdash P :: \Gamma, z : C \qquad \vdash Q :: \Delta, z : C^{\perp}}{\vdash \nu z.(x().P \mid Q) \simeq x().\nu z.(P|Q) :: \Gamma, \Delta, x : \perp}$$

Fig. 7. Observational equivalences arising from elimination of non-principal cuts (commuting conversions)

under a prefix), these are the rules that are taken as the reduction rules of CP by Wadler. They are also the inspiration for our evaluation rules in Fig. 3. However, here these rules are observational equivalences, so we can use them *anywhere* in process to replace two communicating processes with the result of their communication. Figure 7 presents the rules for eliminiating non-principal cuts: (CUT) rule applications where the cut formula is not the most recently introduced one. These rules are also called "commuting conversion" rules because they commute input/output prefixes with applications of the (CUT) rule in order to expose potential interactions. The fact that these are now observational equivalences formalises the informal statement given by Wadler in Sect. 3.6 of [36] that these rules are justified for CP. Note that the semantics we presented in Sect. 2.4 does not make use of commuting conversions. It only requires immediate interactions between process. Since there are no channels left unconnected, there is no way for a process to get stuck.

Permutation of Independent Channels. Figure 8 presents a set of observational equivalence rules arising from permutation of communication along independent channels. We have omitted the type information to save space. The admissibility

$$\vdash \qquad x().x'().P \simeq x'().x().P$$
$$\vdash \qquad x().x'[y'].(P|Q) \simeq x'[y'].(x().P|Q)$$
$$\vdash \qquad x().x'[y'].(P|Q) \simeq x'[y'].(P|x().Q)$$
$$\vdash \qquad x().x'(y').P \simeq x'(y').x().P$$
$$\vdash \qquad x().x'[i].P \simeq x'[i].x().P$$
$$\vdash \qquad x().x'.\mathsf{case}(P,Q) \simeq x'.\mathsf{case}(x().P, x().Q)$$
$$\vdash \qquad x().?x'[y'].P \simeq ?x'[y'].x().P$$
$$\vdash \qquad x[y].(x'[y'].(P|Q)|R) \simeq x'[y'].(x[y].(P|R)|Q)$$
$$\vdash \qquad x[y].(x'[y'].(P|Q)|R) \simeq x'[y'].(P|x[y].(Q|R))$$
$$\vdash \qquad x[y].(P|x'[y'].(Q|R)) \simeq x'[y'].(Q|x[y].(P|R))$$
$$\vdash \qquad x[y].(x'(y').P|Q) \simeq x'(y').x[y].(P|Q)$$
$$\vdash \qquad x[y].(P|x'(y').Q) \simeq x'(y').x[y].(P|Q)$$
$$\vdash \qquad x[y].(x'[i].P|Q) \simeq x'[i].x[y].(P|Q)$$
$$\vdash \qquad x[y].(P|x'[i].Q) \simeq x'[i].x[y].(P|Q)$$
$$\vdash \qquad x[y].(x'.\mathsf{case}(P,Q)|R) \simeq x'.\mathsf{case}(x[y].(P|R), x[y].(Q|R))$$
$$\vdash \qquad x[y].(P|x'.\mathsf{case}(Q,R)) \simeq x'.\mathsf{case}(x[y].(P|Q), x[y].(P|R))$$
$$\vdash \qquad x[y].(?x'[y'].P|Q) \simeq ?x'[y'].x[y].(P|Q)$$
$$\vdash \qquad x[y].(P|?x'[y'].Q) \simeq ?x'[y'].x[y].(P|Q)$$
$$\vdash \qquad x(y).x'(y').P \simeq x'(y').x(y).P$$
$$\vdash \qquad x(y).x'[i].P \simeq x'[i].x(y).P$$
$$\vdash \qquad x(y).x'.\mathsf{case}(P,Q) \simeq x'.\mathsf{case}(x(y).P, x(y).Q)$$
$$\vdash \qquad x(y).?x'[y'].P \simeq ?x'[y'].x(y).P$$
$$\vdash \qquad x[i].x'[j].P \simeq x'[j].x[i].P$$
$$\vdash \qquad x[i].x'.\mathsf{case}(P,Q) \simeq x'.\mathsf{case}(x[i].P|x[i].Q)$$
$$\vdash \qquad x[i].?x'[y'].P \simeq ?x'[y'].x[i].P$$
$$\vdash x.\mathsf{case}(x'.\mathsf{case}(P,Q), x'.\mathsf{case}(R,S)) \simeq x'.\mathsf{case}(x.\mathsf{case}(P,R), x.\mathsf{case}(Q,S))$$
$$\vdash \qquad x.\mathsf{case}(?x'[y'].P, ?x'[y'].Q) \simeq ?x'[y'].x.\mathsf{case}(P,Q)$$
$$\vdash \qquad ?x[y].?x'[y'].P \simeq ?x'[y'].?x[y].P$$

Fig. 8. Permutation of communication along independent channels

of these rules is an indication of the relative weakness of CP contexts to make observations on a process. If a process has a access to a pair of channels, the processes connected to the other ends of those channels must be independent, and so cannot communicate between themselves to discover which one was communicated with first. This is why the denotational semantics of CP that we defined in Sect. 3 does not explain processes' behaviour in terms of traces as is more common when giving denotation semantics to process calculi [30]. The typing constraints of CP mean that there is no global notion of time: the only way that a CP process can "know" the past from the future is by receiving a bit of information via the (&) rule. Everything else that a CP process does is pre-ordained by its type.

There are a large number of equations in Fig. 8 due to the need to account for the permutation of each kind of prefix with itself and with every other prefix. The ($\otimes$) rule is particularly bad due to the presence of two sub-processes, either of which may do perform the permuted action.

6   Related Work

Wadler's papers introducing CP, [35, 36], contain discussions of work related to the formulation of CP as a session-typed language derived from CLL, and how this relates to session types. Here, we discuss work related to logical relations and observational equivalences for session-typed calculi, and the use of denotational semantics for analysing the proofs of CLL.

Just as the Iron Curtain during the Cold War lead to the same work being done twice, once in the East and once in the West, the existence of two logically-based session-typed concurrency formalisms, one based on Intuitionistic Linear Logic (ILL) [9], and one based on Classical Linear Logic, means that analogous work is performed on both sides. (Indeed, ILL has both left and right rules for each connective, meaning that working with ILL-based formalisms already doubles the amount of work one needs to do.) Notions of observational equivalence and logical relations for πDILL have already been studied by Pérez et al. [27]. Pérez et al. use logical relations to prove strong normalisation and confluence for their session-typed calculus based on ILL, and define a notion of observational equivalence between session-typed processes, based on bisimulation. They prove observational equivalences based on the (CUT)-elimination rules of their calculus, analogous to ones we proved in the previous section.

As we noted in the introduction Pérez et al. define an LTS over stuck processes with one free output channel. They use this to coinductively define their notion of observational equivalence. This means that to prove individual equivalences requires the construction of the appropriate bisimulation relation. In contrast, our denotational technique for proving equivalences is much more elementary, involving only simple set theoretic reasoning. Moreover, their technique requires additional proofs that their definition of observational equivalence is a congruence, a fact that is immediate in our definition.

Pérez et al. go further than we have done in also proving that their calculus is strongly normalising and confluent, using a logical relations based proof. As we discussed in Sect. 3.4, it is possible to use a coherence space semantics to prove determinacy, and we conjecture that totality spaces can prove termination.

$\perp\perp$-closed relations are a standard feature of proofs in the meta-theory of Linear Logic: for example weak normalisation proofs by Girard [16] and Baelde [5] and strong normalisation proofs by Accattoli [3]. They have also been used for parametricity results in polymorphically typed π-calculi [8]. An innovation in this paper is the use of Kripke $\perp\perp$-closed relations to account for the contexts Θ describing the possible observations on configurations.

7   Conclusions and Future Work

We have introduced an operational semantics for Wadler's CP calculus that agrees with the standard relational semantics of CLL proofs. We have been able to show that the (CUT)-elimination rules of CLL are precisely observational equivalences with respect to our operational semantics. We view this work as a crucial step in treating CP as a foundational language of structured communication. We now highlight some areas of research that we have opened up.

Refined Denotational Semantics for CP. As we discussed in Sect. 3.4, there is a close connection between semantics of CLL that assign cliques to proofs and the operational properties of the corresponding processes. Further refinements of the relational semantics, beyond coherence spaces, such as Loader's totality spaces [22] and Ehrhard's Finiteness spaces [13], should yield insights into the operational behaviour of CP and its extensions with features such as nondeterminism. Laird et al. [19]'s weighted relational semantics interprets processes as semiring-valued matrices. This could be used to model a variant of CP with complexity measures. Probabilistic Coherence Spaces, introduced by Danos and Ehrhard [11], are another refinement that model probabilistic computation.

Recursive Types for CP. In this paper, we have only investigated the basic features of CP. Extensions of CP with recursive types, based on the work in CLL by Baelde [5], have been carried out by Lindley and Morris [21]. Extension of our operational semantics and the denotational semantics with recursive types is an essential step in turning CP into a more realistic language for structured communication. Constructing concurrency features on CP may be possible by allowing racy interleaving of clients and servers expressive via recursive types.

Dependent Types for CP. More ambitiously, we intend to extend CP with dependent types. Dependent types for logically-based session-typed calculi have already been investigated by Toninho et al. [33] and Toninho and Yoshida [34]. However, these calculi enforce a strict separation between data and communication: there are session types $\Pi x{:}\tau.A(x)$ and $\Sigma x{:}\tau.A(x)$ which correspond to receiving or transmitting a value of *value* type τ. Taking inspiration from McBride's investigation of the combination of linear and dependent types [24], we envisage a more general notion of session-dependent session type $(x : A) \triangleright B$, where the value of x in B is determined by the actual observed data transferred in the session described by A. This type is a dependent generalisation of Retoré's "before" connective [29]. To make this idea work, we need a notion of observed communication in CP, which the observed communication semantics proposed in this paper provides.

Acknowledgements. Thanks to Sam Lindley, J. Garrett Morris, Conor McBride and Phil Wadler for helpful discussions and comments on this paper. This work was partly funded by a Science Faculty Starter Grant from the University of Strathclyde.

References

1. Abramsky, S.: Computational interpretations of linear logic. Theor. Comput. Sci. **111**, 3–57 (1993)
2. Abramsky, S.: Proofs as processes. Theor. Comput. Sci. **135**(1), 5–9 (1992)

3. Accattoli, B.: Linear logic and strong normalization. In: 24th International Conference on Rewriting Techniques and Applications, RTA 2013, 24–26 June 2013, Eindhoven, The Netherlands, pp. 39–54 (2013)
4. Atkey, R., Lindley, S., Morris, J.G.: Conflation confers concurrency. In: Lindley, S., McBride, C., Trinder, P., Sannella, D. (eds.) A List of Successes That Can Change the World. LNCS, vol. 9600, pp. 32–55. Springer, Heidelberg (2016). doi:10.1007/978-3-319-30936-1_2
5. Baelde, D.: Least, greatest fixed points in linear logic. ACM Trans. Comput. Logic 13(1), 2:1–2:44 (2012)
6. Barr, M.: *-Autonomous categories and linear logic. Math. Struct. Comput. Sci. 1(2), 159–178 (1991)
7. Bellin, G., Scott, P.J.: On the π-calculus and linear logic. Theoret. Comput. Sci. 135(1), 11–65 (1994)
8. Berger, M., Honda, K., Yoshida, N.: Genericity and the π-calculus. In: Gordon, A.D. (ed.) FoSSaCS 2003. LNCS, vol. 2620, pp. 103–119. Springer, Heidelberg (2003). doi:10.1007/3-540-36576-1_7
9. Caires, L., Pfenning, F.: Session types as intuitionistic linear propositions. In: Gastin, P., Laroussinie, F. (eds.) CONCUR 2010. LNCS, vol. 6269, pp. 222–236. Springer, Heidelberg (2010). doi:10.1007/978-3-642-15375-4_16
10. Curry, H.B.: Functionality in combinatory logic. Proc. Natl. Acad. Sci. 20, 584–590 (1934)
11. Danos, V., Ehrhard, T.: Probabilistic coherence spaces as a model of higher-order probabilistic computation. Inf. Comput. 209(6), 966–991 (2011)
12. Davey, B.A., Priestley, H.A.: Introduction to Lattices and Order, 2nd edn. Cambridge University Press, Cambridge (2002)
13. Ehrhard, T.: Finiteness spaces. Math. Struct. Comput. Sci. 15(4), 615–646 (2005)
14. Ehrhard, T., Laurent, O.: Interpreting a finitary π-calculus in differential interaction nets. Inf. Comput. 208(6), 606–633 (2010)
15. Gay, S.J., Vasconcelos, V.T.: Linear type theory for asynchronous session types. J. Funct. Program. 20(01), 19–50 (2010)
16. Girard, J.-Y.: Linear logic. Theor. Comput. Sci. 50, 1–101 (1987)
17. Honda, K.: Types for dyadic interaction. In: Best, E. (ed.) CONCUR 1993. LNCS, vol. 715, pp. 509–523. Springer, Heidelberg (1993). doi:10.1007/3-540-57208-2_35
18. Howard, W.A.: The formulae-as-types notion of construction. In: Seldin, J.P., Hindley, J.R. (eds.) To H.B. Curry: Essays on Combinatory Logic, Lambda Calculus and Formalism. Academic Press, Boston (1980)
19. Laird, J., Manzonetto, G., McCusker, G., Pagani, M.: Weighted relational models of typed λ-calculi. In: 28th Annual ACM/IEEE Symposium on Logic in Computer Science, LICS 2013, 25–28 June 2013, New Orleans, LA, USA, pp. 301–310 (2013)
20. Lindley, S., Morris, J.G.: A semantics for propositions as sessions. In: Vitek, J. (ed.) ESOP 2015. LNCS, vol. 9032, pp. 560–584. Springer, Heidelberg (2015). doi:10.1007/978-3-662-46669-8_23
21. Lindley, S., Morris, J.G.: Talking bananas: structural recursion for session types. In: ICFP (2016, to appear)
22. Loader, R.: Linear logic, totality and full completeness. In: Proceedings of the Ninth Annual Symposium on Logic in Computer Science (LICS 1994), 4–7 July 1994, Paris, France, pp. 292–298 (1994)
23. Mazza, D.: The true concurrency of differential interaction nets. Math. Struct. Comput. Sci. (2015, to appear)

24. McBride, C.: I got plenty o' nuttin'. In: Lindley, S., McBride, C., Trinder, P., Sannella, D. (eds.) A List of Successes That Can Change the World. LNCS, vol. 9600, pp. 207–233. Springer, Heidelberg (2016). doi:10.1007/978-3-319-30936-1_12
25. Melliès, P.-A.: Categorical semantics of linear logic. In: Curien, P.-L., Herbelin, H., Krivine, J.-L., Melliès, P.-A. (eds.) Interactive Models of Computation and Program Behavior, Number 27 in Panoramas et Synthèses. Société Mathématique de France (2009)
26. Milner, R., Sangiorgi, D.: Barbed bisimulation. In: Kuich, W. (ed.) ICALP 1992. LNCS, vol. 623, pp. 685–695. Springer, Heidelberg (1992). doi:10.1007/3-540-55719-9_114
27. Pérez, J.A., Caires, L., Pfenning, F., Toninho, B.: Linear logical relations and observational equivalences for session-based concurrency. Inf. Comput. **239**, 254–302 (2014)
28. Plotkin, G.D.: LCF considered as a programming language. Theor. Comput. Sci. **5**(3), 223–255 (1977)
29. Retoré, C.: Pomset logic: a non-commutative extension of classical linear logic. In: Groote, P., Roger Hindley, J. (eds.) TLCA 1997. LNCS, vol. 1210, pp. 300–318. Springer, Heidelberg (1997). doi:10.1007/3-540-62688-3_43
30. Roscoe, A.W.: The Theory and Practice of Concurrency. Prentice Hall, Upper Saddle River (1998)
31. Sangiorgi, D., Walker, D.: The π-Calculus - A Theory of Mobile Processes. Cambridge University Press, Cambridge (2001)
32. Stark, I.: A fully abstract domain model for the π-calculus. In: Proceedings of the 11th Annual IEEE Symposium on Logic in Computer Science, 27–30 July 1996, New Brunswick, New Jersey, USA, pp. 36–42 (1996)
33. Toninho, B., Caires, L., Pfenning, F.: Dependent session types via intuitionistic linear type theory. In: Proceedings of the 13th International ACM SIGPLAN Conference on Principles and Practice of Declarative Programming, 20–22 July 2011, Odense, Denmark, pp. 161–172 (2011)
34. Toninho, B., Yoshida, N.: Certifying data in multiparty session types. In: A List of Successes That Can Change the World - Essays Dedicated to Philip Wadler on the Occasion of His 60th Birthday, pp. 433–458 (2016)
35. Wadler, P.: Propositions as sessions. In: Proceedings of the 17th ACM SIGPLAN International Conference on Functional Programming, ICFP 2012. ACM (2012)
36. Wadler, P.: Propositions as sessions. J. Funct. Program. **24**(2–3), 384–418 (2014)

Is Your Software on Dope?
Formal Analysis of Surreptitiously "enhanced" Programs

Pedro R. D'Argenio[1,2]($\boxtimes$), Gilles Barthe[3], Sebastian Biewer[2],
Bernd Finkbeiner[2], and Holger Hermanns[2]

[1] FaMAF, Universidad Nacional de Córdoba – CONICET, Córdoba, Argentina
dargenio@famaf.unc.edu.ar
[2] Computer Science, Saarland Informatics Campus, Saarland University,
Saarbrücken, Germany
[3] IMDEA Software, Madrid, Spain

Abstract. Usually, it is the software manufacturer who employs verification or testing to ensure that the software embedded in a device meets its main objectives. However, these days we are confronted with the situation that economical or technological reasons might make a manufacturer become interested in the software slightly deviating from its main objective for dubious reasons. Examples include lock-in strategies and the NO_x emission scandals in automotive industry. This phenomenon is what we call *software doping*. It is turning more widespread as software is embedded in ever more devices of daily use.

The primary contribution of this article is to provide a hierarchy of simple but solid formal definitions that enable to distinguish whether a program is *clean* or *doped*. Moreover, we show that these characterisations provide an immediate framework for analysis by using already existing verification techniques. We exemplify this by applying self-composition on sequential programs and model checking of HyperLTL formulas on reactive models.

1 Introduction

The Volkswagen exhaust emissions scandal [43] has put *software doping* in the spotlight: Proprietary embedded control software does not always exploit functionality offered by a device in the best interest of the device owner. Instead the software may be tweaked in various manners, driven by interests different from those of the owner or of society. This is indeed a common characteristics for the manner how different manufacturers circumvented [12,25] the diesel emission regulations around the world. The exhaust software was manufactured in such a way that it heavily polluted the environment, unless the software detected the

This work is partly supported by the ERC Grants 683300 (OSARES) and 695614 (POWVER), by the Saarbrücken Graduate School of Computer Science, by the Sino-German CDZ project 1023 (CAP), by ANPCyT PICT-2012-1823, by SeCyT-UNC 05/BP12 and 05/B497, and by the Madrid Region project S2013/ICE-2731 N-GREENS Software-CM.

© Springer-Verlag GmbH Germany 2017
H. Yang (Ed.): ESOP 2017, LNCS 10201, pp. 83–110, 2017.
DOI: 10.1007/978-3-662-54434-1_4

car to be (likely) fixed on a particular test setup used to determine the NO_x footprint data officially published. Phenomena resembling the emission scandal have also been reported in the context of smart phone designs [2], where software was tailored to perform better when detecting it was running a certain benchmark, and otherwise running in lower clock speed. Another smart phone case, disabling the phone [11] via a software update after "non-authorised" repair, has later been undone [36].

Usually, it is the software manufacturer who employs verification or testing to ensure that the software embedded in a device meets its main objectives. However, these days we are confronted with the situation that economical or technological reasons might make a manufacturer become interested in the software slightly deviating from its main objective for dubious reasons. This phenomenon is what we call *software doping*. It is turning more widespread as software is embedded in ever more devices of daily use.

The simplest and likely most common example of software doping (effectuating a customer lock-in strategy [3]) is that of ink printers [42] refusing to work when supplied with a toner or ink cartridge of a third party manufacturer [41], albeit being technically compatible. Similarly, cases are known where laptops refuse to charge [40] the battery if connected to a third-party charger. More subtle variations of this kind of doping just issue a warning message about the risk of using a "foreign" cartridge [20]. In the same vein, it is known that printers emit "low toner" warnings [33] earlier than needed, so as to drive or force the customer into replacing cartridges prematurely. Moreover, there are allegations that software doping has occurred in the context of electronic-voting so as to manipulate the outcome [1]. Tampering with voting machines has been proved a relatively easy task [21]. Common to all these examples is that the software user has little or no control over its execution, and that the functionality in question is against the interests of user or of society.

Despite the apparently pervasive presence of software doping, a systematic investigation or formalisation from the software engineering perspective is not existing. Fragmentary attention has been payed in the security domain with respect to cryptographic protections being sabotaged by insiders [37]. Typical examples are the many known backdoors, including the prominent dual EC deterministic random bit generator standardised by NIST [14]. Software doping however goes far beyond inclusion of backdoors.

Despite the many examples, it is not at all easy to provide a crisp characterisation of what constitutes software doping. This paper explores this issue, and proposes a hierarchy of formal characterisations of software doping. We aim at formulating and enforcing rigid requirements on embedded software driven by public interest, so as to effectively ban software doping. In order to sharpen our intuition, we offer the following initial characterisation attempt [5].

> A software system is doped if the manufacturer has included a hidden functionality in such a way that the resulting behaviour intentionally favors a designated party, against the interest of society or of the software licensee.   (1)

So, a doped software induces behaviour that can not be justified by the interest of the licensee or of society, but instead serves another usually hidden interest. It thereby favors a certain brand, vendor, manufacturer, or other market participant. This happens intentionally, and not by accident. However, the question whether a certain behaviour is intentional or not is very difficult to decide. To illustrate this, we recall that the above mentioned smart phone case, to be specific the iPhone-6, where "non-authorised" repair rendered the phone unusable [11] after an iOS update, seemed to be intentional when it surfaced, but was actually tracked down to a software glitch of the update and fixed later. Notably, if the iOS designers would have had the particular intention to mistreat licensees who went elsewhere for repair, the same behaviour could well have qualified as software doping in the above sense (1). As a result, we will look at software doping according to the above characterisation, keeping in mind the possibility of intentionality but not aiming to capture it in a precise manner.

In our work, we use concise examples that are directly inspired by the real cases reviewed above. They motivate our hierarchy of formal characterisations of *clean* or *doping-free* software.

A core observation will be that software doping can be characterised by considering the program if started from two different but compatible initial states. If the obtained outputs are not compatible, then this implies that the software is *doped*. Thinking in terms of the printer, one would expect that printing with different but compatible cartridges would yield the same printout without any alteration in the observed alerts. As a consequence, the essence of the property of being clean can be cast as a *hyperproperty* [16,17].

We first explore characterisations on sequential software (Sect. 2). We introduce a characterisation that ensures the proper functioning of the system whenever it is confined to standard parameters and inputs. Afterwards, we give two other characterisations that limit the behaviour of the system whenever it goes beyond such standard framework. We then revise these characterisations so as to apply to reactive non-deterministic systems (Sect. 3).

Traditionally hyperproperties require to be analysed in an *ad-hoc* manner depending on the particular property. However, a general framework is provided by techniques based on, e.g., self-composition techniques [6] or specific logic such as HyperLTL [15]. Indeed, we show (Sect. 4) how these properties can be analysed using self-composition on deterministic programs, particularly using weakest precondition reasoning [18], and we do the same (Sect. 5) for reactive systems using HyperLTL. In both settings we demonstrate principal feasibility by presenting verification studies of simple but representative examples.

2   Software Doping on Sequential Programs

Think of a program as a function that accepts some initial parameters and, given some inputs, produces some outputs, maybe in a non-deterministic manner. Thus, a parameterised sequential non-deterministic program is a function $S :$ Param $\rightarrow$ In $\rightarrow 2^{\mathsf{Out}}$, where Param is a set of parameters, each one of them fixing a particular instance of the program S, and In and Out being respectively the sets of inputs accepted by S and outputs produced by S. Notice that for a fixed parameter p and input i $\in$ In, the run of program $S(\mathsf{p})(\mathsf{i})$ may give a set of possible outputs.

procedure PRINTER(*cartridge_info*)
  if TYPE(*cartridge_info*) $\in$ Compatible
  then
    READ(*document*)
    PRINT(*stdout,document*)
  else
    TURNON(*alert_led*)
  end if
end procedure

procedure PRINTER(*cartridge_info*)
  if BRAND(*cartridge_info*) $=$ *my-brand*
  then
    READ(*document*)
    PRINT(*stdout,document*)
  else
    TURNON(*alert_led*)
  end if
end procedure

Fig. 1. A simple printer.

Fig. 2. A doped printer.

To understand a first possible definition, consider the program embedded in a printer (a simple abstraction is given in Fig. 1). This program may check compatibility of the ink or toner cartridge and print whenever the cartridge is compatible. In this case, we can think of the program PRINTER as a function parameterised with the information on the cartridge, that receives a document as input and produces a sequence of pages as outputs whenever the cartridge is compatible, otherwise it turns on an alert led. In this setting, we expect that the printer shows the same input-output behaviour for any compatible cartridge.

A printer manufacturer may manipulate this program in order to favour its own cartridge brand. An obvious way is displayed in Fig. 2. This is a sort of discrimination based on parameter values. Therefore, a first approach to characterising a program as *clean* (or *doping-free*) is that it should behave in a similar way for all parameters of interest. By "similar behaviour" we mean that the visible output should be the same for any given input in two different instances of the same (parameterised) program. Also, by "all parameters of interest", we refer to all parameter values we are interested in. In the case of the printer, we expect that it works with any *compatible* cartridge, but not with every cartridge. Such a compatibility domain defines a first scope within which a software is evaluated to be clean or doped.

Formally, if Plntrs $\subseteq$ Param, we could say that a parameterised program S is clean (or doping-free) if for all pairs of parameters of interest p, p$'$ $\in$ Plntrs and input i $\in$ In, $S(\mathsf{p})(\mathsf{i}) = S(\mathsf{p}')(\mathsf{i})$. Thus, the program of Fig. 1 satisfies this constraint whenever Compatible is the set of parameters of interest (i.e. Compatible = Plntrs). Instead, the program of Fig. 2 would be rejected as *doped* by the previous definition.

We could imagine, nonetheless, that the printer manufacturer may like to provide extra functionalities for its own product which is outside of the standard for compatibility. For instance (and for the sake of this discussion) suppose the printer manufacturer develops a new file format that is more efficient or versatile at the time of printing, but this requires some new technology on the cartridge (we could compare this to the introduction of the postscript language when standard printing was based on dots or ASCII code). The manufacturer still wants to provide the usual functionality for standard file formats that work with standard compatible cartridges and comes up with the program of Fig. 3. Notice that this program does not conform to the specification of a clean program as given above since it behaves differently when a document of the new (non-standard) type is given. This is clearly not in the spirit of the program in Fig. 3 which is actually conforming to the expected requirements.

Thus, our first definition states that a program is *clean* if, for any possible instance from the set of parameters of interest, it exhibits the same visible outputs when supplied with the same input, provided this input complies with a given standard. Formally, we assume a set PIntrs $\subseteq$ Param of parameters of interest and a set StdIn $\subseteq$ In of standard inputs and propose the following definition.

```
procedure PRINTER(cartridge_info)
    if TYPE(cartridge_info) ∈ Compatible then
        READ(document)
        if (¬NEWTYPE(document)
             ∨ SUPPORTSNEWTYPE(cartridge_info))
        then
            PRINT(stdout,document)
        else
            TURNON(alert_led)
        end if
    else
        TURNON(alert_signal)
    end if
end procedure
```

Fig. 3. A clean printer.

Definition 1. *A parameterised program S is* clean *(or* doping-free*) if for all pairs of parameters of interest* $p, p' \in$ PIntrs *and input* $i \in$ In, *if* $i \in$ StdIn *then* $S(p)(i) = S(p')(i)$. *If the program is not clean we will say that it is* doped.

The characterisation given above is based on a comparison of the behaviour of two instances of a program, each of them responding to different parameter values within PIntrs. A second, different characterisation may instead require to compare a reference specification capturing the essence of clean behaviour against any possible instance of the program. The first approach seems more general than the second one in the sense that the specification could be considered as one of the possible instances of the (parameterised) program. However, we can consider a distinguished parameter $\hat{p}$ so that the instance $S(\hat{p})$ is actually the specification of the program, in which case, both definitions turn out to be equivalent. In any case, it is important to observe that the specification may not be available since it is also made by the software manufacturer, and only the expected requirements may be known.

We remark that Definition 1 entails the existence of a contract which defines the set of parameters of interest and the set of standard inputs. In fact, Definition 1 only asserts doping-freedom if the program is well-behaved within such a contract, namely, as long as the parameters are within PIntrs and inputs are within StdIn. A behaviour outside this realm is deemed immediately correct since it is of no interest. This view results too mild in some cases where the change of behaviour of a program between a standard input and a non-standard but yet not-so-different input is extreme.

Consider the electronic control unit (ECU) of a diesel vehicle, in particular its exhaust emission control module. For diesel engines, the controller injects a certain amount of a specific fluid (an aqueous urea solution) into the exhaust pipeline in order to lower mono-nitrogen oxides (NO_x) emissions. We simplify this control problem to a minimal toy example. In Fig. 4 we display a function that reads the *throttle* position and calculates which is the dose of diesel exhaust fluid (DEF) (stored in *def_dose*) that should be injected to reduce the NO_x emission. The last line of the program precisely models the NO_x emission by storing it in the output variable *NOx* after a (made up) calculation directly depending on the *throttle* value and inversely depending on the *def_dose*.

```
procedure EMISSIONCONTROL()
    READ(throttle)
    def_dose := SCRMODEL(throttle)
    NOx := throttle³ / (k · def_dose)
end procedure
```

Fig. 4. A simple emission control.

The Volkswagen emission scandal arose precisely because their software was instrumented so that it works as expected *only if* operating in or very close to the lab testing conditions [19]. For our simplified example, this behaviour is exemplified by the algorithm of Fig. 5. Of course, the real case was less simplistic. Precisely, in this setting, the lab conditions define the set of standard inputs, i.e., the set StdIn is actually ThrottleTestValues and, as a consequence, a software like this one trivially meets the characterisation of *clean* given in Definition 1. However, this unit is intentionally programmed to defy the regulations when being unobserved and hence it falls directly within our intuition of what a doped software is (see (1)).

```
procedure EMISSIONCONTROL()
    READ(throttle)
    if throttle ∈ ThrottleTestValues then
        def_dose := SCRMODEL(throttle)
    else
        def_dose := ALTSCRMODEL(throttle)
    end if
    NOx := throttle³ / (k · def_dose)
end procedure
```

Fig. 5. A doped emission control.

The spirit of the emission tests is to verify that the amount of NO_x in the car exhaust gas does not exceed a given threshold *in general*. Thus, one would expect that if the input values of the EMISSIONCONTROL function deviates within "reasonable distance" from the *standard* input values provided during the lab emission test, the amount of NO_x found in the exhaust gas is still within the regulated threshold, or at least it does not exceed it more than a "reasonable amount". A similar rationale could be applied for regulation of other systems such as speed limit controllers in scooters and electric bikes.

Therefore, we need to introduce two notions of distance $d_{In} : (In \times In) \to \mathbb{R}_{\geq 0}$ and $d_{Out} : (Out \times Out) \to \mathbb{R}_{\geq 0}$ on inputs and outputs respectively. In principle, we do not require them to be metrics, but they need to be commutative and satisfy that $d_{In}(i, i) = d_{Out}(o, o) = 0$ for all $i \in In$ and $o \in Out$. Since programs are non-deterministic, we need to lift the output distance to sets of outputs and for that we will use the Hausdorff lifting which, as we will see, is exactly what we need. Given a distance d, the Hausdorff lifting $\mathcal{H}(d)$ is defined by

$$\mathcal{H}(d)(A, B) = \max \big\{ \sup_{a \in A} \inf_{b \in B} d(a, b), \sup_{b \in B} \inf_{a \in A} d(a, b) \big\} \qquad (2)$$

Based on this, we provide a new definition that considers two parameters: parameter κ_i refers to the acceptable distance an input may deviate from the norm to be still considered, and parameter κ_o that tells how far apart outputs are allowed to be in case their respective inputs are within κ_i distance.

Definition 2. *A parameterised program S is robustly clean if for all pairs of parameters of interest* $\mathsf{p}, \mathsf{p}' \in \mathsf{PIntrs}$ *and inputs* $\mathsf{i}, \mathsf{i}' \in \mathsf{In}$, *if* $\mathsf{i} \in \mathsf{StdIn}$ *is a standard input and* $d_{\mathsf{In}}(\mathsf{i}, \mathsf{i}') \leq \kappa_i$ *then* $\mathcal{H}(d_{\mathsf{Out}})(S(\mathsf{p})(\mathsf{i}), S(\mathsf{p}')(\mathsf{i}')) \leq \kappa_o$.

Requiring that $\mathcal{H}(d_{\mathsf{Out}})(S(\mathsf{p})(\mathsf{i}), S(\mathsf{p}')(\mathsf{i}')) \leq \kappa_o$ is equivalent to demand that

1. for all $\mathsf{o} \in S(\mathsf{p})(\mathsf{i})$ there exists $\mathsf{o}' \in S(\mathsf{p}')(\mathsf{i}')$ such that $d_{\mathsf{Out}}(\mathsf{o}, \mathsf{o}') \leq \kappa_o$, and
2. for all $\mathsf{o}' \in S(\mathsf{p}')(\mathsf{i}')$ there exists $\mathsf{o} \in S(\mathsf{p})(\mathsf{i})$ such that $d_{\mathsf{Out}}(\mathsf{o}, \mathsf{o}') \leq \kappa_o$.

Notice that this is what we actually need for the non-deterministic case: each output of one of the program instances should be matched within "reasonable distance" by some output of the other program instance.

Notice that i' does not need to satisfy StdIn, but it will be considered as long as it is within κ_i distance of any input satisfying StdIn. In such a case, outputs generated by $S(\mathsf{p}')(\mathsf{i}')$ will be requested to be within κ_o distance of some output generated by the respective execution induced by a standard input. In addition, notice that if the program S is deterministic and terminating we could simply write that $d_{\mathsf{Out}}(S(\mathsf{p})(\mathsf{i}), S(\mathsf{p}')(\mathsf{i}')) \leq \kappa_o$.

The concept of robustly clean programs generalises that of clean programs. Indeed, by taking $d_{\mathsf{In}}(\mathsf{i}, \mathsf{i}) = 0$ and $d_{\mathsf{In}}(\mathsf{i}, \mathsf{i}') > \kappa_i$ for all $\mathsf{i} \neq \mathsf{i}'$, and $d_{\mathsf{Out}}(\mathsf{o}, \mathsf{o}) = 0$ and $d_{\mathsf{Out}}(\mathsf{o}, \mathsf{o}') > \kappa_o$ for all $\mathsf{o} \neq \mathsf{o}'$, we see that Definition 1 is subsumed by Definition 2. Also, notice that the tolerance parameters κ_i and κ_o are values that should be provided as well as the notions of distance d_{In} and d_{Out}, and, together with the set PIntrs of parameters of interest and the set StdIn of standard inputs, are part of the contract that ensures that the software is robustly clean. Moreover, the limitation to these tolerance values has to do with the fact that, beyond it, particular requirements (e.g. safety) may arise. For instance, a smart battery may stop accepting charge if the current emitted by a standardised but foreign charger is higher than "reasonable" (i.e. than the tolerance values); however, it may still proceed in case it is dealing with a charger of the same brand for which it may know that it can resort to a customised protocol allowing ultra-fast charging in a safe manner.

Example 3. We remark that Definition 2 will actually detect as doped the program of Fig. 5 for appropriate distances d_{In} and d_{Out} and tolerance parameters κ_i and κ_o. Indeed, suppose that $\mathrm{SCRMODEL}(x) = x^2$, $\mathrm{ALTSCRMODEL}(x) = x$, and $\mathsf{k} = 2$. To check if the programs are robustly clean, take $\mathsf{In} = (0, 2]$ (these are the values that variable *throttle* takes), $\mathsf{StdIn} = (0, 1]$, let the distances d_{In} and d_{Out} be the absolute values of the differences of the values that take *throttle* and *NOx*, respectively, and let $\kappa_i = 2$ and $\kappa_o = 1$. With this setting, the program of Fig. 4 is robustly clean while the program of Fig. 5 is not.

Definition 2 can be further generalised by adjusting to a precise desired granularity given by a function $f : \mathbb{R} \to \mathbb{R} \cup \{\infty\}$ that relates the distances of the input with the distances of the outputs as follows.

Definition 4. *A parameterised program S is f-clean if for all pairs of parameters of interest* $\mathsf{p}, \mathsf{p}' \in \mathsf{PIntrs}$ *and inputs* $\mathsf{i}, \mathsf{i}' \in \mathsf{In}$, *if* $i \in \mathsf{StdIn}$ *is a standard input then* $\mathcal{H}(d_{\mathsf{Out}})(S(\mathsf{p})(\mathsf{i}), S(\mathsf{p}')(\mathsf{i}')) \leq f(d_{\mathsf{In}}(\mathsf{i}, \mathsf{i}'))$.

Like for Definition 2, the definition of f-clean does not require i' to satisfy StdIn. Moreover, notice that it is important that f can map into ∞, in which case it means that input i' becomes irrelevant to the property. Also here the Hausdorff distance is elegantly encoding the requirement that

1. for all $\mathsf{o} \in S(\mathsf{p})(\mathsf{i})$ there exists $\mathsf{o}' \in S(\mathsf{p}')(\mathsf{i}')$ s.t. $d_{\mathsf{Out}}(\mathsf{o}, \mathsf{o}') \leq f(d_{\mathsf{In}}(\mathsf{i}, \mathsf{i}'))$, and
2. for all $\mathsf{o}' \in S(\mathsf{p}')(\mathsf{i}')$ there exists $\mathsf{o} \in S(\mathsf{p})(\mathsf{i})$ s.t. $d_{\mathsf{Out}}(\mathsf{o}, \mathsf{o}') \leq f(d_{\mathsf{In}}(\mathsf{i}, \mathsf{i}'))$.

This definition is strictly more general than Definition 2, which can be seen by taking f defined by $f(x) = \kappa_{\mathsf{o}}$ whenever $x \leq \kappa_{\mathsf{i}}$ and $f(x) = \infty$ otherwise. (Notice here the use of ∞.) Also, if the program S is deterministic, we could simply require that $d_{\mathsf{Out}}(S(\mathsf{p})(\mathsf{i}), S(\mathsf{p}')(\mathsf{i}')) \leq f(d_{\mathsf{In}}(\mathsf{i}, \mathsf{i}'))$.

In this new definition, the bounding function f, together with the distances d_{In} and d_{Out}, the set PIntrs of parameters of interest and the set StdIn of standard inputs, are part of the contract that ensures that the software is f-clean.

Example 5. For the example of the emission control take the setting as in Example 3 and let $f(x) = x/2$. Then the program of Fig. 4 is f-clean while the program of Fig. 5 is not.

We remark that the notion of f-clean strictly relates the distance of the input values with the distance of the output values. Thus, e.g., the accepted distance on the outputs may grow according the distance of the input grows. Compare it to the notion of robustly clean in which the accepted distance on the outputs is only bounded by a constant (κ_{o}), regardless of the proximity of the inputs (which is only observed w.r.t. to constant κ_{i}).

3 Software Doping on Reactive Programs

Though we use the Volkswagen ECU case study as motivation for introducing Definitions 2 and 4, this program is inherently reactive: the DEF dosage depends not only of the current inputs but also on the current state (which in turn is set according to previous inputs). Therefore, in this section, we revise the definitions given in the previous section within the framework of reactive programs.

We consider a parameterised reactive program as a function $S : \mathsf{Param} \to \mathsf{In}^{\omega} \to 2^{(\mathsf{Out}^{\omega})}$ so that any instance of the program reacts to the k-th input in the input sequence producing the k-th output in each respective output sequence. Thus each instance of the program can be seen, for instance, as a (non-deterministic) Mealy or Moore machine. In this setting, we require that $\mathsf{StdIn} \subseteq \mathsf{In}^{\omega}$. Thus, the definition of a clean reactive program strongly resembles Definition 1.

Definition 6. *A parameterised reactive program S is* clean *if for all pairs of parameters of interest* $\mathsf{p}, \mathsf{p}' \in \mathsf{PIntrs}$ *and input* $\mathsf{i} \in \mathsf{In}^\omega$, *if* $\mathsf{i} \in \mathsf{StdIn}$ *then* $S(\mathsf{p})(\mathsf{i}) = S(\mathsf{p}')(\mathsf{i})$.

Naively, we may think that the definition of robustly clean may be also reused as given in Definition 2 by considering metrics on ω-traces. Unfortunately this definition does not work as expected: suppose two input sequences in In^ω that only differ by a single input in some late k-th position but originates a distance larger than κ_i. Now the program under study may become clean even if the respective outputs differ enormously at an early k'-th position $(k' < k)$. Notice that there is no justification for such early difference on the output, since the input sequences are the same up to position k'.

In fact, we notice that the property of being clean is of a safety nature: if there is a point in a pair of executions in which the program is detected to be doped, there is no extension of such executions that can correct it and make the program clean. In the observation above, the k'-th prefix of the trace should be considered the bad prefix and the program deemed as doped.

Therefore, we consider distances on finite traces: $d_{\mathsf{In}} : (\mathsf{In}^* \times \mathsf{In}^*) \to \mathbb{R}_{\geq 0}$ and $d_{\mathsf{Out}} : (\mathsf{Out}^* \times \mathsf{Out}^*) \to \mathbb{R}_{\geq 0}$. Now, we provide a definition of robustly clean on reactive programs that ensures that, as long as all j-th prefix of a given input sequence, with $j \leq k$, are within κ_i distance, the k-th prefix of the output sequence are within κ_o distance, for any $k \geq 0$. In the following definition, we denote with $\mathsf{i}[..k]$ the k-th prefix of the input sequence i (and similarly for output sequences).

Definition 7. *A parameterised reactive program S is* robustly clean *if for all pairs of parameters of interest* $\mathsf{p}, \mathsf{p}' \in \mathsf{PIntrs}$ *and input sequences* $\mathsf{i}, \mathsf{i}' \in \mathsf{In}^\omega$, *if* $\mathsf{i} \in \mathsf{StdIn}$ *then, for all $k \geq 0$ the following must hold*

$$(\forall j \leq k : d_{\mathsf{In}}(\mathsf{i}[..j], \mathsf{i}'[..j]) \leq \kappa_i) \to \mathcal{H}(d_{\mathsf{Out}})(S(\mathsf{p})(\mathsf{i})[..k], S(\mathsf{p}')(\mathsf{i}')[..k]) \leq \kappa_o,$$

where $S(\mathsf{p})(\mathsf{i})[..k] = \{\mathsf{o}[..k] \mid \mathsf{o} \in S(\mathsf{p})(\mathsf{i})\}$ *and similarly for* $S(\mathsf{p}')(\mathsf{i}')[..k]$.

By having as precondition that $d_{\mathsf{In}}(\mathsf{i}[..j], \mathsf{i}'[..j]) \leq \kappa_i$ for all $j \leq k$, this definition considers the fact that once one instance of the program deviates too much from the normal behaviour (i.e. beyond κ_i distance at the input), this instance is not obliged any longer to meet (within κ_o distance) the output, even if later inputs get closer again. This enables robustly clean programs to stop if an input outside the standard domain may result harmful for the system. Also, notice that, by considering the conditions through all k-th prefixes the definition encompasses the safety nature of the robustly cleanness property.

Example 8. A slightly more realistic version of the emission control system on the ECU is given in Fig. 6. It is a closed loop where the calculation of the DEF dosage also depends on the previous reading of NO_x. Moreover, the DEF dosage does not affect deterministically in the NO_x emission. Instead, there is a margin of error on the NO_x emission which is represented by the factor λ and the non-deterministic assignment of variable NOx in the penultimate line within the loop.

This non-deterministic assignment is an (admittedly unrealistic) abstraction of the chemical reaction between the exhaust gases and the DEF dosage. Figure 7 gives the version of the emission control system instrumenting the cheating hack. We define the selective catalytic reduction (SCR) models as follows:

```
procedure EMISSIONCONTROL()
    NOx := 0
    loop
        READ(throttle)
        def_dose := SCRMODEL(throttle, NOx)
        NOx :∈ [(1 − λ) throttle³/(k·def_dose), (1 + λ) throttle³/(k·def_dose)]
        OUTPUT(NOx)
    end loop
end procedure
```

Fig. 6. An emission control (reactive).

$$\text{SCRMODEL}(x, n) = \begin{cases} x^2 & \text{if } k \cdot n \leq x \\ (1 + \lambda) \cdot x^2 & \text{otherwise} \end{cases}$$

where $\lambda = 0.1$ and $k = 2$, and $\text{ALTSCRMODEL}(x, n) = x$ (i.e., it ignores the feedback of the NO_x emission resulting in the same ALTSCRMODEL as in Example 3). We also take $\ln = (0, 2]$ (recall that these are the values that variable *throttle* takes). The idea of the feedback in SCRMODEL is that if the previous emission was higher than expected with the planned current dosage, then the actual current dosage is an extra λ portion above the planned dosage.

For the contract required by robustly cleanness, we let $\text{StdIn} = (0, 1]^\omega$ and define $d_{\ln}(i, i') = |\text{last}(i) - \text{last}(i')|$ and similarly $d_{\text{Out}}(o, o') = |\text{last}(o) - \text{last}(o')|$, where $\text{last}(t)$ is the last element of the finite trace t. We take $\kappa_i = 2$ and $\kappa_o = 1.1$. (κ_o needs to be a little larger than in Example 3 due to the non-deterministic assignment to NOx.)

In Sect. 6 we will use a model checking tool to prove that the algorithm in Fig. 6 is robustly clean, while the algorithm of Fig. 7 is not.

```
procedure EMISSIONCONTROL()
    NOx := 0
    loop
        READ(throttle)
        if throttle ∈ ThrottleTestValues then
            def_dose := SCRMODEL(throttle, NOx)
        else
            def_dose := ALTSCRMODEL(throttle, NOx)
        end if
        NOx :∈ [(1 − λ) throttle³/(k·def_dose), (1 + λ) throttle³/(k·def_dose)]
        OUTPUT(NOx)
    end loop
end procedure
```

Fig. 7. A doped emission control (reactive).

As before, Definition 7 can be further generalised by adjusting to a precise desired granularity given by a function $f : \mathbb{R} \to \mathbb{R} \cup \{\infty\}$ that relates the distances of the input with the distances of the outputs as follows.

Definition 9. *A parameterised reactive program S is f-clean if for all pairs of parameters of interest* $\mathsf{p}, \mathsf{p}' \in \mathsf{PIntrs}$ *and input sequences* $\mathsf{i}, \mathsf{i}' \in \ln^\omega$, *if* $\mathsf{i} \in \mathsf{StdIn}$ *then for all* $k \geq 0$, $\mathcal{H}(d_{\text{Out}})(S(\mathsf{p})(\mathsf{i})[..k], S(\mathsf{p}')(\mathsf{i}')[..k]) \leq f(d_{\ln}(\mathsf{i}[..k], \mathsf{i}'[..k]))$.

Like for Definition 7, the definition of f-cleanness also considers distance on prefixes to ensure that major differences in late inputs do not impact on differences of early outputs, capturing also the safety nature of the property.

We observe that Definition 9 is more general than Definition 7. As before, define f by $f(x) = \kappa_o$ whenever $x \leq 1$ and $f(x) = \infty$ otherwise, but also redefine the metric on the input domain as follows:

$$
d_{\mathsf{In}}^{\mathrm{new}}(i[..k], i'[..k]) = \begin{cases} 0 & \text{if } i[..k] = i'[..k] \\ 1 & \text{if either } i \in \mathsf{StdIn} \text{ or } i' \in \mathsf{StdIn}, i[..k] \neq i'[..k] \\ & \text{and } d_{\mathsf{In}}(i[..j], i'[..j]) \leq \kappa_i \text{ for all } 0 \leq j \leq k \\ 2 & \text{otherwise} \end{cases}
$$

for all $i, i' \in \mathsf{In}$ and $k \geq 0$.

Example 10. For the example of the emission control take the setting as in Example 8 and let $f(x) = x/2 + 0.3$. The variation of f w.r.t. Example 5 is necessary to cope with the non-determinism introduced in these models. With this setting, in Sect. 6 we will check that the program of Fig. 6 is f-clean while the program of Fig. 7 is not.

4   Analysis Through Self-composition

In this section we will focus on sequential deterministic programs and we will see them in the usual way: as state transformers. Thus, if $\mu, \mu' : \mathsf{Var} \to \mathsf{Val}$ are states mapping the variables of a program into values within their domain, we denote with $(S, \mu) \Downarrow \mu'$ that a program S, initially taking values according to μ, executes and terminates in state μ'. We indicate with $(S, \mu) \Downarrow \perp$ that the program S starting at state μ does not terminate. As usual, we denote by $\mu \models \phi$ that a predicate ϕ holds on a state μ.

In this new setting, and restricting to deterministic programs, Definition 1 could be alternatively formulated as in Proposition 11. For this, we will assume that S contains sets of variables $\vec{x}_p$, $\vec{x}_i$, and $\vec{x}_o$ which are respectively parameter variables, input variables and output variables. Moreover, let PIntrs and StdIn be predicates on states containing only program variables in $\vec{x}_p$ and $\vec{x}_i$, respectively. They characterise the set of parameters of interest and the set of standard inputs. Now, we can state,

Proposition 11. *A sequential and deterministic program S is clean if and only if for all states μ_1, μ_2 and μ'_1 such that $\mu_1 \models \mathsf{PIntrs} \wedge \mathsf{StdIn}$, $\mu_2 \models \mathsf{PIntrs} \wedge \mathsf{StdIn}$, $\mu_1(\vec{x}_i) = \mu_2(\vec{x}_i)$ and $(S, \mu_1) \Downarrow \mu'_1$, it holds that $(S, \mu_2) \Downarrow \mu'_2$ and $\mu'_1(\vec{x}_o) = \mu'_2(\vec{x}_o)$ for some μ'_2.*

The proof of the proposition is straightforward since it is basically a notation change, hence we omit it. Also, notice that we omit any explicit reference to non-terminating programs. This is not necessary due to the symmetric nature of the predicates.

In the nomenclature of [7] relations

$$\mathcal{I} = \{(\mu_1, \mu_2) \mid \mu_1 \models \mathsf{PIntrs} \wedge \mathsf{StdIn},$$
$$\mu_2 \models \mathsf{PIntrs} \wedge \mathsf{StdIn}, \text{ and } \mu_1(\vec{x}_i) = \mu_2(\vec{x}_i)\}$$
$$\mathcal{I}' = \{(\mu_1, \mu_2) \mid \mu_1(\vec{x}_o) = \mu_2(\vec{x}_o)\}$$

are called *indistinguishable criteria*[1], and if $(\mu_1, \mu_2) \in \mathcal{I}$ then we say that μ_1 and μ_2 are $\mathcal{I}$-*indistinguishable*[2]. Similarly, for $\mathcal{I}'$. Thus, Proposition 11 characterises what in [7] is called *termination-sensitive* $(\mathcal{I}, \mathcal{I}')$-*security* and, by [7, Proposition 3], the property of cleanness can be analysed using the weakest (conservative) precondition (wp) [18] through self-composition.

Proposition 12. *Let $[\vec{x}/\vec{x}']$ indicate the substitution of each variable x by variable x'. Then a deterministic program S is clean if and only if*

$$\left(\begin{matrix} (\mathsf{PIntrs} \wedge \mathsf{StdIn}) \wedge (\mathsf{PIntrs} \wedge \mathsf{StdIn})[\vec{x}/\vec{x}'] \\ \wedge \vec{x}_i = \vec{x}'_i \wedge \mathrm{wp}(S, \mathit{true}) \end{matrix} \right) \Rightarrow \mathrm{wp}(S; S[\vec{x}/\vec{x}'], \vec{x}_o = \vec{x}'_o).$$

The term $\mathrm{wp}(S, \mathsf{true})$ in the antecedent of the implication is the weakest precondition that ensures that program S terminates. It is necessary in the predicate, otherwise it could become false only because program S does not terminate.

With the same setting as before, and taking d_{In}, d_{Out}, κ_i and κ_o as for Definition 2, we obtain an alternative definition of robustly cleanness for deterministic programs.

Proposition 13. *A sequential and deterministic program S is robustly clean if and only if for all states μ_1, μ_2, and μ' such that $\mu_1 \models \mathsf{PIntrs} \wedge \mathsf{StdIn}$, $\mu_2 \models \mathsf{PIntrs}$, and $d_{\mathsf{In}}(\mu_1(\vec{x}_i), \mu_2(\vec{x}_i)) \leq \kappa_i$, the following two conditions hold:*

1. *if $(S, \mu_1) \Downarrow \mu'$, then $(S, \mu_2) \Downarrow \mu'_2$ and $d_{\mathsf{Out}}(\mu'(\vec{x}_o), \mu'_2(\vec{x}_o)) \leq \kappa_o$ for some μ'_2; and*
2. *if $(S, \mu_2) \Downarrow \mu'$, then $(S, \mu_1) \Downarrow \mu'_1$ and $d_{\mathsf{Out}}(\mu'_1(\vec{x}_o), \mu'(\vec{x}_o)) \leq \kappa_o$ for some μ'_1.*

In this case, the indistinguishability criteria are

$$\mathcal{I} = \{(\mu_1, \mu_2) \mid \mu_1 \models \mathsf{PIntrs} \wedge \mathsf{StdIn}, \mu_2 \models \mathsf{PIntrs}, \text{ and } d_{\mathsf{In}}(\mu_1(\vec{x}_i), \mu_2(\vec{x}_i)) \leq \kappa_i\}$$
$$\mathcal{I}' = \{(\mu_1, \mu_2) \mid d_{\mathsf{Out}}(\mu_1(\vec{x}_o), \mu_2(\vec{x}_o)) \leq \kappa_o\}$$

Notice that $\mathcal{I}$ is not symmetric. Then the first item of Proposition 13 characterises termination-sensitive $(\mathcal{I}, \mathcal{I}')$-security while the second item characterises termination-sensitive $(\mathcal{I}^{-1}, \mathcal{I}')$-security. Using again [7, Proposition 3], the property of robustly cleanness can be analysed using wp through self-composition.

---

[1] In this definition, states should actually be considered as tuples of values rather than state mappings in order to exactly match the definitions of [7, Sect. 3].

[2] Also, to strictly follow notation in [7, Sect. 3] we should have written $\mu_1 \sim^{\mathcal{I}}_{id} \mu_2$ instead of $(\mu_1, \mu_2) \in \mathcal{I}$.

Proposition 14. *A deterministic program S is robustly clean if and only if*

$$\mathsf{PIntrs} \wedge \mathsf{StdIn} \wedge \mathsf{PIntrs}[\vec{x}/\vec{x}'] \wedge d_{\mathsf{In}}(\vec{x}_i, \vec{x}'_i) \le \kappa_i$$

$$\Rightarrow \left(\begin{array}{l} \mathrm{wp}(S, \textit{true}) \Rightarrow \mathrm{wp}(S; S[\vec{x}/\vec{x}'], d_{\mathsf{Out}}(\vec{x}_o, \vec{x}'_o) \le \kappa_o) \\ \wedge \; \mathrm{wp}(S[\vec{x}/\vec{x}'], \textit{true}) \Rightarrow \mathrm{wp}(S[\vec{x}/\vec{x}']; S, d_{\mathsf{Out}}(\vec{x}_o, \vec{x}'_o) \le \kappa_o) \end{array} \right)$$

Proceeding in a similar manner, we can also obtain an alternative definition of f-cleanness for deterministic programs.

Proposition 15. *A sequential and deterministic program S is f-clean if and only if for all states μ_1, μ_2, and μ' such that $\mu_1 \models \mathsf{PIntrs} \wedge \mathsf{StdIn}$, and $\mu_2 \models \mathsf{PIntrs}$, the following two conditions hold:*

1. *if $(S, \mu_1)\Downarrow\mu'$, then $(S, \mu_2)\Downarrow\mu'_2$ and $d_{\mathsf{Out}}(\mu'(\vec{x}_o), \mu'_2(\vec{x}_o)) \le f(d_{\mathsf{In}}(\mu_1(\vec{x}_i), \mu_2(\vec{x}_i)))$ for some μ'_2; and*
2. *if $(S, \mu_2)\Downarrow\mu'$, then $(S, \mu_1)\Downarrow\mu'_1$ and $d_{\mathsf{Out}}(\mu'_1(\vec{x}_o), \mu'(\vec{x}_o)) \le f(d_{\mathsf{In}}(\mu_1(\vec{x}_i), \mu_2(\vec{x}_i)))$ for some μ'_1.*

Notice that the term $f(d_{\mathsf{In}}(\mu_1(\vec{x}_i), \mu_2(\vec{x}_i)))$ appears in the conclusion of the implications of both items. This may look unexpected since it seems to be related to the input requirements rather than the output requirements, in particular because it refers to the input states. This makes this case a little less obvious than the previous one. To overcome this situation, we introduce a constant $Y \in \mathbb{R}_{\ge 0}$ which we assume universally quantified. Using this, we define the following indistinguishability criteria

$$\mathcal{I}_Y = \{(\mu_1, \mu_2) \mid \mu_1 \models \mathsf{PIntrs} \wedge \mathsf{StdIn},$$
$$\mu_2 \models \mathsf{PIntrs}, \text{ and } f(d_{\mathsf{In}}(\mu_1(\vec{x}_i), \mu_2(\vec{x}_i))) = Y\}$$
$$\mathcal{I}'_Y = \{(\mu_1, \mu_2) \mid d_{\mathsf{Out}}(\mu_1(\vec{x}_o), \mu_2(\vec{x}_o)) \le Y\}$$

By using this, by Proposition 15, we have that S is f-clean if and only if for every $Y \in \mathbb{R}_{\ge 0}$, and for all states μ_1, μ_2, and μ' such that $(\mu_1, \mu_2) \in \mathcal{I}_Y$

1. if $(S, \mu_1) \Downarrow \mu'$, then $(S, \mu_2) \Downarrow \mu'_2$ and $(\mu', \mu'_2) \in \mathcal{I}'_Y$ for some μ'_2; and
2. if $(S, \mu_2) \Downarrow \mu'$, then $(S, \mu_1) \Downarrow \mu'_1$ and $(\mu'_1, \mu') \in \mathcal{I}'_Y$ for some μ'_1.

With this new definition, and taking into account again the asymmetry of $\mathcal{I}_Y$, the first item characterises termination-sensitive $(\mathcal{I}_Y, \mathcal{I}'_Y)$-security while the second one characterises termination-sensitive $(\mathcal{I}_Y^{-1}, \mathcal{I}'_Y)$-security. From this and [7, Prop. 3], the property of f-cleanness can be analysed using wp and self-composition.

Proposition 16. *A deterministic program S is f-clean if and only if for all $Y \in \mathbb{R}_{\ge 0}$*

$$\mathsf{PIntrs} \wedge \mathsf{StdIn} \wedge \mathsf{PIntrs}[\vec{x}/\vec{x}'] \wedge f(d_i(\vec{x}_i, \vec{x}'_i)) = Y$$

$$\Rightarrow \left(\begin{array}{l} \mathrm{wp}(S, \textit{true}) \Rightarrow \mathrm{wp}(S; S[\vec{x}/\vec{x}'], d_{\mathsf{Out}}(\vec{x}_o, \vec{x}'_o) \le Y \\ \wedge \; \mathrm{wp}(S[\vec{x}/\vec{x}'], \textit{true}) \Rightarrow \mathrm{wp}(S[\vec{x}/\vec{x}']; S, d_{\mathsf{Out}}(\vec{x}_o, \vec{x}'_o) \le Y \end{array} \right)$$

$$\mathrm{wp}(x := e, Q) = Q[e/x]$$
$$\mathrm{wp}(\mathbf{if}\ b\ \mathbf{then}\ S_1\ \mathbf{else}\ S_2\ \mathbf{end\ if}, Q) = b \Rightarrow \mathrm{wp}(S_1, Q) \wedge \neg b \Rightarrow \mathrm{wp}(S_2, Q)$$
$$\mathrm{wp}(S_1; S_2, Q) = \mathrm{wp}(S_1, \mathrm{wp}(S_2, Q))$$
$$\mathrm{wp}(\mathbf{while}\ b\ \mathbf{do}\ S\ \mathbf{end\ do}, Q) = \exists k : k \geq 0 : H_k(Q)$$

$$\text{where } H_0(Q) = \neg b \wedge Q \text{ and } H_{k+1}(Q) = (b \wedge \mathrm{wp}(S, H_k(Q))) \vee H_0(Q)$$

Fig. 8. Equations for the wp calculus

Example 17. In this example, we use Proposition 16 to prove correct our statements in Example 3. First, we recall the definition of wp in Fig. 8, and rewrite the programs in Figs. 4 and 5 with all functions and values properly instantiated in the way we need it here (see Figs. 9 and 10).

On the one hand, none of the programs have parameters, then PIntrs = true. On the other hand, StdIn = ($thrtl \in (0, 1]$). Since wp(EC, true) = true we have to prove that

$def\_dose := thrtl^2$
$NOx := thrtl^3 / (2 \cdot def\_dose)$

Fig. 9. Program EC.

$$thrtl \in (0, 1] \wedge \left(\frac{|thrtl - thrtl'|}{2} = Y \right)$$
$$\Rightarrow \left(\begin{array}{c} \mathrm{wp}(\mathrm{EC}; \mathrm{EC}', |NOx - NOx'| \leq Y) \\ \wedge\, \mathrm{wp}(\mathrm{EC}'; \mathrm{EC}, |NOx - NOx'| \leq Y) \end{array} \right) \tag{3}$$

if $thrtl \in$ ThrottleTestValues
then
    $def\_dose := thrtl^2$
else
    $def\_dose := thrtl$
end if
$NOx := thrtl^3 / (2 \cdot def\_dose)$

Fig. 10. Program AEC.

where EC' is another instance of EC with every program variable x renamed by x'. Moreover, function f and distances d_{In} and d_{Out} are already instantiated. It is not difficult to verify that $\mathrm{wp}(\mathrm{EC}; \mathrm{EC}', |NOx - NOx'| \leq Y) \equiv \left(\frac{|thrtl - thrtl'|}{2} \leq Y \right)$ and $\mathrm{wp}(\mathrm{EC}'; \mathrm{EC}, |NOx - NOx'| \leq Y) \equiv \left(\frac{|thrtl' - thrtl|}{2} \leq Y \right)$ from which the implication follows and hence EC is f-clean.

For AEC we also have that wp(AEC, true) = true and hence we have to prove a formula similar to 3. In this case, wp(AEC; AEC', $|NOx - NOx'| \leq Y$) is

$$(thrtl \in (0, 1] \wedge thrtl' \in (0, 1]) \Rightarrow \frac{|thrtl - thrtl'|}{2} \leq Y$$
$$\wedge\, (thrtl \in (0, 1] \wedge thrtl' \notin (0, 1]) \Rightarrow \frac{|thrtl - thrtl'^2|}{2} \leq Y$$
$$\wedge\, (thrtl \notin (0, 1] \wedge thrtl' \in (0, 1]) \Rightarrow \frac{|thrtl^2 - thrtl'|}{2} \leq Y$$
$$\wedge\, (thrtl \notin (0, 1] \wedge thrtl' \notin (0, 1]) \Rightarrow \frac{|thrtl^2 - thrtl'^2|}{2} \leq Y$$

The predicate is the same for wp(AEC'; AEC, $|NOx - NOx'| \leq Y$), since $|a - b| = |b - a|$. Then, the predicate

$$\left(thrtl \in (0, 1] \wedge \frac{|thrtl - thrtl'|}{2} = Y \right) \Rightarrow \left(\begin{array}{c} \mathrm{wp}(\mathrm{AEC}; \mathrm{AEC}', |NOx - NOx'| \leq Y) \\ \wedge\, \mathrm{wp}(\mathrm{AEC}'; \mathrm{AEC}, |NOx - NOx'| \leq Y) \end{array} \right)$$

is equivalent to

$$\left(thrtl \in (0,1] \wedge \frac{|thrtl - thrtl'|}{2} = Y \right) \Rightarrow \left(\begin{array}{l} thrtl' \in (0,1] \Rightarrow \frac{|thrtl - thrtl'|}{2} \leq Y \\ \wedge \; thrtl' \notin (0,1] \Rightarrow \frac{|thrtl - thrtl'^2|}{2} \leq Y \end{array} \right)$$

which can be proved false if, e.g., $thrtl = 1$ and $thrtl' = 1.5$.

Notwithstanding the simplicity of the previous example, the technique can be applied to complex programs including loops. We decided to keep it simple as it is not our intention to show the power of wp, but the applicability of our definition.

We could profit from [7] for the use of other verification techniques, including separation logic and model checking where the properties can be expressed in terms of LTL and CTL. Particularly, CTL permits the encoding of the full non-deterministic properties given in Sect. 2. We will not dwell on this since in the next section we explore the encoding of the reactive properties through a more general setting.

5   Analysis of Reactive Programs with HyperLTL

HyperLTL [15] is a temporal logic for the specification of hyperproperties of reactive systems. HyperLTL extends linear-time temporal logic (LTL) with trace quantifiers and trace variables, which allow the logic to refer to multiple traces at the same time. The problem of model checking a HyperLTL formula over a finite-state model is decidable [24]. In this section, we focus on reactive non-deterministic programs and use HyperLTL to encode the different definitions of clean reactive programs given in Sect. 3. In the following, we interpret a program as a set $S \subseteq (2^{\mathsf{AP}})^\omega$ of infinite traces over a set AP of atomic propositions.

Let π be a *trace variable* from a set $\mathcal{V}$ of trace variables. A *HyperLTL formula* is defined by the following grammar:

$$\begin{array}{ll} \psi ::= \exists \pi. \psi \mid \forall \pi. \psi \mid \phi \\ \phi ::= a_\pi \mid \neg \phi \mid \phi \vee \phi \mid \mathsf{X} \phi \mid \phi \, \mathsf{U} \, \phi \end{array} \tag{4}$$

The quantifiers $\exists$ and $\forall$ quantify existentially and universally, respectively, over the set of traces. For example, the formula $\forall \pi. \exists \pi'. \phi$ means that for every trace π there exists another trace π' such that ϕ holds over the pair of traces. If no universal quantifier occurs in the scope of an existential quantifier, and no existential quantifiers occurs in the scope of a universal quantifier, we call the formula *alternation-free*. In order to refer to the values of the atomic propositions in the different traces, the atomic propositions are indexed with trace variables: for some atomic proposition $a \in \mathsf{AP}$ and some trace variable $\pi \in \mathcal{V}$, a_π states that a holds in the initial position of trace π. The temporal operators and Boolean connectives are interpreted as usual. In particular, $\mathsf{X}\phi$ means that ϕ holds in the next state of every trace under consideration. Likewise, $\phi \, \mathsf{U} \, \phi'$ means that ϕ' eventually holds in every trace under consideration at the same point in time, provided ϕ holds in every previous instant in all such traces. We also use the standard derived operators: $\mathsf{F}\phi \equiv \mathsf{true}\,\mathsf{U}\,\phi$, $\mathsf{G}\phi \equiv \neg\mathsf{F}\neg\phi$, and $\phi\,\mathsf{W}\,\phi' \equiv \neg(\neg\phi'\,\mathsf{U}\,(\neg\phi \wedge \neg\phi'))$.

A *trace assignment* is a partial function $\Pi : \mathcal{V} \to (2^{\mathsf{AP}})^\omega$ that assigns traces to variables. Let $\Pi[\pi \mapsto t]$ denote the same function as Π except that π is mapped to the trace t. For $k \in \mathbb{N}$, let $t[k]$, $t[k..]$, and $t[..k]$ denote respectively the k-th element of t, the k-th suffix of t, and the k-th prefix of t. The trace assignment suffix $\Pi[k..]$ is defined by $\Pi[k..](\pi) = \Pi(\pi)[k..]$. By $\Pi \models_S \psi$ we mean that formula ϕ is satisfied by the program S under the trace assignment Π. Satisfaction is recursively defined as follows.

$$
\begin{array}{lll}
\Pi \models_S \exists\pi.\,\psi & \text{iff} & \Pi[\pi \mapsto t] \models_S \psi \text{ for some } t \in S \\
\Pi \models_S \forall\pi.\,\psi & \text{iff} & \Pi[\pi \mapsto t] \models_S \psi \text{ for every } t \in S \\
\Pi \models_S a_\pi & \text{iff} & a \in \Pi(\pi)[0] \\
\Pi \models_S \neg\phi & \text{iff} & \Pi \not\models_S \phi \\
\Pi \models_S \phi_1 \vee \phi_2 & \text{iff} & \Pi \models_S \phi_1 \text{ or } \Pi \models_S \phi_2 \\
\Pi \models_S \mathsf{X}\phi & \text{iff} & \Pi[1..] \models_S \phi \\
\Pi \models_S \phi_1 \,\mathsf{U}\, \phi_2 & \text{iff} & \text{there exists } k \geq 0 \text{ s.t. } \Pi[k..] \models_S \phi_2 \text{ and} \\
& & \quad \text{for all } 0 \leq j < k, \Pi[j..] \models_S \phi_1
\end{array}
$$

We say that a program S *satisfies* a HyperLTL formula ψ if it is satisfied under the empty trace assignment, that is, if $\varnothing \models_S \psi$.

In the following, we give the different characterisations of cleanness for reactive programs in terms of HyperLTL. For this, let $\mathsf{AP} = \mathsf{AP_p} \cup \mathsf{AP_i} \cup \mathsf{AP_o}$ where $\mathsf{AP_p}$, $\mathsf{AP_i}$, and $\mathsf{AP_o}$ are the atomic propositions that define the parameter values, the input values, and the output values respectively. Thus, we take $\mathsf{Param} = 2^{\mathsf{AP_p}}$, $\mathsf{In} = 2^{\mathsf{AP_i}}$ and $\mathsf{Out} = 2^{\mathsf{AP_o}}$. Therefore, a program $S \subseteq (2^{\mathsf{AP}})^\omega$ can be seen as a function $\hat{S} : \mathsf{Param} \to \mathsf{In}^\omega \to 2^{(\mathsf{Out}^\omega)}$ where

$$
t \in S \quad \text{if and only if} \quad (t \downarrow \mathsf{AP_o}) \in \hat{S}(t[0] \cap \mathsf{AP_p})(t \downarrow \mathsf{AP_i}), \tag{5}
$$

with $t \downarrow A$ defined by $(t \downarrow A)[k] = t[k] \cap A$ for all $k \in \mathbb{N}$.

For the propositions appearing in the rest of this sections, we will assume that distances between traces are defined only according to its last element. That is, for the distance $d_{\mathsf{In}} : (\mathsf{In}^* \times \mathsf{In}^*) \to \mathbb{R}_{\geq 0}$ there exists a distance $\hat{d}_{\mathsf{In}} : (\mathsf{In} \times \mathsf{In}) \to \mathbb{R}_{\geq 0}$ such that $d_{\mathsf{In}}(i, i') = \hat{d}_{\mathsf{In}}(\mathrm{last}(i), \mathrm{last}(i'))$ for every $i, i' \in \mathsf{In}^*$, and similarly for $d_{\mathsf{Out}} : (\mathsf{Out}^* \times \mathsf{Out}^*) \to \mathbb{R}_{\geq 0}$. Let us call these type of distances *past-forgetful*. Moreover, we will need the abbreviations given in Table 1 for a clear presentation of the formulas.

The set of parameters of interest $\mathsf{PIntrs} \subseteq \mathsf{Param}$ defines a Boolean formula which we ambiguously call PIntrs. Also, we let StdIn be an LTL formula with atomic propositions in $\mathsf{AP_i}$, that is, a formula obtained with the grammar in the second line of (4) where atomic propositions have the form $a \in \mathsf{AP_i}$ (instead of a_π). Thus StdIn characterises the set of all input sequences through an LTL formula. With StdIn_π we represent the HyperLTL formula that is exactly like StdIn but where each occurrence of $a \in \mathsf{AP_i}$ has been replaced by a_π. Likewise, we let PIntrs_π represent the Boolean formula that is exactly like PIntrs with each occurrence of $a \in \mathsf{AP_p}$ replaced by a_π. We are now in conditions to state the characterisation of a clean program in terms of HyperLTL.

Table 1. Syntactic sugar for comparisons between traces

$$\mathsf{p}_\pi = \mathsf{p}_{\pi'} \quad \text{iff} \quad \bigwedge_{a \in \mathsf{AP_p}} a_\pi \leftrightarrow a_{\pi'} \qquad \hat{d}_{\mathsf{In}}(\mathsf{i}_\pi, \mathsf{i}_{\pi'}) \le \kappa_i \quad \text{iff} \quad \bigvee_{\substack{i,i' \in \mathsf{In} \\ \hat{d}(i,i') \le \kappa_i}} \bigwedge_{a \in i} a_\pi \wedge \bigwedge_{a \in i'} a_{\pi'}$$

$$\mathsf{i}_\pi = \mathsf{i}_{\pi'} \quad \text{iff} \quad \bigwedge_{a \in \mathsf{AP_i}} a_\pi \leftrightarrow a_{\pi'}$$

$$\mathsf{o}_\pi = \mathsf{o}_{\pi'} \quad \text{iff} \quad \bigwedge_{a \in \mathsf{AP_o}} a_\pi \leftrightarrow a_{\pi'} \qquad \hat{d}_{\mathsf{Out}}(\mathsf{o}_\pi, \mathsf{o}_{\pi'}) \le \kappa_o \quad \text{iff} \quad \bigvee_{\substack{o,o' \in \mathsf{Out} \\ \hat{d}(o,o') \le \kappa_o}} \bigwedge_{a \in o} a_\pi \wedge \bigwedge_{a \in o'} a_{\pi'}$$

$$\hat{d}_{\mathsf{Out}}(\mathsf{o}_\pi, \mathsf{o}_{\pi'}) \le f(\hat{d}_{\mathsf{In}}(\mathsf{i}_\pi, \mathsf{i}_{\pi'})) \quad \text{iff} \quad \bigvee_{\substack{o,o' \in \mathsf{Out}, i,i' \in \mathsf{In} \\ \hat{d}(o,o') \le f(\hat{d}(i,i'))}} \bigwedge_{a \in i} a_\pi \wedge \bigwedge_{a \in i'} a_{\pi'} \wedge \bigwedge_{a \in o} a_\pi \wedge \bigwedge_{a \in o'} a_{\pi'}$$

Proposition 18. *A reactive program S is clean if and only if it satisfies the HyperLTL formula*

$$\forall \pi_1. \forall \pi_2. \exists \pi_2'.(\mathsf{PIntrs}_{\pi_1} \wedge \mathsf{PIntrs}_{\pi_2} \wedge \mathsf{StdIn}_{\pi_1})$$
$$\rightarrow \left(\mathsf{p}_{\pi_2} = \mathsf{p}_{\pi_2'} \wedge \mathsf{G}(\mathsf{i}_{\pi_1} = \mathsf{i}_{\pi_2'} \wedge \mathsf{o}_{\pi_1} = \mathsf{o}_{\pi_2'}) \right) \tag{6}$$

As it is given, the formula actually states that

$$\forall \mathsf{p}_1 : \forall \mathsf{p}_2 : \forall i : \mathsf{p}_1, \mathsf{p}_2 \in \mathsf{PIntrs} \wedge i \in \mathsf{StdIn} : \hat{S}(\mathsf{p}_1)(i) \subseteq \hat{S}(\mathsf{p}_2)(i)$$

Because of the symmetry of this definition (namely, interchanging p_1 and p_2), this is indeed equivalent to Definition 6. Notice that in (6), π_2 quantifies universally the parameter of the second instance, while π_2' represents the existence of the output sequence in such instance. The proofs of Propositions 18 to 20 follow the same structures. So we only provide the proof of Proposition 19 which is the most involved.

In fact, Proposition 19 below states the characterisation of a robustly clean program in terms of two HyperLTL formulas (or as a single HyperLTL formula by taking the conjunction).

Proposition 19. *A reactive program S is robustly clean under past-forgetful distances d_{In} and d_{Out} if and only if S satisfies the following two HyperLTL formulas*

$$\forall \pi_1. \forall \pi_2. \exists \pi_2'.$$
$$(\mathsf{PIntrs}_{\pi_1} \wedge \mathsf{PIntrs}_{\pi_2} \wedge \mathsf{StdIn}_{\pi_1})$$
$$\rightarrow \left(\mathsf{p}_{\pi_2} = \mathsf{p}_{\pi_2'} \wedge \mathsf{G}(\mathsf{i}_{\pi_2} = \mathsf{i}_{\pi_2'}) \wedge \left((\hat{d}_{\mathsf{Out}}(\mathsf{o}_{\pi_1}, \mathsf{o}_{\pi_2'}) \le \kappa_o) \ \mathsf{W} \ (\hat{d}_{\mathsf{In}}(\mathsf{i}_{\pi_1}, \mathsf{i}_{\pi_2'}) > \kappa_i) \right) \right)$$
$$\forall \pi_1. \forall \pi_2. \exists \pi_1'.$$
$$(\mathsf{PIntrs}_{\pi_1} \wedge \mathsf{PIntrs}_{\pi_2} \wedge \mathsf{StdIn}_{\pi_1})$$
$$\rightarrow \left(\mathsf{p}_{\pi_1} = \mathsf{p}_{\pi_1'} \wedge \mathsf{G}(\mathsf{i}_{\pi_1} = \mathsf{i}_{\pi_1'}) \wedge \left((\hat{d}_{\mathsf{Out}}(\mathsf{o}_{\pi_1'}, \mathsf{o}_{\pi_2}) \le \kappa_o) \ \mathsf{W} \ (\hat{d}_{\mathsf{In}}(\mathsf{i}_{\pi_1'}, \mathsf{i}_{\pi_2}) > \kappa_i) \right) \right)$$
$$\tag{7}$$

The difference between the first and second formula is subtle, but reflects the fact that, while the first formula has the universal quantification on the outputs of the program that takes standard input and the existential quantification on the program that may deviate, the second one works in the other way around. Thus each of the formulas capture each of the sup-inf terms in the definition of Hausdorff distance (see (2)). To notice this, follow the existentially quantified variable (π'_2 for the first formula, and π'_1 for the second one). Also, the weak until operator W has exactly the behaviour that we need to represent the interaction between the distances of inputs and the distances of outputs. The semantics of $\phi \, \mathsf{W} \, \psi$ is defined by

$$t \models \phi \, \mathsf{W} \, \psi \text{ iff } \quad \forall k \geq 0 : (\forall j \leq k : t[j..] \models \neg \psi) \to t[k..] \models \phi \qquad (8)$$

Next, we prove Proposition 19.

Proof. We only prove that the first formula captures the bound on the left sup-inf term of the definition of Hausdorff distance (see eq. (2)) in Definition 7. The other condition is proved in the same way and corresponds to the other sup-inf term of the Hausdorff distance. Taking into account the semantics of the weak until operator given in Eq. 8, the semantics of HyperLTL in general and using abbreviations in Table 1, formula 7 is equivalent to the following statement

$$\forall t_1 \in S : \forall t_2 \in S : \exists t'_2 \in S :$$
$$(t_1 \models \mathsf{PIntrs} \wedge t_2 \models \mathsf{PIntrs} \wedge t_1 \models \mathsf{StdIn})$$
$$\to \Big((t_2[0] \cap \mathsf{AP_p}) = (t'_2[0] \cap \mathsf{AP_p}) \wedge (\forall j \geq 0 : t_2[j] \cap \mathsf{AP_i} = t'_2[j] \cap \mathsf{AP_i})$$
$$\wedge \forall k \geq 0 : (\forall j \leq k : \hat{d}_{\mathsf{In}}(t_1[j] \cap \mathsf{AP_i}, t'_2[j] \cap \mathsf{AP_i}) \leq \kappa_i)$$
$$\to \hat{d}_{\mathsf{Out}}(t_1[k] \cap \mathsf{AP_o}, t'_2[k] \cap \mathsf{AP_o}) \leq \kappa_o \Big)$$

By applying some definitions and notation changes, this is equivalent to

$$\forall t_1 \in S : \forall t_2 \in S : \exists t'_2 \in S :$$
$$((t_1[0] \cap \mathsf{AP_p}) \in \mathsf{PIntrs} \wedge (t_2[0] \cap \mathsf{AP_p}) \in \mathsf{PIntrs} \wedge (t_1 \downarrow \mathsf{AP_i}) \in \mathsf{StdIn})$$
$$\to \Big((t_2[0] \cap \mathsf{AP_p}) = (t'_2[0] \cap \mathsf{AP_p}) \wedge (t_2 \downarrow \mathsf{AP_i}) = (t'_2 \downarrow \mathsf{AP_i})$$
$$\wedge \forall k \geq 0 : (\forall j \leq k : \hat{d}_{\mathsf{In}}(t_1[j] \cap \mathsf{AP_i}, t'_2[j] \cap \mathsf{AP_i}) \leq \kappa_i)$$
$$\to \hat{d}_{\mathsf{Out}}(t_1[k] \cap \mathsf{AP_o}, t'_2[k] \cap \mathsf{AP_o}) \leq \kappa_o \Big)$$

which, by logic manipulation, is equivalent to

$$\forall \mathsf{p_1} : \forall \mathsf{p_2} : \forall \mathsf{i_1} : \forall \mathsf{i_2} : \forall \mathsf{o_1} :$$
$$\Big(\exists t_1 \in S : \exists t_2 \in S :$$
$$(\mathsf{p_1} = (t_1[0] \cap \mathsf{AP_p}) \in \mathsf{PIntrs}) \wedge (\mathsf{p_2} = (t_2[0] \cap \mathsf{AP_p}) \in \mathsf{PIntrs})$$
$$\wedge \mathsf{i_1} = (t_1 \downarrow \mathsf{AP_i}) \wedge \mathsf{i_2} = (t_2 \downarrow \mathsf{AP_i}) \wedge \mathsf{o_1} = (t_1 \downarrow \mathsf{AP_o}) \wedge \mathsf{i_1} \in \mathsf{StdIn} \Big)$$

$\rightarrow \exists o_2 : \exists t'_2 \in S :$

$$\left(p_2 = (t'_2[0] \cap AP_p) \wedge i_2 = (t'_2 \downarrow AP_i) \wedge o_2 = (t'_2 \downarrow AP_o) \right.$$

$$\left. \wedge \forall k \geq 0 : (\forall j \leq k : \hat{d}_{In}(i_1[j], i_2[j]) \leq \kappa_i) \rightarrow \hat{d}_{Out}(o_1[k], o_2[k]) \leq \kappa_o \right)$$

By (5) and the fact that distances are past-forgetful, the previous equation is equivalent to

$\forall p_1 : \forall p_2 : \forall i_1 : \forall i_2 : \forall o_1 :$

$$\left(p_1, p_2 \in PIntrs \wedge i_1 \in StdIn \wedge \forall k \geq 0 : (\forall j \leq k : d_{In}(i_1[..j], i_2[..j]) \leq \kappa_i) \right.$$

$$\left. \wedge o_1 \in \hat{S}(p_1)(i_1) \right) \rightarrow \left(\exists o_2 \in \hat{S}(p_2)(i_2) : d_{Out}(o_1[..k], o_2[..k]) \leq \kappa_o \right)$$

which in turn corresponds to bounding the left sup-inf term of the Hausdorff distance (see (2)) in Definition 7,

$\forall p_1 : \forall p_2 : \forall i_1 : \forall i_2 :$

$$\left(p_1, p_2 \in PIntrs \wedge i_1 \in StdIn \wedge \forall k \geq 0 : (\forall j \leq k : d_{In}(i_1[..j], i_2[..j]) \leq \kappa_i) \right)$$

$$\rightarrow \left(\sup_{o_1 \in \hat{S}(p_1)(i_1)} \inf_{o_2 \in \hat{S}(p_2)(i_2)} d_{Out}(o_1[..k], o_2[..k]) \right) \leq \kappa_o$$

thus proving this part of the proposition.   □

Finally, we also give the characterisation of an f-clean program in terms of HyperLTL.

Proposition 20. *A reactive program S is f-clean under past-forgetful distances d_{In} and d_{Out} if and only if S satisfies the following two HyperLTL formulas*

$\forall \pi_1. \forall \pi_2. \exists \pi'_2.$

   $(PIntrs_{\pi_1} \wedge PIntrs_{\pi_2} \wedge StdIn_{\pi_1})$

$$\rightarrow \left(p_{\pi_2} = p_{\pi'_2} \wedge G(i_{\pi_2} = i_{\pi'_2}) \wedge G\left(\hat{d}_{Out}(o_{\pi_1}, o_{\pi'_2}) \leq f(\hat{d}_{In}(i_{\pi_1}, i_{\pi'_2})) \right) \right)$$

$\forall \pi_1. \forall \pi_2. \exists \pi'_1.$

   $(PIntrs_{\pi_1} \wedge PIntrs_{\pi_2} \wedge StdIn_{\pi_1})$

$$\rightarrow \left(p_{\pi_1} = p_{\pi'_1} \wedge G(i_{\pi_1} = i_{\pi'_1}) \wedge G\left(\hat{d}_{Out}(o_{\pi'_1}, o_{\pi_2}) \leq f(\hat{d}_{In}(i_{\pi'_1}, i_{\pi_2})) \right) \right) \quad (9)$$

As before, the difference between the first and second formula is subtle and can be noticed again by following the existentially quantified variables in each of the formulas.

We remark that the HyperLTL characterisations presented in Propositions 19 and 20 can be extended to any distance of bounded memory, that is, distances such that $d(t, t') = d(t[k..], t'[k..])$ for every finite traces t and t' and a fixed bound $k \in \mathbb{N}$. The solution proceeds by basically using the same formulas on an expanded and annotated model (with the expected exponential blow up w.r.t. to the original one).

Example 21. In our running example of the emission control system (see Examples 8 and 10), the property of robustly cleanness reduces to checking formula

$$\forall \pi_1. \forall \pi_2. \exists \pi_2'.$$

$$\mathsf{StdIn}_{\pi_1} \rightarrow \left(\mathsf{G}(t_{\pi_2} = t_{\pi_2'}) \wedge \left((\hat{d}_{\mathsf{Out}}(n_{\pi_1}, n_{\pi_2'}) \le \kappa_\mathsf{o}) \mathsf{W} (\hat{d}_{\mathsf{In}}(t_{\pi_1}, t_{\pi_2'}) > \kappa_\mathsf{i}) \right) \right)$$

$$(10)$$

and the obvious symmetric formula. For readability reasons, we shorthandedly write t for *thrtl* and n for *NOx*. Notice that any reference to parameters disappears since the emission control system does not have parameters, and the set of standard inputs is characterised by the LTL formula $\mathsf{StdIn} \equiv \mathsf{G}(t \in (0, 1])$. Likewise, we can verify that the model of the emission control system is f-clean through the formula

$$\forall \pi_1. \forall \pi_2. \exists \pi_2'.$$

$$\mathsf{StdIn}_{\pi_1} \rightarrow \left(\mathsf{G}(t_{\pi_2} = t_{\pi_2'}) \wedge \mathsf{G} \left(\hat{d}_{\mathsf{Out}}(n_{\pi_1}, n_{\pi_2'}) \le f(\hat{d}_{\mathsf{In}}(t_{\pi_1}, t_{\pi_2'})) \right) \right)$$

$$(11)$$

and the symmetric formula.

6 Experimental Results

We verified the cleanness of the emission control system using the HyperLTL model checker MCHyper [24]. The input to the model checker is a description of the system as an Aiger circuit and a hyperproperty specified as an alternation-free HyperLTL formula. Since the HyperLTL formulas from the previous section are of the form $\forall \pi_1 \forall \pi_2 \exists \pi_2' \dots$, and are, hence, not alternation-free, MCHyper cannot check these formulas directly. However, it is possible to prove or disprove such formulas by strengthening the formulas and their negations manually into alternation-free formulas that are accepted by MCHyper.

In order to prove that program EC in Fig. 9 is robustly clean, we strengthen formula (10) by substituting π_2 for the existentially quantified variable π_2'. The resulting formula is alternation-free:

$$\forall \pi_1. \forall \pi_2. \mathsf{StdIn}_{\pi_1} \rightarrow \left((\hat{d}_{\mathsf{Out}}(n_{\pi_1}, n_{\pi_2}) \le \kappa_\mathsf{o}) \mathsf{W} (\hat{d}_{\mathsf{In}}(t_{\pi_1}, t_{\pi_2}) > \kappa_\mathsf{i}) \right) \qquad (12)$$

MCHyper confirms that program EC satisfies (12). The program thus also satisfies (10). Notice that we had obtained the same formula if we would have started from the formula symmetric to (10).

To prove that program AEC in Fig. 10 is doped with respect to (10), we negate (10) and obtain

$$\exists \pi_1. \exists \pi_2. \forall \pi_2'.$$

$$\neg \left(\mathsf{StdIn}_{\pi_1} \rightarrow \left(\mathsf{G}(t_{\pi_2} = t_{\pi_2'}) \wedge \left((\hat{d}_{\mathsf{Out}}(n_{\pi_1}, n_{\pi_2'}) \le \kappa_\mathsf{o}) \mathsf{W} (\hat{d}_{\mathsf{In}}(t_{\pi_1}, t_{\pi_2'}) > \kappa_\mathsf{i}) \right) \right) \right)$$

This formula is of the form $\exists \pi_1. \exists \pi_2. \forall \pi_2'. \ldots$ and, hence, again not alternation-free. We replace the two existential quantifiers with universal quantifiers and restrict the quantification to two specific throttle values, a for π_1 and b for π_2:

$$\forall \pi_1. \forall \pi_2. \forall \pi_2'.$$
$$G(t_{\pi_1} = a \wedge t_{\pi_2} = b) \rightarrow$$
$$\neg\left(\mathsf{StdIn}_{\pi_1} \rightarrow \left(G(t_{\pi_2} = t_{\pi_2'}) \wedge \left((\hat{d}_{\mathsf{Out}}(n_{\pi_1}, n_{\pi_2'}) \leq \kappa_{\mathsf{o}}) \; W \; (\hat{d}_{\mathsf{In}}(t_{\pi_1}, t_{\pi_2'}) > \kappa_{\mathsf{i}}) \right) \right) \right)$$

$$(13a)$$

This transformation is sound as long as there actually exist traces with throttle values a and b. We establish this by checking, separately, that the following existential formula is satisfied:

$$\exists \pi_1. \exists \pi_2. G(t_{\pi_1} = a \wedge t_{\pi_2} = b) \tag{14}$$

MCHyper confirms the satisfaction of both formulas, which proves that (10) is violated by program AEC. Precisely, the counterexample that shows the violation of (10) is any pair of traces π_1 and π_2 that makes $G(t_{\pi_1} = a \wedge t_{\pi_2} = b)$ true in (14). We proceed similarly for the formula symmetric to (10) obtaining two formulas just as before which are also satisfied by AEC and hence the original formula is not. Also, we follow a similar process to prove that EC is f-clean but AEC is not.

Table 2. Experimental results from the verification of robust cleanness of EC and AEC

Program	NO$_x$	Model size	Circuit size		Property	Time
	Step	#transitions	#latches	#gates		(sec.)
EC	0.05	1436	17	9749	(12)	0.92
	0.00625	60648	23	505123	(12)	22.19
AEC	0.05	3756	19	27574	(13a) $a = 0.1$	1.62
					(13b) $a = 0.1$	1.6
					(13a) $a = 1$	1.68
					(13b) $a = 1$	1.56
	0.00625	175944	25	1623679	(13a) $a = 0.1$	102.07
					(13b) $a = 0.1$	96.3
					(13a) $a = 1$	97.67
					(13b) $a = 1$	92.8

Table 2 shows experimental results obtained with MCHyper[3] version 0.91 for the verification of robustly cleanness. The Aiger models were constructed by discretizing the values of the throttle and the NO$_x$. We show results from two different models, where the values of the throttle was discretised in steps of 0.1

---

[3] https://www.react.uni-saarland.de/tools/mchyper/.

units in both models and the values of the NO_x in steps of 0.05 and 0.00625. All experiments were run under OS X "El Capitan" (10.11.6) on a MacBook Air with a 1.7GHz Intel Core i5 and 4GB 1333MHz DDR3. In Table 2, the model size is given in terms of the number of transitions, while the size of the Aiger circuit encoding the model prepared for the property is given in terms of the number of latches and gates. The specification checked by MCHyper is the formula indicated in the property column. Formula (13b) is the formula symmetric to (13a). For the throttle values a and b in formulas (13a) and (13b), we chose $b = 2$ and let a vary as specified in the property column. Table 3 shows similar experimental results for the verification of f-cleanness. With (12′), (13a′), and (13b′) we indicate the similar variations to (12), (13a), and (13b) required to verify (11). Model checking takes less than two seconds for the coarse discretisation and about two minutes for the fine discretisation.

Table 3. Experimental results from the verification of f-cleanness of EC and AEC

Program	NO_x step	Model size #transitions	Circuit size #latches	#gates	Property	Time (sec.)
EC	0.05	1436	5	9869	(12′)	1.08
	0.00625	60648	8	505285	(12′)	21.74
AEC	0.05	3756	6	27708	(13a′) $a = 0.1$	1.71
					(13b′) $a = 0.1$	1.72
					(13a′) $a = 1$	1.72
					(13b′) $a = 1$	1.77
	0.00625	175944	9	1623855	(13a′) $a = 0.1$	95.29
					(13b′) $a = 0.1$	97.48
					(13a′) $a = 1$	95.57
					(13b′) $a = 1$	95.5

7   A Comprehensive Characterisation

If we concretely focus on the contract between the society or the licensee, and the software manufacturer, we can think in a more general but precise definition. It emerges by noticing that there is a partition on the set of inputs in three sets, each one of them fulfilling a different role within the contract:

1. The set StdIn of *standard inputs*. For these inputs, the program is expected to work exactly as regulated. It is the case, e.g., of the inputs defining the tests for the NO_x emission. Thus, it is expected that the program complies to Definition 1 when provided only with inputs in StdIn.

2. The set Comm of *committed inputs* such that Comm∩StdIn = ∅. These inputs
   are expected to be close according to a distance to StdIn and are not strictly
   regulated. However, it is expected that the manufacturer commits to respect
   certain bounds on the outputs. This would correspond to the inputs that do
   not behave exactly like the tests for the NO_x emission, but yet define "reasonable behaviour" of the car on the road. The behaviour of the program under
   this set of inputs can be characterised either by Definition 2 or Definition 4.
3. All other inputs are supposed to be anomalous and expected to be significantly distant from the standard inputs. In our emission control example,
   this can occur, e.g., if the car is climbing a steep mountain or speeding up
   in a highway. In this realm the only expectation is that the behaviour of the
   output is continuous with respect to the input.

Bearing this partition in mind, we propose the following general definition.

Definition 22. *A parameterised program S is* clean *(or* doping-free*) if for all
pairs of parameters of interest* p, p′ ∈ Plntrs *and inputs* i, i′ ∈ In,

1. *if* i ∈ StdIn *then* $S(p)(i) = S(p')(i)$;
2. *if* i ∈ StdIn *and* i′ ∈ Comm *then* $\mathcal{H}(d_{Out})(S(p)(i), S(p')(i')) \leq f(d_{In}(i, i'))$.
3. *for every* $\epsilon > 0$ *there exists* $\delta > 0$ *such that for all* i′ ∉ StdIn ∪ Comm *and*
   i ∈ In, $d_{In}(i, i') < \delta$ *implies* $\mathcal{H}(d_{Out})(S(p)(i), S(p')(i')) < \epsilon$.

Notice that, while Plntrs, StdIn, Comm, d_{In}, d_{Out}, and f are part of the
contract entailed by the definition, ϵ and δ in item 3 are not since they are
quantified (universally and existentially, resp.) in the definition. In this case,
we choose for item 3 to require that the program S is uniformly continuous in
In \ (StdIn ∪ Comm). However, we could have opted for stronger requirements
such as Lipschitz continuity. The chosen type of continuity would also be part
of the contract. Notice that this is the only case in which we require continuity.
Instead, discontinuities are allowed in cases 1 and 2 as long as the conditions
are respected since they may be part of the specification. In particular, notice
that f could be *any* function. Obviously, a similar definition can be obtained for
reactive systems.

We remark that cases 1 and 2 can be verified, as we showed in the paper. We
have not yet explored the verification of case 3.

8 Related Work

The term "software doping" has being coined by the press about a year ago
and, after the Volkswagen exhaust emissions scandal, the elephant in the room
became unavoidable: software developers introduce code intended to deceive [28].
Recently, a special session at ISOLA 2016 was devoted to this topic [34]. In [9],
Baum attacks the problem from a philosophical point of view and elaborates on
the ethics of it. In [5], we provided a first discussion of the problem and some
informal characterisations hinting at the formal proposal of this paper. Though

all these works point out the need for a technical attack on the problem, none of them provide a formal proposal.

Similar to software doping, backdoored software is a class of software that does not act in the best interest of users; see for instance the recent analysis in [37]. The primary emphasis of backdoored software is on leaking confidential information while guaranteeing functionality.

Dope-freedom in sequential programs is strongly related to abstract non-intereference [6,26] as already disussed in Sect. 4. More generally, our notions of dope-freedom are hyperproperties [16], a general class that encompasses notions across different domains, in particular non-interference in security [39], robustness (a.k.a. stability) in cyber-physical systems [13], and truthfulness in algorithmic game theory [8]. There exist several methods for verifying hyperproperties, including relational and Cartesian Hoare logics [10,38,44], self-composition and product programs constructions [4,7], temporal logics [15,23,24], or games [35]. These techniques greatly vary in their completeness, efficiency, and scalability.

Another worthwhile direction to study is the use of program equivalence analysis [22,27] for the analysis of cleanness.

9   Concluding Remarks

This article has focused on a serious and yet long overlooked problem, arising if software developers intentionally and silently deviate from the intended objective of the developed software. A notorious reason behind such deviations are simple and blunt lock-in strategies, so as to bind the software licensee to a certain product or product family. However, the motivations can be more diverse and obscure. As the software manufacturer has full control over the development process, the deviation can be subtle and surreptitiously introduced in a way that the fact that the program does not quite conform to the expected requirements may go well unnoticed.

We have pioneered the formalisation of this problem domain by offering several formal characterisations of software doping. These can serve as a framework for establishing a contract between the interested parties, namely the society or the licensee, and the software manufacturer, so as to avoid and eventually ban the development of doped programs.

We have also reported on the use of existing theories and tools at hand to demonstrate that the formal characterisation can indeed be analysed in various ways. In particular, the application of the self-composition technique opens many research directions for further analysis of software doping as it has been widely studied in the area of security [29,31], semantic differences [32] and cross or relative verification [30].

As we have demonstrated, the use of HyperLTL enables the automatic analysis of reactive models with respect to software doping. However, the complexity of this technique imposes some serious limits on its applicability. Thus, further studies in this direction are needed in order to enable analysis of reactive models of relatively large size, or alternatively to analyse the program code directly.

We believe our characterisations provide a first solid step to understand software doping and that our result opens a large umbrella of new possibilities, both in the direction of more dedicated characterisations as well as specifically tailored analysis techniques. For instance, the idea of dealing with distances and thresholds already rises the question of whether such distances could be quantified by probabilities. Also, the NO_x emission example would immediately suggest that the technique should also be addressed with testing. Moreover, the fact that the characterisations are hyperproperties also invites us to investigate for static analysis of source code based on type systems, abstraction techniques, etc.

Acknowledgement. We would like to thank the Dependable Systems and Software Group (Saarland University) for a fruitful discussion during an early presentation of this work, and Nicolás Wolovick for drawing our attention to electronic voting.

References

1. Agorist, M.: WATCH: computer programmer testifies he helped rig voting machines. MintPress News (2016) http://www.mintpressnews.com/214505-2/214505/. Accessed 13 Jan 2017
2. AppleInsider: Galaxy S4 on steroids: Samsung caught doping in benchmarks (2013). http://forums.appleinsider.com/discussion/158782/galaxy-s-4-on-steroids-samsung-caught-doping-in-benchmarks. Accessed 13 Jan 2017
3. Arthur, W.B.: Competing technologies, increasing returns, and lock-in by historical events. Econ. J. **99**(394), 116–131 (1989). http://www.jstor.org/stable/2234208
4. Barthe, G., Crespo, J.M., Kunz, C.: Relational verification using product programs. In: Butler, M., Schulte, W. (eds.) FM 2011. LNCS, vol. 6664, pp. 200–214. Springer, Heidelberg (2011). doi:10.1007/978-3-642-21437-0_17
5. Barthe, G., D'Argenio, P.R., Finkbeiner, B., Hermanns, H.: Facets of software doping. In: Margaria, T., Steffen, B. (eds.) ISoLA 2016. LNCS, vol. 9953, pp. 601–608. Springer, Heidelberg (2016). doi:10.1007/978-3-319-47169-3_46
6. Barthe, G., D'Argenio, P.R., Rezk, T.: Secure information flow by self-composition. In: CSFW-17, pp. 100–114. IEEE Computer Society (2004). http://doi.ieeecomputersociety.org/10.1109/CSFW.2004.17
7. Barthe, G., D'Argenio, P.R., Rezk, T.: Secure information flow by self-composition. Math. Struct. Comput. Sci. **21**(6), 1207–1252 (2011). http://dx.doi.org/10.1017/S0960129511000193
8. Barthe, G., Gaboardi, M., Arias, E.J.G., Hsu, J., Roth, A., Strub, P.: Higher-order approximate relational refinement types for mechanism design and differential privacy. In: Rajamani, S.K., Walker, D. (eds.) POPL 2015, pp. 55–68. ACM (2015). http://doi.acm.org/10.1145/2676726.2677000
9. Baum, K.: What the hack is wrong with software doping? In: Margaria, T., Steffen, B. (eds.) ISoLA 2016. LNCS, vol. 9953, pp. 633–647. Springer, Heidelberg (2016). doi:10.1007/978-3-319-47169-3_49
10. Benton, N.: Simple relational correctness proofs for static analyses and program transformations. In: Jones, N.D., Leroy, X. (eds.) POPL 2004, pp. 14–25. ACM Press (2004). http://doi.acm.org/10.1145/964001.964003

11. Brignall, M.: 'Error 53' fury mounts as Apple software update threatens to kill your iPhone 6. The Guardian (2010). https://www.theguardian.com/money/2016/feb/05/error-53-apple-iphone-software-update-handset-worthless-third-party-repair. Accessed 13 Jan 2017
12. Carrel, P., Bryan, V., Croft, A.: Germany asks Opel for more information in Zafira emissions probe. Reuters (2016). http://www.reuters.com/article/us-volkswagen-emissions-germany-opel-idUSKCN0Y92GI. Accessed 13 Jan 2017
13. Chaudhuri, S., Gulwani, S., Lublinerman, R.: Continuity analysis of programs. In: Hermenegildo, M.V., Palsberg, J. (eds.) POPL 2010, pp. 57–70 (2010). http://doi.acm.org/10.1145/1706299.1706308
14. Checkoway, S., Niederhagen, R., Everspaugh, A., Green, M., Lange, T., Ristenpart, T., Bernstein, D.J., Maskiewicz, J., Shacham, H., Fredrikson, M.: On the practical exploitability of dual EC in TLS implementations. In: Fu, K., Jung, J. (eds.) 23rd USENIX Security Symposium. pp. 319–335. USENIX Association (2014). https://www.usenix.org/conference/usenixsecurity14/technical-sessions/presentation/checkoway
15. Clarkson, M.R., Finkbeiner, B., Koleini, M., Micinski, K.K., Rabe, M.N., Sánchez, C.: Temporal logics for hyperproperties. In: Abadi, M., Kremer, S. (eds.) POST 2014. LNCS, vol. 8414, pp. 265–284. Springer, Heidelberg (2014). doi:10.1007/978-3-642-54792-8_15
16. Clarkson, M.R., Schneider, F.B.: Hyperproperties. In: CSF 2008, pp. 51–65 (2008). http://dx.doi.org/10.1109/CSF.2008.7
17. Clarkson, M.R., Schneider, F.B.: Hyperproperties. J. Comput. Secur. 18(6), 1157–1210 (2010). http://dx.doi.org/10.3233/JCS-2009-0393
18. Dijkstra, E.: A Discipline of Programming. Prentice Hall PTR, Upper Saddle River (1997)
19. Domke, F., Lange, D.: The exhaust emissions scandal ("Dieselgate"). In: 30th Chaos Communication Congress (2015). https://events.ccc.de/congress/2015/Fahrplan/events/7331.html. Accessed 13 Jan 2017
20. Dvorak, J.C.: The secret printer companies are keeping from you. PC Mag UK (2012). http://uk.pcmag.com/printers/60628/opinion/the-secret-printer-companies-are-keeping-from-you. Accessed 13 Jan 2017
21. Feldman, A.J., Halderman, J.A., Felten, E.W.: Security analysis of the Diebold AccuVote-ts voting machine. In: Martinez, R., Wagner, D. (eds.) 2007 USENIX/ACCURATE Electronic Voting Technology Workshop, EVT 2007. USENIX Association (2007). https://www.usenix.org/conference/evt-07/security-analysis-diebold-accuvote-ts-voting-machine
22. Felsing, D., Grebing, S., Klebanov, V., Rümmer, P., Ulbrich, M.: Automating regression verification. In: Crnkovic, I., Chechik, M., Grünbacher, P. (eds.) ASE 2014, pp. 349–360. ACM (2014). http://doi.acm.org/10.1145/2642937.2642987
23. Finkbeiner, B., Hahn, C.: Deciding Hyperproperties. In: Desharnais, J., Jagadeesan, R. (eds.) CONCUR 2016. LIPIcs, vol. 59, pp. 13:1–13:14. Schloss Dagstuhl-Leibniz-Zentrum fuer Informatik (2016). http://drops.dagstuhl.de/opus/volltexte/2016/6170
24. Finkbeiner, B., Rabe, M.N., Sánchez, C.: Algorithms for model checking HyperLTL and HyperCTL*. In: Kroening, D., Păsăreanu, C.S. (eds.) CAV 2015. LNCS, vol. 9206, pp. 30–48. Springer, Heidelberg (2015). doi:10.1007/978-3-319-21690-4_3
25. Flak, A., Taylor, E., Wacket, M., Eckert, V., Stonestreet, J.: Test of fiat diesel model shows irregular emissions: Bild am Sonntag. Reuters (2016). http://www.reuters.com/article/us-fiat-emissions-germany-idUSKCN0XL0MT. Accessed 13 Jan 2017

26. Giacobazzi, R., Mastroeni, I.: Abstract non-interference: parameterizing non-interference by abstract interpretation. In: Jones, N.D., Leroy, X. (eds.) POPL 2004, pp. 186–197. ACM (2004). http://doi.acm.org/10.1145/964001.964017
27. Godlin, B., Strichman, O.: Regression verification: proving the equivalence of similar programs. Softw. Test. Verif. Reliab. **23**(3), 241–258 (2013)
28. Hatton, L., van Genuchten, M.: When software crosses a line. IEEE Softw. **33**(1), 29–31 (2016). http://dx.doi.org/10.1109/MS.2016.6
29. Hawblitzel, C., Howell, J., Kapritsos, M., Lorch, J.R., Parno, B., Roberts, M.L., Setty, S.T.V., Zill, B.: IronFleet: proving practical distributed systems correct. In: Miller, E.L., Hand, S. (eds.) SOSP 2015, pp. 1–17. ACM (2015). http://doi.acm.org/10.1145/2815400.2815428
30. Hawblitzel, C., Lahiri, S.K., Pawar, K., Hashmi, H., Gokbulut, S., Fernando, L., Detlefs, D., Wadsworth, S.: Will you still compile me tomorrow? Static cross-version compiler validation. In: Meyer, B., Baresi, L., Mezini, M. (eds.) ESEC/FSE 2013, pp. 191–201 (2013). http://doi.acm.org/10.1145/2491411.2491442
31. Kovács, M., Seidl, H., Finkbeiner, B.: Relational abstract interpretation for the verification of 2-hypersafety properties. In: Sadeghi, A., Gligor, V.D., Yung, M. (eds.) CCS 2013, pp. 211–222. ACM (2013). http://doi.acm.org/10.1145/2508859.2516721
32. Lahiri, S.K., Hawblitzel, C., Kawaguchi, M., Rebêlo, H.: SYMDIFF: a language-agnostic semantic diff tool for imperative programs. In: Madhusudan, P., Seshia, S.A. (eds.) CAV 2012. LNCS, vol. 7358, pp. 712–717. Springer, Heidelberg (2012). doi:10.1007/978-3-642-31424-7_54
33. Manjoo, F.: Take that, stupid printer! Slate (2008). http://www.slate.com/articles/technology/technology/2008/08/take_that_stupid_printer.html. Accessed 13 Jan 2017
34. Margaria, T., Steffen, B. (eds.): ISoLA 2016. LNCS, vol. 9953. Springer, Heidelberg (2016)
35. Milushev, D., Clarke, D.: Incremental hyperproperty model checking via games. In: Riis Nielson, H., Gollmann, D. (eds.) NordSec 2013. LNCS, vol. 8208, pp. 247–262. Springer, Heidelberg (2013). doi:10.1007/978-3-642-41488-6_17
36. Panzarino, M.: Apple apologizes and updates iOS to restore iPhones disabled by error 53. TechCrunch (2016). https://techcrunch.com/2016/02/18/apple-apologizes-and-updates-ios-to-restore-iphones-disabled-by-error-53/. Accessed 13 Jan 2017
37. Schneier, B., Fredrikson, M., Kohno, T., Ristenpart, T.: Surreptitiously weakening cryptographic systems. IACR Cryptology ePrint Archive 2015, 97 (2015). http://eprint.iacr.org/2015/097
38. Sousa, M., Dillig, I.: Cartesian Hoare logic for verifying k-safety properties. In: Krintz, C., Berger, E. (eds.) PLDI 2016, pp. 57–69. ACM (2016). http://doi.acm.org/10.1145/2908080.2908092
39. Terauchi, T., Aiken, A.: Secure information flow as a safety problem. In: Hankin, C., Siveroni, I. (eds.) SAS 2005. LNCS, vol. 3672, pp. 352–367. Springer, Heidelberg (2005). doi:10.1007/11547662_24
40. Tritech Computer Solutions: Dell laptops reject third-party batteries and AC adapters/chargers. Hardware vendor lock-in? https://nctritech.wordpress.com/2010/01/26/dell-laptops-reject-third-party-batteries-and-ac-adapterschargers-hardware-vendor-lock-in/ (2010). Accessed 13 Jan 2017

41. Waller, K.: Has a printer update rendered your cartridges redundant? Which? (2016). https://conversation.which.co.uk/technology/printer-software-update-thi rd-party-printer-ink/. Accessed 13 Jan 2017
42. Waste Ink: Epson firmware update = no to compatibles. http://www.wasteink.co. uk/epson-firmware-update-compatible-problem/ (2012). Accessed 13 Jan 2017
43. Wikipedia: Volkswagen emissions scandal. Wikipedia, The Free Encyclopedia (2016). https://en.wikipedia.org/wiki/Volkswagen_emissions_scandal. Accessed 13 Jan 2017
44. Yang, H.: Relational separation logic. Theor. Comput. Sci. **375**(1–3), 308–334 (2007). http://dx.doi.org/10.1016/j.tcs.2006.12.036

Friends with Benefits

Implementing Corecursion in Foundational Proof Assistants

Jasmin Christian Blanchette[1,2]([envelope]), Aymeric Bouzy[3], Andreas Lochbihler[4], Andrei Popescu[5,6], and Dmitriy Traytel[4]([envelope])

[1] Vrije Universiteit Amsterdam, Amsterdam, The Netherlands
j.c.blanchette@vu.nl
[2] Inria Nancy – Grand Est, Nancy, France
[3] Laboratoire d'informatique, École Polytechnique, Palaiseau, France
[4] Department of Computer Science, Institute of Information Security,
ETH Zürich, Switzerland
traytel@inf.ethz.ch
[5] Department of Computer Science, Middlesex University, London, UK
[6] Institute of Mathematics Simion Stoilow of the Romanian Academy,
Bucharest, Romania

Abstract. We introduce AmiCo, a tool that extends a proof assistant, Isabelle/HOL, with flexible function definitions well beyond primitive corecursion. All definitions are certified by the assistant's inference kernel to guard against inconsistencies. A central notion is that of *friends*: functions that preserve the productivity of their arguments and that are allowed in corecursive call contexts. As new friends are registered, corecursion benefits by becoming more expressive. We describe this process and its implementation, from the user's specification to the synthesis of a higher-order definition to the registration of a friend. We show some substantial case studies where our approach makes a difference.

1 Introduction

Codatatypes and corecursion are emerging as a major methodology for programming with infinite objects. Unlike in traditional lazy functional programming, codatatypes support *total (co)programming* [1,8,30,68], where the defined functions have a simple set-theoretic semantics and productivity is guaranteed. The proof assistants Agda [19], Coq [12], and Matita [7] have been supporting this methodology for years.

By contrast, proof assistants based on higher-order logic (HOL), such as HOL4 [64], HOL Light [32], and Isabelle/HOL [56], have traditionally provided only datatypes. Isabelle/HOL is the first of these systems to also offer codatatypes. It took two years, and about 24 000 lines of Standard ML, to move from an understanding of the mathematics [18,67] to an implementation that automates the process of checking high-level user specifications and producing the necessary corecursion and coinduction theorems [16].

© Springer-Verlag GmbH Germany 2017
H. Yang (Ed.): ESOP 2017, LNCS 10201, pp. 111–140, 2017.
DOI: 10.1007/978-3-662-54434-1_5

There are important differences between Isabelle/HOL and type theory systems such as Coq in the way they handle corecursion. Consider the codatatype of streams given by

codatatype α stream $=$ (shd: α) $\lhd$ (stl: α stream)

where $\lhd$ (written infix) is the constructor, and shd and stl are the head and tail selectors, respectively. In Coq, a definition such as

```
corec natsFrom : nat → nat stream where
  natsFrom n = n ⊲ natsFrom (n + 1)
```

which introduces the function $n \mapsto n \lhd n + 1 \lhd n + 2 \lhd \cdots$, is accepted after a syntactic check that detects the $\lhd$-guardedness of the corecursive call. In Isabelle, this check is replaced by a deeper analysis. The `primcorec` command [16] transforms a user specification into a *blueprint* object: the coalgebra $b = \lambda n.\ (n, n{+}1)$. Then natsFrom is defined as $\mathsf{corec}_{\mathsf{stream}}\ b$, where $\mathsf{corec}_{\mathsf{stream}}$ is the fixed primitive corecursive combinator for α stream. Finally, the user specification is derived as a theorem from the definition and the characteristic equation of the corecursor.

Unlike in type theories, where (co)datatypes and (co)recursion are built-in, the HOL philosophy is to reduce every new construction to the core logic. This usually requires a lot of implementation work but guarantees that definitions introduce no inconsistencies. Since codatatypes and corecursion are derived concepts, there is no a priori restriction on the expressiveness of user specifications other than expressiveness of HOL itself.

Consider a variant of natsFrom, where the function add1 : nat $\rightarrow$ nat stream $\rightarrow$ nat stream adds 1 to each element of a stream:

```
corec natsFrom : nat → nat stream where
  natsFrom n = n ⊲ add1 (natsFrom n)
```

Coq's syntactic check fails on add1. After all, add1 could explore the tail of its argument before it produces a constructor, hence blocking productivity and leading to underspecification or inconsistency.

Isabelle's bookkeeping allows for more nuances. Suppose add1 has been defined as

```
corec add1 : nat stream → nat stream where
  add1 ns = (shd ns + 1) ⊲ add1 (stl ns)
```

When analyzing add1's specification, the `corec` command synthesizes its definition as a blueprint b. This definition can then be proved to be *friendly*, hence acceptable in corecursive call contexts when defining other functions. Functions with friendly definitions are called friendly, or *friends*. These functions preserve productivity by consuming at most one constructor when producing one.

Our previous work [17] presented the category theory underlying friends, based on more expressive blueprints than the one shown above for primitive corecursion. We now introduce a tool, AmiCo, that automates the process of applying and incrementally improving corecursion.

To demonstrate AmiCo's expressiveness and convenience, we used it to formalize eight case studies in Isabelle, featuring a variety of codatatypes and corecursion styles (Sect. 2). A few of these examples required ingenuity and suggest directions for future work. Most of the examples fall in the executable framework of Isabelle, which allows for code extraction to Haskell via Isabelle's code generator. One of them pushes the boundary of executability, integrating friends in the quantitative world of probabilities.

At the low level, the *corecursion state* summarizes what the system knows at a given point, including the set of available friends and a corecursor *up to* friends (Sect. 3). Polymorphism complicates the picture, because some friends may be available only for specific instances of a polymorphic codatatype. To each corecursor corresponds a coinduction principle up to friends and a uniqueness theorem that can be used to reason about corecursive functions. All of the constructions and theorems are derived from first principles, without requiring new axioms or extensions of the logic. This *foundational approach* prevents the introduction of inconsistencies, such as those that have affected the termination and productivity checkers of Agda and Coq in recent years.

The user interacts with our tool via the following commands to the proof assistant (Sect. 4). The `corec` command defines a function f by extracting a blueprint *b* from a user's specification, defining f using *b* and a corecursor, and deriving the original specification from the characteristic property of the corecursor. Moreover, `corec` supports mixed recursion–corecursion specifications, exploiting proof assistant infrastructure for terminating (well-founded) recursion. Semantic proof obligations, notably termination, are either discharged automatically or presented to the user. Specifying the `friend` option to `corec` additionally registers f as a friend, enriching the corecursor state. Another command, `friend_of_corec`, registers existing functions as friendly. Friendliness amounts to the relational parametricity [60, 69] of a selected part of the definition [17], which in this paper we call a *surface*. The tool synthesizes the surface, and the parametricity proof is again either discharged automatically or presented to the user.

AmiCo is a significant piece of engineering, at about 7000 lines of Standard ML code (Sect. 5). It subsumes a crude prototype [17] based on a shell script and template files that automated the corecursor derivation but left the blueprint and surface synthesis problems to the user. Our tool is available as part of the official Isabelle2016-1 release. The formalized examples and case studies are provided in an archive [14].

The contributions of this paper are the following:

- We describe our tool's design, algorithms, and implementation as a foundational extension of Isabelle/HOL, taking the form of the `corec`, `friend_of_corec`, `corecursive` and `coinduction_upto` commands and the *corec_unique* proof method.
- We apply our tool to a wide range of case studies, most of which are either beyond the reach of competing systems or would require type annotations and additional proofs.

More details, including thorough descriptions and proofs of correctness for the surface synthesis algorithm and the mixed recursion–corecursion pipeline, are included in a technical report [15]. Although our tool works for Isabelle, the same methodology is immediately applicable to any prover in the HOL family (including HOL4, HOL Light, HOL Zero [6], and HOL-Omega [34]), whose users represent about half of the proof assistant community. Moreover, a similar methodology is in principle applicable to provers based on type theory, such as Agda, Coq, and Matita (Sect. 6).

Conventions. We recall the syntax relevant for this paper, relying on the standard set-theoretic interpretation of HOL [27].

We fix infinite sets of type variables $\alpha, \beta, \ldots$ and term variables $x, y, \ldots$ and a higher-order signature, consisting of a set of type constructors including bool and the binary constructors for functions ($\rightarrow$), products ($\times$), and sums ($+$). Types σ, τ are defined using type variables and applying type constructors, normally written postfix. Isabelle /HOL supports Haskell-style type classes, with :: expressing class membership (e.g., int :: ring).

Moreover, we assume a set of polymorphic constants c, f, g, $\ldots$ with declared types, including equality $= : \alpha \rightarrow \alpha \rightarrow$ bool, left and right product projections fst and snd, and left and right sum embeddings Inl and Inr. Terms t are built from constants c and variables x by means of typed λ-abstraction and application. Polymorphic constants and terms will be freely used in contexts that require a less general type.

2   Motivating Examples

We apply AmiCo to eight case studies to demonstrate its benefits—in particular, the flexibility that friends provide and reasoning by uniqueness (of solutions to corecursive equations). The first four examples demonstrate the flexibility that friends provide. The third one also features reasoning by uniqueness. The fourth example crucially relies on a form of nested corecursion where the operator under definition must be recognized as a friend. The fifth through seventh examples mix recursion with corecursion and discuss the associated proof techniques. The last example, about a probabilistic process calculus, takes our tool to its limits: We discuss how to support corecursion through monadic sequencing and mix unbounded recursion with corecursion. All eight formalizations are available online [14], together with our earlier stream examples [17].

Since all examples are taken from the literature, we focus on the formalization with AmiCo. No detailed understanding is needed to see that they fit within the friends framework. Background information can be found in the referenced works.

Remarkably, none of the eight examples work with Coq's or Matita's standard mechanisms. Sized types in Agda [4] can cope with the first six but fail on the last two: In one case a function must inspect an infinite list unboundedly deeply, and in the other case the codatatype cannot even be defined in Agda. The Dafny verifier, which also provides codatatypes [46], supports only the seventh case study.

2.1   Coinductive Languages

Rutten [62] views formal languages as infinite tries, i.e., prefix trees branching over the alphabet with boolean labels at the nodes indicating whether the path from the root denotes a word in the language. The type α lang features corecursion through the right-hand side of the function arrow ($\rightarrow$).

    `codatatype` α lang $=$ Lang $(o :$ bool$) (\delta : \alpha \rightarrow \alpha$ lang$)$

Traytel [66] has formalized tries in Isabelle using a codatatype, defined regular operations on them as corecursive functions, and proved by coinduction that the defined operations form a Kleene algebra. Because Isabelle offered only primitive corecursion when this formalization was developed, the definition of concatenation, iteration, and shuffle product was tedious, spanning more than a hundred lines.

    Corecursion up to friends eliminates this tedium. The following extract from an Isabelle formalization is all that is needed to define the main operations on languages:

    `corec (friend)` $+ : \alpha$ lang $\rightarrow \alpha$ lang $\rightarrow \alpha$ lang `where`
      $L + K =$ Lang $(o\ L \vee o\ K) (\lambda a.\ \delta\ L\ a + \delta\ K\ a)$

    `corec (friend)` $\cdot : \alpha$ lang $\rightarrow \alpha$ lang $\rightarrow \alpha$ lang `where`
      $L \cdot K =$ Lang $(o\ L \wedge o\ K) (\lambda a.$ if $o\ L$ then $(\delta\ L\ a \cdot K) + \delta\ K\ a$ else $\delta\ L\ a \cdot K)$

    `corec (friend)` $* : \alpha$ lang $\rightarrow \alpha$ lang `where`
      $L^* =$ Lang True $(\lambda a.\ \delta\ L\ a \cdot L^*)$

    `corec (friend)` $\parallel : \alpha$ lang $\rightarrow \alpha$ lang $\rightarrow \alpha$ lang `where`
      $L \parallel K =$ Lang $(o\ L \wedge o\ K) (\lambda a.\ (\delta\ L\ a \cdot K) + (L \cdot \delta\ K\ a))$

Concatenation ($\cdot$) and shuffle product ($\parallel$) are corecursive up to alternation ($+$), and iteration ($*$) is corecursive up to concatenation ($\cdot$). All four definitions use an alternative λ-based syntax for performing corecursion under the right-hand side of $\rightarrow$, instead of applying the functorial action map$_\rightarrow$ $= \circ$ (composition) associated with $\rightarrow$.

    The `corec` command is provided by AmiCo, whereas `codatatype` and `primcorec` (Sect. 3.2) has been part of Isabelle since 2013. The `friend` option registers the defined functions as friends and automatically discharges the emerging proof obligations, which ensure that friends consume at most one constructor to produce one constructor.

    Proving equalities on tries conveniently works by coinduction up to congruence (Sect. 3.7). Already before `corec`'s existence, Traytel was able to write automatic one-line proofs such as

    `lemma` $K \cdot (L + M) = K \cdot L + K \cdot M$
      `by` (*coinduction arbitrary: K L M rule: +.coinduct*) *auto*

The *coinduction* proof method [16] instantiates the bisimulation witness of the given coinduction rule before applying it backwards. Without `corec`, the rule $+.coinduct$ of coinduction up to congruence had to be stated and proved manually, including the manual inductive definition of the congruence closure under $+$.

Overall, the usage of `corec` compressed Traytel's development from 750 to 600 lines of Isabelle text. In Agda, Abel [3] has formalized Traytel's work up to proving the recursion equation $L^* = \varepsilon + L \cdot L^*$ for iteration (*) in 219 lines of Agda text, which correspond to 125 lines in our version. His definitions are as concise as ours, but his proofs require more manual steps.

2.2 Knuth–Morris–Pratt String Matching

Building on the trie view of formal languages, van Laarhoven [44] discovered a concise formulation of the Knuth–Morris–Pratt algorithm [41] for finding one string in another:

> is-substring-of xs ys = match (mk-table xs) ys
> match t xs = (o t $\vee$ ($xs \neq$ [] $\wedge$ match (δ t (hd x) (tl xs))))
> mk-table xs = let table = tab xs ($\lambda\_.$ table) in table
> tab [] f = Lang True f
> tab ($x \lhd xs$) f = Lang False ($\lambda c.$ if $c = x$ then tab xs (δ (f x)) else f c)

Here, we overload the stream constructor $\lhd$ for finite lists; hd and tl are the selectors. In our context, table : α lang is the most interesting definition because it corecurses through tab. Since there is no constructor guard, table would appear not to be productive. However, the constructor is merely hidden in tab and can be pulled out by unrolling the definition of tab as follows.

As the first step, we register Δ defined by Δ xs $f = \delta$ (tab xs f) as a friend, using the `friend_of_corec` command provided by our tool. The registration of an existing function as a friend requires us to supply an equation with a constructor-guarded right-hand side and to prove the equation and the parametricity of the destructor-free part of the right-hand side, called the surface (Sect. 3.4). Then the definition of table corecurses through Δ. Finally, we derive the original specification by unrolling the definition. We can use the derived specification in the proofs, because proofs in HOL do not depend on the actual definition (unlike in type theory).

> `corec tab` : α list $\rightarrow$ ($\alpha \rightarrow \alpha$ lang) $\rightarrow \alpha$ lang `where`
>   tab xs f = Lang (xs = []) ($\lambda c.$ if xs = [] $\vee$ hd $xs \neq c$ then f c else tab (tl xs) (δ (f c)))
>
> `definition` Δ : α list $\rightarrow$ ($\alpha \rightarrow \alpha$ lang) $\rightarrow \alpha \rightarrow \alpha$ lang `where`
> Δ xs f = δ (tab xs f)
>
> `friend_of_corec` Δ `where`
> Δ xs f c = Lang
>   (if xs = [] $\vee$ hd $xs \neq c$ then o (f x) else tl xs = [])
>   (if xs = [] $\vee$ hd $xs \neq c$ then δ (f x) else Δ (tl xs) (δ (f c)))
>   ⟨two-line proof of the equation and of parametricity⟩
>
> `context fixes` xs : α list `begin`
>   `corec table` : α lang `where`
>   table = Lang (xs = []) (Δ xs ($\lambda\_.$ table))

```
    lemma table = tab xs (λ_. table)
      ⟨one-line proof⟩
end
```

2.3   The Stern–Brocot Tree

The next application involves infinite trees of rational numbers. It is based on Hinze's work on the Stern–Brocot and Bird trees [33] and the Isabelle formalization by Gammie and Lochbihler [25]. It illustrates reasoning by uniqueness (Sect. 3.7).

The Stern–Brocot tree contains all the rational numbers in their lowest terms. It is an infinite binary tree frac tree of formal fractions frac = nat × nat. Each node is labeled with the mediant of its rightmost and leftmost ancestors, where mediant (a, c) $(b, d) = (a + b, c + d)$. Gammie and Lochbihler define the tree via an iterative helper function.

  codatatype α tree = Node (root: α) (left: α tree) (right: α tree)

  primcorec stern-brocot-gen : frac → frac → frac tree where
    stern-brocot-gen l u =
      let m=mediant l u in Node m (stern-brocot-gen l m) (stern-brocot-gen m u)

  definition stern-brocot : frac tree where
    stern-brocot = stern-brocot-gen $(0, 1)$ $(1, 0)$

Using AmiCo, we can directly formalize Hinze's corecursive specification of the tree, where nxt $(m, n) = (m + n, n)$ and swap $(m, n) = (n, m)$. The tree is corecursive up to the two friends suc and $1 / t$.

  corec (friend) suc : frac tree → frac tree where
    suc t = Node (nxt (root t)) (suc (left t)) (suc (right t))

  corec (friend) $1 / \_$: frac tree → frac tree where
    $1 / t$ = Node (swap (root t)) (1 / left t) (1 / right t)

  corec stern-brocot : frac tree where
    stern-brocot = Node $(1, 1)$ (1 / (suc (1 / stern-brocot))) (suc stern-brocot)

Without the iterative detour, the proofs, too, become more direct as the statements need not be generalized for the iterative helper function. For example, Hinze relies on the uniqueness principle to show that a loopless linearization stream stern-brocot of the tree yields Dijkstra's fusc function [23] given by

$$\text{fusc} = 1 \lhd \text{fusc}' \qquad \text{fusc}' = 1 \lhd (\text{fusc} + \text{fusc}' - 2 \cdot (\text{fusc mod fusc}'))$$

where all arithmetic operations are lifted to streams elementwise—e.g., $xs + ys = \text{map}_{\text{stream}} (+) (xs \mathbin{\text{\textit{z}}} ys)$, where $\textit{z}$ zips two streams. We define fusc and stream as follows. To avoid the mutual corecursion, we inline fusc in fusc' for the definition with corec, after having registered the arithmetic operations as friends:

corec fusc$'$: nat stream where
    fusc$'$ = $1 \lhd ((1 \lhd$ fusc$') +$ fusc$' - 2 \cdot ((1 \lhd$ fusc$')$ mod fusc$'))$

definition fusc : nat stream where
    fusc = $1 \lhd$ fusc$'$

corec chop : α tree $\rightarrow$ α tree where
    chop (Node $x\ l\ r$) = Node (root l) r (chop l)

corec stream : α tree $\rightarrow$ α stream where
    stream t = root $t \lhd$ stream (chop t)

Hinze proves that stream stern-brocot equals fusc ℓ fusc$'$ by showing that both satisfy the corecursion equation $x = (1, 1) \lhd$ map$_{stream}$ step x, where step $(m, n) = (n, m + n - 2 \cdot (m \bmod n))$. This equation yields the loopless algorithm, because siterate step $(1, 1)$ satisfies it as well, where siterate is defined by

primcorec siterate : $(\alpha \rightarrow \alpha) \rightarrow \alpha \rightarrow \alpha$ stream where
    siterate $f\ x$ = $x \lhd$ siterate $f\ (f\ x)$

Our tool generates a proof rule for uniqueness of solutions to the recursion equation (Sect. 3.7). We conduct the equivalence proofs using this rule.

For another example, all rational numbers also occur in the Bird tree given by

corec bird : frac tree where
    bird = Node $(1, 1)$ (1 / suc bird) (suc (1 / bird))

It satisfies 1 / bird = mirror bird, where mirror corecursively swaps all subtrees. Again, we prove this identity by showing that both sides satisfy the corecursion equation $x =$ Node $(1, 1)$ (suc $(1 / x)$) $(1 /$ suc $x)$. This equation does not correspond to any function defined with corec, but we can derive its uniqueness principle using our proof method *corec_unique* without defining the function. The Isabelle proof is quite concise:

let $?H = \lambda x$. Node $(1, 1)$ (suc $(1 / x)$) $(1 /$ suc $x)$
have mb: mirror bird = $?H$ (mirror bird)   by (*rule* tree.*expand*) ...
have *unique*: $\forall t.\ t = ?H\ t \longrightarrow t =$ mirror bird by *corec_unique* (*fact mb*)
have 1 / bird = $?H$ (1 / bird)   by (*rule* tree.*expand*) ...
then show 1 / bird = mirror bird   by (*rule unique*)

No coinduction is needed: The identities are proved by expanding the definitions a finite number of times (once each here). We also show that odd-mirror bird = stern-brocot by uniqueness, where odd-mirror swaps the subtrees only at levels of odd depth.

Gammie and Lochbihler manually derive each uniqueness rule using a separate coinduction proof. For odd-mirror alone, the proof requires 25 lines. With AmiCo's *corec_unique* proof method, such proofs are automatic.

2.4   Breadth-First Tree Labeling

Abel and Pientka [4] demonstrate the expressive power of sized types in Agda with the example of labeling the nodes of an infinite binary tree in breadth-first order, which they adapted from Jones and Gibbons [39]. The function bfs takes a stream of streams of labels as input and labels the nodes at depth i according to a prefix of the ith input stream. It also outputs the streams of unused labels. Then bf ties the knot by feeding the unused labels back into bfs :

bfs $((x \lhd xs) \lhd ys) =$
   let $(l, ys') =$ bfs $ys; (r, ys'') =$ bfs ys' in (Node $x\ l\ r,\ xs \lhd ys'')$

bf $xs =$ let $(t, lbls) =$ bfs $(xs \lhd lbls)$ in t

Because bfs returns a pair, we define the two projections separately and derive the original specification for bfs trivially from the definitions. One of the corecursive calls to bfs_2 occurs in the context of bfs_2 itself—it is "self-friendly" (Sect. 4.2).

corec (friend) $\mathsf{bfs}_2 : \alpha$ stream stream $\rightarrow \alpha$ stream stream
   where $\mathsf{bfs}_2 ((x \lhd xs) \lhd ys) = xs \lhd \mathsf{bfs}_2 (\mathsf{bfs}_2\ ys)$

corec $\mathsf{bfs}_1 : \alpha$ stream stream $\rightarrow \alpha$ tree where
   $\mathsf{bfs}_1 ((x \lhd xs) \lhd ys) =$ Node x $(\mathsf{bfs}_1\ ys)$ $(\mathsf{bfs}_1 (\mathsf{bfs}_2\ ys))$

definition bfs : α stream $\rightarrow \alpha$ tree where
   bfs $xss = (\mathsf{bfs}_1\ xss, \mathsf{bfs}_2\ xss)$

corec labels : α stream $\rightarrow \alpha$ stream stream where
   labels $xs = \mathsf{bfs}_2 (xs \lhd$ labels $xs)$

definition bf : α stream $\rightarrow \alpha$ tree where
   bf $xs = \mathsf{bfs}_1 (xs \lhd$ labels $xs)$

For comparison, Abel's and Pientka's formalization in Agda is of similar size, but the user must provide some size hints for the corecursive calls.

2.5   Stream Processors

Stream processors are a standard example of mixed fixpoints:

datatype (α, β, δ) $\mathsf{sp}_\mu =$ Get $(\alpha \rightarrow (\alpha, \beta, \delta)\ \mathsf{sp}_\mu)$ | Put $\beta\ \delta$
codatatype (α, β) $\mathsf{sp}_\nu =$ In (out: $(\alpha, \beta, (\alpha, \beta)\ \mathsf{sp}_\nu)\ \mathsf{sp}_\mu)$

When defining functions on these objects, we previously had to break them into a recursive and a corecursive part, using Isabelle's primcorec command for the latter [16]. Since our tool supports mixed recursion–corecursion, we can now express functions on stream processors more directly.

We present two functions. The first one runs a stream processor:

corecursive run : (α, β) $\mathsf{sp}_\nu \rightarrow \alpha$ stream $\rightarrow \beta$ stream where
   run $sp\ s =$ case out sp of
       Get $f \Rightarrow$ run (In $(f$ (shd $s)))$ (stl s)
       | Put $b\ sp \Rightarrow b \lhd$ run $sp\ s$
   ⟨two-line termination proof⟩

The second function, ∘∘, composes two stream processors:

```
corec (friend) get where
  get f = In (Get (λa. out (f a)))

corecursive ∘∘ : (β, γ) sp_ν → (α, β) sp_ν → (α, γ) sp_ν where
  sp ∘∘ sp' = case (out sp, out sp') of
    (Put b sp, _) ⇒ In (Put b (sp ∘∘ sp'))
  | (Get f, Put b sp') ⇒ In (f b) ∘∘ sp'
  | (_, Get f') ⇒ get (λa. sp ∘∘ In (f' a))
  ⟨two-line termination proof⟩
```

The selector out in the noncorecursive friend get is legal, because get also adds a constructor. In both cases, the **corecursive** command emits a termination proof obligation, which we discharged in two lines, using the same techniques as when defining recursive functions. This command is equivalent to **corec**, except that it lets the user discharge proof obligations instead of applying some standard proof automation.

2.6 A Calculator

Next, we formalize a calculator example by Hur et al. [37]. The calculator inputs a number, computes the double of the sum of all inputs, and outputs the current value of the sum. When the input is 0, the calculator counts down to 0 and starts again. Hur et al. implement two versions, f and g, in a programming language embedded deeply in Coq and prove that f simulates g using parameterized coinduction.

We model the calculator in a shallow fashion as a function from the current sum to a stream processor for nats. Let calc abbreviate $nat \rightarrow (nat, nat)$ sp_ν. We can write the program directly as a function and very closely to its specification [37, Fig. 2]. In f and g, the corecursion goes through the friends get and restart, and the constructor guard is hidden in the abbreviation put x sp = In (Put x sp).

```
corec (friend) restart : calc → calc where
  restart h n = if n > 0 then put n (restart h (n − 1)) else h 0

corec f : calc where
  f n = put n (get (λv. if v ≠ 0 then f (2 · v + n) else restart f (v + n)))

corec g : calc where
  g m = put (2 · m) (get (λv. if v = 0 then restart g (2 · m) else g (v + m)))
```

Our task is to prove that g m simulates f $(2 \cdot m)$. In fact, the two can even be proved to be bisimilar. In our shallow embedding, bisimilarity coincides with equality. We can prove g m = f $(2 \cdot m)$ by coinduction with the rule generated for the friends get and restart.

2.7 Lazy List Filtering

A classic example requiring a mix of recursion and corecursion is filtering on lazy lists. Given the polymorphic type of lazy lists

codatatype α llist $= [] \mid$ (lhd: α) $\lhd$ (ltl: α llist)

the task is to define the function lfilter : $(\alpha \to$ bool$) \to \alpha$ llist $\to \alpha$ llist that retains only the elements that satisfy the given predicate. Paulson [58] defined lfilter using an inductive search predicate. His development culminates in a proof of

$$\text{lfilter } P \circ \text{lfilter } Q = \text{lfilter } (\lambda x.\ P\ x \wedge Q\ x) \qquad (1)$$

In Dafny, Leino [45] suggests a definition that mixes recursion and corecursion. We can easily replicate Leino's definition in Isabelle, where **set** converts lazy lists to sets:

corecursive lfilter : $(\alpha \to$ bool$) \to \alpha$ llist $\to \alpha$ llist **where**
   lfilter P $xs =$ if $\forall x \in$ set $xs.\ \neg\ P\ x$ then $[]$
                else if P (lhd xs) then lhd $xs \lhd$ lfilter P (ltl xs)
                else lfilter P (ltl xs)
   ⟨13-line termination proof⟩

The nonexecutability of the infinite $\forall$ quantifier in the 'if' condition is unproblematic in HOL, which has no built-in notion of computation. Lochbihler and Hölzl [48] define lfilter as a least fixpoint in the prefix order on llist. Using five properties, they substantiate that fixpoint induction leads to shorter proofs than Paulson's approach.

We show how to prove three of their properties using our definition, namely (1) and

$$\text{lfilter } P\ xs = [] \longleftrightarrow (\forall x \in \text{set } xs.\ \neg\ P\ xs) \qquad (2)$$

$$\text{set } (\text{lfilter } P\ xs) = \text{set } xs \cap \{x \mid P\ x\} \qquad (3)$$

We start with (2). We prove the interesting direction, $\longrightarrow$, by induction on $x \in$ set xs, where the inductive cases are solved automatically. For (3), the $\supseteq$ direction is also a simple induction on **set**. The other direction requires two nested inductions: first on $x \in$ set (lfilter $P\ xs$) and then a well-founded induction on the termination argument for the recursion in lfilter. Finally, we prove (1) using the uniqueness principle. We first derive the uniqueness rule for lfilter by a coinduction with a nested induction; this approach reflects the mixed recursive-corecursive definition of lfilter, which nests recursion inside corecursion.

lemma *lfilter_unique*:
   $(\forall xs.\ f\ xs =$ if $\forall x \in$ set $xs.\ \neg\ P\ x$ then $[]$
                 else if P (lhd xs) then lhd $xs \lhd f$ (ltl xs)
                 else f (ltl xs)) $\longrightarrow$
      $f = $ lfilter P

(Our tool does not yet generate uniqueness rules for mixed recursive–corecursive definitions.) Then the proof of (1) is automatic:

> **lemma** lfilter P ∘ lfilter Q = lfilter ($\lambda x.\ P\ x \wedge Q\ x$)
>   **by** (*rule lfilter_unique*) (*auto elim*: llist.set_cases)

Alternatively, we could have proved (1) by coinduction with a nested induction on the termination argument. The uniqueness principle works well because it incorporates both the coinduction and the induction. This underlines that uniqueness can be an elegant proof principle for mixed recursive–corecursive definitions, despite being much weaker than coinduction in the purely corecursive case. Compared with Lochbihler and Hölzl's proofs by fixpoint induction, our proofs are roughly of the same length, but **corecursive** eliminates the need for the lengthy setup for the domain theory.

2.8 Generative Probabilistic Values

Our final example relies on a codatatype that fully exploits Isabelle's modular datatype architecture built on bounded natural functors (Sect. 3.1) and that cannot be defined easily, if at all, in other systems. This example is covered in more detail in the report [15].

Lochbihler [47] proposes generative probabilistic values (GPVs) as a semantic domain for probabilistic input–output systems. Conceptually, each GPV chooses probabilistically between failing, terminating with a result of type α, and continuing by producing an output γ and transitioning into a reactive probabilistic value (RPV), which waits for a response ρ of the environment before moving to the generative successor state. Lochbihler models GPVs as a codatatype (α, γ, ρ) gpv. He also defines a monadic language on GPVs similar to a coroutine monad and an operation inline for composing GPVs with environment converters. The definition of inline poses two challenges. First, it corecurses through the monadic sequencing operation $(\ggeq)_{\text{gpv}} : (\beta, \gamma, \rho)\ \text{gpv} \to (\beta \to (\alpha, \gamma, \rho)\ \text{gpv}) \to (\alpha, \gamma, \rho)\ \text{gpv}$. Due to HOL restrictions, all type variables in a friend's signature must show up in the resulting codatatype, which is not the case for $(\ggeq)_{\text{gpv}}$. To work around this, we define a copy gpv′ of gpv with a phantom type parameter β, register $(\ggeq)_{\text{gpv'}}$ as a friend, and define inline in terms of its copy on gpv′. Second, inline recurses in a non-well-founded manner through the environment converter. Since our tool supports only mixing with well-founded recursion, we mimic the tool's internal behavior using a least fixpoint operator.

Initially, Lochbihler had manually derived the coinduction rule up to $\ggeq_{\text{gpv}}$, which our tool now generates. However, because of the copied type, our reformulation ended up roughly as complicated as the original. Moreover, we noted that coinduction up to congruence works only for equality; for user-defined predicates (e.g., typing judgments), the coinduction rule must still be derived manually. But even though this case study is not conclusive, it demonstrates the flexibility of the framework.

3 The Low Level: Corecursor States

Starting from the primitive corecursor provided by Isabelle [16], our tool derives corecursors up to larger and larger sets of friends. The corecursion state includes the set of friends $\mathcal{F}$ and the corecursor $\text{corec}_{\mathcal{F}}$. Four operations manipulate states:

- BASE gives the first nonprimitive corecursor by registering the first friends—the constructors (Sect. 3.3);
- STEP incorporates a new friend into the corecursor (Sect. 3.4);
- MERGE combines two existing sets of friends (Sect. 3.5);
- INSTANTIATE specializes the corecursor type (Sect. 3.6).

The operations BASE and STEP have already been described in detail and with many examples in our previous paper [17]. Here, we give a brief, self-contained account of them. MERGE and INSTANTIATE are new operations whose need became apparent in the course of implementation.

3.1 Bounded Natural Functors

The mathematics behind our tool assumes that the considered type constructors are both functors and relators, that they include basic functors such as identity, constant, sum, and product, and that they are closed under least and greatest fixpoints (initial algebras and final coalgebras). The tool satisfies this requirement by employing Isabelle's infrastructure for bounded natural functors (BNFs) [16,67]. For example, the codatatype α stream is defined as the greatest solution to the fixpoint equation $\beta \cong \alpha \times \beta$, where both the right-hand side $\alpha \times \beta$ and the resulting type α stream are BNFs.

BNFs have both a functor and a relator structure. If K is a unary type constructor, we assume the existence of polymorphic constants for the functorial action, or map function, $\text{map}_K : (\alpha \rightarrow \beta) \rightarrow \alpha\ K \rightarrow \beta\ K$ and the relational action, or relator, $\text{rel}_K : (\alpha \rightarrow \beta \rightarrow \text{bool}) \rightarrow \alpha\ K \rightarrow \beta\ K \rightarrow \text{bool}$, and similarly for n-ary type constructors. For finite lists, map_{list} is the familiar map function, and given a relation r, $\text{rel}_{\text{list}}\ r$ relates two lists of the same length and with r-related elements positionwise. While the BNFs are functors on their covariant positions, the relator structure covers contravariant positions as well.

We assume that some of the polymorphic constants are known to be (relationally) *parametric* in some type variables, in the standard sense [60]. For example, if K is a ternary relator and $c : (\alpha, \beta, \gamma)\ K$, then c is parametric in β if $\text{rel}_K\ (=)\ r\ (=)\ c\ c$ holds for all $r : \beta \rightarrow \beta' \rightarrow \text{bool}$. In a slight departure from standard practice, if a term does not depend on a type variable α, we consider it parametric in α. The map function of a BNF is parametric in all its type variables. By contrast, $= : \alpha \rightarrow \alpha \rightarrow \text{bool}$ is not parametric in α.

3.2 Codatatypes and Primitive Corecursion

We fix a codatatype J. In general, J may depend on some type variables, but we leave this dependency implicit for now. While J also may have multiple, curried constructors, it is viewed at the low level as a codatatype with a single constructor $\text{ctor}_J : J \, K_{\text{ctor}} \to J$ and a destructor $\text{dtor}_J : J \to J \, K_{\text{ctor}}$:

$$\texttt{codatatype } J = \text{ctor}_J \, (\text{dtor}_J : J \, K_{\text{ctor}})$$

The mutually inverse constructor and destructor establish the isomorphism between J and $J \, K_{\text{ctor}}$. For streams, we have $\beta \, K_{\text{ctor}} = \alpha \times \beta$, $\text{ctor} \, (h, t) = h \lhd t$, and dtor $xs = (\text{shd } xs, \text{stl } xs)$. Low-level constructors and destructors combine several high-level constructors and destructors in one constant each. Internally, the $\texttt{codatatype}$ command works on the low level, providing the high-level constructors as syntactic sugar [16].

In addition, the $\texttt{codatatype}$ command derives a primitive corecursor corec_J : $(\alpha \to \alpha \, K_{\text{ctor}}) \to \alpha \to J$ characterized by the equation $\text{corec}_J \, b = \text{ctor} \circ \text{map}_{K_{\text{ctor}}} (\text{corec}_J \, b) \circ b$. The $\texttt{primcorec}$ command, provided by Isabelle, reduces a primitively corecursive specification to a plain, acyclic definition expressed using this corecursor.

3.3 Corecursion up to Constructors

We call blueprints the arguments passed to corecursors. When defining a corecursive function f, a *blueprint* for f is produced, and f is defined as the corecursor applied to the blueprint. The expressiveness of a corecursor is indicated by the codomain of its blueprint argument. The blueprint passed to the primitive corecursor must return an $\alpha \, K_{\text{ctor}}$ value—e.g., a pair $(m, x) : \text{nat} \times \alpha$ for streams of natural numbers. The remaining corecursion structure is fixed: After producing m, we proceed corecursively with x. We cannot produce two numbers before proceeding corecursively—to do so, the blueprint would have to return $(m, (n, x)) : \text{nat} \times (\text{nat} \times \alpha)$.

Our first strengthening of the corecursor allows an arbitrary number of constructors before proceeding corecursively. This process takes a codatatype J and produces an initial corecursion state $\langle \mathcal{F}, \Sigma_{\mathcal{F}}, \text{corec}_{\mathcal{F}} \rangle$, where $\mathcal{F}$ is a set of known friends, $\Sigma_{\mathcal{F}}$ is a BNF that incorporates the type signatures of known friends, and $\text{corec}_{\mathcal{F}}$ is a corecursor. We omit the set-of-friends index whenever it is clear from the context. The initial state knows only one friend, ctor.

> BASE : $J \rightsquigarrow \langle \mathcal{F}, \Sigma_{\mathcal{F}}, \text{corec}_{\mathcal{F}} \rangle$ where
> $\mathcal{F} = \{\text{ctor}\} \qquad \alpha \, \Sigma_{\mathcal{F}} = \alpha \, K_{\text{ctor}} \qquad \text{corec}_{\mathcal{F}} : (\alpha \to \alpha \, \Sigma_{\mathcal{F}}^{+}) \to \alpha \to J$

Let us define the type $\alpha \, \Sigma_{\mathcal{F}}^{+}$ used for the corecursor. First, we let $\alpha \, \Sigma_{\mathcal{F}}^{*}$ be the free monad of Σ extended with J-constant leaves:

$$\texttt{datatype } \alpha \, \Sigma_{\mathcal{F}}^{*} = \text{Oper} \, ((\alpha \, \Sigma_{\mathcal{F}}^{*}) \, \Sigma_{\mathcal{F}}) \mid \text{Var} \, \alpha \mid \text{Cst} \, J$$

Inhabitants of $\alpha \, \Sigma_{\mathcal{F}}^{*}$ are *(formal) expressions* built from variable or constant leaf nodes (Var or Cst) and a syntactic representation of the constants in $\mathcal{F}$. Writing $\boxed{\text{ctor}}$ for Oper $: (\alpha \, \Sigma_{\mathcal{F}}^{*}) \, K_{\text{ctor}} \to \alpha \, \Sigma_{\mathcal{F}}^{*}$, we can build expressions such as $\boxed{\text{ctor}} \, (1, \text{Var} \, (x : \alpha))$ and $\boxed{\text{ctor}} \, (2, \boxed{\text{ctor}} \, (3, \text{Cst} \, (xs : J)))$. The type $\alpha \, \Sigma_{\mathcal{F}}^{+}$, of *guarded expressions*, is similar to $\alpha\,\Sigma_{\mathcal{F}}^*$, except that it requires at least one $\boxed{\mathsf{ctor}}$ guard on every path to a Var. Formally, $\alpha\,\Sigma_{\mathcal{F}}^+$ is defined as $((\alpha\,\Sigma_{\mathcal{F}}^*)\,\mathsf{K}_{\mathsf{ctor}})\,\Sigma_{\mathcal{F}}^*$, so that $\mathsf{K}_{\mathsf{ctor}}$ marks the guards. To simplify notation, we will pretend that $\alpha\,\Sigma_{\mathcal{F}}^+ \subseteq \alpha\,\Sigma_{\mathcal{F}}^*$.

Guarded variable leaves represent corecursive calls. Constant leaves allow us to stop the corecursion with an immediate result of type J. The polymorphism of Σ^* is crucial. If we instantiate α to J, we can evaluate formal expressions with the function eval : $\mathsf{J}\,\Sigma^* \to \mathsf{J}$ given by eval $(\boxed{\mathsf{ctor}}\;x) = $ ctor $(\mathsf{map}_{\mathsf{K}_{\mathsf{ctor}}}$ eval $x)$, eval $(\mathsf{Var}\;t) = t$, and eval $(\mathsf{Cst}\;t) = t$. We also write eval for other versions of the operator (e.g., for $\mathsf{J}\,\Sigma^+$).

The corecursor's argument, the blueprint, returns guarded expressions consisting of one or more applications of $\boxed{\mathsf{ctor}}$ before proceeding corecursively. Proceeding corecursively means applying the corecursor to all variable leaves and evaluating the resulting expression. Formally:

$$\mathsf{corec}_{\mathcal{F}}\;b = \mathsf{eval}\circ\mathsf{map}_{\Sigma_{\mathcal{F}}^+}\,(\mathsf{corec}_{\mathcal{F}}\;b)\circ b$$

3.4 Adding New Friends

Corecursors can be strengthened to allow friendly functions to surround the context of the corecursive call. At the low level, we consider only uncurried functions.

A function f : $\mathsf{J}\,\mathsf{K}_{\mathsf{f}} \to \mathsf{J}$ is friendly if it consumes at most one constructor before producing at least one constructor. Friendliness is captured by a mixture of two syntactic constraints and the semantic requirement of parametricity of a certain term, called the *surface*. The syntactic constraints amount to requiring that f is *expressible* using $\mathsf{corec}_{\mathcal{F}}$, irrespective of its actual definition.

Specifically, f must be equal to $\mathsf{corec}_{\mathcal{F}}\;b$ for some blueprint b : $\mathsf{J}\,\mathsf{K}_{\mathsf{f}} \to (\mathsf{J}\,\mathsf{K}_{\mathsf{f}})\,\Sigma^+$ that has the guarding constructor at the outermost position, and this object must be decomposable as $b = s\circ\mathsf{map}_{\mathsf{K}_{\mathsf{f}}}\langle\mathsf{id},\mathsf{dtor}\rangle$ for some s : $(\alpha\times\alpha\,\mathsf{K}_{\mathsf{ctor}})\,\mathsf{K}_{\mathsf{f}} \to \alpha\,\Sigma^+$. The convolution operator $\langle f,g\rangle:\alpha\to\beta\times\gamma$ combines two functions $f:\alpha\to\beta$ and $g:\alpha\to\gamma$.

We call s the *surface* of b because it captures b's superficial layer while abstracting the application of the destructor. The surface s is more polymorphic than needed by the equation it has to satisfy. Moreover, s must be parametric in α. The decomposition, together with parametricity, ensures that friendly functions apply dtor at most once to their arguments and do not look any deeper—the "consumes at most one constructor" property.

STEP : $\langle\mathcal{F},\Sigma_{\mathcal{F}},\mathsf{corec}_{\mathcal{F}}\rangle$ and f : $\mathsf{J}\,\mathsf{K}_{\mathsf{f}}\to\mathsf{J}$ friendly $\rightsquigarrow \langle\mathcal{F}',\Sigma_{\mathcal{F}'},\mathsf{corec}_{\mathcal{F}'}\rangle$ where
$\mathcal{F}' = \mathcal{F}\cup\{\mathsf{f}\}$ $\alpha\,\Sigma_{\mathcal{F}'} = \alpha\,\Sigma_{\mathcal{F}}+\alpha\,\mathsf{K}_{\mathsf{f}}$ $\mathsf{corec}_{\mathcal{F}'}:(\alpha\to\alpha\,\Sigma_{\mathcal{F}'}^+)\to\alpha\to\mathsf{J}$

The return type of blueprints corresponding to $\mathsf{corec}_{\mathcal{F}'}$ is $\Sigma_{\mathcal{F}'}^+$, where $\Sigma_{\mathcal{F}'}$ extends $\Sigma_{\mathcal{F}}$ with K_{f}. The type $\Sigma_{\mathcal{F}'}^+$ allows all guarded expressions of the previous corecursor but may also refer to f. The syntactic representations $\boxed{\mathsf{g}}:\alpha\,\Sigma_{\mathcal{F}}^*\,\mathsf{K}_{\mathsf{g}}\to\alpha\,\Sigma_{\mathcal{F}}^*$ of old friends $\mathsf{g}\in\mathcal{F}$ must be lifted to the type $(\alpha\,\Sigma_{\mathcal{F}'}^*)\,\mathsf{K}_{\mathsf{g}}\to\alpha\,\Sigma_{\mathcal{F}'}^*$, which is straightforward. In the sequel, we will reuse the notation $\boxed{\text{g}}$ for the lifted syntactic representations. In addition to $\boxed{\text{g}}$, new expressions are allowed to freely use the syntactic representation $\boxed{\text{f}} : (\alpha\, \Sigma^*_{\mathcal{F}'})\, \mathsf{K}_\mathsf{f} \to \alpha\, \Sigma^*_{\mathcal{F}'}$ of the new friend f, defined as $\boxed{\text{f}} = \mathsf{Oper} \circ \mathsf{Inr}$. Like for $\boxed{\text{ctor}}$, we have eval $(\boxed{\text{f}}\, x) = \mathsf{f}\, (\mathsf{map}_{\mathsf{K}_\mathsf{f}}\, \mathsf{eval}\, x)$. As before, we have $\mathsf{corec}_{\mathcal{F}'}\, b = \mathsf{eval} \circ \mathsf{map}_{\Sigma^+_{\mathcal{F}'}}\, (\mathsf{corec}_{\mathcal{F}'}\, b) \circ b$.

Consider the corecursive specification of pointwise addition on streams of numbers, where $\alpha\, \mathsf{K}_{\mathsf{ctor}}$ is $\mathsf{nat} \times \alpha$ and dtor $xs = (\mathsf{shd}\, xs, \mathsf{stl}\, xs)$:

$$xs \oplus ys = (\mathsf{shd}\, xs + \mathsf{shd}\, ys) \lhd (\mathsf{stl}\, xs \oplus \mathsf{stl}\, ys)$$

To make sense of this specification, we take $\alpha\, \mathsf{K}_\oplus$ to be $\alpha \times \alpha$ and define $\oplus$ as $\mathsf{corec}_{\mathcal{F}}\, b$, where the blueprint b is

$$\lambda p.\ (\mathsf{shd}\, (\mathsf{fst}\, p) + \mathsf{shd}\, (\mathsf{snd}\, p)) \boxed{\lhd} \mathsf{Var}\, (\mathsf{stl}\, (\mathsf{fst}\, p), \mathsf{stl}\, (\mathsf{snd}\, p))$$

To register $\oplus$ as friendly, we must decompose b as $s \circ \mathsf{map}_{\mathsf{K}_\oplus}\, \langle \mathsf{id}, \mathsf{dtor}\rangle$. Expanding the definition of $\mathsf{map}_{\mathsf{K}_\oplus}$, we get

$$\mathsf{map}_{\mathsf{K}_\oplus}\, \langle \mathsf{id}, \mathsf{dtor}\rangle$$
$$= \lambda p.\ ((\mathsf{fst}\, p, \mathsf{dtor}\, (\mathsf{fst}\, p)), (\mathsf{snd}\, p, \mathsf{dtor}\, (\mathsf{snd}\, p)))$$
$$= \lambda p.\ ((\mathsf{fst}\, p, (\mathsf{shd}\, (\mathsf{fst}\, p), \mathsf{stl}\, (\mathsf{fst}\, p))), (\mathsf{snd}\, p, (\mathsf{shd}\, (\mathsf{snd}\, p), \mathsf{stl}\, (\mathsf{snd}\, p))))$$

It is easy to see that the following term is a suitable surface s:

$$\lambda p'.\ (\mathsf{fst}\, (\mathsf{snd}\, (\mathsf{fst}\, p')) + \mathsf{fst}\, (\mathsf{snd}\, (\mathsf{snd}\, p'))) \boxed{\lhd} \mathsf{Var}\, (\mathsf{snd}\, (\mathsf{snd}\, (\mathsf{fst}\, p')), \mathsf{snd}\, (\mathsf{snd}\, (\mathsf{snd}\, p')))$$

In Sect. 4, we give more details on how the system synthesizes blueprints and surfaces.

3.5 Merging Corecursion States

Most formalizations are not linear. A module may import several other modules, giving rise to a directed acyclic graph of dependencies. We can reach a situation where the codatatype has been defined in module A; its corecursor has been extended with two different sets of friends $\mathcal{F}_B$ and $\mathcal{F}_C$ in modules B and C, each importing A; and finally module D, which imports B and C, requires a corecursor that mixes friends from $\mathcal{F}_B$ and $\mathcal{F}_C$. To support this scenario, we need an operation that merges two corecursion states.

$\textsc{Merge}:$ $\langle \mathcal{F}_1, \Sigma_{\mathcal{F}_1}, \mathsf{corec}_{\mathcal{F}_1}\rangle$ and $\langle \mathcal{F}_2, \Sigma_{\mathcal{F}_2}, \mathsf{corec}_{\mathcal{F}_2}\rangle \rightsquigarrow \langle \mathcal{F}, \Sigma_{\mathcal{F}}, \mathsf{corec}_{\mathcal{F}}\rangle$ where
$\mathcal{F} = \mathcal{F}_1 \cup \mathcal{F}_2$ $\alpha\, \Sigma_{\mathcal{F}} = \alpha\, \Sigma_{\mathcal{F}_1} + \alpha\, \Sigma_{\mathcal{F}_2}$ $\mathsf{corec}_{\mathcal{F}} : (\alpha \to \alpha\, \Sigma^+_{\mathcal{F}}) \to \alpha \to J$

The return type of blueprints for $\mathsf{corec}_{\mathcal{F}}$ is $\Sigma^+_{\mathcal{F}}$, where $\Sigma_{\mathcal{F}}$ is the sum of the two input signatures $\Sigma_{\mathcal{F}_1}$ and $\Sigma_{\mathcal{F}_2}$. By lifting the syntactic representations of old friends using overloading, we establish the invariant that for each $\mathsf{f} \in \mathcal{F}$ of a corecursor state, there is a syntactic representation $\boxed{\text{f}} : \Sigma^+_{\mathcal{F}}\, \mathsf{K}_\mathsf{f} \to \Sigma^+_{\mathcal{F}}$. The function eval is then defined in the usual way and constitutes the main ingredient in the definition of $\mathsf{corec}_{\mathcal{F}}$ with the usual characteristic equation. For operations $\mathsf{f} \in \Sigma_{\mathcal{F}_1} \cap \Sigma_{\mathcal{F}_2}$, two syntactic representations are available; we arbitrarily choose the one inherited from $\Sigma_{\mathcal{F}_1}$.

3.6   Type Instantiation

We have so far ignored the potential polymorphism of J. Consider $J = \alpha$ stream. The operations on corecursor states allow friends of type $(\alpha \text{ stream}) K \rightarrow \alpha$ stream but not $(\text{nat stream}) K \rightarrow \text{nat stream}$. To allow friends for nat stream, we must keep track of specialized corecursors. First, we need an operation for instantiating corecursor states.

$$\text{INSTANTIATE} : \quad \langle F, \Sigma_{\mathcal{F}}, \text{corec}_{\mathcal{F}} \rangle \rightsquigarrow \langle F[\overline{\sigma}/\overline{\alpha}], \Sigma_{\mathcal{F}}[\overline{\sigma}/\overline{\alpha}], \text{corec}_{\mathcal{F}}[\overline{\sigma}/\overline{\alpha}] \rangle$$

Once we have derived a specific corecursor for nat stream, we can extend it with friends of type $(\text{nat stream}) K \rightarrow \text{nat stream}$. Such friends cannot be added to the polymorphic corecursor, but the other direction works: Any friend of a polymorphic corecursor is also a friend of a specialized corecursor. Accordingly, we maintain a Pareto optimal subset of corecursor state instances $\{\langle \mathcal{F}_S, \Sigma_{\mathcal{F}_S}, \text{corec}_{\mathcal{F}_S} \rangle \mid S \leq J\}$, where $\sigma' \leq \sigma$ denotes that the type σ' can be obtained from the type σ by applying a type substitution.

More specific corecursors are stored only if they have more friends: For each pair of corecursor instances for S_1 and S_2 contained in the Pareto set, we have $\mathcal{F}_{S_1} \supset \mathcal{F}_{S_2}$ whenever $S_1 < S_2$. All the corecursors in the Pareto set are kept up to date. If we add a friend to a corecursor instance for S from the set via STEP, it is also propagated to all instances S' of S by applying INSTANTIATE to the output of STEP and combining the result with the existing corecursor state for S' via MERGE. When analyzing a user specification, corec selects the most specific applicable corecursor.

Eagerly computing the entire Pareto set is exponentially expensive. Consider a codatatype $(\alpha, \beta, \gamma) J$ and the friends f for $(\text{nat}, \beta, \gamma) J$, g for $(\alpha, \beta :: \text{ring}, \gamma) J$, and h for $(\alpha, \beta, \text{bool}) J$. The set would contain eight corecursors, each with a different subset of $\{f, g, h\}$ as friends. To avoid such an explosion, we settle for a lazy derivation strategy. In the above example, the corecursor for $(\text{nat}, \beta :: \text{constring}, \text{bool}) J$, with f, g, h as friends, is derived only if a definition needs it.

3.7   Reasoning Principles

The primary activity of a working formalizer is to develop proofs. To conveniently reason about nonprimitively corecursive functions, corec provides two reasoning principles: coinduction up to congruence and a uniqueness theorem.

Coinduction up to Congruence. Codatatypes are equipped with a coinduction principle. Coinduction reduces the task of proving equality between two inhabitants l and r of a codatatype to the task of exhibiting a relation R which relates l and r and is closed under application of destructors. A relation closed under destructors is called a *bisimulation*. The codatatype command derives a plain coinduction rule. The rule for stream follows:

$$\frac{R\, l\, r \quad \forall xs\, xs'.R\ xs\ xs' \rightarrow \text{shd } xs = \text{shd } xs' \wedge R(\text{stl } xs)(\text{stl } xs')}{l = r}$$

To reason about functions that are corecursive up to a set of friends, a principle of coinduction up to congruence of friends is crucial. For a corecursor with friends $\mathcal{F}$, our tool derives a rule that is identical to the standard rule except with $R^{\mathcal{F}}$ (stl xs) (stl xs') instead of R (stl xs) (stl xs'), where $R^{\mathcal{F}}$ denotes the congruence closure of the relation R with respect to the friendly operations $\mathcal{F}$.

After registering a binary $\oplus$ on nat stream as friendly, the introduction rules for the inductively defined congruence closure include

$$\frac{x = x' \quad R^{\mathcal{F}} \, xs \, xs'}{R^{\mathcal{F}} \, (x \lhd xs) \, (x' \lhd xs')} \qquad \frac{R^{\mathcal{F}} \, xs \, xs' \quad R^{\mathcal{F}} \, ys \, ys'}{R^{\mathcal{F}} \, (xs \oplus ys) \, (xs' \oplus ys')}$$

Since the tool maintains a set of incomparable corecursors, there is also a set of coinduction principles and a set of sets of introduction rules. The `corec` command orders the set of coinduction principles by increasing generality, which works well with Isabelle's philosophy of applying the first rule that matches.

In some circumstances, it may be necessary to reason about the union of friends associated with several incomparable corecursors. To continue with the example from Sect. 3.6, suppose we want to prove a formula about (nat, β :: ring, bool) J by coinduction up to f, g, h before the corresponding corecursor has been derived. Users can derive it and the associated coinduction principle by invoking a dedicated command:

    coinduction_upto (nat, β :: ring, bool) J

Uniqueness Principles. It is sometimes possible to achieve better automation by employing a more specialized proof method than coinduction. Uniqueness principles exploit the property that the corecursor is the unique solution to a fixpoint equation:

$$h = \mathsf{eval} \circ \mathsf{map}_{\Sigma+} \, h \circ b \longrightarrow h = \mathsf{corec}_{\mathcal{F}} \, b$$

This rule can be seen as a less powerful version of coinduction, where the bisimulation relation has been preinstantiated. In category-theoretic terms, the existence and uniqueness of a solution means that we maintain on J a completely iterative algebra [51] (whose signature is gradually incremented with each additional friend).

For concrete functions defined with `corec`, uniqueness rules can be made even more precise by instantiating the blueprint b. For example, the pointwise addition on streams from Sect. 3.4

    corec $\oplus$: nat stream $\rightarrow$ nat stream $\rightarrow$ nat stream where
    $xs \oplus ys = (\mathsf{shd} \, xs + \mathsf{shd} \, ys) \lhd (\mathsf{stl} \, xs \oplus \mathsf{stl} \, ys)$

yields the following uniqueness principle:

$$(\forall xs \, ys. \, h \, xs \, ys = (\mathsf{shd} \, xs + \mathsf{shd} \, ys) \lhd h \, (\mathsf{stl} \, xs) \, (\mathsf{stl} \, ys)) \longrightarrow h = \oplus$$

Reasoning by uniqueness is not restricted to functions defined with `corec`. Suppose $t \, \overline{x}$ is an arbitrary term depending on a list of free variables $\overline{x}$. The *corec_unique* proof method, also provided by our tool, transforms proof obligations of the form

$$(\forall \overline{x}. \ h \ \overline{x} = H \ \overline{x} \ h) \longrightarrow h \ \overline{x} = t \ \overline{x}$$

into $\forall \overline{x}. \ t \ \overline{x} = H \ \overline{x} \ t$. The higher-order functional H must be such that the equation $h \ \overline{x} = H \ \overline{x} \ h$ would be a valid `corec` specification (but without nested calls to h or unguarded calls). Internally, *corec_unique* extracts the blueprint b from $H \ \overline{x} \ h$ as if it would define h with $\mathsf{corec}_{\mathcal{F}}$ and uses the uniqueness principle for $\mathsf{corec}_{\mathcal{F}}$ instantiated with b to achieve the described transformation.

4   The High Level: From Commands to Definitions

AmiCo's two main commands `corec` (Sect. 4.1) and `friend_of_corec` (Sect. 4.2) introduce corecursive functions and register friends. We describe synthesis algorithms for any codatatype as implemented in the tool. We also show how to capture the "consumes at most one constructor, produces at least one constructor" contract of friends.

4.1   Defining Corecursive Functions

The `corec` command reduces the user's corecursive equation to non(co)recursive primitives, so as to guard against inconsistencies. To this end, the command engages in a chain of definitions and proofs. Recall the general context:

- The codatatype J is defined as a fixpoint of a type constructor $\alpha \ \mathsf{K_{ctor}}$ equipped with constructor ctor and destructor dtor.
- The current set of friends $\mathcal{F}$ contains ctor and has a signature $\Sigma_{\mathcal{F}}$ (or Σ). Each friend $\mathsf{f} \in \mathcal{F}$ of type J $\mathsf{K_f} \rightarrow$ J has a companion syntactic expression $\boxed{\mathsf{f}} : (\alpha \ \Sigma^*) \ \mathsf{K_f} \rightarrow \alpha \ \Sigma^*$.
- The corecursor up to $\mathcal{F}$ is $\mathsf{corec}_{\mathcal{F}} : (\alpha \rightarrow \alpha \ \Sigma^+) \rightarrow \alpha \rightarrow$ J.

In general, J may be polymorphic and f may take more than one argument, but these are minor orthogonal concerns here. As before, we write $\alpha \ \Sigma^*$ for the type of formal expressions built from α-leaves and friend symbols $\boxed{\mathsf{f}}$, and $\alpha \ \Sigma^+$ for $\boxed{\mathsf{ctor}}$-guarded formal expressions. For $\alpha = $ J, we can evaluate the formal expressions into elements of J, by replacing each $\boxed{\mathsf{f}}$ with f and omitting the Var and Cst constructors. Finally, we write eval for the evaluation functions of various types of symbolic expressions to J.

Consider the command

`corec g : A → J where g` $x = u_{\mathsf{g},x}$

where $u_{\mathsf{g},x} : $ J is a term that may refer to g and x. The first task of `corec` is to synthesize a blueprint object $b : \mathsf{A} \rightarrow \mathsf{A} \ \Sigma^+$ such that

$$\mathsf{eval} \ (\mathsf{map}_{\Sigma+} h \ (b \ x)) = u_{h,x} \tag{4}$$

holds for all $h : \mathsf{A} \to \mathsf{J}$. This equation states that the synthesized blueprint must produce, by evaluation, the concrete right-hand side of the user equation. The unknown function h represents corecursive calls, which will be instantiated to g once g is defined. To the occurrences of h in $u_{h,x}$ correspond occurrences of Var in b.

Equipped with a blueprint, we define $\mathsf{g} = \mathsf{corec}_{\mathcal{F}}\ b$ and derive the user equation:

$$
\begin{aligned}
\mathsf{g}\ x &= \mathsf{corec}_{\mathcal{F}}\ b\ x && \{\text{by definition of } \mathsf{g}\} \\
&= \mathsf{eval}\ (\mathsf{map}_{\Sigma+}(\mathsf{corec}\ b)\ (b\ x)) && \{\text{by } \mathsf{corec}_{\mathcal{F}}\text{'s equation}\} \\
&= \mathsf{eval}\ (\mathsf{map}_{\Sigma+}\mathsf{g}\ (b\ x)) && \{\text{by definition of } \mathsf{g}\} \\
&= u_{\mathsf{g},x} && \{\text{by equation (4) with } \mathsf{g} \text{ for } h\}
\end{aligned}
$$

Blueprint Synthesis. The blueprint synthesis proceeds by a straightforward syntactic analysis, similar to the one used for primitive corecursion [16]. We illustrate it with an example. Consider the definition of $\oplus$ from Sect. 3.4. Ignoring currying, the function has type (nat stream) $\mathsf{K}_\oplus \to$ nat stream, with $\alpha\ \mathsf{K}_\oplus = \alpha \times \alpha$. The term b is synthesized by processing the right-hand side of the corecursive equation for $\oplus$. After removing the syntactic sugar, we obtain the following term, highlighting the corecursive call:

$$
\lambda p.\ (\mathsf{shd}\ (\mathsf{fst}\ p) + \mathsf{shd}\ (\mathsf{snd}\ p)) \lhd (\mathsf{stl}\ (\mathsf{fst}\ p) \boxed{\oplus} \mathsf{stl}\ (\mathsf{snd}\ p))
$$

The blueprint is derived from this term by replacing the constructor guard $\lhd = \mathsf{ctor}_{\mathsf{stream}}$ and the friends with their syntactic counterparts and the corecursive call with a variable leaf:

$$
b = \lambda p.\ (\mathsf{s}hd\ (\mathsf{f}st\ p) + \mathsf{s}hd\ (\mathsf{s}nd\ p)) \boxed{\lhd} \mathsf{Var}\ (\mathsf{s}tl\ (\mathsf{f}st\ p), \mathsf{s}tl\ (\mathsf{s}nd\ p))
$$

Synthesis will fail if after the indicated replacements the result does not have the desired type (here, nat $\to$ nat Σ^+). If we omit '(shd (fst p) + shd (snd p)) $\lhd$' in the definition, the type of b becomes nat $\to$ nat Σ^*, reflecting the lack of a guard. Another cause of failure is the presence of unfriendly operators in the call context. Once b has been produced, **corec** proves that $\oplus$ satisfies the user equation we started with.

Mixed Recursion–Corecursion. If a self-call is not guarded, **corec** still gives it a chance, since it could be a terminating *recursive* call. As an example, the following definition computes all the odd numbers greater than 1 arising in the Collatz sequence:

corec collatz : nat $\to$ nat llist **where**
collatz n = if $n \leq 1$ then [] else if **even** n then $\boxed{\text{collatz } \frac{n}{2}}$ else $n \lhd$ collatz $(3 \cdot n + 1)$

The highlighted call is not guarded. Yet, it will eventually lead to a guarded call, since repeatedly halving a positive even number must at some point yield an odd number. The unguarded call yields a recursive specification of the blueprint b, which is resolved automatically by the termination prover.

By writing `corecursive` instead of `corec`, the user takes responsibility for proving termination. A manual proof was necessary for lfilter in Sect. 2.7, whose blueprint satisfies the recursion

$b\ (P, xs) =$ if $\forall x \in$ set $xs.\ \neg\ P\ x$ then $\boxed{[]}$
  else if P (lhd xs) then lhd xs $\boxed{\lhd}$ Var $(P,$ ltl $xs)$
  else $\boxed{b\ (P,\ \text{ltl}\ xs)}$

Termination is shown by providing a suitable well-founded relation, which exists because ltl xs is closer than xs to the next element that satisfies the predicate P.

Like the corecursive calls, the recursive calls may be surrounded only by friendly operations (or by parametric operators such as 'case', 'if', and 'let'). Thus, the following specification is rejected—and rightly so, since the unfriendly stl cancels the corecursive guard that is reached when recursion terminates.

`corec collapz : nat → nat llist where collapz` $n =$
  if $n = 0$ then $[]$ else if `even` n then $\boxed{\text{stl (collapz } \tfrac{n}{2})}$ else $n \lhd$ collapz $(3 \cdot n + 1)$

4.2 Registering New Friendly Operations

The command

`corec (friend) g : J K → J where g` $x = u_{g,x}$

defines g and registers it as a friend. The domain is viewed abstractly as a type constructor K applied to the codatatype J.

The command first synthesizes the blueprint $b :$ J K $\rightarrow$ J Σ^+, similarly to the case of plain corecursive definitions. However, this time the type Σ is not $\Sigma_{\mathcal{F}}$, but $\Sigma_{\mathcal{F}} +$ K. Thus, Σ^+ mixes freely the type K with the components K_f of $\Sigma_{\mathcal{F}}$, which caters for *self-friendship* (as in the bfs$_2$ example from Sect. 2.4): g can be defined making use of itself as a friend (in addition to the already registered friends).

The next step is to synthesize a surface s from the blueprint b. Recall from Sect. 3.4 that a corecursively defined operator is friendly if its blueprint b can be decomposed as $s \circ \text{map}_K \langle \text{id}, \text{dtor} \rangle$, where $s : (\alpha \times \alpha\ K_{\text{ctor}})$ K $\rightarrow \alpha\ \Sigma^+$ is parametric in α.

Once the surface s has been synthesized, proved parametric, and proved to be in the desired relationship with b, the tool invokes the STEP operation (Sect. 3.4), enriching the corecursion state with the function defined by b as a new friend, called g.

Alternatively, users can register arbitrary functions as friends:

`friend_of_corec g : J K → J where g` $x = u_{g,x}$

The user must then prove the equation g $x = u_{g,x}$. The command extracts a blueprint from it and proceeds with the surface synthesis in the same way as `corec (friend)`.

Surface Synthesis Algorithm. The synthesis of the surface from the blueprint proceeds by the context-dependent replacement of some constants with terms.

AmiCo performs the replacements in a logical-relation fashion, guided by type inference.

We start with $b : \mathsf{J}\,\mathsf{K} \to \mathsf{J}\,\Sigma^+$ and need to synthesize $s : (\alpha \times \alpha\,\mathsf{K}_{\mathsf{ctor}})\,\mathsf{K} \to \alpha\,\Sigma^+$ such that s is parametric in α and $b = s \circ \mathsf{map}_\mathsf{K}\,\langle\mathsf{id}, \mathsf{dtor}\rangle$. We traverse b recursively and collect context information about the appropriate replacements. The technical report describes the algorithm in detail. Here, we illustrate it on an example.

Consider the definition of a function that interleaves a nonempty list of streams:

corec (friend) inter : (nat stream) nelist $\to$ nat stream where
    inter xss = shd (hd xss) $\lhd$ inter (tl xss $\rhd$ stl (hd xss))

Here, β nelist is the type of nonempty lists with head and tail selectors hd : β nelist $\to \beta$ and tl : β nelist $\to \beta$ list and $\rhd : \beta$ list $\to \beta \to \beta$ nelist is defined such that $xs \rhd y$ appends y to xs. We have $\mathsf{J} =$ nat stream and $\mathsf{K} =$ nelist. The blueprint is

$$b = \lambda xss.\ \mathsf{shd}\ (\mathsf{hd}\ xss)\ \boxed{\lhd}\ \mathsf{Var}\ (\mathsf{tl}\ xss \rhd \mathsf{stl}\ (\mathsf{hd}\ xss))$$

From this, the tool synthesizes the surface

$$s = \lambda xss'.\ (\mathsf{fst} \circ \mathsf{snd})\ (\mathsf{hd}\ xss')\boxed{\lhd}\ \mathsf{Var}\ ((\mathsf{map}_{\mathsf{list}}\ \mathsf{fst} \circ \mathsf{tl})\ xss' \rhd (\mathsf{snd} \circ \mathsf{snd})\ (\mathsf{hd}\ xss'))$$

When transforming the blueprint $b :$ (nat stream) nelist $\to$ (nat stream) Σ^+ into the surface $s : (\alpha \times (\mathsf{nat} \times \alpha))$ nelist $\to \alpha\,\Sigma^+$, the selectors shd and stl are replaced by suitable compositions. One of the other constants, tl, is composed with a mapping of fst. The treatment of constants is determined by their position relative to the input variables (here, xss) and by whether the input is eventually consumed by a destructor-like operator on J (here, shd and stl). Bindings can also carry consumption information—from the outer context to within their scope— as in the following variant of inter:

corec (friend) inter$'$: (nat stream) nelist $\to$ nat stream where
    inter$'$ xss = case hd xss of $x \lhd xs \Rightarrow x \lhd$ inter$'$ (tl xss $\rhd$ xs)

The case expression is syntactic sugar for a .case$_{\mathsf{stream}}$ combinator. The desugared blueprint and surface constants are

$$b = \lambda xss.\ \mathsf{case}_{\mathsf{stream}}\ (\mathsf{hd}\ xss)\ (\lambda x\ xs.\ x\ \boxed{\lhd}\ \mathsf{Var}\ (\mathsf{tl}\ xss \rhd xs))$$
$$s = \lambda xss'.\ (\mathsf{case}_{\mathsf{prod}} \circ \mathsf{snd})\ (\mathsf{hd}\ xss')(\lambda x'\,xs'.\ x'\ \boxed{\lhd}\ \mathsf{Var}((\mathsf{map}_{\mathsf{list}}\ \mathsf{fst} \circ \mathsf{tl})\,xss' \rhd xs'))$$

The case operator for streams is processed specially, because just like shd and stl it consumes the input. The expression in the scope of the inner λ of the blueprint contains two variables—xss and xs—that have nat stream in their type. Due to the outer context, they must be treated differently: xss as an unconsumed input (which tells us to process the surrounding constant tl) and xs as a consumed input (which tells us to leave the surrounding constant $\rhd$ unchanged). The selectors and case operators for J can also be applied indirectly, via mapping (e.g., $\mathsf{map}_{\mathsf{nelist}}$ stl xss).

5   Implementation in Isabelle/HOL

The implementation of AmiCo followed the same general strategy as that of most other definitional mechanisms for Isabelle:

1. We started from an abstract formalized example consisting of a manual construction of the BASE and STEP corecursors and the corresponding reasoning principles.
2. We streamlined the formal developments, eliminating about 1000 lines of Isabelle definitions and proofs—to simplify the implementation and improve performance.
3. We formalized the new MERGE operation in the same style as BASE and STEP.
4. We developed Standard ML functions to perform the corecursor state operations for arbitrary codatatypes and friendly functions.
5. We implemented, also in Standard ML, the commands that process user specifications and interact with the corecursor state.

HOL's type system cannot express quantification over arbitrary BNFs, thus the need for ML code to repeat the corecursor derivations for each new codatatype or friend. With the foundational approach, not only the corecursors and their characteristic theorems are produced but also all the intermediate objects and lemmas, to reach the highest level of trustworthiness. Assuming the proof assistant's inference kernel is correct, bugs in our tool can lead at most to run-time failures, never to logical inconsistencies.

The code for step 4 essentially constructs the low-level types, terms, and lemma statements presented in Sect. 3 and proves the lemmas using dedicated *tactics*—ML programs that generalize the proofs from the formalization. In principle, the tactics always succeed. The code for step 5 analyses the user's specification and synthesizes blueprints and surfaces, as exemplified in Sect. 4. It reuses `primcorec`'s parsing combinators [16] for recognizing map functions and other syntactic conveniences, such as the use of λs as an alternative to ∘ for corecursing under →, as seen in Sect. 2.1.

The archive accompanying this paper [14] contains instructions that explain where to find the code and the users' manual and how to run the code.

6   Related Work and Discussion

This work combines the safety of foundational approaches to function definitions with an expressive flavor of corecursion and mixed recursion–corecursion. It continues a program of integrating category theory insight into proof assistant technology [16–18,67]. There is a lot of related work on corecursion and productivity, both theoretical and applied to proof assistants and functional programming languages.

Theory of (Co)recursion. AmiCo incorporates category theory from many sources, notably Milius et al. [52] for corecursion up-to and Rot et al. [61] for coinduction up-to. Our earlier papers [17,67] discuss further theoretical sources.

AmiCo implements the first general, provably sound, and fully automatic method for mixing recursive and corecursive calls in function definitions. The idea of mixing recursion and corecursion appears in Bertot [11] for the stream filter, and a generalization is sketched in Bertot and Komendantskaya [13] for corecursion up to constructors. Leino's Dafny tool [46] was the first to offer such a mixture for general codatatypes, which turned out to be unsound and was subsequently restricted to the sound but limited fragment of tail recursion.

Corecursion in Other Proof Assistants. Coq supports productivity by a syntactic guardedness check, based on the pioneering work of Giménez [26]. Mini-Agda [2] and Agda implement a more flexible approach to productivity due to Abel et al. [3,5], based on sized types and copatterns. Coq's guardedness check allows, in our terminology, only the constructors as friends [21]. By contrast, Agda's productivity checker is more expressive than AmiCo's, because sized types can capture more precise contracts than the "consumes at most one constructor, produces at least one constructor" criterion. For example, a Fibonacci stream definition such as fib = 0 ◁ 1 ◁ (fib + stl fib) can be made to work in Agda, but is rejected by AmiCo because stl is not a friend. As mentioned in Sect. 2.4, this flexibility comes at a price: The user must encode the productivity argument in the function's type, leading to additional proof obligations.

CIRC [50] is a theorem prover designed for automating coinduction via sound circular reasoning. It bears similarity with both Coq's Paco and our AmiCo. Its freezing operators are an antidote to what we would call the absence of friendship: Equality is no longer a congruence, hence equational reasoning is frozen at unfriendly locations.

Foundational Function Definitions. AmiCo's commands and proof methods fill a gap in Isabelle/HOL's coinductive offering. They complement codatatype, primcorec, and *coinduction* [16], allowing users to define nonprimitive corecursive and mixed recursive–corecursive functions. Being foundational, our work offers a strong protection against inconsistency by reducing circular fixpoint definitions issued by the user to low-level acyclic definitions in the core logic. This approach has a long tradition.

Most systems belonging to the HOL family include a counterpart to the primrec command of Isabelle, which synthesizes the argument to a primitive recursor. Isabelle/HOL is the only HOL system that also supports codatatypes and primcorec [16]. Isabelle/ZF, for Zermelo–Fraenkel set theory, provides (co)datatype and primrec [57] commands, but no high-level mechanisms for defining corecursive functions.

For nonprimitively recursive functions over datatypes, Slind's TFL package for HOL4 and Isabelle/HOL [63] and Krauss's function command for Isabelle/HOL [42] are the state of the art. Krauss developed the partial_function command for defining monadic functions [43]. Definitional mechanisms based on the Knaster–Tarski fixpoint theorems were also developed for (co)inductive predicates [31,57]. HOLCF, a library for domain theory, offers a fixrec command for defining continuous functions [35].

Our handling of friends can be seen as a round trip between a shallow and a deep embedding that resembles normalization by evaluation [9] (but starting from the shallow side). Initially, the user specification contains shallow (semantic) friends. For identifying the involved corecursion as sound, the tool reifies the friends into deep (syntactic) friends, which make up the blueprint. Then the deep friends are "reflected" back into their shallow versions by the evaluation function eval : J Σ^* → J. A similar technique is used by Myreen in HOL4 for verification and synthesis of functional programs [55].

In Agda, Coq, and Matita, the definitional mechanisms for (co)recursion are built into the system. In contrast, Lean axiomatizes only the recursor [54]. The distinguishing features of AmiCo are its dynamicity and high level of automation. The derived corecursors and coinduction principles are updated with new ones each time a friend is registered. This permits reuse both internally (resulting in lighter constructions) and at the user level (resulting in fewer proof obligations).

Code Extraction. Isabelle's code generator [29] extracts Haskell code from an executable fragment of HOL, mapping HOL (co)datatypes to lazy Haskell datatypes and HOL functions to Haskell functions. Seven out of our eight case studies fall into this fragment; the extracted code is part of the archive [14]. Only the filter function on lazy lists is clearly not computable (Sect. 2.7). In particular, extraction works for Lochbihler's probabilistic calculus (Sect. 2.8) which involves the type spmf of discrete subprobability distributions. Verified data refinement in the code generator makes it possible to implement such BNFs in terms of datatypes, e.g., spmf as associative lists similar to Erwig's and Kollmansberger's PFP library [24]. Thus, we can extract code for GPVs and their operations like inlining. Lochbihler and Züst [49] used an earlier version of the calculus to implement a core of the Transport Layer Security (TLS) protocol in HOL.

Certified Lazy Programming. Our tool and the examples are a first step towards a framework for friendship-based certified programming: Programs are written in the executable fragment, verified in Isabelle, and extracted to Haskell. AmiCo ensures that corecursive definitions are productive and facilitates coinductive proofs by providing strong coinduction rules. Productivity and termination of the extracted code are guaranteed if the whole program is specified in HOL exclusively with datatypes, codatatypes, recursive functions with the `function` command, and corecursive functions with `corec`, and no custom congruence rules for higher-order operators have been used. The technical report [15, Sect. 6] explains why these restrictions are necessary.

If the restrictions are met, the program clearly lies within the executable fragment and the code extracted from the definitions yields the higher-order rewrite system which the termination prover and AmiCo have checked. In particular, these restrictions exclude the noncomputable filter function on lazy lists (Sect. 2.7), with the test $\forall n \in$ set $xs. \neg P\ n$.

A challenge will be to extend these guarantees to Isabelle's modular architecture. Having been designed with only partial correctness in mind, the code extractor can be customized to execute arbitrary (proved) equations— which can easily break productivity and termination. A similar issue occurs with `friend_of_corec`, which cares only about semantic properties of the friend to be. For example, we can specify the identity function id on streams by id $(x \lhd y \lhd xs) = x \lhd y \lhd xs$ and register it as a friend with the derived equation id $x = $ shd $x \lhd$ stl x. Consequently, AmiCo accepts the definition natsFrom $n = n \lhd$ id (natsFrom $(n + 1)$), but the extracted Haskell code diverges. To avoid these problems, we would have to (re)check productivity and termination on the equations used for extraction. In this scenario, AmiCo can be used to distinguish recursive from corecursive calls in a set of (co)recursive equations, and synthesize sufficient conditions for the function being productive and the recursion terminating, and automatically prove them (using Isabelle's parametricity [36] and termination provers [20]).

AmiCo Beyond Higher-Order Logic. The techniques implemented in our tool are applicable beyond Isabelle/HOL. In principle, nothing stands in the way of AgdamiCo, AmiCoq, or MatitamiCo. Danielsson [22] and Thibodeau et al. [65] showed that similar approaches work in type theory; what is missing is a tool design and implementation. AmiCo relies on parametricity, which is now understood for dependent types [10].

In Agda, parametricity could be encoded with sized types, and AgdamiCo could be a foundational tool that automatically adds suitable sized types for justifying the definition and erases them from the end product. Coq includes a parametricity-tracking tool [40] that could form the basis of AmiCoq. The Paco library by Hur et al. [37] facilitates coinductive proofs based on parameterized coinduction [53,70]. Recent work by Pous [59] includes a framework to combine proofs by induction and coinduction. An AmiCoq would catch up on the corecursion definition front, going beyond what is possible with the *cofix* tactic [21]. On the proof front, AmiCoq would provide a substantial entry into Paco's knowledge base: For any codatatype J with destructor dtor : $J \to J\,K$, all registered friends are, in Paco's terminology, respectful up-to functions for the monotonic operator $\lambda r\; x\; y.$ rel$_K$ r (dtor x) (dtor y), whose greatest fixpoint is the equality on J.

A more lightweight application of our methodology would be an AmiCo for Haskell or for more specialized languages such as CoCaml [38]. In these languages, parametricity is ensured by the computational model. An automatic tool that embodies AmiCo's principles could analyze a Haskell program and prove it total. For CoCaml, which is total, a tool could offer more flexibility when writing corecursive programs.

Surface Synthesis Beyond Corecursion. The notion of extracting a parametric component with suitable properties can be useful in other contexts than corecursion. In the programming-by-examples paradigm [28], one needs to choose between several synthesized programs whose behavior matches a set of input–output instances. These criteria tend to prefer programs that are highly parametric. A notion of degree of parametricity does not exist in the literature but could be expressed as the size of a parametric surface, for a suitable notion of surface, where $\langle$id, dtor$\rangle$ is replaced by domain specific functions and fst by their left inverses.

Acknowledgment. Martin Desharnais spent months extending Isabelle's `codatatype` command to generate a wealth of theorems, many of which were useful when implementing AmiCo. Lorenz Panny developed `primcorec`, whose code provided valuable building blocks. Mathias Fleury, Mark Summerfield, Daniel Wand, and the anonymous reviewers suggested many textual improvements. We thank them all. Blanchette is supported by the European Research Council (ERC) starting grant Matryoshka (713999). Lochbihler is supported by the Swiss National Science Foundation (SNSF) grant "Formalising Computational Soundness for Protocol Implementations" (153217). Popescu is supported by the UK Engineering and Physical Sciences Research Council (EPSRC) starting grant "VOWS: Verification of Web-based Systems" (EP/N019547/1). The authors are listed in alphabetical order.

References

1. Abbott, M., Altenkirch, T., Ghani, N.: Containers: constructing strictly positive types. Theor. Comput. Sci. **342**(1), 3–27 (2005)
2. Abel, A.: MiniAgda: integrating sized and dependent types. In: Bove, A., Komendantskaya, E., Niqui, M. (eds.) PAR 2010. EPTCS, vol. 43, pp. 14–28 (2010)
3. Abel, A.: Compositional coinduction with sized types. In: Hasuo, I. (ed.) CMCS 2016. LNCS, vol. 9608, pp. 5–10. Springer, Heidelberg (2016). doi:10.1007/978-3-319-40370-0_2
4. Abel, A., Pientka, B.: Well-founded recursion with copatterns and sized types. J. Funct. Program. **26**, e2 (2016)
5. Abel, A., Pientka, B., Thibodeau, D., Setzer, A.: Copatterns: programming infinite structures by observations. In: Giacobazzi, R., Cousot, R. (eds.) POPL 2013, pp. 27–38. ACM (2013)
6. Adams, M.: Introducing HOL Zero. In: Fukuda, K., Hoeven, J., Joswig, M., Takayama, N. (eds.) ICMS 2010. LNCS, vol. 6327, pp. 142–143. Springer, Heidelberg (2010). doi:10.1007/978-3-642-15582-6_25
7. Asperti, A., Ricciotti, W., Sacerdoti Coen, C., Tassi, E.: The Matita interactive theorem prover. In: Bjørner, N., Sofronie-Stokkermans, V. (eds.) CADE 2011. LNCS (LNAI), vol. 6803, pp. 64–69. Springer, Heidelberg (2011). doi:10.1007/978-3-642-22438-6_7
8. Atkey, R., McBride, C.: Productive coprogramming with guarded recursion. In: Morrisett, G., Uustalu, T. (eds.) ICFP 2013, pp. 197–208. ACM (2013)
9. Berger, U., Schwichtenberg, H.: An inverse of the evaluation functional for typed lambda-calculus. In: LICS 1991, pp. 203–211. IEEE Computer Society (1991)
10. Bernardy, J.P., Jansson, P., Paterson, R.: Proofs for free: parametricity for dependent types. J. Funct. Program. **22**(2), 107–152 (2012)
11. Bertot, Y.: Filters on coinductive streams, an application to Eratosthenes' sieve. In: Urzyczyn, P. (ed.) TLCA 2005. LNCS, vol. 3461, pp. 102–115. Springer, Heidelberg (2005). doi:10.1007/11417170_9
12. Bertot, Y., Casteran, P.: Interactive Theorem Proving and Program Development–Coq'Art: The Calculus of Inductive Constructions. Texts in Theoretical Computer Science. Springer, Heidelberg (2004)
13. Bertot, Y., Komendantskaya, E.: Inductive and coinductive components of corecursive functions in Coq. Electr. Notes Theor. Comput. Sci. **203**(5), 25–47 (2008)
14. Blanchette, J.C., Bouzy, A., Lochbihler, A., Popescu, A., Traytel, D.: Archive associated with this paper. http://matryoshka.gforge.inria.fr/pubs/amico_material.tar.gz
15. Blanchette, J.C., Bouzy, A., Lochbihler, A., Popescu, A., Traytel, D.: Friends with benefits: implementing corecursion in foundational proof assistants. Technical report (2017). http://matryoshka.gforge.inria.fr/pubs/amico_report.pdf

16. Blanchette, J.C., Hölzl, J., Lochbihler, A., Panny, L., Popescu, A., Traytel, D.: Truly modular (co)datatypes for Isabelle/HOL. In: Klein, G., Gamboa, R. (eds.) ITP 2014. LNCS, vol. 8558, pp. 93–110. Springer, Heidelberg (2014). doi:10.1007/978-3-319-08970-6_7

17. Blanchette, J.C., Popescu, A., Traytel, D.: Foundational extensible corecursion: a proof assistant perspective. In: Fisher, K., Reppy, J.H. (eds.) ICFP 2015, pp. 192–204. ACM (2015)

18. Blanchette, J.C., Popescu, A., Traytel, D.: Witnessing (co)datatypes. In: Vitek, J. (ed.) ESOP 2015. LNCS, vol. 9032, pp. 359–382. Springer, Heidelberg (2015). doi:10.1007/978-3-662-46669-8_15

19. Bove, A., Dybjer, P., Norell, U.: A brief overview of Agda – a functional language with dependent types. In: Berghofer, S., Nipkow, T., Urban, C., Wenzel, M. (eds.) TPHOLs 2009. LNCS, vol. 5674, pp. 73–78. Springer, Heidelberg (2009). doi:10.1007/978-3-642-03359-9_6

20. Bulwahn, L., Krauss, A., Nipkow, T.: Finding lexicographic orders for termination proofs in Isabelle/HOL. In: Schneider, K., Brandt, J. (eds.) TPHOLs 2007. LNCS, vol. 4732, pp. 38–53. Springer, Heidelberg (2007). doi:10.1007/978-3-540-74591-4_5

21. Chlipala, A.: Certified Programming with Dependent Types—A Pragmatic Introduction to the Coq Proof Assistant. MIT Press, Cambridge (2013)

22. Danielsson, N.A.: Beating the productivity checker using embedded languages. In: Bove, A., Komendantskaya, E., Niqui, M. (eds.) PAR 2010. EPTCS, vol. 43, pp. 29–48 (2010)

23. Dijkstra, E.W.: An exercise for Dr. R. M. Burstall. In: Dijkstra, E.W. (ed.) Selected Writings on Computing: A Personal Perspective, pp. 215–216. Texts and Monographs in Computer Science. Springer, Heidelberg (1982)

24. Erwig, M., Kollmansberger, S.: Probabilistic functional programming in Haskell. J. Funct. Programm. **16**(1), 21–34 (2006)

25. Gammie, P., Lochbihler, A.: The Stern-Brocot tree. Archive of Formal Proofs (2015). https://www.isa-afp.org/entries/Stern_Brocot.shtml

26. Giménez, E.: Codifying guarded definitions with recursive schemes. In: Dybjer, P., Nordström, B., Smith, J. (eds.) TYPES 1994. LNCS, vol. 996, pp. 39–59. Springer, Heidelberg (1995). doi:10.1007/3-540-60579-7_3

27. Gordon, M.J.C., Melham, T.F.: Introduction to HOL: A Theorem Proving Environment for Higher Order Logic. Cambridge University Press, Cambridge (1993)

28. Gulwani, S.: Programming by examples—and its applications in data wrangling. In: Dependable Software Systems Engineering. NATO Science for Peace and Security Series D: Information and Communication Security, vol. 45, pp. 137–158. IOS Press (2016)

29. Haftmann, F., Nipkow, T.: Code generation via higher-order rewrite systems. In: Blume, M., Kobayashi, N., Vidal, G. (eds.) FLOPS 2010. LNCS, vol. 6009, pp. 103–117. Springer, Heidelberg (2010). doi:10.1007/978-3-642-12251-4_9

30. Hagino, T.: A categorical programming language. Ph.D. thesis, University of Edinburgh (1987)

31. Harrison, J.: Inductive definitions: automation and application. In: Thomas Schubert, E., Windley, P.J., Alves-Foss, J. (eds.) TPHOLs 1995. LNCS, vol. 971, pp. 200–213. Springer, Heidelberg (1995). doi:10.1007/3-540-60275-5_66

32. Harrison, J.: HOL Light: an overview. In: Berghofer, S., Nipkow, T., Urban, C., Wenzel, M. (eds.) TPHOLs 2009. LNCS, vol. 5674, pp. 60–66. Springer, Heidelberg (2009). doi:10.1007/978-3-642-03359-9_4

33. Hinze, R.: The Bird tree. J. Func. Programm. **19**(5), 491–508 (2009)

34. Homeier, P.V.: The HOL-Omega logic. In: Berghofer, S., Nipkow, T., Urban, C., Wenzel, M. (eds.) TPHOLs 2009. LNCS, vol. 5674, pp. 244–259. Springer, Heidelberg (2009). doi:10.1007/978-3-642-03359-9_18

35. Huffman, B.: HOLCF '11: a definitional domain theory for verifying functional programs. Ph.D. thesis, Portland State University (2012)

36. Huffman, B., Kunčar, O.: Lifting and transfer: a modular design for quotients in Isabelle/HOL. In: Gonthier, G., Norrish, M. (eds.) CPP 2013. LNCS, vol. 8307, pp. 131–146. Springer, Heidelberg (2013). doi:10.1007/978-3-319-03545-1_9

37. Hur, C.K., Neis, G., Dreyer, D., Vafeiadis, V.: The power of parameterization in coinductive proof. In: Giacobazzi, R., Cousot, R. (eds.) POPL 2013, pp. 193–206. ACM (2013)

38. Jeannin, J.-B., Kozen, D., Silva, A.: Language constructs for non-well-founded computation. In: Felleisen, M., Gardner, P. (eds.) ESOP 2013. LNCS, vol. 7792, pp. 61–80. Springer, Heidelberg (2013). doi:10.1007/978-3-642-37036-6_4

39. Jones, G., Gibbons, J.: Linear-time breadth-first tree algorithms: an exercise in the arithmetic of folds and zips. Technical report 71, Computer Science Department, University of Auckland (1993)

40. Keller, C., Lasson, M.: Parametricity in an impredicative sort. In: Cégielski, P., Durand, A. (eds.) CSL 2012. LIPIcs, vol. 16, pp. 381–395. Schloss Dagstuhl–Leibniz-Zentrum für Informatik (2012)

41. Knuth, D.E., Morris, J.H., Pratt, V.R.: Fast pattern matching in strings. SIAM J. Comput. 6(2), 323–350 (1977)

42. Krauss, A.: Partial recursive functions in higher-order logic. In: Furbach, U., Shankar, N. (eds.) IJCAR 2006. LNCS (LNAI), vol. 4130, pp. 589–603. Springer, Heidelberg (2006). doi:10.1007/11814771_48

43. Krauss, A.: Recursive definitions of monadic functions. In: Bove, A., Komendantskaya, E., Niqui, M. (eds.) PAR 2010. EPTCS, vol. 43, pp. 1–13 (2010)

44. van Laarhoven, T.: Knuth-Morris-Pratt in Haskell (2007). http://www.twanvl.nl/blog/haskell/Knuth-Morris-Pratt-in-Haskell

45. Leino, K.R.M.: Automating theorem proving with SMT. In: Blazy, S., Paulin-Mohring, C., Pichardie, D. (eds.) ITP 2013. LNCS, vol. 7998, pp. 2–16. Springer, Heidelberg (2013). doi:10.1007/978-3-642-39634-2_2

46. Leino, K.R.M., Moskal, M.: Co-induction simply: automatic co-inductive proofs in a program verifier. In: Jones, C., Pihlajasaari, P., Sun, J. (eds.) FM 2014. LNCS, vol. 8442, pp. 382–398. Springer, Heidelberg (2014). doi:10.1007/978-3-319-06410-9_27

47. Lochbihler, A.: Probabilistic functions and cryptographic oracles in higher order logic. In: Thiemann, P. (ed.) ESOP 2016. LNCS, vol. 9632, pp. 503–531. Springer, Heidelberg (2016). doi:10.1007/978-3-662-49498-1_20

48. Lochbihler, A., Hölzl, J.: Recursive functions on lazy lists via domains and topologies. In: Klein, G., Gamboa, R. (eds.) ITP 2014. LNCS, vol. 8558, pp. 341–357. Springer, Heidelberg (2014). doi:10.1007/978-3-319-08970-6_22

49. Lochbihler, A., Züst, M.: Programming TLS in Isabelle/HOL. Isabelle Workshop 2014 (2014). https://www.ethz.ch/content/dam/ethz/special-interest/infk/inst-infsec/information-security-group-dam/research/publications/pub2014/lochbihler14iw.pdf

50. Lucanu, D., Goriac, E.-I., Caltais, G., Roşu, G.: CIRC: a behavioral verification tool based on circular coinduction. In: Kurz, A., Lenisa, M., Tarlecki, A. (eds.) CALCO 2009. LNCS, vol. 5728, pp. 433–442. Springer, Heidelberg (2009). doi:10.1007/978-3-642-03741-2_30

51. Milius, S.: Completely iterative algebras and completely iterative monads. Inf. Comput. **196**(1), 1–41 (2005)
52. Milius, S., Moss, L.S., Schwencke, D.: Abstract GSOS rules and a modular treatment of recursive definitions. Log. Meth. Comput. Sci. **9**(3:28), 1–52 (2013)
53. Moss, L.S.: Parametric corecursion. Theor. Comput. Sci. **260**(1–2), 139–163 (2001)
54. de Moura, L., Kong, S., Avigad, J., van Doorn, F., von Raumer, J.: The Lean theorem prover (system description). In: Felty, A.P., Middeldorp, A. (eds.) CADE 2015. LNCS (LNAI), vol. 9195, pp. 378–388. Springer, Heidelberg (2015). doi:10.1007/978-3-319-21401-6_26
55. Myreen, M.O.: Functional programs: conversions between deep and shallow embeddings. In: Beringer, L., Felty, A. (eds.) ITP 2012. LNCS, vol. 7406, pp. 412–417. Springer, Heidelberg (2012). doi:10.1007/978-3-642-32347-8_29
56. Nipkow, T., Paulson, L.C., Wenzel, M.: Isabelle/HOL: A Proof Assistant for Higher-Order Logic. Springer, Heidelberg (2002)
57. Paulson, L.C.: A fixedpoint approach to implementing (co)inductive definitions. In: Bundy, A. (ed.) CADE 1994. LNCS, vol. 814, pp. 148–161. Springer, Heidelberg (1994). doi:10.1007/3-540-58156-1_11
58. Paulson, L.C.: Mechanizing coinduction and corecursion in higher-order logic. J. Log. Comput. **7**(2), 175–204 (1997)
59. Pous, D.: Coinduction all the way up. In: Grohe, M., Koskinen, E., Shankar, N. (eds.) LICS 2016, pp. 307–316. ACM (2016)
60. Reynolds, J.C.: Types, abstraction and parametric polymorphism. In: Mason, R.E.A. (ed.) IFIP 1983, pp. 513–523. North-Holland/IFIP (1983)
61. Rot, J., Bonsangue, M., Rutten, J.: Coalgebraic bisimulation-up-to. In: Emde Boas, P., Groen, F.C.A., Italiano, G.F., Nawrocki, J., Sack, H. (eds.) SOFSEM 2013. LNCS, vol. 7741, pp. 369–381. Springer, Heidelberg (2013). doi:10.1007/978-3-642-35843-2_32
62. Rutten, J.J.M.M.: Automata and coinduction (an exercise in coalgebra). In: Sangiorgi, D., Simone, R. (eds.) CONCUR 1998. LNCS, vol. 1466, pp. 194–218. Springer, Heidelberg (1998). doi:10.1007/BFb0055624
63. Slind, K.: Function definition in higher-order logic. In: Goos, G., Hartmanis, J., Leeuwen, J., Wright, J., Grundy, J., Harrison, J. (eds.) TPHOLs 1996. LNCS, vol. 1125, pp. 381–397. Springer, Heidelberg (1996). doi:10.1007/BFb0105417
64. Slind, K., Norrish, M.: A brief overview of HOL4. In: Mohamed, O.A., Muñoz, C., Tahar, S. (eds.) TPHOLs 2008. LNCS, vol. 5170, pp. 28–32. Springer, Heidelberg (2008). doi:10.1007/978-3-540-71067-7_6
65. Thibodeau, D., Cave, A., Pientka, B.: Indexed codata types. In: Sumii, E. (ed.) ICFP 2016. ACM (2016)
66. Traytel, D.: Formal languages, formally and coinductively. In: Kesner, D., Pientka, B. (eds.) FSCD. LIPIcs, vol. 52, pp. 31:1–31:17. Schloss Dagstuhl–Leibniz-Zentrum für Informatik (2016)
67. Traytel, D., Popescu, A., Blanchette, J.C.: Foundational, compositional (co)datatypes for higher-order logic: category theory applied to theorem proving. In: LICS 2012, pp. 596–605. IEEE Computer Society (2012)
68. Turner, D.A.: Elementary strong functional programming. In: Hartel, P.H., Plasmeijer, R. (eds.) FPLE 1995. LNCS, vol. 1022, pp. 1–13. Springer, Heidelberg (1995). doi:10.1007/3-540-60675-0_35
69. Wadler, P.: Theorems for free! In: Stoy, J.E. (ed.) FPCA 1989, pp. 347–359. ACM (1989)
70. Winskel, G.: A note on model checking the modal ν-calculus. Theor. Comput. Sci. **83**(1), 157–167 (1991)

Confluence of Graph Rewriting with Interfaces

Filippo Bonchi[1], Fabio Gadducci[2], Aleks Kissinger[3], Paweł Sobociński[4],
and Fabio Zanasi[5(✉)]

[1] CNRS, ENS de Lyon, Lyon, France
[2] University of Pisa, Pisa, Italy
[3] Radboud University Nijmegen, Nijmegen, The Netherlands
[4] University of Southampton, Southampton, UK
[5] University College London, London, UK
f.zanasi@ucl.ac.uk

Abstract. For terminating double-pushout (DPO) graph rewriting systems confluence is, in general, undecidable. We show that confluence *is* decidable for an extension of DPO rewriting to graphs *with interfaces*. This variant is important due to it being closely related to rewriting of string diagrams. We show that our result extends, under mild conditions, to decidability of confluence for terminating rewriting systems of string diagrams in symmetric monoidal categories.

Keywords: Confluence · DPO rewriting systems · Adhesive categories · PROPs · String diagrams

1   Introduction

Confluence and termination are some of the most important properties of rewriting systems. For *term* rewriting, both confluence [3] and termination [27] are, in general, undecidable. However, for systems known to be terminating, confluence is decidable. The key, celebrated property observed by Knuth and Bendix [33] is that the system is confluent exactly when *all its critical pairs are joinable*.

In recent years, an increasing amount of attention has been given to rewriting structures that are richer than mere terms, many of which can be seen as various flavours (including higher-dimensional) of graphs. Here, unfortunately, the status of confluence is murky because old certainties of critical pair analysis fail: Plump [42], working in the well-established framework of the double-pushout (DPO) graph rewriting mechanism [20], showed that joinability of critical pairs *does not* entail confluence, and that confluence of terminating DPO rewriting systems is, in general, undecidable.

In this paper we focus on an extension of DPO, called *DPO with interfaces*. This variant has emerged in several research threads, including rewriting with borrowed contexts [19], encodings of process calculi [5,24], connecting DPO rewriting systems with computads in cospans categories [25,44] and, more recently, for checking the equivalence of terms of symmetric monoidal theories

© Springer-Verlag GmbH Germany 2017
H. Yang (Ed.): ESOP 2017, LNCS 10201, pp. 141–169, 2017.
DOI: 10.1007/978-3-662-54434-1_6

[4]. Our key observation is that for DPO rewriting with interfaces, the Knuth-Bendix property holds and therefore confluence of a terminating system can be decided by checking whether its critical pairs are joinable. More precisely, if some mild assumptions related to the computability of performing rewriting steps on the underlying notion of term are satisfied, our result holds for the most general venue available for DPO rewriting, namely, adhesive categories [34].

Our results do not falsify Plump's: in DPO with interfaces, rather than rewriting graphs, one rewrites graph morphisms $J \to G$, thought of as a graph G with interface J. The latter allows one to "glue" G to other graphs, analogously to how variables allow a single term to apply to a variety of contexts via substitution. Plump's result, in the light of our analysis, states that it is undecidable to check whether rewriting is confluent for all morphisms $0 \to G$. Intuitively, the failure of Knuth-Bendix for such morphisms is due to the loss of expressive power of critical pairs, when deprived of an interface.

This reveals an attractive analogy with term rewriting: morphisms $0 \to G$ – representing graphs that cannot be non-trivially attached to other graphs, since they have an empty interface – correspond to *ground terms*, that cannot be extended since they have no variables. Now, the property that Plump showed to be undecidable should be compared to *ground confluence* for term rewriting [40], i.e., confluence with respect to all ground terms. And in fact, this property is undecidable for terminating term rewriting systems [30]. Summarising, for both term and DPO rewriting with interfaces, confluence of terminating rewriting systems is decidable, while ground confluence is not.

	Terminating term rewriting system	Terminating DPO system
Ground confluence	Undecidable (Kapur et al. [30])	Undecidable (Plump [42])
Confluence	Decidable (Knuth and Bendix [33])	Decidable (this paper)

Our interest in DPO rewriting with interfaces is motivated by *symmetric monoidal theories* (SMTs) that appear in different fields of computer science, like concurrency theory [11,37,47], quantum information [15,16], and systems theory [1,6,7,23], just to mention a few. The terms of an SMT enjoy an efficient graphical representation by means of *string diagrams* [29,45], in the sense that structural equations are "baked into" the representation. Rewriting at the diagrammatic level can be used to determine equality of terms, i.e. the word problem for an SMT. While rewriting of string diagrams has been broadly studied from a foundational point of view (e.g. using *computads* [48] or *polygraphs* [12]), its *implementation* has thus far received less attention.

In [4] we showed that rewriting of string diagrams, representing terms of an SMT, can be soundly and effectively encoded into DPO rewriting with interfaces. This enables us to reuse the main result of this paper to study confluence of rewriting of string diagrams. This problem is known to be particularly challenging: for example a directed form of the Yang-Baxter equation generates infinitely many critical pairs [35,39].

We show that this issue can be avoided by using DPO with interfaces, and that confluence is decidable. We identify two classes of terminating rewriting systems for which confluence can be decided by means of critical pair analysis. The first one concerns SMTs containing a *special Frobenius structure* [14] (yielding categories alternatively called *well-supported compact closed* [13], *p-* and *dgs-monoidal* [9,25], or recently *hypergraph* categories [22,31]). For arbitrary SMTs, not necessarily equipped with a special Frobenius structure, we identify a second class of rewriting systems for which confluence can be decided. The rules of these systems need to satisfy a simple condition that we call *left-connectedness*. Many rewriting systems arising from SMTs (e.g., [21,26,35]), including aforementioned Yang-Baxter rule, enjoy this property. Amongst these, we consider a rewriting system for *non-commutative bimonoids* that has been shown to be terminating in [4]. We exploit our approach to prove that it is also confluent and thus conclude that equivalence of non-commutative bimonoids is decidable.

Related Work. For ordinary DPO rewriting, a variant of the Knuth-Bendix property holds with respect to a stronger notion of joinability for critical pairs [42]. Moreover, confluence is decidable whenever all critical pairs satisfy a certain syntactic condition called coverability [43]. Both these results however refer to confluence for graphs without interfaces, namely ground confluence. Instead, our same notion of confluence has been studied in [8] in the setting of Milner's reactive systems. By instantiating Proposition 22 in [8] to the category of input-linear cospans (of hypergraphs) and by using the results relating borrowed context DPO rewriting with reactive systems over cospans in [46], one obtains a variant of our Theorem 19. One restriction of that approach is that the matches are required to be mono, which rules out our applications to SMTs.

2   Background

Notation. The composition of arrows $f\colon a \to b$, $g\colon b \to c$ in a category $\mathbb{C}$ is written as $f\,;g$. For $\mathbb{C}$ symmetric monoidal, $\oplus$ is its monoidal product and $\sigma_{a,b}\colon a \oplus b \to b \oplus a$ is the symmetry for objects $a, b \in \mathbb{C}$.

2.1   DPO Rewriting

Adhesive Categories and (Typed) Hypergraphs. In order not to restrict ourselves to any one concrete model of graphs, we work with adhesive categories [34]. Adhesive categories are relevant because they have well-behaved pushouts along monomorphisms, and for this reason they are convenient as ambient categories for DPO rewriting.

An important example is the category of finite directed hypergraphs **Hyp**. An object G of **Hyp** is a hypergraph with finite set of *nodes* $G_\star$ and for each $k, l \in \mathbb{N}$ finite set of *hyperedges* $G_{k,l}$ with k (ordered) sources and l (ordered) targets, i.e. for each $0 \le i < k$ there is the ith source map $s_i\colon G_{k,l} \to G_\star$, and for each $0 \le j < l$, the jth target map $t_j\colon G_{k,l} \to G_\star$. The arrows of

Hyp are homomorphisms: functions $G_\star \to H_\star$ such that for each k, l, $G_{k,l} \to H_{k,l}$ they respect the source and target maps in the obvious way. The seasoned reader will recognise **Hyp** as a presheaf topos, and as such, it is adhesive [34]. We shall visualise hypergraphs as follows: • is a node and ⊐⊐⊏ is an hyperedge, with ordered tentacles attached to the left boundary linking to sources and those on the right linking to targets. An example is on the right.

A signature Σ consists of a set of *generators* $o: n \to m$ with arity n and coarity m where $m, n \in \mathbb{N}$. Any signature Σ can be considered as a hypergraph with a single node, in the obvious way. We can then express Σ-typed hypergraphs as the objects of the slice category $\mathbf{Hyp}/\Sigma$, denoted by $\mathbf{Hyp}_\Sigma$, which is adhesive, since adhesive categories are closed under slice [34]. Σ-typed hypergraphs are drawn by labeling hyperedges with generators in Σ, as on the right.

DPO Rewriting. We recall the DPO approach [20] to rewriting in an adhesive category $\mathbb{C}$. A *DPO rule* is a span $L \leftarrow K \to R$ in $\mathbb{C}$. A *DPO system* $\mathcal{R}$ is a finite set of DPO rules. Given objects G and H in $\mathbb{C}$, we say that G *rewrites* into H —notation $G \Rightarrow_\mathcal{R} H$— if there esist $L \leftarrow K \to R$ in $\mathcal{R}$, object C and morphisms such that the squares below are pushouts. A *derivation* from G into H is a sequence of such rewriting steps.

$$
\begin{array}{ccccc}
L & \longleftarrow & K & \longrightarrow & R \\
{\scriptstyle m}\downarrow {\scriptstyle \lnot} & & \downarrow & & {\scriptstyle \ulcorner}\downarrow \\
G & \longleftarrow & C & \longrightarrow & H
\end{array}
$$

The arrow $m: L \to G$ is called a *match* of L in G. A rule $L \leftarrow K \to R$ is said to be *left-linear* if the morphism $K \to L$ is mono. In this case, the matching m fully determines the graphs C and H, i.e., for fixed a rule and a matching there is a unique H such that $G \Rightarrow_\mathcal{R} H$. Here, by unique, we mean unique up-to isomorphism. More generally, the rewriting steps will always be *up-to iso*: in a step $G \Rightarrow_\mathcal{R} H$, G and H should not be thought of as single graphs but rather as equivalence classes of isomorphic graphs.

Undecidability of Confluence. In DPO rewriting, the confluence of terminating systems is not decidable, even if we restrict to left-linear rules.

Theorem 1 [42]. *Confluence of terminating DPO systems over* $\mathbf{Hyp}_\Sigma$ *is undecidable.*

Indeed, critical pair analysis for traditional DPO systems fails: for terminating DPO systems, joinability of critical pairs does not necessarily imply confluence.

Definition 2 (Pre-critical pair and joinability). *Let $\mathcal{R}$ be a DPO system with rules $L_1 \leftarrow K_1 \to R_1$ and $L_2 \leftarrow K_2 \to R_2$. Consider two derivations with common source S*

$$R_1 \longleftarrow K_1 \longrightarrow L_1 \quad \overset{f_1}{\searrow} \quad \overset{f_2}{\swarrow} \quad L_2 \longleftarrow K_2 \longrightarrow R_2$$

$$H_1 \longleftarrow C_1 \longrightarrow S \longleftarrow C_2 \longrightarrow H_2$$

We say that $H_1 \Leftarrow S \Rightarrow H_2$ *is a* pre-critical pair *if* $[f_1, f_2]: L_1 + L_2 \to S$ *is epi; it is* joinable *if there exists* W *such that* $H_1 \Rightarrow^* W \,^*\!\Leftarrow H_2$.

Intuitively, in a pre-critical pair S should not be bigger than $L_1 + L_2$. In a critical pair, L_1 and L_2 must additionally overlap in S, so that the two rewriting steps are not *parallel independent* (see e.g. [17]). For the purposes of this paper, this restriction is immaterial. We stick to pre-critical pairs in our results, as proofs are less tedious. However, for the sake of succinctness, most of the examples only display the critical pairs. For a pre-critical pair which is *not* a critical pair, see for instance the first picture of Sect. 5.

Example 3 [42]. Consider a DPO system $\mathcal{R}$ consisting of the following two rules, where we labeled nodes with numbers in order to make the graph morphisms explicit.

Amongst the several pre-critical pairs, only the following two have non-trivial overlap.

Both are obviously joinable. However, $\mathcal{R}$ is not confluent, as witnessed by the following

DPO Rewriting with Interfaces. Morphisms $G \leftarrow J$ will play a special role in our exposition. When $\mathbb{C}$ is $\mathbf{Hyp}_\Sigma$, we will call them *(hyper)graphs with interface*. The intuition is that G is a hypergraph and J is an interface that allows G to be "glued" to a context.

Given $G \leftarrow J$ and $H \leftarrow J$ in $\mathbb{C}$, G *rewrites into* H *with interface* J — notation $(G \leftarrow J) \Rightarrow_\mathcal{R} (H \leftarrow J)$ — if there exist rule $L \leftarrow K \to R$ in $\mathcal{R}$, object C and morphisms such that the diagram below commutes and the squares are pushouts.

$$L \longleftarrow K \longrightarrow R$$
$$m\downarrow \quad \quad \downarrow \quad \quad \downarrow$$
$$G \longleftarrow C \longrightarrow H$$
$$\nwarrow \quad \uparrow \quad \nearrow$$
$$J$$

Hence, the interface J is preserved by individual rewriting steps.

When $\mathbb{C}$ has an initial object 0 (for instance, in $\mathbf{Hyp}_\Sigma$ 0 is the empty hypergraph), ordinary DPO rewriting can be considered as a special case, by taking J to be 0.

Like for traditional DPO, rewriting steps are modulo isomorphism: $G_1 \leftarrow J : f_1$ and $G_2 \leftarrow J : f_2$ are isomorphic if there is an isomorphism $\varphi \colon G_1 \to G_2$ with $f_1 ; \varphi = f_2$.

Example 4. Consider the system $\mathcal{R}$ from Example 3 and $\boxed{\overset{0}{\bullet}-\!\boxed{a}\!-\!\overset{1}{\bullet}} \leftarrow \boxed{\overset{0}{\bullet}\ \overset{1}{\bullet}}$, a graph with interface (henceforth depicted in grey). It is the source of two rewriting steps

$$\left(\boxed{\overset{b}{\bullet}}_{0}\ \overset{1}{\bullet} \leftarrow \boxed{\overset{0}{\bullet}\ \overset{1}{\bullet}} \right) \quad \Leftarrow \quad \left(\boxed{\overset{0}{\bullet}-\!\boxed{a}\!-\!\overset{1}{\bullet}} \leftarrow \boxed{\overset{0}{\bullet}\ \overset{1}{\bullet}} \right) \quad \Rightarrow \quad \left(\boxed{\overset{0}{\bullet}\ \overset{b}{\bigtriangledown}_{1}} \leftarrow \boxed{\overset{0}{\bullet}\ \overset{1}{\bullet}} \right) \quad (1)$$

that are *not* joinable. Intuitively, the main difference with Example 3 is that here the interface $\{0,1\}$ allows one to "look inside" the graph and distinguish between the two nodes. Notice that if (1) were considered as a critical pair, the counterexample of Plump [42] (Example 3) would not work. This is the starting observation for our work: in Sect. 3 we will introduce pre-critical pairs for rewriting with interfaces and we will show that, as in term rewriting, joinability of pre-critical pairs entails confluence.

2.2 PROP Rewriting

SMTs and PROPs. A uniform way to express an algebraic structure within a symmetric monoidal category is with a *symmetric monoidal theory* (SMT). A (one-sorted) SMT is a pair (Σ, E) where Σ is a *signature* defined as in Sect. 2.1. The set of Σ-terms is obtained by combining generators in Σ, the *unit* $id \colon 1 \to 1$ and the *symmetry* $\sigma_{1,1} \colon 2 \to 2$ with ; and $\oplus$. That means, given Σ-terms $t \colon k \to l$, $u \colon l \to m$, $v \colon m \to n$, one constructs new Σ-terms $t ; u \colon k \to m$ and $t \oplus v \colon k + m \to l + n$. The set E of *equations* contains pairs (t, t') of Σ-terms, with the requirement that t and t' have the same arity and coarity.

Fig. 1. The equations E_F of special Frobenius monoids.

Just as ordinary (cartesian) algebraic theories have a categorical rendition as Lawvere categories [28], the corresponding (linear[1]) notion for SMTs is a

---

[1] In the sense that variables can neither be copied, nor discarded.

PROP [36] (**pro**duct and **p**ermutation category). A PROP is a symmetric strict monoidal category with objects the natural numbers, where $\oplus$ on objects is addition. Morphisms between PROPs are identity-on-objects strict symmetric monoidal functors. PROPs and their morphisms form a category **PROP**. Any SMT (Σ, E) freely generates a PROP by letting the arrows $n \to m$ be the Σ-terms $n \to m$ modulo the laws of symmetric monoidal categories and the (smallest congruence containing the) equations $t = t'$ for any $(t, t') \in E$.

We write $\mathbf{S}_\Sigma$ to denote the PROP freely generated by $(\Sigma, \varnothing)$. There is a graphical representation of the arrows of $\mathbf{S}_\Sigma$ as string diagrams, which we now sketch, referring to [45] for the details. A Σ-term $n \to m$ is pictured as a box with n ports on the left and m ports on the right, which are ordered and referred to with top-down enumerations $1, \dots, n$ and $1, \dots, m$. Compositions via ; and $\oplus$ are drawn respectively as horizontal and vertical juxtaposition, that means, $t \,;\, s$ is drawn $\boxed{t}\boxed{s}$ and $t \oplus s$ is drawn $\genfrac{}{}{0pt}{}{\boxed{t}}{\boxed{s}}$. There are specific diagrams for the Σ-terms responsible for the symmetries: these are $id_1 \colon 1 \to 1$, represented as $\dashv\vdash$, the symmetry $\sigma_{1,1} \colon 1 + 1 \to 1 + 1$, represented as $\boxtimes$, and the unit object for $\oplus$, that is, $id_0 \colon 0 \to 0$, whose representation is an empty diagram $\boxed{}$. Graphical representation for arbitrary identities id_n and symmetries $\sigma_{n,m}$ are generated using the pasting rules for ; and $\oplus$. It will be sometimes convenient to represent id_n with the shorthand diagram $\boxed{n}$ and, similarly, $t \colon n \to m$ with $\overset{n}{\underset{}{\boxed{t}}}\!{}^{m}$.

Example 5.

(a) A basic example is the theory (Σ_M, E_M) of *commutative monoids*. The signature Σ_M contains two generators: *multiplication* — which we depict $\boxed{\mathrel{\rhd}\!\!-} \colon 2 \to 1$ — and *unit*, represented as $\boxed{-\!\bullet} \colon 0 \to 1$. Equations in E_M are given in the leftmost column of Fig. 1: they assert commutativity, associativity and unitality.

(b) An SMT that plays a key role in our exposition is the theory (Σ_F, E_F) of *special Frobenius monoids*. The signature Σ_F is as follows and E_F is depicted in Fig. 1.

$$\{\boxed{\mathrel{\rhd}\!\!-} \colon 2 \to 1, \; \boxed{-\!\bullet} \colon 0 \to 1, \; \boxed{-\!\!\lhd} \colon 1 \to 2, \; \boxed{\bullet\!-} \colon 1 \to 0\}$$

E_F includes the theory of commutative monoids in the leftmost column. Dually, the equations in the middle column assert that $\boxed{-\!\!\lhd}$ and $\boxed{\bullet\!-}$ form a cocommutative comonoid. Finally, the two rightmost equations describe an interaction between these two structures. We call **Frob** the PROP freely generated by (Σ_F, E_F).

(c) The theory of *non-commutative bimonoids* has signature Σ_{NB}

$$\{\boxed{\mathrel{\rhd}\!\!-} \colon 2 \to 1, \; \boxed{\circ\!-} \colon 0 \to 1, \; \boxed{-\!\!\lhd} \colon 1 \to 2, \; \boxed{-\!\circ} \colon 1 \to 0\}$$

and the following equations E_{NB}.

$$\text{[diagram equations]}$$

We call **NB** the PROP freely generated from (Σ_{NB}, E_{NB}). In [4], we showed that the rewriting system that is obtained by orienting the equalities from left to right terminates. In this paper, we will show that is also confluent. For this, it will be convenient to use μ, η, ν, ϵ, respectively, to refer to the generators in Σ_{NB}.

Rewriting in a PROP. Fix an arbitrary PROP **X**. A rewriting *rule* is a pair $\langle l, r \rangle$ where $l, r\colon i \to j$ in **X** have the same domain and codomain. We say that $i \to j$ is the rule's *type* and sometimes write $\langle l, r \rangle\colon (i, j)$. A *rewriting system* $\mathcal{R}$ is a finite set of rules. Given two arrows $d, e\colon n \to m$ in **X**, $d \rightsquigarrow_{\mathcal{R}} e$ iff $\exists \langle l, r \rangle\colon (i, j) \in \mathcal{R}, c_1\colon n \to k + i, c_2\colon k + j \to n$ such that $d = c_1\,;\,(id_k \oplus l)\,;\,c_2$ and $e = c_1\,;\,(id_k \oplus r)\,;\,c_2$, i.e., diagrammatically

$$n\text{—}\boxed{d}\text{—}m = n\text{—}\boxed{c_1}{}_i\boxed{l}{}_j\boxed{c_2}\text{—}m \qquad n\text{—}\boxed{e}\text{—}m = n\text{—}\boxed{c_1}{}_i\boxed{r}{}_j\boxed{c_2}\text{—}m .$$

The following well-known example illustrates the subtlety of critical pair analysis when rewriting in monoidal categories.

Example 6 (From [35], see also [39]). Fix $\Sigma = \{\gamma\colon 2 \to 2\}$ and consider the rewriting system on $\mathbf{S}_\Sigma$ consisting of the following rule:

$$\text{[diagram]} \rightsquigarrow \text{[diagram]} \qquad (2)$$

A critical pair analysis yields an infinite number of critical pairs. Indeed, as shown in [35,39], any diagram $\phi : 1 + m \to 1 + n$ that does not decompose non-trivially into $\phi = \mu + \nu$ for some μ, ν yields a critical pair

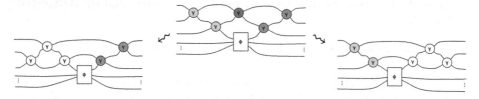

in which clearly there are two embeddings of the left-hand side of (2) (depicted in blue and yellow, respectively, in a colour version of the paper) with an overlap (in green).

In [38] this problem was solved by freely adding duals to monoidal categories. In Sect. 4, we will show another solution based on our earlier work [4]: a translation from PROPs to DPO rewriting with interfaces. The example below anticipates this encoding. It will be useful as a running example for the next section, which is devoted to critical pair analysis and confluence in DPO rewriting with interfaces.

Example 7. Treating the rewriting system of Example 6 as DPO system over **Hyp**$_\Sigma$ with $\gamma : 2 \to 2 \in \Sigma$ yields the following DPO rules.

Below, we give a DPO derivation with interface (in grey), corresponding to a critical pair from the family identified in Example 6.

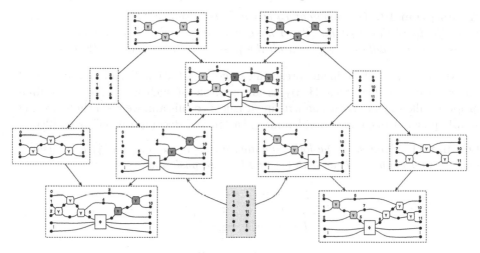

3   Confluence for DPO Rewriting with Interfaces

Differently from Definition 2, when considering pre-critical pairs in the setting of DPO with interfaces, the interface of the pre-critical pair plays a crucial role.

Definition 8 (Pre-critical pair with interface). *Let $\mathcal{R}$ be a DPO system with rules $L_1 \leftarrow K_1 \to R_1$ and $L_2 \leftarrow K_2 \to R_2$. Consider two derivations with source $S \leftarrow J$*

$$
\begin{array}{ccccccccc}
R_1 & \longleftarrow & K_1 & \longrightarrow & L_1 & & L_2 & \longleftarrow & K_2 & \longrightarrow & R_2 \\
\downarrow & \ulcorner & \downarrow & & & {\scriptstyle f_1}\searrow & \swarrow{\scriptstyle f_2} & & \downarrow & \ulcorner & \downarrow \\
H_1 & \longleftarrow & C_1 & & \longrightarrow & & S & \longleftarrow & & C_2 & \longrightarrow & H_2 \\
\end{array}
\qquad (3)
$$

$$(\dagger) \qquad J$$

We say that $(H_1 \leftarrow J) \Leftarrow (S \leftarrow J) \Rightarrow (H_2 \leftarrow J)$ is a pre-critical pair if $[f_1, f_2]: L_1 + L_2 \to S$ is epi and $(\dagger)$ is a pullback; it is joinable if there exists $W \leftarrow J$ such that $(H_1 \leftarrow J) \Rightarrow^* (W \leftarrow J) {}^*\!\!\Leftarrow (H_2 \leftarrow J)$.

Definition 8 augments Definition 2 with the interface J, given by "intersecting" C_1 and C_2. Intuitively, J is the largest interface that allows both the rewriting steps.

Example 9. Consider the pair of rewriting steps (1) in Example 4. This is a pre-critical pair: the reader can check that the interface is indeed a pullback, constructed as in (†). Observe moreover that this pair is *not* joinable.

Plump's Example 3 shows that in ordinary DPO, joinability of pre-critical pairs does not imply confluence. Our Example 9 shows that the argument does not work for DPO with interfaces. Indeed, as we shall see in Theorem 19, in the presence of interfaces joinability suffices for confluence. To prove it, we assume the following.

Assumption 10. *Our ambient category $\mathbb{C}$ is assumed (1) to possess an epi-mono factorisation system, (2) to have binary coproducts, pushouts and pullbacks, (3) to be adhesive (4) with all the pushouts stable under pullbacks.*

All of the above hold in any presheaf category. Additionally, all four are closed under slice. It follows that $\mathbf{Hyp}_\Sigma$ is an example of such a category. The final property allows us to treat non left-linear rules: to this aim we need the following simple pushout decomposition lemma (aka "mixed decomposition" from [2]).

Lemma 11. *Suppose in the following diagram m is mono, (†) + (‡) is a pushout and (‡) is a pullback. Then both (†) and (‡) are pushouts.*

$$
\begin{array}{ccccc}
K & \longrightarrow & C' & \longrightarrow & C \\
\downarrow & (\dagger) & \downarrow & (\ddagger) & \downarrow \\
L & \longrightarrow & G' & \xrightarrow{m} & G
\end{array}
\tag{4}
$$

The following construction mimics [18]. It allows us to restrict –or "clip"– a DPO rewriting step with match $f\colon L \to G$ to any subobject of G' through which f factors.

Construction 12 (One-step clipping). *Suppose we have a DPO rewriting step as below left, together with factorisation $L \to G' \xrightarrow{m} G$ where m is mono. As shown below right, we get C' by pulling back $G' \to G \leftarrow C$ and $K \to C'$ by the universal property.*

$$
\begin{array}{ccccc}
& L & \longleftarrow K & \longrightarrow R \\
\nearrow & \downarrow & \downarrow & \downarrow \\
G' & & & \\
m\searrow & \downarrow & \downarrow & \downarrow \\
& G & \longleftarrow C & \longrightarrow H
\end{array}
\qquad
\begin{array}{ccccc}
& L & \longleftarrow K & \longrightarrow R \\
\nearrow & \downarrow & \nearrow & \downarrow \\
G' & \longleftarrow C' & & \\
m\searrow & \downarrow \searrow & \downarrow & \downarrow \\
& G & \longleftarrow C & \longrightarrow H
\end{array}
$$

By Lemma 11 the two leftmost squares are both pushouts. Next, H' is the pushout of $C' \leftarrow K \to R$ and $H' \to H$ follows from its universal property.

$$
\begin{array}{cccccc}
& L & \longleftarrow & K & \longrightarrow & R \\
\nearrow & \downarrow & \nearrow & \downarrow & \nearrow & \downarrow \\
G' & \longleftarrow C' & \longrightarrow & H' & & \\
m\searrow & \downarrow \searrow & \downarrow & \downarrow \searrow & \downarrow \\
& G & \longleftarrow & C & \longrightarrow & H
\end{array}
$$

By pushout pasting also the bottom-rightmost square is a pushout. Finally, observe that $C' \to C$ is mono since it is the pullback of m along $C \to G$. This means that each of the two squares in diagram below is, as well as being a pushout, also a pullback, since each is a pushout along a mono in an adhesive category.

$$
\begin{array}{ccccc}
G' & \longleftarrow & C' & \longrightarrow & H' \\
m\downarrow & & \downarrow & & \downarrow \\
G & \longleftarrow & C & \longrightarrow & H
\end{array}
$$

Example 13. We use the clipping construction to restrict pairs of derivations with common source into pre-critical pairs. For example, consider the two DPO rewriting rules illustrated in Example 7. We can factorise the two matches through their common image, and clip, as illustrated below.

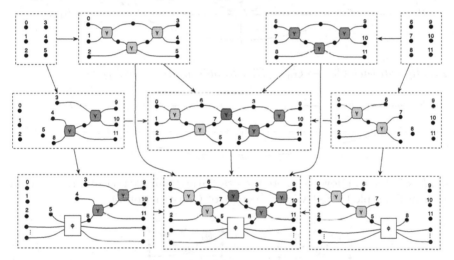

Note that the clipped derivations result with the two matches being jointly epi, which is one of the properties of a pre-critical pair. This generalises: given two rewriting steps with common source $(G_{1,1} \leftarrow I) \Leftarrow (G_0 \leftarrow I) \Rightarrow (G_{1,2} \leftarrow I)$, next construction produces a pre-critical pair $(G'_{1,1} \leftarrow J') \Leftarrow (G_0' \leftarrow J') \Rightarrow (G'_{1,2} \leftarrow J')$ using clipping.

Construction 14 (Pre-critical pair extraction). *Start with two rewrites from $G_0 \leftarrow I$*

$$
\begin{array}{ccccccccc}
R_{1,1} & \longleftarrow & K_{1,1} & \longrightarrow & L_{1,1} & & L_{1,2} & \longleftarrow & K_{1,2} & \longrightarrow & R_{1,2} \\
\downarrow & \ulcorner & \downarrow & & & f_1 \quad f_2 & & & \downarrow & \urcorner & \downarrow \\
G_{1,1} & \longleftarrow & C_{1,1} & \longrightarrow & & G_0 & & \longleftarrow & C_{1,2} & \longrightarrow & G_{1,2}
\end{array}
$$

and factorise $[f_1, f_2] \colon L_{1,1} + L_{1,2} \to G_0$ *to obtain*

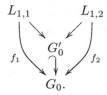

Next apply Construction 12 twice, obtaining

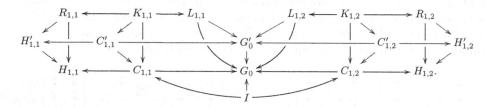

Finally pull back $C'_{1,1} \to G'_0 \leftarrow C'_{1,2}$ *to obtain pre-critical pair*

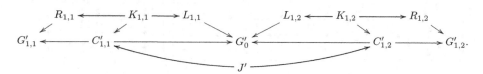

Example 15. We can now complete the pre-critical pair extraction process, commenced in Example 13, following the steps of Construction 14.

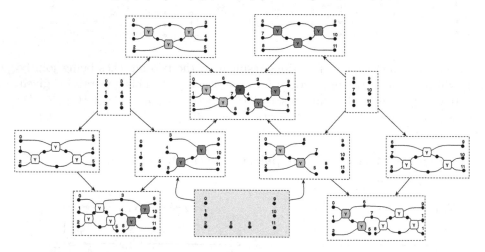

Construction 14 means that we are able to extract a pre-critical pair from two rewriting steps with common source. If the pre-critical pair is joinable, we would then like to embed the joining derivations to the original context.

The following is a useful step in this direction. Assuming a mono $G'_0 \to G_0$, it allows us to extend a derivation from $G'_0 \leftarrow J'$ to a corresponding one from $G_0 \leftarrow J$, if we can obtain G_0 by glueing G'_0 and some context C_0 along J'. Stated more formally, we want the following diagram commute and (†) be a pushout.

$$\begin{array}{ccc} J' & \longrightarrow & G'_0 \\ \downarrow & (\dagger) & \downarrow \\ J & \longrightarrow C_0 \longrightarrow & G_0 \end{array} \tag{5}$$

Construction 16 (Embedding). *The extended derivation is constructed as in the commuting diagram below, where each square is a pushout diagram.*

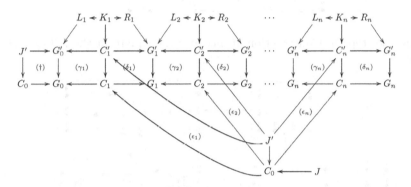

We shall now explain each of the components. The upper row of pushouts together with morphisms $J' \to C'_i$ witnesses the original derivation $(G'_0 \leftarrow J') \Rightarrow^* (G'_n \leftarrow J')$.

For $i = 1 \dots n$, (ϵ_i) is formed as the pushout of $C_0 \leftarrow J' \to C'_i$ and (δ_i) as the pushout of $C_i \leftarrow C'_i \to G'_i$, as shown in the diagram below.

$$\begin{array}{ccc} J' & \longrightarrow C'_i \longrightarrow & G'_i \\ \downarrow & (\epsilon_i) \quad \downarrow \quad (\delta_i) & \downarrow \\ C_0 & \longrightarrow C_i \longrightarrow & G_i \end{array} \tag{6}$$

It remains to construct pushouts (γ_i), which is done in the following diagram.

$$\begin{array}{ccc} J' & \longrightarrow & G'_{i-1} \\ & \searrow \; C'_i \; \nearrow & \\ \downarrow & (\epsilon_i) \;\; \vee \;\; (\gamma_i) & \downarrow \\ & \nearrow \; C_i \; \dashrightarrow & \\ C_0 & \longrightarrow & G_{i-1} \end{array} \tag{7}$$

The exterior square in (7) is a pushout: for $i = 1$ it is (†) from (5), while for $i \geq 2$ it is obtained by composing (ϵ_{i-1}) and (δ_{i-1}) from (6). The universal property of (ϵ_i) yields the morphism $C_i \to G_{i-1}$. By pushout decomposition, the diagram (γ_i) is a pushout.

Example 17. In Example 15 we saw two derivations from

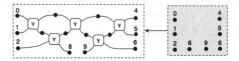

These can be extended to

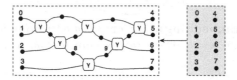

following the steps in Construction 16 because the square in the following is a pushout.

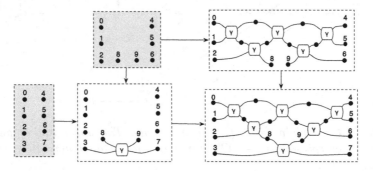

Constructions 14 and 16 are the main ingredients for showing the Knuth-Bendix property for DPO with interfaces. Before we prove it, we need one technical lemma from the theory of adhesive categories.

Lemma 18. *Consider the cube on the right, where the top and bottom faces are pullbacks, the rear faces are both pullbacks and pushouts, and m is mono. Then, the front faces are also pushouts.*

$$
\begin{array}{ccc}
& G_0' \longleftarrow C_{1,2}' \\
C_{1,1}' \longleftarrow J' \\
& G_0 \longleftarrow C_{1,2} \\
C_{1,1} \longleftarrow J
\end{array}
$$

Theorem 19 (Local confluence). *For a DPO system with interfaces, if all pre-critical pairs are joinable then rewriting is locally confluent: given $(G_{1,1} \leftarrow I) \Leftarrow (G_0 \leftarrow I) \Rightarrow (G_{1,2} \leftarrow I)$, there exists $W \leftarrow I$ such that*

$$
\begin{array}{c}
(G_0 \leftarrow I) \\
(G_{1,1} \leftarrow I) \qquad (G_{1,2} \leftarrow I) \\
(W \leftarrow I).
\end{array}
$$

Proof. Following the steps of Construction 14, we obtain a pre-critical pair

$$(G'_{1,1} \leftarrow J') \Leftarrow (G'_0 \leftarrow J') \Rightarrow (G'_{1,2} \leftarrow J')$$

Because pre-critical pairs are by assumption joinable we have derivations

$$(G'_{1,1} \leftarrow J') \Rightarrow^* (W' \xleftarrow{\beta'} J')^* \Leftarrow (G'_{1,2} \leftarrow J').$$

Suppose w.l.o.g. that the leftmost derivation requires n steps and the rightmost m. To keep the notation consistent with Construction 16, we fix notation $G'_{n,1} := W' =: G'_{m,2}$.

Now let J be the pullback object of $C_{1,1} \to G_0 \leftarrow C_{1,2}$. By the universal property, we obtain maps $\iota: I \to J$ and $\xi: J' \to J$.

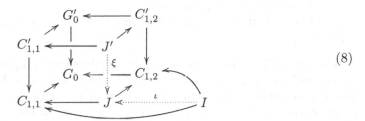

$$(8)$$

Recall by Construction 12 that the rear faces of (8) are both pullbacks and pushouts. Then, by Lemma 18, the square on the right is a pushout.

$$\begin{array}{ccc} J' & \to & G'_0 \\ \downarrow & (\dagger) & \downarrow \\ J & \to & G_0 \end{array}$$

We are now in position to apply Construction 16 by taking $C_0 = J$, which yields

$$(G_0 \leftarrow J) \Rightarrow (G_{1,1} \leftarrow J) \Rightarrow^* (G_{n,1} \xleftarrow{\beta_1} J)$$

extending $(G'_0 \leftarrow J') \Rightarrow (G'_{1,1} \leftarrow J') \Rightarrow^* (G'_{n,1} \xleftarrow{\beta'} J')$ and

$$(G_0 \leftarrow J) \Rightarrow (G_{1,2} \leftarrow J) \Rightarrow^* (G_{m,2} \xleftarrow{\beta_2} J)$$

extending $(G'_0 \leftarrow J') \Rightarrow (G'_{1,1} \leftarrow J') \Rightarrow^* (G'_{m,2} \xleftarrow{\beta'} J')$.

The next step is to prove that $(G_{n,1} \xleftarrow{\beta_1} J) \cong (G_{m,2} \xleftarrow{\beta_2} J)$. To see this, it is enough to observe that both the following squares are pushouts of $J \xleftarrow{\xi} J' \xrightarrow{\beta'} W' = G'_{n,1} = G'_{m,2}$.

$$\begin{array}{ccc} J' & \xrightarrow{\beta'} & G'_{n,1} \\ \xi\downarrow & & \downarrow \\ J & \xrightarrow{\beta_1} & G_{n,1} \end{array} \qquad \begin{array}{ccc} J' & \xrightarrow{\beta'} & G'_{m,2} \\ \xi\downarrow & & \downarrow \\ J & \xrightarrow{\beta_2} & G_{m,2} \end{array}$$

Indeed, the leftmost is a pushout by composition of squares (ϵ_n) and (δ_n) in the embedding construction and the rightmost by composition of (ϵ_m) and (δ_m).

To complete the proof, it remains to show that, in the above derivations, interface J extends to interface I as in the statement of the theorem. But this trivially holds by precomposing with $\iota \colon I \to J$.   □

We are now ready to give our decidability result. To formulate it at the level of generality of adhesive categories we need some additional definitions.

A *quotient* of an object X is an equivalence class of epis with domain X. Two epis $e_1 : X \to X_1$, $e_2 \colon X \to X_2$ are equivalent when there exists isomorphism $\varphi \colon X_1 \to X_2$ such that $e_1 \,;\, \varphi = e_2$. Note that quotient is the dual of *subobject*.

A DPO rewriting system with interfaces is *computable* when

- pullbacks are computable,
- for every pairs of rules $L_i \leftarrow K_i \to R_i$, $L_j \leftarrow K_j \to R_j$, the set of quotients of $L_i + L_j$ is finite and computable,
- for all $G \leftarrow J$, it is possible to compute every $H \leftarrow J$ such that $(G \leftarrow J) \Rightarrow (H \leftarrow J)$.

Computability refers to the possibility of effectively computing each rewriting step as well as to have a finite number of pre-critical pairs. More precisely, the first two conditions ensure that the set of all pre-critical pairs is finite (since every objects has finitely many quotients) and each of them can be computed, while the last one ensures that any possible rewriting step can also be computed. Thus, these assumptions rule out the rewriting of infinite structures, singleing out instead those structures where it is reasonable to apply the DPO mechanism, like finite hypergraphs in $\mathbf{Hyp}_\Sigma$, which are exactly what is needed for implementing rewriting of SMTs.

Corollary 20. *For a computable terminating DPO system with interfaces, confluence is decidable.*

Proof. By Theorem 19, if all pre-critical pairs are joinable then the system is confluent. If not all pre-critical pairs are joinable, then at least one pair witnesses the fact that the system is not confluent. Therefore, to decide confluence, it is enough to check that all pre-critical pairs are joinable.

Since the system is computable, there are only finitely many pre-critical pairs and these can be computed. For each pair, one can decide joinability: indeed each rewriting step can be computed (since the system is computable) and there are only finitely many $(H \leftarrow J)$ such that $(G \leftarrow J) \Rightarrow^* (H \leftarrow J)$ (since the system is terminating).   □

It is worth to remark that this result is not in conflict with Theorem 1: Corollary 20 refers to confluence of all hypergraphs with interfaces $G \leftarrow J$. The property that Theorem 1 states as undecidable is whether the rewriting is confluent for all *hypergraphs with empty interface* $G \leftarrow 0$. Observe that the restriction to hypergraphs with empty interface would make the above proof fail: a non-joinable pre-critical pair $(S \leftarrow J)$, with J non empty, does not witness that rewriting is not confluent for all $G \leftarrow 0$.

A similar problem arises with term rewriting, when restricting to confluence of *ground terms* [30]. As an example consider the following term rewriting system defined on the signature with two unary symbols, f and g, and one constant c.

$$f(g(f(x))) \to x \qquad f(c) \to c \qquad g(c) \to c$$

The critical pair $f(g(x)) \leftarrow f(g(f(g(f(x))))) \to g(f(x))$ is not joinable, but the system is obviously ground confluent, as every ground term will eventually rewrite into c.

Our work therefore allows one to view Theorem 1 in a new light: as hypergraphs with empty interface are morally the graphical analogous of ground terms, we can say that ground confluence is not decidable for DPO rewriting with interfaces.

4 Confluence for PROP Rewriting

As emphasised in the introduction, a major reason for interest in DPO rewriting with interfaces is that PROP rewriting (Sect. 2.2) may be interpreted therein. In this section we investigate how our confluence result behaves with respect to this interpretation. The outcome is that confluence is decidable for terminating PROP rewriting systems, where terms are taken modulo a chosen special Frobenius structure (Corollary 28). For arbitrary symmetric monoidal theories, confluence is also decidable, provided that certain additional conditions hold (Corollary 41).

4.1 From PROPs to Frobenius Termgraphs

In this subsection we report a result from [4] that is crucial for the encoding of PROP rewriting into DPO rewriting with interfaces in $\mathbf{Hyp}_\Sigma$ (cf. Sect. 2.1).

First, we obtain our domain of interpretation by restricting the category $\mathsf{Csp}(\mathbf{Hyp}_\Sigma)$ with arrows the cospans $G_1 \leftarrow G_2 \to G_3$ of Σ-hypergraphs to those with G_1, G_3 discrete.

Definition 21 (Frobenius termgraphs). *Any $k \in \mathbb{N}$ can be seen as a discrete hypergraph with k vertices. The objects of the PROP $\mathbf{FTerm}_\Sigma$ of Σ-Frobenius termgraphs are natural numbers and arrows $n \to m$ are cospans $n \xrightarrow{f} G \xleftarrow{g} m$ in $\mathbf{Hyp}_\Sigma$ (where n, m are considered as hypergraphs). $\mathbf{FTerm}_\Sigma$, therefore, is a full subcategory of $\mathsf{Csp}(\mathbf{Hyp}_\Sigma)$.*

Explicitly, composition in $\mathbf{FTerm}_\Sigma$ is defined by pushout as in $\mathsf{Csp}(\mathbf{Hyp}_\Sigma)$ and the monoidal product $\oplus$ by coproduct in $\mathbf{Hyp}_\Sigma$. The idea behind the discreteness restriction is that f and g tell what are the "left and right dangling wires" in the string diagram encoded by G. In pictures, we shall represent n and m as actual discrete graphs— with n and m nodes respectively— and use number labels (and sometimes colours, whenever available to the reader) to help visualise how they get mapped to nodes of G.

Given a signature Σ, we define a PROP morphism $\|\cdot\|\colon \mathbf{S}_\Sigma \to \mathbf{FTerm}_\Sigma$. Since $\mathbf{S}_\Sigma$ is the PROP freely generated by an SMT with no equations, it suffices to define $\|\cdot\|$ on the generators: for each $o\colon n \to m$ in Σ, we let $\|o\|$ be the following cospan of type $n \to m$.

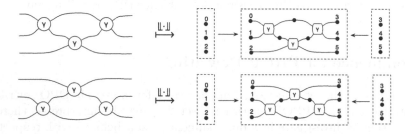

Example 22. The two sides of the PROP rewriting rule (2) (Example 6) get interpreted as the following cospans in $\mathbf{FTerm}_\Sigma$.

Proposition 23 [4]. $\|\cdot\|\colon \mathbf{S}_\Sigma \to \mathbf{FTerm}_\Sigma$ *is faithful.*

The encoding $\|\cdot\|$ is an important part of Theorem 24 below. This is a pivotal result in our exposition, as it serves as a bridge between algebraic and combinatorial structures. Indeed, it provides a presentation, by means of generators and equations, for the PROP $\mathbf{FTerm}_\Sigma$: the disjoint union of the SMTs of $\mathbf{S}_\Sigma$ and **Frob**.

Theorem 24 [4]. *There is an isomorphism of PROPs* $\Phi\colon \mathbf{S}_\Sigma + \mathbf{Frob} \xrightarrow{\cong} \mathbf{FTerm}_\Sigma$.

The isomorphism Φ is given as $[\|\cdot\|, \psi]\colon \mathbf{S}_\Sigma + \mathbf{Frob} \to \mathbf{FTerm}_\Sigma$, where $\psi\colon \mathbf{Frob} \to \mathbf{FTerm}_\Sigma$ is the unique PROP morphism mapping the generators of **Frob** as follows

The special role played by **Frob** is what justifies the terminology *Frobenius termgraph*: it is used to model those features of the graph domain that are not part of the syntactic domain, e.g. the ability of building a "feedback loop" around some $\alpha\colon 1 \to 1$ in Σ.

4.2   Confluence for Rewriting in $\mathbf{S}_\Sigma + \mathbf{Frob}$

We can use Theorem 24 to apply results for graphs with interfaces to $\mathbf{S}_\Sigma + \mathbf{Frob}$. First, one can turn the cospan $n \xrightarrow{i} G \xleftarrow{o} m = \Phi(d)$ interpreting a string diagram d into a graph with interface, which is defined as

$$\ulcorner n \xrightarrow{i} G \xleftarrow{o} m \urcorner := G \xleftarrow{[i,o]} n + m.$$

For a system $\mathcal{R}$ we define the rewriting system $\ulcorner\Phi(\mathcal{R})\urcorner$ in $\mathbf{FTerm}_\Sigma$ as

$$\{\langle \ulcorner\Phi(l)\urcorner, \ulcorner\Phi(r)\urcorner \rangle \mid \langle l, r \rangle \in \mathcal{R}\}.$$

Example 25. The PROP rewriting system $\mathcal{R}$ of Example 6 consists of just a single rule, let us call it $\langle d, e \rangle$. The resulting DPO rewriting system with interfaces $\ulcorner\Phi(\mathcal{R})\urcorner$ is then presented in Example 7. Also, Example 22 is an intermediate step of this transformation, as it shows the cospans $\lfloor\lfloor c \rfloor\rfloor = \Phi(c)$ and $\lfloor\lfloor d \rfloor\rfloor = \Phi(d)$. One can obtain both graphs with interfaces $\ulcorner\Phi(c)\urcorner$ and $\ulcorner\Phi(d)\urcorner$ by "folding" the domain/codomain of the cospans into the interface of Example 7.

Observe that a rule in $\ulcorner\Phi(\mathcal{R})\urcorner$ just consists of a pair of hypergraphs with a common interface, i.e., it is a DPO rule of the form $L \leftarrow n+m \rightarrow R$. Thus, PROP rewriting in $\mathbf{FTerm}_\Sigma$ coincides with DPO rewriting with interfaces: together with Theorem 24, this correspondence yields the following result.

Theorem 26 [4]. *Let $\mathcal{R}$ be a rewriting system on $\mathbf{S}_\Sigma + \mathbf{Frob}$.*

1. *If $d \leadsto_\mathcal{R} e$, then $\ulcorner\Phi(d)\urcorner \Rightarrow_{\ulcorner\Phi(\mathcal{R})\urcorner} \ulcorner\Phi(e)\urcorner$.*
2. *If $\ulcorner\Phi(d)\urcorner \Rightarrow_{\ulcorner\Phi(\mathcal{R})\urcorner} (H \leftarrow J)$, then $\exists e$ such that $\ulcorner\Phi(e)\urcorner \cong (H \leftarrow J)$ and $d \leadsto_\mathcal{R} e$.*

One can read Theorem 26 as: DPO rewriting with interfaces is sound and complete for any symmetric monoidal theory with a chosen special Frobenius structure, i.e. one of shape $(\Sigma + \Sigma_F, E + E_F)$, with (Σ_F, E_F) the SMT of **Frob**. There are various relevant such theories in the literature, such as the ZX-calculus [15], the calculus of signal flow graphs [6], the calculus of stateless connectors [10] and monoidal computer [41].

The combination of the result above with Theorem 19 is however not sufficient for ensuring the decidability of the confluence for a terminating rewriting system $\mathcal{R}$ on $\mathbf{S}_\Sigma + \mathbf{Frob}$. Indeed, Theorem 19 and Theorem 26 ensure that if all the pre-critical pairs in $\ulcorner\Phi(\mathcal{R})\urcorner$ are joinable, then the rewriting in $\mathcal{R}$ is confluent. However, for the decidability of confluence in $\mathcal{R}$ the reverse is also needed: if one pre-critical pair in $\ulcorner\Phi(\mathcal{R})\urcorner$ is not joinable, then $\mathcal{R}$ should not be confluent. To conclude this fact, it is enough to check that all pre-critical pairs of $\ulcorner\Phi(\mathcal{R})\urcorner$ lay in the image of $\ulcorner\Phi(\cdot)\urcorner$, i.e., that they all have discrete interfaces. The key observation is given by the lemma below.

Lemma 27 (Pre-critical pair with discrete interface). *Consider a pre-critical pair in $\mathbf{Hyp}_\Sigma$ as in (3), Definition 8. If both K_1 and K_2 are discrete, so is the interface J.*

Proof. For $i = 1, 2$, since K_i is discrete, the hyperedges of C_i are exactly those of G_i that are not in $f_i(L_i)$. Since $[f_1, f_2] \colon L_1 + L_2 \to S$ is epi, all the hyperedges of G are either in $f_1(L_1)$ or $f_2(L_2)$. Therefore, J cannot contain any hyperedge. $\square$

Since in every rule $L \leftarrow K \to R$ in $\ulcorner \Phi(\mathcal{R}) \urcorner$, K is discrete, from Lemma 27 and Theorem 19 we derive the following result.

Corollary 28. *Confluence is decidable for terminating rewriting systems on* $\mathbf{S}_\Sigma + \mathbf{Frob}$.

Proof. To decide confluence of a rewriting system $\mathcal{R}$ on $\mathbf{S}_\Sigma + \mathbf{Frob}$, it is enough to check whether all pre-critical pairs in $\ulcorner \Phi(\mathcal{R}) \urcorner$ are joinable. Indeed, if all pre-critical pairs are joinable, then $\leadsto_{\mathcal{R}}$ is confluent by Theorems 19 and 26. For the other direction, suppose that there exists a pre-critical pair $_{\ulcorner \Phi(\mathcal{R}) \urcorner} \!\!\Leftarrow (S \leftarrow J) \Rightarrow_{\ulcorner \Phi(\mathcal{R}) \urcorner}$ that is not joinable. By construction, in every rule $L \leftarrow K \to R$ in $\ulcorner \Phi(\mathcal{R}) \urcorner$, K is discrete. Therefore, by Lemma 27, also J is discrete. This is the key fact to entail that there exists d in $\mathbf{S}_\Sigma + \mathbf{Frob}$, such that $\ulcorner \Phi(d) \urcorner = (S \leftarrow J)$. By Theorem 26, d witnesses that $\leadsto_{\mathcal{R}}$ is not confluent.

Now, if $\mathcal{R}$ is terminating, then by Theorem 26, also $\ulcorner \Phi(\mathcal{R}) \urcorner$ is terminating. The latter is also computable and therefore joinability of pre-critical pairs of $\ulcorner \Phi(\mathcal{R}) \urcorner$ can easily be decided by following the steps in the second part of the proof of Corollary 20. $\square$

4.3   Confluence for Left-Connected Rewriting in $\mathbf{S}_\Sigma$

So far, we have shown a procedure to decide confluence for rewriting on $\mathbf{S}_\Sigma + \mathbf{Frob}$. In order to study PROP rewriting in absence of a chosen Frobenius structure, we focus on component $\llbracket \cdot \rrbracket \colon \mathbf{S}_\Sigma \to \mathbf{FTerm}_\Sigma$ of the isomorphism Φ.

We first recall from [4] a combinatorial characterisation of the image of $\llbracket \cdot \rrbracket$. It is based on a few preliminary definitions. We call a sequence of hyperedges $e_1, e_2, \ldots, e_n$ a *directed path* if at least one target of e_k is a source for e_{k+1} and a *directed cycle* if additionally at least one target of e_n is a source for e_1. The *in-degree* of a node v in an hypergraph G is the number of pairs (h, i) where h is an hyperedge with v as its i-th target. Similarly, the *out-degree* of v is the number of pairs (h, j) where h is an hyperedge with v as its j-th source. We call *input* nodes those with in-degree 0, *output* nodes those with out-degree 0, and *internal* nodes the others. We write $\mathrm{in}(G)$ for the set of inputs and $\mathrm{out}(G)$ for the set of outputs.

Definition 29. *An hypergraph G is monogamous directed acyclic (mda) if*

1. *it contains no directed cycle (directed acyclicity) and*
2. *every node has at most in- and out-degree 1 (monogamy).*

A cospan $n \xrightarrow{f} G \xleftarrow{g} m$ in $\mathbf{FTerm}_\Sigma$ is monogamous directed acyclic when G is an mda-hypergraph, f is mono and its image is $\mathrm{in}(G)$, g is mono and its image is $\mathrm{out}(G)$.

Example 30. The following four cospans are *not* monogamous.

$$[\overset{0}{\bullet}] \to [\overset{0}{\bullet}\hspace{-2pt}\rightarrowtriangle\hspace{-2pt}\overset{1}{\bullet}] \leftarrow [\overset{1}{\bullet}] \qquad [\overset{}{\bullet}] \to [\overset{0}{\bullet}\hspace{-2pt}\rightarrowtriangle\hspace{-2pt}\overset{1}{\bullet}] \leftarrow [\overset{1}{\bullet}] \qquad [\overset{}{\bullet}] \to [\ldots] \leftarrow [\ldots] \qquad [\overset{}{\bullet}] \to [\overset{0}{\bullet}\hspace{-2pt}\rightarrowtriangle\hspace{-2pt}\overset{1}{\bullet}] \leftarrow [\overset{}{\bullet}]$$

Theorem 31 [4]. $n \to G \leftarrow m$ in $\mathbf{FTerm}_\Sigma$ *is in the image of $\lfloor\lfloor \cdot \rfloor\rfloor$ iff it is mda.*

As for a graph with interface $G \xleftarrow{f} J$, we call it monogamous directed acyclic if so is G and the image of f coincides with $\mathrm{in}(G) + \mathrm{out}(G)$. This means that there exists a cospan $n \xrightarrow{i} G \xleftarrow{o} m$ such that $\ulcorner n \xrightarrow{i} G \xleftarrow{o} m \urcorner = G \xleftarrow{f} J$, i.e., $J = n + m$ and $f = [i, o]$.

We are now in position to interpret PROP rewriting for $\mathbf{S}_\Sigma$ in DPO-rewriting for mda-hypergraphs with interfaces, via the mapping $\llbracket \cdot \rrbracket \overset{\mathrm{def}}{=} \ulcorner \lfloor\lfloor \cdot \rfloor\rfloor \urcorner$ that takes string diagrams to mda hypergraphs with interfaces.

As shown in [4], this interpretation is generally *unsound*. There are two main reasons, which we illustrate in the next two examples. They motivate our restriction to PROP rewriting systems that make the interpretation sound, in Definition 34 below.

Example 32. Consider $\Sigma = \{\alpha_1 \colon 0 \to 1, \alpha_2 \colon 1 \to 0, \alpha_3 \colon 1 \to 1\}$ and the PROP rewriting system $\mathcal{R} = \{ \overset{}{\rule{1cm}{0.4pt}} \rightsquigarrow \overset{}{-\boxed{\alpha_3}-} \}$ on $\mathbf{S}_\Sigma$. In $\mathbf{FTerm}_\Sigma$, $\llbracket \mathcal{R} \rrbracket$ is given by the DPO rule of mda-hypergraphs with interface $[\overset{}{\bullet^{0,1}}] \xleftarrow{} [0\bullet \;\; \bullet 1] \xrightarrow{} [0\bullet\boxed{\alpha_3}\bullet 1]$. The rule is not left-linear and therefore pushout complements are not necessarily unique for the application of this rule, as witnessed by the following two DPO rewriting steps.

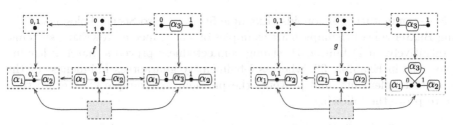

The different outcome is due to the fact that f maps 0 to the leftmost and 1 to the rightmost node, whereas g swaps the assignments. Even though both rewriting steps could be mimicked at the syntactic level in $\mathbf{S}_\Sigma + \mathbf{Frob}$ (as guaranteed by Theorem 26, cf. [4, Ex. 4.8]), the rightmost one is illegal for $\mathcal{R}$ in $\mathbf{S}_\Sigma$.

Example 33. Take $\Sigma = \{\alpha_1 \colon 1 \to 2, \alpha_2 \colon 2 \to 1, \alpha_3 \colon 1 \to 1, \alpha_4 \colon 1 \to 1\}$ and a PROP rewriting system $\mathcal{R}$ on $\mathbf{S}_\Sigma$ given by the rewriting rule below left, interpreted in $\llbracket \mathcal{R} \rrbracket$ as below right. The next line introduces a diagram c of $\mathbf{S}_\Sigma$ and its interpretation.

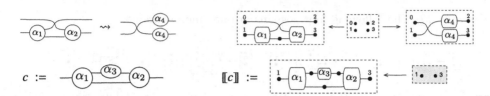

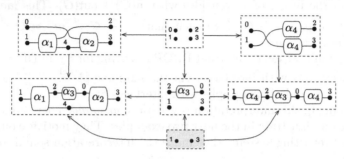

Now, the left-hand side of the rule in $\mathcal{R}$ cannot be matched in c. However, their interpretation in $\mathbf{FTerm}_\Sigma$ yields a legal DPO rewriting step as below.

The two examples motivate the following definition.

Definition 34. *An mda-hypergraph G is strongly connected if for every input $x \in \mathsf{in}(G)$ and output $y \in \mathsf{out}(G)$, there exists a directed path from x to y. A DPO system with interface is called left-connected if it is left-linear and, for every rule $L \leftarrow K \rightarrow R$, $L \leftarrow K$ and $R \leftarrow K$ are mda-hypergraphs with interface and L is strongly connected. We call a PROP rewriting system $\mathcal{R}$ on $\mathbf{S}_\Sigma$ left-connected if $\llbracket \mathcal{R} \rrbracket$ is left-connected.*

Non-commutative bimonoids (Example 5(c), see also Sect. 5 below) and the Yang-Baxter rule of Example 6 are examples of left-connected rewriting systems.

Intuitively, in Definition 34, strong connectedness prevents matches leaving "holes", as in Example 33, whereas left-linearity guarantees uniqueness of the pushout complements, and prevents the problem in Example 32. We are then able to prove the following.

Theorem 35. *Let $\mathcal{R}$ be a left-connected rewriting system on $\mathbf{S}_\Sigma$.*

1. *If $d \rightsquigarrow_\mathcal{R} e$, then $\llbracket d \rrbracket \Rightarrow_{\llbracket \mathcal{R} \rrbracket} \llbracket e \rrbracket$.*
2. *If $\llbracket d \rrbracket \Rightarrow_{\llbracket \mathcal{R} \rrbracket} (H \leftarrow J)$, then $\exists e$ such that $\llbracket e \rrbracket \cong (H \leftarrow J)$ and $d \rightsquigarrow_\mathcal{R} e$.*

Remark 36. For confluence, restricting to left-linearity is not particularly harmful. Indeed, an mda-hypergraph with interface $G \leftarrow J$ is not mono iff G has one node that is both input and output, i.e., an isolated node. A rule with a strongly connected $L \leftarrow K$ is not left-linear precisely when L is discrete, with a single node. Such a rule cannot be part of a terminating system, i.e. one where local confluence implies confluence.

The above theorem allows us to use DPO rewriting with interfaces as a mechanism for rewriting $\mathbf{S}_\Sigma$. The last ingredient that we need for confluence is a suitable notion of pre-critical pair. One cannot simply reuse Definition 8. Indeed, we want to enforce that the common source $S \leftarrow J$ (cf. (3)) of the two derivations is an mda-hypergraph with interfaces, so that it is in the image of $\lfloor\cdot\rfloor$ and we can reason about pre-critical pairs 'syntactically' in $\mathbf{S}_\Sigma$. However, while Lemma 27 guarantees that this is always the case for rewriting systems on $\mathbf{S}_\Sigma + \mathbf{Frob}$, with Definition 8 this is not guaranteed for $\mathbf{S}_\Sigma$ even in presence of left-connected rules, as shown by the two examples below.

Example 37. We concoct a pre-critical pair by instantiating (3) as shown below.

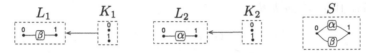

Although $L_1 \leftarrow K_1$ and $L_2 \leftarrow K_2$ are left-hand sides of left-connected rules, S is *not* monogamous, thus this pre-critical pair does not correspond to anything in the syntax.

Example 38. Even if we restrict to left-connected rules with an mda-hypergraph, defining the interface J by pullback as in Definition 34 may not yield an mda-hypergraph with interface. Here is an example, where two rules match in an mda-hypergraph G, but the interface contains one extra node 4 which is neither an input nor an output of G.

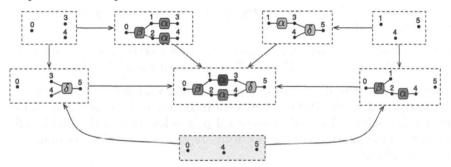

The previous two examples motivate the following definition.

Definition 39 (Mda pre-critical pair). *Let $\mathcal{R}$ be a left-connected DPO system containing the rules $L_1 \leftarrow K_1 \rightarrow R_1$ and $L_2 \leftarrow K_2 \rightarrow R_2$. Consider the following derivations with common source $S \leftarrow J$.*

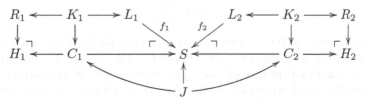

We say that $(H_1 \leftarrow J) \Leftarrow (S \leftarrow J) \Rightarrow (H_2 \leftarrow J)$ is an mda pre-critical pair if $[f_1, f_2]\colon L_1 + L_2 \to S$ is epi and $S \leftarrow J$ is an mda-hypergraph with interface; it is joinable if there exists an mda-hypergraph with interface $W \leftarrow J$ such that $(H_1 \leftarrow J) \Rightarrow^* (W \leftarrow J) \; ^*\!\!\Leftarrow (H_2 \leftarrow J)$.

We will drop the prefix mda, when there is no risk of confusion with Definition 8. We are now in position to state the confluence theorem for left-connected systems.

Theorem 40 (Local confluence for left-connected systems). *For a left-connected DPO system with interfaces, if all mda pre-critical pairs are joinable then rewriting is locally confluent: given an mda-hypergraph with interface $G_0 \leftarrow I$ and $(G_{1,1} \leftarrow I) \Leftarrow (G_0 \leftarrow I) \Rightarrow (G_{1,2} \leftarrow I)$, there exists an mda-hypergraph with interface $W \leftarrow I$ such that*

$$
\begin{array}{ccc}
 & (G_0 \leftarrow I) & \\
 \swArrow & & \seArrow \\
(G_{1,1} \leftarrow I) & & (G_{1,2} \leftarrow I) \\
 \underset{*}{\seArrow} & & \underset{*}{\swArrow} \\
 & (W \leftarrow I). &
\end{array}
$$

The proof of Theorem 40 follows steps analogous to the one of Theorem 19. The essential difference is that mda pre-critical pairs now have interfaces that are not necessarily pullbacks. The assumption of left-connectedness is, nevertheless, enough to ensure that the fundamental pieces, Constructions 14 and 16, can be reproduced.

Corollary 41. *Let $\mathcal{R}$ be a terminating left-connected rewriting system on $\mathbf{S}_\Sigma$. Then confluence of $\leadsto_\mathcal{R}$ is decidable.*

Proof. By Theorem 35 and 40, it is enough to check whether pre-critical pairs in $[\![\mathcal{R}]\!]$ are joinable. This is decidable since $\mathcal{R}$ is terminating and $[\![\mathcal{R}]\!]$ is computable. $\square$

Example 42. The PROP rewriting system $\mathcal{R}$ of Example 6 is left-connected. Once interpreted as the DPO system with interfaces of Example 7, we can do critical pair analysis. The mda pre-critical pair below (where the middle grey graph acts as the interface for the rewriting steps) is not joinable, meaning that $\mathcal{R}$ is not confluent.

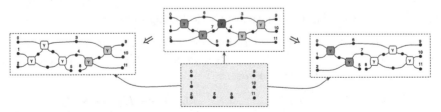

We emphasise that the decision procedure relies on the fact that there are only *finitely many* pre-critical pairs to consider — the above one being the only to feature a nontrivial overlap of rule applications. This is in contrast with a naive, 'syntactic' analysis, which as we observe in Example 6 yields infinitely many pre-critical pairs for $\mathcal{R}$.

We will devote the next section to a positive example of our confluence result.

5   Case Study: Non-commutative Bimonoids

We conclude with an application of the left-connected case, showing confluence of the theory **NB** of non-commutative bimonoids (Example 5(c)). Below is the interpretation of the theory as a DPO system $[\![\mathcal{R}_{\mathbf{NB}}]\!]$, which was shown to be terminating in [4].

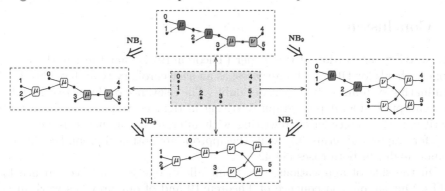

Given that the system is terminating, it suffices to show local confluence. Observe that $[\![\mathcal{R}_{\mathbf{NB}}]\!]$ is left-connected: monogamicity is ensured by the fact that it is in the image of $[\![\ ]\!]$; strong connectedness and left-linearity hold by inspection of the set of rules. We can thus use Theorem 40 and local confluence follows from joinability of the pre-critical pairs. Among them, the pairs without overlap of rule applications pose no problem: they are trivially joinable in one step, by applying the other rule. One example is given below, with the middle grey graph acting as the interface for all depicted derivation steps.

Thus we confine ourselves to analysing actual critical pairs, with overlapping rule applications. One such pair is given below, also involving rules **NB₁** and **NB₉**. Again, we show how it is joined, with the interface of each step drawn in the centre.

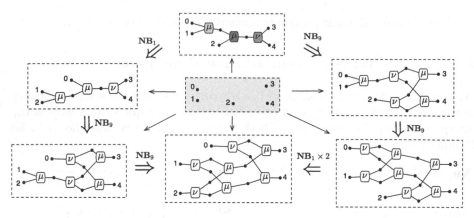

Overall there are 22 critical pairs to consider. For space reasons, for each of them we only show the graph exhibiting the overlap. It is straightforward to check that the corresponding pairs are all joinable.

We can thereby conclude that **NB** is a confluent rewriting system. Since it is also terminating, equivalence of terms in **NB** is decidable by means of rewriting. Note that, by virtue of Corollary 41, the above pre-critical pair analysis can be automated.

6   Conclusion

The starting observation of this paper (Theorem 19) is that the Knuth-Bendix property holds for DPO with interfaces; as an easy corollary (Corollary 20), for a terminating system, confluence is decidable. The relevance of this is two-fold. On the conceptual side, it puts graph rewriting in tight correspondence with term rewriting: when considering rewriting with interfaces, confluence is decidable both for graphs and terms [33], while the appropriate notion of ground confluence is undecidable in both cases [30, 42].

On the side of applications, our result allows one to study confluence for SMTs. One simple consequence of Theorem 19 and of our previous work in [4] is that, for all those SMTs including a special Frobenius structure – which are already commonplace in computer science [1, 6, 7, 10, 11, 15, 16, 23, 47] – local confluence can be checked by means of critical pair analysis. Moreover, when termination is guaranteed, confluence can be decided automatically (Corollary 28).

An analogous result (Corollary 41) holds for those SMTs that do not include a special Frobenius structure, but whose set of rules satisfies the left-connected conditions. Hence it applies to a variety of other non-Frobenius theories, such as those in [21,26,35]. In both cases, these decision procedures are amenable to implementation in string diagram rewriting tools like Quantomatic [32] (via an encoding of hypergraphs) or directly in hypergraph-based rewriting tools.

Acknowledgment. Aleks Kissinger and Fabio Zanasi acknowledge support from the ERC under the European Union's Seventh Framework Programme (FP7/2007-2013)/ERC grant no. 320571. The work of Filippo Bonchi has been partly supported by the project ANR-16-CE25-0011 REPAS and Labex MILYON/ANR-10-LABX-0070. The work of Fabio Gadducci has been partly supported by the project PRA_2016_64 "Through the fog" funded by the University of Pisa.

References

1. Baez, J., Erbele, J.: Categories in control. Theory Appl. Categ. **30**, 836–881 (2015)
2. Baldan, P., Gadducci, F., Sobociński, P.: Adhesivity is not enough: local church-rosser revisited. In: Murlak, F., Sankowski, P. (eds.) MFCS 2011. LNCS, vol. 6907, pp. 48–59. Springer, Heidelberg (2011). doi:10.1007/978-3-642-22993-0_8
3. Bauer, G., Otto, F.: Finite complete rewriting systems and the complexity of the word problem. Acta Inform. **21**(5), 521–540 (1984)
4. Bonchi, F., Gadducci, F., Kissinger, A., Sobociński, P., Zanasi, F.: Rewriting modulo symmetric monoidal structure. In: LiCS 2016, pp. 710–719. ACM (2016)
5. Bonchi, F., Gadducci, F., König, B.: Synthesising CCS bisimulation using graph rewriting. Inf. Comput. **207**(1), 14–40 (2009)
6. Bonchi, F., Sobociński, P., Zanasi, F.: A categorical semantics of signal flow graphs. In: Baldan, P., Gorla, D. (eds.) CONCUR 2014. LNCS, vol. 8704, pp. 435–450. Springer, Heidelberg (2014). doi:10.1007/978-3-662-44584-6_30
7. Bonchi, F., Sobocinski, P., Zanasi, F.: Full abstraction for signal flow graphs. In: POPL 2015, pp. 515–526. ACM (2015)
8. Bruggink, H.J.S., Cauderlier, R., Hülsbusch, M., König, B.: Conditional reactive systems. In: FSTTCS 2011, LIPIcs, vol. 13, pp. 191–203. Schloss Dagstuhl - Leibniz-Zentrum für Informatik (2011)
9. Bruni, R., Gadducci, F., Montanari, U.: Normal forms for algebras of connection. Theor. Comput. Sci. **286**(2), 247–292 (2002)
10. Bruni, R., Lanese, I., Montanari, U.: A basic algebra of stateless connectors. Theor. Comput. Sci. **366**(1–2), 98–120 (2006)
11. Bruni, R., Melgratti, H., Montanari, U.: A connector algebra for P/T nets interactions. In: Katoen, J.-P., König, B. (eds.) CONCUR 2011. LNCS, vol. 6901, pp. 312–326. Springer, Heidelberg (2011). doi:10.1007/978-3-642-23217-6_21
12. Burroni, A.: Higher dimensional word problems with applications to equational logic. Theor. Comput. Sci. **115**(1), 43–62 (1993)
13. Carboni, A.: Matrices, relations, and group representations. J. Algebra **136**(1), 497–529 (1991)
14. Carboni, A., Walters, R.F.C.: Cartesian bicategories I. J. Pure Appl. Algebra **49**(1–2), 11–32 (1987)
15. Coecke, B., Duncan, R.: Interacting quantum observables. In: Aceto, L., Damgård, I., Goldberg, L.A., Halldórsson, M.M., Ingólfsdóttir, A., Walukiewicz, I. (eds.) ICALP 2008. LNCS, vol. 5126, pp. 298–310. Springer, Heidelberg (2008). doi:10.1007/978-3-540-70583-3_25

16. Coecke, B., Duncan, R., Kissinger, A., Wang, Q.: Strong complementarity and non-locality in categorical quantum mechanics. In: LiCS 2012, pp. 245–254. ACM (2012)

17. Corradini, A.: On the definition of parallel independence in the algebraic approaches to graph transformation. In: Milazzo, P., Varró, D., Wimmer, M. (eds.) STAF 2016. LNCS, vol. 9946, pp. 101–111. Springer, Heidelberg (2016). doi:10. 1007/978-3-319-50230-4_8

18. Ehrig, H., Habel, A., Padberg, J., Prange, U.: Adhesive high-level replacement categories and systems. In: Ehrig, H., Engels, G., Parisi-Presicce, F., Rozenberg, G. (eds.) ICGT 2004. LNCS, vol. 3256, pp. 144–160. Springer, Heidelberg (2004). doi:10.1007/978-3-540-30203-2_12

19. Ehrig, H., König, B.: Deriving bisimulation congruences in the DPO approach to graph rewriting. In: Walukiewicz, I. (ed.) FoSSaCS 2004. LNCS, vol. 2987, pp. 151–166. Springer, Heidelberg (2004). doi:10.1007/978-3-540-24727-2_12

20. Ehrig, H., Kreowski, H.-J.: Parallelism of manipulations in multidimensional information structures. In: Mazurkiewicz, A. (ed.) MFCS 1976. LNCS, vol. 45, pp. 284–293. Springer, Heidelberg (1976). doi:10.1007/3-540-07854-1_188

21. Fiore, M., Devesas Campos, M.: The algebra of directed acyclic graphs. In: Coecke, B., Ong, L., Panangaden, P. (eds.) Computation, Logic, Games, and Quantum Foundations. The Many Facets of Samson Abramsky. LNCS, vol. 7860, pp. 37–51. Springer, Heidelberg (2013). doi:10.1007/978-3-642-38164-5_4

22. Fong, B.: Decorated cospans. Theory Appl. Categ. 30(33), 1096–1120 (2015)

23. Fong, B., Rapisarda, P., Sobociński, P.: A categorical approach to open interconnected dynamical systems. In: LiCS 2016, pp. 495–504. ACM (2016)

24. Gadducci, F.: Graph rewriting for the π-calculus. Math. Struct. Comput. Sci. 17(3), 407–437 (2007)

25. Gadducci, F., Heckel, R.: An inductive view of graph transformation. In: Presicce, F.P. (ed.) WADT 1997. LNCS, vol. 1376, pp. 223–237. Springer, Heidelberg (1998). doi:10.1007/3-540-64299-4_36

26. Ghica, D.R.: Diagrammatic reasoning for delay-insensitive asynchronous circuits. In: Coecke, B., Ong, L., Panangaden, P. (eds.) Computation, Logic, Games, and Quantum Foundations. The Many Facets of Samson Abramsky. LNCS, vol. 7860, pp. 52–68. Springer, Heidelberg (2013). doi:10.1007/978-3-642-38164-5_5

27. Huet, G., Lankford, D.: On the uniform halting problem for term rewriting systems. Technical report 283, IRIA (1978)

28. Hyland, M., Power, J.: Lawvere theories and monads. In: Plotkin Festschrift, ENTCS, vol. 172, pp. 437–458. Elsevier, Amsterdam (2007)

29. Joyal, A., Street, R.: The geometry of tensor calculus, I. Adv. Math. 88(1), 55–112 (1991)

30. Kapur, D., Narendran, P., Otto, F.: On ground-confluence of term rewriting systems. Inf. Comput. 86(1), 14–31 (1990)

31. Kissinger, A.: Finite matrices are complete for (dagger)-hypergraph categories. arXiv:1406.5942 [math.CT]

32. Kissinger, A., Zamdzhiev, V.: Quantomatic: a proof assistant for diagrammatic reasoning. In: Felty, A.P., Middeldorp, A. (eds.) CADE 2015. LNCS (LNAI), vol. 9195, pp. 326–336. Springer, Heidelberg (2015). doi:10.1007/978-3-319-21401-6_22

33. Knuth, D.E., Bendix, P.B.: Simple word problems in universal algebras. In: Computational Problems in Abstract Algebra, pp. 263–297. Pergamon Press (1970)

34. Lack, S., Sobociński, P.: Adhesive and quasiadhesive categories. Theor. Inf. Appl. 39(3), 511–546 (2005)

35. Lafont, Y.: Towards an algebraic theory of Boolean circuits. J. Pure Appl. Algebra **184**(2–3), 257–310 (2003)
36. MacLane, S.: Categorical algebra. Bull. Am. Math. Soc. **71**(1), 40–106 (1965)
37. Meseguer, J., Montanari, U.: Petri nets are monoids. Inf. Comput. **88**(2), 105–155 (1990)
38. Mimram, S.: Computing critical pairs in 2-dimensional rewriting systems. In: RTA, LIPIcs, vol. 6, pp. 227–242. Schloss Dagstuhl - Leibniz-Zentrum für Informatik (2010)
39. Mimram, S.: Towards 3-dimensional rewriting theory. Logical Methods Comput. Sci. **10**(2:1), 1–47 (2014)
40. Padawitz, P.: New results on completeness and consistency of abstract data types. In: Dembiński, P. (ed.) MFCS 1980. LNCS, vol. 88, pp. 460–473. Springer, Heidelberg (1980). doi:10.1007/BFb0022525
41. Pavlovic, D.: Monoidal computer I: basic computability by string diagrams. Inf. Comput. **226**, 94–116 (2013)
42. Plump, D.: Hypergraph rewriting: critical pairs and undecidability of confluence. In: Term Graph Rewriting: Theory and Practice, pp. 201–213. Wiley (1993)
43. Plump, D.: Checking graph-transformation systems for confluence. In: Manipulation of Graphs, Algebras and Pictures, ECEASST, vol. 26. EASST (2010)
44. Sassone, V., Sobociński, P.: Reactive systems over cospans. In: LiCS 2005, pp. 311–320. ACM (2005)
45. Selinger, P.: A survey of graphical languages for monoidal categories. In: Coecke, B. (ed.) New Structures for Physics. LNP, vol. 813, pp. 289–355. Springer, Heidelberg (2011)
46. Sobociński, P.: Deriving process congruences from reaction rules. Ph.D. thesis, BRICS, University of Aarhus (2004)
47. Sobociński, P., Stephens, O.: A programming language for spatial distribution of net systems. In: Ciardo, G., Kindler, E. (eds.) PETRI NETS 2014. LNCS, vol. 8489, pp. 150–169. Springer, Heidelberg (2014). doi:10.1007/978-3-319-07734-5_9
48. Street, R.: Limits indexed by category-valued 2-functors. J. Pure Appl. Algebra **8**(2), 149–181 (1976)

Verifying Robustness of Event-Driven Asynchronous Programs Against Concurrency

Ahmed Bouajjani[1], Michael Emmi[2], Constantin Enea[1],
Burcu Kulahcioglu Ozkan[3]([⊠]), and Serdar Tasiran[3]

[1] Université Paris Diderot, Paris, France
[2] Nokia Bell Labs, Murray Hill, NJ, USA
[3] Koç University, Istanbul, Turkey
bkulahcioglu@ku.edu.tr

Abstract. We define a correctness criterion, called *robustness against concurrency*, for a class of event-driven asynchronous programs that are at the basis of modern UI frameworks in Android, iOS, and Javascript. A program is robust when all possible behaviors admitted by the program under arbitrary procedure and event interleavings are admitted even if asynchronous procedures (respectively, events) are assumed to execute serially, one after the other, accessing shared memory in isolation. We characterize robustness as a conjunction of two correctness criteria: *event-serializability* (i.e., events can be seen as atomic) and *event-determinism* (executions within each event are insensitive to the interleavings between concurrent tasks dynamically spawned by the event). Then, we provide efficient algorithms for checking these two criteria based on polynomial reductions to reachability problems in sequential programs. This result is surprising because it allows to avoid explicit handling of all concurrent executions in the analysis, which leads to an important gain in complexity. We demonstrate via case studies on Android apps that the typical mistakes programmers make are captured as robustness violations, and that violations can be detected efficiently using our approach.

1 Introduction

Asynchronous event-driven programming is a widely adopted style for building responsive and efficient software. It allows programmers to use asynchronous procedure calls that are stored for later executions, in contrast with synchronous procedure calls that must be executed immediately. Asynchronous calls are essential for event-driven programming where they correspond to callbacks handling the occurrences of external events. In particular, modern user interface (UI) frameworks in Android, iOS, and Javascript, are instances of asynchronous event-driven programming. These frameworks dedicate a distinguished main thread,

This work is supported in part by the European Research Council (ERC) under the European Union's Horizon 2020 research and innovation programme (grant agreement No. 678177).

© Springer-Verlag GmbH Germany 2017
H. Yang (Ed.): ESOP 2017, LNCS 10201, pp. 170–200, 2017.
DOI: 10.1007/978-3-662-54434-1_7

called UI thread, to handling user interface events. Since responsiveness to user events is a key concern, common practice is to let the UI thread perform only short-running work in response to each event, delegating to asynchronous tasks the more computationally demanding part of the work. These asynchronous tasks are in general executed in parallel on different background threads, depending on the computational resources available on the execution platform.

The apparent simplicity of UI programming models is somewhat deceptive. The difficulty of writing safe programs given the concurrency of the underlying execution platform is still all there. A formal programming abstraction that is simple, yet exposes both the potential benefits and the dangers of the UI frameworks would go a long way in simplifying the job of programmers. Programs written against this abstraction would then be insensitive to implementation and platform changes (e.g., automatic load balancing). Indeed, the choice of parameters such as the number of possible threads running in parallel, the dispatching policy of pending tasks over these threads, the scheduling policy for executing shared-memory concurrent tasks, etc., should be transparent to programmers, and the semantics of a program should be independent from this choice. Therefore the conformance to this abstraction (i.e., a program can be soundly abstracted according it) would be a highly desirable correctness criterion.

The objectives of our work are (1) to provide such a programming abstraction that leads to a suitable correctness criterion for event-driven shared memory asynchronous programs, and (2) to provide efficient algorithms for verifying that a program is correct w.r.t. this criterion.

The programming abstraction we consider compares two semantics, the *multi-thread* and the *single-thread* semantics:

- The multi-thread semantics reflects the concurrency of the actual program: The main (UI) thread and asynchronous tasks posted to background threads interact over the shared memory in a concurrent way. No limit on the number of tasks, no limit on the number of threads, and no restriction on the dispatching and scheduling policies are assumed.
- The single-thread semantics is a reference model where a program is supposed to run on a single thread handling user events in a serial manner, one after the other. Each event is handled by executing its corresponding code including the created asynchronous tasks until completion. The asynchronous tasks created by an event handler (and recursively, by its callee) are executed asynchronously (once the execution of the creator finishes) serially and in the order of their invocation.

While the multi-thread semantics provides greater performance and responsiveness, the single-thread semantics is simpler to apprehend. The inherent non-determinism due to concurrency and asynchronous task dispatching from the multi-thread semantics is not present in the context of the single-thread one.

We consider that a desirable property of a program is that its multi-thread semantics is a *refinement* of its single-thread semantics in the sense that the sets of observable reachable states of the program w.r.t. both semantics are exactly the same. A program that satisfies this refinement condition is said to be *robust against concurrency* (or simply *robust*). In fact, robustness violations correspond to "concurrency bugs", i.e., violations that are due to parallelization of tasks, and that do not show up when tasks are executed in a serial manner.

Then, let us focus now on the problem of verifying the robustness of a given program. We show in this paper that, surprisingly, for the class of UI event-driven asynchronous programs, this problem can be reduced in linear time to the state reachability problem in *sequential programs*. This means that the robustness of such a concurrent program can be checked in polynomial time on an (instrumented) *sequential* version of the program, without exploring all its concurrent executions. Let us describe the way we achieve that.

First, we show that robustness against concurrency can be characterized as the conjunction of *event-serializability* and *event determinism*, which are variants of the classical notions of serializability and determinism, adapted to our context. Intuitively, since the single-thread semantics defines a unique execution, given a set of external events (partially ordered w.r.t. some causality relation imposed by the environment), then (1) the executions of the event handlers must be serializable (to an order compatible with their causality relation), i.e., the execution of each event handler and its subtasks can be seen as an atomic transaction, and (2) the execution of each event handler is deterministic, i.e., it always leads to the same state, for any possible scheduling of its parallel subtasks.

To search efficiently for event-serializability and event-determinism violations, we make use of *conflict-based approximations* in the style of [27], called conflict-serializability and conflict-determinism, respectively. Indeed, these conflict-based criteria do not take into account actual data values, but rather syntactical dependencies between operations (e.g., writing to the same variable), which makes them stronger, but also "easier" to check, while still accurate enough for catching real bugs, introducing rarely false positives, as our experiments show. We reduce verifying conflict event-serializability and conflict event-determinism to detecting cycles in appropriately defined dependency (or happen-before) relations between concurrent events and asynchronous procedure invocations, respectively. Our key contribution is that these cycle detections can be done by reasoning about the computations of *sequential programs* instead of concurrent programs, avoiding explicit encodings of (potentially unbounded) sets of pending tasks and exploring all their possible interleavings. Let us explain this in more details.

An event handler is conflict-deterministic when all its executions have conflict-preserving permutations where tasks are executed serially in the same order as in the single-thread semantics. Scheduling tasks in this order corresponds to the DFS (Depth First Search) traversal of the call-tree of tasks (representing the relation caller-callee). We show that detecting a conflict-determinism violation, i.e., an asynchronous execution with no serial DFS counterpart, can be done by reasoning about an instrumented version of the procedural program obtained from the code of the event handler by roughly, turning pasynchronous calls to synchronous ones. This instrumented program simulates *borderline violations*, if any, i.e., violations where removing the last action leads to a correct execution. We show that the amount of auxiliary memory needed to witness such violations is finite (and small). Moreover, such violations are "almost" asynchronous executions where tasks are scheduled serially according to the DFS traversal of the call-tree. Such executions can be simulated using synchronous procedure calls because roughly, the latter are also initiated according to the DFS traversal of the call-tree. However, they are interleaved in a different way compared to the asynchronous calls and the event handler must undergo a syntactic transformation described in Sect. 6.3.

As for conflict-serializability, a first issue in checking it is that event handlers may consist of different concurrently-executing tasks. This issue is solved by assuming that the conflict-determinism check is done a-priori. If this check fails then the program is not robust and otherwise, checking conflict-serializability can assume sequential event handlers which are in fact the instrumented procedural programs used in the conflict-determinism check.

Even assuming sequential event handlers, general results about conflict-serializability state that this problem is PSPACE-complete for a fixed number of threads [6,15], and EXPSPACE-complete for an unbounded number of threads [10] (assuming a fixed data domain and absence of recursive procedure calls). However, we prove that, in the programming model we consider in this paper, the problem of checking conflict-serializability is *polynomial!* This result relies on two facts: (1) there is only one distinguished thread, the UI thread, for which the order in which procedure invocations are executed is relevant, and (2) we assume that each asynchronous task executed in the background (not on the UI thread) is running on a fresh thread. This assumption is valid since background threads are not manipulated explicitly by the programmer but by the runtime, and therefore, we need to consider the situation where concurrency is maximal.

In fact, we show that when events are conflict-deterministic, the problem of checking conflict-serializability can also be reduced to a reachability problem in a sequential program. Again, we prove that it is sufficient to focus on a particular class of (borderline) violations of conflict-serializability. Then, we show that detecting these violations can be done by reasoning about the executions of a program where events are executed in a sequential manner, in any order (chosen nondeterministically), and where the tasks generated by each event are executed as in the single-thread semantics. For that, we define an instrumentation of that program that consists in simulating the delaying effects of the multi-thread semantics, guessing the actions involved in the violation and tracking the dependencies between them in order to check the correctness of the guess (that they indeed form a cycle). The cycle detection in the case of conflict-serializability is technically more complex than in the case of conflict-determinism. But still, a crucial point in the reduction is that we do not need to store the whole cycle during the search, but it is enough to maintain a fixed number of variables to traverse the elements of this cycle. This leads to a polynomial reduction of the conflict-robustness problem to a reachability problem in a sequential program.

Our reductions hold regardless of the used data domain, for programs with recursive procedure calls, and unbounded numbers of events and tasks. These reductions allow to leverage existing analysis tools for sequential programs to check conflict-robustness. When the data domain is bounded, we obtain a polynomial-time algorithm for checking conflict-robustness for UI event-driven asynchronous programs (with recursive procedure calls, and unboundedly many events and tasks).

We validate our approach on a set of real-life applications, showing that with few exceptions all detected robustness violations are undesirable behaviours. Interestingly, the use of conflict versions of the correctness criteria characterizing robustness is efficient and quite accurate, producing only few false positives (that can be eliminated easily).

Finally, let us mention that our work also leads to an efficient approach for verifying functional correctness of UI event-driven asynchronous programs that consists in reducing this problem to two separate problems: (1) showing that the program is functionally correct w.r.t the single-thread semantics, and (2) showing that it is robust against concurrency. Both of these problems can indeed be solved efficiently by considering only particular types of computations that are captured by sequential programs.

To summarize, our contributions are:

- Introduction of the notion of robustness against concurrency that provides a programming abstraction for event-driven asynchronous programs, and its characterization as the conjunction of event-serializability and event-determinism.
- Efficient algorithms for checking robustness based on reductions from conflict event-serializability and conflict event-determinism to state reachability problems in sequential programs. Decidability and complexity results for verifying robustness in the case of finite data domains.
- Experimentations showing the relevance of our correctness criteria and the efficiency of our approach.

2   Motivating Examples

We demonstrate the relevance of robustness using several excerpts from Android applications. To argue that robustness is not too strong as a requirement, we discuss two concurrency bugs reported in open-source repositories that are also robustness violations, more precisely, event-serializability and event-determinism violations. We also provide a typical example of a robust program.

2.1   A Violation to Event Serializability

```
ActionEditText msgTxt;
boolean onKey(...) {
    // actions on UI thread
    new SendTask().execute();
}

void onDoubleClicked(String name){
    text += "␣" + name;
    msgTxt.setText(text);
}

class SendTask extends AsyncTask {
void onPreExecute(){
    e.command = msgTxt.getText();
}
void doInBackground(..) {
    write msgTxt.getText() into JSON obj
    /* corrected version:
    write e.command into JSON obj */
}
}
```

Fig. 1. A program with an event-serializability violation.

Figure 1 lists a real code excerpt from the Android IrcCloud app [2] for chatting on the IRC. Under the concrete multi-thread semantics, the user event of pressing the "send" key is handled by the procedure onKey. Actions associated with this event handler include actions performed by onKey on the main (UI) thread, actions performed by SendTask.onPreExecute() on the UI thread before the actions performed asynchronously on a background thread by SendTasks's doInBackground procedure. Another event handler in this example is onDoubleClicked, which appends to the message text the name name of the user whose name is clicked on. The multi-thread semantics allows interference between the two event handlers, onDoubleClicked can interleave with doInBackground. In contrast, the single-thread semantics allows no such interference. The event handlers and the asynchronous tasks they create are executed entirely on the UI thread, and all the tasks created by onKey are executed before any other event handler invocation.

This program is not robust and a violation can be generated under the following scenario. Suppose that the user types "Hello", presses "send", and then double-clicks on another IRC user's name. Under the multi-thread semantics, onDoubleClicked may start running on the UI thread while SendTask.doInBackground is in progress. These two procedures' accesses can interfere with each other. In particular, the ordering of msgTxt.getText() with respect to the appending of name to msgTxt determines whether "Hello" or "Hello foo" gets sent on the network. Moreover, since onKey first records msg.getText() to a field e.command, an execution of these two events can end in a program state in which e.command contains "Hello" while msgTxt contains "Hello foo". This end state is not possible with *any* execution of these two event handlers under the single-thread semantics, where the event handlers are executed serially one after the other. This is a violation to event serializability. Actually, this behavior was reported as a bug, and the code was updated [1] so that e.command (instead of msgTxt, which may have changed) is written into a JSON object and sent on the network. It was the designers' intent for the entire event handling code for the "send" key to appear atomic. With this modification the program becomes robust.

2.2   A Violation to Event Determinism

```
void iconPackUpdated(){
 new Thread( new Runnable(){
  void run() {
   ..
   mAdapter=new AppRowAdapter(..);
  } } ).start();
 new Handler().postDelayed(
  new Runnable() {
   void run() {
    ..
    if(setAdapter)
     listView.setAdapter(mAdapter);
    ..
    mAdapter.notifyDataSetChanged();
   } }, 1000);
}
```

Fig. 2. A program with an event-determinism violation.

Figure 2 lists an event handler called iconPackUpdated which creates an asynchronous task (the first runnable to be executed by the created thread) to initialize the mAdapter object. Then it creates another task, to be run by the UI thread, that uses mAdapter to update the list view of displayed icons. In an effort to ensure that the second task runs after the first task completes, the programmer posts the second task after a second's delay.

Under the concrete multi-thread semantics, it is possible for the first task not to complete even after a second. In this case, the second runnable code will produce a null pointer exception, while in other schedules, the code works as intended. Although the programmer had intended a deterministic outcome there are executions with different outcomes, including errors. Therefore, this event handler is not event-deterministic, and not robust.

2.3   A Robust Program

The program in Fig. 3 has two event handlers searchForNews and showDetail which can be invoked by the user to search for news containing a keyword and to display the details of a selected news respectively.

The procedure searchForNews creates two AsyncTask objects SearchTask and SaveTask whose execute method will invoke asynchronously doInBackground followed by onPostExecute, in the case of the former. Under the multi-thread semantics, doInBackground is invoked on a new thread and onPostExecute is invoked

```
// Event 1
void searchForNews(String key) {
 new SearchTask.execute(key);
 new SaveTask.execute(key); }

// Event 2
void showDetail(int id) {
 // show detail of the idth news
 new DownloadTask.execute(id); }

class SaveTask extends AsyncTask {
 void doInBackground(String key) {
  // write key to the database } }
```

```
class SearchTask extends AsyncTask {
 List result = null;
 void doInBackground(String key) {
  result = ...
 // get from the network
 }
 void onPostExecute() {
  list = result;
  // display the list of titles } }

class DownloadTask extends AsyncTask {
 String content = null;
 void doInBackground(int id) {
  content = ... // get from the network
 }
 void onPostExecute() {
  // display the content } }
```

Fig. 3. A robust program.

on the main thread. When the user input to search for news is triggered, the invocation `doInBackground` of `searchTask` connects to the network, searches for the keyword and fetches the list of resulting news titles. Then, the invocation `onPostExecute` displays the list of titles to the user. `SaveTask` saves the keyword to a database representing the search history in the background. The background tasks `SearchTask.doInBackground` and `SaveTask.doInBackground` might interfere but any interleaving produces the same result, i.e., `searchForNews` is deterministic.

The second event, to show the details of a title, can be triggered once the list of titles are displayed on the screen. It invokes an asynchronous task to download the contents of the news in the background and then displays it. In this case, the tasks are executed in a fixed order and the event is trivially deterministic.

Concerning serializability, the invocation of `SaveTask` in the first event and the second event might interleave (under the concrete semantics). However, assuming that the second event is triggered once the results are displayed, any such interleaving results in the same state as a serial execution of these events.

3   Programs

In order to give a generic definition of robustness, which doesn't depend on any particular asynchronous-programming platform or syntax, we frame our discussion around the abstract notion of programs defined in Sect. 3.1. Two alternative multi-thread and single-thread semantics to programs are given in Sects. 3.2 and 3.3. We consider programs that are *data-deterministic*, in the sense that the evaluation of every (Boolean) expression is uniquely determined by the variable valuation.

3.1   Asynchronous Event-Driven Programs

We define an event handler as a procedure which is invoked in response to a user or a system input. For simplicity, we assume that inputs can arrive in any order. Event handlers may have some asynchronous invocations of other procedures, to be executed later on the same thread or on a background thread.

We fix sets G and L of global and local program states. Local states $\ell \in L$ represent the code and data of an asynchronous procedure or event-handler invocation, including the code and data of all nested synchronous procedure calls. A program is defined as a mapping between pairs of global and local states which gives the semantics of each statement in the code of a procedure (the association between threads, local states, and procedure invocations is defined in Sects. 3.2 and 3.3). To formalize the conflict-based approximation of robustness, this mapping associates with each statement a label called *program action* that records the set of variables read or written and the asynchronous invocations in that statement. An *event set* $E \subset L$ is a set of local states; each $e \in E$ represents the code and data for a single event handler invocation (called event for short).

$$x := y \quad y := x \quad \textbf{assume}\, y \quad \textbf{call}\, p(y) \quad \textbf{async}[w]\, p(y) \quad \textbf{return}$$

Fig. 4. A canonical program syntax. The metavariables x and y range over global and local variable names, respectively, p ranges over procedure names, and w over the symbols "main" and "any".

Formally, let $X = \{\text{rd}(x), \text{wr}(x) : x \in \ldots\}$ be the set of memory accesses, $W = \{\text{main}, \text{any}\}$ the set of invocation places, and $B = \{\text{invoke}(\ell, w) : \ell \in L, w \in W\} \cup \{\text{return}\} \cup X \cup \{\varepsilon\}$ the set of program actions, where ε represents irrelevant program actions. The $\text{rd}(x)$ and $\text{wr}(x)$ represent read and write accesses to variable x; $\text{invoke}(\ell, w)$ represents an asynchronous invocation whose initial local state is ℓ; the invocation is to be run on a distinguished main thread when $w = \text{main}$, and on an arbitrary thread when $w = \text{any}$. Finally, the return program action represents the return from an asynchronous procedure invocation.

A *program* $P : G \times L \to G \times L \times B$ maps global states $g \in G$ and local states $\ell \in L$ to new states and program actions; each $P(g, \ell)$ represents a single program transition. We assume that when b is an asynchronous invocation or return program action and $P(g, \ell) = \langle g', \_, b \rangle$ then $g = g'$.

Canonical Program Syntax. Supposing that the global states $g \in G$ are maps from program variables x to values $g(x)$, and that local states $\ell \in L$ map program variables y to values $\ell(y)$ and a program counter variable pc to program statements $\ell(\text{pc})$, we give an interpretation to the canonical program syntax listed in Fig. 4. We assume atomicity of the statements at the bytecode level. For simplicity, we omit the interpretation of synchronous procedure calls $\textbf{call}\, p(y)$ which is defined as usual. For instance, writing ℓ^+ to denote $\ell[\text{pc} \mapsto \ell(\text{pc}) + 1]$, then $P(g, \ell)$ is

- $\langle g[x \mapsto \ell(y)], \ell^+, \text{wr}(x) \rangle$ when $\ell(\text{pc})$ is a global-variable write $x := y$,
- $\langle g, \ell^+[y \mapsto g(x)], \text{rd}(x) \rangle$ when $\ell(\text{pc})$ is a global-variable read $y := x$,
- $\langle g, \ell^+, \text{rd}(y) \rangle$ when $\ell(\text{pc})$ is $\textbf{assume}(y)$ and $\ell(y) \neq 0$,
- $\langle g, \ell, \varepsilon \rangle$ when $\ell(\text{pc})$ is $\textbf{assume}(y)$ and $\ell(y) = 0$,
- $\langle g, \ell^+, \text{invoke}(\ell', w) \rangle$ when $\ell(\text{pc})$ is an asynchronous invocation $\textbf{async}[w]\, p(y)$, where ℓ' maps the parameters of procedure p to the invocation arguments y and pc to the initial statement of p, and
- $\langle g, \ell, \text{return} \rangle$ when $\ell(\text{pc})$ is the $\textbf{return}$ statement.

The semantics of other statements, including if-then-else conditionals, while loops, or goto statements, etc. (we assume that Boolean conditions use only local variables), is standard, and yield the empty program action ε.

An event is called *sequential* when its code doesn't contain asynchronous invocations $\textbf{async}[w]\, p(y)$. Also, a program P with event set E is called *sequential* when every event $e \in E$ is sequential. Otherwise, P is called *concurrent*.

3.2 Multi-thread Asynchronous Semantics

Our multi-thread semantics maximizes the set of possible program behaviors by allowing events to interleave and interfere with each other. It dispatches the event handlers serially on the main thread but allows the asynchronous procedure invocations to execute on separate threads, not necessarily in invocation order. Configurations of the multi-thread semantics thus maintain sets of running procedure invocations as well as an unordered queue of pending invocations, and invocations are associated with events and threads.

To characterize executions by the event-serializability and event-determinism criteria, we expose the following set A of actions in execution traces:

$$A = \{\mathrm{start}(j), \mathrm{end}(j) : j \in \mathbb{N}\} \cup X \cup \{\mathrm{invoke}(i), \mathrm{begin}(i), \mathrm{return}(i) : i \in \mathbb{N}\}$$

By convention, we denote asynchronous procedure invocation, event, and thread identifiers, respectively, with the symbols i, j, k. The $\mathrm{start}(j)$ and $\mathrm{end}(j)$ actions represent the start and end of event j; the $\mathrm{invoke}(i)$, $\mathrm{begin}(i)$, and $\mathrm{return}(i)$ actions represent an asynchronous procedure invocation (when it is added to the queue of pending invocations), the start of i's execution (when it is removed from the queue), and return of i, respectively. The set X of memory accesses is defined as in the program actions of Sect. 3.1.

A *task* $u = \langle \ell, i, j, k \rangle$ is a local state $\ell \in L$ along with invocation, event and thread identifiers $i, j, k \in \mathbb{N}$, and U denotes the set of tasks. We write $\mathrm{invoc}(u)$, $\mathrm{event}(u)$, and $\mathrm{thread}(u)$ to refer to i, j, and k, respectively. A *configuration* $c = \langle g, t, q \rangle$ is a global state $g \in G$ along with sets $t, q \subseteq U$ of running and waiting tasks such that: (1) invocation identifiers are unique, i.e., $\mathrm{invoc}(u_1) \neq \mathrm{invoc}(u_2)$ for all $u_1 \neq u_2 \in t \cup q$, and (2) threads run one task at a time, i.e., $\mathrm{thread}(u_1) \neq \mathrm{thread}(u_2)$ for all $u_1 \neq u_2 \in t$. The set of configurations is denoted by C_m. We say that a thread k is *idle* in c when $k \notin \{\mathrm{thread}(u) : u \in t\}$, and that an identifier i, j, k is *fresh* when $i, j, k \notin \{\alpha(u) : u \in (t \cup q)\}$ for $\alpha \in \{\mathrm{invoc}, \mathrm{event}, \mathrm{thread}\}$, respectively. A configuration is *idle* when all threads are *idle*.

The transition function $\rightarrow$ in Fig. 5 is determined by a program P and event set E, and maps a configuration $c_1 \in C_m$ and thread identifier $k \in \mathbb{N}$ to another configuration $c_2 \in C_m$ and label $\lambda = \langle i, j, a \rangle$ where i and j are invocation and event identifiers, and $a \in A$ is an action—we write $\mathrm{invoc}(\lambda)$, $\mathrm{event}(\lambda)$, and $\mathrm{act}(\lambda)$ to refer to i, j, and a, respectively. EVENT transitions mark the beginnings of events. We assume that all events are initiated on thread 0, which is also referred to as the *main* thread. Also, for simplicity, we assume that events

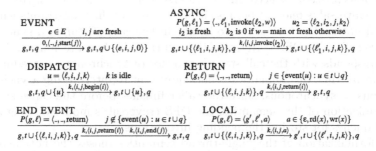

Fig. 5. The multi-thread transition function $\rightarrow$ for a program P with event set E.

can be initiated arbitrarily at any time. Adding causality constraints between events, e.g., one event can be initiated only when a certain action has been executed, is possible but tedious. ASYNC transitions create pending asynchronous invocations, DISPATCH transitions begin the execution of pending invocations, and RETURN transitions signal their end (the condition in the right ensures that this is not a return from an event). END EVENT transitions mark the end of an event and by an abuse of notation, they map c_1 and k to a configuration c_2 and two labels, return(i) denoting the end of the asynchronous invocation and end(j) denoting the end of the event. All other transitions are LOCAL.

An *execution* of a program P under the multi-thread semantics with event set E to configuration c_n is a configuration sequence $c_0 c_1 \ldots c_n$ such that $c_m \xrightarrow{k_m, \lambda_{m+1}} c_{m+1}$ for $0 \leq m < n$. We say that c_n is reachable in P with E under the multi-thread semantics, and we call the sequence $\lambda_1 \ldots \lambda_n$ the *trace* of $c_0 c_1 \ldots c_n$. The *reachable states* of P with E, denoted $R_m(P, E)$, is the set of global states in reachable idle configurations. The set of traces of P with E under the multi-thread semantics is denoted by $[\![P, E]\!]_m$. We may omit P when it is understood from the context, and write $[\![E]\!]_m$ instead of $[\![P, E]\!]_m$.

The *call tree* of a trace τ is a ranked tree $CallTree_\tau = \langle V, E, O \rangle$ where V are the invocation identifiers in τ, and the set of edges E contains an edge from i_1 to i_2 whenever i_2 is invoked by i_1, i.e., τ contains a label $\langle i_1, \_, \text{invoke}(i_2) \rangle$. The function $O : E \to \mathbb{N}$ labels each edge (i_1, i_2) with an integer n whenever i_2 is the nth invocation made by i_1, i.e., $\langle i_1, \_, \text{invoke}(i_2) \rangle$ is the nth label of the form $\langle i_1, \_, \text{invoke}(\_) \rangle$ occurring in τ (reading τ from left to right).

3.3 Single-Thread Asynchronous Semantics

Conversely to the multi-thread semantics of Sect. 3.2, our single-thread semantics minimizes the set of possible program behaviors by executing all events and asynchronous invocations on the main thread, the asynchronous procedure invocations being executed in a *fixed* order.

We explain the order in which asynchronous invocations are executed using the event handler searchForNews in Fig. 3. This event handler is supposed to add the keyword to the search history only after the fetching of the news containing that keyword succeeds. This expectation corresponds to executing the asynchronous procedures according to the DFS traversal of the call tree. In general, this traversal is relevant because it preserves causality constraints which are imprinted in the structure of the code, like in the case of standard synchronous procedure calls. The DFS traversal of the call tree also has a technical advantage as it corresponds with the call stack semantics of synchronous procedure calls. Note however that this semantics is not equivalent to interpreting asynchronous invocations as synchronous, since the caller finishes before the callee starts. In the formalization of this semantics, the DFS traversal is modeled using a stack of FIFO queues for storing the pending invocations.

The formalization of the single-thread semantics reuses the notions of task and label in Sect. 3.2. Let U_0 be the set of tasks $u = \langle \ell, i, j, 0 \rangle$ executing on thread 0. We overload the term *configuration* which in this context is a tuple

$$\textbf{EVENT} \quad \frac{e \in E \qquad i,j \text{ are fresh}}{g,\bot,\varepsilon \xrightarrow{0,\langle -,j,\text{start}(j)\rangle} g,\bot,\langle e,i,j,0\rangle}$$

$$\textbf{END EVENT} \quad \frac{P(g,\ell) = \langle -,-,\text{return}\rangle}{g,\langle \ell,i,j,k\rangle,\varepsilon \xrightarrow{k,\langle i,j,\text{return}(i)\rangle\ k,\langle i,j,\text{end}(j)\rangle} g,\bot,\varepsilon}$$

$$\textbf{ASYNC} \quad \frac{P(g,\ell_1) = \langle -,\ell_1',\text{invoke}(\ell_2,w)\rangle \quad u_2 = \langle \ell_2,i_2,j,0\rangle \quad i_2 \text{ is fresh}}{g,\langle \ell_1,i,j,k\rangle,q\cdot f \xrightarrow{0,\langle i,j,\text{invoke}(i_2)\rangle} g,\langle \ell_1',i,j,k\rangle,q\cdot(f\circ i_2)}$$

$$\textbf{DISPATCH} \quad \frac{u = \langle \ell,i,j,k\rangle \quad f = u\circ f' \quad q' \text{ is } \langle\rangle \text{ if } f' = \langle\rangle \text{ or } f'\cdot\langle\rangle, \text{ otherwise}}{g,\bot,q\cdot f \xrightarrow{0,\langle i,j,\text{begin}(i)\rangle} g,u,q\cdot q'}$$

$$\textbf{RETURN} \quad \frac{P(g,\ell) = \langle -,-,\text{return}\rangle \quad j \in \{\text{event}(u) : u \in q\}}{g,\langle \ell,i,j,k\rangle,q \xrightarrow{k,\langle i,j,\text{return}(i)\rangle} g,\bot,\overline{q}}$$

$$\textbf{LOCAL} \quad \frac{P(g,\ell) = \langle g',\ell',a\rangle \quad a \in \{\varepsilon,\text{rd}(x),\text{wr}(x)\}}{g,\langle \ell,i,j,k\rangle,q \xrightarrow{k,\langle i,j,a\rangle} g',\langle \ell',i,j,k\rangle,q}$$

Fig. 6. The single-thread transition function $\Rightarrow$ for a program P with events E (ε and $\langle\rangle$ are the empty sequence and tuple, resp.,). Also, f and f' are tuples, and $\overline{q}$ is obtained by popping a queue from q if this queue is empty, or $\overline{q} = q$, otherwise.

$c = \langle g,u,q\rangle$ where $g \in G$, $u \in (U_0 \cup \{\bot\})$ is a possibly-empty task placeholder (at most one task is running at any moment), and $q \in (\text{Tuples}(U_0))^*$ is a sequence of tuples of tasks (a tuple, resp., a sequence, denotes a FIFO queue, resp., a stack). C_s is the set of configurations of the single-thread semantics. We call $c \in C_s$ *idle* if $u = \bot$.

The transition function $\Rightarrow$ in Fig. 6 is essentially a restriction of $\rightarrow$ where all the procedures run on the main thread, an event begins when there are no pending invocations, and the rules ASYNC and DISPATCH use a stack of FIFO queues for storing pending invocations. The effect of pushing/popping a queue to the stack or enqueuing/dequeueing a task to a queue is represented using the concatenation operation $\cdot$, resp.,$\circ$, for sequences, resp., tuples. Every task created by ASYNC is posted to the *main* thread and it is enqueued in the queue on the top of the stack q. DISPATCH dequeues a pending task from the queue f on the top of q, and pushes a new *empty* queue to q (for storing the tasks created during the newly started invocation) if f doesn't become empty. Moreover, the rules RETURN and END EVENT pop the queue on the top of q if it is empty.

An *execution* of a program P under the single-thread semantics with event set E to configuration c_n is a sequence $c_0c_1\ldots c_n$ s.t. $c_m \xrightarrow{0,\lambda_{m+1}} c_{m+1}$ for $0 \le m < n$. We say that c_n is *reachable* in P with E under the single-thread semantics, and we call the sequence $\lambda_1\ldots\lambda_n$ the *trace* of $c_0c_1\ldots c_n$. The *reachable states* of P with E, denoted $R_s(P,E)$, is the set of global states reachable in idle configurations.

The set of traces of P with E under the single-thread semantics is denoted by $[\![P,E]\!]_s$ (P may be omitted when it is understood from the context).

4 Robustness of Asynchronous Programs

Our robustness criterion is defined as the equality of the single-thread and multi-thread semantics of a program, and decomposed into two independently-checkable criteria, event serializability and event determinism.

Given a program P with event set E, each execution under the single-thread semantics can be simulated by an execution under the multi-thread semantics: the latter corresponds to a special scheduling policy that consists in executing all tasks created by an event before starting executing tasks corresponding to another event, and moreover, tasks are executed atomically, in the order given by the DFS traversal of the call tree. This implies that the multi-thread semantics is a relaxation of the single-thread semantics, and therefore, $R_s(P, E) \subseteq R_m(P, E)$. The reverse direction is the most interesting one:

Definition 1 (Robustness). *A program P with events E is robust against concurrency (or simply robust) when all reachable states in the multi-thread semantics are also reachable in the single-thread semantics: $R_m(P, E) \subseteq R_s(P, E)$.*

Robustness means that for the considered program, the concurrency introduced by the multi-thread semantics does not modify the set of observable states, i.e., $R_m(P, E) = R_s(P, E)$. We introduce in the following two correctness criteria that capture precisely the notion of robustness.

We say an execution with trace $\lambda_1 \cdots \lambda_n$ is *event-serial* when for all $n_1 < n_3$, if $\text{act}(\lambda_{n_1}) = \text{start}(j)$ and $\text{act}(\lambda_{n_3}) = \text{start}(j')$, then there is n_2 such that $n_1 < n_2 < n_3$ and $\text{act}(\lambda_{n_2}) = \text{end}(j)$.

Definition 2 (Event-serializability). *A program P with events E is event-serializable if every global state in $R_m(P, E)$ can be reached by an event-serial execution[1].*

Given an event e, an *e-execution starting from global state g_0* is a g_0-initialized execution (according to the multi-thread semantics) with trace $\lambda_1 \cdots \lambda_n$ such that (1) $\text{act}(\lambda_1) = \text{start}(j)$, (2) $\text{act}(\lambda_n) = \text{end}(j)$, for some j, and (3) for every $m \in \mathbb{N}$ such that $1 < m < n$, $\text{act}(\lambda_m)$ is neither a start nor an end action. Intuitively, we consider executions of individual events, from their starting point until the completion of all the tasks they have created. Then, let $R_m(P, g_0, e)$ be the set of global states in final configurations of e-executions starting from g_0. Notice that e-executions from g_0 differ by the scheduling order of the tasks created by e that are running in parallel on different threads.

Definition 3 (Event-determinism). *An event e of a program P is deterministic if for every global state g_0, the set $R_m(P, g_0, e)$ is a singleton or empty. A program P with events E is event-deterministic, if every $e \in E$ is deterministic.*

Notice that our notion of determinism is defined for events that are running alone, without interference of other events.

Theorem 1. *A program is robust against asynchrony if and only if it is event-serializable and event-deterministic.*

---

[1] For simplicity, we have ignored the set of events which are executed when comparing global state reached by aribitrary and event-serial executions, resp. Reaching a global state using the same set of events is easy to formalize but tedious.

5   Conflict Robustness

Following an idea introduced in the context of database transactions [27], we define a syntactic, conservative notion of *conflict robustness* that is the conjunction of two properties: *conflict-event serializability* and *conflict-event determinism*.

5.1   Conflict-Event Serializability

Let $\prec \subseteq A \times A$ be a *conflict relation* that relates any two actions a, a' accessing the same variable, i.e., $a, a' \in \{\mathrm{rd}(x), \mathrm{wr}(x)\}$ for some x, one of them being a write. A trace is conflict-event serializable iff the "conflict-event graph" which tracks the conflict relation between concurrent events is acyclic.

Formally, the *conflict-event graph* of a trace τ is the directed graph $EvG_\tau = \langle V, E \rangle$ whose nodes V are the event identifiers of τ, and which contains an edge from j_1 to j_2 when τ contains a pair of labels λ_1 and λ_2 such that λ_1 occurs before λ_2, $act(\lambda_1) \prec act(\lambda_2)$, $event(\lambda_1) = j_1$, and $event(\lambda_2) = j_2$.

Definition 4. *A trace τ is called conflict-event serializable when EvG_τ is acyclic. A program P with event set E is conflict-event serializable iff every trace in $[\![P, E]\!]_m$ is conflict serializable.*

A permutation τ' of a trace τ is *conflict-preserving* when every pair λ_1, λ_2 of labels in τ appear in the same order in τ' whenever $act(\lambda_1) \prec act(\lambda_2)$. Note that a conflict-preserving permutation τ' leads to the same global state as the original trace τ. *From now on, whenever we use permutation we mean conflict-preserving permutation.* A trace τ is conflict-event serializable iff it is a conflict-preserving permutation of an event-serial trace.

Theorem 2. *A program P with event set E is event-serializable when it is conflict-event serializable.*

5.2   Conflict Determinism

We define *conflict determinism*, which is also based on the acyclicity of a certain class of "conflict graphs", called *conflict-invocation graphs*. These graphs represent the conflicts between the asynchronous invocations, but also the order in which these invocations would be executed under the single-thread semantics, i.e., the DFS traversal of the call tree. If the conflict-invocation graph of every trace τ of an event e is acyclic, then e is deterministic because every trace τ is a conflict-preserving permutation of the trace t_0 corresponding to the single-thread semantics, and thus leads to the same global state as t_0.

Given a trace τ, let $<_{dfs}$ be the total order between the invocation identifiers in τ defined by the DFS traversal of $CallTree_\tau$. The *conflict-invocation graph* of a trace τ is the directed graph $InvG(\tau) = \langle V, E \rangle$ whose nodes V are the asynchronous invocation identifiers in τ, and which contains an edge from i_1 to i_2 when $i_1 <_{dfs} i_2$, or τ contains a pair of labels λ_1 and λ_2 of i_1 and i_2, resp., such that $act(\lambda_1) \prec act(\lambda_2)$ and λ_1 occurs before λ_2.

Definition 5. *A trace* τ *is DFS-serial iff* $InvG(\tau)$ *is acyclic. An event* e *is* conflict-deterministic *iff every trace in* $[\![e]\!]_m$ *is DFS-serial.*

A trace τ is called *invocation-serial* iff for every three labels $\lambda_1, \lambda_2, \lambda_3$ occurring in τ in this order, if $invoc(\lambda_1) = invoc(\lambda_3)$, then $invoc(\lambda_1) = invoc(\lambda_2)$. For an event e, a DFS-serial trace τ in $[\![e]\!]_m$ is a permutation of an invocation-serial trace $\tau_0 \in [\![e]\!]_m$ where $invoc(\lambda_1) <_{dfs} invoc(\lambda_2)$ for every two labels λ_1 and λ_2 occurring in this order in τ_0.

Theorem 3. *An event is deterministic when it is conflict-deterministic.*

6   Checking Conflict Determinism

We reduce the problem of checking conflict determinism of an event to a reachability problem in a *sequential* program. We present the reduction in two steps. First, conflict determinism of an event interpreted under the multi-thread semantics, whose asynchronous invocations run concurrently, is reduced to a reachability problem in a program running on the single-thread semantics, where asynchronous invocations are executed serially (Sects. 6.1 and 6.2). The latter is then reduced to a reachability problem in a sequential program (Sect. 6.3).

This reduction uses the fact that a certain class of conflict determinism violations can be simulated by a sequential program up to conflict-preserving permutations of actions (note that any conflict-preserving permutation of a violation is also a violation). This class of violations called *borderline violations* are minimal in the sense that removing the last action leads to a correct trace. Besides the simulation, we show that fixed-size additional memory is required to witness the conflicts inducing a cycle in the conflict invocation graph.

Definition 6 (Borderline Conflict Determinism Violation). *A trace* τ *is a* borderline violation *to conflict determinism if it is not DFS-serial but every strict prefix of* τ *is DFS-serial.*

For instance, the trace τ_1 given in Fig. 7(a) contains a borderline violation. This trace is generated by an event e that invokes two procedures p and q in this order, each procedure on a different thread. The only conflict between memory accesses is that between the $wr(x)$ actions in q and resp., p. The conflict-invocation graph of τ_1 contains a cycle between the invocations of p and q: the edge from the invocation of p to that of q is implied by the fact that p is invoked before q within the same procedure (we have "$p <_{dfs} q$"), and the edge in the other direction exists because q writes to the variable x before p does. The trace τ_1 until after the second $wr(x)$ is a borderline violation since its maximal strict prefix (without the second $wr(x)$) is DFS-serial. The last label of a borderline violation τ, in this example $wr(x)$, is called the *pivot* of τ. The label of τ which precedes and conflicts with its pivot and which induces the cycle in its conflict-invocation graph is called the *root* of τ. Formally, if i_1 is the invocation containing the pivot of τ, the root of τ is an action conflicting with the pivot and which is included in an invocation i_2 such that $i_1 <_{dfs} i_2$. For the trace in Fig. 7(a), the root is the action $wr(x)$ in the invocation of q.

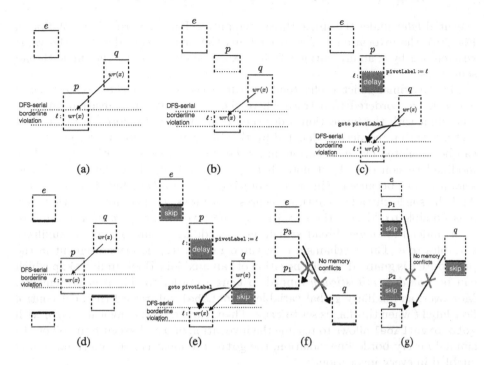

Fig. 7. Simulating borderline conflict determinism violations on the single-thread semantics. The event e makes two fresh thread asynchronous invocations to p and q in this order. Boxes represent sequences of trace labels ordered from top to bottom. Actions of the same thread are aligned vertically. The arrows represents transition label conflicts. For readability, we omit the event and task identifiers in the trace labels and keep only the memory accesses. The grey blocks labeled by delay, resp., skip, denote sequences of actions that are delayed, resp., skipped.

6.1 Simulating Borderline Violations

We define a code-to-code translation from an event e to an event $\mathsf{detStr}^-(e)$ which simulates[2] permutations of every DFS-serial or borderline violation trace in $[\![e]\!]_m$. The event $\mathsf{detStr}^-(e)$ uses additional non-deterministically enabled statements to simulate the particular interleavings present in those traces. The instrumentation required to witness violations is introduced in Sect. 6.2.

Overview. We give an informal description of the translation using as examples the traces pictured in Fig. 7.

Delaying the Pivot. We first explain the simulation of the invocation that contains the pivot, which may interfere with invocations that are supposed to be

---

[2] We refer to the standard notion of (stuttering) simulation where (sequences of) transitions in $\mathsf{detStr}^-(e)$ are mapped to transitions of e.

executed *later* under the single-thread semantics. For the borderline violation in Fig. 7(a), the invocation of p that contains the pivot $wr(x)$ destroys the value written to x by q, an invocation which is executed after p under the single-thread semantics.

The maximal strict prefix (ending before the second $wr(x)$) is DFS-serial and can be reordered to a trace where the order between transition labels is consistent with the invocation order (i.e., e before p and before q). Figure 7(b) pictures such a reordering, denoted by τ_1'. Our goal is to show that the trace τ_1' can be simulated by an execution under the single-thread semantics of a slightly modified version of e. First note that τ_1' is not admitted by the single-thread semantics of e because the invocation of p is only *partially* included in this prefix. And the single-thread semantics executes every task until completion. However, it is possible to "delay" the execution of the pivot $wr(x)$ in p until q finishes, even under the single-thread semantics, by adding a suitable set of auxiliary variables to e. This mechanism is pictured in Fig. 7(c). Every statement in the procedure p is guarded by (the negation of) an auxiliary Boolean flag skip which can be *non-deterministically* flipped to true in order to skip over statements. Moreover, an auxiliary global variable pivotLabel will record the next control flow label ℓ when this flag is set to true. Then, extending the invocation of q with goto pivotLabel allows to resume the invocation of p and execute the pivot. To simulate every borderline violation, the goto statement is non-deterministically enabled in every invocation.

Incomplete Invocations. While the violation in Fig. 7(a) includes only one incomplete invocation (the one containing the pivot) this is not always the case. A borderline violation may contain unboundedly-many other incomplete invocations. For instance, the violation in Fig. 7(d) includes incomplete invocations of e and q (they finish after the pivot). Should the simulation of this borderline violation execute e and q entirely, the pivot may never be enabled. The correct simulation, pictured in Fig. 7(e), will make use of the same mechanism based on the Boolean flag skip in order to skip over statements in e and q. In general, an invocation can be skipped in its entirety. This simulation also shows that the goto statement can be executed after an incomplete invocation.

Main Thread Invocations. The last issue concerns the main thread which has the particularity of being able to execute more than one invocation (all the other threads execute a single invocation). It executes invocations serially and only the last one may be incomplete. For instance, consider the DFS-serial trace τ_3 pictured in Fig. 7(f). This is the trace of an event e that invokes p_1, q, p_2, and p_3, in this order, and except q all the tasks are assigned to the main thread. Since p_1 is invoked before p_3, a DFS-serial permutation τ_3' of τ_3 contains the *incomplete* invocation of p_1 before the *complete* invocation of p_3, as shown in Fig. 7(g). None of the semantics we defined allows such traces. The problem is that both invocations are executed by the main thread which has to complete a task before executing another one. Our simulation will however admit such traces but it will verify that they are conflict-preserving permutations of valid traces. This verification procedure (included in the definition of $\mathsf{detStr}^-(e)$) checks that the conflict invocation graph doesn't contain a path of *memory conflicts*, i.e., conflicts induced by read and write accesses, from the incomplete invocation on the main thread to any future complete invocation on the same thread. Let us consider again the trace τ_3 in Fig. 7(f). Since τ_3 is DFS-serial, its conflict invocation graph doesn't contain paths of memory conflicts from p_3 to any other invocation ordered before p_3 in the DFS traversal of the call tree. This includes the incomplete invocation p_1 and q. For the permutation τ_3', this implies that its conflict invocation graph contains no paths of memory conflicts from p_1 to p_3. When a trace satisfies this condition, i.e., an incomplete invocation on the main thread doesn't conflict with a future complete invocation on the same thread, all the complete invocations on the main thread can be reordered before the incomplete one (preserving the order between conflicting trace labels) and this results in a valid trace (under the multi-thread semantics). The simulation of τ_3' on the single-thread semantics, pictured in Fig. 7(g), enables this verification procedure during the invocation of p_1 because it is executed on the main thread and it skips over statements. It is also possible that other invocations on the main thread, e.g., p_2, are skipped *entirely*.

Notations. We introduce several notations used in the definition of $\mathsf{detStr}^-(e)$. This event is obtained by rewriting every statement s of a procedure transitively invoked by e to a code fragment $s_1; \mathtt{if}(c)$ $\mathtt{then}$ $s; s_2$ where s_1 and s_2 are statements and c is a Boolean expression. We use before(s), guard(s), and after(s) to refer to s_1, c, and s_2, respectively. For every statement s, $\ell(s)$ denotes the control flow label of s, that can be used for instance in goto statements. Also, $rdSet(s)$, resp., $wrSet(s)$, is the set of global variables read, resp., written, by s. We have $wrSet(s) = \{x\}$ and $rdSet(s) = \emptyset$ when s is $x := y$, and $wrSet(s) = \emptyset$ and $rdSet(s) = \{x\}$ when s is $y := x$. Otherwise, $rdSet(s) = wrSet(s) = \emptyset$.

We assume that every procedure p is augmented with two local variables $\mathtt{rdSetProc}$ and $\mathtt{wrSetProc}$ tracking the global variables read and written by p, respectively ($rdSet(s)$ and $wrSet(s)$ are added to $\mathtt{rdSetProc}$ and $\mathtt{wrSetProc}$, respectively, after every statement s that gets executed).

The instrumentation uses the non-deterministic choice denoted by $*$ (formally, $*$ is a distinguished Boolean variable that evaluates non-deterministically to $\mathtt{true}$ or $\mathtt{false}$). To refer to the different non-deterministic choices in the instrumentation, we may index them with natural numbers.

To reduce clutter in the instrumentation, we use $[\, s \,]_{\mathtt{ev}}(\mathtt{b})$ to denote a statement s that is executed at most once during the execution of the event and the Boolean variable $\mathtt{b}$ is set to $\mathtt{true}$ when s gets executed.

For an event e, let $\mathcal{P}(e)$ be the set of the procedures possibly invoked by e, which is defined inductively by: (1) $e \in \mathcal{P}(e)$ and (2) for every $p \in \mathcal{P}(e)$, if $\mathtt{async}[w]$ $q(y)$ occurs syntactically in the code of e, then $q \in \mathcal{P}(e)$. Also, let $\mathcal{P}_0(e)$ be the subset of $\mathcal{P}(e)$ consisting of procedures posted to the main thread, i.e., in the previous inductive definition, we take $w = \mathtt{main}$. W.l.o.g. we assume that the procedures in $\mathcal{P}_0(e)$ are distinct from the procedures q contained in asynchronous invocations "$\mathtt{async}[\mathtt{any}]$ $q(\ldots)$" executed on other threads.

All the Boolean variables added by the instrumentation are initially $\mathtt{false}$.

Defining the Instrumentation

Dealing with Fresh Thread Invocations. To simulate incomplete invocations executed by threads other than the main thread, every procedure in $\mathcal{P}(e) \setminus \mathcal{P}_0(e)$ is augmented with a Boolean flag `skip` that is non-deterministically set to `true`. Once `skip` is set to `true`, the rest of statements are skipped and the first skipped statement *may* be chosen as the pivot and its label stored in `pivotLabel`. The pivot may get executed non-deterministically at a later time.

The program instrumentation to simulate borderline violations is given in Fig. 8a. For every statement s of procedure $p \in \mathcal{P}(e) \setminus \mathcal{P}_0(e)$, guard($s$) and before($s$) are defined respectively at lines 1 and 4 where `skip` is a local variable and `pivotLabel` is a global variable.

Dealing with Main Thread Invocations. For procedures in $\mathcal{P}_0(e)$, the instrumentation ensures that at most one invocation of such a procedure is incomplete, and also, that the invocation graph contains no path of memory conflicts from such an incomplete invocation to any future complete invocation of a procedure in $\mathcal{P}_0(e)$. Such paths of memory conflicts may cross invocations of procedures which are not in $\mathcal{P}_0(e)$, therefore the instrumentation of the latter must also be modified.

To simulate an incomplete invocation on the main thread, for every statement s of a procedure $p \in \mathcal{P}_0(e)$, before(s) is defined as in line 15 in Fig. 8a where `skip` is a Boolean local variable. As for invocations executed on other threads, the first skipped statement may be chosen as the pivot. To be able to track

```
 1    // guard(s) for p ∈ P(e) \ P₀(e):
 2    !skip
 3
 4    // before(s) for p ∈ P(e) \ P₀(e):
 5    if ( !skip & *₁ ) then
 6       skip := true
 7       if ( *₂ ) then
 8          [pivotLabel := ℓ(s)]_ev(pivotSet)
 9    if ( skip & pivotSet & *₃) then
10       [goto pivotLabel]_ev(gotoDone)
11
12    // guard(s) for p ∈ P₀(e):
13    ! skipProc & ! skip
14
15    // before(s) for p ∈ P(e):
16    if ( *₄ ) then
17       [skip := true]_ev(skipMainSet)
18       rdSetGlobal := rdSetProc
19       wrSetGlobal := wrSetProc
20       if ( *₅ ) then
21          [pivotLabel := ℓ(s)]_ev(pivotSet)
```

```
22    // at the beginning of each p ∈ P(e):
23    if ( *₆ ) then skipProc := true
24    validMain := false
25
26    // after(s) for p ∈ P(e), after(s):
27    if ( skipMainSet & ( rdSetGlobal ∩ wrSetProc ≠ ∅
28       | wrSetGlobal ∩ rdSetProc ≠ ∅
29       | wrSetGlobal ∩ wrSetProc ≠ ∅
30       | conflictDetected)) then
31       rdSetGlobal := rdSetGlobal ∪ rdSetProc
32       wrSetGlobal := wrSetGlobal ∪ wrSetProc
33       conflictDetected := true
34
35    // at the end of each p ∈ P(e):
36    if ( skipMainSet & ! skipProc & ! skip ) then
37       assume ! conflictDetected
38       validMain := true
39    if ( pivotSet & *₇ ) then
40       [goto pivotLabel]_ev(gotoDone)
```

(a) Simulating Borderline Violations

```
41    // added to before(s):
42    if (!skip & pivotSet & *) then
43       [rootLabel := ℓ(s)]_ev(rootSet)
```

```
44    // added to after(s):
45    if (conflict(pivotLabel,rootLabel) & pivotLabel == ℓ(s)
46       & gotoDone & rootSet ) then error := true;
```

(b) Witnessing Borderline Violations

Fig. 8. Instrumentation for checking conflict-determinism.

paths of memory conflicts, the variables read and written during the incomplete invocation are stored in the global variables rdSetGlobal and wrSetGlobal, respectively. For invocations of procedures $p \in \mathcal{P}_0(e)$, skip can be set to true at most once during the execution of the event.

Other tasks posted to the main thread can be skipped entirely or executed completely, by setting a local flag skipProc. When they are executed completely, a global Boolean flag validMain is used to witness that they are not the destination of a path of memory conflicts as explained above. At the beginning of each procedure, validMain is reset to false as shown at line 22. Then, guard(s) of every statement s of a procedure $p \in \mathcal{P}_0(e)$ checks for skipProc as in line 13.

Once an incomplete invocation on the main thread is present, i.e., skipMainSet is true, the procedure for checking the absence of paths of memory conflicts is enabled. For every statement s of every procedure $p \in \mathcal{P}(e)$, after(s) is set as in line 26 where conflictDetected is a Boolean local variable. This conditional checks whether the current procedure conflicts with the incomplete invocation or transitively, with all the other invocations that conflict with the latter. If this is the case, then its set of memory accesses is continuously added to the global sets rdSetGlobal and wrSetGlobal of memory accesses.

When a main thread invocation finishes, if it has been executed completely and if it follows an incomplete main thread invocation, the instrumentation checks for absence of paths of memory conflicts and may non-deterministically execute the pivot. The code at line 35 is added at the end of every $p \in \mathcal{P}_0(e)$.

Relationship Between e and detStr$^-(e)$. The following result expresses the relationship between the original event e and detStr$^-(e)$. It shows that the single-thread semantics of detStr$^-(e)$ simulates permutations of all the DFS-serial traces and borderline violations of e under the multi-thread semantics (modulo a thread id renaming). Moreover, every trace of detStr$^-(e)$ under the single-thread semantics where the last value of validMain is true, this set of traces being denoted by $[\![\text{detStr}^-(e)]\!]_s^{\text{validMain}}$, corresponds to a trace of e under the multi-thread semantics (modulo the instrumentation added in detStr$^-(e)$ and a thread id renaming). For a trace τ of detStr$^-(e)$, $\overline{\tau}$ is the trace obtained from τ by erasing all transition labels corresponding to statements added by the instrumentation. For readability, we ignore the issue of renaming thread ids.

Theorem 4. *For every trace τ_1 in $[\![e]\!]_m$, if τ_1 is DFS-serial or a borderline conflict determinism violation, then there exists a trace τ_2 in $[\![\text{detStr}^-(e)]\!]_s$ such that $\tau_1' = \overline{\tau_2}$ is a conflict-preserving permutation of τ_1. Moreover, for every trace τ_1 in $[\![\text{detStr}^-(e)]\!]_s^{\text{validMain}}$ there exists a trace τ_2 in $[\![e]\!]_m$ such that $\tau_2 = \overline{\tau_1}$.*

6.2   Witnessing Borderline Violations

The instrumentation used to verify that a trace is indeed a borderline violation consists in guessing a candidate for the root and then, when the pivot gets executed, checking whether it conflicts with the chosen candidate. For instance, if we consider the single-thread semantics simulation in Fig. 7(c), the action

$wr(x)$ in q is guessed as the root and its label is stored in an auxiliary variable `rootLabel`. This label is used to check that the root candidate conflicts with the pivot when the latter is executed. The root must be chosen after the pivot in order to guarantee that this leads to a cycle in the conflict invocation graph (i.e., the DFS traversal of the call tree orders the invocation containing the pivot before the one containing the root).

We define a new event $\mathsf{detStr}(e)$ that sets an `error` flag to `true` whenever the current trace is not DFS serial and the root and pivot candidates are valid. This event is obtained from $\mathsf{detStr}^-(e)$ by adding two global variables `error` and `rootLabel`, and:

- Concatenating the code at line 41 in Fig. 8b to before(s). This allows to non-deterministically choose s to be the root of the violation. In order to avoid choosing the pivot after the root, we must also replace $*_2$ and $*_5$ in $\mathsf{detStr}^-(e)$ with ! `rootSet` & $*_2$ and ! `rootSet` & $*_5$, respectively.
- Concatenating the code at line 44 in Fig. 8b to after(s) where

$$conflict(\texttt{pivotLabel}, \texttt{rootLabel}) ::= rdSet(\ell^{-1}(\texttt{pivotLabel})) \cap wrSet(\ell^{-1}(\texttt{rootLabel})) \neq \emptyset$$
$$\| rdSet(\ell^{-1}(\texttt{rootLabel})) \cap wrSet(\ell^{-1}(\texttt{pivotLabel})) \neq \emptyset$$
$$\| wrSet(\ell^{-1}(\texttt{rootLabel})) \cap wrSet(\ell^{-1}(\texttt{pivotLabel})) \neq \emptyset$$

This allows to validate that the root does indeed conflict with the pivot, once the latter gets executed. If the conflict is validated, then `error` is set to `true`.

Since the added instrumentation only reads variables of $\mathsf{detStr}^-(e)$, the new event $\mathsf{detStr}(e)$ still satisfies the claim in Theorem 4.

Theorem 5. *An event e (under the multi-thread semantics) satisfies conflict determinism iff the program $\mathsf{detStr}(e)$ under the single-thread semantics does not reach a state where* `error = true`.

For complexity, $\mathsf{detStr}(e)$ can be constructed in linear time and its number of variables increases linearly in the number of variables and procedures of e.

6.3   Reduction to the Procedural Semantics

As a continuation to Theorem 5, we define a code-to-code translation from an event e to a *sequential* event $\mathsf{seq}(e)$ such that $\mathsf{seq}(e)$ admits exactly the set of traces of e under the <u>single-thread</u> semantics[3].

Single-Thread Semantics vs Procedural Semantics. Essentially, $\mathsf{seq}(e)$ is obtained from e by rewriting asynchronous procedure invocations to regular procedure

---

[3] Modulo the omission of the labels invoke(i), begin(i), return(i) related to asynchronous invocations.

calls. However, this rewriting can't be applied directly because of the following issue. Consider a procedure p invoking another procedure q. If the invocation of q is asynchronous, the single-thread semantics executes p completely before starting q. Under the procedural semantics, when q is invoked using a regular procedure call, the execution of p is blocked when q is invoked and resumed when q is completed. For instance, consider the event:

```
procedure e₁(){y:=1;async[main] p();y:=2;} procedure p(){y:=3;}
```

Executing e_1 on the single-thread semantics, we get the sequence of assignments y := 1, y := 2, y := 3. Rewriting `async[main]` $p()$ to a regular procedure call call $p()$, we get an event that executes y := 1, y := 3, y := 2 in this order.

This issue doesn't exist if all the asynchronous invocations occur at the end of the procedures. For instance consider the following event e_2:

```
procedure e₂(){x:=1;async[main] p();}  procedure q()  {x:=3;}
procedure p(){x:=2;async[main] q();}
```

Rewriting every `async[main]` _ to a procedure call `call` _, we get an event that executes the assignments on x in exactly the same order as e_2 under the single-thread semantics. This holds because the single-thread semantics executes the asynchronous invocations according to the DFS traversal of the call tree, which corresponds to the "stack" semantics of procedure calls.

Therefore, the event $\mathsf{seq}(e)$ is obtained in two steps. A first translation is used to move all asynchronous invocations at the end of the procedures. This results in an event having exactly the same single-thread semantics as the original one. Then, we replace every asynchronous invocation with a procedure call.

Defining $\mathsf{seq}(e)$. The event e is extended with auxiliary data structures that store the names and the inputs of the asynchronous invocations. Using these data structures, all the invocations are delayed till the end of the encompassing procedure. Thus,

- each procedure p is extended with an auxiliary local variable `invocList` which stores a list of procedure names and inputs,
- when an asynchronous procedure q is invoked in p with inputs y, the procedure name q together with its parameters y is appended to the local variable `invocList` of p without invoking q,
- before returning from a procedure p, all the procedures stored in `invocList` are invoked in the order they are recorded.

For the event e_1, this boils down to simply moving the invocation in e_1 at the end (i.e., after y := 1). It is easy to see that the obtained event has the same single-thread semantics as the original event.

Let $\mathsf{seq}(e)$ be the event obtained from e by applying the transformation above and then, replacing every asynchronous invocation $\mathtt{async}[w]\ p(y)$ with $\mathtt{call}$ $p(y)$.

For an event e, we overload the equality relation between traces $\tau_1 \in [\![e]\!]_s$ and $\tau_2 \in [\![\mathsf{seq}(e)]\!]_s$ as follows: $\tau_1 = \tau_2$ iff removing the labels $\mathsf{invoke}(i)$, $\mathsf{begin}(i)$, $\mathsf{return}(i)$ with $i \in \mathbb{N}$ from τ_1, and the transition labels corresponding to statements added by the instrumentation from τ_2, we get the same trace.

A sequential program Seq has the same set of traces under the multi-thread and the single-thread semantics, so its set of traces is denoted $[\![\mathsf{Seq}]\!]$.

Theorem 6. *For any event e, $[\![e]\!]_s = [\![\mathsf{seq}(e)]\!]$.*

For an event e, let $\mathsf{detSeq}(e) = \mathsf{seq}(\mathsf{detStr}(e))$. By Theorem 6, $\mathsf{detSeq}(e)$ still satisfies the claim in Theorem 4. The following is a direct consequence of Theorems 5 and 6.

Corollary 1. *An event e (under the multi-thread semantics) satisfies conflict determinism iff the sequential event $\mathsf{detSeq}(e)$ does not reach a state where error = true.*

Concerning complexity, let e be an event where each procedure invokes at most k other procedures, for some fixed k. Then, the time complexity of constructing $\mathsf{detSeq}(e)$ and its number of variables are quadratic in the number of variables and procedures of e and k.

7   Checking Conflict Robustness

Building on the reduction of conflict determinism to reachability in sequential programs, we show that a similar reduction can be obtained for conflict robustness. This reduction is based on two facts: (1) incomplete executions of conflict-deterministic events can be simulated by a sequential program, which has been proved in Sect. 6, and (2) conflict serializability for a set of conflict deterministic events can be again reduced to reachability in sequential programs. To prove the latter we use the concept of borderline violation, this time for conflict serializability. We show that interleavings corresponding to such violations can be simulated by a sequential program. This program behaves like a "most-general client" of the event-based program in the sense that it executes an arbitrary set of events, in an arbitrary order, but serially without interference from others. We show that the memory required to track the conflicts which induce a cycle in the conflict graph is of *bounded* size, although the conflict graph cycles are of unbounded size in general.

Definition 7 (Borderline Conflict Serializability Violation). *A trace t is a borderline violation to conflict serializability if it is not conflict serializable but every strict prefix of τ is conflict serializable.*

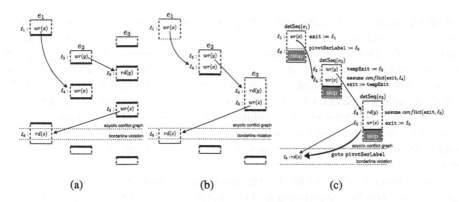

Fig. 9. Simulating borderline conflict serializability violations with a sequential program. Boxes represent sequences of trace labels ordered from top to bottom. Actions of the same event are aligned vertically. The arrows represent all the conflicts in the trace. The grey blocks labeled by delay, resp., skip, denote sequences of actions that are delayed, resp., skipped.

The trace τ_1 in Fig. 9(a) contains a borderline violation. Its conflict-event graph contains a cycle between the three events e_1, e_2, and e_3. The prefix of τ_1 ending just before $rd(z)$ satisfies conflict serializability. The last label of a borderline violation τ is called the *pivot* of τ (in this example $rd(z)$) and the event that contains the pivot is called the *delayed event* of τ (in this example e_1).

Simulating Borderline Violations. For a set of conflict-deterministic events E, we define a code-to-code translation to a set of sequential events that simulates every conflict-serializable trace and every borderline serializability violation of E under the multi-thread semantics.

As for conflict determinism, the maximal *strict* prefix of a borderline violation can be reordered to a trace where events are executed serially, but *possibly not until completion* (because it satisfies conflict serializability). Such a reordering for the trace τ_1 is given in Fig. 9(b). This reordering can be simulated by a sequential program that executes the conflict determinism instrumentations $\mathsf{detSeq}(e_i)$ with $i \in [1,3]$ instead of the original events, as shown in Fig. 9(c). The sequential program chooses non-deterministically the delayed event, in this case e_1, and the pivot, and stores the latter in an auxiliary variable `pivotSerLabel` when leaving the delayed event. While executing other possibly incomplete events using the skipping mechanism introduced for conflict determinism, it may non-deterministically choose to execute goto `pivotSerLabel`, in this case after e_3.

Witnessing Borderline Violations. To establish that a trace is indeed a borderline violation, the instrumentation guesses for each event a statement called *exit point* which conflicts with an action of a future event and a statement called *entry point* which conflicts with the currently recorded exit point of a previous event. The conflict is validated each time an entry point is chosen. This instrumentation is demonstrated in Fig. 9(c). For instance, while simulating e_1, $wr(x)$ is guessed as the exit point and its label is recorded in the auxiliary exit variable. During the simulation of e_2, $wr(x)$ is guessed as the entry point and the conflict is validated. As the simulation of e_2 shows, the exit point may occur before the entry point. In this case, the instrumentation uses an additional variable tempExit to store the exit point of the current event until the conflict with a previous event is validated. Once the conflict is confirmed the value of tempExit is copied to exit. Since the conflicts must form a path in the conflict event graph, there is no need to recall more than one exit point at a time.

The instrumentation added for checking conflict robustness is similar to the one used for conflict determinism. Let $\mathsf{robSeq}(e)$ denote the sequential event obtained from $\mathsf{detSeq}(e)$ by adding this instrumentation. For an event set E, let $\mathsf{robSeq}(E) = \{\mathsf{robSeq}(e) : e \in E\}$.

Then, let $\mathsf{robSeq}(E)$ be the set of events $\mathsf{robSeq}(e)$ with $e \in E$.

Theorem 7. *A program P with events E satisfies conflict robustness iff* $\mathsf{robSeq}(E)$ *doesn't reach a state where* error = true.

For complexity, $\mathsf{robSeq}(E)$ can be constructed in linear time and the number of additional variables is linear in the number of procedures in $\mathsf{detSeq}(E)$. The complexity of checking conflict robustness is given by the following theorem.

Theorem 8. *Checking conflict robustness of a program P with events E, a fixed number of variables which are all Boolean, and a fixed number of procedures, each procedure containing a fixed number of asynchronous invocations, is polynomial time decidable.*

8   Experimental Evaluation

The goal of our experimental work [5] is to show that (i) event-serializability and event-determinism violations correspond to actual bugs, and (ii) detecting these violations using the reduction to reachability in sequential programs is feasible.

We use the Soot framework [7] to implement the instrumentation required for robustness checking. The reachability of the error state in the instrumented sequential program is verified using Java Path Finder (JPF) [4].

We applied the conflict-robustness checking algorithm to a set of Android apps from the FDroid [3] repository. The application code for reflection, dependency to external libraries (e.g., for http connection, analytics tracker, maps), and the code which only effects the display (e.g., displaying web pages, animation, custom graphics) is eliminated. The remaining code factors out the variables that does not effect the concurrent behavior of the program and keeps the program logic.

We define an event as a procedure which is invoked by the Android app in order to initialize an activity, in response to an user input (e.g., clicking on a button, writing text, navigating back) or a system input (e.g., location change, network disconnect). Our tool receives as input a driver class which initiates the application and invokes a set of events. The tool checks conflict-robustness for the set of executions defined by the driver class. In our experiments, we take into consideration causality constraints between events, e.g., the event handler of a UI component can not be invoked if it is not visible on the screen.

8.1 Event-Determinism Experiments

Table 1. Experimental data for conflict determinism. The last column lists whether the event is found conflict deterministic.

Application	Event handler	#inst	#c	#m	#r/w	#(*)	t(m:s)	Det?
aarddict	Create activity	1307780	177	3016	90	1428	0:01	Y
	Lookup word	77203	222	3604	60	103	<1 s	Y
	Scan sd	21334	167	2941	15	21	<1 s	Y
apphangar	Select item	58908	222	3560	48	70	<1 s	Y
	Update icon pack	13308927	264	4004	95	28833	00:33	N
bookworm	Generate cover	34528	194	2928	30	41	<1 s	Y
	Retrieve cover	36789	213	3440	31	41	<1 s	Y
	Save edits	63017	189	3015	108	158	<1 s	Y
	Search book	53250	185	3012	50	69	<1 s	Y
grtgtfs	Fav stops	53995	162	2885	142	113	<1 s	Y
	Process bustimes	65945	159	2749	105	168	<1 s	Y
	Search route	55077	167	2968	34	67	<1 s	Y
	Search stop	56742	168	2968	52	75	0:01	Y
irccloud	Save prefs	103344	293	3478	18	15	<1 s	Y
	Save settings	102868	293	3478	17	13	<1 s	Y
	Select buffer	136224103	379	4330	761	260605	8:04	Y
	Send message	162682	356	4140	171	77	<1 s	Y
vlille	Load stations	971665	404	5808	236	131	0:01	Y
	Load favorites	9583	141	2400	37	0	<1 s	Y
	Update stations	975974	416	5905	265	131	0:01	Y

Table 1 lists the experimental data related to conflict-deterministic checking. Related to the size of the event handlers, we list the number of analyzed instructions (#inst), loaded classes (#c) and methods (#m). The analysis time is affected by the number of resolved non-deterministic data choices (#(*)), the number of asynchronous invocations, whether the instrumented read/write accesses are made in these invocations, and the execution time of the analyzed program.

We have applied our algorithm to various event handlers and all but one are found to be deterministic. A determinism violation is found in `iconPackUpdated` benchmark as explained in Sect. 2. The pivot of the violation is a write access to the `mAdapter` variable by a procedure running in the background, and the root is a read on the same variable made by a procedure running on the main thread.

8.2 Event-Serializability Experiments

Table 2 shows experimental data for conflict-serializability checking.

True Bugs. Four of the benchmarks had traces with conflict serializability violations which we concluded were true bugs (and true event-serializability violations) after examining the code and the consequences of these violations.

196   A. Bouajjani et al.

Table 2. Experimental data for conflict serializability. The last two columns say whether the example is serializable and whether a violation is not spurious.

Application	Seq.	#inst	#c	#m	#r/w	# (*)	t(m:s)	Ser?	Bug?
aarddict	1	1084371993	224	3620	154	1764359	23:12	N	Y
	2	101776570	169	2957	100	195370	1:42	N	Y
bookworm	1	22701600	183	2801	202	77614	0:42	Y	-
	2	19179949	183	2801	201	61896	0:33	Y	-
	3	1094300968	189	3016	286	3494089	33:51	Y	-
	4	3547795	188	3029	131	15961	0:08	N	Y
grtgtfs	1	74082801	168	2969	123	279857	2:04	Y	-
	2	-	-	-	149	-	>1 h	-	-
	3	1130239	139	2692	77	4712	0:02	Y	-
	4	60736622	170	2984	161	163236	1:21	N	N
irccloud	1	33713083	293	3479	141	147000	2:55	Y	-
	2	1761539	293	3479	140	7851	0:10	Y	-
	3	171715464	294	3485	147	534338	08:51	Y	-
	4	-	-	-	-	2110	>1 h	-	-
	5	-	-	-	-	902	>1 h	-	-
	6	54556857	358	4165	849	208076	5:28	N	Y
	7	11104756	357	4154	833	39599	0:59	N	Y
vlille	1	48935337	406	5824	286	134461	3:05	N	Y
	2	394535226	406	5824	292	1319041	28:52	N	N

The violation in `aarddict` app occurs between the initialization of the activity (initializes the UI components and starts the dictionary service to load the dictionaries) and an event handler to lookup a word. The lookup cannot retrieve the requested word if the service gets initialized after the lookup. The pivot of the serializability violation is a write access to a variable `dictionaryService` in an asynchronous procedure invoked on the main thread that conflicts with the asynchronous procedure invoked on a background thread by the second event handler. We detected an event serializability violation in the `bookworm` app between the events dealing with user inputs to search for a book and navigating back to the previous screen. In this violation, while the first event handler performs the search in the background and not yet updated the `currSearchTerm` variable, the second event handler saves the stale `currSearchTerm` value in the cache. The pivot of the violation is a write access to the current search term in an asynchronous procedure invoked on the background thread. A violation detected in the `irccloud` app is presented in Sect. 2, which causes the app to send wrong messages. The pivot is a read access to the message text in an asynchronous procedure invoked on a background thread that conflicts with a write access in the double click event. A similar violation occurs in another user input sequence where the user types some text after pressing the "send" key. In the `vlille` benchmark, the serializability violation in the first line occurs when the user removes an item from the favorites list while the items are being loaded. The app throws an exception when the removal in the second event handler interleaves with the asynchronous procedure in the background.

Avoidable False Alarms. In the `grtftfs` benchmark, the conflict-serializability violation is *not* a bug or a serializability violation. (Conflict-serializability is stronger than serializability.) This violation is triggered by making two queries one after another. In an execution where the second event handler overwrites the query before the first event handler reads it in the background, both asynchronous procedures end up performing the same, later search. While technically this is not a serializability violation, we believe it is worthwhile to report conflict-serializability violations to the programmer, because fixing them would lead to improved code.

Inter-related Events. Some event handlers intervene the execution of another event by design. For such inter-related events, the event-serializability violation might not be a bug. The `vlille` benchmark has such an example (the second row on the table). In this scenario, the user navigates back while the app is loading a list of items asynchronously in a background thread. The event handler for back navigation sets the `mCancelled` flag of the `AsyncTask`. If this flag is set, the first event handler does not invoke the `AsyncTask`'s asynchronous `onPostExecute` procedure. Our techniques can be modified to consider inter-related events and task cancellation, but we leave this for future work.

9   Related Work

The UI framework in Android has been the focus of much work. Most existing tools for detecting concurrency errors investigate race detection [8,21,25]. Race conditions are low-level symptoms for a much broader class of concurrent programs which are often not indicative of actual programming errors. In this paper, we attempt to characterize and detect higher-level concurrency errors in Android programs. Robustness violations are incomparable with data-race freedom violations. Data races do not generally imply cyclic data dependencies among events, and cyclic data dependencies do not imply data races: e.g., surrounding each individual memory access within a cycle by a common lock eliminates possible races, but preserves cycles. Furthermore, checking conflict robustness is fundamentally more efficient than checking for data race freedom. Conflict event serializability requires tracking events, while data race freedom requires tracking individual program actions like reads and writes, which greatly outnumber events. Moreover, conflict robustness reduces to reachability in *sequential* programs, yielding significantly lower asymptotic complexity.

Recent work [29] proposes a static analysis to detect "anomalies" in event driven programs, i.e. accesses to the same memory location by more than one event handlers. Since many events access shared memory locations, this approach produces many false alarms, but programs without anomalies are conflict-event serializable. The works in [23,24] refactor applications by moving long running jobs to asynchronous tasks and transform improperly-used asynchrony constructs into correct constructs. Ensuring transformed asynchronous tasks do not race with their callers lends support to our work as it guarantees event-determinism.

The works in [12–14,26] target exploring interesting subsets of executions and schedules for asynchronous programs, that offer a large coverage of the execution space. This is orthogonal to the focus of our paper which is to investigate correctness criteria.

Conflict serializability [27] has been introduced in the context of databases and since then used as a tractable approximation of atomicity. We use serializability to formalize the fact that event handlers behave as if they were executed in isolation, without interference from others. While in other uses of serializability the transactions are sequential, in our case a single invocation of an event handler consists of several asynchronous procedures that can interleave arbitrarily in between them. Farzan and Madhusudan [15,16] and Bouajjani et al. [10] investigate decision procedures for conflict serializability of finite-state concurrent models while checking serializability in general has been approached using both static, e.g., [18,20,32,34], and dynamic tools, e.g., [17,19,30,33].

Determinism has been largely advocated in the context of concurrent programs, e.g., [9,31], since it simplifies the debugging and verification process. Prior work has introduced static verification techniques, e.g., [22] but also dynamic analyses based on testing, e.g., [11,28]. Differently from prior work, we provide a methodology for checking determinism of event-driven asynchronous programs that ultimately reduces to a reachability problem in a sequential program.

References

1. https://github.com/irccloud/android/commit/c81f3374
2. http://github.com/irccloud/android/tree/9e2f5cf04e
3. F-Droid - Free and Open Source App Repository. http://f-droid.org/
4. Java pathfinder. http://babelfish.arc.nasa.gov/trac/jpf/
5. https://github.com/burcuku/async-robustness-checker
6. Alur, R., McMillan, K.L., Peled, D.: Model-checking of correctness conditions for concurrent objects. Inf. Comput. **160**(1–2), 167–188 (2000)
7. Arzt, S., Rasthofer, S., Bodden, E.: Instrumenting android and Java applications as easy as abc. In: Legay, A., Bensalem, S. (eds.) RV 2013. LNCS, vol. 8174, pp. 364–381. Springer, Heidelberg (2013). doi:10.1007/978-3-642-40787-1_26
8. Bielik, P., Raychev, V., Vechev. M.: Scalable race detection for android applications. In: Proceedings of ACM SIGPLAN International Conference on Object-Oriented Programming, Systems, Languages, and Applications, OOPSLA 2015, NY, USA, pp. 332–348. ACM (2015)
9. Bocchino, Jr. R.L., Adve, V.S., Adve, S.V., Snir, M.: Parallel programming must be deterministic by default. In: Proceedings of 1st USENIX Conference on Hot Topics in Parallelism, HotPar 2009, CA, USA (2009)
10. Bouajjani, A., Emmi, M., Enea, C., Hamza, J.: Verifying concurrent programs against sequential specifications. In: Felleisen, M., Gardner, P. (eds.) ESOP 2013. LNCS, vol. 7792, pp. 290–309. Springer, Heidelberg (2013). doi:10.1007/978-3-642-37036-6_17
11. Burnim, J., Sen, K.: Asserting and checking determinism for multithreaded programs. Commun. ACM **53**(6), 97–105 (2010)
12. Emmi, M., Qadeer, S., Rakamarić, Z.: Delay-bounded scheduling. SIGPLAN Not. **46**(1), 411–422 (2011). ISSN 0362-1340
13. Emmi, M., Lal, A., Qadeer, S.: Asynchronous programs with prioritized task-buffers. In: Proceedings of International Symposium on Foundations of Software Engineering, FSE 2012, pp. 48:1–48:11. ACM (2012)
14. Emmi, M., Ozkan, B.K., Tasiran, S.: Exploiting synchronization in the analysis of shared-memory asynchronous programs. In: Proceedings of International SPIN Symposium on Model Checking of Software, pp. 20–29. ACM (2014)
15. Farzan, A., Madhusudan, P.: Monitoring atomicity in concurrent programs. In: Gupta, A., Malik, S. (eds.) CAV 2008. LNCS, vol. 5123, pp. 52–65. Springer, Heidelberg (2008). doi:10.1007/978-3-540-70545-1_8

16. Farzan, A., Madhusudan, P.: The complexity of predicting atomicity violations. In: Kowalewski, S., Philippou, A. (eds.) TACAS 2009. LNCS, vol. 5505, pp. 155–169. Springer, Heidelberg (2009). doi:10.1007/978-3-642-00768-2_14

17. Flanagan, C., Freund, S.N.: Atomizer: a dynamic atomicity checker for multi-threaded programs. Sci. Comput. Program. **71**(2), 89–109 (2008)

18. Flanagan, C., Freund, S.N., Lifshin, M., Qadeer, S.: Types for atomicity: static checking and inference for Java. ACM Trans. Program. Lang. Syst. **30**(4), 20 (2008)

19. Flanagan, C., Freund, S.N., Yi, J.: Velodrome: a sound and complete dynamic atomicity checker for multithreaded programs. In: Proceedings of ACM SIGPLAN Conference on Programming Language Design and Implementation, pp. 293–303 (2008)

20. Hatcliff, J., Robby, Dwyer, M.B.: Verifying atomicity specifications for concurrent object-oriented software using model-checking. In: Steffen, B., Levi, G. (eds.) VMCAI 2004. LNCS, vol. 2937, pp. 175–190. Springer, Heidelberg (2004). doi:10.1007/978-3-540-24622-0_16

21. Hsiao, C.-H., Yu, J., Narayanasamy, S., Kong, Z., Pereira, C.L., Pokam, G.A., Chen, P.M., Flinn, J.: Race detection for event-driven mobile applications. In: Proceedings of 35th ACM SIGPLAN Conference on Programming Language Design and Implementation, PLDI 2014, pp. 326–336. ACM (2014)

22. Bocchino Jr. R.L., Adve, V.S., Dig, D., Adve, S.V., Heumann, S., Komuravelli, R., Overbey, J., Simmons, P., Sung, H. and Vakilian, M.: A type and effect system for deterministic parallel Java. In: Proceedings of OOPSLA, pp. 97–116 (2009)

23. Lin, Y., Ra, C., Dig, D.: Retrofitting concurrency for android applications through refactoring. In: Proceedings of International Symposium on Foundations of Software Engineering, FSE 2014, NY, USA, pp. 341–352. ACM (2014)

24. Lin, Y., Okur, S., Dig, D.: Study and refactoring of android asynchronous programming. In: Proceedings of ASE (2015)

25. Maiya, P., Kanade, A., Majumdar, R.: Race detection for android applications. In: Proceedings of 35th ACM SIGPLAN Conference on Programming Language Design and Implementation, PLDI 2014, pp. 316–325. ACM (2014)

26. Ozkan, B.K., Emmi, M., Tasiran, S.: Systematic asynchrony bug exploration for android apps. In: Computer Aided Verification - 27th International Conference, CAV 2015, San Francisco, CA, USA, pp. 455–461 (2015)

27. Papadimitriou, C.H.: The serializability of concurrent database updates. J. ACM **26**(4), 631–653 (1979)

28. Sadowski, C., Freund, S.N., Flanagan, C.: SingleTrack: a dynamic determinism checker for multithreaded programs. In: Castagna, G. (ed.) ESOP 2009. LNCS, vol. 5502, pp. 394–409. Springer, Heidelberg (2009). doi:10.1007/978-3-642-00590-9_28

29. Safi, G., Shahbazian, A., Halfond, W.G.J., Medvidovic, N.: Detecting event anomalies in event-based systems. In: Proceedings of International Symposium on Foundations of Software Engineering FSE, pp. 25–37. ACM (2015)

30. Sinha, A., Malik, S., Wang, C., Gupta, A.: Predicting serializability violations: SMT-based search vs. DPOR-based search. In: Hardware and Software: Verification and Testing - 7th International Haifa Verification Conference, HVC 2011, Haifa, Israel, Revised Selected Papers, pp. 95–114 (2011)

31. Steele, Jr. G.L.: Making asynchronous parallelism safe for the world. In: Proceedings of 17th ACM SIGPLAN-SIGACT Symposium on Principles of Programming Languages, POPL 1990, NY, USA, pp. 218–231. ACM (1990)

32. von Praun, C., Gross, T.R.: Static detection of atomicity violations in object-oriented programs. J. Object Technol. **3**(6), 103–122 (2004)

33. Wang, L., Stoller, S.D.: Runtime analysis of atomicity for multithreaded programs. IEEE Trans. Softw. Eng. **32**(2), 93–110 (2006)
34. Yi, J., Disney, T., Freund, S.N., Flanagan, C.: Cooperative types for controlling thread interference in Java. In: International Symposium on Software Testing and Analysis, ISSTA, pp. 232–242 (2012)

Incremental Update for Graph Rewriting

Pierre Boutillier[1], Thomas Ehrhard[2], and Jean Krivine[2]([✉])

[1] Harvard Medical School, 200 Longwood Avenue,
Warren Alpert Building 513, Boston, MA 02115, USA
[2] IRIF and CNRS, IRIF - Université Paris Diderot - Case 7014,
8, place Aurélie Nemours, 75205 Paris Cedex 13, France
Jean.Krivine@irif.fr

Abstract. Graph rewriting formalisms are well-established models for the representation of biological systems such as protein-protein interaction networks. The combinatorial complexity of these models usually prevents any explicit representation of the variables of the system, and one has to rely on stochastic simulations in order to sample the possible trajectories of the underlying Markov chain. The bottleneck of stochastic simulation algorithms is the update of the propensity function that describes the probability that a given rule is to be applied next. In this paper we present an algorithm based on a data structure, called extension basis, that can be used to update the counts of predefined graph observables after a rule of the model has been applied. Extension basis are obtained by static analysis of the graph rewriting rule set. It is derived from the construction of a qualitative domain for graphs and the correctness of the procedure is proven using a purely domain theoretic argument.

1 Introduction

1.1 Combinatorial Models in Systems Biology

As the quest for a cure for cancer is progressing through the era of high throughput experiments, the attention of biologists has turned to the study of a collection of signaling pathways, which are suspected to be involved in the development of tumors.

These pathways can be viewed as channels that propagate, via protein-protein interactions, the information received by the cell at its surface down to the nucleus in order to trigger the appropriate genetic response. This simplified view is challenged by the observation that most of these signaling cascades share components, such as kinases (which tend to propagate the signal) and phosphatases (which have the opposite effect). This implies that signaling cascades not only propagate information, but have also evolved to implement robust probabilistic "protocols" to trigger appropriate responses in the presence of various (possibly conflicting) inputs [1].

As cancer is now believed to be caused by a deregulation of such protocols, usually after some genes coding for the production of signaling components have

© Springer-Verlag GmbH Germany 2017
H. Yang (Ed.): ESOP 2017, LNCS 10201, pp. 201–228, 2017.
DOI: 10.1007/978-3-662-54434-1_8

mutated, systems biologists are accumulating immense collections of biological facts about proteins involved in cell signaling[1]. The hope of such data accumulation is to be able to identify possible targets for chemotherapy that would be specialized to a specific oncogenic mutation.

Although biological data are being massively produced thanks to high throughput experiments, the production of comprehensive models of cell signaling is lagging. One of the reasons for the unequal race between data production and data integration is the difficulty to make large combinatorial models executable.

1.2 Rule-Based Modeling

Site (or port) graph rewriting techniques, also called *rule-based modeling* [2,3], provide an efficient representation formalism to model protein-protein interactions in the context of cell-signaling. In these approaches, a cell state is abstracted as a graph, the nodes of which correspond to elementary molecular agents (typically proteins). Edges of site graphs connect nodes through named sites (sometimes called ports) that denote a physical contacts between agents. Biological mechanisms of action are interpreted as rewriting rules given as pairs of (site) graphs patterns.

Importantly, rules are applied following a stochastic strategy, also known as SSA or Gillespie's algorithm for rule-based formalisms [4]. KaSim [5] and NFSim [6] are two efficient rule-based simulators that implement this algorithm.

A critical part of the stochastic rewriting procedure is the maintenance, after each rewriting event, of all possible matches that rules may have in the current state of the system, which is a (large) site graph called *mixture*[2]. This number determines the probability that a rule is to be applied next. In general we call *observables* the graph patterns the matches of which need to be updated after each rewriting event. If all rules's left hand sides are mandatory observables, any biologically relevant observation the modeler wishes to track over time has to be declared as an observable as well.

1.3 Rewrite and Update

Beside the initialization phase where all observable matches are identified in the initial graph, observable matches need to be updated after a state change. The update phase can be split into two steps: the *negative update* in which observable matches that no longer hold in the new state are removed, and the *positive update* in which observable matches that have been created by a rule application should be added.

---

[1] More than 18,000 papers mentioning the protein EGFR, a major signaling protein, either in their title or abstract have been published since 2012. For the year 2015 only there are nearly 5,000 papers for EGFR (source pubmed).

[2] To fix the intuition, let us say that a realistic model of cell signaling would have a few million agents of about a hundred protein types, and several hundreds of rewrite rules, possibly thousands when refinements are automatically generated.

Contrarily to multiset rewriting, in graph rewriting the effect of a rule on a mixture cannot be statically determined. Once a rule has been applied it is necessary to explore the vicinity of the modification to detect potential new or obsolete matches. During this exploration, one may restrict to searching for graph patterns that have a chance to be added (resp. removed) by the modification. In the algorithm presented in Ref. [4], a relation called *activation* (resp. *inhibition*) is computed statically during the initialization phase of a simulation. After a rule r has been applied, the algorithm will look for new instances of observable o only if r activates o. Similarly, a given instance of an observable o' may disappear after the application of r only if r inhibits o'.

There are two essential problems left aside by this simple update method: first, knowing that a new instance of an observable might be created (or deleted) as a consequence of a rewrite does entail one knows in how many *ways* this observable can be found. In particular when dealing with a large amount of possible symmetries, there might be several *equivalent* ways to find a new match. So the first problem to deal with is of combinatorial nature: we wish to statically identify all the *different* manners an observable can be discovered, starting the exploration from a particular sub-graph of this observable (which corresponds to part that may be created or erased by a rewrite). The second issue is to avoid having redundant explorations of the graph after a rewrite: with the classical method sketched above, each observable activated (or inhibited) by the occurrence of a rule need to be searched for. Yet several observables might share sub-graphs. This is particularly true in models that present a lot of refinements of the same rule [7]. In other terms, we wish to design an update method that factors explorations of the graph that can be shared by several observables.

1.4 Outline

This paper presents a novel method for incremental graph rewriting that addresses both issues listed above. We first introduce a *domain of concrete graphs* (Sect. 2), which can be tuned to various types of graphs and, importantly for the application case of this work, to site-graphs.

This domain will serve as mathematical foundation in order to specify the *incremental update function* (Sect. 3).

We will then describe *extension bases* (Sect. 4), which can be viewed as a representation of the activation and inhibition relations taking into account sharing and conflict between observables.

These extension bases enable us to implement our incremental update procedure (Sect. 5), and we eventually check that the method is correct using the domain theoretic argument developed in Sect. 3.

2   Concrete Domain

Graph terms can be viewed in two different manners: observables of the system (for instance the left hand sides of the rules) are understood as *abstract* graphs, while the graph representing the state that is to be rewritten is *concrete*. In abstract graphs, nodes identifiers are used up-to consistent renaming, and two isomorphic observables denote in fact *the same* observable, for instance any graph in the shape of a triangle or a rectangle (see right figures).

The state of the rewriting system, however, can be viewed as a concrete graph in the sense that its nodes are used as a reference to track (potentially isomorphic) observables.

Thus, observable *instances* in the state are concrete: a new instance may appear in the state although isomorphic instances existed before.

Since the present work deals with the problem of updating observable instances in a graph state, following a rewriting event, we begin by establishing a simple mathematical framework, which enables us to describe in an extensional fashion, the universe in which concrete graphs live.

2.1   Graphs as Sets

Let $\mathcal{N}$ be a countable set of *nodes* with meta-variables $\{u, v, \dots\}$. *Edges* $\mathcal{E} \subseteq \mathcal{P}_2(\mathcal{N})$ are unordered pairs of nodes with meta-variables $\{e, e' \dots\}$. We say that e and e' are *connected*, whenever $e \cap e' \neq \emptyset$. We use meta-variables $G, H, \dots$ to denotes elements of $\mathcal{P}(\mathcal{E})$.

We consider a *coherence* predicate $\mathsf{Coh} : \mathcal{P}(\mathcal{E}) \to 2$, which is downward closed by inclusion, i.e. $\mathsf{Coh}\ G$ and $H \subseteq G$ implies $\mathsf{Coh}\ H$. A *concrete graph* is a coherent element of $\mathcal{P}(\mathcal{E})$. We use $\mathcal{G} \subseteq \mathcal{P}(\mathcal{E})$ to denote the set of concrete graphs, i.e. $\mathcal{G} =_{\mathsf{def}} \{G \in \mathcal{P}(\mathcal{E}) \mid \mathsf{Coh}\ G\}$ and for all $G \in \mathcal{G}$, we use the notation $|G| =_{\mathsf{def}} \bigcup \{e \in G\}$.

Concrete graphs and set inclusion form the *concrete domain* of coherent graphs. Note that $\mathcal{G}$ is an instance of Girard's qualitative domain [8]. For all $\mathcal{H} \subseteq \mathcal{G}$, we use $\uparrow\mathcal{H}$ and $\downarrow\mathcal{H}$ to denote the upper and lower sets of $\mathcal{H}$ in $\mathcal{G}$. Note that in particular $\downarrow\{G\} = \mathcal{P}(G)$.

For all graphs G, H we say that G is more *abstract* than H (resp. more *concrete*) whenever $G \subseteq H$ (resp. $H \subseteq G$).

Kappa Graphs. Since efficient Kappa graph rewriting is the main motivation of the present work, we spend some time now to describe Kappa and show how the formalism fits into our general framework.

Kappa graphs are particular kinds of coherent graphs where a node denotes a protein patch, which can either be *free* (i.e. not connected to any other protein) or in *contact* with another protein patch. We encode this by adding a bit of structure to nodes, taking $\mathcal{N} \subseteq \mathcal{A} \times \mathbb{N}$ where $\mathcal{A} =_{\mathsf{def}} \{a, b, \dots\}$ is a countable set of *agents* (protein individuals) that are *sorted* by the map $\kappa : \mathcal{A} \to \mathsf{K}$, where $\mathsf{K} = \{A, B, C, \dots, \mathbf{free}\}$ is a finite set of node *kinds* (the biological name of the protein) with a distinguished element $\mathbf{free}$. Therefore in Kappa, a node is of the form $u = (a, i)$ where $i \in \mathbb{N}$ is called the *site* of agent a (a patch of a). A *signature* $\Sigma : \mathsf{K} \to \mathbb{N}$ maps a kind to a (finite) sequence of *sites* identified by natural numbers, with $\Sigma(\mathbf{free}) =_{\mathsf{def}} 1$.

The coherence relation for Kappa is $\mathsf{Coh} =_{\mathsf{def}} \mathsf{Sorted} \wedge \mathsf{ConfFree}$, where:

$$\mathsf{Sorted}(G) =_{\mathsf{def}} \forall e \in G.\,((a, i) \in e \implies i \leq (\Sigma \circ \kappa)a)$$
$$\mathsf{ConfFree}(G) =_{\mathsf{def}} \forall e, e' \in G.\,(e = e' \vee e \cap e' = \emptyset)$$

We picture on the right an example of a Kappa graph. Nodes (small circles) sharing an agent are depicted attached to the same large circle, named after the kind of the agent. The node $(b, 1)$ that is connected to a $\mathbf{free}$ node encodes the fact that this protein patch is available for a future interaction. The corresponding graph is obtained as the union of $\{\{(a, 1), (b, 0)\}, \{(b, 1), (c, 0)\}\}$ and $\{\{(a', 1), (b', 0)\}, \{(b', 1), (c', 0)\}\}$.

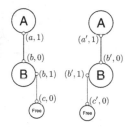

2.2   Effects

In the graph rewriting literature, techniques to decide whether a rule can be applied to a graph come in various flavors [9–11]. In the present work, we do not need to discuss this problem and focus on what happens after a rule has been applied to a graph: we call this the *effect* of a rewrite. The only important point here is that we only consider deterministic effects. For the reader knowledgeable in graph rewriting techniques, they correspond to effects induced by double pushout rewriting [9], where the only way to delete a node is to explicitly delete all edges in which the node appears.

The *effect*, $\eta, \eta', \dots$, of a rewrite can be decomposed as a triple of the form $(G, H^-, H^+) \in \mathcal{G}^3$ where G is the sub-graph that is *tested* by η, and where H^- and H^+ are respectively the *abstraction* and *concretization* steps of η. Intuitively, G are the edges that are required for the rewrite to take place (the match of the left hand side of a rule), H^- and H^+ are the edges that are respectively removed and added during the rewrite step. We do not consider *side-effects*, i.e. those that do not satisfy $H^- \subseteq G$. An effect $\eta = (G, H^-, H^+)$ *occurs* on a graph K if:

- It is *valid*, i.e.: $G \subseteq K$
- It is *visible*, i.e.: $K \cap H^+ = \emptyset$
- It is *defined*, i.e.: $(K \backslash H^-) \cup H^+ \in \mathcal{G}$

For all such effect η and graph K, we define $\eta \cdot K =_{\mathsf{def}} (K \backslash H^-) \cup H^+$. For all effect $\eta = (G, H^-, H^+)$ and for all graph K in which η occurs, we define

$\mathsf{pre}(\eta) =_{\mathsf{def}} G$, the set of edges that are necessarily present in K. Similarly we define $\mathsf{post}(\eta) =_{\mathsf{def}} (G \backslash H^-) \cup H^+$ which is the set of edges that are necessarily present in $\eta \cdot K$. For the remaining of the paper we only discuss defined effects which are both valid and visible[3].

Kappa Effects. To conclude this section and in order to illustrate effects in the context of Kappa, we show below an effect η and its occurrence in the graph K (Fig. 1).

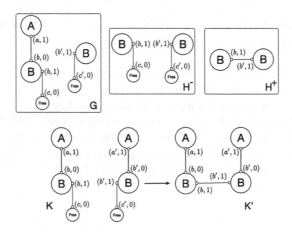

Fig. 1. Illustrating effect in Kappa: $\eta = (G, H^-, H^+)$ occurs in K, with $K' = \eta \cdot K$.

2.3 The Update Problem

Let Φ denote the set of possible effects over graphs in $\mathcal{G}$ and consider a fixed set $\mathcal{O} \subseteq \mathcal{G}$ of *observable* graphs. Let $\mathsf{Obs} : \mathcal{G} \to \mathcal{P}(\mathcal{O})$ be the *observation map* defined as $\mathsf{Obs}\ G =_{\mathsf{def}} \{O \in \mathcal{O} \mid O \subseteq G\}$.

A *macroscopic effect* $\aleph \in \mathcal{P}(\mathcal{O}) \times \mathcal{P}(\mathcal{O})$ is a pair of observable sets $\aleph = \langle \Omega^-, \Omega^+ \rangle$ satisfying $\Omega^- \cap \Omega^+ = \emptyset$. For all $\mathcal{O}' \subseteq \mathcal{O}$, we define $\aleph \odot \mathcal{O}' =_{\mathsf{def}} (\mathcal{O}' \backslash \Omega^-) \cup \Omega^+$. Intuitively a macroscopic effect describes the set of observables that should be removed (in Ω^-) and added (in Ω^+) after a rewrite has occurred.

We are now in position to state the *incremental update problem*: let K be a graph and η an effect such that $\eta \cdot K$ is defined. We wish to define a function

$$\Delta : \Phi \to \mathcal{G} \to \mathcal{P}(\mathcal{O}) \times \mathcal{P}(\mathcal{O})$$

that satisfies the following equation:

$$(\Delta\ \eta\ K) \odot (\mathsf{Obs}\ K) = \mathsf{Obs}\ (\eta \cdot K) \tag{1}$$

---

[3] All rewriting techniques satisfy these properties, although only double pushout guarantees the absence of side effect.

Application. Whenever all possible effects $\eta \in \Phi$ satisfy $\mathsf{pre}(\eta) \in \mathcal{O}$, and given the set $\mathcal{O}_K$ of observables that have an occurrence in a graph K, the a priori costly function $\mathsf{Obs}\ (\eta \cdot K)$ can be evaluated by computing $(\Delta\ \eta\ K) \odot (\mathsf{Obs}\ K)$. This is a property that is desirable for any efficient implementation of the stochastic simulation algorithm (SSA) [4], in which $\mathcal{O}_K$ needs to be updated after each rewrite step in order to evaluate the propensity function.

The function Δ will be characterized as a fixpoint of an incremental (one-step) update function on a particular directed sub-domain of $\mathcal{G}$. We turn now to its specification.

3   Exploration Domains

During a sequence of rewrites $K_0, K_1, \ldots, K_n$, the effect $\eta_i = (G_i, H_i^-, H_i^+)$ that occurs during the transition from K_i to K_{i+1} provides the starting point of the update procedure: the observables that should disappear are those that are above H_i^- and below K_i, while the observables that should appear are at those above H_i^+ and below K_{i+1} (see the diagram on the right). Notice that both observables O_4 and O_5 are above H_i^+ but only O_4 is also in $\downarrow\{K_{i+1}\}$. In this case O_5 is not created by the effect and we call it a false positive. In the same example, the instance O_3 is preserved by the effect, as a consequence it cannot be above either H_i^- or H_i^+.

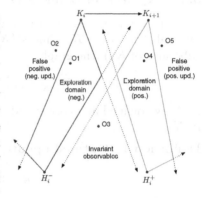

In the following of this section we assume a fixed graph K and an effect $\eta =_{\mathsf{def}} (G, H_\eta^-, H_\eta^+)$ such that $\eta \cdot K$ is defined. In order to emphasize the symmetry between positive and negative update, we introduce the notation $K^- =_{\mathsf{def}} K$, $K^+ =_{\mathsf{def}} \eta \cdot K$, $\pi_\eta^- =_{\mathsf{def}} \mathsf{pre}(\eta)$ and $\pi_\eta^+ =_{\mathsf{def}} \mathsf{post}(\eta)$ (see Sect. 2.2). In the following, the informal superscript $\_^\varepsilon$ can be replaced globally by either $\_^-$ or $\_^+$ in order to specialize the mathematical description to the negative or positive update.

3.1   Observable Witnesses

Define first the set of *witness* graphs $(W, W', \ldots)$, the presence of which will serve as a proof of negative or positive update of an observable, induced by the occurrence of η:

$$\mathcal{W}_\eta^\varepsilon =_{\mathsf{def}} \{W \in \mathcal{G} \mid \exists O \in \mathcal{O}, O \cap H_\eta^\varepsilon \neq \emptyset \wedge W = O \cup \pi_\eta^\varepsilon\}$$

For all $W \in \mathcal{W}_\eta^\varepsilon$, we say that W is an η-*witness* of $O \in \mathcal{O}$ if $O \cap H_\eta^\varepsilon \neq \emptyset$ and $W = O \cup \pi_\eta^\varepsilon$ and we write $W \rhd_\eta^\varepsilon O$. Notice that W may be the η-witness of several observables.

Proposition 1. *For all* $W \in \mathcal{W}_\eta^-$ *and* $O \in \mathcal{O}$ *such that* $W \rhd_\eta^- O$:

$$W \subseteq K^- \iff O \in (\text{Obs } K^-) \wedge O \notin (\text{Obs } K^+) \tag{2}$$

Similarly, for all $W \in \mathcal{W}_\eta^+$ *and* $O \in \mathcal{O}$ *such that* $W \rhd_\eta^+ O$:

$$W \subseteq K^+ \iff O \notin (\text{Obs } K^-) \wedge O \in (\text{Obs } K^+) \tag{3}$$

Proposition 1 guarantees that after η has occurred on K, it is sufficient to extend the graph π_η^ε with edges taken from K^ε in order to reach a witness in $\mathcal{W}_\eta^\varepsilon$. For each $W \subseteq K^\varepsilon$ that are more concrete than π_η^ε, the observable $O \in \mathcal{O}$ that satisfies $W \rhd_\eta^\varepsilon O$ is (positively or negatively) updated.

3.2   Exploration Boundaries

The updatable witnesses after the occurrence of η are the witnesses that are more abstract than K^ε. Since $\downarrow\{K^\varepsilon\}$ forms a complete lattice (it is simply the sub-parts of K^ε), the graph:

$$\widehat{W}_{\eta,K}^\varepsilon =_{\text{def}} \bigcup\{W \in \mathcal{W}_\eta^\varepsilon \mid W \subseteq K^\varepsilon\}$$

is always defined and corresponds to the union of all witnesses that are present in K^ε.

Definition 1 (Optimal update domain). *We call:*

$$\mathcal{X}_{\eta,K}^\varepsilon =_{\text{def}} \downarrow\{\widehat{W}_{\eta,K}^\varepsilon\} \cap \uparrow\{\pi_\eta^\varepsilon\}$$

the optimal *(negative or positive) update domain for* η *and* K.

Proposition 2. *For all witness* $W \in \mathcal{W}_\eta^\varepsilon$, $W \subseteq K^\varepsilon$ *if and only if* $W \in \mathcal{X}_{\eta,K}^\varepsilon$.

Proposition 2 indicates that after an effect η has occurred, $\mathcal{X}_{\eta,K}^\varepsilon$ is the smallest domain one needs to explore in order to discover all updatable witnesses. Yet, one cannot hope that a realistic update procedure stays within the boundaries of $\mathcal{X}_{\eta,K}^\varepsilon$ because some witnesses may seem to be updatable given π_η^ε, but are in fact not reachable within K^ε (they are the false positives, discussed in the introduction of this section). The remaining of this section is dedicated to the specification of the directed set that is being explored during the update procedure, and that is defined as an over-approximation of $\mathcal{X}_{\eta,K}^\varepsilon$.

We first define the η-*domain* which is coarsening of the optimal update domain:

Definition 2 (η-Domain). *For all* $\mathcal{H} \subseteq \mathcal{G}$, *we define the* $\cup$-*closure of* $\mathcal{H}$, *written* $\uparrow^\cup \mathcal{H}$, *as:*

$$\uparrow^\cup \mathcal{H} =_{\text{def}} \max\{G \in \mathcal{G} \mid G = \bigcup_i H_i \in \mathcal{H}\}$$

where for all $\mathcal{H} \subseteq \mathcal{G}$, $\max \mathcal{H}$ *is the set of maximal graphs in* $\mathcal{H}$. *We use this construction to define the* η-domain:

$$\mathcal{D}^\varepsilon(\eta) =_{\text{def}} \downarrow(\uparrow^\cup \mathcal{W}_\eta^\varepsilon) \cap \uparrow\{\pi_\eta^\varepsilon\}$$

Notice that $\uparrow^{\cup} \mathcal{H} = \bigcup \mathcal{H}$ when $\mathcal{H}$ has a supremum.

Contrary to the optimal update domain $\mathcal{X}_{\eta,K}^{\varepsilon}$ (Definition 1), the η-domain $\mathcal{D}^{\varepsilon}(\eta)$ is independent of K^{ε}. By itself it is not a correct over-approximation of the optimal update domain, since it is not in general a directed set. However we get a fine grained approximation of the optimal update domain when one restricts (on the fly) explorations of $\mathcal{D}^{\varepsilon}(\eta)$ to graphs that are also below K^{ε} (see Fig. 2 for illustration):

Proposition 3 (Over-approximation). *For all effect η and graph K such that η occurs on K, the following directed sets are ordered by inclusion:*

$$\mathcal{X}_{\eta,K}^{\varepsilon} \subseteq (\mathcal{D}^{\varepsilon}(\eta) \cap \downarrow\{K^{\varepsilon}\}) \subseteq \downarrow\{K^{\varepsilon}\} \tag{4}$$

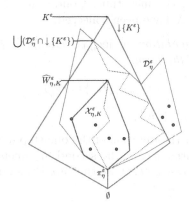

Fig. 2. An exploration of $\mathcal{X}_{\eta,K}^{\varepsilon}$ (leftmost dotted line) and an exploration of $\mathcal{D}^{\varepsilon}(\eta) \cap \downarrow\{K^{\varepsilon}\}$ (rightmost dotted line). Circles denote witnesses. In the first exploration all edges that are added along the exploration belong to a witness that is also within K^{ε}. The exploration stops exactly at the supremum of all reachable witnesses, i.e. the sup of the optimal update domain (Definition 1). The rightmost exploration correspond to a path where edges are added only if the resulting graph belong to the η-domain $\mathcal{D}^{\varepsilon}(\eta)$ (Definition 2) and is present in $\downarrow\{K^{\varepsilon}\}$. The difference between the endpoints of the rightmost and leftmost explorations corresponds to the edges that have been inspected with no corresponding updatable witness.

3.3   Specifying the Incremental Update Function

We have now everything in place to specify the incremental update function Δ of Sect. 3. In order to do so, we require that a call to $(\Delta\ \eta\ K)$ be the fixpoint of a *one-step exploration function* that we specify now. Consider a function $\mathsf{inc}_{\eta,K}^{\varepsilon}$:

$$\mathsf{inc}_{\eta,K}^{\varepsilon} : \mathcal{D}^{\varepsilon}(\eta) \times \mathcal{P}(\mathcal{W}_{\eta}^{\varepsilon}) \to \mathcal{D}^{\varepsilon}(\eta) \times \mathcal{P}(\mathcal{W}_{\eta}^{\varepsilon})$$

such that whenever

$$\mathrm{inc}^{\varepsilon}_{\eta,K}\langle X, \mathcal{R}\rangle = \langle X', \mathcal{R}'\rangle$$

the following properties hold:

$$
\begin{aligned}
& X' = X \cup G \text{ if there exists } G \subseteq K^{\varepsilon} \text{ satisfying } G \cap X = \emptyset \text{ and } G \in \mathcal{D}^{\varepsilon}(\eta) \\
& X' = X \qquad \text{otherwise}
\end{aligned}
\tag{5}
$$

$$\mathcal{R}' = \{W \in \mathcal{W}^{\varepsilon}_{\eta} \mid W \subseteq X\} \tag{6}$$

Intuitively, the first argument of the function is a graph X (for *explored*) corresponding the current endpoint of the exploration of $\mathcal{D}^{\varepsilon}(\eta) \cap {\downarrow}\{K^{\varepsilon}\}$. The second argument $\mathcal{R}$ (for *reached*) correspond to the set of observable witnesses that have been discovered so far. Condition (5) ensures that the explored subgraph X of K^{ε} grows uniformly, and inside the boundaries of $\mathcal{D}^{\varepsilon}(\eta)$ until it reaches its supremum. In the meantime, Condition 6 is making sure that all witnesses that are below X have been collected.

Lemma 1. *Any implementation of* $\mathrm{inc}^{\varepsilon}_{\eta,K}$ *satisfying the above specification admits a least fixpoint of the form:*

$$\langle \mathsf{T}^{\varepsilon}_{\eta,K}, {\downarrow}\{K^{\varepsilon}\} \cap \mathcal{W}^{\varepsilon}_{\eta}\rangle$$

where $\mathsf{T}^{\varepsilon}_{\eta,K} =_{\mathsf{def}} \bigcup(\mathcal{D}^{\varepsilon}(\eta) \cap {\downarrow}\{K^{\varepsilon}\})$.

Lemma 1 ensures that the iteration of the one-step incremental update function terminates and returns a pair, the second argument of which is precisely the set of updatable witnesses, i.e. those that are the same time above π^{ε}_{η} and a sub-graph of K^{ε}.

Definition 3 (Incremental update function). *For all effect η and all graph K such that $\eta \cdot K$, and all correct implementation of* $\mathrm{inc}^{\varepsilon}_{\eta,K}$*, let:*

$$
\begin{aligned}
(\mathrm{inc}^{-}_{\eta,K})^{\omega}\langle \mathrm{pre}(\eta), \emptyset\rangle &= \langle \_, \mathcal{R}^{-}\rangle \\
(\mathrm{inc}^{+}_{\eta,K})^{\omega}\langle \mathrm{post}(\eta), \emptyset\rangle &= \langle \_, \mathcal{R}^{+}\rangle
\end{aligned}
$$

let also $\Omega^{\varepsilon} : \mathcal{P}(\mathcal{W}^{\varepsilon}_{\eta}) \to \mathcal{P}(\mathcal{O})$ *be:*

$$\Omega^{\varepsilon} \, \mathcal{R} =_{\mathsf{def}} \{O \in \mathcal{O} \mid \exists W \in \mathcal{R}.W \rhd^{\varepsilon}_{\eta} O\}$$

we define the incremental update function *as:*

$$\Delta \, \eta \, K =_{\mathsf{def}} \langle (\Omega^{-} \, \mathcal{R}^{-}), (\Omega^{+} \, \mathcal{R}^{+})\rangle$$

Theorem 1. *For all effect η and all graph K such that $\eta \cdot K$,*

$$(\Delta \, \eta \, K) \odot (\mathsf{Obs} \, K) = (\mathsf{Obs} \, \eta \cdot K)$$

Theorem 1 concludes this section by stating that, provided our one-step incremental update function satisfies its specification, its fixpoint correspond to the macroscopic effect $\langle \Omega^{-}, \Omega^{+}\rangle$ that we are looking for.

4   Abstraction

Although $\mathcal{D}^{\varepsilon}(\eta)$ is an invariant domain, it cannot be used as a data structure *per se* (it is an infinite object). For the update algorithm we use a data structure that can be viewed as a quotient of $\mathcal{D}^{\varepsilon}(\eta)$ in which isomorphic graphs are identified. This quotienting of the concrete domain is naturally described using a categorical terminology.

4.1   Graph: a category of graphs

A graph *homomorphism*, $f : G \to H$, is an injective function on nodes $f : |G| \to |H|$ that preserves edges, i.e.:

$$\{u,v\} \in G \implies \{f(u), f(v)\} \in H$$

We call Graph the category that has graphs as objects and we use $\mathsf{Hom}(\mathcal{G})$ to denote the set of its arrows. We use $\phi, \psi, \dots$ for graph *isomorphisms*.

A Category for Kappa Graphs. In order to tune Graph to Kappa we require that morphisms should be injective on agents and preserve sorting, i.e. $\kappa \circ f = \kappa$ (see Fig. 5 for an example).

Property 1 (Pullbacks). For all co-span:

$$\boldsymbol{f} : \langle f_1 : G_1 \to H, f_2 : G_2 \to H \rangle$$

there is a unique span:

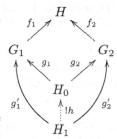

$$\mathsf{pb}(\boldsymbol{f}) : \langle g_1 : H_0 \to G_1, g_2 : H_0 \to G_2 \rangle$$

satisfying $f_1 g_1 = f_2 g_2$ and such that for any alternative span $\boldsymbol{g}'$ there is a unique morphism h that makes the right diagram commute.

We follow now the relative pushout terminology introduced in the context of bigraphical reactive systems [12]. A span:

$$\boldsymbol{f} : \langle f_1 : H \to G_1, f_2 : H \to G_2 \rangle$$

admits a *bound*:

$$\boldsymbol{g} : \langle g_1 : G_1 \to H', g_2 : G_2 \to H' \rangle$$

whenever $g_1 f_1 = g_2 f_2$. Given a span $\boldsymbol{f}$ and a bound $\boldsymbol{g}$, we say that $\boldsymbol{f}$ has a bound:

$$\boldsymbol{h} : \langle h_1 : G_1 \to H'', h_2 : G_2 \to H'' \rangle$$

relative to $\boldsymbol{g}$, if there exists a morphism $h : H'' \to H'$ such that $h h_1 = g_1$ and $h h_2 = g_2$. We call the triple $(h, \boldsymbol{h})$ a $\boldsymbol{g}$-*relative bound* of $\boldsymbol{f}$.

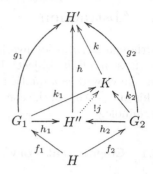

Property 2 (Relative pushout). A span f that admits bound g also admits a *best* g-relative bound (h, h) such that for all alternative g-relative bound (k, k), there exists a unique morphism j such that $jh_1 = k_1$ and $jh_2 = k_2$. This best g-relative bound (h, h) is called a *g-relative pushout* for f (see right diagram).

Note in particular that if (h, h) is a g-relative pushout for f, then h is a bound for f. So in the above diagram we have that $(\mathrm{id}_{H''}, h)$ is an h-relative pushout for f and we simply say that h is an *idem pushout* for f, written $\mathsf{IPO}_f(g)$.

Define the *multi-pushout* of a span f as the set of its idem pushouts, i.e.:

$$\mathsf{Mpo}(f) =_{\mathrm{def}} \{g \mid \mathsf{IPO}_f(g)\}$$

The following proposition states that any bound for a span f factors uniquely (up-to iso) through one member of $\mathsf{Mpo}(f)$. In other words, elements of the multi-pushout of f are either isomorphic, or conflicting.

Proposition 4. *Let g be a bound for f. For all $h, h' \in \mathsf{Mpo}(f)$ if there exists k, k' such that $khf = k'h'f = gf$ then there exists a unique iso ϕ such that $\phi hf = h'f$.*

Proof. (sketch). The proof is a straightforward application of the relative pushout properties. Since both h and h' are g-relative pushouts, there is a unique morphism j and a unique morphism j' such that $jhf = h'f$ and $hf = j'h'f$. Since j and j' are injective they are also isos.   □

We will need one final construction which defines the *gluings* of two graphs. It is obtained by first using the pullback construction, and then building a multi-pushout:

Definition 4 (gluing). *Let:*

$$\mathsf{Inter}(G, H) =_{\mathrm{def}} \{f \colon \langle f_1 : I \to G, f_2 : I \to H \rangle \mid I \neq \emptyset \wedge \exists g \ s.t \ f = \mathsf{pb}(g)\}$$

We define:

$$\mathsf{Gluings}(G, H) =_{\mathrm{def}} \bigcup_{f \in \mathsf{Inter}(G,H)} \mathsf{Mpo}(f)$$

We conclude this section by illustrating Fig. 3, the concept of multi-pushout in the context of Kappa, previously described in Ref. [13].

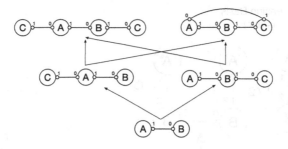

Fig. 3. The multi-pushout of the lower span contains 2 possible bounds (up-to iso). All closed diagrams are commuting.

4.2 Extension and Matching

We wish now to define a way to capture a notion of "abstract exploration". Such exploration is defined by means of *extension steps* (see Definition 7 of this section) along a statically computed "chart", called an *extension basis*. We illustrate Fig. 4 the main ideas of this extension basis. In order to *build* an extension basis, we need a first notion of morphism equivalence called *extension equivalence* that equates morphisms that denote the same "way" of discovering a graph starting from a smaller one. In order to *use* the extension basis during the update procedure we need a second notion of equivalence called *matching equivalence* that equates morphisms that denote the same instance (or match) of a graph into the concrete state. With extension and matching morphisms, we define a procedure, called extension step, that produces an exploration of the concrete domain, which is at the core of the update procedure (see Fig. 4 for an example).

Definition 5 (Extension equivalence). *Two morphisms* $f : G \to H$ *and* $g : G \to H'$ *are equivalent with respect to* extension, *written* $f \sim_{\mathsf{ext}} g$, *if there exists an iso* $\phi : H \to H'$ *that makes the right diagram commutes. Whenever* $f \sim_{\mathsf{ext}} g$ *we say that* f *and* g *denote the same* extension.

$$\begin{array}{ccc} & f & \\ G & \longrightarrow & H \\ g & \searrow & \downarrow \phi \\ & & H' \end{array}$$

Extension classes come with the dual notion of *matching classes* that enables one to count different instances of a graph into another one.

Definition 6 (Matching equivalence). *Two morphisms* $f : G \to H$ *and* $g : G' \to H$ *are equivalent with respect to* matching, *written* $f \sim_{\mathsf{mat}} g$, *if there exists an iso* $\phi : G \to G'$ *that makes the right diagram commutes. Whenever* $f \sim_{\mathsf{mat}} g$ *we say that* f *and* g *denote the same* match.

$$\begin{array}{ccc} & f & \\ G & \longrightarrow & H \\ \phi \downarrow & \nearrow & \\ G' & g & \end{array}$$

Another way to describe matching equivalence between f and g is that their codomain coincide:

Property 3. Two morphisms $f : G \to H$ and $g : G' \to H$ are matching equivalent if and only if $f(G) = g(G')$.

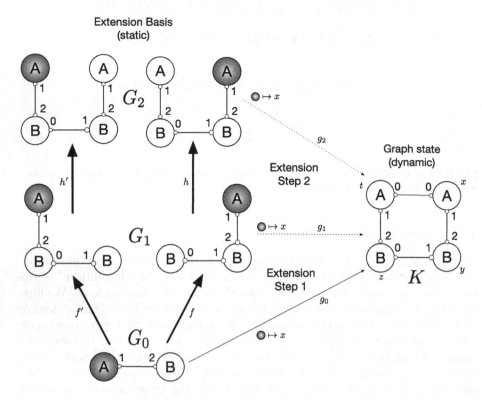

Fig. 4. An extension basis (thick arrows) describing how to "discover" G_1 and G_2 starting from G_0. The colored A node helps tracking the identity of A through the basis: note here that the basis has two distinct ways of discovering G_1 from G_0, each of which has its own extension into G_2. Given an initial match g_0 into K, one may extend g_0 into g_1 through f, and then g_1 into g_2 through the extension h. Note that f' fails to extend g_0 in K.

For all $f \in \mathsf{Hom}(\mathcal{G})$, for all $g, h \in \mathsf{Hom}(\mathcal{G})$, we say that g is *extended* by f into h, whenever $g = hf$. We say that the extension is *trivial* when f is an iso.

Importantly, two maps $g : G \to K$ and $g' : G \to K$ denoting the *same* match can be respectively extended by a map $f : G \to H$ into *distinct* matches of H into K (Fig. 6, left diagram). Similarly, two *distinct* matches $g : G \to K$ and $g' : G \to K$ might be extended by $f : G \to H$ into maps that denote the *same* match (Fig. 6, right diagram).

Definition 7 (Extension step). *Let* $\Gamma \subseteq \mathsf{Hom}(G, K)$ *and* $\Gamma' \subseteq \mathsf{Hom}(H, K)$ *for some* $G, H, K \in \mathcal{G}$. *For all* $\mathcal{F} \subseteq \mathsf{Hom}(\mathcal{G})$, *the pair* (Γ, Γ') *defines an* $\mathcal{F}$-*extension step if* $\Gamma' = Ext_{\mathcal{F}, K}(\Gamma)$ *with:*

$$Ext_{\mathcal{F}, K}(\Gamma) =_{\mathsf{def}} \{h : H \to K \mid \exists (f : G \to H) \in \mathcal{F}, \exists g \in \Gamma : g = hf\}$$

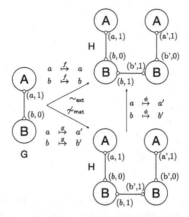

Fig. 5. Two morphisms f and g that belong to the same extension class (since $f = \phi g$) but define two distinct matchings of G in H (there is no iso ψ such that $f = g\psi$).

For all set $\mathcal{S}$ and $\approx \subseteq \mathcal{S} \times \mathcal{S}$ an equivalence relation over elements of $\mathcal{S}$, we define:

$$[\mathcal{S}]_\approx =_{\mathsf{def}} \{\mathcal{S}' \subseteq \mathcal{S} \mid \forall s \in \mathcal{S}, \exists! s' \in \mathcal{S}' : s \approx s'\}$$

Definition 8 (Extension basis). *Consider a set of morphisms $\mathcal{F} \subseteq \mathrm{Hom}(\mathcal{G})$. We say that $\mathcal{F}$ is an* extension basis *if it satisfies $[\mathcal{F}]_{\mathsf{ext}} = \{\mathcal{F}\}$.*

In Definition 7, $\mathit{Ext}_{\mathcal{F},K}(\varGamma)$ extends an arbitrary set of maps $\varGamma$ into *all* possible extensions of $g \in \varGamma$ by a map in $\mathcal{F}$. This raises two issues: first, we wish to build extension steps between sets of *matches* into K and not all equivalent ways of denoting the same match. So one may wonder what one obtains if, instead of computing $\mathit{Ext}_{\mathcal{F},K}(\varGamma)$, one were to compute $\mathit{Ext}_{\mathcal{F},K}(\varGamma')$ for some $\varGamma' \in [\varGamma]_{\mathsf{mat}}$. Second, the set $\mathcal{F}$ might be arbitrarily large, and we wish to compute the same extension step with a smaller set of maps.

The Extension theorem below provides an answer to these two issues: computing $\mathit{Ext}_{\mathcal{F},K}(\varGamma)$ is essentially equivalent to computing $\mathit{Ext}_{\mathcal{F}',K}(\varGamma')$ if one picks $\mathcal{F}' \in [\mathcal{F}]_{\mathsf{ext}}$ and $\varGamma' \in [\varGamma]_{\mathsf{mat}}$.

Theorem 2 (Extension). *Let $\mathcal{F} \subseteq \mathrm{Hom}(G, H)$, and $\varGamma \subseteq \mathrm{Hom}(G, K)$. For all $\varGamma' \in [\varGamma]_{\mathsf{mat}}$, for all extension basis $\mathcal{F}' \in [\mathcal{F}]_{\mathsf{ext}}$, we have:*

$$\mathit{Ext}_{\mathcal{F}',K}(\varGamma') = \emptyset \iff \mathit{Ext}_{\mathcal{F},K}(\varGamma) = \emptyset \qquad (7)$$

$$[\mathit{Ext}_{\mathcal{F}',K}(\varGamma')]_{\mathsf{mat}} \subseteq [\mathit{Ext}_{\mathcal{F},K}(\varGamma)]_{\mathsf{mat}} \qquad (8)$$

Importantly, replacing $\mathcal{F}$ by an arbitrary extension basis and $\varGamma$ by an arbitrary member of $[\varGamma]_{\mathsf{mat}}$ is not a neutral operation with respect to extension step. However the resulting set of maps is *indistinguishable* from $\mathit{Ext}_{\mathcal{F},K}(\varGamma)$ if one equates matching equivalent maps.

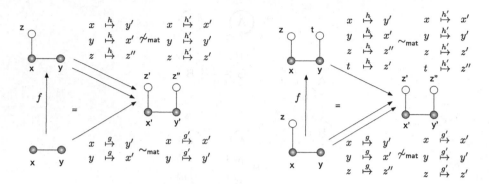

Fig. 6. Left diagram (loosing symmetry): two equivalent matches g and g' can be extended by f into two distinct matches. Right diagram (gaining symmetry): two distinct matches g and g' can be extended by f into the same match.

Notice also that although $[\Gamma']_{\text{mat}} = \{\Gamma'\}$ (Γ' is already stripped of any redundant map), in general $[Ext_{\mathcal{F}',K}(\Gamma')]_{\text{mat}} \neq \{Ext_{\mathcal{F}',K}(\Gamma')\}$ because one extension step, even using purely non equivalent extensions, may produce matching-equivalent maps (see Fig. 6, right example). However we can prove that it is not possible to extend the same map g into two matching-equivalent h and h' unless one has used extension-equivalent maps to do so:

Proposition 5. *Consider the commuting diagram on the right, if there exists an iso $\phi : H \to H'$ such that $h = h'\phi$, then $\phi f = f'$. As a consequence $h \sim_{\text{mat}} h' \implies f \sim_{\text{ext}} f'$.*

Proof. By hypothesis we have $hf = h'f'$. Suppose we have $h = h'\phi$ for some iso ϕ. So we have $h'\phi f = h'f'$ by substituting h in the hypothesis. Since h' is injective, we deduce $\phi f = f'$ and $f \sim_{\text{ext}} f'$ follows by Definition 5.   □

In combination with the example of Fig. 6 (right diagram), this proposition essentially guarantees that, when using an extension basis, the only way to produce matching-equivalent extensions is to start from two maps that were not matching equivalent. This remark will become handy when we describe our update algorithm in Sect. 5.

4.3   Proof of the Extension Theorem

We begin by a lemma that shows one cannot lose any match into K after the extension step if one disregards extension-equivalent maps in $\mathcal{F}$:

Lemma 2. *Consider the commuting diagram on the right, if there exists an iso $\phi : H \to H'$ such that $f' = \phi f$, then there exists $h'' \sim_{\text{mat}} h'$ such that $g = h''f$.*

Eventually we need a Lemma that shows it is also not possible to lose a match into K after the extension step, if one disregards matching-equivalent maps in Γ.

Lemma 3. *Let $g : G \to K$, $f : G \to H$ and $h : H \to K$ an f-extension of g. The following proposition holds:*

$$\forall g' \sim_{\mathsf{mat}} g, \exists h' \sim_{\mathsf{mat}} h \text{ s.t either } \begin{cases} g' = h'f \text{ or} \\ \exists f' \not\sim_{\mathsf{ext}} f \text{ s.t } g' = h'f' \end{cases}$$

We are now in position to prove the Extension Theorem.

Proof (Theorem 2). We first prove Eq. (7).

– Suppose $Ext_{\mathcal{F}',K}(\Gamma') = \emptyset$, by definition this implies:

$$\{h \mid \exists f \in \mathcal{F}' : hf \in \Gamma'\} = \emptyset$$

This can be either true because $\Gamma' = \emptyset$ (point 1) or because no f in $\mathcal{F}'$ satisfies $hf \in \Gamma'$ for some h (point 2).
  1. Since $\Gamma' = \emptyset$ and $\Gamma' \in [\Gamma]_{\mathsf{mat}}$, we have that $\Gamma = \emptyset$. In turn, this entails that $Ext_{\mathcal{F},K}(\Gamma) = \emptyset$.
  2. Looking for a contradiction, suppose that some $f \in \mathcal{F}$ is such that $hf \in \Gamma$ for some h. Since we supposed that no $f \in \mathcal{F}'$ satisfies $hf \in \Gamma'$ necessarily $f \notin \mathcal{F}'$. But since $\mathcal{F}' \in [\mathcal{F}]_{\mathsf{ext}}$ there exists $f' \in \mathcal{F}'$ such that $f' \sim_{\mathsf{ext}} f$. According to Lemma 2, there exists $h' \sim_{\mathsf{mat}} h$ such that $h'f' \in \Gamma'$ which entails a contradiction. Therefore no f in $\mathcal{F}$ satisfies $hf \in \Gamma$ for any h and $\Gamma = \emptyset$.
– Suppose that $Ext_{\mathcal{F},K}(\Gamma) = \emptyset$. Since $\Gamma' \subseteq \Gamma$ it follows immediately that $Ext_{\mathcal{F}',K}(\Gamma') \subseteq Ext_{\mathcal{F}',K}(\Gamma')$ and hence $Ext_{\mathcal{F}',K}(\Gamma') = \emptyset$. □

We now prove Eq. (8). Note that it is equivalent to proving:

$$\forall h \in Ext_{\mathcal{F},K}(\Gamma), h \notin Ext_{\mathcal{F}',K}(\Gamma') \implies \exists h' \sim_{\mathsf{mat}} h : h' \in Ext_{\mathcal{F}',K}(\Gamma') \tag{9}$$

So let us suppose there is some h such that $h \in Ext_{\mathcal{F},K}(\Gamma)$ and $h \notin Ext_{\mathcal{F}',K}(\Gamma')$. Recall that $h \in Ext_{\mathcal{F},K}(\Gamma)$ implies that $hf \in \Gamma$ for some $f \in \mathcal{F}$. In addition, $h \notin Ext_{\mathcal{F}',K}(\Gamma')$ implies that for all $f' \in \mathcal{F}'$, $hf' \notin \Gamma'$. Now there are several cases to consider:

– $f \in \mathcal{F}'$ and $hf \in \Gamma'$. This would imply that $h \in Ext_{\mathcal{F}',K}(\Gamma')$ which would contradict our hypothesis.
– $f \in \mathcal{F}'$ and $hf \notin \Gamma'$. Since $\Gamma' \in [\Gamma]_{\mathsf{mat}}$ we know there exists $g \in \Gamma'$ such that $g \sim_{\mathsf{mat}} hf$. We apply Lemma 3 to deduce that there exists $h' \sim_{\mathsf{mat}} h$ and f' such that $h'f' = g$. Still according to Lemma 3, either $f' = f$ (point 1) or $f' \not\sim_{\mathsf{ext}} f$ (point 2).
  1. Since $f \in \mathcal{F}'$ we have that $h' \in Ext_{\mathcal{F}',K}(\Gamma')$.

2. Since $\mathcal{F}' \in [\mathcal{F}]_{\text{ext}}$, $f' \not\sim_{\text{ext}} f$ implies there is $f'' \sim_{\text{ext}} f'$ such that $f'' \in \mathcal{F}'$. We apply Lemma 2 to deduce that there exists $h'' \sim_{\text{mat}} h'$ such that $f'' h'' \in \Gamma'$. By transitivity of $\sim_{\text{mat}}$ we have $h'' \sim_{\text{mat}} h$ and we do have $h'' \in Ext_{\mathcal{F}',K}(\Gamma')$.

– $f \notin \mathcal{F}'$ and $hf \in \Gamma'$. Since $\mathcal{F}' \in [\mathcal{F}]_{\text{ext}}$ we know there exists $f' \in \mathcal{F}'$ that satisfies $f' \sim_{\text{ext}} f$. We apply Lemma 2 to deduce that there is $h' \sim_{\text{mat}} h$ such that $h' f' \in \Gamma'$. It entails that $h' \in Ext_{\mathcal{F}',K}(\Gamma')$.

– $f \notin \mathcal{F}'$ and $hf \notin \Gamma'$ and we proceed by combining the arguments of the two previous points.   □

5   The Update Algorithm

In this section we show how to utilize extension bases and extension steps to implement the incremental update function specified in Sect. 3. We describe Fig. 7 the interplay of extension steps and exploration of the concrete domain.

Fig. 7. Extension steps and domain exploration. The occurrence of η on K provides a map $g : G_0 \rightarrow K$ and the concrete identity of G_0 in K. The algorithm looks for all possible extension steps above G_0 in the statically computed basis. The extensions that succeed are represented with plain line arrows. Those that fail are represented with dotted line arrows. For instance no extension step is able to provide a match for G_4 in K.

5.1   Abstract Effects

Graph rewriting systems are given as a set of rewriting rules of the form

$$r : L \rightharpoonup R$$

where r is a partial map between $L \in \mathcal{G}$ and $R \in \mathcal{G}$. Formally such a partial map is given as a span $r = \langle \text{lhs} : D \rightarrow L, \text{rhs} : D \rightarrow R \rangle$ where $D \in \mathcal{G}$ is the domain of definition of r and lhs (resp. rhs) stands for the left hand side map of r (resp. right hand side). For all such span r, we define:

$$H_r^+ =_{\mathsf{def}} R \backslash \mathsf{rhs}(D) \qquad H_r^- =_{\mathsf{def}} L \backslash \mathsf{lhs}(D)$$

Definition 9 (abstract effect). *Let r be a rule. The* abstract effect *of r, written $\eta_r^\sharp$, is the pair of maps:*

$$\eta_r^\sharp =_{\mathsf{def}} \langle f_r^- : H_r^- \to L, f_r^+ : H_r^+ \to R \rangle$$

where f_r^ε is the identity on its domain.

We give Fig. 8 an example of the derivation of an abstract effect from a Kappa rule.

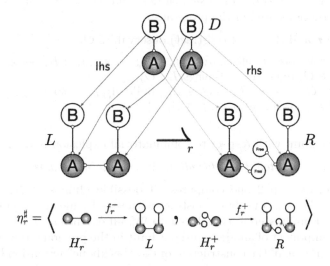

Fig. 8. Deriving an abstract effect from a Kappa rule. The Kappa rule is given as a partial map $r : L \rightharpoonup R$ (upper part). The corresponding abstract effect is a pair of maps (f_r^-, f_r^+) describing respectively the edges that are removed and added by the rule.

Definition 10 (K-occurrence). *Consider an abstract effect*

$$\eta_r^\sharp = \langle f_r^- : H_r^- \to L, f_r^+ : H_r^+ \to R \rangle$$

For all concrete state K, a K-occurrence $m_{K,r}$ of $\eta_r^\sharp$ is a pair of maps:

$$m_{K,r} =_{\mathsf{def}} (g^- : L \to K, g^+ : R \to K)$$

and we write $m_{K,r}(\eta_r^\sharp) = \eta$ whenever:

$$\eta = (g^-(L), g^- f_r^-(H_r^-), g^+ f_r^+(H_r^+))$$

5.2 Extension Basis Synthesis

Recall from Sect. 2.3 that we consider a set $\mathcal{O} \subseteq \mathcal{G}$ of *observable graphs*. Since the observables (including any match of the left hand sides of a rule) are intentionally given as a finite set of abstract graphs (see Sect. 2), we may assume that every elements of $[\mathcal{O}]_{\mathsf{iso}}$ is finite, where $\sim_{\mathsf{iso}}$ is the graph isomorphism equivalence relation. Let us thus consider an arbitrary $\hat{\mathcal{O}} \subseteq \mathcal{G}$ such that $\hat{\mathcal{O}} \in [\mathcal{O}]_{\mathsf{iso}}$.

For all rule r, we define now the procedure to build a *negative and positive r-extension basis*, respectively $\mathfrak{B}_r^+ \subseteq \mathsf{Hom}(\mathcal{G})$ and $\mathfrak{B}_r^- \subseteq \mathsf{Hom}(\mathcal{G})$.

Similarly to Sect. 3 we adopt the following naming convention: for all $r : L \rightharpoonup R$ we write $\pi_r^+ =_{\mathsf{def}} R$ and $\pi_r^- =_{\mathsf{def}} L$ and the superscript $\_^\varepsilon$ should be globally replaced by either $\_^+$ or $\_^-$ to specialize a definition to the positive or negative update.

Procedure 1: *"Backbone" extension basis synthesis* (see Sect. 4.1 for the categorical constructions used in the procedure).

Input: a rule r and the set of (abstract) observables $\hat{\mathcal{O}}$.

1. Compute the abstract effect $\eta_r^\sharp = \langle f_r^- : H_r^- \to \pi_r^-, f_r^+ : H_r^+ \to \pi_r^+ \rangle$
2. For all $O \in \hat{\mathcal{O}}$, build $\Lambda_O^\varepsilon \in [\mathsf{Gluings}(H_r^\varepsilon, O)]_{\mathsf{ext}}$
3. For all $\langle f : O \to G, h : H_r^\varepsilon \to G \rangle \in \Lambda_O^\varepsilon$, build $\Lambda_{O,h}^\varepsilon \in [\mathsf{Mpo}(h, f_r^\varepsilon)]_{\mathsf{ext}}$
4. $\mathfrak{B}_r^\varepsilon =_{\mathsf{def}} \{f \mid \exists O, \exists h, \exists g \text{ s.t } \langle g, f \rangle \in \Lambda_{O,h}^\varepsilon\}$
5. return $\mathfrak{B}_r^\varepsilon$

An important point with respect to combinatorial explosion is the following:

Proposition 6. *At step 3 and for all h, $\Lambda_{O,h}^\varepsilon$ contains at most one element.*

In a nutshell, at step 2 one computes all possible gluings of H_r^ε with some observable O. At step 3 we build abstract witnesses by means of multi-pushout construction. Finally step 4 assembles into $\mathfrak{B}_r^\varepsilon$ all extensions $f : \pi_r^\varepsilon \to W$ that are the left component of an idem-pushout built in the previous step. We provide and example, Fig. 9, of the construction of the "backbone" extension basis in the context of Kappa.

We call this extension basis a "backbone" because it only contains direct extensions from π_r^ε to some witness. We will see shortly how to enrich this backbone basis into a new basis that takes into account sharing between witnesses.

In the meantime, we may readily state a lemma that guarantees that extensions steps along $\mathfrak{B}_r^\varepsilon$ produce concrete witnesses. Consider a basis $\mathfrak{B}_r^\varepsilon$ build from a rule r and a set of abstract observables following Procedure 1. Recall that any K-occurrence of $\eta_r^\sharp$ is a pair of maps (g_0^-, g_0^+) that identify the edges that are respectively removed and added in K. Whenever the $\mathfrak{B}_r^\varepsilon$-extension of $\{g_0^\varepsilon\}$ (see Definition 7) builds a non empty set Γ of witness matches into K, then those matches indeed provide η-witnesses (see Sect. 3.1) that are also below K^ε.

Lemma 4 (Soundness). *Let r be a rule with an abstract effect $\eta_r^\sharp$. Let also $m_{K,r} =_{\mathsf{def}} (g_0^-, g_0^+)$ be a K-occurrence of r with $\eta = m_{K,r}(\eta_r^\sharp)$ a concrete effect. For all $(h : W \to K) \in Ext_{\mathfrak{B}_r^\varepsilon, K^\varepsilon}(\{g_0^\varepsilon\})$, there exists $f_K : O \to K$ such that:*

$$h(W) \rhd_\eta^\varepsilon f_K(O)$$

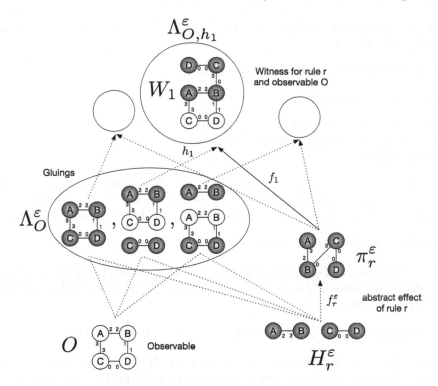

Fig. 9. Construction of the "backbone" extension basis $\mathfrak{B}_r^\varepsilon = \{f_1\}$. Grey coloring of nodes helps tracking nodes of H_r^ε through the morphisms (all closed diagrams are commuting). In dotted line, the maps that are used for the construction of the basis but that are not morphisms of $\mathfrak{B}_r^\varepsilon$. Consistently with Proposition 6, the multi-pushouts in the upper part of the diagram have at most one element ($\Lambda_{O,h_1}^\varepsilon = \{W_1\}$, the other gluings are incompatible with π_r^ε).

A simple saturation procedure enables one to add sharing between graphs of the "backbone" extension basis we have constructed so far:

Procedure 2: *Add sharing to an extension basis.*

Input: an extension basis $\mathfrak{B}$.

1. if there exists $f, f' \in \mathfrak{B}$ and $g, h, h' \notin \mathfrak{B}$ such that $f = hg$ and $f' = h'g$ then $\mathfrak{B} = \mathfrak{B} \cup \{g, h, h'\}$ and go to 1.
2. else return $\mathfrak{B}$.

 We write $G <_{\mathfrak{B}}^1 H$ if there exists $f \in \mathfrak{B}$ such that $f : G \to H$. The relation $\leq_{\mathfrak{B}}$ is the transitive and reflexive closure of $<_{\mathfrak{B}}^1$ and denotes a partial order.

5.3   Implementing the Incremental Update Function

This section is dedicated to the implementation of the incremental update function, according to the specification that was given Sect. 3.3. The algorithm relies on a pre-computation of the r-extension bases (with sharing) of all rule r contained in the rule set:

Procedure 3: *Compute the extension bases.*

Input: a finite rule set $\mathcal{R}$.

1. For all $r \in \mathcal{R}$, build $\mathfrak{B}_r^\varepsilon$ following Procedure 1.
2. For all $\mathfrak{B}_r^\varepsilon$, add sharing following Procedure 2.
3. return $\bigcup_r \{\mathfrak{B}_r^\varepsilon\}$.

Each time a rule r is applied to a graph K, one obtains the corresponding K-occurrence $m_{K,r} = (g_0^+ : \pi_r^+ \to K, g_0^+ : \pi_r^+ \to K)$. We use g_0^ε as an input to the update procedure, which is a breadth-first traversal of the extension basis $\mathfrak{B}_r^\varepsilon$:

Procedure 4: *Incremental update.*

Input: a basis $\mathfrak{B}_r^\varepsilon$, *a* K-*occurrence* $g_0^\varepsilon : \pi_r^\varepsilon \to K$ *of* $\eta_r^\sharp$, *and a predicate* $w : \mathcal{G} \to 2$ *such that* $w(G)$ *holds if* G *is an abstract witness of* $\mathfrak{B}_r^\varepsilon$. *For all set of morphisms* $\mathcal{F} \subseteq \mathfrak{B}_r^\varepsilon$ *we define:*

$$\min(\mathcal{F}) =_{\mathsf{def}} \{f \in \mathcal{F} \mid f : G \to H \wedge \forall (g : G' \to H') \in \mathcal{F} : H' \not\leq_\mathfrak{B} H\}$$

1. Initialize $\gamma : \mathcal{G} \to \mathcal{P}(\mathsf{Hom}(\mathcal{G}))$ as $\gamma(G) := \emptyset$ for all $G \neq \pi_r^\varepsilon$ and $\gamma(\pi_r^\varepsilon) := \{g_0\}$
2. $\mathcal{F} := \emptyset$ (for the extensions yet to explore), $x := \pi_r^\varepsilon$ (for the current point in the basis) and $\mathcal{W} := \emptyset$ (for the reached witnesses).
3. if $w(x)$ then $\mathcal{W} := \mathcal{W} \cup \{x\}$
4. for all $(f : x \to G) \in \mathfrak{B}_r^\varepsilon$ do $\mathcal{F} := \mathcal{F} \cup \{f\}$
5. if $\mathcal{F} \neq \emptyset$ then
6.   choose $(f : G \to H) \in \min(\mathcal{F})$
7. $\gamma(H) := [\gamma(H) \cup Ext_{\{f\},K^\varepsilon}(\gamma(G))]_{\mathsf{mat}}$
8. $\mathcal{F} := \mathcal{F}\backslash\{f\}$ and $x := H$
9.   go to step 3.
10. else return $\mathcal{W}_{\eta,K}^\varepsilon$ where:

$$\mathcal{W}_{\eta,K}^\varepsilon := \bigcup \{W \mid \exists G \in \mathcal{W}, \exists g \in \gamma(G) : g(G) = W\}.$$

The procedure builds the function γ that maps the graphs of the basis to the matches they have in K. Initially only π_r^ε has a match given by g_0^ε and γ is updated at step 7 each time an extension step is performed. We give Fig. 10 an example of the construction of the map γ for a specific extension basis.

We conclude this section by proving that the above procedure complies with the specification of the incremental update function given Sect. 3.3.

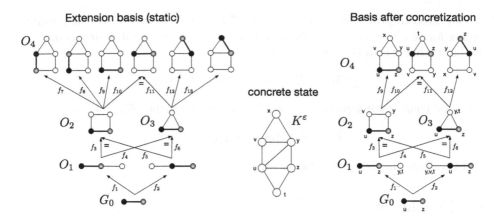

Fig. 10. An extension basis (left) for the observables O_1 (line), O_2 (square), O_3 (triangle) and O_4 (house) and $\pi_r^\varepsilon = H^\varepsilon = G_0$ (creation or deletion of a single edge). A concrete graph state K^ε (middle) and a representation of the final γ map (right). The concretization is performed using the initial match $G_0 \mapsto \{u, z\}$ (the edge $\{u, z\}$ of K^ε has been created or deleted by the effect occurrence). Colored nodes help tracking the identity of the nodes of G_0 (all closed diagrams are commuting). Overall 5 new instances of O_1 were found, 1 instance of O_2, 2 instances of O_3 and 3 instances of O_4.

5.4 Correctness Proof

We essentially need to follow the guidelines of Sect. 3.3. Let:

$$X(\gamma) =_{\text{def}} \bigcup \{H \mid \exists (g : G \to K) \in \gamma(G) : g(G) = H\}$$

and

$$\mathcal{R}(\gamma, \mathcal{W}) =_{\text{def}} \bigcup \{H \mid \exists W \in \mathcal{W}, \exists g \in \gamma(W) : g(W) = H\}$$

We write $\text{inc}_{\eta, K}^\varepsilon(X_0, \mathcal{R}_0) = (X_1, \mathcal{R}_1)$ if at step 3 we have $X(\gamma) = X_0$ and $\mathcal{R}(\gamma, \mathcal{W}) = \mathcal{R}_0$ and the next values of $X(\gamma)$ and $\mathcal{R}(\gamma, \mathcal{W})$ are respectively X_1 and $\mathcal{R}_1$.

We begin by proving that $\text{inc}_{\eta, K}^\varepsilon(X_0, \mathcal{R}_0) = (X_1, \mathcal{R}_1)$ satisfies the requirements for X_i. After one loop of the procedure we have two cases:

- if Step 5 was satisfied, then at step 7, $X_1 = X_0 \cup X$ where:

$$X = \bigcup \{G' \subseteq K^\varepsilon \mid \exists g \in \gamma(H) : G' = g(H)\}$$

by construction $X \subseteq K^\varepsilon$ and $X \cap X_0 \neq \emptyset$ since a new extension step has been performed. Furthermore $X \in \mathcal{D}^\varepsilon(\eta)$ by construction of the basis: it is either itself an abstract witness or it is below some other witnesses. Therefore we satisfy Eq. (5) (Sect. 3.3).
- if Step 10 was satisfied then $X_0 = X_1$ since γ is not modified.

We need to prove now that $\mathrm{inc}_{\eta,K}^{\varepsilon}(X_0, \mathcal{R}_0) = (X_1, \mathcal{R}_1)$ satisfies the requirements for $\mathcal{R}_i$. The only step where $\mathcal{W}$ is modified is at step 3. Using Lemma 4 we know that for all $G \in \mathcal{W}$, we have:

$$g : W \to K \in \gamma(G) \implies g(W) \rhd_{\eta}^{\varepsilon} O$$

for some concrete observable $O \subseteq K^{\varepsilon}$. Thus we have either $\mathcal{R}_0 = \mathcal{R}_1$ or:

$$\mathcal{R}_1 = \mathcal{R}_0 \cup \{g(W) \mid g(W) \rhd_{\eta}^{\varepsilon} O\}$$

and therefore the Eq. (6) is also satisfied. $\square$

6   Conclusion

We have investigated in this paper the problem of efficiently updating observable counts in a graph after a rewrite step has occurred. We believe our approach has several merits.

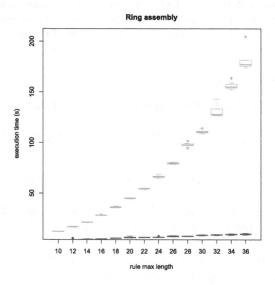

Fig. 11. A comparison between the average time of KaSim 3 runs (in red) vs. KaSim 4 runs (in blue) on successive variants of the "ring assembly" model. KaSim 4. Scales linearly with the maximal size of the largest observable (the left hand side of the largest rule), while KaSim 3. Scales with the total number of rules in each model. (Color figure online)

The first one is of methodological nature: to our knowledge it is the first attempt to describe a problem that is usually treated in a purely algorithmic fashion [14], using domain theoretic arguments for proofs and categorical constructions for the implementation. In particular algorithmic approaches tend to consider quite concrete graphs, represented by their adjacency matrices, while graph rewriting literature uses morphisms to track node identity. We have seen here that it is possible to conciliate both worlds through the interplay between extension maps and matchings.

The second merit is of qualitative nature. The incremental update procedure that is described in this paper has been implemented in the version 4.x of KaSim, a stochastic simulator for the rewriting of Kappa models. We show Fig. 11 a comparison between runs of KaSim 3 vs. 4. On variations of the "ring assembly model" that is designed to highlight the benefits of sub-graph sharing: the number of rules each variants of the model has, grows exponentially with the size of their largest left hand side: each variant of the model is characterized by the length of a ring-like graph it is trying to form. The first variant is forming all rings up-to length 10, while the last variant is forming all rings up-to length 36. Forming all possible rings up-to length n requires $!n$ rules, and the largest left hand side of these rules has length n.

As usual there are multiple continuations of this work one may envision. Just to mention a promising one, it would be interesting to see what happens if instead of incrementally maintaining $\mathcal{O}_K$ (the observable that are present in state K) one were to maintain $\downarrow\mathcal{O}_K$. In theory one could benefit from having partial observables already explored in order to minimize what remains to be discovered after an effect has occurred. From an implementation point of view this may lead to potentially memory intensive data structures but to very minimalist update phases.

Acknowledgments. This work was supported by the ANR grant ICEBERG (ANR-10-BINF-0006) and is partially sponsored by the Defense Advanced Research Projects Agency (DARPA) and the U.S. Army Research Office under grant number W911NF-14-1-0367. The views, opinions, and/or findings contained in this paper are those of the authors and should not be interpreted as representing the official views or policies, either expressed or implied, of the Defense Advanced Research Projects Agency or the Department of Defense.

Appendix

Proofs Omitted in Section 3

Proof (Proposition 1). We first prove Eq. (2), $\Rightarrow$. By unfolding the def. of $W \rhd_\eta^- O$ and by $W \subseteq K$ we have $O \cup \mathsf{pre}(\eta) \subseteq K$. As a consequence, $O \subseteq K$ and by def. of Obs (Sect. 3) we have $O \in (\mathsf{Obs}\ K)$. Still by definition of $W \rhd_\eta O$ we have $O \cap H_\eta^- \neq \emptyset$ (i). By def. of $\eta \cdot K$ (Sect. 2.2) we have $O \backslash H_\eta^- \cup H_\eta^+ \subseteq \eta \cdot K$ (ii). In addition $H_\eta^- \cap H_\eta^+ = \emptyset$. By (i) and (ii) we have $O \nsubseteq \eta \cdot K$ and consequently $O \notin (\mathsf{Obs}\ \eta \cdot K)$.

We now prove Eq. (2), $\Leftarrow$. By def. $W = O \cup \mathsf{pre}(\eta)$ (i), and by hyp. we have $O \in (\mathsf{Obs}\ K)$ implies $O \subseteq K$ (ii). Moreover since $\eta \cdot K$ is defined we have $\mathsf{pre}(\eta) \subseteq K$ (iii). From (i)–(iii) we get $O \cup \mathsf{pre}(\eta) \subseteq K$. In order to conclude that $W = O \cup \mathsf{pre}(\eta) \in \mathcal{W}_\eta^-$ we need to additionally show that $O \cap H_\eta^- \neq \emptyset$.

Since $O \notin (\mathrm{Obs}\ \eta \cdot K)$ and $O \in (\mathrm{Obs}\ K)$ we have $O \nsubseteq (O \backslash H_\eta^- \cup H_\eta^+)$ (iv). Since $H_\eta^- \cap H_\eta^+ = \emptyset$ by def. of η, the only possibility to satisfy (iv) is $O \cap H_\eta^- \neq \emptyset$. $\square$

Proofs Omitted in Section 4

Proof (Lemma 2). It suffices to take $h'' = h'\phi$ which, by Definition 6 implies that $h'' \sim_{\mathsf{mat}} h'$. By hypothesis we have $g = h'f'$ and $f' = \phi f$. From these equalities we get $g = h'\phi f$. By substituting $h'\phi$ by h'' we obtain $g = h''f$. $\square$

Proofs Omitted in Section 5

Proof (Lemma 3). By hypothesis we start from the following commuting diagram:

Since $g' \sim_{\mathsf{mat}} g$, by Definition 6, we have $g = g'\phi$ for some iso ϕ. We have two cases:

$$
\begin{array}{ccc}
H & \xrightarrow{\ h\ } & \\
f \big\uparrow \ \ = & & K \\
G & \xrightarrow{\ g\ } &
\end{array}
$$

- either f is ϕ-preserving and there exists an iso ψ such that $f\phi = \psi f$. Then by construction $h\psi^{-1}f = g'$ and we can conclude by noticing that $h' =_{\mathsf{def}} h\psi^{-1} \sim_{\mathsf{mat}} h$ (by Definition 6).
- or f is not ϕ-preserving and there is no iso ψ such that $f\phi = \psi f$. It entails that $f\phi \nsim_{\mathsf{ext}} f$ (by Definition 5) and (by symmetry) $f' =_{\mathsf{def}} f\phi^{-1} \nsim_{\mathsf{ext}} f$. Now we can conclude, since by construction $hf' = g'$. $\square$

Proof (Proposition 6). We have the following diagram:

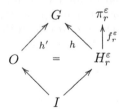

where $\boldsymbol{h} = \langle h', h \rangle$ is a gluing of O and H_r^ε. Now the procedure attempts to build the multi-pushout of the span $\boldsymbol{f} = \langle h, f_r^\varepsilon \rangle$. Suppose it has at least two elements, we have the following diagram:

$$
\begin{array}{ccc}
U & \xleftarrow{\ \ } & U' \\
i \big\uparrow \ \diagup_{j} \ \ _{k} \diagdown \ \big\uparrow l & & \\
G & = & \pi_r^\varepsilon \\
h' \diagup \ \ h \diagdown & & \big\uparrow f_r^\varepsilon \\
O \ \ = & & H_r^\varepsilon \\
& \diagdown \quad \diagup & \\
& I &
\end{array}
$$

where $\langle ih', kf_r^\varepsilon \rangle$ and $\langle jh', lf_r^\varepsilon \rangle$ are bounds for $\boldsymbol{h} = \langle h, h' \rangle$. By construction $\boldsymbol{h}$ is a relative pushout, therefore, by Proposition 4, there exists an iso $\phi : U \rightarrow U'$ that equates the bounds $\langle i, k \rangle$ and $\langle j, l \rangle$. This would entail $i \sim_{\text{ext}} j$ which contradicts the hypothesis. $\qquad\qquad\qquad\qquad\qquad\qquad\qquad\qquad\qquad\qquad\qquad\qquad\qquad\qquad\qquad\square$

Proof (Lemma 4). Recall from Sect. 3.1 that a (concrete) η-witness W for a (concrete) observable O must satisfy:

$$O \cap H_\eta^\varepsilon \neq \emptyset \wedge W = O \cup \pi_\eta^\varepsilon \qquad\qquad (10)$$

By construction of the basis, and using the hypothesis of the lemma we have the following diagram:

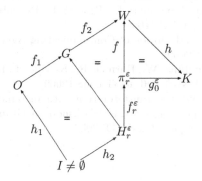

We take $f_K =_{\text{def}} hf_2 f_1$, $g^\varepsilon = g_0^\varepsilon f_r^\varepsilon$, and we have:

$$f_K(O) \cap g^\varepsilon(H_r^\varepsilon) = g^\varepsilon h_2(I) = f_K h_1(I) \neq \emptyset$$

and

$$h(W) = f_K(O) \cup g_0^\varepsilon(\pi_r^\varepsilon) = f_K(O) \cup \pi_\eta$$

which verifies Eq. (10). $\qquad\qquad\qquad\qquad\qquad\qquad\qquad\qquad\qquad\qquad\qquad\qquad\qquad\quad\square$

References

1. Rowland, M.A., Deeds, E.J.: Crosstalk and the evolution of specificity in two-component signaling. PNAS **111**(25), 9325 (2014)
2. Danos, V., Feret, J., Fontana, W., Harmer, R., Krivine, J.: Rule-based modelling of cellular signalling. In: Caires, L., Vasconcelos, V.T. (eds.) CONCUR 2007. LNCS, vol. 4703, pp. 17–41. Springer, Heidelberg (2007). doi:10.1007/978-3-540-74407-8_3
3. Faeder, J.R., Blinov, M.L., Hlavacek, W.S.: Rule-based modeling of biochemical systems with bionetgen. Methods Mol. Biol. **500**, 113–167 (2009)
4. Danos, V., Feret, J., Fontana, W., Krivine, J.: Scalable simulation of cellular signaling networks. In: Shao, Z. (ed.) APLAS 2007. LNCS, vol. 4807, pp. 139–157. Springer, Heidelberg (2007). doi:10.1007/978-3-540-76637-7_10
5. Boutillier, P., Feret, J., Krivine, J. (2008). https://github.com/kappa-dev/kasim

6. Sneddon, M.W., Faeder, J.R., Emonet, T.: Efficient modeling, simulation and coarse-graining of biological complexity with NFsim. Nat. Methods **8**, 177–183 (2011)
7. Danos, V., Heckel, R., Sobocinski, P.: Transformation and refinement of rigid structures. In: Giese, H., König, B. (eds.) ICGT 2014. LNCS, vol. 8571, pp. 146–160. Springer, Heidelberg (2014). doi:10.1007/978-3-319-09108-2_10
8. Girard, J.-Y.: The system F of variable types fifteen years after. Theor. Comput. Sci. **45**, 159–192 (1986)
9. Ehrig, H., Pfender, M., Schneider, H.J.: Graph grammars: an algebraic approach. In: Proceedings of IEEE Conference on Automata and Switching Theory, pp. 167–180 (1973)
10. Raoult, J.C.: On graph rewriting. TCS **32**, 1–24 (1984)
11. Corradini, A., Heindel, T., Hermann, F., König, B.: Sesqui-pushout rewriting. In: Corradini, A., Ehrig, H., Montanari, U., Ribeiro, L., Rozenberg, G. (eds.) Proceedings of ICGT 2006, pp. 30–45 (2006)
12. Milner, R.: The Space and Motion of Communicating Agents. Cambridge University Press, Cambridge (2009)
13. Feret, J., Danos, V., Fontana, W., Harmer, R., Krivine, J.: Internal coarse-graining of molecular systems. PNAS **106**, 6453–6458 (2009)
14. Varró, G., Varró, D.: Graph transformation with incremental updates. ENTCS **109**, 71–83 (2004). Proceedings of the Workshop on Graph Transformation and Visual Modelling Techniques (GT-VMT 2004)

Linearity, Control Effects, and Behavioral Types

Luís Caires[1] and Jorge A. Pérez[2]($\boxtimes$)

[1] NOVA LINCS and Departamento de Informática, FCT,
Universidade Nova de Lisboa, Lisbon, Portugal
[2] University of Groningen & CWI, Amsterdam, The Netherlands
j.a.perez@rug.nl

Abstract. Mainstream programming idioms intensively rely on state mutation, sharing, and concurrency. Designing type systems for handling and disciplining such idioms is challenging, due to long known conflicts between internal non-determinism, linearity, and control effects such as exceptions. In this paper, we present the first type system that accommodates non-deterministic and abortable behaviors in the setting of session-based concurrent programs. Remarkably, our type system builds on a Curry-Howard correspondence with (classical) linear logic conservatively extended with two dual modalities capturing an additive (co)monad, and provides a first example of a Curry-Howard interpretation of a realistic programming language with built-in internal non-determinism. Thanks to its deep logical foundations, our system elegantly addresses several well-known tensions between control, linearity, and non-determinism: globally, it enforces progress and fidelity; locally, it allows the specification of non-deterministic and abortable computations. The expressivity of our system is illustrated by several examples, including a typed encoding of a higher-order functional language with threads, session channels, non-determinism, and exceptions.

1 Introduction

In this paper, we study a principled, typeful foundation to represent a relevant class of control effects within a behavioral type system for stateful concurrent programs. Sophisticated structural type systems have shaped mainstream static type checking for a long time now, and are fairly complete tools to discipline and effectively check programs that manipulate pure values. Unfortunately, the same cannot be said for most mainstream programming idioms, which intensively rely on state mutation, sharing, and often concurrency, about which "standard" type systems are quite silent.

Interactive concurrent systems need to manipulate stateful resources, ranging from basic memory references and passive objects (such as files, locks, and communication channels) to dynamic entities (such as threads or web references) typically subject to linearity constraints. To extend type-based verification techniques to this challenging setting, substructural type systems, based on various forms of linearity and affinity, have been increasingly investigated [31,35,45–47], and start to make their way towards practical adoption. Recent examples include

© Springer-Verlag GmbH Germany 2017
H. Yang (Ed.): ESOP 2017, LNCS 10201, pp. 229–259, 2017.
DOI: 10.1007/978-3-662-54434-1_9

```
LET a = Ref() IN LET b = Ref() IN        LET a = Ref() IN LET b = Ref() IN
LET x1 = f() IN                          LET x1 = f() IN
LET a' = write a x1 IN                   LET x2 = g() IN
LET x2 = g() IN                          LET a' = write a x1 IN
LET b' = write b x2 IN (free a'; free b')  LET b' = write b x2 IN (free a'; free b')
```

Fig. 1. Two code snippets.

Mozilla's Rust, but also embeddings of session types in target languages without linear types [32,41]. Some approaches use types to model states (cf. assertions); examples include typestate and several affine, linear, and stateful type systems, see, e.g., [20,31,33]. In other works, types are used to model behaviors (cf. processes); examples in this line include session types and usage types such as, e.g., [27,28,34], often referred to as *behavioral types* [29].

Linear types are in general very expressive, and the fine-grained specifications of usage types that they typically support may simultaneously bring a benefit and a curse. In particular, a still open issue is how to seamlessly combine linearity with many other useful programming mechanisms—a prominent example being the interaction of linearity with non-determinism and control effects, such as exceptions and (linear) continuations. The general issue is that by their very essence control effects (and associated programming language constructs) conflict with the linear, stateful usage discipline of values manipulated by programs, which makes it difficult to statically check programs. For example, when a communication channel is aborted, any linear values held by a channel client continuation must be aborted as well (which may not be always possible), or passed away to some candidate consumer code in scope. Likewise, after an exception is raised, it is not always clear how to safely discard a continuation holding linear values, nor how to proceed after the exception is caught. This situation is already present in non-deterministic programs where subexpressions may return more than one result, or even no result at all (e.g., "fail"), as in the non-deterministic monad.

These challenges and conflicts are illustrated by the examples in Fig. 1, adapted from [46], which we express in an idealized linear functional language. The *Ref* function is assumed to return a stateful fresh value r that may either be initially discarded, or subject to a strictly linear protocol consisting of a *write r x* operation followed by a *free r* operation. We use a common idiom when programming with usage types, in which an operation f acting on a linear value a that needs to be used according to a stateful protocol would be called as $a' = (f a)$, where a' refers to the new state of a (which gets "consumed" in the call $(f\ a)$). So, in our examples, failure to call *free r* after $r' = write\ r\ x$ may result in, say, a memory leak. Now, in Fig. 1(left), if for some reason the call $f()$ raises an exception, the continuation will be safely aborted, but if $f()$ succeeds and the call $g()$ raises an exception instead, the resulting behavior would be ill-defined, as the required execution of *free a'* will be discarded. On the other

LET log = FORK l. RECV(l, m_1); RECV(l, m_2); CLOSE? l IN

LET res = FORK f. RECV($f, code$); SEND($f, qs(code)$); RECV(f, bk); CLOSE? f IN

    SEND(res, QU2112); RECV(res, qss);

        TRY

            LET log = $Check\ log\ qss$ IN

                SEND($res, bkok$); SEND(log, "ok"); CLOSE! log; CLOSE! res

            CATCH $logc$. SEND($logc$, "$fail$"); CLOSE! $logc$

Fig. 2. Code snippet for the server example.

hand, consider the slightly different code snippet in Fig. 1(right): even assuming that $f()$ or $g()$ may raise an exception, there will be no value usage violations, since both a and b will still be in their initially discardable state at such stage. A suitable typing discipline should deem the left snippet unsafe but the right snippet safe, taking into account the interference between control effects and the linear usage behavior of values in scope.

For a further example, consider the slightly more involved scenario given in Fig. 2, which involves concurrent communication and explicit exception handling. Our idealized linear functional language is now assumed to include the ability to fork threads, and manipulate session typed communication channels. In the first line of Fig. 2, a thread representing a logging server is forked: the fork primitive FORK $l.e$ spawns a thread with body e accessing one endpoint of session channel l, and returns the other endpoint (bound to log) to the caller. The logging server receives precisely two messages, whose payload is a string, and closes the connection. Then another concurrent thread is spawned, mocking a resource allocation service: it receives a resource code, returns the quality of service constraints, and receives some reservation information bk.

The server at channel res is used by client code that first sends a resource code QU2112, receives a quality of service qss spec, and then calls a conformance checking operation $Check$ which, crucially, may raise an exception:

LET $Check$ = $\lambda l.\lambda x$.SEND(l, "$checkin$"); if $Valid(x)$ then l else THROW (l) IN ...

All interactions between client and server are meant to be logged, so channel log is also passed to the $Check$ function together with the quality of service specification.

The overall expected behavior would be as follows. If $Valid()$ returns true, then $Check$ succeeds and the client will proceed booking the resource; however, if $Check$ raises an exception, the continuation will be discarded and the exception handler invoked. In this case, the continuation of the resource allocation thread at the other endpoint will also need to be aborted. If the overall ongoing (linear) session between client and server could be safely discarded at that particular stage of the protocol, then the overall behavior may be deemed safe, even if the log could not be safely aborted, since the linear outstanding interaction on the log endpoint will be performed anyway by the exception handler. Indeed, notice that the *log* is linearly passed to the exception handler as *logc*. Again, a suitable typing discipline combining effects and linearity should be able to express the assumptions underlying the reasoning above, and deem the code snippet safe, under the stated assumptions, but unsafe if the client server session is not safely abortable exactly before the RECV(f, bk) interaction (cf. Line 2 in Fig. 2). Moreover, any such typing discipline should also be compatible with internal non-determinism, in the sense that if the result of *Valid*() is non-deterministic, then the resulting computation must be soundly typed for any alternative result, including the degenerate situation in which no value at all is returned, and the rest of the computation needs to safely abort, including, in that extreme case, the exception handler code itself!

The main goal of the paper is to investigate a principled foundation to express, reason and type-check a wide class of control effects in the context of a linear behavioral type system. Crucially, our approach builds on prior work on Curry-Howard correspondences between session types and various fragments of linear logic; our type system is a conservative extension of a standard system of classical linear logic. By approaching a Curry-Howard correspondence from the programming language perspective (in the spirit of, e.g., [5,6,18]), we introduce two new dual logical modalities—monadic $\&A$ and co-monadic $\oplus A$—with associated programming constructs and proof reductions. As is often the case for type systems motivated by Curry-Howard correspondences, our system ensures global progress and usage/session protocol fidelity. Moreover, it is intrinsically compatible with all other logically motivated constructs and methods introduced in prior/related work, such as behavioral polymorphism [10,48], logical relations [37], dependent types [42], higher-order code mobility [44], and multiparty protocols [9,16].

It turns out that our new modalities $\&A$ and $\oplus A$ suffice to express general forms of internal non-determinism, and, importantly, include failure—an explicitly typed form of affinity—as a special case. These two modalities can be seen as an additional pair of linear logic exponentials, and as such obey the basic monadic/co-monadic laws. However, while the standard linear logic modalities $!A$ and $?A$ encapsulate contraction and weakening, $\&A$ and $\oplus A$ encapsulate non-determinism and failure, in a sense to be made precise below. Although related to the non-deterministic monad and to well-known powerdomain models of non-determinism [39], a key novelty of our work is the perfect Curry-Howard match between proof reductions associated to the $\&A$ and $\oplus A$ modalities and sensible operational rules. This correspondence allows us to state cut-elimination, and to naturally derive key properties with practical impact (e.g., lock freedom, fidelity, and strong normalization), while supporting natural effectful programming idioms and powerful reasoning techniques (such as logical relations).

We will illustrate through examples how expressive linear usage protocols involving effects may be compiled down to the basic linear logic system extended with these two primitives and associated programming constructs. We will present our basic results and examples for a canonical session-based π-calculus model realizing a Curry-Howard interpretation of session types as linear logic propositions. As is well-known, the π-calculus is a complete foundational model, able to represent, e.g., general concurrent computation, higher-order data, and object-oriented features [40]. Hence, our development is carried out in the setting of most higher-level programming languages. In particular, we will use this process model as target language in a typed encoding of an effectful linear higher-order functional language with threads, session-typed channels, non-determinism, and exceptions, allowing us to show typings for the above examples.

Structure of the Paper. Next, Sect. 2 presents our Curry-Howard interpretation of session types for concurrent processes via examples. Sect. 3 establishes meta-theoretical results for typed processes: cut elimination (Theorem 3.1), type preservation (Theorem 3.2), progress (Theorem 3.3). Also, a postponing result (Theorem 3.5) connects our process model with the (non confluent) non-determinism typical of process calculi. Sect. 4 encodes λ^{exc} (a linear, higher-order functional language with concurrency and exceptions) into session-typed processes. λ^{exc} is the reference language for the motivating examples above. Theorem 4.1 ensures that our encoding preserves typing; therefore, all results in Sect. 3 will carry over to λ^{exc}. In Sect. 5 we discuss related works, and Sect. 6 concludes.

2 The Core Language and Its Type System

We base our development on a standard session-typed π-calculus, a core language in which general higher-order concurrent programs may be modeled and analyzed [40]. The (binary) session discipline [27,28] applies to pairs of name passing processes that communicate through point-to-point channels. In this setting, interaction between processes always occur in matching pairs: when one partner sends, the other receives; when one partner offers a selection, the other chooses; when a partner closes the session, the other must acknowledge—no further interactions may occur on the same channel. Sessions are initiated when a participant invokes a server, which acts as a shared provider, with the capability of unboundedly spawning fresh sessions between the invoking client and the newly created service instance process. A service name may be publicly shared by any clients in the environment. A session-based system exhibits concurrency and parallelism because many sessions may be executing simultaneously and independently. No races in communications within a session (or even between different sessions) can occur. Both session and server names may be passed around in communications. Session channels are subject to a linear usage discipline, conforming to a specific state dependent protocol, while server channels can be freely shared, and used by an arbitrary number of concurrent clients that can call on them for spawning new session instances.

Next we gradually introduce the ingredients of our typed process model (syntax, semantics, session types and their linear logic interpretation), which are summarized in Fig. 3. This presentation allows us to better motivate and describe the key novelty in this paper—the(dual) types for non-deterministic behaviors in sessions.

Caires and Pfenning [11] introduced a type system for π-calculus processes that corresponds to a linear logic proof system, revealing the first Curry-Howard interpretation of session types as linear logic propositions. Unlike traditional session type systems, Curry-Howard interpretations of behavioral types ensure global progress (i.e., well-typed processes never get stuck), livelock-freedom, and confluence (up to $\equiv$), and may be developed within intuitionistic [11,13] or classical linear logic [13,48], with certain subtle differences in expressiveness. Our system extends the presentation Σ_2 of classical linear logic [1] with mix principles and, crucially, with new exponential modalities $\oplus A$ and $\&A$, which will be interpreted as (dual) types for non-deterministic sessions.

Definition 2.1 (Types). *Types (A, B, C) are given by*

$$A, B ::= \perp \mid 1 \mid !A \mid ?A \mid A \otimes B \mid A \,\wp\, B \mid A \oplus B \mid A \,\&\, B \mid \oplus A \mid \&A$$

In examples we will also assume given some basic (data) types (e.g., naturals, strings, etc.), but will not elaborate the nature of such basic types (see, e.g., [42]). Despite notational similarity, there is no ambiguity between our new (unary) modalities $\oplus A$ and $\&A$ and standard linear logic (binary) operators for additive disjunction and conjunction.

For any type A, we define its dual $\overline{A}$, where $\overline{(\cdot)}$ corresponds to linear logic negation $(\cdot)^{\perp}$, following standard de Morgan-like laws. Intuitively, the type of a session endpoint is the dual of the type of the opposite endpoint.

Definition 2.2 (Duality). *The duality relation on types is given by:*

$$\overline{1} = \perp \quad \overline{!A} = ?\overline{A} \quad \overline{A \otimes B} = \overline{A} \,\wp\, \overline{B} \quad \overline{A \oplus B} = \overline{A} \,\&\, \overline{B} \quad \overline{\oplus A} = \&\overline{A}$$
$$\overline{\perp} = 1 \quad \overline{?A} = !\overline{A} \quad \overline{A \,\wp\, B} = \overline{A} \otimes \overline{B} \quad \overline{A \,\&\, B} = \overline{A} \oplus \overline{B} \quad \overline{\&A} = \oplus\overline{A}$$

Typing judgments have the form $P \vdash \Delta; \Theta$, where P is a program term, Δ is the linear context and Θ is the unrestricted context, along the lines of DILL [4] and Σ_2 [1]. Both contexts are assignments of types to (channel) names $x, y, z, \ldots$. We write '$\cdot$' to denote empty typing environments. After erasing the term P, our judgment corresponds exactly to a logical sequent in the classical linear logic Σ_2 of [1]. Remarkably, this formulation naturally supports a Curry-Howard interpretation for the exponentials $!A$ and $?A$ in terms of standard (π-calculus) semantics for lazy replication [11,13].

2.1 Reduction Semantics

The operational semantics of our session calculus is defined by a relation of reduction (denoted $P \to Q$) that expresses dynamic evolution, and a relation of structural congruence (denoted $P \equiv Q$), which equates processes with the same spatial (or static) structure. This semantics exhibits a precise correspondence with cut elimination at the logic level. While most cut-reduction steps directly correspond to process reductions, other cut-reduction steps are better expressed in the process world as structural congruence principles or as behavioral equivalences; this applies similarly to the so-called commuting conversions, which are known to capture typed behavioral equivalences [37].

To describe reductions and conversions on proof trees (which correspond to typing derivations), we introduce a simple algebraic notation. For each typing rule (T*) with k premises $d_1, \ldots, d_k$ we denote by $T^*(p_1, p_2, \ldots)$ the derivation obtained by applying rule (T*) to the derivations $p_1, \ldots, p_k$. If the proof rule binds names $\tilde{x}$ in the conclusion (as in, e.g., cut), we would then write $T^*(\tilde{x})(p_1, p_2, \ldots)$ to make this binding explicit.

2.2 Basic Typing Rules, Congruence Rules, and Reduction Rules

The parallel composition of processes is typed in our system by rules corresponding to the cut and mix principles (dependent and independent composition, respectively).

$$\frac{P \vdash \Delta; \Theta \quad Q \vdash \Delta'; \Theta}{P \mid Q \vdash \Delta, \Delta'; \Theta} \ (T\mid) \quad \frac{P \vdash \Delta, x{:}\overline{A}; \Theta \quad Q \vdash \Delta', x{:}A; \Theta}{(\nu x)(P \mid Q) \vdash \Delta, \Delta'; \Theta} \ (Tcut) \quad \frac{}{\mathbf{0} \vdash ; \Theta} \ (T{\cdot})$$

The mix rule $(T\mid)$ types the composition of two processes that do not share linear names; P and Q run in parallel but do not interact. The cut rule (Tcut) types the composition of P and Q while establishing a binary session between them using a single linear channel x; each process holds one of the two (dual) endpoints x of a session of type A and $\overline{A}$. This channel is kept private to the composition by the restriction operator $(\nu x)(\ldots)$ so that the newly established session will not be affected by interferences. Rule $(T{\cdot})$ allows the inactive process $\mathbf{0}$ to be introduced. Neutrality of $\mathbf{0}$ is expressed by the conversion $T\mid(T{\cdot}, D) \cong D$ at the level of proofs, which corresponds exactly to the usual structural congruence principle $\mathbf{0} \mid P \equiv P$ (we consider here a conversion, not a computational reduction, since it does not involve any process interaction). We take process terms up to basic structural congruence principles, namely we assume that $- \mid -$ is commutative and associative with unit $\mathbf{0}$, etc. This way, e.g., $P \mid Q$ and $Q \mid P$ denote the same process, i.e., the (unique) parallel composition of P and Q. Thus, Rule (Tcut) is symmetric w.r.t. its premises: if $\text{Tcut}(D_1, D_2)$ is a derivation then $\text{Tcut}(D_2, D_1)$ is the same derivation; we then also consider the conversion $\text{Tcut}(D_1, D_2) \cong \text{Tcut}(D_2, D_1)$.

Session Send and Receive. Session-typed processes communicate by sending and receiving messages according to some session discipline. The message payload can be a value of some primitive data type or a session channel; we focus here on the general case of session passing (delegation). Type $A \otimes B$ is the type of a session that first sends a session of type A and then continues as a session of type B. As such, it corresponds to the session type $!A.B$ of [27]. Dually, $A \,\invamp\, B$ is the type of a session that first receives a session of type A and then continues as a session of type B; it thus corresponds to the session type $?\overline{A}.B$. Hence, the session type $?A.B$ corresponds to the linear type $A \multimap B$. We have the following typing rules for send $A \otimes B$ and receive $A \,\wp\, B$.

$$\frac{P \vdash \Delta, y{:}A; \Theta \quad Q \vdash \Delta', x{:}B; \Theta}{\overline{x}(y).(P \mid Q) \vdash \Delta, \Delta', x{:}A \otimes B; \Theta} \ (\mathrm{T}\otimes) \qquad \frac{R \vdash \Gamma, y{:}C, x{:}D; \Theta}{x(y).R \vdash \Gamma, x{:}C \,\wp\, D; \Theta} \ (\mathrm{T}\wp)$$

An output process is then of the form $\overline{x}(y).M$, where y is a freshly created name. The behavior of such an output process is to send session y on x and then proceed as defined by M. In our typed language, the output continuation M has the form $P \mid Q$, where P defines the behavior of the session y being sent and Q the behavior of the continuation session on x. An input process is of the form $x(y).R$, a process that receives on session x a session n, passed in parameter y, and then proceeds as specified by R. The continuation R will use the received session but also any other open sessions (including x). Notice that y is bound both in $\overline{x}(y).M$ and in $x(y).R$, and so only fresh names can be sent in output processes; this corresponds to the *internal mobility* discipline [7], without loss of expressiveness. The associated principal cut reduction corresponds to process communication, where $C = \overline{A}$, $D = \overline{B}$, expressed by

$$\mathsf{Tcut}(x)(\mathsf{T}\otimes(y)(D_1, D_2), \mathsf{T}\wp(y)(D_3)) \to \mathsf{Tcut}(x)(\mathsf{Tcut}(y)(D_1, D_3), D_2)$$

This reduction exactly captures (bound output) communication in the π-calculus

$$(\nu x)(\overline{x}(y).M \mid x(y).R) \to (\nu x)(\nu y)(M \mid R)$$

where we write $M \equiv P \mid Q$. Although $- \mid -$ is commutative there is no ambiguity in Rule $(\mathrm{T}\otimes)$: P and Q are the split of M typed by $P \vdash \Delta, y{:}A; \Theta$ and $Q \vdash \Delta', x{:}B; \Theta$, respectively, and Δ and Δ' are the split of the linear context in the conclusion. The multiplicative units $\bot$ and $\mathbf{1}$ type session termination actions as seen from each endpoint; no partner can further use a closed session.

$$\frac{}{x.\overline{\mathsf{close}} \vdash x{:}\mathbf{1}; \Theta} \ (\mathrm{T}1) \qquad \frac{P \vdash \Delta; \Theta}{x.\mathsf{close}; P \vdash x{:}\bot, \Delta; \Theta} \ (\mathrm{T}\bot)$$

The associated principal cut reduction corresponds to session termination, which we define at the level of processes and proof trees respectively by the rules

$$(\nu x)(x.\overline{\mathsf{close}} \mid x.\mathsf{close}; P) \to P \quad \mathsf{Tcut}(x)(\mathrm{T}1, \mathrm{T}\bot(D)) \to D$$

Types $\mathbf{1}$ and $\bot$ correspond to the single type **end** in usual session types, and usually have a silent interpretation. In the presence of mix principles, as we consider here, propositions $\bot \multimap \mathbf{1}$ and $\mathbf{1} \multimap \bot$ are valid. Considering $\bot = \mathbf{1}$, we could define a single type '$\bullet$' as standing for "both" $\mathbf{1}$ or $\bot$, where $\overline{\bullet} = \bullet$. (Recall that $A \multimap B \triangleq \overline{A} \,\wp\, B$.)

Session Offer and Choice. The linear type $A \oplus B$ types a session that first *chooses* (from the dual partner menu) either "left" or "right", and then continues as a session of type A or B, depending on the choice. This type is the binary version of the session type $\oplus_{i \in I}\{l_i{:}A_i\}$ (labeled internal choice). The linear type $A\&B$ types a session that first *offers* both "left" or "right" menu options and then continues as a session of type A or B, depending on the choice made by the partner. Thus, $A\&B$ is the binary version of the session type $\&_{i \in I}\{l_i{:}A_i\}$ (labeled external choice). Offers and choices are typed by the additive linear conjunction and disjunction $\&$ and $\oplus$, as defined by the rules:

$$\frac{R \vdash \Delta, x{:}A; \Theta}{x.\mathtt{inl}; R \vdash \Delta, x{:}A \oplus B; \Theta} \ (\mathrm{T}\oplus_1) \qquad\qquad \frac{R \vdash \Delta, x{:}B; \Theta}{x.\mathtt{inr}; R \vdash \Delta, x{:}A \oplus B; \Theta} \ (\mathrm{T}\oplus_2)$$

$$\frac{P \vdash \Delta, x{:}A; \Theta \quad Q \vdash \Delta, x{:}B; \Theta}{x.\mathtt{case}(P, Q) \vdash \Delta, x{:}A \& B; \Theta} \ (\mathrm{T}\&)$$

The associated principal cut reductions correspond to the process and proof reductions

$$(\nu x)(x.\mathtt{case}(P, Q) \mid x.\mathtt{inl}; R) \to (\nu x)(P \mid R)$$
$$(\nu x)(x.\mathtt{case}(P, Q) \mid x.\mathtt{inr}; R) \to (\nu x)(Q \mid R)$$
$$\mathrm{Tcut}(x)(\mathrm{T}\&(D_1, D_2), \mathrm{T}\oplus_1(D_3)) \to \mathrm{Tcut}(x)(D_1, D_3)$$
$$\mathrm{Tcut}(x)(\mathrm{T}\&(D_1, D_2), \mathrm{T}\oplus_2(D_3)) \to \mathrm{Tcut}(x)(D_2, D_3)$$

In examples we may consider n-ary labeled sums, close to usual session types constructs:

$$\frac{R \vdash \Delta, x{:}A; \Theta}{x.l_i; R \vdash \Delta, x{:} \oplus_{i \in I}\{l_i : A_i\}; \Theta} \qquad \frac{P_i \vdash \Delta, x{:}A_i; \Theta \quad (\text{all } i \in I)}{x.\mathtt{case}_{i \in I}(l_i.P_i) \vdash \Delta, x{:} \&_{i \in I}\{l_i : A_i\}; \Theta}$$

with associated principal cut reduction expressed by

$$(\nu x)(x.\mathtt{case}_{i \in I}(l_i.P_i) \mid x.l_i; R) \to (\nu x)(P_i \mid R)$$

Example 2.3 (Movie Server (1)). Consider a toy scenario involving a movie server and some clients. We first model a single session (on channel s) established between client $Alice(s)$ and server instance $SBody(s)$. The server session offers two options: "buy movie" ($\mathtt{inl}$), and "preview trailer" ($\mathtt{inr}$). Alice selects the "preview" option from the server menu, and plays the corresponding protocol. Consider now the following terms:

$$SBody(s) \triangleq s.\mathtt{case}(s(title).s(card).s\langle movie \rangle.s.\overline{\mathtt{close}}, s(title).s\langle trailer \rangle.s.\overline{\mathtt{close}})$$

$$Alice(s) \triangleq s.\mathtt{inr}; s\langle \text{"mullholanddrive"} \rangle.s(preview).s.\mathtt{close}; 0$$

$$System_1 \triangleq (\nu s)(SBody(s) \mid Alice(s))$$

Assume some given basic types for movie titles (T), credit card data (C) and movie files M, which are self-dual (since they do not type communication capabilities but values of basic types). We can then provide the following types and derivable type assignments for the various system components as follows:

$$SBT \triangleq (T \multimap C \multimap M \otimes 1) \& (T \multimap M \otimes 1)$$
$$SBody(s) \vdash s : SBT \; ; \cdot \qquad Alice(s) \vdash s : \overline{SBT} \; ; \cdot$$

We would then have $System_1 \vdash \cdot \; ; \cdot$. While the type of the server endpoint is SBT, the type of a client endpoint would be $\overline{SBT} = (T \otimes C \otimes M \multimap \bot) \oplus (T \otimes M \multimap \bot)$. □

Shared Service Definition and Invocation. Shared service definition and invocation are typed by the linear logic exponentials ! and ?. Type $!A$ types a shared channel that persistently offers a replicated service which whenever invoked spawns a fresh session of type A (from the server's perspective). Dually, type $?A$ types a shared channel on which requests to a persistently replicated service of type A can be unboundedly issued (from the client's perspective). We consider the following typing rules:

$$\frac{P \vdash \Delta; x{:}A, \Theta}{P \vdash \Delta, x{:}?A; \Theta} \; (\text{T?}) \qquad \frac{Q \vdash y{:}A; \Theta}{!x(y).Q \vdash x{:}!A; \Theta} \; (\text{T!}) \qquad \frac{P \vdash \Delta, y{:}A; x{:}A, \Theta}{\overline{x}?(y).P \vdash \Delta; x{:}A, \Theta} \; (\text{Tcopy})$$

The associated principal cut reduction corresponds to shared service invocation

$$(\nu x)(!x(y).Q \mid \overline{x}?(y).P) \rightarrow (\nu x)(!x(y).Q \mid (\nu y)(P \mid Q))$$

This operational interpretation of the rules for $!A$ and $?A$ (cf. [1,4,38], implementing "lazy" contraction) exactly coincides with the usual interpretation of lazy replication. Notice that Rule (T?) is silent on the term assignment: it implements a bookkeeping device to move the typed channel $x{:}?A$ to the unrestricted context, and does not induce a computational effect (e.g., as exchange is also implicitly handled).

As our typing judgments have two different regions, linear and exponential, two cut rules are required [4], one for cutting a linear (session) channel in the linear context (Rule (Tcut), already presented in Sect. 2.2), and the following rule, for cutting an unrestricted (shared) channel in the exponential context [4,38]:

$$\frac{P \vdash y{:}\overline{A}; \Theta \quad Q \vdash \Delta; x{:}A, \Theta}{(\nu x)(!x(y).P \mid Q) \vdash \Delta; \Theta} \; (\text{Tcut}^?)$$

For typing "source programs" only the linear Rule (Tcut) is required, but Rule (Tcut$^?$) is required for cut-elimination; hence, Rule (Tcut$^?$) is a "runtime" typing rule. The principal reduction above is expressed at the level of proofs by

$$\text{Tcut}(x)(\text{T!}(y)(D_1), \text{Tcopy}(y)(D_2)) \rightarrow \text{Tcut}_?(xy)(D_1, \text{Tcut}(y)(D_1, D_2))$$

Example 2.4 (Movie Server (2)). We illustrate the usage of $!A$ and $?A$ types using a shared movie server, which may answer requests from an unbounded number of clients; here we use just two concurrent clients, *SAlice* and *SBob*. Alice still selects the "preview trailer" option as in Example 2.3, but Bob selects the "buy movie" option. Recall the definitions of processes $SBody(s)$ and $Alice(s)$ and type SBT from Example 2.3.

$MOVIES(srv) \triangleq \,!srv(s).SBody(s)$

$\quad Bob(s) \triangleq s.\texttt{inl};\overline{s}(\text{``}inception\text{''}).\overline{s}(bobscard).s(mpeg).s.\texttt{close};\mathbf{0}$

$SAlice(srv) \triangleq \overline{srv}(s).Alice(s) \qquad SBob(srv) \triangleq \overline{srv}(s).Bob(s)$

$\quad System_2 \triangleq (\nu srv)(MOVIES(srv) \mid SAlice(srv) \mid SBob(srv))$

The following typing judgments are derivable:

$MOVIES(srv) \vdash srv :\, !SBT \; ; \; \cdot \qquad SAlice(srv) \vdash \cdot \; ; srv : \overline{SBT}$

$SBob(srv) \vdash \cdot \; ; srv : \overline{SBT} \qquad \qquad Alice(srv) \mid Bob(srv) \vdash srv :\, ?\overline{SBT}; \; \cdot$

We can obtain $System_2 \vdash \cdot; \cdot$ as follows: we first use the (mix) Rule (T $\mid$) to compose the two clients; then, Rule (T?) is used to merge the shared endpoints under the explicit type $?\overline{SBT}$; finally, the clients are composed with the server using Rule (Tcut). $\qquad\qquad\square$

Identity. We interpret the identity axiom by the *forwarder process* $[x \leftrightarrow y]$ [12,48], which denotes a bidirectional (linear) link between sessions x and y, giving a logical justification to a known concept in π-calculi (cf. [24]). The forwarder at type A is typed

$$[x \leftrightarrow y] \vdash x{:}A, y{:}\overline{A}; \Theta \; (\text{Tid})$$

The associated cut reduction $(\nu x)(P \mid [x \leftrightarrow y]) \rightarrow P\{y/x\}$ (where y is not free in P) is akin to the application of an explicit substitution. It is known since [30] that linear forwarders can simulate substitution in the sense of the above reduction rule. We also introduce $[x \leftrightarrow y] \equiv [y \leftrightarrow x]$ as a structural congruence axiom, as a direct consequence of (implicit) exchange in the typing context. While a well-typed copycat process F_A without forwarder links can be easily constructed for any concrete type A by η-expansion (see [13]) the primitive forwarder is important when considering polymorphism [10]. It also allows us to represent the "free" output construct $x\langle y \rangle.P$ (where y is a free channel name in scope) by $\overline{x}(z).([y \leftrightarrow z] \mid P)$ (cf. [7]).

2.3   Non-determinism and Failure

The developments of this paper focus on the challenge of expressing fundamental primitives for non-deterministic behavior—including the special important case of abortable behavior—in the setting of our Curry-Howard correspondence for session types.

It is often believed that a Curry-Howard interpretation of a programming language is hard to reconcile with true (so-called internal) non-determinism in computation, since reduction steps should express at most behavioral equivalences on processes, via proof identities, which are inherently confluent from an operational viewpoint. However, it is clear, at least from work on denotational semantics and functional programming, that non-determinism can be handled equationally by working on the powerdomain of computation results. In the logical setting, developments on differential linear logic [22] also require the interpretation domain for proofs to be closed under a (formal) notion of "sum", which could be interpreted as non-deterministic choice. Although partially inspired by such approaches, our proposal picks a fairly different road, which turns out to lead to the first example of a Curry-Howard interpretation of a realistic programming language with built-in internal non-determinism.

It is well-known after Girard that the linear logic exponential modalities $!A$ and $?A$, which have been used above to model the type of shared channel names, are not uniquely defined by their standard proof rules: not surprisingly, if one adds additional operators defined by the same rules, we obtain independent monad/comonad pairs. We exploit this fact to our advantage, noting that it allows us to modularly add new "exponential" modalities to the base logical system, defined by identical proof rules (in Girard's original formulation), without semantically interfering with the existing ones. Any such pair of connectives (say, $\&A$ and $\oplus A$) will yield a dual monad/comonad pair defined by the fundamental principles (in a simplified form):

$$\frac{\vdash \Delta, A}{\vdash \Delta, \&A} \qquad \frac{\vdash \&\Delta, A}{\vdash \&\Delta, \oplus A}$$

For the usual modalities $!A$ and $?A$, additional specific rules for $?A$ define the intended semantics of the linear logic exponentials, which encapsulate the structural principles of weakening and contraction:

$$\frac{\vdash \Delta}{\vdash \Delta, ?A} \qquad \frac{\vdash \Delta, ?A, ?A}{\vdash \Delta, ?A}$$

These observations suggest a logically justified methodology for adding new monadic operators to the basic linear logic framework, by means of independent monad/comonad pairs in which the monad semantics is defined by specific additional logical principles. We develop our type system on top of (classical) linear logic, conservatively extended with two operators capturing a (co)monad defined by (a refined version of the) following principles, which can be verified to be sound for an (additive) monad $\&-$ and comonad $\oplus-$.

$$\frac{\vdash \Delta, A}{\vdash \Delta, \&A} \qquad \frac{\vdash \&\Delta, A}{\vdash \&\Delta, \oplus A} \qquad \frac{\vdash}{\vdash \&A} \qquad \frac{\vdash \&\Delta \quad \vdash \&\Delta}{\vdash \&\Delta}$$

The resulting proof (and type) system provides a Curry-Howard interpretation of a realistic programming language with built-in internal non-determinism and failure.

Getting back to the presentation of our type system, we capture non-deterministic behavior in the type structure by operators $\&A$ and $\oplus A$ related by duality $(\overline{\&A} = \oplus \overline{A})$ and defined by the following rules:

$$\frac{P \vdash \Delta, x{:}A; \Theta}{x.\overline{\mathsf{some}}; P \vdash \Delta, x{:}\&A; \Theta} \ (\mathrm{T}\&_d^x) \qquad \frac{}{x.\overline{\mathsf{none}} \vdash x{:}\&A; \Theta} \ (\mathrm{T}\&^x)$$

$$\frac{P \vdash \overline{w}{:}\&\Delta, x{:}A; \Theta}{x.\mathsf{some}_{\overline{w}}; P \vdash \overline{w}{:}\&\Delta, x{:}\oplus A; \Theta} \ (\mathrm{T}\oplus_w^x) \qquad \frac{P \vdash \&\Delta; \Theta \quad Q \vdash \&\Delta; \Theta}{P \oplus Q \vdash \&\Delta; \Theta} \ (\mathrm{T}\&)$$

Intuitively, $\&A$ is the type of a session that *may produce* a behavior of type A: this potential is made concrete in Rule $(\mathrm{T}\&_d^x)$ where the behavior $x{:}A$ is indeed available (some), whereas Rule $(\mathrm{T}\&^x)$ describes the case in which $x:A$ is not available (none). Dually, the type $\oplus A$ is the type of a session that *may consume* a behavior of type A. Rule $(\mathrm{T}\oplus_{\overline{w}}^x)$ accounts for the possibility of not being able to consume an A by considering sessions different from x as potentially not available (i.e., abortable - cf. $\overline{w}{:}\&\Delta$ in the rule, where $\overline{w}$ denotes a sequence $w_1, \ldots, w_n$ of names). Rule $(\mathrm{T}\&)$ expresses non-deterministic choice. While it may be seem to correspond to a formal sum of proofs (cf. [22]), in our case it corresponds exactly to non-deterministic choice $P \oplus Q$ of processes[1], and can only be used inside the monad $\&A$. The principal cut reductions are:

$$\mathrm{Tcut}(x)(\mathrm{T}\&_d^x(D_1), \mathrm{T}\oplus_{\overline{w}}^x(D_2)) \to \mathrm{Tcut}(x)(D_1, D_2)$$
$$\mathrm{Tcut}(x)(\mathrm{T}\&^x, \mathrm{T}\oplus_{\overline{w}}^x(D_2)) \to \mathrm{T} \mid (\mathrm{T}\&^{w_1}, \cdots, \mathrm{T}\&^{w_i})$$

At the level of the process interpretation, these reduction rules are expressed by

$$(\nu x)(x.\overline{\mathrm{some}}; P \mid x.\mathrm{some}_{\overline{w}}; Q) \to (\nu x)(P \mid Q)$$
$$(\nu x)(x.\overline{\mathrm{none}} \mid x.\mathrm{some}_{\overline{w}}; Q) \to w_1.\overline{\mathrm{none}} \mid \cdots \mid w_n.\overline{\mathrm{none}}$$

Notice how the reduction for $\overline{\mathrm{none}}$ safely discards the continuation Q. We also consider the following proof conversion (and corresponding process congruence) that expresses the distribution of parallel composition over internal choice:

$$\mathrm{Tcut}(x)(\mathrm{T}\&(D_1, D_2), D_3) \equiv \mathrm{T}\&(\mathrm{Tcut}(x)(D_1, D_3), \mathrm{Tcut}(x)(D_2, D_3))$$
$$(\nu x)(P \mid (Q \oplus R)) \equiv (\nu x)(P \mid Q) \oplus (\nu x)(P \mid R)$$

Notice that, in principle, the two computational reduction rules above could be formally used to express the reduction rules for the "sharing" exponentials (cf. [48]) in presentations of linear logic with explicit weakening and dereliction rules, instead of the DILL-style presentation we have adopted here. Indeed, we prefer the DILL-style presentation as it more tightly express the behavior of sharing present in traditional session types. On the other hand, together with the conversion principle just shown, the primitives and reduction rules just presented turn out to be quite adequate to express the behavior of non-determinism and failure.

Before closing the section, we discuss examples that use $\oplus A$ and $\&A$ types.

Example 2.5 (Movie Server (3)). Getting back to our movie server scenario we illustrate how to model a system with a client $Randy(s)$ that non-deterministically decides between either buying a movie or just seeing its trailer. Recalling process definitions for $SBody(s)$, $Alice(s)$, and $Bob(s)$ from Examples 2.3 and 2.4, we would have:

$$Randy(s) \triangleq s.\overline{\mathrm{some}}; Alice(s) \oplus s.\overline{\mathrm{some}}; Bob(s)$$

$$USystem \triangleq (\nu s)(s.\mathrm{some}_\emptyset; SBody(s) \mid Randy(s))$$

---

[1] We use $\oplus$ for denoting internal non-determinism in processes since this is rather standard; indeed, this notation goes back at least to De Nicola and Hennessy [19].

where the suitable types and type assignments are now given by

$$Randy(s) \vdash s : \& \overline{SBT} \; ; \; \cdot \qquad s.\text{some}_\emptyset; SBody(s) \vdash s : \oplus SBT \; ; \; \cdot$$

Process $Randy(s)$ is typed by using Rule $(\text{T}\&_d^s)$ on each individual client; then, using Rule $(\text{T}\&)$ one would obtain a typed non-deterministic choice between them. The server is typed using Rule $(\text{T}\oplus_{\overline{w}}^s)$ with $\overline{w} = \emptyset$, for there are no sessions (besides s) in the linear context (recall that $SBody(s) \vdash s : SBT \; ; \cdot$). This way, we derive $USystem \vdash \cdot \; ; \; \cdot$. $\qquad \square$

Interestingly, the non-deterministic choices enabled at the level of types by $\&A$ and $\oplus A$ (and at the process level by $\oplus$) are completely orthogonal to the usual deterministic choices enabled by labeled internal and external choices. The following example illustrates the pleasant interaction between deterministic and non-deterministic choices:

Example 2.6 (Movie Server (4)). Consider now a variant of the movie server that logs the request made by the client on a log service l of (boolean) type $\mathbf{B} = \mathbf{1} \oplus \mathbf{1}$. We extend the process $SBody(s)$ from Example 2.3 as follows:

$$SBodyL(s) \triangleq s.\text{case}(s(title).s(card).s\langle movie\rangle.s.\overline{\text{close}} \mid l.\text{inl}; l.\overline{\text{close}},$$
$$s(title).s\langle trailer\rangle.s.\overline{\text{close}} \mid l.\text{inr}; l.\overline{\text{close}})$$

We may provide a typing $SBodyL(s) \vdash s{:}SBT, l{:}\mathbf{B} \; ; \cdot$ which cannot be composed with the non-deterministic client $Randy(s)$ from Example 2.5. However, process

$$s.\text{some}_l; l.\overline{\text{some}}; SBodyL(s)$$

may now be composed with client process $Randy(s)$ as

$$ULSystem \triangleq (\nu s)(s.\text{some}; l.\overline{\text{some}}; SBodyL(s) \mid Randy(s))$$

Now we may derive: $l.\overline{\text{some}}; SBodyL(s) \vdash s{:}SBT, l{:}\&\mathbf{B} \; ; \cdot$ and

$$s.\text{some}_l; l.\overline{\text{some}}; SBodyL(s) \vdash s : \oplus \ SBT, l{:}\&\mathbf{B} \; ; \cdot \qquad ULSystem \vdash l{:}\&\mathbf{B} \; ; \cdot$$

Writing $P \Rightarrow Q$ to denote the reflexive-transitive closure of $P \rightarrow Q$, we obtain the reduction sequence $ULSystem \Rightarrow (l.\text{inr}; l.\overline{\text{close}} \oplus l.\text{inl}; l.\overline{\text{close}})$.

Notice that the visible behavior of log channel l in $ULSystem$ must be given the non-deterministic type $\&\mathbf{B}$: there is no typing $ULSystem \vdash l{:}\mathbf{B}$, since the resulting interaction is essentially non-deterministic. $\qquad \square$

In our system, the ability of representing (internal) non-determinism is intrinsically tied to that of describing, in a completely logically motivated manner, abortable behaviors as typical of programming constructs such as exceptions and compensations [23]. Our following example illustrates this distinctive aspect of our model.

Example 2.7 (Movie Server (5)). To consider the possibility of modeling failure, we introduce the code for a "faulty" client, that non-deterministically behaves like $Bob(s)$ (cf. Example 2.4) or does not produce any behavior at all. Consider the non-deterministic server $SBodyNDL(s)$ from Example 2.6; we may now have:

$$Buzz(s) \triangleq s.\overline{\mathtt{some}}; Bob(s) \oplus s.\overline{\mathtt{none}} \qquad Buzz(s) \vdash s : \&\overline{SBT} \; ; \cdot$$
$$(\nu s)(SBodyNDL(s) \mid Buzz(s)) \vdash l{:}\&\mathbf{B} \; ; \cdot$$

Notice how failure of sub-computations propagates inside the monad $\&-$, encapsulated in a hereditarily safe way. Here, we have the reduction sequence

$$(\nu s)(SBodyNDL(s) \mid Buzz(s)) \Rightarrow (l.\overline{\mathtt{none}} \oplus l.\mathtt{inl}; l.\overline{\mathtt{close}})$$

reflecting that the composed system either aborts or chooses $l.\mathtt{inl}$ on the log. $\square$

We now illustrate how systems encapsulating non-deterministic behavior can nevertheless be given a globally deterministic type, thus showing that internal non-determinism and failure are not visible as long as they are typed by "plain" deterministic types.

Example 2.8. Consider the following processes and typings:

$Some(y) \triangleq y.\overline{\mathtt{some}}; y.\mathtt{inl}; y.\overline{\mathtt{close}} \oplus y.\overline{\mathtt{some}}; y.\mathtt{inr}; y.\overline{\mathtt{close}}$
$Prod \triangleq \overline{x}(y).(Some(y) \mid x.\mathtt{close}; b\langle\text{"}done\text{"}\rangle.b.\overline{\mathtt{close}})$
$Cons \triangleq x(u).(u.\mathtt{some}; u.\mathtt{case}(u.\mathtt{close}; 0, u.\mathtt{close}; 0) \mid x.\overline{\mathtt{close}})$
$Blob \triangleq (\nu x)(Prod \mid Cons)$
$Some(y) \vdash y : \&\mathbf{B} \qquad Prod \vdash x : (\&\mathbf{B}) \otimes \bot, b : Str \otimes 1 \qquad Cons \vdash x{:}(\oplus\overline{\mathbf{B}}) \,\wp\, 1$

Notice that the although the producer process $Prod$ sends a non-deterministic boolean to the consumer process $Cons$, the type of the composed system $Blob$ is $b : Str \otimes 1$, a deterministic type. In fact, we may easily verify that $Blob \Rightarrow b\langle\text{"}done\text{"}\rangle.b.\overline{\mathtt{close}}$. $\square$

Figure 3 summarizes our process language, and associated reduction and structural congruence relations. The main properties of our system will be established next.

3 Main Results

We collect in this section main sanity results for our non-deterministic linear logic-based type system for session process behavior. First, our system enjoys the cut-elimination property. Cut elimination may be derived given a suitable congruence $\cong_s$ on processes consisting of reduction (computational conversions), structural congruence (structural conversions), and some key commuting conversions (cf. [11,13,37]).

Theorem 3.1 (Cut Elimination). *If $P \vdash \Delta; \Theta$ then there is a process Q such that $P \cong_s Q$ and $Q \vdash \Delta; \Theta$ is derivable without using rules (Tcut) and (Tcut?).*

(Processes)

$$P ::= [x \leftrightarrow y] \mid P \mid Q \mid (\nu y)P \mid \mathbf{0}$$
$$\mid \overline{x}(y).P \mid x(y).P \mid \overline{x}?(y).P \mid !x(y).P$$
$$\mid x.\mathsf{case}(P,Q) \mid x.\mathsf{inr}; P \mid x.\mathsf{inl}; P \mid x.\overline{\mathsf{close}} \mid x.\mathsf{close}; P$$
$$\mid P \oplus Q \mid x.\overline{\mathsf{some}}; P \mid x.\overline{\mathsf{none}}; P \mid x.\mathsf{some}_{\overline{w}}; P$$

(Reduction - Contextual Congruence Rules omitted)

$$\overline{x}(y).Q \mid x(y).P \to (\nu y)(Q \mid P) \qquad \overline{x}?(y).Q \mid !x(y).P \to (\nu y)(Q \mid P) \mid !x(y).P$$

$$x.\mathsf{inr}; P \mid x.\mathsf{case}(Q,R) \to P \mid R \qquad x.\mathsf{inl}; P \mid x.\mathsf{case}(Q,R) \to P \mid Q$$

$$(\nu x)([x \leftrightarrow y] \mid P) \to P\{y/x\} \qquad x.\overline{\mathsf{some}}; P \mid x.\mathsf{some}_{\overline{w}}; Q \to P \mid Q$$

$$x.\overline{\mathsf{close}} \mid x.\mathsf{close}; P \to P \qquad x.\overline{\mathsf{none}} \mid x.\mathsf{some}_{\overline{w}}; Q \to w_1.\overline{\mathsf{none}} \mid \dots \mid w_n.\overline{\mathsf{none}}$$

$$P \to Q \Rightarrow (\nu y)P \to (\nu y)Q \qquad P \equiv P', P' \to Q', Q' \equiv Q \Rightarrow P \to Q$$

$$Q \to Q' \Rightarrow P \mid Q \to P \mid Q' \qquad Q \to Q' \Rightarrow P \oplus Q \to P \oplus Q'$$

(Structural Congruence - Contextual Congruence Rules omitted)

$$P \mid \mathbf{0} \equiv P \qquad P \equiv_\alpha Q \Rightarrow P \equiv Q \qquad (\nu x)\mathbf{0} \equiv \mathbf{0} \qquad P \mid Q \equiv Q \mid P$$

$$P \mid (Q \mid R) \equiv (P \mid Q) \mid R \qquad x \notin \mathit{fn}(P) \Rightarrow P \mid (\nu x)Q \equiv (\nu x)(P \mid Q)$$

$$[x \leftrightarrow y] \equiv [y \leftrightarrow x] \qquad (\nu x)(\nu y)P \equiv (\nu y)(\nu x)P \qquad \mathbf{0} \oplus \mathbf{0} \equiv \mathbf{0} \qquad P \oplus Q \equiv Q \oplus P$$

$$P \oplus (Q \oplus R) \equiv (P \oplus Q) \oplus R \qquad (\nu x)(P \mid (Q \oplus R)) \equiv (\nu x)(P \mid Q) \oplus (\nu x)(P \mid R)$$

Fig. 3. The process language.

The proof is an extension of the proof for classical linear logic with mix, but considering the new reductions and conversions introduced above for revealing and reducing principal cuts involving the $\&A$ and $\oplus A$ modalities.

Then, we may state type safety, witnessed by theorems of type preservation and global progress for closed systems. Type preservation states that the observable interface of a system is invariant under reduction.

Theorem 3.2 (Type Preservation). *If $P \vdash \Delta; \Theta$ and $P \to Q$ then $Q \vdash \Delta; \Theta$.*

Proof. (Sketch) By induction on typing derivations, and case analysis on reduction steps. In each case, the result easily follows, given that reductions come from well-defined proof conversions, which by construction preserve typing. ∎

Unlike standard type systems for session types, our logical interpretation satisfies *global progress*, meaning that well-typed processes never get stuck on pending linear communications. More precisely, we say that a process P is *live*, noted $live(P)$, if and only if $P \equiv C[\pi.Q]$ where $C[-]$ is a static context (e.g. a process term context in which the hole is not behind an action prefix, but only under parallel composition $- \mid -$, name restriction $(\nu x)-$, or sum $- \oplus -$ operators) and $\pi.Q$ is not a replicated process (i.e., π is a session input, output, offer, choice, or non-deterministic action). We then have:

Theorem 3.3 (Progress). *If $P \vdash ; \Theta$ and $live(P)$ then there is Q such that $P \to Q$.*

Proof. (Sketch) By induction on the typing derivation. Our proof relies on a contextual progress lemma, which uses a labeled transition system for processes, compatible with reduction (cf. [13]). This lemma yields a more general progress property for processes with free linear channels that transition by means of immediate external interactions. It extends Lemma 4.3 in [13] (which holds for a language without non-determinism) as follows: If $P \vdash \Delta; \Theta$ and $live(P)$ then either (1) there is Q such that $P \rightarrow Q$ or (2) there are P_i ($i = 1..n$) such that $P \equiv \oplus P_i$ and for all P_i there exist Q_i and α such that $P_i \overset{\alpha}{\rightarrow} Q_i$. The proof of this extended lemma is by induction on derivations.   ∎

We now discuss additional results that clarify some key features of the our type system. We say that a process P is *prime* if it is not structurally congruent to a process of the form $Q \oplus R$ with non-trivial (i.e., equivalent to **0**) Q and R. We can then prove:

Proposition 3.4. *Let $P \vdash \Delta; \Theta$ where types in $\Delta; \Theta$ are deterministic (do not contain $\&A$ or $\oplus A$ types at the top level), and let $P \Rightarrow Q \nrightarrow$. Then Q is prime.*

Proof. (Sketch) By induction on the typing derivation.   ∎

Based on a logical system in which reduction matches cut-elimination, it turns out that typing in our system enforces confluence and also strong normalization. These results can be established using (linear) logical relations, as developed in [37]. Intuitively, confluence holds because non-determinism is captured equationally without losing information, by means of delaying choice in processes $P \oplus Q$, which express sets of alternative states. Still, it is interesting to relate our system with standard process calculi which explicitly commit non-deterministic states into alternative components. For that purpose, we investigate the extension of the reduction relation in Fig. 3 with non-confluent rules for internal choice, standard in process calculi but clearly incompatible with any Curry-Howard interpretation, namely $P \oplus Q \rightarrow P$ and $P \oplus Q \rightarrow Q$. We denote by $P \rightarrow_c Q$ (and $P \Rightarrow_c Q$) the extended reduction relation, which can be proven to still satisfy preservation and progress in the sense of Theorems 3.2 and 3.3. We may then show the following property, expressing postponing of internal non-deterministic collapse of non-deterministic states into prime states.

Theorem 3.5 (Postponing). *Let $P \vdash \Delta; \Theta$. We have*

1. *If $P \Rightarrow P_1 \oplus \ldots \oplus P_n \nrightarrow$ with P_i prime for all i, then $P \Rightarrow_c P_i$ for all $0 < i \leq n$.*
2. *Let $\mathcal{C} = \{P_i \mid P \Rightarrow_c P_i \nrightarrow_c$ and P_i is prime $\}$. Then $\mathcal{C}$ is finite up to $\equiv$, with $\#\mathcal{C} = n$, and for all $0 < i \leq n$, $P \Rightarrow P_1 \oplus \ldots \oplus P_n \rightarrow_c P_i$.*

Proof. 1. Trivial by definition. 2. By induction on the reduction sequence, using the fact that we may commute $\Rightarrow$ reduction steps backwards with $\Rightarrow_c$ reduction steps.   ∎

Theorem 3.5(2) shows that no information is lost by $\Rightarrow$ with respect to the (standard) non-deterministic (and non-confluent) semantics of internal choice

$P \oplus Q$ expressed by $\Rightarrow_c$. We may therefore tightly relate our system, based on a logically motivated reduction relation, with a standard non-confluent reduction relation including rules for internal choice, in the sense that the former precisely captures the multiset of observable alternatives defined by the latter, while preserving compositional and equational reasoning about system behavior as expected from a Curry-Howard interpretation.

4   Higher-Order Concurrency, Non Determinism, and Exceptions

We illustrate the expressive power of our typed process model by embedding λ^{exc}, a linear higher-order functional, concurrent programming language with concurrency, non-determinism—including failure—, and exceptions. Defined by a typed compositional encoding, this embedding allows us to showcase the generality of our developments and the relevance of our Curry-Howard correspondence in a broader setting; it will also enable us to give a rigorous footing to our motivating examples (cf. Figs. 1 and 2).

The Target Calculus. λ^{exc} is a typed call-by-value functional calculus, defined by the grammar below. We use $e, e', \ldots$ to range over expressions; $v, v', \ldots$ to range over values; $x, y, z, \ldots$ to range over variables; $c, c', \ldots$ to range over channels, and T, U, A, B to range over types. The syntax of values, expressions, and types (T) is as follows:

$$
\begin{aligned}
v &::= x \mid * \mid \lambda z.e \mid \langle\!\langle v \rangle\!\rangle \\
e &::= v \mid (f\,x) \mid \mathsf{LET}\, a = e_1 \,\mathsf{IN}\, e_2 \\
&\quad \mid\ \mathsf{TRY}\, e_1 \,\mathsf{CATCH}\, z.\, e_2 \mid \mathsf{THROW}\, z \\
&\quad \mid\ \mathsf{LIFT}\, e \mid \mathsf{SOME}\,!\, z; e \mid \mathsf{SOME}\,?\, z; e \mid \mathsf{NONE}\,!\, z; e \mid e_1 \oplus e_2 \\
&\quad \mid\ \mathsf{FORK}\, c.e \mid \mathsf{SEND}(c, e_1); e_2 \mid \mathsf{RECV}(c, z); e \mid \mathsf{CLOSE}\,!\, c; e \mid \mathsf{CLOSE}\,?\, c \\
T &::= \mathbf{unit} \mid A \xrightarrow{T} B \mid A \xrightarrow{0} B \mid !T.T' \mid ?T.T' \mid \mathsf{end}_! \mid \mathsf{end}_? \mid \oplus T \mid \&T
\end{aligned}
$$

We say expressions are *effectful* if they can raise an exception, and *pure* otherwise. Besides the unit type, types for λ^{exc} include (linear) arrow types of two forms: $A \xrightarrow{0} B$ is the type of functions that do not raise exceptions, whereas $A \xrightarrow{T} B$ is the type of functions that may raise an exception of type T. We also have session types $!T.T'$ and $?T.T'$ for output and input channel-based communication. Types for labeled selection and choice are not included but can be easily accommodated. Types $\mathsf{end}_!$ and $\mathsf{end}_?$ denote the dual views of terminated endpoints. Furthermore, we have types $\oplus T$ and $\&T$ for expressions that may produce and consume values of a type T, respectively. We write S, S' to denote the session fragment of the type structure (i.e., no unit nor arrow types). On this fragment, we assume a duality relation, denoted $\overline{S}$, defined as expected. The type syntax does not include general (non-linear) functional values nor shared sessions; the integration of these constructs is orthogonal and unsurprising.

As values, we consider variables, abstractions, and the unit value $*$; we also have the *abortable value* $\langle\!\langle v \rangle\!\rangle$, which represents discardable (affine) values: given a value v of type T, value $\langle\!\langle v \rangle\!\rangle$ will be of type $\oplus T$. For convenience, the language is let-expanded; as a result, application is of the form $(f\,x)$, for variables f and x. Expressions also include a try-catch construct for scoped exceptions, with the expected meaning, and a construct for raising/throwing exceptions with an explicit value. The key features of the process model in Sect. 2 appear as expressions that may produce a value of a certain type and one construct that may consume a value of a certain type. Non-deterministic choices between two expressions are also supported. Concurrency is enabled by spawning threads, using a forking construct. Moreover, λ^{exc} includes expressions for channel-based communication, enabling the exchange of values of any type (including channels).

As mentioned above, the intended operational model for λ^{exc} is call-by-value; rather than directly giving the operational semantics for the language, we first delineate its behavior via a type system and then give its semantics indirectly, via a type respecting encoding into the basic type system introduced in Sect. 2.

The type system we consider here is actually a type-and-effect system in which the effect represents the type of the exception that can be raised by the typed expression. Judgments are then the form $\mathsf{D} \vdash^U e : T$: under an environment D (a set of typing assignments), the expression e has return type T, while the effect type U is either 0 (the expression is pure) or T (the expected type of exceptions).

The typing rules for λ^{exc} are shown in Fig. 4. Rule (ABS) types abstractions; it decrees that the type of the exception possibly raised by the abstraction body will be used as the effect associated to the arrow type. Rule (PRO) types abortable values $\langle\!\langle v \rangle\!\rangle$, as motivated earlier: it closely follows the principles of Rule $(\mathsf{T}\oplus\frac{x}{w})$ for session-based processes; in particular, it requires all free variables in v to be abortable (cf. the premise $\oplus\mathsf{D}$). Rule (LIFT) allows to cast an (trivially) effecful expression from a pure one.

There are three typing rules for let expressions $\mathsf{LET}\,a = e_1\,\mathsf{IN}\,e_2$; the actual rule used depends on the exceptions possibly raised by its constituent subexpressions e_1 and e_2. Rule (LET1) is used when both e_1 and e_2 are effectful. Observe that e_2 must be typable in an abortable environment, in order to safely account for an exception raised in e_1. Rule (LET2) handles the case in which both e_1 and e_2 are pure, while Rule (LET3) covers the case in which only e_1 is pure. These three typing rules are crucial to isolate effects and to exploit the combination of pure with effectful computations.

Rule (TRY) types the construct $\mathsf{TRY}\,e_1\,\mathsf{CATCH}\,x.\,e_2$; the type of the exception possibly raised by e_1 must match with the type of x in e_2. Notice that e_1 and e_2 must be of the same type (T in the rule). Rule (THROW) ensures that the type of the thrown value is propagated as an effect. Rule (FORK) captures the essence of thread spawning for communication types, creating a new (linear) session channel where one endpoint is handed to the thread body and the other endpoint returned by the fork operation. Rules (CLOSE1) and (CLOSE2) type session channel closing operations; Rules (SEND) and (RECV) type operations for sending and receiving values along session channels.

$$\text{VAR} \quad \frac{}{x : T \vdash^U x : T} \qquad \text{ABS} \quad \frac{D, x : A \vdash^U e : B}{D \vdash^{U'} \lambda x.e : A \xrightarrow{U} B} \qquad \text{APP} \quad \frac{D \vdash^U f : A \xrightarrow{U} B \quad D' \vdash^V a : A}{D, D' \vdash^U (f\,a) : B} \qquad \text{UNIT} \quad \frac{}{\vdash^U * : \text{unit}}$$

$$\text{PRO} \quad \frac{\oplus D \vdash^0 v : T}{\oplus D \vdash^0 \langle\!\langle v \rangle\!\rangle : \oplus T} \qquad \text{LIFT} \quad \frac{D \vdash^0 e : B}{D \vdash^T \text{LIFT}\, e : B} \qquad \text{LET1} \quad \frac{D_1 \vdash^T e_1 : A \qquad \oplus D_2, a{:}A \vdash^T e_2 : B}{D_1, \oplus D_2 \vdash^T \text{LET}\, a = e_1 \text{ IN}\, e_2 : B}$$

$$\text{LET2} \quad \frac{D_1 \vdash^0 e_1 : A \qquad D_2, a{:}A \vdash^0 e_2 : B}{D_1, D_2 \vdash^0 \text{LET}\, a = e_1 \text{ IN}\, e_2 : B} \qquad \text{LET3} \quad \frac{D_1 \vdash^0 e_1 : A \qquad D_2, a{:}A \vdash^T e_2{:}B}{D_1, D_2 \vdash^T \text{LET}\, a = e_1 \text{ IN}\, e_2 : B}$$

$$\text{TRY} \quad \frac{D_1 \vdash^U e_1 : T \qquad x : U \vdash^0 e_2 : T}{D_1 \vdash^0 \text{TRY}\, e_1 \text{ CATCH}\, x.e_2 : T} \qquad \text{THROW} \quad \frac{D \vdash^0 z : T}{D \vdash^T \text{THROW}\, z : U} \qquad \text{FORK} \quad \frac{D, x : \overline{S} \vdash^0 e : \text{unit}}{D \vdash^0 \text{FORK}\, x.e : S}$$

$$\text{CLOSE1} \quad \frac{}{c : \text{end}_? \vdash^T \text{CLOSE}?\, c : \text{unit}} \qquad \text{CLOSE2} \quad \frac{D \vdash^T e : \text{unit}}{D, c : \text{end}_! \vdash^T \text{CLOSE}!\, c; e : \text{unit}}$$

$$\text{SEND} \quad \frac{D \vdash^0 a : T_1 \qquad D', c : S \vdash^U e : T}{D, D', c : !T_1.S \vdash^U \text{SEND}(c, a); e : T} \qquad \text{RECV} \quad \frac{D, z : T_1, c : S \vdash^U e : T}{D, c : ?T_1.S \vdash^U \text{RECV}(c, z); e : T}$$

$$\text{SOME1} \quad \frac{D, z : T_1 \vdash^U e : T}{D, z : \oplus T_1 \vdash^U \text{SOME}!\, z; e : T} \qquad \text{SOME2} \quad \frac{\oplus D, z : T \vdash^0 e : \text{unit}}{\oplus D, z : \& T \vdash^0 \text{SOME}?\, z; e : \text{unit}}$$

$$\text{NONE} \quad \frac{D \vdash^U e : T}{D, z : \oplus T_1 \vdash^U \text{NONE}!\, z; e : T} \qquad \text{NONDET} \quad \frac{\oplus D \vdash^0 e_1 : \text{unit} \qquad \oplus D \vdash^0 e_2 : \text{unit}}{\oplus D \vdash^0 e_1 \oplus e_2 : \text{unit}}$$

Fig. 4. Typing rules for λ^{exc}.

Rule (SOME1) and Rule (SOME2) type the production and consumption of a non-deterministic value as z, respectively. In particular, Rule (SOME2) applies to expressions that do not return values, but that may interact with expressions that do return values via channel-based communication. Notice the similarities between Rules (SOME1) and (SOME2) (for functional expressions) and Rules $(\text{T}\&^x_d)$ and $(\text{T}\oplus^x_w)$ (for process terms), respectively. In the same vein, Rule (NONE) can be seen as the analogue of Rule $(\text{T}\&^x)$ but for abortable expressions in our functional language. Rule (NONDET) enables the non-deterministic choice between two pure expressions that do not return values; this allows us to define, e.g., non-deterministic sessions.

In general, the (two-sided) typing rules in Fig. 4 encompass a notion of duality, in the sense that a connective appearing in the left-hand side of the turnstile in the Fig. 4 corresponds to its dual in the right-hand side of the turnstile. This intuition will be captured in our embedding of functional expressions as processes, detailed next.

Example 4.1. We can now return to the code snippet in Fig. 2 and give some typings using the type structure just introduced. As mentioned in the introduction,

$[\![\mathsf{unit}]\!] = \mathbf{1}$

$[\![A \xrightarrow{0} B]\!] = (\overline{[\![A]\!]} \,\otimes\, ((\uparrow[\![B]\!]) \,\otimes\, \bot))$

$[\![A \xrightarrow{U} B]\!] = (\overline{[\![A]\!]} \,\otimes\, ((\&([\![B]\!] \div \overline{[\![U]\!]})) \,\otimes\, (([\![B]\!] \boxplus [\![U]\!]) \,\otimes\, \bot)))$

$[\![!T_1.T_2]\!] = [\![T_1]\!] \otimes \overline{[\![T_2]\!]}$ $[\![?T_1.T_2]\!] = [\![T_1]\!] \,\otimes\, [\![T_2]\!]$

$[\![\oplus T]\!] = \oplus[\![T]\!]$ $[\![\& T]\!] = \&[\![T]\!]$ $[\![\mathsf{end}_!]\!] = \bot$ $[\![\mathsf{end}_?]\!] = \mathbf{1}$

Fig. 5. Encoding of λ^{exc} types into logical propositions.

there is a precise stage of the protocol along (dual) names res and f after which failure is safe. In our type structure we can precisely delineate such a place. We would have:

l : ?string.?string.end$_?$ log : !string.!string.end$_!$

f : ?string.!int.$\oplus$(?string.end$_?$) res : !string.?int.$\&$(!string.end$_!$)

These typings require minor modifications in the code of Fig. 2: we add prefix 'SOME ? f' before 'RECV(f, bk)', and prefix 'SOME ! res' before 'SEND$(res, book)$'.

Embedding λ^{exc} Into Session Typed Processes. We now present a typeful encoding of λ^{exc} into the logically motivated typed process model of Sect. 2, and establish its correctness (Theorem 4.1). The encoding has two main components: the encoding of (functional) types into linear logic based session types, and the encoding of λ^{exc} expressions into (non-deterministic) concurrent processes.

Figure 5 gives the encoding of types. We use the following shorthand notations:

$$\uparrow[\![T]\!] \triangleq [\![T]\!] \otimes \mathbf{1} \tag{1}$$

$$[\![U]\!] \boxplus [\![T]\!] \triangleq ([\![U]\!] \otimes \mathbf{1}) \oplus ([\![T]\!] \otimes \mathbf{1}) \tag{2}$$

$$\&([\![T]\!] \div \overline{[\![U]\!]}) \triangleq \&([\![T]\!] \otimes ((\overline{[\![U]\!]} \boxplus \overline{[\![T]\!]}) \otimes \mathbf{1})) \tag{3}$$

Also, we assume the expected extension of the encoding of types to typing environments: given $\mathsf{D} = x_1{:}T_1, \cdots, x_n{:}T_n$ then $[\![\mathsf{D}]\!] = x_1{:}[\![T_1]\!], \cdots, x_n{:}[\![T_n]\!]$.

The encoding of expressions is typeful: for each typing rule in Fig. 4 we give a corresponding type derivation for session-typed processes. Figures 6 and 7 give a complete account; for readability, in those figures we show only the conclusion (final judgment) in the derivation. Also, we use the following abbreviations for processes:

– we write $y\langle z \rangle.P$ (where z is free in P) for the free output process, represented as $\overline{y}(w).([w \leftrightarrow z] \mid P)$ (cf. Sect. 2);
– we write $y.0; P$ and $y.\overline{0}$ to stand for $y.\mathsf{close}; P$ and $y.\overline{\mathsf{close}}$, respectively;
– we define S_q as the process $q(u).q.0; u.0; \mathbf{0}$. Notice that $\mathsf{S}_q \vdash q : \uparrow[\![\mathsf{unit}]\!]$.

$$\left[\!\!\left[\frac{}{z:T \vdash^0 z:T}\right]\!\!\right]^y = \overline{y\langle z\rangle.y.\overline{0} \vdash z:\overline{\overline{[T]}}, y: \uparrow[T]}$$

$$\left[\!\!\left[\frac{U \neq 0}{z:T \vdash^U z:T}\right]\!\!\right]^{y,x} = \overline{y.\overline{\mathsf{some}}; y\langle z\rangle.y\langle x\rangle.y.\overline{0} \vdash z:\overline{\overline{[T]}}, y:\&([T] \div \overline{[U]}), x:[U] \boxplus [T]}$$

$$\left[\!\!\left[\frac{D, z:A \vdash^0 e:B}{D \vdash^0 \lambda z.e:A \xrightarrow{0} B}\right]\!\!\right]^y = \overline{\overline{y}(f).(y.\overline{0} \mid f(z).f(k).f.0; [e]_k) \vdash \overline{[D]}, y: \uparrow[A \xrightarrow{0} B]}$$

$$\left[\!\!\left[\frac{D, z:A \vdash^U e:B}{D \vdash^0 \lambda z.e:A \xrightarrow{U} B}\right]\!\!\right]^y = \overline{\overline{y}(f).(y.\overline{0} \mid f(z).f(k).f(j).f.0; [e]_{k,j}) \vdash \overline{[D]}, y: \uparrow[A \xrightarrow{U} B]}$$

$$\left[\!\!\left[\frac{D, z:A \vdash^U e:B}{D \vdash^V \lambda z.e:A \xrightarrow{U} B}\right]\!\!\right]^{y,x} = \frac{y.\overline{\mathsf{some}}; \overline{y}(f).(y\langle x\rangle.y.\overline{0} \mid f(z).f(k).f(j).f.0; [e]_{k,j})}{\vdash \overline{[D]}, y:\&([A \xrightarrow{U} B] \div \overline{[V]}), x:[V] \boxplus [A \xrightarrow{U} B]}$$

$$\left[\!\!\left[\frac{D \vdash^U f:A \xrightarrow{T} B \quad D' \vdash^V a:A}{D, D' \vdash^T (f\,a):B}\right]\!\!\right]^{y,x} = \frac{f\langle a\rangle.f\langle y\rangle.f\langle x\rangle.f.\overline{0} \vdash f:[A \xrightarrow{T} B],}{y:\&([B] \div \overline{[T]}), x:[T] \boxplus [B], a:\overline{[A]}}$$

$$\left[\!\!\left[\frac{D \vdash^U f:A \xrightarrow{0} B \quad D' \vdash^V a:A}{D, D' \vdash^0 (f\,a):B}\right]\!\!\right]^y = \overline{f\langle a\rangle.f\langle y\rangle.f\langle x\rangle.f.\overline{0} \vdash f:[A \xrightarrow{0} B], y: \uparrow[B], a:\overline{[A]}}$$

$$\left[\!\!\left[\frac{D_1 \vdash^0 e_1:A \quad D_2, a:A \vdash^0 e_2:B}{D_1, D_2 \vdash^0 \mathsf{LET}\, a = e_1 \mathsf{IN}\, e_2:B}\right]\!\!\right]^y = \overline{(\nu q)([e_1]_q \mid q(a).q.0; [e_2]_y) \vdash \overline{[D_1]}, \overline{[D_2]}, y: \uparrow[B]}$$

$$\left[\!\!\left[\frac{D_1 \vdash^0 e_1:A \quad D_2, a:A \vdash^T e_2:B}{D_1, D_2 \vdash^T \mathsf{LET}\, a = e_1 \mathsf{IN}\, e_2:B}\right]\!\!\right]^{y,x} = \frac{(\nu q)([e_1]_q \mid q(a).q.0; [e_2]_{y,x})}{\vdash \overline{[D_1]}, \overline{[D_2]}, y:\&([B] \div \overline{[T]}), x:[T] \boxplus [B]}$$

$$\left[\!\!\left[\frac{D_1 \vdash^T e_1:A \quad \oplus D_2, a:A \vdash^T e_2:B}{D_1, \oplus D_2 \vdash^T \mathsf{LET}\, a = e_1 \mathsf{IN}\, e_2:B}\right]\!\!\right]^{y,x} = \frac{(\nu q)([e_1]_{q,x} \mid q.\mathsf{some}_D; q(a).q(s).q.0; [e_2]_{y,s})}{\vdash \overline{[D_1]}, \&\overline{[D_2]}, y:\&([B] \div \overline{[T]}), x:[T] \boxplus [B]}$$

$$\left[\!\!\left[\frac{D \vdash^0 e:B}{D \vdash^T \mathsf{LIFT}\, e:B}\right]\!\!\right]^{y,x} = \frac{(\nu q)([e]_q \mid q(v).q.0; y.\overline{\mathsf{some}}; y\langle v\rangle.y\langle x\rangle.y.\overline{0})}{\vdash \overline{[D]}, y:\&([T] \div \overline{[B]}), x:[T] \boxplus [B]}$$

$$\left[\!\!\left[\frac{\oplus D \vdash^0 v:T}{\oplus D \vdash^0 \langle\!\langle v\rangle\!\rangle : \oplus T}\right]\!\!\right]^y = \frac{\overline{y}(z).(z.\mathsf{some}_D; (\nu q)([v]_q \mid q(u).q.0; [u \leftrightarrow z]) \mid y.\overline{0})}{\vdash \&\overline{[D]}, y: \uparrow(\oplus[T])}$$

Fig. 6. Typeful encoding of λ^{exc} terms into basic processes (Part 1).

As usual in encodings of (call-by-value) functional languages into the π-calculus, our encoding of expressions is indexed by names, which are used to interact with the environment; they can be seen as *continuations* or as *locations* where the value returned by an expression will be made available. In our case, these names are related to the effects of the source expression e:

$$\left[\!\!\left[\dfrac{D_1 \vdash^U e_1 : T \quad z : U \vdash^0 e_2 : T}{D_1 \vdash^0 \text{TRY } e_1 \text{ CATCH } z.\, e_2 : T} \right]\!\!\right]_y = \begin{array}{l} (\nu j)((\nu k)([e_1]_{k,j} \mid \\ \quad k.\text{some}_\emptyset; k(u).k(z).k.0; z.\text{inl}; z\langle u\rangle.z.\overline{0}) \mid \\ \quad j.\text{case}(j(u).j.0; y\langle u\rangle.y.\overline{0},\ j(z).j.0; [e_2]_y)) \\ \quad \vdash \overline{[D_1]}, y: \uparrow[T] \end{array}$$

$$\left[\!\!\left[\dfrac{D \vdash^0 z : T}{D \vdash^T \text{THROW } z : U} \right]\!\!\right]_{y,x} = \dfrac{y.\overline{\text{none}} \mid x.\text{inr}; x\langle z\rangle.x.\overline{0}}{\vdash \overline{[D]}, y:\&([T] \div \overline{[U]}), x:[T] \boxplus [U]}$$

$$\left[\!\!\left[\dfrac{D, x : S \vdash^0 e : \textbf{unit}}{D \vdash^0 \text{FORK } x.e : \overline{S}} \right]\!\!\right]_y = \overline{y}(x).((\nu q)([e]_q \mid S_q) \mid y.\overline{0}) \vdash \overline{[D]}, y: \uparrow[\overline{S}]$$

$$\left[\!\!\left[\dfrac{D, z : S \vdash^U e : T}{D, z : \oplus S \vdash^U \text{SOME}!z; e : T} \right]\!\!\right]_{y,x} = \dfrac{z.\overline{\text{some}}; [e]_{y,x} \vdash \overline{[D]}, z:\&[S], y:\&([T] \div \overline{[U]}),}{x:[U] \boxplus [T]}$$

$$\left[\!\!\left[\dfrac{\oplus D, z : S \vdash^0 e : \textbf{unit}}{\oplus D, z : \& S \vdash^0 \text{SOME}?z; e : \textbf{unit}} \right]\!\!\right]_y = \dfrac{z.\text{some}_D; (\nu q)([e]_q \mid S_q) \mid \overline{y}(v).(v.\overline{0} \mid y.\overline{0})}{\vdash \&\overline{[D]}, z: \oplus \overline{[S]}, y: \uparrow[\textbf{unit}]}$$

$$\left[\!\!\left[\dfrac{D \vdash^U e : T}{D, z : \oplus S \vdash^U \text{NONE}!z; e : T} \right]\!\!\right]_{y,x} = \dfrac{z.\overline{\text{none}} \mid [e]_{y,x} \vdash \overline{[D]}, z:\&[S], y:\&([T] \div \overline{[U]}),}{x:[U] \boxplus [T]}$$

$$\left[\!\!\left[\dfrac{D \vdash^0 a : T_1 \quad D', c : T_2 \vdash^U e : T}{D, D', c : !T_1.T_2 \vdash^U \text{SEND}(c,a); e : T} \right]\!\!\right]_{y,x} = \dfrac{c\langle a\rangle.[e]_{y,x} \vdash \overline{[D']}, c:\overline{[T_1]} \otimes \overline{[T_2]},}{y:\&([T] \div \overline{[U]}), x:[U] \boxplus [T], a:\overline{[T_1]}}$$

$$\left[\!\!\left[\dfrac{D, z : T_1, c : T_2 \vdash^U e : T}{D, c : ?T_1.T_2 \vdash^U \text{RECV}(c,z); e : T} \right]\!\!\right]_{y,x} = \dfrac{c(z).[e]_{y,x} \vdash \overline{[D]}, c:\overline{[T_1]} \otimes \overline{[T_2]},}{y:\&([T] \div \overline{[U]}), x:[U] \boxplus [T]}$$

$$\left[\!\!\left[\dfrac{\oplus D \vdash^0 e_1 : \textbf{unit} \quad \oplus D \vdash^0 e_2 : \textbf{unit}}{\oplus D \vdash^0 e_1 \oplus e_2 : \textbf{unit}} \right]\!\!\right]_y = \dfrac{((\nu z)([e_1]_z \mid S_z) \oplus (\nu z)([e_2]_z \mid S_z)) \mid [*]_y}{\vdash \&\overline{[D]}, y: \uparrow[\textbf{unit}]}$$

$$\left[\!\!\left[\dfrac{D \vdash^T e : \textbf{unit}}{D, c : \text{end}_! \vdash^T \text{CLOSE}!c; e : \textbf{unit}} \right]\!\!\right]_{y,x} = \dfrac{c.\overline{0} \mid [e]_{y,x}}{\vdash c:\overline{[\text{end}_!]}, y:\&([\textbf{unit}] \div \overline{[T]}), x:[\textbf{unit}] \boxplus [T]}$$

$$\left[\!\!\left[\dfrac{}{c : \text{end}_? \vdash^T \text{CLOSE}?c : \textbf{unit}} \right]\!\!\right]_{y,x} = \dfrac{c.0; 0 \mid y.\overline{\text{some}}; \overline{y}(r).(r.\overline{0} \mid y\langle x\rangle.y.\overline{0})}{\vdash c:\overline{[\text{end}_?]}, y:\&([\textbf{unit}] \div \overline{[T]}), x:[T] \boxplus [\textbf{unit}]}$$

$$\left[\!\!\left[\dfrac{}{\cdot \vdash^0 * : \textbf{unit}} \right]\!\!\right]_y = \overline{y}(u).(u.\overline{0} \mid y.\overline{0}) \vdash y: \uparrow[\textbf{unit}]$$

Fig. 7. Typeful encoding of λ^{exc} terms into basic processes (Part 2).

- If e is pure then its encoding will be indexed by a single continuation name y. This will be denoted $[e]_y$.
- If e is effectful then its encoding will be indexed by names y and x. This will be denoted $[e]_{y,x}$: name y represents an *non-deterministic* continuation, along which the value to which e reduces *may be produced*; name x represents the continuation to the enclosing try-catch block exception handler.

These intuitive distinctions are made precise in our main technical result, which exploits the shorthand notations (1), (2), and (3) above:

Theorem 4.1 (Typability). *Suppose* $D \vdash^U e : T$. *Then, for some names* y, x, *we have:*

- $[e]_y \vdash \overline{[D]}, y{:} \uparrow [T]$, *if* $U = 0$.
- $[e]_{y,x} \vdash \overline{[D]}, y{:}\&([T] \div \overline{[U]}), x{:}[U] \boxplus [T]$, *if* $U \neq 0$.

Consequently, our source language λ^{exc} (which combines functions, concurrency, non-determinism, and exceptions) will inherit key guarantees from the target process language, namely preservation and global progress (deadlock absence and lock-freedom).

Due to space limitations, in the following we only discuss selected cases of Figs. 6 and 7. As already mentioned, the type of a let expression $\mathsf{LET}\, a = e_1\, \mathsf{IN}\, e_2$ considers different possibilities for the interplay of pure and effectful computations in e_1 and e_2. If both expressions are pure (cf. Rule (LET2)) then the encoding is simple:

$$[\mathsf{LET}\, a = e_1\, \mathsf{IN}\, e_2]_y = (\nu q)([e_1]_q \mid q(a).q.0; [e_2]_y)$$

Since e_1 is pure, we know $[e_1]_q$ will surely produce a value, which will be made available to $[e_2]_y$ along the private (linear) name q. The case in which both e_1 and e_2 may raise exceptions (cf. Rule (LET1)) is more interesting:

$$[\mathsf{LET}\, a = e_1\, \mathsf{IN}\, e_2]_{y,x} = (\nu q)([e_1]_{q,x} \mid q.\mathsf{some}_D; q(a).q(s).q.0; [e_2]_{y,s})$$

In this case, since e_1 may raise an exception, we account for this possibility via the prefix $q.\mathsf{some}_D$, which requires all values (including sessions) in $[e_2]_{y,s}$ (excepting a) to be in abortable state. The production of a value within $[e_1]_{q,x}$ will be signaled by a prefix $q.\overline{\mathsf{some}}$, while throwing of an exception will be signaled by a prefix $q.\overline{\mathsf{none}}$ (see next). Therefore, if $[e_1]_{q,x}$ produces a value ($q.\overline{\mathsf{some}}$ is executed) then this value will be passed to $[e_2]_{q,s}$ using the private name q; subsequently, the reference to the enclosing try-block x will also be passed to $[e_2]_{q,s}$ as parameter s, exploiting linearity of name-passing (delegation). Otherwise, if $[e_1]_{q,x}$ ever raises an exception ($q.\overline{\mathsf{none}}$ is executed) then all the values in D will be safely and hereditarily discarded.

The encoding of values takes into account that a value may occur in an abortable context. The encoding of a variable z of type T is as follows:

$$[z]_y = y\langle z \rangle . y . \overline{0} \qquad\qquad [z]_{y,x} = y.\overline{\mathsf{some}}; y\langle z \rangle . y\langle x \rangle . y . \overline{0}$$

If z occurs in a pure context/expression, then its encoding, given on the left, is standard; name y will have type $\uparrow [T]$ (cf. (1)). Otherwise, if z occurs in an effectful (abortable) context, then its encoding, given on the right, first announces the production of a value using prefix $y.\overline{\mathsf{some}}$; after z is sent along y, name x (representing the continuation of the enclosing try-catch block exception handler) will be sent along y. The type of x will be $[U] \boxplus [T]$, where U is the type of the enclosing exception (cf. (2)). Thus, intuitively, x encompasses the potential for a normal execution ($\llbracket T \rrbracket$) but also contains information on the (exceptional) behavior to be triggered upon failure ($\llbracket U \rrbracket$). A more concrete justification for the typing $x{:}\llbracket U \rrbracket \boxplus \llbracket T \rrbracket$ will become apparent next, when discussing the deterministic choice that underlies the encoding of try-catch and throw expressions.

To encode an abstraction $\lambda z.e$, we distinguish several cases, depending on whether e and $\lambda z.e$ are effectful or not. The simplest case is when both e and $\lambda z.e$ are pure:

$$[\lambda z.e]_y = \overline{y}(f).(y.\overline{0} \mid f(z).f(k).f.0; [e]_k)$$

We follow closely known encodings of λ-calculus in the π-calculus, here adapted to a linear setting in which the continuation y and the reference to the function body f are session-typed [43]. When both $\lambda z.e$ and e are effectful we follow a similar principle:

$$[\lambda z.e]_{y,x} = y.\overline{\text{some}}; \overline{y}(f).(y\langle x\rangle.y.\overline{0} \mid f(z).f(k).f(j).f.0; [e]_{k,j})$$

The prefix $y.\overline{\text{some}}$ declares the production of a value, namely the reference to the function body f. An invocation to f must supply the parameter of the function (z) but also the continuations k and j, to be linearly used by the encoding $[e]_{k,j}$.

The encoding of applications goes hand in hand with the encoding of let expressions. Given the let-expanded semantics (which forces an expression's context to deal with potentially abortable expressions), the encoding of applications $(f\, a)$ is simple:

$$[(f\, a)]_{y,x} = f\langle a\rangle.f\langle y\rangle.f\langle x\rangle.f.\overline{0}$$

We may now discuss the encodings of try-catch and throw expressions:

$$[\text{TRY } e_1 \text{ CATCH } z.\, e_2]_y = (\nu j)((\nu k)([e_1]_{k,j} \mid \underbrace{k.\text{some}_\emptyset; k(u).k(z).k.0; z.\text{inl}; z\langle u\rangle.z.\overline{0})}_{\text{(I)}} \mid$$

$$\underbrace{j.\text{case}(j(u).j.0; y\langle u\rangle.y.\overline{0}\, ,\ j(z).j.0; [e_2]_y))}_{\text{(II)}}$$

$$[\text{THROW } z]_{y,x} = y.\overline{\text{none}} \mid x.\text{inr}; x\langle z\rangle.x.\overline{0}$$

The encoding of TRY e_1 CATCH $z.\, e_2$ is in two parts, denoted (I) and (II) above. Part (I) concerns normal behaviors only; Part (II) concerns normal and exceptional behaviors:

– If e_1 does not raise an exception then $[e_1]_{k,j}$ will trigger a prefix $k.\overline{\text{some}}$, which will synchronize with Part (I). Subsequently, the obtained value and the reference to the enclosing exception block will be passed around; in this case, z will be substituted by j, and the prefix $j.\text{inl}$ will synchronize with the choice on j (Part (II)) to send the resulting value along y. This choice discards the right branch containing $[e_2]_y$.

- If e_1 raises an exception then, because of the encoding of throw, process $[e_1]_{k,j}$ will trigger a prefix $k.\overline{\mathsf{none}}$ which will synchronize with Part (I). As a result, the remaining behavior on k and z will be discarded. However, the choice on j (Part (II)) will continue to be available: this is used by the encoding of throw, which by executing $j.\mathsf{inr}$ will select the right branch of Part (II). The value raised by the exception will be then passed to $[e_2]_y$, which can now be executed.

Our encoding of try-catch therefore elegantly amalgamates the key features of our process model: most notably, the presence of abortable behaviors in a pleasant coexistence with non-abortable behaviors, and the interplay between non-deterministic and deterministic choices—indeed, it is the deterministic choice that underlies the exception mechanism what ultimately justifies the type $[U] \boxplus [T]$ for x, given in (2).

In the typed model presented here (and its encoding into processes), we consider try-catch constructs $\mathsf{TRY}\ e_1\ \mathsf{CATCH}\ z.\,e_2$ in which e_2 is pure (cf. Fig. 4). However, there is no fundamental obstacle to address the general case in which both e_1 and e_2 may raise exceptions; the encoding given in Fig. 7 can be extended following expected lines.

Constructs for non-deterministic behaviors have fairly straightforward encodings:

$$[\mathsf{SOME}\,!\,z; e]_{y,x} = z.\overline{\mathsf{some}}; [e]_{y,x} \qquad [\mathsf{NONE}\,!\,z; e]_{y,x} = z.\overline{\mathsf{none}} \mid [e]_{y,x}$$

$$[\mathsf{SOME}\,?\,z; e]_{y,x} = z.\mathsf{some}_D; (\nu q)([e]_q \mid S_q) \mid \overline{y}(v).(v.\overline{0} \mid y.\overline{0})$$

In $[\mathsf{SOME}\,?\,z; e]_{y,x}$, notice that typing ensures that e does not return a value; also, set D enables to safely discard behaviors in e in the event of an exception. Given the conditions ensured by typing, the encoding of non-deterministic choices is unsurprising:

$$[e_1 \oplus e_2]_y = ((\nu z)([e_1]_z \mid S_z) \oplus (\nu z)([e_2]_z \mid S_z)) \mid [*]_y$$

In essence, processes S_z consume the (unit) value produced by $[e_1]_y$ and $[e_2]_y$ through z. The resulting processes can then be composed first in a non-deterministic choice, and then in an independent parallel composition with $[*]_y$. It would not be hard to extend this encoding to handle the general case in which e_1 and e_2 may raise exceptions and return values different from $\mathbf{unit}$. To that end, typing should ensure that e_1 and e_2 are each typable in an abortable context (cf. Rule (T&)), but also that the name representing the continuation to the enclosing exception handlers (i.e., x) is given an abortable type.

5   Further Related Work

In the purely functional (and sequential) programming setting, control operators have been given Curry-Howard interpretations in the context of classical logic [2,26,36]. To our best knowledge, this paper presents the first attempt at tackling state-aware concurrent programming features, involving linearity (our main focus herein), while building on a Curry-Howard interpretation of classical linear logic as session types. A very tentative sketch of some ideas behind this work was presented at Cardelli's Fest [8]; here we provide a complete account of non-determinism and failure, introduce new computational primitives, present associated results, and provide non-trivial examples, including the typeful embedding of a realistic functional, concurrent language with exceptions.

The tensions between affinity, linearity and control effects have been widely investigated in different settings, and already referred in the introduction. The work [45] considers a form of affinity in stateful settings (including session types) and explores how to safely interface an affine language with a conventional one. We share several high level aims with [45], although following a fundamentally different approach, and obtaining results of different relevance; in particular, we consider a unified (concurrent) language that admits a fundamental Curry-Howard correspondence with linear logic, and offers strong guarantees by static typing such as deadlock-freedom. Within the session types literature, the interplay of session types and functional languages (including encodings of functional calculi) has received much attention (see, e.g., [25,32,35,48]) but non-determinism/failure do not seem to have been addressed. The paper [35] relates effect and session type systems, but effects such as exceptions are not addressed. A work exploring affinity in session calculi is [34]. Existing works on exception mechanisms for session types impose severe syntactic restrictions to typable programs and/or do not ensure progress: this observation applies to models of interactional exceptions and interruptible sessions based on both binary sessions (cf. [15]) and multiparty sessions (cf. [14,21]). Further work is required to connect our process model (based on binary session types) with multiparty structured interactions with exceptions/interruptions, following logic-based relationships between binary and multiparty session types [9].

Also related are [3,17]. The work in [3] explores forms of non-determinism and failure via the conflation of additive connectives. This is quite different from our approach, which is based on a new pair of monadic/comonadic connectives, fully justified by a Curry-Howard interpretation and expressive enough to represent forms of affinity and exceptions. The work in [17] does have non-determinism at the level of processes, but its expressiveness is not analyzed, and non-determinism at the level of types is not addressed. In contrast, we provide types for non-determinism via specific connectives in the context of a Curry-Howard correspondence, and exploit the expressiveness of the non-deterministic process model by modeling a realistic functional language.

As explained in the introduction, a main aim of this work is not just to propose yet another point in the design space solution for exceptions, affinity, or linearity. Instead, we show how a small set of logically motivated primitives is expressive enough to model fairly general notions of (controlled) affinity and non-determinism in higher-order concurrent programs (including exception handling) while preserving all the fundamental properties of a Curry-Howard interpretation for linear logic. We leave for future work a deeper study of the expressiveness of our model, as exceptions and compensations are key programming abstractions in models of service-oriented computing (see, e.g., [23]).

6 Concluding Remarks

We have presented the first type system that accommodates non-deterministic and abortable behaviors within session-based concurrent programs while building on a Curry-Howard correspondence with linear logic. Conceptually simple, our approach conservatively extends classical linear logic with two dual modal connectives, related to linear logic exponentials, but that express non-determinism and failure rather than sharing.

We have shown that our type system enforces progress and session fidelity; its underlying operational semantics, based on Curry-Howard principles, is actually compatible with standard non-confluent formulations of internal non-determinism for process algebra, in the sense of our postponing result (Theorem 3.5). Our system is very expressive, as illustrated by several examples, including a typed embedding of a higher-order linear functional language with threads, sessions, non-determinism, and exceptions.

We have not discussed the presence of intuitionistic (unrestricted) types in the functional language of Sect. 4, as the main focus in the paper is on linearity and its challenging combination with non-determinism and failure. The combination of these ingredients with general (non-linear) functional values and shared sessions would be as expected, resulting from the type discipline of the interpretation of the exponentials in the basic model. Also, key properties of our type system such as strong normalization and confluence can be established along predictable lines [37]. A further advantage of our approach is its natural compatibility with other extensions to the basic framework, for example behavioral polymorphism [10]. Another interesting direction for future work is to better understand the behavioral equivalences induced by our interpretation.

Acknowledgments. Thanks to the anonymous reviewers for useful remarks and suggestions. This work has been partially sponsored by FCT PEst/UID/ CEC/04516/2013; by FCT CLAY PTDC/EEI-CTP/4293/2014; by EU COST Actions IC1201 (BETTY), IC1402 (ARVI), and IC1405 (Reversible Computation); and by CNRS PICS project 07313 (SuCCeSS).

References

1. Andreoli, J.-M.: Logic programming with focusing proofs in linear logic. J. Log. Comput. **2**(3), 297–347 (1992)
2. Ariola, Z.M., Herbelin, H.: Minimal classical logic and control operators. In: Baeten, J.C.M., Lenstra, J.K., Parrow, J., Woeginger, G.J. (eds.) ICALP 2003. LNCS, vol. 2719, pp. 871–885. Springer, Heidelberg (2003). doi:10.1007/ 3-540-45061-0_68

3. Atkey, R., Lindley, S., Morris, J.G.: Conflation confers concurrency. In: Lindley, S., McBride, C., Trinder, P., Sannella, D. (eds.) A List of Successes That Can Change the World. LNCS, vol. 9600, pp. 32–55. Springer, Heidelberg (2016). doi:10.1007/978-3-319-30936-1_2
4. Barber, A.: Dual intuitionistic linear logic. Technical report LFCS-96-347 University of Edinburgh (1996)
5. Benton, P.N., Bierman, G.M., de Paiva, V.: Computational types from a logical perspective. J. Funct. Program. **8**(2), 177–193 (1998)
6. Benton, N., Bierman, G., Paiva, V., Hyland, M.: A term calculus for intuitionistic linear logic. In: Bezem, M., Groote, J.F. (eds.) TLCA 1993. LNCS, vol. 664, pp. 75–90. Springer, Heidelberg (1993). doi:10.1007/BFb0037099
7. Boreale, M.: On the expressiveness of internal mobility in name-passing calculi. Theor. Comput. Sci. **195**(2), 205–226 (1998)
8. Caires, L.: Types and logic, concurrency and non-determinism. In: Abadi, M., Gardner, P., Gordon, A.D., Mardare, R. (eds.) Essays for the Luca Cardelli Fest, pp. 69–83. Microsoft Research TR MSR-TR–104 (2014)
9. Caires, L., Pérez, J.A.: Multiparty session types within a canonical binary theory, and beyond. In: Albert, E., Lanese, I. (eds.) FORTE 2016. LNCS, vol. 9688, pp. 74–95. Springer, Heidelberg (2016). doi:10.1007/978-3-319-39570-8_6
10. Caires, L., Pérez, J.A., Pfenning, F., Toninho, B.: Behavioral polymorphism and parametricity in session-based communication. In: Felleisen, M., Gardner, P. (eds.) ESOP 2013. LNCS, vol. 7792, pp. 330–349. Springer, Heidelberg (2013). doi:10.1007/978-3-642-37036-6_19
11. Caires, L., Pfenning, F.: Session types as intuitionistic linear propositions. In: Gastin, P., Laroussinie, F. (eds.) CONCUR 2010. LNCS, vol. 6269, pp. 222–236. Springer, Heidelberg (2010). doi:10.1007/978-3-642-15375-4_16
12. Caires, L., Pfenning, F., Toninho, B.: Towards concurrent type theory. In: Types in Language Design and Implementation, pp. 1–12 (2012)
13. Caires, L., Pfenning, F., Toninho, B.: Linear logic propositions as session types. Math. Struct. Comput. Sci. **26**(03), 367–423 (2016)
14. Capecchi, S., Giachino, E., Yoshida, N.: Global escape in multiparty sessions. Math. Struct. Comput. Sci. **26**(2), 156–205 (2016)
15. Carbone, M., Honda, K., Yoshida, N.: Structured interactional exceptions in session types. In: Breugel, F., Chechik, M. (eds.) CONCUR 2008. LNCS, vol. 5201, pp. 402–417. Springer, Heidelberg (2008). doi:10.1007/978-3-540-85361-9_32
16. Carbone, M., Lindley, S., Montesi, F., Schürmann, C., Wadler, P.: Coherence generalises duality: a logical explanation of multiparty session types. In: CONCUR 2016, pp. 3:1–33:15 (2016)
17. Carbone, M., Montesi, F., Schürmann, C., Yoshida, N.: Multiparty session types as coherence proofs. In: Proceedings of CONCUR 2015. LIPIcs, vol. 42, pp. 412–426. Schloss Dagstuhl (2015)
18. Cardelli, L.: Typeful Programming. IFIP State-of-the-Art Reports: Formal Description of Programming Concepts, pp. 431–507 (1991)
19. Nicola, R., Hennessy, M.: CCS without τ's. In: Ehrig, H., Kowalski, R., Levi, G., Montanari, U. (eds.) CAAP 1987. LNCS, vol. 249, pp. 138–152. Springer, Heidelberg (1987). doi:10.1007/3-540-17660-8_53
20. DeLine, R., Fähndrich, M.: Typestates for objects. In: Odersky, M. (ed.) ECOOP 2004. LNCS, vol. 3086, pp. 465–490. Springer, Heidelberg (2004). doi:10.1007/978-3-540-24851-4_21

21. Demangeon, R., Honda, K., Hu, R., Neykova, R., Yoshida, N.: Practical interruptible conversations: distributed dynamic verification with multiparty session types and python. Formal Methods Syst. Des. **46**(3), 197–225 (2015)
22. Ehrhard, T., Regnier, L.: Differential interaction nets. Theor. Comput. Sci. **364**(2), 166–195 (2006)
23. Ferreira, C., Lanese, I., Ravara, A., Vieira, H.T., Zavattaro, G.: Advanced mechanisms for service combination and transactions. In: Wirsing, M., Hölzl, M. (eds.) Rigorous Software Engineering for Service-Oriented Systems. LNCS, vol. 6582, pp. 302–325. Springer, Heidelberg (2011). doi:10.1007/978-3-642-20401-2_14
24. Gardner, P., Laneve, C., Wischik, L.: Linear forwarders. Inf. Comput. **205**(10), 1526–1550 (2007)
25. Gay, S., Vasconcelos, V.T.: Linear type theory for asynchronous session types. J. Funct. Program. **20**(1), 19–50 (2010)
26. Griffin, T.: A formulae-as-types notion of control. In: POPL 1990, pp. 47–58 (1990)
27. Honda, K.: Types for dyadic interaction. In: Best, E. (ed.) CONCUR 1993. LNCS, vol. 715, pp. 509–523. Springer, Heidelberg (1993). doi:10.1007/3-540-57208-2_35
28. Honda, K., Vasconcelos, V.T., Kubo, M.: Language primitives and type discipline for structured communication-based programming. In: Hankin, C. (ed.) ESOP 1998. LNCS, vol. 1381, pp. 122–138. Springer, Heidelberg (1998). doi:10.1007/BFb0053567
29. Hüttel, H., Lanese, I., Vasconcelos, V.T., Caires, L., et al.: Foundations of session types and behavioural contracts. ACM Comput. Surv. **49**(1), 3 (2016)
30. Kobayashi, N., Pierce, B.C., Turner, D.N.: Linearity and the pi-calculus. In: 23rd Symposium on Principles of Programming Languages, POPL 1996, pp. 358–371. ACM (1996)
31. Krishnaswami, N.R., Turon, A., Dreyer, D., Garg, D.: Superficially substructural types. In: ICFP 2012, pp. 41–54 (2012)
32. Lindley, S., Morris, J.G.: Embedding session types in Haskell. In: 9th International Symposium on Haskell, Haskell 2016, pp. 133–145 (2016)
33. Militão, F., Aldrich, J., Caires, L.: Rely-guarantee protocols. In: Jones, R. (ed.) ECOOP 2014. LNCS, vol. 8586, pp. 334–359. Springer, Heidelberg (2014). doi:10.1007/978-3-662-44202-9_14
34. Mostrous, D., Vasconcelos, V.T.: Affine sessions. In: Kühn, E., Pugliese, R. (eds.) COORDINATION 2014. LNCS, vol. 8459, pp. 115–130. Springer, Heidelberg (2014). doi:10.1007/978-3-662-43376-8_8
35. Orchard, D.A., Yoshida, N.: Effects as sessions, sessions as effects. In: Proceedings of the POPL 2016, pp. 568–581. ACM (2016)
36. Parigot, M.: $\lambda\mu$-calculus: an algorithmic interpretation of classical natural deduction. In: Voronkov, A. (ed.) LPAR 1992. LNCS, vol. 624, pp. 190–201. Springer, Heidelberg (1992). doi:10.1007/BFb0013061
37. Pérez, J.A., Caires, L., Pfenning, F., Toninho, B.: Linear logical relations for session-based concurrency. In: Seidl, H. (ed.) ESOP 2012. LNCS, vol. 7211, pp. 539–558. Springer, Heidelberg (2012). doi:10.1007/978-3-642-28869-2_27
38. Pfenning, F.: Structural cut elimination. In: 10th Annual IEEE Symposium on Logic in Computer Science, LICS 1995, pp. 156–166. IEEE Computer Society (1995)
39. Plotkin, G.D.: A powerdomain construction. SIAM J. Comput. **5**(3), 452–487 (1976)
40. Sangiorgi, D., Walker, D.: The π-Calculus: A Theory of Mobile Processes. Cambridge University Press, Cambridge (2001)

41. Scalas, A., Yoshida, N.: Lightweight session programming in scala. In: 30th European Conference on Object-Oriented Programming, ECOOP 2016, pp. 21:1–21:28 (2016)
42. Toninho, B., Caires, L., Pfenning, F.: Dependent session types via intuitionistic linear type theory. In: PPDP 2011, pp. 161–172 (2011)
43. Toninho, B., Caires, L., Pfenning, F.: Functions as session-typed processes. In: Birkedal, L. (ed.) FoSSaCS 2012. LNCS, vol. 7213, pp. 346–360. Springer, Heidelberg (2012). doi:10.1007/978-3-642-28729-9_23
44. Toninho, B., Caires, L., Pfenning, F.: Higher-order processes, functions, and sessions: a monadic integration. In: Felleisen, M., Gardner, P. (eds.) ESOP 2013. LNCS, vol. 7792, pp. 350–369. Springer, Heidelberg (2013). doi:10.1007/978-3-642-37036-6_20
45. Tov, J.A., Pucella, R.: Stateful contracts for affine types. In: Gordon, A.D. (ed.) ESOP 2010. LNCS, vol. 6012, pp. 550–569. Springer, Heidelberg (2010). doi:10.1007/978-3-642-11957-6_29
46. Tov, J.A., Pucella, R.: A theory of substructural types and control. In: OOPSLA 2011, pp. 625–642 (2011)
47. Tov, J.A., Pucella, R.: Practical affine types. In: POPL 2011, pp. 447–458 (2011)
48. Wadler, P.: Propositions as sessions. In: ICFP 2012, pp. 273–286. ACM (2012)

Temporary Read-Only Permissions
for Separation Logic

Arthur Charguéraud[1,2] and François Pottier[1(✉)]

[1] Inria, Paris, France
francois.pottier@inria.fr
[2] ICube – CNRS, Université de Strasbourg, Strasbourg, France

Abstract. We present an extension of Separation Logic with a general mechanism for temporarily converting any assertion (or "permission") to a read-only form. No accounting is required: our read-only permissions can be freely duplicated and discarded. We argue that, in circumstances where mutable data structures are temporarily accessed only for reading, our read-only permissions enable more concise specifications and proofs. The metatheory of our proposal is verified in Coq.

1 Introduction

Separation Logic [30] offers a natural and effective framework for proving the correctness of imperative programs that manipulate the heap. It is exploited in many implemented program verification systems, ranging from fully automated systems, such as Infer [9], through semi-interactive systems, such as Smallfoot [4], jStar [15], and VeriFast [22], to fully interactive systems (embedded within a proof assistant), such as the Verified Software Toolchain [1] and Charge! [3], to cite just a few. The CFML system, developed by the first author [10,11], can be viewed as a member of the latter category. We have used it to verify many sequential data structures and algorithms, representing several thousand lines of OCaml code.

1.1 Redundancy in Specifications

Our experience with Separation Logic at scale in CFML leads us to observe that many specifications suffer from a somewhat unpleasant degree of verbosity, which results from a frequent need to repeat part of the precondition in the postcondition. This repetition is evident already in the Separation Logic axiom for dereferencing a pointer:

TRADITIONAL READ AXIOM
$$\{l \hookrightarrow v\} \, (\mathsf{get}\, l) \, \{\lambda y. \, [y = v] \star l \hookrightarrow v\}$$

This axiom states that "if initially the memory location l stores the value v, then dereferencing l yields the value v *and, after this operation, l still stores v.*"

This research was partly supported by the French National Research Agency (ANR) under the grant ANR-15-CE25-0008.

H. Yang (Ed.): ESOP 2017, LNCS 10201, pp. 260–286, 2017.
DOI: 10.1007/978-3-662-54434-1_10

Arguably, to a human reader, the last part of this statement may seem obvious, even though it is not formally redundant.

Beginning with this axiom, this redundancy contaminates the entire system. It arises not only when a single memory cell is read, but, more generally, every time a data structure is accessed for reading. To illustrate this, consider a function *array_concat* that expects (pointers to) two arrays a_1 and a_2 and returns (a pointer to) a new array a_3 whose content is the concatenation of the contents of a_1 and a_2. Its specification in Separation Logic would be as follows:

$$\{a_1 \rightsquigarrow \mathsf{Array}\, L_1 \star a_2 \rightsquigarrow \mathsf{Array}\, L_2\} \tag{1}$$
$$(array\_concat\, a_1\, a_2)$$
$$\{\lambda a_3.\ a_3 \rightsquigarrow \mathsf{Array}\,(L_1 + \!\!+ L_2) \star a_1 \rightsquigarrow \mathsf{Array}\, L_1 \star a_2 \rightsquigarrow \mathsf{Array}\, L_2\}$$

We assume that $a \rightsquigarrow \mathsf{Array}\, L$ asserts the existence (and unique ownership) of an array at address a whose content is given by the list L. A separating conjunction $\star$ is used in the precondition to require that a_1 and a_2 be disjoint arrays. Its use in the postcondition guarantees that a_3 is disjoint with a_1 and a_2. In this specification, again, the fact that the arrays a_1 and a_2 are unaffected must be explicitly stated as part of the postcondition, making the specification seem verbose.

Ideally, we would like to write a more succinct specification, which directly expresses the idea that the arrays a_1 and a_2 are only read by *array_concat*, even though they are mutable arrays. Such a specification could be as follows, where "RO" is a read-only modality, whose exact meaning remains to be explained:

$$\{\mathsf{RO}(a_1 \rightsquigarrow \mathsf{Array}\, L_1) \star \mathsf{RO}(a_2 \rightsquigarrow \mathsf{Array}\, L_2)\} \tag{2}$$
$$(array\_concat\, a_1\, a_2)$$
$$\{\lambda a_3.\ a_3 \rightsquigarrow \mathsf{Array}\,(L_1 + \!\!+ L_2)\}$$

The idea is, because only read access to a_1 and a_2 is granted, these arrays cannot be modified or deallocated by the call *array_concat* $a_1\, a_2$. Therefore, the postcondition need not say anything about these arrays: that would be redundant.

1.2   Can "RO" Be Interpreted by Macro-Expansion?

At this point, the reader may wonder whether the meaning of "RO" could be explained by a simple macro-expansion process. That is, assuming that "RO" is allowed to appear only at the top level of the precondition, the Hoare triple $\{\mathsf{RO}(H_1)\star H_2\}\ t\ \{Q\}$ could be viewed as syntactic sugar for $\{H_1\star H_2\}\ t\ \{H_1\star Q\}$. Such sugar is easy to implement; in fact, CFML offers it, under the notation "INV", for "invariant". However, this naïve interpretation suffers from several shortcomings, which can be summarized as follows:

1. It reduces apparent redundancy in specifications, but does not eliminate the corresponding redundancy in proofs.
2. It does not allow read-only state to be aliased.
3. It leads to deceptively weak specifications.
4. It can lead to unusably weak specifications.

In the following, we expand on each of these points.

Shortcoming 1: Does Not Reduce Proof Effort. Under the naïve interpretation of "RO" as macro-expansion, the Hoare triple $\{RO(H_1) \star H_2\}\ t\ \{Q\}$ is just syntactic sugar. The presence or absence of this sugar has no effect on the proof obligations that the user must fulfill. Even though the sugar hides the presence of the conjunct H_1 in the postcondition, it really is still there. So, the user must prove that H_1 holds upon termination of the command t. This might take several proof steps: for example, several predicate definitions might need to be folded. In other words, the issue that we would like to address is not just undesired verbosity; it is also undesired work.

In this paper, we intend to give direct semantic meaning to "RO". In this approach, $\{RO(H_1) \star H_2\}\ t\ \{Q\}$ is an ordinary Hoare triple, whose postcondition does not mention H_1. Thus, there is no need for the user to argue that H_1 holds upon termination. The proof effort is therefore reduced.

Shortcoming 2: Does Not Allow Aliasing Read-Only State. Under the naïve interpretation of "RO", our proposed specification of *array_concat* (2) is just sugar for the obvious specification (1), therefore means that *array_concat* must be applied to two disjoint arrays. Yet, in reality, a call of the form "*array_concat a a*" is safe and makes sense. To allow it, one could prove another specification for *array_concat*, dealing specifically with the case where an array is concatenated with itself:

$$\{a \rightsquigarrow \mathsf{Array}\, L\} \tag{3}$$
$$(array\_concat\ a\ a)$$
$$\{\lambda a_3.\ a_3 \rightsquigarrow \mathsf{Array}\, (L \mathbin{+\!\!+} L) \star a \rightsquigarrow \mathsf{Array}\, L\}$$

However, that would imply extra work: firstly, when *array_concat* is defined, as its code must be verified twice; secondly, when it is invoked, as the user may need to indicate which of the two specifications (1) and (3) should be used.

In this paper, we define the meaning of "RO" in such a way that every read-only assertion is duplicable: that is, $RO(H)$ entails $RO(H) \star RO(H)$. Thanks to this property, our proposed specification of *array_concat* (2) allows justifying the call "*array_concat a a*". In fact, under our reasoning rules, specification (2) subsumes both of the specifications (1) and (3) that one would need in the absence of read-only assertions.

Shortcoming 3: Deceptively Weak. Under the naïve interpretation of "RO" as macro-expansion, the Hoare triple $\{RO(H_1) \star H_2\}\ t\ \{Q\}$ does not guarantee that the memory covered by H_1 is unaffected by the execution of the command t. Instead, it means only that H_1 still holds upon termination of t. To see this, imagine that the assertion $h \rightsquigarrow \mathsf{HashTable}\, M$ means "the hash table at address h currently represents the dictionary M". A function *population*, which returns the number of entries in a hash table, could have the following specification:

$$\{RO(h \rightsquigarrow \mathsf{HashTable}\, M)\}\ (population\ h)\ \{\lambda y.\ [y = \mathsf{card}\, M]\} \tag{4}$$

Under the macro-expansion interpretation, this specification guarantees that $h \rightsquigarrow \mathsf{HashTable}\, M$ is preserved, so, after a call to *population*, the table h still represents the dictionary M. Somewhat subtly, this does not guarantee that the concrete data structure is unchanged. In fact, a function *resize*, which doubles the physical size of the table and profoundly affects its organization in memory, would admit a similar specification:

$$\{\mathsf{RO}(h \rightsquigarrow \mathsf{HashTable}\,M)\}\ (resize\ h)\ \{\lambda().\ []\} \tag{5}$$

In this paper, we define the meaning of "RO" in such a way that it really means "read-only". Therefore, the above specification of *population* (4) acquires stronger meaning, and guarantees that *population* does not modify the hash table. The specification of *resize* (5) similarly acquires stronger meaning, and can no longer be established, since *resize* does modify the hash table. A valid specification of *resize* is $\{h \rightsquigarrow \mathsf{HashTable}\,M\}\ (resize\ h)\ \{\lambda().\ h \rightsquigarrow \mathsf{HashTable}\,M\}$.

Shortcoming 4: Unusably Weak. The weakness of the above specifications is not only somewhat unexpected and deceptive: there are in fact situations where it is problematic.

Imagine that a hash table is internally represented as a record of several fields, among which is a *data* field, holding a pointer to an array. The abstract predicate $h \rightsquigarrow \mathsf{HashTable}\,M$ might then be defined as follows:

$$h \rightsquigarrow \mathsf{HashTable}\,M := \tag{6}$$
$$\exists a.\ \exists L.\ (h \rightsquigarrow \{data = a; \dots\} \star a \rightsquigarrow \mathsf{Array}\,L \star \dots)$$

Suppose we wish to verify an operation *foo*, inside the "hash table" module, whose code begins as follows:

```
let foo h =
  let d = h.data in        – read the address of the array
  let p = population h in   – call population
  ...
```

A proof outline for this function must begin as follows:

```
1  let foo h =
2    {h ⤳ HashTable M}                              – foo's precondition
3    {h ⤳ {data = a; ...} ⋆ a ⤳ Array L ⋆ ...}      – by unfolding
4    let d = h.data in
5    {h ⤳ {data = a; ...} ⋆ a ⤳ Array L ⋆ ... ⋆ [d = a]}  – by reading
6    {h ⤳ HashTable M ⋆ [d = a]}                    – by folding
7    let p = population h in
8    {h ⤳ HashTable M ⋆ [d = a] ⋆ [p = #M]}
9    ...
```

At line 3, we unfold $h \rightsquigarrow \mathsf{HashTable}\,M$. Two auxiliary variables, a and L, are introduced at this point; their scope extends to the end of the proof outline. This unfolding step is mandatory: indeed, the read instruction at line 4 requires $h \rightsquigarrow \{data = a; \dots\}$. This instruction produces the pure assertion $[d = a]$, which together with the assertion $h \rightsquigarrow \{data = a; \dots\}$ means that d is the current value of the field $h.data$.

At line 6, we fold $h \rightsquigarrow \mathsf{HashTable}\,M$. This is mandatory: indeed, under the naïve interpretation of "RO", the precondition of the call "*population h*" is $h \rightsquigarrow \mathsf{HashTable}\,M$. Unfortunately, this folding step is harmful: it causes us to lose $h \rightsquigarrow \{data = a; \ldots\}$ and thereby to forget that d is the current value of the field $h.data$. (The equation $d = a$ remains true, but becomes useless.) Yet, in reality, this fact is preserved through the call, which does not modify the hash table.

In summary, because the specification of *population* (4) is too weak, calling *population* at line 7 causes us to lose the benefit of the read instruction at line 4. In this particular example, one could work around the problem by exchanging the two instructions. In general, though, it might not be possible or desirable to modify the code so as to facilitate the proof. Another work-around is to equip *population* with a lower-level specification, where the predicate HashTable is manually unfolded.

We have demonstrated that, under the naïve interpretation, the specification of *population* (4) can be unsuitable for use inside the "hash table" abstraction.

In this paper, we define the meaning of "RO" in such a way that all of the information that is available at line 5 is preserved through the call to *population*. This is explained later on (Sect. 2.5).

1.3   Towards True Read-Only Permissions

The question that we wish to address is: what is a simple extension of sequential Separation Logic with duplicable temporary read-only permissions[1] for mutable data?

We should stress that we are primarily interested in a logic of sequential programs. We do discuss structured parallelism and shared-memory concurrency near the end of the paper (Sect. 6.2).

We should also emphasize that we are not interested in read permissions for permanently immutable data, which are a different concept. Such permissions can be found, for instance, in Mezzo [2], and could be introduced in Separation Logic, if desired. They, too, grant read access only, and are duplicable. Mezzo allows converting a unique read-write permission to a duplicable read permission, but not the other way around: the transition from mutable to immutable state is irrevocable. Mezzo has no mechanism for obtaining a temporary read-only view of a mutable data structure.

Finally, we should say a word of fractional permissions (which are discussed in greater depth in Sect. 5.4). Fractional permissions [6] can be used to obtain temporary read-only views of mutable data. A fraction that is strictly less than 1 grants read-only access, and, by joining all shares so as to recover the fraction 1, a unique read-write access permission can be recovered. Nevertheless, fractional permissions are not what we seek. They do not address our shortcoming 1: their use requires work that we wish to avoid, namely "accounting" (arithmetic reasoning) as well as (universal and existential) quantification over fraction variables.

---

[1] Following Boyland [6], Balabonski *et al.* [2], and others, we use the words "assertion" and "permission" interchangeably.

Furthermore, whereas $\mathsf{RO}(h \leadsto \mathsf{HashTable}\,M)$ is a well-formed permission in our logic, in most systems of fractional permissions, $\frac{1}{2}(h \leadsto \mathsf{HashTable}\,M)$ is not well-formed. The systems that do allow this kind of "scaling", such as Boyland's [7], do so at the cost of restricting disjunction and existential quantification so that they are "precise".

In this paper, we answer the above question. We introduce a generic assertion transformer, "RO". For any assertion H, it is permitted to form the assertion $\mathsf{RO}(H)$, which offers read-only access to the memory covered by H. For instance, $\mathsf{RO}(x \hookrightarrow v)$ offers read-only access to the memory cell at address x. The temporary conversion from a permission H to its read-only counterpart $\mathsf{RO}(H)$ is performed within a lexically-delimited scope, via a "read-only frame rule". Upon entry into the scope, H is replaced with $\mathsf{RO}(H)$. Within the scope, $\mathsf{RO}(H)$ can be duplicated if desired, and some copies can be discarded; there is no need to keep track of all shares and recombine them so as to regain a full permission. Upon exit of the scope, the permission H re-appears.

The rest of the paper is organized as follows. First, we review our additions to Separation Logic (Sect. 2). Then, we give a formal, self-contained presentation of our logic (Sect. 3) and of its model, which we use to establish the soundness of the logic (Sect. 4). The soundness proof is formalized in Coq and can be found online [12]. Then, we review some of the related work (Sect. 5), discuss some potential applications and extensions of our logic (Sect. 6), and conclude (Sect. 7).

2 Overview

In this section, we describe our additions to Separation Logic, with which we assume a basic level of familiarity. The following sections describe our logic (Sect. 3) and its model (Sect. 4) in full, and may serve as a reference.

2.1 A "Read-Only" Modality

To begin with, we introduce read-only permissions in the syntax of permissions. Informally, the permission $\mathsf{RO}(H)$ controls the same heap fragment as the permission H, but can be used only for reading. A more precise understanding of the meaning of "RO" is given by the semantic model (Sect. 4.1).

The "RO" modality enjoys several important properties, shown in Fig. 1, where the symbol $\triangleright$ denotes entailment. When applied to a pure assertion $[P]$, "RO" vanishes. It can be pushed into a separating conjunction: $\mathsf{RO}(H_1 \star H_2)$ entails $\mathsf{RO}(H_1) \star \mathsf{RO}(H_2)$. The reverse entailment is false[2]. Because of this, one might worry that exploiting the entailment $\mathsf{RO}(H_1 \star H_2) \triangleright \mathsf{RO}(H_1) \star \mathsf{RO}(H_2)$ causes a loss of information. This is true, but if that is a problem, then one can exploit the equality $\mathsf{RO}(H_1 \star H_2) = \mathsf{RO}(H_1 \star H_2) \star \mathsf{RO}(H_1) \star \mathsf{RO}(H_2)$

---

[2] If it were true, then we would have the following chain of equalities: $\mathsf{RO}(l \hookrightarrow v) = \mathsf{RO}(l \hookrightarrow v) \star \mathsf{RO}(l \hookrightarrow v) = \mathsf{RO}(l \hookrightarrow v \star l \hookrightarrow v) = \mathsf{RO}([\mathsf{False}]) = [\mathsf{False}]$.

$$RO([P]) = [P]$$
$$RO(H_1 \star H_2) \rhd RO(H_1) \star RO(H_2) \qquad \text{(the reverse is false)}$$
$$RO(H_1 \lor H_2) = RO(H_1) \lor RO(H_2)$$
$$RO(\exists x.\, H) = \exists x.\, RO(H)$$
$$RO(RO(H)) = RO(H)$$
$$RO(H) \rhd RO(H') \qquad \text{if } H \rhd H'$$
$$RO(H) = RO(H) \star RO(H)$$

Fig. 1. Properties of RO

instead. "RO" commutes with disjunction and existential quantification. "RO" is idempotent[3]. A read-only permission for a single cell of memory, $RO(l \hookrightarrow v)$, cannot be rewritten into a simpler form, which is why there is no equation for it in Fig. 1. It can be exploited via the new read axiom (Sect. 2.4). The last two lines of Fig. 1 respectively state that "RO" is covariant and that read-only permissions are duplicable.

Together, these rules allow pushing "RO" into composite permissions. For instance, if $h \rightsquigarrow \mathsf{HashTable}\, M$ is defined as before (Sect. 1, (6)), then the read-only permission $RO(h \rightsquigarrow \mathsf{HashTable}\, M)$ entails:

$$\exists a.\, \exists L.\ (RO(h \rightsquigarrow \{data = a; \ldots\}) \star RO(a \rightsquigarrow \mathsf{Array}\, L) \star RO(\ldots))$$

In other words, "read-only access to a hash table" implies read-only access to the component objects of the table, as expected.

2.2 A Read-Only Frame Rule

To guarantee the soundness of our extension of Separation Logic with read-only permissions, we must enforce one key metatheoretical invariant, namely: a memory location is never governed at the same time by a read-write permission and by a read permission. Indeed, if two such permissions were allowed to coexist, the read-write permission by itself would allow writing a new value to this memory location. The read permission would not be updated (it could be framed out, hence invisible, during the write) and would therefore become stale (that is, carry out-of-date information about the value stored at this location). That would be unsound.

In order to forbid the co-existence of read-write and read-only permissions for a single location, we propose enforcing the following informal rules:

1. Read-only permissions obey a lexical scope (or "block") discipline.
2. Upon entry into a block, a permission H can be replaced with its read-only counterpart $RO(H)$.
3. Upon exit of this block, the permission H reappears.
4. No read-only permissions are allowed to exit the block.

---

[3] In practice, this property should not be useful, because permissions of the form $RO(RO(H))$ never appear: the read-only frame rule (Sect. 2.2) is formulated in such a way that it cannot give rise to such a permission.

$$\text{normal } [P] \qquad \text{normal } (x \hookrightarrow v) \qquad \frac{\text{normal } H_1 \qquad \text{normal } H_2}{\text{normal } (H_1 \star H_2)}$$

$$\frac{\text{normal } H_1 \qquad \text{normal } H_2}{\text{normal } (H_1 \vee H_2)} \qquad \frac{\forall x. \text{ normal } H}{\text{normal } (\exists x.\, H)}$$

Fig. 2. Properties of normal

Roughly speaking, there is no danger of co-existence between read-write and read permissions when a block is entered, because H is removed at the same time $\mathsf{RO}(H)$ is introduced. There is no danger either when this block is exited, even though H reappears, because no read-only permissions are allowed to exit.

Technically, all four informal rules above take the form of a single reasoning rule, the "read-only frame rule", which subsumes the frame rule of Separation Logic. The frame rule allows an assertion H' to become hidden inside a block: H' disappears upon entry, and reappears upon exit of the block. The read-only frame rule does this as well, and in addition, makes the read-only permission $\mathsf{RO}(H')$ available within the block. In our system, the two rules are as follows:

FRAME RULE
$$\frac{\{H\}\, t\, \{Q\} \qquad \text{normal } H'}{\{H \star H'\}\, t\, \{Q \star H'\}}$$

READ-ONLY FRAME RULE
$$\frac{\{H \star \mathsf{RO}(H')\}\, t\, \{Q\} \qquad \text{normal } H'}{\{H \star H'\}\, t\, \{Q \star H'\}}$$

The frame rule (above, left) is in fact just a special case of the read-only frame rule (above, right). Indeed, a read-only permission can be discarded at any time (using rule DISCARD-PRE from Fig. 4). Thus, the frame rule can be derived by applying the read-only frame rule and immediately discarding $\mathsf{RO}(H')$.

Both rules above have the side condition normal H', which requires H' to be "normal". Its role is to ensure that "no read-only permissions are allowed to exit the block". "Normality" can be understood in several ways:

1. A syntactic understanding is that a permission is "normal" if "RO" does not occur in it. This view is supported by the rules in Fig. 2. The one thing to remark about these rules is that there is no rule whose conclusion is normal$(\mathsf{RO}(H))$.
2. A semantic understanding is given when we set up a model of our logic (Sect. 4.1). There, we define what it means for a heap, where each memory location is marked either as read-write or as read-only, to satisfy a permission. Then, a permission is "normal" if a heap that satisfies it cannot contain any read-only memory locations.

Because of the normality condition in the read-only frame rule, a Hoare triple $\{H\}\,t\,\{Q\}$ typically[4] has a normal postcondition Q. This means that read-only permissions can only be "passed down", from caller to callee. They cannot be "passed back up", from callee to caller.

2.3   A Framed Sequencing Rule

The sequencing rule of Separation Logic (below, left) remains sound in our logic. However, in a setting where postconditions must be normal (or are typically normal), this rule is weaker than desired: it does not allow read-only permissions to be distributed into its second premise. Indeed, suppose Q' is normal, as it is the postcondition of the first premise. Unfortunately, Q' is also the precondition of the second premise. This means that no read-only permissions are available in the proof of t_2. Yet, in practice, it is useful and desirable to be able to thread one or more read-only permissions through a sequence of instructions. We remedy the problem by giving a slightly generalized sequencing rule (below, right), which allows an arbitrary permission H' to be framed out of t_1 and therefore passed directly to t_2.

$$
\begin{array}{cc}
\text{TRADITIONAL SEQUENCING RULE} & \text{FRAMED SEQUENCING RULE} \\[4pt]
\dfrac{\{H\}\,t_1\,\{Q'\} \qquad \{Q'\}\,t_2\,\{Q\}}{\{H\}\,(t_1\,;\,t_2)\,\{Q\}} & \dfrac{\{H\}\,t_1\,\{Q'\} \qquad \{Q' \star H'\}\,t_2\,\{Q\}}{\{H \star H'\}\,(t_1\,;\,t_2)\,\{Q\}}
\end{array}
$$

In Separation Logic, the "framed sequencing rule" can be derived from the sequencing rule and the frame rule. Here, conversely, it is viewed as a primitive reasoning rule; the traditional sequencing rule can be derived from it, if desired.

When a read-only permission is available at the beginning of a sequence of instructions, it is in fact available to every instruction in the sequence. This is expressed by the following rule, which can be derived from the framed sequencing rule, the rule of consequence, and from the fact that read-only permissions are duplicable.

$$
\begin{array}{c}
\text{READ-ONLY SEQUENCING RULE} \\[4pt]
\dfrac{\{H \star \mathsf{RO}(H')\}\,t_1\,\{Q'\} \qquad \{Q' \star \mathsf{RO}(H')\}\,t_2\,\{Q\}}{\{H \star \mathsf{RO}(H')\}\,(t_1\,;\,t_2)\,\{Q\}}
\end{array}
$$

2.4   A New Read Axiom

The axiom for reading a memory cell must be generalized so as to accept a read-only permission (instead of a read-write permission) as proof that reading is permitted. The traditional axiom (below, left) requires a read-write permission $l \hookrightarrow v$, which it returns. The new axiom (below, right) requires a read-only permission $\mathsf{RO}(l \hookrightarrow v)$, which it discards.

---

[4] If we restricted the rule of CONSEQUENCE in Fig. 4 by adding the side condition normal Q, then we would be able to prove that every triple $\{H\}\,t\,\{Q\}$ that can be established using the reasoning rules has a normal postcondition Q. We did not restrict the rule of consequence in this way because this is technically not necessary.

TRADITIONAL READ AXIOM $\quad\quad\quad\quad$ NEW READ AXIOM

$\{l \hookrightarrow v\}\ (\mathsf{get}\, l)\ \{\lambda y.\ [y = v] \star l \hookrightarrow v\} \quad\quad \{\mathsf{RO}(l \hookrightarrow v)\}\ (\mathsf{get}\, l)\ \{\lambda y.\ [y = v]\}$

The traditional read axiom remains sound, and can in fact be derived from the new read axiom and the read-only frame rule.

2.5   Illustration

Recall the hypothetical operation *foo* that was used earlier (Sect. 1.2) to illustrate our claim that faking read-only permissions by macro-expansion is unsatisfactory. Let us carry out this proof again, this time with our read-only permissions. As before, we assume that *population* requires read access to the hash table. This is expressed by specification (4), which we repeat here:

$$\{\mathsf{RO}(h \rightsquigarrow \mathsf{HashTable}\, M)\}\ (population\ h)\ \{\lambda y.\ [y = \#M]\}$$

We will use the following derived rule, which follows from the read-only frame rule, the rule of consequence, and the fact that "RO" is covariant:

READ-ONLY FRAME RULE (WITH CONSEQUENCE)

$$\frac{H' \vartriangleright H'' \quad\quad \{H \star \mathsf{RO}(H'')\}\ t\ \{Q\} \quad\quad \text{normal}\, H'}{\{H \star H'\}\ t\ \{Q \star H'\}}$$

This rule differs from the read-only frame rule in that, instead of introducing $\mathsf{RO}(H')$, this rule introduces $\mathsf{RO}(H'')$, where H'' is logically weaker than H'. Nevertheless, upon exit, the permission H' is recovered.

We can now give a new proof outline for *foo*:

```
1   let foo h =
2     {h ⤳ HashTable M}
3     {h ⤳ {data = a;...} ⋆ a ⤳ Array L ⋆ ...}
4     let d = h.data in
5     {h ⤳ {data = a;...} ⋆ a ⤳ Array L ⋆ ... ⋆ [d = a]}
6     {RO(h ⤳ HashTable M) ⋆ [d = a]}
      – by the read-only frame rule (with consequence)
7     let p = population h in
8     {h ⤳ {data = a;...} ⋆ a ⤳ Array L ⋆ ... ⋆ [d = a] ⋆ [p = #M]}
9     ...
```

Up to and including line 5, the outline is the same as in our previous attempt. At this point, in order to justify the call to *population*, we wish to obtain the read-only permission $\mathsf{RO}(h \rightsquigarrow \mathsf{HashTable}\, M)$. This is done by applying the read-only frame rule (with consequence) around the call. We exploit the entailment $(h \rightsquigarrow \{data = a;...\} \star a \rightsquigarrow \mathsf{Array}\, L \star ...) \vartriangleright (h \rightsquigarrow \mathsf{HashTable}\, M)$, which corresponds to folding the HashTable predicate. Thus, for the duration of the call, we obtain the read-only permission $\mathsf{RO}(h \rightsquigarrow \mathsf{HashTable}\, M)$. After the call, the more precise, unfolded, read-write permission $h \rightsquigarrow \{data = a;...\} \star a \rightsquigarrow \mathsf{Array}\, L \star ...$ reappears. The loss of information in our first proof outline (Sect. 1.2) no longer occurs here.

3   Logic

In this section, we give a formal presentation of Separation Logic with read-only permissions. We present the syntax of programs, the syntax of assertions, and the reasoning rules. This is all a user of the logic needs to know. The semantic model and the proof of soundness come in the next section (Sect. 4).

$$
\text{EVAL-VAL} \atop v/m \Downarrow v/m
$$

$$
\text{EVAL-IF} \\
\dfrac{\begin{array}{l} n \neq 0 \,\wedge\, t_1/m \Downarrow v'/m' \\ \vee \quad n = 0 \,\wedge\, t_2/m \Downarrow v'/m' \end{array}}{(\text{if } n \text{ then } t_1 \text{ else } t_2)/m \Downarrow v'/m'}
$$

$$
\text{EVAL-LET} \\
\dfrac{\begin{array}{l} t_1/m \Downarrow v_1/m' \\ ([v_1/x]\, t_2)/m' \Downarrow v/m'' \end{array}}{(\text{let } x = t_1 \text{ in } t_2)/m \Downarrow v/m''}
$$

$$
\text{EVAL-APP} \\
\dfrac{\begin{array}{c} v_1 = \mu f.\lambda x.t \\ ([v_1/f]\,[v_2/x]\, t)/m \Downarrow v'/m' \end{array}}{(v_1\, v_2)/m \Downarrow v'/m'}
$$

$$
\text{EVAL-REF} \\
\dfrac{l \notin \mathsf{dom}\, m \qquad m' = m \uplus (l \mapsto v)}{(\mathsf{ref}\, v)/m \Downarrow l/m'}
$$

$$
\text{EVAL-GET} \\
\dfrac{l \in \mathsf{dom}\, m \qquad v = m[l]}{(\mathsf{get}\, l)/m \Downarrow v/m}
$$

$$
\text{EVAL-SET} \\
\dfrac{l \in \mathsf{dom}\, m \qquad m' = m[l := v]}{(\mathsf{set}\, l\, v)/m \Downarrow ()/m'}
$$

Fig. 3. Big-step evaluation

3.1   Calculus

Our programming language is a λ-calculus with references. Its syntax is as follows:

$$
v := x \mid () \mid n \mid l \mid \mu f.\lambda x.t
$$
$$
t := v \mid \text{if } v \text{ then } t_1 \text{ else } t_2 \mid \text{let } x = t_1 \text{ in } t_2 \mid (v\, v) \mid \mathsf{ref}\, v \mid \mathsf{get}\, v \mid \mathsf{set}\, v\, v
$$

A value v is either a variable x, the unit value $()$, an integer constant n, a memory location l, or a recursive function $\mu f.\lambda x.t$. A term t is either a value, a conditional construct, a sequencing construct, a function call, or a primitive instruction for allocating, reading, or writing a reference.

The big-step evaluation judgement (Fig. 3) takes the form $t/m \Downarrow v/m'$, and asserts that the evaluation of the term t in the memory m terminates and produces the value v in the memory m'. A memory is a finite map of locations to values.

3.2   Permissions

The syntax of permissions, also known as assertions, is as follows:

$$
H := [P] \mid l \hookrightarrow v \mid H_1 \star H_2 \mid H_1 \mathbin{\lor\!\!\!\lor} H_2 \mid \exists x.\, H \mid \mathrm{RO}(H)
$$

All of these constructs are standard, except for $RO(H)$, which represents a read-only form of the permission H. The pure assertion $[P]$ is true of an empty heap, provided the proposition P holds. P is expressed in the metalanguage; in our Coq formalisation, it is an arbitrary proposition of type Prop. In particular, a Hoare triple $\{H\}\, t\, \{Q\}$ (defined later on) is a proposition: this is important, as it allows reasoning about first-class functions. The empty permission $[\,]$ can be viewed as syntactic sugar for [True]. The permission $l \hookrightarrow v$ grants unique read-write access to the reference cell at address l, and asserts that this cell currently contains the value v. Separating conjunction $\star$, disjunction $\lor$, and existential quantification are standard. We omit ordinary conjunction $\land$, partly because we do not use it in practice when carrying out proofs in CFML, partly because we did not have time to study whether the rule of conjunction holds in our logic.

From a syntactic standpoint, a "normal" permission is one that does not contain any occurrences of "RO". (Recall Fig. 2.)

As usual in Separation Logic, permissions are equipped with an entailment relation, written $H_1 \triangleright H_2$ ("H_1 entails H_2"). It is a partial order. (In particular, it is antisymmetric: we view two propositions that entail each other as equal.) The standard connectives of Separation Logic enjoy their usual properties, which, for the sake of brevity, we do not repeat. (For instance, separating conjunction is associative, commutative, and admits $[\,]$ as a unit.) In addition, read-only permissions satisfy the laws of Fig. 1, which have been explained earlier (Sect. 2.1).

3.3   Reasoning Rules

As usual in Separation Logic, a Hoare triple takes the form $\{H\}\, t\, \{\lambda y.\, H'\}$ where H and H' are permissions and t is a term. The precondition H expresses requirements on the initial state; the postcondition $\lambda y.\, H'$ offers guarantees about the result y of the computation and about the final state. We write Q for a postcondition $\lambda y.\, H'$. For greater readability, we write $Q \star H'$ for $\lambda y.\, (Q\, y \star H')$. We write $Q \lor Q'$ as a shorthand for $\lambda y.\, (Q\, y) \lor (Q'\, y)$. We write $Q \triangleright Q'$ as a shorthand for $\forall y.\, (Q\, y) \triangleright (Q'\, y)$.

We adopt a total correctness interpretation, whereby a triple $\{H\}\, t\, \{\lambda y.\, H'\}$ guarantees that (under the precondition H) the evaluation of t terminates. This is arbitrary: our read-only permissions would work equally well in a partial correctness setting.

The reasoning rules, by which Hoare triples can be established, are divided in two groups: structural (or non-syntax-directed) rules (Fig. 4) and syntax-directed rules (Fig. 5).

Among the structural rules, the only nonstandard rule is the READ-ONLY FRAME RULE, which has been explained earlier (Sect. 2.2). The rule of CONSEQUENCE allows exploiting entailment to strengthen the precondition and weaken the postcondition. The rules DISCARD-PRE and DISCARD-POST allow discarding part of the pre- or postcondition. (The rule of consequence cannot be used for this purpose: for instance, $x \hookrightarrow v$ does not entail $[\,]$.) The permission GC controls what permissions can be discarded. Here, we let GC stand for $\exists H.\, H$:

READ-ONLY FRAME RULE

$$\frac{\{H \star \mathsf{RO}(H')\}\, t\, \{Q\} \qquad \text{normal } H'}{\{H \star H'\}\, t\, \{Q \star H'\}}$$

CONSEQUENCE

$$\frac{H \rhd H' \qquad \{H'\}\, t\, \{Q'\} \qquad Q' \rhd Q}{\{H\}\, t\, \{Q\}}$$

DISCARD-PRE

$$\frac{\{H\}\, t\, \{Q\}}{\{H \star \mathsf{GC}\}\, t\, \{Q\}}$$

DISCARD-POST

$$\frac{\{H\}\, t\, \{Q \star \mathsf{GC}\}}{\{H\}\, t\, \{Q\}}$$

EXTRACT-PROP

$$\frac{P \Rightarrow \{H\}\, t\, \{Q\}}{\{[P] \star H\}\, t\, \{Q\}}$$

EXTRACT-OR

$$\frac{\{H_1\}\, t\, \{Q\} \qquad \{H_2\}\, t\, \{Q\}}{\{H_1 \lor H_2\}\, t\, \{Q\}}$$

EXTRACT-EXISTS

$$\frac{\forall x.\ \{H\}\, t\, \{Q\}}{\{\exists x.\, H\}\, t\, \{Q\}}$$

Fig. 4. Reasoning rules (structural)

VAL

$$\{[\,]\}\, v\, \{\lambda y.\ [y = v]\}$$

IF

$$\frac{n \neq 0 \Rightarrow \{H\}\, t_1\, \{Q\} \qquad n = 0 \Rightarrow \{H\}\, t_2\, \{Q\}}{\{H\}\ (\text{if } n \text{ then } t_1 \text{ else } t_2)\ \{Q\}}$$

FRAMED SEQUENCING RULE (LET)

$$\frac{\{H\}\, t_1\, \{Q'\} \qquad \forall x.\ \{Q'\, x \star H'\}\, t_2\, \{Q\}}{\{H \star H'\}\ (\text{let } x = t_1 \text{ in } t_2)\ \{Q\}}$$

APP

$$\frac{v_1 = \mu f.\lambda x.t \qquad \{H\}\ ([v_1/f]\,[v_2/x]\,t)\ \{Q\}}{\{H\}\ (v_1\, v_2)\ \{Q\}}$$

REF

$$\{[\,]\}\ (\mathsf{ref}\, v)\ \{\lambda y.\ \exists l.\ [y = l] \star l \hookrightarrow v\}$$

NEW READ AXIOM (GET)

$$\{\mathsf{RO}(l \hookrightarrow v)\}\ (\mathsf{get}\, l)\ \{\lambda y.\ [y = v]\}$$

SET

$$\{l \hookrightarrow v'\}\ (\mathsf{set}\, l\, v)\ \{\lambda y.\ l \hookrightarrow v\}$$

Fig. 5. Reasoning rules (syntax-directed)

this means that any permission can be discarded[5]. The last three rules in Fig. 4 are elimination rules for pure assertions, disjunction, and existential quantification. Note that the standard symmetric rule of disjunction, shown below, follows directly from the rules EXTRACT-OR and CONSEQUENCE.

DISJUNCTION

$$\frac{\{H_1\}\, t\, \{Q_1\} \qquad \{H_2\}\, t\, \{Q_2\}}{\{H_1 \lor H_2\}\, t\, \{Q_1 \lor Q_2\}}$$

The syntax-directed reasoning rules appear in Fig. 5. They are standard, except for the FRAMED SEQUENCING RULE and the NEW READ AXIOM, which have been explained earlier (Sects. 2.3 and 2.4).

---

[5] $\exists H.\, H$ is equivalent to true. If the programming language had explicit deallocation instead of garbage collection, one might wish to define GC as $\exists H.\, \mathsf{RO}(H)$, which means that read-only permissions can be implicitly discarded, but read-write permissions cannot. This restriction would be necessary in order to enforce "complete collection", that is, to ensure that every reference cell is eventually deallocated.

The implications in the premises of EXTRACT-PROP and IF and the universal quantifiers in the premises of EXTRACT-EXISTS and FRAMED SEQUENCING RULE are part of the metalanguage (which, in our formalization, is Coq). Thus, in reality, we work with assertions of the form $\forall \Gamma.\ \{H\}\ t\ \{Q\}$, where Γ represents a metalevel hypothesis.

3.4   Treatment of Variables and Functions

Our treatment of variables, as well as the manner in which we reason about functions, may seem somewhat mysterious or unusual. We briefly explain them here. This material is entirely independent of the issue of read-only permissions, so this section may safely be skipped by a reader who wishes to focus on read-only permissions.

In the paper presentation, we identify program variables with the variables of the metalanguage. For example, in the FRAMED SEQUENCING RULE, the name x that occurs in the conclusion let $x = t_1$ in t_2 denotes a program variable, while the name x that is universally quantified in the second premise denotes a variable of the metalanguage.

In our Coq formalization, we clearly distinguish between program variables and metavariables. On the one hand, program variables are explicitly represented as identifiers (which may be implemented as integers or as strings). They are explicitly embedded in the syntax of values. The type of values, Val, is inductively defined (this is a "deep embedding"). On the other hand, metavariables are not "represented as" anything. They are just Coq variables of type Val, that is, they stand for an unknown value. To bridge the gap between program variables and metavariables, a substitution is necessary. For example, in Coq, the FRAMED SEQUENCING RULE is formalized as follows:

$$\forall x t_1 t_2 H H' Q Q'.\quad \{H\}\, t_1\, \{Q'\}$$
$$\wedge\ (\forall X.\ \{Q'\, X \star H'\}\ ([X/x]\, t_2)\ \{Q\})$$
$$\Rightarrow \{H \star H'\}\ (\text{let } x = t_1 \text{ in } t_2)\ \{Q\}$$

Note how, in the second premise, a metavariable X (of type Val) is substituted for the program variable x in the term t_2. The metavariable X denotes the runtime value of the program variable x.

As one descends into the syntax of a term, metavariables are substituted for program variables, as explained above. Thus, one can never reach a leaf that is an occurrence of a program variable x! If a leaf labeled x originally existed in the term, it must be replaced with a value X when the binder for x is entered.

This explains a surprising feature of our reasoning rules, which is that they do not allow reasoning about terms that have free program variables. The rule IF, for instance, allows reasoning about a term of the form (if n then t_1 else t_2), where n is a literal integer value. It does not allow reasoning about (if x then t_1 else t_2), where x is a program variable. As argued above, this is not a problem. Similarly, APP expects the value v_1 to be a λ-abstraction; it does not allow v_1 to be a program variable. NEW READ AXIOM and SET expect the first argument of get and set to be a literal memory location; it cannot be a program variable.

Another possibly mysterious aspect of our presentation is the treatment of functions. In apparence, our only means of reasoning about functions is the rule APP, which states that, in order to reason about a call to a literal function (a λ-abstraction), one should substitute the actual arguments for the formal parameters in the function's body, and reason about the term thus obtained. At first, this may not seem modular: in Hoare logic, one expects to first assign a specification to each function, then check that each function body satisfies its specification, under the assumption that each function call satisfies its specification. In a total correctness setting, one must also establish termination.

It turns out that, by virtue of the power of the metalanguage, this style of reasoning is in fact possible, based on the rules that we have given. We cannot explain everything here, but present one rule for reasoning about the definition and uses of a (possibly recursive) function. This rule can be derived from the rules that we have given. It is as follows:

$$
\left(\begin{array}{c} \forall S.\forall F. \end{array} \left(\left(\begin{array}{c} \forall X H' Q'. \quad \{H'\} \left([F/f] [X/x] t_1 \right) \{Q'\} \\ \Rightarrow \{H'\} \left(F X \right) \{Q'\} \end{array} \right) \Rightarrow S F \right) \right)
$$
$$
\wedge \; (S F \Rightarrow \{H\} \left([F/f] t_2 \right) \{Q\})
$$
$$
\Rightarrow \{H\} \left(\text{let } f = \mu f.\lambda x.t_1 \text{ in } t_2 \right) \{Q\}
$$

This rule provides a way of establishing a Hoare triple about a term of the form let $f = \mu f.\lambda x.t_1$ in t_2. In order to establish such a triple, it suffices to:

1. Pick a specification S, whose type is Val $\rightarrow$ Prop. This is typically a Hoare triple, which represents a specification of the function $\mu f.\lambda x.t_1$.
2. Establish the desired triple about the term t_2, under the assumption that the function satisfies the specification S. (This is the third line above.) In doing so, one does not have access to the code of the function: it is represented by a metavariable F about which nothing is known but the hypothesis $S F$.
3. Prove that the function satisfies the specification S. (These are the first two lines above.) The function is still represented by a metavariable F. This time, one has access to the hypothesis that invoking F is equivalent to executing the function body t_1, under a substitution of actual arguments for formal parameters. If the function $\mu f.\lambda x.t_1$ is recursive, then this proof must involve induction (which is carried out in the metalanguage).

4   Model

In this section, we establish the soundness of our extension of Separation Logic. We first provide a concrete model of permissions, then give an interpretation of triples with respect to which each of the reasoning rules is proved sound.

4.1   A Model of Permissions

In traditional Separation Logic, a permission is interpreted as a predicate over heaps, also known as heap fragments. There, a "heap" coincides with what we

Two memories m_1 and m_2 have disjoint domains:
$$m_1 \perp m_2 \;\equiv\; \mathbf{dom}\,m_1 \cap \mathbf{dom}\,m_2 = \varnothing$$
Two memories r_1 and r_2 agree on the intersection of their domains:
$$\mathbf{agree}\;r_1\;r_2 \;\equiv\; \forall l v_1 v_2.\; (l, v_1) \in r_1 \wedge (l, v_2) \in r_2 \Rightarrow v_1 = v_2$$
Two heaps h_1 and h_2 are compatible:
$$\mathbf{compatible}\;h_1\;h_2 \;\equiv\; (\mathbf{agree}\;h_1.\mathsf{r}\;h_2.\mathsf{r}) \wedge (h_1.\mathsf{f} \perp h_2.\mathsf{f} \perp (h_1.\mathsf{r} \cup h_2.\mathsf{r}))$$
The composition of two compatible heaps h_1 and h_2:
$$h_1 + h_2 \;\equiv\; ((h_1.\mathsf{f} \uplus h_2.\mathsf{f}), (h_1.\mathsf{r} \cup h_2.\mathsf{r}))$$

Fig. 6. Compatibility and composition of heaps

$$
\begin{aligned}
[P] &\equiv \lambda h.\; (h.\mathsf{f} = \varnothing) \wedge (h.\mathsf{r} = \varnothing) \wedge P \\
l \hookrightarrow v &\equiv \lambda h.\; (h.\mathsf{f} = (l \mapsto v)) \wedge (h.\mathsf{r} = \varnothing) \\
H_1 \star H_2 &\equiv \lambda h.\; \exists h_1 h_2.\; \mathbf{compatible}\;h_1\;h_2 \wedge (h = h_1 + h_2) \wedge H_1\,h_1 \wedge H_2\,h_2 \\
H_1 \vee H_2 &\equiv \lambda h.\; H_1\,h \vee H_2\,h \\
\exists x.\,H &\equiv \lambda h.\; \exists x.\,H\,h \\
\mathsf{RO}(H) &\equiv \lambda h.\; (h.\mathsf{f} = \varnothing) \wedge \exists h'.\; (h.\mathsf{r} = h'.\mathsf{f} \uplus h'.\mathsf{r}) \wedge H\,h' \\
\mathsf{normal}(H) &\equiv \forall h.\; H\,h \Rightarrow h.\mathsf{r} = \varnothing \\
H_1 \rhd H_2 &\equiv \forall h.\; H_1\,h \Rightarrow H_2\,h
\end{aligned}
$$

Fig. 7. Interpretation of permissions

have called a "memory", that is, a finite map of memory locations to values. Then, famously, a separating conjunction $H_1 \star H_2$ is satisfied by a heap h if and only if h is the disjoint union of two subheaps that respectively satisfy H_1 and H_2.

In the following, we need a slightly more complex model, where a "heap" is a richer object than a "memory". Whereas a memory maps locations to values, a heap must additionally map memory locations to access rights: that is, it must keep track of which memory locations are considered accessible for reading and writing and which memory locations are accessible only for reading. A permission remains interpreted as a predicate over heaps.

We let a "heap" be a pair (f, r) of two memories f and r whose domains are disjoint[6]. (We let f and r range over memories.) The memory f represents the memory cells that are fully accessible, that is, accessible for reading and writing. The memory r represents the memory cells that are accessible only for reading. We note that there exist other (isomorphic) concrete representations of heaps: for instance, we could have defined a heap as a map of memory locations to pairs of a value and an access right (either "read-write" or "read-only").

We let h range over heaps. We write $h.\mathsf{f}$ for the first component of the pair h (that is, the read-write memory) and $h.\mathsf{r}$ for its second component (the read-only memory).

---

[6] Technically, in Coq, a heap is defined as a pair (f, r) accompanied with a proof that f and r have disjoint domains. Thus, whenever in the paper we assemble a heap (f, r), we have an implicit obligation to prove $\mathbf{dom}\,f \cap \mathbf{dom}\,r = \varnothing$.

In traditional Separation Logic, two heaps are compatible (that is, can be composed) if and only if they have disjoint domains, and their composition is just their union. Here, because heaps contain information about access rights, we need slightly more complex notions of compatibility and composition of heaps. These notions are defined in Fig. 6. We first introduce a few notations. We write $m_1 \perp m_2$ when the memories m_1 and m_2 have disjoint domains. By extension, we write $m_1 \perp m_2 \perp m_3$ when the memories m_1, m_2 and m_3 have pairwise disjoint domains. We write agree r_1 r_2 when the memories r_1 and r_2 agree where their domains overlap.

These notations allow us to succinctly state when two heaps h_1 and h_2 are compatible. First, the read-only components of h_1 and h_2 must agree where their domains overlap. Second, the read-write component of h_1, the read-write component of h_2, and the combined read-only components of h_1 and h_2 must have pairwise disjoint domains. When two heaps h_1 and h_2 are compatible, they can be composed. Composition is performed component-wise, that is, by taking the (disjoint) union of the read-write components and the (compatible) union of the read-only components. (The hypothesis that h_1 and h_2 are compatible is used to meet the proof obligation that $h_1 + h_2$ is a well-formed heap whose read-write and read-only components have disjoint domains.) Composition, where defined, is associative and commutative.

The interpretation of permissions appears in Fig. 7. The interpretation of the standard permission forms is essentially standard: superficial adaptations are required to deal with the fact that a heap is a pair of a read-write memory and a read-only memory. The permission $[P]$ is satisfied by a heap whose read-write and read-only components are both empty, provided the proposition P holds. The permission $l \hookrightarrow v$ is satisfied by a heap whose read-write component is a singleton memory $(l \mapsto v)$ and whose read-only component is empty. The permission $H_1 \star H_2$ is satisfied by a heap h if and only if h is the composition of two (compatible) subheaps h_1 and h_2 which respectively satisfy H_1 and H_2. The interpretation of disjunction and existential quantification is standard.

A key aspect is the interpretation of $\mathsf{RO}(H)$. A human-readable, yet relatively accurate rendering of the formal meaning of $\mathsf{RO}(H)$ is as follows: "we do not have write access to any memory locations, but if we did have read-write (instead of read-only) access to certain locations, then H would hold". Technically, this is expressed as follows. The permission $\mathsf{RO}(H)$ is satisfied by a heap h if (1) the read-write component of h is empty and (2) the read-only component of h is of the form $h'.\mathsf{f} \uplus h'.\mathsf{r}$, where h' satisfies H. Thus, "RO" is a modality: it changes the "world" (the heap) with respect to which H is interpreted. In the outside world h, everything must be marked as read-only, whereas in the inside world h', some locations may be marked as read-write.

As explained earlier (Sect. 2.2), the meaning of normal H is defined as follows: a permission H is normal if and only if every heap h that satisfies it has an empty read-only component.

Entailment is defined in a standard way: $H_1 \rhd H_2$ holds if every heap that satisfies H_1 also satisfies H_2.

Lemma 1. *The above definitions validate the laws listed in Figs. 1 and 2.*

4.2 A Model of Triples

We now wish to assign an interpretation to a Hoare triple of the form $\{H\}\,t\,\{Q\}$. Then, each of the reasoning rules of the logic can be proved sound, independently, by checking that it is a valid lemma. Before giving this interpretation, a couple of auxiliary definitions are needed.

First, if h is a heap, let $\lfloor h \rfloor$ be the memory $h.\mathsf{f} \uplus h.\mathsf{r}$. That is, $\lfloor h \rfloor$ is the memory obtained by forgetting the distinction between read-write and read-only locations in the heap h. This definition serves as a link between memories, which exist at runtime (they appear in the operational semantics: see Fig. 3), and heaps, which additionally contain access right information. This information does not exist at runtime: it is "ghost" data.

Second, if H is a permission, let on-some-rw-frag(H) stand for the permission (that is, the predicate over heaps) that holds of a heap h if and only if h is the composition of two heaps h_1 and h_2, where h_1 has an empty read-only component and satisfies H. In mathematical notation:

$$\text{on-some-rw-frag}(H) \equiv$$
$$\lambda h.\, \exists h_1 h_2.\, \text{compatible } h_1\, h_2 \wedge h = h_1 + h_2 \wedge h_1.\mathsf{r} = \varnothing \wedge H\, h_1$$

Intuitively, on-some-rw-frag$(H)\,h$ asserts that H holds of a fragment of h whose read-only component is empty. This definition is used in the following to precisely express the meaning of postconditions, which in reality do not apply to the whole final heap, but to some fragment of the final heap whose read-only component is empty, or equivalently, to "some read-write fragment" of the final heap.

The interpretation of triples is now defined as follows:

Definition 1 (Interpretation of triples). *A semantic Hoare triple $\{H\}\,t\,\{Q\}$ is a short-hand for the following statement:*

$$\forall h_1 h_2.\, \left\{ \begin{array}{l} \textit{compatible } h_1\, h_2 \\ H\, h_1 \end{array} \right. \Rightarrow \exists v h_1'.\, \left\{ \begin{array}{l} \textit{compatible } h_1'\, h_2 \\ t/\lfloor h_1 + h_2 \rfloor \Downarrow v/\lfloor h_1' + h_2 \rfloor \\ h_1'.\mathsf{r} = h_1.\mathsf{r} \\ \textit{on-some-rw-frag}(Q\, v)\, h_1' \end{array} \right.$$

In order to understand this definition, it is useful to first read the special case where the heap h_2 is empty:

$$\forall h_1.\, H\, h_1 \Rightarrow \exists v h_1'.\, \left\{ \begin{array}{l} t/\lfloor h_1 \rfloor \Downarrow v/\lfloor h_1' \rfloor \\ h_1'.\mathsf{r} = h_1.\mathsf{r} \\ \textit{on-some-rw-frag}(Q\, v)\, h_1' \end{array} \right.$$

This may be read as follows. Let h_1 be an arbitrary initial heap that satisfies the permission H. Then, the term t, placed in the memory $\lfloor h_1 \rfloor$, runs safely and terminates, returning a value v in a final memory that can be described as $\lfloor h_1' \rfloor$, for some heap h_1'. The heap h_1' obeys the constraint $h_1'.\mathsf{r} = h_1.\mathsf{r}$, which

A. Charguéraud and F. Pottier

means that the set of all read-only locations is unchanged[7] and that the content of these locations is unchanged as well. Last, the permission $Q\,v$ is satisfied by some read-write fragment of the heap h'_1[8].

In the general case, where h_2 is an arbitrary heap, the definition of $\{H\}\,t\,\{Q\}$ states that the execution of the term t cannot affect a subheap h_2 which t "does not know about". Thus, running t in an initial heap $\lfloor h_1 + h_2 \rfloor$ must yield a final heap of the form $\lfloor h'_1 + h_2 \rfloor$. This requirement has the effect of "building the frame rule into the interpretation of triples". It is standard [14, Definition 11]. We note that the memories $\lfloor h_1 \rfloor$ and $\lfloor h_2 \rfloor$ are not necessarily disjoint: indeed, the read-only components of the heaps h_1 and h_2 may have overlapping domains.

Theorem 1 (Soundness). *The above definition of triples validates all of the reasoning rules of Figs. 4 and 5.*

Proof. We refer the reader to our Coq formalization [12]. □

5 Related Work

5.1 The C/C++ "const" Modifier

The C and C++ languages provide a type qualifier, const, which, when applied to the type of a pointer, makes this pointer usable only for reading. For example, a pointer of type const int* offers read access to an integer memory cell, but does not allow mutating this cell. A pointer of type int* can be implicitly converted to a pointer of type const int*.

The const qualifier arguably suffers from at least two important defects. First, as aliasing is not restricted, the above conversion rule immediately implies that a single pointer can perfectly well be stored at the same time in two distinct variables of types const int* and int*. Thus, although const prevents writing (through this pointer), it does not guarantee that the memory cell cannot be written (through an alias). Second, const does not take effect "in depth". If t has type const tree*, for instance, then t->left has type tree*, as opposed to const tree*. Thus, the const qualifier, applied to the type tree*, does not forbid modifications to the tree.

For these reasons, when a function expects a const pointer to a mutable data structure, one cannot be certain that this data structure is unaffected by a call to this function. In contrast, our read-only permissions do offer such a guarantee.

---

[7] That is, no read-write locations become read-only, or vice-versa. This reflects the fact that "RO" permissions appear and disappear following a lexical scope discipline. As a consequence, any newly-allocated memory cells must be marked read-write in h'_1.

[8] The operator on-some-rw-frag is used here for two reasons. First, in the presence of the rules DISCARD-PRE and DISCARD-POST, which discard arbitrary permissions, one cannot expect the postcondition $Q\,v$ to be satisfied by the whole final heap h'_1. Instead, one should expect $Q\,v$ to be satisfied by a fragment of h'_1. Second, $Q\,v$ is typically a normal permission, which can be satisfied only by a heap whose read-only component is empty. So, one may expect that $Q\,v$ is satisfied by a "read-write" fragment of h'_1.

5.2   The "Read-Only Frame" Connective

Jensen *et al.* [23] present a Separation Logic for "low-level" code. It is "high-level" in the sense that, even though machine code does not have a built-in notion of function, the logic offers structured reasoning rules, including first- and higher-order frame rules. The logic is stratified: assertions and specifications form two distinct levels. At the specification level, one finds a "frame" connective $\otimes$ and a "read-only frame" connective $\oslash$.

When applied to the specification of a first-order function, the "frame" connective has analogous effect to the "macro-expansion" scheme that was discussed earlier (Sect. 1.2): framing such a specification S with an assertion R amounts to applying $\_\ast R$ to the pre- and postcondition. Thus, if R is (say) $h \rightsquigarrow \mathsf{HashTable}\, M$, then the specification $S \otimes R$ states that h must remain a valid hash table that represents the dictionary M, but does not require that the table be unchanged: it could, for instance, be resized.

The "read-only frame" connective $\oslash$ is stronger: the specification $S \oslash R$ requires not just that the assertion R be preserved, but that the concrete heap fragment that satisfies R be left in its initial state. It is defined on top of the "frame" connective by bounded quantification. A typical use is to indicate that the code of a function (which, in this machine model, is stored in memory) must be accessible for reading, and is not modified when the function is called. Jensen *et al.*'s "read-only frame" connective allows "read-only" memory to be temporarily modified, as long as its initial state is restored upon exit. Therefore, it is quite different from our read-only permissions, which at the same time impose a restriction and offer a guarantee: they prevent the current function from modifying the "read-only" memory, and they guarantee that a callee cannot modify it either. Furthermore, our read-only permissions can be duplicated and discarded, whereas Jensen *et al.*'s "read-only frame" connective exists at the specification level: they have no read-only assertions.

5.3   Thoughts About Lexical Scope

The read-only frame rule takes advantage of lexical scope: it applies to a code block with well-defined entry and exit points, and governs how permissions are transformed when control enters and exits this block. Upon entry, a read-write permission is transformed to a read-only permission; upon exit, no read-only permissions are allowed to go through, and the original read-write permission reappears. The soundness of this rule relies on the fact that read-only permissions cannot escape through side channels[9].

There are several type systems and program logics in the literature which rely on lexical scope in a similar manner, sometimes for the same purpose (that

---

[9] For instance, we do not have concurrency, so a read-only permission cannot be transmitted to another thread via a synchronization operation. Furthermore, unlike Mezzo [2], we do not allow a closure to capture a duplicable permission, so a read-only permission cannot escape by becoming hidden in a closure.

is, to temporarily allow shared read-only access to a mutable data structure), sometimes for other purposes.

Wadler's "let!" construct [32, Sect. 4], for instance, is explicitly designed to allow temporary shared read-only access to a "linear value", that is, in our terminology, a uniquely-owned, mutable data structure. The "let!' rule changes the type of a variable x from T outside the block to $!T$ inside the block, which means that x temporarily becomes shareable and accessible only for reading. In order to ensure that no component of x is accessed for reading after the block is exited, Wadler requires a stronger property, namely that no component of x is accessible through the result value. Furthermore, in order to enforce this property, he imposes an even more conservative condition, namely that the result type U be "safe for T". In comparison, things are simpler for us. Separation Logic distinguishes values and permissions: thus, we do not care if a value (the address of x, or of a component of x) escapes, as long as no read permission escapes. Furthermore, in our setting, it is easy to enforce the latter condition. Technically, the side condition "normal H'" in the READ-ONLY FRAME RULE plays this role. At a high level, this side condition implies that read-only permissions appear only in preconditions, never in postconditions. In Wadler's system, in contrast, the "!" modality describes both inputs and outputs, and describes both permanently-immutable and temporarily-read-only data, so things are less clear-cut.

In Vault [17], the "focus" mechanism temporarily yields a unique read-write permission for an object that inhabits a region (therefore, can be aliased, so normally would be accessible only for reading). Meanwhile, the permission to access this region is removed. This is essentially the dual of the problem that we are addressing! In the case of "focus", it is comparatively easy to ensure that the temporary read-write permission does not escape: as this is a unique permission, it suffices to require it upon exit. For the same reason, it is possible to relax the lexical scope restriction by using an explicit linear implication [17, Sect. 6]. Boyland and Retert's explanation of "borrowing" [8] is also in terms of "focus".

Gordon et al. [18] describe a variant of C# where four kinds of references are distinguished, namely: ordinary writable references; readable references, which come with no write permission and no guarantee; immutable references, which come with a guarantee that nobody has (or will ever have) write permission; and isolated references, which form a unique entry point into a cluster of objects. Quite strikingly, the system does not require any accounting. Lexical scope is exploited in several interesting ways. In particular, the "isolation recovery" rule states that, if, upon entry into a block, only isolated and immutable references are available, and if, upon exit of that block, a single writable reference is available, then this reference can safely be viewed as isolated. (The soundness of this rule relies on the fact that there are no mutable global variables.) This rule may seem superficially analogous to the read-only frame rule, in that a unique permission is lost and recovered. It is unclear to us whether there is a deeper connection. The system has a typing rule for structured parallelism and allows a mutable data structure to be temporarily shared (for reading) by several threads.

Gordon *et al.*'s work is part of a line of research on "reference immutability", where type qualifiers are used to control object mutation. We refer to the reader to Gordon *et al.*'s paper [18] and to Potanin *et al.*'s survey [27]. Coblenz *et al.*'s recent study of language support for immutability [13] is also of interest.

Rust [31] has lexically-scoped "borrows", including "immutable borrows", during which multiple temporary read-only pointers into a uniquely-owned mutable data structure can be created. The borrowing discipline does not require any counting, but involves "lifetimes", a form of region variables. Lifetimes can often be hidden in the surface syntax, but must sometimes be exposed to the programmer. In contrast, our read-only permissions require neither counting nor region variables. Reed [29] offers a tentative formal description of Rust's borrowing discipline.

5.4   Fractional Permissions

Fractional permissions were introduced by Boyland [6] with the specific purpose of enabling temporary shared read-only access to a data structure. They have been integrated into several variants of Concurrent Separation Logic [5,19,21] and generalized in several ways, e.g., by replacing fractions with more abstract "shares" [16]. They are available in several program verification tools, including VeriFast [22], Chalice [20,24], and the Verified Software Toolchain [1].

In its simplest incarnation, a fractional permission takes the form $l \overset{\alpha}{\hookrightarrow} v$, where α is a rational number in the range $(0, 1]$. If α is 1, then this permission grants unique read-write access to the memory location l; if α is less than 1, then it grants shared read access. The following conversion rule allows splitting and joining fractional permissions:

$$(l \overset{\alpha+\beta}{\hookrightarrow} v) = (l \overset{\alpha}{\hookrightarrow} v) \star (l \overset{\beta}{\hookrightarrow} v) \qquad \text{when } \alpha, \beta, (\alpha + \beta) \in (0, 1]$$

Thanks to this rule, one can transition from a regime where a single thread has read-write access to a regime where several threads have read-only access, and back. Fractional permissions are not duplicable, and must not be carelessly discarded: indeed, in order to move back from read-only regime to read-write regime, one must prove that "no share has been lost" and that the fraction 1 has been recovered. This requires "accounting", that is, arithmetic reasoning, as well as returning fractional permissions in postconditions. In contrast, our proposal is less expressive in some ways (for instance, it does not support unstructured concurrency; see Sect. 6.2) but does not require accounting: our read-only permissions can be freely duplicated and discarded.

Fractional permissions also allow expressing a form of irrevocable (as opposed to temporary) read-only permissions. Define $(l \overset{ro}{\hookrightarrow} v)$ as follows:

$$(l \overset{ro}{\hookrightarrow} v) = \exists \alpha \in (0, 1). \ (l \overset{\alpha}{\hookrightarrow} v)$$

From this definition, it follows that $(l \overset{ro}{\hookrightarrow} v)$ is duplicable. It also follows that $(l \overset{1}{\hookrightarrow} v)$ can be converted to $(l \overset{ro}{\hookrightarrow} v)$, but not the other way around: the transition from read-write to read-only mode, in this case, is permanent.

In the systems of fractional permissions mentioned above, the fraction α is built into the points-to assertion $l \stackrel{\alpha}{\hookrightarrow} v$. Boyland [7] studies a more general idea, "scaling", where any permission H can be scaled by a fraction: that is, $H ::= \alpha.H$ is part of the syntax of permissions. Scaling seems a desirable feature, as it allows expressing read-only access to an abstract data structure, as in, say, $\frac{1}{2}(h \rightsquigarrow \mathsf{HashTable}\,M)$, which is impossible when scaling is built into points-to assertions. However, scaling exhibits a problematic interaction with disjunction and existential quantification. Boyland shows that "reasoning with a fractional unrestricted existential is unsound" [7, Sect. 5.4]. In short, it seems difficult to find a model that validates both of the laws $(\alpha.H) \star (\beta.H) = (\alpha + \beta).H$ and $\alpha.(\exists x.\,H) = \exists x.\,(\alpha.H)$. Indeed, under these laws, $\frac{1}{2}.(l_1 \hookrightarrow v) \star \frac{1}{2}.(l_2 \hookrightarrow v)$ entails $\exists l.\,(1.(l \hookrightarrow v))$, which does not make intuitive sense. Boyland escapes this problem by restricting the existential quantifier so that it is precise: the construct $\exists x.\,H$ is replaced with $\exists y.\,(x \hookrightarrow y \star H)$. In contrast, our read-only permissions do not require any such restriction, yet do support "scaling", in the sense that "RO" can be applied to an arbitrary permission: $\mathsf{RO}(H)$ is well-formed and has well-defined meaning for every H.

Chalice offers "abstract read permissions" [20], an elaborate layer of syntactic sugar above fractional permissions. An abstract read permission, which could be written $l \stackrel{rd}{\hookrightarrow} v$, is translated to a fractional permission $l \stackrel{\epsilon}{\hookrightarrow} v$, where the variable ϵ stands for an unknown fraction. The variable ϵ is suitably quantified: for instance, if this abstract read permission appears in a method specification, then ϵ is universally quantified in front of this specification [20, Sect. 4.1]. The system is powerful enough to automatically introduce and instantiate quantifiers and automatically split and join fractional permissions where needed. Unfortunately, because abstract read permissions are just fractional permissions, they are not duplicable, and they must not be carelessly discarded: they must be returned (or transferred to some other thread) so that the fraction 1 can eventually be recovered. Also, it is not known to us whether abstract read permissions can be explained to the programmer in a direct manner, without reference to fractional permissions.

In a somewhat related vein, Aldrich *et al.* [25] propose a type system where (among other features) out of a "unique" reference, any number of "local immutable" references can be temporarily "borrowed". The type system internally relies on integer accounting, but this is hidden from the user.

6 Potential Applications and Extensions

6.1 Where Read-Only Permissions Could (or Could Not) Help

The second author has specified and proved an OCaml implementation of hash tables [28], in Separation Logic, using the first author's tool, CFML. Iterating on a hash table is possible either via a higher-order function, `HashTable.iter`, or via "cascades", a form of iterators, built by the function `HashTable.cascade`.

In either case, the specification should ideally be stated in such a way that the consumer has read-only access to the table while iteration is in progress. For this purpose, the abstract predicate $h \rightsquigarrow \mathsf{HashTable}\, M$, which gives unique read-write access, is not appropriate. A finer-grained predicate, $h \rightsquigarrow \mathsf{HashTableInState}\, M\, s$, is introduced, where s is an abstract name for the current concrete state of the table. Then, a function that does not modify the table, like *population*, requires the permission $h \rightsquigarrow \mathsf{HashTableInState}\, M\, s$ and returns it. (It is polymorphic in s.) In contrast, a function that does modify the table, like *resize*, also requires $h \rightsquigarrow \mathsf{HashTableInState}\, M\, s$, but returns $\exists s'.\, h \rightsquigarrow \mathsf{HashTableInState}\, M\, s'$. In fact, because $h \rightsquigarrow \mathsf{HashTable}\, M$ is an abbreviation for $\exists s.\, h \rightsquigarrow \mathsf{HashTableInState}\, M\, s$, one can simply say that *resize* requires and returns $h \rightsquigarrow \mathsf{HashTable}\, M$.

The specification of `HashTable.iter` (not shown here) involves universal quantification over s and the predicate $h \rightsquigarrow \mathsf{HashTableInState}\, M\, s$. This allows expressing the fact that `iter` does not modify the table and requires the function that it receives as an argument to not modify it either. Read-only permissions, if implemented in CFML, would help simplify this specification. It would be sufficient to state that `iter` requires the permission $\mathsf{RO}(h \rightsquigarrow \mathsf{HashTable}\, M)$ and passes it on to the function that it receives as an argument.

The specification of `HashTable.cascade` (not shown either) also exploits s in order to express the fact that the iterator returned by `cascade` remains valid as long as the hash table is not modified. Unfortunately, because our read-only permissions have lexical scope, they cannot help state a simpler specification. Indeed, the iterator outlives the call to `cascade`: it still needs read access after this call is finished.

6.2 Parallelism and Concurrency

We believe that our read-only permissions remain sound when the calculus is extended with "structured parallelism", that is, with a term construct $t ::= (t \parallel t)$ for evaluating two terms in parallel. The parallel composition rule of Concurrent Separation Logic [26] can be used:

$$\text{PARALLEL COMPOSITION}$$
$$\frac{\{H_1\}\, t_1\, \{Q_1\} \qquad \{H_2\}\, t_2\, \{Q_2\}}{\{H_1 \star H_2\}\, (t_1 \parallel t_2)\, \{Q_1 \star Q_2\}}$$

Because read-only permissions are duplicable, this rule, combined with the rule of consequence, allows read access to be shared between the threads t_1 and t_2. That is, the following rule is derivable:

$$\text{PARALLEL COMPOSITION WITH SHARED READ}$$
$$\frac{\{H_1 \star \mathsf{RO}(H')\}\, t_1\, \{Q_1\} \qquad \{H_2 \star \mathsf{RO}(H')\}\, t_2\, \{Q_2\}}{\{H_1 \star H_2 \star \mathsf{RO}(H')\}\, (t_1 \parallel t_2)\, \{Q_1 \star Q_2\}}$$

This rule can be used to share read access between any number of threads. By combining it with the read-only frame rule, one obtains the following rule, which allows a mutable data structure (represented by the permission H') to temporarily be made accessible for reading to several threads and to become again accessible for reading and writing once these threads are finished:

PARALLEL COMPOSITION WITH TEMPORARY SHARED READ

$$\frac{\{H_1 \star \mathsf{RO}(H')\}\, t_1\, \{Q_1\} \qquad \{H_2 \star \mathsf{RO}(H')\}\, t_2\, \{Q_2\} \qquad \mathsf{normal}\ H'}{\{H_1 \star H_2 \star H'\}\, (t_1 \parallel t_2)\, \{Q_1 \star Q_2 \star H'\}}$$

At present, we do not have a proof that the PARALLEL COMPOSITION rule is sound. Our current proof technique apparently cannot easily accommodate it, primarily because it is based on a big-step operational semantics (Fig. 3), which (to the best of our knowledge) cannot be easily extended to support parallel composition ($t_1 \parallel t_2$).

These remarks lead to several questions. Could Separation Logic with read-only permissions be proved sound, based on a small-step operational semantics? Could the logic and its proof then be extended with support for structured parallelism? There seems to be no reason why they could not, but this requires further research.

Another question arises: could Separation Logic with read-only permissions be extended so as to support unstructured parallelism, that is, shared-memory concurrency with explicit threads and synchronization facilities, such as locks and channels? We do not have an answer. We know that naïvely transmitting a read-only permission from one thread to another would be unsound. So, probably, the logic would have to be made more complex, perhaps by explicitly annotating read-only permissions with "lifetime" information. Whether this can be done while preserving the simplicity of the approach is an open question. After all, the whole approach is worthwhile only as long as it remains significantly simpler than fractional permissions (Sect. 5.4), which offer a well-understood solution to this problem.

7   Conclusion

We have extended sequential Separation Logic with a simple form of temporary read-only permissions. We have argued that they can (at least in some situations) express more concise, more accurate, more useful specifications and give rise to simpler proofs. Our proposal involves very few additions to Separation Logic, namely the "RO" modality; the read-only frame rule, which subsumes the frame rule; and a generalized sequencing rule. We have given semantic meaning to read-only permissions and to Hoare triples in terms of heaps that include "ghost" access rights information. We have formalized the logic and its proof of soundness in Coq. We hope to implement read-only permissions in CFML [11] in the future.

References

1. Appel, A.W.: Verified software toolchain. In: Barthe, G. (ed.) ESOP 2011. LNCS, vol. 6602, pp. 1–17. Springer, Heidelberg (2011). doi:10.1007/978-3-642-19718-5_1
2. Balabonski, T., Pottier, F., Protzenko, J.: The design and formalization of Mezzo, a permission-based programming language. ACM Trans. Program. Lang. Syst. 38(4), 14:1–14:94 (2016)

3. Bengtson, J., Jensen, J.B., Birkedal, L.: Charge! A framework for higher-order separation logic in Coq. In: Interactive Theorem Proving (ITP), pp. 315–331 (2012)
4. Berdine, J., Calcagno, C., O'Hearn, P.W.: Smallfoot: modular automatic assertion checking with separation logic. In: Boer, F.S., Bonsangue, M.M., Graf, S., Roever, W.-P. (eds.) FMCO 2005. LNCS, vol. 4111, pp. 115–137. Springer, Heidelberg (2006). doi:10.1007/11804192_6
5. Bornat, R., Calcagno, C., O'Hearn, P., Parkinson, M.: Permission accounting in separation logic. In: Principles of Programming Languages (POPL), pp. 259–270 (2005)
6. Boyland, J.: Checking interference with fractional permissions. In: Cousot, R. (ed.) SAS 2003. LNCS, vol. 2694, pp. 55–72. Springer, Heidelberg (2003). doi:10.1007/3-540-44898-5_4
7. Boyland, J.T.: Semantics of fractional permissions with nesting. ACM Trans. Program. Lang. Syst. **32**(6), 22:1–22:33 (2010)
8. Boyland, J.T., Retert, W.: Connecting effects and uniqueness with adoption. In: Principles of Programming Languages (POPL), pp. 283–295 (2005)
9. Calcagno, C., Distefano, D.: Infer: an automatic program verifier for memory safety of C programs. In: Bobaru, M., Havelund, K., Holzmann, G.J., Joshi, R. (eds.) NFM 2011. LNCS, vol. 6617, pp. 459–465. Springer, Heidelberg (2011). doi:10.1007/978-3-642-20398-5_33
10. Charguéraud, A.: Characteristic formulae for mechanized program verification. Ph.D. thesis, Université Paris 7 (2010)
11. Charguéraud, A.: Characteristic formulae for the verification of imperative programs (2013, unpublished). http://www.chargueraud.org/research/2013/cf/cf.pdf
12. Charguéraud, A., Pottier, F.: Self-contained archive (2017). http://gallium.inria.fr/~fpottier/dev/seplogics/
13. Coblenz, M.J., Sunshine, J., Aldrich, J., Myers, B.A., Weber, S., Shull, F.: Exploring language support for immutability. In: International Conference on Software Engineering (ICSE), pp. 736–747 (2016)
14. Dinsdale-Young, T., Birkedal, L., Gardner, P., Parkinson, M.J., Yang, H.: Views: compositional reasoning for concurrent programs. In: Principles of Programming Languages (POPL), pp. 287–300 (2013)
15. Distefano, D., Parkinson, M.J.: jStar: towards practical verification for Java. In: Object-Oriented Programming, Systems, Languages, and Applications (OOPSLA), pp. 213–226 (2008)
16. Dockins, R., Hobor, A., Appel, A.W.: A fresh look at separation algebras and share accounting. In: Hu, Z. (ed.) APLAS 2009. LNCS, vol. 5904, pp. 161–177. Springer, Heidelberg (2009). doi:10.1007/978-3-642-10672-9_13
17. Fähndrich, M., DeLine, R.: Adoption and focus: practical linear types for imperative programming. In: Programming Language Design and Implementation (PLDI), pp. 13–24 (2002)
18. Gordon, C.S., Parkinson, M.J., Parsons, J., Bromfield, A., Duffy, J.: Uniqueness and reference immutability for safe parallelism. In: Object-Oriented Programming, Systems, Languages, and Applications (OOPSLA), pp. 21–40 (2012)
19. Gotsman, A., Berdine, J., Cook, B., Rinetzky, N., Sagiv, M.: Local reasoning for storable locks and threads. Technical report MSR-TR-2007-39, Microsoft Research (2007)
20. Heule, S., Leino, K.R.M., Müller, P., Summers, A.J.: Abstract read permissions: fractional permissions without the fractions. In: Giacobazzi, R., Berdine, J., Mastroeni, I. (eds.) VMCAI 2013. LNCS, vol. 7737, pp. 315–334. Springer, Heidelberg (2013). doi:10.1007/978-3-642-35873-9_20

21. Hobor, A., Appel, A.W., Nardelli, F.Z.: Oracle semantics for concurrent separation logic. In: Drossopoulou, S. (ed.) ESOP 2008. LNCS, vol. 4960, pp. 353–367. Springer, Heidelberg (2008). doi:10.1007/978-3-540-78739-6_27
22. Jacobs, B., Piessens, F.: The VeriFast program verifier. Technical report CW-520, Department of Computer Science, Katholieke Universiteit Leuven (2008)
23. Jensen, J.B., Benton, N., Kennedy, A.: High-level separation logic for low-level code. In: Principles of Programming Languages (POPL), pp. 301–314 (2013)
24. Leino, K.R.M., Müller, P.: A basis for verifying multi-threaded programs. In: Castagna, G. (ed.) ESOP 2009. LNCS, vol. 5502, pp. 378–393. Springer, Heidelberg (2009). doi:10.1007/978-3-642-00590-9_27
25. Naden, K., Bocchino, R., Aldrich, J., Bierhoff, K.: A type system for borrowing permissions. In: Principles of Programming Languages (POPL), pp. 557–570 (2012)
26. O'Hearn, P.W.: Resources, concurrency and local reasoning. Theor. Comput. Sci. **375**(1–3), 271–307 (2007)
27. Potanin, A., Östlund, J., Zibin, Y., Ernst, M.D.: Immutability. In: Clarke, D., Noble, J., Wrigstad, T. (eds.) Aliasing in Object-Oriented Programming. Types, Analysis and Verification. LNCS, vol. 7850, pp. 233–269. Springer, Heidelberg (2013). doi:10.1007/978-3-642-36946-9_9
28. Pottier, F.: Verifying a hash table and its iterators in higher-order separation logic. In: Certified Programs and Proofs (CPP), pp. 3–16 (2017)
29. Reed, E.: Patina: a formalization of the rust programming language. Technical report UW-CSE-15-03-02, University of Washington (2015)
30. Reynolds, J.C.: Separation logic: a logic for shared mutable data structures. In: Logic in Computer Science (LICS), pp. 55–74 (2002)
31. The Mozilla Foundation: The Rust programming language (2014)
32. Wadler, P.: Linear types can change the world! In: Broy, M., Jones, C. (eds.) Programming Concepts and Methods, North Holland (1990)

Faster Algorithms for
Weighted Recursive State Machines

Krishnendu Chatterjee[1], Bernhard Kragl[1]([✉]),
Samarth Mishra[2], and Andreas Pavlogiannis[1]

[1] IST Austria, Klosterneuburg, Austria
bkragl@ist.ac.at
[2] IIT Bombay, Mumbai, India

Abstract. Pushdown systems (PDSs) and recursive state machines (RSMs), which are linearly equivalent, are standard models for interprocedural analysis. Yet RSMs are more convenient as they (a) explicitly model function calls and returns, and (b) specify many natural parameters for algorithmic analysis, e.g., the number of entries and exits. We consider a general framework where RSM transitions are labeled from a semiring and path properties are algebraic with semiring operations, which can model, e.g., interprocedural reachability and dataflow analysis problems.

Our main contributions are new algorithms for several fundamental problems. As compared to a direct translation of RSMs to PDSs and the best-known existing bounds of PDSs, our analysis algorithm improves the complexity for finite-height semirings (that subsumes reachability and standard dataflow properties). We further consider the problem of extracting distance values from the representation structures computed by our algorithm, and give efficient algorithms that distinguish the complexity of a one-time preprocessing from the complexity of each individual query. Another advantage of our algorithm is that our improvements carry over to the concurrent setting, where we improve the best-known complexity for the context-bounded analysis of concurrent RSMs. Finally, we provide a prototype implementation that gives a significant speed-up on several benchmarks from the SLAM/SDV project.

1 Introduction

Interprocedural Analysis. One of the classical algorithmic analysis problems in programming languages is the interprocedural analysis. The problem is at the heart of several key applications, ranging from alias analysis, to data dependencies (modification and reference side effect), to constant propagation, to live and use analysis [10, 14–16, 18, 19, 24, 32, 35]. In seminal works [32, 35] it was shown that a large class of interprocedural dataflow analysis problems can be solved in polynomial time.

Models for Interprocedural Analysis. Two standard models for interprocedural analysis are *pushdown systems* (or finite automata with stacks) and

© Springer-Verlag GmbH Germany 2017
H. Yang (Ed.): ESOP 2017, LNCS 10201, pp. 287–313, 2017.
DOI: 10.1007/978-3-662-54434-1_11

recursive state machines (RSMs) [4,5]. An RSM is a formal model for control flow graphs of programs with recursion. We consider RSMs that consist of modules, one for each method or function that has a number of entry nodes and a number of exit nodes, and each module contains boxes that represent calls to other modules. A special case of RSMs with a single entry and a single exit node for every module (*SESE RSMs*, aka *supergraph* in [32]) has also been considered. While pushdown systems and RSMs are linearly equivalent (i.e., there is a linear translation from one model to the other and vice versa), there are two distinct advantages of RSMs. First, the model of RSMs closely resembles the problems of programming languages with explicit function calls and returns, and hence even its special cases such as SESE RSMs has been considered to model many applications. Second, the model of RSMs provides many parameters, such as the number of entry and exit nodes, and the number of modules, and better algorithms can be developed by considering that some parameters are small. Typically the SESE RSMs can model data-independent interprocedural analysis, whereas general RSMs can model data dependency as well. For most applications, the number of entries and exits of a module, usually represents the input parameters of the module.

Semiring Framework. We consider a general framework to express computation properties of RSMs where the transitions of an RSM are labeled from a semiring. The labels are referred to as weights. A *computation* of an RSM executes transitions between configurations consisting of a node (representing the current control state) and a stack of boxes (representing the current calling context). To express properties of interest we need to define how to assign weights to computations, i.e., to accumulate weights *along* a computation, and how to assign weights to sets of computations, i.e., to combine weights *across* a set of computations. The weight of a given computation is the semiring product of the weights on the individual transitions of the computation, and the weight of a given set of computations is the semiring plus of the weights of the individual computations in the set. For example, (i) with the Boolean semiring (with semiring product as AND, and semiring plus as OR) we express the reachability property; (ii) with a Dataflow semiring we can express problems from dataflow analysis. One class of such problems is given by the IFDS/IDE framework [32,35] that considers the propagation of dataflow facts along distributive dataflow functions (note that the IFDS/IDE framework only considers SESE RSMs). Hence the large and important class of dataflow analysis problems that can be expressed in the IFDS/IDE framework can also be expressed in our framework. Pushdown systems with semiring weights have also been extensively considered in the literature [20,22,33,34].

Problems Considered. We consider the following basic *distance problems*.

– *Configuration distance.* Given a set of *source* configurations and a *target* configuration, the *configuration distance* is the weight of the set of computations that start at some source configuration and end in the target configuration. In the *configuration distance problem* the input is a set of source configurations and the output is the configuration distance to all reachable configurations.

- *Superconfiguration distance.* We also consider a related problem of *superconfiguration distance*. A *superconfiguration* represents a sequence of modules, rather than a sequence of invocations. Intuitively, it does not consider the sequence of function calls, but only which functions were invoked. This is a coarser notion than configurations and allows for fast overapproximation. The superconfiguration distance problem is then similar to the configuration distance problem, with configurations replaced by superconfigurations.
- *Node distance.* Given a set of source configurations and a target node, the *node distance* is the weight of the set of computations that start at some source configuration and end in a configuration with the target node (with arbitrary stack). In the *node distance problem* the input is a set of source configurations and the output is the node distance to all reachable nodes.

Symbolic Representation. A core ingredient for solving distance problems is the symbolic representation of sets of RSM configurations and their manipulation. Given a symbolic representation of the set of initial configurations, we provide a two step approach to solve the distance problems. In step one we compute a symbolic representation of the set of all configurations reachable from the initial configurations. Furthermore, the transitions in the representation are annotated with appropriate semiring weights to capture the various distances described above. In step two we query the computed representation for the required distances. Thus we make the important distinction between the complexity of a *one-time* preprocessing and the complexity of every *individual query*.

Concurrent RSMs. While reachability is the most basic property, the study of pushdown systems and RSMs with the semiring framework is the fundamental quantitative extension of the basic problem. An orthogonal fundamental extension is to study the reachability property in a *concurrent* setting, rather than the sequential setting. However, the reachability problem in concurrent RSMs (equivalently concurrent pushdown systems) is undecidable [31]. A very relevant problem to study in the concurrent setting is to consider context-bounded reachability, where at most k context switches are allowed. The context-bounded reachability problem is both decidable [29] and practically relevant [26,27].

Previous Results. Many previous results have been established for pushdown systems, and the translation of RSMs to pushdown systems implies that similar results carry over to RSMs as well. We describe the most relevant previous results with respect to our results. For an RSM $\mathcal{R}$, let $|\mathcal{R}|$ denote its size, θ_e and θ_x the maximum number of entries and exits, respectively, and f the number of modules. The existing results for weighted pushdown systems over semirings of height H [34,36] along with the linear translation of RSMs to pushdown systems [4] gives an $O(H \cdot |\mathcal{R}| \cdot \theta_e \cdot \theta_x \cdot f)$-time algorithm for the configuration and node distance problems for RSMs. The previous results for context-bounded reachability of concurrent pushdown systems [29] applied to concurrent RSMs gives the following complexity bound: $O(|\mathcal{R}^{\|}|^5 \cdot \theta_x^{\|}{}^5 \cdot n^k \cdot |G|^k)$, where $|\mathcal{R}^{\|}|$ is the size of the concurrent RSM, $\theta_x^{\|}$ is the number of exit nodes, n is the number of component RSMs, G is the global part of the concurrent RSM, and k is the bound on the number of context switches.

Table 1. Asymptotic time complexity of computing configuration automata.

	Sequential		Concurrent	
Existing	$H \cdot |\mathcal{R}| \cdot \theta_e \cdot \theta_x \cdot f$	[34,36]	$|\mathcal{R}^{\|}|^5 \cdot \theta_x^{\|\,5} \cdot n^k \cdot |G|^k$	[29]
Our result	$H \cdot (|\mathcal{R}| \cdot \theta_e + |Call| \cdot \theta_e \cdot \theta_x)$	[Theorem 1]	$|\mathcal{R}^{\|}| \cdot \theta_e^{\|} \cdot \theta_x^{\|} \cdot n^k \cdot |G|^{k+2}$	[Theorem 7]

Table 2. Asymptotic time complexity of answering a configuration/superconfiguration distance query of size n. Preprocess time refers to additional preprocessing after the configuration automaton is constructed.

Semiring					RSM		
General	Boolean	Constant size	Size $|D|^a$			Sparse[b]	
Query	Query	Query	Preprocess	Query	Preprocess		Query
$n \cdot \theta_e^2$	$|\mathcal{R}| \cdot \theta_e \cdot \frac{n}{\log n}$	$n \cdot \frac{\theta_e^2}{\log \theta_e}$	$|\mathcal{R}| \cdot \theta_e^{1+\varepsilon \cdot \log |D|}$	$n \cdot \frac{\theta_e^2}{\varepsilon^2 \cdot \log^2 \theta_e}$	$|\mathcal{R}| \cdot \theta_e^{\omega-1} \cdot x$	$n \cdot$	$\frac{\theta_e^2}{\log x}$

^{a} For any fixed $\varepsilon > 0$.
^{b} In a sparse RSM every module only calls a constant number of other modules, and the result applies only to superconfiguration distances. The parameter x has to satisfy $x = O(\text{poly}(|\mathcal{R}|))$, and ω is the smallest constant required for multiplying two square matrices of size $m \times m$ in time $O(m^\omega)$ (currently $\omega \simeq 2.372$).

Our Contributions. Our main contributions are as follows:

1. *Finite-height semirings.* We present an algorithm for computing configuration and node distance problems for RSMs over semirings with finite height H with running time $O(H \cdot (|\mathcal{R}| \cdot \theta_e + |Call| \cdot \theta_e \cdot \theta_x))$, where $|Call|$ is the number of call nodes. The algorithm we present constructs the symbolic representations from which the distances can be extracted. Thus our algorithm improves the current best-known algorithms by a factor of $\Omega((|\mathcal{R}| \cdot f)/(\theta_x + |Call|))$ (Table 1) (also see Remark 3 for details).

2. *Distance queries.* Once a symbolic representation is constructed, it can be used for extracting distances. We present algorithms which given a configuration query of size n, return the distance in $O(n \cdot \theta_e^2)$ time. Furthermore, we present several improvements for the case when the semiring has a small domain. Finally, we show that when the RSM has a sparse call graph, we can obtain a range of tradeoffs between preprocessing and querying times. Our results on distance queries are summarized in Table 2.

3. *Concurrent RSMs.* For the context-bounded reachability of concurrent RSMs we present an algorithm with time bound $O(|\mathcal{R}^{\|}| \cdot \theta_e^{\|} \cdot \theta_x^{\|} \cdot n^k \cdot |G|^{k+2})$. Thus our algorithm significantly improves the current best-known algorithm (Table 1).

4. *Experimental results.* We experiment with a basic prototype implementation for our algorithms. Our implementation is an explicit (rather than symbolic) one. We compare our implementation with jMoped [1], which is a leading and mature tool for weighted pushdown systems, on several real-world benchmarks coming from the SLAM/SDV project [6,7]. We consider the basic reachability property (representative for finite-height semirings) for the sequential setting. Our experimental results show that our algorithm provides significant improvements on the benchmarks compared to jMoped.

Technical Contribution. The main technical contributions are as follows:

- We show how to combine (i) the notion of *configuration automata* as a *symbolic* representation structure for sets of configurations, and (ii) entry-to-exit *summaries* to avoid redundant computations, and obtain an efficient dynamic programming algorithm for various distance problems in RSMs over finite-height semirings.
- Configuration and superconfiguration distances are extracted using graph traversal of configuration automata. When the semiring has small domain, we obtain several speedups by exploiting advances in matrix-vector multiplication. Finally, the speedup of superconfiguration distance extraction on sparse RSMs is achieved by devising a Four-Russians type of algorithm, which spends some polynomial preprocessing time in order to allow compressing the query input in blocks of logarithmic length.

All proofs are provided in our technical report [12].

2   Preliminaries

In this section we present the necessary definitions of recursive state machines (RSMs) where every transition is labeled with a value (or weight) from an appropriate domain (semiring). Then we formally state the problems we study on weighted RSMs.

Semirings. An *idempotent semiring* is a quintuple $\langle D, \oplus, \otimes, \overline{0}, \overline{1} \rangle$, where D is a set called the *domain*, $\overline{0}$ and $\overline{1}$ are elements of D, and $\oplus$ (the *combine* operation) and $\otimes$ (the *extend* operation) are binary operators on D such that

1. $\langle D, \oplus, \overline{0} \rangle$ is an idempotent commutative monoid with neutral element $\overline{0}$,
2. $\langle D, \otimes, \overline{1} \rangle$ is a monoid with neutral element $\overline{1}$,
3. $\otimes$ distributes over $\oplus$,
4. $\overline{0}$ is an annihilator for $\otimes$, i.e., $a \otimes \overline{0} = \overline{0} \otimes a = \overline{0}$ for all $a \in D$.

An idempotent semiring has a canonical partial order $\sqsubseteq$, defined by

$$a \sqsubseteq b \iff a \oplus b = a.$$

Furthermore, this partial order is *monotonic*, i.e., for all $a, b, c \in D$

$$a \sqsubseteq b \implies a \oplus c \sqsubseteq b \oplus c,$$
$$a \sqsubseteq b \implies a \otimes c \sqsubseteq b \otimes c,$$
$$a \sqsubseteq b \implies c \otimes a \sqsubseteq c \otimes b.$$

The *height* H of an idempotent semiring is the length of the longest descending chain in $\sqsubseteq$. In the rest of the paper we will only write semiring to mean an idempotent finite-height semiring.

Remark 1. Instead of finite height, the more general *descending chain condition* would be sufficient for our purposes. This only requires that there are no infinite descending chains in $\sqsubseteq$, but there is not necessarily a finite height H.

Recursive State Machines (informally). Intuitively, an RSM is a collection of finite automata, called modules, such that computations consist of ordinary local transitions within a module as well as calls to other modules, and returns from other modules. For this, every module has a well-defined interface of entry and exit nodes. Calls to other modules are represented by boxes, which have call and return nodes corresponding to the respective entry and exit nodes of the called module.

Unlike pushdown automata (PDAs), there is no explicit stack manipulation in RSMs. Instead a call stack is maintained implicitly along computations as follows. When a call node of a box is reached, the control is passed to the respective entry node of the called module and the box is pushed onto the top of the stack. When an exit node of a module is reached, a box is popped off from the top of the stack and the control is passed to the corresponding return node of the box. Hence, the stack is a sequence of boxes representing the current calling context and a configuration in a computation of an RSM is a node together with a sequence of boxes.

Recursive State Machines (formally). A *recursive state machine (RSM)* over a semiring $\langle D, \oplus, \otimes, \overline{0}, \overline{1} \rangle$ is a tuple $\mathcal{R} = \langle \mathcal{M}_1, \ldots, \mathcal{M}_k \rangle$, where every *module* $\mathcal{M}_i = \langle B_i, Y_i, N_i, \delta_i, w_i \rangle$ is given by

- a finite set B_i of *boxes*,
- a mapping $Y_i : B_i \mapsto \{1, \ldots, k\}$,
- a finite set $N_i = In_i \cup En_i \cup Ex_i \cup Call_i \cup Ret_i$ of *nodes*, partitioned into
  - *internal* nodes In_i,
  - *entry* nodes En_i,
  - *exit* nodes Ex_i,
  - *call* nodes $Call_i = \{\langle b, e \rangle \mid b \in B_i \text{ and } e \in En_{Y_i(b)}\}$,
  - *return* nodes $Ret_i = \{\langle b, x \rangle \mid b \in B_i \text{ and } x \in Ex_{Y_i(b)}\}$,
- a *transition relation* $\delta_i \subseteq (In_i \cup En_i \cup Ret_i) \times (In_i \cup Ex_i \cup Call_i)$,
- a *weight function* $w_i : \delta_i \mapsto D$, with $w_i(u, x) = \overline{1}$ for every exit node $x \in Ex_i$.

We write B for $\bigcup_{i=1}^{k} B_i$, and similarly for N, In, En, Ex, $Call$, Ret, δ, w. To measure the size of an RSM we let $|\mathcal{R}| = \max(|N|, \sum_i |\delta_i|)$. A major source of complexity in analysis problems for RSMs is the number of entry and exit nodes of the modules. Throughout the paper we express complexity with respect to the *entry bound* $\theta_e = \max_{1 \leq i \leq k} |En_i|$ and the *exit bound* $\theta_x = \max_{1 \leq i \leq k} |Ex_i|$, i.e., the maximum number of entries and exits, respectively, over all modules. Note that the restriction on the weight function to assign weight $\overline{1}$ to every transition to an exit node is wlog, as any weighted RSM that does not respect this can be turned into an equivalent one that does, with only a constant factor increase in its size.

Stacks. A *stack* is a sequence of boxes $S = b_1 \ldots b_r$, where the first box denotes the top of the stack; and ε is the empty stack. The *height* of S is $|S| = r$, i.e., the number of boxes it contains. For a box b and a stack S, we denote with bS the concatenation of b and S, i.e., a push of b onto the top of S.

Configurations and Transitions. A *configuration of an RSM* $\mathcal{R}$ is a tuple $\langle u, S \rangle$, where $u \in In \cup En \cup Ret$ is an internal, entry, or return node, and S is a stack. For $S = b_1 \ldots b_r$, where $b_i \in B_{j_i}$ for $1 \leq i \leq r$ and some j_i, we require that $Y_{j_i}(b_i) = j_{i-1}$ for $1 < i \leq r$, as well as $u \in N_{Y_{j_1}(b_1)}$. This corresponds to the case where the control is inside the module of node u, which was entered via box b_1 from module $\mathcal{M}_{j_1}$, which was entered via box b_2 from module $\mathcal{M}_{j_2}$, and so on.

We define a transition relation $\Rightarrow$ over configurations and a corresponding weight function $w : \Rightarrow \mapsto D$, such that $\langle u, S \rangle \Rightarrow \langle u', S' \rangle$ with $w(\langle u, S \rangle, \langle u', S' \rangle) = v$ if and only if there exists a transition $t \in \delta_i$ in $\mathcal{R}$ with $w_i(t) = v$ and one of the following holds:

1. *Internal transition:* $u' \in In_i$, $t = \langle u, u' \rangle$, and $S' = S$.
2. *Call transition:* $u' = e \in En_{Y_i(b)}$ for some box $b \in B_i$, $t = \langle u, \langle b, e \rangle \rangle$, and $S' = bS$.
3. *Return transition:* $u' = \langle b, x \rangle \in R_i$ for some box $b \in B_i$ and exit node $x \in Ex_{Y_i(b)}$, $t = \langle u, x \rangle$, and $S = bS'$.

Note that we follow the convention that a call immediately enters the called module and a return immediately returns to the calling module. Hence, the node of a configuration can be an internal node, an entry node, or a return node, but not a call node or an exit node.

Computations. A *computation* of an RSM $\mathcal{R}$ is a sequence of configurations $\pi = c_1, \ldots, c_n$, such that $c_i \Rightarrow c_{i+1}$ for every $1 \leq i < n$. We say that π is a computation from c_1 to c_n, of length $|\pi| = n - 1$, and of weight $\otimes(\pi) = \bigotimes_{i=1}^{n-1} w(c_i, c_{i+1})$ (the empty extend is $\bar{1}$). We write $\pi : c \Rightarrow^* c'$ to denote that π is a computation from c to c' of any length. A computation $\pi : c \Rightarrow^* c'$ is called *non-decreasing* if the stack height of every configuration of π is at least as large as that of c (in other words, the top stack symbol of c is never popped in π). The computation π is called *same-context* if it is non-decreasing, and c and c' have the same stack height. A computation that cannot be extended by any transition is called a *halting* computation. For a set of computations Π we define its weight as $\bigoplus(\Pi) = \bigoplus_{\pi \in \Pi} \otimes(\pi)$ (the empty combine is $\bar{0}$). For a configuration c and a set of configurations R we denote by $\Pi(R, c)$ the set of all computations from any configuration in R to c. Here, and for similar purposes below, we will use the convention to write $\Pi(c, c')$ instead of $\Pi(\{c\}, c')$.

Example 1. Figure 1 shows an RSM $\mathcal{R} = \langle \mathcal{M}_1, \mathcal{M}_2 \rangle$ that consists of two modules $\mathcal{M}_1$ and $\mathcal{M}_2$. The modules are mutually recursive, since box b_1 of module $\mathcal{M}_1$ calls module $\mathcal{M}_2$, and box b_2 of module $\mathcal{M}_2$ calls module $\mathcal{M}_1$. A possible computation of $\mathcal{R}$ is

$$
\begin{aligned}
&\langle e_1^1, \varepsilon \rangle \xRightarrow{w_1} \langle e_2, b_1 \rangle \xRightarrow{w_5} \langle e_1^1, b_2 b_1 \rangle \xRightarrow{w_1} \langle e_2, b_1 b_2 b_1 \rangle \xRightarrow{w_6} \langle e_1^2, b_2 b_1 b_2 b_1 \rangle \xRightarrow{w_3} \\
&\langle u_1, b_2 b_1 b_2 b_1 \rangle \xRightarrow{w_4} \langle \langle b_2, x_1 \rangle, b_1 b_2 b_1 \rangle \xRightarrow{w_7} \langle \langle b_1, x_2 \rangle, b_2 b_1 \rangle \xRightarrow{w_3} \langle u_1, b_2 b_1 \rangle \xRightarrow{w_4} \quad (1) \\
&\langle \langle b_2, x_1 \rangle, b_1 \rangle \xRightarrow{w_7} \langle \langle b_1, x_2 \rangle, \varepsilon \rangle \xRightarrow{w_3} \langle u_1, \varepsilon \rangle.
\end{aligned}
$$

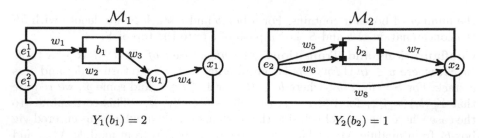

Fig. 1. Example of a weighted RSM that consists of two modules with mutual recursion.

Distance Problems. Given a set of configurations R, the set of configurations that are *reachable* from R is

$$post^*(R) = \{c \mid \exists c_0 \in R : c_0 \Rightarrow^* c\}.$$

Instead of mere reachability, we are interested in the following distance metrics that aggregate over computations from R using the semiring combine and hence are expressed as semiring values.

– *Configuration distance.* The *configuration distance* from R to c is defined as

$$d(R, c) = \bigoplus(\Pi(R, c)).$$

That is, we take the combine over the weights of all computations from a configuration in R to c. Naturally, for configurations c not reachable from R we have $d(R, c) = \bar{0}$.

– *Superconfiguration distance.* A *superstack* is a sequence of modules $\overline{S} = \mathcal{M}_1 \ldots \mathcal{M}_r$. A stack $S = b_1 \ldots b_r$ *refines* $\overline{S}$ if $b_i \in B_i$ for all $1 \leq i \leq r$, i.e., the i-th box of S belongs to the i-th module of $\overline{S}$. A *superconfiguration* of $\mathcal{R}$ is a tuple $\langle u, \overline{S} \rangle$. Let $[\![\langle u, \overline{S} \rangle]\!] = \{\langle u, S \rangle \mid S \text{ refines } \overline{S}\}$. The *superconfiguration distance* from R to a superconfiguration $\overline{c}$ is defined as

$$d(R, \overline{c}) = \bigoplus_{c \in [\![\overline{c}]\!]} d(R, c)$$

The superconfiguration distance is only concerned with the sequence of modules that have been used to reach the node u, rather than the concrete sequence of boxes as in the configuration distance. This is a coarser notion than configuration and allows for fast overapproximation.

– *Node and same-context distance.* The *node distance* of a node u from R is defined as

$$d(R, u) = \bigoplus_{c = \langle u, S \rangle} d(R, c)$$

where S ranges over stacks of $\mathcal{R}$. Finally, the *same-context node distance* of a node u in module $\mathcal{M}_i$ is defined as

$$d(\mathcal{M}_i, u) = \bigoplus_{e \in En_i} d(\langle e, \varepsilon \rangle, \langle u, \varepsilon \rangle).$$

Intuitively, the node distance minimizes over all possible ways (i.e., stack sequences) to reach a node, and the same-context problem considers nodes in the same module that can be reached with empty stack.

Relevance. We discuss the relevance of the model and the problems we consider in program analysis. A prime application area of our framework is the analysis of procedural programs. Computations in an RSM correspond to the interprocedurally valid paths of a program. The distance values defined above allow to obtain information at different levels of granularity, depending on the requirement for a particular analysis. MEME (multi-entry, multi-exit) RSMs naturally arise in the model checking of procedural programs, where every node represents a combination of control location and data. Checking for reachability, usually of an error state, requires only the simple Boolean semiring. On the other hand, interprocedural data flow analysis problems, like in IFDS/IDE, are usually cast on SESE (single-entry, single-exit) RSMs (the control flow graph of the program) using richer semirings. Our framework captures both of these important applications, and furthermore allows a hybrid approach of modeling program information both in the state space of the RSM as well as in the semiring.

3   Configuration Distance Algorithm

In this section we present an algorithm which takes as input an RSM $\mathcal{R}$ and a representation of a *regular set* of configurations R, and computes a representation of the set of reachable configurations $post^*(R)$ that allows the extraction of the distance metrics defined above. In Sect. 3.1 we introduce configuration automata as representation structures for regular sets of configurations. In Sect. 3.2 we present an algorithm for RSMs over finite-height semirings. The algorithm saturates the input configuration automaton with additional transitions and assigns the correct weights via a dynamic programming approach that gradually relaxes transition weights from an initial overapproximation. We exploit the monotonicity property in idempotent semirings which allows to factor the computation into subproblems, and hence corresponds to the *optimal substructure* property of dynamic programming. Although a transition might have to be processed multiple times, the finite height of the semiring prevents a transition from being relaxed indefinitely. Here we show that the final configuration automata constructed by our algorithms correctly capture configuration distances. The extraction of distance values is considered in Sect. 4.

3.1   Configuration Automata

In general, like R, the set $post^*(R)$ is infinite. Hence we make use of a representation of regular sets of configurations as the language accepted by configuration automata, defined below. The main feature of a regular set of configurations R is its closure under $post^*$. That is, $post^*(R)$ is also a regular set of configurations and can be represented by a configuration automaton.

Intuition. Every state in a configuration automaton corresponds to a node in the RSM. In order to represent arbitrary regular sets of configurations we must allow the replication of states with the same node. Therefore we annotate every state with a *mark* (see Remark 2 for details). Transitions are of two types: (i) ε-transitions pointing from a node u to an entry node e and labeled with ε, denoting that a computation reaching u entered the module of u via entry e, and (ii) b-transitions pointing from an entry node e to another entry node e' and labeled with a box b, corresponding to a call transition $\langle u, \langle b, e \rangle \rangle$ in the module of e' in the RSM. Reading the labels along a path in the automaton yields a stack.

In addition to the labeling with boxes we label every transition of a configuration automaton with a semiring value. In the final configuration automata constructed by our algorithms, every run generates a configuration c and thereby captures a certain subset $\Pi \subseteq \Pi(R, c)$ of computations from the initial set of configurations R to c. The weight of the run equals the combine over the weight of the computations in Π. The combine over the weights of all runs in the automaton that generate c equals the combine over the weights of all computations from R to c, i.e., the configuration distance $d(R, c)$. Since the transitions in a configuration automaton are essentially reversed transitions of the RSM (and the extend operation is not commutative), the weight of a run is given by the extend of the transitions in reversed order.

Configuration Automata. Let $\mathbb{M}$ be a countably infinite set of *marks*. A *configuration automaton for an RSM* $\mathcal{R}$, also called an *$\mathcal{R}$-automaton*, is a weighted finite automaton $\mathcal{C} = \langle Q, B, \to, I, F, \ell \rangle$, where

- $Q \subseteq (In \cup En \cup Ret) \times \mathbb{M}$ is a finite set of *states*,
- B (the boxes of $\mathcal{R}$) is the transition alphabet,
- $\to \subseteq Q \times (B \cup \{\varepsilon\}) \times Q$ is a transition relation, such that every transition has one of the following forms:
  - *b-transition:* $\langle e, m_e \rangle \xrightarrow{b} \langle e', m_{e'} \rangle$, where $b \in B_i$ for some i, $e \in En_{Y_i(b)}$, and $e' \in En_i$,
  - *ε-transition:* $\langle u, m_u \rangle \xrightarrow{\varepsilon} \langle e, m_e \rangle$, where $e \in En_i$ for some i, and either $u \in In_i \cup Ret_i$, or $u = e$,
- $I \subseteq Q$ is a set of *initial states*,
- $F \subseteq Q$ and $F \subseteq En \times \mathbb{M}$ is a set of *final states*,
- $\ell : \to \mapsto D$ is a *weight function* that assigns a semiring weight to every transition.

Remark 2 (Marks). The marks in the states of a configuration automaton are introduced to support the general setting of representing an arbitrary set of configurations, e.g., with stacks that are not even reachable in the RSM. Since every state is tied to an RSM node, the marks allow to have multiple "copies" of the same node in unrelated parts of the automaton. Furthermore, our algorithm (Sect. 3.2) introduces a *fresh mark* to recognize when it can safely store *entry-to-exit summaries*. For the common setting of starting the analysis from the entry nodes of a main module with empty stack, marks are not necessary and can be elided.

Runs and Regular sets of Configurations. A *run* of a configuration automaton $\mathcal{C}$ is a sequence $\lambda = t_1, \ldots, t_n$, such that there are states $q_1, \ldots, q_{n+1}$ and each $t_i = q_i \xrightarrow{\sigma_i} q_{i+1}$ is a transition of $\mathcal{C}$ labeled with σ_i. We say that λ is a run from q_1 to q_{n+1}, of length $|\lambda| = n$, labeled by $S = \sigma_1 \ldots \sigma_n$, and of weight $\otimes(\lambda) = \bigotimes_{i=n}^{1} \ell(t_i)$ (note that the weights of the transitions are extended in reverse order). We write $\lambda : q \xrightarrow{S/v}{}^* q'$ to denote that λ is a run from q to q' of any length labeled by S and of weight v. We will also use the notation without v if we are not interested in the weight. The run λ is *accepting* if $q \in I$ and $q' \in F$. A configuration $\langle u, S \rangle$ is *accepted* by $\mathcal{C}$ if there is an accepting run $\lambda : \langle u, m \rangle \xrightarrow{S}{}^* q_f$ for some mark $m \in \mathbb{M}$, and additionally $\otimes(\lambda) \neq \bar{0}$. We say that two runs are *equivalent* if they accept the same configuration with the same weight. For technical convenience we consider that for every state $\langle e, m_e \rangle$ with entry node $e \in En$ there is an ε-self-loop $\langle e, m_e \rangle \xrightarrow{\varepsilon} \langle e, m_e \rangle$ with weight $\bar{1}$.

The set of all configurations accepted by $\mathcal{C}$ is denoted by $\mathcal{L}(\mathcal{C})$. A set of configurations R is called *regular* if there exists an $\mathcal{R}$-automaton $\mathcal{C}$ such that $\mathcal{L}(\mathcal{C}) = R$. For a configuration c let $\Lambda(c)$ be the set of all accepting runs of c and define $\mathcal{C}(c) = \bigoplus_{\lambda \in \Lambda(c)} \otimes(\lambda)$ the weight that $\mathcal{C}$ assigns to c.

We note that, despite the imposed syntactic restrictions, our definition of configuration automata is most general in the following sense.

Proposition 1. *Let R be a set of configurations such that their string representations is a regular language. Then there exists a configuration automaton $\mathcal{C}$ such that $\mathcal{L}(\mathcal{C}) = R$.*

3.2   Algorithm for Finite-Height Semirings

In the following we present algorithm `ConfDist` for computing the set $post^*(R)$ of a regular set of configurations R. The algorithm operates on an $\mathcal{R}$-automaton $\mathcal{C}$ with $\mathcal{L}(\mathcal{C}) = R$. In the end, it has constructed an $\mathcal{R}$-automaton $\mathcal{C}_{post^*}$ such that $\mathcal{L}(\mathcal{C}_{post^*}) = post^*(R)$. Moreover, the configuration distance $d(R, c)$ from R to any configuration c can be obtained from the labels of $\mathcal{C}_{post^*}$ as $\mathcal{C}_{post^*}(c)$. A computation is called *initialized*, if its first configuration is accepted by the initial configuration automaton $\mathcal{C}$.

Key Technical Contribution. In this work we consider the configuration distance computation. Using the notion of configuration automata as a *symbolic* representation structure for regular sets of configurations, the solution of the configuration distance problem has been previously studied in the setting of (weighted) pushdown systems [9,34,36]. One of the main algorithmic ideas for the efficient RSM reachability algorithm of [4] is to expand RSM transitions and use entry-to-exit *summaries* to avoid traversing a module more than once. However, the algorithm in [4] is limited to the node reachability problem. We combine the symbolic representation of configuration automata, along with the summarization principle, to obtain an efficient algorithm for the general configuration distance problem on RSMs.

Intuitive Description of ConfDist. The intuition behind our algorithm is very simple: it performs a forward search in the RSM. In every iteration it picks a frontier node u and extends the already discovered computations to u with the outgoing transitions from u. Depending on the type of outgoing transitions, a new node discovered and added to the frontier can be (a) an internal node by following an internal transition, (b) the entry node of another module by following a call transition, and (c) a return node corresponding to a previously discovered call by following an exit transition.

In summary, the algorithm simply follows interprocedural paths. However, the crux to achieve our complexity is to keep summaries of paths through a module. Whenever we discovered a full (interprocedural) path from an entry e to an exit x, we keep its weight as an upper bound. Now any subsequently discovered call reaching e does not need to continue the search from e, but short-circuits to x by using the stored summary.

Preprocessing. In order to ease the formal presentation of the algorithm, we consider the following preprocessing on the initial configuration automaton $\mathcal{C}$. Let $M \subseteq \mathbb{M}$ be the set of marks in the initial automaton and $\widehat{m} \in \mathbb{M} \setminus M$ a *fresh mark*.

1. For every node $u \in In \cup En \cup Ret$, we add a new state $\langle u, \widehat{m} \rangle$ marked with the fresh mark. Additionally, all these new states are declared initial.
2. For every initial state $\langle u, m_u \rangle \in I$ such that there is a call transition $t = \langle u, \langle b, e \rangle \rangle \in \delta_i$ in $\mathcal{R}$, for every state $\langle e', m_{e'} \rangle$ where e' is an entry node of the same module as u, we add a b-transition $\langle e, \widehat{m} \rangle \xrightarrow{b} \langle e, m_{e'} \rangle$ with weight $\overline{0}$.
3. For every state $\langle e, m_e \rangle$ with entry node $e \in En_i$ and every internal or return node $u \in In_i \cup Ret_i$ in the same module as e, we add an ε-transition $\langle u, \widehat{m} \rangle \xrightarrow{\varepsilon} \langle e, m_e \rangle$ with weight $\overline{0}$.

Essentially the preprocessing a priori adds to $\mathcal{C}$ all possible states and transitions, so that the algorithm only has to relax those transitions (i.e., without adding them first). Note that the preprocessing only provides for an easier presentation of our algorithm. Indeed, in practice it would be impractical to do the full preprocessing and thus our implementation adds states and transitions to the automaton on the fly.

Technical Description of ConfDist. We present a detailed explanation of the algorithm supporting the formal description given in Algorithm 1. We require that every transition in the input configuration automaton $\mathcal{C}$ has weight $\overline{1}$, since the configurations in $\mathcal{L}(\mathcal{C})$ should not contribute any initial weight to the configuration distance. The algorithm maintains a *worklist* WL of weighted transitions either of the form $\langle u, m_u \rangle \xrightarrow{\varepsilon} \langle e, m_e \rangle$ or $\langle e, m_e \rangle \xrightarrow{b} \langle e', m_{e'} \rangle$, and a *summary function* sum $: (En \times \mathbb{M}) \times Ex \mapsto D$. Initially, the worklist contains all such transitions where the source state $\langle u, m_u \rangle$ is an initial state in I, and sum is all $\overline{0}$. In every iteration a transition $t_{\mathcal{C}}$ is extracted from the worklist and processed as follows. Since every accepting run starting with $t_{\mathcal{C}}$ corresponds to a reachable configuration $\langle u, S \rangle$ (where S varies over different runs), every transition $t_{\mathcal{R}} = \langle u, u' \rangle$ in $\mathcal{R}$ gives rise to another reachable configuration. More precisely, the run corresponds to a set of computations reaching $\langle u, S \rangle$ from the initial

$$t_{\mathcal{R}} = \langle u, u' \rangle$$

$$\langle u, m_u \rangle \xrightarrow{\varepsilon} \langle e, m_e \rangle \dashrightarrow^{S}$$
$$\overset{\varepsilon}{\nearrow}$$
$$\langle u', \widehat{m} \rangle$$

(a) Internal transition (Lines 8–9)

$$t_{\mathcal{R}} = \langle u, \langle b, e' \rangle \rangle$$

$$\langle u, m_u \rangle \xrightarrow{\varepsilon} \langle e, m_e \rangle \dashrightarrow^{S}$$
$$\overset{b}{\nearrow}$$
$$\langle e', \widehat{m} \rangle$$

(b) Call transition (Lines 10–12)

$$t_{\mathcal{R}} = \langle u, x \rangle$$

$$\langle u, m_u \rangle \xrightarrow{\varepsilon} \langle e, m_e \rangle \xrightarrow{b} \langle e', m_{e'} \rangle \dashrightarrow^{S'}$$
$$\overset{\varepsilon}{\nearrow}$$
$$\langle \langle b, x \rangle, \widehat{m} \rangle$$

(c) Exit transition (Lines 13–17)

$$\mathsf{sum}(\langle e, \widehat{m} \rangle, x)$$

$$\langle e, \widehat{m} \rangle \xrightarrow{b} \langle e', m_{e'} \rangle \dashrightarrow^{S}$$
$$\overset{\varepsilon}{\nearrow}$$
$$\langle \langle b, x \rangle, \widehat{m} \rangle$$

(d) Using summary (Lines 18–21)

Fig. 2. Relaxation steps of `ConfDist`.

set of configurations, and $t_{\mathcal{R}}$ allows to extend these computations by one step. The algorithm incorporates the newly discovered computations by relaxing a transition as follows, illustrated in Fig. 2.

1. If $t_{\mathcal{C}}$ is of the form $\langle u, m_u \rangle \xrightarrow{\varepsilon} \langle e, m_e \rangle$, then:
   (a) If u' is an internal node then the algorithm captures the internal transition $\langle u, S \rangle \Rightarrow \langle u', S \rangle$ by relaxing the transition $\langle u', \widehat{m} \rangle \xrightarrow{\varepsilon} \langle e, m_e \rangle$ using the weights $\ell(t_{\mathcal{C}})$ and $w(t_{\mathcal{R}})$.
   (b) If u' is a call node $\langle b, e' \rangle$ then the transition $\langle e', \widehat{m} \rangle \xrightarrow{b} \langle e, m_e \rangle$ is relaxed with the new weight $\ell(t_{\mathcal{C}}) \otimes w(t_{\mathcal{R}})$. Furthermore, an ε-self-loop is stored in the worklist to continue exploration from the called entry node e'.
   (c) If u' is an exit node x then the algorithm relaxes $\mathsf{sum}(\langle e, m_e \rangle, x)$ if a smaller computation to x has been discovered. Note that for $m_e = \widehat{m}$ this corresponds to valid entry-to-exit computations from e to x. If another call to e is discovered later, the summary is used to avoid traversing the module again. For $m_e \neq \widehat{m}$ the summary does not necessarily correspond to valid entry-to-exit computations (e.g., because node u was provided as an initial configuration) and is only stored to avoid redundant work. For a return transition from $\langle u, S \rangle$ the stack S has to be non-empty. The algorithm looks for all possible boxes b at the top of S by going along a b-transition from $\langle e, m_e \rangle$ to a state $\langle e', m_{e'} \rangle$. Then for any $S = bS'$, relaxing the transition $\langle \langle b, x \rangle, \widehat{m} \rangle \xrightarrow{\varepsilon} \langle e', m_{e'} \rangle$ captures the return transition $\langle u, S \rangle \Rightarrow \langle \langle b, x \rangle, S' \rangle$. Note that here we make use of the fact that the return transition itself has weight $\overline{1}$.
2. If $t_{\mathcal{C}}$ is of the form $\langle e, m_e \rangle \xrightarrow{b} \langle e', m_{e'} \rangle$, then:
   (d) for every exit node x in the module of e the summary function is used to relax the weight of the transition $\langle \langle b, x \rangle, \widehat{m} \rangle \xrightarrow{\varepsilon} \langle e', m_{e'} \rangle$ to the value $\ell(t_{\mathcal{C}}) \otimes \mathsf{sum}(\langle e, \widehat{m} \rangle, x)$.

Algorithm 1: ConfDist

Input: RSM $\mathcal{R}$ and $\mathcal{R}$-automaton $\mathcal{C}$ with $\ell(t) = \overline{1}$ for all transitions t in $\mathcal{C}$
Output: $\mathcal{R}$-automaton $\mathcal{C}_{post^*}$ with $\mathcal{C}_{post^*}(c) = d(\mathcal{L}(\mathcal{C}), c)$ for all configurations c

1   preprocess $\mathcal{C}$ as described in the main text
    // Initialization of worklist and summary function
2   $\mathsf{WL} := \{t = q \xrightarrow{\varepsilon} q' \mid q \in I \text{ and } \ell(t) = \overline{1}\}$
3   $\mathsf{sum}(\langle e, m_e \rangle, x) := \overline{0}$ for all states $\langle e, m_e \rangle$ and $x \in Ex$
    // Main loop
4   **while** $\mathsf{WL} \neq \emptyset$ **do**
5   extract $t_{\mathcal{C}}$ from WL
6   **if** $t_{\mathcal{C}} = \langle u, m_u \rangle \xrightarrow{\varepsilon} \langle e, m_e \rangle$ **then**
7   let $\mathcal{M}_i$ be the module of node u
        // Internal transitions from u
8   **foreach** $t_{\mathcal{R}} = \langle u, u' \rangle \in \delta_i$ where $u' \in In_i$ **do**
9            $\mathtt{Relax}(\langle u', \widehat{m} \rangle \xrightarrow{\varepsilon} \langle e, m_e \rangle, \ell(t_{\mathcal{C}}) \otimes w_i(t_{\mathcal{R}}))$

        // Call transitions from u
10   **foreach** $t_{\mathcal{R}} = \langle u, \langle b, e' \rangle \rangle \in \delta_i$ **do**
11           $\mathtt{Relax}(\langle e', \widehat{m} \rangle \xrightarrow{b} \langle e, m_e \rangle, \ell(t_{\mathcal{C}}) \otimes w_i(t_{\mathcal{R}}))$
12   add $\langle e', \widehat{m} \rangle \xrightarrow{\varepsilon} \langle e', \widehat{m} \rangle$ to WL, if it was never added before

        // Exit transitions from u
13   **foreach** $t_{\mathcal{R}} = \langle u, x \rangle \in \delta_i$ where $x \in Ex_i$ **do**
14   **if** $\mathsf{sum}(\langle e, m_e \rangle, x) \not\sqsubseteq \ell(t_{\mathcal{C}})$ **then**
15             $\mathsf{sum}(\langle e, m_e \rangle, x) := \mathsf{sum}(\langle e, m_e \rangle, x) \oplus \ell(t_{\mathcal{C}})$
16   **foreach** $\langle e, m_e \rangle \xrightarrow{b/v} \langle e', m_{e'} \rangle$ **do**
17               $\mathtt{Relax}(\langle \langle b, x \rangle, \widehat{m} \rangle \xrightarrow{\varepsilon} \langle e', m_{e'} \rangle, v \otimes \mathsf{sum}(\langle e, m_e \rangle, x))$

18   **else if** $t_{\mathcal{C}} = \langle e, m_e \rangle \xrightarrow{b} \langle e', m_{e'} \rangle$ **then**
19   let $\mathcal{M}_i$ be the module of node e
        // Using entry-to-exit summaries
20   **foreach** $x \in Ex_i$ **do**
21           $\mathtt{Relax}(\langle \langle b, x \rangle, \widehat{m} \rangle \xrightarrow{\varepsilon} \langle e', m_{e'} \rangle, \ell(t_{\mathcal{C}}) \otimes \mathsf{sum}(\langle e, \widehat{m} \rangle, x))$

22   **Procedure** $\mathtt{Relax}(t, v)$
23   **if** $\ell(t) \neq \ell(t) \oplus v$ **then**
24         $\ell(t) := \ell(t) \oplus v$
25   add t to WL

The initial states of $\mathcal{C}_{post^*}$ are the initial states of $\mathcal{C}$ together with all states with the fresh mark added in the preprocessing. The final states of $\mathcal{C}_{post^*}$ are the unmodified final states of $\mathcal{C}$.

Example 2. In Fig. 3 we illustrate an execution of ConfDist for the reachability problem in the RSM from Fig. 1. The reader can verify that every configuration in the example computation (1) is accepted by a run of the constructed automaton.

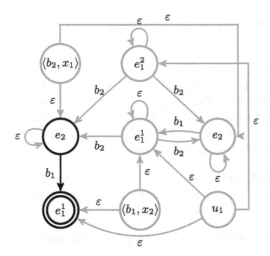

Fig. 3. The configuration automaton $\mathcal{C}_{post*}$ constructed by `ConfDist` for the RSM in Fig. 1 over the Boolean semiring $\langle\langle 0, 1\rangle, \vee, \wedge, 0, 1\rangle$, expressing the reachability problem. The initial input automaton $\mathcal{C}$ is given by the black states, whereas the gray states represent the newly added states with the fresh mark $\widehat{m}$. The black/gray color gives a similar distinction for the transitions (i.e., the gray transitions have been added by the algorithm). The set of initial states of $\mathcal{C}$ is $I = \{e_1^1, e_2\}$, and the set of final states is the singleton set $F = \{e_1^1\}$. Transitions added in the preprocessing phase with value $\bar{0}$ are not shown.

Correctness. In the following we outline the correctness of the algorithm. We start with a simple observation about the shape of runs in the constructed configuration automaton.

Proposition 2. *For every accepting run λ there exists an equivalent accepting run λ' that starts with an ε-transition followed by only b-transitions. Furthermore, all but the first state contain an entry node.*

The following three lemmas capture the correctness of `ConfDist`. We start with completeness, namely that the distance computed for any configuration c is at most the actual distance from the initial set of configurations $\mathcal{L}(\mathcal{C})$ to c. The proof relies on showing that for any initialized computation $\pi : \langle u, S\rangle \Rightarrow^* \langle u', S'\rangle$ there is a run λ accepting $\langle u', S'\rangle$ such that $\otimes(\lambda) \sqsubseteq \otimes(\pi)$, and follows an induction on the length $|\pi|$.

Lemma 1 (Completeness). *For every configuration c we have $\mathcal{C}_{post*}(c) \sqsubseteq d(\mathcal{L}(\mathcal{C}), c)$.*

We now turn our attention to soundness, namely that the distance computed for any configuration c is at least the actual distance from the initial set of configurations $\mathcal{L}(\mathcal{C})$ to c. The proof is established via a set of interdependent invariants that state that the algorithm maintains sound entry-to-exit summaries and any run in the automaton has a weight that is witnessed by a set of computations.

Lemma 2 (Soundness). *For every configuration c we have $d(\mathcal{L}(\mathcal{C}), c) \sqsubseteq \mathcal{C}_{post^*}(c)$.*

Complexity. Finally, we turn our attention to the complexity analysis of the algorithm, which is done by bounding the number of times the algorithm can perform a relaxation step. The complexity bound is based on the height of the semiring H, which implies that every transition can be relaxed at most H times. The contribution of the size of the initial automaton $\mathcal{C}$ in the complexity is captured by the number of initial marks κ.

Lemma 3 (Complexity). *Let κ be the number of distinct marks $m \in \mathbb{M}$ of the initial automaton $\mathcal{C}$. Algorithm* `ConfDist` *constructs $\mathcal{C}_{post^*}$ in time $O(H \cdot (|\mathcal{R}| \cdot \theta_e \cdot \kappa^2 + |Call| \cdot \theta_e \cdot \theta_x \cdot \kappa^3))$, and $\mathcal{C}_{post^*}$ has $O(|\mathcal{R}| \cdot \theta_e \cdot \kappa^2)$ transitions.*

We summarize the results of this section in the following theorem.

Theorem 1. *Let $\mathcal{R}$ be an RSM over a semiring of height H, and $\mathcal{C}$ an $\mathcal{R}$-automaton with κ marks. Algorithm* `ConfDist` *constructs in $O(H \cdot (|\mathcal{R}| \cdot \theta_e \cdot \kappa^2 + |Call| \cdot \theta_e \cdot \theta_x \cdot \kappa^3))$ time an $\mathcal{R}$-automaton $\mathcal{C}_{post^*}$ with $\kappa + 1$ marks, such that $d(\mathcal{L}(\mathcal{C}), c) = \mathcal{C}_{post^*}(c)$ for every configuration c.*

Remark 3 (Comparison with existing work). We now relate Theorem 1 with the existing work for computing configuration distance (often called generalized reachability in the literature) in weighted pushdown systems *(WPDS)* [34,36]. For simplicity we assume that the initial automaton is of constant size. A formal description of WPDS is omitted; the reader can refer to [4,34]. Let $\mathcal{P}$ be a WPDS where:

1. $n_{\mathcal{P}}$ is the number of states
2. n_{Δ} is the size of the transition relation
3. n_{sp} is the number of different pairs $\langle p', \gamma' \rangle$ such that there is a transition of the form $\langle p, \gamma \rangle \rightarrow \langle p', \gamma' \gamma'' \rangle$ (i.e., from some state p with γ on the top of the stack, the WPDS $\mathcal{P}$ (i) transitions to state p', (ii) swaps γ and γ'', and (iii) pushes γ' on the top of the stack).

As shown in [34], given a WPDS $\mathcal{P}$ with weights from a semiring with height H, together with a corresponding automaton $\mathcal{C}^{\mathcal{P}}$ that encodes configurations of $\mathcal{P}$, an automaton $\mathcal{C}^{\mathcal{P}}_{post^*}$ can be constructed as a solution to the configuration distance problem for $\mathcal{P}$. For ease of presentation we focus on the common case where $\mathcal{C}^{\mathcal{P}}$ has constant size (e.g., for encoding an initial configuration of $\mathcal{P}$ with empty stack). Then the time required to construct $\mathcal{C}^{\mathcal{P}}_{post^*}$ is $O(H \cdot n_{\mathcal{P}} \cdot n_{\Delta} \cdot n_{\mathsf{sp}})$ [34,36].

A direct consequence of [4, Theorem 1] is that an RSM $\mathcal{R}$ and a configuration automaton $\mathcal{C}^{\mathcal{R}}$ can be converted to an equivalent PDS $\mathcal{P}$ and configuration automaton $\mathcal{C}^{\mathcal{P}}$, and vice versa, such that the following equalities hold:

$$|\mathcal{R}| = \Theta(n_{\Delta}); \quad \theta_x = \Theta(n_{\mathcal{P}}); \quad f \cdot \theta_e = \Theta(n_{\mathsf{sp}}),$$

where f represents the number of modules. Hence, the bound we obtain by translating the input RSM to a WPDS and using the algorithm of [34,36] is $O(H \cdot |\mathcal{R}| \cdot \theta_e \cdot \theta_x \cdot f)$. Our complexity bound on Theorem 1 is better by a factor $\Omega((|\mathcal{R}| \cdot f)/(\theta_x + |Call|))$. Moreover, to verify such improvements, we have also constructed a family of dense RSMs, and apply our algorithm, and compare against the jMoped implementation of the existing algorithms, and observe a linear speed-up (see Sect. 6.1 for details).

The above analysis considers an explicit model, where $\mathcal{R}$ comprises two parts, a program control-flow graph $\mathcal{R}_{CFG}$ and the set of all data valuations V, where $|V| = \theta_e = \theta_x$. Hence, $|\mathcal{R}| = |\mathcal{R}_{CFG}| \cdot |V|^2$. In a symbolic model, where all the data valuations are tracked on the semiring, the input RSM is a factor $|V|^2$ smaller (i.e., the contribution of the data valuation to $|\mathcal{R}|$), and $\theta_e = \theta_x = 1$. However, now each semiring operation incurs a factor $|V|^2$ increase in time cost, and the height of the semiring increases by a factor $|V|^2$ as well, in the worst case. Hence, existing symbolic approaches for PDSs have the same worst-case time complexity as the explicit one, and our comparison applies to these as well. For further discussion on symbolic extensions of our algorithm we refer to our technical report [12].

4   Distance Extraction

The algorithm presented in Sect. 3 takes as input a weighted RSM $\mathcal{R}$ over a semiring and a configuration automaton $\mathcal{C}$ that represents a regular set R of configurations of $\mathcal{R}$, and outputs an automaton $\mathcal{C}_{post*}$ that encodes the distance $d(R, c)$ to every configuration c. We now discuss the algorithmic problem of extracting such distances from $\mathcal{C}_{post*}$, and present fast algorithms for this problem. First we will consider the general case for RSMs over an arbitrary semiring. Then we present several improvements for special cases, like RSMs over a semiring with small domain, or sparse RSMs. As the correctness of the constructions is straightforward, our attention will be on the complexity.

4.1   Distances over General Semirings

Configuration Distances. Given a configuration $c = \langle u, S \rangle$, $S = b_1 \ldots b_{|S|}$, the task is to extract $d(R, c) = \bigoplus(\Pi(R, c))$. This is done by a dynamic-programming style algorithm, which computes iteratively for every prefix $b_1 \ldots b_i$ of S and state $\langle e, m_e \rangle$ with $e \in En_j$ and $b_i \in B_j$, the weight

$$w_{\langle e, m_e \rangle} = \bigoplus \{ \otimes(\lambda) \mid \lambda : \langle u, m_u \rangle \xrightarrow{b_1 \ldots b_i}{}^* \langle e, m_e \rangle \}.$$

Since there are $O(\kappa^2 \cdot \theta_e^2)$ transitions labeled with b_i, every iteration requires $O(\kappa^2 \cdot \theta_e^2)$ time, and the total time for computing $d(R, c)$ is $O(|S| \cdot \kappa^2 \cdot \theta_e^2)$.

Superconfiguration Distances. Given a superconfiguration $\bar{c} = \langle u, \bar{S} \rangle$, $\bar{S} = \mathcal{M}_1 \ldots \mathcal{M}_{|\bar{S}|}$, the task is to extract $d(R, \bar{c}) = \bigoplus_{c \in [\![\langle u, \bar{S} \rangle]\!]} d(R, c)$. To handle such queries, we perform a one-time preprocessing of $\mathcal{C}_{post*}$, so that the transitions are labeled with modules instead of boxes. That is, we create an automaton $\overline{\mathcal{C}}_{post*}$, initially identical to $\mathcal{C}_{post*}$. Then we add a transition $t = \langle e, m_e \rangle \xrightarrow{\mathcal{M}} \langle e', m_{e'} \rangle$, with $\mathcal{M}$ being the module of e', if there exists a b-transition $\langle e, m_e \rangle \xrightarrow{b} \langle e', m_{e'} \rangle$ in $\mathcal{C}_{post*}$. The weight function $\overline{\ell}$ of $\overline{\mathcal{C}}_{post*}$ is such that the weight of the transition t is

$$\overline{\ell}(t) = \bigoplus_{t':\langle e,m_e \rangle \xrightarrow{b} \langle e',m_{e'} \rangle} \ell(t')$$

where t' ranges over transitions of $\mathcal{C}_{post*}$. This construction requires linear time in the number of b-transitions of $\mathcal{C}_{post*}$, i.e., $O(|\mathcal{R}| \cdot \theta_e)$. It is straightforward to see that

$$\bigoplus_{\overline{\lambda}:\langle u,m_u \rangle \xrightarrow{\overline{S}}* q_f} \overline{\ell}(\lambda) = \bigoplus_{\lambda:\langle u,m_u \rangle \xrightarrow{S}* q_f} \ell(\lambda)$$

where $\overline{\lambda}$ and λ range over accepting runs of $\overline{\mathcal{C}}_{post*}$ and $\mathcal{C}_{post*}$ respectively, and S refines $\overline{S}$. Then, given a superconfiguration $\overline{c} = \langle u, \overline{S} \rangle$, the extraction of $d(R, \overline{c})$ is done similarly to the configuration distance extraction, in $O(|S| \cdot \kappa^2 \cdot \theta_e^2)$ time.

Node Distances. For node distances, the task is to compute $d(R, u) = \bigoplus_{c=\langle u,S \rangle} d(R, c)$ for every node u of $\mathcal{R}$. This reduces to treating the automaton $\mathcal{C}_{post*}$ as a graph G, and solving a traditional single-source distance problem, where the source set contains all states with old marks (i.e., old states that appear in the initial automaton $\mathcal{C}$). This requires $O(H \cdot |\mathcal{C}_{post*}|)$ time for semirings of height H. An informal argument for these bounds is to observe that G can be itself encoded by a SESE RSM $\mathcal{R}_G$ with a single module, where the entry represents the source set of nodes with old marks. Then, running ConfDist for the corresponding semiring, we obtain a solution to the single-source distance problem in the aforementioned times, as established in Theorem 1. Finally, computing same-context node distances requires $O(|\mathcal{R}| \cdot \theta)$ time in total (i.e., for all nodes). Hence, regardless of the semiring, all node distances can be computed with no overhead, i.e., within the time bounds required for constructing the respective configuration automaton $\mathcal{C}_{post*}$. The following theorem summarizes the complexity bounds that we obtain for the various distance extraction problems.

Theorem 2 (Distance extraction). *Let $\mathcal{R}$ be an RSM over a semiring of height H and $\mathcal{C}$ an $\mathcal{R}$-automaton with κ marks. After $O(H \cdot |\mathcal{R}| \cdot \theta_e \cdot \theta_x \cdot \kappa^3)$ preprocessing time*

1. *configuration and superconfiguration distance queries $\langle u, S \rangle$ are answered in $O(|S| \cdot \theta_e^2 \cdot \kappa^2)$ time;*
2. *node distance queries are answered in $O(1)$ time.*

4.2   Distances over Semirings with Small Domain

We now turn our attention to configuration and superconfiguration distance extraction for the case of semirings with small domains D. Such semirings express a range of important problems, with reachability being the most well-known (expressed on the Boolean semiring with $|D| = 2$). We harness algorithmic advancements on the matrix-vector multiplication problem and Four-Russians-style algorithms to obtain better bounds on the distance extraction problem.

Recall that given a box b, the configuration automaton $\mathcal{C}_{post*}$ has at most $(\theta_e \cdot \kappa)^2$ transitions labeled with b. Such transitions can be represented by a matrix $A_b \in D^{(\theta_e \cdot \kappa) \times (\theta_e \cdot \kappa)}$. Additionally, for every internal node u we have one matrix $A_u \in D^{(\kappa) \times (\theta_e \cdot \kappa)}$ that captures the weights of all transitions of the form $\langle u, m_u \rangle \xrightarrow{\varepsilon} \langle e, m_e \rangle$. Then, answering a configuration distance query $\langle u, S \rangle$ with $S = b_1, \ldots, b_{|S|}$ amounts to evaluating the expression

$$\overline{1}_\kappa \cdot A_u \cdot A_{b_1} \cdots A_{b_{|S|}} \cdot \overline{1}_{\kappa \cdot \theta_e}^\top \qquad (2)$$

where $\overline{1}_z$ is a row vector of $\overline{1}$s and size z, $\cdot^\top$ denotes the transpose, and matrix multiplication is taken over the semiring. The situation is similar in the case of superconfiguration distances, where we have one matrix $A_{\mathcal{M}, \mathcal{M}'}$ for each pair of modules $\mathcal{M}, \mathcal{M}'$ such that $\mathcal{M}$ invokes $\mathcal{M}'$.

Evaluating Eq. (2) from left to right (or right to left) yields a sequence of matrix-vector multiplications. The following two theorems use the results of [25, 37] on matrix-vector multiplications to provide a speedup on the distance extraction problem when the semiring has constant size $|D| = O(1)$.

Theorem 3 (Mailman's speedup [25]). *Let $\mathcal{R}$ be an RSM over a semiring of constant size, and $\mathcal{C}$ an $\mathcal{R}$-automaton with κ marks. After $O(|\mathcal{R}| \cdot \theta_e \cdot \theta_x \cdot \kappa^3)$ preprocessing time, configuration and superconfiguration distance queries $\langle u, S \rangle$ are answered in $O\left(|S| \cdot \frac{\theta_e^2 \cdot \kappa^2}{\log(\theta_e \cdot \kappa)}\right)$ time.*

Theorem 4 (Williams's speedup [37]). *Let $\mathcal{R}$ be an RSM over a semiring of size $|D|$, and $\mathcal{C}$ an $\mathcal{R}$-automaton with κ marks. For any fixed $\varepsilon > 0$, let $X = |\mathcal{R}| \cdot \theta_e \cdot \theta_x \cdot \kappa^3$ and $Z = |\mathcal{R}| \cdot \kappa \cdot (\theta_e \cdot \kappa)^{1 + \varepsilon \log_2 |D|}$. After $O(\max(X, Z))$ preprocessing time, configuration and superconfiguration distance queries $\langle u, S \rangle$ are answered in $O\left(|S| \cdot \frac{\theta_e^2 \cdot \kappa^2}{\varepsilon^2 \cdot \log^2(\theta_e \cdot \kappa)}\right)$ time.*

Finally, using the Four-Russians technique for parsing on non-deterministic automata [28], we obtain the following speedup for the case of reachability. We note that although the alphabet is not of constant size (i.e., the number of boxes is generally non-constant) this poses no overhead, as long as comparing two boxes for equality requires constant time (which is the case in the standard RAM model).

Theorem 5 (Four-Russians speedup [28]). *Let $\mathcal{R}$ be an RSM over a binary semiring, and $\mathcal{C}$ an $\mathcal{R}$-automaton with κ marks. After $O(|\mathcal{R}| \cdot \theta_e \cdot \theta_x \cdot \kappa^3)$ pre-processing time, configuration and superconfiguration distance queries $\langle u, S \rangle$ are answered in $O\left(|\mathcal{R}| \cdot \theta_e \cdot \kappa^2 \cdot \frac{|S|}{\log(|S|)}\right)$ time.*

4.3   A Speedup for Sparse RSMs

We call an RSM $\mathcal{R}$ *sparse* if there is a constant bound r such that for all modules $\mathcal{M}_i$ we have $|\{Y_i(b) \mid b \in B_i\}| \leq r$ i.e., every module invokes at most r other modules (although $\mathcal{M}_i$ can have arbitrarily many boxes). Typical call-graphs of most programs are very sparse, e.g., typical call graphs of thousands of nodes have average degree at most eight [8,30]. Hence, an RSM modeling a typical program is expected to comprise thousands of modules, while the average module invokes a small number of other modules. Although this does not imply a constant bound on the number of invoked modules, such an assumption provides a good theoretical basis for the analysis of typical programs.

Our goal is to provide a speedup for extracting superconfiguration distances w.r.t. a sparse RSM. This is achieved by an additional polynomial-time preprocessing, which then allows to process a distance query in blocks of logarithmic size, and thus offers a speedup of the same order.

Given an RSM $\mathcal{R}$ of k modules and an integer z, there exist at most $k \cdot r^z$ valid module sequences $\mathcal{M}_1 \ldots, \mathcal{M}_{z+1}$ which can appear as a substring in a module sequence $\overline{S}$ which is refined by some stack S. Recall the definition of the matrices $A_{\mathcal{M},\mathcal{M}'} \in D^{(\theta_e \cdot \kappa) \times (\theta_e \cdot \kappa)}$ from Sect. 4.2. For every valid sequence of $z+1$ modules $s = \mathcal{M}_1 \ldots, \mathcal{M}_{z+1}$, we construct a matrix $A_s = A_{\mathcal{M}_1,\mathcal{M}_2} \cdot A_{\mathcal{M}_2,\mathcal{M}_3} \cdots A_{\mathcal{M}_z,\mathcal{M}_{z+1}}$ in total time

$$k \cdot (\theta_e \cdot \kappa)^\omega \sum_{i=1}^{z} r^i = O\left(|\mathcal{R}| \cdot \theta_e^{\omega-1} \kappa^\omega \cdot r^z\right) \tag{3}$$

where $(\theta_e \cdot \kappa)^\omega = \Omega(\theta^2 \cdot \kappa^2)$ is time require to multiply two $D^{(\theta_e \cdot \kappa) \times (\theta_e \cdot \kappa)}$ matrices (currently $\omega \simeq 2.372$, due to [38]).

Observe that as long as $z = O(\log|\mathcal{R}|)$, there are polynomially many such sequences s, and thus each one can be indexed in $O(1)$ time on the standard RAM model. Then a superconfiguration distance query $\langle u, S \rangle$ can be answered by grouping S in $\lceil \frac{|S|}{z} \rceil$ blocks of size z each, and for each such block s multiply with matrix A_s.

Theorem 6 (Sparsity speedup). *Let $\mathcal{R}$ be a sparse RSM over a semiring of height H, and $\mathcal{C}$ an $\mathcal{R}$-automaton with κ marks. Let $X = H \cdot |\mathcal{R}| \cdot \theta_e \cdot \theta_x \cdot \kappa^3$, and given an integer parameter $x = O(\text{poly} |\mathcal{R}|)$, let $Z = |\mathcal{R}| \cdot \theta_e^{\omega-1} \kappa^\omega \cdot x$. After $O(\max(X, Z))$ preprocessing time, superconfiguration distance queries $\langle u, S \rangle$ are answered in $O\left(|S| \cdot \left\lceil \frac{\theta_e^2 \cdot \kappa^2}{\log x} \right\rceil\right)$ time.*

By varying the parameter z, Theorem 6 provides a tradeoff between preprocessing and query times. Finally, the presented method can be combined with the preprocessing on constant-size semirings of Sect. 4.2 which leads to a $\Theta(\log z)$ factor improvement on the query times of Theorems 3, 4 and 5.

5   Context-Bounded Reachability in Concurrent Recursive State Machines

Context bounding, i.e., limiting the number of context switches considered during state space exploration, is an effective technique for systematic analysis of concurrent programs. The context-bounded reachability problem in concurrent pushdown systems has been studied in [29]. In this section we phrase the context-bounded reachability problem over concurrent RSMs and show that the procedure of [29] using our algorithm ConfDist together with the results of the previous sections give a better time complexity for the problem. As the section follows closely the well-known framework of concurrent pushdown systems [29], we keep the description brief.

Concurrent RSMs. A *concurrent RSM (CRSM)* $\mathcal{R}^{\|}$ is a collection of RSMs $\mathcal{R}_i$ equipped with a finite set of *global states* G used for communication between the RSMs. To this end, the semantics of RSMs is lifted to $\mathcal{R}_i$-configurations of the form $\langle g, u_i, S_i \rangle$, carrying an additional global state $g \in G$. Then, a *global configuration* of $\mathcal{R}^{\|}$ is a tuple $\langle g, \langle u_1, S_1 \rangle, \ldots, \langle u_n, S_n \rangle \rangle$, where $\langle g, u_i, S_i \rangle$ are configurations of $\mathcal{R}_i$, respectively. The semantics of $\mathcal{R}^{\|}$ over global configurations is the standard interleaving semantics, i.e., in each step some RSM $\mathcal{R}_i$ modifies the global state and its local configuration, while the local configuration of every other RSM remains unchanged.

Context-Bounded Reachability. For a positive natural number k and a fixed initial global configuration c, the *k-bounded reachability problem* asks for all global configurations c' such that there is a computation from c to c' that switches control between RSMs at most $k - 1$ times.

An Algorithm for Context-Bounded Reachability. The procedure of [29] for solving the k-bounded reachability problem for *concurrent pushdown systems (CPDSs)* systematically performs $post^*$ operations on the reachable configuration set of every constituent PDS, while capturing all possible interleavings within k context switches. The k-bounded reachability problem for CRSMs can be solved with an almost identical procedure, replacing the black-box invocations of the PDS reachability algorithm of [36] with our algorithm ConfDist. However, using our algorithm for each $post^*$ operation, we obtain a complexity improvement over the method of [29].

Key Complexity Improvement. The key advantage of our algorithm as compared to [29] is as follows: in the algorithm of [29], in each iteration the configuration automata, used to represent the reachable configurations of each component RSM, grows by a cubic term; in contrast, replacing with our algorithm the configuration automata grows only by a linear term in each iteration. This comes from the fact that in our configuration automata every state corresponds to a node of the RSM, whereas such strong correspondence does not hold for the configuration automata of [29].

Theorem 7. *For a concurrent RSM $\mathcal{R}^{\|}$, and a bound k, the procedure of [29, Figure 2] using ConfDist for performing post* operations correctly solves the k-bounded reachability problem and requires $O(|\mathcal{R}^{\|}| \cdot \theta_e^{\|} \cdot \theta_x^{\|} \cdot n^k \cdot |G|^{k+2})$ time.*

Compared to Theorem 7, solving the CRSM problem by translation to a CPDS and using the algorithm of [29] gives the bound $O(|\mathcal{R}^{\|}|^5 \cdot \theta_x^{\| \ 5} \cdot n^k \cdot |G|^k)$. Conversely, solving the CPDS problem by translation to a CRSM and using our algorithm gives an improvement by a factor $\Omega(|\mathcal{P}^{\parallel}|^3/|G|^2)$. We refer to our technical report [12] for a detailed discussion.

6   Experimental Results

In this section we empirically demonstrate the algorithmic improvements achieved by our RSM-based algorithm over existing PDS-based algorithms on interprocedural program analysis problems. The main goal is to demonstrate the improvements in algorithmic ideas rather than implementation details and engineering aspects. In particular, we implemented our algorithm ConfDist in a prototype tool and compared its efficiency against jMoped [1], which implements the algorithms of [34,36] and is a leading tool for the analysis of weighted pushdown systems. In all cases we used an explicit representation of data valuations on the nodes of RSMs, as opposed to a symbolic semiring representation. All experiments were run on a machine with an Intel Xeon CPU and a memory limit of 80 GB. We first present our result on a synthetic example to verify the algorithmic improvements on a constructed family, and then present results on real-world benchmarks.

6.1   A Family of Dense RSMs

For our first experiments we constructed a family of dense RSMs that can be scaled in size. The purpose of this experiments is to verify that (i) our algorithm indeed achieves a speedup over the algorithms of [34,36], and (ii) the speedup scales with the size of the input to ensure that improvements on real-world benchmarks are not due to implementation details, such as the used data types. Let $\mathcal{R}_n$ be a single-module RSM that consists of n entries and n exits, and a single box which makes a recursive call. The transition relation is $\delta = (En \times (Call \cup Ex)) \cup (Ret \times Ex)$,

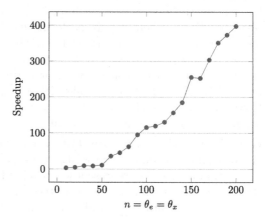

Fig. 4. Speedup of our algorithm over the algorithms of [34,36] implemented by jMoped on the RSM family $\mathcal{R}_n$.

i.e., every entry node connects to every call and exit node, and every return node connects to every exit node. Hence $|\mathcal{R}_n| = n^2$. The transition weights are irrelevant, as we will focus on reachability. The initial configuration automaton $\mathcal{C}$ contains a single entry state. We considered $\mathcal{R}_n$ with n in the range from 10 to 200. For each RSM, we used the standard translation to a PDS [4], and then applied our tool and jMoped to compute a configuration automaton that represents $post^*(\mathcal{L}(\mathcal{C}))$. Figure 4 depicts the obtained speedup, which scales linearly with n. We have also experimented with other similar synthetic RSMs with different means of scaling; and in all cases the obtained speedups have the same qualitative behavior. This confirms the theoretical algorithmic improvements of our algorithm on the synthetic benchmarks.

6.2   Boolean Programs from SLAM/SDV

Benchmarks. For our second experiments we used the collection of Boolean programs distributed as part of the SLAM/SDV project [6,7]. These programs are the final abstractions in the verification of Windows device drivers, and thus they represent RSMs obtained from real-world programs. From the Boolean programs we obtained RSMs where every node represents a control location together with a valuation of Boolean variables, and call/entry and exit/return nodes model the parameter passing between functions. Thus, the RSMs are naturally multi-entry-multi-exit. Overall we obtained 73 RSMs, which correspond to the largest Boolean programs possible to handle explicitly.

Evaluation. To ensure a fair performance comparison, we applied two preprocessing steps to the benchmark RSMs.

– First, to ensure that both tools compute the same result without any potential unnecessary work, we restricted the state space of the RSMs to the interprocedurally reachable states.
– Second, to focus on the performance of interprocedural analysis, we eliminated all internal nodes by computing the intraprocedural transitive closure within every RSM module.

The above two transformations ensure preprocessing steps like removal of unreachable states and intraprocedural analysis is already done, and we compare the interprocedural algorithmic aspects of the algorithms. For each RSM, we used the standard translation to a PDS [4], and then applied our tool and jMoped to compute a configuration automaton that represents $post^*(\mathcal{L}(\mathcal{C}))$, where $\mathcal{C}$ is an initial configuration automaton that contains the entry states of the main module. Table 3 shows for every benchmark the number of RSM transitions (Trans.), their ratio to nodes (D), the runtime for computing the intraprocedural transitive closure (TC), the runtime of jMoped (jMop), the runtime of our tool (Ours), and the speedup our tool achieved over jMoped (SpUp).

Out tool clearly outperforms jMoped on every benchmark, with speedups from 3.94 up to 28.48. The runtimes of our tool range from 0.13 to 33.96 s, while the runtimes of jMoped range from 1.03 to 950.82 s. Thus, our experiments show that also for real-world examples our algorithm successfully exploits the structure of procedural programs preserved in RSMs. This shows the potential of our algorithm for building program analysis tools.

Note that the benchmark RSMs are quite large, with millions of nodes and transitions, which even a basic implementation of our algorithm handled quite efficiently. Moreover, in our experiments we observed that our tool uses considerably less memory than jMoped. While we set 80 GB as the memory limit, the

Table 3. Comparison of our tool against jMoped. Runtimes are given in seconds. The names of all benchmarks are given in our technical report [12].

#	Trans.	D	TC	jMop	Ours	SpUp	#	Trans.	D	TC	jMop	Ours	SpUp
1	246,101	1.9	1.18	1.10	0.28	3.94	38	14,473,411	1.5	9.68	53.38	7.49	7.13
2	216,021	0.8	0.70	1.03	0.26	3.96	39	11,616,241	3.3	19.59	42.73	5.54	7.71
3	593,041	1.5	1.05	2.05	0.49	4.19	40	300,401	2.6	0.74	1.05	0.14	7.79
4	1,043,217	1.2	3.01	4.67	1.11	4.20	41	1,916,064	2.3	3.38	10.83	1.39	7.80
5	329,088	1.4	1.41	1.43	0.34	4.24	42	216,070	1.7	0.56	1.37	0.17	7.83
6	10,281,149	3.0	11.36	52.00	10.61	4.90	43	1,293,130	2.3	2.06	5.44	0.69	7.92
7	908,092	1.7	2.04	3.31	0.65	5.08	44	8,364,920	2.1	6.31	32.95	4.09	8.05
8	969,388	2.2	2.00	33.71	6.60	5.11	45	18,733,065	4.9	10.84	62.14	7.63	8.15
9	298,126	1.5	0.68	1.31	0.25	5.23	46	5,373,059	6.4	8.66	18.20	2.17	8.38
10	1,780,776	1.3	5.82	6.44	1.20	5.35	47	1,342,348	1.6	4.75	5.02	0.58	8.73
11	163,853	1.4	0.33	1.03	0.19	5.35	48	779,369	7.2	1.94	6.73	0.77	8.75
12	205,608	1.0	0.50	4.62	0.86	5.36	49	18,812,123	4.9	8.87	63.86	6.99	9.14
13	28,568,561	1.7	23.21	102.54	18.82	5.45	50	40,025,428	6.3	36.49	310.16	33.07	9.38
14	21,911,277	1.8	15.79	80.41	14.64	5.49	51	2,503,668	15.3	21.53	10.17	1.08	9.44
15	2,453,881	1.5	4.54	9.57	1.72	5.55	52	40,084,249	6.2	36.37	320.70	33.96	9.44
16	5,833,574	1.8	6.97	21.14	3.80	5.56	53	4,852,736	6.5	4.14	17.68	1.83	9.64
17	332,768	0.8	0.77	2.28	0.41	5.59	54	18,520,461	5.4	8.96	60.24	6.21	9.69
18	1,782,697	1.3	5.79	6.70	1.20	5.60	55	6,796,783	7.0	9.78	21.33	2.16	9.87
19	246,127	1.9	1.31	1.36	0.24	5.63	56	40,026,391	6.3	35.69	327.66	33.05	9.91
20	21,648,560	1.8	15.50	79.45	14.01	5.67	57	805,305	4.7	1.66	8.14	0.80	10.17
21	7,033,834	2.1	8.23	23.97	4.21	5.70	58	4,532,440	26.4	7.49	33.46	3.15	10.61
22	28,944,391	1.7	24.26	105.00	18.15	5.78	59	18,374,693	5.8	8.99	60.54	5.52	10.96
23	464,004	1.7	0.75	2.17	0.37	5.83	60	1,284,096	5.9	1.53	48.54	4.39	11.05
24	424,916	1.6	1.20	2.94	0.49	5.96	61	3,862,954	6.3	3.44	12.94	1.14	11.38
25	22,186,326	1.6	17.77	63.27	10.56	5.99	62	52,269,131	3.4	44.45	177.98	15.53	11.46
26	11,719,007	5.2	20.36	52.29	8.55	6.11	63	130,721	2.2	0.43	1.55	0.13	11.52
27	2,989,001	1.4	3.55	11.04	1.80	6.12	64	545,063	16.4	6.88	2.27	0.16	13.85
28	1,952,647	1.3	3.83	7.98	1.30	6.13	65	545,046	16.4	6.78	2.17	0.15	14.04
29	7,970,359	3.2	4.04	30.16	4.70	6.42	66	829,090	12.3	9.60	3.40	0.24	14.17
30	682,435	2.1	2.14	4.88	0.76	6.42	67	63,918,783	267.0	115.87	244.01	16.00	15.25
31	9,480,799	4.9	17.23	44.34	6.77	6.55	68	20,382,912	3.3	15.78	76.69	4.80	15.98
32	845,867	2.4	1.59	3.22	0.48	6.67	69	29,689,784	6.2	11.18	120.82	7.16	16.88
33	953,420	3.1	1.22	4.51	0.67	6.77	70	2,619,392	5.2	3.48	660.92	31.62	20.90
34	1,205,731	2.0	3.31	4.68	0.68	6.84	71	2,575,360	5.7	3.03	589.87	25.69	22.96
35	754,270	1.7	4.25	22.28	3.23	6.90	72	2,639,872	5.0	3.17	816.08	29.93	27.27
36	1,463,749	2.0	2.38	6.10	0.88	6.95	73	2,691,072	4.5	3.43	950.82	33.39	28.48
37	434,884	5.8	6.85	1.90	0.27	7.10							

peak memory consumption of jMoped was 72 GB, whereas our tool solved all benchmarks with less than 32 GB memory.

6.3   Discussion

In our experiments we compared the implementation of our algorithm with jMoped on sequential RSM analysis in an explicit setting. While our algorithm can be made symbolic in a straightforward way, a symbolic implementation and efficiency for large symbolic domains involve significant engineering efforts. Moreover, the main goal of our work is to compare the algorithmic improvements over the existing approaches, which is best demonstrated in an explicit setting, since in the explicit setting the improvements are algorithmic rather than due to implementation details of symbolic data-structures. Our experimental results show the potential of the new algorithmic ideas, and investigating the applicability of them with a symbolic implementation is a subject of future work.

7   Related Work

Sequential Setting. Pushdown systems are very well studied for interprocedural analysis [10,32,35]. While the most basic problem is reachability, the weighted pushdown systems (i.e., pushdown systems enriched with semiring) can express several basic dataflow properties, and other relevant problems in interprocedural program analysis [20,22,33,34]. Hence weighted pushdown systems have been studied in many different contexts, such as [13,17,32,35], and tools have been developed, such as Moped [2], jMoped [1], and WALi [3]. The more convenient model of RSMs was introduced and studied in [4], which on the one hand explicitly models the function calls and returns, and on the other hand specifies many natural parameters for algorithmic analysis. In this work, we improve the fundamental algorithms for RSMs over finite-height semirings, as compared to the bounds obtained by translating RSMs to pushdown systems and applying the best-known bounds for the pushdown case. Along with general RSMs, special cases of SESE RSMs have also been considered, such as RSMs with constant treewidth, and only same context queries [11] (i.e., computation of node distances between nodes of the same module). Our results apply to the general case of all RSMs and are not restricted to any special types of queries.

Concurrent Setting. The problem of reachability in concurrent pushdown systems (or concurrent RSMs) is again a fundamental problem in program analysis, which allows for the interprocedural analysis in a concurrent setting. However, the problem is undecidable [31]. Motivated by practical problems, where bugs are discovered with few context switches, the context-bounded reachability problem, where there can be at most k context switches have been considered for concurrent pushdown systems [21,23,26,27,29] as well as related models of asynchronous pushdown networks [9]. We present a new algorithm for concurrent pushdown systems and concurrent RSMs which improves the existing complexity when the size of the global component is small.

8   Conclusion

In this work we consider RSMs, a fundamental model for interprocedural analysis, with path properties expressed over finite-height semirings, that can express a large class of properties for program analysis. We present algorithms that improve the previous algorithms, both in the sequential as well as in the concurrent setting. Moreover, along with our algorithm, we present new methods to extract distances from the data-structure (configuration automata) that the algorithm constructs. We present a prototype implementation for sequential RSMs in an explicit setting that provides significant improvements for real-world programs obtained from SLAM/SDV benchmarks. Our results show the potential of the new algorithmic ideas. There are several interesting directions of future work. A symbolic implementation is a direction for future work. Another direction of future work is to explore the new algorithmic ideas in the concurrent setting in practice.

Acknowledgments. This research was supported in part by the Austrian Science Fund (FWF) under grants S11402-N23, S11407-N23, P23499-N23, and Z211-N23, and by the European Research Council (ERC) under grant 279307.

References

1. jMoped 2.0. https://www7.in.tum.de/tools/jmoped/
2. Moped. http://www2.informatik.uni-stuttgart.de/fmi/szs/tools/moped/
3. WALi. https://research.cs.wisc.edu/wpis/wpds/
4. Alur, R., Benedikt, M., Etessami, K., Godefroid, P., Reps, T.W., Yannakakis, M.: Analysis of recursive state machines. ACM Trans. Program. Lang. Syst. **27**(4), 786–818 (2005)
5. Alur, R., Bouajjani, A., Esparza, J.: Model checking procedural programs. In: Clarke, E.M., Henzinger, T.A., Veith, H., Bloem, R. (eds.) Handbook of Model Checking. Springer, Heidelberg (2016)
6. Ball, T., Bounimova, E., Levin, V., Kumar, R., Lichtenberg, J.: The static driver verifier research platform. In: Touili, T., Cook, B., Jackson, P. (eds.) CAV 2010. LNCS, vol. 6174, pp. 119–122. Springer, Heidelberg (2010). doi:10.1007/978-3-642-14295-6_11
7. Ball, T., Rajamani, S.K.: Bebop: a symbolic model checker for boolean programs. In: Havelund, K., Penix, J., Visser, W. (eds.) SPIN 2000. LNCS, vol. 1885, pp. 113–130. Springer, Heidelberg (2000). doi:10.1007/10722468_7
8. Bhattacharya, P., Iliofotou, M., Neamtiu, I., Faloutsos, M.: Graph-based analysis and prediction for software evolution. In: ICSE (2012)
9. Bouajjani, A., Esparza, J., Schwoon, S., Strejček, J.: Reachability analysis of multithreaded software with asynchronous communication. In: Sarukkai, S., Sen, S. (eds.) FSTTCS 2005. LNCS, vol. 3821, pp. 348–359. Springer, Heidelberg (2005). doi:10.1007/11590156_28
10. Callahan, D., Cooper, K.D., Kennedy, K., Torczon, L.: Interprocedural constant propagation. In: CC (1986)
11. Chatterjee, K., Ibsen-Jensen, R., Pavlogiannis, A., Goyal, P.: Faster algorithms for algebraic path properties in recursive state machines with constant treewidth. In: POPL (2015)
12. Chatterjee, K., Kragl, B., Mishra, S., Pavlogiannis, A.: Faster algorithms for weighted recursive state machines. Technical report arXiv:1701.04914 [cs.PL] (2017)
13. Chaudhuri, S.: Subcubic algorithms for recursive state machines. In: POPL (2008)
14. Cousot, P., Cousot, R.: Static determination of dynamic properties of recursive procedures. In: IFIP Conference on Formal Description of Programming Concepts (1977)
15. Giegerich, R., Möncke, U., Wilhelm, R.: Invariance of approximate semantics with respect to program transformations. In: Brauer, W. (ed.) ECI 1981, vol. 50, pp. 1–10. Springer, Heidelberg (1981)
16. Grove, D., Torczon, L.: Interprocedural constant propagation: a study of jump function implementation. In: PLDI (1993)
17. Horwitz, S., Reps, T., Sagiv, M.: Demand interprocedural dataflow analysis. SIGSOFT Softw. Eng. Notes **20**(4), 104–115 (1995)
18. Knoop, J., Steffen, B.: The interprocedural coincidence theorem. In: Kastens, U., Pfahler, P. (eds.) CC 1992. LNCS, vol. 641, pp. 125–140. Springer, Heidelberg (1992). doi:10.1007/3-540-55984-1_13

19. Knoop, J., Steffen, B., Vollmer, J.: Parallelism for free: efficient and optimal bitvector analyses for parallel programs. ACM Trans. Program. Lang. Syst. **18**(3), 268–299 (1996)
20. Lal, A., Reps, T.: Solving multiple dataflow queries using WPDSs. In: Alpuente, M., Vidal, G. (eds.) SAS 2008. LNCS, vol. 5079, pp. 93–109. Springer, Heidelberg (2008). doi:10.1007/978-3-540-69166-2_7
21. Lal, A., Reps, T.W.: Reducing concurrent analysis under a context bound to sequential analysis. Formal Methods Syst. Des. **35**(1), 73–97 (2009)
22. Lal, A., Reps, T., Balakrishnan, G.: Extended weighted pushdown systems. In: Etessami, K., Rajamani, S.K. (eds.) CAV 2005. LNCS, vol. 3576, pp. 434–448. Springer, Heidelberg (2005). doi:10.1007/11513988_44
23. Lal, A., Touili, T., Kidd, N., Reps, T.: Interprocedural analysis of concurrent programs under a context bound. In: Ramakrishnan, C.R., Rehof, J. (eds.) TACAS 2008. LNCS, vol. 4963, pp. 282–298. Springer, Heidelberg (2008). doi:10.1007/978-3-540-78800-3_20
24. Landi, W., Ryder, B.G.: Pointer-induced aliasing: a problem classification. In: POPL (1991)
25. Liberty, E., Zucker, S.W.: The mailman algorithm: a note on matrix-vector multiplication. Inf. Process. Lett. **109**(3), 179–182 (2009)
26. Musuvathi, M., Qadeer, S.: Iterative context bounding for systematic testing of multithreaded programs. In: PLDI (2007)
27. Musuvathi, M., Qadeer, S., Ball, T., Basler, G., Nainar, P.A., Neamtiu, I.: Finding and reproducing heisenbugs in concurrent programs. In: OSDI (2008)
28. Myers, G.: A four russians algorithm for regular expression pattern matching. J. ACM **39**(2), 430–448 (1992)
29. Qadeer, S., Rehof, J.: Context-bounded model checking of concurrent software. In: Halbwachs, N., Zuck, L.D. (eds.) TACAS 2005. LNCS, vol. 3440, pp. 93–107. Springer, Heidelberg (2005). doi:10.1007/978-3-540-31980-1_7
30. Yu, Q., Guan, X., Zheng, Q., Liu, T., Zhou, J., Li, J.: Calling network: a new method for modeling software runtime behaviors. ACM SIGSOFT Softw. Eng. Notes **40**(1), 1–8 (2015)
31. Ramalingam, G.: Context-sensitive synchronization-sensitive analysis is undecidable. ACM Trans. Program. Lang. Syst. **22**(2), 416–430 (2000)
32. Reps, T., Horwitz, S., Sagiv, M.: Precise interprocedural dataflow analysis via graph reachability. In: POPL (1995)
33. Reps, T., Lal, A., Kidd, N.: Program analysis using weighted pushdown systems. In: Arvind, V., Prasad, S. (eds.) FSTTCS 2007. LNCS, vol. 4855, pp. 23–51. Springer, Heidelberg (2007). doi:10.1007/978-3-540-77050-3_4
34. Reps, T.W., Schwoon, S., Jha, S., Melski, D.: Weighted pushdown systems and their application to interprocedural dataflow analysis. Sci. Comput. Program. **58**(1–2), 206–263 (2005)
35. Sagiv, M., Reps, T., Horwitz, S.: Precise interprocedural dataflow analysis with applications to constant propagation. Theor. Comput. Sci. **167**(1), 131–170 (1996)
36. Schwoon, S.: Model-checking pushdown systems. Ph.D. thesis, Technische Universität München (2002)
37. Williams, R.: Matrix-vector multiplication in sub-quadratic time (some preprocessing required). In: SODA (2007)
38. Williams, V.V.: Multiplying matrices faster than Coppersmith-Winograd. In: STOC (2012)

ML and Extended Branching VASS

Conrad Cotton-Barratt[1]([⊠]), Andrzej S. Murawski[2], and C.-H. Luke Ong[1]

[1] University of Oxford, Oxford, UK
conrad.cotton-barratt@cs.ox.ac.uk
[2] University of Warwick, Coventry, UK
a.murawski@warwick.ac.uk

Abstract. We prove that the observational equivalence problem for a finitary fragment of ML is recursively equivalent to the reachability problem for extended branching vector addition systems with states (EBVASS). Our proof uses the fully abstract game semantics of the language. We introduce a new class of automata, VPCMA, as a representation of the game semantics. VPCMA are a version of class memory automata equipped with a visibly pushdown stack; they serve as a bridge enabling interreducibility of decision problems between the game semantics and EBVASS. The results of this paper complete our programme to give an automata classification of the ML types with respect to the observational equivalence problem for closed terms.

1 Introduction

RML is a prototypical call-by-value functional language with state [3], which may be viewed as the canonical restriction of Standard ML to ground-type references. This paper is about the decidability of observational equivalence of finitary RML. Recall that two terms-in-context are *observationally* (or *contextually*) *equivalent*, written $\Gamma \vdash M \cong N$, if they are interchangeable in all program contexts without causing any observable difference in the computational outcome. Observational equivalence is a compelling notion of program equality, but it is hard to reason about because of the universal quantification over program contexts. Our ultimate goal is to completely classify the decidable fragments of finitary RML, and characterise each fragment by an appropriate class of automata. In the case of finitary Idealized Algol [27] – the call-by-name counterpart of RML, the decidability of observational equivalence depends on the type-theoretic order [21] of the terms. By contrast, the decidability of RML terms is not neatly characterised by order: there are undecidable fragments of terms-in-context of order as low as 2 [20], amidst interesting decidable fragments at each of orders 1 to 4. Indeed, as we shall see, there is a pair of second-order types[1] with opposite decidability status but which differs only in the ordering of their argument types.

Let $\mathcal{L}$ be a collection of finitary RML terms-in-context. The observational equivalence problem asks: given two terms-in-context $(i = 1, 2)$

$$x_1 : \theta_1, \cdots, x_k : \theta_k \vdash M_i : \theta$$

---

[1] Namely, unit → (unit → unit) → unit *vs* (unit → unit) → unit → unit.

© Springer-Verlag GmbH Germany 2017
H. Yang (Ed.): ESOP 2017, LNCS 10201, pp. 314–340, 2017.
DOI: 10.1007/978-3-662-54434-1_12

from $\mathcal{L}$, are they observationally equivalent? Unsurprisingly the general problem is undecidable [20]. However decidability has been established for certain fragments, which we present in Fig. 1 by listing for each fragment the shapes of types allowable on the LHS and RHS of the turnstile, where β is a base type.[2]

Shape	LHS Type, θ_i	RHS Type, θ
I [9]	$(\beta \to \beta) \to \cdots \to (\beta \to \beta) \to \beta$	$\beta \to \cdots \to \beta$
II [15]	$((\beta \to \cdots \to \beta) \to \beta) \to \cdots \to ((\beta \to \cdots \to \beta) \to \beta) \to \beta$	$(\beta \to \cdots \to \beta) \to \beta$

Fig. 1. Two decidable fragments of finitary RML

Note that (the RHS type) θ of shape I ranges over all first-order types; and θ of shape II admits the simplest second-order types. Because [9] also establishes undecidability for the second-order type $\theta = (\text{unit} \to \text{unit}) \to \text{unit} \to \text{unit}$ and the simplest third-order type $\theta = ((\text{unit} \to \text{unit}) \to \text{unit}) \to \text{unit}$, as far as closed terms are concerned, the only unclassified cases are second-order types of the shape

$$\underbrace{\beta \to \cdots \to \beta}_{m} \to \underbrace{(\beta \to \cdots \to \beta)}_{n} \to \beta \tag{1}$$

where $m \geq 1$ and $n \geq 2$. These types are the subject of this paper.

Our main contribution concerns the closed terms of types of the shape

$$\beta \to (\beta \to \cdots \to \beta) \to \beta \tag{2}$$

and relates their observational equivalence problem to the reachability problem for *extended branching vector addition systems with states* (EBVASS) [17], whose decidability status is, to our knowledge, unknown. Our result applies not only to closed terms but also to the fragment RML$_{\text{EBVASS}}$ (Definition 4) of open terms of type (2) in which free variables are subject to certain type constraints. Our main result is the following

Theorem 1. *Observational equivalence for the terms-in-context in* RML$_{\text{EBVASS}}$ *is recursively equivalent to the reachability problem for extended branching vector addition systems.*

Our second result (Theorem 23) is that the reachability problem for *reset vector addition systems with states* [5] is reducible to the observational equivalence of closed terms of type $\beta \to \beta \to (\beta \to \beta) \to \beta$. It follows that the observational equivalence of closed terms of all of the remaining types of the shape (1), i.e., where $m, n \geq 2$, is undecidable.

In the following, we discuss the key ideas behind the main results. Like the earlier results [9,15], Theorems 1 and 23 are proved by appealing to the

---

[2] For the sake of clarity, we do not list types with int ref and the corresponding constraints. They are analogous to treating int ref as $\beta \to \beta$.

game semantics for RML [3,13], which is *fully abstract*, i.e., the equational theory induced by the semantics coincides with observational equivalence. In game
semantics [1,16], player P takes the viewpoint of the term-in-context, and player
O takes the viewpoint of the program context or environment. Thus a term-in-
context, $\Gamma \vdash M : \theta$ with $\Gamma = x_1 : \theta_1, \cdots, x_n : \theta_n$, is interpreted as a P-strategy
$[\![\Gamma \vdash M : \theta]\!]$ in the prearena $[\![\theta_1, \cdots, \theta_n \vdash \theta]\!]$. A play is a sequence of moves,
made alternately by O and P, such that each non-initial move has a justification
pointer to some earlier move. Thanks to the fully abstract game semantics of
RML [3,13], observational equivalence is characterised by *complete plays*, i.e.,
$\Gamma \vdash M \cong N$ holds iff the respective P-strategies, $[\![\Gamma \vdash M : \theta]\!]$ and $[\![\Gamma \vdash N : \theta]\!]$,
contain the same set of complete plays. Strategies may be viewed as highly
constrained processes, and are amenable to automata-theoretic representations.
The main technical challenge, however, lies in the encoding of the justification
pointers of the plays.

In recent work [8,9], we considered finitary RML terms-in-context with types
of shape I (see Fig. 1). To represent the plays in the game semantics of such terms,
we need to encode O-pointers (i.e. justification pointers from O-moves), which
is tricky because O-moves are controlled by the environment rather than the
term. It turns out that the game semantics of these terms are representable as
nested data class memory automata (NDCMA) [10], which are a variant of *class
memory automata* [6] whose data values exhibit a tree structure, reflecting the
tree structure of the threads in the plays.

Because of the type constraints, a play (in the strategy denotation) of a
term in RML$_{\text{EBVASS}}$ may be viewed as an interleaving of "visibly pushdown"
threads, subject to the global well-bracketing condition. (See Sect. 3 for an explanation.) In order to model such plays, we introduce *visibly pushdown class memory automata* (VPCMA), which naturally augment class memory automata with
a stack and follow a visibly pushdown discipline, but also add data values to the
stack so that matching push- and pop-moves must share the same data value.
To give a clear representation of the game semantics, we introduce a slight variant of VPCMA with a run-time constraint on the words accepted, called *scoping
VPCMA* (SVPCMA). This constraint prevents data values from being read once
the stack element that was at the top of the stack when the data value was first
read in the run has been popped off the stack. Although these two models are
expressively different, they have equivalent emptiness problems.

Unlike in class memory automata (CMA), weakness[3] does not affect the
hardness of the emptiness problem for VPCMA, as the stack can be used to
check the local acceptance condition. However, like CMA, weakness does help
with the closure properties of the languages recognised. The closure properties
of these automata are the same as for normal CMA [9]: weak deterministic
VPCMA are closed under union, intersection and complementation; similarly
for SVPCMA. We show that the complete plays in the game semantics of each
RML$_{\text{EBVASS}}$ term-in-context are representable as a weak deterministic SVPCMA

---

[3] *Weak* class memory automata [8,9] are class memory automata in which the local
acceptance condition is dropped.

(Lemma 14). Thanks to the closure property of SVPCMA, it then follows that RML$_{\text{EBVASS}}$ observational equivalence is reducible to the emptiness problem for VPCMA (Theorem 13).

Finally and most importantly, we show (Theorems 20 and 22) that the emptiness problem for VPCMA (equivalently for SVPCMA) is equivalent to the reachability problem for extended branching VASS (EBVASS) [17], the decidability of which remains an open problem. In particular, reachability in EBVASS is a harder problem than the long-standing open problem of reachability in BVASS (equivalently, provability in multiplicative exponential linear logic) [11], which is known to be non-elementary [19].

In summary, the results complete our programme to give an automata classification of the ML types with respect to the observational equivalence problem for closed terms of finitary RML. We tabulate our findings as follows:

Order	Type	Automata/status
1	unit $\to \cdots \to$ unit	NDCMA/decidable [9,14]
2	(unit $\to \cdots \to$ unit) $\to$ unit	VPA/decidable [15]
2	unit $\to$ (unit $\to \cdots \to$ unit) $\to$ unit	EBVASS (this paper)
2	unit $\to$ unit $\to$ (unit $\to$ unit) $\to$ unit	Undecidable (this paper)
2	(unit $\to$ unit) $\to$ unit $\to$ unit	Undecidable [9]
3	((unit $\to$ unit) $\to$ unit) $\to$ unit	Undecidable [9]

Related Work. Hopkins and Murawski [14] used deterministic class memory automata to recognise the strategies of RML terms of a first-order type with certain constraints on the types of their free variables. Building on this idea, strategies of terms-in-context with shape-I types (Fig. 1) are shown to be representable as NDCMA [9]. Automata over an infinite alphabet (specifically, pushdown register automata) have also been applied to game semantics [24,25] for a different purpose, namely, to model generation of fresh names in fragments of ML [25] and Java [22]. When extended with name storage, observational equivalence of terms-in-context with types in RML$_{\text{EBVASS}}$ becomes undecidable [25]; in particular, this is already the case for closed terms of type unit $\to$ unit $\to$ unit.

Outline. In Sect. 2 we define the syntax and operational semantics of RML and the fragment RML$_{\text{EBVASS}}$. In Sect. 3 we present the game semantics for RML. The automata models, VPMCA and SVPCMA, are then presented in Sect. 4, where we show that their emptiness problems are interreducible, and discuss their closure properties. In Sect. 5 we show that the complete plays in the game semantics of RML$_{\text{EBVASS}}$-terms are representable as weak deterministic SVPCMA. Consequently the observational equivalence of RML$_{\text{EBVASS}}$-terms is reducible to the emptiness problem of SVPCMA (and equivalently to that of VPCMA). Reducibility in the opposite direction is then shown in Sect. 6. In Sect. 7 we introduce EBVASS and show that its reachability problem and the emptiness problem for VPCMA are interreducible. Finally, in Sect. 8, we show that observational equivalence for closed terms of type unit $\to$ unit $\to$ (unit $\to$ unit) $\to$ unit is undecidable.

2   A Stateful Call-by-Value Functional Language RML

RML is a call-by-value functional language with state [3]. Its types are generated from ground types of int and unit, which represent integers and commands respectively, and the variable type int ref. As the int and unit types will be very similar in their behaviour for our purposes, we will often use β to range over int and unit. Types are then constructed from these in the normal way, using the $\to$ operator:

$$\theta ::= \text{int} \mid \text{unit} \mid \text{int ref} \mid \theta \to \theta.$$

The *order* of a type is given by: $\mathbf{ord}(\text{int}) = \mathbf{ord}(\text{unit}) := 0$, $\mathbf{ord}(\text{int ref}) := 1$, and $\mathbf{ord}(\theta \to \theta') := max(\mathbf{ord}(\theta) + 1, \mathbf{ord}(\theta'))$. In order to eliminate obvious sources of undecidability, we consider *finitary* RML, with finite ground types (int $=$ $\{0, \cdots, \text{max}\}$), and iteration instead of recursion. The syntax and typing rules of RML terms are given by induction over the rules in Fig. 2. Note that although we only include arithmetic operations **succ**() and **pred**(), other operations are easily definable using case distinction, because we work with finite int. We will write **let** $x = M$ **in** N as syntactic sugar for $(\lambda x.N)M$, and $M; N$ for **let** $x = M$ **in** N where x is chosen to be fresh in N.

$$\frac{}{\Gamma \vdash () : \text{unit}} \qquad \frac{i \in \{0, \cdots, \text{max}\}}{\Gamma \vdash i : \text{int}} \qquad \frac{}{\Gamma, x : \theta \vdash x : \theta}$$

$$\frac{\Gamma \vdash M : \text{int}}{\Gamma \vdash \mathbf{succ}(M) : \text{int}} \qquad \frac{\Gamma \vdash M : \text{int}}{\Gamma \vdash \mathbf{pred}(M) : \text{int}}$$

$$\frac{\Gamma \vdash M : \text{int} \quad \Gamma \vdash M_0 : \theta \quad \Gamma \vdash M_1 : \theta}{\Gamma \vdash \mathbf{if}\ M\ \mathbf{then}\ M_1\ \mathbf{else}\ M_0 : \theta}$$

$$\frac{\Gamma \vdash M : \text{int ref}}{\Gamma \vdash !M : \text{int}} \qquad \frac{\Gamma \vdash M : \text{int ref} \quad \Gamma \vdash N : \text{int}}{\Gamma \vdash M := N : \text{unit}} \qquad \frac{\Gamma \vdash M : \text{int}}{\Gamma \vdash \mathbf{ref}\ M : \text{int ref}}$$

$$\frac{\Gamma \vdash M : \text{unit} \to \text{int} \quad \Gamma \vdash N : \text{int} \to \text{unit}}{\Gamma \vdash \mathbf{mkvar}(M, N) : \text{int ref}} \qquad \frac{\Gamma \vdash M : \text{int} \quad \Gamma \vdash N : \text{unit}}{\Gamma \vdash \mathbf{while}\ M\ \mathbf{do}\ N : \text{unit}}$$

$$\frac{\Gamma \vdash M : \theta \to \theta' \quad \Gamma \vdash N : \theta}{\Gamma \vdash MN : \theta'} \qquad \frac{\Gamma, x : \theta \vdash M : \theta'}{\Gamma \vdash \lambda x^\theta.M : \theta \to \theta'}$$

Fig. 2. Syntax of finitary RML

The operational semantics of the language is presented as a "big-step" relation that uses *stores* [3] to capture the behaviour of variables. Let L range over a countable set of *locations*, then a store is just a partial function $s : L \to \mathbb{N}_{\leq max}$. For $l \in L$ and $i \in \{0, \cdots, max\}$, we write $s[l \mapsto i]$ for the store obtained from s by making l map to i, and for a store s we write $dom(s)$ for the value in L on which s is defined. The reduction rules are defined inductively on pairs (s, M) where s is a store, by the rules presented in Fig. 3. We assume $max + 1 = max$ and $0 - 1 = 0$. These reductions reduce terms to *canonical forms*, V, which can be the empty command (), a constant integer i, a location l, a lambda-abstraction term $\lambda x.M$, or a *bad-variable construct* using canonical forms inside, $\mathbf{mkvar}(V_1, V_2)$.

$$\frac{}{s, V \Downarrow s, V} \qquad \frac{s, M \Downarrow s', i}{s, \mathbf{succ}(M) \Downarrow s', i+1} \qquad \frac{s, M \Downarrow s', i}{s, \mathbf{pred}(M) \Downarrow s', i-1}$$

$$\frac{s, M \Downarrow s', 0 \quad s', N_1 \Downarrow s'', V}{s, \mathbf{if}\ M\ \mathbf{then}\ N_0\ \mathbf{else}\ N_1 \Downarrow s'', V} \qquad \frac{s, M \Downarrow s', n+1 \quad s', N_0 \Downarrow s'', V}{s, \mathbf{if}\ M\ \mathbf{then}\ N_0\ \mathbf{else}\ N_1 \Downarrow s'', V}$$

$$\frac{s, M \Downarrow s', n}{s, \mathbf{ref}\ M \Downarrow s'[l \mapsto n], l}\ l \notin dom(s) \qquad \frac{s, M \Downarrow s', l}{s, !M \Downarrow s', s'(l)}$$

$$\frac{s, M \Downarrow s', l \quad s', N \Downarrow s'', n}{s, M := N \Downarrow s''[l \mapsto n], ()} \qquad \frac{s, M \Downarrow s', \mathbf{mkvar}(V_0, V_1) \quad s', V_0() \Downarrow s'', V}{s, !M \Downarrow s'', V}$$

$$\frac{s, M \Downarrow s', \mathbf{mkvar}(V_0, V_1) \quad s', N \Downarrow s'', n \quad s'', V_1 n \Downarrow s''', V}{s, M := N \Downarrow s''', V}$$

$$\frac{s, M \Downarrow s', V_1 \quad s', N \Downarrow s'', V_2}{s, \mathbf{mkvar}(M, N) \Downarrow s'', \mathbf{mkvar}(V_1, V_2)} \qquad \frac{s, M \Downarrow s', 0}{s, \mathbf{while}\ M\ \mathbf{do}\ N \Downarrow s', ()}$$

$$\frac{s, M \Downarrow s', n \quad s', N \Downarrow s'', () \quad s'', \mathbf{while}\ M\ \mathbf{do}\ N \Downarrow s''', ()}{s, \mathbf{while}\ M\ \mathbf{do}\ N \Downarrow s''', ()}\ n \neq 0$$

$$\frac{s, M \Downarrow s', \lambda x.M' \quad s', N \Downarrow s'', V \quad s'', M'[V/x] \Downarrow s''', V'}{s, MN \Downarrow s''', V'}$$

Fig. 3. Operational semantics of RML

Observational equivalence (OE), also known as contextual equivalence, is the problem of whether two program-fragments are interchangeable without causing any changes to the observable computational outcome. We give a formal definition in Definition 2. OE is a natural notion of program equivalence, a key problem in verification [12].

Definition 2. *Given an RML term M, we write $M\Downarrow$ if there exist s and V such that $\emptyset, M \Downarrow s, V$ (where $\emptyset$ is the empty store).*
We say two terms $\Gamma \vdash M : \theta$ and $\Gamma \vdash N : \theta$ are observationally equivalent if for all contexts $C[-]$ such that $\Gamma \vdash C[M], C[N] : \mathsf{unit}$, $C[M] \Downarrow$ iff $C[N] \Downarrow$.

Remark 3. RML is similar to Reduced ML [26], the restriction of Standard ML to ground-type references, but is augmented with a "bad-variable" constructor in the sense of Reynolds [27] (in the absence of the constructor, the equality test is definable). In the presence of int ref, RML is generally more discriminating then Reduced ML. However observational equivalence of RML coincides with that of Reduced ML on types in which all occurrences (if any) of int ref are positive. The semantics of int ref-types in Reduced ML is much subtler, though, and its analysis requires one to use carefully tailored store annotations in the corresponding game semantics [23].

Definition 4. *The fragment* $\mathrm{RML}_{\mathrm{EBVASS}}$ *consists of finitary RML terms-in-context of the form,* $x_1 : \theta_3, \ldots, x_n : \theta_3 \vdash M : \theta_0 \to \theta_2$*, where*

$$\theta_0 ::= \text{unit} \mid \text{int} \qquad\qquad \theta_1 ::= \theta_0 \mid \theta_0 \to \theta_1 \mid \text{int ref}$$
$$\theta_2 ::= \theta_0 \mid \theta_1 \to \theta_0 \mid \text{int ref} \qquad \theta_3 ::= \theta_0 \mid \theta_2 \to \theta_3 \mid \text{int ref}$$

Example 5. The following term $\vdash M : \text{int} \to (\text{int} \to \text{int}) \to \text{int}$ is in $\mathrm{RML}_{\mathrm{EBVASS}}$.

$$\lambda x^{\text{int}}. \; \textbf{let } \mathrm{m} = \textbf{ref}(0)$$
$$\textbf{in } \lambda f^{\text{int} \to \text{int}}. \; \textbf{assert}(\text{even}(!m)); \; \textbf{if } \text{even}(x) \; \textbf{then } m := 1;$$
$$\textbf{let } \text{y=f(x)} \; \textbf{in } m := x; \; y$$

We write **assert**(M) for **if** M **then** $()$ **else** Ω, where Ω is the divergent term **while** 1 **do** $()$. When applied to an integer x, the term yields a function of type $(\text{int} \to \text{int}) \to \text{int}$, which will apply its argument (a function $f : \text{int} \to \text{int}$) to x. However, owing to the assertion and the side effects, the behaviour of $M\,x$ is quite different from $\lambda f^{\text{int} \to \text{int}}.f\,x$. If x is even then only sequential (non-overlapping) uses of the function will be allowed. Thus, **let** $g = M\,0$ **in** (**let** $a = g(\lambda x^{\text{int}}.0)$ **in** $g(\lambda y^{\text{int}}.0)$) terminates, whereas **let** $g = M\,0$ **in** $g(\lambda x^{\text{int}}.g(\lambda y^{\text{int}}.0))$ diverges. In contrast, when x is odd, $M\,x$ can only be called in a nested way and new calls become forbidden as soon as the first call returns. Thus, a typical usage pattern consists of a series of nested calls (of arbitrary depth) followed by the same number of returns. Consequently, **let** $g = M\,1$ **in** $g(\lambda x^{\text{int}}.g(\lambda y^{\text{int}}.0))$ terminates, whereas **let** $g = M\,1$ **in** (**let** $a = g(\lambda x^{\text{int}}.0)$ **in** $g(\lambda y^{\text{int}}.0)$) diverges.

3   Game Semantics of RML

We use a presentation of call-by-value game semantics in the style of Honda and Yoshida [13], as opposed to Abramsky and McCusker's isomorphic model [3], as Honda and Yoshida's more concrete constructions lend themselves more easily to recognition by automata. We recall the following presentation of the game semantics for RML from [15].

An *arena* A is a triple $(M_A, \vdash_A, \lambda_A)$ where M_A is a set of *moves* where $I_A \subseteq M_A$ consists of *initial* moves, $\vdash_A \subseteq M_A \times (M_A \backslash I_A)$ is called the *enabling relation*, and $\lambda_A : M_A \to \{O, P\} \times \{Q, A\}$ a labelling function such that for all $i_A \in I_A$ we have $\lambda_A(i_A) = (P, A)$, and if $m \vdash_A m'$ then $(\pi_1 \circ \lambda_A)(m) \neq (\pi_1 \circ \lambda_A)(m')$ and $(\pi_2 \circ \lambda_A)(m') = A \Rightarrow (\pi_2 \circ \lambda_A)(m) = Q$. The function λ_A labels moves as belonging to either *Opponent* or *Proponent* and as being either a *Question* or an *Answer*. Note that answers are always enabled by questions, but questions can be enabled by either a question or an answer. We will use arenas to model types. However, the actual games will be played over *prearenas*, which are defined in the same way except that initial moves are O-questions.

Three basic arenas are 0 (the empty arena), 1 (the arena containing a single initial move $\bullet$), and $\mathbb{Z}$ (has integers as moves, all of which are initial P-answers). In all cases, the enabling relation is empty. The constructions on arenas are defined in Figs. 4 and 5, where the lines represent enabling. Here we use $\overline{I_A}$ as an abbreviation for $M_A \backslash I_A$, and $\overline{\lambda_A}$ for the O/P-complement of λ_A. Intuitively $A \otimes B$ is the union of the arenas A and B, but with the initial moves combined pairwise. $A \Rightarrow B$ is slightly more complex. First we add a new initial move, $\bullet$. We take the O/P-complement of A, change the initial moves into questions, and set them to now be justified by $\bullet$. Finally, we take B and set its initial moves to be justified by A's initial moves. The final construction, $A \to B$, takes two arenas A and B and produces a prearena, as shown below. This is essentially the same as $A \Rightarrow B$ without the initial move $\bullet$.

$$M_{A \Rightarrow B} = \{\bullet\} \uplus M_A \uplus M_B \qquad M_{A \otimes B} = I_A \times I_B \uplus \overline{I_A} \uplus \overline{I_B}$$

$$I_{A \Rightarrow B} = \{\bullet\} \qquad\qquad I_{A \otimes B} = I_A \times I_B$$

$$\lambda_{A \Rightarrow B} = m \mapsto \begin{cases} PA & \text{if } m = \bullet \\ OQ & \text{if } m \in I_A \\ \overline{\lambda_A}(m) & \text{if } m \in \overline{I_A} \\ \lambda_B(m) & \text{if } m \in M_B \end{cases} \qquad \lambda_{A \otimes B} = m \mapsto \begin{cases} PA & \text{if } m \in I_A \times I_B \\ \lambda_A(m) & \text{if } m \in \overline{I_A} \\ \lambda_B(m) & \text{if } m \in \overline{I_B} \end{cases}$$

$$\vdash_{A \Rightarrow B} = \{(\bullet, i_A) | i_A \in I_A\} \qquad \vdash_{A \otimes B} = \{((i_A, i_B), m) | i_A \in I_A \wedge i_B \in I_B$$
$$\uplus \{(i_A, i_B) | i_A \in I_A, i_B \in I_B\} \qquad\qquad \wedge (i_A \vdash_A m \vee i_B \vdash_B m)\}$$
$$\cup \vdash_A \cup \vdash_B \qquad\qquad\qquad \cup (\vdash_A \cap (\overline{I_A} \times \overline{I_A}))$$
$$\qquad\qquad\qquad\qquad \cup (\vdash_B \cap (\overline{I_B} \times \overline{I_B}))$$

$$M_{A \to B} = M_A \uplus M_B \qquad \lambda_{A \to B}(m) = \begin{cases} OQ & \text{if } m \in I_A \\ \overline{\lambda_A}(m) & \text{if } m \in \overline{I_A} \\ \lambda_B(m) & \text{if } m \in M_B \end{cases}$$

$$I_{A \to B} = I_A \qquad\qquad \vdash_{A \to B} = \{(i_A, i_B) | i_A \in I_A, i_B \in I_B\} \cup \vdash_A \cup \vdash_B$$

Fig. 4. Arena and prearena constructions: definitions

We intend arenas to represent types, in particular $[\![\text{unit}]\!] = 1$, $[\![\text{int}]\!] = \mathbb{Z}$ (or a finite subset of $\mathbb{Z}$ for RML_f), $[\![\text{int ref}]\!] = [\![\text{unit} \to \text{int}]\!] \otimes [\![\text{int} \to \text{unit}]\!]$ and $[\![\theta_1 \to \theta_2]\!] = [\![\theta_1]\!] \Rightarrow [\![\theta_2]\!]$. A term-in-context $x_1 : \theta_1, \ldots, x_n : \theta_n \vdash M : \theta$ will be represented by a *strategy* for the prearena $[\![\theta_1]\!] \otimes \ldots \otimes [\![\theta_n]\!] \to [\![\theta]\!]$.

A *justified sequence* in a prearena A is a sequence of moves from A in which the first move is initial and all other moves m are equipped with a pointer to an earlier move m', such that $m' \vdash_A m$. A *play* s is a justified sequence which additionally satisfies the standard conditions of Alternation, Well-Bracketing, and Visibility [3]. A *strategy* σ for prearena A is a non-empty, even-prefix-closed set of plays from A, satisfying the determinism condition: if $s\,m_1, s\,m_2 \in \sigma$ then $s\,m_1 = s\,m_2$. We can think of a strategy as being a playbook telling P how to respond by mapping odd-length plays to moves. A play is *complete* if all questions have been answered. Note that (unlike in the call-by-name case) a complete play is not necessarily maximal. We denote the set of complete plays in strategy σ by **comp**(σ).

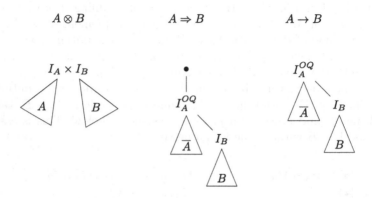

$$A \otimes B \qquad\qquad A \Rightarrow B \qquad\qquad A \to B$$

Fig. 5. Arena and prearena constructions, pictorially

In the game model of RML, a term-in-context $x_1 : \theta_1, \ldots, x_n : \theta_n \vdash M : \theta$ is interpreted by a strategy of the prearena $[\![\theta_1]\!] \otimes \ldots \otimes [\![\theta_n]\!] \to [\![\theta]\!]$. These strategies are defined by recursion over the syntax of the term. Free identifiers $x : \theta \vdash x : \theta$ are interpreted as *copy-cat* strategies where P always copies O's move into the other copy of $[\![\theta]\!]$, $\lambda x.M$ allows multiple copies of $[\![M]\!]$ to be run, application MN requires a form of parallel composition plus hiding and the other constructions can be interpreted using special strategies. The game-semantic model is fully abstract in the following sense.

Theorem 6 (Abramsky and McCusker [2,3]). *If $\Gamma \vdash M : \theta$ and $\Gamma \vdash N : \theta$ are RML terms then $\Gamma \vdash M \cong N$ iff* **comp**$([\![M]\!]) = $ **comp**$([\![N]\!])$.

To represent the game semantics for the fragment RML$_{\mathrm{EBVASS}}$, we need an automaton over an infinite alphabet which is equipped with a visibly pushdown stack. The shape of the prearenas for terms-in-context in this fragment is shown in Fig. 6.

Remark 7. We describe the intuitive meaning of various moves from the Figure. q_0 starts the evaluation of the term. a_0 stands for successful evaluation. q_1 invokes the resultant function with a base-type argument, while a_1 means that a value of type $(\beta \to \cdots \to \beta) \to \beta$ was generated. q_2 then corresponds to calling the value on a function argument, $q_*^1, a_*^1, \ldots, q_*^{m-1}, a_*^{m-1}$ represent interaction with that argument, while a_2 means that the call has returned.

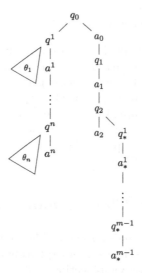

Fig. 6. Shape of prearena for $\theta_1 \to \cdots \to \theta_n \to \beta \vdash \beta \to (\beta_1 \to \cdots \to \beta_m) \to \beta$

Next we analyse the shape of non-empty complete plays in such arenas. At the beginning, each such play will contain a segment $q_0\, s\, a_0$ where s contains moves originating from the left-hand side of the arena. The unique occurrence of a_0 can be used to justify subsequent occurrences of q_1, each of which will have to be answered with a_1. Note that, due to the visibility condition, the moves between q_1 and the corresponding a_1 can only come from the left-hand side of the arena. It will be useful to think of each $q_1\,a_1$-pair as defining a thread of play (moves made between q_1 and a_1 can then be said to occur in that thread).

Further, each a_1 can be used to justify subsequent occurrences of q_2, which we may think of as starting a subthread of the corresponding thread $q_1\,a_1$. Note that in this case the justification pointer from q_2 is crucial in linking the q_2-subthread to the corresponding thread determined by $q_1\,a_1$. We give a sample play below, which represents the interaction of the term $\lambda x^{\text{unit}}.\lambda f^{\text{unit}\to\text{unit}}.fx$ with context **let** $g = [\,]$ **in let** $f_1 = g()$ **in let** $f_2 = g()$ **in** $f_1(\lambda x^{\text{unit}}.\textbf{let } f_3 = g() \textbf{ in } ())$.

$$q_0 \quad a_0 \quad q_1 \quad a_1 \quad q_1 \quad a_1 \quad q_2 \quad q_*^1 \quad q_1 \quad a_1 \quad a_*^1 \quad a_2$$

Observe that due to the well-bracketing condition and the availability of q_*^i moves, each thread can have a pushdown character. Thus, a play becomes an interleaving of pushdown threads subject to the global well-bracketing condition. This interleaving may switch between threads after any a_1, a_2, or q_*^i-move. Where a q_*^i-move is made, the corresponding q_2-subthread can only be returned to subject to the stack discipline. Furthermore, whenever O has the opportunity to start a new thread – after an a_1, a_2, or q_*^i-move, it can also create a new q_2-subthread by pointing at a visible occurrence of a_1. Later on we shall introduce an automata-theoretic model over infinite alphabets, called VPCMA, to capture such scenarios. The preceding play will correspond to the following data word

$$(q_0, n_0)(a_0, n_0)(q_1, n_1)(a_1, n_1)(q_1, n_2)(a_1, n_2)(q_2, n_1)(q_*^1, n_1)(q_1, n_3)(a_1, n_3)(a_*^1, n_1)(a_2, n_1)$$

where n_1, n_2, n_3 are elements of the infinite alphabet playing the rôle of thread identifiers (technically, they represent pointers from q_2).

There is one more complication due to the visibility condition. Note that once a_2 is played, it will remove the third $q_1 a_1$ segment from the O-view and will effectively prevent the thread from generating future q_2-subthreads. Thus, the visibility condition restricts the way in which threads can be revisited to be compatible with the stack discipline. This constraint will motivate a variant of VPCMA, called *scoping VPCMA*.

4   Visibly Pushdown Class Memory Automata

In this section we introduce *visibly pushdown class memory automata* (VPCMA), which will be a convenient mechanism for capturing the game-semantic scenarios discussed at the end of the previous section.

VPCMA are a formalism over *data words*, i.e., elements of $(\Sigma \times \mathcal{D})^*$ where Σ is a finite alphabet of *data tags* and $\mathcal{D}$ is an infinite set of *data values*. VPCMA combine ideas from class memory automata (CMA) [7] and visibly pushdown automata (VPA) [4]. As with CMA, our VPCMA will have a class memory function that, for each data value seen in the run, will remember the state in which the data value was last seen. Following VPA, the input alphabet Σ will be partitioned into Σ_{push}, Σ_{pop}, and Σ_{noop}, which determine the kind of stack action that is performed once letters from $\Sigma \times \mathcal{D}$ are being read. Stack actions will use elements of $\Gamma \times \mathcal{D}$, where Γ is a finite stack alphabet. The only subtlety in how these two kinds of automata are combined is in the contents of the stack: whenever an element of $\mathcal{D}$ will be involved in a push or pop, we shall require that it be equal to the element of $\mathcal{D}$ that is currently read by the machine. Thus, matching push- and pop-moves will always read the same data value. The data values on the stack can only be used in enforcing that the same data value that pushed an element to the stack is used to pop it off the stack.

Definition 8 (VPCMA). *Let $\Sigma = \Sigma_{\text{push}} + \Sigma_{\text{pop}} + \Sigma_{\text{noop}}$ be finite and $Q_\perp = Q + \{\perp\}$. Fix an infinite dataset $\mathcal{D}$. A visibly pushdown class memory automaton is a tuple $\langle Q, \Sigma, \Gamma, \Delta, q_0, F_G, F_L \rangle$, where Q is a finite set of states, $q_0 \in Q$ is the initial state, $F_G \subseteq F_L \subseteq Q$ are sets of globally and locally accepting states respectively, Γ a finite stack alphabet and Δ is the transition relation, where:*

$$\Delta \subseteq (Q \times Q_\perp \times (\Sigma_{\text{push}} \cup \Sigma_{\text{pop}}) \times \Gamma \times Q) \cup (Q \times Q_\perp \times \Sigma_{\text{noop}} \times Q).$$

We explain the workings of a VPCMA below. A configuration is a triple (q, f, S) where $q \in Q$ is the current state, $f : \mathcal{D} \to Q_\perp$ is a *class memory function*, and $S \in (\mathcal{D} \times \Gamma)^*$ is the stack. The initial configuration is (q_0, f_0, ϵ) where f_0 maps all data values to $\perp$. A configuration (q, f, S) is *accepting* if $q \in F_G$, $f(d) \in F_L \cup \{\perp\}$ for all $d \in \mathcal{D}$, and $S = \epsilon$. On reading an input letter $(a, d) \in \Sigma \times \mathcal{D}$ whilst in configuration (q, f, S) the automaton can follow transitions as follows:

– if $a \in \Sigma_{\text{push}}$ the automaton can follow a transition $(q, f(d), a, \gamma, q')$ to configuration $(q', f[d \mapsto q'], S \cdot (d, \gamma))$.
– if $a \in \Sigma_{\text{pop}}$ and $S = S' \cdot (d, \gamma)$ the automaton can follow a transition $(q, f(d), a, \gamma, q')$ to configuration $(q', f[d \mapsto q'], S')$.
– if $a \in \Sigma_{\text{noop}}$ the automaton can follow a transition $(q, f(d), a, q')$ to configuration $(q', f[d \mapsto q'], S)$.

Acceptance of words is then defined in the normal way, with a word being accepted just if there is a run of the word from the initial configuration to an accepting configuration. Determinism is also defined in the normal way. That is, a VPCMA is deterministic just if the following conditions all hold:

(i) $(q, s, a_{\text{push}}, \gamma, p), (q, s, a_{\text{push}}, \gamma', p') \in \Delta \Rightarrow \gamma = \gamma', p = p'$;
(ii) $(q, s, a_{\text{pop}}, \gamma, p), (q, s, a_{\text{pop}}, \gamma, p') \in \Delta \Rightarrow p = p'$; and
(iii) $(q, s, a_{\text{noop}}, p), (q, s, a_{\text{noop}}, p') \in \Delta \Rightarrow p = p'$.

In our translation from RML, we shall rely on *weak VPCMA*, in which all states are locally accepting, i.e. $F_L = Q$. Then a configuration is final if a global accepting state has been reached and the stack is empty. Although for class memory automata (CMA), there is a significant gap between the complexity of normal CMA and weak CMA emptiness (corresponding essentially to the difference between reachability and coverability in vector addition systems) [10], there is no similar gap for VPCMA. The emptiness problem for VPCMA can be easily reduced to that for weak VPCMA by constructing, for a given VPCMA, a weak VPCMA which will at the very beginning guess all the data values to be used in an accepting run, push them on the stack one by one and, at the very end, verify the local acceptance conditions for each data value during pops.

Proposition 9. *Emptiness of VPCMA can be reduced to emptiness of weak VPCMA.*

Using standard product constructions, in the same way as for weak CMA [10], one can show that weak VPCMA are closed under union and intersection. Deterministic weak VPCMA are also closed under complementation (by reversing accepting states) but the complement needs to be taken with respect to the set of "well-bracketed" words generated by the grammar

$$W ::= \quad \epsilon \quad | \quad (a_{\text{noop}}, d) \cdot W \quad | \quad (a_{\text{push}}, d) \cdot W \cdot (a_{\text{pop}}, d) \cdot W$$

where d ranges over $\mathcal{D}$, and a_{push}, a_{pop}, and a_{noop} range over Σ_{push}, Σ_{pop}, and Σ_{noop} respectively. The closure properties make it possible to reduce deterministic VPCMA inclusion and equivalence to VPCMA emptiness.

We wrap this section up with the introduction of a special kind of VPCMA, called *scoping* VPCMA (SVPCMA). This variant is meant to reflect the shape of plays analysed at the end of Sect. 3 particularly well. Its definition is identical to that of VPCMA. The difference is in how the runs are defined, and as a result in the languages recognised. For SVPCMA, a configuration keeps track not just of the current state, class memory function, and stack, but also of a set of "visible" data values. The idea is that when a data value is first read after a push-move but before that move's corresponding pop-move, this data value will only be usable until that pop-move – preventing the data value from "leaking" into other parts of the run. Consequently, a tree hierarchy is imposed on the use of data values. Although this may seem a substantial restriction at first, scoping VPCMA turn out to have identical algorithmic properties to normal VPCMA.

Definition 10. *A scoping VPCMA (SVPCMA) is a tuple $\langle Q, \Sigma, \Gamma, \Delta, q_0, F_G, F_L \rangle$ of the same construction as a VPCMA.*

In contrast to VPCMA configuration, an SVPCMA configuration is a tuple (q, f, V, S) where q and f are states and class memory functions as before, $V \subset_{\text{fin}} \mathcal{D}$ is the set of visible data values, and $S \in (\mathcal{D} \times \Gamma \times \mathcal{P}_{\text{fin}}(\mathcal{D}))^*$. The initial configuration is $(q_0, f_0, \emptyset, \epsilon)$, and a configuration is accepting just in the conditions set for normal VPCMA (i.e. no restrictions on V). On reading an input letter (a, d) whilst in configuration (q, f, V, S), if $f(d) = \bot$ or $d \in V$ the automaton can follow transitions as follows:

- if $a \in \Sigma_{\text{push}}$ the automaton can follow a transition $(q, f(d), a, \gamma, q')$ to configuration $(q', f[d \mapsto q'], V \cup \{d\}, S \cdot (d, \gamma, V \cup \{d\}))$.
- if $a \in \Sigma_{\text{pop}}$ and $S = S' \cdot (d, \gamma, V')$ the automaton can follow a transition $(q, f(d), a, \gamma, q')$ to configuration $(q', f[d \mapsto q'], V', S')$.
- if $a \in \Sigma_{\text{noop}}$ the automaton can follow a transition $(q, f(d), a, q')$ to configuration $(q', f[d \mapsto q'], V \cup \{d\}, S)$.

Note that if $f(d) \neq \bot$ and $d \notin V$, the automaton cannot transition!

Weakness and determinism for SVPCMA are defined in the usual way. And we can obtain the same result collapsing weakness as for normal VPCMA:

Proposition 11. *Emptiness of SVPCMA can be reduced to emptiness of weak SVPCMA.*

Proof (Sketch). The idea for this construction is similar to that for VPCMA, but this time we cannot just read all of the data values at the start of the run, and check them at the end. Instead, whenever a new data value would be introduced we first introduce it with a push-move; and when that value is popped, we check that it is in a locally accepting state, and prevent it from being used again.

Similarly, all of the closure constructions that work for VPCMA also work for SVPCMA (though this time closure is with respect to well-bracketed words that are consistent with the SVPCMA restriction). In any case, the equivalence problem for deterministic SVPCMA can also be reduced to SVPCMA emptiness.

Next we discuss why the emptiness problems for VPCMA and SVPCMA are interreducible. Owing to the defining restriction for SVPCMA, not all languages recognisable by VPCMA are recognisable by SVPCMA, and vice versa. Hence, there cannot be effective translations between VPCMA and SVPCMA that preserve recognisability. However, we have

Proposition 12. *VPCMA and SVPCMA emptiness problems are interreducible.*

Proof. To reduce emptiness of VPCMA to that of SVPCMA we employ a similar trick to that used to reduce VPCMA to weak VPCMA: we begin by having the automaton read all of the data values that are going to be used in the run, then running the automaton as normal, with calls for fresh data values replaced with calls for data values seen at the start of the run.

To reduce emptiness of SVPCMA to that of VPCMA we employ a similar trick to that used to reduce SVPCMA to weak SVPCMA: whenever a data value is first read we insert a dummy push-move, which must be popped before any containing push-move is popped. When the dummy push-move is popped, we prevent that data value from being read again.

In Sect. 7 we show that VPCMA (SVPCMA) emptiness is recursively equivalent to reachability in extended branching VASS [17]. In the next section, we use SVPCMA to represent the game semantics of RML_{EBVASS}.

5 RML_{EBVASS} to VPCMA

In this section we prove

Theorem 13. *Observational equivalence of* RML_{EBVASS}*-terms is reducible to the emptiness problem for VPCMA.*

The result, in conjunction with results of Sect. 7 will imply the left-to-right implication in Theorem 1. To establish Theorem 13, we rely on the following crucial lemma.

Lemma 14. *For any* RML_{EBVASS}*-term* $\Gamma \vdash M$*, there exists a weak deterministic SVPCMA* $\mathcal{A}^M$ *whose language is a faithful representation of* $\mathbf{comp}(\llbracket \Gamma \vdash M \rrbracket)$*.*

As discussed in Sect. 4, SVPCMA equivalence can be reduced to VPCMA emptiness, so the Lemma implies Theorem 13. We shall prove the Lemma by induction for terms in canonical form.

Definition 15. *An* RML *term is in* canonical form *if it is generated by the following grammar:*

$$
\begin{aligned}
\mathbb{C} ::= \ &() \mid i \mid x^\beta \mid \mathbf{succ}(x^\beta) \mid \mathbf{pred}(x^\beta) \mid \mathbf{if}\, x^\beta \,\mathbf{then}\,\mathbb{C}\,\mathbf{else}\,\mathbb{C} \mid \\
&x^{\mathsf{int\ ref}} := y^{\mathsf{int}} \mid !x^{\mathsf{int\ ref}} \mid \mathbf{let}\, x = \mathbf{ref}\, 0\,\mathbf{in}\,\mathbb{C} \mid \mathbf{mkvar}(\lambda u^{\mathsf{unit}}.\mathbb{C}, \lambda v^{\mathsf{int}}.\mathbb{C}) \mid \\
&\mathbf{while}\,\mathbb{C}\,\mathbf{do}\,\mathbb{C} \mid \lambda x^\theta.\mathbb{C} \mid \mathbf{let}\, x^\beta = \mathbb{C}\,\mathbf{in}\,\mathbb{C} \mid \mathbf{let}\, x = z\, y^\beta\,\mathbf{in}\,\mathbb{C} \mid \\
&\mathbf{let}\, x = z\, (\lambda x^\theta.\mathbb{C})\,\mathbf{in}\,\mathbb{C} \mid \mathbf{let}\, x = z\,\mathbf{mkvar}(\lambda u^{\mathsf{unit}}.\mathbb{C}, \lambda v^{\mathsf{int}}.\mathbb{C})\,\mathbf{in}\,\mathbb{C}
\end{aligned}
$$

It can be shown [14] that, for any RML term $\Gamma \vdash M : \theta$ there is a term $\Gamma \vdash N : \theta$ in canonical form, effectively constructible from M, such that $\llbracket \Gamma \vdash M \rrbracket = \llbracket \Gamma \vdash N \rrbracket$ (for the most part, the conversions involve let-commutations and β-reduction).

Next we explain how justification pointers from games will be handled. Pointers from answers need not be represented explicitly, because they can be reconstructed uniquely from the underlying sequences of moves via the Well-Bracketing condition. Pointers from questions may need to be represented, but sometimes they too are uniquely recoverable thanks to the Visibility condition, when at most one justifier is guaranteed to occur in the relevant view. For O-questions, this was always the case in the fragment considered in [15], called the *O-strict fragment*. RML_{EBVASS} is an extension of that fragment and some O-pointers will need to be represented explicitly, but fortunately these are only pointers from moves marked q_2 in Fig. 6. As already hinted at the end of Sect. 3, we shall use data values to handle the issue as follows.

- The unique q_0-move, and each q_1-move will take a fresh data value.
- All a_i-moves will take the same data value as their justifying q_i-move.
- Each q_2-move, and all hereditarily justified moves, will take the same data value as their justifying a_1-move.
- Each move corresponding to the types of free variables in the term will take the same data value as the preceding move.

Because q_2-moves are labelled with the same data value as their justifiers, the problematic O-pointers are clearly represented by the above scheme. As concerns P-pointers, there are also cases in which pointers from P-moves have to be represented explicitly, because there may be two potential justifiers in the relevant P-view. Fortunately, the problems are of the same kind as those for the O-strict fragment and can be handled using the marking technique used in [15,18].

Next we discuss the automata constructions, focussing on the new cases with respect to [15], i.e. when the term is of type $\beta \to (\beta \to \cdots \to \beta) \to \beta$. In other cases, i.e. (), i, x^β, $\mathbf{succ}(x^\beta)$, $\mathbf{pred}(x^\beta)$, if x^β then $\mathbb{C}$ else $\mathbb{C}$, $x^{\mathsf{int\ ref}} := y^{\mathsf{int}}$, $!x^{\mathsf{int\ ref}}$, and $\mathbf{mkvar}(\lambda x^{\mathsf{unit}}.\mathbb{C}, \lambda y^{\mathsf{int}}.\mathbb{C})$, while $\mathbb{C}$ do $\mathbb{C}$ we can rely on the constructions from [15], as they produce visibly pushdown automata, which can be easily be upgraded to SVPCMA by annotating each move with a dummy data value. $\lambda x.M$ The most important case is that of λ-abstraction. In the case where $\lambda x.M$ is not of type $\beta \to (\beta \to \cdots \to \beta) \to \beta$, this has already been covered by the VPA constructions. We therefore can assume this is the final lambda abstraction in the term, and so x is of type $\beta \in \{\mathsf{int}, \mathsf{unit}\}$ and M's type is of the shape $(\beta \to \cdots \to \beta) \to \beta$.

Then the key idea of this construction is that the strategy for $\lambda x.M$, after the unique a_0-move, is an interleaving of multiple strategies for M. Since we can handle M with a VPA [15], each q_1-move corresponds to starting a new VPA running. SVPCMA allow us to simulate multiple VPAs, each identified by its own data value. The well-bracketing constraint on plays is enforced by the single stack discipline of the SVPCMA, while the visibility condition on O-pointers is checked by the scoping restriction on SVPCMA.

Before we give the formal definition of the SVPCMA for $\lambda x.M$, we analyse the plays in $[\![\lambda x.M]\!]$ in more detail. O starts by playing an initial move γ, to which P plays the unique response a_0. O then starts a q_1-thread with a move i_x corresponding to the value of x. Play then in that thread continues as in $[\![M]\!]$ with initial move (γ, i_x). However, at any point after P has played an a_1, q_*^j, or a_2 move, O may switch to another thread (new or existing), subject to that thread (i.e. the $q_1 \frown a_1$ moves of that thread) being visible.

For the construction, we know that there is a family of VPA, $(\mathcal{A}_i^M)$, where $\mathcal{A}_i^M$ recognises the complete plays from $[\![M]\!]$ that start with initial move i (the move i is omitted). We note that these initial moves have an x-component, as x is a free variable of ground type in M, hence we can think of the initial moves as having the form (γ, i_x), where i_x is the part that corresponds to x. We make a further assumption on the $(\mathcal{A}_i^M)$, that the states reachable by following a transition with a Σ-label corresponding to a a_1, q_*^j, or a_2 move can only be reached by following transitions with those Σ-labels. We write N_i for these states. (Note that it is straightforward to convert a VPA without this property to one with it.) Further we note that these states, due to the plays possible, will only have no-op and pop transitions from them.

Hence we construct the automata $(\mathcal{A}_\gamma^{\lambda x.M})$ as follows.

- The set of states of $\mathcal{A}_\gamma^{\lambda x.M}$ is formed of two new states, (1) and (2) together with the disjoint union of the states from each $\mathcal{A}_{(\gamma, i_x)}^M$ (for each possible value i_x).
- The initial state is the new state (1).
- The set of globally accepting states is the union of the sets of accepting states from each $\mathcal{A}_{(\gamma, i_x)}^M$ together with the new state (2).
- The transitions are defined as follows:
  - There is a (no-op) transition $(1) \xrightarrow{a_0, \perp} (2)$
  - For each i_x there is a (no-op) transition $(2) \xrightarrow{i_x, \perp} q_{i_x}$ where q_{i_x} is the initial state of $\mathcal{A}_{(\gamma, i_x)}^M$
  - For each $\mathcal{A}_{(\gamma, i_x)}^M$:
    * For each no-op transition $q_1 \xrightarrow{m} q_2$ inside $\mathcal{A}_{(\gamma, i_x)}^M$, there is a (no-op) transition $q_1 \xrightarrow{m, q_1} q_2$
    * For each push/pop transition $q_1 \xrightarrow{m, \sigma} q_2$ inside $\mathcal{A}_{(\gamma, i_x)}^M$, there is a (push/pop resp.) transition $q_1 \xrightarrow{m, q_1, \sigma} q_2$
  - For each state q_1, q_2 in $\bigcup_{i_x} N_{(\gamma, i_x)}$ and each no-op transition $q_2 \xrightarrow{m} q_3$ in the constituent automaton there is a transition $q_1 \xrightarrow{m, q_2} q_3$. Similarly for each pop transition $q_2 \xrightarrow{a, \sigma} q_3$ we have the transition $q_1 \xrightarrow{a, q_2, \sigma} q_3$. This allows for changing between threads at the appropriate points.

The remaining cases concern $\mathbf{let}\, x = \ldots \mathbf{in}\, M$ and adaptations of the corresponding cases in the O-strict constructions in the O-strict case [14,15]. Crucially, whilst these constructions all allow the "interruption" of $[\![M]\!]$ to make plays corresponding to x, the strategy for x can be recognised by a normal VPA and so the interruptions do not disturb the data value being used. Hence the adaptations from the O-strict case are straightforward. We discuss two of the cases in more detail.

$\mathbf{let}\, x = \mathbf{ref}\, 0 \,\mathbf{in}\, M$ The states of $\mathcal{A}_\gamma^{\mathbf{let}\, x = \mathbf{ref}\, 0\, M}$ is equal to the states of $\mathcal{A}_\gamma^M$ crossed with the finitary fragment of $\mathbb{N}$ being used. We refer to the new finitary fragment as the x-component of the state. The new initial state is the old initial state with x-component 0. Transitions are generally preserved, without altering the x-component, except $write_x(i)$-transitions now change the x-component to i, and answers to $read_x$-transitions must match the current x-component (other answer transitions are removed). For every (maximal) sequence of x-transitions out of a state, we now replace that sequence with a silent transition, which we then eliminate (and alter the required signature of the data value accordingly). Since the data value being read cannot change in sequences of x-transitions, this is a straightforward operation.

let $x^\beta = N$ **in** M $[\![\mathbf{let}\, x^\beta = N\, \mathbf{in}\, M]\!]$ first evaluates N, i.e. runs as $[\![N]\!]$ until a value is returned for x, then begins running as $[\![M]\!]$ in which that value of x was provided in the first move.

Since N is of type β, there are VPA $(\mathcal{A}^N_\gamma)$ representing $[\![\Gamma \vdash N]\!]$. Further since x is free in M the initial moves in M have an x-component, so we have a family of SVPCMA $(\mathcal{A}^M_{(\gamma, i_x)})$. The automata construction for the term is then a fairly straightforward concatenation of the the automata for N and M, with which copy of $\mathcal{A}^M$ used being determined by the outcome of $\mathcal{A}^N$. The only difficulty is adding the data values to the automaton for N, but this is straightforward as only one data value is used for the entire run of N.

6   VPCMA to RML_{EBVASS}

So far we have shown that observational equivalence of terms in RML_{EBVASS} is reducible to emptiness of SVPCMA. In this section we show that the converse is also true.

To reduce SVPCMA emptiness to observational equivalence of RML_{EBVASS}-terms, we will first alter the given SVPCMA to make the reduction to RML-terms easier. We already saw, in Sect. 4, that given an SVPCMA it is possible to construct a weak SVPCMA with equivalent emptiness problem.

Now, given a weak SVPCMA $\mathcal{A}$, by doubling the states and stack alphabet, it is straightforward to construct another weak SVPCMA, $\mathcal{A}'$, recognising the same languages as $\mathcal{A}$ such that whether or not the stack is empty is stored in the state of the automaton. Hence, the emptiness of $\mathcal{A}'$ is determined just by whether or not a globally accepting state is reachable.

How then, do we construct the RML terms from $\mathcal{A}'$? We shall represent each data value by a single $q_1\,\overline{a}_1$-thread. Hence, a transition reading a new data value will be represented by O playing q_1 and P responding with a_1. The class memory function's value for this data value will then be stored in a local variable with suitable scope. Noop-moves not taking a fresh data value can then be made by playing $q_2\,\overline{a}_2$-moves justified by the $q_1\,\overline{a}_1$ corresponding to the data value. When the q_2-move is played, the term can update the class memory function as required.

Push-moves will be represented by $q_2\,\overline{q}_*$-moves, with the stack letter stored locally. If the push-move introduces a fresh data value, the $q_1\,\overline{a}_1$-thread must be created first, and then immediately followed by the $q_2\,\overline{q}_*$-moves. Pop-moves will be represented by $a_* a_2$ pairs. Note that the Well-Bracketing condition will enforce the stack discipline during the simulation. Furthermore, as we saw in the previous section, the visibility condition of the plays will correspond precisely to the scoping condition of SVPCMA, that restricts use of data values first seen inside pushes.

In the term, we will need O to choose which transition is fired next. We will do this by alternating O's plays between those that correspond to transitions of the SVPCMA as described already, and a simple q_1-move that provides as int-input, which transition will be fired next. The term, using a global variable, can keep track of whether the next O-move should be providing input, or simulating a transition.

Using these ideas, we prove that the representation scheme can be implemented using RML$_{\text{EBVASS}}$-terms.

Proposition 16. *Given a weak SVPCMA such that the automaton can only arrive at a final state with an empty stack, there are* RML$_{\text{EBVASS}}$-*terms*

$$\vdash M, N : \mathsf{int} \to (\mathsf{unit} \to \mathsf{unit}) \to \mathsf{unit}$$

such that the language recognised by the automaton is non-empty iff M and N are not observationally equivalent.

The only difference between M and N above is that one of them will diverge on reaching the final state whereas the other will carry on simulating the last step. In the above we have used an int-type, to make it easy for P to ask the environment (O) which transition should be fired next. We note that we could have used only unit-types, using a different scheme for O-choices. For example, at the very beginning we could introduce as many $q_1\frown a_1$ segments as there are transitions and O-choice could be represented by playing a $q_2\frown a_2$ justified by one of the a_1 (so O-choice would be represented by the choice of a justifer, one of the special a_1's). Thus, the result can also be shown to hold for $\mathsf{unit} \to (\mathsf{unit} \to \mathsf{unit}) \to \mathsf{unit}$.

Thus we have shown that RML$_{\text{EBVASS}}$ observational equivalence and VPCMA emptiness are recursively equivalent.

7   VPCMA and EBVASS

In this section we show that VPCMA emptiness and EBVASS reachability are interreducible. We first review *extended branching VASS* (EBVASS), which were introduced in [17] to analyse a two-variable fragment of first-order logic over data trees, and shown to be equivalent to a form of data tree automaton.

EBVASS are slightly more powerful than *branching VASS* (BVASS) [11], whose reachability problem is not known to be decidable. Thus, we begin our review with BVASS, which extend VASS where, in addition to the standard transitions affecting the counter values and the state, there are "split" transitions, which split the current counter values into two copies of the current VASS, each copy then transitioning to a pre-given state. These copies must then complete their runs independently. Formally:

Definition 17 (BVASS). *A (top-down) branching vector addition system with states (BVASS) is a tuple $(Q, q_0, L, k, \Delta_u, \Delta_s)$ where Q is a finite set of states, $q_0 \in Q$ is the initial (root) state, $L \subseteq Q$ is the set of target (leaf) states, $k \in \mathbb{N}$ is the number of counters (dimension of the BVASS), and Δ_u and Δ_s are the unary and split transition relations respectively. The unary and split relations are of the forms:*

$$\Delta_u \subseteq (Q \times \mathbb{N}^k) \times (Q \times \mathbb{N}^k) \qquad \Delta_s \subseteq (Q \times \mathbb{N}^k) \times (Q \times \mathbb{N}^k) \times (Q \times \mathbb{N}^k)$$

We may write unary transitions, $(q_1, \bar{v}_1, q_2, \bar{v}_2) \in \Delta_u$, and split transitions, $(q_1, \bar{v}_1, q_2, \bar{v}_2, q_3, \bar{v}_3) \in \Delta_s$, in the following ways:

$$(unary) \quad \frac{q_1, \bar{v} + \bar{v}_1}{q_2, \bar{v} + \bar{v}_2} \qquad (split) \quad \frac{q_1, \bar{v} + \bar{v}' + \bar{v}_1}{q_2, \bar{v} + \bar{v}_2 \qquad q_3, \bar{v}' + \bar{v}_3}$$

These representations reflect the runs of BVASS, which we now define. A configuration of a BVASS is a pair $(q, \bar{v})$ where $q \in Q$ and $\bar{v} \in \mathbb{N}^k$. A run of a BVASS is a (finite) tree labelled with configurations, such that each node has at most two children, with the following conditions:

- if a node labelled with $(q, \bar{v})$ has precisely one child node, then there is a transition $(q, \bar{u}_1, q', \bar{u}_2) \in \Delta_u$ such that $\bar{v} - \bar{u}_1 \in \mathbb{N}^k$ and the child node is labelled with $(q', \bar{v} - \bar{u}_1 + \bar{u}_2)$.
- if a node labelled with $(q, \bar{v})$ has two child nodes, then there is a transition $(q, \bar{u}_1, q', \bar{u}_2, q'', \bar{u}_3) \in \Delta_s$ such that there exist $\bar{v}_1, \bar{v}_2 \in \mathbb{N}^k$ such that $\bar{v} = \bar{v}_1 + \bar{v}_2 + \bar{u}_1$ and the left child node is labelled $(q', \bar{v}_1 + \bar{u}_2)$ and the right child node is labelled $(q'', \bar{v}_2 + \bar{u}_3)$.

A run is *accepting* just if every leaf node's label is $(q, \bar{0})$ for some $q \in L$. The reachability problem asks whether there is an accepting run of the BVASS with root configuration $(q_0, \bar{0})$.

We note that this is a strong form of BVASS, where several operations may be performed in one step: multiple increments and decrements. It is possible for unary transitions to be able to only make a single increment or decrement, and for split transitions to make no increments or decrements. It is clear that this more powerful presentation does not change the power of the model, but it allows us a slightly more concise reduction from VPCMA.

We now move to give a definition of EBVASS. These were introduced in [17], and extend BVASS with the ability to split counters in more complex ways when a split transition is made.

Definition 18 (EBVASS). *An extended branching vector addition system with states (EBVASS) is a tuple $(Q, q_0, L, k, \Delta_u, \Delta_s, C)$ where $(Q, q_0, L, k, \Delta_u, \Delta_s)$ is a BVASS and $C \subseteq \{1, \ldots, k\}^3$ is the set of constraints.*

Each constraint (i, j, k) can fire *any* number of times when a split transition is made, and for each time it fires it will decrement the ith counter (pre-splitting), and then increment the jth counter in the left-hand branch and the kth counter in the right-hand branch. Formally, this means that runs are again finite labelled trees, with the rules for single-child nodes as for BVASS, but the following extended rule for nodes with two children.

- Suppose $C = \{c_1, \ldots, c_m\}$. If a node labelled $(q, \bar{v})$ has two child nodes then there is a transition $(q, \bar{u}_1, q', \bar{u}_2, q'', \bar{u}_3) \in \Delta_s$, $n_1, \ldots, n_m \in \mathbb{N}$, and $\bar{v}_1, \bar{v}_2 \in \mathbb{N}^k$ such that $\bar{v} = \bar{v}_1 + \bar{v}_2 + \Sigma(n_i \cdot \bar{e}_{\pi_1(c_i)})$, and the left child node is labelled $(q', \bar{v}_1 + \Sigma(n_i \cdot \bar{e}_{\pi_2(c_i)}))$, and the right child node is labelled $(q'', \bar{v}_2 + \Sigma(n_i \cdot \bar{e}_{\pi_3(c_i)}))$, where the vector $\bar{e}_l \in \mathbb{Z}^k$ is 1 in position l and 0 elsewhere.

Again, a run is accepting just if each leaf node is labelled with a configuration $(q, \bar{0})$ where $q \in L$, and the *reachability problem* asks whether there is an accepting run with root node labelled $(q_0, \bar{0})$.

Remark 19. We work with a top-down version of EBVASS, as this formulation is more convenient for capturing the correspondence with VPCMA. In the language of [17, Sect. 5], our definition of runs corresponds to the non-commutative treatment of constraints.

7.1   From VPCMA to EBVASS

Theorem 20. *The emptiness problem for VPCMA is reducible to the reachability problem for EBVASS.*

We first give the central ideas behind the reduction.

- The states of the EBVASS will correspond to pairs of states of the VPCMA. If a position in the tree has a configuration with state (q, q') this will mean that the subtree under this position represents a stack-neutral run of the VPCMA from state q to q', i.e. all elements pushed on the stack will subsequently be removed.
- The counters in the EBVASS will correspond to pairs of states of the VPCMA. Each increment of a counter corresponding to the pair (q, q') in a position in a tree will (roughly) mean that there is a data value d with $f(d) = q$ that becomes a data value with $f(d) = q'$ within that subtree (and this needs to be borne out within the subtree).
- No-op moves in the VPCMA will be modelled by unary transitions in the EBVASS, adjusting the current state and counters appropriately.
- Push and pop moves will be modelled by split-transitions, with a single split-transition representing both the push and the pop move. The left-hand branch will correspond to the part of the run between the push and pop moves, whilst the right-hand branch corresponds to the moves after. Constraints allow data values to be split into what happens to them within the branch and what happens to them after.

We now give a formal account of the reduction. W.l.o.g. (Proposition 9) we work with weak VPCMA. Suppose $\mathcal{A} = \langle Q, \Sigma, \Gamma, \Delta, q_0, \{q_f\} \rangle$ is a weak

VPCMA[4]. We shall construct an EBVASS $\mathcal{E}_\mathcal{A}$ such that its reachability problem is a yes-instance iff $\mathcal{L}(\mathcal{A}) \neq \emptyset$ as follows.

We let the set of states of $\mathcal{E}_\mathcal{A}$ be $P = Q \times Q$, the initial state (q_0, q_f), the set of leaf states $L = \{(q,q) : q \in Q\}$. We set the number of counters $k = |Q_\perp \times Q|$, with a counter corresponding to each pair $(q, q') \in Q_\perp \times Q$. For each such pair, we use the notation $c_{q,q'}$ for the counter corresponding to that pair, and $\bar{e}_{q,q'}$ for the vector in $\mathbb{Z}^k$ with a 1 in position $c_{q,q'}$ and 0 elsewhere. The set of constraints contains $(c_{q,q''}, c_{q,q'}, c_{q',q''})$ for each $q, q', q'' \in Q_\perp$.

The transition relation for $\mathcal{E}_\mathcal{A}$ is given as follows:

- For each transition $(q, s, a, q') \in \Delta$, where $a \in \Sigma_{\text{noop}}$, we have:

$$(\text{NO-OP}) \quad \frac{(q,p), \bar{v} + \bar{e}_{s,s'}}{(q',p), \bar{v} + \bar{e}_{q',s'}}$$

- For each pair of transitions (q_1, s, a, γ, q_2) and $(q_3, s', b, \gamma, q_4)$ where $a \in \Sigma_{\text{push}}$ and $b \in \Sigma_{\text{pop}}$, we have:

$$(\text{PUSH-POP}) \quad \frac{(q_1, p), \bar{v}_1 + \bar{v}_2 + \bar{e}_{s,s''}}{(q_2, q_3), \bar{v}_1 + \bar{e}_{q_2,s'} \qquad (q_4, p), \bar{v}_2 + \bar{e}_{q_4,s''}}$$

(Note that the above is a slight abuse of notation: split rules cannot also include increments[5]. However, it is straightforward to implement the above using unary transitions before and after the split, though to do this additional states must be introduced to keep track - we leave this out for clarity.)
- For every $x \in Q \times Q$ and $q \in Q$ we have the rule

$$(\text{DECREMENT}) \quad \frac{x, \bar{v} + \bar{e}_{q,q}}{x, \bar{v}}$$

(This rule allows counters corresponding to data values which have "reached their required destination" to be decremented.)
- For every $x \in Q \times Q$ and $q \in Q$:

$$(\text{INCREMENT}) \quad \frac{x, \bar{v}}{x, \bar{v} + \bar{e}_{\perp,q}}$$

(This rule makes it possible to add a new class along with its evolution profile, from $\perp$ to some state q.)

One can show that $\mathcal{L}(\mathcal{A}) \neq \emptyset$ iff there is a run of $\mathcal{E}_\mathcal{A}$ reaching the target configurations.

---

[4] We assume the set of globally accepting states to be a singleton merely for convenience - it is trivial to adjust.

[5] Actually there is another abuse of notation: the $\bar{v}_1$ and $\bar{v}_2$ may be altered by the constraints yet that is not mentioned in the rule.

7.2   From **EBVASS** to **SVPCMA**

Here we show that VPCMA emptiness is at least as hard as the reachability problem for EBVASS. W.l.o.g. (Proposition 12) we do this by reducing EBVASS reachability to SVPCMA emptiness. The key idea is that words over a pushdown alphabet can be viewed as trees by viewing them as their construction trees when generated by the grammar:

$$W ::= \epsilon \mid a_{\text{noop}} \cdot W \mid a_{\text{push}} \cdot W \cdot a_{\text{pop}} \cdot W$$

Hence, a push-pop pair of moves correspond to a split-transition of the EBVASS, with the word occurring between the push and pop-moves corresponding to the left-hand branch, and the word after the pop-move corresponding to the right-hand branch. Our reduction argument will represent counter values as the number of data values with an appropriate class memory function value, and the EBVASS state can simply be stored as the SVPCMA state. The scoping visibility condition on runs will prevent increments made in the left-hand branch (from some split) being used in the right-hand branch. The only difficulty in the reduction is the handling of constraints: but for this we can use the stack again. After the push-move of a split-transition, we will be able to fire transitions corresponding to the constraints. Given a constraint (i, j, k) the corresponding push transition will take a data value where the class memory function remembers it as belonging to counter i, change it to belong to counter j, and put on the stack the fact that, when popped, it needs to be returned to counter k. Then, when we come to do the pop-transition corresponding to the split, we must first perform the pop-transitions corresponding to all the counters that were split by the constraints.

Remark 21. 1. Class memory functions are normally of the form $f : \mathcal{D} \to Q_\perp$. In our encoding we shall use a special set Lab of *labels* to keep track of local behaviour and will rely on functions $f : \mathcal{D} \to \text{Lab}_\perp$ instead. Accordingly, our VPCMA will have a transition relation of the form

$$\Delta \subseteq Q \times \text{Lab}_\perp \times (\Sigma_{\text{push}} \cup \Sigma_{\text{pop}}) \times \Gamma \times Q \times \text{Lab} \ \cup \ Q \times \text{Lab}_\perp \times \Sigma_{\text{noop}} \times Q \times \text{Lab}.$$

Note that the above can be easily accommodated by the standard definition by extending the set of states.

2. When we introduced EBVASS, we gave them the power to perform multiple increments and decrements in one transition. While this was useful in reducing VPCMA to EBVASS, we will now find it useful to simply permit a single increment or decrement in unary transitions, and decouple increments/decrements from split transitions.

In our reduction data values will be used to store the counter information. That is, the value of a counter will be represented by the number of data values that the class memory function assigns a label corresponding to that counter (we use the labels $1, \ldots, n$ for the n counters). When a counter is incremented, a fresh data value is read, and given the appropriate label. When a counter is decremented, a data value with the label corresponding to that counter has its label changed to done. The fact that all increments have been decremented by the end of the run is then checked by the local acceptance condition.

To model constraints, after a push-transition corresponding to a split, we shall allow several more push-transitions corresponding to firings of the constraints. Firing a transition corresponding to a constraint (i, j, k) will take a data value with current label i, give it label j, and put a letter k on the stack. Then, when the corresponding pop-move is made, the label will be changed from done to k. The shape of the parts of the automaton corresponding to a split transition $\delta = (q, q', q'')$ is shown below

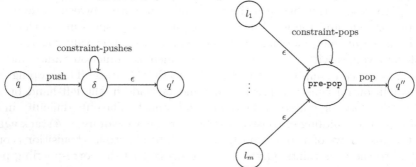

There is a slight subtlety in the above, which is that in an EBVASS all constraints are fired simultaneously at a split transition, not sequentially. Hence we should be sure that the same data value cannot be used to fire two constraints at the same split. Fortunately, this is already prevented, as if two such constraints were fired, when it came to make the corresponding pop-transitions, the first would fire correctly, but then the second could not because the data value would not have the done-label.

Thus, given an EBVASS $\mathcal{B} = (Q, q_0, L, n, \Delta_u, \Delta_s, C)$, we construct a SVPCMA $\mathcal{A}_\mathcal{B}$ as follows:

- The set of states of $\mathcal{A}_\mathcal{B}$ is $Q \uplus \Delta_s \uplus \{\textsf{pre-pop}\}$, where q_0 is initial;
- $\textsf{Lab} = \{1, \ldots, n\} \cup \{\textsf{done}, \textsf{split}\}$ and $\Gamma = Q \uplus \{1, \ldots, k\}$;
- $\Sigma = (\Delta_s \uplus C) + \{\textsf{split-pop}, \textsf{constraint-pop}\} + (\Delta_u \uplus \{\epsilon\})$;
- The set of globally accepting states is L;
- The set of locally accepting labels is $\{\textsf{done}\}$; and
- The transition relation is constructed as follows:
  - for each (unary) increment transition $\delta \in \Delta_u$ of the form $q \xrightarrow{+e_i} q'$ we have the transition $(q, \bot, \delta, q', i)$;
  - for each (unary) decrement transition $\delta \in \Delta_u$ of the form $q \xrightarrow{-e_i} q'$ we have the transition $(q, i, \delta, q', \textsf{done})$;
  - for each split transition $\delta \in \Delta_s$ of the form $q \to q' + q''$ we have the push-transition $(q, \bot, \delta, q'', \delta, \textsf{split})$, and the silent transition $\delta \xrightarrow{\epsilon} q'$;
  - for each $\delta \in \Delta_s$ and constraint $(i, j, k) \in C$ we have the push-transition $(\delta, i, (i, j, k), k, \delta, j)$;
  - for each $i \in \{1, \ldots, n\}$ we have the pop-transition $(\textsf{pre-pop}, \textsf{done}, \textsf{constraint-pop}, i, \textsf{pre-pop}, i)$;

- for each $l \in L$ we have the silent transition $l \xrightarrow{\epsilon}$ pre-pop;
- finally, for each $q \in Q$ we have the pop-transition (pre-pop, split, split-pop, $q, q,$ done).

Theorem 22. *The reachability problem for EBVASS is reducible to the emptiness problem for SVPCMA.*

8 Undecidability for unit $\to$ unit $\to$ (unit $\to$ unit) $\to$ unit

Here we show, by reduction from reachability in reset VASS [5], that observational equivalence in finitary RML is undecidable for closed terms of type unit $\to$ unit $\to$ (unit $\to$ unit) $\to$ unit. Observe that the arena used for modelling closed terms of this above has the following move structure: $q_0 \vdash a_0 \vdash q_1 \vdash a_1 \vdash q_2 \vdash a_2 \vdash q_3 \vdash a_3$ and $q_3 \vdash q_4 \vdash a_4$. Next we discuss how plays over the arena can be used to simulate reset VASS.

- The simulation will begin with $q_0 \ a_0 \ q_1 \ a_1 \ q_2 \ a_2 \ q_3 \ q_4$. This yields a play with pending questions q_3, q_4, which will block the formation of complete plays until the two questions are answered. We will take advantage of these questions at the very end of the simulation to check whether the simulation has reached an accepting state (if so, they will be answered).
  After the initialising segment discussed above, we shall have k segments $q_1 \ a_1$, where k is the number of counters. Each segment $q_1 \ a_1$ is used to represent a single counter and its identity as well as status (active or reset) will be stored in a local variable.
- Counter increments for counter j will be modelled with $q_2 \ a_2 \ q_3 \ q_4$, where q_2 is justified by the occurrence of a_1 corresponding to the jth counter. Each such segment will be equipped with a local variable that records the fact that the segment stores a singleton value of the relevant counter. The $q_3 q_4$ moves are intended to contribute pending questions to the play (to create stack structure) and guarantee that a complete play can be formed only after the questions have been answered. In the final stage of the simulation, we shall use the need to answer these questions to check whether all increments have been matched by decrements (unless the counter has been reset in the meantime).
- Decrements will be represented by $q_3 \ a_3$, where q_3 is justified by a_2 from a segment corresponding to an (unreset) increment of the same counter. The local variable recording the singleton value will then be modified to reflect the fact that the value has been spent.
- Resets will be simulated by $q_2 \ a_2$, where q_2 is justified by $q_1 a_1$ corresponding to the relevant counter. Its status will be updated to inactive and the $q_1 a_1$ segment will not be used by the translation any more. However, in order to allow for further operations on the same counter, we shall create a new $q_1 \ a_1$ segment, which will be used as a target when simulating subsequent decrements.

– Zero testing, to be performed at the very end, will be triggered by O playing a_4 in response to the most recent q_4 used for modelling increments. If the corresponding $q_3 q_4$ segment corresponds to a counter value that has been reset or decremented then a_3 will be played (otherwise the simulation will break - P will not respond). Finally, if all $q_3 q_4$ corresponding to increments have been answered in this way, the first $q_3 q_4$ segment will become pending. If O then plays a_4 then P will reply with a_3 iff the simulation has reached a final state.

Our main result is that, for any reset VASS, it is possible to build RML terms whose game semantics represents the reset VASS in the sense sketched above. This leads to:

Theorem 23. *Given a reset VASS $\mathcal{A} = (Q, k, \Delta_i \cup \Delta_d \cup \Delta_0, q_0)$ and target state $q_f \in Q$, there are RML-terms $\vdash M, M' :$ unit $\to$ unit $\to$ (unit $\to$ unit) $\to$ unit such that $M \cong M'$ iff there is a run of $\mathcal{A}$ reaching configuration $(q_f, \bar{0})$.*

As before, the only difference between M and M' is the place where final-state detection takes place: M will then terminate, wheereas M' will diverge.

Conclusion and Further Directions

For all types, we have a result giving the decidability status of a finitary RML fragment containing closed terms of that type, with the exception of the types in RML$_{\text{EBVASS}}$, for which we know observational equivalence is equivalent to EBVASS reachability. Clearly the open question of the decidability of EBVASS reachability, which seems interesting for its own sake, is especially important to us. More broadly, we do not yet have a complete classification of which types on the LHS of the turnstile give undecidability or decidability, nor a complete picture of which combinations of LHS and RHS types remain decidable. Settling these remaining questions would be a natural next step.

Acknowledgments. We are grateful to the anonymous reviewers for numerous constructive suggestions and to Ranko Lazić for discussions on VASS.

References

1. Abramsky, S., Jagadeesan, R., Malacaria, P.: Full abstraction for PCF. Inf. Comput. **163**(2), 409–470 (2000)
2. Abramsky, S., McCusker, G.: Linearity, sharing and state: a fully abstract game semantics for idealized Algol with active expressions. Electr. Notes Theor. Comput. Sci. **3**, 2–14 (1996)
3. Abramsky, S., McCusker, G.: Call-by-value games. In: Nielsen, M., Thomas, W. (eds.) CSL 1997. LNCS, vol. 1414, pp. 1–17. Springer, Heidelberg (1998). doi:10.1007/BFb0028004
4. Alur, R., Madhusudan, P.: Visibly pushdown languages. In: STOC, pp. 202–211. ACM (2004)
5. Araki, T., Kasami, T.: Some decision problems related to the reachability problem for petri nets. Theor. Comput. Sci. **3**(1), 85–104 (1976)

6. Björklund, H., Schwentick, T.: On notions of regularity for data languages. In: Csuhaj-Varjú, E., Ésik, Z. (eds.) FCT 2007. LNCS, vol. 4639, pp. 88–99. Springer, Heidelberg (2007). doi:10.1007/978-3-540-74240-1_9

7. Björklund, H., Schwentick, T.: On notions of regularity for data languages. Theor. Comput. Sci. **411**(4–5), 702–715 (2010)

8. Cotton-Barratt, C.: Using class memory automata in algorithmic game semantics. Ph.D. thesis, University of Oxford (submitted, 2016)

9. Cotton-Barratt, C., Hopkins, D., Murawski, A.S., Ong, C.-H.L.: Fragments of ML decidable by nested data class memory automata. In: Pitts, A. (ed.) FoSSaCS 2015. LNCS, vol. 9034, pp. 249–263. Springer, Heidelberg (2015). doi:10.1007/978-3-662-46678-0_16

10. Cotton-Barratt, C., Murawski, A.S., Ong, C.-H.L.: Weak and nested class memory automata. In: Dediu, A.-H., Formenti, E., Martín-Vide, C., Truthe, B. (eds.) LATA 2015. LNCS, vol. 8977, pp. 188–199. Springer, Cham (2015). doi:10.1007/978-3-319-15579-1_14

11. de Groote, P., Guillaume, B., Salvati, S.: Vector addition tree automata. In: LICS, pp. 64–73. IEEE Computer Society (2004)

12. Godlin, B., Strichman, O.: Regression verification. In: DAC, pp. 466–471. ACM (2009)

13. Honda, K., Yoshida, N.: Game-theoretic analysis of call-by-value computation. Theor. Comput. Sci. **221**(1–2), 393–456 (1999)

14. Hopkins, D.: Game semantics based equivalence checking of higher-order programs. Ph.D. thesis, Department of Computer Science, University of Oxford (2012)

15. Hopkins, D., Murawski, A.S., Ong, C.-H.L.: A fragment of ML decidable by visibly pushdown automata. In: Aceto, L., Henzinger, M., Sgall, J. (eds.) ICALP 2011. LNCS, vol. 6756, pp. 149–161. Springer, Heidelberg (2011). doi:10.1007/978-3-642-22012-8_11

16. Hyland, J.M.E., Ong, C.-H.L.: On full abstraction for PCF: I, II, and III. Inf. Comput. **163**(2), 285–408 (2000)

17. Jacquemard, F., Segoufin, L., Dimino, J.: FO2($<$ +1, $\sim$) on data trees, data tree automata and branching vector addition systems. Logical Methods Comput. Sci. **12**(2), 1–28 (2016)

18. Lazić, R., Murawski, A.S.: Contextual approximation and higher-order procedures. In: Jacobs, B., Löding, C. (eds.) FoSSaCS 2016. LNCS, vol. 9634, pp. 162–179. Springer, Heidelberg (2016). doi:10.1007/978-3-662-49630-5_10

19. Lazic, R., Schmitz, S.: Nonelementary complexities for branching VASS, MELL, and extensions. ACM Trans. Comput. Log. **16**(3), 20:1–20:30 (2015)

20. Murawski, A.S.: Functions with local state: regularity and undecidability. Theor. Comput. Sci. **338**(1/3), 315–349 (2005)

21. Murawski, A.S., Ong, C.-H.L., Walukiewicz, I.: Idealized Algol with ground recursion, and DPDA equivalence. In: Caires, L., Italiano, G.F., Monteiro, L., Palamidessi, C., Yung, M. (eds.) ICALP 2005. LNCS, vol. 3580, pp. 917–929. Springer, Heidelberg (2005). doi:10.1007/11523468_74

22. Murawski, A.S., Ramsay, S.J., Tzevelekos, N.: Game semantic analysis of equivalence in IMJ. In: Finkbeiner, B., Pu, G., Zhang, L. (eds.) ATVA 2015. LNCS, vol. 9364, pp. 411–428. Springer, Cham (2015). doi:10.1007/978-3-319-24953-7_30

23. Murawski, A.S., Tzevelekos, N.: Full abstraction for reduced ML. In: Alfaro, L. (ed.) FoSSaCS 2009. LNCS, vol. 5504, pp. 32–47. Springer, Heidelberg (2009). doi:10.1007/978-3-642-00596-1_4

24. Murawski, A.S., Tzevelekos, N.: Algorithmic nominal game semantics. In: Barthe, G. (ed.) ESOP 2011. LNCS, vol. 6602, pp. 419–438. Springer, Heidelberg (2011). doi:10.1007/978-3-642-19718-5_22
25. Murawski, A.S., Tzevelekos, N.: Algorithmic games for full ground references. In: Czumaj, A., Mehlhorn, K., Pitts, A., Wattenhofer, R. (eds.) ICALP 2012. LNCS, vol. 7392, pp. 312–324. Springer, Heidelberg (2012). doi:10.1007/978-3-642-31585-5_30
26. Pitts, A.M., Stark, I.D.B.: Operational reasoning for functions with local state. In: Higher Order Operational Techniques in Semantics, pp. 227–273. Cambridge University Press (1998)
27. Reynolds, J.C.: The essence of ALGOL. In: Proceedings of the International Symposium on Algorithmic Languages. Elsevier Science Inc. (1981)

Metric Reasoning About λ-Terms: The General Case

Raphaëlle Crubillé[1] and Ugo Dal Lago[2,3(✉)]

[1] IRIF, Université Denis Diderot - Paris 7, Paris, France
rcrubille@pps.univ-paris-diderot.fr
[2] Università di Bologna, Bologna, Italy
ugo.dallago@unibo.it
[3] Inria, Sophia Antipolis, France

Abstract. In any setting in which observable properties have a quantitative flavor, it is natural to compare computational objects by way of *metrics* rather than *equivalences* or *partial orders*. This holds, in particular, for probabilistic higher-order programs. A natural notion of comparison, then, becomes context *distance*, the metric analogue of Morris' context *equivalence*. In this paper, we analyze the main properties of the context distance in fully-fledged probabilistic λ-calculi, this way going beyond the state of the art, in which only affine calculi were considered. We first of all study to which extent the context distance trivializes, giving a sufficient condition for trivialization. We then characterize context distance by way of a coinductively-defined, *tuple-based* notion of distance in one of those calculi, called $\Lambda_!^{\oplus}$. We finally derive pseudometrics for call-by-name and call-by-value probabilistic λ-calculi, and prove them fully-abstract.

1 Introduction

Probability theory offers computer science models which enable system abstraction (at the price of introducing uncertainty), but which can also be seen as a *a way to compute*, like in randomized computation. Domains in which probabilistic models play a key role include machine learning [27], robotics [34], and linguistics [24]. In cryptography, on the other hand, having access to a source of uniform randomness is essential to achieve security, e.g., in the public key setting [20]. This has stimulated the development of concrete and abstract programming languages, which most often are extensions of their deterministic siblings. Among the many ways probabilistic choice can be captured in programming, the simplest one consists in endowing the language of programs with an operator modeling the flipping of a fair coin. This renders program evaluation a probabilistic process, and under mild assumptions the language becomes universal for

This work is partially supported by the ANR projects 12IS02001 PACE, 14CE250005 ELICA, and 16CE250011 REPAS.

© Springer-Verlag GmbH Germany 2017
H. Yang (Ed.): ESOP 2017, LNCS 10201, pp. 341–367, 2017.
DOI: 10.1007/978-3-662-54434-1_13

probabilistic computation. Particularly fruitful in this sense has been the line of work on the functional paradigm, both at a theoretical [22, 26, 29] and at a more practical level [21].

We are still far, however, from a satisfactory understanding of higher-order probabilistic computation. As an example, little is known about how much of the classic, beautiful, theory underlying the λ-calculus [1] can be lifted to probabilistic λ-calculi, although the latter have been known from forty years now [30]. Until the beginning of this decade, indeed, most investigations were directed towards domain theory, which has been proved to be much more involved in presence of probabilistic choice than in a deterministic scenario [23]. In the last ten years, however, some promising results have appeared. As an example, both quantitative semantics and applicative bisimilarity have been shown to coincide with context equivalence for certain kinds of probabilistic λ-calculi [5, 14]. This not only provides us with new proof methodologies for program equivalence, but also sheds new light on the very nature of probabilistic higher-order computation. As an example, recent results tell us that program equivalence in presence of probabilistic choice lies somehow in between determinism and non-determinism [5].

But are equivalences the most proper way to compare terms? Actually, this really depends on what the underlying observable is. If observables are boolean, then equivalences (and preorders) are indeed natural choices: two programs are dubbed equivalent if they give rise to the same observable (of which there are just two!) in any context. If, on the other hand, the observable is an element of a metric space, which happens for example when we observe (the probability of) convergence in a probabilistic setting, one may wonder whether replacing equivalences with metrics makes sense. This is a question that has recently been given a positive answer in the *affine* setting [6], i.e., in a λ-calculus in which copying is simply not available. More specifically, a notion of context distance has been shown to model differences between terms satisfactorily, and has also been shown to be characterized by notions of trace metrics, and to be approximated from below by behavioral metrics.

Affine λ-calculi are very poor in terms of the computations they are able to model. Measuring the distance between terms in presence of copying, however, is bound to be problematic. On the one hand, allowing contexts to copy their argument has the potential risk of *trivializing* the underlying metric. On the other hand, finding handier characterizations of the obtained notion of metric in the style of behavioral or trace metrics is inherently hard. A more thorough discussion on these issues can be found in Sect. 2 below.

In this paper, we attack the problem of analyzing the distance between λ-terms in its full generality. More specifically, the contributions of this paper are fourfold:

- First of all, we define a linear probabilistic λ-calculus, called $\Lambda_\oplus^{!,\|}$, in which copying and a nonstandard construct, namely Plotkin's parallel disjunction, are both available. A very liberal type system prevents deadlocks, but nevertheless leaves the expressive power of the calculus very high. This choice has been motivated by our will to put ourselves in the most general setting, so as to be able to talk about different fragments. The calculus is endowed with a notion of context distance, in Morris' style. This is covered in Sect. 3 below.

- We study trivialization of the obtained notion(s) of metric for different fragments of $\Lambda_{\oplus}^{!,\|}$, showing that both parallel disjunction and strong normalization give us precisely the kind of discriminating power we need to arbitrarily amplify distances, while in the most natural fragment, namely $\Lambda_{\oplus}^{!}$, trivialization does *not* hold. This is the subject of Sect. 4.

- In Sect. 5, we prove that context distance can be characterized as a co-inductively-defined distance on a labeled Markov chain of *tuples*. The way (tuples of) terms interact with their environment makes proofs of soundness laborious and different from their affine counterparts from [6]. An up-to-context notion of bisimulation is proved to be sound, and to be quite useful when evaluating the distance between concrete programs.

- Finally, we show that the results from Sect. 5 can be lifted back to ordinary probabilistic λ-calculi from the literature [5,10]. Both when call-by-name evaluation and call-by-value are considered, our framework can be naturally adapted, and helps in facilitating concrete proofs. This is in Sect. 6.

More details can be found in a long version of this paper, available online [7].

2   Metrics and Trivialization, Informally

The easiest way to render the pure λ-calculus a universal probabilistic computation model [10] consists in endowing it with a binary construct ⊕ for probabilistic choice. The term $M \oplus N$ evolves as either M or N, each with probability $\frac{1}{2}$. The obtained calculus can be given meaning by an operational semantics which puts terms in correspondence with *distributions of* values. The natural notion of observation, at least in an untyped setting like the one we will consider in this paper, is thus the *probability of convergence* of the observed term M, which will be denoted as $\sum_{[\![M]\!]}$. One could then define a notion of *context equivalence* following Morris' pattern, and stipulate that two terms M and N should be equivalent whenever they terminate with *exactly* the same probability when put in *any* context:

$$M \equiv N \iff \forall C. \sum_{[\![C[M]]\!]} = \sum_{[\![C[N]]\!]}.$$

The anatomy of the obtained notion of equivalence has been recently studied extensively, the by-products of this study being powerful techniques for it in the style of bisimilarity and logical relations [3,5,9].

As observed by various authors (see, e.g., [25] for a nice account), probabilistic programs and processes are naturally compared by *metrics* rather than *equivalences*: the latter do not give any quantitative information about *how different* two non-equivalent programs are. Given that the underlying notion of observation is inherently quantitative, on the other hand, generalizing context equivalence to a *pseudometric* turns out to be relatively simple:

$$\delta(M, N) = \sup_C \left| \sum_{[\![C[M]]\!]} - \sum_{[\![C[N]]\!]} \right|.$$

Observe that the obtained notion of context *distance* between two terms is a real number between 0 and 1, which is minimal precisely when the considered terms are context equivalent. It is the least discriminating pseudometric which is non-expansive and adequate, and as such it provides some quite precise information about how far the two argument programs are, observationally. A similar notion has recently been studied by the authors [6], but only in a purely affine setting.

Let us now consider two prototypical examples of non-equivalent terms, namely $I = \lambda x.x$ (the identity) and Ω (the always-divergent term). The context distance $\delta^c(I, \Omega)$ between them is maximal: when applied, e.g., to the trivial context $[\cdot]$, they converge with probability 1 and 0, respectively. A term which is conceptually "in the middle" of them is $M = I \oplus \Omega$. Indeed, in a purely affine λ-calculus, $\delta^c(I, M) = \delta^c(M, \Omega) = \frac{1}{2}$.

If we render the three terms duplicable (by putting them in the scope of a !-operator), however, the situation becomes much more complicated. Consider the terms $!I$ and $!(I \oplus \Omega)$. One can easily define a family of contexts $\{C_n\}_{n \in \mathbb{N}}$ such that the probability of convergence of $C_n[!I]$ and $C_n[!(I \oplus \Omega)]$ tend to 1 and 0 (respectively) when n tends to infinity. It suffices to take C_n as $(\lambda! x.\ \underbrace{x \ldots x}_{n \text{ times}})[\cdot]$.

Allowing contexts to have the capability to duplicate their argument seems to mean that they can arbitrarily *amplify* distances. Indeed, the argument above also works when $(I \oplus \Omega)$ is replaced by any term which behaves as Ω with probability ε and as I with probability $1 - \varepsilon$, provided of course $\varepsilon > 0$. But how about $!\Omega$ and $!(I \oplus \Omega)$? Are they at maximal distance, i.e. is it that $\delta^c(!\Omega, !(I \oplus \Omega)) = 1$? Apparently, this is *not* the case. The previously defined contexts C_n cannot amplify the "linear" distance between the two terms above, namely $\frac{1}{2}$, up to 1. But what is the distance between $!\Omega$ and $!(I \oplus \Omega)$, then? Evaluating it is hard, since you need to consider all contexts, which do not have a nice structure. In Sect. 5, we will introduce a different, better behaved, notion of distance, this way being able to prove that, indeed, $\delta^c(!\Omega, !(I \oplus \Omega)) = \frac{1}{2}$.

All this hints at even more difficult examples, like the one in which $M_\varepsilon = !(\Omega \oplus^\varepsilon I)$, where $\oplus^\varepsilon$ is the natural generalization of $\oplus$ to a possibly unfair coin flip, and one is interested in evaluating $\delta^c(M_\varepsilon, M_\mu)$. In that case, we can easily see that the "linear" distance between them is $|\varepsilon - \mu|$. In some cases, it is possible to amplify it: the most natural way is again to consider the contexts C_n defined above. Indeed, we see that the probabilities of convergence of $C_n[M_\varepsilon]$ and $C_n[M_\mu]$ are ε^n and μ^n, respectively. It follows that $\delta^c(M_\varepsilon, M_\mu) \geq \sup_{n \in \mathbb{N}} |\varepsilon^n - \mu^n|$. For some ε and μ (for example if $\varepsilon + \mu > 1$), the context distance can be greater than $|\varepsilon - \mu|$. But there is no easy way to know *how far* amplification can lead us. The terms M_ε and M_μ will be running examples in the course of this paper. Despite their simplicity, evaluating the distance between them is quite challenging.

We are also going to consider the case in which contexts can evaluate terms *in parallel*, converging if and only if at least one of the copies converges. This behavior is not expressible in the usual λ-calculus, but is captured by well-known constructs and in particular by Plotkin's parallel disjunction [28]. In Sect. 4 below, we prove that all this is not accidental: the presence of parallel disjunction turns a non-trivializing metric into a trivializing one. The proof of it, by the way, relies on building certain amplifying contexts which are then shown to be universal using tools from functional analysis.

3   A Linear Probabilistic λ-Calculus

In this section, we present the syntax and operational semantics of our language $\Lambda_\oplus^{!,\|}$, on which we will later define metrics. $\Lambda_\oplus^{!,\|}$ is a probabilistic and linear λ-calculus, designed not only to allow copying, but to have a better control on it. It is based on a probabilistic variation of the calculus defined in [33], whose main feature is to never reduce inside exponential boxes. As we will see in Sect. 6, the calculus is capable of encoding both call-by-value and call-by-name fully-fledged probabilistic λ-calculi. We add a parallel disjunction construct to the calculus, being inspired by Plotkin's parallel disjunction [28]. Noticeably, it has been recently shown [8] that adding parallel disjunction to a (non-linear) λ-calculus increases the expressive power of contexts to the point of enabling coincidence between the contextual preorder and applicative similarity. The choice of studying a very general calculus is motivated by our desire to be as general as possible. This being said, many of our results hold only in *absence* of parallel disjunction.

Definition 1. *We assume a countable set of variables $\mathscr{X}$. The set of terms of $\Lambda_\oplus^{!,\|}$ (denoted $\mathscr{T}$) is defined by the following grammar:*

$$M \in \mathscr{T} ::= x \mid MM \mid \lambda x.M \mid \lambda !x.M \mid !M \mid M \oplus M$$
$$\mid \; ([M \parallel M] \rightarrowtail M),$$

where $x \in \mathscr{X}$. The fragment of $\Lambda_\oplus^{!,\|}$ without the $([\cdot \parallel \cdot] \rightarrowtail \cdot)$ construct will be indicated as $\Lambda_\oplus^!$. Values are those terms derived from the following grammar:

$$V \in \mathscr{V} ::= \lambda x.M \mid \lambda !x.M \mid !M.$$

As already mentioned, $M \oplus N$ can evolve to either M or N, each with probability $\frac{1}{2}$. The term $!M$ is a duplicable version of M, often called an *(exponential) box*. We have two distinct abstraction operators: $\lambda x.M$ is a *linear* abstraction, while the *non-linear* abstraction $\lambda !x.M$ requires exponential boxes as arguments. The term $([M \parallel N] \rightarrowtail L)$ behaves as L if either M or N converges. Please observe that both abstractions and boxes are values—our notion of reduction is *weak* and *surface* [33].

We are now going to define an operational semantics for the closed terms of $\Lambda_\oplus^{!,\|}$ in a way similar to the one developed for a (non-linear) λ-calculus in [10]. We need to first define a family of *approximation semantics*, and then to take the semantics of a term as the least upper bound of all its approximations. The approximation semantics relation is denoted $M \Rightarrow \mathcal{D}$, where M is a closed term of $\Lambda_\oplus^{!,\|}$, and $\mathcal{D}$ is a *(sub)distribution on values* with finite support, i.e., a function from $\mathcal{V}$ to $\mathbb{R}_{[0,1]}$ which sums to a real number $\sum_{\mathcal{D}} \leq 1$. For any distribution $\mathcal{D}$ on a set X, we call *support of* $\mathcal{D}$, and we note $S(\mathcal{D})$, the set $\{x \in X \mid \mathcal{D}(x) > 0\}$. We say that $\mathcal{D}$ is *finite* if $S(\mathcal{D})$ is a finite set.

The rules deriving the approximation semantics relation are given in Fig. 1, and are based on the notion of an *evaluation context*, which is an expression generated from the following grammar:

$$E ::= [\cdot] \mid EV \mid ME \mid ([M \parallel E] \rightarrowtail N) \mid ([E \parallel M] \rightarrowtail N).$$

As usual, $E[M]$ stands for the term obtained by filling the sole occurrence of $[\cdot]$ in E with M. In Fig. 1 and elsewhere in this paper, we indicate the distribution assigning probability p_i to V_i for every $i \in \{1, \ldots, n\}$ as $\{V_1^{p_1}, \ldots, V_n^{p_n}\}$. We proceed similarly for the expression $\{V_i^{p_i}\}_{i \in I}$, where I is any countable index set. Observe how we first define a one-step reduction relation $\cdot \rightarrow \cdot$ between closed terms and *sequences* of terms, only later extending it to a small-step reduction relation $\cdot \Rightarrow \cdot$ between closed terms and *distributions* on values. A reduction step can be a linear or non-linear β-reduction, or a probabilistic choice. Moreover, there can be more than one active redex in any closed term M, due to the presence of parallel disjunction. For any term M, the set of sub-distributions $\mathcal{D}$ such that $M \Rightarrow \mathcal{D}$ is a countable directed set. Since the set of sub-distributions (with potentially infinite support) is an ω-complete partial order, we can define the *semantics* of a term M as $[\![M]\!] = \sup\{\mathcal{D} \mid M \Rightarrow \mathcal{D}\}$. We could also define alternatively a big-step semantics, again in the same way as that of the probabilistic λ-calculus considered in [10].

$$\frac{}{M \oplus N \hookrightarrow M, N} \qquad \frac{}{(\lambda x.M)V \hookrightarrow M\{x/V\}} \qquad \frac{}{(\lambda!x.M)!N \hookrightarrow M\{x/N\}}$$

$$\frac{}{([V \parallel M] \rightarrowtail N) \hookrightarrow N} \qquad \frac{}{([M \parallel V] \rightarrowtail N) \hookrightarrow N} \qquad \frac{M \hookrightarrow N_1, \ldots, N_n}{E[M] \rightarrow E[N_1], \ldots E[N_n]}$$

$$\frac{}{V \Rightarrow \{V^1\}} \qquad \frac{}{M \Rightarrow \emptyset} \qquad \frac{M \rightarrow N_1, \ldots, N_n \qquad (N_i \Rightarrow \mathcal{D}_i)_{1 \leq i \leq n}}{M \Rightarrow \sum_{1 \leq i \leq n} \frac{1}{n} \cdot \mathcal{D}_i}$$

Fig. 1. Approximation semantics for $\Lambda_\oplus^!$

Not all irreducible terms are values in $\Lambda_\oplus^{!,\parallel}$, e.g. $(\lambda!x.x)(\lambda x.x)$. We thus need a *type-system* which guarantees the absence of deadlocks. Since we want to be as general as possible, we consider recursive types as formulated in [2], which are expressive enough to type the image of the embeddings we will study in Sect. 6. The grammar of *types* is the following:

$$\sigma \in \mathscr{A} ::= \alpha \mid \mu\alpha.\sigma \multimap \sigma \mid \mu\alpha.!\sigma \mid \sigma \multimap \sigma \mid !\sigma$$

$$\frac{}{\mu\alpha.\sigma \multimap \tau =^{\mathscr{A}} \sigma[\alpha \to (\mu\alpha.\sigma \multimap \tau)] \multimap \tau[\alpha \to (\mu\alpha.\sigma \multimap \tau)]}$$

$$\frac{}{\mu\alpha.!\sigma =^{\mathscr{A}} !(\sigma[\alpha \to \mu\alpha.!\sigma])} \qquad \frac{\sigma =^{\mathscr{A}} \gamma[\alpha \to \sigma] \qquad \tau =^{\mathscr{A}} \gamma[\alpha \to \tau]}{\sigma =^{\mathscr{A}} \tau}$$

Fig. 2. Equality of types

Types are defined up to the equality $=^{\mathscr{A}}$, defined in Fig. 2. $\sigma[\alpha \to \tau]$ stands for the type obtained by substituting all free occurrences of α by τ in σ. An *environment* is a set of expressions in the form $x : \sigma$ or $!x :!\sigma$ in which any variable occurs at most once. Environments are often indicated with metavariables like $!\Gamma$, which stands for an environment in which all variables occur as $!x$, or Δ in which, on the contrary, variables can *only* occur with the shape x, so that Δ is of the form $x_1 : \sigma_1, \ldots, x_n : \sigma_n$. *Typing judgments* are thus of the form $!\Gamma, \Delta \vdash M : \sigma$. The typing system is given in Fig. 3. The role of this type system is *not* to guarantee termination, but rather to guarantee a form of type soundness:

Lemma 1. *If $\vdash M : \sigma$ and $M \Rightarrow \mathcal{D}$, then $\vdash V : \sigma$ for every V in the support of $\mathcal{D}$. Moreover, if $\vdash M : \sigma$ and M is irreducible (i.e. $M \not\to N$ for every N), then M is value.*

$$\frac{}{!\Gamma, !x :!\sigma \vdash x : \sigma} \qquad \frac{}{!\Gamma, x : \sigma \vdash x : \sigma} \qquad \frac{!\Gamma, x : \sigma, \Delta \vdash M : \tau}{!\Gamma, \Delta \vdash \lambda x.M : \sigma \multimap \tau}$$

$$\frac{!x :!\sigma, !\Gamma, \Delta \vdash M : \tau}{!\Gamma, \Delta \vdash \lambda !x.M :!\sigma \multimap \tau} \qquad \frac{!\Gamma, \Delta \vdash M : \sigma \multimap \tau \qquad !\Gamma, \Theta \vdash N : \sigma}{!\Gamma, \Delta, \Theta \vdash MN : \tau}$$

$$\frac{!\Gamma \vdash M : \sigma}{!\Gamma \vdash !M :!\sigma} \qquad \frac{!\Gamma, \Delta \vdash M : \sigma \qquad !\Gamma, \Delta \vdash N : \sigma}{!\Gamma, \Delta \vdash M \oplus N : \sigma}$$

$$\frac{!\Gamma, \Delta \vdash M : \sigma \qquad !\Gamma, \Theta \vdash N : \sigma \qquad !\Gamma, \Xi \vdash L : \tau}{!\Gamma, \Delta, \Theta, \Xi \vdash ([M \parallel N] \rightarrowtail L) : \tau}$$

Fig. 3. Typing rules

Example 1. The term $I = \lambda x.x$ can be typed as $\vdash I : \sigma \multimap \sigma$ for every $\sigma \in \mathscr{A}$. We define $\Omega_!$ to be the term $(\lambda !x.x!x)(!(\lambda !x.x!x))$, which is the counterpart in our linear calculus of the prototypical diverging term of the λ-calculus, namely $\Omega = (\lambda x.xx)(\lambda x.xx)$. We can type this divergent term with any possible type: indeed, if we take $\tau ::= \mu\alpha.!\alpha \multimap \sigma$, then $\tau =^{\mathscr{A}} !\tau \multimap \sigma$ and $\vdash \lambda !x.x!x : \sigma$. Using that, we can see that $\vdash \Omega_! : \sigma$ for every type σ. We will see in Sect. 6 that, more generally, there are several ways to turn any pure λ-term M into a $\Lambda_\oplus^!$ term in such a way as to obtain meaningful typing and semantics: $\Lambda_\oplus^!$ is actually at least as powerful as the usual untyped probabilistic λ-calculus [10].

Termination could in principle be guaranteed if one considers *strictly positive* types, as we will do in Sect. 4.1 below. Let $\mathbb{D}$ be the set of dyadic numbers (i.e. those rational numbers in the form $\frac{n}{2^m}$ (with $n, m \in \mathbb{N}$ and $n \leq 2^m$). It is easy to derive, for every $\varepsilon \in \mathbb{D}$, a new binary operator on terms $\cdot \oplus^\varepsilon \cdot$ such that $[\![M \oplus^\varepsilon N]\!] = (1 - \varepsilon)[\![M]\!] + \varepsilon [\![N]\!]$ for every closed M, N.

Example 2. We define here a family of terms that we use as a running example. We consider terms of the form $M_\varepsilon = !(\Omega_! \oplus^\varepsilon I)$, for $\varepsilon \in \mathbb{D}$. It holds that $\vdash M_\varepsilon : !(\sigma \multimap \sigma)$ for every σ. M_ε corresponds to a duplicable term, each copy of which behaves as I with probability ε, and does not terminate with probability $1 - \varepsilon$.

3.1   Some Useful Terminology and Notation

In this paper, we will make heavy use of sequences of terms and types. It is thus convenient to introduce some terminology and notation about them.

A finite (ordered) sequence whose elements are $e_1, \ldots, e_n$ will be indicated as $\boldsymbol{e} = [e_1, \ldots, e_n]$, and called an *$n$-sequence*. Metavariables for sequences are boldface variations of the metavariables for their elements. Whenever $E = \{i_1, \ldots, i_m\} \subseteq \{1, \ldots, n\}$ and $i_1 < \ldots < i_m$, the sub-sequence $[e_{i_1}, \ldots, e_{i_m}]$ of an n-sequence $\boldsymbol{e}$ will be indicated as $\boldsymbol{e}_E$. If the above holds, E will be called an *n-set*. If $\boldsymbol{e}$ is an n-sequence, and φ is a permutation on $\{1, \ldots, n\}$, we note $\boldsymbol{e}_\varphi$ the n-sequence $[e_{\varphi(1)}, \ldots, e_{\varphi(n)}]$. We can turn an n-sequence into an $(n+1)$-sequence by adding an element at the end: this is the role of the semicolon operator. We denote by $[e^n]$ the n-sequence in which all components are equal to e.

Whenever this does not cause ambiguity, notations like the ones above will be used in conjunction with syntactic constructions. For example, if $\boldsymbol{\sigma}$ is an n-sequence of types, then $!\boldsymbol{\sigma}$ stands for the sequence $[!\sigma_1, \ldots, !\sigma_n]$. As another example, if $\boldsymbol{\sigma}$ is an n-sequence of types and E is an n-set, then $\boldsymbol{x}_E : \boldsymbol{\sigma}_E$ stands for the environment assigning type σ_i to x_i for every $i \in E$. As a final example, if $\boldsymbol{M}$ is an n-sequence of terms and $\boldsymbol{\sigma}$ is an n-sequence of types, $\vdash \boldsymbol{M} : \boldsymbol{\sigma}$ holds iff $\vdash M_i : \sigma_i$ is provable for every $i \in \{1, \ldots, n\}$.

3.2   Context Distance

A *context of type σ for terms of type τ* is a term C which can be typed as $hole : \tau \vdash C : \sigma$, where $hole$ is a distinguished variable. $\mathcal{C}_\sigma^\tau$ collects all such terms. If $C \in \mathcal{C}_\sigma^\tau$ and M is a closed term of type τ, then the closed term $C\{hole/M\}$ has type σ and is often indicated as $C[M]$.

The *context distance* [6] is the natural quantitative refinement of context equivalence. Intuitively, it corresponds to the maximum separation that contexts can induce between two terms. Following [6], we take as observable the probability of convergence: for any term M, we define its *observable* $\mathrm{Obs}(M)$ as $\sum_{[\![M]\!]}$. Then, for any terms M, N such that $\vdash M : \sigma$ and $\vdash N : \sigma$, we define:

$$\delta^c_{\sigma,!,\|}(M,N) = \sup_{C \in \mathcal{C}^\tau_\sigma} |\mathrm{Obs}(C[M]) - \mathrm{Obs}(C[N])|.$$

Please observe that this distance is a pseudometric, and that moreover we can recover context equivalence by considering its *kernel*, that is the set of pairs of terms which are at distance 0. The binary operator $\delta^c_{\sigma,!}$ is defined similarly, but referring to terms (and contexts) from $\Lambda^!_\oplus$.

Example 3. What can we say about $\delta^c_{\sigma,!,\|}(M_\varepsilon, M_\mu)$? Not much apparently, since *all* contexts should be considered. Even if we put ourselves in the fragment $\Lambda^!_\oplus$, the best we can do is to conclude that $\delta^c_{\sigma,!}(M,N) \geq \sup_{n \in \mathbb{N}} |\varepsilon^n - \mu^n|$, as explained in Sect. 2.

4   On Trivialization

As we have already mentioned, there can well be classes of terms such that the context distance collapses to context equivalence, due to the copying abilities of the language. The question of trivialization can in fact be seen as a question about the expressive power of contexts: given two duplicable terms, how much can a context amplify the observable differences between their behaviors?

More precisely, we would like to identify *trivializing* fragments of $\Lambda^{!,\|}_\oplus$, that is to say fragments such that for any pair of duplicable terms, their context distance (with respect to the fragment) is either 0 or 1. This is not the case in $\Lambda^!_\oplus$ (see Example 8 below).

In fact, a sufficient condition to trivialization is to require the existence of *amplification contexts*: for every observable type σ, for every $\alpha, \beta \in [0,1]$ distinct, for every $\gamma > 0$, we want to have a context $C^{\alpha,\beta,\gamma}_\sigma$ such that:

$$\left.\begin{array}{r}\vdash M, N : \sigma \\ \mathrm{Obs}(M) = \alpha \\ \mathrm{Obs}(N) = \beta\end{array}\right\} \Rightarrow \left|\mathrm{Obs}(C^{\alpha,\beta,\gamma}_\sigma[!M]) - \mathrm{Obs}(C^{\alpha,\beta,\gamma}_\sigma[!N])\right| \geq 1 - \gamma.$$

Fact 1. *Any fragment of $\Lambda^{!,\|}_\oplus$ admitting all amplifications contexts trivializes.*

4.1   Strictly Positive Types

First, let us consider the case of the fragment $\Lambda^{!,\downarrow}_\oplus$ of $\Lambda^!_\oplus$ obtained by considering strictly positive types, only (in a similar way to [2]), and by dropping parallel disjunction. Every term M of $\Lambda^{!,\downarrow}_\oplus$ is terminating (i.e. $\sum[\![M]\!] = 1$), so we need to adapt our notion of observation: we define the type $\mathbb{B} = !\alpha \multimap !\alpha \multimap \alpha$, which can be seen as boolean type using a variant of the usual boolean encoding in λ-calculi. Our new notion of observation, defined only at type $\mathbb{B}$, is $\mathrm{Obs}(M) = \sum_{[\![M!I!\Omega_I]\!]}$, which corresponds to the probability that M evaluates to **true**. While this notion of observation uses the full power of $\Lambda^!_\oplus$, the context distance $\delta^c_{!,\downarrow}$ based on it only consider contexts in $\Lambda^{!,\downarrow}_\oplus$.

Theorem 1. $\delta^c_{!,\downarrow}$ *trivializes.*

The proof of Theorem 1 is based on the construction of amplification contexts. We are going to use Bernstein constructive proof of the Stone–Weierstrass theorem. Indeed, Bernstein showed that for every continuous function $f : [0,1] \rightarrow \mathbb{R}$, the following sequence of polynomials converges uniformly towards f:

$$P_n^f(x) = \sum_{0 \le k \le n} f\left(\frac{k}{n}\right) \cdot B_k^n(x), \text{ where } B_k^n(x) = \binom{n}{k} \cdot x^k \cdot (1-x)^{n-k}.$$

Let us consider the following continuous function: we fix $f(\alpha) = 0$, $f(\beta) = 1$, and f defined elsewhere in such a way that it is continuous, that it has values in $[0,1]$, and that moreover $f(\mathbb{Q}) \subseteq \mathbb{Q}$. We can easily implement P_n^f by a context, i.e. define C such that for every M, $\mathrm{Obs}(C[M]) = P_n^f(\mathrm{Obs}(M))$. In $\Lambda^{!,\downarrow}_\oplus$, we can indeed copy an argument n times, then evaluate it, and then for every k between 0 and n, if the number of **trues** obtained is exactly k, return the term **false** $\oplus^{f(\frac{k}{n})}$ **true** (that corresponds to a term returning **true** with probability $f\left(\frac{k}{n}\right)$). Please observe that this construction works only because in $\Lambda^{!,\downarrow}_\oplus$ all terms converge with probability 1.

4.2   Parallel Disjunction

As we have seen, trivialization can be enforced by restricting the class of terms, but we can also take the opposite road, namely increasing the discriminating power of contexts. Indeed, consider the full language $\Lambda^{!,\|}_\oplus$, with the usual notion of observation.

We can first see how parallel disjunction increases the expressive power of the calculus on a simple example. Consider the following two terms: $M = {!}\Omega_!$ and $N = {!}(\Omega_! \oplus I)$. We will see later that these two terms are the simplest example of non-trivialization in $\Lambda^!_\oplus$: indeed $\delta^c_{!(\tau \multimap \tau),!}(M,N) = \frac{1}{2}$, while $\delta^c_{!(\tau \multimap \tau),!,\|}(M,N) = 1$. In $\Lambda^{!,\|}_\oplus$, we are able to define a family of contexts $(C_n)_{n \in \mathbb{N}}$ as follows:

$$C_n = (\lambda!x. \, ([x \, \| \, ([x \, \| \, \ldots] \rightarrowtail I)] \rightarrowtail I)) \, [\cdot].$$

Essentially, C_n makes n copies of its argument, and then converges towards I if *at least* one of these copies itself converges. When we apply the context C_n to M and N, we can see that the convergence probability of $C_n[M]$ is always 0 independently of n, whereas the convergence probability of $C_n[N]$ tends towards 1 when n tends to infinity.

Theorem 2. $\delta^c_{!,\|}$ *trivializes.*

The proof is based on the construction of amplification contexts $C_\sigma^{\alpha,\beta,\gamma}$. If $\max(\alpha,\beta) = 1$, we can extend the informal argument from Sect. 2, by taking contexts that copy an arbitrary number of times their argument. If $\min(\alpha,\beta) = 0$, we can use the same idea as in the example above, by taking contexts that do an arbitrary number of disjunctions. What remains to be done to obtain the trivialization result is treating the case in which $0 < \alpha,\beta < 1$. The overall idea is to somehow mix the contexts we use in the previous cases. More precisely, we define a family of contexts $(C_n^m)_{n,m\in\mathbb{N}}$ as follows:

$$C_n^m = \lambda!y.\left(\bigwedge^n(\bigvee^m(y,\ldots,y),\ldots,\bigvee^m(y,\ldots,y))\right)[\cdot]$$

where

$$\bigvee^n(M_1,\ldots M_n) = ([M_1 \parallel ([M_2 \parallel \ldots] \rightarrowtail I)] \rightarrowtail I) ;$$
$$\bigwedge^n(M_1 \ldots M_n) = (\lambda z_1.\lambda z_2.\ldots.\lambda y.(yz_1\ldots z_n))M_1\ldots M_n.$$

The term $\bigvee^n(M_1,\ldots,M_n)$ behaves as a n-ary disjunction: it terminates if *at least one* of the M_i terminates. On the other hand, $\bigwedge^n(M_1,\ldots,M_n)$ can be seen as a n-ary conjunction: it terminates if *all* the M_i terminates. The contexts C_n^α compute m-ary conjunctions of n-ary disjunctions. Now, let ι be such that $\alpha < \iota < \beta$. We need to show that for every n, we can choose $m(n,\iota) \in \mathbb{N}$ such that:

$$\lim_{n\to\infty} \mathrm{Obs}(C_n^{m(n,\iota)}[!M]) = \begin{cases} 1 \text{ if } \mathrm{Obs}(M) > \iota; \\ 0 \text{ if } \mathrm{Obs}(M) < \iota. \end{cases} .$$

We can express this problem purely in terms of functional analysis, by observing that $\mathrm{Obs}(C_n^m[!M]) = (1-(1-\mathrm{Obs}(M))^m)^n$. Then the result is proved by applying the dominated convergence theorem to a well-chosen sequence of functions.

5   Tuples and Full Abstraction

This section is structured as follows: first, we define a labeled Markov chain (LMC) which expresses the semantics of our calculus in an interactive way, and then we use it to give a coinductively-defined notion of distance on a labeled transition system (LTS) of *distributions*, which coincides with the context distance defined in Sect. 3.2. We are not considering parallel disjunction here: the motivations for that should be clear from Theorem 2.

5.1   A Labeled Markov Chain over Tuples

Labeled Markov chains are the probabilistic analogues to labeled transition systems. Formally, a LMC is a triple $\mathscr{M} = (\mathcal{S},\mathcal{A},\mathcal{P})$, where $\mathcal{S}$ is a countable set of states, $\mathcal{A}$ is a countable set of *labels*, and $\mathcal{P} : \mathcal{S} \times \mathcal{A} \to \mathrm{Distr}(\mathcal{S})$ is a *transition probability matrix* (where $\mathrm{Distr}(X)$ is the set of all distributions over X).

Following [9], the interactive behavior of probabilistic λ-terms can be represented by a LMC whose states are the terms of the language, whose actions are values, and where performing the action V starting from a state M corresponds to applying the value V to M. This approach is bound *not* to work in presence of pairs when metrics take the place of equivalences, due to the unsoundness of projective actions. In [6], this observation led us to introduce a new LMC whose states are *tuples* of terms, and whose actions include one *splitting* a pair: $\mathcal{P}([\langle M, N \rangle])(\mathrm{destruct}) = \{[M, N]^1\}$. This turns out to work well in an affine setting [6]. We are going to define a LMC $\mathcal{M}_\oplus^! = (\mathcal{S}_{\mathcal{M}_\oplus^!}, \mathcal{A}_{\mathcal{M}_\oplus^!}, \mathcal{P}_{\mathcal{M}_\oplus^!})$ which is an extension of the one from [6], and which is adapted to a language with copying capabilities. The idea is to treat exponentials in the spirit of Milner's Law: $!A \multimap A \otimes !A$.

States. *Tuples* are pairs of the form $K = (\boldsymbol{M}, \boldsymbol{V})$ where $\boldsymbol{M}$ and $\boldsymbol{V}$ are a sequence of terms and values, respectively. The set of all such tuples is indicated as $\mathcal{U}$. The first component of a tuple is called its *exponential part*, while the second one is called its *linear part*. We write $\vdash (\boldsymbol{M}, \boldsymbol{V}) : (\boldsymbol{\sigma}, \boldsymbol{\tau})$ if $\vdash \boldsymbol{M} : \boldsymbol{\sigma}$ and $\vdash \boldsymbol{V} : \boldsymbol{\tau}$. We note $\mathbf{T}$ the set of pairs $A = (\boldsymbol{\sigma}, \boldsymbol{\tau})$, and we call *tuple types* the elements of $\mathbf{T}$. Moreover, we say that $(\boldsymbol{\sigma}, \boldsymbol{\tau})$ is a (n, m) *tuple type* if $\boldsymbol{\sigma}$ and $\boldsymbol{\tau}$ are, respectively, an n-sequence and an m-sequence. To any term M, we associate a tuple in a natural way: we note $\dot{M}$ the tuple $([\,], [M])$, and similarly if σ is a type, we indicate the tuple type $([\,], [\sigma])$ as $\dot{\sigma}$. Please observe that if $\vdash M : \sigma$, then it holds that $\vdash \dot{M} : \dot{\sigma}$.

A sequence of the form $(E, F, \boldsymbol{\sigma}, \boldsymbol{\tau}, M, \gamma)$ is said to be an *applicative typing judgment* when $\boldsymbol{\sigma}$ and $\boldsymbol{\tau}$ are, respectively, an n-sequence and an m-sequence of types, E and F are respectively an n-set and an m-set, and moreover it holds that $!\boldsymbol{x}_E : !\boldsymbol{\sigma}_E, \boldsymbol{y}_F : \boldsymbol{\tau}_F \vdash M : \gamma$. Intuitively, this means that if we have a tuple $K = (\boldsymbol{N}, \boldsymbol{V})$ of type $(\boldsymbol{\sigma}, \boldsymbol{\tau})$, we can replace free variables of M by *some* of the terms from K. More precisely, we can replace variables in linear position by the V_i with $i \in F$, and variables in non linear position by N_j, with $j \in E$. We note as $M[K]$ the closed term of type γ that we obtain this way. We note $\mathcal{J}$ the set of all applicative typing judgments. We are specially interested in those judgments $(E, F, \boldsymbol{\sigma}, \boldsymbol{\tau}, M, \gamma)$ in $\mathcal{J}$ such that for every tuple K, the resulting term $M[K]$ is a *value*: that is when either $M = y_i$ for a $i \in \mathbb{N}$, or M is of the form $\lambda z.N$, $\lambda!z.N$, or $!N$. We note $\mathcal{J}^{\mathcal{V}}$ the set of those judgments.

We are now in a position to define $\mathcal{M}_\oplus^!$ formally. The set of its states is indeed defined as $\mathcal{S}_{\mathcal{M}_\oplus^!} = \{(K, A) \mid K \in \mathcal{U}, A \in \mathbf{T}, \vdash K : A\}$.

Labels and Transitions. How do states in $\mathcal{S}_{\mathcal{M}_\oplus^!}$ interact with the environment? This is captured by the labels in $\mathcal{A}_{\mathcal{M}_\oplus^!}$, and the associated probability matrix. We define $\mathcal{A}_{\mathcal{M}_\oplus^!}$ as the disjoint union of $\mathcal{A}_?$, $\mathcal{A}_!$ and $\mathcal{A}_@$, where:

$$\mathcal{A}_! = \mathcal{A}_? = \{i \mid i \in \mathbb{N}\}; \qquad \mathcal{A}_@ = \{(\kappa, i) \mid i \in \mathbb{N}, \kappa \in \mathcal{J}^{\mathcal{V}}\}.$$

In order to distinguish actions in $\mathcal{A}_!$ and $\mathcal{A}_?$, we write the action $i \in \mathbb{N}$ as $(?^i)$ if it comes from $\mathcal{A}_?$, and as $(!^i)$ if it comes from $\mathcal{A}_!$. The action $(\kappa, i) \in \mathcal{A}_@$ is often indicated as $@_\kappa^i$. The probability matrix $\mathcal{P}_{\mathscr{M}_\oplus^!}$ is defined formally in Fig. 4. We give below some intuitions about it. The general idea is that $\mathscr{M}_\oplus^!$ is designed to express every possible effect that a context can have on tuples. $\mathcal{A}_?$ and $\mathcal{A}_!$ are designed to model copying capabilities, while $\mathcal{A}_@$ corresponds to applicative interactions.

Actions in $\mathcal{A}_?$ take any term of the form $!M$ from the linear part of the underlying tuple, unbox it and transfer M to the exponential part of the tuple. Please observe that this action is in fact deterministic: the resulting tuple is uniquely determined. Labels in $\mathcal{A}_!$, on the other hand, model the act of *copying* terms in the exponential part. We call its elements *Milner's actions*. More specifically, the action $(!^i)$ takes the i-th term in the exponential part of the tuple, makes a copy of it, evaluates it and adds the result to the linear part. Please observe that, contrary to $(?^i)$, this action can have a probabilistic outcome: the transferred term is evaluated.

Labels in $\mathcal{A}_@$ are analogues of the applicative actions from applicative bisimulation over terms (see, e.g. [9]). As such, they model environments passing arguments to programs. Here, we have to adapt this idea to our tuple framework: indeed, we can see the tuple as a collection of programs available to the environment, who is free to choose *with which* of the programs to interact with by passing it an argument. This argument, however, could depend on other components of the tuple, which need to be removed from it if lying in its linear part. Finally, please observe that all this should respect types. Labels in $\mathcal{A}_@$ are indeed defined as a pair of an index i corresponding to the position in the tuple of the term the environment chooses, and an applicative typing judgment, used to specify the argument. Please observe that in the definition of the probability matrix for applicative actions, in Fig. 4, the condition on i implies that the i-th linear component of the tuple is not used to construct the argument term.

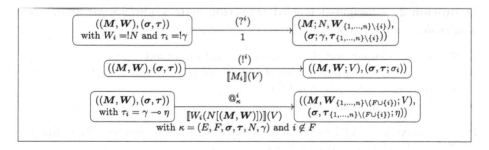

Fig. 4. Definition of $\mathcal{P}_{\mathscr{M}_\oplus^!}$

Example 4. We give in Fig. 5 a fragment of $\mathscr{M}_\oplus^!$ illustrating our definitions on an example. Let τ be an element of $\mathscr{A}$. We consider terms of the form

$M_\varepsilon = !(\Omega_1 \oplus^\varepsilon I)$, for $\varepsilon \in \mathbb{D}$ and we look at *some* of the possible evolutions in $\mathscr{M}^!_\oplus$ from the associated state $(\dot{M}_\varepsilon, !(\tau \multimap \tau)) = ([], [M_\varepsilon]), ([], [!(\tau \multimap \tau)])$. In Fig. 5, we denote by σ the type $\tau \multimap \tau$.

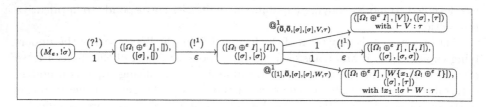

Fig. 5. A fragment of $\mathcal{P}_{\mathscr{M}^!_\oplus}$

5.2   Distributions as States

Now that we have a LMC $\mathcal{P}_{\mathscr{M}^!_\oplus}$ modeling interaction between (tuple of) terms and their environment, we could define notions of metrics following one of the abstract definitions from the literature, e.g. by defining the *trace distance* or the *behavioral distance* between terms. This is, by the way, the approach followed in [6]. We prefer, however, to first turn $\mathcal{P}_{\mathscr{M}^!_\oplus}$ into a transition system $\mathscr{L}^!_\oplus$ whose states are *distributions* of tuples. This supports both a simple, coinductive presentation of the trace distance, but also up-to techniques, as we will see in Sect. 5.5 below. Both will be very convenient when evaluating the distance between concrete terms, and in particular for our running example.

It turns out that the usual notion of LTS is not sufficient for our purposes, since it lacks a way to *expose* the observables of each state, i.e., its sum. We thus adopt the following definition:

Definition 2. *A* weighted labeled transition system *(WLTS for short) is a quadruple in the form* $\mathscr{L} = (\mathcal{S}, \mathcal{A}, \dot\rightarrow, w)$ *where:*

- $\mathcal{S}$ *is a set of states and* $\mathcal{A}$ *is a countable set of actions,*
- $\dot\rightarrow$ *is a transition function such that, for every* $t \in \mathcal{S}$ *and* $a \in \mathcal{A}$, *there exists at most one* $s \in \mathcal{S}$ *such that* $t \xrightarrow{a} s$,
- $w : \mathcal{S} \rightarrow [0, 1]$ *is a function.*

Please observe how WLTSs are *deterministic* transition systems. We define the WLTS $\mathscr{L}^!_\oplus$ by the equations of Fig. 6.

If $t = (\mathcal{D}, A)$ is in $\mathcal{S}_{\mathscr{L}^!_\oplus}$, we say that t is a A-state. It is easy to check that $\mathscr{L}^!_\oplus$ is nothing more than the natural way to turn $\mathcal{P}_{\mathscr{M}^!_\oplus}$ into a deterministic transition system. We illustrate this idea in Fig. 7, by giving a fragment of $\mathscr{L}^!_\oplus$ corresponding to (part of) the fragment of $\mathscr{M}^!_\oplus$ given in Example 4.

$$S_{\mathscr{L}_\oplus^!} = \bigcup_{A \in \mathbf{T}} (\text{Distr}(\{K \mid\vdash K : A\}) \times \{A\}) \qquad A_{\mathscr{L}_\oplus^!} = A_{\mathscr{M}_\oplus^!} \cup \{A \mid A \in \mathbf{T}\} \qquad w(\mathcal{D}, A) = \sum_{\mathcal{D}}$$

$$(\mathcal{D}, A) \xrightarrow{A} (\mathcal{D}, A) \text{ for } A \in \mathbf{T} \qquad (\mathcal{D}, A) \xrightarrow{a} \sum_{K \in \mathscr{U}} \mathcal{D}(K) \cdot \mathcal{P}_{\mathscr{M}_\oplus^!}((K, A))(a) \text{ for } a \in A_{\mathscr{M}_\oplus^!}.$$

Fig. 6. The WLTS $\mathscr{L}_\oplus^! = (S_{\mathscr{L}_\oplus^!}, A_{\mathscr{L}_\oplus^!}, \rightarrow, w)$

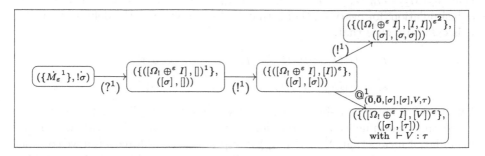

Fig. 7. A fragment of $\mathscr{L}_\oplus^!$

5.3 A Coinductively-Defined Metric

Following Desharnais et al. [13], we use a quantitative notion of bisimulation on $\mathscr{L}_\oplus^!$ to define a distance between terms. The idea is to stipulate that, for any $\varepsilon \in [0, 1]$, a relation R is an ε-bisimulation if it is, somehow, ε-*close to a bisimulation*. The distance between two states t and s is just the smallest ε such that t and s are ε-bisimilar. However, while in [13] the notion of ε-bisimulation is *local*, we want it to be more restricted by the *global* deviation we may accept considering arbitrary sequences of actions.

Definition 3. *Let $\mathscr{L} = (S, A, \rightarrow, w)$ be a WLTS. Let R be a symmetric and reflexive relation on S, and $\varepsilon \in [0, 1]$. R is a ε-bisimulation whenever the following two conditions hold:*

- *if $t R s$, and $t \xrightarrow{a} u$, then there exists v such that $s \xrightarrow{a} v$, and it holds that $u R v$.*
- *if $t R s$, then $|w(t) - w(s)| \leq \varepsilon$.*

For every $\varepsilon \in [0, 1]$, there exists a largest ε-bisimulation, that we indicate as R^ε. Please observe that it is not an equivalence relation (since it is not transitive). We can now define a metric on S: $\delta_{\mathscr{L}}^b(t, s) = \inf \{\varepsilon \mid t R^\varepsilon s\}$. The greatest lower bound is in fact reached as a $\delta_{\mathscr{L}}^b(t, s)$-bisimulation [7].

How can we turn $\delta_{\mathscr{L}}^b$ into a metric on *terms*? The idea is to consider the distributions on *tuples* one naturally gets when evaluating the term. To every term M of type σ, we define $\hat{s}_\sigma(M) \in S_{\mathscr{L}_\oplus^!}$ as $(\{\dot{V}^{[\![M]\!](V)}\}_{V \in \mathscr{V}}, \dot{\sigma})$.

Definition 4. *For every terms M and N such that $\vdash M : \sigma$ and $\vdash N : \sigma$, we set $\delta_{\sigma, !}^b(M, N) = \delta_{\mathscr{L}_\oplus^!}^b(\hat{s}_\sigma(M), \hat{s}_\sigma(N))$.*

Example 5. Consider again the terms M_ε and M_μ from Example 2. We fix a type τ, and define $\sigma = \tau \multimap \tau$. As mentioned in Example 2, it holds that $\vdash M_\varepsilon :!\sigma$. Let now ε, μ, α be in $[0,1]$, and let R be any α-bisimulation, such that $\hat{s}_{!\sigma}(M_\varepsilon)\, R\, \hat{s}_{!\sigma}(M_\mu)$. Let $\{t_i\}_{i \in \mathbb{N}}$ and $\{s_i\}_{i \in \mathbb{N}}$ be families from $\mathcal{S}_{\mathcal{L}^!_\oplus}$ such that $\hat{s}_{!\sigma}(M_\varepsilon) \overset{(?^1)}{\rightarrow} t_0 \overset{(!^1)}{\rightarrow} \ldots \overset{(!^1)}{\rightarrow} t_i \ldots$ and $\hat{s}_{!\sigma}(M_\mu) \overset{(?^1)}{\rightarrow} s_0 \overset{(!^1)}{\rightarrow} \ldots \overset{(!^1)}{\rightarrow} s_i \ldots$. Since R is an α-bisimulation, for every i, it holds that $t_i\, R\, s_i$. Looking at the definition of $\mathcal{L}^!_\oplus$, it is easy to realize that:

$$t_i = \{([\Omega_! \oplus^\varepsilon I], [I, \ldots, I]), ([\sigma], [\sigma, \ldots, \sigma])^{\varepsilon^i}\}_{i \in \mathbb{N}};$$

$$s_i = \{([\Omega_! \oplus^\mu I], [I, \ldots, I]), ([\sigma], [\sigma, \ldots, \sigma])^{\mu^i}\}_{i \in \mathbb{N}}.$$

By the definition of an α-bisimulation, we see that this implies that $\alpha \geq |\varepsilon^i - \mu^i|$. Since this reasoning can be done for every α such that M_ε and M_μ are α-bisimilar, it means that: $\delta^b_{!\sigma,!}(M_\varepsilon, M_\mu) \geq \sup_{i \in \mathbb{N}} |\varepsilon^i - \mu^i|$. Moreover, if we consider the special case where $\varepsilon = 0$, we can actually construct a μ-bisimulation by taking

$$R = (\hat{s}_{!\sigma}(M_0), \hat{s}_{!\sigma}(M_\mu)) \cup \{(t_0, s_0)\} \cup \{((0, A), (\mathcal{D}, A) \mid \textstyle\sum_\mathcal{D} \leq \mu\}.$$

We can easily check that R is indeed a μ-bisimulation, which tells us that $\delta^b_{!\sigma,!}(M_0, M_\mu) = \mu$.

5.4   Full Abstraction

In this section, we prove that $\delta^b_{\sigma,!}$ coincides with $\delta^c_{\sigma,!}$. We first of all show that the metric $\delta^b_{\sigma,!}$ is *sound* with respect to $\delta^c_{\sigma,!}$, i.e. that $\delta^b_{\sigma,!}$ discriminates at least as much as $\delta^c_{\sigma,!}$:

Theorem 3 (Soundness). *For any terms M and N of $\Lambda^!_\oplus$, such that $\vdash M : \sigma$ and $\vdash N : \sigma$, it holds that $\delta^c_{\sigma,!}(M, N) \leq \delta^b_{\sigma,!}(M, N)$.*

Please remember that our definition of the tuple distance is based on the notion of ε-bisimulation. Proving the soundness theorem, thus, requires us to show that for any terms M and N of type σ such that $\hat{s}_\sigma(M)$ and $\hat{s}_\sigma(N)$ are ε-bisimilar, and for any context C, it holds that $|\sum_{[\![C[M]]\!]} - \sum_{[\![C[N]]\!]}| \leq \varepsilon$. Our proof strategy is based on the fact that we can decompose every evaluation path of a term in the form $C[L]$ into *external* reduction steps (that is, steps that do *not* affect L), and *internal* reduction steps (that is, reduction steps affecting L, but which can be shown to correspond *only* to actions from $\mathcal{L}^!_\oplus$). Intuitively, if we reduce in parallel $C[M]$ and $C[N]$, we are going to have steps where only the context is modified (and the modification does not depend on whether we are considering the first program or the second), and steps where the internal part is modified, but these steps cannot induce too much of a difference between the two programs, since the two internal terms are ε-bisimilar.

We first of all need to generalize the notion of context to deal with tuples rather than with terms. In particular, we need contexts with multiple holes having types which match those of the tuple (or, more precisely, the A-state) they are meant to be paired with. More formally:

Definition 5 (Tuple Contexts). *Tuple contexts are triples of the form* (C, A, γ)*, where* C *is an open term,* $A = (\boldsymbol{\sigma}, \boldsymbol{\tau})$ *is a* (n, m)*-tuple type, and* γ *is a type such that* $!\boldsymbol{x}_{\{1,\ldots,n\}} : !\boldsymbol{\sigma}, \boldsymbol{y}_{\{1,\ldots,m\}} : \boldsymbol{\tau} \vdash C : \gamma$*. We note* $\mathscr{C}^{\mathbf{T}}$ *the set of tuple contexts. A tuple context* (C, A, γ) *is said to be an* open value *if* C *is of one of the following four forms:* $\lambda x.M$*,* $\lambda!x.M$*,* $!M$*,* y_i *(where* $i \in \mathbb{N}$*).*

We now want to define *when* a tuple context and an A-state can be paired together, and the operational semantics of such an object, which will be derived from that of $\varLambda^!_\oplus$-terms. This is the purpose of the following definition:

Definition 6 (Tuple Context Pairs). *We say that a pair* $u = (C, t)$ *is a* tuple context pair *iff* $t = (A, \mathcal{D})$ *is an* A*-state, and* $\exists \gamma \in \mathscr{A}, (C, A, \gamma) \in \mathscr{C}^{\mathbf{T}}$*. We indicate as* $\mathbf{C} \times \boldsymbol{\Delta}(\mathscr{U})$ *the set of tuple context pairs. Moreover, given such a pair* $u = (C, (A, \mathcal{D}))$*, we define* $\boldsymbol{F}(u)$ *as the (potentially infinite) distribution over* $\mathscr{T}$ *given by:*

$$\boldsymbol{F}(u) = \{C\{\boldsymbol{x}/\boldsymbol{M}\}\{\boldsymbol{y}/\boldsymbol{N}\}^{\mathcal{D}(\boldsymbol{M},\boldsymbol{N})}\}_{(\boldsymbol{M},\boldsymbol{N})\in S(\mathcal{D})}.$$

Giving a notion of context distance for A-states is now quite easy and natural, since we know how contexts for such objects look like. For the sake of being as general as possible, this notion of a distance is parametric on a set of tuple contexts $\mathscr{C} \subseteq \mathscr{C}^{\mathbf{T}}$.

Definition 7. *Let* $\mathscr{C} \subseteq \mathscr{C}^{\mathbf{T}}$*,* $A \in \mathbf{T}$*, and* t, s *be two* A*-states. We define:*

$$\delta^c_\mathscr{C}(t, s) = \sup_{(C, A, \sigma) \in \mathscr{C}} \left| \sum_{[\![\boldsymbol{F}(C,t)]\!]} - \sum_{[\![\boldsymbol{F}(C,s)]\!]} \right|$$

Unsurprisingly, the context distance between terms equals $\delta^c_{\mathscr{C}^{\mathbf{T}}}$ when applied to A-states obtained through $\hat{s}_\sigma(\cdot)$:

Proposition 1. *If* $\vdash M, N : \sigma$*, then* $\delta^c_{\sigma,!}(M, N) = \delta^c_{\mathscr{C}^{\mathbf{T}}}(\hat{s}_\sigma(M), \hat{s}_\sigma(N))$*.*

But why did we introduce $\mathbf{C} \times \boldsymbol{\Delta}(\mathscr{U})$? Actually, these pairs allow a fine analysis of how tuples behave when put in a context, which in turn is precisely what we need to prove Theorem 3. This analysis, however, is not possible without endowing $\mathbf{C} \times \boldsymbol{\Delta}(\mathscr{U})$ itself with an operational semantics, which is precisely what we are going to do in the next paragraphs.

Two relations need to be defined. On the one hand, we need a one-step *labeled* transition relation $\rightarrow_{\mathbf{C} \times \boldsymbol{\Delta}(\mathscr{U})}$ which turns an element of $\mathbf{C} \times \boldsymbol{\Delta}(\mathscr{U})$ into a distribution over $\mathbf{C} \times \boldsymbol{\Delta}(\mathscr{U})$ by performing an action. Intuitively, one step of reduction in $\rightarrow_{\mathbf{C} \times \boldsymbol{\Delta}(\mathscr{U})}$ corresponds to *at most* one step of reduction in $\mathscr{L}^!_\oplus$. If that step exists, (i.e. if the *term* is reduced) then the label is the same, and otherwise (i.e., if only the *context* is reduced) the label is just τ. We also need a multi-step approximation semantics $\Rightarrow_{\mathbf{C} \times \boldsymbol{\Delta}(\mathscr{U})}$ between elements of $\mathbf{C} \times \boldsymbol{\Delta}(\mathscr{U})$ and subdistributions over the same set. The latter is based on the former, and both are formally defined in Fig. 8, where

$$(E[(\lambda z.N)M], t) \xrightarrow{\tau}_{\mathbf{C}\times\Delta(\mathscr{U})} \{(E[N\{z/M\}], t)^1\} \qquad (E[(\lambda!z.N)!M], t) \xrightarrow{\tau}_{\mathbf{C}\times\Delta(\mathscr{U})} \{(E[N\{z/M\}], t)^1\}$$

$$(E[M \oplus N], t) \xrightarrow{\tau}_{\mathbf{C}\times\Delta(\mathscr{U})} \{(E[M], t)^{1/2}\} + \{(E[N], t)^{1/2}\}$$

$$\frac{t \xrightarrow{(!^j)} s}{(E[x_j], t) \xrightarrow{(!^j)}_{\mathbf{C}\times\Delta(\mathscr{U})} \{(E[y_{m+1}], s)^1\}} \qquad \frac{t \xrightarrow{(?^j)} s \qquad C = E[(\lambda!z.N)!x_{n+1}]_{\text{remove}(\{j\})}}{(E[(\lambda!z.N)y_j], t) \xrightarrow{(?^j)}_{\mathbf{C}\times\Delta(\mathscr{U})} \{(C, s)^1\}}$$

$$\frac{t \xrightarrow{@^j_\$} s \qquad \begin{array}{c} t = (\mathcal{D}, A) \wedge A = \sigma, \tau \\ \tau_j = \eta \multimap \iota \end{array} \qquad \begin{array}{c} \kappa = (\{1,\dots,n\}, F, \sigma, \tau, V, \eta) \in \mathscr{J}^{\mathscr{V}} \\ j \notin F \end{array}}{(E[y_j V], t) \xrightarrow{@^j_\$}_{\mathbf{C}\times\Delta(\mathscr{U})} \{((E[y_{m+1}])_{\text{remove}(F\cup\{j\})}, s)^1\}}$$

$$\frac{h \text{ in normal form for } \to_{\mathbf{C}\times\Delta(\mathscr{U})}}{h \Rightarrow_{\mathbf{C}\times\Delta(\mathscr{U})} \{t^1\}} \qquad \overline{h \Rightarrow_{\mathbf{C}\times\Delta(\mathscr{U})} 0} \qquad \frac{h \xrightarrow{a}_{\mathbf{C}\times\Delta(\mathscr{U})} \mathcal{D} \qquad k \Rightarrow_{\mathbf{C}\times\Delta(\mathscr{U})} \mathcal{E}_k}{h \Rightarrow_{\mathbf{C}\times\Delta(\mathscr{U})} \sum_{k\in S(\mathcal{D})} \mathcal{D}(k) \cdot \mathcal{E}_k}$$

Fig. 8. Rules for $\Rightarrow_{\mathbf{C}\times\Delta(\mathscr{U})}$

- E is an evaluation context;
- t is an (n, m)-state from $S_{\mathscr{L}^!_\oplus}$;
- h is a tuple-context pair from $\mathbf{C} \times \Delta(\mathscr{U})$;
- For every context C, $C_{\text{remove}(E)}$ stands for the context

$$C\{y_1/y_{1-\#\{j|j\in E \wedge j<1\}}\} \cdots \{y_n/y_{n-\#\{j|j\in E \wedge j<n\}}\}$$

We first show that this definition can indeed be related to the usual semantics for terms. This takes the form of the following lemma:

Lemma 2. *Let be* $u \in \mathbf{C} \times \Delta(\mathscr{U})$. *Then:*

- $\{\mathcal{D} \mid u \Rightarrow_{\mathbf{C}\times\Delta(\mathscr{U})}\mathcal{D}\}$ *is a directed set. We define* $[\![u]\!]^{\mathbf{C}\times\Delta(\mathscr{U})}$ *as its least upper bound;*
- $F(\cdot) : Distr(\mathbf{C} \times \Delta(\mathscr{U})) \to Distr(\mathscr{T})$ *is continuous;*
- $[\![F(u)]\!] = F([\![u]\!]^{\mathbf{C}\times\Delta(\mathscr{U})})$.

Before proceeding, we need to understand how any reflexive and symmetric relation on $\mathbf{C} \times \Delta(\mathscr{U})$ can be turned into a relation on *distributions* on $\mathbf{C} \times \Delta(\mathscr{U})$. If R is a reflexive and symmetric relation on $\mathbf{C} \times \Delta(\mathscr{U})$, we lift it to distributions over $\mathbf{C} \times \Delta(\mathscr{U})$ by stipulating that $\mathcal{D} \, R \, \mathcal{E}$ whenever there exists a countable set I, a family $(p_i)_{i\in I}$ of positive reals of sum smaller than 1, and families $(h_i)_{i\in I}, (k_i)_{i\in I}$ in $\mathbf{C} \times \Delta(\mathscr{U})$, such that $\mathcal{D} = \{h_i^{p_i}\}_{i\in I}$, $\mathcal{E} = \{k_i^{p_i}\}_{i\in I}$, and moreover $h_i \, R \, k_i$ for every $i \in I$.

We now want to precisely capture *when* a relation on $\mathbf{C} \times \Delta(\mathscr{U})$ can be used to evaluate the distance between tuple-context pairs.

Definition 8. *Let R be a reflexive and symmetric relation on $\mathbf{C} \times \mathbf{\Delta}(\mathscr{U})$.*

- *We say that R is preserved by $\rightarrow_{\mathbf{C} \times \mathbf{\Delta}(\mathscr{U})}$ if, for any $h, k \in \mathbf{C} \times \mathbf{\Delta}(\mathscr{U})$ such that $h \, R \, k$, if $h \xrightarrow{a}_{\mathbf{C} \times \mathbf{\Delta}(\mathscr{U})} \mathcal{D}$, then there exists $\mathcal{E}$ such that $k \xrightarrow{a}_{\mathbf{C} \times \mathbf{\Delta}(\mathscr{U})} \mathcal{E}$, and that $\mathcal{D} \, R \, \mathcal{E}$.*
- *We say that R is ε-bounding if $h \, R \, k$ implies $|\sum_{F(h)} - \sum_{F(k)}| \leq \varepsilon$.*
- *Let $\mathscr{C}$ be a set of tuple contexts, and $t, s \in \mathcal{S}_{\mathscr{L}^!_\oplus}$ be two A-states. We say that R is $\mathscr{C}$-closed with respect to t and s if, for every C and γ such that $(C, A, \gamma) \in \mathscr{C}$, it holds that $(C, t) \, R \, (C, s)$.*

Please observe how any relation preserving $\rightarrow_{\mathbf{C} \times \mathbf{\Delta}(\mathscr{U})}$ and being ε-bounding can be seen somehow as an ε-bisimulation, but on tuple-context pairs. The way we defined the lifting, however, makes it even a *stronger* notion, i.e., the ideal candidate for an intermediate step towards Soundness.

As a first step, the conditions from Definition 8 are enough to guarantee that two terms are at context distance at most ε.

Proposition 2. *Let M, N be two terms of type σ. Suppose there exists a reflexive and symmetric relation R on $\mathbf{C} \times \mathbf{\Delta}(\mathscr{U})$, which is preserved by $\rightarrow_{\mathbf{C} \times \mathbf{\Delta}(\mathscr{U})}$, ε-bounding, and $\mathscr{C}^{\mathbf{T}}$-closed with respect to $\hat{s}_\sigma(M)$ and $\hat{s}_\sigma(N)$. Then $\delta^c_{\sigma,!}(M, N) \leq \varepsilon$.*

What remains to be done, then, is to show that if two terms are related by R^ε, then they themselves satisfy Definition 8. Compulsory to that is showing that any ε-bisimulation can at least be turned into a relation on $\mathbf{C} \times \mathbf{\Delta}(\mathscr{U})$. We need to do that, in particular, in a way guaranteeing the $\mathscr{C}$-closure of the resulting relation, and thus considering all possible tuple contexts from $\mathscr{C}$:

Definition 9. *Let R be a reflexive and symmetric relation on $\mathcal{S}_{\mathscr{L}^!_\oplus}$. Let be $\mathscr{C}$ a set of tuple contexts. We define its* contextual lifting *to $\mathbf{C} \times \mathbf{\Delta}(\mathscr{U})$ with respect to $\mathscr{C}$ as the following binary relation on $\mathbf{C} \times \mathbf{\Delta}(\mathscr{U})$:*

$$\widehat{R}^{\mathscr{C}}_A = \bigcup_{(C,A,\sigma) \in \mathscr{C}} \{((C,t),(C,s)) \mid t, s \, A\text{-states}, \, t \, R \, s\}; \qquad \widehat{R}^{\mathscr{C}} = \bigcup_{A \in \mathbf{T}} \widehat{R}^{\mathscr{C}}_A.$$

The following result tells us that, indeed, any ε-bisimulation can be turned into a relation satisfying Definition 8:

Proposition 3. *Let R be an ε-bisimulation. Then $\widehat{R}^{\mathscr{C}^{\mathbf{T}}}$ is preserved by $\rightarrow_{\mathbf{C} \times \mathbf{\Delta}(\mathscr{U})}$ and ε-bounding, and $\mathscr{C}^{\mathbf{T}}$-closed with respect to every t, s such that $t \, R \, s$.*

We are finally ready to give a proof of soundness:

Proof (of Theorem 3). Consider two terms M and N of type σ. Let ε be $\delta^b_{\sigma,!}(M, N)$. We take R^ε (defined in Definition 3 as the largest ε-bisimulation), and we see that $\hat{s}_\sigma(M) \, R^\varepsilon \, \hat{s}_\sigma(N)$. Proposition 3 tells us that we can apply Proposition 2 to M, N, and $\widehat{(R^\varepsilon)}^{\mathscr{C}^{\mathbf{T}}}$. Doing so we obtain that $\delta^c_{\sigma,!}(M, N) \leq \varepsilon$, which is the thesis. $\qquad\square$

We can actually show (see [7]) that $\delta^b_{\sigma,!}$ is also complete with respect to the contextual distance:

Theorem 4 (Full Abstraction). *For every* σ, $\delta^c_{\sigma,!} = \delta^b_{\sigma,!}$.

5.5 On an Up-to-Context Technique

As we have just shown, context distance can be characterized as a coinductively-defined metric, which turns out to be useful when evaluating the distance between terms. In this section, we will go even further, and show how an *up-to-context* [31] notion of ε-bisimulation is precisely what we need to handle our running example.

We first of all need to generalize our definition of a tuple: an *open tuple* is a pair (M, N), where M and N are sequences of (not necessarily closed) typable terms.

Definition 10. *If* $K = (M, N)$ *is an open tuple, and* $A = (\gamma, \eta)$ *is a tuple type, we say that* (σ, τ, K, A) *is a* substitution judgment *iff:*

- $!x :!\sigma \vdash M_i : \gamma_i$;
- *if* n *and* m *are such that* τ *is a* n-sequence, and N *a* m-sequence, then there exists a partition $\{E_1, \ldots E_m\}$ of $\{1, \ldots, n\}$ such that $y_{E_j} : \tau_{E_j} \vdash N_j : \eta_j$ for every $j \in \{1, \ldots, m\}$.*

$\mathscr{J}^{\text{subst}}$ *is the set of all substitution judgments.*

If $\kappa = (\sigma, \tau, K, A) \in \mathscr{J}^{\text{subst}}$, and $H \in \mathscr{U}$ is of type (σ, τ), then there is a natural way to form a tuple $\kappa[H]$, namely by substituting the free variables of K by the components of H. In the following, we restrict $\mathscr{J}^{\text{subst}}$ to those judgments κ such that for every H, terms in the linear part of $\kappa[H]$ are values. Observe that we always have $\vdash \kappa[H] : A$. We extend the notation $\kappa[H]$ to distributions over $\mathscr{U}$: if $\mathcal{D}$ is a distribution over tuples of type (σ, τ), we note $\kappa[\mathcal{D}] = \{\kappa[H]^{\mathcal{D}(H)}\}_{H \in \mathscr{U}}$, which is a distribution over tuples of type A. Moreover, we want to be able to apply our substitution judgments to the states of $\mathscr{L}^!_{\oplus}$. If $t = (\mathcal{D}, (\sigma, \tau)) \in S_{\mathscr{L}^!_{\oplus}}$, and $\kappa = (\sigma, \tau, K, A)$, the state of $\mathscr{L}^!_{\oplus}$ defined by $(\kappa[\mathcal{D}], A)$ will be often indicated as $\kappa[t]$.

Example 6. We illustrate on a simple example the use of substitution judgments. Let be τ any type. Consider $\sigma = [\tau \multimap \tau]$, and $\tau = []$. Moreover, let $K = ([x_1], [I])$ and $A = ([\tau \multimap \tau], [\tau \multimap \tau])$. Then $\kappa = (\sigma, \tau, K, A)$ is a substitution judgment. We consider now a tuple of type (σ, τ). In fact, we take here a tuple that will be useful in order to analyze our running example: $H = ([\Omega_! \oplus^\varepsilon I], [])$. By substituting H in κ, we obtain $\kappa[H] = ([\Omega_! \oplus^\varepsilon I], [I])$, and we can see easily that we obtain indeed a tuple of type A.

The main idea behind up-to-context bisimulation is to allow for the freedom of discarding any context when proving a relation to be a bisimulation. This is captured by the following definition:

Definition 11. *Let R be a relation on $\mathcal{S}_{\mathscr{L}_{\oplus}^!}$. R is an ε-bisimulation up-to-context if for every t and s such that $t\,R\,s$, the following holds:*

- *there exists $C \in \mathbf{T}$ such that $t = (\mathcal{D}, C)$, $s = (\mathcal{E}, C)$, and $|\sum_{\mathcal{D}} - \sum_{\mathcal{E}}| \leq \varepsilon$.*
- *for any $a \in \mathcal{A}_{\mathscr{M}_{\oplus}^!}$, if $t\xrightarrow{a}u = (\mathcal{D}, A)$ and $s\xrightarrow{a}v = (\mathcal{E}, A)$, then there exists a finite set $I \subseteq \mathbb{N}$ such that:*
    - *there is a family of rationals $(p_i)_{i \in I}$ such that $\sum_{i \in I} p_i \leq 1$;*
    - *there are families $\boldsymbol{\sigma}^i$, $\boldsymbol{\tau}^i$, and K^i, such that $\kappa_i = (\boldsymbol{\sigma}^i, \boldsymbol{\tau}^i, K^i, A)$ is a substitution judgment for every $i \in I$;*
    - *there are distributions over tuples $\mathcal{D}_i$, $\mathcal{E}_i$ such that $(\mathcal{D}_i, B_i)\,R\,(\mathcal{E}_i, B_i)$;*
  and moreover $\mathcal{D} = \sum_{i \in I} p_i \cdot \kappa_i[\mathcal{D}_i]$, and $\mathcal{E} = \sum_{i \in I} p_i \cdot \kappa_i[\mathcal{E}_i]$.

The proof method we just introduced is indeed quite useful when handling our running example.

Example 7. We show that up-to bisimulations can handle our running example. Please recall the definition of M_ε given in Example 2. First, we can see that, for every a, for every type τ, $\hat{s}_{!(\tau \multimap \tau)}(M_a) = (\{([]\,, [!\Omega_! \oplus^a I])^1\}, ([]\,, [!\tau \multimap \tau]))$. We define a relation R on $\mathcal{S}_{\mathscr{L}_{\oplus}^!}$ containing $(\hat{s}_{!(\tau \multimap \tau)}(M_\varepsilon), \hat{s}_{!(\tau \multimap \tau)}(M_\mu))$, and we show that it is a γ-bisimulation up-to-context for an appropriate γ. In order to simplify the notations, we define $B = ([\tau \multimap \tau], [])$, and $t_n, s_n \in \mathcal{S}_{\mathscr{L}_{\oplus}^!}$ as:

$$t_n = (\{([(\Omega_! \oplus^\varepsilon I)], [])^{(\varepsilon^n)}\}, B), \qquad s_n = (\{([(\Omega_! \oplus^\mu I)], [])^{(\mu^n)}\}, B).$$

Then, we define the relation R as $R = \{(\hat{s}_\sigma(M), \hat{s}_\sigma(N))\} \cup \{(t_n, s_n) \mid n \in \mathbb{N}\}$. One can check that R is indeed a γ-bisimulation up-to-context (where $\gamma = \sup_{n \in \mathbb{N}} |\varepsilon^n - \mu^n|$) by carefully analyzing [7] every possible action. The proof is based on the following observations:

- The only action starting from $\hat{s}_\sigma(M)$ or $\hat{s}_\sigma(N)$ is $a = (?^1)$, passing a term to the exponential part of the tuple, then we end up in t_0 and s_0 respectively.
- If we start from t_n or s_n, the only relevant action is Milner's action $a = (!^1)$, consisting in taking a copy of the term in the exponential part, evaluating it, and putting the result in the linear part. We can see (using the substitution judgment κ defined in Example 6), that $t_n\xrightarrow{a}\kappa[t_{n+1}]$, and similarly $s_n\xrightarrow{a}\kappa[s_{n+1}]$, and the result follows.

Bisimulations up-to-context would be useless without a correctness result such as the following one:

Theorem 5. *If R is an ε-bisimulation up-to context, then $R \subseteq R^\varepsilon$.*

The proof is an extension of that of Theorem 3 (although technically more involved), and can be found in [7].

Example 8. We can exploit the soundness of up-to-context bisimulation to obtain the contextual distance for our running example. This allows us to conclude that $\delta^c_{!(\tau \multimap \tau), !}(M_\varepsilon, M_\mu) = \sup_{n \in \mathbb{N}} |\varepsilon^n - \mu^n|$. The context distance between M_ε and M_μ is thus *strictly* between 0 and 1 whenever $0 < |\varepsilon - \mu| < 1$.

6   Probabilistic λ-Calculi, in Perspective

The calculus $\Lambda_\oplus^{!,\|}$ we analyzed in this paper is, at least apparently, nonstandard, given the presence of parallel disjunction, but also because of the linear refinement it is based on. In this section, we will reconcile what we have done so far with calculi in the literature, and in particular with untyped probabilistic λ-calculi akin to those studied, e.g., in [5,9].

We consider a language $\Lambda_\oplus$ defined by the following grammar:

$$M \in \Lambda_\oplus ::= x \mid MM \mid \lambda x.M \mid M \oplus M.$$

6.1   On Stable Fragments of $\mathscr{M}_\oplus^!$

Our objective in this section is to characterize various notions of context distance for $\Lambda_\oplus$ by way of appropriate embeddings into $\Lambda_\oplus^!$, and thus by the LMC $\mathscr{M}_\oplus^!$. It is quite convenient, then, to understand when any fragment of $\mathscr{M}_\oplus^!$ is sufficiently *robust* so as to be somehow self-contained:

Definition 12. *We say that the pair $(\hat{S}, \hat{A})$, where $\hat{S} \subseteq S_{\mathscr{M}_\oplus^!}$, and $\hat{A} \subseteq \mathbf{T} \times A_{\mathscr{M}_\oplus^!}$ is a stable fragment of $\mathscr{M}_\oplus^!$ iff for every pair $(A, a) \in \hat{A}$, for every A-state t, and for every $s \in S$ such that $\mathcal{P}_{\mathscr{M}_\oplus^!}(t, a, s) > 0$, it holds that $s \in \hat{S}$.*

Using a stable fragment of $\mathscr{M}_\oplus^!$, we can restrict the WLTS $\mathscr{L}_\oplus^!$ in a meaningful way. The idea is that we only consider some of the states of $\mathscr{L}_\oplus^!$, and we are able to choose the possible actions depending on the type of the state of $\mathscr{L}_\oplus^!$ we consider.

Definition 13. *If $\mathscr{F} = (\hat{S}, \hat{A})$ is a stable fragment of $\mathscr{M}_\oplus^!$, we define a WLTS by $\mathscr{L}_\mathscr{F} = (S_{\mathscr{L}_\mathscr{F}}, A_{\mathscr{L}_\mathscr{F}}, \dot{\rightarrow}_\mathscr{F}, w_\mathscr{F})$, as*

$$S_{\mathscr{L}_\mathscr{F}} = \bigcup_{A \in \mathbf{T}} Distr(\{K \mid (K, A) \in \hat{S}\}) \times \{A\}; \qquad A_{\mathscr{L}_\mathscr{F}} = \bigcup_{(A,a) \in \hat{A}} \{a\} \cup \mathbf{T};$$

$$\dot{\rightarrow}_\mathscr{F} = \dot{\rightarrow} \cap \{((\mathcal{D}, A), a, s) \mid S(\mathcal{D}) \subseteq \hat{S}, (A, a) \in \hat{A}\};$$

and $w_\mathscr{F}$ is defined as expected.

We want to be able to define a notion of distance on a *fragment* of the original language $\Lambda_\oplus^!$, so that it verifies the soundness property for a *restricted* set of contexts. To do that, we need the restricted set of contexts $\mathscr{C}$ to be preserved by the stable fragment:

Definition 14. *Let $\mathscr{F} = (\hat{S}, \hat{A})$ be a stable fragment of $\mathscr{M}_\oplus^!$. Let $\mathscr{C}$ be a set of tuple contexts. We say that $\mathscr{C}$ is preserved by $\mathscr{F}$ if the following holds: for any $(C, A, \gamma) \in \mathscr{C}$ that is not an open value and for any A-state t in $S_{\mathscr{L}_\mathscr{F}}$, there exists a such that $(A, a) \in \hat{A} \bigcup (\mathbf{T} \times \{\tau\})$, $(C, t) \xrightarrow{a}_{\mathbf{C} \times \Delta(\mathscr{U})} \mathcal{E}$, and moreover:*

$$S(\mathcal{E}) \subseteq \bigcup_{B \in \mathbf{T}} \{(D, s) \mid s \text{ a } B\text{-state} \wedge \exists \eta \text{ s.t. } (D, B, \eta) \in \mathscr{C}\}$$

We are now able to provide guarantees that the contextual distance $\delta_{\mathscr{C}}^{c}$ with respect to our restricted set of contexts $\mathscr{C}$ is smaller that the distance defined on the WLTS $\mathscr{L}_{\mathscr{F}}$ induced by our stable fragment $\mathscr{F}$. This is the spirit of the following proposition.

Proposition 4. *Let $\mathscr{F} = (\hat{\mathcal{S}}, \hat{\mathcal{A}})$ be a stable fragment of $\mathscr{M}_{\oplus}^{!}$, $\mathscr{C}$ be a set of tuple contexts preserved by $\mathscr{F}$, and $t, s \in \mathcal{S}_{\mathscr{L}_{\mathscr{F}}}$. Then $\delta_{\mathscr{C}}^{c}(t, s) \leq \delta_{\mathscr{L}_{\mathscr{F}}}^{b}(t, s)$.*

In the following, we make use of Proposition 4 on stable fragments corresponding to embeddings of $\Lambda_{\oplus}$ into $\Lambda_{\oplus}^{!}$. We will consider two different encodings depending on the underlying notion of evaluation.

6.2   Call-by-Name

$\Lambda_{\oplus}$ can first of all be endowed with call-by-name semantics, as in Fig. 9. We use it to define an approximation semantics exactly in the same way as in Fig. 1, and we take as usual the semantics of a term to be the least upper bound of its approximated semantics. Moreover, we denote by $\delta_{\mathrm{cbn}}^{c}$ the context distance on $\Lambda_{\oplus}$, defined the natural way. We are going, in the remainder of this section, to use our results about $\Lambda_{\oplus}^{!}$ to obtain a characterization of $\delta_{\mathrm{cbn}}^{c}$.

$$E ::= [\cdot] \mid EM \qquad \overline{M \oplus N \hookrightarrow M, N} \qquad \overline{(\lambda x.M)N \hookrightarrow M\{x/N\}} \qquad \frac{M \hookrightarrow N_1, \ldots, N_n}{E[M] \to E[N_1], \ldots E[N_n]}$$

Fig. 9. One-step call-by-name semantics

The Call-By-Name Embedding. Girard's translation [19] gives us an embedding $\langle \cdot \rangle^{\mathrm{cbn}} : \Lambda_{\oplus} \to \Lambda_{\oplus}^{!}$, defined as follows:

$$\langle x \rangle^{\mathrm{cbn}} = x \qquad\qquad \langle \lambda x.M \rangle^{\mathrm{cbn}} = \lambda!x.\langle M \rangle^{\mathrm{cbn}}$$
$$\langle MN \rangle^{\mathrm{cbn}} = \langle M \rangle^{\mathrm{cbn}}!\langle N \rangle^{\mathrm{cbn}} \qquad \langle M \oplus N \rangle^{\mathrm{cbn}} = \langle M \rangle^{\mathrm{cbn}} \oplus \langle N \rangle^{\mathrm{cbn}}$$

Please observe that $\langle \cdot \rangle^{\mathrm{cbn}}$ respects typing in the sense that, when we define $\sigma^{\mathrm{cbn}} = \mu\alpha.!\alpha \multimap \alpha$, it holds that for every term M of $\Lambda_{\oplus}$ whose free variables are in $\{x_1, \ldots, x_n\}$, we can show that $!x_1 :!\sigma^{\mathrm{cbn}}, \ldots, !x_n :!\sigma^{\mathrm{cbn}} \vdash \langle M \rangle^{\mathrm{cbn}} : \sigma^{\mathrm{cbn}}$.

Metrics for $\Lambda_{\oplus}$. It is very tempting to define a metric on $\Lambda_{\oplus}$ just as follows: $\delta_{\mathrm{cbn}}^{b}(M, N) = \delta_{!\sigma^{\mathrm{cbn}},!}^{b}(!\langle M \rangle^{\mathrm{cbn}}, !\langle N \rangle^{\mathrm{cbn}})$. We can easily see that it is sound with respect to the context distance for $\Lambda_{\oplus}$, since any context of this language can be seen, through $\langle \cdot \rangle^{\mathrm{cbn}}$, as a context in $\Lambda_{\oplus}^{!}$. However, it is not complete, as shown by the following example:

Example 9. We consider $M = \Omega \oplus (\lambda x.\Omega)$ and $N = (\lambda x.\Omega)$. We can see that $\delta_{!\sigma^{\mathrm{cbn}},!}^{b}(!\langle M \rangle^{\mathrm{cbn}}, !\langle N \rangle^{\mathrm{cbn}}) = 1$: indeed, when we define a sequence of $\Lambda_{\oplus}^{!}$-contexts by $C_n = \lambda!x. ((\lambda y_1. \ldots \lambda y_n.(\lambda z.zy_1, \ldots y_n))x \ldots x) []$, we see that $\mathrm{Obs}(!\langle M \rangle^{\mathrm{cbn}}) = 1/2^n$ while $\mathrm{Obs}(!\langle N \rangle^{\mathrm{cbn}}) = 1$. But those contexts C_n have more expressive power than any context in $\langle \Lambda_{\oplus} \rangle^{\mathrm{cbn}}$, since they do something that none of the contexts from $\Lambda_\oplus$ can do: they evaluate a copy of the term, and then shift their focus to *another* copy of the term. It can be seen in the embedding: a term in $\langle\Lambda_\oplus\rangle^{cbn}$ never has several redexes in linear position. It can actually be shown (see [7]) that $\delta^c_{cbn}(M,N) = \frac{1}{2} < \delta^b_{cbn}(M,N)$.

The way out consists in using the notion of stable fragment to refine the Markov Chain $\mathcal{M}^!_\oplus$ by keeping only the states and actions we are interested in.

Definition 15. *We define a stable fragment $\mathscr{F}^{cbn}$ as specified in Fig. 10, and a distance δ_{cbn} on $\Lambda_\oplus$ as $\delta_{cbn}(M,N) = \delta^b_{\mathscr{L}_{\mathscr{F}^{cbn}}}(\hat{s}^{cbn}(M), \hat{s}^{cbn}(N))$, where $\hat{s}^{cbn}(M) = (\{([\langle M\rangle^{cbn}], [])^1\}, A^0)$.*

$$A^0 = ([\sigma^{cbn}], []) \qquad A^1 = ([\sigma^{cbn}], [\sigma^{cbn}]) \qquad \hat{U}^{cbn}(M) = (([\langle M\rangle^{cbn}], []), A^0)$$

$$S_{\mathcal{M}^{cbn}_\oplus} = \left(\left\{\hat{U}^{cbn}(M) \mid M \in \Lambda_\oplus\right\} \cup \left\{([\langle M\rangle^{cbn}], [\langle V\rangle^{cbn}]), A^1 \mid M \in \Lambda_\oplus, V \in \Lambda_\oplus \text{ a value }\right\}\right) \cap S_{\mathcal{M}^!_\oplus}$$

$$\mathscr{J}^\gamma_{cbn} = \mathscr{J}^\gamma \cap \{(E, F, \sigma, \tau, M, \gamma), M \in \langle\Lambda_\oplus\rangle^{cbn}\}$$

$$A_{\mathcal{M}^{cbn}_\oplus} = \{A^1\} \times \{@^1_\kappa \mid \kappa \in \mathscr{J}^\gamma_{cbn}\} \cup \{A^0\} \times A_!$$

Fig. 10. The stable fragment $\mathscr{F}^{cbn} = (S_{\mathcal{M}^{cbn}_\oplus}, A_{\mathcal{M}^{cbn}_\oplus})$.

We need now to define a set of tuple contexts preserved by $\mathscr{F}^{cbn}$, the aim of applying Proposition 4.

Definition 16. *$\mathscr{C}_{cbn}$ is the smallest set of tuple contexts such that:*

- *If $M \in \Lambda_\oplus$ with $FV(M) \subseteq \{x_1\}$, then $(\langle M\rangle^{cbn}, A^0, \sigma^{cbn}) \in \mathscr{C}_{cbn}$;*
- *If $(C, A^0, \sigma^{cbn}) \in \mathscr{C}_{cbn}$, and $C = E[x_1]$, it holds that $(E[y_1], A^1, \sigma^{cbn}) \in \mathscr{C}_{cbn}$.*

$\mathscr{C}_{cbn}$ is designed to allow us to link δ^c_{cbn} and $\delta^c_{\mathscr{C}_{cbn}}$: for any $M, N \in \Lambda_\oplus$ closed terms, it holds that $\delta^c_{cbn}(M,N) = \delta^c_{\mathscr{C}_{cbn}}(\hat{s}^{cbn}(M), \hat{s}^{cbn}(N))$. Moreover, $\mathscr{C}_{cbn}$ is preserved by the stable fragment $\mathscr{F}^{cbn}$ (the proof can be found in [7]).

Theorem 6 (Call-by-Name Full Abstraction). *δ^c_{cbn} and δ_{cbn} coincide.*

Proof. We first show that δ_{cbn} is at least as discriminating δ^c_{cbn}. Let be $M, N \in \Lambda_\oplus$. By definition of $\mathscr{L}_{\mathscr{F}^{cbn}}$, we know that $\hat{s}^{cbn}(M), \hat{s}^{cbn}(N) \in S_{\mathscr{L}_{\mathscr{F}^{cbn}}}$. Moreover, we know that $\mathscr{C}_{cbn}$ is preserved by $\mathscr{F}^{cbn}$. So we can apply Proposition 4, and we see that $\delta^c_{\mathscr{C}_{cbn}}(\hat{s}^{cbn}(M), \hat{s}^{cbn}(N)) \leq \delta_{cbn}(M,N)$, and soundness follows. When proving completeness part, we rely on an "intrinsic" characterization of δ_{cbn}. The details can be found in [7]. □

6.3 Call-by-Value

In a similar way, we can endow $\Lambda_\oplus$ with a call-by-value semantics, and embed it into $\Lambda^!_\oplus$. We are then able to define a suitable fragment of $\mathcal{M}^!_\oplus$, a suitable set of tuple contexts preserving it, and a characterization of a call-by-value context distance for $\Lambda_\oplus$ follows [7]. While the construction of the stable fragment (and the set of tuple contexts to consider) are more involved than in the call-by-name case, we noticed that the characterization we obtain seems to have some similarities with the way environmental bisimulation for a call-by-value probabilistic λ-calculus was defined in [32].

7   Related Work

This is definitely *not* the first work on metrics in the context of programming languages semantics. A very nice introduction to the topic, together with a comprehensive (although outdated) list of references can be found in [35]. One of the many uses of metrics is as an alternative to order-theoretic semantics. This has also been applied to higher-order languages, and to *deterministic* PCF [15].

If one focuses on probabilistic programming languages, the first attempts at using metrics as a way to measure "how far" two programs are, algebraically or behaviorally, are due to Giacalone et al. [18], and Desharnais et al. [11,12], who both consider process algebras in the style of Milner's CCS. Most of further work in this direction has focused on concurrent specifications. Among the recent advances in this direction (and without any hope of being comprehensive), we can cite Gebler et al.'s work on uniform continuity as a way to enforce compositionality in metric reasoning [16,17]. Great inspiration for this work came from the many contributions on metrics for labeled Markov chains and processes appeared in the last twenty years (e.g. [13,36]).

8   Conclusions

We have shown *how* the context distance can be characterized so as to simplify concrete proofs, and *to which extent* this metric trivializes. All this has been done in a universal linear λ-calculus for probabilistic computation. This clarifies to which extent refining equivalences into metrics is worth in such a scenario. The tuple-based techniques in Sect. 5.5 are potentially very interesting in view of possible applications to cryptography, as hinted in [4]. This is indeed what we are working on currently.

References

1. Barendregt, H.P.: The Lambda Calculus - Its Syntax and Semantics. Studies in Logic and the Foundations of Mathematics, vol. 103. North-Holland, Amsterdam (1984)
2. Barendregt, H.P., Dekkers, W., Statman, R.: Lambda Calculus with Types. Perspectives in Logic. Cambridge University Press, Cambridge (2013)
3. Bizjak, A., Birkedal, L.: Step-indexed logical relations for probability. In: Pitts, A. (ed.) FoSSaCS 2015. LNCS, vol. 9034, pp. 279–294. Springer, Heidelberg (2015). doi:10.1007/978-3-662-46678-0_18

4. Cappai, A., Dal Lago, U.: On equivalences, metrics, and polynomial time. In: Kosowski, A., Walukiewicz, I. (eds.) FCT 2015. LNCS, vol. 9210, pp. 311–323. Springer, Cham (2015). doi:10.1007/978-3-319-22177-9_24

5. Crubillé, R., Dal Lago, U.: On probabilistic applicative bisimulation and call-by-value λ-calculi. In: Shao, Z. (ed.) ESOP 2014. LNCS, vol. 8410, pp. 209–228. Springer, Heidelberg (2014). doi:10.1007/978-3-642-54833-8_12

6. Crubillé, R., Dal Lago, U.: Metric reasoning about λ-terms: the affine case. In: Proceedings of LICS, pp. 633–644 (2015)

7. Crubillé, R., Dal Lago, U.: Metric reasoning about λ-terms: the general case (long version) (2016). http://arxiv.org/abs/1701.05521

8. Crubillé, R., Dal Lago, U., Sangiorgi, D., Vignudelli, V.: On applicative similarity, sequentiality, and full abstraction. In: Meyer, R., Platzer, A., Wehrheim, H. (eds.) Correct System Design. LNCS, vol. 9360, pp. 65–82. Springer, Heidelberg (2015). doi:10.1007/978-3-319-23506-6_7

9. Dal Lago, U., Sangiorgi, D., Alberti, M.: On coinductive equivalences for higher-order probabilistic functional programs. In: Proceedings of POPL, pp. 297–308 (2014)

10. Dal Lago, U., Zorzi, M.: Probabilistic operational semantics for the lambda calculus. RAIRO Theor. Inform. Appl. **46**(3), 413–450 (2012)

11. Desharnais, J., Gupta, V., Jagadeesan, R., Panangaden, P.: Metrics for labeled Markov systems. In: Baeten, J.C.M., Mauw, S. (eds.) CONCUR 1999. LNCS, vol. 1664, pp. 258–273. Springer, Heidelberg (1999). doi:10.1007/3-540-48320-9_19

12. Desharnais, J., Jagadeesan, R., Gupta, V., Panangaden, P.: The metric analogue of weak bisimulation for probabilistic processes. In: Proceedings of LICS, pp. 413–422 (2002)

13. Desharnais, J., Laviolette, F., Tracol, M.: Approximate analysis of probabilistic processes: logic, simulation and games. In: Proceedings of QEST, pp. 264–273 (2008)

14. Ehrhard, T., Tasson, C., Pagani, M.: Probabilistic coherence spaces are fully abstract for probabilistic PCF. In: Proceedings of POPL, pp. 309–320 (2014)

15. Escardo, M.: A metric model of PCF. In: Proceedings of the Workshop on Realizability Semantics and Applications (1999). http://www.cs.bham.ac.uk/~mhe/papers/metricpcf.pdf

16. Gebler, D., Larsen, K.G., Tini, S.: Compositional metric reasoning with probabilistic process calculi. In: Pitts, A. (ed.) FoSSaCS 2015. LNCS, vol. 9034, pp. 230–245. Springer, Heidelberg (2015). doi:10.1007/978-3-662-46678-0_15

17. Gebler, D., Tini, S.: SOS specifications of probabilistic systems by uniformly continuous operators. In: Proceedings of CONCUR, pp. 155–168 (2015)

18. Giacalone, A., Jou, C.C., Smolka, S.A.: Algebraic reasoning for probabilistic concurrent systems. In: Proceedings of IFIP TC2, pp. 443–458. North-Holland (1990)

19. Girard, J.: Linear logic. Theor. Comput. Sci. **50**, 1–102 (1987)

20. Goldwasser, S., Micali, S.: Probabilistic encryption. J. Comput. Syst. Sci. **28**(2), 270–299 (1984)

21. Goodman, N.D., Mansinghka, V.K., Roy, D.M., Bonawitz, K., Tenenbaum, J.B.: Church: a language for generative models. In: UAI 2008, pp. 220–229 (2008)

22. Jones, C., Plotkin, G.D.: A probabilistic powerdomain of evaluations. In: Proceedings of LICS, pp. 186–195 (1989)

23. Jung, A., Tix, R.: The troublesome probabilistic powerdomain. Electron. Notes Theor. Comput. Sci. **13**, 70–91 (1998)

24. Manning, C.D., Schütze, H.: Foundations of Statistical Natural Language Processing, vol. 999. MIT Press, Cambridge (1999)

25. Mardare, R.: Logical foundations of metric behavioural theory for Markov processes. Doctoral thesis (2016, in preparation)
26. Park, S., Pfenning, F., Thrun, S.: A probabilistic language based on sampling functions. ACM Trans. Program. Lang. Syst. **31**(1), 4 (2008)
27. Pearl, J.: Probabilistic Reasoning in Intelligent Systems: Networks of Plausible Inference. Morgan Kaufmann, San Francisco (1988)
28. Plotkin, G.D.: LCF considered as a programming language. Theor. Comput. Sci. **5**(3), 223–255 (1977)
29. Ramsey, N., Pfeffer, A.: Stochastic lambda calculus and monads of probability distributions. In: Proceedings of POPL, pp. 154–165 (2002)
30. Saheb-Djahromi, N.: Probabilistic LCF. In: Winkowski, J. (ed.) MFCS 1978. LNCS, vol. 64, pp. 442–451. Springer, Heidelberg (1978). doi:10.1007/3-540-08921-7_92
31. Sangiorgi, D.: On the bisimulation proof method. Math. Struct. Comput. Sci. **8**, 447–479 (1998)
32. Sangiorgi, D., Vignudelli, V.: Environmental bisimulations for probabilistic higher-order languages. In: Proceedings of the 43rd Annual ACM SIGPLAN-SIGACT Symposium on Principles of Programming Languages, POPL 2016, St. Petersburg, FL, USA, 20–22 January 2016, pp. 595–607 (2016)
33. Simpson, A.: Reduction in a linear lambda-calculus with applications to operational semantics. In: Giesl, J. (ed.) RTA 2005. LNCS, vol. 3467, pp. 219–234. Springer, Heidelberg (2005). doi:10.1007/978-3-540-32033-3_17
34. Thrun, S.: Robotic mapping: a survey. Explor. Artif. Intell. New Millenn. **1**, 1–35 (2002)
35. van Breugel, F.: An introduction to metric semantics: operational and denotational models for programming and specification languages. Theor. Comput. Sci. **258**(1–2), 1–98 (2001)
36. van Breugel, F., Worrell, J.: A behavioural pseudometric for probabilistic transition systems. Theor. Comput. Sci. **331**(1), 115–142 (2005)

Contextual Equivalence for Probabilistic Programs with Continuous Random Variables and Scoring

Ryan Culpepper[✉] and Andrew Cobb[✉]

Northeastern University, Boston, USA
{ryanc,acobb}@ccs.neu.edu

Abstract. We present a logical relation for proving contextual equivalence in a probabilistic programming language (PPL) with continuous random variables and with a scoring operation for expressing observations and soft constraints.

Our PPL model is based on a big-step operational semantics that represents an idealized sampler with likelihood weighting. The semantics treats probabilistic non-determinism as a deterministic process guided by a source of entropy. We derive a measure on result values by aggregating (that is, integrating) the behavior of the operational semantics over the entropy space. Contextual equivalence is defined in terms of these measures, taking real events as observable behavior.

We define a logical relation and prove it sound with respect to contextual equivalence. We demonstrate the utility of the logical relation by using it to prove several useful examples of equivalences, including the equivalence of a β_v-redex and its contractum and a general form of expression re-ordering. The latter equivalence is sound for the sampling and scoring effects of probabilistic programming but not for effects like mutation or control.

1 Introduction

A universal probabilistic programming language (PPL) consists of a general-purpose language extended with two probabilistic features: the ability to make non-deterministic (probabilistic) choices and the ability to adjust the likelihood of the current execution, usually used to model conditioning. Programs that use these features in a principled way express probabilistic models, and the execution of such programs corresponds to Bayesian inference.

Universal PPLs include Church [8] and its descendants [13,22] as well as other systems and models [2,3,10,16,18,20]. In contrast, other PPLs [4,12,14,17] limit

This material is based upon work sponsored by the Air Force Research Laboratory (AFRL) and the Defense Advanced Research Projects Agency (DARPA) under Contract No. FA8750-14-C-0002. The views expressed are those of the authors and do not reflect the official policy or position of the Department of Defense or the U.S. Government.

© Springer-Verlag GmbH Germany 2017
H. Yang (Ed.): ESOP 2017, LNCS 10201, pp. 368–392, 2017.
DOI: 10.1007/978-3-662-54434-1_14

programs to more constrained structures that can be translated to intermediate representations such as Bayes nets or factor graphs.

PPLs can also be divided into those that support continuous random choices and those that support only discrete choices. Most probabilistic programming systems designed for actual use support continuous random variables, and some implement inference algorithms specialized for continuous random variables [4,21]. On the other hand, much of the literature on the semantics of PPLs has focused on discrete choice—particularly the literature on techniques for proving program equivalence such as logical relations [1] and bisimulation [19]. The semantics that do address continuous random variables and scoring [3,20] do not focus on contextual equivalence.

This paper addresses the issue of contextual equivalence in a PPL with real arithmetic, continuous random variables, and an explicit scoring operation for expressing observations and soft constraints. We present a model of such a PPL with a big-step operational semantics based on an idealized sampler with likelihood weighting; the program's evaluation is guided by a supply of random numbers from an "entropy space." Based on the operational semantics we construct a measure on the possible results of the program, and we define contextual equivalence in terms of these measures. Finally, we construct a binary logical relation, prove it sound with respect to contextual equivalence, and demonstrate proofs that conversions such as β_v and expression reordering respect contextual equivalence.

Our language and semantics are similar to that of Borgström et al. [3], except our language is simply typed and our treatment of entropy involves splitting rather than concatenating variable-length sequences. Our entropy structure reflects the independence of subexpression evaluations and simplifies the decomposition of value measures into nested integrals.

Compared with semantics for traditional languages, our model of probabilistic programming is further from the world of computable programming languages so that it can be closer to the world of measures and integration, the foundations of probability theory. It is "syntactic" rather than "denotational" in the sense that the notion of "value" includes λ-expressions rather than mathematical functions, but on the other hand these syntactic values can contain arbitrary real numbers in their bodies, and our semantics defines and manipulates measures over spaces of such values. We do not address computability in this paper, but we hope our efforts can be reconciled with previous work on incorporating the real numbers into programming languages [6,7,9].

We have formalized the language and logical relation in Coq, based on a high-level axiomatization of measures, integration, and entropy. We have formally proven the soundness of the logical relation as well as some of its applications, including β_v and restricted forms of expression reordering. The formalization can be found at

https://github.com/cobbal/ppl-ctx-equiv-coq/tree/esop-2017.

The rest of this paper is organized as follows: Sect. 2 introduces probabilistic programming with some example models expressed in our core PPL. Section 3 reviews some relevant definitions and facts from measure theory. Section 4 presents our PPL model, including its syntax, operational semantics, measure semantics, and notion of contextual equivalence. In Sect. 5 we develop a logical relation and show that it is sound with respect to contextual equivalence. Section 6 proves several useful equivalences using using the machinery provided by the logical relation.

2   Probabilistic Programming

In a probabilistic program, random variables are created implicitly as the result of stochastic effects, and dependence between random variables is determined by the flow of values from one random variable to another. Random variables need not correspond to program variables. For example, the following two programs both represent the sum of two random variables distributed uniformly on the unit interval:

– **let** $x =$ **sample**, $y =$ **sample in** $x + y$
– **sample** + **sample**

We write **sample** for the effectful expression that creates a new independent random variable distributed uniformly on the unit interval $[0, 1]$.

Values distributed according to other real-valued distributions can be obtained from a standard uniform by applying the inverse of the distribution's *cumulative distribution function* (CDF). For example, normalinvcdf(**sample**) produces a value from the standard normal distribution, with mean 0 and standard deviation 1. The familiar parameterized normal can then be defined by scaling and shifting as follows:

normal m $s \triangleq m + s *$ normalinvcdf(**sample**)

The parameters of a normal random variable can of course depend on other random variables. For example,

$m =$ **normal** 0 *wide*
$f\_ =$ **normal** m *narrow*

defines f as a function that returns random points—a fresh one each time it is called. The points are concentrated narrowly around some common point, randomly chosen once and shared. (We write $f\_$ to emphasize that f ignores its argument.)

The other feature offered by PPLs is some way of expressing *conditioning* on observed evidence. We introduce conditioning via a hypothetical **observe** form. Consider m from the program above. Our *prior belief* about m is that it is somewhere in a wide vicinity of 0. Suppose we amend the program by adding the following observations, however:

observe 9.3 **from** $f\_$
observe 8.9 **from** $f\_$
observe 9.1 **from** $f\_$

Given those observations, you might suspect that m is in a fairly narrow region around 9. Bayes' Law quantifies that belief as the *posterior distribution* on m, defined in terms of the prior and the observed evidence.

$$p(m|data) \propto p(m) \cdot p(data|m)$$

That is the essence of Bayesian inference: calculating updated distributions on "causes" given observed "effects" and a probabilistic model that relates them.

Some PPLs [5, 13, 15] provide an **observe**-like form to handle conditioning; they vary in what kinds of expressions can occur in the right-hand side of the observation. Other PPLs provide a more primitive facility, called **factor** or **score**, which takes a real number and uses it to scale the likelihood of the current values of all random variables. To represent an observation, one simply calls **factor** with $p(data|x)$; of course, if one is observing the result of a computation, one has to compute the correct probability density. For example, the first observation above would be translated as

factor (normalpdf((9.3 $-$ m) $\div$ narrow) $\div$ narrow)

The normalpdf operation computes the *probability density function* density of a standard normal, so to calculate the density for a scaled and shifted normal, we must invert the translation by subtracting the mean and dividing by the scale (*narrow*). Then, since probability densities are *derivatives*, to get the correct density of **normal** m narrow we must divide by the (absolute value of) the derivative of the translation function from the standard normal—that accounts for the second division by *narrow*.

3   Measures and Integration

This section reviews some basic definitions, theorems, and notations from measure theory. We assume that the reader is familiar with the basic notions of measure theory, including measurable spaces, σ-algebras, measures, and Lebesgue integration—that is, the notion of integrating a function with respect to a measure, not necessarily the Lebesgue measure on $\mathbb{R}$.

We write $\mathbb{R}^{\geq 0}$ for the non-negative reals—that is, $[0, \infty)$—and $\mathbb{R}^+$ for the non-negative reals extended with infinity—that is, $[0, \infty]$.

A measure $\mu : \Sigma_X \to \mathbb{R}^+$ on the measurable space (X, Σ_X) is *finite* if $\mu(X)$ is finite. It is σ-finite if X is the union of countably many X_i and $\mu(X_i)$ is finite for each X_i.

We write $\int_A f(x)\ \mu(dx)$ for the integral of the measurable function $f : X \to \mathbb{R}$ on the region $A \subseteq X$ with respect to the measure $\mu : \Sigma_X \to \mathbb{R}^+$. We occasionally abbreviate this to $\int_A f\ d\mu$ if omitting the variable of integration is convenient. We omit the region of integration A when it is the whole space X.

We rely on the following lemmas concerning the equality of integrals. Tonelli's theorem allows changing the order of integration of non-negative functions. Since all of our integrands are non-negative, it suits our needs better than Fubini's theorem. In particular, Tonelli's theorem holds even when the functions can attain infinite values as well as when the integrals are infinite.

Lemma 1 (Tonelli). *If (X, Σ_X) and (Y, Σ_Y) are measurable spaces and μ_X and μ_Y are σ-finite measures on X and Y, respectively, and $f : X \times Y \to \mathbb{R}^+$ is measurable, then*

$$\int_X \left(\int_Y f(x,y)\, \mu_Y(dy) \right) \mu_X(dx) = \int_Y \left(\int_X f(x,y)\, \mu_X(dx) \right) \mu_Y(dy)$$

The other main lemma we rely on equates two integrals when the functions and measures may not be the same but are nonetheless related. In particular, there must be a relation such that the measures agree on related sets and the functions have related pre-images—that is, the relation specifies a "coarser" structure on which the measures and functions agree. This lemma is essential for showing the observable equivalence of measures derived from syntactically different expressions.

Lemma 2 (Coarsening). *Let (X, Σ_X) be a measurable space, $M \subseteq (\Sigma_X \times \Sigma_X)$ be a binary relation on measurable sets, $\mu_1, \mu_2 : \Sigma_X \to \mathbb{R}^+$ be measures on X, and $f_1, f_2 : X \to \mathbb{R}^+$ be measurable functions on X. If the measures agree on M-related sets and if the functions have M-related pre-images—that is,*

- *$\forall (A_1, A_2) \in M, \ \mu_1(A_1) = \mu_2(A_2)$*
- *$\forall B \in \Sigma_\mathbb{R}, \ (f_1^{-1}(B), f_2^{-1}(B)) \in M$*

then their corresponding integrals are equal:

$$\int f_1 \, d\mu_1 = \int f_2 \, d\mu_2$$

Proof. Together the two conditions imply that

$$\forall B \in \Sigma_\mathbb{R}, \ \mu_1(f_1^{-1}(B)) = \mu_2(f_2^{-1}(B))$$

We apply this equality after rewriting the integrals using the "layer cake" perspective to make the pre-images explicit [11].

$$\int f_1 \, d\mu_1 = \int_0^\infty \mu_1(f_1^{-1}([t, \infty]))\, dt$$
$$= \int_0^\infty \mu_2(f_2^{-1}([t, \infty]))\, dt$$
$$= \int f_2 \, d\mu_2$$

□

Even though in the proof we immediately dispense with the intermediate relation M, we find it useful in the applications of the lemma to identify the relationship that justifies the agreement of the functions and measures.

A useful special case of Lemma 2 is when the measures are the same and the relation is equality of measure.

Lemma 3. *Let $f, g : X \to \mathbb{R}^+$ and let μ_X be a measure on X. If $\forall B \in \Sigma_\mathbb{R}, \ \mu_X(f^{-1}(B)) = \mu_X(g^{-1}(B))$, then $\int f \, d\mu = \int g \, d\mu$.*

Proof. Special case of Lemma 2.

□

$$e ::= r \mid x \mid \lambda x : \tau.\, e \mid e\, e \mid op^n(e_1, \cdots, e_n) \mid \textbf{sample} \mid \textbf{factor } e$$
$$v ::= r \mid x \mid \lambda x : \tau.\, e$$
$$r \in \mathbb{R}$$
$$op^1 ::= \log \mid \exp \mid \text{normalpdf} \mid \text{normalinvcdf} \mid \cdots$$
$$op^2 ::= + \mid - \mid * \mid \div \mid \cdots$$

$$\tau ::= \mathbb{R} \mid \tau \to \tau$$

Fig. 1. Syntax

$$\frac{}{\Gamma \vdash r : \mathbb{R}} \qquad \frac{\Gamma(x) = \tau}{\Gamma \vdash x : \tau} \qquad \frac{\Gamma[x \mapsto \tau'] \vdash e : \tau}{\Gamma \vdash (\lambda x : \tau'.\, e) : \tau' \to \tau} \qquad \frac{\Gamma \vdash e : \tau' \to \tau \qquad \Gamma \vdash e' : \tau'}{\Gamma \vdash e\, e' : \tau}$$

$$\frac{op^n : (\tau_1, \cdots, \tau_n) \to \tau \qquad \Gamma \vdash e_i : \tau_i}{\Gamma \vdash op^n(e_1, \cdots, e_n) : \tau} \qquad \frac{}{\Gamma \vdash \textbf{sample} : \mathbb{R}} \qquad \frac{\Gamma \vdash e : \mathbb{R}}{\Gamma \vdash \textbf{factor } e : \mathbb{R}}$$

$$\log, \exp, \text{normalpdf}, \text{normalinvcdf} : (\mathbb{R}) \to \mathbb{R}$$
$$+, -, *, \div : (\mathbb{R}, \mathbb{R}) \to \mathbb{R}$$

Fig. 2. Type rules

4   Syntax and Semantics

This section presents the syntax and semantics of a language for probabilistic programming, based on a functional core extended with real arithmetic and stochastic effects.

We define the semantics of this language in two stages. We first define a big-step evaluation relation based on an idealized sampler with likelihood weighting; the evaluation rules consult an "entropy source" which determines the random behavior of a program. From this sampling semantics we then construct an aggregate view of the program as a *measure* on syntactic values. Contextual equivalence is defined in terms of these value measures.

4.1   Syntax

Figure 1 presents the syntax of our core probabilistic programming language. The language consists of a simply-typed lambda calculus extended with real arithmetic and two effects: a **sample** form for random behavior and a **factor** form for expressing observations and soft constraints. Figure 2 gives the type rules for the language.

The **sample** form returns a real number uniformly distributed between 0 and 1. We assume inverse-CDF and PDF operations—used to produce samples and score observations, respectively—for every primitive real-valued distribution of interest. Recall from Sect. 2 that sampling a normal random variable is accomplished as follows:

normal $m\ s \triangleq m + s *$ normalinvcdf(**sample**)

and observing a normal random variable is expressed thus:

factor (normalpdf(($data - m$) $\div$ s) $\div$ s)

A Note on Notation: We drop the type annotations on bound variables when they are obvious from the context, and we use syntactic sugar for local bindings and sequencing; for example, we write

let $x =$ **sample in factor** $1 \div x$; x

instead of

$(\lambda x : \mathbb{R}.\ ((\lambda \_ : \mathbb{R}.\ x)\ (\textbf{factor}\ 1 \div X)))$ **sample**

4.2 Evaluation Relation

If we interpret evaluation as idealized importance sampling, the evaluation relation tells us how to produce a single sample given the initial state of the random number generator. Evaluation is defined via the judgment

$$\sigma \vdash e \Downarrow v, w$$

where $\sigma \in \mathbb{S}$ is an entropy source, e is the expression to evaluate, v is the resulting value, and $w \in \mathbb{R}^{\geq 0}$ is the likelihood weight (Fig. 3).

The σ argument acts as the source of randomness—evaluation is a deterministic function of e and σ. Rather than threading σ through evaluation like a store, rules with multiple sub-derivations split the entropy. The indexed family of functions $\pi_i : \mathbb{S} \to \mathbb{S}$ splits the entropy source into independent pieces and $\pi_U : \mathbb{S} \to [0, 1]$ extracts a real number on the unit interval. We discuss the structure of the entropy space further in Sect. 4.3.

The result of evaluation is a closed value: either a real number or a closed λ-expression. Let $[\![\tau]\!]$ be the set of all closed values of type τ. We consider $[\![\tau]\!]$ a measurable space with a σ-algebra $\Sigma_{[\![\tau]\!]}$. See the comments on measurability at the end of this section. Note that the σ-algebras for function types are defined on syntactic values, not for mathematical functions, so we avoid the issues concerning measurable function spaces [20].

The evaluation rules for the language's functional fragment are unsurprising. For simple expressions, the entropy is ignored and the likelihood weight is 1. For compound expressions, the entropy is split and sent to sub-expression evaluations, and the resulting weights are multiplied together. We assume a partial function δ that interprets the primitive operations.[1] For example, $\delta(+, 1, 2) = 3$ and $\delta(\div, 4, 0)$ is undefined.

The rule for **sample** extracts a real number uniformly distributed on the unit interval $[0, 1]$. The **factor** form evaluates its subexpression and interprets it as a

---

[1] No relation to the Dirac measure, also often written δ.

CONST
$$\overline{\sigma \vdash r \Downarrow r, 1}$$

LAM
$$\overline{\sigma \vdash \lambda x. e \Downarrow \lambda x. e, 1}$$

APP
$$\frac{\pi_1(\sigma) \vdash e_1 \Downarrow \lambda x. e_b, w_1 \qquad \pi_2(\sigma) \vdash e_2 \Downarrow v_2, w_2 \qquad \pi_3(\sigma) \vdash e_b\,[x \mapsto v_2] \Downarrow v, w_3}{\sigma \vdash e_1\ e_2 \Downarrow v, w_1 \cdot w_2 \cdot w_3}$$

PRIMOP
$$\frac{\pi_i(\sigma) \vdash e_i \Downarrow v_i, w_i \qquad v = \delta(op^n, v_1, \cdots, v_n) \qquad w = \prod_{i=1}^{n} w_i}{\sigma \vdash op^n(e_1, \cdots, e_n) \Downarrow v, w}$$

SAMPLE
$$\frac{r = \pi_U(\sigma)}{\sigma \vdash \textbf{sample} \Downarrow r, 1}$$

FACTOR
$$\frac{\sigma \vdash e \Downarrow r, w \qquad r > 0}{\sigma \vdash \textbf{factor}\ e \Downarrow r, r \cdot w}$$

Fig. 3. Evaluation rules

likelihood weight to be factored into the weight of the current execution—but only if it is positive.

There are two ways evaluation can fail:

- the argument to **factor** is zero or negative
- the δ function is undefined for an operation with a particular set of arguments, such as for $1 \div 0$ or $\log(-5)$

The semantics does not distinguish these situations; in both cases, no evaluation derivation tree exists for that particular combination of σ and e.

4.3 Entropy Space

The evaluation relation of Sect. 4.2 represents evaluation of a probabilistic program as a deterministic partial function of points in an entropy space $\mathbb{S}$. To capture the meaning of a program, we must consider the aggregate behavior over the entire entropy space. That requires integration, which in turn requires a measurable space $(\Sigma_\mathbb{S})$ and a base measure on entropy $(\mu_\mathbb{S} : \Sigma_\mathbb{S} \to \mathbb{R}^+)$.

The entropy space must support our formulation of evaluation, which roughly corresponds to the following transformation:

$$\begin{matrix} & & \sigma \sim \mu_\mathbb{S} \\ x_1 \sim D_1 & & x_1 = \text{invcdf}_{D_1}(\pi_1(\sigma)) \\ \vdots & \Rightarrow & \vdots \\ x_n \sim D_n & & x_n = \text{invcdf}_{D_n}(\pi_n(\sigma)) \end{matrix}$$

The entropy space and its associated functions are ours to choose, provided they satisfy the following criteria:

- It must be a probability space. That is, $\mu_{\mathbb{S}}(\mathbb{S}) = 1$.
- It must be able to represent common real-valued random variables. It is sufficient to support a *standard uniform*—that is, a random variable uniformly distributed on the interval $[0, 1]$. Other distributions can be represented via the inverse-CDF transformation.
- It must support multiple *independent* random variables. That is, the entropy space must be isomorphic—in a measure-preserving way—to products of itself: $\mathbb{S} \cong \mathbb{S}^2 \cong \mathbb{S}^n \quad (n \geq 1)$.

The following specification formalizes these criteria.

Definition 4 (Entropy). $(\mathbb{S}, \Sigma_{\mathbb{S}})$ *is a measurable space with measure* $\mu_{\mathbb{S}}$: $\Sigma_{\mathbb{S}} \to \mathbb{R}^+$ *and functions*

$$\pi_U : \mathbb{S} \to [0, 1]$$
$$\pi_L, \pi_R : \mathbb{S} \to \mathbb{S}$$

such that the following integral equations hold:

- $\mu_{\mathbb{S}}(\mathbb{S}) = 1$, *and thus for all* $k \in \mathbb{R}^+$, $\int k \, \mu_{\mathbb{S}}(d\sigma) = k$,
- *for all measurable functions* $f : [0, 1] \to \mathbb{R}^+$,

$$\int f(\pi_U(\sigma)) \, \mu_{\mathbb{S}}(d\sigma) = \int_{[0,1]} f(x) \, \lambda(dx)$$

  where λ *is the Lebesgue measure, and*
- *for all measurable functions* $g : \mathbb{S} \times \mathbb{S} \to \mathbb{R}^+$,

$$\int g(\pi_L(\sigma), \pi_R(\sigma)) \, \mu_{\mathbb{S}}(d\sigma) = \iint g(\sigma_1, \sigma_2) \, \mu_{\mathbb{S}}(d\sigma_1) \, \mu_{\mathbb{S}}(d\sigma_2)$$

That is, π_U interprets the entropy as a standard uniform random variable, and π_L and π_R split the entropy into a pair of independent parts and return the first or second part, respectively. We generalize from two-way splits to indexed splits via the following family of functions:

Definition 5 (π_i). *Let* $\pi_i : \mathbb{S} \to \mathbb{S}$ *be the family of functions defined thus:*

$$\pi_1(\sigma) = \pi_L(\sigma)$$
$$\pi_{n+1}(\sigma) = \pi_n(\pi_R(\sigma))$$

Definition 5 is "wasteful"—for any $n \in \mathbb{N}$, using only $\pi_1(\sigma)$ through $\pi_n(\sigma)$ discards part of the entropy—but that does not cause problems, because the wasted entropy is independent and thus integrates away. Thus the a generalized entropy-splitting identity holds for measurable $f : \mathbb{S}^n \to \mathbb{R}^+$:

$$\int f(\pi_1(\sigma), \cdots, \pi_n(\sigma)) \, \mu_{\mathbb{S}}(d\sigma) = \int \cdots \int f(\sigma_1, \cdots, \sigma_n) \, \mu_{\mathbb{S}}(d\sigma_1) \cdots \mu_{\mathbb{S}}(d\sigma_n)$$

Our preferred concrete representation of $\mathbb{S}$ is the countable product of unit intervals, $[0,1]^\omega$, sometimes called the Hilbert cube. The π_L, π_R, and π_U functions are defined as follows:

$$\pi_L(\langle u_0, u_1, u_2, u_3, \dots \rangle) = \langle u_0, u_2, \dots \rangle$$
$$\pi_R(\langle u_0, u_1, u_2, u_3, \dots \rangle) = \langle u_1, u_3, \dots \rangle$$
$$\pi_U(\langle u_0, u_1, u_2, u_3, \dots \rangle) = u_0$$

The σ-algebra $\Sigma_\mathbb{S}$ is the Borel algebra of the product topology (cf Tychonoff's Theorem). The basis of the product topology is the set of products of intervals, only finitely many of which are not the whole unit interval $U = [0,1]$:

$$\left\{ \left(\prod_{i=1}^{k}(a_i, b_i) \right) \times U^\omega \quad | \quad 0 \le a_i \le b_i \le 1, k \in \mathbb{N} \right\}$$

We define the measure $\mu_\mathbb{S}$ on a basis element as follows:

$$\mu_\mathbb{S}\left(\left(\prod_{i=1}^{k}(a_i, b_i) \right) \times U^\omega \right) = \prod_{i=1}^{k}(b_i - a_i)$$

That uniquely determines the measure $\mu_\mathbb{S} : \Sigma_\mathbb{S} \to \mathbb{R}^+$ by the Carathéodory extension theorem.

Another representation of entropy is the Borel space on $[0,1]$ with (restricted) Lebesgue measure and bit-splitting π_L and π_R. In fact, both of these representations are examples of *standard atomless probability spaces*, and all such spaces are isomorphic (modulo null sets). In the rest of the paper, we rely only on the guarantees of Definition 4, not on the precise representation of $\mathbb{S}$.

4.4   Measure Semantics

We represent the aggregate behavior of a closed expression as a measure, obtained by integrating the behavior of the evaluation relation over the entropy space. If $\vdash e : \tau$ then $\mu_e : \Sigma_{[\![\tau]\!]} \to \mathbb{R}^+$ is the *value measure of e*, defined as follows:

Definition 6 (Value Measure)

$$\mu_e(V) = \int \text{evalin}(e, V, \sigma) \, \mu_\mathbb{S}(d\sigma)$$

$$\text{evalin}(e, V, \sigma) = \mathbb{I}_V(\text{ev}(e, \sigma)) \cdot \text{ew}(e, \sigma)$$

$$\text{ev}(e, \sigma) = \begin{cases} v & \text{if } \sigma \vdash e \Downarrow v, w \\ \bot & \text{otherwise} \end{cases}$$

$$\text{ew}(e, \sigma) = \begin{cases} w & \text{if } \sigma \vdash e \Downarrow v, w \\ 0 & \text{otherwise} \end{cases}$$

The evaluation relation $\sigma \vdash e \Downarrow v, w$ is a partial function of (σ, e)—non-deterministic behavior is represented as deterministic dependence on the entropy σ. From this partial function we define a total evaluation function $\mathrm{ev}(e, \sigma)$ and a total weighting function $\mathrm{ew}(e, \sigma)$. The $\mathrm{evalin}(e, V, \sigma)$ function takes a measurable outcome set of interest and checks whether the result of evaluation falls within that set. If so, it produces the weight of the evaluation; otherwise, it produces 0. We write $\mathbb{I}_X$ for the indicator function for X, which returns 1 if its argument is in X and 0 otherwise.

Integrating $\mathrm{evalin}(e, V, \sigma)$ over the entire entropy space yields the value measure μ_e. Strictly speaking, the definition above defines μ_e as a measure on $[\![\tau]\!]_\bot$, but since $\mathrm{ev}(e, \sigma) = \bot$ only when $\mathrm{ew}(e, \sigma) = 0$, μ_e never assigns any weight to $\bot$ and thus we can consider it a measure on $[\![\tau]\!]$.

The following theorem shows that the value measure is an adequate representation of the behavior of a program.

Theorem 7. *Let* $f : [\![\tau]\!] \to \mathbb{R}^+$ *be measurable, and let* $\vdash e : \tau$. *Then*

$$\int f(v) \, \mu_e(dv) = \int f(\mathrm{ev}(e, \sigma)) \cdot \mathrm{ew}(e, \sigma) \, \mu_{\mathbb{S}}(d\sigma)$$

Proof. First consider the case where f is an indicator function $\mathbb{I}_X$:

$$\int f(v) \, \mu_e(dv) = \int \mathbb{I}_X(v) \, \mu_e(dv) \qquad\qquad (f = \mathbb{I}_X)$$

$$= \mu_e(X) \qquad\qquad \text{(integral of indicator function)}$$

$$= \int \mathbb{I}_X(\mathrm{ev}(e, \sigma)) \cdot \mathrm{ew}(e, \sigma) \, \mu_{\mathbb{S}}(d\sigma) \qquad\qquad \text{(Definition 6)}$$

$$= \int f(\mathrm{ev}(e, \sigma)) \cdot \mathrm{ew}(e, \sigma) \, \mu_{\mathbb{S}}(d\sigma) \qquad\qquad (f = \mathbb{I}_X)$$

The equality extends to simple functions—linear combinations of characteristic functions—by the linearity of integration and to measurable functions as the suprema of sets of simple functions. □

Measurability. For the integral defining $\mu_e(V)$ to be well-defined, evalin (e, V, σ) must be measurable when considered as a function of σ. Furthermore, in later proofs we will need the $\mathrm{ev}(\cdot, \cdot)$ and $\mathrm{ew}(\cdot, \cdot)$ functions to be measurable with respect to the product space on their arguments. More precisely, if we consider a type-indexed family of functions

$$\mathrm{ev}_\tau : \mathrm{Expr}[\![\tau]\!] \times \mathbb{S} \to [\![\tau]\!]$$

then we need each ev_τ to be measurable in $\Sigma_{[\![\tau]\!]}$ with respect to the product measurable space $\Sigma_{\mathrm{Expr}[\![\tau]\!]} \times \Sigma_{\mathbb{S}}$, and likewise for ew_τ. Note that the space of values $[\![\tau]\!]$ is a subset of the expressions $\mathrm{Expr}[\![\tau]\!]$, so we can take $\Sigma_{[\![\tau]\!]}$ to be $\Sigma_{\mathrm{Expr}[\![\tau]\!]}$ restricted to the values. But we must still define $\Sigma_{\mathrm{Expr}[\![\tau]\!]}$ and show the functions are measurable.

We do not present a direct proof of measurability in this paper. Instead, we rely again on Borgström et al. [3]: we treat their language, for which they have proven measurability, as a meta-language. Interpreters for the ev and ew functions of our language can be written as terms in this meta-language, and thus their measurability result can be carried over to our language. We take $\mathbb{S} = [0,1]$ and extend the meta-language with the measurable functions π_L, π_R, and π_U. The definition of $\Sigma_{\mathrm{Expr}[\![\tau]\!]}$ is induced by the encoding function that represents our object terms as values in their meta-language and the structure of their measurable space of expressions.

4.5   Digression: Interpretation of Probabilistic Programs

In general, the goal of a probabilistic programming language is to interpret programs as probability distributions.

If a program's value measure is finite and non-zero, then it can be normalized to yield a probability distribution. The following examples explore different classes of such programs:

- Continuous measures: **sample**, normalinvcdf(**sample**), etc.
- Discrete measures: **if sample** < 0.2 **then** 1 **else** 0
- Sub-probability measures:

   let $x =$ normalinvcdf(**sample**) **in if** $x < 0$ **then factor** 0 **else** x

- Mixtures of discrete and continuous: for example,

   let $x =$ **sample in if** $x < 0.5$ **then** 0 **else** x

   has a point mass at 0 and is continuous on (0.5, 1).

Our language, however, includes programs that have no interpretation as distributions:

- Zero measure: **factor** 0
- Infinite (but σ-finite) measures. For example,

   let $x =$ **sample in factor** $(1 \div x)$; x

   has infinite measure because $\int_0^1 \frac{1}{x}\, dx$ is infinite. But the measure is σ-finite because each interval $[\frac{1}{n}, 1]$ has finite measure and the union of all such intervals covers $(0,1]$, the support of the measure.
- Non-σ-finite measures. For example,

   let $x =$ **sample in factor** $(1 \div x)$; 0

   has $\mu(0) = \infty$. (We conjecture that all value measures definable in this language are either σ-finite or have a point with infinite weight.)

$$C ::= [\,] \mid \lambda x : \tau.\, C \mid C\; e \mid e\; C \mid op(e, \cdots, C, e, \cdots) \mid \textbf{factor}\; C$$

$$\overline{[\,] : \emptyset} \qquad\qquad \frac{C : \Gamma}{(\lambda x : \tau.\, C) : \Gamma[x \mapsto \tau]}$$

$$\frac{C : \Gamma}{C\; e : \Gamma} \qquad \frac{C : \Gamma}{e\; C : \Gamma} \qquad \frac{C : \Gamma}{op(e, \cdots, C, e, \cdots) : \Gamma} \qquad \frac{C : \Gamma}{\textbf{factor}\; C : \Gamma}$$

Fig. 4. Contexts

Zero measures indicate unsatisfiable constraints; more precisely, the set of successful evaluations may not be empty, merely measure zero.

Infinite value measures arise only from the use of **factor**; the value measure of a program that does not contain **factor** is always a sub-probability measure. It may not be a probability measure—recall that $1 \div 0$ and **factor** 0 both cause execution to fail. We could eliminate infinite-measure programs by sacrificing expressiveness. For example, if the valid arguments to **factor** were restricted to the range $(0, 1]$, as in Börgstrom et al. [3], only sub-probability measures would be expressible. But there are good reasons to allow **factor** with numbers greater than 1, such as representing the observation of a normal random variable with a small variance—perhaps a variance computed from another random variable. There is no simple syntactic rule that excludes the infinite-measure programs above without also excluding some useful applications of **factor**.

Note that the theorems in this paper apply to *all* programs, regardless of whether they can be interpreted as probability distributions. In particular, we apply Lemma 1 (Tonelli) only to integrals over $\mu_{\mathbb{S}}$, which is finite.

4.6   Contextual Equivalence

Two expressions are contextually equivalent ($=_{\text{ctx}}$) if for all closing program contexts C their observable aggregate behavior is the same. We take *programs* to be real-valued closed expressions; their *observable behavior* consists of their value measures ($\Sigma_{\mathbb{R}} \to \mathbb{R}^+$).

Figure 4 defines contexts and their relationship with type environments. The relation $C : \Gamma$ means that C provides bindings satisfying Γ to the expression placed in its hole.

Definition 8 (Contextual equivalence) *If $\Gamma \vdash e_1 : \tau$ and $\Gamma \vdash e_2 : \tau$, then e_1 and e_2 are contextually equivalent ($e_1 =_{\text{ctx}}^{\Gamma} e_2$) if and only if for all contexts C such that $C : \Gamma$ and $\vdash C[e_1] : \mathbb{R}$ and $\vdash C[e_2] : \mathbb{R}$ and for all measurable sets $A \in \Sigma_{\mathbb{R}}$,*

$$\mu_{C[e_1]}(A) = \mu_{C[e_2]}(A)$$

Instances of contextual equivalence are difficult to prove directly because of the quantification over all syntactic contexts.

Definition 9 ($\approx$)

$$\Gamma \vdash e_1 \approx e_2 : \tau \iff \forall(\gamma_1, \gamma_2) \in \mathcal{G}[\![\Gamma]\!], \ (e_1 \cdot \gamma_1, e_2 \cdot \gamma_2) \in \mathcal{E}[\![\tau]\!]$$

$$(r_1, r_2) \in \mathcal{V}[\![\mathbb{R}]\!] \iff r_1 = r_2$$
$$(\lambda x. e_1, \lambda x. e_2) \in \mathcal{V}[\![\tau_1 \to \tau_2]\!] \iff \forall(v_1, v_2) \in \mathcal{V}[\![\tau_1]\!], \ (e_1\,[x \mapsto v_1]\,, e_2\,[x \mapsto v_2]) \in \mathcal{E}[\![\tau_2]\!]$$

$$(\gamma_1, \gamma_2) \in \mathcal{G}[\![\Gamma]\!] \iff \gamma_1 \models \Gamma \ \wedge \ \gamma_2 \models \Gamma \ \wedge \ \forall x \in \mathrm{dom}(\Gamma), \ (\gamma_1(x), \gamma_2(x)) \in \mathcal{V}[\![\Gamma(x)]\!]$$

$$(e_1, e_2) \in \mathcal{E}[\![\tau]\!] \iff \forall(A_1, A_2) \in \mathcal{A}[\![\tau]\!], \ \mu_{e_1}(A_1) = \mu_{e_2}(A_2)$$

$$(A_1, A_2) \in \mathcal{A}[\![\tau]\!] \iff A_1, A_2 \in \Sigma_{[\![\tau]\!]} \ \wedge \ \forall(v_1, v_2) \in \mathcal{V}[\![\tau]\!], \ (v_1 \in A_1 \iff v_2 \in A_2)$$

Fig. 5. Logical relation and auxiliary relations

5 A Logical Relation for Contextual Equivalence

In this section we develop a logical relation for proving expressions contextually equivalent. Membership in the logical relation implies contextual equivalence but is easier to prove directly. We prove soundness via compatibility lemmas, one for each kind of compound expression. The fundamental property (a form of reflexivity) enables simplifications to the logical relation that we take advantage of in Sect. 6 when applying the relation to particular equivalences.

Figure 5 defines the relation

$$\Gamma \vdash e_1 \approx e_2 : \tau$$

and its auxiliary relations (Definition 9). In a deterministic language, we would construct the relation so that two expressions are related if they produce related values when evaluated with related substitutions. In our probabilistic language, two expressions are related if they have related *value measures* when evaluated with related substitutions. (The notation $e \cdot \gamma$ indicates the substitution γ applied to the expression e.)

The $\approx$ relation depends on the following auxiliary relations:

- $\mathcal{V}[\![\tau]\!]$ relates closed values of type τ. Real values are related if they are identical, and functions are related if they take related inputs to related evaluation configurations ($\mathcal{E}[\![\tau]\!]$).
- $\mathcal{G}[\![\Gamma]\!]$ relates substitutions. Variables are mapped to related values.
- $\mathcal{E}[\![\tau]\!]$ relates closed expressions. Expressions are related if their value measures agree on measurable sets related by $\mathcal{A}[\![\tau]\!]$.
- $\mathcal{A}[\![\tau]\!]$ relates measurable sets of values.

When comparing value measures, we must not demand complete equality of the measures; instead, we only require that they agree on $\mathcal{V}[\![\tau]\!]$-closed measurable value sets. To see why, consider the expressions $\lambda x.\, x + 2$ and $\lambda x.\, x + 1 + 1$. As values, they are related by $\mathcal{V}[\![\mathbb{R} \to \mathbb{R}]\!]$. As expressions, we want them to be related by $\mathcal{E}[\![\mathbb{R} \to \mathbb{R}]\!]$, but their value measures are not identical; they are Dirac measures on different—but related—syntactic values. In particular:

- $\mu_{\lambda x.\, x+2}(\{\lambda x.\, x + 2\}) = 1$, but
- $\mu_{\lambda x.\, x+1+1}(\{\lambda x.\, x + 2\}) = 0$

The solution is to compare measures only on related measurable sets. For every value in the set given to the first measure, we must include every related value in the set given to the second measure (and vice versa). This relaxation on measure equivalence preserves the spirit of "related computations produce related results."

Lemma 10 (Symmetry and transitivity). $\mathcal{V}[\![\tau]\!]$, $\mathcal{G}[\![\Gamma]\!]$, $\mathcal{E}[\![\tau]\!]$, $\mathcal{A}[\![\tau]\!]$, and $\approx$ are symmetric and transitive.

Proof. The symmetry and transitivity of $\approx$ and $\mathcal{G}$ follow from that of $\mathcal{E}$ and $\mathcal{V}$.

We prove symmetry and transitivity of $\mathcal{V}[\![\tau]\!]$, $\mathcal{E}[\![\tau]\!]$, and $\mathcal{A}[\![\tau]\!]$ simultaneously by induction on τ. For a given τ, the properties of $\mathcal{E}[\![\tau]\!]$ and $\mathcal{A}[\![\tau]\!]$ follow from $\mathcal{V}[\![\tau]\!]$. The $\mathbb{R}$ case is trivial. Transitivity for $\mathcal{V}[\![\tau' \to \tau]\!]$ is subtle; given $(v_1, v_3) \in \mathcal{V}[\![\tau']\!]$, we must find a v_2 such that $(v_1, v_2) \in \mathcal{V}[\![\tau']\!]$ and $(v_2, v_3) \in \mathcal{V}[\![\tau']\!]$ in order to use transitivity of $\mathcal{E}[\![\tau]\!]$ (induction hypothesis). But we can use symmetry and transitivity of $\mathcal{V}[\![\tau']\!]$ (also induction hypotheses) to show $(v_1, v_1) \in \mathcal{V}[\![\tau']\!]$, so v_1 is a suitable value for v_2. $\qquad\square$

The reflexivity of $\mathcal{V}$, $\mathcal{E}$, $\mathcal{G}$, and $\approx$ is harder to prove. In fact, it is a corollary of the fundamental property of the logical relation (Theorem 15).

5.1   Compatibility Lemmas

The compatibility lemmas show that expression pairs built from related components are themselves related. Equivalently, they allow the substitution of related expressions in single-frame contexts. Given the compatibility lemmas, soundness with respect to contextual equivalence with arbitrary contexts is a short inductive hop away.

Lemma 11 (Lambda Compatibility).

$$\frac{\Gamma, x : \tau' \vdash e_1 \approx e_2 : \tau}{\Gamma \vdash (\lambda x : \tau'.\, e_1) \approx (\lambda x : \tau'.\, e_2) : \tau' \to \tau}$$

Proof. Let $(\gamma_1, \gamma_2) \in \mathcal{G}[\![\Gamma]\!]$. We must prove that $\lambda x.\, e_i \cdot \gamma_i$ are in $\mathcal{E}[\![\tau' \to \tau]\!]$—that is, the corresponding value measures $\mu_{\lambda x.\, e_i \cdot \gamma_i}$ agree on all $(A_1, A_2) \in \mathcal{A}[\![\tau' \to \tau]\!]$.

The value measure $\mu_{\lambda x.\, e_i \cdot \gamma_i}$ is concentrated at $\lambda x.\, e_i \cdot \gamma_i$ with weight 1, so the measures are related if those closures are related in $\mathcal{V}[\![\tau' \to \tau]\!]$. That in turn requires that $(e_i \cdot \gamma_i)\, [x \mapsto v_i]$ be related in $\mathcal{E}[\![\tau]\!]$ for $(v_1, v_2) \in \mathcal{V}[\![\tau']\!]$. That follows from $\Gamma, x : \tau' \vdash e_1 \approx e_2 : \tau$, instantiated at $[\gamma_i, x \mapsto v_i]$. $\qquad\square$

Lemma 12 (App Compatibility).

$$\frac{\Gamma \vdash e_1 \approx e_2 : \tau' \rightarrow \tau \quad \Gamma \vdash e_1' \approx e_2' : \tau'}{\Gamma \vdash e_1 \ e_1' \approx e_2 \ e_2' : \tau}$$

Proof. By the premises, the $\mu_{e_i \cdot \gamma_i}$ measures agree on $\mathcal{A}[\![\tau' \rightarrow \tau]\!]$, and the $\mu_{e_i' \cdot \gamma_i}$ measures agree on $\mathcal{A}[\![\tau']\!]$. Our strategy is to use Lemma 2 (Coarsening) to rewrite the integrals after unpacking the definition of the value measures and the APP rule. The applyin function defined as follows

$$\text{applyin}(\lambda x. \, e, v', A, \sigma) = \text{evalin}(e \, [x \mapsto v'] \, , A, \sigma)$$

is useful for expressing the unfolding of the APP rule.

Let $(\gamma_1, \gamma_2) \in \mathcal{G}[\![\Gamma]\!]$. We must prove the expressions $(e_i \ e_i') \cdot \gamma_i$ are in $\mathcal{E}[\![\tau]\!]$.

After unfolding $\mathcal{E}$ and introducing $(A_1, A_2) \in \mathcal{A}[\![\tau]\!]$, we must show the corresponding value measures agree:

$$\mu_{(e_1 \ e_1') \cdot \gamma_1}(A_1) = \mu_{(e_2 \ e_2') \cdot \gamma_2}(A_2)$$

We rewrite each side as follows:

$$\mu_{(e_i \ e_i') \cdot \gamma_i}(A_i)$$

$$= \int \text{evalin}((e_i \ e_i') \cdot \gamma_i, A_i, \sigma) \ \mu_{\mathbb{S}}(d\sigma) \qquad \text{(by Definition 6)}$$

$$= \int \text{applyin}(\text{ev}(e_i \cdot \gamma_i, \pi_1(\sigma)), \text{ev}(e_i' \cdot \gamma_i, \pi_2(\sigma)), A_i, \pi_3(\sigma)) \qquad \text{(by APP)}$$
$$\cdot \text{ew}(e_i \cdot \gamma_i, \pi_1(\sigma)) \cdot \text{ew}(e_i' \cdot \gamma_i, \pi_2(\sigma)) \ \mu_{\mathbb{S}}(d\sigma)$$

$$= \iiint \text{applyin}(\text{ev}(e_i \cdot \gamma_i, \sigma_1), \text{ev}(e_i' \cdot \gamma_i, \sigma_2), A_i, \sigma_3)$$
$$\cdot \text{ew}(e_i \cdot \gamma_i, \sigma_1) \cdot \text{ew}(e_i' \cdot \gamma_i, \sigma_2) \ \mu_{\mathbb{S}}(d\sigma_3) \ \mu_{\mathbb{S}}(d\sigma_2) \ \mu_{\mathbb{S}}(d\sigma_1)$$
$$\qquad \text{(by Proposition 4)}$$

$$= \iiint \text{applyin}(v, v', A_i, \sigma_3) \ \mu_{\mathbb{S}}(d\sigma_3) \ \mu_{e_i' \cdot \gamma_i}(dv') \ \mu_{e_i \cdot \gamma_i}(dv) \quad \text{(by Theorem 7)}$$

After rewriting both sides, we have the goal

$$\iiint \text{applyin}(v, v', A_1, \sigma) \ \mu_{\mathbb{S}}(d\sigma) \ \mu_{e_1' \cdot \gamma_1}(dv') \ \mu_{e_1 \cdot \gamma_1}(dv)$$

$$= \iiint \text{applyin}(v, v', A_2, \sigma) \ \mu_{\mathbb{S}}(d\sigma) \ \mu_{e_2' \cdot \gamma_2}(dv') \ \mu_{e_2 \cdot \gamma_2}(dv)$$

We show this equality via Lemma 2 (Coarsening) using the binary relation $\mathcal{A}[\![\tau' \rightarrow \tau]\!]$. By the induction hypothesis we have that $\mu_{e_1 \cdot \gamma_1}, \mu_{e_2 \cdot \gamma_2}$ agree on sets in $\mathcal{A}[\![\tau' \rightarrow \tau]\!]$. That leaves one other premise to discharge: the functions must have related pre-images. Let $B \in \Sigma_{\mathbb{R}}$. We must show the pre-images are related by $\mathcal{A}[\![\tau' \to \tau]\!]$, where each pre-image is

$$\left(v \mapsto \iint \text{applyin}(v, v', A_i, \sigma) \; \mu_{\mathbb{S}}(d\sigma) \; \mu_{e'_i \cdot \gamma_i}(dv') \right)^{-1} (B)$$

To show that the function pre-images are in $\mathcal{A}[\![\tau' \to \tau]\!]$, we show something stronger: for related values the function values are the same.

Let $(v_1, v_2) \in \mathcal{V}[\![\tau' \to \tau]\!]$. We will show that

$$\iint \text{applyin}(v_1, v', A_1, \sigma) \; \mu_{\mathbb{S}}(d\sigma) \; \mu_{e'_1 \cdot \gamma_i}(dv')$$
$$= \iint \text{applyin}(v_2, v', A_2, \sigma) \; \mu_{\mathbb{S}}(d\sigma) \; \mu_{e'_2 \cdot \gamma_i}(dv')$$

We show this by again applying Lemma 2 (Coarsening), this time with the relation $\mathcal{A}[\![\tau']\!]$. Again, the induction hypothesis tells us that the measures $\mu_{e'_i \cdot \gamma_i}$ agree on sets in $\mathcal{A}[\![\tau']\!]$. We follow the same strategy for showing the function pre-images related. Let $(v'_1, v'_2) \in \mathcal{V}[\![\tau']\!]$. We must show

$$\int \text{applyin}(v_1, v'_1, A_1, \sigma) \; \mu_{\mathbb{S}}(d\sigma) = \int \text{applyin}(v_2, v'_2, A_2, \sigma) \; \mu_{\mathbb{S}}(d\sigma)$$

Since $v_1, v_2 : \tau' \to \tau$, they must be abstractions. Let $v_1 = \lambda x : \tau'. e''_1$ and likewise for v_2. Then the goal reduces to

$$\int \text{evalin}(e''_1 [x \mapsto v'_1], A_1, \sigma) \; \mu_{\mathbb{S}}(d\sigma) = \int \text{evalin}(e''_2 [x \mapsto v'_2], A_2, \sigma) \; \mu_{\mathbb{S}}(d\sigma)$$

That is, by the definition of value measure, the following:

$$\mu_{e''_1[x \mapsto v'_1]}(A_1) = \mu_{e''_2[x \mapsto v'_2]}(A_2)$$

That follows from $(v_1, v_2) \in \mathcal{V}[\![\tau' \to \tau]\!]$ and the definitions of $\mathcal{V}$ and $\mathcal{E}$. □

Lemma 13 (Op Compatibility).

$$\frac{\Gamma \vdash e_i \approx e'_i : \tau_i \qquad op^n : (\tau_1, \cdots, \tau_n) \to \tau}{\Gamma \vdash op^n(e_1, \cdots, e_n) \approx op^n(e'_1, \cdots, e'_n) : \tau}$$

Proof. Similar to but simpler than Lemma 12. Since all operations take real-valued arguments, this proof does not rely on Lemma 2. We rely on the fact that δ, the function that interprets primitive operations, takes related arguments to related results, which holds trivially because reals are related only when they are identical. □

Lemma 14 (Factor Compatibility).

$$\frac{\Gamma \vdash e \approx e' : \mathbb{R}}{\Gamma \vdash \textbf{factor } e \approx \textbf{factor } e' : \mathbb{R}}$$

Proof. Similar to Lemma 13. □

5.2   Fundamental Property

Theorem 15 (Fundamental Property). *If $\Gamma \vdash e : \tau$ then $\Gamma \vdash e \approx e : \tau$.*

Proof. By induction on $\Gamma \vdash e : \tau$.

- **Case** x. Let $(\gamma_1, \gamma_2) \in \mathcal{G}[\![\Gamma]\!]$. We must prove the value measures $\mu_{x \cdot \gamma_i}$ agree on related $(A_1, A_2) \in \mathcal{A}[\![\tau]\!]$. The measures are concentrated on $\gamma_i(x)$ with weight 1, so they agree if those values are related by $\mathcal{V}[\![\tau]\!]$, which they do because the substitutions are related by $\mathcal{G}[\![\Gamma]\!]$.
- **Case** r. The value measures are identical Dirac measures concentrated at r.
- **Case sample.** The value measures are identical.
- **Case** $\lambda x : \tau_1 . e_2$. By Lemma 11.
- **Case** $e\, e'$. By Lemma 12.
- **Case** $op^n(e_1, \cdots, e_n)$. By Lemma 13.
- **Case factor** e. By Lemma 14.

□

Corollary 16 (Reflexivity). $\mathcal{V}[\![\tau]\!]$, $\mathcal{G}[\![\Gamma]\!]$, *and* $\mathcal{E}[\![\tau]\!]$ *are reflexive.*

One consequence of the fundamental property is that the $\mathcal{A}[\![\tau]\!]$, a binary relation on measurable sets, is the least reflexive relation on measurable sets closed under the $\mathcal{V}[\![\tau]\!]$ relation. We define $\mathcal{A}'[\![\tau]\!]$ as the collection of $\mathcal{V}[\![\tau]\!]$-closed measurable sets. To show two expressions related by $\mathcal{E}[\![\tau]\!]$ it is sufficient to compare their corresponding measures applied to sets in $\mathcal{A}'[\![\tau]\!]$.

Definition 17.

$$A \in \mathcal{A}'[\![\tau]\!] \iff A \in \Sigma_{[\![\tau]\!]} \wedge \forall (v_1, v_2) \in \mathcal{V}[\![\tau]\!], \ (v_1 \in A \iff v_2 \in A)$$

Lemma 18. *If* $(A_1, A_2) \in \mathcal{A}[\![\tau]\!]$ *then* $A_1 = A_2$, *and if* $A \in \mathcal{A}'[\![\tau]\!]$ *then* $(A, A) \in \mathcal{A}[\![\tau]\!]$.

Proof. By reflexivity of $\mathcal{V}$. □

Corollary 19.

$$(e_1, e_2) \in \mathcal{E}[\![\tau]\!] \iff \forall A \in \mathcal{A}'[\![\tau]\!], \ \mu_{e_1}(A) = \mu_{e_2}(A)$$

Another consequence of the fundamental property is that to prove two expressions related by $\approx$ it suffices to show that they are $\mathcal{E}[\![\tau]\!]$-related when paired with the same arbitrary substitution.

Lemma 20 (Same Substitution Suffices). *If* $\Gamma \vdash e_1 : \tau$ *and* $\Gamma \vdash e_2 : \tau$, *and if* $(e_1 \cdot \gamma, e_2 \cdot \gamma) \in \mathcal{E}[\![\tau]\!]$ *for all* $\gamma \models \Gamma$, *then* $\Gamma \vdash e_1 \approx e_2 : \tau$.

Proof. Let $(\gamma_1, \gamma_2) \in \mathcal{G}[\![\Gamma]\!]$; we must show $(e_1 \cdot \gamma_1, e_2 \cdot \gamma_2) \in \mathcal{E}[\![\tau]\!]$. The premise gives us $(e_1 \cdot \gamma_1, e_2 \cdot \gamma_1) \in \mathcal{E}[\![\tau]\!]$, and we have $(e_2 \cdot \gamma_1, e_2 \cdot \gamma_2) \in \mathcal{E}[\![\tau]\!]$ from the fundamental property (Theorem 15) for e_2. Finally, transitivity (Lemma 10) yields $(e_1 \cdot \gamma_1, e_2 \cdot \gamma_2) \in \mathcal{E}[\![\tau]\!]$. □

Together, Lemmas 19 and 20 simplify the task of proving instances of $\approx$ via arguments about the shape of big-step evaluations and entropy pre-images, as we will see in Sect. 6.

5.3 Soundness

The logical relation is sound with respect to contextual equivalence.

Theorem 21 (Soundness). *If $\Gamma \vdash e_1 \approx e_2 : \tau$, then $e_1 =_{\text{ctx}}^{\Gamma} e_2$.*

Proof. First show $\vdash C[e_1] \approx C[e_2] : \mathbb{R}$ by induction on C, using the compatibility Lemmas (11–14). Then unfold the definitions of $\approx$ and $\mathcal{E}[\![\mathbb{R}]\!]$ to get the equivalence of the measures.   □

In the next section, we demonstrate the utility of the logical relation by proving a few example equivalences.

6 Proving Equivalences

Having shown that $\approx$ is sound with respect to $=_{\text{ctx}}$, we can now prove instances of contextual equivalence by proving instances of the $\approx$ relation in lieu of thinking about arbitrary real-typed syntactic contexts.

Specific equivalence proofs fall into two classes, which we characterize as structural and deep based on the kind of reasoning involved. Structural equivalences include β_v and commutativity of expressions. In a structural equivalence, the same evaluations happen, just in different regions of the entropy space because the access patterns have been shuffled around. Deep equivalences include conjugacy relationships and other facts about probability distributions; they involve interactions between intermediate measures and mathematical operations. Deep equivalences are a lightweight form of denotational reasoning restricted to the ground type $\mathbb{R}$.

6.1 Structural Equivalences

The first equivalence we prove is β_v, the workhorse of call-by-value functional programming. Unrestricted β conversions (call-by-name) do not preserve equivalence in this language, of course, because they can duplicate (or eliminate) effects. But there is another subset of β conversions, which we call β_S, that moves arbitrary effectful expressions around while avoiding duplication. In particular, β_S permits the reordering of expressions in a way that is unsound for languages with mutation and many other effects but sound for probabilistic programming.

Theorem 22 (β_v). *If $\Gamma \vdash (\lambda x.\, e)\, v : \tau$, then $\Gamma \vdash (\lambda x.\, e)\, v \approx e[x \mapsto v] : \tau$.*

We present two proofs of this theorem. The first proof shows a correspondence between evaluation derivations for the redex and contractum.

Proof (by derivation correspondence). For simplicity we assume that the bound variables of $\lambda x.\, e$ are unique and distinct from the domain of Γ; thus the substitution $e\,[x \mapsto v]$ does not need to rename variables to avoid capturing free references in v.

Let $\gamma \models \Gamma$ and let $A \in \mathcal{A}'[\![\tau]\!]$. By Lemmas 19 and 20, it is sufficient to show that

$$\mu_{((\lambda x.\, e)\ v)\cdot\gamma}(A) = \mu_{(e[x \mapsto v])\cdot\gamma}(A)$$

that is,

$$\int \mathrm{evalin}(((\lambda x.\, e)\ v) \cdot \gamma, A, \sigma)\ \mu_{\mathbb{S}}(d\sigma) = \int \mathrm{evalin}((e\,[x \mapsto v]) \cdot \gamma, A, \sigma)\ \mu_{\mathbb{S}}(d\sigma)$$

By Lemma 3, it suffices to show that for all $W \in \Sigma_{\mathbb{R}}$, the entropy pre-images have the same measure. That is,

$$\mu_{\mathbb{S}}(\mathrm{evalin}(((\lambda x.\, e)\ v) \cdot \gamma, A, \cdot)^{-1}(W)) = \mu_{\mathbb{S}}(\mathrm{evalin}((e\,[x \mapsto v]) \cdot \gamma, A, \cdot)^{-1}(W))$$

Every evaluation of $((\lambda x.\, e)\ v) \cdot \gamma$ has the following form:

$$\pi_1(\sigma) \vdash \lambda x.\, e \cdot \gamma \Downarrow \lambda x.\, e \cdot \gamma, 1$$

$$
\cfrac{\pi_2(\sigma) \vdash v \cdot \gamma \Downarrow v \cdot \gamma, 1 \qquad \cfrac{\cfrac{\sigma' \vdash v \cdot \gamma \Downarrow v \cdot \gamma, 1}{\vdots}}{\pi_3(\sigma) \vdash (e\,[x \mapsto v]) \cdot \gamma \Downarrow v_r, w}\ ^{\Delta_1}}{\sigma \vdash ((\lambda x.\, e)\ v) \cdot \gamma \Downarrow v_r, w}
$$

The application of the λ-expression and the syntactic value argument are both trivial. The evaluation of the body expression depends on e; it contains zero or more leaf evaluations of x yielding $v \cdot \gamma$. These leaf evaluations ignore their entropy argument and have weight 1. We refer to the structure of the e evaluation as Δ_1.

Likewise, every evaluation derivation of $(e\,[x \mapsto v]) \cdot \gamma$ has the following form:

$$
\cfrac{\cfrac{\sigma'' \vdash v \cdot \gamma \Downarrow v \cdot \gamma, 1}{\vdots}}{\sigma \vdash (e\,[x \mapsto v]) \cdot \gamma \Downarrow v_r, w}\ ^{\Delta_2}
$$

Δ_2 has exactly the same structure as Δ_1. Consequently, the two expressions evaluate the same if Δ_1 and Δ_2 receive the same entropy. In short:

$$\sigma \vdash ((\lambda x.\, e)\ v) \cdot \gamma \Downarrow v_r, w \quad \Longleftrightarrow \quad \pi_3(\sigma) \vdash (e\,[x \mapsto v]) \cdot \gamma \Downarrow v_r, w$$

Let $S_1, S_2 \subseteq \mathbb{S}$ be the entropy pre-images of the two expressions:

$$S_1 = \mathrm{evalin}(((\lambda x.\, e)\ v) \cdot \gamma, A, \cdot)^{-1}(W)$$
$$S_2 = \mathrm{evalin}((e\,[x \mapsto v]) \cdot \gamma, A, \cdot)^{-1}(W)$$

We conclude that $S_1 = \pi_3^{-1}(S_2)$ and thus the pre-images have the same measure. $\qquad\square$

The second proof rewrites the measure of the redex into that of the contractum using integral identities.

Proof (by integral rewriting). As in the first proof, let $\gamma \models \Gamma$ and $A \in \mathcal{A}'[\![\tau]\!]$. It will be sufficient to show that

$$\mu_{((\lambda x.\, e)\ v)\cdot\gamma}(A) = \mu_{(e[x\mapsto v])\cdot\gamma}(A)$$

Using the same steps as in Lemma 12, we can express the value measure of an application as an integral by the value measures of its subexpressions.

$$\mu_{((\lambda x.\, e)\ v)\cdot\gamma}(A) = \iiint \mathrm{applyin}(v', v'', A, \sigma)\ \mu_{\mathbb{S}}(d\sigma)\ \mu_{v\cdot\gamma}(dv'')\ \mu_{\lambda x.\, e\cdot\gamma}(dv')$$

Both the subexpressions $\lambda x.\, e \cdot \gamma$ and $v \cdot \gamma$ are values, so their value measures are Dirac. We complete the proof using the fact that integration by a Dirac measure is equivalent to substitution.

$$= \iiint \mathrm{applyin}(v', v'', A, \sigma)\ \mu_{\mathbb{S}}(d\sigma)\ \mathrm{dirac}_{v\cdot\gamma}(dv'')\ \mathrm{dirac}_{\lambda x.\, e\cdot\gamma}(dv')$$

$$= \int \mathrm{applyin}(\lambda x.\, e \cdot \gamma, v \cdot \gamma, A, \sigma)\ \mu_{\mathbb{S}}(d\sigma) \qquad \text{(integration by Dirac)}$$

$$= \int \mathrm{evalin}((e\,[x \mapsto v]) \cdot \gamma, A, \sigma)\ \mu_{\mathbb{S}}(d\sigma) \qquad \text{(definition of applyin)}$$

$$= \mu_{(e[x\mapsto v])\cdot\gamma}(A) \qquad \text{(definition of } \mu_e)$$

$$\square$$

The second equivalence concerns reordering expression evaluations. In probabilistic programming, **factor** and **factor** effects can be reordered, as long as they are not duplicated or eliminated. We define simple contexts, a generalization of evaluation contexts, as a class of contexts that an expression may be moved through without changing the number of times it is evaluated.

Definition 23 (Simple Contexts).

$$S ::= [\,]\ |\ S\ e\ |\ e\ S\ |\ (\lambda x.\, S)\ e\ |\ op(e, \cdots, S, e, \cdots)\ |\ \textbf{factor } S$$

Note that $(\lambda x.\, S)\ e$ can also be written **let** $x = e$ **in** S.

Theorem 24 (Substitution into Simple Context). *If* $\Gamma \vdash (\lambda x.\, S[x])\ e : \tau$ *and* x *does not occur free in* S, *then* $\Gamma \vdash (\lambda x.\, S[x])\ e \approx S[e] : \tau$.

Proof. We can prove the following equivalence for a context S^1 consisting of a single frame, such as $([\,]\ e)$. For all λ-values f where $\Gamma \vdash S^1[f\ e] : \tau$,

$$\Gamma \vdash (\lambda x.\, S^1[f\ x])\ e \approx S^1[f\ e] : \tau$$

The proof is similar to that of Theorem 22, but see also below.

The proof for arbitrary S contexts proceeds by induction on S. The base case, $\Gamma \vdash (\lambda x.\, x)\ e \approx e : \tau$, is easily proven directly. For the inductive case:

$$\Gamma \vdash (\lambda x.\, S^1[S[x]])\ e \approx (\lambda x.\, S^1[(\lambda y.\, S[y])\ x])\ e \qquad \text{(by Theorem 22)}$$
$$\approx S^1[(\lambda y.\, S[y])\ e] \qquad \text{(by single-frame case)}$$
$$\approx S^1[S[e]] \qquad \text{(by IH and compatibility of } S^1)$$

$$\square$$

The β_S and β_v theorems together show that the following terms are equivalent:

- **let** $x = e1,\ y = e2$ **in** *body*
- **let** $y = e2,\ x = e1$ **in** *body*

First *e2* is lifted to the outside with β_S to get **let** $z = e2,\ x = e1,\ y = z$ **in** *body*. Then *y* is replaced with *z* in *body* using β_v. Finally, the outer *z* is renamed back to *y*.

This reordering can also be shown directly, and the proof is similar to the $S^1 = (\lambda x.\,[\,])\ e$ case above but simpler to present. It involves a generalization of Lemma 1 (Tonelli).

We first apply the technique from the the second proof of Theorem 22 to express substitution as integration by value measures.

$$\mu_{(\lambda x.\,(\lambda y.\, e_3)\ e_2)\ e_1}(A) = \int \mu_{((\lambda y.\, e_3)\ e_2)[x \mapsto v_1]}(A)\ \mu_{e_1}(dv_1)$$
$$= \iint \mu_{e_3[x \mapsto v_1, y \mapsto v_2]}(A)\ \mu_{e_2}(dv_2)\ \mu_{e_1}(dv_1)$$

Doing the same to the other side, we now need to show that the order of integration is interchangable:

$$\iint \mu_{e_3[x \mapsto v_1, y \mapsto v_2]}(A)\ \mu_{e_2}(dv_2)\ \mu_{e_1}(dv_1) = \iint \mu_{e_3[y \mapsto v_2, x \mapsto v_1]}(A)\ \mu_{e_1}(dv_1)\ \mu_{e_2}(dv_2)$$

Since μ_{e_1} and μ_{e_2} may not be σ-finite we cannot immediately apply Lemma 1. Lemma 25 shows exchangability for value measures and completes the proof.

Lemma 25 (μ_e interchangable). *If $\vdash e_1 : \tau_1$ and $\vdash e_2 : \tau_2$ then for all measurable $f : [\![\tau_1]\!] \times [\![\tau_2]\!] \to \mathbb{R}^+$,*

$$\iint f(v_1, v_2)\ \mu_{e_2}(dv_2)\ \mu_{e_1}(dv_1) = \iint f(v_1, v_2)\ \mu_{e_1}(dv_1)\ \mu_{e_2}(dv_2)$$

Proof. Since integrals about μ_e can be expressed in terms of the σ-finite $\mu_{\mathbb{S}}$, we can apply Lemma 1 (Tonelli) once we have exposed the underlying measures.

$$\iint f(v_1, v_2)\, \mu_{e_2}(dv_2)\, \mu_{e_1}(dv_1)$$

$$= \iint f(\mathrm{ev}(v_1, \sigma_1), \mathrm{ev}(v_2, \sigma_2)) \cdot \mathrm{ew}(v_2, \sigma_2)\, \mu_{\mathbb{S}}(d\sigma_2) \cdot \mathrm{ew}(v_1, \sigma_1)\, \mu_{\mathbb{S}}(d\sigma_1)$$

$$\text{(Theorem 7)}$$

$$= \iint f(\mathrm{ev}(v_1, \sigma_1), \mathrm{ev}(v_2, \sigma_2)) \cdot \mathrm{ew}(v_2, \sigma_2) \cdot \mathrm{ew}(v_1, \sigma_1)\, \mu_{\mathbb{S}}(d\sigma_2)\, \mu_{\mathbb{S}}(d\sigma_1)$$

$$\text{(linearity of integration)}$$

$$= \iint f(\mathrm{ev}(v_1, \sigma_1), \mathrm{ev}(v_2, \sigma_2)) \cdot \mathrm{ew}(v_1, \sigma_1) \cdot \mathrm{ew}(v_2, \sigma_2)\, \mu_{\mathbb{S}}(d\sigma_1)\, \mu_{\mathbb{S}}(d\sigma_2)$$

$$\text{(Lemma 1)}$$

$$= \iint f(v_1, v_2)\, \mu_{e_1}(dv_1)\, \mu_{e_2}\, dv_2$$

$\square$

6.2 Deep Equivalences

In contrast to structural equivalences such as β_v, deep equivalences rely on the specific computations being performed and mathematical relationships between them. They generally concern only expressions of ground type ($\mathbb{R}$). Proving them requires "locally denotational" reasoning about expressions and the real-valued measures (or measure kernels, when free variables are present) they represent.

For example, the following theorem encodes the fact that the sum of two normally-distributed random variables is normally distributed.

Theorem 26 (Sum of normals with variable parameters). *Let*

$$e_1 = \mathbf{normal}\ x_{m_1}\ x_{s_1} + \mathbf{normal}\ x_{m_2}\ x_{s_2}$$

$$e_2 = \mathbf{normal}\ (x_{m_1} + x_{m_2})\ \sqrt{x_{s_1}^2 + x_{s_2}^2}$$

and let $\Gamma(x_{m_1}) = \Gamma(x_{m_2}) = \Gamma(x_{s_1}) = \Gamma(x_{s_2}) = \mathbb{R}$. *Then* $\Gamma \vdash e_1 \approx e_2 : \mathbb{R}$.

Proof. Let $(\gamma_1, \gamma_2) \in \mathcal{G}[\![\Gamma]\!]$. Since x_{m_1}, x_{m_2}, x_s have ground type, the substitutions agree on their values: let $m_1 = \gamma_1(x_{m_1}) = \gamma_2(x_{m_1})$ and likewise for m_2, s_1, and s_2.

We must show $(e_1 \cdot \gamma_1, e_2 \cdot \gamma_2) \in \mathcal{E}[\![\mathbb{R}]\!]$; that is, $\mu_{e_1 \cdot \gamma_1}(A) = \mu_{e_2 \cdot \gamma_2}(A)$ for all $A \in \Sigma_{\mathbb{R}}$. The value measures of the **normal** expressions are actually the measures of normally-distributed random variables. This reasoning relies on the meaning assigned to the normalinvcdf operation as well as $+$ and $*$; recall that

normal $m\ s \triangleq m + s * \mathsf{normalinvcdf}(\mathbf{sample})$

Then we apply the fact from probability that the sum of two normal random variables is a normal random variable. $\square$

6.3   Combining Equivalences

The transitivity of the logical relation permits equivalence proofs to be decomposed into smaller, simpler steps, using the compatibility lemmas to focus in and rewrite subexpressions of the main expression of interest.

Theorem 27 (Sum of normals). *Let*

$$e_1 = \textbf{normal } e_{m_1} \ e_{s_1} + \textbf{normal } x_{m_2} \ e_{s_1}$$

$$e_2 = \textbf{normal } (e_{m_1} + e_{m_2}) \ \sqrt{e_{s_1}^2 + e_{s_2}^2}$$

and let $\Gamma \vdash e_1 : \mathbb{R}$ and $\Gamma \vdash e_2 : \mathbb{R}$. Then $\Gamma \vdash e_1 \approx e_2 : \mathbb{R}$.

Proof. This theorem is just like Theorem 26 except with expressions instead of variables for the parameters to the normal distributions. We use β_S (Theorem 24) "in reverse" to move the expressions out and replace them with variables, then we apply the variable case (Theorem 26), then we use β_S again to move the parameter expressions back in.   ⊓

7   Conclusion

We have defined a logical relation to help prove expressions contextually equivalent in a probabilistic programming language with continuous random variables and a scoring operation. We have proven it sound and demonstrated its usefulness with a number of applications to both structural equivalences like β_v and deep equivalences like the sum of normals.

Acknowledgments. We thank Amal Ahmed for her guidance on logical relations, and we thank Theophilos Giannakopoulos, Mitch Wand, and Olin Shivers for many helpful discussions and suggestions.

References

1. Bizjak, A., Birkedal, L.: Step-indexed logical relations for probability. In: Pitts, A. (ed.) FoSSaCS 2015. LNCS, vol. 9034, pp. 279–294. Springer, Heidelberg (2015). doi:10.1007/978-3-662-46678-0_18
2. Borgström, J., Gordon, A.D., Greenberg, M., Margetson, J., Gael, J.V.: Measure transformer semantics for Bayesian machine learning. Log. Methods Comput. Sci. **9**(3) (2013)
3. Borgström, J., Lago, U.D., Gordon, A.D., Szymczak, M.: A lambda-calculus foundation for universal probabilistic programming. In: Conference Record of 21st ACM International Conference on Functional Programming, September 2016
4. Carpenter, B., Gelman, A., Hoffman, M., Lee, D., Goodrich, B., Betancourt, M., Brubaker, M.A., Guo, J., Li, P., Riddell, A.: Stan: a probabilistic programming language. J. Stat. Softw. **20**, 1–30 (2016)
5. Culpepper, R.: Gamble (2015). https://github.com/rmculpepper/gamble

6. Edalat, A., Escardó, M.H.: Integration in real PCF. Inf. Comput. **160**(1), 128–166 (2000)
7. Escardó, M.H.: PCF extended with real numbers. Theoret. Comput. Sci. **162**(1), 79–115 (1996)
8. Goodman, N.D., Mansinghka, V.K., Roy, D.M., Bonawitz, K., Tenenbaum, J.B.: Church: a language for generative models. In: UAI, pp. 220–229 (2008)
9. Huang, D., Morrisett, G.: An application of computable distributions to the semantics of probabilistic programming languages. In: Thiemann, P. (ed.) ESOP 2016. LNCS, vol. 9632, pp. 337–363. Springer, Heidelberg (2016). doi:10.1007/978-3-662-49498-1_14
10. Kiselyov, O., Shan, C.: Embedded probabilistic programming. In: Taha, W.M. (ed.) DSL 2009. LNCS, vol. 5658, pp. 360–384. Springer, Heidelberg (2009). doi:10.1007/978-3-642-03034-5_17
11. Lieb, E.H., Loss, M.: Analysis. Graduate Studies in Mathematics, vol. 14. American Mathematical Society, Providence (1997)
12. Lunn, D.J., Thomas, A., Best, N., Spiegelhalter, D.: Winbugs - a Bayesian modelling framework: concepts, structure, and extensibility. Stat. Comput. **10**(4), 325–337 (2000)
13. Mansinghka, V., Selsam, D., Perov, Y.: Venture: a higher-order probabilistic programming platform with programmable inference, March 2014. http://arxiv.org/abs/1404.0099
14. Minka, T., Winn, J., Guiver, J., Webster, S., Zaykov, Y., Yangel, B., Spengler, A., Bronskill, J.: Infer.NET 2.6. Microsoft Research Cambridge (2014). http://research.microsoft.com/infernet
15. Narayanan, P., Carette, J., Romano, W., Shan, C., Zinkov, R.: Probabilistic inference by program transformation in hakaru (system description). In: Kiselyov, O., King, A. (eds.) FLOPS 2016. LNCS, vol. 9613, pp. 62–79. Springer, Heidelberg (2016). doi:10.1007/978-3-319-29604-3_5
16. Park, S., Pfenning, F., Thrun, S.: A probabilistic language based on sampling functions. ACM Trans. Program. Lang. Syst. **31**(1), 4:1–4:46 (2008)
17. Pfeffer, A.: Figaro: an object-oriented probabilistic programming language. Technical report, Charles River Analytics (2009)
18. Ramsey, N., Pfeffer, A.: Stochastic lambda calculus and monads of probability distributions. In: Conference Record of 29th ACM Symposium on Principles of Programming Languages, pp. 154–165 (2002)
19. Sangiorgi, D., Vignudelli, V.: Environmental bisimulations for probabilistic higher-order languages. In: Conference Record of 43rd ACM Symposium on Principles of Programming Languages, POPL 2016, pp. 595–607 (2016)
20. Staton, S., Yang, H., Heunen, C., Kammar, O., Wood, F.: Semantics for probabilistic programming: higher-order functions, continuous distributions, and soft constraints. In: Proceedings of 31st IEEE Symposium on Logic in Computer Science (2016)
21. Wingate, D., Goodman, N.D., Stuhlmüller, A., Siskind, J.M.: Nonstandard interpretations of probabilistic programs for efficient inference. In: Advances in Neural Information Processing Systems, vol. 24 (2011)
22. Wood, F., van de Meent, J.W., Mansinghka, V.: A new approach to probabilistic programming inference. In: Proceedings of 17th International Conference on Artificial Intelligence and Statistics, pp. 1024–1032 (2014)

Probabilistic Termination
by Monadic Affine Sized Typing

Ugo Dal Lago[1,2(⊠)] and Charles Grellois[2]

[1] University of Bologna, Bologna, Italy
ugo.dallago@unibo.it
[2] Inria, Sophia Antipolis, France
charles.grellois@inria.fr

Abstract. We introduce a system of monadic affine sized types, which substantially generalise usual sized types, and allows this way to capture probabilistic higher-order programs which terminate almost surely. Going beyond plain, strong normalisation without losing soundness turns out to be a hard task, which cannot be accomplished without a richer, quantitative notion of types, but also without imposing some affinity constraints. The proposed type system is powerful enough to type classic examples of probabilistically terminating programs such as random walks. The way typable programs are proved to be almost surely terminating is based on reducibility, but requires a substantial adaptation of the technique.

1 Introduction

Probabilistic models are more and more pervasive in computer science [1–3]. Moreover, the concept of algorithm, originally assuming determinism, has been relaxed so as to allow probabilistic evolution since the very early days of theoretical computer science [4]. All this has given impetus to research on probabilistic programming languages, which however have been studied at a large scale only in the last twenty years, following advances in randomized computation [5], cryptographic protocol verification [6,7], and machine learning [8]. Probabilistic programs can be seen as ordinary programs in which specific instructions are provided to make the program evolve probabilistically rather than deterministically. The typical example are instructions for sampling from a given distribution toolset, or for performing probabilistic choice.

One of the most crucial properties a program should satisfy is *termination*: the execution process should be guaranteed to end. In (non)deterministic computation, this is easy to formalize, since any possible computation path is only considered qualitatively, and termination is a Boolean predicate on programs: any non-deterministic program either terminates – in must or may sense – or it

---

This work is partially supported by the ANR projects 12IS02001 PACE and 14CE250005 ELICA.

H. Yang (Ed.): ESOP 2017, LNCS 10201, pp. 393–419, 2017.
DOI: 10.1007/978-3-662-54434-1_15

does not. In probabilistic programs, on the other hand, any terminating computation path is attributed a probability, and thus termination becomes a *quantitative* property. It is therefore natural to consider a program terminating when its terminating paths form a set of measure one or, equivalently, when it terminates with maximal probability. This is dubbed "almost sure termination" (AST for short) in the literature [9], and many techniques for automatically and semi-automatically checking programs for AST have been introduced in the last years [10–13]. All of them, however, focus on imperative programs; while probabilistic functional programming languages are nowadays among the most successful ones in the realm of probabilistic programming [8]. It is not clear at all whether the existing techniques for imperative languages could be easily applied to functional ones, especially when higher-order functions are involved.

In this paper, we introduce a system of monadic affine sized types for a simple probabilistic λ-calculus with recursion and show that it guarantees the AST property for all typable programs. The type system, described in Sect. 4, can be seen as a non-trivial variation on Hughes et al.'s sized types [14], whose main novelties are the following:

- Types are generalised so as to be *monadic*, this way encapsulating the kind of information we need to type non-trivial examples. This information, in particular, is taken advantage of when typing recursive programs.
- Typing rules are *affine*: higher-order variables cannot be freely duplicated. This is quite similar to what happens when characterising polynomial time functions by restricting higher-order languages akin to the λ-calculus [15]. Without affinity, the type system is bound to be unsound for AST.

The necessity of both these variations is discussed in Sect. 2 below. The main result of this paper is that typability in monadic affine sized types entails AST, a property which is proved using an adaptation of the Girard-Tait reducibility technique [16]. This adaptation is technically involved, as it needs substantial modifications allowing to deal with possibly infinite and probabilistic computations. In particular, every reducibility set must be parameterized by a quantitative parameter p guaranteeing that terms belonging to this set terminate with probability at least p. The idea of parameterizing such sets already appears in work by the Dal Lago and Hofmann [17], in which a notion of realizability parameterized by resource monoids is considered. These realizability models are however studied in relation to linear logic and to the complexity of normalisation, and do not fit as such to our setting, even if they provided some crucial inspiration. In our approach, the fact that recursively-defined terms are AST comes from a continuity argument on this parameter: we can prove, by unfolding such terms, that they terminate with probability p for every $p < 1$, and continuity then allows to take the limit and deduce that they are AST. This soundness result is technically speaking the main contribution of this paper, and is described in Sect. 5.

An extended version with more details and proofs is available [18].

1.1   Related Works

Sized types have been originally introduced by Hughes et al. [14] in the context of reactive programming. A series of papers by Barthe et al. [19–21] presents sized types in a way similar to the one we will adopt here, although still for a deterministic functional language. Contrary to the other works on sized types, their type system is proved to admit a decidable type inference, see the unpublished tutorial [20]. Abel developed independently of Barthe and colleagues a similar type system featuring size informations [22]. These three lines of work allow polymorphism, arbitrary inductive data constructors, and ordinal sizes, so that data such as infinite trees can be manipulated. These three features will be absent of our system, in order to focus the challenge on the treatment of probabilistic recursive programs. Another interesting approach is the one of Xi's Dependent ML [23], in which a system of lightweight dependent types allows a more liberal treatment of the notion of size, over which arithmetic or conditional operations may in particular be applied. Termination is ensured by checking during typing that a given metrics decreases during recursive calls. This system is well-adapted for practical termination checking and can be extended with mutual recursion, inductive types and polymorphism, but does not feature ordinal sizes. See [22] for a detailed comparison of the previously cited systems. Some works along these lines are able to deal with coinductive data, as well as inductive ones [14,19,22]. They are related to Amadio and Coupet-Grimal's work on guarded types ensuring productivity of infinite structures such as streams [24]. None of these works deal with probabilistic computation, and in particular with almost sure termination.

There has been a lot of interest, recently, about probabilistic termination as a verification problem in the context of imperative programming [10–13]. All of them deal, invariably, with some form of while-style language without higher-order functions. A possible approach is to reduce AST for probabilistic programs to termination of non-deterministic programs [10]. Another one is to extend the concept of ranking function to the probabilistic case. Bournez and Garnier obtained in this way the notion of Lyapunov ranking function [25], but such functions capture a notion more restrictive than AST: *positive* almost sure termination, meaning that the program is AST and terminates in expected finite time. To capture AST, the notion of ranking supermartingale [26] has been used. Note that the use of ranking supermartingales allows to deal with programs which are both probabilistic and non-deterministic [11,13] and even to reason about programs with real-valued variables [12].

Some recent work by Cappai et al. [27,28] introduce type systems ensuring that all typable programs can be evaluated in probabilistic polynomial time. This is too restrictive for our purposes. On the one hand, we aim at termination, and restricting to polynomial time algorithms would be an overkill. On the other hand, the above-mentioned type systems guarantee that the length of *all* probabilistic branches are uniformly bounded (by the same polynomial). In our setting, this would restrict the focus to terms in which infinite computations are forbidden, while we simply want the set of such computations to have probability

0. In fact, the results we present in this paper can be seen as a first step towards a type system characterizing average polynomial time, in the style of implicit computational complexity [29].

2 Why is Monadic Affine Typing Necessary?

In this section, we justify the design choices that guided us in the development of our type system. As we will see, the nature of AST requires a significant and non-trivial extension of the system of sized types originally introduced to ensure termination in the deterministic case [14].

Sized Types for Deterministic Programs. The simply-typed λ-calculus endowed with a typed recursion operator letrec and appropriate constructs for the natural numbers, sometimes called PCF, is already Turing-complete, so that there is no hope to prove it strongly normalizing. Sized types [14] refine the simple type system by enriching base types with annotations, so as to ensure the termination of any recursive definition. Let us explain the idea of sizes in the simple, yet informative case in which the base type is Nat. Sizes are defined by the grammar

$$\mathfrak{s} \ ::= \ \mathsf{i} \ \mid \ \infty \ \mid \ \widehat{\mathfrak{s}}$$

where i is a size variable and $\widehat{\mathfrak{s}}$ is the successor of the size $\mathfrak{s}$—with $\widehat{\infty} = \infty$. These sizes permit to consider decorations $\mathsf{Nat}^{\mathfrak{s}}$ of the base type Nat, whose elements are natural numbers of size at most $\mathfrak{s}$. The type system ensures that the only constant value of type $\mathsf{Nat}^{\widehat{\mathsf{i}}}$ is 0, that the only constant values of type $\mathsf{Nat}^{\widehat{\widehat{\mathsf{i}}}}$ are 0 or $1 = \mathsf{S}\ 0$, and so on. The type Nat^{∞} is the one of all natural numbers, and is therefore often denoted as Nat.

The crucial rule of the sized type system, which we present here following Barthe et al. [19], allows one to type recursive definitions as follows:

$$\frac{\Gamma, f \ : \ \mathsf{Nat}^{\mathsf{i}} \to \sigma \vdash M \ : \ \mathsf{Nat}^{\widehat{\mathsf{i}}} \to \sigma[\widehat{\mathsf{i}}/\mathsf{i}] \qquad \mathsf{i}\ \mathrm{pos}\ \sigma}{\Gamma \vdash \mathsf{letrec}\ f \ = \ M \ : \ \mathsf{Nat}^{\mathfrak{s}} \to \sigma[\mathfrak{s}/\mathsf{i}]} \tag{1}$$

This typing rule ensures that, to recursively define the function $f = M$, the term M taking an input of size $\widehat{\mathsf{i}}$ calls f on inputs of *strictly lesser* size i. This is for instance the case when typing the program

$$M_{DBL} \ = \ \mathsf{letrec}\ f \ = \ \lambda x.\mathsf{case}\ x\ \mathsf{of}\ \left\{ \mathsf{S} \to \lambda y.\mathsf{S}\ \mathsf{S}\ (f\ y)\ \mid\ 0 \to 0 \right\}$$

computing recursively the double of an input integer, as the hypothesis of the fixpoint rule in a typing derivation of M_{DBL} is

$$f \ : \ \mathsf{Nat}^{\mathsf{i}} \to \mathsf{Nat} \vdash \lambda x.\mathsf{case}\ x\ \mathsf{of}\ \left\{ \mathsf{S} \to \lambda y.\mathsf{S}\ \mathsf{S}\ (f\ y)\ \mid\ 0 \to 0 \right\} \ : \ \mathsf{Nat}^{\widehat{\mathsf{i}}} \to \mathsf{Nat}$$

The fact that f is called on an input y of strictly lesser size i is ensured by the rule typing the case construction:

$$\frac{\Gamma \vdash x \ : \ \mathsf{Nat}^{\widehat{\mathsf{i}}} \qquad \Gamma \vdash \lambda y.\mathsf{S}\ \mathsf{S}\ (f\ y) \ : \ \mathsf{Nat}^{\mathsf{i}} \to \mathsf{Nat} \qquad \Gamma \vdash 0 \ : \ \mathsf{Nat}}{\Gamma \vdash \mathsf{case}\ x\ \mathsf{of}\ \left\{ \mathsf{S} \to \lambda y.\mathsf{S}\ \mathsf{S}\ (f\ y)\ \mid\ 0 \to 0 \right\} \ : \ \mathsf{Nat}}$$

where $\Gamma = f : \mathsf{Nat}^i \to \mathsf{Nat},\ x : \mathsf{Nat}^{\widehat{i}}$. The soundness of sized types for strong normalization allows to conclude that M_{DBL} is indeed SN.

A Naïve Generalization to Probabilistic Terms. The aim of this paper is to obtain a probabilistic, *quantitative* counterpart to this soundness result for sized types. Note that unlike the result for sized types, which was focusing on *all* reduction strategies of terms, we only consider a *call-by-value* calculus[1]. Terms can now contain a probabilistic choice operator $\oplus_p$, such that $M \oplus_p N$ reduces to the term M with probability $p \in \mathbb{R}_{[0,1]}$, and to N with probability $1 - p$. The language and its operational semantics will be defined more extensively in Sect. 3. Suppose for the moment that we type the choice operator in a naïve way:

$$\text{Choice} \quad \frac{\Gamma \vdash M : \sigma \qquad \Gamma \vdash N : \sigma}{\Gamma \vdash M \oplus_p N : \sigma}$$

On the one hand, the original system of sized types features subtyping, which allows some flexibility to "unify" the types of M and N to σ. On the other hand, it is easy to realise that *all* probabilistic branches would have to be terminating, without any hope of capturing interesting AST programs: nothing has been done to capture the *quantitative* nature of probabilistic termination. An instance of a term which is not strongly normalizing but which is almost-surely terminating— meaning that it normalizes with probability 1—is

$$M_{BIAS} = \left(\mathsf{letrec}\ f = \lambda x.\mathsf{case}\ x\ \mathsf{of}\ \left\{ \mathsf{S} \to \lambda y.f(y) \oplus_{\frac{2}{3}} (f(\mathsf{S}\,\mathsf{S}\,y)))\ \mid\ 0 \to 0 \right\} \right)\ \underline{n} \quad (2)$$

simulating a *biased random walk* which, on $x = m+1$, goes to m with probability $\frac{2}{3}$ and to $m + 2$ with probability $\frac{1}{3}$. The naïve generalization of the sized type system only allows us to type the body of the recursive definition as follows:

$$f :\ \mathsf{Nat}^{\widehat{i}} \to \mathsf{Nat}^\infty\ \vdash\ \lambda y.f(y) \oplus_{\frac{2}{3}} (f(\mathsf{S}\,\mathsf{S}\,y)))\ :\ \mathsf{Nat}^{\widehat{i}} \to \mathsf{Nat}^\infty \quad (3)$$

and thus does not allow us to deduce any relevant information on the *quantitative* termination of this term: nothing tells us that the recursive call $f(\mathsf{S}\,\mathsf{S}\,y)$ is performed with a relatively low probability.

A Monadic Type System. Along the evaluation of M_{BIAS}, there is *indeed* a quantity which decreases during each recursive call to the function f: the *average* size of the input on which the call is performed. Indeed, on an input of size $\widehat{i}$, f calls itself on an input of smaller size i with probability $\frac{2}{3}$, and on an input of greater size $\widehat{\widehat{i}}$ with probability only $\frac{1}{3}$. To capture such a relevant *quantitative* information on the recursive calls of f, and with the aim to capture almost sure termination, we introduce a *monadic* type system, in which *distributions of types* can be used to type in a finer way the functions to be used recursively. Contexts $\Gamma \mid \Theta$ will be generated by a context Γ attributing sized types to any number

---

[1] Please notice that choosing a reduction strategy is crucial in a probabilistic setting, otherwise one risks getting nasty forms of non-confluence [30].

of variables, while Θ will attribute a *distribution* of sized types to at most *one* variable—typically the one we want to use to recursively define a function. In such a context, terms will be typed by a distribution type, formed by combining the Dirac distributions of types introduced in the Axiom rules using the following rule for probabilistic choice:

$$\text{Choice} \quad \frac{\Gamma \mid \Theta \vdash M : \mu \qquad \Gamma \mid \Psi \vdash N : \nu \qquad \langle \mu \rangle = \langle \nu \rangle}{\Gamma \mid \Theta \oplus_p \Psi \vdash M \oplus_p N : \mu \oplus_p \nu}$$

The guard condition $\langle \mu \rangle = \langle \nu \rangle$ ensures that μ and ν are distributions of types decorating of the *same* simple type. Without this condition, there is no hope to aim for a decidable type inference algorithm.

The Fixpoint Rule. Using these monadic types, instead of the insufficiently informative typing (3), we can derive the sequent

$$f : \left\{ \left(\mathsf{Nat}^i \to \mathsf{Nat}^\infty \right)^{\frac{2}{3}}, \left(\mathsf{Nat}^{\widehat{i}} \to \mathsf{Nat}^\infty \right)^{\frac{1}{3}} \right\} \vdash \lambda y. f(y) \oplus_{\frac{2}{3}} (f(\mathsf{S}\,\mathsf{S}\,y))) \ : \ \mathsf{Nat}^{\widehat{i}} \to \mathsf{Nat}^\infty \quad (4)$$

in which the type of f contains finer information on the sizes of arguments over which it is called recursively, and with which probability. This information enables us to perform a first switch from a qualitative to a quantitative notion of termination: we will adapt the hypothesis

$$\Gamma, f : \mathsf{Nat}^i \to \sigma \vdash M : \mathsf{Nat}^{\widehat{i}} \to \sigma[\widehat{i}/i] \quad (5)$$

of the original fix rule (1) of sized types, expressing that f is called on an argument of size one less than the one on which M is called, to a condition meaning that there is probability 1 to call f on arguments of a lesser size *after enough iterations of recursive calls*. We therefore define a random walk associated to the distribution type μ of f, the *sized walk* associated to μ, and which is as follows for the typing (4):

- the random walk starts on 1, corresponding to the size $\widehat{i}$,
- on an integer $n + 1$, the random walk jumps to n with probability $\frac{2}{3}$ and to $n + 2$ with probability $\frac{1}{3}$,
- 0 is stationary: on it, the random walk loops.

This random walk – as all sized walks will be – is an instance of *one-counter Markov decision problem* [31], so that it is decidable in polynomial time whether the walk reaches 0 with probability 1. We will therefore replace the hypothesis (5) of the letrec rule by the quantitative counterpart we just sketched, obtaining

$$\text{letrec} \quad \frac{\left\{ (\mathsf{Nat}^{s_j} \to \nu[s_j/i])^{p_j} \ \mid \ j \in \mathcal{J} \right\} \text{Induces an AST sized walk} \qquad \Gamma \mid f : \left\{ (\mathsf{Nat}^{s_j} \to \nu[s_j/i])^{p_j} \ \mid \ j \in \mathcal{J} \right\} \vdash V : \mathsf{Nat}^{\widehat{i}} \to \nu[\widehat{i}/i]}{\Gamma, \Delta \mid \Theta \vdash \text{letrec } f = V : \mathsf{Nat}^r \to \nu[r/i]}$$

where we omit two additional technical conditions to be found in Sect. 4 and which justify the weakening on contexts incorporated to this rule. The resulting type system allows to type a varieties of examples, among which the following program computing the geometric distribution over the natural numbers:

$$M_{EXP} = \left(\text{letrec } f = \lambda x.x \oplus_{\frac{1}{2}} S (f\, x)\right) 0 \tag{6}$$

and for which the decreasing quantity is the size of the set of probabilistic branches of the term making recursive calls to f. Another example is the unbiased random walk

$$M_{UNB} = \left(\text{letrec } f = \lambda x.\text{case } x \text{ of } \left\{S \to \lambda y.f(y) \oplus_{\frac{1}{2}} (f(S\,S\,y))) \mid 0 \to 0\right\}\right) \underline{n} \tag{7}$$

for which there is no clear notion of decreasing measure during recursive calls, but which yet terminates almost surely, as witnessed by the sized walk associated to an appropriate derivation in the sized type system. We therefore claim that the use of this external guard condition on associated sized walks, allowing us to give a general condition of termination, is satisfying as it both captures an interesting class of examples, and is computable in polynomial time.

In Sect. 5, we prove that this shift from a qualitative to a quantitative hypothesis in the type system results in a shift from the soundness for strong normalization of the original sized type system to a soundness for its quantitative counterpart: *almost-sure termination*.

Why Affinity? To ensure the soundness of the letrec rule, we need one more structural restriction on the type system. For the sized walk argument to be adequate, we must ensure that the recursive calls of f are indeed precisely modelled by the sized walk, and this is not the case when considering for instance the following term:

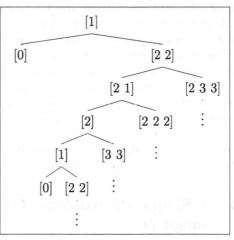

Fig. 1. A tree of recursive calls.

$$M_{NAFF} = \left(\text{letrec } f = \lambda x.\text{case } x \text{ of } \left\{S \to \lambda y.f(y) \oplus_{\frac{2}{3}} (f(S\,S\,y); f(S\,S\,y)) \mid 0 \to 0\right\}\right) \underline{n} \tag{8}$$

where the sequential composition ; is defined in this call-by-value calculus as $M\,;\,N = (\lambda x.\lambda y.0)\, M\, N$. Note that M_{NAFF} calls recursively f *twice* in the right branch of its probabilistic choice, and is not therefore modelled appropriately by the sized walk associated to its type. In fact, we would need a generalized notion of random walk to model the recursive calls of this process; it would be a random walk on *stacks* of integers. In the case where $n = 1$, the recursive calls to f can indeed be represented by a tree of stacks as depicted in Fig. 1, where leftmost edges have probability $\frac{2}{3}$ and rightmost ones $\frac{1}{3}$. The root indicates that the first call on f was on the integer 1. From it, there is either a call of f on 0 which terminates, or *two* calls on 2 which are put into a stack of calls, and so on. We could prove that, without the *affine* restriction we are about to formulate, the term M_{NAFF} is typable with monadic sized types and the fixpoint rule we just designed. However, this term is not almost-surely terminating. Notice, indeed, that the *sum* of the integers appearing in a stack labelling a node of the tree in Fig. 1 decreases by 1 when the left edge of probability $\frac{2}{3}$ is taken, and increases by *at least* 3 when the right edge of probability $\frac{1}{3}$ is taken. It follows that the expected increase of the sum of the elements of the stack during one step is at least $-1 \times \frac{2}{3} + 3 \times \frac{1}{3} = \frac{1}{3} > 0$. This implies that the probability that f is called on an input of size 0 after enough iterations is strictly less than 1, so that the term M_{NAFF} cannot be almost surely terminating.

Such general random processes have stacks as states and are rather complex to analyse. To the best of the authors' knowledge, they do not seem to have been considered in the literature. We also believe that the complexity of determining whether 0 can be reached almost surely in such a process, if decidable, would be very high. This leads us to the design of an *affine* type system, in which the management of contexts ensures that a given probabilistic branch of a term may only use at most once a given higher-order symbol. We do not however formulate restrictions on variables of simple type Nat, as affinity is only used on the letrec rule and thus on higher-order symbols. Remark that this is in the spirit of certain systems from implicit computational complexity [15, 32].

Another restriction imposed by this reduction of almost-sure termination checking for higher-order programs to almost-sure termination checking for one-counter Markov decision processes is the fact that we do not allow a general form of nested recursion. This restriction is encoded in the system by allowing *at most* one variable to have a distribution of types in the context. It follows that programs making use of mutual recursion can not be typed in this system.

3   A Simple Probabilistic Functional Programming Language

We consider the language $\lambda_\oplus$, which is an extension of the λ-calculus with recursion, constructors for the natural numbers, and a choice operator. In this section, we introduce this language and its operational semantics, and use them to define the crucial notion of *almost-sure termination*.

Terms and Values. Given a set of variables $\mathcal{X}$, terms and values of the language $\lambda_\oplus$ are defined by mutual induction as follows:

Terms: $M, N, \ldots \quad ::= \quad V \mid V\,W \mid \mathsf{let}\ x = M\ \mathsf{in}\ N \mid M \oplus_p N$
$\mid\ \mathsf{case}\ V\ \mathsf{of}\ \{\mathsf{S} \to W \mid 0 \to Z\}$

Values: $V, W, Z, \ldots \quad ::= \quad x \mid 0 \mid \mathsf{S}\,V \mid \lambda x.M \mid \mathsf{letrec}\ f = V$

where $x, f \in \mathcal{X}$, $p \in\ ]0, 1[$. When $p = \frac{1}{2}$, we often write $\oplus$ as a shorthand for $\oplus_{\frac{1}{2}}$. The set of terms is denoted $\Lambda_\oplus$ and the set of values is denoted $\Lambda_\oplus^V$.

Terms of the calculus are assumed to be in A-normal form [33]. This allows to formulate crucial definitions in a simpler way, concentrating in the Let construct the study of the probabilistic behaviour of terms. We claim that all traditional constructions can be encoded in this formalism. For instance, the usual application M N of two terms can be harmlessly recovered via the encoding let x = M in (let y = N in x y). In the sequel, we write c $\overrightarrow{V}$ when a value may be either 0 or of the shape S V.

Term Distributions. The introduction of a probabilistic choice operator in the syntax leads to a *probabilistic* reduction relation. It is therefore meaningful to consider the (operational) semantics of a term as a *distribution* of values modelling the outcome of *all* the finite probabilistic reduction paths of the term. For instance, the term M_{EXP} defined in (6) evaluates to the term distribution assigning probability $\frac{1}{2^{n+1}}$ to the value n. Let us define this notion more formally:

Definition 1 (Distribution). *A distribution on X is a function $\mathscr{D}$: X → $[0,1]$ satisfying the constraint $\sum \mathscr{D} = \sum_{x \in X} \mathscr{D}(x) \leq 1$, where $\sum \mathscr{D}$ is called the* sum *of the distribution $\mathscr{D}$. We say that $\mathscr{D}$ is* proper *precisely when $\sum \mathscr{D} = 1$. We denote by $\mathcal{P}$ the set of all distributions, would they be proper or not. We define the support $\mathsf{S}(\mathscr{D})$ of a distribution $\mathscr{D}$ as: $\mathsf{S}(\mathscr{D}) = \{x \in X \mid \mathscr{D}(x) > 0\}$. When $\mathsf{S}(\mathscr{D})$ consists only of closed terms, we say that $\mathscr{D}$ is a* closed *distribution. When it is finite, we say that $\mathscr{D}$ is a* finite *distribution. We call* Dirac *a proper distribution $\mathscr{D}$ such that $\mathsf{S}(\mathscr{D})$ is a singleton. We denote by 0 the null distribution, mapping every term to the probability 0.*

When $X = \Lambda_\oplus$, we say that $\mathscr{D}$ is a *term distribution.* In the sequel, we will use a more practical notion of *representation* of distributions, which enumerates the terms with their probabilities as a family of assignments. For technical reasons, notably related to the subject reduction property, we will also need *pseudo-representations*, which are essentially multiset-like decompositions of the representation of a distribution.

Definition 2 (Representations and Pseudo-Representations). *Let $\mathscr{D} \in \mathcal{P}$ be of support $\{x_i \mid i \in \mathcal{I}\}$, where $x_i = x_j$ implies $i = j$ for every $i, j \in \mathcal{I}$. The* representation *of $\mathscr{D}$ is the set $\mathscr{D} = \left\{ x_i^{\mathscr{D}(x_i)} \mid i \in \mathcal{I} \right\}$ where $x_i^{\mathscr{D}(x_i)}$ is just an intuitive way to write the pair $(x_i, \mathscr{D}(x_i))$. A* pseudo-representation *of $\mathscr{D}$ is any multiset $\left[y_j^{P_j} \mid j \in \mathcal{J} \right]$ such that*

$$\forall j \in \mathcal{J}, \quad y_j \in \mathsf{S}(\mathscr{D}) \qquad \forall i \in \mathcal{I}, \quad \mathscr{D}(x_i) = \sum_{y_j = x_i} p_j.$$

By abuse of notation, we will simply write $\mathscr{D} = \left[y_j^{P_j} \mid j \in \mathcal{J} \right]$ to mean that $\mathscr{D}$ admits $\left[y_j^{P_j} \mid j \in \mathcal{J} \right]$ as pseudo-representation. Any distribution has a canonical pseudo-representation obtained by simply replacing the set-theoretic notation with the multiset-theoretic one.

Distributions support operations like affine combinations and sums – the latter being only a partial operation. We extend these operations to (pseudo)-representations, in a natural way. Distributions, endowed with the pointwise partial-order $\preccurlyeq$, form an ω-CPO, but not a lattice, since the join of two distributions is not guaranteed to exist.

Definition 3 (Value Decomposition of a Term Distribution). *Let $\mathscr{D}$ be a term distribution. We write its value decomposition as $\mathscr{D} \overset{VD}{=} \mathscr{D}_{|V} + \mathscr{D}_{|T}$, where $\mathscr{D}_{|V}$ is the maximal subdistribution of $\mathscr{D}$ whose support consists of values, and $\mathscr{D}_{|T} = \mathscr{D} - \mathscr{D}_{|V}$ is the subdistribution of "non-values" contained in $\mathscr{D}$.*

Operational Semantics. The semantics of a term will be the value distribution to which it reduces via the probabilistic reduction relation, iterated up to the limit. As a first step, we define the call-by-value reduction relation $\rightarrow_v \subseteq \mathcal{P} \times \mathcal{P}$ on Fig. 2. Note that we write Dirac distributions simply as terms on the left side of $\rightarrow_v$, to improve readability. As usual, we denote by $\rightarrow_v^n$ the n-th iterate of the relation $\rightarrow_v$, with $\rightarrow_v^0$ being the identity relation. We then define the relation $\Rightarrow_v^n$ as follows. Let $\mathscr{D} \rightarrow_v^n \mathscr{E} \overset{VD}{=} \mathscr{E}_{|V} + \mathscr{E}_{|T}$. Then $\mathscr{D} \Rightarrow_v^n \mathscr{E}_{|V}$. Note that, for every $n \in \mathbb{N}$ and $\mathscr{D} \in \mathcal{P}$, there is a unique distribution $\mathscr{E}$ such that $\mathscr{D} \rightarrow_v^n \mathscr{E}$. Moreover, $\mathscr{E}_{|V}$ is the only distribution such that $\mathscr{D} \Rightarrow_v^n \mathscr{E}_{|V}$.

Lemma 1. *Let $n, m \in \mathbb{N}$ with $n < m$. Let $\mathscr{D}_n$ (resp $\mathscr{D}_m$) be the distribution such that $M \Rightarrow_v^n \mathscr{D}_n$ (resp $M \Rightarrow_v^m \mathscr{D}_m$). Then $\mathscr{D}_n \preccurlyeq \mathscr{D}_m$.*

Definition 4 (Semantics of a Term, of a Distribution). *The semantics of a distribution $\mathscr{D}$ is the distribution $[\![\mathscr{D}]\!] = \sup_{n \in \mathbb{N}} (\{\mathscr{D}_n \mid \mathscr{D} \Rightarrow_v^n \mathscr{D}_n\})$. This supremum exists thanks to Lemma 1, combined with the fact that $(\mathcal{P}, \preccurlyeq)$ is an ω-CPO. We define the semantics of a term M as $[\![M]\!] = [\![\{M^1\}]\!]$.*

We now have all the ingredients required to define the central concept of this paper, the one of almost-surely terminating term:

Definition 5 (Almost-Sure Termination). *We say that a term M is almost-surely terminating precisely when $\sum [\![M]\!] = 1$.*

4   Monadic Affine Sized Typing

Following the discussion from Sect. 2, we introduce in this section a non-trivial lifting of sized types to our probabilistic setting. As a first step, we design an *affine* simple type system for $\lambda_\oplus$. This means that no higher-order variable may be used more than once in the same probabilistic branch. However, variables of base type Nat may be used freely. In spite of this restriction, the resulting system allows to type terms corresponding to any probabilistic Turing machine. In Sect. 4.2, we introduce a more sophisticated type system, which will be *monadic* and affine, and which will be sound for almost-sure termination as we prove in Sect. 5.

$$\overline{\text{let } x \,=\, V \text{ in } M \,\,\to_v\,\, \{\,(M[V/x])^1\,\}} \qquad \overline{(\lambda x.M)\ V \,\,\to_v\,\, \{\,(M[V/x])^1\,\}}$$

$$\overline{M \,\oplus_p\, N \,\,\to_v\,\, \{\,M^p,\, N^{1-p}\,\}}$$

$$\frac{M \,\to_v\, \{\,L_i^{p_i} \mid i \in \mathcal{I}\,\}}{\text{let } x \,=\, M \text{ in } N \,\,\to_v\,\, \{\,(\text{let } x \,=\, L_i \text{ in } N)^{p_i} \mid i \in \mathcal{I}\,\}}$$

$$\overline{\text{case S } V \text{ of } \{\, S \to W \mid 0 \to Z\,\} \,\,\to_v\,\, \{\,(W\ V)^1\,\}}$$

$$\overline{\text{case 0 of } \{\, S \to W \mid 0 \to Z\,\} \,\,\to_v\,\, \{\,(Z)^1\,\}}$$

$$\overline{(\text{letrec } f \,=\, V)\left(c\ \overrightarrow{W}\right) \,\,\to_v\,\, \left\{\,\left(V[(\text{letrec } f \,=\, V)/f]\left(c\ \overrightarrow{W}\right)\right)^1\,\right\}}$$

$$\frac{\mathscr{D} \,\stackrel{VD}{=}\, \{\,M_j^{p_j} \mid j \in \mathcal{J}\,\} + \mathscr{D}_{|V} \qquad \forall j \in \mathcal{J},\ M_j \,\to_v\, \mathscr{E}_j}{\mathscr{D} \,\to_v\, \left(\sum_{j \in \mathcal{J}} p_j \cdot \mathscr{E}_j\right) + \mathscr{D}_{|V}}$$

Fig. 2. Call-by-value reduction relation $\to_v$ on distributions.

4.1   Affine Simple Types for $\lambda_\oplus$

The terms of the language $\lambda_\oplus$ can be typed using a variant of the simple types of the λ-calculus, extended to type letrec and $\oplus_p$, but also restricted to an *affine* management of contexts. Recall that the constraint of affinity ensures that a given higher-order symbol is used at most *once* in a probabilistic branch. We define simple types over the base type Nat in the usual way: $\kappa, \kappa', \ldots ::= \text{Nat} \mid \kappa \to \kappa'$ where, by convention, the arrow associates to the right. Contexts $\Gamma, \Delta, \ldots$ are sequences of simply-typed variables $x :: \kappa$. We write sequents as $\Gamma \vdash M :: \kappa$ to distinguish these sequents from the ones using distribution types appearing later in this section. Before giving the rules of the type system, we need to define two policies for contracting contexts: an affine and a general one.

Context Contraction. Contexts can be combined in two different ways. On the one hand, one can form the *non-affine contraction* $\Gamma \cup \Delta$ of two contexts, for which Γ and Δ are allowed to share some variables, but these variables must be attributed the *same type* in both contexts. On the other hand, one can form the *affine contraction* $\Gamma \uplus \Delta$, in which variables in common between Γ and Δ must be attributed the type Nat.

$$\text{Var} \quad \overline{\Gamma, x :: \kappa \vdash x :: \kappa} \qquad \frac{\Gamma \vdash V :: \mathsf{Nat}}{\Gamma \vdash S\,V :: \mathsf{Nat}} \qquad \overline{\Gamma \vdash 0 :: \mathsf{Nat}}$$

$$\lambda \quad \frac{\Gamma, x :: \kappa \vdash M :: \kappa'}{\Gamma \vdash \lambda x.M :: \kappa \to \kappa'} \qquad \frac{\Gamma \vdash V :: \kappa \to \kappa' \qquad \Delta \vdash W :: \kappa}{\Gamma \uplus \Delta \vdash V\,W :: \kappa'} \quad \text{App}$$

$$\text{Choice} \quad \frac{\Gamma \vdash M :: \kappa \qquad \Delta \vdash N :: \kappa}{\Gamma \cup \Delta \vdash M \oplus_p N :: \kappa}$$

$$\text{Let} \quad \frac{\Gamma \vdash M :: \kappa \qquad \Delta, x :: \kappa \vdash N :: \kappa'}{\Gamma \uplus \Delta \vdash \mathsf{let}\ x\ =\ M\ \mathsf{in}\ N :: \kappa'}$$

$$\text{Case} \quad \frac{\Gamma \vdash V :: \mathsf{Nat} \qquad \Delta \vdash W :: \mathsf{Nat} \to \kappa \qquad \Delta \vdash Z :: \kappa}{\Gamma \uplus \Delta \vdash \mathsf{case}\ V\ \mathsf{of}\ \{\,S \to W \mid 0 \to Z\,\} :: \kappa}$$

$$\text{letrec} \quad \frac{\Gamma, f :: \mathsf{Nat} \to \kappa \vdash V :: \mathsf{Nat} \to \kappa \qquad \forall x \in \Gamma,\ x :: \mathsf{Nat}}{\Gamma \vdash \mathsf{letrec}\ f\ =\ V :: \mathsf{Nat} \to \kappa}$$

Fig. 3. Affine simple types for $\lambda_\oplus$.

The Affine Type System. The affine simple type system is then defined in Fig. 3. All the rules are quite standard. Higher-order variables can occur at most once in any probabilistic branch because all binary typing rules – except probabilistic choice – treat contexts affinely. We set $\Lambda_\oplus^V(\Gamma, \kappa) = \{V \in \Lambda_\oplus^V \mid \Gamma \vdash V :: \kappa\}$ and $\Lambda_\oplus(\Gamma, \kappa) = \{M \in \Lambda_\oplus \mid \Gamma \vdash M :: \kappa\}$. We simply write $\Lambda_\oplus^V(\kappa) = \Lambda_\oplus^V(\emptyset, \kappa)$ and $\Lambda_\oplus(\kappa) = \Lambda_\oplus(\emptyset, \kappa)$ when the terms or values are closed. These closed, typable terms enjoy subject reduction and the progress property.

4.2   Monadic Affine Sized Types

This section is devoted to giving the basic definitions and results about monadic affine sized types (MASTs, for short), which can be seen as decorations of the affine simple types with some *size information*.

Sized Types. We consider a set $\mathcal{S}$ of *size variables*, denoted $\mathsf{i}, \mathsf{j}, \ldots$ and define *sizes* (called *stages* in [19]) as:

$$\mathfrak{s}, \mathfrak{r} \ ::= \ \mathsf{i} \ \mid \ \infty \ \mid \ \widehat{\mathfrak{s}}$$

where $\widehat{\ }$ denotes the *successor* operation. We denote the iterations of $\widehat{\ }$ as follows: $\widehat{\widehat{\mathfrak{s}}}$ is denoted $\widehat{\mathfrak{s}}^2$, $\widehat{\widehat{\widehat{\mathfrak{s}}}}$ is denoted $\widehat{\mathfrak{s}}^3$, and so on. By definition, at most one variable $\mathsf{i} \in \mathcal{S}$ appears in a given size $\mathfrak{s}$. We call it its *spine variable*, denoted as $\mathrm{spine}(\mathfrak{s})$. We write $\mathrm{spine}(\mathfrak{s}) = \emptyset$ when there is no variable in $\mathfrak{s}$. An order $\preccurlyeq$ on sizes can be defined as follows:

$$\frac{}{\mathfrak{s} \preccurlyeq \mathfrak{s}} \qquad \frac{\mathfrak{s} \preccurlyeq \mathfrak{r} \qquad \mathfrak{r} \preccurlyeq \mathfrak{t}}{\mathfrak{s} \preccurlyeq \mathfrak{t}} \qquad \frac{}{\mathfrak{s} \preccurlyeq \widehat{\mathfrak{s}}} \qquad \frac{}{\mathfrak{s} \preccurlyeq \infty}$$

Notice that these rules imply notably that $\widehat{\infty}$ is equivalent to ∞, i.e., $\widehat{\infty} \preccurlyeq \infty$ and $\infty \preccurlyeq \widehat{\infty}$. We consider sizes modulo this equivalence. We can now define sized types and distribution types by mutual induction, calling distributions of (sized) types the distributions over the set of sized types:

Definition 6 (Sized Types, Distribution Types). *Sized types and distribution types are defined by mutual induction, contextually with the function $\langle \cdot \rangle$ which maps any sized or distribution type to its* underlying *affine type.*

Sized types:	$\sigma, \tau ::= \sigma \to \mu \mid \mathsf{Nat}^{\mathfrak{s}}$
Distribution types:	$\mu, \nu ::= \left\{ \sigma_i^{P_i} \mid i \in \mathcal{I} \right\},$
Underlying map:	$\langle \sigma \to \mu \rangle = \langle \sigma \rangle \to \langle \mu \rangle$
	$\langle \mathsf{Nat}^{\mathfrak{s}} \rangle = \mathsf{Nat}$

$$\left\langle \left\{ \sigma_i^{P_i} \mid i \in \mathcal{I} \right\} \right\rangle = \langle \sigma_j \rangle$$

For distribution types we require additionally that $\sum_{i \in \mathcal{I}} p_i \leq 1$, that $\mathcal{I}$ is a finite non-empty set, and that $\langle \sigma_i \rangle = \langle \sigma_j \rangle$ for every $i, j \in \mathcal{I}$. In the last equation, j is any element of $\mathcal{I}$.

The definition of sized types is *monadic* in that a higher-order sized type is of the shape $\sigma \to \mu$ where σ is again a sized type, and μ is a *distribution* of sized types.

Contexts and Operations on Them. Contexts are sequences of variables together with a sized type, and at most one distinguished variable with a distribution type:

Definition 7 (Contexts). *Contexts are of the shape $\Gamma \mid \Theta$, with*

Sized contexts:	$\Gamma, \Delta, \ldots ::= \emptyset \mid x : \sigma, \Gamma \ (x \notin dom(\Gamma))$
Distribution contexts:	$\Theta, \Psi, \ldots ::= \emptyset \mid x : \mu$

As usual, we define the domain *$dom(\Gamma)$ of a sized context Γ by induction: $dom(\emptyset) = \emptyset$ and $dom(x : \sigma, \Gamma) = \{x\} \uplus dom(\Gamma)$. We proceed similarly for the domain $dom(\Theta)$ of a distribution context Θ. When a sized context $\Gamma = x_1 : \sigma_1, \ldots, x_n : \sigma_n \ (n \geq 1)$ is such that there is a simple type κ with $\forall i \in \{1, \ldots, n\}, \ \langle \sigma_i \rangle = \kappa$, we say that Γ is* uniform *of simple type κ. We write this as $\langle \Gamma \rangle = \kappa$.*

We write Γ, Δ for the disjoint union *of these sized contexts: it is defined whenever $dom(\Gamma) \cap dom(\Delta) = \emptyset$. We proceed similarly for Θ, Ψ, but note that due to the restriction on the cardinality of such contexts, there is the additional requirement that $\Theta = \emptyset$ or $\Psi = \emptyset$.*

We finally define contexts as pairs $\Gamma \mid \Theta$ of a sized context and of a distribution context, with the constraint that $dom(\Gamma) \cap dom(\Theta) = \emptyset$.

Definition 8 (Probabilistic Sum). *Let μ and ν be two distribution types. We define their probabilistic sum $\mu \oplus_p \nu$ as the distribution type $p \cdot \mu + (1-p) \cdot \nu$. We extend this operation to a* partial *operation on distribution contexts:*

- *For two distribution types μ and ν such that $\langle \mu \rangle = \langle \nu \rangle$, we define $(x : \mu) \oplus_p (x : \nu) = x : \mu \oplus_p \nu$,*
- *$(x : \mu) \oplus_p \emptyset = x : p \cdot \mu$,*
- *$\emptyset \oplus_p (x : \mu) = x : (1-p) \cdot \mu$,*
- *In any other case, the operation is undefined.*

Definition 9 (Weighted Sum of Distribution Contexts). *Let $(\Theta_i)_{i \in \mathcal{I}}$ be a non-empty family of distribution contexts and $(p_i)_{i \in \mathcal{I}}$ be a family of reals of $[0,1]$. We define the weighted sum $\sum_{i \in \mathcal{I}} p_i \cdot \Theta_i$ as the distribution context $x : \sum_{i \in \mathcal{I}} p_i \cdot \mu_i$ when the following conditions are met:*

1. *$\exists x, \quad \forall i \in \mathcal{I}, \ \Theta_i = x : \mu_i$,*
2. *$\forall (i,j) \in \mathcal{I}^2, \ \langle \Theta_i \rangle = \langle \Theta_j \rangle$,*
3. *and $\sum_{i \in \mathcal{I}} p_i \le 1$,*

In any other case, the operation is undefined.

We define the substitution $[\mathfrak{r}/i]$ of a size variable in a size or in a sized or distribution type in the expected way; see the long version [18] for details. A subtyping relation allows to lift the order $\preccurlyeq$ on sizes to monadic sized types:

Definition 10 (Subtyping). *We define the subtyping relation $\sqsubseteq$ on sized types and distribution types as follows:*

$$\frac{}{\sigma \sqsubseteq \sigma} \qquad \frac{\mathfrak{s} \preccurlyeq \mathfrak{t}}{\mathsf{Nat}^{\mathfrak{s}} \sqsubseteq \mathsf{Nat}^{\mathfrak{t}}} \qquad \frac{\tau \sqsubseteq \sigma \qquad \mu \sqsubseteq \nu}{\sigma \to \mu \sqsubseteq \tau \to \nu}$$

$$\frac{\exists f : \mathcal{I} \to \mathcal{J}, \ \left(\forall i \in \mathcal{I}, \ \sigma_i \sqsubseteq \tau_{f(i)} \right) \ and \ \left(\forall j \in \mathcal{J}, \ \sum_{i \in f^{-1}(j)} p_i \le p'_j \right)}{\left\{ \sigma_i^{P_i} \ \middle| \ i \in \mathcal{I} \right\} \sqsubseteq \left\{ \tau_j^{P'_j} \ \middle| \ j \in \mathcal{J} \right\}}$$

Sized Walks and Distribution Types. As we explained in Sect. 2, the rule typing letrec in the monadic, affine type system relies on an external decision procedure, computable in polynomial time. This procedure ensures that the *sized walk*—a particular instance of *one-counter Markov decision process* (OC-MDP, see [31]), but which does not make use of non-determinism—associated to the type of the recursive function of interest indeed ensures almost sure termination. Let us now define the sized walk associated to a distribution type μ. For the precise connection with OC-MDPs, see the long version [18].

Definition 11 (Sized Walk). *Let $\mathcal{I} \subseteq_{fin} \mathbb{N}$ be a finite set of integers. Let $\{p_i\}_{i \in \mathcal{I}}$ be such that $\sum_{i \in \mathcal{I}} p_i \le 1$. These parameters define a Markov chain whose set of states is $\mathbb{N}$ and whose transition relation is defined as follows:*

- *the state $0 \in \mathbb{N}$ is stationary (i.e. one goes from 0 to 0 with probability 1),*
- *from the state $s + 1 \in \mathbb{N}$ one moves:*
  - *to the state $s + i$ with probability p_i, for every $i \in \mathcal{I}$;*
  - *to 0 with probability $1 - \left(\sum_{i \in \mathcal{I}} p_i \right)$.*

We call this Markov chain the sized walk *on* $\mathbb{N}$ *associated to* $\left(\mathcal{I}, (p_i)_{i \in \mathcal{I}}\right)$. *A sized walk is* almost surely terminating *when it reaches* 0 *with probability* 1 *from any initial state.*

Notably, checking whether a sized walk is terminating is relatively easy:

Proposition 1 (Decidability of AST for Sized Walks). *It is decidable in polynomial time whether a sized walk is AST.*

Proof. By encoding sized walks into OC-MDPs, which enjoy this property [31]. See the long version [18]. ∎

Definition 12 (From Types to Sized Walks). *Consider a distribution type* $\mu = \left\{ (\mathsf{Nat}^{\mathfrak{s}_j} \to \nu_j)^{P_j} \mid j \in \mathcal{J} \right\}$ *such that* $\forall j \in \mathcal{J}$, $\mathrm{spine}(\mathfrak{s}_j) = \mathtt{i}$. *Then* μ *induces a sized walk, defined as follows. First, by definition,* $\mathfrak{s}_j$ *must be of the shape* $\widehat{\mathtt{i}}^{k_j}$ *with* $k_j \geq 0$ *for every* $j \in \mathcal{J}$. *We set* $\mathcal{I} = \left\{ K_j \mid j \in \mathcal{J} \right\}$ *and* $q_{K_j} = p_j$ *for every* $j \in \mathcal{J}$. *The sized walk induced by the distribution type* μ *is then the sized walk associated to* $\left(\mathcal{I}, (q_i)_{i \in \mathcal{I}}\right)$.

Example 1. Let $\mu = \left\{ \left(\mathsf{Nat}^{\mathtt{i}} \to \mathsf{Nat}^{\infty}\right)^{\frac{1}{2}}, \left(\mathsf{Nat}^{\widehat{\mathtt{i}}^2} \to \mathsf{Nat}^{\infty}\right)^{\frac{1}{3}} \right\}$. Then the induced sized walk is the one associated to $\left(\{0, 2\}, (p_0 = \frac{1}{2}, p_2 = \frac{1}{3})\right)$. In other words, it is the random walk on $\mathbb{N}$ which is stationary on 0, and which on non-null integers $i + 1$ moves to i with probability $\frac{1}{2}$, to $i + 2$ with probability $\frac{1}{3}$, and jumps to 0 with probability $\frac{1}{6}$. Note that the type μ, and therefore the associated sized walk, models a recursive function which calls itself on a size lesser by one unit with probability $\frac{1}{2}$, on a size greater by one unit with probability $\frac{1}{3}$, and which does not call itself with probability $\frac{1}{6}$.

Typing Rules. Judgements are of the shape $\Gamma \mid \Theta \vdash M : \mu$. When a distribution $\mu = \left\{ \sigma^1 \right\}$ is Dirac, we simply write it σ. The type system is defined in Fig. 4. As earlier, we define sets of typable terms, and set $\Lambda_{\oplus}^{\mathfrak{s}, V}(\Gamma \mid \Theta, \sigma) = \left\{ V \mid \Gamma \mid \Theta \vdash V : \sigma \right\}$, and $\Lambda_{\oplus}^{\mathfrak{s}}(\Gamma \mid \Theta, \mu) = \left\{ M \mid \Gamma \mid \Theta \vdash M : \mu \right\}$. We abbreviate $\Lambda_{\oplus}^{\mathfrak{s}, V}(\emptyset \mid \emptyset, \sigma)$ as $\Lambda_{\oplus}^{\mathfrak{s}, V}(\sigma)$ and $\Lambda_{\oplus}^{\mathfrak{s}}(\emptyset \mid \emptyset, \sigma)$ as $\Lambda_{\oplus}^{\mathfrak{s}}(\sigma)$.

This sized type system is a refinement of the affine simple type system for $\lambda_{\oplus}$: if $x_1 : \sigma_1, \ldots, x_n : \sigma_n \mid f : \mu \vdash M : \nu$, then it is easily checked that $x_1 :: \langle \sigma_1 \rangle, \ldots, x_n :: \langle \sigma_n \rangle, f :: \langle \mu \rangle \vdash M :: \langle \nu \rangle$.

Lemma 2 (Properties of Distribution Types).

- $\Gamma \mid \Theta \vdash V : \mu \implies \mu$ *is Dirac.*
- $\Gamma \mid \Theta \vdash M : \mu \implies \mu$ *is proper.*

Subject Reduction for Monadic Affine Sized Types. The type system enjoys a form of subject reduction adapted to the probabilistic case and more specifically

$$\text{Var} \quad \frac{}{\Gamma, x : \sigma \mid \Theta \vdash x : \sigma} \qquad \frac{}{\Gamma \mid x : \sigma \vdash x : \sigma} \quad \text{Var'}$$

$$\text{Succ} \quad \frac{\Gamma \mid \Theta \vdash V : \mathsf{Nat}^{\mathfrak{s}}}{\Gamma \mid \Theta \vdash \mathsf{S}\, V : \mathsf{Nat}^{\widehat{\mathfrak{s}}}} \qquad \frac{}{\Gamma \mid \Theta \vdash 0 : \mathsf{Nat}^{\widehat{\mathfrak{s}}}} \quad \text{Zero}$$

$$\lambda \quad \frac{\Gamma, x : \sigma \mid \Theta \vdash M : \mu}{\Gamma \mid \Theta \vdash \lambda x.M : \sigma \to \mu} \qquad \frac{\Gamma \mid \Theta \vdash M : \mu \qquad \mu \sqsubseteq \nu}{\Gamma \mid \Theta \vdash M : \nu} \quad \text{Sub}$$

$$\text{App} \quad \frac{\Gamma, \Delta \mid \Theta \vdash V : \sigma \to \mu \qquad \Gamma, \Xi \mid \Psi \vdash W : \sigma \qquad \langle \Gamma \rangle = \mathsf{Nat}}{\Gamma, \Delta, \Xi \mid \Theta, \Psi \vdash V\,W : \mu}$$

$$\text{Choice} \quad \frac{\Gamma \mid \Theta \vdash M : \mu \qquad \Gamma \mid \Psi \vdash N : \nu \qquad \langle \mu \rangle = \langle \nu \rangle}{\Gamma \mid \Theta \oplus_p \Psi \vdash M \oplus_p N : \mu \oplus_p \nu}$$

$$\text{Let} \quad \frac{\Gamma, \Delta \mid \Theta \vdash M : \left\{ \sigma_i^{p_i} \mid i \in \mathcal{I} \right\} \qquad \langle \Gamma \rangle = \mathsf{Nat} \qquad \Gamma, \Xi, x : \sigma_i \mid \Psi_i \vdash N : \mu_i \quad (\forall i \in \mathcal{I})}{\Gamma, \Delta, \Xi \mid \Theta, \left(\sum_{i \in \mathcal{I}} p_i \cdot \Psi_i \right) \vdash \mathsf{let}\; x = M \;\mathsf{in}\; N : \sum_{i \in \mathcal{I}} p_i \cdot \mu_i}$$

$$\text{Case} \quad \frac{\Gamma \mid \emptyset \vdash V : \mathsf{Nat}^{\widehat{\mathfrak{s}}} \qquad \Delta \mid \Theta \vdash W : \mathsf{Nat}^{\mathfrak{s}} \to \mu \qquad \Delta \mid \Theta \vdash Z : \mu}{\Gamma, \Delta \mid \Theta \vdash \mathsf{case}\; V \;\mathsf{of}\; \{ \mathsf{S} \to W \mid 0 \to Z \} : \mu}$$

$$\langle \Gamma \rangle = \mathsf{Nat}$$
$$i \notin \Gamma \text{ and } i \text{ positive in } \nu \text{ and } \forall j \in \mathcal{J}, \text{ spine}\,(\mathfrak{s}_j) = i$$
$$\left\{ (\mathsf{Nat}^{\mathfrak{s}_j} \to \nu[\mathfrak{s}_j/i])^{p_j} \mid j \in \mathcal{J} \right\} \text{ induces an AST sized walk}$$

$$\text{letrec} \quad \frac{\Gamma \mid f : \left\{ (\mathsf{Nat}^{\mathfrak{s}_j} \to \nu[\mathfrak{s}_j/i])^{p_j} \mid j \in \mathcal{J} \right\} \vdash V : \mathsf{Nat}^{\widehat{i}} \to \nu[\widehat{i}/i]}{\Gamma, \Delta \mid \Theta \vdash \mathsf{letrec}\; f = V : \mathsf{Nat}^{\mathfrak{r}} \to \nu[\mathfrak{r}/i]}$$

Fig. 4. Affine distribution types for $\lambda_{\oplus}$.

to the fact that terms reduce to *distributions* of terms. Let us sketch the idea of this adapted subject reduction property on an example. Remark that the type system allows us to derive the sequent

$$\emptyset \mid \emptyset \vdash 0 \oplus 0 : \left\{ \left(\mathsf{Nat}^{\widehat{\mathfrak{s}}} \right)^{\frac{1}{2}}, \left(\mathsf{Nat}^{\widehat{\mathfrak{r}}} \right)^{\frac{1}{2}} \right\} \tag{9}$$

where this distribution type is formed by typing a copy of 0 with $\mathsf{Nat}^{\widehat{\mathfrak{s}}}$ and the other with $\mathsf{Nat}^{\widehat{\mathfrak{r}}}$. Then, the term $0 \oplus 0$ reduces to $\left\{ 0^{\frac{1}{2}} \right\} + \left\{ 0^{\frac{1}{2}} \right\} = \left\{ 0^1 \right\} = [\![0 \oplus 0]\!]$: the operational semantics collapses the two copies of 0 appearing during the reduction. However, in the spirit of the usual subject reduction for deterministic languages, we would like to type the two copies of 0 appearing during the reduction with different types. We therefore use the notion of *pseudo-representation*: $\left[0^{\frac{1}{2}}, 0^{\frac{1}{2}} \right]$ is a pseudo-representation of $[\![0 \oplus 0]\!]$, and we attribute the type $\mathsf{Nat}^{\widehat{\mathsf{s}}}$ to the first element of this pseudo-representation and the type $\mathsf{Nat}^{\widehat{\widehat{\mathsf{f}}}}$ to the other, obtaining the following *closed distribution of typed terms*:

$$\left\{ \left(0 : \mathsf{Nat}^{\widehat{\mathsf{s}}} \right)^{\frac{1}{2}}, \left(0 : \mathsf{Nat}^{\widehat{\widehat{\mathsf{f}}}} \right)^{\frac{1}{2}} \right\} \tag{10}$$

We can then compute the *average* type of (10), which we call the *expectation type* of this closed distribution of typed terms:

$$\frac{1}{2} \cdot \left\{ \left(\mathsf{Nat}^{\widehat{\mathsf{s}}} \right)^1 \right\} + \frac{1}{2} \cdot \left\{ \left(\mathsf{Nat}^{\widehat{\widehat{\mathsf{f}}}} \right)^1 \right\} = \left\{ \left(\mathsf{Nat}^{\widehat{\mathsf{s}}} \right)^{\frac{1}{2}}, \left(\mathsf{Nat}^{\widehat{\widehat{\mathsf{f}}}} \right)^{\frac{1}{2}} \right\}$$

Remark that it coincides with the type of the initial term (9). This will be our result of subject reduction: when a closed term M of distribution type μ reduces to a distribution $\mathscr{D}$ of terms, we can type all the terms appearing in a pseudo-representation of $\mathscr{D}$ to obtain a closed distribution of typed terms whose expectation type is μ. Let us now introduce the definitions necessary to the formal statement of the subject reduction property.

Definition 13 (Distributions of Distribution Types, of Typed Terms).

- A distribution of distribution types *is a distribution $\mathscr{D}$ over the set of distribution types, and such that $\mu, \nu \in \mathsf{S}(\mathscr{D}) \Rightarrow \langle \mu \rangle = \langle \nu \rangle$.*
- A distribution of typed terms, *or typed distribution, is a distribution of typing sequents which are derivable in the monadic, affine sized type system. The representation of such a distribution has thus the following form: $\left\{ (\Gamma_i \,|\, \Theta_i \vdash M_i : \mu_i)^{P_i} \mid i \in \mathcal{I} \right\}$. In the sequel, we restrict to the uniform case in which all the terms appearing in the sequents are typed with distribution types of the same fixed underlying type.*
- A distribution of closed typed terms, *or closed typed distribution, is a typed distribution in which all contexts are $\emptyset \,|\, \emptyset$. In this case, we simply write the representation of the distribution as $\left\{ (M_i : \mu_i)^{P_i} \mid i \in \mathcal{I} \right\}$, or even as $(M_i : \mu_i)^{P_i}$ when the indexing is clear from context. We write pseudo-representations in a similar way.*

Definition 14 (Expectation Types). *Let $(M_i : \mu_i)^{P_i}$ be a closed typed distribution. We define its expectation type as the distribution type $\mathbb{E}\left((M_i : \mu_i)^{P_i} \right) = \sum_{i \in \mathcal{I}} p_i \mu_i.$*

We can now state the main lemma of subject reduction:

Lemma 3 (Subject Reduction, Fundamental Lemma). *Let $M \in \Lambda_{\oplus}^{\mathsf{s}}(\mu)$ and $\mathscr{D}$ be the unique closed term distribution such that $M \to_v \mathscr{D}$. Then there exists a closed typed distribution $\left\{ (L_j : \nu_j)^{P_j} \mid j \in \mathcal{J} \right\}$ such that*

- $\mathbb{E}\left((L_j \,:\, \nu_j)^{P_j}\right) \;=\; \mu,$
- $\left[(L_j)^{P_j} \;\mid\; j \in \mathcal{J} \right]$ *is a pseudo-representation of* $\mathscr{D}$.

Note that the condition on expectations implies that $\bigcup_{j \in \mathcal{J}} \mathsf{S}(\nu_j) \;=\; \mathsf{S}(\mu)$.

The proof of this result, and its generalization to the iterated reduction of closed typed distributions, appear in the long version. They allow us to deduce the following property on the operational semantics of $\lambda_\oplus$-terms:

Theorem 1 (Subject Reduction). *Let* $M \in \Lambda_\oplus^{\mathfrak{s}}(\mu)$. *Then there exists a closed typed distribution* $\left\{ (W_j \,:\, \sigma_j)^{P_j} \;\mid\; j \in \mathcal{J} \right\}$ *such that*

- $\mathbb{E}\left((W_j \,:\, \sigma_j)^{P_j}\right) \;\preccurlyeq\; \mu,$
- *and that* $\left[(W_j)^{P_j} \;\mid\; j \in \mathcal{J} \right]$ *is a pseudo-representation of* $[\![M]\!]$.

Note that $\mathbb{E}\left((W_j \,:\, \sigma_j)^{P_j}\right) \;\preccurlyeq\; \mu$ since the semantics of a term may not be a proper distribution at this stage. In fact, it will follow from the soundness theorem of Sect. 5 that the typability of M implies that $\sum [\![M]\!] = 1$ and thus that the previous statement is an equality.

5   Typability Implies Termination: Reducibility Strikes Again

This section is technically the most advanced one of the paper, and proves that the typing discipline we have introduced indeed enforces almost sure termination. As already mentioned, the technique we will employ is a substantial generalisation of Girard-Tait's reducibility. In particular, reducibility must be made quantitative, in that terms can be said to be reducible *with a certain probability*. This means that reducibility sets will be defined as sets parameterised by a real number p, called the *degree of reducibility* of the set. As Lemma 4 will emphasize, this degree of reducibility ensures that terms contained in a reducibility set parameterised by p terminate with probability at least p. These "intermediate" degrees of reducibility are required to handle the fixpoint construction, and show that recursively-defined terms that are typable are indeed AST—that is, that they belong to the appropriate reducibility set, parameterised by 1.

The first preliminary notion we need is that of a size environment:

Definition 15 (Size Environment). *A size environment is any function* ρ *from* $\mathcal{S}$ *to* $\mathbb{N} \cup \{\infty\}$. *Given a size environment* ρ *and a size expression* $\mathfrak{s}$, *there is a naturally defined element of* $\mathbb{N} \cup \{\infty\}$, *which we indicate as* $[\![\mathfrak{s}]\!]_\rho$:

- $[\![\widehat{\mathfrak{i}^n}]\!]_\rho \;=\; \rho(\mathfrak{i}) + n,$
- $[\![\infty]\!]_\rho \;=\; \infty.$

In other words, the purpose of size environments is to give a semantic meaning to size expressions. Our reducibility sets will be parameterised not only on a probability, but also on a size environment.

Definition 16 (Reducibility Sets).

- *For values of simple type* Nat, *we define the reducibility sets*

$$\mathsf{VRed}^p_{\mathsf{Nat}^s,\rho} \;=\; \left\{ \mathsf{S}^n\, 0 \;\mid\; p > 0 \Longrightarrow n < [\![s]\!]_\rho \right\}.$$

- *Values of higher-order type are in a reducibility set when their applications to appropriate values are reducible terms, with an adequate degree of reducibility:*

$$\mathsf{VRed}^p_{\sigma \to \mu,\rho} \;=\; \left\{ V \in \Lambda^V_\oplus(\langle \sigma \to \mu \rangle) \;\mid\; \forall q \in (0,1], \quad \forall W \in \mathsf{VRed}^q_{\sigma,\rho}, \atop V\, W \in \mathsf{TRed}^{pq}_{\mu,\rho} \right\}$$

- *Distributions of values are reducible with degree p when they consist of values which are themselves globally reducible "enough". Formally, $\mathsf{DRed}^p_{\mu,\rho}$ is the set of finite distributions of values – in the sense that they have a finite support – admitting a pseudo-representation $\mathscr{D} = \left[(V_i)^{P_i} \;\mid\; i \in \mathcal{I} \right]$ such that, setting $\mu = \left\{ (\sigma_j)^{P'_j} \;\mid\; j \in \mathcal{J} \right\}$, there exists a family $(p_{ij})_{i \in \mathcal{I}, j \in \mathcal{J}} \in [0,1]^{|\mathcal{I}| \times |\mathcal{J}|}$ of probabilities and a family $(q_{ij})_{i \in \mathcal{I}, j \in \mathcal{J}} \in [0,1]^{|\mathcal{I}| \times |\mathcal{J}|}$ of degrees of reducibility, satisfying:*
  1. $\forall i \in \mathcal{I}, \quad \forall j \in \mathcal{J}, \quad V_i \in \mathsf{VRed}^{q_{ij}}_{\sigma_j,\rho}$,
  2. $\forall i \in \mathcal{I}, \quad \sum_{j \in \mathcal{J}} p_{ij} = p_i$,
  3. $\forall j \in \mathcal{J}, \quad \sum_{i \in \mathcal{I}} p_{ij} = \mu(\sigma_j)$,
  4. $p \leq \sum_{i \in \mathcal{I}} \sum_{j \in \mathcal{J}} q_{ij} p_{ij}$.

  Note that (2) and (3) imply that $\sum \mathscr{D} = \sum \mu$. We say that $\left[(V_i)^{P_i} \;\mid\; i \in \mathcal{I} \right]$ witnesses that $\mathscr{D} \in \mathsf{DRed}^p_{\mu,\rho}$.

- *A term is reducible with degree p when its finite approximations compute distributions of values of degree of reducibility arbitrarily close to p:*

$$\mathsf{TRed}^p_{\mu,\rho} \;=\; \left\{ M \in \Lambda_\oplus(\langle \mu \rangle) \;\mid\; \forall 0 \leq r < p, \quad \exists \nu_r \preccurlyeq \mu, \quad \exists n_r \in \mathbb{N}, \atop M \Rrightarrow^{n_r}_v \mathscr{D}_r \text{ and } \mathscr{D}_r \in \mathsf{DRed}^r_{\nu_r,\rho} \right\}$$

Note that here, unlike to the case of DRed, *the fact that $M \in \Lambda_\oplus(\langle \mu \rangle)$ implies that μ is proper.*

The first thing to observe about reducibility sets as given in Definition 16 is that they only deal with closed terms, and not with arbitrary terms. As such, we cannot rely *directly* on them when proving AST for typable terms, at least if we want to prove it by induction on the structure of type derivations. We will therefore define in the sequel an extension of these sets to open terms, which will be based on these sets of closed terms, and therefore enjoy similar properties. The following lemma, relatively easy to prove, is crucial for the understanding of the reducibility sets, for that it shows that the degree of reducibility of a term gives information on the sum of its operational semantics:

Lemma 4 (Reducibility and Termination).

- *Let $\mathscr{D} \in \mathsf{DRed}^p_{\mu,\rho}$. Then $\sum \mathscr{D} \geq p$.*
- *Let $M \in \mathsf{TRed}^p_{\mu,\rho}$. Then $\sum \llbracket M \rrbracket \geq p$.*

It follows from this lemma that terms with degree of reducibility 1 are AST:

Corollary 1 (Reducibility and AST). *Let $M \in \mathsf{TRed}^1_{\mu,\rho}$. Then M is AST.*

Fundamental Properties. Before embarking in the proof that typability implies reducibility, it is convenient to prove some fundamental properties of reducibility sets, which inform us about how these sets are structured, and which will be crucial in the sequel. First of all, if the degree of reducibility p is 0, then no assumption is made on the probability of termination of terms, distributions or values. It follows that the three kinds of reducibility sets collapse to the set of all affinely simply typable terms, distributions or values:

Lemma 5 (Candidates of Null Reducibility).

- *If $V \in \Lambda^V_\oplus(\kappa)$, then $V \in \mathsf{VRed}^0_{\sigma,\rho}$ for every σ such that $\langle \sigma \rangle = \kappa$ and every size environment ρ.*
- *Let $\mathscr{D} = \left\{ (V_i)^{P_i} \mid i \in \mathcal{I} \right\}$ be a finite distribution of values. If $\forall i \in \mathcal{I}$, $V_i \in \Lambda^V_\oplus(\kappa)$, then $\mathscr{D} \in \mathsf{DRed}^0_{\mu,\rho}$ for every μ such that $\langle \mu \rangle = \kappa$ and $\sum \mu = \sum \mathscr{D}$ and every ρ.*
- *If $M \in \Lambda_\oplus(\kappa)$, then $M \in \mathsf{TRed}^0_{\mu,\rho}$ for μ such that $\langle \mu \rangle = \kappa$ and every ρ.*

As p gives us a lower bound on the sum of the semantics of terms, it is easily guessed that a term having degree of reducibility p must also have degree of reducibility $q < p$. The following lemma makes this statement precise:

Lemma 6 (Downward Closure). *Let σ be a sized type, μ be a distribution type and ρ be a size environment. Let $0 \leq q < p \leq 1$. Then:*

- *For any value V, $V \in \mathsf{VRed}^p_{\sigma,\rho} \implies V \in \mathsf{VRed}^q_{\sigma,\rho}$,*
- *For any finite distribution of values $\mathscr{D}$, $\mathscr{D} \in \mathsf{DRed}^p_{\mu,\rho} \implies \mathscr{D} \in \mathsf{DRed}^q_{\mu,\rho}$,*
- *For any term M, $M \in \mathsf{TRed}^p_{\mu,\rho} \implies M \in \mathsf{TRed}^q_{\mu,\rho}$.*

To analyse the letrec construction, we will prove that, for every $\varepsilon \in (0, 1]$, performing enough unfoldings of the fixpoint allows to prove that the recursively-defined term is in a reducibility set parameterised by $1 - \varepsilon$. We will be able to conclude on the AST nature of recursive constructions using the following continuity lemma, proved using the theory of linear programming [18]:

Lemma 7 (Continuity). *Let σ be a sized type, μ be a distribution type and ρ be a size environment. Let $p \in (0, 1]$. Then:*

- $\mathsf{VRed}^p_{\sigma,\rho} = \bigcap_{0 < q < p} \mathsf{VRed}^q_{\sigma,\rho}$,
- $\mathsf{DRed}^p_{\mu,\rho} = \bigcap_{0 < q < p} \mathsf{DRed}^q_{\mu,\rho}$,
- $\mathsf{TRed}^p_{\mu,\rho} = \bigcap_{0 < q < p} \mathsf{TRed}^q_{\mu,\rho}$.

The last fundamental property about reducibility sets which will be crucial to treat the recursive case is the following, stating that the sizes appearing in a sized type may be recovered in the reducibility set by using an appropriate semantics of the size variables, and conversely:

Lemma 8 (Size Commutation). *Let* i *be a size variable,* $\mathfrak{s}$ *be a size such that* $\mathfrak{s} = \infty$ *or that* $\mathrm{spine}\,(\mathfrak{s}) \neq i$ *and* ρ *be a size environment. Then:*

- $\mathsf{VRed}^p_{\sigma[\mathfrak{s}/i],\rho} \;=\; \mathsf{VRed}^p_{\sigma,\rho[i \mapsto [\![\mathfrak{s}]\!]_\rho]},$
- $\mathsf{DRed}^p_{\mu[\mathfrak{s}/i],\rho} \;=\; \mathsf{DRed}^p_{\mu,\rho[i \mapsto [\![\mathfrak{s}]\!]_\rho]},$
- $\mathsf{TRed}^p_{\mu[\mathfrak{s}/i],\rho} \;=\; \mathsf{TRed}^p_{\mu,\rho[i \mapsto [\![\mathfrak{s}]\!]_\rho]}.$

Unfoldings. The most difficult step in proving all typable terms to be reducible is, unexpectedly, proving that terms involving *recursion* are reducible whenever their respective *unfoldings* are. This very natural concept expresses simply that any term in the form letrec $f = W$ is assumed to compute the fixpoint of the function defined by W.

Definition 17 (n-Unfolding). *Suppose that* $V = (\text{letrec } f = W)$ *is closed, then the* n-unfolding *of* V *is:*

- V *if* $n = 0$;
- $W[Z/f]$ *if* $n = m + 1$ *and* Z *is the* m-unfolding *of* V.

We write the set of unfoldings of V *as* $\mathrm{Unfold}\,(V)$. *Note that if* V *admits a simple type, then all its unfoldings have this same simple type as well. In the sequel, we implicitly consider that* V *is simply typed.*

Any unfolding of $V = (\text{letrec } f = W)$ should behave like V itself: all unfoldings of V should be equivalent. This, however, cannot be proved using simply the operational semantics. It requires some work, and techniques akin to logical relations, to prove (see [18]) this behavioural equivalence between a recursive definition and its unfoldings.

Proposition 2 (Reducibility is Stable by Unfolding). *Let* $n \in \mathbb{N}$ *and* $V = (\text{letrec } f = W)$ *be a closed value. Suppose that* Z *is the* n-unfolding *of* V. *Then* $V \in \mathsf{VRed}^p_{\mathsf{Nat}^\mathfrak{s} \to \mu,\rho}$ *if and only if* $Z \in \mathsf{VRed}^p_{\mathsf{Nat}^\mathfrak{s} \to \mu,\rho}.$

Extension to Open Terms. We are now ready to extend the notion of reducibility set from the realm of *closed* terms to the one of *open* terms. This turns out to be subtle. The guiding intuition is that one would like to define a term M with free variables in $\overrightarrow{x}$ to be reducible iff any closure $M[\overrightarrow{V}/\overrightarrow{x}]$ is itself reducible in the sense of Definition 16. What happens, however, to the underlying degree of reducibility p? How do we relate the degrees of reducibility of $\overrightarrow{V}$ with the one of $M[\overrightarrow{V}/\overrightarrow{x}]$? The answer is contained in the following definition:

Definition 18 (Reducibility Sets for Open Terms). *Suppose that* Γ *is a sized context in the form* $x_1 : \sigma_1, \ldots, x_n : \sigma_n$, *and that* y *is a variable distinct from* $x_1, \ldots, x_n$. *Then we define the following sets of terms and values:*

$$\mathsf{OTRed}_{\mu,\rho}^{\Gamma\,|\,\emptyset} \;=\; \Big\{ M \;\Big|\; \forall (q_i)_i \in [0,1]^n, \;\; \forall (V_1, \ldots, V_n) \in \prod_{i=1}^n \mathsf{VRed}_{\sigma_i,\rho}^{q_i}, \\ M[\vec{V}/\vec{x}] \in \mathsf{TRed}_{\mu,\rho}^{\prod_{i=1}^N q_i} \Big\}$$

$$\mathsf{OVRed}_{\mu,\rho}^{\Gamma\,|\,\emptyset} \;=\; \Big\{ W \;\Big|\; \forall (q_i)_i \in [0,1]^n, \;\; \forall (V_1, \ldots, V_n) \in \prod_{i=1}^n \mathsf{VRed}_{\sigma_i,\rho}^{q_i}, \\ W[\vec{V}/\vec{x}] \in \mathsf{VRed}_{\mu,\rho}^{\prod_{i=1}^N q_i} \Big\}$$

$$\mathsf{OTRed}_{\mu,\rho}^{\Gamma\,|\,y:\{\tau_j^{P_j}\}_{j\in\mathcal{J}}} \;=\; \Big\{ M \;\Big|\; \forall (q_i)_i \in [0,1]^n, \;\; \forall \vec{V} \in \prod_{i=1}^n \mathsf{VRed}_{\sigma_i,\rho}^{q_i}, \\ \forall \big(q_j'\big)_j \in [0,1]^{\mathcal{J}}, \;\; \forall W \in \bigcap_{j\in\mathcal{J}} \mathsf{VRed}_{\tau_j,\rho}^{q_j'}, \\ M[\vec{V}, W/\vec{x}, y] \in \mathsf{TRed}_{\mu,\rho}^{\alpha} \Big\}$$

$$\mathsf{OVRed}_{\mu,\rho}^{\Gamma\,|\,y:\{\tau_j^{P_j}\}_{j\in\mathcal{J}}} \;=\; \Big\{ Z \;\Big|\; \forall (q_i)_i \in [0,1]^n, \;\; \forall \vec{V} \in \prod_{i=1}^n \mathsf{VRed}_{\sigma_i,\rho}^{q_i}, \\ \forall \big(q_j'\big)_j \in [0,1]^{\mathcal{J}}, \;\; \forall W \in \bigcap_{j\in\mathcal{J}} \mathsf{VRed}_{\tau_j,\rho}^{q_j'}, \\ Z[\vec{V}, W/\vec{x}, y] \in \mathsf{VRed}_{\mu,\rho}^{\alpha} \Big\}$$

where $\alpha = \left(\prod_{i=1}^n q_i\right)\left(\left(\sum_{j\in\mathcal{J}} p_j q_j'\right) + 1 - \left(\sum_{j\in\mathcal{J}} p_j\right)\right)$ is called the degree of reducibility. Note that these sets extend the ones for closed terms: in particular, $\mathsf{OTRed}_{\mu,\rho}^{\emptyset\,|\,\emptyset} = \mathsf{TRed}_{\mu,\rho}^1$.

Lemma 9 (Reducible Values are Reducible Terms). *For every* Γ, Θ, σ *and* ρ, $V \in \mathsf{OVRed}_{\sigma,\rho}^{\Gamma\,|\,\Theta}$ *if and only if* $V \in \mathsf{OTRed}_{\{\sigma^1\},\rho}^{\Gamma\,|\,\Theta}$. *An immediate consequence is that* $\mathsf{OVRed}_{\sigma,\rho}^{\Gamma\,|\,\Theta} \subseteq \mathsf{OTRed}_{\{\sigma^1\},\rho}^{\Gamma\,|\,\Theta}$.

Reducibility and Sized Walks. To handle the fixpoint rule, we need to relate the notion of sized walk which guards it with the reducibility sets, and in particular with the degrees of reducibility we can attribute to recursively-defined terms.

Definition 19 (Probabilities of Convergence in Finite Time). *Let us consider a sized walk. We define the associated probabilities of convergence in finite time* $(Pr_{n,m})_{n\in\mathbb{N},m\in\mathbb{N}}$ *as follows:* $\forall n \in \mathbb{N}, \;\; \forall m \in \mathbb{N}$, *the real number* $Pr_{n,m}$ *is defined as the probability that, starting from* m, *the sized walk reaches* 0 *in at most* n *steps.*

The point is that, for an AST sized walk, the more we iterate, the closer we get to reaching 0 in finite time n with probability 1.

Lemma 10 (Finite Approximations of AST). *Let* $m \in \mathbb{N}$ *and* $\varepsilon \in (0,1]$. *Consider a sized walk, and its associated probabilities of convergence in finite time* $(Pr_{n,m})_{n\in\mathbb{N},m\in\mathbb{N}}$. *If the sized walk is AST, there exists* $n \in \mathbb{N}$ *such that* $Pr_{n,m} \geq 1 - \varepsilon$.

The following lemma is the crucial result relating sized walks with the reducibility sets. It proves that, when the sized walk is AST, and after substitution of the variables of the context by reducible values in the recursively-defined term, we can prove the degree of reducibility to be any probability $Pr_{n,m}$ of convergence in finite time.

Lemma 11 (Convergence in Finite Time and letrec). *Consider the distribution type* $\mu = \big\{ (\mathsf{Nat}^{s_j} \to \nu[s_j/i])^{p_j} \mid j \in \mathcal{J} \big\}$. *Let* Γ *be the sized context* $x_1 : \mathsf{Nat}^{r_1}, \ldots, x_l : \mathsf{Nat}^{r_l}$. *Suppose that* $\Gamma \mid f : \mu \vdash V : \mathsf{Nat}^{\widehat{i}} \to \nu[\widehat{i}/i]$ *and that* μ *induces an AST sized walk. Denote* $(Pr_{n,m})_{n \in \mathbb{N}, m \in \mathbb{N}}$ *its associated probabilities of convergence in finite time. Suppose that* $V \in \mathsf{OVRed}_{\mathsf{Nat}^{\widehat{i}} \to \nu[\widehat{i}/i], \rho}^{\Gamma \mid f : \mu}$ *for every* ρ.
Let $\overrightarrow{W} \in \prod_{i=1}^l \mathsf{VRed}_{\mathsf{Nat}^{r_i}, \rho}^1$, *then for every* $(n, m) \in \mathbb{N}^2$, *we have that*

$$\mathsf{letrec}\ f = V[\overrightarrow{W}/\overrightarrow{x}] \in \mathsf{VRed}_{\mathsf{Nat}^i \to \nu, \rho[i \mapsto m]}^{Pr_{n,m}}$$

Proof. We give a sketch of the proof, to be found in the long version [18]. The proof is by recurrence on n. The main case relies on the decomposition $Pr_{n+1,m'+1} = \sum_{j \in \mathcal{J}} p_j Pr_{N,m'+k_j} + 1 - \big(\sum_{j \in \mathcal{J}} p_j\big)$. The induction hypothesis allows then to state that for every $j \in \mathcal{J}$ we have $\mathsf{letrec}\ f = V[\overrightarrow{W}/\overrightarrow{x}] \in \mathsf{VRed}_{\mathsf{Nat}^i \to \nu, \rho[i \mapsto m'+k_j]}^{Pr_{n,m'+k_j}}$. We use the Size Commutation lemma (Lemma 8) to obtain that $\mathsf{letrec}\ f = V[\overrightarrow{W}/\overrightarrow{x}]$ is in an appropriate intersection of reducibility sets, and the hypothesis that $V \in \mathsf{OVRed}_{\mathsf{Nat}^{\widehat{i}} \to \nu[\widehat{i}/i], \rho[i \mapsto m']}^{\Gamma \mid f : \mu}$ then implies that $V[\overrightarrow{W}, \mathsf{letrec}\ f = V[\overrightarrow{W}/\overrightarrow{x}]/\overrightarrow{x}, f] \in \mathsf{VRed}_{\mathsf{Nat}^i \to \nu, \rho[i \mapsto m'+1]}^{Pr_{n+1,m'+1}}$, using the Size Commutation lemma once again. As this term is an unfolding of $\mathsf{letrec}\ f = V[\overrightarrow{W}/\overrightarrow{x}]$, we conclude using Proposition 2. □

When $m = \infty$, the previous lemma does not allow to conclude, and an additional argument is required. Indeed, it does not make sense to consider a sized walk beginning from ∞: the meaning of this size is in fact *any integer*, not the ordinal ω. The following lemma justifies this vision by proving that, if a term is in a reducibility set for any finite interpretation of a size, then it is also in the set where the size is interpreted as ∞.

Lemma 12 (Reducibility for Infinite Sizes). *Suppose that* i pos ν *and that* W *is the value* $\mathsf{letrec}\ f = V$. *If* $W \in \mathsf{VRed}_{\mathsf{Nat}^i \to \nu, \rho[i \mapsto n]}^p$ *for every* $n \in \mathbb{N}$, *then* $W \in \mathsf{VRed}_{\mathsf{Nat}^i \to \nu, \rho[i \mapsto \infty]}^p$.

All these fundamental lemmas allow us to prove the following proposition, which expresses that all typable terms are reducible and is the key step towards the fact that typability implies AST:

Proposition 3 (Typing Soundness). *If* $\Gamma \mid \Theta \vdash M : \mu$, *then* $M \in \mathsf{OTRed}_{\mu, \rho}^{\Gamma \mid \Theta}$ *for every* ρ. *Similarly, if* $\Gamma \mid \Theta \vdash V : \sigma$, *then* $V \in \mathsf{OVRed}_{\sigma, \rho}^{\Gamma \mid \Theta}$ *for every* ρ.

Proof. We proceed by induction on the derivation of the sequent $\Gamma \mid \Theta \vdash M : \mu$. When $M = V$ is a value, we know by Lemma 2 that $\mu = \{ \sigma^1 \}$; and we prove that $V \in \mathsf{OVRed}_{\sigma, \rho}^{\Gamma \mid \Theta}$ for every ρ. By Lemma 9 we obtain that $V \in \mathsf{OTRed}_{\mu, \rho}^{\Gamma \mid \Theta}$ for every ρ. We proceed by case analysis on the last rule of the derivation:

- letrec: Suppose that $\Gamma, \Delta \mid \Theta \vdash \mathsf{letrec}\ f = V : \mathsf{Nat}^r \to \nu[r/i]$. We treat the case where $\Delta = \Theta = \emptyset$. The general case is easily deduced using the downward-closure of the reducibility sets (Lemma 6). Let $\Gamma = x_1 :$ $\mathsf{Nat}^{\mathfrak{r}_1}, \ldots, x_n : \mathsf{Nat}^{\mathfrak{r}_n}$. We need to prove that, for every family $(q_i)_i \in [0,1]^n$ and every $(W_1, \ldots, W_n) \in \prod_{i=1}^n \mathsf{VRed}^{Q_i}_{\mathsf{Nat}^{\mathfrak{r}_i}, \rho}$, we have

$$(\mathsf{letrec}\ f\ =\ V)\,[\overrightarrow{W}/\overrightarrow{x}]\ =\ \left(\mathsf{letrec}\ f\ =\ V[\overrightarrow{W}/\overrightarrow{x}]\right)\ \in\ \mathsf{VRed}^{\prod_{i=1}^n q_i}_{\mathsf{Nat}^{\mathfrak{r}} \to \nu[\mathfrak{r}/\mathfrak{i}], \rho}$$

If there exists $i \in \mathcal{I}$ such that $q_i = 0$, the result is immediate as the term is simply-typed and Lemma 5 applies. Else, for every $i \in \mathcal{I}$, we have by definition that $\mathsf{VRed}^{q_i}_{\mathsf{Nat}^{\mathfrak{r}_i}, \rho} = \mathsf{VRed}^1_{\mathsf{Nat}^{\mathfrak{r}_i}, \rho}$. Since the sets VRed are downward-closed (Lemma 6), it is in fact enough to prove that for every $(W_1, \ldots, W_n) \in \prod_{i=1}^n \mathsf{VRed}^1_{\mathsf{Nat}^{\mathfrak{r}_i}, \rho}$, we have

$$\mathsf{letrec}\ f\ =\ V[\overrightarrow{W}/\overrightarrow{x}]\ \in\ \mathsf{VRed}^1_{\mathsf{Nat}^{\mathfrak{r}} \to \nu[\mathfrak{r}/\mathfrak{i}], \rho}$$

Moreover, by size commutation (Lemma 8),

$$\mathsf{VRed}^1_{\mathsf{Nat}^{\mathfrak{r}} \to \nu[\mathfrak{r}/\mathfrak{i}], \rho}\ =\ \mathsf{VRed}^1_{\mathsf{Nat}^{\mathfrak{i}} \to \nu, \rho[\mathfrak{i} \mapsto [\![\mathfrak{r}]\!]_\rho]}$$

Let us therefore prove the stronger fact that, for *every* integer $m \in \mathbb{N} \cup \{\infty\}$,

$$\mathsf{letrec}\ f\ =\ V[\overrightarrow{W}/\overrightarrow{x}]\ \in\ \mathsf{VRed}^1_{\mathsf{Nat}^{\mathfrak{i}} \to \nu, \rho[\mathfrak{i} \mapsto m]}$$

Now, the typing derivation gives us that $\Gamma \mid f : \mu \vdash V : \mathsf{Nat}^{\widehat{\mathfrak{i}}} \to \nu[\widehat{\mathfrak{i}}/\mathfrak{i}]$ and that μ induces an AST sized walk. Denote $(Pr_{n,m})_{n \in \mathbb{N}, m \in \mathbb{N}}$ its associated probabilities of convergence in finite time. By induction hypothesis, $V \in \mathsf{OVRed}^{\Gamma \mid f : \mu}_{\mathsf{Nat}^{\widehat{\mathfrak{i}}} \to \nu[\widehat{\mathfrak{i}}/\mathfrak{i}], \rho}$ for every ρ and we can apply Lemma 11. It follows that, for every $(n, m) \in \mathbb{N}$,

$$\mathsf{letrec}\ f\ =\ V[\overrightarrow{W}/\overrightarrow{x}]\ \in\ \mathsf{VRed}^{Pr_{n,m}}_{\mathsf{Nat}^{\mathfrak{i}} \to \nu, \rho[\mathfrak{i} \mapsto m]}$$

Let $\varepsilon \in (0,1)$. By Lemma 10, there exists $n \in \mathbb{N}$ such that $Pr_{n,m} \geq 1 - \varepsilon$. Using downward closure (Lemma 6) and quantifying over all the ε, we obtain

$$\mathsf{letrec}\ f\ =\ V[\overrightarrow{W}/\overrightarrow{x}]\ \in\ \bigcap_{0 < \varepsilon < 1} \mathsf{VRed}^{1 - \varepsilon}_{\mathsf{Nat}^{\mathfrak{i}} \to \nu, \rho[\mathfrak{i} \mapsto m]}$$

so that, by continuity of VRed (Lemma 7), we obtain

$$\mathsf{letrec}\ f\ =\ V[\overrightarrow{W}/\overrightarrow{x}]\ \in\ \mathsf{VRed}^1_{\mathsf{Nat}^{\mathfrak{i}} \to \nu, \rho[\mathfrak{i} \mapsto m]} \tag{11}$$

for every $m \in \mathbb{N}$, allowing us to conclude. It remains however to treat the case where $m = \infty$. Since $\mathfrak{i}$ pos ν and that (11) holds for every $m \in \mathbb{N}$, Lemma 12 applies and we obtain the result.

• **Other cases:** the other cases are treated in the long version [18].   □

This proposition, together with the definition of OTRed, implies the main result of the paper, namely that typability implies almost-sure termination:

Theorem 2. *Suppose that* $M \in \Lambda_\oplus^{\mathrm{s}}(\mu)$. *Then* M *is AST.*

Proof. Suppose that $M \in \Lambda_\oplus^{\mathrm{s}}(\mu)$, then by Proposition 3 we have $M \in \mathsf{OTRed}_{\mu,\rho}^{\emptyset\,|\,\emptyset}$ for every ρ. By definition, $\mathsf{OTRed}_{\mu,\rho}^{\emptyset\,|\,\emptyset} = \mathsf{TRed}_{\mu,\rho}^{1}$. Corollary 1 then implies that M is AST.

6   Conclusions and Perspectives

We presented a type system for an affine, simply-typed λ-calculus enriched with a probabilistic choice operator, constructors for the natural numbers, and recursion. This affinity constraint implies that a given higher-order variable may occur (freely) at most once in any probabilistic branch of a program. The type system we designed decorates the affine simple types with *size information*, allowing to incorporate in the types relevant information about the recursive behaviour of the functions contained in the program. A guard condition on the typing rule for letrec, formulated with reference to an appropriate Markov chain, ensures that typable terms are AST. The proof of soundness of this type system for AST relies on a quantitative extension of the reducibility method, to accommodate sets of candidates to the infinitary and probabilistic nature of the computations we consider.

A first natural question is the one of the decidability of type inference for our system. In the deterministic case, this question was only addressed by Barthe and colleagues in an unpublished tutorial [20], and their solution is technically involved, especially when it comes to dealing with the fixpoint rule. We believe that their approach could be extended to our system of monadic sized types, and hope that it could provide a decidable type inference procedure for it. However, this extension will certainly be challenging, as we need to appropriately infer distribution types associated with AST sized walks in the letrec rule.

Another perspective would be to study the general, *non-affine* case. This is challenging, for two reasons. First, the system of size annotations needs to be more expressive in order to distinguish between various occurrences of a same function symbol in a same probabilistic branch. A solution would be to use the combined power of dependent types – which already allowed Xi to formulate an interesting type system for termination in the deterministic case [23] – and of linearity: we could use *linear dependent types* [34] to formulate an extension of the monadic sized type system keeping track of *how many* recursive calls are performed, and of the size of *each* recursive argument. The second challenge would then be to associate, in the typing rule for letrec, this information contained in linear dependent types with an appropriate random process. This random process should be kept decidable to guarantee that at least *derivation* checking can be automated, and there will probably be a trade-off between the duplication power we allow in programs and the complexity of deciding AST for the guard in the letrec rule.

The extension of our type system to deal with general inductive datatypes is essentially straightforward. Other perspectives would be to enrich the type system so as to be able to treat coinductive data, polymorphic types, or ordinal sizes, three features present in most system of sized types dealing with the traditional deterministic case, but which we chose not to address in this paper to focus on the already complex task of accommodating sized types to a probabilistic and higher-order framework.

References

1. Manning, C.D., Schütze, H.: Foundations of Statistical Natural Language Processing. MIT Press, Cambridge (2001)
2. Pearl, J.: Probabilistic Reasoning in Intelligent Systems - Networks of Plausible Inference. Morgan Kaufmann Series in Representation and Reasoning. Morgan Kaufmann, Burlington (1989)
3. Thrun, S.: Robotic mapping: a survey. In: Exploring Artificial Intelligence in the New Millenium, Morgan Kaufmann (2002)
4. de Leeuw, K., Moore, E.F., Shannon, C.E., Shapiro, N.: Computability by probabilistic machines. Automata Studies **34**, 183–212 (1956)
5. Motwani, R., Raghavan, P.: Randomized Algorithms. Cambridge University Press, Cambridge (1995)
6. Barthe, G., Grégoire, B., Béguelin, S.Z.: Formal certification of code-based cryptographic proofs. In: Shao, Z., Pierce, B.C. (eds.) POPL 2009, pp. 90–101. ACM (2009)
7. Barthe, G., Grégoire, B., Heraud, S., Béguelin, S.Z.: Computer-aided security proofs for the working cryptographer. In: Rogaway, P. (ed.) CRYPTO 2011. LNCS, vol. 6841, pp. 71–90. Springer, Heidelberg (2011). doi:10.1007/978-3-642-22792-9_5
8. Goodman, N.D., Mansinghka, V.K., Roy, D.M., Bonawitz, K., Tenenbaum, J.B.: Church: a language for generative models. In: McAllester, D.A., Myllymäki, P. (eds.) UAI 2008, pp. 220–229. AUAI Press (2008)
9. Bournez, O., Kirchner, C.: Probabilistic rewrite strategies. applications to ELAN. In: Tison, S. (ed.) RTA 2002. LNCS, vol. 2378, pp. 252–266. Springer, Heidelberg (2002). doi:10.1007/3-540-45610-4_18
10. Esparza, J., Gaiser, A., Kiefer, S.: Proving termination of probabilistic programs using patterns. In: Madhusudan, P., Seshia, S.A. (eds.) CAV 2012. LNCS, vol. 7358, pp. 123–138. Springer, Heidelberg (2012). doi:10.1007/978-3-642-31424-7_14
11. Fioriti, L.M.F., Hermanns, H.: Probabilistic termination: soundness, completeness, and compositionality. In: Rajamani, S.K., Walker, D. (eds.) POPL 2015, pp. 489–501. ACM (2015)
12. Chatterjee, K., Fu, H., Novotný, P., Hasheminezhad, R.: Algorithmic analysis of qualitative and quantitative termination problems for affine probabilistic programs. In: Bodík, R., Majumdar, R. (eds.) POPL 2016, pp. 327–342. ACM (2016)
13. Chatterjee, K., Fu, H., Goharshady, A.K.: Termination analysis of probabilistic programs through Positivstellensatz's. In: Chaudhuri, S., Farzan, A. (eds.) CAV 2016. LNCS, vol. 9779, pp. 3–22. Springer, Heidelberg (2016). doi:10.1007/978-3-319-41528-4_1
14. Hughes, J., Pareto, L., Sabry, A.: Proving the correctness of reactive systems using sized types. In: Boehm, H. Jr., Shackle, G.L.S. (eds.) POPL 1996, pp. 410–423. ACM Press (1996)

15. Hofmann, M.: A mixed modal/linear lambda calculus with applications to Bellantoni-Cook safe recursion. In: Nielsen, M., Thomas, W. (eds.) CSL 1997. LNCS, vol. 1414, pp. 275–294. Springer, Heidelberg (1998). doi:10.1007/BFb0028020

16. Girard, J.Y., Taylor, P., Lafont, Y.: Proofs and Types. Cambridge University Press, New York (1989)

17. Dal Lago, U., Hofmann, M.: Realizability models and implicit complexity. Theoret. Comput. Sci. **412**(20), 2029–2047 (2011)

18. Dal Lago, U., Grellois, C.: Probabilistic termination by monadic affine sized typing (long version) (2016). https://arxiv.org/abs/1701.04089

19. Barthe, G., Frade, M.J., Giménez, E., Pinto, L., Uustalu, T.: Type-based termination of recursive definitions. MSCS **14**(1), 97–141 (2004)

20. Barthe, G., Grégoire, B., Riba, C.: A tutorial on type-based termination. In: Bove, A., Barbosa, L.S., Pardo, A., Pinto, J.S. (eds.) LerNet 2008. LNCS, vol. 5520, pp. 100–152. Springer, Heidelberg (2009). doi:10.1007/978-3-642-03153-3_3

21. Barthe, G., Grégoire, B., Riba, C.: Type-based termination with sized products. In: Kaminski, M., Martini, S. (eds.) CSL 2008. LNCS, vol. 5213, pp. 493–507. Springer, Heidelberg (2008). doi:10.1007/978-3-540-87531-4_35

22. Abel, A.: Termination checking with types. ITA **38**(4), 277–319 (2004)

23. Xi, H.: Dependent types for program termination verification. High.-Order Symb. Comput. **15**(1), 91–131 (2002)

24. Amadio, R.M., Coupet-Grimal, S.: Analysis of a guard condition in type theory. In: Nivat, M. (ed.) FoSSaCS 1998. LNCS, vol. 1378, pp. 48–62. Springer, Heidelberg (1998). doi:10.1007/BFb0053541

25. Bournez, O., Garnier, F.: Proving positive almost-sure termination. In: Giesl, J. (ed.) RTA 2005. LNCS, vol. 3467, pp. 323–337. Springer, Heidelberg (2005). doi:10.1007/978-3-540-32033-3_24

26. Chakarov, A., Sankaranarayanan, S.: Probabilistic program analysis with martingales. In: Sharygina, N., Veith, H. (eds.) CAV 2013. LNCS, vol. 8044, pp. 511–526. Springer, Heidelberg (2013). doi:10.1007/978-3-642-39799-8_34

27. Cappai, A., Dal Lago, U.: On equivalences, metrics, and polynomial time. In: Kosowski, A., Walukiewicz, I. (eds.) FCT 2015. LNCS, vol. 9210, pp. 311–323. Springer, Cham (2015). doi:10.1007/978-3-319-22177-9_24

28. Dal Lago, U., Parisen Toldin, P.: A higher-order characterization of probabilistic polynomial time. Inf. Comput. **241**, 114–141 (2015)

29. Dal Lago, U.: A short introduction to implicit computational complexity. In: Bezhanishvili, N., Goranko, V. (eds.) ESSLLI 2010-2011. LNCS, vol. 7388, pp. 89–109. Springer, Heidelberg (2012). doi:10.1007/978-3-642-31485-8_3

30. Dal Lago, U., Zorzi, M.: Probabilistic operational semantics for the lambda calculus. RAIRO - Theoret. Inf. Appl. **46**(3), 413–450 (2012)

31. Brázdil, T., Brožek, V., Etessami, K., Kučera, A., Wojtczak, D.: One-counter Markov decision processes. In: 21st ACM-SIAM Symposium on Discrete Algorithms (2010)

32. Dal Lago, U.: The geometry of linear higher-order recursion. In: LICS 2005, pp. 366–375. IEEE Computer Society (2005)

33. Sabry, A., Felleisen, M.: Reasoning about programs in continuation-passing style. LISP Symb. Comput. **6**(3–4), 289–360 (1993)

34. Dal Lago, U., Gaboardi, M.: Linear dependent types and relative completeness. In: LICS 2011, pp. 133–142. IEEE Computer Society (2011)

CAPER

Automatic Verification for Fine-Grained Concurrency

Thomas Dinsdale-Young[1]([✉]), Pedro da Rocha Pinto[2],
Kristoffer Just Andersen[1], and Lars Birkedal[1]

[1] Aarhus University, Aarhus, Denmark
{tyoung,kja,birkedal}@cs.au.dk
[2] Imperial College London, London, UK
pmd09@doc.ic.ac.uk

Abstract. Recent program logics based on separation logic emphasise a modular approach to proving functional correctness for fine-grained concurrent programs. However, these logics have no automation support. In this paper, we present CAPER, a prototype tool for automated reasoning in such a logic. CAPER is based on symbolic execution, integrating reasoning about interference on shared data and about ghost resources that are used to mediate this interference. This enables CAPER to verify the functional correctness of fine-grained concurrent algorithms.

1 Introduction

In recent years, much progress has been made in developing program logics for verifying the functional correctness of concurrent programs [7,10,19,29,32], with emphasis on fine-grained concurrent data structures. Reasoning about such programs is challenging since data is concurrently accessed by multiple threads: the reasoning must correctly account for interference between threads, which can often be subtle. Recent program logics address this challenge by using *resources* that are associated with some form of *protocol* for accessing shared data.

The concept of heap-as-resource was a fundamental innovation of separation logic [26]. It is possible to specify and verify a piece of code in terms of the resources that it uses. Further resources, which are preserved by the code, can be added by framing, provided that they are disjoint. Concurrent separation logic (CSL) [23] uses the observation that threads operating on disjoint resources do not interfere. This is embodied in the disjoint concurrency proof rule:

$$\frac{\{p_1\}\ c_1\ \{q_1\} \qquad \{p_2\}\ c_2\ \{q_2\}}{\{p_1 * p_2\}\ c_1 \| c_2\ \{q_1 * q_2\}}.$$

The *separating conjunction* connective '$*$' in the assertion $p_1 * p_2$ asserts that both p_1 and p_2 hold but for disjoint portions of the heap. In separation logic, the primitive resources are heap cells, represented $x \mapsto y$, meaning the heap at address x holds value y. A thread that owns a heap cell has an exclusive right to read, modify or dispose of it. The separating conjunction $x \mapsto y * y \mapsto z$ enforces disjointness: it requires x and y to be different addresses in the heap.

© Springer-Verlag GmbH Germany 2017
H. Yang (Ed.): ESOP 2017, LNCS 10201, pp. 420–447, 2017.
DOI: 10.1007/978-3-662-54434-1_16

In fine-grained concurrent algorithms, however, threads use *shared* data, so a more flexible concept of resources is required. *Shared regions* [10] are one approach to this. A shared region encapsulates some underlying (concrete) resources, which may be accessed by multiple threads when they perform atomic operations. The region enforces a protocol that determines how threads can mutate the encapsulated resources. The region is associated with abstract resources called *guards* that determine the role that a thread can play in the protocol. Importantly, these resources determine what knowledge a thread can have about the region that is *stable* — i.e., continues to hold under the actions of other threads.

For example, consider a region that encapsulates a heap cell at address x. Associated with this region are two guards INC and DEC. The protocol states that a thread with the INC guard can increase the value stored at x, and a thread with the DEC guard can decrease the value stored at x. A thread holding the INC guard can know that the value at x is *at most* the last value it observed; without the DEC guard, a thread cannot know that the value will not be decreased by another thread. Conversely, a thread holding the DEC guard can know a lower bound on the value at x. A thread that holds both guards can change the value arbitrarily and know it precisely, much as if it had the resource $x \mapsto y$ itself.

In this paper we present CAPER, a novel tool for automatic verification of fine-grained concurrent programs using separation logic. To verify a program, the user specifies the types of shared regions, defining their guards and protocols, and provides specifications for functions (and loop invariants) that use these regions. CAPER uses a *region-aware* symbolic execution (Sect. 3.3) to verify the code, in the tradition of SmallFoot [1]. The key novelties of CAPER's approach are:

- the use of *guard algebras* (Sect. 3.1) as a mechanism for representing and reasoning automatically about abstract resources, while supporting a range of concurrency verification patterns;
- techniques for automatically reasoning about interference on shared regions (Sect. 3.2), in particular, accounting for transitivity; and
- heuristics for non-deterministic proof search (Sect. 4), including the novel use of abduction to infer abstract updates to shared regions and guards.

We introduce our approach by considering a number of examples in Sect. 2. We emphasise that these examples are complete and self-contained — CAPER can verify them without additional input. In Sect. 5 we evaluate CAPER, reporting results for a range of examples. We discuss related work in Sect. 6 before concluding with remarks on future directions in Sect. 7.

The CAPER tool is implemented in Haskell, and uses Z3 [8] and (optionally) E [27] to discharge proof obligations. The source code and examples are available [11], as is a soundness proof of the separation logic underlying CAPER [12].

2 Motivating Examples

We begin by considering a series of examples that illustrate the programs and specifications that CAPER is designed to prove. In each case, we discuss how

CAPER handles the example and why. In later sections, we will describe the rules and algorithms that underlie CAPER in more detail. For each example, we give the *complete* source file, which CAPER verifies with no further annotation.

2.1 Spin Lock

Figure 1 shows a typical annotated source file for CAPER, which implements a simple fine-grained concurrent data structure: a spin lock. Note that &*& is CAPER syntax for ∗ — separating conjunction.

Lines 1–11 define a *region type*, SLock, for spin locks. There are two kinds of assertions associated with regions, and their shape is dictated by region type definitions. SLock(r,x,s) is the assertion representing knowledge of a region r of type SLock with parameter x in abstract state s. The second are guard assertions of the form r@(G), meaning we hold the guard G for region r.

examples/recursive/SpinLock.t

```
1   region SLock(r,x) {
2      guards %LOCK * UNLOCK;
3      interpretation {
4         0 : x ↦ 0 &*& r@UNLOCK;
5         1 : x ↦ 1;
6      }
7      actions {
8         LOCK[_] : 0 ⤳ 1;
9         UNLOCK : 1 ⤳ 0;
10     }
11  }
12  function makeLock()
13     requires true;
14     ensures SLock(r,ret,0) &*& r@LOCK[1p]; {
15        v := alloc(1);
16        [v] := 0;
17        return v;
18  }
19  function acquire(x)
20     requires SLock(r,x,_) &*& r@LOCK[p];
21     ensures SLock(r,x,1) &*& r@(LOCK[p] * UNLOCK); {
22        b := CAS(x, 0, 1);
23        if (b = 0) {
24           acquire(x);
25        }
26  }
27  function release(x)
28     requires SLock(r,x,1) &*& r@UNLOCK;
29     ensures SLock(r,x,_); {
30        [x] := 0;
31  }
```

Fig. 1. CAPER listing for a spin lock implementation.

Line 2 is a *guard algebra* declaration, indicating the guards associated with a given region type, and how they compose. There are two kinds of guard associated with SLock regions: LOCK guards, which are used to acquire the lock, and may be subdivided to allow multiple threads to compete for the lock (indicated by % in the guards declaration); and UNLOCK guards, which are used to release the lock, and are exclusive — only a thread holding the lock owns the UNLOCK guard.

Lines 3–6 declare a *region interpretation*: the resources held by the region when in each abstract state. SLock regions have two states: 0 represents that the lock is *available*, which is indicated concretely by the heap cell x $\mapsto$ 0; 1 represents that the lock has been *acquired*, which is indicated concretely by the heap cell x $\mapsto$ 1. In the *available* state the UNLOCK guard belongs to the region — a thread that transitions to the acquired state obtains this guard.

Finally, lines 7–10 declare the *actions* — the protocol governing the shared region. This embodies both the updates allowed for a given thread and the interference a thread must anticipate from the environment. A thread can transition an SLock region from abstract state 0 (available) to 1 (acquired) if it holds the LOCK[p] guard for any p. Similarly, a thread can transition an SLock region from acquired to available if it holds the UNLOCK guard.

The makeLock function allocates a new spin lock. It has the precondition true since it does not require any resources. In the postcondition, the function returns an SLock region with full permission to its LOCK guard (expressed by r@(LOCK[1p])). The logical variable r holds the identifier for the region, which is used to relate assertions that refer to the same region; it is implicitly existentially quantified as it occurs in the postcondition but neither in the precondition nor as a parameter to the function. The logical variable ret binds the return value, which is the address of the lock. When CAPER symbolically executes the function body, at the return it has the resource v $\mapsto$ 0 but requires SLock(r, v, 0). This missing resource is abduced: CAPER backtracks searching for a place where it could have obtained the missing resource. CAPER thus tries to construct the region before executing the return statement. Constructing the region consists of creating a fresh region identifier and adding the full guards for the region to the symbolic state (in this case LOCK[1p] * UNLOCK); the resources belonging to the region according to the interpretation are consumed (removed from the symbolic state). This is successful for the interpretation 0, leaving the guard LOCK[1p] for the new region. CAPER can then successfully symbolically execute the return statement, since it has the resources required by the postcondition.

The acquire function attempts to acquire the lock. The precondition asserts that the spin lock is in an unknown state and that we have permission to acquire the lock in the form of the LOCK[p] guard. The postcondition asserts that the lock is in the acquired state (indicated by the 1 in the SLock predicate) and that we retain the LOCK[p] guard but have also acquired the UNLOCK guard.

The lock is acquired by performing an atomic compare-and-set (CAS) operation, which attempts to set the value stored at address x from 0 to 1. In symbolically executing the CAS, CAPER determines that it needs to open the region because it does not have x $\mapsto$ −. In opening the region, CAPER branches on the interpretation of the region; it must show that both cases are correct. The CAS itself also introduces branches depending on whether it failed; these are quickly pruned as the CAS cannot fail if the region is in state 0, nor succeed if it is in state 1. Immediately after the atomic CAS, CAPER must close the region. It does so by non-deterministically choosing among the interpretations.

If the initial state was 1, the CAS fails and CAPER closes with state 1. Since the state is unchanged, this 'update' is permitted. After the atomic operation, CAPER must stabilise the region; since the thread does not own the UNLOCK guard, another thread could transition the region to state 0. Consequently, after the CAS, CAPER does not know which state the region is in. Since the CAS fails, the if condition succeeds. CAPER then makes the recursive call to acquire using the specification, which allows it to obtain the postcondition in the end.

If the initial state was 0, the CAS succeeds and CAPER closes with state 1. In doing so, the UNLOCK guard is acquired, since it is part of the interpretation of state 0, but not of state 1. CAPER must then check that the update from state 0 to 1 is permitted by the available guards, LOCK[p] * UNLOCK, which it is. After the CAS, the thread owns the UNLOCK guard so no other thread can change the state of the region, and so it is stable in state 1. The result of a successful CAS is 1, so CAPER does not symbolically execute the body of the if in this case, and proceeds to check the postcondition, which is successful.

The verification of the release function proceeds along similar lines.

2.2   Ticket Lock

Figure 2 shows a CAPER listing for a ticket lock. A ticket lock comprises two counters: the first records the next available ticket and the second records the ticket which currently holds the lock. (Note that the lock is "available" when the two counters are equal — i.e. the ticket holding the lock is the next available ticket.) To acquire the lock, a thread obtains a ticket by incrementing the first counter and waiting until the second counter reaches the value of the ticket it obtained. To release the lock, a thread simply increments the second counter.

In CAPER, a ticket lock is captured by a TLock region, defined in lines 1–9 of Fig. 2. In contrast to the SLock region, a TLock region has an infinite number of states: there is an abstract state for each integer n. The abstract state n of a TLock region represents the ticket that currently holds the lock. The guards associated with a TLock region represent the tickets: there is a unique guard TICKET(n) for each integer n. (This is indicated by the # in the guards declaration.) The region interpretation of state n ensures that:

- the first counter (x) is the next available ticket number, m, which is at least n;
- the second counter (x+1) is n, the lock-holding ticket number;
- all TICKET resources from m up belong to the region. (A set of indexed resources is expressed with a set-builder-style notation, as in TICKET{k|k≥m}.)

Note that m is implicitly existentially quantified in the interpretation.

A thread may acquire a ticket by incrementing the next-available-ticket counter and removing the corresponding TICKET guard from the region. Doing so does not affect the abstract state of the region, and can, therefore, happen at any time (no guards are required to do so). In order to increment the lock-holding-ticket counter, a thread must hold the TICKET(n) resource for the current value of the counter, n. We might, therefore, expect the actions declaration to be:

```
8    actions {
9       TICKET(n) : n ⤳ n + 1;
10   }
```

This action declaration is, however, problematic for automation. Between symbolically executing atomic actions, CAPER widens the set of possible abstract states for each region according to the *rely* relation for that region type. Suppose a TLock region is initially in state 0. If the thread does not hold the TICKET(0) guard, CAPER must add the state 1 to the possible state set. If the thread does not hold TICKET(1), CAPER must add the state 2, and so on. In general, we cannot expect this widening process to terminate, so we must consider a *transitively-closed* rely relation. CAPER cannot, in general, compute the transitive closure, but it *is* possible to *check* that a given actions declaration is transitively closed. We address this in Sect. 3.2. The proposed action declaration is, however, not transitive, since transitions from 0 to 1 and from 1 to 2 are possible, but the transitive transition from 0 to 2 is not possible in one step.

examples/iterative/TickLock.t

```
1    region TLock(r,x) {
2       guards #TICKET;
3       interpretation {
4          n : x ↦ m &*& (x + 1) ↦ n &*& r@TICKET{ k | k ≥ m } &*& m ≥ n;
5       }
6       actions {
7          n < m | TICKET{ k | n ≤ k, k < m } : n ⤳ m;
8       }
9    }
10   function acquire(x)
11      requires TLock(r,x,_);
12      ensures TLock(r,x,n) &*& r@TICKET(n); {
13        do {
14           t := [x + 0];
15           b := CAS(x + 0, t, t + 1);
16        }
17          invariant TLock(r,x,ni) &*& (b=0 ? true : r@TICKET(t) &*& t ≥ ni);
18        while (b = 0);
19        do {
20           v := [x + 1];
21        }
22          invariant TLock(r,x,ni) &*& r@TICKET(t) &*& t ≥ ni &*& ni ≥ v;
23        while (v < t);
24   }
25   function release(x)
26      requires TLock(r,x,n) &*& r@TICKET(n);
27      ensures TLock(r,x,_); {
28        v := [x + 1];
29        [x + 1] := v + 1;
30   }
```

Fig. 2. CAPER listing for a ticket lock implementation.

Instead, we use the `actions` declaration in Fig. 2, which *is* transitively closed. It remedies the problem with the simple version by generalising from a single increment to allow multiple increments. This is achieved by placing a condition on the transition that $n \rightsquigarrow m$ is only permitted when $n<m$, enforcing that the counter can only increase, as indicated before the vertical bar in the `actions` declaration. The guard `TICKET{k|n≤k,k<m}` denotes the set of all guards `TICKET(k)` for k between n and m-1 inclusive. This ensures that a thread can increment the counter past k only when it holds the `TICKET(`k`)` guard. For example, a thread holding `TICKET(n)` can transition the `TLock` region from abstract state n to n+1.

The precondition of `acquire` asserts that the ticket lock exists in some arbitrary abstract state. The postcondition ensures that the lock is in some state n and that the guard `TICKET(n)` has been acquired. The function contains two loops and CAPER requires that we provide an invariant for each. The first loop, lines 13–18, increments the next available ticket. The invariant states that the region is in some state `ni` and that once the CAS succeeds (b = 1) we have the `TICKET(t)` guard and t is at least `ni`; the conditional is expressed using the C-like `_?_:_` notation. Similarly to the `acquire` operation for the spin lock, CAPER opens the region when symbolically executing the CAS operation. Since there is only one clause in the `TLock` region interpretation, CAPER considers one generic case, rather than branching as in the spin lock. Immediately after symbolically executing the CAS operation, CAPER needs to close the region. If the CAS succeeds CAPER knows that the next available ticket m is t+1. Hence the guard `TICKET(t)` is not included in the set of guards `TICKET{k|k≥m}` needed for closing the region, so CAPER can transfer the guard `TICKET(t)` out of the `TLock` region. The next loop, lines 19–23, spins until the acquired ticket becomes the lock-holding ticket. CAPER proceeds similarly to the first loop. After the loop, the invariant and failed loop test are sufficient to establish the postcondition.

The precondition of the `release` function expresses that the lock-holding ticket of the region is n and that we hold that ticket. Because we hold the guard `TICKET(n)`, we can make a transition from abstract state n to abstract state n+1. No other thread can make a transition, since to transition from n to m one needs to hold all the guards from n to m-1. Therefore, there is no interference from other threads on the second counter and we can update it without using a CAS loop. After the read on line 28, CAPER knows that v holds value n by opening the region. To execute the write on line 29, CAPER again opens the region in state n. CAPER closes the region in a new state n_1, which must be the value of the x+1 counter, i.e. $n_1 = n + 1$. The value of m is unchanged, but CAPER must establish that $m \geq n_1 = n + 1$, which follows from the fact that $m \geq n$ and that `TICKET(n)` (from the thread) is disjoint from `TICKET{k|k≥m}` (from the region). CAPER must also establish that the transition $n \rightsquigarrow n+1$ is permitted by the actions for the available guards, which it is.

Client. Figure 3 shows an implementation of a simple client using the ticket lock. Here, the `Client(r,x,s,z)` region uses a ticket lock region `TLock(s,z)` to maintain the lock invariant that two cells, x and x+1, have the same value.

examples/iterative/TickLockClient.t

```
 1  region Client(r,x,s,z) {
 2    guards 0;
 3    interpretation {
 4      0 : TLock(s,z,k) &*& (x ↦ a &*& (x+1) ↦ a ∨ s@TICKET(k));
 5    }
 6    actions {}
 7  }
 8  function set(x,z,w)
 9    requires Client(r,x,s,z,0) &*& TLock(s,z,_);
10    ensures Client(r,x,s,z,0) &*& TLock(s,z,_); {
11      acquire(z);
12      [x] := w;
13      [x + 1] := w;
14      release(z);
15  }
```

Fig. 3. A CAPER listing of a client of the ticket lock.

The disjunction with the guard s@TICKET(k) makes it possible to temporarily break the invariant. The function set(x,z,w) sets the value of the two shared memory cells to w. Lines 12–13 are a critical section protected by the ticket lock. Note that the invariant is temporarily broken between the two writes.

In symbolically executing the call to acquire in line 11, CAPER uses the postcondition of acquire to obtain s@TICKET(k) and TLock(s,z,k) for some k. When CAPER symbolically executes line 12, it opens the Client region and must consider each of the disjuncts of the interpretation. It finds that the right-hand disjunct is not possible as we already hold the TICKET guard for the current abstract state k of the lock. Hence it obtains the points-to assertions for x and x+1, and can perform the write to x. Since the values stored at x and x+1 are now different, CAPER can only close the region by transferring s@TICKET(k) to the region. When CAPER symbolically executes line 13, it again opens the Client region. This time it finds that the region holds s@TICKET(k) since we have the points-to predicates. After the assignment, the values stored at x and x+1 are the same, and CAPER can close the region while leaving us with the s@TICKET(k) resource which CAPER then uses to satisfy the precondition of release.

2.3   Stack-Based Bag

Figure 4 shows a CAPER implementation of a concurrent bag based on Treiber's stack [31]. The stack is lock-free, and uses CAS operations to manipulate the head of a linked-list structure. To push a new item, a thread constructs a new head node and atomically updates the head pointer of the bag. When popping an item, a thread anticipates what the head node is before atomically updating the head pointer. In both cases, the function of the atomic compare-and-swap operation is to ensure that no other thread has manipulated the bag between operations. Unlike the preceding examples, the heap is fundamental to the implementation.

The specification is parametrised by an *abstract predicate* [2,24] bagInvariant (line 1). The idea is that adding an item v to the bag requires

examples/recursive/BagStack.t

```
1   predicate bagInvariant(v);
2   region Bag(r,x) {
3     guards 0;
4     interpretation {
5       0 : x ↦ y &*& BagList(s,y,_,_,0) &*& s@OWN;
6     }
7     actions {}
8   }
9   region BagList(s,y,v,z) {
10    guards OWN;
11    interpretation {
12      0 : y = 0 ? true : y ↦ v &*& y+1 ↦ z
13            &*& BagList(t,z,_,_,0) &*& t@OWN &*& bagInvariant(v);
14      1 : s@OWN &*& y ↦ v &*& y+1 ↦ z &*& BagList(t,z,_,_,_);
15    }
16    actions {
17      OWN : 0 ⤳ 1;
18    }
19  }
20  function push(x,v)
21    requires Bag(r,x,0) &*& bagInvariant(v);
22    ensures Bag(r,x,0); {
23      y := alloc(2); [y] := v;
24      innerPush(x,y);
25  }
26  function innerPush(x,y)
27    requires Bag(r,x,0) &*& y ↦ v &*& y+1 ↦ _ &*& bagInvariant(v);
28    ensures Bag(r,x,0); {
29      t := [x];
30      [y + 1] := t;
31      cr := CAS(x,t,y);
32      if (cr = 0) {
33        innerPush(x, y);
34      }
35  }
36  function pop(x)
37    requires Bag(r,x,0);
38    ensures ret = 0 ? Bag(r,x,0) : Bag(r,x,0) &*& bagInvariant(ret); {
39      t := [x];
40      if (t = 0) { return 0; }
41      t2 := [t + 1];
42      cr := popCAS(x,t,t2);
43      if (cr = 0) { ret := pop(x); return ret; }
44      ret := [t];
45      return ret;
46  }
47  function popCAS(x,t,t2)
48    requires Bag(r,x,0) &*& BagList(rt,t,v,t2,_)
49          &*& BagList(rt2,t2,_,_,_) &*& t != 0;
50    ensures ret = 0 ∨ bagInvariant(v); {
51      cr := CAS(x,t,t2); return cr;
52  }
```

Fig. 4. CAPER listing for a concurrent bag implementation.

transferring ownership of the predicate $\text{bagInvariant}(v)$ to the bag, which is returned when the item is removed. Clients can decide how to instantiate bagInvariant.

In Caper, the head pointer and the linked-list nodes are encapsulated by separate regions: Bag and BagList, respectively. Note that there is an apparent hierarchy between Bag and BagList regions: a Bag refers to a BagList, which may, in turn, refer to another BagList and so on. In this way, we can use regions to model inductive data structures such as linked lists. While regions can fulfil a similar role to inductive predicates, they are semantically distinct. Regions are shared globally, and so may refer to each other in arbitrary, even cyclical ways. Although it appears as though the regions are nested, semantically all regions exist at the same level. In this example, we achieve a hierarchy through ownership of guards: the top-level Bag holds the OWN guard for the first BagList, which holds the OWN guard for the second, and so on.

A Bag region is simple, in that it has no guards and is always in one abstract state. It simply permits sharing of the resources it holds. The interpretation of abstract state 0 of a region Bag(r,x) holds a pointer to the first, possibly null, linked-list node at x in addition to its OWN guard.

The BagList(s,y,v,z) region type represents a list node (or a null terminator) with payload value v at address y and a pointer to the successor z at y+1. A BagList region is in one of two states, depending on whether it belongs to the bag or not. Abstract state 0 means that the region belongs to the bag, in which case it can represent either a null-pointer terminating the list or a list node with a value and successor, represented by another BagList region. The region also holds the OWN guard to the successor and the bagInvariant predicate for its value. The abstract state 1 represents a list node that has been popped. The interpretation therefore includes the region's own OWN guard and knowledge of the successor, but *not* the successor's OWN guard or the bagInvariant predicate.

Since the bag can be used concurrently, we do not specify exactly which elements it contains at a given time. Instead, our specification of push and pop focuses on ownership transfer of elements pushed to and popped from the bag.

The precondition of push asserts only knowledge of the bag and ownership of the bagInvariant for the value v to be put in the bag. In the postcondition, the bagInvariant resource is absent, as it is transferred to the bag. The push function allocates a new list node and then delegates to a CAS loop in innerPush.

The specification of innerPush is similar to that of push, but the precondition requires the list node that is to be pushed. Note that the successor of the node, y+1, is initially undetermined. In lines 29–30, innerPush loads the current head of the list into the tail pointer of the new node via the variable t. To do so, Caper opens the Bag region, getting access to x, and closes it again. The observed value is then written as the successor of the new node, at address y+1, without opening any regions. To account for the head of the stack having changed since it was read, a CAS is used to update the head pointer. To symbolically execute the CAS in line 31, Caper again opens the Bag region. If successful, it must close and restore the Bag region. This means a new BagList region in state 0 must be created for the new head. Upon creation, CAPER creates the OWN guard for the new region, which is given to the Bag region, closing it in state 0. If the CAS does not succeed, it means another thread updated the stack between lines 29 and 31, and innerPush recursively tries again.

The specification of the pop function states that, from a Bag, pop produces either null (0), in case the bag is empty, or a value satisfying the bagInvariant predicate. The idea is that the concrete value comes from the underlying linked list, and the corresponding bagInvariant(v) predicate is removed from a BagList region. The pop function attempts to CAS the head pointer of the bag to the successor of the first link, effectively removing the first element from the bag. It first reads the head pointer into t, which requires opening the Bag region. At this point, we obtain the BagList region, which can be freely duplicated, although the OWN guard remains in the Bag region. After the Bag region is closed again, we must stabilise the BagList region to account for the fact that another thread could remove the head node from the stack. That is, its abstract state could now be 0 or 1. If the head pointer was 0, then the bag was empty and so 0 is returned. Otherwise, t points to a node, and line 41 reads its successor pointer into t2. This involves opening the BagList region previously obtained. It is not necessary to open the Bag region again at this stage. The call to popCAS at line 42 attempts to update the head node to the successor of the head node. We give this CAS operation a specification (lines 48–50) to assist CAPER. To symbolically execute that CAS, CAPER opens the Bag region containing x and the OWN guard for the BagList region for the head of the stack. The BagList region for the previously seen head (with region identifier rt) and the BagList region for the current head (if it is different) are also opened. CAPER determines that the CAS can only succeed if these two regions are the same. In this case, the bagInvariant is transferred to the thread, the OWN guard for the successor is transferred to the Bag region, and the OWN guard for the head is transferred to its own BagList region. In this process, the state of the BagList region for the old head is updated from 0 to 1. This is allowed since we have access to its OWN guard. If the CAS fails, nothing is changed and the pop is retried. On success, the return value is read from the BagList region that is now in state 1. This value corresponds to the previously-obtained bagInvariant predicate.

3   Proof System

CAPER's proof system is based on the logic of CAP [10], using improvements from iCAP [29] and TaDA [7]. The logic is a separation logic with shared regions.

Each shared region has a unique *region identifier*. A region has an associated *region type*, which determines the resources and protocol associated with the region. Region types $\mathbf{T}(r, \bar{x})$ are parametrised, with the first parameter (r) always being the region identifier. A region also has an *abstract state*. In CAPER's logic, *region assertions* describe the type and state of a region. The region assertion $\mathbf{T}(r, \bar{x}, y)$ asserts the existence of a region with identifier r and type $\mathbf{T}(r, \bar{x})$ in abstract state y. Region assertions are freely duplicable; i.e., they satisfy the equivalence: $\mathbf{T}(r,\bar{x},y) \iff \mathbf{T}(r,\bar{x},y) * \mathbf{T}(r,\bar{x},y)$. Moreover, region assertions with the same region identifier must agree on the region type and abstract state: $\mathbf{T}(r,\bar{x},y) * \mathbf{T}'(r,\bar{x}',y') \implies (\mathbf{T},\bar{x},y) = (\mathbf{T}',\bar{x}',y')$.

Shared regions are also associated with (ghost) resources called *guards*. Which guards can be associated with a region, as well as their significance and behaviour is determined by the type of the region. Guards are interpreted as elements of a partial commutative monoid (PCM), referred to as a *guard algebra*. That is, they have a partial composition operator that is associative, commutative and has a unit. This is sufficient for them to behave as separation logic resources (see e.g. [9]). In CAPER's logic, *guard assertions* assert ownership of guard resources. The guard assertion $r@(G_1 * \ldots * G_n)$ asserts ownership of the guards $G_1, \ldots, G_n$ associated with region identifier r. Guard assertions are not in general duplicable, but they distribute with respect to $*$: $r@(G_1 * G_2) \iff r@G_1 * r@G_2$.

The region type determines how a shared region is used. A region type definition determines the following properties of regions of that type: the guard algebra associated with the region; the abstract states of the region and their concrete *interpretation*; and the *actions* that can be used to update the state of the region, and which guards are required in order to perform each action. Region type definitions determine two derived relations, Rely and Guar (for *guarantee*), which are defined in Fig. 5, based on the actions for the region types. The relation $\text{Rely}(\mathbf{T}(r,\bar{x}), G)$ consists of all state transitions that a thread's environment may make to a region of type $\mathbf{T}(r,\bar{x})$, if the thread owns guard G. The relation $\text{Guar}(\mathbf{T}(r,\bar{x}), G)$ consists of all state transitions that a thread itself may make to a region of type $\mathbf{T}(r,\bar{x})$, if it owns guard G.

$$\frac{(P(\bar{z})|G : e_1(\bar{z}) \rightsquigarrow e_2(\bar{z})) \in \text{Actions}(\mathbf{T}(r,\bar{x})) \qquad P(\bar{w})}{(e_1(\bar{w}), e_2(\bar{w})) \in \text{Guar}(\mathbf{T}(r,\bar{x}), G)} \qquad \frac{}{(x,x) \in \text{Guar}(\mathbf{T}(r,\bar{x}), G)}$$

$$\frac{(x,y), (y,z) \in \text{Guar}(\mathbf{T}(r,\bar{x}), G)}{(x,z) \in \text{Guar}(\mathbf{T}(r,\bar{x}), G)} (\dagger) \qquad \frac{(x,y) \in \text{Guar}(\mathbf{T}(r,\bar{x}), G)}{(x,y) \in \text{Guar}(\mathbf{T}(r,\bar{x}), G * G')}$$

$$\frac{(P(\bar{z})|G : e_1(\bar{z}) \rightsquigarrow e_2(\bar{z})) \in \text{Actions}(\mathbf{T}(r,\bar{x})) \qquad P(w) \qquad G * G' \text{ defined}}{(e_1(\bar{w}), e_2(\bar{w})) \in \text{Rely}(\mathbf{T}(r,\bar{x}), G')}$$

$$\frac{(x,y), (y,z) \in \text{Rely}(\mathbf{T}(r,\bar{x}), G)}{(x,z) \in \text{Rely}(\mathbf{T}(r,\bar{x}), G)} (\dagger) \qquad \frac{(x,y) \in \text{Rely}(\mathbf{T}(r,\bar{x}), G * G')}{(x,y) \in \text{Rely}(\mathbf{T}(r,\bar{x}), G)}$$

$$\frac{}{(x,x) \in \text{Rely}(\mathbf{T}(r,\bar{x}), G)}$$

Fig. 5. Rules defining the Guar and Rely relations.

3.1 Guards

The underlying logic of CAPER permits the guard algebra for a region to be an arbitrary PCM. However, in order to reason automatically about guards, CAPER must be able to effectively compute solutions to certain problems within the PCM. To this end, CAPER provides a number of constructors for guard algebras for which these problems are soluble. These constructors are inspired by common patterns in concurrency verification, and are useful for many examples. The three automation problems are as follows.

Frame Inference. Given guard assertions A and B, find a C (if it exists) such that A ⊢ B * C. This problem has two applications: 1. Computing the Guar relation requires determining if the guard currently available to the thread (A) entails the guard required to perform some action (B); 2. At call sites, returns and when closing regions, symbolic execution consumes assertions (i.e. checks that the assertion holds and removes the corresponding resources from the symbolic state). Frame inference (for guards) does this for guard assertions.

Composition and Compatibility. Given guard assertions A and B, determine their composition A*B and the condition for it being defined. Whether it is defined will be a pure assertion on the free variables of A and B. This also has two applications: 1. Computing the Rely relation requires determining when the guard currently owned by the thread (A) is compatible with the guard required to perform some action (B); 2. At entry points, after calls and when opening regions, symbolic execution produces assertions (i.e. adds resources and assumptions corresponding to the assertion to the symbolic state). Composition does this for guards.

Least Upper-Bounds. Given guard assertions A and B, compute C such that C ⊢ A, C ⊢ B and for any D with D ⊢ A and D ⊢ B, D ⊢ C. This is used to compose two actions, which will be guarded by the least upper-bound of the two guards.

Supported Guard Algebras. We present the guard algebras that are supported by CAPER. Each guard algebra has a maximal element, the *full guard*, which is generated for a region when it is initially created.

Trivial Guard Algebra. The trivial guard algebra, 0 in CAPER syntax, consists of one element which is the unit. This algebra is used when a region has no roles associated with it: it can be used in the same way by all threads at all times.

All-or-Nothing Guard Algebra. An all-or-nothing guard algebra consists of a single element distinct from the unit, which is the full guard. In CAPER syntax, this algebra is represented by the name chosen for the point; for instance, GUARD would be the all-or-nothing algebra with point GUARD.

Permissions Guard Algebra. A permissions guard algebra %GUARD has the full resource GUARD[1p] which can be subdivided into smaller permissions GUARD[π]. The typical model for permissions is as fractions in the interval [0, 1]. This allows for (non-zero) permissions to be split arbitrarily often. CAPER implements a different theory of permissions. This theory also allows arbitrary splitting, but also requires that GUARD[π] * GUARD[π] is undefined for any non-zero π.

The theory can be encoded into the theory of *atomless Boolean algebras* — a Boolean algebra is said to be atomless if for all $a > \bot$ there exists a' with $a > a' > \bot$. The encoding defines the PCM operator as $p_1 * p_2 = p_1 \vee p_2$ if $p_1 \wedge p_2 = \bot$ (and undefined otherwise). Conveniently, the first-order theory of atomless Boolean algebras is complete and therefore decidable (initially reported by Tarski [30], proved by Ershov [15], and see e.g. [6] for details).

CAPER implements three different proof procedures for the theory of permissions. One uses the encoding with Boolean algebras and passes the problem to the first-order theorem prover E [27]. A second checks for the satisfiability of a first-order permissions formula directly. The third encodes the satisfiability problem with bit-vectors and passes it to the SMT solver Z3 [8]. Dockins et al. [13] previously proposed a tree-share model of permissions, which is also a model of this theory. Le et al. [20] have developed decision procedures for entailment checking based on this model, which could also be used by CAPER.

Counting Guard Algebra. A counting guard algebra |GUARD| consists of *counting guards* similar to the counting permissions of Bornat et al. [3]. For $n \geq 0$, GUARD$|n|$ expresses n counting guards. An *authority guard* tracks the number of counting guards that have been issued. For $n \geq 0$, GUARD$|-1 - n|$ expresses the authority guard with n counting guards issued. The PCM operator is defined as:

$$\text{GUARD}|n| * \text{GUARD}|m| = \text{GUARD}|n + m| \quad \text{if } (n \geq 0 \wedge m \geq 0) \vee$$
$$(n < 0 \wedge m \geq 0 \wedge n + m < 0) \vee (n \geq 0 \wedge m < 0 \wedge n + m < 0).$$

This ensures that the authority is unique (e.g. GUARD$|-1|$ * GUARD$|-2|$ is undefined) and that owning GUARD$|-1|$, which is the full guard, guarantees that no other thread may have a counting guard.

Indexed Guard Algebra. An indexed guard algebra #GUARD consists of sets of individual guards GUARD(n) where n ranges over integers. A set of such individual guards is expressed using a set-builder notation: GUARD$\{x \mid P\}$ describes the set of all guards GUARD(x) for which P holds of x. The full guard is GUARD$\{x \mid \text{true}\}$. The notation GUARD(n) is syntax for GUARD$\{x \mid x = n\}$. The PCM operator is defined as GUARDS_1 * GUARDS_2 = GUARD$(S_1 \cup S_2)$ if $S_1 \cap S_2 = \emptyset$.

The automation problems reduce to testing conditions concerning sets, specifically set inclusion. Sets in CAPER are not first-class entities: they are always described by a logical predicate that is a (quantifier-free) arithmetic formula. For sets characterised in this way, set inclusion can be characterised as: $\{x \mid P\} \subseteq \{x \mid Q\} \iff \forall x. P \Rightarrow Q$. Advanced SMT solvers, such as Z3 [8], have support for first-order quantification, and CAPER exploits this facility to handle the verification conditions concerning set inclusion.

Product Guard Algebra Construction. Given guard algebras M and N, the product construction $M * N$ consists of pairs $(m, n) \in M \times N$, where the PCM operation is defined pointwise: $(m_1, n_1) * (m_2, n_2) = (m_1 * m_2, n_1 * n_2)$. The unit is the pair of units and the full resource is the pair of full resources.

Sum Guard Algebra Construction. Given guard algebras M and N, the sum construction $M + N$ is the discriminated (or disjoint) union of M and N, up to identifying the units and identifying the full resources of the two PCMs. The PCM operation embeds the operations of each of the constituent PCMs, with composition between elements of different PCMs undefined.

Within the CAPER implementation, guards are represented as maps from guard names to parameters that depend on the guard type. For this to work, CAPER disallows multiple guards with the same name in a guard algebra definition. For instance, INSERT * %INSERT is not legal. The sum construction is implemented by rewriting where necessary by the identities the construction introduces.

3.2   Interference Reasoning

There are two sides to interference: on one side, a thread should only perform actions that are anticipated by the environment, expressed by the Guar relation; on the other, a thread must anticipate all actions that the environment could perform, expressed by the Rely relation. Each time a thread updates a region, it must ensure that the update is permitted by the Guar with respect to the guards it owns (initially) for that region. Moreover, the symbolic state between operations and frames for non-atomic operations must be *stabilised* by closing the set of states they might be in under the Rely relation. CAPER must therefore be able to compute with these relations effectively.

The biggest obstacle to effective computation is that the relations are transitively closed. Transitivity is necessary, at least for Rely, since the environment may take arbitrarily many steps in between the commands of a thread. However, computing the transitive closure in general is a difficult problem. For instance, consider a region that has the (unguarded) action : $n \rightsquigarrow n + 1$. From this action, we should infer the relation $\{(n, m) \mid n \le m\}$, as the reflexive-transitive closure of $\{(n, n + 1) \mid n \in \mathbb{Z}\}$. It is generally beyond the ability of SMT solvers to compute transitive closures, although some (limited) approaches have been proposed [14].

CAPER employs two techniques to deal with the transitive closure problem. This first is that, if the state space of the region is finite, then it is possible to compute the transitive closure directly. CAPER uses a variant of the Floyd-Warshall algorithm [16] for computing shortest paths in a weighted graph. The 'weights' are constraints (first-order formulae) with conjunction as the 'addition' operation and disjunction as the 'minimum' operation.

The second technique is to add composed actions until the set of actions is transitively closed. When the actions are transitively closed, the Rely and Guar relations can be computed without further accounting for transitivity (i.e. the (†) rules in Fig. 5 can be ignored). For two actions $P \mid G : e_1 \rightsquigarrow e_2$ and $P' \mid G' : e_1' \rightsquigarrow e_2'$ (assuming the only common variables are region parameters) their composition is $P, P', e_2 = e_1' \mid G \sqcup G' : e_1 \rightsquigarrow e_2'$ where $\sqcup$ is the least-upper-bound operation on guards. Using frame inference for guards, we can check if one action subsumes another — that is, whether any transition permitted by the second is also permitted by the first.

CAPER uses the following process to reach a transitive set of actions. First, consider the composition of each pair of actions currently in the set and determine if it is subsumed by any action in the set. If all compositions are already subsumed then the set is transitive. Otherwise, add all compositions that are not subsumed and repeat. Since this process is not guaranteed to terminate (for example, for $n \rightsquigarrow n + 1$), CAPER will give up after a fixed number of iterations fail to reach a transitive set. Note that adding composite actions does not change the Rely and Guar relations, since these are defined to be transitively closed.

If CAPER is unable to reach a transitive set of actions, the Rely relation is over-approximated by the universal relation, while the Guar is under-approximated. This is sound, since CAPER can prove strictly less in such circumstances, although the over-approximation is generally too much to prove many examples.

It is often practical to represent the transition system for a region type in a way that CAPER can determine its transitive closure. For example, instead of the action : $n \rightsquigarrow n + 1$ we can give the action $n < m \mid : n \rightsquigarrow m$, which CAPER can prove subsumes composition with itself. Since CAPER tries to find a transitive closure, it is often unnecessary to provide a set of actions that is transitively closed. For instance, given the actions $0 \leq n$, $n < m \mid A : n \rightsquigarrow -m$ and $0 < n \mid B : -n \rightsquigarrow n$, CAPER adds the following actions to reach a transitive closure:

$$0 \leq n, \ n < m \mid A * B : n \rightsquigarrow m;$$
$$0 < n, \ n < m \mid A * B : -n \rightsquigarrow -m;$$
$$0 < n, \ n < m \mid A * B : -n \rightsquigarrow m;$$

3.3 Symbolic Execution

CAPER's proof system is based on symbolic execution, where programs are interpreted over a domain of symbolic states. Symbolic states represent separation logic assertions, but are distinct from the syntactic assertions of the CAPER input language. To verify that code satisfies a specification, the code is symbolically executed from a symbolic state corresponding to the precondition. The symbolic execution may be non-deterministic — for instance, to account for conditional statements — and so produces a set of resulting symbolic states. If each of these symbolic states entails the postcondition, then the code satisfies the specification.

A symbolic state $S = (\Delta, \Pi, \Sigma, \Xi, \Upsilon) \in$ SState consists of:

- $\Delta \in$ VarCtx = SVar $\rightharpoonup_{\text{fin}}$ Sort, a *variable context* associating logical sorts with symbolic variables;
- $\Pi \in$ Pure = Cond*, a context of *pure conditions* (over the symbolic variables) representing logical assumptions;
- $\Sigma \in$ Preds = Pred*, a context of *predicates* (over the symbolic variables) representing owned resources;
- $\Xi \in$ Regions = RId $\rightharpoonup_{\text{fin}}$ RType$_\perp \times$ Exp$_\perp \times$ Guard, a finite map of region identifiers to an (optional) region type, an (optional) expression representing

the state of the region, and an guard expression representing the owned guards for the region;
- $\Upsilon \in$ ProgVars = ProgVar $\rightharpoonup_{\mathrm{fin}}$ Exp, a map from program variables to expressions representing their current values.

We take the set of symbolic variables SVar to be countably infinite. Symbolic variables are considered distinct from program variables (ProgVar), which occur in the syntax of the program code (Stmt), and assertion variables (AssnVar), which occur in syntactic assertions (Assn). Currently, the set of sorts supported by CAPER is Sort = {**Val, Perm, RId**}. That is, a variable can represent a program value (i.e. an integer), a permission, or a region identifier.

We do not formally define the syntax of (symbolic) expressions (Exp) and conditions (Cond). Expressions include symbolic variables, as well as arithmetic operators and operators on permissions. Conditions include a number of relational propositions over expressions, such as equality and inequality ($<$). They can also express rely and guarantee relations and inclusions between sets. A context of pure conditions is a sequence of conditions, interpreted as a conjunction. Symbolic execution generates entailments between contexts of conditions as verification conditions. The practical limitation on conditions is that these entailments should be checkable automatically by means of provers such as SMT solvers.

A (spatial) predicate $P(\bar{e}) \in$ Pred consists of a predicate name P and a list of expressions $\bar{e}$. Two types of predicates are given special treatment and have their own syntax: individual heap cells $a \mapsto b$ (where a is the address and b the value stored), and blocks of heap cells $a \mapsto \#\mathrm{cells}(n)$ (where a is the starting address and n is the number of consecutive heap cells). All other predicates are abstract.

A region map associates region identifiers with knowledge and resources for the given region. The knowledge consists of the type of the region, which is a pair of a region type name and list of expressions representing the parameters, and an expression describing the current state of the region. The resources consist of a guard. It is possible to have a guard for a region without knowing the type or state of the region, so these two components can be unspecified ($\perp$).

Figure 6 gives the correctness judgement for functions that forms the basis of CAPER's proof system. The judgement is parametrised by a context of region declarations Ψ, and a context of function specifications Φ. (Both contexts are left implicit in the sub-judgements.) The conditions break down into four key steps:

1. A symbolic state is generated corresponding to the function's precondition A_{pre}. This is captured by the judgement $produce(A_{\mathrm{pre}}, \gamma) : (\Delta, \varepsilon, \varepsilon, \emptyset) \rightsquigarrow \mathbb{S}_0$ which adds resources and assumptions to an initially empty symbolic state.
2. The body of the function is symbolically executed. This is captured by the judgement $\vdash C : (\Delta_0, \Pi_0, \Sigma_0, \Xi_0, [\bar{x} \mapsto \gamma(\bar{x})]) \rightsquigarrow \mathbb{S}_1$.
3. The regions of the resulting symbolic states are stabilised to account for possible interference from other threads. This is captured by the judgement

$$\frac{\mathrm{dom}(\gamma) = S \qquad \mathrm{range}(\gamma) = \Gamma \qquad \forall x, y \in S.\, \gamma(x) = \gamma(y) \implies x = y \qquad \Delta \cap \Gamma = \emptyset}{\mathit{freshSub}(\Delta, \Gamma, S, \gamma)}$$

$$\frac{\begin{array}{c} s_1', \ldots, s_n' \notin \Delta \qquad \Xi = [r_1 \mapsto (t_1, s_1, G_1), \ldots, r_n \mapsto (t_n, s_n, G_n)] \\ P = (s_1, s_1') \in \mathrm{Rely}(t_1, G_1); \ldots ; (s_n, s_n') \in \mathrm{Rely}(t_n, G_n) \\ \Xi' = [r_1 \mapsto (t_1, s_1', G_1), \ldots, r_n \mapsto (t_n, s_n', G_n)] \end{array}}{\mathit{stabilise}(\Delta, \Xi, s_1' : \mathbf{Val}; \ldots ; s_n' : \mathbf{Val}, P, \Xi')}$$

$$\frac{\begin{array}{c} \Phi(f) = (\bar{x}, A_{\mathrm{pre}}, A_{\mathrm{post}}) \\ \mathit{freshSub}(\varepsilon, \Delta, \mathrm{vars}(A_{\mathrm{pre}}) \cup \bar{x}, \gamma) \qquad \mathit{produce}(A_{\mathrm{pre}}, \gamma) : (\Delta, \varepsilon, \varepsilon, \emptyset) \rightsquigarrow \mathbb{S}_0 \\ \forall (\Delta_0, \Pi_0, \Sigma_0, \Xi_0) \in \mathbb{S}_0.\, \exists \mathbb{S}_1. \vdash C : (\Delta_0, \Pi_0, \Sigma_0, \Xi_0, [\bar{x} \mapsto \gamma(\bar{x})]) \rightsquigarrow \mathbb{S}_1 \\ \forall (\Delta_1, \Pi_1, \Sigma_1, \Xi_1, \Upsilon_1) \in \mathbb{S}_1.\, \exists \Delta_1', \Pi_1', \Xi_1'.\, \mathit{stabilise}(\Delta_1, \Xi_1, \Delta_1', \Pi_1', \Xi_1') \\ \exists \Gamma_1, \gamma'.\, \mathit{freshSub}(\Delta_1; \Delta_1', \Gamma_1, \mathrm{vars}(A_{\mathrm{post}}) \setminus (\mathrm{vars}(A_{\mathrm{pre}}) \cup \bar{x}), \gamma') \\ \exists \mathbb{S}_2.\, \mathit{consume}(A_{\mathrm{post}}, \gamma \cup \gamma') : (\Delta_1; \Delta_1', \Pi_1; \Pi_1', \Gamma_1, \varepsilon, \Sigma_1, \Xi_1') \rightsquigarrow \mathbb{S}_2 \\ \forall (\Delta_2, \Pi_2, \Gamma_2, P_2, \Sigma_2, \Xi_2) \in \mathbb{S}_2.\, \Delta_2, \Pi_2 \vdash \Gamma_2, P_2 \end{array}}{\Psi, \Phi \vdash \texttt{function } f(\bar{x})\{C\}}$$

Fig. 6. Function correctness judgement.

$\mathit{stabilise}(\Delta_1, \Xi_1, \Delta_1', \Pi_1', \Xi_1')$. (Note that stabilisation also occurs at each interleaving step in the symbolic execution.)

4. Each final symbolic state is checked against the postcondition. This is captured by the judgement $\mathit{consume}(A_{\mathrm{post}}, \gamma \cup \gamma') : (\Delta_1, \Pi_1, \Gamma, \varepsilon, \Sigma_1, \Xi_1) \rightsquigarrow \mathbb{S}_2$ which removes resources and generates verification conditions that are sufficient for the symbolic state to entail the postcondition. These verification conditions are checked by the judgement $\Delta_2, \Pi_2 \vdash \Gamma_2, P_2$.

Step 1 uses the judgement $\mathit{produce} \subseteq (\mathsf{Assn} \times (\mathsf{AssnVar} \rightharpoonup \mathsf{Exp})) \times \overline{\mathsf{SState}} \times \mathcal{P}(\overline{\mathsf{SState}})$, where $\overline{\mathsf{SState}} = \mathsf{VarCtx} \times \mathsf{Pure} \times \mathsf{Preds} \times \mathsf{Regions}$. The $\mathit{produce}$ judgement (we adopt the produce/consume nomenclature of Verifast [18]) adds resources and assumptions to the symbolic state corresponding to a given syntactic assertion. It is parametrised by a substitution from assertion variables to expressions. In producing the precondition, this substitution maps the assertion variables occurring in the precondition and the function parameters (treated as assertion variables) to fresh symbolic variables. This is captured by the $\mathit{freshSub}$ judgement. These fresh symbolic variables are bound in the initial variable context (Δ), while the initial context of conditions (ε), context of predicates (ε) and region map ($\emptyset$) are all empty. The judgement produces a set of symbolic states (sans program variable context). This set should be interpreted disjunctively: each of the symbolic states is possible after producing the assertion.

Step 2 uses the symbolic execution judgement: $(\vdash - : - \rightsquigarrow -) \subseteq \mathsf{Stmt} \times \mathsf{SState} \times \mathcal{P}(\mathsf{SState})$. This judgement updates the symbolic state according to the symbolic execution rules for program statements. The initial program variable context is given by mapping the function parameters $\bar{x}$ (treated as program variables) to the corresponding logical expressions $\gamma(\bar{x})$.

Step 3 uses the judgement $\mathit{stabilise} \subseteq \mathsf{VarCtx} \times \mathsf{Regions} \times \mathsf{VarCtx} \times \mathsf{Pure} \times \mathsf{Regions}$. This judgement relates an initial region map (in a given context) with a new region map that accounts for interference, with an extended context and additional pure conditions. The judgement is defined by the rule given in Fig. 6. This rule creates a fresh variable (s_i') to represent the new state of each region and asserts that it is related to the old state (s_i) in accordance with the rely relation for the given region. To account for the region type or state being unknown, we extend the definition of Rely with the following two rules:

$$\frac{}{(x,y) \in \text{Rely}(\bot, G)} \qquad \frac{}{(\bot, y) \in \text{Rely}(\mathbf{T}(r, \bar{x}), G)}$$

Step 4 uses the judgement $consume \subseteq (\text{Assn} \times (\text{AssnVar} \rightharpoonup \text{Exp})) \times \widehat{\text{SState}} \times \mathcal{P}(\widehat{\text{SState}})$, where $\widehat{\text{SState}} = \text{VarCtx} \times \text{Pure} \times \text{VarCtx} \times \text{Pure} \times \text{Preds} \times \text{Regions}$. The *consume* judgement removes resources and adds assertions to the symbolic state. The symbolic state is extended with a second variable context representing existentially quantified variables and a second context of pure conditions representing logical assertions. As an example, consuming the assertion x $\mapsto$ 2 where the predicates include $a \mapsto b$ can remove that predicate, adding the assertions $[\![x]\!]_\gamma = a$ and $2 = b$ (where γ is the assertion variable substitution). Any assertion variables occurring in the postcondition that are neither parameters of the function nor occur in the precondition are treated as existentially quantified. The *freshSub* judgement is used again to generate a context and substitution for these variables.

It remains to check that the assertions arising from consuming the postcondition follow from the assumptions. This is achieved with the entailment judgement: $(-, - \vdash -, -) \subseteq \text{VarCtx} \times \text{Pure} \times \text{VarCtx} \times \text{Pure}$. The judgement is defined by:

$$\Delta, \Pi \vdash \Gamma, P \overset{\text{def}}{\iff} \forall \delta \in [\![\Delta]\!] . [\![\Pi]\!]_\delta \implies \exists \delta' \in [\![\Gamma]\!] . [\![P]\!]_{\delta \cup \delta'}$$

Here, $[\![\Delta]\!]$ is the set of variable assignments agreeing with context Δ and $[\![\Pi]\!]_\delta$ is the valuation of the conjunction of the conditions Π in the variable assignment δ.

The Produce Judgement. The rules for the *produce* judgement are given in Fig. 7. The rules follow the syntax of the assertion to be produced. For a separating conjunction (&*&), first the left assertion is produced and then the right. Producing a conditional expression (?:) introduces non-determinism: we generate cases for whether the condition is true or false. For the true case, the first assertion is produced together with the condition; for the false case, the second assertion is produced together with the negated condition. Note that this non-determinism is demonic, in that the proof must deal with all cases. Producing a pure assertion simply adds it to the logical assumptions (interpreting the assertion variables through the substitution γ). Producing a predicate assertion adds it to the predicate context. As a special case, the points-to predicate also adds logical assumptions, expressed by $\mathcal{C}_{\text{cell}}$, which express that addresses must be positive and no two cells can have the same address (we elide the formal definition here).

The remaining two rules concern regions: producing a region and a guard assertion respectively. In each case, a region descriptor r_0 is created — in the first

$$\frac{\begin{array}{c} produce(A_1,\gamma) : S \rightsquigarrow \{S_i\}_{i \in I} \\ \forall i \in I.\, produce(A_2,\gamma) : S_i \rightsquigarrow \{S_{i,j}\}_{j \in J_i} \end{array}}{produce(A_1 \,\&*\&\, A_2,\gamma) : S \rightsquigarrow \{S_{i,j} \mid i \in I, j \in J_i\}}$$

$$\frac{\begin{array}{c} produce(A_1,\gamma) : (\Delta, \Pi; [\![p]\!]_\gamma, \Sigma, \Xi) \rightsquigarrow \mathbb{S}_1 \\ produce(A_2,\gamma) : (\Delta, \Pi; \neg [\![p]\!]_\gamma, \Sigma, \Xi) \rightsquigarrow \mathbb{S}_2 \end{array}}{produce(p \,?\, A_1 : A_2,\gamma) : (\Delta, \Pi, \Sigma, \Xi) \rightsquigarrow \mathbb{S}_1 \cup \mathbb{S}_2}$$

$$\frac{}{produce(p,\gamma) : (\Delta, \Pi, \Sigma, \Xi) \rightsquigarrow (\Delta, \Pi; [\![p]\!]_\gamma, \Sigma, \Xi)}$$

$$\frac{}{produce(P(\bar{e}),\gamma) : (\Delta, \Pi, \Sigma, \Xi) \rightsquigarrow (\Delta, \Pi, \Sigma; P([\![\bar{e}]\!]_\gamma), \Xi)}$$

$$\frac{}{produce(e_1 \mapsto e_2,\gamma) : (\Delta, \Pi, \Sigma, \Xi) \rightsquigarrow (\Delta, \Pi; \mathcal{C}_{\mathrm{cell}}([\![e_1]\!]_\gamma, \Sigma), \Sigma; [\![e_1]\!]_\gamma \mapsto [\![e_2]\!]_\gamma, \Xi)}$$

$$\frac{\begin{array}{c} r_0 = (\mathbf{T}([\![z,\bar{e}]\!]_\gamma), [\![s]\!]_\gamma, 0) \qquad \mathbb{S}_1 = \mathrm{rmerge}(\Delta, \Pi, \Sigma, \Xi, [\![z]\!]_\gamma, r_0) \\ i \notin \mathrm{dom}(\Xi) \qquad \mathbb{S}_2 = \mathrm{rnew}(\Delta, \Pi, \Sigma, \Xi, [\![z]\!]_\gamma, r_0, i) \end{array}}{produce(\mathbf{T}(z,\bar{e},s),\gamma) : (\Delta, \Pi, \Sigma, \Xi) \rightsquigarrow \mathbb{S}_1 \cup \mathbb{S}_2}$$

$$\frac{\begin{array}{c} r_0 = (\bot, \bot, [\![G]\!]_\gamma) \qquad \mathbb{S}_1 = \mathrm{rmerge}(\Delta, \Pi, \Sigma, \Xi, [\![z]\!]_\gamma, r_0) \\ i \notin \mathrm{dom}(\Xi) \qquad \mathbb{S}_2 = \mathrm{rnew}(\Delta, \Pi, \Sigma, \Xi, [\![z]\!]_\gamma, r_0, i) \end{array}}{produce(z@(G),\gamma) : (\Delta, \Pi, \Sigma, \Xi) \rightsquigarrow \mathbb{S}_1 \cup \mathbb{S}_2}$$

$$\mathrm{rmerge}(\Delta, \Pi, \Sigma, \Xi, a, r_0) =$$
$$\{(\Delta, \Pi; a = i'; \Pi', \Sigma, \Xi[i' \mapsto r']) \mid \exists r.\, \Xi(i) = r \wedge mergeRegion(r, r_0, \Pi', r')\}$$

$$\mathrm{rnew}(\Delta, \Pi, \Sigma, \Xi, a, r_0, i) = \{(\Delta, \Pi; a = i; \bigwedge \{i \neq i' \mid i' \in \mathrm{dom}(\Xi)\}, \Sigma, \Xi[i \mapsto r_0])\}$$

Fig. 7. Selected rules for the *produce* judgement.

case, including the region type and state but the empty guard, and in the second case, including a guard but no region type or state. We non-deterministically consider two cases: when the region identified by z already exists in the symbolic state, and when it represents a completely fresh region. The first case is handled by rmerge, which non-deterministically merges the region with one of the existing regions. The second case is handled by rnew, which associates the region with a fresh identifier (i) and adds assumptions that this is distinct from all other identifiers. Merging regions is governed by the *mergeRegion* judgement, which combines two region descriptors into one, producing a series of assumptions that are necessary for the merger to be well-defined. We elide the details here.

The Consume Judgement. A selection of rules for the *consume* judgement are given in Fig. 8. Unlike with *produce*, the syntax of the assertion may not uniquely determine which rule to apply. For instance, there are two rules for consuming a conditional assertion. The first rule consumes the conditional by consuming either the condition and the first assertion or the negated condition and the second assertion. (This are somewhat analogous to the ∨-introduction rules of natural deduction.) The second rule non-deterministically *assumes* the truth or

$$\frac{(A,q) \in \{(A_1, [\![p]\!]_\gamma), (A_2, \neg [\![p]\!]_\gamma)\} \qquad consume(A, \gamma) : (\Delta, \Pi, \Gamma, P; q, \Sigma, \Xi) \rightsquigarrow \mathbb{S}}{consume(p \ ? \ A_1 \ : \ A_2, \gamma) : (\Delta, \Pi, \Gamma, P, \Sigma, \Xi) \rightsquigarrow \mathbb{S}}$$

$$\frac{fv([\![p]\!]_\gamma) \subseteq \Delta \qquad consume(A_1, \gamma) : (\Delta, \Pi; [\![p]\!]_\gamma, \Gamma, P, \Sigma, \Xi) \rightsquigarrow \mathbb{S}_1 \qquad consume(A_2, \gamma) : (\Delta, \Pi; \neg [\![p]\!]_\gamma, \Gamma, P, \Sigma, \Xi) \rightsquigarrow \mathbb{S}_2}{consume(p \ ? \ A_1 \ : \ A_2, \gamma) : (\Delta, \Pi, \Gamma, P, \Sigma, \Xi) \rightsquigarrow \mathbb{S}_1 \cup \mathbb{S}_2}$$

$$\frac{\Xi(i) = ((R, \bar{x}), s, G) \qquad s \neq \bot}{consume(R(r, \bar{e}, a), \gamma) : (\Delta, \Pi, \Gamma, P, \Sigma, \Xi) \rightsquigarrow \{(\Delta, \Pi, \Gamma, P; [\![r]\!]_\gamma = i; [\![r, \bar{e}]\!]_\gamma = \bar{x}; [\![a]\!]_\gamma = s, \Sigma, \Xi)\}}$$

$$\frac{\Xi(i) = (t, s, H) \qquad takeGuard(\Delta, t, H, [\![G]\!]_\gamma, \Gamma', F, P')}{consume(r@G, \gamma) : (\Delta, \Pi, \Gamma, P, \Sigma, \Xi) \rightsquigarrow \{(\Delta, \Pi, \Gamma; \Gamma', P; P', \Sigma, \Xi[i \mapsto (t, s, F)])\}}$$

Fig. 8. Selected rules for the *consume* judgement.

falsity of the condition, consuming the first or second assertion in the respective case. This requires that only assumption variables can occur in the condition $(fv([\![p]\!]_\gamma) \subseteq \Delta)$, since otherwise the context of assumptions would be ill-formed. Here, we are exploiting the law of the excluded middle for pure assertion p: that is $p \lor \neg p$ holds. Consuming a region assertion asserts that there is a corresponding region with the specified type and state. Consuming a guard assertion makes use of the judgement $takeGuard(\Delta, t, H, G, \Gamma, P, F)$, which expresses that guard G can be removed from guard H leaving the frame F, under conditions P, given the region type t. Frame inference is used to discharge $takeGuard$ obligations.

The Symbolic Execution Judgement. The symbolic execution judgement expresses how executing a program statement affects the symbolic state. Most of the symbolic execution rules are standard, except that when statements are sequenced together, the intermediate symbolic state is stabilised (using the *stabilise* judgement). The other novelty is the symbolic execution of atomic statements (read, write and CAS operations), which require access to the shared regions. The symbolic execution rule is given in Fig. 9. It consists of six steps:

1. Regions are opened with the *openRegions* judgement. This is based on the *open* judgement, which opens a single region by producing its interpretation (by case analysis on the possible interpretations).
2. The atomic statement is symbolically executed with the *atomic* judgement. This cannot affect the shared regions.
3. The regions are updated with the *updateRegions* judgement. This applies the *update* judgement to each of the regions, updating the state arbitrarily in a manner that is consistent with the guarantee for the available guard.
4. New regions may be created with the *createRegions* judgement. These regions must be distinct from the existing ones, and will be created along with the full guard for the region type. At this point, these new regions are open.

$$\Xi(r) = (\mathbf{T}(\bar{x}), s, G)$$
$$\Psi_{\mathrm{I}}(\mathbf{T}) = \{(P_i, e_i, A_i)\}_{i \in I} \qquad \forall i \in I.\, freshSub(\Delta, \Gamma_i, \mathrm{vars}(P_i, e_i, A_i), \gamma_i)$$
$$\frac{\forall i \in I.\, produce(A_i, \gamma_i) : (\Delta; \Gamma_i, \Pi; [\![\Psi_{\mathrm{P}}(\mathbf{T})]\!]_{\gamma_i} = \bar{x}; s = [\![e_i]\!]_{\gamma_i}\,; [\![P_i]\!]_{\gamma_i}, \Sigma, \Xi) \rightsquigarrow \mathbb{S}_i}{open(r) : (\Delta, \Pi, \Sigma, \Xi) \rightsquigarrow \bigcup \{\mathbb{S}_i\}_{i \in I}}$$

$$\frac{\Xi(r) = (\mathbf{T}(\bar{x}), s, G) \qquad s' \notin \Delta \qquad \Gamma = (s' : \mathbf{Val}) \qquad P = ((s, s') \in \mathrm{Guar}_{\Psi}(\mathbf{T}(\bar{x}), G))}{update(r, \Delta, \Xi, \Gamma, P, \Xi[r \mapsto (\mathbf{T}(\bar{x}), s', G)])}$$

$$\Xi(r) = (\mathbf{T}(\bar{x}), s, G)$$
$$(P_0, e_0, A_0) \in \Psi_{\mathrm{I}}(\mathbf{T}) \qquad freshSub(\Delta, \Gamma, \Gamma_0, \mathrm{vars}(P_0, e_0, A_0), \gamma)$$
$$\frac{consume(A_0, \gamma) : (\Delta, \Pi, \Gamma; \Gamma_0, P; [\![\Psi_{\mathrm{P}}(\mathbf{T})]\!]_{\gamma} = \bar{x}; s = [\![e_0]\!]_{\gamma}\,; [\![P_0]\!]_{\gamma}, \Sigma, \Xi) \rightsquigarrow \mathbb{S}}{close(r) : (\Delta, \Pi, \Gamma, P, \Sigma, \Xi) \rightsquigarrow \mathbb{S}}$$

$$openRegions : (\Delta, \Pi, \Sigma, \Xi, \varepsilon) \rightsquigarrow \mathbb{S}$$
$$\forall (\Delta_1, \Pi_1, \Sigma_1, \Xi_1, \bar{r}) \in \mathbb{S}.\, \exists \mathbb{S}_1.\, atomic(\alpha) : (\Delta_1, \Pi_1, \Sigma_1, \Upsilon) \rightsquigarrow \mathbb{S}_1$$
$$\forall (\Delta_2, \Pi_2, \Sigma_2, \Upsilon_2) \in \mathbb{S}_1.\, \exists \Gamma_2, P_2, \Xi_2.\, updateRegions(\bar{r}, \Delta_2, \Xi_1, \Gamma_2, P_2, \Xi_2)$$
$$\exists \bar{s}, \Gamma_2', P_2', \Xi_2'.\, createRegions(\bar{s}, \Delta_2; \Gamma_2, \Xi_2, \Gamma_2', P_2', \Xi_2')$$
$$\exists \mathbb{S}_2.\, closeRegions(\bar{s}, \bar{r}) : (\Delta_2, \Pi_2, \Gamma_2; \Gamma_2', P_2; P_2', \Sigma_2, \Xi_2') \rightsquigarrow \mathbb{S}_2$$
$$\frac{\forall (\Delta_3, \Pi_3, \Gamma_3, P_3, \Sigma_3, \Xi_3) \in \mathbb{S}_3.\, (\Delta_3, \Pi_3 \vdash \Gamma_3, P_3) \wedge (\Delta_3; \Gamma_3, \Pi_3; P_3, \Sigma_3, \Xi_3, \Upsilon_2) \in \mathbb{S}_3}{\vdash \langle \alpha \rangle : (\Delta, \Pi, \Sigma, \Xi, \Upsilon) \rightsquigarrow \mathbb{S}_3}$$

Fig. 9. Symbolic execution rule for atomic statements.

5. All of the open regions are closed with the *closeRegions* judgement. This applies *close* for each region, which consumes the interpretation.
6. The generated assertions are checked to follow from the assumptions, and the assertions are treated as assumptions in the new symbolic state.

4 Proof Search

The success of separation logic as a basis for symbolic execution is in part due to its determinacy: given a precondition and a program statement, it is feasible to compute the strongest postcondition or determine that the program might fault. Concurrent separation logics, however, depend on auxiliary state, such as CAPER's regions and guards, which can introduce non-determinism since the program itself does not specify how the auxiliary state should be updated. For instance, when closing a region, CAPER may have more than one valid choice for the region state. Consequently, non-determinism is fundamental to CAPER's design and backtracking is used to resolve the non-deterministic choices in the proof search. This non-determinism is used in: consuming conditional or disjunctive assertions; determining which heap cell, region or predicate to consume; choosing which regions to open; determining which state interpretation to close a region with; and determining how to rewrite guards.

Since non-determinism introduces branching, which can be detrimental to performance, CAPER uses some heuristics in an effort to prune or avoid bad branches. For instance, when consuming a heap cell, if there is a cell whose address matches syntactically (e.g. consuming $x \mapsto z$ in a symbolic state with $x \mapsto 2$) CAPER will not consider other cases, which would be eliminated by a later SMT call. Another example is that CAPER prioritises opening *different* regions over opening *more* regions. Opening a region typically involves case analysis, and so opening multiple regions can lead to bad performance when it is not required.

It is important to note that choices by the user can significantly affect CAPER's level of non-determinism. For instance, if the abstract state of a region is determined exactly by the concrete state, CAPER will consider fewer possibilities than if a region can be in multiple states for the same concrete state.

There are a some non-deterministic choices that should not generally be considered as options everywhere they could be allowed. One of these is region creation: at any point it is legal to create a new region, provided the appropriate resources are available. It would quickly make proof search intractable if CAPER considered all possible ways of creating regions at all times. On the other hand, there is a good indicator for when creating a region will be helpful: when CAPER fails to consume a region assertion. CAPER's backtracking mechanism includes handlers that introduce additional non-determinism in response to specific failures. In particular, a failure to consume a region assertion will be handled by attempting to create an appropriate region.

This behaviour is a form of abductive reasoning: the general reasoning principle of inferring explanatory hypotheses from a goal. Abduction has previously been applied to automatically derive separation logic specifications [4]. Our approach differs in that we infer missing updates to auxiliary state rather than missing resources in the precondition.

A further application of abduction in CAPER is in handling existential logical variables. Consuming an assertion may introduce a new (existential) logical variable with some constraints. CAPER calls the prover to check that these constraints are satisfiable; thereafter, CAPER only knows that the variable satisfies these constraints. If, later in the symbolic execution, CAPER requires the variable to satisfy additional constraints, then the proof may fail even if there was a witness satisfying these constraints. The constraints are therefore abductively propagated back to where the variable was introduced, and the proof is retried. Since CAPER then knows that the additional constraints are satisfied, it can successfully discharge them when they arise.

5   Evaluation

We have successfully applied CAPER to verify a number of concurrent algorithms. In Sect. 2, we discussed the spin lock and ticket lock, whose specifications guarantee mutual exclusion. We have verified a reader-writer lock, whose specification permits multiple readers or a single writer to enter their critical sections concurrently. This example uses counting permissions, but we have also verified a bounded version that does not. We have also verified a number of counter implementations with specifications that enforce monotonicity (CASCounter, BoundedCounter and IncDec), and an atomic reference counter (ReferenceCount). We have verified a library for joining on forked threads and a client that waits for the child thread to terminate before presenting the work done by the child. We have also verified a synchronisation barrier and a client that uses it to synchronise threads incrementing and decrementing a counter. Finally, we have verified two implementations of a bag: the stack of Sect. 2.3, and a concurrent queue. We summarise these examples in Table 1, which shows the number of lines of code and annotation and verification times for recursive and iterative versions of each example. By default, CAPER can create up to two regions at a time (-c 2) and open up to two regions (-o 2). The BagStack and Queue examples require opening up to three regions. The BarrierClient requires creating no regions, because of an issue with CAPER's failure handling implementation.

Table 1. Examples (recursive/iterative).

Name	Code (lines)	Annotations (lines)	Time (s)
SpinLock	17/17	17/18	0.21/0.35
TicketLock(Client)	33 (41)/24 (32)	19 (29)/17 (27)	0.77 (0.82)/2.22 (2.23)
ReadWriteLock	36/37	25/28	3.32/15.98
BoundedReadWriteLock	55/57	36/41	31.01/127.34
CASCounter	20/20	15/16	0.08/0.14
BoundedCounter	25/25	20/21	4.01/20.14
IncDec	29/29	19/21	0.10/0.36
ReferenceCount	31/30	22/24	0.22/0.73
ForkJoin(Client)	17 (32)/17 (32)	16 (30)/17 (31)	0.05 (0.07)/0.07 (0.09)
Barrier(Client[a])	71 (127)/77 (130)	31 (60)/35 (67)	28.22 (30.50)/26.96 (31.44)
BagStack[b]	35/30	26/26	3.22/11.98
Queue[c]	60/58	37/38	177.33/179.82

[a] flags: -c 0   [b] flags: -c 1 -o 3   [c] flags: -c 2 -o 3

From the verification times, we can observe that the versions that use loops tend to take longer than the recursive versions. This is due to case analysis which propagates through loops, but is abstracted in function calls. The high verification times for the bounded examples are largely due to CAPER computing transitive closures for finite-state regions. The barrier example also takes significant time to compute the transitive closure of an infinite-state region. The BagStack and Queue use nested regions, and Queue has a complicated transition system, which combine to give a long verification time.

There are three key areas where CAPER could use significant improvement. Firstly, proof search could be improved, for instance by directing the choice of regions to open and abstracting multiple branches into one. Currently, successful proofs may take some time and failing proofs take even longer. Secondly, CAPER heuristics used in abduction require improvement, including loop invariants, this should allow more algorithms to be proved. Thirdly, CAPER's annotations limit the expressivity of specifications to some extent. For instance, there is no support for regions with abstract states other than integers. Despite these limitations, we believe that CAPER demonstrates the viability of our approach, and provides a good basis for further investigation.

6   Related Work

CAPER is a tool for automating proofs in a concurrent separation logic with shared regions, aimed at proving functional correctness for fine-grained concurrent algorithms. The logic is in the spirit of concurrent abstract predicates (CAP) [10] taking inspiration from recent developments in concurrent separation logic such as iCAP [29], TaDA [7], Views [9], CaReSL [32], FCSL [22] and Iris [19].

Smallfoot [1] pioneered symbolic execution for separation logic. While it can prove functional correctness, it has limited support for concurrency and so cannot prove fine-grained concurrent algorithms.

SmallfootRG [5] extended Smallfoot to the more expressive logic RGSep [33]. The tool uses shared resources that are annotated with invariants and actions that can be performed over these resources. The actions that can be performed are not guarded, which leads to very weak specifications: it can prove memory safety, but not functional correctness. The abstraction of stabilisation employed by SmallfootRG is different than the transitivity-based technique of CAPER. SmallfootRG uses abstract interpretation to weaken assertions such that they are stable, where the abstract domain is based on symbolic assertions. Requiring (or ensuring) that a set of actions is transitively closed can be seen as an abstraction that terminates in a single step.

CAVE [34] built on SmallfootRG's action inference to prove linearisability [17] of concurrent data structures. That is, CAVE can prove that the operations of a concurrent data structure are atomic with respect to each other, and satisfy an abstract functional specification. CAPER cannot yet prove linearisability, although it could in future support abstract atomicity in the style of TaDA [7]. On the other hand, CAVE cannot prove functional correctness of non-linearisable examples such as a spin lock.

Other mechanised — but not automatic — approaches based on separation logic include Verifast [18] and the Coq mechanisation of fine-grained concurrent separation logic [22,28]. Both approaches support an expressive assertion language, including higher-order predicates. They are able to prove functional correctness properties for fine-grained concurrent programs. Direct comparisons are, however, difficult. Programs and specifications need adaptation, often more than simple translation, resulting in different and sometimes weaker specifications. This is due in part to a smaller core set of operations and in part to a lack of features and expressivity of logic. However, when examples are comparable, the annotation overhead of the CAPER examples is lower, often significantly. For example, the spin lock requires 87 lines of annotation in Verifast, compared to 18 in CAPER, while the ticket lock requires 123 lines compared to 17. Verifast takes 0.11 s to check each of these examples.

Viper [21] is a verification infrastructure for program verification based on permissions. It supports an expressive permission model that includes fractional permissions and symbolic permissions. It would be interesting to develop a front end for Viper that implements CAPER's verification approach. A challenging issue is whether (and how) the non-deterministic proof search can be encoded in Viper's intermediate language.

7 Conclusions

We have presented CAPER, the first automatic proof tool for a separation logic with CAP-style shared regions, and discussed the significant innovations that it involves. As a prototype, CAPER provides a foundation for exploring the possibilities for automation with such a logic. Support for a number of different features will significantly increase the scope of examples that CAPER can handle. We anticipate adding support for the following: additional guard algebra constructions; richer logical data types, such as sets and inductive data types; support for abstract and inductive predicates; and support for separation at the level of abstract states in the spirit of FCSL [22] and CoLoSL [25]. We would like to investigate inferring loop invariants and other annotations. We would like to make CAPER more usable by providing proofs and failed proofs in a format that can easily be navigated and interpreted by a user. To this end, CAPER already provides an interactive proof mode that allows a user to drive the proof search. This enables exploration of, in particular, failing proofs, which has proven valuable in development of the tool and the accompanying examples. A further goal is to put CAPER on a rigorous footing by formalising its logic in a proof assistant (such as Coq) and using CAPER to generate program proofs that can be checked in the proof assistant or by a verified checker.

Acknowledgements. We thank the anonymous referees for useful feedback. This research was supported by the "ModuRes" Sapere Aude Advanced Grant from The Danish Council for Independent Research for the Natural Sciences (FNU), the "Automated Verification for Concurrent Programs" Individual Postdoc Grant from The Danish Council for Independent Research for Technology and Production Sciences (FTP), and the EPSRC Programme Grants EP/H008373/1 and EP/K008528/1.

References

1. Berdine, J., Calcagno, C., O'Hearn, P.W.: Smallfoot: modular automatic assertion checking with separation logic. In: Boer, F.S., Bonsangue, M.M., Graf, S., Roever, W.-P. (eds.) FMCO 2005. LNCS, vol. 4111, pp. 115–137. Springer, Heidelberg (2006). doi:10.1007/11804192_6
2. Biering, B., Birkedal, L., Torp-Smith, N.: BI hyperdoctrines and higher-order separation logic. In: Sagiv, M. (ed.) ESOP 2005. LNCS, vol. 3444, pp. 233–247. Springer, Heidelberg (2005). doi:10.1007/978-3-540-31987-0_17
3. Bornat, R., Calcagno, C., O'Hearn, P., Parkinson, M.: Permission accounting in separation logic. In: POPL, pp. 259–270 (2005)

4. Calcagno, C., Distefano, D., O'Hearn, P., Yang, H.: Compositional shape analysis by means of bi-abduction. In: Proceedings of the 36th Annual ACM SIGPLAN-SIGACT Symposium on Principles of Programming Languages, POPL 2009, New York, pp. 289–300 (2009). http://doi.acm.org/10.1145/1480881.1480917
5. Calcagno, C., Parkinson, M., Vafeiadis, V.: Modular safety checking for fine-grained concurrency. In: Nielson, H.R., Filé, G. (eds.) SAS 2007. LNCS, vol. 4634, pp. 233–248. Springer, Heidelberg (2007). doi:10.1007/978-3-540-74061-2_15
6. Chang, C.C., Keisler, H.J.: Model Theory. Studies in Logic and the Foundations of Mathematics. Elsevier Science, Amsterdam (1990)
7. da Rocha Pinto, P., Dinsdale-Young, T., Gardner, P.: TaDA: a logic for time and data abstraction. In: Jones, R. (ed.) ECOOP 2014. LNCS, vol. 8586, pp. 207–231. Springer, Heidelberg (2014). doi:10.1007/978-3-662-44202-9_9
8. de Moura, L., Bjørner, N.: Z3: an efficient SMT solver. In: Ramakrishnan, C.R., Rehof, J. (eds.) TACAS 2008. LNCS, vol. 4963, pp. 337–340. Springer, Heidelberg (2008). doi:10.1007/978-3-540-78800-3_24
9. Dinsdale-Young, T., Birkedal, L., Gardner, P., Parkinson, M., Yang, H.: Views: compositional reasoning for concurrent programs. In: POPL, pp. 287–300 (2013)
10. Dinsdale-Young, T., Dodds, M., Gardner, P., Parkinson, M.J., Vafeiadis, V.: Concurrent abstract predicates. In: D'Hondt, T. (ed.) ECOOP 2010. LNCS, vol. 6183, pp. 504–528. Springer, Heidelberg (2010). doi:10.1007/978-3-642-14107-2_24
11. Dinsdale-Young, T., da Rocha Pinto, P., Andersen, K.J.: Caper (source code). https://github.com/caper-tool/caper
12. Dinsdale-Young, T., da Rocha Pinto, P., Andersen, K.J., Birkedal, L.: Caper, automatic verification with concurrent abstract predicates. Technical Appendix: Program logic (2016). http://cs.au.dk/~kja/papers/caper-esop.17/techreport.pdf
13. Dockins, R., Hobor, A., Appel, A.W.: A fresh look at separation algebras and share accounting. In: Hu, Z. (ed.) APLAS 2009. LNCS, vol. 5904, pp. 161–177. Springer, Heidelberg (2009). doi:10.1007/978-3-642-10672-9_13
14. El Ghazi, A.A., Taghdiri, M., Herda, M.: First-order transitive closure axiomatization via iterative invariant injections. In: Havelund, K., Holzmann, G., Joshi, R. (eds.) NFM 2015. LNCS, vol. 9058, pp. 143–157. Springer, Heidelberg (2015). doi:10.1007/978-3-319-17524-9_11
15. Ershov, Y.L.: Decidability of the elementary theory of distributive lattices with relative complements and the theory of filters. Algebra i Logika 3, 17–38 (1964)
16. Floyd, R.W.: Algorithm 97: shortest path. Commun. ACM 5(6), 345 (1962). http://doi.acm.org/10.1145/367766.368168
17. Herlihy, M.P., Wing, J.M.: Linearizability: a correctness condition for concurrent objects. ACM Trans. Program. Lang. Syst. 12(3), 463–492 (1990)
18. Jacobs, B., Smans, J., Philippaerts, P., Vogels, F., Penninckx, W., Piessens, F.: VeriFast: a powerful, sound, predictable, fast verifier for C and Java. In: Bobaru, M., Havelund, K., Holzmann, G.J., Joshi, R. (eds.) NFM 2011. LNCS, vol. 6617, pp. 41–55. Springer, Heidelberg (2011). doi:10.1007/978-3-642-20398-5_4
19. Jung, R., Swasey, D., Sieczkowski, F., Svendsen, K., Turon, A., Birkedal, L., Dreyer, D.: Iris: monoids and invariants as an orthogonal basis for concurrent reasoning. In: POPL, pp. 637–650 (2015)
20. Le, X.B., Gherghina, C., Hobor, A.: Decision procedures over sophisticated fractional permissions. In: Jhala, R., Igarashi, A. (eds.) APLAS 2012. LNCS, vol. 7705, pp. 368–385. Springer, Heidelberg (2012). doi:10.1007/978-3-642-35182-2_26

21. Müller, P., Schwerhoff, M., Summers, A.J.: Viper: a verification infrastructure for permission-based reasoning. In: Jobstmann, B., Leino, K. (eds.) Verification, Model Checking, and Abstract Interpretation. LNCS, vol. 9583, pp. 41–62. Springer, Heidelberg (2016). doi:10.1007/978-3-662-49122-5_2

22. Nanevski, A., Ley-Wild, R., Sergey, I., Delbianco, G.A.: Communicating state transition systems for fine-grained concurrent resources. In: Shao, Z. (ed.) ESOP 2014. LNCS, vol. 8410, pp. 290–310. Springer, Heidelberg (2014). doi:10.1007/978-3-642-54833-8_16

23. O'Hearn, P.W.: Resources, concurrency and local reasoning. Theor. Comput. Sci. **375**(1–3), 271–307 (2007)

24. Parkinson, M.J., Bierman, G.M.: Separation logic and abstraction. In: POPL (2005)

25. Raad, A., Villard, J., Gardner, P.: CoLoSL: concurrent local subjective logic. In: Vitek, J. (ed.) ESOP 2015. LNCS, vol. 9032, pp. 710–735. Springer, Heidelberg (2015). doi:10.1007/978-3-662-46669-8_29

26. Reynolds, J.C.: Separation logic: a logic for shared mutable data structures. In: 2002 Proceedings of 17th Annual IEEE Symposium on Logic in Computer Science, pp. 55–74. IEEE (2002)

27. Schulz, S.: System description: E 1.8. logic for programming. In: McMillan, K., Middeldorp, A., Voronkov, A. (eds.) Logic for Programming, Artificial Intelligence, and Reasoning, LPAR 2013, LNCS, vol. 8312, pp. 735–743. Springer, Berlin (2013). doi:10.1007/978-3-642-45221-5_49

28. Sergey, I., Nanevski, A., Banerjee, A.: Mechanized verification of fine-grained concurrent programs. In: 36th ACM SIGPLAN International Conference on Programming Language Design and Implementation (PLDI 2015) (2015)

29. Svendsen, K., Birkedal, L.: Impredicative concurrent abstract predicates. In: Shao, Z. (ed.) ESOP 2014. LNCS, vol. 8410, pp. 149–168. Springer, Heidelberg (2014). doi:10.1007/978-3-642-54833-8_9

30. Tarski, A.: Arithmetical classes and types of Boolean algebras. Bull. Am. Math. Soc. **55**, 63 (1949)

31. Treiber, R.K.: Systems programming: coping with parallelism. Technical report RJ 5118, IBM Almaden Research Center, April 1986

32. Turon, A., Dreyer, D., Birkedal, L.: Unifying refinement and hoare-style reasoning in a logic for higher-order concurrency. In: ICFP, pp. 377–390 (2013)

33. Vafeiadis, V.: Modular fine-grained concurrency verification. Ph.D. thesis, University of Cambridge, Computer Laboratory (2008)

34. Vafeiadis, V.: Automatically proving linearizability. In: Touili, T., Cook, B., Jackson, P. (eds.) CAV 2010. LNCS, vol. 6174, pp. 450–464. Springer, Heidelberg (2010). doi:10.1007/978-3-642-14295-6_40

Tackling Real-Life Relaxed Concurrency with FSL++

Marko Doko$^{(\boxtimes)}$ and Viktor Vafeiadis

Max Planck Institute for Software Systems (MPI-SWS),
Kaiserslautern, Germany
mdoko@mpi-sws.org

Abstract. We extend fenced separation logic (FSL), a program logic for reasoning about C11 relaxed access and memory fences. Our extensions to FSL allow us to handle concurrent algorithms appearing in practice. New features added to FSL allow for reasoning about concurrent non-atomic reads, atomic updates, ownership transfer via release sequences, and ghost state. As a demonstration of power of the extended FSL, we verify correctness of the atomic reference counter (ARC), a standard library of the Rust programing language, whose implementation relies heavily on advanced features of the C11 memory model. Soundness of FSL and its extensions, as well as the correctness proof of ARC have been established in Coq.

1 Introduction

Most formal verification work on multithreaded programs with concurrent accesses to shared memory assumes that programs follow the *sequentially consistent* model of execution [22]. In this model, the executions of a concurrent program consist of all possible interleavings of the actions of its threads.

Even though sequential consistency is a simple and intuitive concurrency model, it does not match the real world. In practice, no hardware provides us with a sequentially consistent execution environment. In order to improve performance or conserve energy, modern hardware implementations give us what is known as *weak memory* models; that is, models of concurrency providing weaker guarantees than sequential consistency. As a result, most of the verification techniques developed for sequential consistency are inapplicable to weak memory models.

In this paper, we will focus on the C11 weak memory model. This software-level model was introduced by the 2011 C and C++ standards [15,16] as an abstraction over the various different hardware memory models, and provides various low-level primitives for developing efficient concurrent programs. These low-level primitives are slowly gaining adoption not only in C and C++, but are also being incorporated in other programming languages such as Java and Rust.

As the adoption of C11-style weak memory primitives grows, so does the importance of being able to verify correctness of algorithms that use them. Currently, the most successful logic for reasoning about the C11 memory model

© Springer-Verlag GmbH Germany 2017
H. Yang (Ed.): ESOP 2017, LNCS 10201, pp. 448–475, 2017.
DOI: 10.1007/978-3-662-54434-1_17

is GPS [34], which has, for instance, been used to verify an implementation of the read-copy-update (RCU) algorithm [33], a synchronization mechanism used in the Linux kernel. GPS, however, has an important limitation: namely, it can reason only about the *release-acquire* fragment of the C11 memory model, which leaves programs that use *relaxed* operations (i.e., operations weaker than release-acquire ones) completely out of the reach of GPS. One such algorithm is the *atomic reference counter* (ARC) [1], which we will verify in this paper.

ARC is a part of the standard library of the Rust programming language [2] and provides an interface for concurrent access to a shared data structure. The shared structure can be read by multiple threads, but cannot be modified. ARC ensures that the shared data structure will be deallocated once no reader needs to access the data structure any more. Features present in ARC, which are unsupported by GPS, include *relaxed memory accesses* and *memory fences*.

There is a logic that can deal with both relaxed accesses and memory fences: *fenced separation logic* (FSL) [13]. Unfortunately, even though FSL supports relaxed accesses and memory fences, it lacks some key features which makes it inapplicable beyond simple "toy" examples.

In this work, we extend FSL to make it applicable to real world examples, using ARC as a demonstration of its abilities. Specifically, we extend FSL with three new features:

- partial read *permissions* for non-atomic accesses [8,10],
- support for *compare-and-swap* (CAS) operations, and
- *ghost state* [12,18,23],

all of which are actually needed for proving ARC correct.

Among these three features, the most interesting is ghost state because it interacts with the other FSL features in novel and interesting ways. Ghost state represents supplementary logical resources not used by the program, but only by the user of the logic in order to establish program's correctness.

Ghost state interacts with FSL's ability to transfer ownership of resources between threads. For soundness purposes, transferring a resource from one thread to another cannot happen by simply writing or reading a shared variable; it requires some form of additional synchronization: either a memory fence or a special type of memory access, which essentially incorporates a fence.

A key observation that we made, however, is that ghost state may be soundly transferred between threads under weaker conditions than the other types of resources owned by threads. In particular, it may be transferred by simple non-synchronizing memory accesses! In essence, this is sound because unlike other resources such as $x \mapsto 5$, owning some ghost state does not provide additional power to a thread to perform an action; it only allows us to deduce that certain interference patterns between threads are not possible. As such, the soundness proof can impose slightly weaker conditions that allow two threads to occasionally own the same ghost state resource simultaneously.

At this point, it is worth noting that the soundness proof of FSL assumes a standard strengthening of the C11 model which disables some compiler optimizations (namely, read-write reordering). This strengthening of the C11 model—though standard and partly necessary for performing any kind of formal reasoning about the model—has interesting implications for the soundness of ghost state, which we will discuss in Sect. 5.2.

With FSL strengthened in this way, we are able to *formally verify an implementation of ARC* that uses the same pattern of atomic accesses and memory fences as the one that can be found in the standard library of Rust. Both the soundness proof of the new features of FSL and the formal correctness proof of ARC have been fully mechanized in Coq. The complete Coq development, together with our online appendix, is available at http://plv.mpi-sws.org/fsl/.

As a rough measure of the effort required to extend the FSL with the features mentioned above, we can look at the size of the Coq development. The size of the soundness proof for FSL is approximately 17.6 KLOC (thousand lines of code), while the soundness proof for FSL++ consists of around 22.7 KLOC representing an increase in size of about 30%. Another 2000 lines were required to complete the verification of ARC, out of which 800 belong to generic auxiliary lemmas, while the remaining 1200 closely follow the correctness proof outlined in Sect. 4.

```
new(v){                          drop(a){
    a = alloc();                     t = fetch_and_add_rel(a.count, -1);
    a.data = v;                      if(t == 1){
    a.count_rlx = 1;                     fence_acq;
    return a;                            free(a);
}                                    }
                                 }

read(a){                         clone(a){
    return a.data;                   fetch_and_add_rlx(a.count, 1);
}                                }
```

Fig. 1. Atomic reference counter implementation.

2   Atomic Reference Counter

Before going into FSL and its extensions, let us first have a look at the ARC algorithm, as we will use its features to motivate our extensions of FSL.

2.1   The Algorithm

Our ARC implementation is given in Fig. 1 and consists of four functions: new, read, drop, and clone. To gain a basic understanding of the algorithm, we can ignore the **rel**, acq, and rlx annotations, as well as any **fence** instructions.

Function new(v) creates a new ARC object a, sets its **data** field to v, and the **count** field to 1. The **data** field holds the value that can be accessed through the ARC object, and **count** counts the number of references to the ARC object.

Function read(v) simply returns the value stored in the ARC object.

Function `clone(a)` operationally just increments the reference counter by one using an atomic *fetch-and-add* instruction. Semantically, `clone` gives us another reference to the ARC object (hence the increment of the counter), which can now also be used to access the value stored in the ARC object. After calling `clone` we can, for example, create a new thread, let it read from one ARC reference, and keep the other reference available for ourselves.

Function `drop(a)` disposes of a reference to the ARC object `a`. If there are still multiple references to the ARC object, `drop` only decreases the reference counter. On the other hand, if the counter gets decremented from one to zero (i.e., there are no more references to the ARC object), `drop` also deallocates the ARC object.

$$\{\mathsf{emp}\} \; \mathbf{new}(v) \; \{a. \; \mathsf{ARC}(a, v)\}$$
$$\{\mathsf{ARC}(a, v)\} \; \mathbf{read}(a) \; \{y. \; y = v \land \mathsf{ARC}(a, v)\}$$
$$\{\mathsf{ARC}(a, v)\} \mathbf{clone}(a) \{\mathsf{ARC}(a, v) * \mathsf{ARC}(a, v)\}$$
$$\{\mathsf{ARC}(a, v)\} \; \mathbf{drop}(a) \; \{\mathsf{emp}\}$$

Fig. 2. ARC specification in separation logic.

The intended use of the ARC library can be succinctly expressed in terms of separation logic in Fig. 2. In this specification, $\mathsf{ARC}(a, v)$ represents the permission to run functions that access the ARC object a. This permission is created by the function `new`, duplicated by `clone`, and destroyed by `drop`.

2.2   Why Is ARC Correct?

Let us now consider why ARC is correct. Before attempting to answer this question, we should first ask ourselves, what is the correctness criterion for this algorithm? In other words, what should its specification in Fig. 2 achieve?

For the algorithm to operate correctly, we are primarily interested in memory safety. We have to ensure that the deallocation does not happen until all the threads are done with reading the value stored in the ARC object. More precisely, the read of the `data` field in the `read` function should not race with the deallocation that happens in the `drop` function.

Additionally, the deallocation should not be attempted twice. For this particular algorithm, it is quite easy to see that is not the case: deallocation happens only once, when the reference counter drops to zero.

In remainder of this section, we therefore focus on the first property.

Sequential Consistency. From the perspective of the *interleaving semantics* (a.k.a. *sequential consistency*), the situation is quite clear. Recall that the deallocation happens when `drop` decrements the reference counter to zero. This means that all the ARC objects that have been produced (by either `new` or `clone`) have also been disposed of by `drop`. Obviously, no call to `read` can be made any more, since we no longer have any ARC objects available.

Weak Memory. When moving to weak memory models, such as C11, the reasoning becomes significantly more complex. In what follows, we are going to give a simplified presentation of the C11 model, focusing on the features used in the ARC algorithm. Complete presentations of the C11 model can be found in [6, 35].

The C11 model presents executions as graphs where nodes (also called *events*) represent memory accesses. Events (i.e., memory accesses and fences) can be either reads (R), writes (W), updates (U), or fences (F). Reads and writes can be of atomic or non-atomic kind, while updates represent atomic read-modify-write instructions, such as compare-and-swap or fetch-and-add, and can thus be only of atomic kind.

Having a data race on non-atomic accesses is considered to be a programming error, while racing on atomic access is allowed. Atomic accesses provide us with mechanisms to implement synchronization among different threads. How effective an atomic access is in enforcing synchronization depends on its type. Types of atomic accesses are: *relaxed* (rlx), which can be applied to any atomic access; *release* (**rel**), for writes and updates; *acquire* (acq), for reads and updates; and *acquire-release* (acq_rel) for updates only.

For us, the most important question about the C11 model is, *how do we know when one event precedes another in a given execution?*

Put simply, the C11 model specifies that the events in different threads are happening concurrently, and the only way to be sure that two events from different threads are happening in some definite order is to have one of them "see" the other through the process of *synchronization*. In other words, in order to show that an event *a* happens before another event *b*, we have to be able to start at *a*, and eventually reach *b* by following thread execution "downstream", and the only time we are allowed to move from one thread to another is at the synchronization points.

Some simple ways to achieve synchronization are depicted in Fig. 3. Synchronization always connects a *release event* (event of a **rel** or acq_rel type) with an *acquire event* (event of an acq or acq_rel type), and always happens as consequence of a read. In Fig. 3a we see the simplest case of synchronization, which happens immediately when an acquire read reads from a release write. In the other three situations in Fig. 3, relaxed accesses are helped along by fences (which can be of a **rel**, acq, or acq_rel kind) in order to achieve synchronization. Note that in these three cases, synchronization does not occur immediately as the read happens, but is delayed until all the required fences come into play.

Looking back at the ARC algorithm in Fig. 1 we can see that it uses relaxed accesses in the new and clone functions, while the function drop features a release access and an acquire fence. Instead of being regular reads or writes, fetch_and_add instructions are *atomic update* events, which act as both reads and writes. A release update (such as the one inside drop) acts as a release write and a relaxed read, while relaxed updates are relaxed as both reads and writes.

In order to get an intuitive understanding of the synchronization strategy employed by the ARC algorithm, we will have a look at the example execution

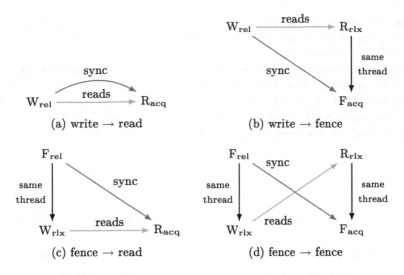

Fig. 3. Basic release-acquire synchronization.

presented in Fig. 4. The underlined **drop** function is the one that does the deallocation. To ensure absence of data races, all other drop functions should synchronize with **drop**. This suffices to ensure the absence of races, because we know by the intended use of the ARC library that every **read** will be followed by some **drop**.

One of these synchronizations happens according to Fig. 3b, as the **drop** at node b reads from the **drop** at node c. For the other synchronization between nodes a and b, however, the mechanisms presented in Fig. 3 are just not enough.

The problem we are facing with achieving the other synchronization is that so far presented synchronization mechanisms allow an acquire construct to

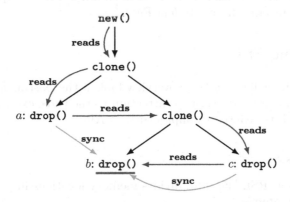

Fig. 4. An example execution of the ARC algorithm.

synchronize only with one other thread. What we need is some mechanism that will allow the single acquire fence in the whole ARC algorithm to synchronize with multiple release writes.

In order to synchronize all threads before deallocation, ARC exploits a more advanced synchronization technique provided by C11 called *release sequences*. Simply stated, to trigger synchronization between two threads it is not necessary for one to read directly from the other (as in Fig. 3), but there can be a reading chain (through atomic updates) from one thread to the other.

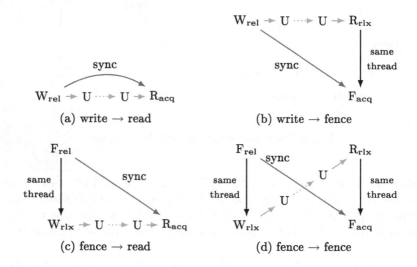

Fig. 5. Synchronization through release sequences.

Figure 5 depicts the four generalized versions of the cases in Fig. 3. We can now see that the synchronization mechanism shown in Fig. 5b explains the problematic synchronization from a to b in Fig. 4.

3   Extending FSL

In this section, we will first take an overview look at the existing features of FSL, after which we are going to turn our attention to the three extensions necessary for applying FSL to realistic examples such as ARC.

3.1   FSL Basics

Like its precursor, RSL [35], FSL divides memory locations into two categories: *atomic* and *non-atomic*.

Non-atomic locations are the ones that are used for "regular" accesses (i.e., we use non-atomic accesses whenever we are not implementing a synchronization mechanism). FSL ensures that there will be no data races on non-atomic accesses. For reasoning about non-atomic accesses, FSL provides the standard separation logic rules [26, 29].

Atomic accesses are the more interesting ones. As we have already seen in Sect. 2.2, atomic accesses come in four modes ($\mathrm{acq\_rel}$, rel, acq, and rlx), and are used to create synchronization between threads. In the rest of this subsection, we will focus our attention on FSL rules regarding atomic accesses.

From the perspective of FSL, atomic accesses are used to transfer ownership between threads. Threads can give up ownership of certain resources by writing to an atomic location, after which another thread can pick up that resource by reading from the same location. Resources are transferred through write-read pairs, and the rules of the logic make sure that the transferred resources are not used until the threads in question synchronize.

In what follows, for the sake of clarity, we are going to present slightly simplified FSL rules. A complete presentation of FSL can be found in [13].

FSL Triples. FSL triples are of the form $\{P\} E \{v.Q\}$, where P and Q are assertions denoting the precondition and the postcondition of the expression E. In the postcondition, the variable v binds the return value of E. In cases where the postcondition does not depend on the return value, the v binder may be omitted.

Release Writes. The easiest way to transfer away a resource is to do a release write. Since the release write is both the point of origin of ownership transfer, as well as the point of origin of synchronization (see Fig. 3a and b), we can simply transfer the resource we want without any further complications. This is summarized in the following rule.

$$\left\{\mathsf{Rel}(\ell, \mathcal{Q}) * \mathcal{Q}(v)\right\} [\ell]_{\mathbf{rel}} := v \left\{\mathsf{Rel}(\ell, \mathcal{Q})\right\} \qquad \text{(W-REL)}$$

In the precondition, the assertion $\mathsf{Rel}(\ell, \mathcal{Q})$ grants us permission to write to the atomic location ℓ. $\mathcal{Q}$ is a mapping from values to assertions, specifying which resource we have to give up when writing which value. In particular, if we want to store the value v into ℓ, we have to give up the ownership of the resource $\mathcal{Q}(v)$. As we can see from the postcondition, once the write is done, we no longer have the access to the resource $\mathcal{Q}(v)$, which can now be obtained by readers.

Relaxed Writes. Resources can also be sent away by doing a relaxed write, but only if the write is helped along by a release fence, as in Fig. 3c and d. Our ownership transfer strategy is somewhat more involved in this case. By doing a relaxed write, we can only transfer resources that have been "prepared" before the release fence took effect. In other words, the resources sent away by the relaxed write should not be accessed in between the fence and the write. The following two rules describe this situation.

$$\{P\} \, \mathtt{fence_{rel}} \, \{\triangle P\} \qquad \text{(F-REL)}$$

$$\left\{\mathsf{Rel}(\ell,\mathcal{Q}) * \triangle\, \mathcal{Q}(v)\right\} [\ell]_{\mathrm{rlx}} := v \left\{\mathsf{Rel}(\ell,\mathcal{Q})\right\} \qquad \text{(W-RLX)}$$

When executing a release fence, we can put any resource under the $\triangle$ modality. The assertion $\triangle P$ says, "P has been made ready for transfer and it may not be accessed any more." The (W-RLX) rule differs from the (W-REL) rule only in the appearance of $\triangle$ in the precondition. Essentially, we execute a relaxed write the same way we do a release write, with one important difference: a resource transferred away by the relaxed write has to be under the $\triangle$ modality, ensuring that a release fence has been placed before the write.

Acquire Reads. Acquire reads function as end points of both resource transfer and synchronization (see Fig. 3a and c). For this reason, resource acquisition by acquire reads is quite simple.

$$\left\{\mathsf{Acq}(\ell,\mathcal{Q})\right\} [\ell]_{\mathrm{acq}} \left\{v.\, \mathcal{Q}(v)\right\} \qquad \text{(R-ACQ)}$$

The assertion $\mathsf{Acq}(\ell,\mathcal{Q})$ allows a thread to perform the acquire read. Again, $\mathcal{Q}$ is a mapping from values to assertions. From the perspective of a read, this mapping tells us which resource will be acquired when reading which value. In particular, if the value read is v, then the resource acquired is $\mathcal{Q}(v)$.

Relaxed Reads. When acquiring ownership via relaxed read, we have to wait for a subsequent acquire fence to synchronize with the thread we are reading from (see Fig. 3b and d). Only after synchronization are we allowed to use the acquired resource. The following two rules represent this case.

$$\left\{\mathsf{Acq}(\ell,\mathcal{Q})\right\} [\ell]_{\mathrm{rlx}} \left\{v.\, \nabla\mathcal{Q}(v)\right\} \qquad \text{(R-RLX)}$$

$$\left\{\nabla P\right\} \mathtt{fence}_{\mathrm{acq}} \left\{P\right\} \qquad \text{(F-ACQ)}$$

The resource acquired in the (R-ACQ) rule is placed under the ∇ modality. The assertion ∇P simply means "P cannot be used before an acquire fence has been reached." The (F-ACQ) rule tells us that the acquire fence makes resources hidden behind the ∇ modality usable.

Allocation of Atomics. The Rel and Acq permissions are generated when a new atomic variable is allocated. At the point of allocation, we can freely choose the mapping $\mathcal{Q}$ which governs the ownership transfer through the newly allocated variable.

$$\frac{\mathcal{Q}\colon \textit{Values} \to \textit{Assertions}}{\left\{\mathsf{emp}\right\} \mathbf{alloc}() \left\{\ell.\, \mathsf{Rel}(\ell,\mathcal{Q}) * \mathsf{Acq}(\ell,\mathcal{Q})\right\}} \qquad \text{(A-AT)}$$

These are all the rules regarding ownership transfer through atomic accesses in FSL. Let us now turn our attention to the three extensions which will allow us to verify ARC.

3.2 Partial Permissions for Non-atomics

Basic FSL does not support reasoning about programs with concurrent read accesses to non-atomic locations. On the other hand, ARC is a library specifically used to allow concurrent reads of a shared resource. Therefore, this is the first gap that needs to be bridged in order to successfully verify programs like ARC.

To enable reasoning about concurrent non-atomic reads, we outfitted FSL with partial permissions [8,10] for non-atomic locations. In order to execute a write, the full permission is needed, while reading is possible with a partial permission. The rules of the logic make sure that the full permission cannot concurrently coexists with a partial one, nor can there exists more than one full permission at a time. As a result, there cannot be any read-write or write-write races on non-atomic locations.

Formally, permission structures are tuples $(M, \oplus, \varepsilon, \mathbb{1})$, where $(M, \oplus)$ forms a partial commutative monoid with ε as the neutral element, and $\mathbb{1} \in M \setminus \{\varepsilon\}$ is a 'maximal' element of the monoid composable only with the neutral element, i.e., $\mathbb{1} \oplus q$ is undefined for every $q \in M \setminus \{\varepsilon\}$.

To write to a location ℓ, one must have the full permission $\ell \mapsto -$; while to read from ℓ, having a permission $\ell \xmapsto{q} v$ for any $q \in M \setminus \{\varepsilon\}$ suffices. Assertion $\ell \xmapsto{\varepsilon} -$ is taken to be equivalent with the empty resource emp. Separating conjunction respects the composition operation on the monoid:

$$\ell \xmapsto{p} v * \ell \xmapsto{q} v \iff \begin{cases} \ell \xmapsto{p \oplus q} v & \text{if } p \oplus q \text{ is defined} \\ \text{false} & \text{otherwise.} \end{cases}$$

The most well known permission model, which is incidentally also the one used in the correctness proof of ARC, is the model of *fractional permissions* [10]. In this model, permissions are fractions in the interval $[0, 1]$, $\varepsilon = 0$, $\mathbb{1} = 1$, and composition is defined by

$$p \oplus q = \begin{cases} p + q & \text{if } p + q \in [0, 1] \\ \textbf{undefined} & \text{otherwise.} \end{cases}$$

Our proof of soundness is not dependent on fractional permissions, but is parametric in the permission structure for non-atomic accesses, which allows for greater flexibility when designing proofs that require partial permissions.

3.3 Compare-and-Swap Rules

Another problem we are facing when verifying ARC is the presence of atomic update operations (`fetch_and_add` instructions), for which no support is provided in FSL. We provide the rules for compare-and-swap (CAS), a basic atomic update instruction, which can be used to implement other, more advanced ones, such as `fetch_and_add`.

Details of the implementation of `fetch_and_add` using CAS, and the corresponding FSL specification for `fetch_and_add` can be found in Sect. 4.3.

The CAS instruction $\mathsf{CAS}_\tau(\ell, v, v')$ reads the location ℓ, and if the value read is v it updates it atomically to v'. If CAS reads some value other than v, then the update is not executed. In any case, CAS returns the value read. Parameter τ tells us the type of update event generated by the successful CAS operation. The possible values of τ are $\mathrm{rlx}, \mathbf{rel}, \mathrm{acq}$, and $\mathrm{acq\_rel}$.

Recall that update actions act as both reads and writes. When reading, the update is treated as an acquire read action if it is of acq or $\mathrm{acq\_rel}$ kind, and as a relaxed read otherwise. Acting as a writer, the update is treated as a release write if it is of $\mathbf{rel}$ or $\mathrm{acq\_rel}$ kind, and as a relaxed write otherwise.

FSL [13] provides no CAS rules, but its predecessor RSL [35] does. The CAS rule provided by RSL only supports ownership transfer by $\mathrm{acq\_rel}$ CASes, and does not allow any ownership transfer over release sequences. Ownership transfer using release sequences and multiple types of CASes is necessary to verify complex algorithms such as ARC. Therefore, it is necessary to augment FSL with stronger CAS rules than the one present in RSL.

In what follows, we will present the new rules regarding CAS instructions. Here, as in Sect. 3.1, we are presenting a simplified version of the rules. For full rules, we refer the reader to the appendix.

We will start the presentation of the CAS rules with a simplified version of the rule for the strongest type of CAS instruction, the $\mathrm{acq\_rel}$ CAS.

$$
\frac{\begin{array}{c} \mathcal{Q}(v) \ \Rightarrow A * T \\ P * T \Rightarrow \mathcal{Q}(v') \end{array}}{\{\mathsf{U}(\ell, \mathcal{Q}) * P\} \, \mathsf{CAS}_{\mathrm{acq\_rel}}(\ell, v, v') \left\{ \begin{array}{l} a. \, (a = v \wedge A) \\ \vee \, (a \neq v \wedge \mathsf{U}(\ell, \mathcal{Q}) * P) \end{array} \right\}} \quad (\text{CAS-AR}^*)
$$

In the precondition we have assertion $\mathsf{U}(\ell, \mathcal{Q})$, which gives us the permission to execute CAS on the location ℓ. As in Rel and Acq assertions, $\mathcal{Q}$ is a mapping from values to assertions, telling us what resource we can get by reading a value, and which resource we have to send away when writing a value. The remaining component in the precondition is P, the resource we want to transfer away upon a successful CAS operation.

If the CAS fails (i.e., the value read, a, is different from v), then no resource transfer happens, and in the postcondition we are left with the same resources we had in the precondition.

In the case of a successful CAS (i.e., the value read was v), we have at our disposal the resource $\mathcal{Q}(v)$. According to the first premise of the rule, we have to split $\mathcal{Q}(v)$ into two parts, A, and T. Resource A is the part that we are going to acquire and keep it for ourselves in the postcondition. Resource T will remain in the invariant $\mathcal{Q}$. The second premise requires that the resource P (which we have in our precondition) together with the resource T (which we left behind when acquiring ownership) are enough to satisfy $\mathcal{Q}(v')$, thus reestablishing the invariant for the newly written value.

The (CAS-AR*) is a useful rule as it stands, but can still be strengthened. The opportunity for strengthening lies in the second premise of the (CAS-AR*) rule. If, in addition to merely reestablishing the invariant, we manage to prove some additional facts, we can carry those facts into the postcondition. The strengthened rule is

$$\frac{\begin{array}{c} \mathcal{Q}(v) \Rightarrow \exists z.\ \mathcal{A}(z) * \mathcal{T}(z) \\ \forall z.\ (P * \mathcal{T}(z) \Rightarrow \mathcal{Q}(v') \wedge \varphi(z)) \\ \forall z.\ \mathsf{pure}(\varphi(z)) \end{array}}{\left\{\mathsf{U}(\ell,\mathcal{Q}) * P\right\} \mathsf{CAS}_{\mathrm{acq\_rel}}(\ell,v,v') \left\{\begin{array}{l} a.\ (a = v \wedge \exists z.\ \mathcal{A}(z) \wedge \varphi(z)) \\ \vee\ (a \neq v \wedge \mathsf{U}(\ell,\mathcal{Q}) * P) \end{array}\right\}} \,. \quad \text{(CAS-AR)}$$

Instead of assertions A and T, the rule now features mappings $\mathcal{A}$ and $\mathcal{T}$ from values to assertions. The first premise asks us to split $\mathcal{Q}(v)$ into $\mathcal{A}(z)$ and $\mathcal{T}(z)$, for some value z. The second premise requires that from $P * \mathcal{T}(z)$ we prove not only $\mathcal{Q}(v')$, but also some fact about z, which then gets carried over to the postcondition. Lastly, it is required for $\varphi(z)$ to be *pure*, meaning that the assertion $\varphi(z)$ is a logical fact about z, and is not saying anything about the ownership of resources or the state of the heap.

Rules for the other types of CAS accesses are all a slight modification of the (CAS-AR) rule. Modifications are in the same vein as the ones that get us from (R-ACQ) and (W-REL) to (R-RLX) and (W-RLX). Namely, where the access type gets relaxed, $\triangle$ and $\triangledown$ modalities take over in order to ensure that proper fences have been placed.

Since the premises in (CAS-REL), (CAS-ACQ), and (CAS-RLX) are the same as in (CAS-AR), we will avoid repeating them.

$$\left\{\mathsf{U}(\ell,\mathcal{Q}) * P\right\}\mathsf{CAS}_{\mathbf{rel}}(\ell,v,v') \left\{\begin{array}{l} a.\ (a = v \wedge \exists z.\ \triangledown\mathcal{A}(z) \wedge \varphi(z)) \\ \vee\ (a \neq v \wedge \mathsf{U}(\ell,\mathcal{Q}) * P) \end{array}\right\} \quad \text{(CAS-REL)}$$

$$\left\{\mathsf{U}(\ell,\mathcal{Q}) * \triangle P\right\}\mathsf{CAS}_{\mathrm{acq}}(\ell,v,v') \left\{\begin{array}{l} a.\ (a = v \wedge \exists z.\ \mathcal{A}(z) \wedge \varphi(z)) \\ \vee\ (a \neq v \wedge \mathsf{U}(\ell,\mathcal{Q}) * \triangle P) \end{array}\right\} \quad \text{(CAS-ACQ)}$$

$$\left\{\mathsf{U}(\ell,\mathcal{Q}) * \triangle P\right\}\mathsf{CAS}_{\mathrm{rlx}}(\ell,v,v') \left\{\begin{array}{l} a.\ (a = v \wedge \exists z.\ \triangledown\mathcal{A}(z) \wedge \varphi(z)) \\ \vee\ (a \neq v \wedge \mathsf{U}(\ell,\mathcal{Q}) * \triangle P) \end{array}\right\} \quad \text{(CAS-RLX)}$$

Release CAS is treated as a release write and a relaxed read. Therefore, in (CAS-REL) we can send away P without any problems, but the acquired resource has to be placed under the $\triangledown$ modality, requiring us to use an acquire fence before accessing the resource.

Acquire CAS is a relaxed write and an acquire read. Because of this, in (CAS-ACQ) the resource we are trying to transfer away is under the $\triangle$ modality, requiring a release fence before the CAS. On the other hand, the resource we acquire is immediately usable.

Relaxed CAS is relaxed as both read and write. This is reflected in the (CAS-RLX) rule by having both modalities in play.

Note that simple CAS rules in the style of (CAS-AR*) can be derived from the more general ones for any type of CAS. We simply need to choose $\mathcal{A}$ and $\mathcal{T}$ such that they do not depend on z, and set $\varphi(z)$ to always be true.

Remark 1 (About the CAS rule strengthening). The strengthening was motivated by the ARC proof. The ARC algorithm can be proven correct using just the simple CAS rules that do not contain the "z parametrization". The proof using the simple CAS rules requires the use of additional ghost state (see Sect. 3.4), and is in general more complicated compared to the proof presented in Sect. 4.

Remark 2 (About the soundness of the CAS rules). The soundness of FSL++'s CAS rules (even the simple ones) depends heavily on release sequences (Fig. 5). Specifically, the rules allow us to split the invariant of the value read $\mathcal{Q}(v)$ into two parts and take out only the $\mathcal{A}(z)$ part, while using the $\mathcal{T}(z)$ part to reestablish the invariant for the new value written. In essence, the $\mathcal{T}(z)$ part of $\mathcal{Q}(v)$ is being sent down the chain of updates reading from each other, and can be picked up at any later point.

It is interesting to note that as long as we are working within the release-acquire fragment of the C11 model (i.e., all writes are of **rel** type, all reads are of acq type, and all updates are of acq_rel type), the soundness of the split does not depend on release sequences, because every act of reading causes synchronization to happen.

On the other hand, in the presence of the relaxed accesses, release sequences are required to establish the soundness of the split even for the (CAS-AR) rule.

Remark 3 (Soundness of the RSL-style CAS rule). A variant of the RSL's CAS rule is admissible in FSL++. The difference is that we would now require the release permission to be present in the precondition, unlike in RSL, where it could be a part of the acquired resource. This is not an important restriction, because (due to the duplicability of release permissions) any RSL proof that uses the CAS rule can be modified to include the release permission in the precondition.

The last CAS rule (CAS-$\perp$) allows us to quickly conclude that a successful CAS cannot happen in the situation where we own a resource which is incompatible with the resources which would be acquired by a successful CAS operation.

$$\frac{\mathcal{Q}(v) * P \Rightarrow \mathsf{false} \quad \tau \in \{\mathrm{rlx}, \mathbf{rel}, \mathrm{acq}, \mathrm{acq\_rel}\}}{\{\mathsf{U}(\ell, \mathcal{Q}) * P\}\, \mathsf{CAS}_\tau(\ell, v, v')\, \{a.\, a \neq v \wedge \mathsf{U}(\ell, \mathcal{Q}) * P\}} \quad \text{(CAS-$\perp$)}$$

The U permission is obtained upon allocation in a similar fashion as the Rel and Acq permissions.

$$\frac{\mathcal{Q}\colon Values \to Assertions}{\{\mathsf{emp}\}\, \mathbf{alloc}()\, \{\ell.\, \mathsf{U}(\ell, \mathcal{Q})\}} \quad \text{(A-AT-U)}$$

Finally, we would like to bring your attention to several useful properties of the update permission U. It is duplicable, and it interacts with the Rel and Acq permissions, allowing us to perform not only updates, but also reads and writes, when holding an update permission.

$$\mathsf{U}(\ell, \mathcal{Q}) \iff \mathsf{U}(\ell, \mathcal{Q}) * \mathsf{U}(\ell, \mathcal{Q}) \qquad \text{(U-SPLIT)}$$

$$\mathsf{U}(\ell, \mathcal{Q}) \iff \mathsf{U}(\ell, \mathcal{Q}) * \mathsf{Rel}(\ell, \mathcal{Q}) \qquad \text{(U-REL-SPLIT)}$$

$$\mathsf{U}(\ell, \mathcal{Q}) \iff \mathsf{U}(\ell, \mathcal{Q}) * \mathsf{Acq}(\ell, \lambda v.\mathsf{emp}) \qquad \text{(U-ACQ-SPLIT)}$$

According to (U-REL-SPLIT), when holding the $\mathsf{U}(\ell, \mathcal{Q})$, we also have $\mathsf{Rel}(\ell, \mathcal{Q})$, allowing us to write to ℓ using the appropriate atomic write rule. On the other hand, (U-ACQ-SPLIT) tells us that we are allowed to read when holding the $\mathsf{U}(\ell, \mathcal{Q})$ permission, but we cannot gain any ownership (more precisely, no matter the value read, the acquired resource will always be the empty resource emp).

3.4 Ghost State

Even though we are now able to reason about both concurrent non-atomic reads, and atomic update operations, we still do not have sufficient reasoning power to verify the correctness of ARC.

To see what are we lacking, we will turn our attention to the `clone` function (see Fig. 1). Our desired specification from Fig. 2 tells us that starting with one $\mathsf{ARC}(a, v)$ resource, after executing `clone(a)`, we will have that permission duplicated.

The only thing `clone` does is to increment the reference counter by one. The obvious way to get the additional ARC permission would be to acquire it from the invariant governing the reference counter, via the (CAS-RLX) rule. Unfortunately, any resource acquired that way would be protected by the $\triangledown$ modality, and there is no acquire fence to make the resource usable. In short, `clone` function cannot acquire any ownership, since it does not synchronize with any other thread.

So, if we cannot acquire any ownership when executing `clone`, what can we do? One possibility is to somehow duplicate the $\mathsf{ARC}(a, v)$ permission we already have. This would not require us to acquire any ownership, but it also makes the act of incrementing the counter superfluous. If we can simply duplicate the $\mathsf{ARC}(a, v)$ permission, what is the point in having the `clone` function at all?

If we want to verify ARC, we have to be able to remember the fact that `clone` produced another instance of the $\mathsf{ARC}(a, v)$ resource (i.e., the reference counter was incremented), without the `clone` function acquiring any additional resources. To achieve this reasoning, we employ *ghost state* [12, 18, 23, 34], a very useful feature of program logics that is often used for logical "accounting" without changing the program state.

The way to think of the ghost state is as if we have at our disposal locations that are never accessed by our program. Those locations carry *ghost resources*, which cannot influence the behavior of the program, since they are never accessed by the program, but can help us in reasoning.

In a proof, ghosts can be simply introduced whenever the need for them arises using the (GHOST-INTRO) rule.

$$\frac{\{P\}\,C\,\{Q\}}{\{P\}\,C\,\left\{Q * \exists \gamma. \boxed{\gamma : g}\right\}} \qquad \text{(GHOST-INTRO)}$$

The assertion $\boxed{\gamma : g}$ means that the ghost location γ carries the ghost resource g. Ghost resources (on a single location) have to form a *partial commutative monoid* (PCM). The composition operation ($\oplus$) of the PCM connects the ghost resources to the separating conjunction of FSL.

$$\boxed{\gamma : g} * \boxed{\gamma : g'} \iff \begin{cases} \boxed{\gamma : g \oplus g'} & \text{if } g \oplus g' \text{ is defined,} \\ \text{false} & \text{otherwise.} \end{cases} \qquad \text{(GHOST-\ast)}$$

The most important feature of ghost state from the perspective of the verification of ARC is ability to transfer ownership of ghosts without the need for synchronization. This is achieved by having the ghost state be agnostic with respect to the $\triangle$ and $\triangledown$ modalities.

$$\boxed{\gamma : \varepsilon} \iff \triangle \boxed{\gamma : \varepsilon} \iff \triangledown \boxed{\gamma : \varepsilon} \qquad \text{(GHOST-MOD)}$$

Intuitively, it is not a problem to define the ghost state in such a way to have the (GHOST-MOD) equivalences hold, because the ghost state is not accessed by the program. The principal duty of the $\triangle$ and $\triangledown$ modalities is to ensure proper placement of fences in order to avoid any data races on non-atomic accesses. Since the ghost state is never accessed, it cannot be involved in any data races, and is therefore free to ignore modalities.

4   Verification of ARC

In this section, we will use FSL to verify the ARC algorithm from Fig. 1. Since FSL does not have support for deallocation, we treat the call to the `free` function as a no-operation. For further discussion about handling deallocation see Sect. 5.3.

The following theorem contains the formal correctness statement for ARC.

Theorem 1 (Correctness of ARC). *There exists a predicate* $\mathsf{ARC}_{\gamma,\delta}$, *parametrized by two ghost locations* γ *and* δ, *such that the following holds*

$$
\begin{aligned}
\{\mathsf{emp}\} \quad &\mathtt{new}(v) \quad \{a.\, \exists \gamma, \delta.\, \mathsf{ARC}_{\gamma,\delta}(a,v)\} \\
\{\mathsf{ARC}_{\gamma,\delta}(a,v)\} \quad &\mathtt{read}(a) \quad \{y.\, y = v \wedge \mathsf{ARC}_{\gamma,\delta}(a,v)\} \\
\{\mathsf{ARC}_{\gamma,\delta}(a,v)\} \quad &\mathtt{clone}(a) \quad \{y.\, y \neq 0 \wedge \mathsf{ARC}_{\gamma,\delta}(a,v) * \mathsf{ARC}_{\gamma,\delta}(a,v)\} \\
\{\mathsf{ARC}_{\gamma,\delta}(a,v)\} \quad &\mathtt{drop}(a) \quad \{y.\, (y > 1 \wedge \mathsf{emp}) \vee (y = 1 \wedge a.\mathtt{data} \xmapsto{1} v)\},
\end{aligned}
$$

where the fractional permission structure is used for the non-atomic locations.

The return value of the `clone` and `drop` functions is considered to be the value returned by the `fetch_and_add` instruction within those functions. (Function `fetch_and_add` returns the value before the increment.) In other words, return value y for `clone` means that it incremented the reference counter from y to $y + 1$, and for `drop` it means that the counter was decremented from y to $y - 1$.

Note that the specification of `drop` tells us that in the case where the reference counter was decremented from 1 to 0, we have the full permission on $a.\mathtt{data}$.

When modeling deallocation, having the full permission for a location would be enough to deallocate it.

An additional thing of note is that we prove that the return value of the `clone` and `drop` functions can never be 0. This means that `clone` and `drop` never try to access the ARC object after all the references to it have been dropped.

The rest of this section is devoted to the proof of Theorem 1.

The theorem already states the permission model used for non-atomic locations. We are left with choosing a PCM for the ghost state. Our chosen structure is described in the following lemma.

Lemma 1 (Ghost Monoid). *The structure* $(\mathbb{Q}_{\geq 0} \times \{+, -\}, \oplus)$, *with the partial binary operation* $\oplus$ *defined as*

$$f^+ \oplus q^+ := (f + q)^+$$
$$f^- \oplus q^- := \textbf{undefined}$$
$$f^+ \oplus q^- := q^- \oplus f^+ := \begin{cases} (q - f)^- & \text{if } q - f \geq 0 \\ \textbf{undefined} & \text{otherwise} \end{cases}$$

is a partial commutative monoid, with the neutral element 0^+.

Think of a "positive" ghost assertion $\boxed{\gamma : q^+}$ as having a q amount of some resource, while the "negative" ghost assertion $\boxed{\gamma : q^-}$ counts how much of that resource exists at any given time.

It is important to note that there can exist only one negative ghost assertion at a single point in time, since (according to (GHOST-*)) having more than one would lead to a contradiction.

We can now define the invariant that will govern updates to ARC's reference counting field.

Definition 1 (ARC invariant). *For location* x, *value* v, *and ghost locations* γ *and* δ, *we define the mapping from values to assertions*

$$\mathcal{Q}_{\gamma, \delta, v, x} \overset{\text{def}}{=} \lambda c.\, \textbf{if } c = 0 \textbf{ then } \boxed{\gamma : 0^-} * \boxed{\delta : 0^-}$$
$$\textbf{else } \exists f \in [0, 1].\, x \overset{f}{\mapsto} v * \boxed{\gamma : (c - 1 + f)^-} * \boxed{\delta : (1 - f)^-}.$$

The way to think about the invariant is "if the value of the resource counter is c, then $\mathcal{Q}_{\gamma, \delta, v, x}(c)$ holds." There are two main parts to the $\mathcal{Q}_{\gamma, \delta, v, x}$ invariant.

1. Permissions to access the location x that have been dropped by various threads are collected into the assertion $x \overset{f}{\mapsto} v$.
2. The assertion $\boxed{\gamma : (c - 1 + f)^-}$ counts the number of still active ARC objects created by the `clone` function (this number is $c - 1$), while at the same taking note of the amount of read permissions to x that have been dropped so far (this is represented by f).

The interplay between these two parts is what will enable us to reconstitute the full permission after all the ARC objects have been dropped. How this happens will become clear in Sect. 4.5.

Lastly, the least complicated part of the invariant, the ghost state attached to the ghost location δ, counts how much of the access permission to x is shared by the still active ARC objects. This will be used in Sect. 4.4 and Sect. 4.5 in order to establish that clone and drop never read 0 as the value of the reference counter.

We are now finally at the point where we can define the ARC predicate.

Definition 2 (ARC Predicate). *For ghost locations γ and δ, we define*

$$\mathsf{ARC}_{\gamma,\delta}(a,v) \stackrel{\text{def}}{=} \mathsf{U}(a.\mathit{count}, \mathcal{Q}_{\gamma,\delta,v,a.\mathtt{data}}) *$$
$$\exists q \in \langle 0, 1]. a.\mathit{data} \stackrel{q}{\mapsto} v * \boxed{\gamma : (1-q)^+} * \boxed{\delta : q^+}.$$

The ARC predicate consists of four parts.

1. A permission to execute atomic updates on $a.\mathtt{count}$, as long as we respect the $\mathcal{Q}_{\gamma,\delta,v,a.\mathtt{data}}$ invariant.
2. Some fraction of the access permission to $a.\mathtt{data}$, allowing us to read from it.
3. A ghost $\boxed{\gamma : (1-q)^+}$, designed to help the ARC invariant in keeping track of the number of outstanding ARC objects, and the amount of read permissions to $a.\mathtt{data}$ shared among them.
4. A ghost $\boxed{\delta : q^+}$, designed to make the $\mathsf{ARC}_{\gamma,\delta}(a,v)$ assertion incompatible with the $\mathcal{Q}_{\gamma,\delta,v,a.\mathtt{data}}(0)$ assertion ($q > 0 \wedge \boxed{\delta : q^+} * \boxed{\delta : 0^-} \Rightarrow \mathsf{false}$), therefore making sure we cannot read 0 from $a.\mathtt{count}$.

In what follows, we are going to discuss main points of the proof for each of the functions from the ARC algorithm. Full formal proofs are available in the Coq formalization.

4.1 Function new

In Fig. 6 you can see a simplified version of the proof for the function new.

At the beginning, we have to introduce two ghosts (γ and δ) using the (GHOST-INTRO) rule, as well as allocate a non-atomic location a.data, and an atomic location a.count. We are allocating a.count using the (A-AT-U) rule. Naturally, we will choose the mapping defined in Definition 1 as the invariant governing the a.count location.

The most interesting part of the proof happens when we are executing the relaxed write instruction $a.\mathtt{count}_{\mathrm{rlx}} = 1$. The resources we own as we are about to execute the relaxed write are

$$\mathsf{U}(a.\mathtt{count}, \mathcal{Q}_{\gamma,\delta,v,a.\mathtt{data}}) * a.\mathtt{data} \stackrel{1}{\mapsto} v * \boxed{\gamma : 0^-} * \boxed{\delta : 0^-},$$

$$\{\mathsf{emp}\}$$
$$\mathtt{a\ =\ alloc();}$$
$$\left\{\mathsf{U}(\mathtt{a.count}, \mathcal{Q}_{\gamma,\delta,v,\mathtt{a.data}}) * \mathtt{a.data} \overset{1}{\mapsto} - * \boxed{\gamma : 0^-} * \boxed{\delta : 0^-}\right\}$$
$$\mathtt{a.data\ =\ } v\mathtt{;}$$
$$\left\{\mathsf{U}(\mathtt{a.count}, \mathcal{Q}_{\gamma,\delta,v,\mathtt{a.data}}) * \mathtt{a.data} \overset{1}{\mapsto} v * \boxed{\gamma : 0^-} * \boxed{\delta : 0^-}\right\}$$

$\Downarrow$ (using (GHOST-$*$), and $\mathtt{a.data} \overset{0}{\mapsto} v \iff \mathsf{emp}$)

$$\left\{ \begin{array}{c} \mathsf{U}(\mathtt{a.count}, \mathcal{Q}_{\gamma,\delta,v,\mathtt{a.data}}) * \mathtt{a.data} \overset{1}{\mapsto} v * \mathtt{a.data} \overset{0}{\mapsto} v * \\ \boxed{\gamma : 0^-} * \boxed{\gamma : 0^+} * \boxed{\delta : 1^-} * \boxed{\delta : 1^+} \end{array} \right\}$$

$\Downarrow$ (using (GHOST-MOD), and $\mathsf{emp} \iff \triangle\mathsf{emp}$)

$$\left\{ \begin{array}{c} \mathsf{U}(\mathtt{a.count}, \mathcal{Q}_{\gamma,\delta,v,\mathtt{a.data}}) * \mathtt{a.data} \overset{1}{\mapsto} v * \boxed{\gamma : 0^+} * \boxed{\delta : 1^+} * \\ \triangle\left(\mathtt{a.data} \overset{0}{\mapsto} v * \boxed{\gamma : 0^-} * \boxed{\delta : 1^-}\right) \end{array} \right\}$$

$$\mathtt{a.count_{rlx}\ =\ 1;}$$
$$\left\{\mathsf{U}(\mathtt{a.count}, \mathcal{Q}_{\gamma,\delta,v,\mathtt{a.data}}) * \mathtt{a.data} \overset{1}{\mapsto} v * \boxed{\gamma : 0^+} * \boxed{\delta : 1^+}\right\}$$

$$\mathtt{return\ a;}$$
$$\{\mathsf{ARC}_{\gamma,\delta}(\mathtt{a}, v)\}$$

Fig. 6. Function **new**: proof sketch.

and according to (U-REL-SPLIT) and (W-RLX), in order to execute our relaxed write, we have to send away a resource given by

$$\triangle\mathcal{Q}_{\gamma,\delta,v,\mathtt{a.data}}(1) = \triangle\left(\exists f \in [0,1].\, \mathtt{a.data} \overset{f}{\mapsto} v * \boxed{\gamma : f^-} * \boxed{\delta : (1-f)^-}\right).$$

Since we have not executed a release fence, we can only send away resources that are invariant under the $\triangle$ modality. The only non-ghost resource invariant under $\triangle$ is the empty resource. Therefore, we have to choose f to be 0, in order to exploit the equivalence $\mathtt{a.data} \overset{0}{\mapsto} v \iff \mathsf{emp} \iff \triangle\mathsf{emp}$.

Setting f to 0 dealt with the $\mathtt{a.data} \overset{f}{\mapsto} v$ part of the invariant. We now have to produce the rest of the invariant: the ghosts $\boxed{\gamma : 0^-}$ and $\boxed{\delta : 1^-}$. The γ ghost we already have, and the δ one can be produced using the $\boxed{\delta : 0^-} \iff \boxed{\delta : 1^-} * \boxed{\delta : 1^+}$ equivalence.

Before releasing $\mathtt{a.data} \overset{0}{\mapsto} v * \boxed{\gamma : 0^-} * \boxed{\delta : 1^-}$, we will exploit the $\boxed{\gamma : 0^-} \iff \boxed{\gamma : 0^-} * \boxed{\gamma : 0^+}$ equivalence in order to keep the $\boxed{\gamma : 0^+}$ ghost for ourselves.

We can now finally release the required resource, and what we are left with is $\mathtt{a.data} \overset{1}{\mapsto} v * \boxed{\gamma : 0^+} * \boxed{\delta : 1^+}$, which is exactly the ARC predicate from Definition 2, with the existentially quantified q set to be 1.

4.2 Function read

Verifying read is trivial. The ARC predicate from Definition 2 tells us that we have some positive fraction q of the access permission for a.data, which allows us to execute the non-atomic read and return the value stored in a.data.

4.3 Implementing fetch_and_add

Before continuing with the proofs of clone and drop, let us take a step back and look at the fetch_and_add instruction used in those two functions. As mentioned in Sect. 3.3, fetch_and_add can be implemented using CAS instructions. The implementation of fetch_and_add using CAS is given in Fig. 7, together with the specification that will be used in the next two subsections.

```
fetch_and_add_τ(x, v) {
    do {
        t = x_rlx;
        u = CAS_τ(x, t, t + v);
    } while(t != u);
    return u;
}
```

$$\forall t. (P \iff \mathcal{P}_{\mathrm{send}}(t) * \mathcal{P}_{\mathrm{keep}}(t))$$

$$\forall t. \left(\begin{array}{l} \{\mathsf{U}(\ell, \mathcal{Q}) * \mathcal{P}_{\mathrm{send}}(t)\} \\ \mathsf{CAS}_\tau(x, t, t + \mathbf{v}) \\ \left\{ \begin{array}{l} y. (y = t \wedge \mathcal{R}(t)) \\ \quad \vee (y \neq t \wedge \mathsf{U}(\ell, \mathcal{Q}) * \mathcal{P}_{\mathrm{send}}(t)) \end{array} \right\} \end{array} \right)$$

$$\frac{}{\begin{array}{c} \{\mathsf{U}(\ell, \mathcal{Q}) * P\} \\ \texttt{fetch\_and\_add}_\tau(x, v) \\ \{y. \mathcal{R}(y) * \mathcal{P}_{\mathrm{keep}}(y)\} \end{array}}$$

$$\tau \in \{\mathrm{rlx}, \mathrm{rel}, \mathrm{acq}, \mathrm{acq\_rel}\}$$

Fig. 7. Fetch and add implemented using CAS.

Proving the specification of fetch_and_add correct is simple, and we will not be going into details of it here. On the other hand, the specification looks quite daunting and deserves a closer look.

In the precondition, we are given the update permission $\mathsf{U}(\ell, \mathcal{Q})$ and some resource P.

The first premise of the specification allows us to decide how to split the resource P *depending on the value that we will end up updating*. If the value modified is v, we want to keep the resource $\mathcal{P}_{\mathrm{keep}}(v)$, while sending $\mathcal{P}_{\mathrm{send}}(v)$ away.

The second premise deals with the atomic update of the location ℓ from t to $t + v$. We need to prove that upon successful update we can send away $\mathcal{P}_{\mathrm{send}}(t)$, and acquire $\mathcal{R}(t)$.

After executing the fetch_and_add instruction, in the postcondition we get $\mathcal{R}(y) * \mathcal{P}_{\mathrm{keep}}(y)$, with y being the value stored at the location ℓ prior to the update taking place. $\mathcal{R}(y)$ is what we acquired by updating ℓ, while $\mathcal{P}_{\mathrm{keep}}(y)$ is the part we kept from the original resource P we had in the precondition.

Using the fetch_and_add specification boils down to deciding how we want to split the resource we have for each particular value, and then applying appropriate CAS rules to satisfy the second precondition of the rule.

4.4 Function `clone`

For the `clone` function, we are required to prove two things: (1) executing `clone` produces an additional ARC resource, and (2) `clone` never increments the value of the reference counter from 0 to 1.

First, let us assume that the value read by the `fetch_and_add` is 0. In that case (in accordance with the rule from Fig. 7) we decide to put $\boxed{\delta : q^+}$ into $\mathcal{P}_{\texttt{keep}}$. Since $q > 0$, assertions $\boxed{\delta : q^+}$ and $\mathcal{Q}_{\gamma,\delta,v,\texttt{a.data}}(0) = \boxed{\gamma : 0^-} * \boxed{\delta : 0^-}$ are incompatible $(q > 0 \wedge \boxed{\delta : q^+} * \boxed{\delta : 0^-} \Rightarrow \mathsf{false})$, and we can use the $(\textsc{cas-}\bot)$ rule to conclude that the value 0 could not have been read.

Now that we know that the value read is not 0, we need, in cases where we read some positive value of the reference counter, to somehow produce an additional ARC resource.

When executing `fetch_and_add`, we are going to keep all the resources we have to ourselves, which means that we have to satisfy the invariant for the incremented value using only what is already there in the invariant for the original value. Fortunately, our invariant is designed in such a way that for any $c > 0$, the equivalence $\mathcal{Q}_{\gamma,\delta,v,\texttt{a.data}}(c) \iff \mathcal{Q}_{\gamma,\delta,v,\texttt{a.data}}(c+1) * \boxed{\gamma : 1^+}$ holds. Using this equivalence, when incrementing the reference counter from c to $c+1$, we obtain the ownership of the ghost assertion $\boxed{\gamma : 1^+}$.

Adding the newly acquired ghost resource to the ARC resource we already have allows us to "produce" an additional ARC resource. In order to do that, we have to use the following three equivalences: $\texttt{a.data} \overset{q}{\mapsto} v \iff \texttt{a.data} \overset{\frac{q}{2}}{\mapsto} v *$ $\texttt{a.data} \overset{\frac{q}{2}}{\mapsto} v$, $\boxed{\gamma : (1-q)^+} * \boxed{\gamma : 1^+} \iff \boxed{\gamma : \left(1 - \frac{q}{2}\right)^+} * \boxed{\gamma : \left(1 - \frac{q}{2}\right)^+}$, and $\boxed{\delta : q^+} \iff \boxed{\delta : \frac{q}{2}^+} * \boxed{\delta : \frac{q}{2}^+}$. Using those equivalences, it is easy to see that the implication $\mathsf{ARC}_{\gamma,\delta}(\texttt{a.data}, v) * \boxed{\gamma : 1^+} \Rightarrow \mathsf{ARC}_{\gamma,\delta}(\texttt{a.data}, v) *$ $\mathsf{ARC}_{\gamma,\delta}(\texttt{a.data}, v)$ holds.

Please note the importance of the fact that the only ownership we obtained when updating the counter was of a ghost state. Since we are executing an update of the relaxed kind, any non-ghost resources acquired would be burdened by the $\triangledown$ modality, and thus unusable.

4.5 Function `drop`

When verifying the `drop` function, we can establish that the value of the reference counter is not 0 in exactly the same way we have done it for the `clone` function in Sect. 4.4. We are now left with two distinct cases.

First case is when the decrementing the counter does not bring the counter down to zero, i.e., the value of the counter is being decremented from some value $c > 1$. In this case, we are going to release all the resources held by the ARC predicate, and push them into the invariant. It is easy to see that $\mathcal{Q}_{\gamma,\delta,v,\texttt{a.data}}(c) * \texttt{a.data} \overset{q}{\mapsto} v * \boxed{\gamma : (1-q)^+} * \boxed{\delta : q^+} \Rightarrow \mathcal{Q}_{\gamma,\delta,v,\texttt{a.data}}(c-1)$ holds for any $q \in \langle 0, 1]$ and $c > 1$, which reestablishes the invariant for the decremented value, and leaves us with the empty resource.

Note the importance of the `fetch_and_add` being of the release kind, which (trough the (CAS-REL) rule) enables us to release all the resources we have.

In the second case, the decrement brings the reference count down to 0. Since the value read from the counter is 1, we know that the resource being held by the invariant is $\mathcal{Q}_{\gamma,\delta,v,\text{a.data}}(1) = \text{a.data} \overset{f}{\mapsto} v * \boxed{\gamma : f^-} * \boxed{\delta : (1-f)^-}$, for some fraction $f \in [0, 1]$. We are going to take the read permission to the `data` field out of the invariant, and we are going to release the ghost resources held by the ARC predicate back into the invariant.

The ghost resource held by the ARC predicate is $\boxed{\gamma : (1-q)^+} * \boxed{\delta : q^+}$, for some $q \in \langle 0, 1]$. In order for this assertion to be compatible with $\boxed{\gamma : f^-} * \boxed{\delta : (1-f)^-}$, the resource that is already inside the invariant, it is necessary to have $q + f = 1$, and in that case we have $\boxed{\gamma : (1-q)^+} * \boxed{\delta : q^+} * \boxed{\gamma : f^-} * \boxed{\delta : (1-f)^-} \Rightarrow \boxed{\gamma : 0^-} * \boxed{\delta : 0^-}$, establishing the $\mathcal{Q}_{\gamma,\delta,v,\text{a.data}}(0)$ invariant.

While establishing the $\mathcal{Q}_{\gamma,\delta,v,\text{a.data}}(0)$ invariant, we were also able to prove $q + f = 1$, which is a pure assertion. According to the (CAS-REL) rule, we can use this fact in the postcondition.

After executing the decrement, we have $\text{a.data} \overset{q}{\mapsto} v * \triangledown \text{a.data} \overset{f}{\mapsto} v$ in the postcondition. The f fraction of the access permission, which we obtained from the invariant, is under $\triangledown$, because the `fetch_and_add` was of the release kind, and we still have to wait for the acquire fence in order to use any resources taken from the invariant. Since we are in the case where the original value of the reference counter was 1, the very next instruction is exactly the acquire fence.

After the fence clears the $\triangledown$ modality (F-ACQ), the resource we own is transformed into $\text{a.data} \overset{q}{\mapsto} v * \text{a.data} \overset{f}{\mapsto} v \iff \text{a.data} \overset{q+f}{\mapsto} v \iff \text{a.data} \overset{1}{\mapsto} v$. These equivalences hold because we know $q + f = 1$, as proven earlier.

With this, the proof of Theorem 1 is concluded.

5   Discussion

In this section, we are going to discuss the strengthening of the C11 memory model which is assumed by the FSL soundness proof and how it affects the ARC verification (Sect. 5.1). Further, in Sect. 5.2, we will discuss the necessity of this assumption showing that the logic is unsound in its absence. Finally, in Sect. 5.3 we will talk about a possible way to extend FSL with the support for deallocation.

5.1   The Additional Acyclity Assumption

As mentioned in the introduction, FSL is proven sound with respect to a strengthening of the C11 model. The strengthening is put in place in order to prevent the so called *out-of-thin-air* reads that are allowed by the original C11 model.

$$
\begin{array}{l}
x_{rlx} = 0; \\
y_{rlx} = 0; \\
\texttt{if } (x_{rlx} \texttt{ == 1)} \;\Big\|\; \texttt{if } (y_{rlx} \texttt{ == 1)} \\
\quad y_{rlx} = 1; \qquad\quad x_{rlx} = 1;
\end{array}
$$

(a) C11 model allows $x = y = 1$.

$$
\begin{array}{ccc}
R_{rlx}(x,1) & & R_{rlx}(y,1) \\
\Big\downarrow po & \overset{rf}{\times} & \Big\downarrow po \\
W_{rlx}(y,1) & & W_{rlx}(x,1)
\end{array}
$$

(b) Problematic cyclic execution.

Fig. 8. Out-of-thin-air behavior due to a cycle in the $po \cup rf$ relation.

The problem arises because C11 is very lenient in what kind of cycles are allowed to be formed by the *program order* and *reads from* relations.

- The program order (po) tells us about the ordering of the events within each execution thread. More precisely, $po(a, b)$ means that the events a and b belong to the same thread, and a precedes b.
- The reads from relation (rf) relates writes and reads that read from those writes: $rf(w, r)$ says that the read event r reads the value written by the write event w.

Figure 8a shows a program with an undesirable behavior resulting from a cycle in $po \cup rf$. The C11 model allows the program to set both x and y to 1, due to the allowed "cyclic" execution shown in Fig. 8b.

As noted in [5,35], this kind of behavior inhibits even the simplest forms of thread-local reasoning for relaxed accesses.

The simplest way to rectify the problem of out-of-thin-air behaviors is to forbid cycles in the $po\cup rf$ relation altogether. Forbidding these cycles requires the smallest possible intervention in the C11 model, namely adding just one axiom requiring acyclicity of $po \cup rf$. This is the solution employed by the soundness proofs of both RSL [35], and FSL [13] in order to restore sane reasoning principles for relaxed accesses under the C11 memory model. Apart from being used in RSL and FSL, this "patch" is also advocated by Boehm and Demsky [7].

Requiring $po\cup rf$ to be acyclic, however, does come with some implementation cost. First, it invalidates some compiler optimizations (namely, the reordering of a relaxed store above a relaxed load), and requires a slightly more expensive compilation scheme to the Power and ARM architectures. The problem is that these hardware architectures allow some executions with $po\cup rf$ cycles. Consider, for example, *load buffering*, shown in Fig. 9a. The weak behavior, returning $r = 1$ is forbidden by the strengthened C11 model, but allowed by Power and ARM if the relaxed accesses are compiled to plain loads and stores. Intuitively, the behavior may arise if the hardware reorders the read from x and the write to y in the left thread, which do not depend on each other.

Note that the execution in Fig. 9b, which explains the load buffering behavior, is exactly the same as the execution we deemed undesirable in Fig. 8b. The difference between these two examples is the possibility of reordering two independent instructions in Fig. 9a, while in Fig. 8a the writes depend on the reads, and these dependencies should render any reorderings invalid. The C11 model does not model the dependencies between memory accesses, which makes it unable to differentiate between executions in Figs. 8 and 9.

$$x_{rlx} = 0;$$
$$y_{rlx} = 0;$$
$$r = x_{rlx}; \;\|\; \text{if } (y_{rlx} == 1)$$
$$y_{rlx} = 1; \;\|\; x_{rlx} = 1;$$

(a) We can observe $r = 1$!

$$R_{rlx}(x,1) \qquad R_{rlx}(y,1)$$
$$\text{po} \downarrow \qquad \overset{rf}{\times} \qquad \downarrow \text{po}$$
$$W_{rlx}(y,1) \qquad W_{rlx}(x,1)$$

(b) Cyclic execution explaining $r = 1$.

Fig. 9. Load buffering (allowed on Power and ARM).

As noted by Boehm and Demsky in [7], in order to obtain acyclic $\text{po} \cup \text{rf}$, it is enough to forbid load-to-store reordering. On x86-TSO acyclicity of $\text{po} \cup \text{rf}$ comes at no additional cost, since the architecture does not allow reordering of loads and the subsequent stores. On Power and ARM, load-to-store reordering can be avoided by placing a *false dependency* (i.e., a conditional branch to the next instruction) between every relaxed load and subsequent relaxed stores.

Acyclic $\text{po} \cup \text{rf}$ and ARC. It is interesting to note that with algorithms like ARC, which predominantly use atomic updates, and do not have many atomic reads, ensuring the acyclicity of $\text{po} \cup \text{rf}$ on Power and ARM comes for free.

The reason for this comes from the way atomic update instructions are implemented on Power and ARM [31]. When compiling atomic updates, a conditional branch is placed after the load instruction, which induces a dependency between the load and any subsequent stores. This means that the false dependencies are not necessary when compiling atomic updates.

In the case of ARC, a false dependency needs to be placed after the relaxed read in the implementation of fetch_and_add in Fig. 7. If fetch_and_add is implemented as a primitive, as it actually is in practice, then it comes without the burden of false dependencies. Therefore, there is no additional implementation cost for ensuring that ARC runs under the strengthened C11 model.

5.2   Without the Acyclicity Assumption Ghosts Are Too Strong

Ruling out $\text{po} \cup \text{rf}$ cycles is the simplest but not the only way of ruling out "out-of-thin-air" behaviors. In fact, during the last year, we saw the emergence of several new memory models [17,19,28] aimed at eliminating out-of-thin-air behaviors without completely forbidding cycles within the $\text{po} \cup \text{rf}$ relation. All these models allow the weak behavior of the load buffering program, while forbidding the weak behavior of the version with dependencies in both threads.

Let $\mathcal{Q} := \lambda v.\, v = 0 \vee \lceil \gamma : T \rceil$, and $T \oplus T$ undefined.

$$\left\{ \mathsf{Acq}(x, \mathcal{Q}) * \mathsf{Rel}(y, \mathcal{Q}) * \lceil \gamma : T \rceil \right\}$$
$$\mathbf{r} = \mathbf{x_{rlx}};$$
$$\left\{ \mathsf{Rel}(y, \mathcal{Q}) * \lceil \gamma : T \rceil * (r = 0 \vee \lceil \gamma : T \rceil) \right\}$$
$$\left\{ \mathsf{Rel}(y, \mathcal{Q}) * \lceil \gamma : T \rceil \wedge r = 0 \right\}$$
$$\mathbf{y_{rlx}} = \mathbf{1};$$
$$\{ r = 0 \}$$

$$\{ \mathsf{Acq}(y, \mathcal{Q}) * \mathsf{Rel}(x, \mathcal{Q}) \}$$
$$\texttt{if } (\mathbf{y_{rlx}} \texttt{ == 1})$$
$$\left\{ \mathsf{Rel}(x, \mathcal{Q}) * \lceil \gamma : T \rceil \right\}$$
$$\mathbf{x_{rlx}} = \mathbf{1};$$
$$\{ \mathsf{emp} \}$$

Fig. 10. Using ghosts we can establish absence of load buffering.

We will now show that our extension of FSL with ghost state is unsound with respect to these models. As can be seen in Fig. 10, FSL outfitted with ghost state is strong enough to prove that the weak behavior of the load buffering program does not happen, which in turn means that FSL is not sound for any of the new models which allow that behavior.

The proof uses a single ghost location γ holding a non-duplicable token T. We then use the $\mathcal{Q}(v)$ resource invariant to say that either $v = 0$ or the location owns the token. Since the token is non-duplicable, we thus encode the invariant saying that at most one of x and y can have a non-zero value. Initially, both locations store the value 0, so the ghost token is given to the left thread. Using the token, the first thread can thus assert that $r = 0$, and then use it to write 1 to y. The right thread can conversely gain the token by reading y = 1 and then use it to write 1 to x.

An interesting thing of note is that all the examples (that we are aware of) showing unsoundness of FSL under these new models rely on the use of ghosts, and in the ability to transfer them without any synchronization. In a sense, being able to fully transfer the ownership of the ghost state without any synchronization exposes the acyclicity of the $\mathsf{po} \cup \mathsf{rf}$ relation.

There are thus two main open questions regarding the connection of FSL, and the memory models that do not rely on the acyclic $\mathsf{po} \cup \mathsf{rf}$ assumption.

1. *Is FSL without ghosts sound under any of the models that do not require* $\mathsf{po} \cup \mathsf{rf}$ *to be acyclic?* We strongly suspect that FSL without ghosts is sound under the recent promising model of Kang et al. [19], but proving that this is indeed the case is a highly non-trivial task.
2. In the case of the affirmative answer to the first question, *can we come up with the rules for the ghost state which would allow us to verify algorithms like ARC?* A possibility would be to somehow restrict the (GHOST-MOD) rule so that it may be used only in conjuction with a release write. Such a restriction would preserve the proof of ARC, while ruling out the proof of load buffering. Its soundness with respect to models such as [17,19,28], however, is unclear.

5.3   Deallocation

The proof of soundness of FSL already ensures that if a thread owns the full permission to access a non-atomic location, then there are no other threads that concurrently hold an access permission to the same location. Using this fact, proving that it is safe to deallocate a non-atomic location when holding the full access permission to it is a purely technical matter.

In order to enable deallocation of the atomic locations, we would have to outfit atomic locations with permissions, and show that (for a single location) the full permission cannot coexist concurrently with any other permission. This result should follow from the same line of reasoning as the corresponding result for the non-atomic locations.

In the context of our correctness proof of ARC, the necessary permission for deallocating the atomic variable `a.count` could be obtained in exactly the same way as we obtained the full permission of `a.data` (see Sect. 4.5).

6   Related Work

In this section we would like to call attention to some related work that was not already discussed in Sect. 5. We divide our discussion in two parts: in Sect. 6.1 we discuss other program logics for reasoning about weak memory, and in Sect. 6.2 we turn our attention to some other approaches for establishing program correctness under weak memory.

6.1   Program Logics

Apart from FSL's predecessor, RSL [35], the only other separation logic for the C11 memory model is GPS [34]. Even though GPS handles the ownership transfer in a more flexible way than FSL (using protocols and escrows), GPS is unable to reason about programs that use relaxed memory accesses, such as ARC. The reason for this limitation of GPS is the fact that GPS works under the release-acquire fragment of the C11 memory model.

He et al. [14] have proposed an extension of GPS with FSL-style modalities, to give it support for relaxed accesses and memory fences. As the original FSL, this extension of GPS does not have support for atomic updates, which makes it inapplicable to programs like ARC. Additionally, unlike FSL, this extension of GPS lacks a soundness proof.

It would be interesting to explore adapting GPS-style protocols to FSL, in order to make FSL applicable to an even wider range of programs that require more sophisticated forms of reasoning.

Apart from the separation logics, there is an Owicki-Gries-based logic called OGRA [21] for reasoning about the C11 memory model, but it also handles only the release-acquire fragment of the C11 model. Other program logics for weak memory [30,32] have been focused on the x86-TSO memory model, which is stronger than the one assumed by FSL.

6.2   Other Approaches

Aside from program logics, there are model checking tools for programs with C11-style atomics. Worth noting is CDSCHECKER [25] which includes support for relaxed accesses and memory fences. CDSCHECKER is designed to conduct unit tests on concurrent programs, and cannot be used to verify correctness.

An alternative approach to reasoning about weak memory behaviors is to restore sequential consistency. This can be done by placing fences or stronger atomic accesses in order to eliminate weak behaviors [4,24], or by proving robustness theorems [9,11,20] stating conditions under which programs have no observable weak behaviors. These approaches are not applicable to performance-critical algorithms such as ARC, which are exploiting weak memory consistency. Placing additional fences or using stronger memory accesses to restore sequential consistency would go against the basic design principles of these algorithms.

Recently, Alglave proposed an invariance method for proving program correctness under weak memory [3]. This approach is parametric with the respect to the memory model, and so could be applied to the C11 memory model. It is, however, non-compositional, which makes using it to obtain a correctness proof for the ARC algorithm difficult.

Acknowledgments. We would like to thank Soham Chakraborty, Rayna Dimitrova, Jeehoon Kang, Ori Lahav, Alex Summers, and the ESOP'17 reviewers for their feedback.

References

1. Atomic reference counter (ARC) documentation. https://doc.rust-lang.org/std/sync/struct.Arc.html
2. The Rust programming language. https://www.rust-lang.org/
3. Alglave, J.: Simulation and invariance for weak consistency. In: Rival, X. (ed.) SAS 2016. LNCS, vol. 9837, pp. 3–22. Springer, Heidelberg (2016). doi:10.1007/978-3-662-53413-7_1
4. Alglave, J., Kroening, D., Nimal, V., Poetzl, D.: Don't sit on the fence - a static analysis approach to automatic fence insertion. In: Biere, A., Bloem, R. (eds.) CAV 2014. LNCS, vol. 8559, pp. 508–524. Springer, Heidelberg (2014). doi:10.1007/978-3-319-08867-9_33
5. Batty, M., Dodds, M., Gotsman, A.: Library abstraction for C/C++ concurrency. In: POPL 2013, pp. 235–248. ACM (2013)
6. Batty, M., Owens, S., Sarkar, S., Sewell, P., Weber, T.: Mathematizing C++ concurrency. In: POPL 2011, pp. 55–66. ACM (2011)
7. Boehm, H., Demsky, B.: Outlawing ghosts: avoiding out-of-thin-air results. In: Singer, J., Kulkarni, M., Harris, T. (eds.) MSPC 2014, pp. 7:1–7:6. ACM (2014)
8. Bornat, R., Calcagno, C., O'Hearn, P.W., Parkinson, M.J.: Permission accounting in separation logic. In: POPL 2005, pp. 259–270. ACM (2005)
9. Bouajjani, A., Meyer, R., Möhlmann, E.: Deciding robustness against total store ordering. In: Aceto, L., Henzinger, M., Sgall, J. (eds.) ICALP 2011. LNCS, vol. 6756, pp. 428–440. Springer, Heidelberg (2011). doi:10.1007/978-3-642-22012-8_34

10. Boyland, J.: Checking interference with fractional permissions. In: Cousot, R. (ed.) SAS 2003. LNCS, vol. 2694, pp. 55–72. Springer, Heidelberg (2003). doi:10.1007/3-540-44898-5_4

11. Derevenetc, E., Meyer, R.: Robustness against power is PSpace-complete. In: Esparza, J., Fraigniaud, P., Husfeldt, T., Koutsoupias, E. (eds.) ICALP 2014. LNCS, vol. 8573, pp. 158–170. Springer, Heidelberg (2014). doi:10.1007/978-3-662-43951-7_14

12. Dinsdale-Young, T., Birkedal, L., Gardner, P., Parkinson, M.J., Yang, H.: Views: compositional reasoning for concurrent programs. In: Giacobazzi, R., Cousot, R. (eds.) POPL 2013, pp. 287–300. ACM (2013)

13. Doko, M., Vafeiadis, V.: A program logic for C11 memory fences. In: Jobstmann, B., Leino, K.R.M. (eds.) VMCAI 2016. LNCS, vol. 9583, pp. 413–430. Springer, Heidelberg (2016). doi:10.1007/978-3-662-49122-5_20

14. He, M., Vafeiadis, V., Qin, S., Ferreira, J.F.: Reasoning about fences and relaxed atomics. In: PDP 2016, pp. 520–527. IEEE Computer Society (2016)

15. ISO/IEC 14882:2011: Programming language C++ (2011)

16. ISO/IEC 9899: 2011: Programming language C (2011)

17. Jeffrey, A., Riely, J.: On thin air reads towards an event structures model of relaxed memory. In: LICS 2016, pp. 759–767. ACM (2016)

18. Jensen, J.B., Birkedal, L.: Fictional separation logic. In: Seidl, H. (ed.) ESOP 2012. LNCS, vol. 7211, pp. 377–396. Springer, Heidelberg (2012). doi:10.1007/978-3-642-28869-2_19

19. Kang, J., Hur, C.K., Lahav, O., Vafeiadis, V., Dreyer, D.: A promising semantics for relaxed-memory concurrency. In: POPL 2017, pp. 175–189. ACM (2017)

20. Lahav, O., Giannarakis, N., Vafeiadis, V.: Taming release-acquire consistency. In: Bodík, R., Majumdar, R. (eds.) POPL 2016, pp. 649–662. ACM (2016)

21. Lahav, O., Vafeiadis, V.: Owicki-Gries reasoning for weak memory models. In: Halldórsson, M.M., Iwama, K., Kobayashi, N., Speckmann, B. (eds.) ICALP 2015. LNCS, vol. 9135, pp. 311–323. Springer, Heidelberg (2015). doi:10.1007/978-3-662-47666-6_25

22. Lamport, L.: How to make a multiprocessor computer that correctly executes multiprocess programs. IEEE Trans. Comput. 28(9), 690–691 (1979)

23. Ley-Wild, R., Nanevski, A.: Subjective auxiliary state for coarse-grained concurrency. In: Giacobazzi, R., Cousot, R. (eds.) POPL 2013, pp. 561–574. ACM (2013)

24. Meshman, Y., Rinetzky, N., Yahav, E.: Pattern-based synthesis of synchronization for the C++ memory model. In: Kaivola, R., Wahl, T. (eds.) FMCAD 2015, pp. 120–127. IEEE (2015)

25. Norris, B., Demsky, B.: CDSChecker: Checking concurrent data structures written with C/C++ atomics. In: Hosking, A.L., Eugster, P.T., Lopes, C.V. (eds.) OOPSLA 2013, pp. 131–150. ACM (2013)

26. O'Hearn, P.W.: Resources, concurrency and local reasoning. In: Gardner, P., Yoshida, N. (eds.) CONCUR 2004. LNCS, vol. 3170, pp. 49–67. Springer, Heidelberg (2004). doi:10.1007/978-3-540-28644-8_4

27. O'Hearn, P.W., Yang, H., Reynolds, J.C.: Separation and information hiding. ACM Trans. Program. Lang. Syst. 31(3), 11 (2009)

28. Pichon-Pharabod, J., Sewell, P.: A concurrency semantics for relaxed atomics that permits optimisation and avoids thin-air executions. In: Bodík, R., Majumdar, R. (eds.) POPL 2016, pp. 622–633. ACM (2016)

29. Reynolds, J.C.: Separation logic: a logic for shared mutable data structures. In: LICS 2002, pp. 55–74. IEEE Computer Society (2002)

30. Ridge, T.: A rely-guarantee proof system for x86-TSO. In: Leavens, G.T., O'Hearn, P., Rajamani, S.K. (eds.) VSTTE 2010. LNCS, vol. 6217, pp. 55–70. Springer, Heidelberg (2010). doi:10.1007/978-3-642-15057-9_4

31. Sarkar, S., Memarian, K., Owens, S., Batty, M., Sewell, P., Maranget, L., Alglave, J., Williams, D.: Synchronising C/C++ and power. In: PLDI 2012, pp. 311–322. ACM (2012)

32. Sieczkowski, F., Svendsen, K., Birkedal, L., Pichon-Pharabod, J.: A separation logic for fictional sequential consistency. In: Vitek, J. (ed.) ESOP 2015. LNCS, vol. 9032, pp. 736–761. Springer, Heidelberg (2015). doi:10.1007/978-3-662-46669-8_30

33. Tassarotti, J., Dreyer, D., Vafeiadis, V.: Verifying read-copy-update in a logic for weak memory. In: Grove, D., Blackburn, S. (eds.) PLDI 2015, pp. 110–120. ACM (2015)

34. Turon, A., Vafeiadis, V., Dreyer, D.: GPS: navigating weak-memory with ghosts, protocols, and separation. In: Black, A.P., Millstein, T.D. (eds.) OOPSLA 2014, pp. 691–707. ACM (2014)

35. Vafeiadis, V., Narayan, C.: Relaxed separation logic: a program logic for C11 concurrency. In: Hosking, A.L., Eugster, P.T., Lopes, C.V. (eds.) OOPSLA 2013, pp. 867–884. ACM (2013)

Extensible Datasort Refinements

Jana Dunfield[⊠]

University of British Columbia, Vancouver, Canada
jd169@queensu.ca

Abstract. Refinement types turn typechecking into lightweight verification. The classic form of refinement type is the datasort refinement, in which datasorts identify subclasses of inductive datatypes.

Existing type systems for datasort refinements require that all the refinements of a type be specified when the type is declared; multiple refinements of the same type can be obtained only by duplicating type definitions, and consequently, duplicating code.

We enrich the traditional notion of a signature, which describes the inhabitants of datasorts, to allow *re-refinement* via signature extension, without duplicating definitions. Since arbitrary updates to a signature can invalidate the inversion principles used to check case expressions, we develop a definition of signature well-formedness that ensures that extensions maintain existing inversion principles. This definition allows different parts of a program to extend the same signature in different ways, without conflicting with each other. Each part can be type-checked independently, allowing separate compilation.

1   Introduction

Type systems provide guarantees about run-time behaviour; for example, that a record will not be multiplied by a string. However, the guarantees provided by traditional type systems like Hindley–Milner do not rule out a practically important class of run-time failures: nonexhaustive match exceptions. For example, the type system of Standard ML allows a case expression over lists that omits a branch for the empty list:

```
case elems of head :: tail => head
```

If this expression is evaluated with `elems` bound to the empty list `[]`, the exception `Match` will be raised.

Datasort refinements eliminate this problem: a datasort can express, within the static type system, that `elems` is not empty; therefore, the above case expression will never raise `Match`. Datasorts can also express less shallow properties. For example, the definition in Fig. 1 encodes conjunctive normal form—a formula that consists of (possibly nested) Ands of clauses, where a clause consists of (possibly nested) Ors of literals, where a literal is either a positive literal (a variable) or a negation of a positive literal. A case expression comparing two

© Springer-Verlag GmbH Germany 2017
H. Yang (Ed.): ESOP 2017, LNCS 10201, pp. 476–503, 2017.
DOI: 10.1007/978-3-662-54434-1_18

$$\text{pos-literal} \preceq \text{literal}, \quad \text{literal} \preceq \text{clause}, \quad \text{clause} \preceq \text{cnf},$$

$$
\begin{aligned}
\text{Var} \ &: \ \text{symbol} \to \text{pos-literal}, \\
\text{Not} \ &: \ \text{pos-literal} \to \text{literal}, \\
\text{Or} \ &: \ (\text{clause} * \text{clause}) \to \text{clause}, \\
\text{And} \ &: \ (\text{cnf} * \text{cnf}) \to \text{cnf}
\end{aligned}
$$

Fig. 1. Datasorts for conjunctive normal form

values of type clause would only need branches for Or, Not and Var; the And branch could be omitted, since And does not produce a clause.

Datasorts correspond to regular tree grammars, which can encode various data structure invariants (such as the colour invariant of red-black trees), as well as properties such as CNF and A-normal form. Datasort refinements are less expressive than the "refinement type" systems (such as liquid types) that followed work on index refinements and indexed types; like regular expressions, which "can't count", datasorts cannot count the length of a list or the height of a tree. However, types with datasorts are simpler in some respects; most importantly, types with datasorts never require quantifiers. Avoiding quantifiers, especially existential quantifiers, also avoids many complications in type checking. By analogy, regular expressions cannot solve every problem—but when they *can* solve the problem, they may be the best solution.

The goal of this paper is to make datasort refinements more usable—not by making datasorts express more invariants, but by liberating them from the necessity of a fixed specification (a fixed signature). First, we review the trajectory of research on datasorts.

The first approach to datasort refinements (Freeman and Pfenning 1991; Freeman 1994) extended ML, using abstract interpretation (Cousot and Cousot 1977) to infer refined types. The usual argument in favour of type inference is that it reduces a direct burden on the programmer. When type annotations are boring or self-evident, as they often are in plain ML, this argument is plausible. But datasorts can express more subtle specifications, calling that argument into question. Moreover, inference discourages a form of fine-grained modularity. Just as we expect a module system to support information hiding, so that clients of a module cannot depend on its internal details, a type system should prevent the callers of a function from depending on its internal details. Inferring refinements exposes those details. For example, if a function over lists is written with only nonempty input in mind, the programmer may not have thought about what the function should do for empty input, so the type system shouldn't let the function be applied to an empty list. Finally, inferring all properties means that the inferred refined types can be long, e.g. inferring a 16-part intersection type for a simple function (Freeman and Pfenning 1991, p. 271).

Thus, the second generation of work on datasort refinements (Davies and Pfenning 2000; Davies 2005) used bidirectional typing, rather than inference. Programmers have to write more annotations, but refinement checking will never fabricate unintended invariants. A third generation of work (Dunfield and

Pfenning 2004; Dunfield 2007b) stuck with bidirectional type checking, though this was overdetermined: other features of that type system made inference untenable.

All three generations (and later work by Lovas (2010) on datasorts for LF) shared the constraint that a given datatype could be refined only once. The properties tracked by datasorts could not be subsequently extended; the same set of properties must be used throughout the program. Modular refinement checking could be achieved only by duplicating the type definition and all related code. Separate type-checking of refinements enables simpler reasoning about programs, separate compilation, and faster type-checking (simpler refinement relations lead to simpler case analyses).

The history of pattern typing in case expressions is also worth noting, as formulating pattern typing seems to be the most difficult step in the design of datasort type systems. Freeman supported a form of pattern matching that was oversimplified. Davies implemented the full SML pattern language and formalized most of it, but omitted as-patterns—which become nontrivial when datasort refinements enter the picture.

The system in this paper allows multiple, separately declared refinements of a type by revising a fundamental mechanism of datasort refinements: the signature. Refinements are traditionally described using a *signature* that specifies—for the entire program—which values of a datatype belong to which refinements. For example, the type system can track the parity of bitstrings using the following signature, which says: (1) even and odd are subsorts (subtypes) of the type bits of bitstrings, the (2) empty bitstring has even parity, (3) appending a 1 flips the parity, and (4) appending a 0 preserves parity.

$$\text{even} \preceq \text{bits}, \quad \text{odd} \preceq \text{bits},$$
$$\text{Empty} \; : \; \text{even},$$
$$\text{One} \; : \; (\text{even} \rightarrow \text{odd}) \wedge (\text{odd} \rightarrow \text{even}),$$
$$\text{Zero} \; : \; (\text{even} \rightarrow \text{even}) \wedge (\text{odd} \rightarrow \text{odd})$$

The connective $\wedge$, read "and" or "intersection", denotes conjunction of properties: adding a One makes an even bitstring odd (even $\rightarrow$ odd), *and* makes an odd bitstring even (odd $\rightarrow$ even). Thus, if b is a bitstring known to have odd parity, then appending a 1 yields a bitstring with even parity:

$$\text{b} : \text{odd} \;\vdash\; \text{One}(\text{b}) : \text{even}$$

In some datasort refinement systems (Dunfield 2007b; Lovas 2010), the programmer specifies the refinements by writing a signature like the one above. In the older systems of Freeman and Davies, the programmer writes a regular tree grammar[1], from which the system infers a signature, including the constructor types and the subsort relation:

---

[1] A *regular tree grammar* is like a regular grammar (the class of grammars equivalent to regular expressions), but over trees instead of strings (Comon et al. 2008); the leftmost terminal symbol in a production of a regular grammar corresponds to the symbol at the root of a tree.

$$\text{even} = \text{Empty} \mid \text{Zero}(\text{even}) \mid \text{One}(\text{odd})$$
$$\text{odd} = \text{Zero}(\text{odd}) \mid \text{One}(\text{even})$$

In either design, the typing phase uses the same form of signature. We use the first design, where the programmer gives the signature directly. Giving the signature directly is more expressive, because it enables refinements to carry information not present at run time. For example, we can refine natural numbers by Tainted and Untainted:

$$Z \ : \ \text{nat}, \qquad S : \text{nat} \to \text{nat},$$
$$\text{tainted} \preceq \text{nat}, \ \ \text{untainted} \preceq \text{nat},$$
$$Z \ : \ \text{tainted}, \qquad S : \text{tainted} \to \text{tainted},$$
$$Z \ : \ \text{untainted}, \ \ S : \text{untainted} \to \text{untainted}$$

The sorts tainted and untainted have the same closed inhabitants, but a program cannot directly create an instance of untainted from an instance of tainted:

$$x : \text{tainted} \not\vdash S(x) : \text{untainted}$$

Thus, the two sorts have different *open* inhabitants. This is analogous to dimension typing, where an underlying value is just an integer or float, but the type system tracks that the number is in (for example) metres (Kennedy 1996).

Giving the signature directly allows programmers to choose between a variety of subsorting relationships. For example, to allow untainted data to be used where tainted data is expected, write untainted $\preceq$ tainted. Subsorting can be either *structural* (as the signatures generated from grammars) or *nominal* (as in the example above). In this paper, giving signatures directly is helpful: it enables *extension* of signatures without translating between signatures and grammars.

Contributions. This paper makes the following contributions:

- A language and type system with *extensible signatures* for datasort refinements (Sect. 3). Refinements are extended by *blocks* that are checked to ensure that they do not weaken a sort's inversion principle, which would make typing unsound.
- A new formulation of typing (Sect. 4) for case expressions. This formulation is based on a notion of finding the intersection of a type with a pattern; it concisely models the interesting aspects of realistic ML-style patterns.
- Type (datasort) preservation and progress for the type assignment system, stated in Sect. 6 and proved in Appendix B, with respect to a standard call-by-value operational semantics (Sect. 5).
- A bidirectional type system (Sect. 7), which directly yields an algorithm. We prove that this system is sound (given a bidirectional typing derivation, erasing annotations yields a type assignment derivation) and complete (given any type assignment derivation, annotations can be added to make bidirectional typing succeed).

The appendix, which includes definitions and proofs omitted for space reasons, can be found at http://www.cs.queensu.ca/~jana/papers/extensible/.

2   Datasort Refinements

What are Datasort Refinements? Datasort refinements are a syntactic discipline for enforcing invariants. This is a play on Reynolds's definition of types as a "syntactic discipline for enforcing levels of abstraction" (Reynolds 1983). Datasorts allow programmers to conveniently categorize inductive data, and operations on such data, more precisely than in conventional type systems.

Indexed types and related systems (e.g. liquid types and other "refinement types") also serve that purpose, but datasorts are highly syntactic, whereas indexed types depend on the semantics of a constraint domain. For example, to check the safety of accessing the element at position $2k$ of a 0-based array of length n, an indexed type system must check whether the proposition $2k < n$ is entailed in the theory of integers (under some set of assumptions, e.g. $0 \leq k \leq n/3$). The truth of $2k < n$ depends on the semantics of arithmetic, whereas membership in a datasort only depends on a head constructor and the datasorts of its arguments. Put roughly, datasorts express regular grammars, and indexed types express grammars with more powerful side conditions. (Unrestricted dependent types can express arbitrarily precise side conditions.)

Applications of Datasort Refinements. Datasorts are especially suited to applications of symbolic computing, such as compilers and theorem provers. Compilers usually work with multiple internal languages, from abstract syntax through to intermediate languages. These internal languages may be decomposed into further variants: source ASTs with and without syntactic sugar, A-normal form, and so on. Similarly, theorem provers, SMT solvers, and related tools transform formulas into various normal forms or sublanguages: quantifier-free Boolean formulas, conjunctive normal form, formulas with no free variables, etc. Many such invariants can be expressed by regular tree grammars, and hence by datasorts.

Our extensible refinements offer the ability to use new refinements of a datatype when the need arises, without the need to update a global refinement declaration. For example, we could extend the types in Fig. 1, in which clause contains disjunctions of literals and cnf contains conjunctions of clauses, with a new sort for *conjunctions* of literals:

[everything from Fig. 1]   literal $\preceq$ conj-literal, conj-literal $\preceq$ cnf,
And : (conj-literal $*$ conj-literal) $\rightarrow$ conj-literal

What are Datasort Refinements Not? First, datasorts are not really types, at least not in the sense of Hindley–Milner type systems. A function on bitstrings (Sect. 1) has a best, or principal, type: bits $\rightarrow$ bits. In contrast, such a function may have many refined types (sometimes called *sorts*), depending not only on the way the programmer chose to refine the bits type, but on which possible properties they wish to check. The type, or sort, of a function is a tiny module interface. In a conventional Hindley–Milner type system, there is a best interface (the principal type); with datasorts, the "best" interface is—as with a module interface, which may reveal different aspects of the module—*the one the program-mer thinks best*. Maybe the programmer only cares that the function preserves odd parity, and annotates it with odd → odd; the compiler will reject calls with even bitstrings, even though such a call would be conventionally well-typed.

To infer sorts, as in the original work of Freeman, is like assuming that all declarations in a module should be exposed. (Tools that suggest possible invariants could be useful, just as a tool that suggests possible module interfaces could be useful. But such tools are not the focus of this paper.)

3 A Type System with Extensible Refinements

This section gives our language's syntax, introduces signatures, discusses the introduction and elimination forms for datasorts, and presents the typing rules. The details of typing pattern matching are in Sect. 4.

Term vars. $x, y, \ldots$

Expressions e ::= $x \mid \lambda x.\, e \mid e_1\, e_2 \mid (e_1,\, e_2) \mid c(e) \mid$ case e of ms
$\mid$ declare Σ in e —signature extension (Fig. 4)

Matches ms ::= $\cdot \mid ((p \Rightarrow e) \mid ms)$

Values v ::= $x \mid \lambda x.\, e \mid (v_1,\, v_2) \mid c(v) \mid (v : A)$

Patterns p ::= $\_ \mid \emptyset \mid c(p) \mid (p_1,\, p_2) \mid x$ as $p \mid p_1 \sqcup p_2$

Fig. 2. Expressions

3.1 Syntax

The syntax of expressions (Fig. 2) includes functions $\lambda x.\, e$, function application $e_1\, e_2$, pairs $(e_1,\, e_2)$, constructors $c(e)$, and case expressions. Signatures are extended by declare Σ in e.

Datasorts $s, t, \ldots$

Types A, B, D ::= $1 \mid A \to B \mid A * B \mid s \mid A \wedge B$

Typing contexts Γ ::= $\cdot \mid \Gamma, x : A$

Fig. 3. Types and contexts

Types (Fig. 3), written A and B, include unit (1), function, and product types, along with datasorts s and t. The intersection type $A \wedge B$ represents the conjunction of the two properties denoted by A and B; for example, a function to repeat a bitstring could be checked against type (odd → even) $\wedge$ (even → even): given any bitstring b, the repetition bb has even parity.

3.2 Unrefined Types and Signatures

Our unrefined types τ, in Fig. 4, are very simple: unit 1, functions $\tau_1 \to \tau_2$, products $\tau_1 * \tau_2$, and datatypes d. We assume that each datatype has a known set of constructors: for example, the bitstring type of Sect. 1 has constructors Empty, One and Zero. Refinements don't add constructors; they only refine the types of the given constructors. We assume that each program has some *unrefined signature* $\mathcal{U}$ that gives datatype names (d) and (unrefined) constructor typings $(c : \tau \to d)$. Since this signature is the same throughout a program, we elide it in most judgment forms.

The judgment $\Sigma \vdash A \sqsubseteq \tau$ says that A is a refinement of τ. Both the symbol $\sqsubseteq$ and several of the rules are reminiscent of subtyping, but that is misleading: sorts and types are not in an inclusion relation in the sense of subtyping, because the rule for $\to$ is covariant, not contravariant. Covariance is needed for functions whose domains are nontrivially refined, e.g. odd $\to \cdots$, which is not a subtype of bits $\to \cdots$ because bits $\not\leq$ odd.

Rule $\sqsubseteq\!\wedge$ implements the usual refinement restriction: both parts of an intersection $A_1 \wedge A_2$ must refine the same unrefined type τ.

3.3 Signatures

Refinements are defined by *signatures* Σ (Fig. 4).

Unrefined datatype names d		
Unrefined types	$\tau ::= 1 \mid \tau_1 \to \tau_2 \mid \tau_1 * \tau_2 \mid d$	
Unrefined signatures	$\mathcal{U} ::= \cdot \mid \mathcal{U}, d \mid \mathcal{U}, c : \tau \to d$	

Constructor types	$C ::= A \to s$	
Blocks	$K ::= \cdot$	empty block
	$\mid K, s_1 \preceq s_2$	subsorting declaration
	$\mid K, c : C$	constructor type decl.
Sort sets	$S ::= (s_1 \sqsubseteq d_1, \ldots, s_n \sqsubseteq d_n)$	
Abbrev. sort sets	$S ::= (s_1, \ldots, s_n)$	
Signatures	$\Sigma, \Omega ::= \cdot$	empty signature
	$\mid \Sigma, S\langle K \rangle$	datasort specification

$\boxed{\Sigma \vdash A \sqsubseteq \tau}$ Under signature Σ (and unrefined signature $\mathcal{U}$), type A is a refinement of unrefined type τ

$$\frac{}{\Sigma \vdash 1 \sqsubseteq 1} \;\sqsubseteq 1 \qquad \frac{\Sigma \vdash A_1 \sqsubseteq \tau_1 \quad \Sigma \vdash A_2 \sqsubseteq \tau_2}{\Sigma \vdash (A_1 \to A_2) \sqsubseteq (\tau_1 \to \tau_2)} \;\sqsubseteq\!\to \qquad \frac{\Sigma \vdash A_1 \sqsubseteq \tau_1 \quad \Sigma \vdash A_2 \sqsubseteq \tau_2}{\Sigma \vdash (A_1 * A_2) \sqsubseteq (\tau_1 * \tau_2)} \;\sqsubseteq *$$

$$\frac{(s \sqsubseteq d) \in \Sigma}{\Sigma \vdash s \sqsubseteq d} \;\sqsubseteq\mathsf{Data} \qquad\qquad \frac{\Sigma \vdash A_1 \sqsubseteq \tau \quad \Sigma \vdash A_2 \sqsubseteq \tau}{\Sigma \vdash (A_1 \wedge A_2) \sqsubseteq \tau} \;\sqsubseteq\!\wedge$$

Fig. 4. Unrefined types and signatures, refined signatures, $\sqsubseteq$

$\boxed{\Sigma \vdash A \; type}$ Type A is well-formed

$$\frac{}{\Sigma \vdash 1 \; type} \; \text{WfType1} \qquad \frac{\Sigma \vdash A_1 \; type \qquad \Sigma \vdash A_2 \; type}{\Sigma \vdash A_1 * A_2 \; type} \; \text{WfType*}$$

$$\frac{\Sigma \vdash A_1 \; type \qquad \Sigma \vdash A_2 \; type}{\Sigma \vdash A_1 \to A_2 \; type} \; \text{WfType} \to \qquad \frac{\Sigma \vdash A_1 \; type \quad \Sigma \vdash A_1 \sqsubset \tau \qquad \Sigma \vdash A_2 \; type \quad \Sigma \vdash A_2 \sqsubset \tau}{\Sigma \vdash A_1 \wedge A_2 \; type} \; \text{WfType} \wedge$$

$$\frac{s \in S}{\Sigma, S\langle K \rangle, \Sigma' \vdash s \; type} \; \text{WfTypeSort}$$

$\boxed{\Sigma \vdash c : C \; contype}$ Under (prefix) context Σ, the typing $c : C$ refines a typing in $\mathcal{U}$

$$\frac{\Sigma \vdash A \; type \qquad \Sigma \vdash s \; type \qquad (c : \tau \to d) \in \mathcal{U} \qquad \Sigma \vdash (A \to s) \sqsubset (\tau \to d)}{\Sigma \vdash c : A \to s \; contype} \; \text{ContypeArr}$$

Fig. 5. Type well-formedness

As in past datasort systems, we separate signatures Σ from typing contexts Γ. Typing assumptions over term variables (x, y, etc.) in Γ can mention sorts declared in Σ, but the signature Σ cannot mention the term variables declared in Γ. Thus, our judgment for term typing will have the form $\Sigma; \Gamma \vdash e : A$, where the term e can include constructors declared in Σ and variables declared in Γ, and the type A can include sorts declared in Σ. Some judgments, like subsorting $\Sigma \vdash s \preceq t$ and subtyping $\Sigma \vdash A \leq B$, are independent of variable typing and don't include Γ at all.

Traditional formulations of refinements assume the signature is given once at the beginning of the program. Since the same signature is used throughout a given typing derivation, the signature can be omitted from the typing judgments. In this paper, our goal is to support extensible refinements, where the signature can evolve within a typing derivation; in this respect, the signature is analogous to an ordinary typing context Γ, which is extended in subderivations that type λ-expressions and other binding forms. So the signature must be explicit in our judgment forms (Fig. 5).

Constructor types C are types of the form $A \to s$. In past formulations of datasorts, constructor types in the signature use intersection to represent multiple behaviours. For example, a "one" constructor for bitstrings, which represents appending a 1 bit, takes odd-parity bitstrings to even-parity and vice versa; its type in the signature is the intersection type $(\text{odd} \to \text{even}) \wedge (\text{even} \to \text{odd})$. Such a formulation ensures that the signature has a standard property of (typing) contexts: each data constructor is declared only once; additional behaviours are conjoined (intersected) within a single declaration $c : C_1 \wedge C_2 \wedge \cdots$. In our setting, we must be careful about not only *which* types a constructor has, but *when* those types were declared. The reasons are explained below; for now, just note that we will write something like $c : C_1, \ldots, c : C_2$ rather than $c : C_1 \wedge C_2$.

Structure of Signatures. A signature Σ is a sequence of *blocks* $S\langle K\rangle$ of declarations, where refinements declared in outer scopes in the program appear to the left of those declared in inner scopes.

Writing $(s \sqsubset d)\langle K\rangle$ declares s to be a sort refining some (unrefined) datatype d; however, we usually elide the datatype and write just $s\langle K\rangle$. The declarations K, called the *block* of s, define the values (constructors) of s, and the subsortings for s. Declarations outside this block may declare new subsorts and supersorts of s *only* if doing so would not affect s—for example, adding inhabitants to s via a constructor declaration, or declaring a new subsorting between s and previously declared sorts, would affect s and will be forbidden (via signature well-formedness). The grammar generalizes this construct to multiple sorts, e.g. $(s_1 \sqsubset d_1, s_2 \sqsubset d_2)\langle K\rangle$, abbreviated as $(s_1, s_2)\langle K\rangle$.

Writing $s_1 \preceq s_2$ says that s_1 is a subsort of s_2, and c : C says that constructor c has type C, where C has the form $A \rightarrow s$. A constructor c can be given more than one type: $\Sigma = (s, s_1, s_2)\langle s_1 \preceq s, s_2 \preceq s, c : s_1 \rightarrow s_2, c : s_2 \rightarrow s_1\rangle$.

Adding inhabitants to a sort is only allowed within its block. Thus, the following signature is ill-formed, because $c' : 1 \rightarrow s$ adds the value $c'()$ to s, but $c' : 1 \rightarrow s$ is not within s's block: $s\langle c : s \rightarrow s\rangle$, $t\langle c' : 1 \rightarrow s\rangle$. New sorts can be declared as subsorts and supersorts of each other, and of previously declared sorts: $s\langle c_1 : 1 \rightarrow s, c_2 : 1 \rightarrow s\rangle$, $t\langle t \preceq s, c_2 : 1 \rightarrow t\rangle$.

However, a block cannot modify the subsorting relation between earlier sorts; "backpatching" $s_1 \preceq s_2$ into the first block, through a new intermediate sort t, is not permitted: The signature $\Sigma_* = (s_1, s_2)\langle c : 1 \rightarrow s_1, c : 1 \rightarrow s_2\rangle$, $t\langle s_1 \preceq t, t \preceq s_2\rangle$ is not permitted even though it looks safe: sorts s_1 and s_2 have the same set of inhabitants—the singleton set $\{c()\}$—so the values of s_1 are a subset of the values of s_2. But this fact was not declared in the first block, which is the definition of s_1 and s_2. We assume the declaration of the first block completely reflects the programmer's intent: if they had wanted structural subsorting, rather than nominal subsorting, they should have declared $s_1 \preceq s_2$ in the first block. Allowing backpatching would not violate soundness, but would reduce the power of the type system: nominal subsorting would no longer be supported, since it could be made structural after the fact.

Ordering. A block $S\langle K\rangle$ can refer to the sorts S being defined and to sorts declared to the left. In contrast to block ordering, the order of declarations inside a block doesn't matter.

3.4   Introduction Form

From a type-theoretic perspective, the first questions about a type are: (1) How are the type's inhabitants created? That is, what are the type's introduction rules? (2) How are its inhabitants used? That is, what are its elimination rules? (Gentzen (1934) would ask the questions in this order; the reverse order has been considered by Dummett, among others (Zeilberger 2009).) In our setting, we must also ask: What happens with the introduction and elimination forms when new refinements are introduced?

In the introduction rule—Datal in Fig. 6—the signature Σ is separated from the ordinary context Γ (which contains typing assumptions of the form $x : A$). The typing of c is delegated to its first premise, $\Sigma \vdash c : A \rightarrow s$, so we need a way to derive this judgment. At the top of Fig. 6, we define a single rule ConArr, which looks up the constructor in the signature and weakens the result type (codomain), expressing a subsumption principle. (Since we'll have subsumption as a typing rule, including it here is an unforced choice; its presence is meant to make the metatheory of constructor typing go more smoothly.)

In a system of extensible refinements, adding refinements to a signature should preserve typing. That is, if $\Sigma; \Gamma \vdash e : B$, then $\Sigma, \Sigma'; \Gamma \vdash e : B$. This is a weakening property: we can derive, from the judgment that e has type B under Σ, the logically weaker judgment that e has type B under more assumptions Σ, Σ'. (The signature becomes longer, therefore stronger; but a turnstile is a kind of implication with the signature as antecedent, so the judgment becomes weaker, hence "weakening".) So for the introduction form, we need that if $\Sigma \vdash c : A \rightarrow s$, then $\Sigma, \Sigma' \vdash c : A \rightarrow s$. Under our formulation of the signature, this holds: If $c : A \rightarrow s$, then there exists $(c : A \rightarrow s') \in \Sigma$ such that $s' \preceq s$. Therefore, there exists $(c : A \rightarrow s') \in (\Sigma, \Sigma')$. Likewise, since $\Sigma \vdash s' \preceq s$, we also have $\Sigma, \Sigma' \vdash s' \preceq s$. One cannot use Σ' to withdraw a commitment made in Σ.[2]

3.5   Elimination Form: Case Expressions

Exhaustiveness checking for case expressions assumes complete knowledge about the inhabitants of types. Thus, we must avoid extending a signature in a way that adds inhabitants to previously declared sorts. Consider the case expression case $x :$ empty of Nil() $\Rightarrow$ () which is exhaustive for the signature $\Sigma = (\text{list}, \text{empty})\langle\text{empty} \preceq \text{list}, \text{Nil} : 1\rightarrow\text{empty}, \text{Cons} : \text{list}\rightarrow\text{list}\rangle$ but not for

$$(\Sigma, \Sigma') = (\text{list}, \text{empty})\langle\text{empty} \preceq \text{list}, \text{Nil} : 1\rightarrow\text{empty}, \text{Cons} : \text{list}\rightarrow\text{list}\rangle,$$
$$\langle\text{Cons} : \text{list}\rightarrow\text{empty}\rangle$$

Suppose we type-check the case expression under Σ, but then extend Σ to (Σ, Σ'). Evaluating the above case expression with $x = \text{Cons}(\text{Nil}())$ will "fall off the end". The inversion principle that "every empty has the form Nil()" is valid under Σ, but with the additional type for Cons in Σ', that inversion principle becomes invalid under (Σ, Σ'). Our system will reject the latter signature as ill-formed.

In the following, "up" and "down" are used in the usual sense: a subsort is below its supersort. In Σ', the second constructor type for Cons had a smaller codomain than the first: the second type had empty, instead of list. Varying the codomain downward *can* be sound when the lower codomain is newly defined:

---

[2] Under the traditional formulation where each constructor has just one type in a signature, the relationship between the old signature Σ and the new signature would be slightly more complicated: the old signature might contain $c : C_1$, and the new signature $c : C_1 \wedge C_2$, and we would need to explicitly eliminate the intersection to expose the old type C_1. In our formulation, the new signature appends additional typings for c while keeping the typing $c : C_1$ intact.

$\Sigma, \Sigma'' = \Sigma$, subempty⟨subempty $\preceq$ empty, Nil : 1→subempty⟩. Here, the inversion principle that every empty is Nil is still valid (along with the new inversion principle that every subempty is Nil). We only added information about a new sort subempty, without changing the definition of list and empty.

Moving the Domain Down. Giving a new type whose domain is smaller, but that has the same codomain, is sound but pointless. For example, extending Σ with Cons : empty→list, which is the same as the type Σ has for Cons except that the domain is empty instead of list, is sound. The inversion principle for values v of type list in Σ alone is "either (1) v has the form Nil(), or (2) v has the form Cons(y) where y has type list". Reading off the new inversion principle for list from Σ, Cons : empty→list, we get "either (1) v has the form Nil(), or (2) v has the form Cons(y) where y has type list, or (3) v has the form Cons(y) where y has type empty". Since empty is a subsort of list, part (3) implies part (2), and any case arm that checks under the assumption that y : list must also check under the assumption that y : empty. Here, the new signature is equivalent to Σ alone; the "new" type for Cons is spurious.

Moving the Codomain Up. Symmetrically, giving a new type whose *codomain* gets *larger* is sound but pointless. For example, adding Nil : 1→list to Σ has no effect, because (in the introduction form) we could use the old type Nil : 1 → empty with subsumption (empty $\preceq$ list).

Moving the Domain Up. Making the domain of a constructor *larger* is unsound in general. To show this, we need a different starting signature Σ_2.

$$\Sigma_2 = (\text{list, empty, nonempty})⟨\text{empty} \preceq \text{list, nonempty} \preceq \text{list,}$$
$$\text{Nil : 1→empty, Cons : empty→nonempty}⟩$$

This isn't a very useful signature—it doesn't allow construction of any list with more than one element—but it is illustrative. We can read off from Σ_2 the following inversion principle for values v of sort nonempty: "v has the form Cons(y) where y has type empty". If x : nonempty then Case x of Cons (Nil()) $\Rightarrow$ () is exhaustive under Σ_2. Now, extend Σ_2: $\Sigma_2, \Sigma_2' = \Sigma_2, ⟨\text{Cons : list→nonempty}⟩$. For the signature Σ_2, Σ_2', the inversion principle for nonempty should be "(1) v has the form Cons(y) where y has type empty, or (2) v has the form Cons(y) where y has type list". But there are more values of type list than of type empty. The new inversion principle gives less precise information about the argument y, meaning that the old inversion principle gives *more* precise information than (Σ_2, Σ_2') allows. Concretely, the case expression above was exhaustive under Σ_2, but is not exhaustive under (Σ_2, Σ_2') because Cons(Cons(Nil())) has type list.

The above examples show that signature extension can be sound but useless, unsound, or sound and useful (when the domain and codomain, or just the codomain, are moved down). Ruling out unsoundness will be the main purpose of our type system, where unsoundness includes raising a "match" exception due to a nonexhaustive case. The critical requirement is that each block must not affect previously declared sorts by adding constructors to them, or by adding subsortings between them.

3.6 Typing

Figure 6 gives rules deriving the main typing judgment $\Sigma; \Gamma \vdash e : A$. The variable rule Var, the introduction ($\rightarrow$I) and elimination ($\rightarrow$E) rules for $\rightarrow$, and the introduction rules for the unit type (1I) and products ($*$I) are standard. Products can be eliminated via case e of $(x_1, x_2) \Rightarrow \cdots$, so they need no elimination rule.

Subsumption. A subsumption rule Sub incorporates subtyping, based on the subsort relation $\preceq$; see Sect. 3.7. Several of the subtyping rules express the same properties as elimination rules would; for example, anything of type $A_1 \wedge A_2$ has type A_1 and also type A_2. Consequently, we can omit these elimination rules without losing expressive power.

$$\boxed{\Sigma \vdash c : C} \quad \begin{array}{l} \text{Under signature } \Sigma, \\ \text{constructor } c \text{ has type } C \end{array} \qquad \dfrac{(c : A \rightarrow s') \in \Sigma \quad \Sigma \vdash s' \preceq s}{\Sigma \vdash c : A \rightarrow s} \;\; \text{ConArr}$$

$$\boxed{\Sigma; \Gamma \vdash e : A} \quad \text{Under signature } \Sigma \text{ and context } \Gamma, \text{ expression } e \text{ has type } A$$

$$\dfrac{}{\Sigma; \Gamma, x : A, \Gamma' \vdash x : A} \;\; \text{Var} \qquad \dfrac{\Sigma; \Gamma \vdash e : A \quad \Sigma \vdash A \leq B}{\Sigma; \Gamma \vdash e : B} \;\; \text{Sub}$$

$$\dfrac{\Sigma; \Gamma, x : A \vdash e : B}{\Sigma; \Gamma \vdash (\lambda x. e) : (A \rightarrow B)} \;\; \rightarrow\!\text{I} \qquad \dfrac{\Sigma; \Gamma \vdash e_1 : (A \rightarrow B) \quad \Sigma; \Gamma \vdash e_2 : A}{\Sigma; \Gamma \vdash e_1\, e_2 : B} \;\; \rightarrow\!\text{E}$$

$$\dfrac{\Sigma; \Gamma \vdash v : A_1 \quad \Sigma; \Gamma \vdash v : A_2}{\Sigma; \Gamma \vdash v : (A_1 \wedge A_2)} \;\; \wedge\text{I} \qquad \begin{array}{l} \wedge\text{E}_k \text{ admissible} \\ \text{via Sub} + \leq\!\wedge\text{L}_k \end{array}$$

$$\dfrac{\Sigma; \Gamma \vdash e_1 : A_1 \quad \Sigma; \Gamma \vdash e_2 : A_2}{\Sigma; \Gamma \vdash (e_1, e_2) : A_1 * A_2} \;\; *\text{I} \qquad \begin{array}{l} \text{elimination via DataE} \\ \text{with } (x_1, x_2) \Rightarrow \cdots \end{array}$$

$$\dfrac{}{\Sigma; \Gamma \vdash () : 1} \;\; \text{1I} \qquad \dfrac{\Sigma \vdash c : A \rightarrow s \quad \Sigma; \Gamma \vdash e : A}{\Sigma; \Gamma \vdash c(e) : s} \;\; \text{DataI}$$

$$\dfrac{\Sigma; \Gamma \vdash e : A \quad \Sigma; \Gamma, \_ : A \vdash ms : B}{\Sigma; \Gamma \vdash (\text{case } e \text{ of } ms) : B} \;\; \text{DataE} \qquad \dfrac{(\Sigma, \Sigma')\ sig \quad \Sigma \vdash B\ type \quad \Sigma, \Sigma'; \Gamma \vdash e : B}{\Sigma; \Gamma \vdash (\text{declare } \Sigma' \text{ in } e) : B} \;\; \text{Declare}$$

Fig. 6. Typing rules for constructors and expressions

Intersection. The introduction rule $\wedge$ I corresponds to a binary version of the introduction rule for parametric polymorphism in System F. The restriction to a value v avoids unsoundness in the presence of mutable references (Davies and Pfenning 2000), similar to SML's value restriction for parametric polymorphism (Wright 1995). We omit the elimination rules, which are admissible using Sub and subtyping (Sect. 3.7).

$$\frac{\Sigma;\Gamma \vdash e : A_1 \wedge A_2}{\Sigma;\Gamma \vdash e : A_1} \qquad \frac{\Sigma;\Gamma \vdash e : A_1 \wedge A_2}{\Sigma;\Gamma \vdash e : A_2}$$

Datasorts. Rule DataI introduces a datasort, according to a constructor type found in Σ (via the $\Sigma \vdash c : C$ judgment). Rule DataE examines an expression e of type A and checks matches ms under the assumption that the expression matches the wildcard pattern $\_$; see Sect. 4.

Re-refinement. Rule Declare allows sorts to be declared. Its premises check that (1) the signature Σ' is a valid extension of Σ (see Sect. 3.8); (2) the type B of the expression is well-formed *without* the extension Σ', which prevents sorts declared in Σ' from escaping their scope; (3) that the expression e is well-typed under the extended signature (Σ, Σ').

$$\boxed{\Sigma \vdash A \leq B}\ \text{A is a subtype of B} \qquad\qquad \frac{\Sigma \vdash s \preceq t}{\Sigma \vdash s \leq t}{\leq}\text{Data}$$

$$\frac{}{\Sigma \vdash 1 \leq 1}{\leq}1 \qquad \frac{\Sigma \vdash A_1 \leq B_1 \qquad \Sigma \vdash A_2 \leq B_2}{\Sigma \vdash (A_1 * A_2) \leq (B_1 * B_2)}{\leq}*$$

$$\frac{\Sigma \vdash B_1 \leq A_1 \quad \Sigma \vdash A_2 \leq B_2}{\Sigma \vdash (A_1 \to A_2) \leq (B_1 \to B_2)}{\leq}{\to} \quad \frac{\Sigma \vdash A_k \leq B}{\Sigma \vdash (A_1 \wedge A_2) \leq B}{\leq}{\wedge}L_k \quad \frac{\Sigma \vdash A \leq B_1 \quad \Sigma \vdash A \leq B_2}{\Sigma \vdash A \leq (B_1 \wedge B_2)}{\leq}{\wedge}R$$

Fig. 7. Subtyping

3.7   Subtyping

Our subtyping judgment $\Sigma \vdash A \leq B$ says that all values of type A also have type B. The rules follow the style of Dunfield and Pfenning (2003); in particular, the rules are orthogonal (each rule mentions only one kind of connective) and transitivity is admissible. Instead of an explicit transitivity rule, we bake transitivity into each rule; for example, rule ${\leq}{\wedge}\ L_1$ has a premise $A_1 \leq B$ and conclusion $(A_1 \wedge A_2) \leq B$, rather than just $(A_1 \wedge A_2) \leq A_1$ (with no premises). This makes the rules easier to implement: to decide whether $A \leq C$, we never have to guess a middle type B such that $A \leq B$ and $B \leq C$ (Fig. 7).

3.8   Signature Well-Formedness

A signature is well-formed if standard conditions (e.g. no duplicate declarations of sorts) *and* conservation conditions hold. Reading Fig. 8 from bottom to top, we start with well-formedness of signatures Σ *sig*. For each block $S\langle K \rangle$, rule SigBlock checks that the sorts S are not duplicates $(S \cap \text{dom}(\Sigma) = \emptyset)$, and then checks that (1) subsorting is conserved by K and (2) each element in K is *safe*.

$\boxed{\text{dom}(\Sigma)}$ Domain (declared sorts) of Σ: $\text{dom}(S_1\langle K_1\rangle,\ldots,S_n\langle K_n\rangle) = S_1 \cup \cdots \cup S_n$

$\boxed{\Sigma \vdash s_1 \preceq s_2}$ Sort s_1 is a subsort of s_2

$$\dfrac{}{\Sigma_L, S\langle \ldots, s_1 \preceq s_2, \ldots\rangle, \Sigma_R \vdash s_1 \preceq s_2}\preceq\text{Assum}$$

$$\dfrac{s \in \text{dom}(\Sigma)}{\Sigma \vdash s \preceq s}\preceq\text{Refl} \qquad \dfrac{\Sigma \vdash s_1 \preceq s_2 \qquad \Sigma \vdash s_2 \preceq s_3}{\Sigma \vdash s_1 \preceq s_3}\preceq\text{Trans}$$

$\boxed{\Sigma; S\langle K\rangle \vdash c : C \text{ safe at } t}$ C safely extends a type given by Σ for c

$$\dfrac{(c : A' \to s') \in \Sigma \qquad \begin{array}{c}\Sigma, S\langle K\rangle \vdash s' \preceq t \\ \Sigma, S\langle K\rangle \vdash s \preceq s' \qquad \Sigma, S\langle K\rangle \vdash A \leq A'\end{array}}{\Sigma; S\langle K\rangle \vdash c : A \to s \text{ safe at } t}\text{SafeConAt}$$

$\boxed{\Sigma; S\langle K\rangle \vdash K_{\text{elem}} \text{ safe}}$ $K_{\text{elem}} \in K$ is safe for $\Sigma; S\langle K\rangle$

$$\dfrac{s_1, s_2 \in (\text{dom}(\Sigma) \cup S)}{\Sigma; S\langle K\rangle \vdash s_1 \preceq s_2 \text{ safe}}\text{BlockSubsort} \qquad \dfrac{\begin{array}{c}\Sigma, S\langle K\rangle \vdash c : A \to s \text{ contype} \\ \text{for all } t \in \text{dom}(\Sigma) \\ \text{such that } \Sigma, S\langle K\rangle \vdash s \preceq t, \\ s \in S \qquad \Sigma; S\langle K\rangle \vdash c : A \to s \text{ safe at } t\end{array}}{\Sigma; S\langle K\rangle \vdash c : A \to s \text{ safe}}\text{BlockCon}$$

$\boxed{\Sigma \text{ sig}}$ Signature Σ is well-formed

$$\dfrac{}{\cdot \text{ sig}}\text{SigEmpty}$$

$$\dfrac{\begin{array}{c}\Sigma \text{ sig} \\ (S \cap \text{dom}(\Sigma)) = \emptyset\end{array} \quad \begin{array}{c}\text{for all } t_1, t_2 \in \text{dom}(\Sigma), \\ (\Sigma \vdash t_1 \preceq t_2) \\ \text{iff } (\Sigma, S\langle K\rangle \vdash t_1 \preceq t_2)\end{array} \quad \begin{array}{c}\text{for all } K_{\text{elem}} \in K, \\ \Sigma; S\langle K\rangle \vdash K_{\text{elem}} \text{ safe}\end{array}}{\Sigma, S\langle K\rangle \text{ sig}}\text{SigBlock}$$

Fig. 8. Signature well-formedness and subsorting

(1) Subsorting Preservation. The subsortings declared in K must not affect the subsort relation between sorts previously declared in Σ. The left-to-right direction of this "iff" always holds by weakening: adding to a signature cannot delete edges in the subsort relation. The right-to-left direction is contingent on the contents of K; see signature Σ_* in Sect. 3.3. This premise could also be written as $(\Sigma \vdash \preceq|_{\text{dom}(\Sigma)}) = (\Sigma, S\langle K\rangle \vdash \preceq|_{\text{dom}(\Sigma)})$, where $\preceq|_{\text{dom}(\Sigma)}$ is the $\preceq$ relation restricted to sorts in $\text{dom}(\Sigma)$.

(2a) Subsort Elements. Rule BlockSubsort checks that the subsorts are in scope.

(2b) Constructor Element Safety. Rule BlockCon's first premise checks that $s \in S$. (Certain declarations with $s \notin S$ would be safe, but useless.) Its second premise checks that the constructor type $A \to s$ is well-formed. Finally, for all sorts t that were (1) previously declared (in $\text{dom}(\Sigma)$) and (2) supersorts of the constructor's codomain ($s \preceq t$), the rule checks that the constructor is "safe at t".

The judgment $\Sigma; S\langle K\rangle \vdash c : A \to s \text{ safe at } t$ says that adding the constructor typing $c : A \to s$ does not invalidate Σ's inversion principle for t. Rule SafeConAt checks that signature Σ already has a constructor typing $c : A' \to s'$, where $s' \preceq t$, such that $A \leq A'$. Thus, any value $c(v)$ typed using $c : A \to s$ can already be typed using $c : A' \preceq s'$, which is a subsort of t, so the new constructor typing $c : A \to s$ does not add inhabitants to t.

This check is *not* analogous to function subtyping, because we need covariance $(A \leq A')$, not contravariance. The relation $\sqsubseteq$ (Fig. 4) is a closer analogy.

More subtly, SafeConAt also checks that $s \preceq s'$. Suppose we have the signature $\Sigma = (t, s_1, s_2)\langle s_1 \preceq t, s_2 \preceq t, c_1 : s_1, c_2 : s_2 \rangle$ and extend it with $s\langle s \preceq t, c_1 : s \rangle$. (To focus on the issue at hand, we assume c_1 and c_2 take no arguments.) For the original signature Σ, the inversion principle for t is: If a value v has type t, then either $v = c_1$ and v has type s_1, or $v = c_2$ and v has type s_2. However, under the extended signature, there is a new possibility: v has type s. Merely being inhabited by c_1 is not sufficient to allow s to be a subsort of t.

If, instead, we start with $\Sigma' = (t, s_1, s_2)\langle c_1 : t, s_1 \preceq t, s_2 \preceq t, c_1 : s_1, c_2 : s_2 \rangle$ then the inversion principle for t under Σ' is that v has type s_1, type s_2, *or* type t. Therefore, any case arm whose pattern is x as c_1 must be checked assuming $x : t$. If an expression can be typed assuming $x : t$, then it can be typed assuming $x : t'$ for any $t' \preceq t$, so the inversion principle (again, under Σ' before extension) is equivalent to "v has type t". Extending Σ' with $s\langle s \preceq t, c_1 : s \rangle$ would extend the inversion principle to say "if $v : t$ then v has type t, or v has type s", but since $s \preceq t$ the extended inversion principle is equivalent to that for t under Σ'.

The $s \preceq s'$ premise of SafeConAt is needed to prove the constructor lemma (Lemma 12), which says that a constructor typing in an extended signature must be below a constructor typing in the original signature.

4   Typing Pattern Matching

Pattern matching is how a program gives different answers on different inputs. A key motivation for datasort refinements is to exclude impossible patterns, so that programmers can avoid having to choose between writing impossible case arms (that raise an "impossible" exception) and ignoring nonexhaustiveness warnings. The pattern typing rules must model the relationship between datasorts and the operational semantics of pattern matching. It's no surprise, then, that in datasort refinement systems, case expressions lead to the most interesting typing rules.

The relationship between types and patterns is more involved than with, say, Damas–Milner plus inductive datatypes: with (unrefined) inductive datatypes, all the information needed to check for exhaustiveness (also called coverage) is immediately available as soon as the type of the scrutinee is known. Moreover, types for pattern variables can be "read off" by traversing the pattern top-down, tracking the definition of the scrutinee's inductive datatype. But with datasorts, a set of patterns that looks nonexhaustive at first glance—looking only at the head constructors—may in fact be exhaustive, thanks to the inner patterns.

Giving types to pattern variables is also tricky, because sufficiently precise types may be evident only after examining the whole pattern. For example, when matching x : bits against the pattern y as One(Empty), we shouldn't settle on y : bits because the scrutinee x has type bits; we should descend into the pattern and observe that Empty : even and One : (even $\to$ odd), so y must have type odd.

Restricting the form of case expressions to a single layer of clearly disjoint patterns $c_1(x_1) \mid \ldots \mid c_n(x_n)$ would simplify the rules, at the cost of a big gap between theory and practice: Since real implementations need to support nested patterns, the theory fails to model the real complexities of exhaustiveness checking and pattern variable typing. Giving code examples becomes fraught; either we flatten case expressions (resulting in code explosion), or we handwave a lot.

Another option is to support the full syntax of case expressions, *except for as-patterns*, so that pattern variables occur only at the leaves. If subsorting were always structural, as in Davies's system, we could exploit a handy equivalence between patterns and values: if the pattern is x as $c(p_0)$, let-bind x to $c(p_0)$ inside the case arm, letting rule DataI figure out the type of x. But with nominal subsorting, constructing a value is *not* equivalent; see Davies (2005, pp. 234–235) and Dunfield (2007b, pp. 112–113).

Our approach is to support the full syntax, including as-patterns. This approach was taken by Dunfield (2007b, Chap. 4), but our system seems simpler— partly because (except for signature extension) our type system omits indexed types and union types, but also because we avoid embedding typing derivations inside derivations of pattern typing.

Instead, we confine most of the complexity to a single mechanism: a function called intersect, which returns a set of types (and contexts that type as-variables) that represent the intersection between a type and a pattern. The definition of this function is not trivial, but does not refer to expression-level typing.

4.1   Unrefined Pattern Typing, Match Typing, and Pattern Operations

Figure 9 defines a judgment $\mathcal{U} \vdash p : \tau$ that says that pattern p matches values of unrefined type τ under the unrefined signature $\mathcal{U}$.

Rule DataE for case expressions (Fig. 6) invokes a match typing judgment, $\Sigma; \Gamma; p : A \vdash ms : D$. In this judgment, p is a *residual pattern* that represents the space of possible values. For the first arm in a case expression, no patterns have yet failed to match, so the residual pattern in the premise of DataE is $\_$.

Each arm, of the form $p_1 \Rightarrow e_1$, is checked by rule TypeMs (Fig. 10). The leftmost premises check that the type A corresponds to the pattern type τ. The middle "for all" checks e_1 under various assumptions produced by the intersect

$\boxed{\mathcal{U} \vdash p : \tau}$ Pattern p is suitable for values of unrefined type τ

$$\frac{}{\mathcal{U} \vdash \_ : \tau}\text{ p-Wild} \qquad \frac{\mathcal{U} \vdash p : \tau}{\mathcal{U} \vdash (x \text{ as } p) : \tau}\text{ p-As} \qquad \frac{}{\mathcal{U} \vdash \emptyset : \tau}\text{ p-Empty} \qquad \frac{}{\mathcal{U} \vdash () : 1}\text{ p-Unit}$$

$$\frac{\mathcal{U} \vdash p_1 : \tau \quad \mathcal{U} \vdash p_2 : \tau}{\mathcal{U} \vdash (p_1 \sqcup p_2) : \tau}\text{ p-Or} \qquad \frac{\mathcal{U} \vdash p_1 : \tau_1 \quad \mathcal{U} \vdash p_2 : \tau_2}{\mathcal{U} \vdash (p_1, p_2) : \tau_1 * \tau_2}\text{ p-Pair} \qquad \frac{\mathcal{U} \vdash c : (\tau \to d) \quad \mathcal{U} \vdash p : \tau}{\mathcal{U} \vdash c(p) : d}\text{ p-Con}$$

Fig. 9. Pattern type rules

$$\boxed{\Sigma; \Gamma; p : A \vdash ms : D} \quad \begin{array}{l}\text{For a scrutinee of type A that matches residual pattern p,}\\ \text{check each match in ms against D}\end{array}$$

$$\begin{array}{c}\begin{array}{ccc}\Sigma \vdash A \sqsubseteq \tau \\ \mathcal{U} \vdash p_1 : \tau\end{array} \quad \begin{array}{c}\text{for all } (\Gamma' \vdash B)\\ \in \text{intersect}(\Sigma \vdash A; p \cap p_1):\\ \Sigma; \Gamma, \Gamma' \vdash e_1 : D\end{array} \quad \Sigma; \Gamma; (p \cap \neg p_1) : A \vdash ms : D\\ \hline \Sigma; \Gamma; p : A \vdash \big((p_1 \Rightarrow e_1) \mid ms\big) : D\end{array} \text{TypeMs}$$

$$\dfrac{\text{intersect}(\Sigma \vdash A; p) = \emptyset}{\Sigma; \Gamma; p : A \vdash \emptyset : D} \text{TypeMsEmpty}$$

Fig. 10. Match typing

function (Sect. 4.2) with respect to the pattern $p \cap p_1$, ensuring that if p_1 matches the value at run time, the arm is well-typed. The last premise moves on to the remaining matches; there, we know that the value did not match p_1, so we subtract p_1 from the previous residual pattern p—expressed as $p \cap \neg p_1$. These operations are defined in the appendix (Fig. 13).

When typing reaches the end of the matches, $ms = \emptyset$ in rule TypeMsEmpty, we check that the case expression is exhaustive by checking that intersect returns $\emptyset$. For case expressions that are syntactically exhaustive, such as a case expression over lists that has both Nil and Cons arms, the residual pattern p will be the empty pattern $\emptyset$; the intersect function on an empty pattern returns $\emptyset$.

We define pattern complement $\neg p$ and pattern intersection $p_1 \cap p_2$ in the appendix (Fig. 13). For example, $\neg\_ = \emptyset$. No types appear in these definitions, but the complement of a constructor pattern $c(p_0)$ uses the (implicit) unrefined signature $\mathcal{U}$. Our definition of pattern complement never generates as-patterns, so we need not define intersection for as-patterns.

$$\boxed{\text{intersect}(\Sigma \vdash A; p) = \overrightarrow{B^*}} \quad \begin{array}{l}\text{Intersection of type A with pattern p}\\ \text{where each } B^* \text{ has the form } (\Gamma' \vdash B')\end{array}$$

$$\begin{array}{rcl}\text{intersect}(\Sigma \vdash A; \_) &=& \big\{(\cdot \vdash A)\big\}\\[2pt] \text{intersect}(\Sigma \vdash A; \emptyset) &=& \emptyset\\[2pt] \text{intersect}(\Sigma \vdash A; x \text{ as } p) &=& \big\{(\Gamma', x : B \vdash B) \mid (\Gamma' \vdash B) \in \text{intersect}(\Sigma \vdash A; p)\big\}\\[2pt] \text{intersect}(\Sigma \vdash A; p_1 \sqcup p_2) &=& \text{intersect}(\Sigma \vdash A; p_1) \cup \text{intersect}(\Sigma \vdash A; p_2)\\[2pt] \text{intersect}(\Sigma \vdash A_1 * A_2; (p_1, p_2)) &=& \big\{(\Gamma_1, \Gamma_2 \vdash B_1 * B_2) \mid (\Gamma_1 \vdash B_1) \in \text{intersect}(\Sigma \vdash A_1; p_1)\\ && \quad \text{and } (\Gamma_2 \vdash B_2) \in \text{intersect}(\Sigma \vdash A_2; p_2)\big\}\\[2pt] \text{intersect}(\Sigma \vdash s; c(p_0)) &=& \big\{(\Gamma' \vdash s_c) \mid (c : A_c \to s_c) \in \Sigma \text{ and } \Sigma \vdash s_c \preceq s\\ && \quad \text{and } (\Gamma' \vdash B) \in \text{intersect}(\Sigma \vdash A_c; p_0)\big\}\end{array}$$

Fig. 11. Intersection of a type with a pattern

4.2   The intersect function

We define a function intersect that builds the "intersection" of a type and a pattern. Given a signature Σ, type A and pattern p, the intersect function returns a (possibly empty) set of *tracks* $\{(\Gamma_1' \vdash B_1), \ldots, (\Gamma_n' \vdash B_n)\}$. Each track $(\Gamma' \vdash B)$ has a list of typings Γ' (giving the types of as-variables) and a type B that represents the subset of values inhabiting A that also match p. The union of B_1 through B_n constitutes the intersection of A and p. We call these "tracks" because each one represents a possible shape of the values that match p, and the type-checking "train" must check a given case arm under each track's Γ'.

Many of the clauses in the definition of intersect (see Fig. 10) are straightforward. The intersection of A with the wildcard $\_$ is just $\{(\cdot \vdash A)\}$. Dually, the intersection of A with the empty pattern $\emptyset$ is the empty set. In the same vein, the intersection of A with the or-pattern $p_1 \sqcup p_2$ is the union of two intersections (A with p_1, and A with p_2). The intersection of a product $A_1 * A_2$ with a pair pattern is the union of products of the pointwise intersections.

The most interesting case is when we intersect a sort s with a pattern of the form $c(p_0)$. For this case, intersect iterates through all the constructor declarations in Σ that could have been used to create the given value: those of the form $(c : A_c \to s_c)$ where $s_c \preceq s$. For each such declaration, it calls intersect on A_c and p_0. For each resulting track $(\Gamma' \vdash B)$, it returns a track $(\Gamma' \vdash s_c)$.

Optimization. In practice, it may be necessary to optimize the result of intersect. If $\Sigma = (\text{list}, \text{empty})\langle \text{empty} \preceq \text{list}, \text{Nil} : 1 \to \text{empty}, \text{Cons} : \text{empty} \to \text{list}, \text{Cons} : \text{list} \to \text{list}\rangle$ then intersect$(\Sigma \vdash \text{Cons}(\text{xas}\_); \text{list})$ returns $\{(x : \text{empty} \vdash \text{list}), (x : \text{list} \vdash \text{list})\}$. Since any case arm that checks under $x : \text{list}$ will check under $x : \text{empty}$, there is no point in trying to check under $x : \text{empty}$. Instead, we should check only under $x : \text{list}$. A similar optimization in the Stardust type checker could reduce the size of the set of tracks by "about an order of magnitude" Dunfield (2007b, p.112).

Missing Clauses? As is standard in typed languages, pattern matching doesn't look inside λ, so intersect needs no clause for $\to / \lambda$. If we can't match on an arrow type, we don't need to match on intersections of arrows. The other useful case of intersection is on sorts, $s_1 \wedge s_2$. However, an intersection of sorts can be obtained by declaring a new sort below s_1 and s_2 with the appropriate constructor typings, so we omit such a clause from the definition.

Comparison to an Earlier System. A declarative system of rules in Dunfield (2007b, Chap. 4) appears to be a conservative extension of intersect: the earlier system supports a richer type system, but for the features in common, the information produced is similar to that of intersect. The earlier system was based on a judgment $\Sigma \vdash p \Leftarrow A \rhd (e \Leftarrow D)$. To clarify the connection to the present system, we adjust notation; for example, we make Σ explicit.

The meta-variables Σ, p, and A directly correspond to the arguments to intersect, while e and D correspond to e_1 and D in our rule TypeMs. No meta-variables correspond directly to the tracks in the *result* of intersect, but within

$\Sigma \vdash p \Leftarrow A \rhd (e \Leftarrow B)$, we find subderivations of $B + \Gamma \vdash \text{FORGETTYPE} \rhd e \Leftarrow$
D, where the set of pairs $\langle \Gamma, B \rangle$ indeed correspond to the result of intersect.

Cutting through the differences in the formalism, and omitting rules for unions and other features not present in this paper, the earlier system behaves like intersect. For example, $\langle p_1, p_2 \rangle$ was also handled by considering each component, and assembling all resulting combinations. Perhaps most importantly, $c(p_0)$ was also handled by considering each constructor type in the signature, filtering out inappropriate codomains, and recursing on p_0. A rule for $\wedge$ appears in the declarative system in Dunfield (2007b, Chap. 4), but the rule was never implemented, and seems not to be needed in practice.

Since the information given by the older system is precise enough to check interesting invariants of actual programs, our definition of intersect should also be precise enough.

5   Operational Semantics

We prove our results with respect to a call-by-value, small-step operational semantics. The main judgment form is $e \mapsto e'$, which uses evaluation contexts ε. Stepping case expressions is modelled using a judgment $\text{ms} \mapsto_v e'$, which compares each pattern in ms against the value v being cased upon. This comparison is handled by the judgment p match $v \longrightarrow \theta$, which says that θ is evidence that p matches v (that is, $[\theta]p = v$). The rules are in Fig. 14 in the appendix.

6   Metatheory

This section gives definitions, states some lemmas and theorems, and discusses their significance in proving our main results. For space reasons, we summarize a number of lemmas; their full statements appear in the appendix. All proofs are also relegated to the appendix.

Subtyping and Subsorting. Subtyping is reflexive and transitive (Lemmas (Lemmas 6–7). We define what it means for signature extension to preserve subsorting:

Definition 1 (Preserving subsorting). *Given Σ_1 and Σ_2, we say that Σ_2 preserves subsorting of Σ_1 iff for all sorts $s, t \in \text{dom}(\Sigma_1)$, if $\Sigma_1, \Sigma_2 \vdash s \preceq t$ then $\Sigma_1 \vdash s \preceq t$.*

This definition allows new sorts in $\text{dom}(\Sigma_2)$ to be subsorts or supersorts of the old sorts in $\text{dom}(\Sigma_1)$, provided that the subsort relation between the old sorts doesn't change.

If two signatures do not have subsortings that cross into each other's domain, they are *non-adjacent*; non-adjacent signatures preserve subsorting.

Definition 2 (Non-adjacency). *Two signatures Σ_1 and Σ_2 are non-adjacent iff each signature contains no subsortings of the form $s_1 \preceq s_2$ or $s_2 \preceq s_1$, where $s_1 \in \text{dom}(\Sigma_1)$ and $s_2 \in \text{dom}(\Sigma_2)$.*

Theorem 1 (Non-adjacent preservation).
*If Σ_2 preserves subsorting of Σ_1 and Σ_3 preserves subsorting of Σ_1
and Σ_2 and Σ_3 are non-adjacent then Σ_3 preserves subsorting of (Σ_1, Σ_2).*

Strengthening, Weakening, and Substitution. Theorem 4 (Weakening) will allow
the assumptions in a judgment to be changed in two ways: (1) the signature may
be strengthened by replacing a signature (Σ, Σ') with a signature $(\Sigma, \Omega, \Sigma')$; and
(2) the context may be strengthened by replacing Γ with a context Γ^+ in which
any typing assumption $(x : A) \in \Gamma$ can be replaced with $(x : A^+) \in \Gamma$, if $A \le A^+$.

Repeatedly applying (1) with different Ω leads to a more general notion of
strengthening a signature:

Definition 3. *A signature Σ' is stronger than Σ, written $\Sigma' \le_{\mathsf{sig}} \Sigma$, if Σ' can
be obtained from Σ by inserting entire signatures at any position in Σ.*

We often use the less general notion (inserting a single Ω), which simplifies
proofs. For any result stated less generally, however, the more general strengthening of Definition 3 can be shown by induction on the number of blocks inserted.

Definition 4. *Under Σ, a context Γ' is stronger than Γ, written $\Sigma \vdash \Gamma' \le_{\mathsf{ctx}} \Gamma$,
if for each $(x : A') \in \Gamma'$, there exists $(x : A) \in \Gamma$ such that $\Sigma \vdash A' \le A$.*

Several lemmas show weakening. Lemma 8 says that Σ in $\Sigma \vdash \mathcal{J}$ can be
replaced by a stronger Σ', where $\mathcal{J}$ has the form A *type* or $s_1 \preceq s_2$ or $A \le B$ or
$c : A \to s$ or $A \sqsubset \tau$ or $c : C$. Lemma 9 says that $(\Sigma, \Omega, \Sigma')$ can replace (Σ, Σ')
in $\Sigma, \Sigma'; S\langle K \rangle \vdash c : A \to s$ *safe at* t.Lemma 10 allows the sort t' in the judgment
$\Sigma; S\langle K \rangle \vdash c : A \to s$ *safe at* t' to be replaced by a supersort t.

Using the above lemmas and Theorem 1, we can show that the key judgment
"$\cdots c : A {\to} s$ safe" can be weakened by inserting Ω inside the signature:

Theorem 2 (Weakening 'safe').
*If (Σ, Σ') sig and (Σ, Ω) sig and $\mathsf{dom}(\Sigma') \cap \mathsf{dom}(\Omega) = \emptyset$ and $\mathsf{dom}(\Sigma, \Omega, \Sigma') \cap S = \emptyset$
and K does not mention anything in $\mathsf{dom}(\Omega)$ and $S\langle K \rangle$ preserves subsorting for
(Σ, Σ') and $(c : A \to s) \in K$ and $\Sigma, \Sigma'; S\langle K \rangle \vdash c : A \to s$ safe then $\Sigma, \Omega, \Sigma'; S\langle K \rangle \vdash
c : A \to s$ safe.*

With this additional lemma, we have weakening for the judgments involved
in checking that a signature is well-formed, so we can show that if Σ is safely
extended by Σ' and separately by Ω, then Ω and Σ', together, safely extend Σ.

Theorem 3 (Signature Interleaving).
If (Σ, Σ') sig and (Σ, Ω) sig and $\mathsf{dom}(\Sigma') \cap \mathsf{dom}(\Omega) = \emptyset$ then $(\Sigma, \Omega, \Sigma')$ sig.

Ultimately, we will show type preservation; in the preservation case for the
Declare rule, we extend the signature in a premise. We therefore need to show
that the typing judgment can be weakened. Since the typing rules for matches
involve the intersect function, we need to show that a stronger input to intersect
yields a stronger output; that is, a longer (stronger) signature yields a stronger
type B_+ (a subtype of B) and a stronger context Γ_+ typing as-variables.

Definition 5. *Under a signature* Σ, *a track* $(\Gamma_+ \vdash B_+)$ *is stronger than* $(\Gamma \vdash B)$, *written* $\Sigma \vdash (\Gamma_+ \vdash B_+) \leq_{trk} (\Gamma \vdash B)$, *if and only if* $\Sigma \vdash \Gamma_+ \leq_{ctx} \Gamma$ *and* $\Sigma \vdash B_+ \leq B$.

A set of tracks $\overrightarrow{B^*_+}$ *is stronger than* $\overrightarrow{B^*}$, *written* $\overrightarrow{B^*_+} \leq_{trk} \overrightarrow{B^*}$, *if and only if, for each track* $(\Gamma_+ \vdash B_+) \in \overrightarrow{B^*_+}$, *there exists a track* $(\Gamma \vdash B) \in \overrightarrow{B^*}$ *such that* $(\Gamma_+ \vdash B_+) \leq_{trk} (\Gamma \vdash B) \in \overrightarrow{B^*}$.

Lemma 13 says that the result of intersect on a stronger signature is stronger. We can then show that weakening holds for the typing judgment itself, along with substitution typing (defined in the appendix) and match typing.

Theorem 4 (Weakening).
If (Σ, Σ') *sig*, (Σ, Ω) *sig*, $\mathrm{dom}(\Sigma') \cap \mathrm{dom}(\Omega) = \emptyset$ *and* $\Sigma, \Omega, \Sigma' \vdash \Gamma^+ \leq_{ctx} \Gamma$ *then*

(1) If $\Sigma, \Sigma'; \Gamma \vdash e : A$ *then* $\Sigma, \Omega, \Sigma'; \Gamma^+ \vdash e : A$.
(2) If $\Sigma, \Sigma'; \Gamma \vdash \theta : \Gamma'$ *then* $\Sigma, \Omega, \Sigma'; \Gamma^+ \vdash \theta : \Gamma'$.
(3) If $\Sigma, \Sigma'; \Gamma; p : A \vdash ms : D$ *then* $\Sigma, \Omega, \Sigma'; \Gamma^+; p : A \vdash ms : D$.

Properties of Values. Substitution properties (Lemmas 14 and 15) and inversion (or *canonical forms*) properties (Lemma 16) hold.

Type Preservation and Progress. The last important piece needed for type preservation is that intersect does what it says: if a value v matches p, then v has type B where B is one of the outputs of intersect.

Theorem 5 (Intersect). *If* Σ *sig and* $\Sigma; \cdot \vdash v : A$ *and* $\Sigma \vdash A$ *type and* p *match* $v \longrightarrow \theta$ *and* $\mathrm{intersect}(\Sigma \vdash A; p) = \overrightarrow{B^*}$ *then there exists* $(\Gamma' \vdash B) \in \overrightarrow{B^*}$ *s.t.* $\Sigma; \cdot \vdash v : B$ *and* $\Sigma; \cdot \vdash \theta : \Gamma'$ *where* $\Sigma \vdash B$ *type and* $\Sigma \vdash B \leq A$.

The preservation result allows for a longer signature, to model entering the scope of a declare expression or the arms of a match. We implicitly assume that, in the given typing derivation, all types are well-formed under the local signature: for any subderivation of $\Sigma; \Gamma \vdash e' : B$, it is the case that $\Sigma \vdash B$ *type*.

Theorem 6 (Preservation).
If Σ *sig and* $\Sigma; \cdot \vdash e : A$ *and* $e \mapsto e'$ *then there exists* Σ' *such that* $\Sigma, \Sigma' \vdash e' : A$ *where* (Σ, Σ') *sig*.

Theorem 7 (Progress). *If* Σ *sig and* $\Sigma; \cdot \vdash e : A$ *then* e *is a value or there exists* e' *such that* $e \mapsto e'$.

7   Bidirectional Typing

The type assignment system in Fig. 6 is not syntax-directed, because the rules Sub and $\wedge$I apply to any shape of expression. Nor is the system directed by the syntax of types: rule Sub can conclude $e : B$ for any type B that is a supertype of some other type A. Finally, while the choice to apply rule Data I is guided by the shape of the expression—it must be a constructor application $c(e)$—the resulting sort is not uniquely determined, since the signature can have multiple constructor typings for c.

Fortunately, obtaining an algorithmic system is straightforward, following previous work with datasort refinements and intersection types. We follow the bidirectional typing recipe of Davies and Pfenning (2000); Davies (2005); Dunfield and Pfenning (2004):

1. Split the typing judgment into checking $\Sigma; \Gamma \vdash e \Leftarrow A$ and synthesis $\Sigma; \Gamma \vdash e \Rightarrow A$ judgments. In the checking judgment, the type A is input (it might be given via type annotation); in the synthesis judgment, the type A is output.
2. Allow change of direction: Change the subsumption rule to synthesize a type, then check if it is a subtype of a type being checked against; add an annotation rule that checks e against A in the annotated expression $(e : A)$.
3. In each introduction rule, e.g. $\rightarrow$I, make the conclusion a checking judgment; in each elimination rule, e.g. DataE, make the premise that contains the eliminated connective a synthesis judgment.
4. Make the other judgments in the rules either checking or synthesizing, according to what information is available. For example, the premise of $\rightarrow$I becomes a checking judgment, because we know B from the conclusion.
5. Since the subsumption rule cannot synthesize, add rules such as Syn$\wedge$E$_1$, which were admissible in the type assignment system.

This yields the rules in Fig. 12. (Rules for the match typing judgment $\Sigma; \Gamma; p : A \vdash ms \Leftarrow B$ can be obtained from Fig. 10 by replacing ":" in "$e_1 : D$" and

---

$$\boxed{\Sigma;\Gamma \vdash e \Leftarrow A \quad \Sigma;\Gamma \vdash e \Rightarrow A} \quad \text{Expr. } e \text{ checks against } (\Leftarrow) \text{ / synthesizes } (\Rightarrow) \text{ type } A$$

$$\frac{}{\Sigma;\Gamma,x:A,\Gamma' \vdash x \Rightarrow A}\text{SynVar} \qquad \frac{\Sigma;\Gamma \vdash e \Rightarrow A \quad \Sigma \vdash A \leq B}{\Sigma;\Gamma \vdash e \Leftarrow B}\text{ChkSub} \qquad \frac{A \in \vec{A} \quad \Sigma;\Gamma \vdash e \Leftarrow A}{\Sigma;\Gamma \vdash (e:\vec{A}) \Rightarrow A}\text{SynAnno}$$

$$\frac{\Sigma;\Gamma,x:A \vdash e \Leftarrow B}{\Sigma;\Gamma \vdash (\lambda x.\, e) \Leftarrow (A \rightarrow B)}\text{Chk}\rightarrow\text{I} \qquad \frac{\Sigma;\Gamma \vdash e_1 \Rightarrow (A \rightarrow B) \quad \Sigma;\Gamma \vdash e_2 \Leftarrow A}{\Sigma;\Gamma \vdash e_1\, e_2 \Rightarrow B}\text{Syn}\rightarrow\text{E}$$

$$\frac{\Sigma;\Gamma \vdash v \Leftarrow A_1 \quad \Sigma;\Gamma \vdash v \Leftarrow A_2}{\Sigma;\Gamma \vdash v \Leftarrow (A_1 \wedge A_2)}\text{Chk}\wedge\text{I} \qquad \frac{\Sigma;\Gamma \vdash e \Rightarrow (A_1 \wedge A_2) \quad k \in \{1,2\}}{\Sigma;\Gamma \vdash e \Rightarrow A_k}\text{Syn}\wedge\text{E}_k$$

$$\frac{\Sigma;\Gamma \vdash e_1 \Leftarrow A_1 \quad \Sigma;\Gamma \vdash e_2 \Leftarrow A_2}{\Sigma;\Gamma \vdash (e_1, e_2) \Leftarrow A_1 * A_2}\text{Chk}*\text{I} \qquad \frac{}{\Sigma;\Gamma \vdash () \Leftarrow 1}\text{Chk1I}$$

$$\frac{\Sigma \vdash c:A \rightarrow s \quad \Sigma;\Gamma \vdash e \Leftarrow A}{\Sigma;\Gamma \vdash c(e) \Leftarrow s}\text{ChkDataI} \qquad \frac{\Sigma;\Gamma \vdash e \Rightarrow A \quad \Sigma;\Gamma;\_:A \vdash ms \Leftarrow B}{\Sigma;\Gamma \vdash (\text{case } e \text{ of } ms) \Leftarrow B}\text{ChkDataE}$$

$$\frac{(\Sigma,\Sigma')\; sig \quad \Sigma \vdash B\; type \quad \Sigma,\Sigma';\Gamma \vdash e \Leftarrow B}{\Sigma;\Gamma \vdash (\text{declare } \Sigma' \text{ in } e) \Leftarrow B}\text{ChkDeclare}$$

Fig. 12. Bidirectional typing rules

"ms : D" with "⇐".) While this system is much more algorithmic than Fig. 6, the presence of intersection types requires backtracking: if we apply a function of type (even → odd) ∧ (odd → even), we need to synthesize even → odd first; if we subsequently fail (e.g. if the argument has type odd), we backtrack and try odd → even. Similarly, if the signature contains several typings for a constructor c, we may need to try rule ChkDataI with each typing.

Type-checking for this system is almost certainly PSPACE-complete (Reynolds 1996); however, the experience of Davies (2005) shows that a similar system, differing primarily in whether the signature can be extended, is practical if certain techniques, chiefly memoization, are used.

Using these rules, annotations are required exactly on (1) the entire program e (if e is a checked form, such as a λ) and (2) expressions not in normal form, such as a λ immediately applied to an argument, a recursive function declaration, or a let-binding (assuming the rule for let synthesizes a type for the bound expression). Rules with "more synthesis"—such as a synthesizing version of ∗I— could be added along the lines of previous bidirectional type systems (Xi 1998; Dunfield and Krishnaswami 2013).

Following Davies (2005), an annotation can list several types A. Rule SynAnno chooses one of these, backtracking if necessary. Multiple types may be needed if a λ-term is checked against intersection type: when checking (λx. x) against (even → even) ∧ (odd → odd), the type of x will be even inside the left subderivation of Chk∧I, but odd inside the right subderivation. Thus, if we annotate x with even, the check against odd → odd fails; if we annotate x with odd, the check against even → even fails. For a less contrived example, and for a variant annotation form that reduces backtracking, see Dunfield and Pfenning (2004).

In the appendix, we prove that our bidirectional system is sound and complete with respect to our type assignment system:

Theorem 8 (Bidirectional soundness).
If $\Gamma \vdash e \Leftarrow A$ *or* $\Gamma \vdash e \Rightarrow A$ *then* $\Gamma \vdash |e| : A$ *where* $|e|$ *is* e *with all annotations erased.*

Theorem 9 (Annotatability).
If $\Gamma \vdash e : A$ *then:*

(1) There exists $e_\Leftarrow$ *such that* $|e_\Leftarrow| = e$ *and* $\Gamma \vdash e_\Leftarrow \Leftarrow A$.
(2) There exists $e_\Rightarrow$ *such that* $|e_\Rightarrow| = e$ *and* $\Gamma \vdash e_\Rightarrow \Rightarrow A$.

We also prove that the ⇒ and ⇐ judgments are decidable (Appendix, Theorem 10).

8   Related Work

Datasort Refinements. Freeman and Pfenning (1991) introduced datasort refinements with intersection types, defined the refinement restriction (where A ∧ B is well-formed only if A and B are refinements of the same type), and developed an inference algorithm in the spirit of abstract interpretation. As discussed earlier, the lack of annotations not only makes the types difficult to see, but makes inference prone to finding long, complex types that include accidental invariants.

Davies (2005), building on the type system developed by Davies and Pfenning (2000), used a bidirectional typing algorithm, guided by annotations on redexes. This system supports parametric polymorphism through a front end based on Damas–Milner inference, but—like Freeman's system—does not support extensible refinements. Davies's CIDRE implementation (Davies 2013) goes beyond his formalism by allowing a single type to be refined via multiple declarations, but this has no formal basis; CIDRE appears to simply gather the multiple declarations together, and check the entire program using the combined declaration, even when this violates the expected scoping rules of SML declarations.

Datasort refinements were combined with union types and indexed types by Dunfield and Pfenning (2003, 2004), who noticed the expressive power of nominal subsorting, called "invaluable refinement" (Dunfield 2007b, pp. 113, 220–230).

Giving multiple refinement declarations for a single datatype was mentioned early on, as future work: "embedded refinement type declarations" (Freeman and Pfenning 1991, p. 275); "or even ... declarations that have their scope limited" (Freeman 1994, p. 167); "it does seem desirable to be able to make local datasort declarations" (Davies 2005, p. 245). But the idea seems not to have been pursued.

Logical Frameworks. In the logical framework LF (Harper et al. 1993), data is characterized by declaring constructors with their types. In this respect, our system is closer to LF than to ML: LF doesn't require all of a type's constructors to be declared together. By itself, LF has no need for inversion principles. However, systems such as Twelf (Pfenning and Schürmann 1999), Delphin (Poswolsky and Schürmann 2009) and Beluga (Pientka and Dunfield 2010) use LF as an object-level language but also provide meta-level features. One such feature is coverage (exhaustiveness) checking, which needs inversion principles for LF types. Thus, these systems mark a type as *frozen* when its inversion principle is applied (to process %covers in Twelf, or a case expression in Beluga); they also allow the user to mark types as frozen. These systems lack subtyping and subsorting; once a type is frozen, it is an error to declare a new constructor for it.

Lovas (2010) extended LF with refinements and subsorting, and developed a constraint-based algorithm for signature checking. This work did not consider meta-level features such as coverage checking, so it yields no immediate insights about inversion principles or freezing. Since Lovas's system takes the subsorting relation directly from declarations, rather than by inferring it from a grammar, it supports what Dunfield (2007b) called invaluable refinements; see Lovas's example (Lovas 2010, pp. 145–147).

Indexed Types and Refinement Types. As the second generation of datasort refinements (exemplified by the work of Davies and Pfenning) began, so did a related approach to lightweight type-based verification: *indexed types* or *limited dependent types* (Xi and Pfenning 1999; Xi 1998), in which datatypes are refined by indices drawn from a (possibly infinite) constraint domain. Integers with linear inequalities are the standard example of an index domain; another good example is physical units or dimensions (Dunfield 2007a). More recent work in this vein, such as liquid types (Rondon et al. 2008), uses "refinement types" for a mechanism close to indexed types.

Datasort refinements have always smelled like a special case of indexed types. At the dawn of indexed types (and the second generation of datasort refinements), the relationship was obscured by datasorts' "fellow traveller", intersection types, which were absent from the first indexed type systems, and remain absent from the approaches now called "refinement types". That is, while datasorts themselves strongly resemble a specific form of indices—albeit related by a partial order (subtyping), rather than by equality—and would thus suggest that indexed type systems subsume datasort refinement type systems, the inclusion of intersection types confounds such a comparison. Intersection types *are* present, along with both datasorts and indices, in Dunfield and Pfenning (2003) and Dunfield (2007b); the relationship is less obscured. But no one has given an encoding of types with datasorts into types with indices, intersections or no.

The focus of this paper is a particular kind of *extensibility* of datasort refinements, so it is natural to ask whether indexed types and (latter-day) refinement types have anything similar. Indexed types are not immediately extensible: both Xi's DML and Dunfield's Stardust require that a given datatype be refined exactly once. Thus, a particular list type may carry its length, or the value of its largest element, or the parity of its boolean elements. By refining the type with a tuple of indices, it may also carry combinations of these, such as its length *and* its largest element. Subsequent uses of the type can leave out some of the indices, but the combination must be stated up front.

However, some of the approaches descended from DML, such as liquid types, allow refinement with a predicate that can mention various attributes. These attributes are declared separately from the datatype; adding a new attribute does not invalidate existing code. Abstract refinement types (Vazou et al. 2013) even allow types to quantify over predicates.

Setting aside extensibility, datasort refinements can express certain invariants more clearly and succinctly than indexed types (and their descendants).

Program Analysis. Koot and Hage (2015) formulate a type system that analyzes where exceptions can be raised, including match exceptions raised by nonexhaustive case expressions. This system appears to be less precise than datasorts, but has advantages typical to program analysis: no type annotations are required.

9   Future Work

Modular Refinements. This paper establishes a critical mechanism for extensible refinements, safe signature extension, in the setting of a core language without modules: refinements are lexically scoped. To scale up to a language with modules, we need to ask: what notions of scope are appropriate? For example, a strict λ-calculus interpreter could be refined with a sort val of values, while a lazy interpreter could be refined with a sort whnf of terms in weak head normal form. If every val is a whnf, we might want to have val $\preceq$ whnf. In the present system, these two refinements could be in separate `declare` blocks; in that case, val and whnf could not both be in scope, and the subsorting is not well-formed. Alternatively, one `declare` block could be nested inside the other. In that case, val $\preceq$ whnf could be given in the nested block, since it would not add new subsortings within the outer refinement. In a system with modules, we would likely want to have val $\preceq$ whnf, at least for clients of *both* modules; such backpatching is currently not allowed, but should be safe since the new subsorting crosses two independent signature blocks (the block declaring val and the block declaring whnf) without changing the subsortings within each block.

Type Polymorphism. Standard parametric polymorphism is absent in this paper, but it should be feasible to follow the approach of Davies (2005), as long as the unrefined datatype declarations are not themselves extensible (which would break signature well-formedness, even without polymorphism).

Datasort Polymorphism. Extensible signatures open the door to sort-bounded polymorphism. In our current system, a function that iterates over an abstract syntax tree and α-renames free variables—which would conventionally have the type exp $\to$ exp—must be duplicated, even though the resulting tree has the same shape and the same constructors, and therefore should always produce a tree of the same sort as the input tree (at least, if the free variables are not specified with datasorts). We would like the function to check against a polymorphic type $\forall\alpha\preceq$exp. $\alpha \to \alpha$, which works for any sort α below exp.

We would like to reason "backwards" from a pattern match over a polymorphic sort variable α. For example, if a value of type α matches the pattern Plus(x1, x2), then we know that Plus : $(\alpha_1 * \alpha_2) \to \alpha$ for some sorts α_1 and α_2. The recursive calls on x1 and x2 must preserve the property of being in α_1 and α_2, so Plus(f x1, f x2) has type α, as needed. The mechanisms we have developed may be a good foundation for adding sort-bounded polymorphism: the intersect function would need to return a signature, as well as a context and type, so that the constructor typing Plus : $(\alpha_1 * \alpha_2) \to \alpha$ can be made available.

Implementation. Currently, we have a prototype of a few pieces of the system, including a parser and implementations of the Σ *sig* judgment and the intersect function. Experimenting with these pieces was helpful during the design of the system (and reassured us that the most novel parts of our system can be implemented), but they fall short of a usable implementation.

References

Comon, H., Dauchet, M., Gilleron, R., Jacquemard, F., Lugiez, D., Tison, S., Tommasi, M.: Tree automata techniques and applications (2008). https://gforge.inria.fr/frs/download.php/file/10994/tata.pdf. Accessed 18 Nov 2008

Cousot, P., Cousot, R.: Abstract interpretation: a unified lattice model for static analysis of programs by construction or approximation of fixpoints. In: Principles of Programming Languages, pp. 238–252 (1977)

Davies, R.: Practical refinement-type checking. Ph.D. thesis, Carnegie Mellon University, CMU-CS-05-110 (2005)

Davies, R.: SML checker for intersection and datasort refinements (pronounced "cider") (2013). https://github.com/rowandavies/sml-cidre

Davies, R., Pfenning, F.: Intersection types and computational effects. In: ICFP, pp. 198–208 (2000)

Dunfield, J.: Refined typechecking with stardust. In: Programming Languages Meets Program Verification (PLPV 2007) (2007a)

Dunfield, J.: A unified system of type refinements. Ph.D. thesis, Carnegie Mellon University, CMU-CS-07-129 (2007b)

Dunfield, J., Krishnaswami, N.R.: Complete and easy bidirectional typechecking for higher-rank polymorphism. In: ICFP (2013). arXiv:1306.6032

Dunfield, J., Pfenning, F.: Type assignment for intersections and unions in call-by-value languages. In: Gordon, A.D. (ed.) FoSSaCS 2003. LNCS, vol. 2620, pp. 250–266. Springer, Heidelberg (2003). doi:10.1007/3-540-36576-1_16

Dunfield, J., Pfenning, F.: Tridirectional typechecking. In: Principles of Programming Languages, pp. 281–292 (2004)

Freeman, T.: Refinement types for ML. Ph.D. thesis, Carnegie Mellon University, CMU-CS-94-110 (1994)

Freeman, T., Pfenning, F.: Refinement types for ML. In: Programming Language Design and Implementation, pp. 268–277 (1991)

Gentzen, G.: Untersuchungen über das logische Schließen. Mathematische Zeitschrift **39**, 176–210, 405–431 (1934). English translation, Investigations into logical deduction. In: Szabo, M. (ed.) Collected Papers of Gerhard Gentzen, pp. 68–131. North-Holland (1969)

Harper, R., Honsell, F., Plotkin, G.: A framework for defining logics. J. ACM **40**(1), 143–184 (1993)

Kennedy, A.: Programming languages and dimensions. Ph.D. thesis, University of Cambridge (1996)

Koot, R., Hage, J.: Type-based exception analysis for non-strict higher-order functional languages with imprecise exception semantics. In: Proceedings of the Workshop on Partial Evaluation and Program Manipulation, pp. 127–138 (2015)

Lovas, W.: Refinement types for logical frameworks. Ph.D. thesis, Carnegie Mellon University, CMU-CS-10-138 (2010)

Pfenning, F., Schürmann, C.: System description: Twelf—a meta-logical framework for deductive systems. In: Ganzinger, H. (ed.) CADE 1999. LNCS (LNAI), vol. 1632, pp. 202–206. Springer, Heidelberg (1999). doi:10.1007/3-540-48660-7_14

Pientka, B., Dunfield, J.: Beluga: a framework for programming and reasoning with deductive systems (system description). In: Giesl, J., Hähnle, R. (eds.) IJCAR 2010. LNCS (LNAI), vol. 6173, pp. 15–21. Springer, Heidelberg (2010). doi:10.1007/978-3-642-14203-1_2

Poswolsky, A., Schürmann, C.: System description: Delphin–a functional programming language for deductive systems. In: International Workshop on Logical Frameworks and Meta-Languages: Theory and Practice (LFMTP 2008). Electronic Notes in Theoretical Computer Science, vol. 228, pp. 135–141 (2009)

Reynolds, J.C.: Types, abstraction, and parametric polymorphism. In: Information Processing 83, pp. 513–523. Elsevier (1983). http://www.cs.cmu.edu/afs/cs/user/jcr/ftp/typesabpara.pdf

Reynolds, J.C.: Design of the programming language Forsythe. Technical report CMU-CS-96-146, Carnegie Mellon University (1996)

Rondon, P., Kawaguchi, M., Jhala, R.: Liquid types. In: Programming Language Design and Implementation, pp. 159–169 (2008)

Vazou, N., Rondon, P.M., Jhala, R.: Abstract refinement types. In: Felleisen, M., Gardner, P. (eds.) ESOP 2013. LNCS, vol. 7792, pp. 209–228. Springer, Heidelberg (2013). doi:10.1007/978-3-642-37036-6_13

Wright, A.K.: Simple imperative polymorphism. Lisp Symbolic Comput. **8**(4), 343–355 (1995)

Xi, H.: Dependent types in practical programming. Ph.D. thesis, Carnegie Mellon University (1998)

Xi, H., Pfenning, F.: Dependent types in practical programming. In: Principles of Programming Languages, pp. 214–227 (1999)

Zeilberger, N.: The logical basis of evaluation order and pattern-matching. Ph.D. thesis, Carnegie Mellon University, CMU-CS-09-122 (2009)

Programs Using Syntax with First-Class Binders

Francisco Ferreira[(✉)] and Brigitte Pientka

McGill University, Montreal, Canada
{fferre8,bpientka}@cs.mcgill.ca

Abstract. We present a general methodology for adding support for higher-order abstract syntax definitions and first-class contexts to an existing ML-like language. As a consequence, low-level infrastructure that deals with representing variables and contexts can be factored out. This avoids errors in manipulating low-level operations, eases the task of prototyping program transformations and can have a major impact on the effort and cost of implementing such systems.

We allow programmers to define syntax in a variant of the logical framework LF and to write programs that analyze these syntax trees via pattern matching as part of their favorite ML-like language. The syntax definitions and patterns on syntax trees are then eliminated via a translation using a deep embedding of LF that is defined in ML. We take advantage of GADTs which are frequently supported in ML-like languages to ensure our translation preserves types. The resulting programs can be type checked reusing the ML type checker, and compiled reusing its first-order pattern matching compilation. We have implemented this idea in a prototype written for and in OCaml and demonstrated its effectiveness by implementing a wide range of examples such as type checkers, evaluators, and compilation phases such as CPS translation and closure conversion.

Keywords: Higher-order abstract syntax · Programming with binders · Functional programming · ML

1 Introduction

Writing programs that manipulate other programs is a common activity for a computer scientist, either when implementing interpreters, writing compilers, or analyzing phases for static analysis. This is so common that we have programming languages that specialize in writing these kinds of programs. In particular, ML-like languages are well-suited for this task thanks to recursive data types and pattern matching. However, when we define syntax trees for realistic input languages, there are more things on our wish list: we would like support for representing and manipulating variables and tracking their scope; we want to compare terms up-to α-equivalence (i.e. the renaming of bound variables); we would like to avoid implementing capture avoiding substitutions, which is tedious and error-prone. ML languages typically offer no high-level abstractions or support for manipulating variables and the associated operations on abstract syntax trees.

H. Yang (Ed.): ESOP 2017, LNCS 10201, pp. 504–529, 2017.
DOI: 10.1007/978-3-662-54434-1_19

Over the past decade, there have been several proposals to add support for defining and manipulating syntax trees into existing programming environments. For example: FreshML [22], the related system Romeo [23], and Caml [20] use Nominal Logic [18] as a basis and the Hobbits library for Haskell [25] uses a name based formalism. In this paper, we show how to extend an existing (functional) programming language to define abstract syntax trees with variable binders based on higher-order abstract syntax (HOAS) (sometimes also called λ-trees [11]). Specifically, we allow programmers to define object languages in the simply-typed λ-calculus where programmers use the intentional function space of the simply typed λ-calculus to define binders (as opposed to the extensional function space of ML). Hence, HOAS representations inherit α-renaming from the simply-typed λ-calculus and we can model object-level substitution for HOAS trees using β-reduction in the underlying simply-typed λ-calculus. We further allow programmers to express whether a given sub-tree in the HOAS tree is closed by using the necessity modality of S4 [6]. This additional expressiveness is convenient to describe that sub-trees in our abstract syntax tree are closed.

Our work follows the pioneering work of HOAS representations in the logical framework LF [9]. On the one hand we restrict it to the simply-typed setting to integrate it smoothly into existing simply-typed functional programming languages such as OCaml, and on the other hand we extend its expressiveness by allowing programmers to distinguish between closed and open parts of their syntax trees. As we analyze HOAS trees, we go under binders and our sub-trees may not remain closed. To model the scope of binders in sub-trees we pair a HOAS tree together with its surrounding context of variables following ideas from Beluga [12,15]. In addition, we allow programmers to pattern match on such contextual objects, i.e. an HOAS tree together with its surrounding context.

Our contribution is two-fold: First, we present a general methodology for adding support for HOAS tree definitions and first-class contexts to an existing (simply-typed) programming language. In particular, programmers can define simply-typed HOAS definitions in the syntactic framework (SF) based on modal S4 following [6,12]. In addition, programmers can manipulate and pattern match on well-scoped HOAS trees by embedding HOAS objects together with their surrounding context into the programming language using contextual types [15]. The result is a programming language that can express computations over open HOAS objects. We describe our technique abstractly and generically using a language that we call Core-ML. In particular, we show how Core-ML with first-class support for HOAS definitions and contexts can be translated in into a language Core-ML^{gadt} that supports Generalized Abstract Data Types (GADTs) using a deep (first-order) embedding of SF and first-class contexts (see Fig. 1 for an overview). We further show that our translation preserves types.

Second, we show how this methodology can be realized in OCaml by describing our prototype Babybel [1]. In our implementation of Babybel we take advantage of the sophisticated type system, in particular GADTs, that OCaml provides to ensure our translation is type-preserving. By translating HOAS objects

---

[1] available at www.github.com/fferreira/babybel/.

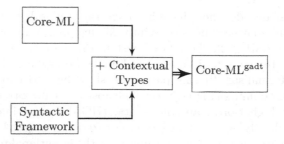

Fig. 1. Adding contextual types to ML

together with their context to a first-order representation in OCaml with GADTs we can also reuse OCaml's first-order pattern matching compilation allowing for a straightforward compilation. Programmers can also exploit OCaml's impure features such as exceptions or references when implementing programs that manipulate HOAS syntax trees. We have used Babybel to implement a type-checker, an evaluator, closure conversion (shown in Sect. 2.3 together with a variable counting example and a syntax desugaring examples), and a continuation passing style translation. These examples demonstrate that our approach allows programmers to write programs that operate over abstract syntax trees in a manner that is safe and effective.

Finally, we would like to stress that our translation which eliminates the language extensions and permits programmers to define, analyze and manipulate HOAS trees is not specific to OCaml or even to simple types in our implementation. The same approach could be implemented in Haskell, and with some care (to be really useful it would need an equational theory for substitutions) this technique can be extended to a dependently typed language.

2   Main Ideas

In this section, we show some examples that illustrate the use of Babybel, our proof of concept implementation where we embed the syntactic framework SF inside OCaml. To smoothly integrate SF into OCaml, Babybel defines a PPX filter (a mechanism for small syntax extensions for OCaml). In particular, we use attributes and quoted strings to implement our syntax extension.

2.1   Example: Removing Syntactic Sugar

In this example, we describe the compact and elegant implementation of a compiler phase that de-sugars programs functional programs with let-expressions by translating them into function applications. We first specify the syntax of a simple functional language that we will transform. To do this we embed the syntax specification using this tag:

    [@@@signature {def| ... |def}]

Inside the **@@@signature** block we will embed our SF specifications.

Our source language is defined using the type `tm`. It consists of constants (written as `cst`), pairs (written as `pair`), functions (built using `lam`), applications (built using `app`), and let-expressions.

```
[@@@signature {def|
tm : type.
cst      : tm.
pair     : tm → tm → tm.
lam      : (tm → tm) → tm.
fst      : tm → tm.
snd      : tm → tm.
letpair  : tm → (tm → tm → tm) → tm.
letv     :  tm → (tm → tm) → tm.
app      : tm → tm → tm.
|def}]
```

Our definition of the source language exploits HOAS using the function space of our syntactic framework SF to represent binders in our object language. For example, the constructor `lam` takes as an argument a term of type `tm → tm`. Similarly, the definition of let-expressions models variable binding by falling back to the function space of our meta-language, in our case the syntactic framework SF. As a consequence, there is no constructor for variables in our syntactic definition and moreover we can reuse the substitution operation from the syntactic framework SF to model substitution in our object language. This avoids building up our own infrastructure for variables bindings.

We now show how to simplify programs written in our source language by replacing uses of `letpair` in terms with projections, and uses of `letv` by β reduction. Note how we use higher-order abstract syntax to represent let-expressions and abstractions.

$$\texttt{letv } M \ (\lambda \texttt{x}.N) \equiv N[M/\texttt{x}]$$
$$\texttt{letpair } M \ (\lambda \texttt{x}.\lambda \texttt{y}. \ N) \equiv N[(\texttt{fst } M \ )/\texttt{x}, (\texttt{snd } M)/\texttt{y}]$$

To implement this simplification phase we implement an OCaml program `rewrite`: it analyzes the structure of our terms, calls itself on the sub-terms, and eliminates the use of the let-expressions into simpler constructs. As we traverse terms, our sub-terms may not remain closed. For simplicity, we use the same language as source and target for our transformation. We therefore specify the type of the function `rewrite` using contextual types pairing the type `tm` together with a context γ in which the term is meaningful inside the tag [`@type .... `].

`rewrite[@type ` $\gamma . [\gamma \vdash$ `tm]`$\to [\gamma \vdash$ `tm]]`

The type can be read: for all contexts γ, given a `tm` object in the context γ, we return a `tm` object in the same context. In general, contextual types associate a context and a type in the syntactic framework SF. For example if we want to specify a term in the empty context we would write [$\vdash$ `tm]` or for a term that depends on some context with at least one variable and potentially more we would write [γ,`x:tm` $\vdash$ `tm]`.

We now implement the function `rewrite` by pattern matching on the structure of a contextual term. In Babybel, contextual terms are written inside boxes (⦇...⦈) and contextual patterns inside (⦇...⦈$_p$).

```
let rec rewrite[@type γ.[γ ⊢ tm]→[γ ⊢ tm]]
= function
| ⦇ cst ⦈ₚ → ⦇cst⦈
| ⦇ pair 'm 'n ⦈ₚ → let mm, nn = rewrite m, rewrite n
                     in ⦇pair 'mm 'nn⦈
| ⦇ fst 'm ⦈ₚ → let mm = rewrite m in ⦇fst 'mm⦈
| ⦇ snd 'm⦈ₚ →  let mm = rewrite m in ⦇snd 'mm⦈
| ⦇ app 'm 'n ⦈ₚ → let mm,nn = rewrite m, rewrite n in
                     ⦇app 'mm 'nn⦈
| ⦇ lam (λx. 'm) ⦈ₚ → let mm = rewrite m in ⦇lam (λx. 'mm)⦈
| ⦇ #x ⦈ₚ → ⦇#x⦈
| ⦇ letpair 'm (λf.λs. 'n) ⦈ₚ → let mm = rewrite m in
                     rewrite ⦇'n [snd 'mm;fst 'mm]⦈
| ⦇ letv 'm (λx. 'n) ⦈ₚ → rewrite ⦇'n['m]⦈
```

Note that we are pattern matching on potentially open terms. Although we do not write the context γ explicitly, in general patterns may mention their context (i.e.: ⦇_ ⊢ cst⦈$_p$ [2]. As a guiding principle, we may omit writing contexts, if they do not mention variables explicitly and are irrelevant at run-time. Inside patterns or terms, we specify incomplete terms using quoted variables (e.g.: 'm). Quoted variables are an 'unboxing' of a computational expression inside the syntactic framework SF. The quote signals that we are mentioning the computational variable inside SF.

The interesting cases are the let-expressions. For them, we perform the rewriting according to the two rules given earlier. The syntax of the substitutions puts in square brackets the terms that will be substituted for the variables. We consider contexts and substitutions ordered, this allows for efficient implementations and more lightweight syntax (e.g.: substitutions omit the name of the variables because contexts are ordered). Importantly, the substitution is an operation that is eagerly applied during run-time and not part of the representation. Consequently, the representation of the terms remains normal and substitutions cannot be written in patterns. We come back to this design decision later.

To translate contextual SF objects and contexts, Babybel takes advantage of OCaml's advanced type system. In particular, we use Generalized Abstract Data Types [4, 26] to index types with the contexts in which they are valid. Type indices, in particular contexts, are then erased at run-time.

2.2   Finding the Path to a Variable

In this example, we compute the path to a specific variable in an abstract syntax tree describing a lambda-term. This will show how to specify particular context

---

[2] The underscore means that there might be a context but we do not bind any variable for it because contexts are not available at run-time.

shapes, how to pattern match on variables, how to manage our contexts, and how the Babybel extensions interact seamlessly with OCaml's impure features. For this example, we concentrate on the fragment of terms that consists only of abstractions and application which we repeat here.

```
[@@@signature {def|
tm : type.
app : tm → tm → tm.
lam : (tm → tm) → tm.
|def}]
```

To find the first occurrence of a particular variable in the HOAS tree, we use backtracking that we implement using the user-defined OCaml exception Not_found. To model the path to a particular variable occurrence in the HOAS tree, we define an OCaml data type step that describes the individual steps we take and finally model a path as a list of individual steps.

```
exception Not_found
type step
= Here   (*the path ends here*)
| AppL   (*take left on app*)
| AppR   (*take right on app*)
| InLam  (*go inside the body of the term*)
type path = step list
```

The main function path_aux takes as input a term that lives in a context with at least one variable and returns a path to the occurrence of the top-most variable or an empty list, if the variable is not used. Its type is:

```
[@type γ. [γ, x:tm ⊢ tm] → path].
```

We again quantify over all contexts γ and require that the input term is meaningful in a context with at least one variable. This specification simply excludes closed terms since there would be no top-most variable. Note also how we mix in the type annotation to this function both contextual types and OCaml data types.

```
let rec path_aux [@type γ.[γ, x:tm ⊢ tm] → path]
= function
| (|_, x ⊢ x|)ₚ→ [Here]
| (|_, x ⊢ #y|)ₚ→ raise Not_found
| (|_, x ⊢ lam (λy. 'm)|)ₚ→ InLam::(path_aux(|_,x,y ⊢ 'm[_;y;x]|))
| (|_, x ⊢ app 'm 'n|)ₚ→ try AppL::(path_aux m)
                         with _ → AppR::(path_aux n)
```

All patterns in this example make the context explicit, as we pattern match on the context to identify whether the variable we encounter refers to the top-most variable declaration in the context. The underscore simply indicates that there might be more variables in the context. The first case, matches against the bound variable x. The second case has a special pattern with the sharp symbol, the pattern #y matches against any variable in the context _, x. Because of the first pattern if it had been x it would have matched the first case. Therefore, it simply raises the exception to backtrack to the last choice we had.

The case for lambda expressions is interesting because the recursive call happens in an extended context. Furthermore, in order to keep the variable we are searching for on top, we need to swap the two top-most variables. For that purpose, we apply the [_ ; y; x] substitution. In this substitution the underscore stands for the identity on the rest of the context, or more precisely, the appropriate shift in our internal representation that relies on de Bruijn encoding. Once elaborated, this substitution becomes [↑2 ; y; x] where the shift by two arises, because we are swapping variables as opposed to instantiating them.

The final case is for applications. We first look on the left side and if that raises an exception we catch it and search again on the right. We again use quoted variables (e.g.: 'm) to bind and refer to ML variables in patterns and terms of the syntactic framework and more generally be able to describe incomplete terms.

```
let get_path [@type γ.[γ, x:tm ⊢ tm] → path]
= fun t → try path_aux t with _ → []
```

The get_path function has the same type as the path_aux function. It simply handles the exception and returns an empty path in case that variable x is not found in the term.

2.3   Closure Conversion

In the final example, we describe the implementation of a naive algorithm for closure conversion for untyped λ-terms following [3]. We take advantage of the syntactic framework SF to represent source terms (using the type family tm) and closure-converted terms (using the type family ctm). In particular, we use SF's closed modality box to ensure that all functions in the target language are closed. This is impossible when we simply use LF as the specification framework for syntax as in [3]. We omit here the definition of lambda-terms, our source language, that was given in the previous section and concentrate on the target language ctm.

```
[@@@signature {def|
ctm: type.   % closed term
btm: type.   % binder term
sub: type.   % environment

capp    : ctm → ctm → ctm.
clam    : {btm} → ctm.
clo     : ctm → sub → ctm.
embed   : ctm → btm.
bind    : (ctm → btm) → btm.

empty   : sub.
dot     : sub → ctm → sub.
|def}]
```

Applications in the target language are defined using the constructor `capp` and simply take two target terms to form an application. Functions (constructor `clam`), however, take a `btm` object wrapped in {} braces. This means that the object inside the braces is closed. The curly braces denote the internal closed modality of the syntactic framework. As the original functions may depend on variables in the environment, we need closures where we pair a function with a substitution that points to the appropriate environment. We define our own substitutions explicitly, because they are part of the target language and the built-in substitution is an operation on terms that is eagerly computed away. Inside the body of the function, we need to bind all the variables from the environment that the body uses such that later we can instantiate them applying the substitution. This is achieved by defining multiple bindings using constructors `bind` and `embed` inside the term.

When writing a function that translates between representations, their open terms depend on contexts that store assumptions of different representations and it is often the case that one needs to relate these contexts. In our example here we define a context relation that keeps the input and output contexts in sync using a GADT data type `rel` in OCaml where we model contexts as types. The relation statically checks correspondence between contexts, but it is also available at run-time (i.e. after type-erasure).

```
type (_ , _) rel  =
    Empty : ([.], [.]) rel
  | Both  : ([γ], [δ]) rel →   ([γ, x:tm], [δ, y:ctm]) rel


exception Error of string

let rec lookup [@type γ δ.[γ ⊢ tm]→(γ, δ) rel→[δ ⊢ ctm]] =
fun t → function
| Both r' → begin match t with
   | ( _,x ⊢ x )ₚ → (_,x ⊢ x)
   | ( _,x ⊢ ##v )ₚ → let v1 = lookup (#v) r'
                      in (_, x ⊢ 'v1 [_])
   | _ → raise Error (''Term that is not a variable'')
| Empty → raise Error (''Term is not a variable'')
end
```

The function `lookup` searches for related variables in the context relation. If we have a source context γ,x:tm and a target context δ,y:ctm, then we consider two variable cases: In the first case, we use matching to check that we are indeed looking for the top-most variable x and we simply return the corresponding target variable. If we encounter a variable from the context, written as ##v, then we recurse in the smaller context stripping off the variable declaration x. Note that ##v denotes a variable from the context _, that is not x, while #v describes a variable from the context _, x, i.e. it could be also x. The recursive call returns the corresponding variable v1 in the target context that does not include the variable declaration x. We hence need to weaken v1 to ensure it is meaningful in the original context. We therefore associate 'v1 with the identity substitution for the appropriate context, namely: [_]. In this case, it will be elaborated into a one variable shift in the internal de Bruijn representation that is used in our implementation. The last case returns an exception whenever we are trying to look up in the context something that is not a variable.

As we cannot express at the moment in the type annotation that the input to the lookup function is indeed only a variable from the context γ and not an arbitrary term, we added another fall-through case for when the context is empty. In this case the input term cannot be a variable, as it would be out of scope.

Finally, we implement the function conv which takes an untyped source term in a context γ and a relation of source and target variables, described by (γ, δ) rel and returns the corresponding target term in the target context δ.

```
let rec close [@type γ δ. (γ, δ) rel→[δ ⊢ btm]→[btm]]
= fun r m → match r with
| Empty → m
| Both r → close r ⦇bind (λx. 'm)⦈

let rec envr [@type γ δ. (γ, δ)rel→[δ ⊢ sub]]
= fun r → match r with
| Empty → ⦇empty⦈
| Both r →
  let s = envr r in ⦇_, x ⊢ dot ('s[_]) x⦈

let rec conv [@type γ δ.(γ, δ)rel→[γ ⊢tm]→[δ ⊢ctm]]
= fun r m → match m with
| ⦇ lam (λx. 'n)  ⦈p →
  let mc = conv (Both r) n in
  let mb = close r ⦇bind(λx. embed 'mc)⦈
  in let s = envr r in ⦇clo (clam {'mb}) 's⦈
| ⦇#x⦈p → lookup ⦇#x⦈ r
| ⦇app 'm 'n⦈p → let mm, nn = conv r m, conv r n in
                 ⦇capp 'mm 'nn⦈
```

The core of the translation is defined in functions conv, envr, and close. The main function is conv. It is implemented by recursion on the source term. There are three cases: (i) source variables simply get translated by looking them up in the context relation, (ii) applications just get recursively translated each term in the application, and (iii) lambda expressions are translated recursively by converting the body of the expression in the extended context (notice the recursive call with Both r) and then turning the lambda expression into a closure.

In the first step we generate the closed body by the function close that adds the multiple binders (constructors bind and embed) and generates the closed term. Note that the return type [btm] of close guarantees that the final result is indeed a closed term, because we omit the context. For clarity, we could have written [⊢ btm].

Finally, the function `envr` computes the substitution (represented by the type `sub`) for the closure.

The implementation of closure conversion shows how to enforce closed terms in the specification, and how to make contexts and their relationships explicit at run-time using OCaml's GADTs. We believe it also illustrates well how HOAS trees can be smoothly manipulated and integrated into OCaml programs that may use effects.

3   Core-ML: A Functional Language with Pattern Matching and Data Types

We now introduce Core-ML, a functional language based on ML with pattern matching and data types. In Sect. 5 we will extend this language to also support contextual types and terms in our syntactic framework SF.

We keep the language design of Core-ML minimal in the interest of clarity. However, our prototype implementation which we describe in Sect. 9 supports interaction with all of OCaml's features such as exceptions, references and GADTs.

$$
\begin{array}{lll}
\text{Types} & \tau ::= D \mid \tau_1 \rightarrow \tau_2 \\
\text{Expressions} & e ::= i \mid \mathtt{fun}\, f(x) = e \mid \mathtt{let}\, x = i\, \mathtt{in}\, e \mid \mathtt{match}\, i\, \mathtt{with}\, \overrightarrow{b} \\
\text{Neutral Exp.} & i ::= i\, .e.\mid C\, \overrightarrow{e} \mid x \mid e : \tau \\
\text{Patterns} & pat ::= C\, \overrightarrow{pat} \mid x \\
\text{Branches} & b ::= \mid pat \mapsto e \\
\text{Contexts} & \Gamma ::= \cdot \mid \Gamma, x : \tau \\
\text{Signature} & \Xi ::= \cdot \mid \Xi, D \mid \Xi, C : \overrightarrow{\tau} \rightarrow D
\end{array}
$$

In Core-ML, we declare data-types by adding type formers (D) and type constructors (C) to the signature (Ξ). Constructors must be fully-applied. In addition all functions are named and recursive. The language supports pattern matching with nested patterns where patterns consist of just variables and fully applied constructors. We assume that all patterns are linear (i.e. each variable occurs at most once) and that they are covering.

The bi-directional typing rules for Core-ML have access to a signature Ξ and are standard (see Fig. 2). For lack of space, we omit the operational semantics which is standard. We also will not address the details of pattern matching compilation but merely state that it is possible to implement it in an efficient manner using decision trees [1].

4   A Syntactic Framework

In this section we describe the Syntactic Framework (SF) based on S4 [6]. Our framework characterizes only normal forms. All computation is delegated to the ML layer, that will perform pattern matching and substitutions on terms.

$\boxed{\Gamma \vdash e \Leftarrow \tau}$: Expression e checks against type τ in context Γ

$$\dfrac{\Gamma, f : \tau \to \tau', x : \tau \vdash e \Leftarrow \tau'}{\Gamma \vdash \mathbf{fun}\, f(x) = e \Leftarrow \tau \to \tau'}\ \text{t-rec} \qquad \dfrac{\Gamma \vdash i \Rightarrow \tau' \quad \Gamma, x : \tau' \vdash e \Leftarrow \tau}{\Gamma \vdash \mathbf{let}\, x = i\ \mathbf{in}\ e \Leftarrow \tau}\ \text{t-let}$$

$$\dfrac{\Gamma \vdash i \Rightarrow \tau' \quad \forall b_k \in \vec{b}\ .\ \Gamma \vdash b_k \Leftarrow \tau' \to \tau}{\Gamma \vdash \mathbf{match}\, i\, \mathbf{with}\ \vec{b} \Leftarrow \tau}\ \text{t-match} \qquad \dfrac{\Gamma \vdash i \Rightarrow \tau' \quad \tau = \tau'}{\Gamma \vdash i \Leftarrow \tau}\ \text{t-emb}$$

$\boxed{\Gamma \vdash i \Rightarrow \tau}$: Neutral expr. i synthesizes type τ in context Γ

$$\dfrac{\Gamma \vdash e \Leftarrow \tau}{\Gamma \vdash e : \tau \Rightarrow \tau}\ \text{t-ann} \qquad \dfrac{\Xi(C) = \vec{\tau} \to D \quad \forall \tau_i \in \vec{\tau}\ .\ \forall e_i \in \vec{e}\ .\ \Gamma \vdash e_i \Leftarrow \tau_i}{\Gamma \vdash C\,\vec{e} \Rightarrow D}\ \text{t-constr}$$

$$\dfrac{\Gamma \vdash i \Rightarrow \tau' \to \tau \quad \Gamma \vdash e \Leftarrow \tau'}{\Gamma \vdash i\,e \Rightarrow \tau}\ \text{t-app} \qquad \dfrac{\Gamma(x) = \tau}{\Gamma \vdash x \Rightarrow \tau}\ \text{t-var}$$

$\boxed{\Gamma \vdash |\ pat \mapsto e \Leftarrow \tau_1 \to \tau_2}$: Branch $|\ pat \mapsto e$ checks against types τ_1 and τ_2 in Γ

$$\dfrac{\vdash pat : \tau' \downarrow \Gamma' \quad \Gamma, \Gamma' \vdash e \Leftarrow \tau}{\Gamma \vdash |\ pat \mapsto e \Leftarrow \tau' \to \tau}\ \text{t-branch}$$

$\boxed{\vdash pat : \tau \downarrow \Gamma}$: Pattern pat is of type τ and binds variables in context Γ

$$\dfrac{}{\vdash x : \tau \downarrow x : \tau}\ \text{t-pat-var}$$

$$\dfrac{\Xi(C) = \vec{\tau} \to D \quad \forall \tau_i \in \vec{\tau}\ .\ \forall pat_i \in \vec{pat}\ .\ \vdash pat_i : \tau_i \downarrow \Gamma_i}{\vdash C\,\vec{pat} : D \downarrow \Gamma_1, ..., \Gamma_i}\ \text{t-pat-con}$$

Fig. 2. Core-ML typing rules

4.1   The Definition of SF

The Syntactic Framework (SF) is a simply typed λ-calculus based on S4 where the type system forces all variables to be of base type, and all constants declared in a signature Σ to be fully applied. This simplifies substitution, as variables of base type cannot be applied to other terms, and in consequence, there is no need for hereditary substitution in the specification language. Finally, the syntactic framework supports the box type to describe closed terms [13]. It can also be viewed as a restricted version of the contextual modality in [12] which could be an interesting extension to our work.

Having closed objects enforced at the specification level is not strictly necessary. However, being able to state that some objects are closed in the specification has two distinct advantages: first, the user can specify some objects as closed so their contexts are always empty. This removes the need for some unnecessary substitutions. Second, it allows us to encode more fine-grained invariants and is hence an important specification tool (i.e. when implementing closure conversion inSect. 2.3).

$$\begin{array}{ll}
\text{Types} & A, B ::= \mathbf{a} \mid A \to B \mid \Box A \\
\text{Terms} & M, N ::= \mathbf{c}\, \overrightarrow{M} \mid \lambda x.M \mid \{M\} \mid x \\
\text{Contexts} & \Psi, \Phi ::= \cdot \mid \Psi, x : \mathbf{a} \\
\text{Signature} & \Sigma ::= \cdot \mid \Sigma, \mathbf{a} : K \mid \Sigma, \mathbf{c} : A
\end{array}$$

Figure 3 shows the typing rules for the syntactic framework. Note that constructors always are fully applied (as per rule t-con), and that all variables are of base type as enforced by rules t-var and t-lam.

$$\boxed{\Psi \vdash M : A} : M \text{ has type } A \text{ in context } \Psi$$

$$\frac{\Psi, x : \mathbf{a} \vdash M : A}{\Psi \vdash \lambda x.M : \mathbf{a} \to A} \ \text{t-lam} \qquad \frac{\cdot \vdash M : A}{\Psi \vdash \{M\} : \Box A} \ \text{t-box} \qquad \frac{\Psi(x) = \mathbf{a}}{\Psi \vdash x : \mathbf{a}} \ \text{t-var}$$

$$\frac{\Sigma(\mathbf{c}) = A \quad \Psi \vdash \overrightarrow{M} : A/\mathbf{a}}{\Psi \vdash \mathbf{c}\, \overrightarrow{M} : \mathbf{a}} \ \text{t-con}$$

$$\boxed{\Psi \vdash \overrightarrow{M} : A/\mathbf{a}} : \text{spine } \overrightarrow{M} \text{ checks against type } A \text{ and has target type } \mathbf{a}$$

$$\frac{}{\Psi \vdash \cdot : \mathbf{a}/\mathbf{a}} \ \text{t-sp-em} \qquad \frac{\Psi \vdash N : A \quad \Psi \vdash \overrightarrow{M} : B/\mathbf{a}}{\Psi \vdash N, \overrightarrow{M} : A \to B/\mathbf{a}} \ \text{t-sp}$$

Fig. 3. Syntactic framework typing

4.2 Contextual Types

We use contextual types to embed possibly open SF objects in Core-ML and ensure that they are well-scoped. Contextual types pair the type A of an SF object together with its surrounding context Ψ in which it makes sense. This follows the design of Beluga [3,15].

$$\begin{array}{ll}
\text{Contextual Types} & U ::= [\Psi \vdash A] \\
\text{Type Erased Contexts} & \hat{\Psi} ::= \cdot \mid \hat{\Psi}, x \\
\text{Contextual Objects} & C ::= [\hat{\Psi} \vdash M]
\end{array}$$

Contextual objects, written as $[\hat{\Psi} \vdash M]$ pair the term M with the variable name context $\hat{\Psi}$ to allow for α-renaming of variables occurring in M. Note how the $\hat{\Psi}$ context just corresponds to the context with the typing assumptions erased.

When we embed contextual objects in a programming language we want to refer to variables and expressions from the ambient language, in order to support incomplete terms. Following [12,15], we extend our syntactic framework SF with two ideas: first, we have incomplete terms with meta-variables to describe holes in terms. As in Beluga, there are two different kinds: *quoted variables* 'u represent a hole in the term that may be filled by an arbitrary term. In contrast, *parameter variables* v represent a hole in a term that may be filled only with some bound variable from the context. Concretely, a parameter variable may be #x and describe any concrete variable from a context Ψ. We may also want to restrict what bound variables a parameter variable describes. For example, if we have two sharp signs (i.e. ##x) the top-most variable declaration is excluded. Intuitively, the number of sharp signs, after the first, in front of x correspond to a weakening (or in de Bruijn lingo the number of shifts). Second, substitution operations allow us to move terms from one context to another.

We hence extend the syntactic framework SF with quoted variables, parameter variables and closures, written as $M[\sigma]_\Psi^\Phi$. We annotate the substitution with its domain and range to simplify the typing rule, however our prototype omits these typing annotations and lets type inference infer them.

$$
\begin{array}{lll}
\text{Parameter Variables} & \text{v} ::= \text{\#x} \mid \text{\#v} \\
\text{Terms} & M ::= \ldots \mid \text{'u} \mid \text{v} \mid M[\sigma]_\Psi^\Phi \\
\text{Substitutions} & \sigma ::= \cdot \mid \sigma, M/x \\
\text{Ambient Ctx.} & \Gamma ::= \ldots \mid \Gamma, \text{u} : [\Psi \vdash \text{a}]
\end{array}
$$

In addition, we extend the context Γ of the ambient language Core-ML to keep track of assumptions that have a contextual type.

Finally, we extend the typing rules of the syntactic framework SF to include quoted variables, parameter variables, closures, and substitutions. We keep all the previous typing rules for SF from Sect. 4 where we thread through the ambient Γ, but the rules remain unchanged otherwise.

$\boxed{\Gamma; \Psi \vdash_v \text{v} : \text{a}}$: Parameter Variable v has type **a** in contexts Ψ and Γ

$$
\frac{\Gamma(x) = [\Psi \vdash \text{a}]}{\Gamma; \Psi \vdash_v \text{\#x} : \text{a}} \text{ t-pvar-v} \qquad \frac{\Gamma; \Psi \vdash_v \text{v} : \text{a}}{\Gamma; \Psi, y : \_ \vdash_v \text{\#v} : \text{a}} \text{ t-pvar-\#}
$$

$\boxed{\Gamma; \Psi \vdash M : A}$: Term M has type A in contexts Ψ and Γ

$$
\frac{\Gamma(\text{u}) = [\Psi \vdash \text{a}]}{\Gamma; \Psi \vdash \text{'u} : \text{a}} \text{ t-qvar} \qquad \frac{\Gamma; \Psi \vdash_v \text{v} : \text{a}}{\Gamma; \Psi \vdash \text{v} : \text{a}} \text{ t-pvar}
$$

$$
\frac{\Gamma; \Psi \vdash \sigma : \Phi \quad \Gamma; \Phi \vdash M : A}{\Gamma; \Psi \vdash M[\sigma]_\Psi^\Phi : A} \text{ t-sub}
$$

$\boxed{\Gamma; \Psi \vdash \sigma : \Psi'}$: Substitution σ has domain Ψ' and range Ψ in the amb. ctx. Γ

$$
\frac{}{\Gamma; \Psi \vdash \cdot : \cdot} \text{ t-empty-sub} \qquad \frac{\Gamma; \Psi \vdash \sigma : \Psi' \quad \Gamma; \Psi \vdash M : \text{a}}{\Gamma; \Psi \vdash \sigma, M/x : (\Psi', x : \text{a})} \text{ t-dot-sub}
$$

The rules for quoted variables (t-qvar) and parameter variables (t-pvar) might seem very restrictive as we can only use a meta-variable of type $\Psi \vdash \text{a}$ in the same context Ψ. As a consequence meta-variables often occur as a closure paired with a substitution (i.e.: $\text{'u}[\sigma]_\Psi^\Phi$). This leads to the following admissible rule:

$$
\frac{\Gamma(\text{u}) = [\Phi \vdash \text{a}] \quad \Delta; \Psi \vdash \sigma : \Phi}{\Gamma; \Psi \vdash \text{'u}[\sigma]_\Psi^\Phi : \text{a}} \text{ t-qvar-adm}
$$

The substitution operation is straightforward to define and we omit it here. The next step is to define the embedding of this framework in a programming language that will provide the computational power to analyze and manipulate contextual objects.

5   Core-ML with Contextual Types

To embed contextual SF objects into Core-ML, we extend the syntax of Core-ML as follows:

Types	$\tau ::= \ldots \mid [\Psi \vdash a]$
Expressions	$e ::= \ldots \mid [\hat{\Psi} \vdash M] \mid \texttt{cmatch}\, e\, \texttt{with}\, \vec{c}$
Patterns	$pat ::= \ldots \mid [\hat{\Psi} \vdash R]$
Contextual Branches	$c ::= \ldots \mid\mid [\Psi \vdash R] \mapsto e$

In particular, we allow programmers to directly pattern match on the syntactic structures they define in SF using the case-expression $\texttt{cmatch}\, e\, \texttt{with}\, \vec{c}$.

5.1   SF Objects as SF Patterns

The grammar of SF patterns follows the grammar of SF objects.

SF Parameter Pattern	$w ::= \texttt{\#p} \mid \texttt{\#w}$
SF Patterns	$R ::= \lambda x.R \mid \{R\} \mid x \mid c\, \vec{R} \mid\, 'u \mid w$

However, there is an important restriction: closures are not allowed in SF patterns. Intuitively this means that all quoted variables are associated with the identity substitution and hence depend on the entire context in which they occur. Parameter variables may be associated with weakening substitutions. This allows us to easily infer the type of quoted variables and parameter variables as we type check a pattern. This is described by the judgment

$$\boxed{\Psi \vdash R : A \downarrow \Gamma} : \text{Pattern } R \text{ has type } A \text{ in } \Psi \text{ and binds } \Gamma$$

We omit these rules as they follow closely the typing rules for SF terms that are given in the previous section. We only show here the interesting rules for parameter patterns. They illustrate the built-in weakening.

$$\boxed{\Psi \vdash_v w : a \downarrow \Gamma} : \text{Parameter Pattern } w \text{ has type } a \text{ in } \Psi \text{ and binds } \Gamma$$

$$\frac{}{\Psi \vdash_v \texttt{\#p} : a \downarrow p : [\Psi \vdash a]}\ \text{tp-pvar} \qquad \frac{\Psi \vdash_v w : a \downarrow \Gamma}{\Psi, y : b \vdash_v \texttt{\#w} : a \downarrow \Gamma}\ \text{tp-pvar-\#}$$

Further, the matching algorithm for SF patterns degenerates to simple first-order matching [17] and can be defined straightforwardly. Because of space constraints, we only describe the successful matching operation. However, it is worth considering the matching rules for parameter patterns. As matching will only consider well-typed terms, we know that in the rules m-pv and m-pv-# the variable x is well-typed in the context $\hat{\Psi}$.

$\boxed{\Gamma; \hat{\Psi} \vdash_v w \doteq x/\rho}$: Param. Pattern w matches var. x from $\hat{\Psi}$ producing ρ.

$$\frac{}{\text{p}: [\Psi \vdash A]; \hat{\Psi} \vdash_v \#\text{p} \doteq x/\cdot, [\hat{\Psi} \vdash x]/\text{p}} \ \text{m-pv} \qquad \frac{x \neq y \quad \Gamma; \hat{\Psi} \vdash_v w \doteq x/\rho}{\Gamma; \widehat{\Psi, y} \vdash_v \#w \doteq x/\rho} \ \text{m-pv-\#}$$

$\boxed{\Gamma; \hat{\Psi} \vdash R \doteq M/\rho}$: M matches pattern R with bound vars. in $\hat{\Psi}$ producing ρ.

$$\frac{\Gamma; \hat{\Psi}, x \vdash R \doteq M/\rho}{\Gamma; \hat{\Psi} \vdash \lambda x.R \doteq \lambda x.M/\rho} \ \text{m-}\lambda \qquad \frac{}{\cdot; \hat{\Psi} \vdash x \doteq x/\cdot} \ \text{m-bv}$$

$$\frac{\Gamma; \cdot \vdash R \doteq M/\rho}{\Gamma; \hat{\Psi} \vdash \{R\} \doteq \{M\}/\rho} \ \text{m-box} \qquad \frac{\text{for all } R_i \in \vec{R} \text{ such as } \Gamma; \hat{\Psi} \vdash R_i \doteq M_i/\rho_i}{\Gamma; \hat{\Psi} \vdash \text{c } \vec{R} \doteq \text{c } \vec{M}/\rho_0, \ldots, \rho_n} \ \text{m-cc}$$

$$\frac{}{\text{u}: [\Psi \vdash A]; \hat{\Psi} \vdash \text{'u} \doteq M/\cdot, [\hat{\Psi} \vdash M]/\text{u}} \ \text{m-cv} \qquad \frac{\Gamma; \hat{\Psi} \vdash_v w \doteq x/\rho}{\Gamma; \hat{\Psi} \vdash w \doteq x/\rho} \ \text{m-pv}$$

Finally, it has another important consequence: closures only appear in the branches of case-expressions. As Core-ML has a call-by-value semantics, we know the instantiations of quoted variables and parameter variables when they appear in the body of a case-expression and all closures can be eliminated by applying the substitution eagerly.

5.2   Typing Rules for Core-ML with Contextual Types

We now add the following typing rules for contextual objects and pattern matching to the typing rules of Core-ML:

$$\frac{\Gamma; \Psi \vdash M : \text{a}}{\Gamma \vdash [\hat{\Psi} \vdash M] \Leftarrow [\Psi \vdash \text{a}]} \ \text{t-ctx-obj}$$

$$\frac{\Gamma \vdash i \Rightarrow [\Psi \vdash \text{a}] \quad \forall b \in \vec{b} \ . \ \Gamma \vdash b \Leftarrow [\Psi \vdash \text{a}] \rightarrow \tau}{\Gamma \vdash \text{cmatch } i \text{ with } \vec{b} \Leftarrow \tau} \ \text{t-cm}$$

$$\frac{\Psi \vdash R : \text{a} \downarrow \Gamma' \quad \Gamma, \Gamma' \vdash e \Leftarrow \tau}{\Gamma \vdash [\Psi \vdash R] \mapsto e \Leftarrow [\Psi \vdash \text{a}] \rightarrow \tau} \ \text{t-cbranch}$$

The typing rule for contextual objects (rule t-ctx-obj) simply invokes the typing judgment for contextual objects. Notice, that we need the context Γ when checking contextual objects, as they may contain quoted variables from Γ.

Extending the operational semantics to handle contextual SF objects is also straightforward.

6   Core-ML with GADTs

So far we reviewed how to support contextual types and contextual objects in a standard functional programming language. This allows us to define syntactic structures with binders and manipulate them with the guarantee that variables will not escape their scopes. This brings some of the benefits of the Beluga system to mainstream languages focusing on writing programs instead of proofs. A naive implementation of this language extension requires augmenting the type checker and operational semantics of the host language. This is a rather significant task – especially if it includes implementing a compiler for the extended language. In this section, we describe how to embed Core-ML with contextual types in a functional language with GADTs, called Core-ML^{gadt}, based on $\lambda_{2,G\mu}$ by Xi et al. [26]. The choice of this target language is motivated by the fact that it is close to what realistic typed languages already offer (e.g.: OCaml and Haskell) and it directly lends itself to an implementation.

Signatures	$\Sigma ::= \cdot \mid \Sigma, D : (*, \ldots, *) \to * \mid C : \forall \overrightarrow{\alpha} . \tau \to D[\overrightarrow{\tau}]$
Types	$\tau ::= D[\overrightarrow{\tau}] \mid \forall \alpha . \tau \mid \tau_1 \to \tau_2 \mid \alpha \mid \tau_1 \times \tau_2$
Expressions	$e ::= x \mid C[\overrightarrow{\tau}] e \mid \text{fix } f : \tau = e \mid e_1 e_2 \mid (e_1, e_2) \mid \lambda x . e$
	$\mid \text{let } x = e_1 \text{ in } e_2 \mid \text{match } e \text{ with } \overrightarrow{b} \mid \varLambda \alpha . e \mid e[\tau] \mid (e_1, e_2)$
Branch	$b ::= pat \mapsto e$
Pattern	$pat ::= x \mid C[\overrightarrow{\alpha}] pat \mid (pat_1, pat_2)$
Exp. Ctx.	$\Gamma ::= \cdot \mid \Gamma, x : \tau$
Type Ctx.	$\Delta ::= \cdot \mid \Delta, \alpha \mid \Delta, \tau_1 \equiv \tau_2$

Core-ML^{gadt} contains polymorphism and GADTs, which makes it a good ersatz OCaml that is still small and easy to reason about. GADTs are particularly convenient, since they allow us to track invariants about our objects in a similar fashion to dependent types. Compared to Core-ML, Core-ML^{gadt}'s signatures now store type constants and constructors that are parametrized by other types. We show the typing judgments for the language in Fig. 4.

The operational semantics is fundamentally the same as the semantics for Core-ML, after all, type information is irrelevant at run-time (i.e. Core-ML^{gadt} has strong type separation). The interested reader can find the operational semantics in [26].

7   Deep Embedding of SF into Core-ML^{gadt}

We now show how to translate objects and types defined in the syntactic framework SF into Core-ML^{gadt} using a deep embedding. We take advantage of the advanced features of Core-ML^{gadt}'s type system to fully type-check the result. Our representation of SF objects and types is inspired by [2] but uses GADTs instead of full dependent types. We add the idea of typed context shifts, that represent weakening, to be able to completely erase types at run-time.

$\boxed{\Delta; \Gamma \vdash e : \tau}$: e is of type τ in contexts Δ and Γ.

$$\frac{\Sigma(C) = \forall \vec{\alpha} \, . \, \tau_1 \to D[\vec{\tau}] \quad \Delta; \Gamma \vdash e : \tau_1[\vec{\tau}] \quad \Delta \vdash \vec{\tau} \, \mathtt{wf}}{\Delta; \Gamma \vdash C \vec{\tau} \, e : D[\vec{\tau}]} \quad \text{g-con}$$

$$\frac{\Delta; \Gamma \vdash e_1 : \tau_1 \to \tau_2 \quad \Delta; \Gamma \vdash e_2 : \tau_1}{\Delta; \Gamma \vdash e_1 \, e_2 : \tau_2} \quad \text{g-app} \qquad \frac{\Delta; \Gamma \vdash e_1 : \tau_1 \quad \Delta; \Gamma \vdash e_1 : \tau_2}{\Delta; \Gamma \vdash (e_1, e_2) : \tau_1 \times \tau_2} \quad \text{g-pair}$$

$$\frac{\Gamma(x) = \tau}{\Delta; \Gamma \vdash x : \tau} \quad \text{g-var} \qquad \frac{\Delta; \Gamma, f : \tau \vdash e : \tau}{\Delta; \Gamma \vdash \mathtt{fix} \, f : \tau = e : \tau} \quad \text{g-fix} \qquad \frac{\Delta; \Gamma, x : \tau_1 \vdash e : \tau_2}{\Delta; \Gamma \vdash \lambda x \, . \, e : \tau_1 \to \tau_2} \quad \text{g-lam}$$

$$\frac{\Delta; \Gamma \vdash e : \forall \alpha \, . \, \tau \quad \Delta; \Gamma \vdash \tau \, \mathtt{wf}}{\Delta; \Gamma \vdash e[\tau] : \tau_1} \quad \text{g-tapp} \qquad \frac{\Delta; \Gamma \vdash e_1 : \tau_1 \quad \Delta; \Gamma, x : \tau_1 \vdash e_2 : \tau}{\Delta; \Gamma \vdash \mathtt{let} \, x = e_1 \, \mathtt{in} \, e_2 : \tau} \quad \text{g-let}$$

$$\frac{\Delta, \alpha; \Gamma \vdash e : \tau}{\Delta; \Gamma \vdash \Lambda \alpha \, . \, e : \tau} \quad \text{g-Lam} \qquad \frac{\Delta; \Gamma \vdash e : \tau_1 \quad \text{for all } i. \Delta; \Gamma \vdash b_i : \tau_1 \to \tau}{\Delta; \Gamma \vdash \mathtt{match} \, e \, \mathtt{with} \, \vec{b} : \tau} \quad \text{g-match}$$

$$\frac{\Delta; \Gamma \vdash pat : \tau \downarrow \Delta'; \Gamma' \quad \Delta, \Delta'; \Gamma, \Gamma' \vdash e : \tau_2}{\Delta; \Gamma \vdash pat \mapsto e : \tau_1 \to \tau_2} \quad \text{g-branch}$$

$\boxed{\Delta_o \vdash pat : \tau \downarrow \Delta; \Gamma}$: pat is of type τ and binds variables in Δ and Γ

$$\frac{\Delta_0 \vdash \tau \, \mathtt{wf}}{\Delta_0 \vdash x : \tau \downarrow \cdot; x : \tau} \quad \text{gp-var}$$

$$\frac{\Delta_0 \vdash pat_1 : \tau_1 \downarrow \Delta_1; \Gamma_1 \quad \Delta_0 \vdash pat_2 : \tau_2 \downarrow \Delta_2; \Gamma_2}{\Delta_0 \vdash (pat_1, pat_2) : \tau_1 \times \tau_2 \downarrow \Delta_1, \Delta_2; \Gamma_1, \Gamma_2} \quad \text{gp-pair}$$

$$\frac{\Sigma(C) = \forall \vec{\alpha} \, . \, \tau \to D[\vec{\tau_1}] \quad \Delta_0, \vec{\alpha}, \vec{\tau_1} \equiv \vec{\tau_2} \vdash pat : \tau \downarrow \Delta; \Gamma}{\Delta_o \vdash C[\vec{\alpha}] \, pat : D[\vec{\tau_2}] \downarrow \vec{\alpha}, \vec{\tau_1} \equiv \vec{\tau_2}, \Delta; \Gamma} \quad \text{gp-con}$$

Fig. 4. The typing of Core-ML^{gadt}

To ensure SF terms are well-scoped and well-typed, we define SF types in Core-ML^{gadt} and index their representations by their type and context. The following types are only used as indices for GADTs. Because of that, they do not have any term constructors.

$$\Sigma = \mathtt{base} : * \to *, \mathtt{arr} : (*, *) \to *, \mathtt{boxed} : * \to *, \mathtt{prod} : (*, *) \to *, \mathtt{unit} : *$$

We define three type families, one for each of SF's type constructors. It is important to note the number of type parameters they require. Base types take one parameter: a type from the signature. Function types simply have a source and target type. Finally, boxes contain just one type.

Terms are also indexed by the contexts in which they are valid. To this effect, we define two types to statically represent contexts. Analogously to the representation of types, these two types are only used statically and there will be no instances at run-time. The type $\mathtt{nil}$ represents an empty context and thus has no parameters. The constructor $\mathtt{cons}$ has two parameters, the first one is the rest of the context and the second one is the type of the top-most variable.

$$\Sigma = \ldots, \mathtt{nil} : *, \mathtt{cons} : (*, *) \to *$$

We show the encoding of well-typed SF objects and types in Fig. 5. Every declaration is parametrized with the type of constructors that the user defined inside of the @@@**signature** blocks.

$\Sigma = \ldots, \mathtt{var} : (*, *) \to *,$

$\mathtt{Top} : \forall \gamma, \alpha . \mathtt{var}[\mathtt{cons}[\gamma, \alpha], \alpha],$

$\mathtt{Pop} : \forall \gamma, \alpha, \beta . \mathtt{var}[\gamma, \alpha] \to \mathtt{var}[\mathtt{cons}[\gamma, \beta], \alpha],$

$\mathtt{tm} : (*, *) \to *, \mathtt{sp} : (*, *, *) \to *$

$\mathtt{Lam} : \forall \gamma, \alpha, \tau . \mathtt{tm}[\mathtt{cons}[\gamma, \mathtt{base}[\alpha]], \tau] \to \mathtt{tm}[\gamma, \mathtt{arr}[\mathtt{base}[\alpha], \tau]],$

$\mathtt{Var} : \forall \gamma, \alpha . \mathtt{var}[\gamma, \alpha] \to \mathtt{tm}[\gamma, \mathtt{base}[\alpha]],$

$\mathtt{Box} : \forall \gamma, \tau . \mathtt{tm}[\cdot, \tau] \to \mathtt{tm}[\gamma, \tau],$

$\mathtt{C} : \forall \gamma, \tau, \alpha . \mathtt{con}[\tau, \alpha] \times \mathtt{tm}[\gamma, \tau] \to \mathtt{tm}[\gamma, \mathtt{base}[\alpha]],$

$\mathtt{Empty} : \forall \gamma, \tau . \mathtt{sp}[\gamma, \tau, \tau],$

$\mathtt{Cons} : \forall \gamma, \tau_1, \tau_2, \tau_3 . \mathtt{tm}[\gamma, \tau_1] \times \mathtt{sp}[\gamma, \tau_2, \tau_3] \to \mathtt{sp}[\gamma, \mathtt{arr}[\tau_1, \tau 2], \tau_3],$

$\mathtt{shift} : (*, *) \to *,$

$\mathtt{Id} : \forall \gamma . \mathtt{shift}[\gamma, \gamma],$

$\mathtt{Suc} : \forall \gamma, \delta, \alpha . \mathtt{shift}[\gamma, \delta] \to \mathtt{shift}[\mathtt{cons}[\gamma, \mathtt{base}[\alpha]], \delta],$

$\mathtt{sub} : (*, *) \to *,$

$\mathtt{Shift} : \forall \gamma, \delta . \mathtt{shift}[\gamma, \delta] \to \mathtt{sub}[\gamma, \delta],$

$\mathtt{Dot} : \forall \gamma, \delta, \tau . \mathtt{sub}[\gamma, \delta] \times \mathtt{tm}[\gamma, \tau] \to \mathtt{sub}[\gamma, \mathtt{cons}[\delta, \tau]]]$

Fig. 5. Syntactic framework definition

The specification takes the form of the type $\mathtt{con} : (*, *) \to *$, where $\mathtt{con}$ is the name of a constructor indexed by the type of its parameters and the base type they produce.

Variables and terms are indexed by two types, the first parameter is always their context and the second is their type. The type $\mathtt{var}$ represents variables with two constructors: $\mathtt{Top}$ represents the variable that was introduced last in the context and if $\mathtt{Top}$ corresponds to the de Bruijn index 0 then the constructor $\mathtt{Pop}$ represents the successor of the variable that it takes as parameter. It is interesting to consider the parameters of these constructors. $\mathtt{Top}$ is simply indexed by its context and type (variables γ and α respectively). On the other hand, $\mathtt{Pop}$ requires three type parameter: the first γ represents a context, α the resulting type of the variable, and β the type of the extension of the context. These parameter make it so that if we apply the constructor $\mathtt{Pop}$ to a variable of type α in context γ, we obtain a variable of type α in the context γ extended with type β.

As mentioned, terms described by the type family $\mathtt{tm}$ are indexed by their context and their type. It is interesting to check in some detail how the indices of the term constructors follow the typing rules from Fig. 3. The constructor for lambda terms (Lam), extends the context γ with base type α and then it produces a term in γ of function type from the base type α to the type of the body τ. The constructor for boxes simply forces its body to be closed by using the context type nil. The constructor Var simply embeds variables as terms. Finally the C constructor has two parameters, one is the name of the constructor from the user's definitions that constrains the type of the second parameter, the other is the term of the appropriated type.

The definition of substitution is a modified presentation of the substitution for well-scoped de Bruijn indices, as for example presented in [2]. We define two types, sub and shift indexed by two contexts, the domain and the range of the substitutions. Substitutions are either a shift (constructor Shift) or the combination of a term for the top-most variable and the rest of the substitution (constructor Dot).

Our implementation differs from Benton et al. [2] in the representation of renamings. Benton et.al define substitutions and renamings, the latter as a way of representing shifts. However to compute a shift, they need the context that they use to index the data-types. Hence, contexts are not erasable during run-time. As we do want contexts to be erasable at run-time, we cannot use renamings. Instead, we replace renamings with typed shifts (defined in type shift), that encode how many variables we are shifting over. This is encoded in the indices of shifts.

Finally, we omit the function implementing the substitution as it is standard We will simply mention that we implement a function apply_sub of type:
$\forall \gamma, \delta, \tau . \, \text{tm}[\gamma, \tau] \rightarrow \text{sub}[\gamma, \delta] \rightarrow \text{tm}[\delta, \tau]$ that applies a substitution moving a term from context γ to context δ.

8   From Core-ML with Contextual Types to Core-ML^{gadt}

In this section, we translate Core-ML with contextual types into Core-ML^{gadt}. Because our embedding of the syntactic framework SF in Core-ML^{gadt} is intrinsically typed, there is no need to extend the type-checker to accommodate contextual objects. Further, recall that we restricted quoted variables and parameter variables such that the matching operation remains first order. In addition, as our deep embedding uses a representation with canonical names (namely de Bruijn indices), we are able to translate pattern matching into Core-ML^{gadt}'s pattern matching; thus there is no need to extend the operational semantics of the language.

The translation we describe in this section provides the footprint of an implementation to directly generate OCaml code, as Core-ML^{gadt} is essentially a subset of OCaml. It therefore shows how to extend a functional programming language such as OCaml with the syntactic framework with minimal impact on OCaml's compiler.

We begin by translating SF types and contexts into Core-ML^{gadt} types. These types are used to index terms in the implementation of SF:

$$\text{SF Types:} \quad \ulcorner \mathbf{a} \to A \urcorner = \mathtt{arr}[\mathbf{a}, \ulcorner A \urcorner]$$
$$\ulcorner \Box A \urcorner = \mathtt{boxed}[\ulcorner A \urcorner]$$
$$\ulcorner \mathbf{a} \urcorner = \mathbf{a}$$

$$\text{SF Contexts:} \quad \ulcorner \cdot \urcorner = \mathtt{nil}[]$$
$$\ulcorner \Psi, x : \mathbf{a} \urcorner = \mathtt{cons}[\ulcorner \Psi \urcorner, \mathbf{a}]$$

The translation of SF terms is directed by their contextual type $\Psi \vdash A$, because it needs the context to perform the translation of names to de Bruijn indices and the types to appropriately index the terms.

$$\text{SF Terms:} \quad \ulcorner \lambda x.M \urcorner_{\Psi \vdash \mathbf{a} \to A} = \mathtt{Lam}[\mathtt{cons}[\ulcorner \Psi \urcorner, \mathbf{a}], \ulcorner A \urcorner]\ulcorner M \urcorner_{\Psi, \mathbf{a} \vdash A}$$
$$\ulcorner \{M\} \urcorner_{\Psi \vdash \Box A} = \mathtt{Box}[\ulcorner \Psi \urcorner, \ulcorner A \urcorner]\ulcorner M \urcorner_{\cdot \vdash A}$$
$$\ulcorner x \urcorner_{\Psi \vdash \mathbf{a}} = \mathtt{Var}[\ulcorner \Psi \urcorner, \mathbf{a}]\ulcorner x \urcorner^{v}_{\Psi}$$
$$\ulcorner \mathbf{c}\,\vec{M} \urcorner_{\Psi \vdash \mathbf{a}} = \mathtt{C}[\ulcorner \Psi \urcorner, \ulcorner A \urcorner, \mathbf{a}](\mathbf{c}, \ulcorner \vec{M} \urcorner_{\Psi \vdash A \downarrow \mathbf{a}})$$
$$\text{with } \Sigma(\mathbf{c}) = A$$
$$\ulcorner M[\sigma]^{\Phi}_{\Psi} \urcorner_{\Psi \vdash A} = \mathtt{apply\_sub}\ulcorner M \urcorner_{\Phi \vdash A}\ulcorner \sigma \urcorner_{\Psi \vdash \Phi}$$
$$\ulcorner {}'u \urcorner_{\Psi \vdash A} = u$$
$$\ulcorner \#v \urcorner_{\Psi \vdash A} = \mathtt{Var}[\ulcorner \Psi \urcorner, \mathbf{a}]\ulcorner v \urcorner_{\Psi \vdash \mathbf{a}}$$
$$\ulcorner N, \vec{M} \urcorner_{\Psi \vdash A \to B \downarrow \mathbf{a}} = \mathtt{Cons}[\ulcorner \Psi \urcorner, \mathtt{arr}[\ulcorner A \urcorner, \ulcorner B \urcorner], \mathbf{a}]$$
$$(\ulcorner N \urcorner_{\Psi \vdash A}, \ulcorner \vec{M} \urcorner_{\Psi \vdash B \downarrow \mathbf{a}})$$
$$\ulcorner \cdot \urcorner_{\Psi \vdash \mathbf{a} \downarrow \mathbf{a}} = \mathtt{Empty}[\ulcorner \psi \urcorner, \mathbf{a}, \mathbf{a}]$$

$$\text{Param. Vars:} \quad \ulcorner x \urcorner_{\Psi \vdash \mathbf{a}} = x$$
$$\ulcorner \#v \urcorner_{\Psi, y : \mathbf{a}' \vdash \mathbf{a}} = \mathtt{Pop}[\ulcorner \Psi \urcorner, \mathbf{a}, \mathbf{a}']\ulcorner v \urcorner_{\Psi \vdash \mathbf{a}}$$

There are three kinds of variables in the syntactic framework SF: bound variables, quoted variables and parameter variables. Each kind requires a different translation strategy. Bound variables are translated into de Bruijn indices where the numbers are encoded using the constructors Top and Pop. Quoted variables are simply translated into the Core-ML^{gadt} variables they quote. And finally the parameter variables are translated into a Var constructor to indicate that the resulting expression is an SF variable, and the shifts (indicated by extra '#') are translated to applications of the constructor Pop.

Notice how substitutions are not part of the representation. They are translated to the eager application of apply_sub, an OCaml function that performs the substitution. Before we call appy_sub we translate the substitution. This amounts to generating the right shift for empty substitutions and otherwise recursively translating the terms and the substitution.

Translating variables requires computing the de Bruijn index with the appropriate type annotations.

We also need to translate SF patterns into Core-ML^{gadt} expressions with the right structure. The special cases are:

- Variables are translated to de Bruijn indexes.
- Quoted variables simply translate to Core-ML^{gadt} variables.
- Parameter variables translate to a pattern that matches only variables by specifying the Var constructor.

The translation of patterns follows the same line as the translation of terms, however, we do not use the indices of type variables in Core-ML^{gadt} patterns. This is indicated by writing an underscore.

$$
\begin{aligned}
\text{SF Patterns:} \quad \ulcorner \lambda x.R \urcorner^{\Gamma}_{\Psi \vdash \mathbf{a} \to A} &= \text{Lam}[\_,\_,\_] \ulcorner R \urcorner^{\Gamma}_{\Psi,\mathbf{a} \vdash A} \\
\ulcorner \{R\} \urcorner^{\Gamma}_{\Psi \vdash \square A} &= \text{Box}[\_,\_] \ulcorner R \urcorner^{\Gamma}_{\cdot \vdash A} \\
\ulcorner x \urcorner^{\cdot}_{\Psi \vdash \mathbf{a}} &= \text{Var}[\_,\_] \ulcorner x \urcorner^{p}_{\Psi} \\
\ulcorner \mathbf{c} \, \vec{R} \urcorner^{\Gamma}_{\Psi \vdash \mathbf{a}} &= \text{C}[\_,\_,\_] \ulcorner \vec{R} \urcorner^{\Gamma}_{\Psi \vdash A \downarrow \mathbf{a}} \qquad \text{with } \Sigma(\mathbf{c}) = A \\
\ulcorner {}^{,}\mathbf{u} \urcorner^{u : \ulcorner \Psi \vdash A \urcorner}_{\Psi \vdash A} &= u \\
\ulcorner \#x \urcorner^{x : \ulcorner \Psi \vdash A \urcorner}_{\Psi \vdash \mathbf{a}} &= \text{Var}[\_,\_]x \\
\ulcorner \#\#x \urcorner^{x : \ulcorner \Psi, y : \vdash A \urcorner}_{\Psi, y : \vdash \mathbf{a}} &= \text{Var}[\_,\_](\text{Pop}[\_,\_,\_]x) \\
\ulcorner R, \vec{R} \urcorner^{\Gamma, \Gamma'}_{\Psi \vdash A \to B \downarrow \mathbf{a}} &= \text{Cons}[\_,\_,\_,\_](\ulcorner R \urcorner^{\Gamma}_{\Psi \vdash A}, \ulcorner \vec{R} \urcorner^{\Gamma'}_{\Psi \vdash B \downarrow \mathbf{a}}) \\
\ulcorner \cdot \urcorner^{\cdot}_{\Psi \vdash \mathbf{a} \downarrow \mathbf{a}} &= \text{Empty}[\_,\_] \\[4pt]
\text{SF Variables:} \quad \ulcorner x \urcorner^{p}_{\Psi, x : \mathbf{a}} &= \text{Top}[\_,\_] \\
\ulcorner y \urcorner^{p}_{\Psi, x : \mathbf{b}} &= \text{Pop}[\_,\_,\_] \ulcorner y \urcorner^{p}_{\Psi}
\end{aligned}
$$

Our main translation of Core-ML to Core-ML^{gadt} uses the following main operations:

$$\ulcorner \tau \urcorner, \ulcorner \Xi \urcorner, \ulcorner \Gamma \urcorner : \text{Translate types, signatures and contexts.}$$
$$\ulcorner e \urcorner_{\Gamma \vdash \tau} : \text{Type directed translation of expressions.}$$
$$\ulcorner pat \urcorner^{\Gamma'}_{\Gamma \vdash \tau} : \text{Translates patterns and outputs } \Gamma' \text{ the}$$
$$\text{context of the bound variables.}$$

The translation of Core-ML expressions into Core-ML^{gadt} directly follows the structure of programs in Core-ML and is type directed to fill in the required types for the Core-ML^{gadt} representation. The translation is as follows:

$$\ulcorner x \urcorner_{\Gamma\vdash\tau} = x$$

$$\ulcorner C\, \vec{e}\, \urcorner_{\Gamma\vdash D} = C[\,]\, \ulcorner \vec{e}\, \urcorner_{\Gamma\vdash\vec{\tau}} \quad \text{with } \Xi(C) = \vec{\tau} \to D$$

$$\ulcorner \mathtt{fun}\, f(x) = e\, \urcorner_{\Gamma\vdash\tau_1\to\tau_2} = \mathtt{fix}\, f : \ulcorner \tau_1 \to \tau_2 \urcorner = \lambda x\,.\, \ulcorner e\, \urcorner_{\Gamma,x:\tau_1\vdash\tau_2}$$

$$\ulcorner i\,.e.\, \urcorner_{\Gamma\vdash\tau} = \ulcorner i\, \urcorner_{\Gamma\vdash\tau_1\to\tau}\, \ulcorner e\, \urcorner_{\Gamma\vdash\tau_1}$$
$$\text{with } \Gamma \vdash i \Rightarrow \tau_1 \to \tau$$

$$\ulcorner \mathtt{let}\, x = i\, \mathtt{in}\,.e.\, \urcorner_{\Gamma\vdash\tau} = \mathtt{let}\, x = \ulcorner i\, \urcorner_{\Gamma\vdash\tau_1}\, \mathtt{in}\, \ulcorner e\, \urcorner_{\Gamma,x:\tau_1\vdash\tau}$$
$$\text{with } \Gamma \vdash i \Rightarrow \tau_1$$

$$\ulcorner \mathtt{match}\, i\, \mathtt{with}\, \vec{b}\, \urcorner_{\Gamma\vdash\tau} = \mathtt{match}\, \ulcorner i\, \urcorner_{\Gamma\vdash\tau_1}\, \mathtt{with}\, \ulcorner \vec{b}\, \urcorner_{\Gamma\vdash\tau_1\to\tau}$$
$$\text{with } \Gamma \vdash i \Rightarrow \tau_1$$

$$\ulcorner e_1,\ldots,e_n\, \urcorner_{\Gamma\vdash\vec{\tau}} = \ulcorner e_1\, \urcorner_{\Gamma\vdash\tau_1},\ldots,\ulcorner e_n\, \urcorner_{\Gamma\vdash\tau_n}$$

$$\ulcorner [\hat{\Psi} \vdash M]\, \urcorner_{\Gamma\vdash[\Psi\vdash A]} = \ulcorner M \urcorner_{\Psi\vdash A}$$

$$\ulcorner \mathtt{cmatch}\, i\, \mathtt{with}\, \vec{c}\, \urcorner_{\Gamma\vdash\tau} = \mathtt{match}\, \ulcorner i\, \urcorner_{\Gamma\vdash[\Psi\vdash A]}\, \mathtt{with}\, \ulcorner \vec{c}\, \urcorner_{\Gamma\vdash[\Psi\vdash A]\to\tau}$$
$$\text{with } \Gamma \vdash i \Rightarrow [\Psi \vdash A]$$

Translating branches and patterns:

Branch: $\quad\quad \ulcorner pat \mapsto e\, \urcorner_{\Gamma\vdash\tau_1\to\tau_2} = \ulcorner pat \urcorner^{\Gamma'}_{\Gamma\vdash\tau_1} \mapsto \ulcorner e\, \urcorner_{\Gamma,\Gamma'\vdash\tau_2}$

Patterns: $\quad\quad \ulcorner x \urcorner^{x:\tau}_{\Gamma\vdash\tau} = x$

$$\ulcorner C\, \overrightarrow{pat}\, \urcorner^{\Gamma'}_{\Gamma\vdash D} = C[]\, \ulcorner \overrightarrow{pat}\, \urcorner^{\Gamma'}_{\Gamma\vdash\vec{\tau}} \quad\quad \text{with } \Xi(C) = \vec{\tau} \to D$$

Finally, we define the translation of branches for $\mathtt{cmatch}\, i\, \mathtt{with}\, \vec{c}$. Note how we use the context generated from the pattern to translate the body of the branch.

$$\ulcorner [\Psi \vdash R] \mapsto e\, \urcorner_{\Gamma\vdash[\Psi\vdash A]\to\tau} = \ulcorner R \urcorner^{\Gamma'}_{\Psi\vdash A} \mapsto \ulcorner e\, \urcorner_{\Gamma,\Gamma'\vdash\tau}$$

Finally we show that the translation from Core-ML with contextual types into Core-ML^{gadt} preserves types.

Theorem 1 (Main).

1. *If* $\Gamma \vdash e \Leftarrow \tau$ *then* $\cdot; \ulcorner\Gamma\urcorner \vdash \ulcorner e \urcorner_{\Gamma\vdash\tau} : \ulcorner\tau\urcorner$.
2. *If* $\Gamma \vdash i \Rightarrow \tau$ *then* $\cdot; \ulcorner\Gamma\urcorner \vdash \ulcorner i \urcorner_{\Gamma\vdash\tau} : \ulcorner\tau\urcorner$.

Our result relies on several lemmas that deal with the other judgments and context lookups:

Lemma 1 (Ambient Context). *If* $\Gamma(u) = [\Psi \vdash a]$ *then* $\ulcorner\Gamma\urcorner(u) = tm[\ulcorner\Psi\urcorner, a]$.

Lemma 2 (Terms).

1. *If* $\Gamma; \Psi \vdash M : A$ *then* $\cdot; \ulcorner\Gamma\urcorner \vdash \ulcorner M\urcorner_{\Psi\vdash A} : \ulcorner\Psi \vdash A\urcorner$.
2. *If* $\Gamma; \Psi \vdash \sigma : \Phi$ *then* $\cdot; \ulcorner\Gamma\urcorner \vdash \ulcorner\sigma\urcorner_{\Psi\vdash\Phi} : \ulcorner\Psi \vdash \Phi\urcorner$

Lemma 3 (Pat.). *If* $\vdash pat : \tau \downarrow \Gamma$ *then* $\cdot \vdash \ulcorner pat\urcorner^{\Gamma}_{\Psi\vdash A} : \ulcorner\tau\urcorner \downarrow \Gamma$.

Lemma 4 (Ctx. Pat.). *If* $\Psi \vdash R : A \downarrow \Gamma$ *then* $\cdot \vdash \ulcorner R\urcorner^{\Gamma}_{\Psi\vdash A} : \ulcorner\Psi \vdash A\urcorner \downarrow \Gamma$.

Given our set-up, the proofs are straightforward by induction on the typing derivation.

9   A Proof of Concept Implementation

In this section, we describe the implementation[3] of Babybel which uses the ideas from previous sections. One major difference is that Babybel translates OCaml programs that use syntax extensions for contextual SF types and terms and translates them into pure OCaml with GADTs. In fact, even our input OCaml programs may use GADTs to for example describe context relations on SF contexts (see also our examples from Sect. 2).

The presence of GADTs in our source language also means that we can specify precise types for functions where we can quantify over contexts. Let's revisit some of the types of the programs that we wrote earlier in Sect. 2:

- `rewrite:`γ. `[`$\gamma \vdash$ `tm]`$\rightarrow$`[`$\gamma \vdash$ `tm]`: In this type we implicitly quantify over all contexts **g** and then we take a potentially open term and return another term in the same context. These constraints imposed in the types are due to being able to index types with types thanks to GADTs.
- `get_path:`γ. `[`γ`,x:tm` $\vdash$ `tm]`$\rightarrow$`path`: In this case we quantify over all contexts, but the input of the function is some term in a non-empty context.
- `conv:`$\gamma\delta$.`(`γ,δ`) rel`$\rightarrow$`[`$\gamma \vdash$ `tm]`$\rightarrow$`[`$\delta \vdash$ `ctm]`:
  This final example shows that we can also use the contexts to index regular OCaml GADTs. In this function we are translating between terms in different representations.
  To be able to translate between these different context representations, it is necessary to establish a relation between these contexts. So we need to define a special OCaml type (i.e.:`rel`) that relates variable to variable in each contexts.

By embedding the SF in OCaml using contextual types, we can combine and use the impure features of OCaml. Our example, in Sect. 2.2 takes advantage of them in our implementation of backtracking with exceptions. Additionally, performing I/O or using references works seamlessly in the prototype.

The presence of GADTs in our target language also makes the actual implementation of Babybel simpler than the theoretical description, as we take advantage of OCaml's built-in type reconstruction. In addition to GADTs, our implementation depends on several OCaml extensions. We use Attributes from Sect. 7.18 of the reference manual [10] and strings to embed the specification of our signature. We use quoted strings from Sect. 7.20 to implement the boxes for terms $(\langle\!\langle \ldots \rangle\!\rangle)$ and patterns $(\langle\!\langle \ldots \rangle\!\rangle_p)$. All these appear as annotations in the internal Abstract Syntax Tree in the compiler implementation. To perform the translation (based on Sect. 8) we define a PPX rewriter as discussed in Sect. 23.1 of the OCaml manual. In our rewriter, we implement a parser for the framework SF and translate all the annotations using our embedding.

10   Related Work

Babybel and the syntactic framework SF are derived from ideas that originated in proof checkers based on the logical framework LF such as the Twelf system [14].

---

[3] Available at www.github.com/fferreira/babybel/.

In the same category are the proof and programming languages Delphin [19] and Beluga [16] that offer a computational language on top of the LF. In many ways, the work that we present in this paper and forms the foundation of Babybel are a distillation of Beluga's ideas applied to a mainstream programming language. As a consequence, we have shown that we can get some of the benefits from Beluga at a much lower cost, since we do not have to build a stand-alone system or extend the compiler of an existing language to support contexts, contextual types and objects.

Our approach of embedding an LF specification language into a host language is in spirit related to the systems Abella [8] and Hybrid [7] that use a two-level approach. In these systems we embed the specification language (typically hereditary harrop formulas) in first-order logic (or a variant of it). While our approach is similar in spirit, we focus on embedding SF specifications into a programming language instead of embedding it into a proof theory. Moreover, our embedding is type preserving by construction.

There are also many approaches and tools that specifically add support for writing programs that manipulate syntax with binders – even if they do not necessarily use HOAS. FreshML [22] and Caml [20] extend OCaml's data types with the ideas of names and binders from nominal logic [18]. In these system, name generation is an effect, and if the user is not careful variables may extrude their scopes. Purity can be enforced by adding a proof system with a decision procedure that statically guarantees that no variable escapes its scope [21]. This adds some complexity to the system. We feel that Babybel's contextual types offer a simpler formalism to deal with bound variables. On the other hand, Babybel's approach does not try to model variables that do not have lexical scope, like top-level definitions. Another related language is Romeo [23] that uses ideas from Pure FreshML to represent binders. Where our system statically catches variables escaping their scope, the Romeo system either throws a run time exception or uses an SMT solver to prove the absence of scoping issues. The Hobbits system for Haskell [25] is implemented in a similar way to ours, using quasi-quoting but they use a different formalism based on the concepts of names and freshness. Last but not least, approaches based on parametric HOAS (PHOAS) [5] also model binding in the object language by re-using the function space of the meta-language. In particular, Washburn and Weirich [24] propose a library that uses catamorphisms to compute over a parametric HOAS representation. This is a powerful approach but requires a different way of implementing recursive functions. A fundamental difference between this line of work and ours, is that in PHOAS functions are extensional, i.e. they are black box functions, while our approach introduces a distinction between an intensional and extensional function space. The intensional function space from SF allows us to model binding and supports pattern matching. The extentional function space allows us to write recursive functions.

11   Conclusion and Future Work

In this work, we describe the syntactic framework SF (a simply typed variant of the logical framework LF with the necessity modality from S4) and explain the embedding of SF into a functional programming language using contextual types. This gives programmers the ability to write programs that manipulate abstract syntax trees with binders while knowing at type checking time that no variables extrude their scope. We also show how to translate the extended language back into a first order representation. For this, we use de Bruijn indices and GADTs to implement the SF in Core-ML^{gadt}. Important characteristics of the embedding are that it preserves the phase separation, making types (and thus contexts) erasable at run-time. This allows pattern matching to remain first-order and thus it is possible to compile with the traditional algorithms.

Finally, we describe Babybel an implementation of these ideas that embeds SF in OCaml using contextual types. The embedding is flexible enough that we can take advantage of the more powerful type system in OCaml to make the extension more powerful. We use GADTs in our examples to express more powerful invariants (e.g. that the translation preserves the context).

In the future, we plan to implement our approach also in other languages. In particular, it would be natural to implement our approach in Haskell. We do not expect that the the type system extensions to GHC pose any challenging issues. Finally, it would be interesting to extend our approach to type systems with dependent types (e.g. Coq or Agda) where we can reason about the programs we write. This extension would require extending SF with theorems about substitutions (e.g. proving that applying an identity substitution does not change a term).

References

1. Augustsson, L.: Compiling pattern matching. In: Jouannaud, J.-P. (ed.) FPCA 1985. LNCS, vol. 201, pp. 368–381. Springer, Heidelberg (1985). doi:10.1007/3-540-15975-4_48
2. Benton, N., Hur, C.K., Kennedy, A.J., McBride, C.: Strongly typed term representations in Coq. J. Autom. Reasoning 49(2), 141–159 (2012)
3. Cave, A., Pientka, B.: Programming with binders and indexed data-types. In: 39th Annual ACM SIGPLAN-SIGACT Symposium on Principles of Programming Languages (POPL 2012), pp. 413–424. ACM Press (2012)
4. Cheney, J., Hinze, R.: First-class phantom types. Technical Report CUCIS TR2003-1901, Cornell University (2003)
5. Chlipala, A.J.: Parametric higher-order abstract syntax for mechanized semantics. In: Hook, J., Thiemann, P. (eds.) 13th ACM SIGPLAN International Conference on Functional Programming (ICFP 2008), pp. 143–156. ACM (2008)
6. Davies, R., Pfenning, F.: A modal analysis of staged computation. J. ACM 48(3), 555–604 (2001)
7. Felty, A., Momigliano, A.: Hybrid: a definitional two-level approach to reasoning with higher-order abstract syntax. J. Autom. Reasoning 48(1), 43–105 (2012)
8. Gacek, A., Miller, D., Nadathur, G.: A two-level logic approach to reasoning about computations. J. Autom. Reasoning 49(2), 241–273 (2012)

9. Harper, R., Honsell, F., Plotkin, G.: A framework for defining logics. J. ACM **40**(1), 143–184 (1993)
10. Leroy, X., Doligez, D., Frisch, A., Garrigue, J., Rémy, D., Vouillon, J.: The OCaml System Release 4.03 - Documentation and user's manual. Institut National de Recherche en Informatique et en Automatique (2016)
11. Miller, D., Palmidessi, C.: Foundational aspects of syntax. ACM Comput. Surv. **31**(3es), 11 (1999)
12. Nanevski, A., Pfenning, F., Pientka, B.: Contextual modal type theory. ACM Trans. Comput. Logic **9**(3), 1–49 (2008)
13. Pfenning, F., Davies, R.: A judgmental reconstruction of modal logic. Math. Struct. Comput. Sci. **11**(4), 511–540 (2001)
14. Pfenning, F., Schürmann, C.: System description: twelf – a meta-logical framework for deductive systems. In: Ganzinger, H. (ed.) CADE 1999. LNCS (LNAI), vol. 1632, pp. 202–206. Springer, Heidelberg (1999). doi:10.1007/3-540-48660-7_14
15. Pientka, B.: A type-theoretic foundation for programming with higher-order abstract syntax and first-class substitutions. In: 35th Annual ACM SIGPLAN-SIGACT Symposium on Principles of Programming Languages (POPL 2008), pp. 371–382. ACM Press (2008)
16. Pientka, B., Cave, A.: Inductive Beluga: programming proofs (system description). In: Felty, A.P., Middeldorp, A. (eds.) CADE 2015. LNCS (LNAI), vol. 9195, pp. 272–281. Springer, Cham (2015). doi:10.1007/978-3-319-21401-6_18
17. Pientka, B., Pfenning, F.: Optimizing higher-order pattern unification. In: Baader, F. (ed.) CADE 2003. LNCS (LNAI), vol. 2741, pp. 473–487. Springer, Heidelberg (2003). doi:10.1007/978-3-540-45085-6_40
18. Pitts, A.: Nominal logic, a first order theory of names and binding. Inf. Comput. **186**(2), 165–193 (2003)
19. Poswolsky, A., Schürmann, C.: System description: Delphin–a functional programming language for deductive systems. In: International Workshop on Logical Frameworks and Meta-Languages: Theory and Practice (LFMTP 2008). Electronic Notes in Theoretical Computer Science (ENTCS), vol. 228, pp. 135–141. Elsevier (2009)
20. Pottier, F.: An overview of Caml. In: proceedings of the ACM-SIGPLAN Workshop on ML (ML 2005). Electronic Notes in Theoretical Computer Science, vol. 148(2), pp. 27–52 (2006)
21. Pottier, F.: Static name control for FreshML. In: 22nd IEEE Symposium on Logic in Computer Science (LICS 2007), pp. 356–365. IEEE Computer Society, July 2007
22. Shinwell, M.R., Pitts, A.M., Gabbay, M.J.: FreshML: programming with binders made simple. In: 8th International Conference on Functional Programming (ICFP 2003), pp. 263–274. ACM Press (2003)
23. Stansifer, P., Wand, M.: Romeo: a system for more flexible binding-safe programming. In: Proceedings of the 19th ACM SIGPLAN International Conference on Functional Programming, ICFP 2014, pp. 53–65 (2014)
24. Washburn, G., Weirich, S.: Boxes go bananas: encoding higher-order abstract syntax with parametric polymorphism. J. Funct. Program. **18**(01), 87–140 (2008)
25. Westbrook, E., Frisby, N., Brauner, P.: Hobbits for Haskell: a library for higher-order encodings in functional programming languages. In: 4th ACM Symposium on Haskell (Haskell 2011), pp. 35–46. ACM (2011)
26. Xi, H., Chen, C., Chen, G.: Guarded recursive datatype constructors. In: 30th ACM SIGPLAN-SIGACT Symposium on Principles of Programming Languages (POPL 2003), pp. 224–235. ACM Press (2003)

LINCX: A Linear Logical Framework with First-Class Contexts

Aina Linn Georges[1](✉), Agata Murawska[2](✉), Shawn Otis[1](✉), and Brigitte Pientka[1](✉)

[1] McGill University, Montreal, QC, Canada
{aina.georges,shawn.otis}@mail.mcgill.ca, bpientka@cs.mcgill.ca
[2] IT University of Copenhagen, Copenhagen, Denmark
agmu@itu.dk

Abstract. Linear logic provides an elegant framework for modelling stateful, imperative and concurrent systems by viewing a context of assumptions as a set of resources. However, mechanizing the meta-theory of such systems remains a challenge, as we need to manage and reason about mixed contexts of linear and intuitionistic assumptions.

We present LINCX, a contextual linear logical framework with first-class mixed contexts. LINCX allows us to model (linear) abstract syntax trees as syntactic structures that may depend on intuitionistic and linear assumptions. It can also serve as a foundation for reasoning about such structures. LINCX extends the linear logical framework LLF with first-class (linear) contexts and an equational theory of context joins that can otherwise be very tedious and intricate to develop. This work may be also viewed as a generalization of contextual LF that supports both intuitionistic and linear variables, functions, and assumptions.

We describe a decidable type-theoretic foundation for LINCX that only characterizes canonical forms and show that our equational theory of context joins is associative and commutative. Finally, we outline how LINCX may serve as a practical foundation for mechanizing the meta-theory of stateful systems.

1 Introduction

Logical frameworks make it easier to mechanize formal systems and proofs about them by providing a single meta-language with abstractions and primitives for common and recurring concepts, like variables and assumptions in proofs. This can have a major impact on the effort and cost of mechanization. By factoring out and abstracting over low-level details, it reduces the time it takes to mechanize formal systems, avoids errors in manipulating low-level operations, and makes the mechanizations themselves easier to maintain. It can also make an enormous difference when it comes to proof checking and constructing meta-theoretic proofs, as we focus on the essential aspect of a proof without getting bogged down in the quagmire of bureaucratic details.

A. Murawska—Supported by grant 10-092309 from the Danish Council for Strategic Research to the *Demtech* project.

H. Yang (Ed.): ESOP 2017, LNCS 10201, pp. 530–555, 2017.
DOI: 10.1007/978-3-662-54434-1_20

The contextual logical framework [20,21], an extension of the logical framework LF [14], is designed to support a broad range of common features that are needed for mechanizations of formal systems. To model variables, assumptions and derivations, programmers can take advantage of higher-order abstract syntax (HOAS) trees; a context of assumptions together with properties about uniqueness of assumptions can be represented abstractly using first-class contexts and context variables [21]; single and simultaneous substitutions together with their equational theory are supported via first-class substitutions [7,8]; finally, derivation trees that depend on a context of assumption can be precisely described via contextual objects [20]. This last aspect is particularly important. By encapsulating and representing derivation trees together with their surrounding context of assumptions, we can analyze and manipulate these rich syntactic structures via pattern matching, and can construct (co)inductive proofs by writing recursive programs about them [6,24]. This leads to a modular and robust design where we cleanly separate the representation of formal systems and derivations from the (co)inductive reasoning about them.

Substructural frameworks such as the linear logical framework LLF [9] provide additional abstractions to elegantly model the behaviour of imperative operations such as updating and deallocating memory [12,30] and concurrent computation (see for example session types [5]). However, it has been very challenging to mechanize proofs about LLF specifications as we must manage mixed contexts of unrestricted and linear assumptions. When constructing a derivation tree, we must often split the linear resources and distribute them to the premises relying on a *context join* operation, written as $\Psi = \Psi_1 \bowtie \Psi_2$. This operation should be commutative and associative. Unrestricted assumptions present in Ψ should be preserved in both contexts Ψ_1 and Ψ_2. The mix of unrestricted and restricted assumptions leads to an intricate equational theory of contexts that often stands in the way of mechanizing linear or separation logics in proof assistants and has spurred the development of specialized tactics [2,16].

Our main contribution is the design of Lincx (read: "lynx"), a contextual linear logical framework with first-class contexts that may contain both intuitionistic and linear assumptions. On the one hand our work extends the linear logical framework LLF with support for first-class linear contexts together with an equational theory of context joins, contextual objects and contextual types; on the other we can view Lincx as a generalization of contextual LF to model not only unrestricted but also linear assumptions. Lincx hence allows us to abstractly represent syntax trees that depend on a mixed context of linear and unrestricted assumptions, and can serve as a foundation for mechanizing the meta-theory of stateful systems where we implement (co)inductive proofs about linear contextual objects by pattern matching following the methodology outlined by Cave and Pientka [6] and Thibodeau et al. [29]. Our main technical contributions are:

(1) A bi-directional decidable type system that only characterizes canonical forms of our linear LF objects. Consequently, exotic terms that do not represent legal objects from our object language are prevented. It is an inherent property of our

design that bound variables cannot escape their scope, and no separate reasoning about scope is required. To achieve this we rely on hereditary substitution to guarantee normal forms are preserved. Equality of two contextual linear LF objects reduces then to syntactic equality (modulo α-renaming).

(2) Definition of first-class (linear) contexts together with an equational theory of context joins. A context in LINCX may contain both unrestricted and linear assumptions. This not only allows for a uniform representation of contexts, but also leads to a uniform representation of simultaneous substitutions. Context variables are indexed and their indices are freely built from elements of an infinite, countable set through a context join operation ($\bowtie$) that is associative, commutative and has a neutral element. This allows a canonical representation of contexts and context joins. In particular, we can consider contexts equivalent modulo associativity and commutativity. This substantially simplifies the meta-theory of LINCX and also directly gives rise to a clean implementation of context joins which we exploit in our mechanization of the meta-theoretic properties of LINCX.

(3) Mechanization of LINCX *together with its meta-theory in the proof assistant* BELUGA [23]. Our development takes advantage of higher-order abstract syntax to model binding structures compactly. We only model linearity constraints separately. We have mechanized our bi-directional type-theoretic foundation together with our equational theory of contexts. In particular, we mechanized all the key properties of our equational theory of context joins and the substitution properties our theory satisfies.

We believe that LINCX is a significant step towards modelling (linear) derivation trees as well-scoped syntactic structures that we can analyze and manipulate via case-analysis and implementing (co)inductive proofs as (co)recursive programs. As it treats contexts, where both unrestricted and linear assumptions live, abstractly and factors out the equational theory of context joins, it eliminates the need for users to explicitly state basic mathematical definitions and lemmas and build up the basic necessary infrastructure. This makes the task easier and lowers the costs and effort required to mechanize properties about imperative and concurrent computations.

2   Motivating Examples

To illustrate how we envision using (linear) contextual objects and (linear) contexts, we implement two program transformations on object languages that exploit linearity. We first represent our object languages in LINCX and then write recursive programs that analyze the syntactic structure of these objects by pattern matching. This highlights the role that contexts and context joins play.

2.1   Example: Code Simplification

To illustrate the challenges that contexts pose in the linear setting, we implement a program that translates linear Mini-ML expressions that feature let-expression into a linear core lambda calculus. We define the linear Mini-ML using the linear type `ml` and our linear core lambda calculus using the linear type `lin` as our target language. We introduce a linear LF type together with its constructors using the keyword **Linear LF**.

```
Linear LF ml : type =              Linear LF lin: type =
  | lam  : (ml -o ml) -o ml          | llam  : (lin -o lin) -o lin
  | app  : ml -o ml -o ml            | lapp  : lin -o lin -o lin
  | letv : ml -o (ml -o ml) -o ml;   ;
```

We use the linear implication `-o` to describe the linear function space and we model variable bindings that arise in abstractions and let-expressions using higher-order abstract syntax, as is common in logical frameworks. This encoding technique exploits the function space provided by LF to model variables. In linear LF it also ensures that bound variables are used only once.

Our goal is to implement a simple translation of Mini-ML expressions to the core linear lambda calculus by eliminating all let-expressions and transforming them into function applications. We thus need to traverse Mini-ML expressions recursively. As we go under an abstraction or a let-expression, our sub-expression will not, however, remain closed. We therefore model a Mini-ML expression together with its surrounding context in which it is meaningful. Our function `trans` takes a Mini-ML expression in a context γ, written as $[\gamma \vdash ml]$, and returns a corresponding expression in the linear lambda calculus in a context δ, an object of type $[\delta \vdash lin]$. More precisely, there exists such a corresponding context δ. Due to linearity, the context of the result of translating a Mini-ML term has the same length as the original context. This invariant is however not explicitly tracked.

We first define the structure of such contexts using context schema declarations. The tag `1` ensures that any declaration of type `ml` in a context of schema `ml_ctx` must be linear. Similarly, any declaration of type `lin` in a context of schema `core_ctx` must be linear.

```
schema ml_ctx   = 1 (ml);
schema core_ctx = 1 (lin);
```

To characterize the result of this translation, we define a recursive type:

```
inductive Result: type = Return : (δ:core_ctx) [δ ⊢ lin] → Result;
```

By writing round parenthesis in $(\delta\text{:core\_ctx})$ we indicate that we do not pass δ explicitly to the constructor `Return`, but it can always be reconstructed. It is merely an annotation declaring the schema of δ.

We now define a recursive function `trans` using the keyword `rec` (see Fig. 1). First, let us highlight some high level principles and concepts that we use. We write $[\Psi \vdash N]$ to describe an expression N that is meaningful in the context Ψ. For example, $[\gamma \vdash lam \ \hat{} \ (\hat{\lambda}x. \ M)]$ denotes a term of type `ml` in the context γ where γ is a context variable that describes contexts abstractly. We call M a meta-variable. It stands for a `ml` term that may depend on the context $\gamma,x{:}ml$. In general, all meta-variables are associated with a stuck substitution, written $N[\sigma]$ or $M[\sigma]$. We usually omit the substitution σ, if it is the identitiy substitution. One substitution that

```
rec trans : (γ:ml_ctx)[γ ⊢ ml] → Result =
fn e ⇒ case e of
| [x̂:ml ⊢ x] ⇒ Return [x̂:lin ⊢ x]

| [γ ⊢ lam ^ (λ̂x. M)] ⇒
    let Return [δ, x̂:lin ⊢ M'] = trans [γ, x̂:ml ⊢ M] in
    Return [δ ⊢ llam ^ (λ̂x. M)]

| [γ(1⋈2) ⊢ app ^ M ^ N] where M:[γ₁ ⊢ ml] and N:[γ₂ ⊢ ml] and γ(1⋈2) = γ₁ ⋈ γ₂ ⇒
    let Return [δ₁ ⊢ M'] = trans [γ₁ ⊢ M] in
    let Return [δ₂ ⊢ N'] = trans [γ₂ ⊢ N] in
        Return [δ(1⋈2) ⊢ lapp ^ M' ^ N'] where δ(1⋈2) = δ₁ ⋈ δ₂

| [γ(1⋈2) ⊢ let ^ M ^ (λ̂x. N)] where M:[γ₁⊢ ml] and N:[γ₂, x̂:ml ⊢ ml]
                                  and γ(1⋈2) = γ₁ ⋈ γ₂ ⇒
    let Return [δ₁ ⊢ M']            = trans [γ₁ ⊢ M] in
    let Return [δ₂, x̂:lin ⊢ N']     = trans [γ₂, x̂:ml ⊢ N] in
        Return [δ(1⋈2) ⊢ lapp ^ (llam ^ (λ̂x. N)) ^ M'] where δ(1⋈2) = δ₁ ⋈ δ₂;
```

Fig. 1. Translation of linear ML-expressions to a linear core language

frequently arises in practice is the empty substitution that is written as [] and maps from the empty context to an unrestricted context Ψ. It hence acts as a weakening substitution.

Our simplification is implemented by pattern matching on [γ ⊢ ml] objects and specifying constraints on contexts. In the variable case, since we have a linear context, we require that x be the only variable in the context[1]. In the lambda case [γ ⊢ lam ^(λ̂x.M)] we write ^ for linear application and linear abstraction. We expect the type of M to be inferred as [γ,x̂:ml ⊢ ml], since we interpret every pattern variable to depend on all its surrounding context unless otherwise specified. We now recursively translate M in the extended context γ, x̂:ml, unpack the result and rebuild the equivalent linear term. Note that we pattern match on the result translating M by writing Result [δ, x̂:lin ⊢ M']. However, we do not necessarily know that the output core_ctx context is of the same length as the input ml_ctx context and hence necessarily has the shape [δ, x̂:lin], as we do not track this invariant explicitly. To write a covering program we would need to return an error, if we would encounter Return [⊢ M'], i.e. a closed term where δ is empty. We omit this case here.

The third and fourth cases are the most interesting ones, as we must split the context. When we analyze for example [γ(1⋈2) ⊢ app ^ M ^N], then M has some type [γ₁ ⊢ ml] and N has some type [γ₂ ⊢ ml] where γ(1⋈2) = γ₁ ⋈ γ₂. We specify these type annotations and context constraints explicitly. Note that we overload the ⋈ symbol in this example: when it occurs as a subscript it is part of the name, while when we write γ₁ ⋈ γ₂ it refers to the operation on contexts. Then we can simply recursively translate M and N and rebuild the final result where we explicitly state δ₁⋈₂ = δ₁ ⋈ δ₂. We proceed similarly to translate recursively every let-expression into a function application.

---

[1] In case we have a mixed context, we could specify instead that the rest of the context is unrestricted, using the keywords where and unr.

Type checking verifies that a given object is well-typed modulo context joins. This is non-trivial. Consider for example $[\delta_{(1\bowtie2)} \vdash \mathtt{lapp} \; \hat{} \; (\mathtt{llam} \; \hat{}(\hat{\lambda}\mathtt{x}. \; \mathtt{N'})) \; \hat{} \; \mathtt{M'}]$ where $\delta_{(1\bowtie2)} = \delta_1 \bowtie \delta_2$. Clearly, we should be able to type check such an example also if the user wrote $\delta = \delta_2 \bowtie \delta_1$. Hence we want our underlying type theory to reason about context constraints modulo associativity and commutativity.

As the astute reader will have noticed, we only allow one context variable in every context, i.e. writing $[\delta_1, \delta_2 \vdash \mathtt{lapp} \; \hat{} \; (\mathtt{llam} \; \hat{} \; (\hat{\lambda}\mathtt{x}. \; \mathtt{N'})) \; \hat{} \; \mathtt{M'}]$ is illegal. Furthermore, we have deliberately chosen the subscripts for our context variables to emphasize their encoding in our underlying theory. Note that all context variables that belong to the same tree of context splits have the same name, but differ in their subscripts. The context variables γ_1 and γ_2 are called *leaf-level context variables*. The context variable $\gamma_{(1\bowtie2)}$ is their direct parent and sits at the root of this tree. One can think of the tree of context joins as an abstraction of the typing derivation. To emphasize this idea, let us consider the following deeply nested pattern: $[\gamma_{((11\bowtie12)\bowtie2)} \vdash \mathtt{lapp} \; \hat{} \; (\mathtt{lapp} \; \hat{} \; (\mathtt{llam} \; \hat{} \; (\hat{\lambda}\mathtt{x}. \; \mathtt{M})) \; \hat{} \; \mathtt{N'}) \; \hat{} \; \mathtt{K}]$ where $\mathtt{M} : [\gamma_{11}, \mathtt{x} \overset{\cdot}{:} \mathtt{ml} \vdash \mathtt{ml}]$, $\mathtt{N} : [\gamma_{12} \vdash \mathtt{ml}]$, and $\mathtt{K} : [\gamma_2 \vdash \mathtt{ml}]$, and where we again encode the splitting of γ in its subscript. Our underlying equational theory of context joins treats $\gamma_{(11\bowtie(12\bowtie2))}$ as equivalent to $\gamma_{((11\bowtie12)\bowtie2)}$ or $\gamma_{((12\bowtie11)\bowtie2)}$ as it takes into account commutativity and associativity. However, it may require us to generate a new intermediate node $\gamma_{(1\bowtie21)}$ and eliminate intermediate nodes (such as $\gamma_{21\bowtie22}$).

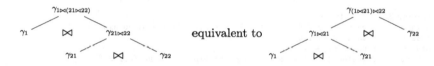

Fig. 2. Context joins

Our encoding of context variables is hence crucial to allow the rearrangement of context constraints, but also to define what it means to instantiate a given context variable such as γ_{21} with a concrete context Ψ. If Ψ contains also unrestricted assumptions then instantiating γ_{21} will have a global effect, as unrestricted assumptions are shared among all nodes in this tree of context joins. This latter complication could possibly be avoided if we separate the context of intuitionistic assumptions and the context of linear assumptions. However, this kind of separation between intuitionistic and linear assumptions is not trivial in the dependently typed setting because linear assumptions may depend on intuitionistic assumptions.

This design of context variables and capturing their dependency is essential to LINCX and to the smooth extension of contextual types to the linear setting. As the leaf-level context variables uniquely describe a context characterized by a tree of context joins, we only track the leaf-level context variables as assumptions while type checking an object, but justify the validity of context variables that occur as interior nodes through the leaf-level variables. We want to emphasize that this kind of encoding of context variables does not need to be exposed to programmers.

2.2   Example: CPS Translation

As a second example, we implement the translation of programs into continuation passing style following Danvy and Filinski [11]. Concretely, we follow closely the existing implementation of type-preserving CPS translation in BELUGA by Belanger et al. [1], but enforce that the continuations are used linearly, an idea from Berdine et al. [3]. Although context splits do not arise in this example, as we only have one linear variable (standing for the continuation) in our context, we include it, to showcase the mix and interplay of intuitionistic and linear function spaces in encoding program transformations.

Our source language is a simple language consisting of natural numbers, functions, applications and let-expressions. We only model well-typed expressions by defining a type source that is indexed by types tp.

```
Linear LF tp : type =      Linear LF source : tp → type =
| nat   : tp               | app   : source (arr S T) → source S → source T
| arr   : tp → tp → tp     | lam   : (source S → source T) → source (arr S T)
;                          | z     : source nat
                           | s     : source nat → source nat;
```

In our target language we distinguish between expressions, characterized by the type exp and values, defined by the type value. Continuations take values as their argument and return an exp. We ensure that each continuation itself is used exactly once by abstracting exp over the linear function space.

```
Linear LF exp : type =
| kapp     : value (arr S T) → value S → (value T → exp) -o exp
| halt     : value S → exp
and value : tp → type =
| klam     : (value S → (value T → exp) -o exp) → value (arr S T)
| kz       : value nat
| ksuc     : value nat → value nat ;
```

We can now define our source and value contexts as unrestricted contexts by marking the schema element with the tag u.

```
schema sctx = u (source T);
schema vctx = u (value T);
```

To guarantee that the resulting expression is well-typed, we define a context relation Ctx_Rel to relate the source context to the value context (see Fig. 3). Notice that we explicitly state that the type s of a source and target expression is closed; it does not depend on γ or δ. To distinguish between objects that depend on their surrounding context and objects that do not, we associate every index and pattern variable with a substitution (the identity substitution by default); if we want to state that a given variable is closed, we associate it with the empty substitution [].

We can now define the translation itself (see Fig. 3). The function cpse takes in a context relation Ctx_Rel [γ] [δ] and a source term of type source s[] that depends on context γ. It then returns the corresponding expression of type exp, depending on context δ extended by a continuation from value s to exp. The fact that the continuation is used only once in exp is enforced by declaring it linear in the

context. The translation proceeds by pattern matching on the source term. We
concentrate here on the interesting cases.

```
data Ctx_Rel: {γ:sctx}{δ:vctx} type =
Nil  : Ctx_Rel [] []
Cons : Ctx_Rel [γ] [δ] → Ctx_Rel [γ, x:source S[]] [δ, v:value S[]] ;

rec cpse:(γ:sctx)(δ:vctx)(S:[ ⊢ tp])
         Ctx_Rel [γ] [δ] → [γ ⊢ source S[]] → [δ, k:value S[] → exp ⊢ exp] =
fn r, e ⇒ case e of
| [γ ⊢ #p] ⇒
    let [δ⊢ #q] = lookup r [γ ⊢ #p] in
      [δ, k:value _ → exp ⊢ k #q]

| [γ ⊢ z] ⇒ let (r : Ctx_Rel [γ] [δ]) = r in [δ,k:value nat → exp ⊢ k kz]

| [γ ⊢ suc N] ⇒
    let [δ,k:value nat → exp ⊢ P] = cpse r [γ ⊢ N] in
      [δ,k:value nat → exp ⊢  P[λp. k (ksuc p)] ]

| [γ ⊢ lam λx. M] ⇒
    let [δ, v:value S[], k:value T[] → exp ⊢ P] = cpse [Cons r] [γ, x:source _ ⊢ M] in
      [δ, k^:value (arr S[] T[]) → exp ⊢ k (klam (λx.λ̂c. P))]

| [γ ⊢ app M N] ⇒
    let [δ, k1:value (arr S[] T[]) → exp ⊢ P] = cpse r [γ ⊢ M] in
    let [δ, k2:value S[]          → exp ⊢ Q] = cpse r [γ ⊢ N] in
      [δ,k:value T[] → exp ⊢ P[λf. Q[λx. kapp f x ^ k]]];
```

Fig. 3. CPS translation

Parameter Variable. If we encounter a variable from the context γ, written as
#p, we look up the corresponding variable #q in the target context δ by using the
context relation and we pass it to the continuation k. We omit here the definition
of the lookup function which is straightforward. We use _ where we believe that
the omitted object can reasonably be inferred. Finally, we note that k #q is well-
typed in the context δ, k:value _ → exp, as k is well-typed in the context that only
contains the declaration k:value _ → exp and #q is well-typed in the context δ.

Constant z. We first retrieve the target context δ to build the final expression by
pattern matching on the context relation r. Then we pass kz to the continuation
k in the context δ,k:value nat → exp. Note that an application k kz is well-typed in
δ,k:value nat → exp, as kz is well-typed in δ, i.e. its unrestricted part.

Lambda Abstraction. To convert functions, we extend the context γ and the
context relation r and convert the term M recursively in the extended context
to obtain the target expression P. We then pass to the continuation k the value
klam λx.λ̂c.P.

Application. Finally, let us consider the the source term app M N. We translate
both M and N recursively to produce the target terms P and Q respectively. We
then substitute for the continuation variable k2 in Q a continuation consuming

the local argument of an application. A continuation is then built from this, expecting the function to which the local argument is applied and substituted for k1 in P producing a well-typed expression, if a continuation for the resulting type s is provided.

We take advantage of our built-in substitution here to reduce any administrative redexes. The term (λx. kapp f x ^ k) that we substitute for references to k2 in Q will be β-reduced wherever that k2 appears in a function call position, such as the function calls introduced in the variable case. We hence reduce administrative redexes using the built-in (linear) LF application.

3   LINCX: A Linear Logical Framework with First-Class Contexts

Throughout this section we gradually introduce LINCX, a contextual linear logical framework with first-class contexts (i.e. context variables) that generalizes the linear logical framework LLF [9] and contextual LF [6]. Figure 4 presents both contextual linear LF (see Sect. 3.1) and its meta-language (see Sect. 3.6).

Contextual Linear LF

Kinds	K	$::=$	$\mathsf{type} \mid \Pi x{:}A.K$
Types	A, B	$::=$	$P \mid \Pi x{:}A.B \mid A \multimap B$
Atomic Types	P, Q	$::=$	$a \cdot S$
Heads	H	$::=$	$x \mid c \mid p[\sigma]$
Spines	S	$::=$	$\epsilon \mid M\,;S \mid M\,\hat{;}\,S$
Atomic Terms	R	$::=$	$H \cdot S \mid u[\sigma]$
Canonical Terms	M, N	$::=$	$R \mid \lambda x.M \mid \widehat{\lambda} x.M$
Variable Declarations	D	$::=$	$x{:}A \mid x\hat{:}A \mid x\dot{:}A$
Contexts	Ψ, Φ	$::=$	$\cdot \mid \psi_m \mid \Psi, D$
Substitutions	σ, τ	$::=$	$\cdot \mid \mathsf{id}_\psi \mid \sigma, M$

Meta-Language

Meta-Variables	X	$::=$	$u \mid p \mid \psi_i$
Meta-Objects	C	$::=$	$\widetilde{\Psi}.R \mid \widetilde{\Psi}.H \mid \Psi$
Context Schema Elem.	E	$::=$	$\lambda(\overrightarrow{x_i{:}A_i}).A \mid \lambda(\overrightarrow{x_i{:}A_i}).\widehat{A}$
Context Schemata	G	$::=$	$E \mid G + E$
Context Var. Indices	m	$::=$	$\epsilon \mid i \mid m \bowtie n$
Meta Types	U	$::=$	$\Psi \vdash P \mid \Psi \vdash \#A \mid G$
Meta-Contexts	Δ	$::=$	$\cdot \mid \Delta, X : U$
Meta-Substitutions	Θ	$::=$	$\cdot \mid \Theta, C/X$

Fig. 4. Contextual linear LF with first-class contexts

3.1   Syntax of Contextual Linear LF

LINCX allows for linear types, written $A \multimap B$, and dependent types $\Pi x{:}A.B$ where x may be unrestricted in B. We follow recent presentations where we only describe canonical LF objects using hereditary substitution.

As usual, our framework supports constants, (linear) functions, and (linear) applications. We only consider objects in η-long β-normal form, as these are the only meaningful terms in a logical framework. While the grammar characterizes objects in β-normal form, the bi-directional typing rules will also ensure that objects are η-long. Normal canonical terms are either intuitionistic lambda abstractions, linear lambda abstractions, or neutral atomic terms. We define (linear) applications as neutral atomic terms using a spine representation [10], as it makes the termination of hereditary substitution easier to establish. For example, instead of $x\, M_1 \ldots M_n$, we write $x \cdot M_1;\ \ldots;\ M_n;\ \epsilon$. The three possible variants of a spine head are: a variable x, a constant c or a parameter variable closure $p[\sigma]$.

Our framework contains *ordinary bound variables* x which may refer to a variable declaration in a context Ψ or may be bound by either the unrestricted or linear lambda-abstraction, or by the dependent type $\Pi x{:}A.B$. Similarly to contextual LF, LINCX also allows two kinds of *contextual variables* as terms. First, the meta-variable u of type $(\Psi \vdash P)$ stands for a general LF object of atomic type P and uses the variables declared in Ψ. Second, the parameter variable p of type $(\Psi \vdash \#A)$ stands for a variable object of type A from the context Ψ. These contextual variables are associated with a postponed substitution σ representing a closure. The intention is to apply σ as soon as we know what u (or p resp.) stands for.

The system has one mixed context Ψ containing both intuitionistic and linear assumptions: $x{:}A$ is an intuitionistic assumption in the context (also called *unrestricted assumption*), $x\hat{\,}{:}A$ represents a linear assumption and $x\check{\,}{:}A$ stands for its dual, an unavailable assumption. It is worth noting that we use $\hat{\,}$ throughout the system description to indicate a linear object – be it term, variable, name etc. Similarly, $\check{\,}$ always denotes an unavailable resource.

In the simultaneous substitution σ, we do not make the domain explicit. Rather, we think of a substitution together with its domain Ψ; the i-th element in σ corresponds to the i-th declaration in Ψ. The expression id_ψ denotes the identity substitution with domain ψ_m for some index m; we write $\cdot$ for the empty substitution. We build substitutions using normal terms M. We must however be careful: note that a variable x is only a normal term if it is of base type. As we push a substitution σ through a λ-abstraction $\lambda x.M$, we need to extend σ with x. The resulting substitution σ, x might not be well-formed, since x might not be of base type and, in fact, we do not know its type. This is taken care of in our definition of substitution, based on contextual LF [7]. As we substitute and replace a context variable with a concrete context, we unfold and generate an (η-expanded) identity substitution for a given context Ψ.

3.2   Contexts and Context Joins

Since linearity introduces context splitting, context maintenance is crucial in any linear system. When we allow for first-class contexts, as we do in LINCX, it becomes much harder: we now need to ensure that, upon instantiation of the context variables, we do not accidentally join two contexts sharing a linear variable. To enforce this in LINCX, we allow for at most one (indexed) context variable per context and use indices to abstractly describe splitting. This lets us generalize the standard equational theory for contexts based on context joins to include context variables.

As mentioned above, contexts in LINCX are mixed. Besides linear and intuitionistic assumptions, we allow for unavailable assumptions following the approach of Schack-Nielsen and Schürmann [27], in order to maintain symmetry when splitting a context: if $\Psi = \Psi_1 \bowtie \Psi_2$, then Ψ_1 and Ψ_2 both contain all the variables declared in Ψ; however, if Ψ_1 contains a linear assumption $x_l^\bullet A$, Ψ_2 will contain its unavailable counterpart $x_l^\bullet A$ (and vice-versa).

To account for context splitting in the presence of context variables, we index the latter. The indices are freely built from elements of an infinite, countable set $\mathcal{I}$, through a join operation ($\bowtie$). It is associative and commutative, with ϵ as its neutral element. In other words, $(\mathcal{I}^*, \bowtie, \epsilon)$ is a (partial) free commutative monoid over $\mathcal{I}$. For our presentation it is important that no element of the monoid is invertible, that is if $m \bowtie n = \epsilon$ then $m = n = \epsilon$. In the process of joining contexts, it is crucial to ensure that each linear variable is used only once: we do not allow a join of $\Psi, x_l^\bullet A$ with $\Phi, x_l^\bullet A$. To express the fact that indices m and n share no elements of $\mathcal{I}$ and hence the join of ψ_m with ψ_n is meaningful, we use the notation $m \perp n$. In fact we will overload $\bowtie$, changing it into a partial operation $m \bowtie n$ that fails when $m \not\perp n$. This is because we want the result of joining two context variables to continue being a correct context upon instantiation. We will come back to this point in Sect. 3.6, when discussing meta-substitution for context variables.

To give more intuition, the implementation of the indices in our formalization of the system is using binary numbers, where $\mathcal{I}$ contains powers of 2, $\bowtie$ is defined as a binary OR and $\epsilon = 0$. $m \perp n$ holds when m and n use different powers of 2 in their binary representation. We can also simply think of indices m as sets of elements from $\mathcal{I}$ with $\bowtie$ being $\cup$ for sets not sharing any elements.

The only context variables tracked in the meta-context Δ are the *leaf-level* context variables ψ_i. We require that these use elements of the carrier set $i \in \mathcal{I}$ as indices. To construct context variables for use in contexts, we combine leaf-level context variables using $\bowtie$ on indices. Consider again the tree describing the context joins (see Fig. 2). In this example, we have the leaf-level context variables γ_1, γ_{21}, and γ_{22}. These are the only context variables we track in the meta-context Δ. Using a binary encoding we would use the subscripts 100, 010 and 001 instead of 1, 21, and 22.

Rules of constructing a well-formed context (Fig. 5) describe four possible initial cases of context construction. First, the empty context, written simply as ·, is well-formed. Next, there are two possibilities why a context denoted

$$\boxed{\Delta \vdash \Psi \ \mathsf{ctx}} \qquad \Psi \text{ is a valid context under meta-context } \Delta$$

$$\frac{}{\Delta \vdash \cdot \ \mathsf{ctx}} \qquad \frac{\psi_i \in \mathsf{dom}(\Delta)}{\Delta \vdash \psi_\epsilon \ \mathsf{ctx}} \qquad \frac{\psi_i \in \mathsf{dom}(\Delta)}{\Delta \vdash \psi_i \ \mathsf{ctx}} \qquad \frac{\Delta \vdash \psi_k \ \mathsf{ctx} \quad \Delta \vdash \psi_l \ \mathsf{ctx} \quad m = k \bowtie l}{\Delta \vdash \psi_m \ \mathsf{ctx}}$$

$$\frac{\Delta \vdash \Psi \ \mathsf{ctx} \quad \Delta; \overline{\Psi} \vdash A \ \mathsf{type} \quad D \in \{x{:}A, x^{\hat{}}{:}A, x^{\hat{}}{:}A\}}{\Delta \vdash \Psi, D \ \mathsf{ctx}}$$

Fig. 5. Well-formed contexts

by a context variable ψ_i is well-formed. If the context variable ψ_i is declared in the meta-context Δ, then it is well-formed and describes a leaf-variable. To guarantee that also context variables that describe intermediate nodes in our context tree are well-formed, we have a composition rule that allows joining two well-formed context variables using $\bowtie$ operation on indices; the restriction we make on $\bowtie$ ensures that they do not share any leaf-level variables. ψ_ϵ forms a well-formed context as long as there is some context variable ψ_i declared in Δ. This is an abstraction that allows us to describe the intuitionistic variables of a context. Finally, the last case for context extensions is straightforward.

In general we write Γ for contexts that do not start with a context variable and Ψ, Γ for the extension of context Ψ by the variable declarations of Γ.

When defining our inference rules, we will often need to access the *intuitionistic part* of a context. Much like in linear LF [9], we introduce the function $\overline{\Psi}$ which is defined as follows:

$$\boxed{\overline{\Psi}} \qquad \text{Intuitionistic part of } \Psi$$

$$\overline{\cdot} = \cdot$$
$$\overline{\psi_m} = \psi_\epsilon$$
$$\overline{\Psi, x{:}A} = \overline{\Psi}, x{:}A$$
$$\overline{\Psi, x^{\hat{}}{:}A} = \overline{\Psi}, x^{\hat{}}{:}A$$
$$\overline{\Psi, x^{\hat{}}{:}A} = \overline{\Psi}, x^{\hat{}}{:}A$$

Note that this function does not remove any variable declarations from Ψ, it simply makes them unavailable. Further, when applying this function to a context variable, it drops all the indices, indicating access to only the shared part of the context variable. After we instantiate ψ_m with a concrete context, we will apply the operation. Extracting the intuitionistic part of a context is hence simply postponed.

Further, we define notation $\mathsf{unr}(\Psi)$ to denote an unrestricted context, i.e. a context that only contains unrestricted assumptions; while $\overline{\Psi}$ drops all linear assumptions, $\mathsf{unr}(\Psi)$ simply verifies that Ψ is a purely intuitionistic context. In other words, $\mathsf{unr}(\Psi)$ holds if and only if $\overline{\Psi} = \Psi$. We omit here its (straightforward) judgmental definition.

The rules for joining contexts (see Fig. 6) follow the approach presented by Schack-Nielsen in his PhD dissertation [26], but are generalized to take into

$$\boxed{\Psi = \Psi_1 \bowtie \Psi_2} \qquad \text{Context } \Psi \text{ is a join of } \Psi_1 \text{ and } \Psi_2$$

$$\frac{}{\cdot = \cdot \bowtie \cdot} \qquad \frac{m = k \bowtie l}{\psi_m = \psi_k \bowtie \psi_l}$$

$$\frac{\Psi = \Psi_1 \bowtie \Psi_2}{\Psi, x{:}A = \Psi_1, x{:}A \bowtie \Psi_2, x{:}A} \qquad \frac{\Psi = \Psi_1 \bowtie \Psi_2}{\Psi, x^{\cdot}_{\cdot}A = \Psi_1, x^{\cdot}_{\cdot}A \bowtie \Psi_2, x^{\cdot}_{\cdot}A}$$

$$\frac{\Psi = \Psi_1 \bowtie \Psi_2}{\Psi, x^{\cdot}_{\cdot}A = \Psi_1, x^{\cdot}_{\cdot}A \bowtie \Psi_2, x^{\cdot}_{\cdot}A} \qquad \frac{\Psi = \Psi_1 \bowtie \Psi_2}{\Psi, x^{\cdot}_{\cdot}A = \Psi_1, x^{\cdot}_{\cdot}A \bowtie \Psi_2, x^{\cdot}_{\cdot}A}$$

Fig. 6. Joining contexts

account context variables. Because of the monoid structure of context variable indices, the description can be quite concise while still preserving the desired properties of this operation. For instance the expected property $\Psi = \Psi \bowtie \overline{\Psi}$ follows, on the context variable level, from ϵ being the neutral element of $\bowtie$. Indeed, for any ψ_m, we have that $\psi_m = \psi_m \bowtie \psi_\epsilon$.

It is also important to note that, thanks to the determinism of $\bowtie$, context joins are unique. In other words, if $\Psi = \Psi_1 \bowtie \Psi_2$ and $\Phi = \Psi_1 \bowtie \Psi_2$, $\Psi = \Phi$. On the other hand, context splitting is non-deterministic: given a context Ψ we have numerous options of splitting it into Ψ_1 and Ψ_2, since each linear variable can go to either of the components.

We finish this section by describing the equational theory of context joins. We expect joining contexts to be a commutative and associative operation, and the unrestricted parts of contexts in the join should be equal. Further, it is always possible to extend a valid join with a ground unrestricted context, and $\overline{\Psi}$ can always be joined with Ψ without changing the result.

Lemma 1 (Theory of context joins).

1. *(Commutativity) If $\Psi = \Psi_1 \bowtie \Psi_2$ then $\Psi = \Psi_2 \bowtie \Psi_1$.*
2. *(Associativity$_1$) If $\Psi = \Psi_1 \bowtie \Psi_2$ and $\Psi_1 = \Psi_{11} \bowtie \Psi_{12}$ then there exists a context Ψ_0 s.t. $\Psi = \Psi_{11} \bowtie \Psi_0$ and $\Psi_0 = \Psi_{12} \bowtie \Psi_2$.*
3. *(Associativity$_2$) If $\Psi = \Psi_1 \bowtie \Psi_2$ and $\Psi_2 = \Psi_{21} \bowtie \Psi_{22}$ then there exists a context Ψ_0 s.t. $\Psi_0 = \Psi_1 \bowtie \Psi_{21}$ and $\Psi = \Psi_0 \bowtie \Psi_{22}$.*
4. *If $\Psi = \Psi_1 \bowtie \Psi_2$ then $\overline{\Psi} = \overline{\Psi_1} = \overline{\Psi_2}$.*
5. *If $\mathsf{unr}(\Gamma)$ and $\Psi = \Psi_1 \bowtie \Psi_2$ then $\Psi, \Gamma = \Psi_1, \Gamma \bowtie \Psi_2, \Gamma$.*
6. *For any Ψ, $\Psi = \Psi \bowtie \overline{\Psi}$.*

We will need these properties to prove lemmas about typing and substitution, specifically for the cases that call for specific context joins.

3.3 Typing for Terms and Substitutions

We now describe the bi-directional typing rules of LINCX terms (see Fig. 7). All typing judgments have access to the meta-context Δ, context Ψ, and to a fixed well-typed signature Σ where we store constants c together with their types and kinds. LINCX objects may depend on variables declared in the context Ψ and a fixed meta-context Δ which contains contextual variables such as meta-variables u, parameter variables p, and context variables. Although the rules are bi-directional, they do not give a direct algorithm, as we need to split a context Ψ into contexts Ψ_1 and Ψ_2 such that $\Psi = \Psi_1 \bowtie \Psi_2$ (see for example the rule for checking $H \cdot S$ against a base type P). This operation is in itself non-deterministic, however since our system is linear there is only one split that makes the components (for example H and S in $H \cdot S$) typecheck.

$$\boxed{\Delta;\Psi \vdash M \Leftarrow A} \qquad \text{Term } M \text{ checks against type } A$$

$$\frac{\Delta;\Psi,x{:}A \vdash M \Leftarrow B}{\Delta;\Psi \vdash \lambda x.M \Leftarrow \Pi x{:}A.B} \qquad \frac{\Delta;\Psi,x\hat{:}A \vdash M \Leftarrow B}{\Delta;\Psi \vdash \widehat{\lambda}x.M \Leftarrow A \multimap B}$$

$$\frac{u : (\Phi \vdash P) \in \Delta \quad \Delta;\Psi \vdash \sigma \Leftarrow \Phi \quad \Delta;\overline{\Psi} \vdash [\sigma]_{\overline{\Phi}}P = Q}{\Delta;\Psi \vdash u[\sigma] \Leftarrow Q}$$

$$\frac{\Delta;\Psi_1 \vdash H \Rightarrow A \quad \Delta;\Psi_2 \vdash S > A \Rightarrow P \quad \Delta;\overline{\Psi} \vdash P = Q \quad \Psi = \Psi_1 \bowtie \Psi_2}{\Delta;\Psi \vdash H \cdot S \Leftarrow Q}$$

$$\boxed{\Delta;\Psi \vdash H \Rightarrow A} \qquad \text{Head } H \text{ synthesizes a type } A$$

$$\frac{c{:}A \in \Sigma \quad \mathsf{unr}(\Psi)}{\Delta;\Psi \vdash c \Rightarrow A} \qquad \frac{p : (\Phi \vdash \#A) \in \Delta \quad \Delta;\Psi \vdash \sigma \Leftarrow \Phi}{\Delta;\Psi \vdash p[\sigma] \Rightarrow [\sigma]_{\overline{\Phi}}A}$$

$$\frac{\mathsf{unr}(\Psi) \quad x{:}A \in \Psi}{\Delta;\Psi \vdash x \Rightarrow A} \qquad \frac{\mathsf{unr}(\Psi_1) \quad \mathsf{unr}(\Psi_2)}{\Delta;\Psi_1,x\hat{:}A,\Psi_2 \vdash x \Rightarrow A}$$

$$\boxed{\Delta;\Psi \vdash S > A \Rightarrow P} \qquad \text{Spine } S \text{ synthesizes type } P$$

$$\frac{\mathsf{unr}(\Psi)}{\Delta;\Psi \vdash \epsilon > P \Rightarrow P} \qquad \frac{\Delta;\overline{\Psi} \vdash M \Leftarrow A \quad \Delta;\Psi \vdash S > [M/x]_A B \Rightarrow P}{\Delta;\Psi \vdash M\,;S > \Pi x{:}A.B \Rightarrow P}$$

$$\frac{\Delta;\Psi_1 \vdash M \Leftarrow A \quad \Delta;\Psi_2 \vdash S > B \Rightarrow P \quad \Psi = \Psi_1 \bowtie \Psi_2}{\Delta;\Psi \vdash M\hat{;}S > A \multimap B \Rightarrow P}$$

Fig. 7. Typing rules for terms

Typing rules presented in Fig. 7 are, perhaps unsurprisingly, a fusion between contextual LF and linear LF. As in contextual LF, the typing for meta-variable closures and parameter variable closures is straightforward. A meta-variable $u :$ $(\Psi \vdash P)$ represents an open LF object (a "hole" in a term). As mentioned earlier it has, associated with it, a postponed substitution σ, applied as soon as u is made concrete. Similarly, a parameter variable $p : (\Psi \vdash \#A)$ represents an LF variable – either an unrestricted or linear one.

As in linear LF, we have two lambda abstraction rules (one introducing intu-itionistic, the other linear assumptions) and two corresponding variable cases.

Moreover, we ensure that types only depend on the unrestricted part of a context when checking that two types are equal. As we rely on hereditary substitutions, this equality check ends up being syntactic equality. Similarly, when we consider a spine $M \, ; S$ and check it against the dependent type $\Pi x{:}A.B$, we make sure that M has type A in the unrestricted context before continuing to check the spine S against $[M/x]_A B$. When we encounter a spine $M \, \overset{\circ}{,} S$ and check it against the linear type $A \multimap B$ in the context Ψ, we must show that there exists a split s.t. $\Psi = \Psi_1 \bowtie \Psi_2$ and then check that the term M has type A in the context Ψ_1 and the remaining spine S is checked against B to synthesize a type P.

$$\boxed{\Delta; \Psi \vdash \sigma \Leftarrow \Phi} \qquad \text{Substitution } \sigma \text{ maps variables in } \Phi \text{ to variables in } \Psi$$

$$\frac{\mathsf{unr}(\Psi)}{\Delta; \Psi \vdash \cdot \Leftarrow \cdot} \qquad \frac{\mathsf{unr}(\Gamma)}{\Delta; \psi_m, \Gamma \vdash \mathsf{id}_\psi \Leftarrow \psi_m}$$

$$\frac{\Delta; \Psi \vdash \sigma \Leftarrow \Phi \quad \Delta; \overline{\Psi} \vdash M \Leftarrow [\sigma]_{\overline{\Phi}} A}{\Delta; \Psi \vdash \sigma, M \Leftarrow \Phi, x{:}A}$$

$$\frac{\Delta; \Psi_1 \vdash \sigma \Leftarrow \Phi \quad \Delta; \Psi_2 \vdash M \Leftarrow [\sigma]_{\overline{\Phi}} A \quad \Psi = \Psi_1 \bowtie \Psi_2}{\Delta; \Psi \vdash \sigma, M \Leftarrow \Phi, x\overset{\circ}{:}A}$$

$$\frac{\Delta; \Psi \vdash \sigma \Leftarrow \Phi \quad \overline{\Psi} = \overline{\Psi'} \quad \Delta; \Psi' \vdash M \Leftarrow [\sigma]_{\overline{\Phi}} A}{\Delta; \Psi \vdash \sigma, M \Leftarrow \Phi, x\overset{\cdot}{:}A}$$

Fig. 8. Typing rules for substitutions

Finally, we consider the typing rules for substitutions, presented in Fig. 8. We exercise care in making sure the range context in the base cases, i.e. where the substitution is empty or the identity, is unrestricted. This guarantees weakening and contraction for unrestricted contexts.

The substitution σ, M is well-typed with domain $\Phi, x{:}A$ and range Ψ, if σ is a substitution from Φ to the context Ψ and in addition M has type $[\sigma]_\Phi A$ in the unrestricted context $\overline{\Psi}$. The substitution σ, M is well-typed with domain $\Phi, x\overset{\circ}{:}A$ and range Ψ, if there exists a context split $\Psi = \Psi_1 \bowtie \Psi_2$ s.t. σ is a substitution with domain Φ and range Ψ_1 and M is a well-typed term in the context Ψ_2. The substitution σ, M is well-typed with domain $\Phi, x\overset{\cdot}{:}A$ and range Ψ, if σ is a substitution from Φ to Ψ and for some context Ψ', $\overline{\Psi} = \overline{\Psi'}$, M is a well-typed term in the context Ψ'. This last rule, extending the substitution domain by an unavailable variable, is perhaps a little surprising. Intuitively we may want to skip the unavailable variable of a substitution. This would however mean that we have to perform not only context splitting, but also substitution splitting when defining the operation of simultaneous substitution. An alternative is to use an arbitrary term M to be substituted for this unavailable variable, as the typing rules ensure it will never actually occur in the term in which we substitute. When establishing termination of type-checking, it is then important that M

type checks in a context that can be generated from the one we already have. We ensure this with a side condition $\overline{\Psi} = \overline{\Psi'}$. By enforcing that the unrestricted parts of Ψ and Ψ' are equal we limit the choices that we have for Ψ' deciding which linear variables to take (linear) and which to drop (unavailable), and deciding on the index of context variable.

When considering an identity substitution id_ψ, we allow for some ambiguity: we can use any ψ_m for both the domain and range of id_ψ. Upon meta-substitution, all instantiations of ψ_m will have the same names and types of variables; the only thing differentiating them will be their status (intuitionistic, linear or unavailable). Since substitutions do not store information about the status of variables they substitute for (this information is available only in the domain and range), the constructed identity substitution will be the same regardless of the initial choice of ψ_m – it will however have a different type.

The observation above has a more general consequence, allowing us to avoid substitution splits when defining the operation of hereditary substitution: if a substitution in LINCX transforms context Φ to context Ψ, it does so also for their unrestricted fragments.

Lemma 2. *If $\Delta; \Psi \vdash \sigma \Leftarrow \Phi$ then $\Delta; \overline{\Psi} \vdash \sigma \Leftarrow \overline{\Phi}$.*

3.4   Hereditary Substitution

Next we will characterise the operation of hereditary substitution, which allows us to consider only normal forms in our grammar and typing rules, making the decidability of type-checking easy to establish.

As usual, we annotate hereditary substitutions with an approximation of the type of the term we substitute for to guarantee termination.

$$\text{Type approximations } \alpha, \beta ::= a \mid \alpha \rightarrow \beta \mid \alpha \multimap \beta$$

We then define the dependency erasure operator $(-)^-$ as follows:

$$\boxed{A^- = \alpha} \qquad \alpha \text{ is a type approximation of } A$$
$$(a \cdot S)^- = a$$
$$(\Pi x{:}A.B)^- = A^- \rightarrow B^-$$
$$(A \multimap B)^- = A^- \multimap B^-$$

We will sometimes tacitly apply the dependency erasure operator $(-)^-$ in the following definitions. Hereditary single substitution for LINCX is standard and closely follows [7], since linearity does not induce any complications. When executing the current substitution would create redexes, we proceed by hereditarily performing another substitution. This reduction operation is defined as:

$$\boxed{\mathsf{reduce}(M:\alpha,S)=N}\quad N \text{ is the result of reducing } M \text{ applied to the spine } S$$

$$\mathsf{reduce}(\lambda x.M:\alpha\to\beta,(N\,;S))=\mathsf{reduce}([N/x]_\alpha M:\beta,S)$$
$$\mathsf{reduce}(\widehat{\lambda} x.M:\alpha\multimap\beta,(N\,\widehat{;}\,S))=\mathsf{reduce}([N/x]_\alpha M:\beta,S)$$
$$\mathsf{reduce}(R:a,\epsilon)\qquad\qquad=R$$
$$\mathsf{reduce}(M:\alpha,S)\qquad\qquad=\bot$$

Termination can be readily established:

Theorem 1 (Termination of hereditary single substitution).
  The hereditary substitutions $[M/x]_\alpha(N)$ and $\mathsf{reduce}(M:\alpha,S)$ terminate, either by failing or successfully producing a result.

The following theorem provides typing for the hereditary substitution. We use J to stand for any of the forms of judgments defined above.

Theorem 2 (Hereditary single substitution property).

1. *If $\Delta;\overline{\Psi}\vdash M\Leftarrow A$ and $\Delta;\Psi,x{:}A\vdash J$ then $\Delta;\Psi\vdash[M/x]_A J$.*
2. *If $\Delta;\Psi_1\vdash M\Leftarrow A$, $\Delta;\Psi_2,x{\widehat{:}}A\vdash J$ and $\Psi=\Psi_1\bowtie\Psi_2$ then $\Delta;\Psi\vdash[M/x]_A J$*
3. *If $\Delta;\Psi_1\vdash M\Leftarrow A$, $\Delta;\Psi_2\vdash S>A\Rightarrow B$, $\Psi=\Psi_1\bowtie\Psi_2$ and $\mathsf{reduce}(M:A^-,S)=M'$ then $\Delta;\Psi\vdash M'\Leftarrow B$*

We can easily generalize hereditary substitution to simultaneous substitution. We focus here on the simultaneous substitution in a canonical terms (see Fig. 9). Hereditary simultaneous substitution relies on a lookup function that is defined below. Note that $(\sigma,M)_{\Psi,x{:}A}(x)=\bot$, since we assume x to be unavailable in the domain of σ.

$$\boxed{\sigma_\Psi(x)}\qquad\text{Variable lookup}$$

$$(\sigma,M)_{\Psi,x:A}(x)=M:A^-$$
$$(\sigma,M)_{\Psi,x\widehat{:}A}(x)=M:A^-$$
$$(\sigma,M)_{\Psi,y:A}(x)=\sigma_\Psi(x)\qquad\text{where }y\neq x$$
$$(\sigma,M)_{\Psi,y\widehat{:}A}(x)=\sigma_\Psi(x)\qquad\text{where }y\neq x$$
$$\sigma_\Psi(x)\qquad\quad=\bot$$

Unlike many previous formulations of contextual LF, we do not allow substitutions to be directly extended with variables. Instead, following Cave and Pientka's more recent approach [7], we require that substitutions must be extended with η-long terms, thus guaranteeing unique normal forms for substitutions. For this reason, we maintain a list of variable names and statuses which are not to be changed, $\widetilde{\Phi}$ in $[\sigma]_\Psi^{\widetilde{\Phi}}$. This list gets extended every time we pass through a lambda expression. We use it when substituting in $y\cdot S$ – if $y\in\widetilde{\Phi}$ or $\widehat{y}\in\widetilde{\Phi}$ we simply leave the head unchanged. It is important to preserve not only the name

$$\boxed{[\sigma]_{\Psi}^{\widetilde{\Phi}}M}$$ Substitution of the variables of Ψ in a canonical term
(leaving elements of $\widetilde{\Phi}$ unchanged)

$$[\sigma]_{\Psi}^{\widetilde{\Phi}}(\lambda y.N) = \lambda y.N' \qquad \text{where } [\sigma]_{\Psi}^{\widetilde{\Phi},y}N = N', \text{ choosing } y \notin \Psi, y \notin \mathsf{FV}(\sigma)$$

$$[\sigma]_{\Psi}^{\widetilde{\Phi}}(\widehat{\lambda} y.N) = \widehat{\lambda} y.N' \qquad \text{where } [\sigma]_{\Psi}^{\widetilde{\Phi},\widetilde{y}}N = N', \text{ choosing } y \notin \Psi, y \notin \mathsf{FV}(\sigma)$$

$$[\sigma]_{\Psi}^{\widetilde{\Phi}}(u[\tau]) = u[\tau'] \qquad \text{where } [\sigma]_{\Psi}^{\widetilde{\Phi}}\tau = \tau'$$

$$[\sigma]_{\Psi}^{\widetilde{\Phi}}(c \cdot S) = c \cdot S' \qquad \text{where } [\sigma]_{\Psi}^{\widetilde{\Phi}}S = S'$$

$$[\sigma]_{\Psi}^{\widetilde{\Phi}}(x \cdot S) = \mathsf{reduce}(M : \alpha, S') \text{ where } \Psi = \Psi_1 \bowtie \Psi_2 \text{ and } x \notin \widetilde{\Phi}$$
$$\text{and } \sigma_{\Psi_1}(x) = M : \alpha \text{ and } [\sigma]_{\Psi_2}^{\widetilde{\Phi}}S = S'$$

$$[\sigma]_{\Psi}^{\widetilde{\Phi}}(y \cdot S) = y \cdot S' \qquad \text{where } y \in \widetilde{\Phi} \text{ and } [\sigma]_{\Psi}^{\widetilde{\Phi}}S = S'$$

$$[\sigma]_{\Psi}^{\widetilde{\Phi}}(y \cdot S) = y \cdot S' \qquad \text{where } \widetilde{y} \in \widetilde{\Phi}, \text{ and } [\sigma]_{\Psi}^{\widetilde{\Phi}\setminus\widetilde{y}}S = S'$$

$$[\sigma]_{\Psi}^{\widetilde{\Phi}}(p[\tau] \cdot S) = p[\tau'] \cdot S' \qquad \text{where } \Psi = \Psi_1 \bowtie \Psi_2, \text{ and } \widetilde{\Phi} = \widetilde{\Phi}_1 \bowtie \widetilde{\Phi}_2$$
$$\text{and } [\sigma]_{\Psi_1}^{\widetilde{\Phi}_1}\tau = \tau' \text{ and } [\sigma]_{\Psi_2}^{\widetilde{\Phi}_2}S = S'$$

Fig. 9. Simultaneous substitution

of the variable, but also its status (linear, intuitionistic or unavailable), since we sometimes have to perform a split on $\widetilde{\Phi}$. Such split works precisely like one on complete contexts, since types play no role in context splitting.

As simultaneous substitution is a transformation of contexts, it is perhaps not surprising that it becomes more complex in the presence of context splitting. Consider for instance the case where we push the substitution σ through an expression $p[\tau] \cdot S$. While σ has domain Ψ (and is ignoring variables from $\widetilde{\Phi}$) and $p[\tau] \cdot S$ is well-typed in (Ψ, Φ), the closure $p[\tau]$ is well-typed in a context (Ψ_1, Φ_1) and the spine S is well-typed in a context (Ψ_2, Φ_2) where $\Psi = \Psi_1 \bowtie \Psi_2$ and $\Phi = \Phi_1 \bowtie \Phi_2$. As a consequence, $[\sigma]_{\Psi}^{\widetilde{\Phi}}\tau$ and $[\sigma]_{\Psi}^{\widetilde{\Phi}}S$ would be ill-typed, however $[\sigma]_{\Psi_1}^{\widetilde{\Phi_1}}\tau$ and $[\sigma]_{\Psi_2}^{\widetilde{\Phi_2}}S$ will work well. Notice that it is only the domain of the substitution that we need to split, not the substitution itself.

Similarly to the case for hereditary single substitution, the theorem below provides typing for simultaneous substitution.

Theorem 3 (Simultaneous substitution property).
If $\Delta; \Psi \vdash J$ and $\Delta; \Phi \vdash \sigma \Leftarrow \Psi$ then $\Delta; \Phi \vdash [\sigma]_{\Psi}J$.

3.5 Decidability of Type Checking in Contextual Linear LF

In order to establish a decidability result for type checking, we observe that the typing judgments are syntax directed. Further, when a context split is necessary (e.g. when checking $\Delta, \Psi \vdash \sigma, M \Leftarrow \Phi, x{:}A$), it is possible to enumerate all the possible correct splits (all Ψ_1, Ψ_2 such that $\Psi = \Psi_1 \bowtie \Psi_2$). For exactly one of them it will hold that $\Delta; \Psi_1 \vdash \sigma \Leftarrow \Phi$ and $\Delta; \Psi_2 \vdash M \Leftarrow [\sigma]_{\overline{\Phi}}A$. Finally, in the $\Delta, \Psi \vdash \sigma, M \Leftarrow \Phi, x{:}A$ case, thanks to explicit mention of all the variables (including unavailable ones), we can enlist all possible contexts Ψ' well-formed under Δ and such that $\overline{\Psi} = \overline{\Psi'}$.

Theorem 4 (Decidability of type checking). *Type checking is decidable.*

3.6 LINCX's Meta-Language

To use contextual linear LF as an index language in BELUGA, we have to be able to lift LINCX objects to meta-types and meta-objects and the definition of the meta-substitution operation. We are basing our presentation on one for contextual LF [6].

Figure 4 presents the meta-language of LINCX. Meta-objects are either contextual objects or contexts. The former may be instantiations to parameter variables $p : (\Psi \vdash \#A)$ or meta-variables $u : (\Psi \vdash P)$. These objects are written $\widetilde{\Psi}.R$ where $\widetilde{\Psi}$ denotes a list of variables obtained by dropping all the type information from the declaration, but retaining the information about variable status (intuitionistic, linear or unavailable).

$$\boxed{\widetilde{\Psi}} \qquad \text{Name and status of variables from } \Psi$$

$$\widetilde{\cdot} = \cdot$$
$$\widetilde{\psi_m} = \psi_m$$
$$\widetilde{\Psi, x{:}A} = \widetilde{\Psi}, x$$
$$\widetilde{\Psi, x{\hat{:}}A} = \widetilde{\Psi}, \widehat{x}$$
$$\widetilde{\Psi, x{\check{:}}A} = \widetilde{\Psi}, \check{x}$$

Contexts as meta-objects are used to instantiate context variables $\psi_i : G$. When constructing those we must exercise caution, as we need to ensure that no linear variable is used in two contexts that are, at any point, joined. At the same time, instantiations for context variables differing only in the index (ψ_i and ψ_j) have to use precisely the same variable names and their unrestricted fragments have to be equal. It is also important to ensure that the constructed context is of a correct schema G. Schemas describe possible shapes of contexts, and each schema element can be either linear ($\lambda(\overrightarrow{x_i{:}A_i}).\widehat{A}$) or intuitionistic ($\lambda(\overrightarrow{x_i{:}A_i}).A$). This can be extended to also allow combinations of linear and intuitionistic schema elements.

We now give rules for a well-formed meta-context Δ (see Fig. 10). It is defined on the structure of Δ and is mostly straightforward. As usual, we assume the

$$\boxed{\vdash \Delta \text{ mctx}} \qquad \Delta \text{ is a valid meta-context}$$

$$\frac{}{\vdash \cdot \text{ mctx}} \qquad \frac{\vdash \Delta \text{ mctx} \quad \Delta; \overline{\Psi} \vdash P \text{ type}}{\vdash \Delta, u : (\Psi \vdash P) \text{ mctx}}$$

$$\frac{\vdash \Delta \text{ mctx} \quad \Delta; \overline{\Psi} \vdash A \text{ type}}{\vdash \Delta, p : (\Psi \vdash \#A) \text{ mctx}} \qquad \frac{\vdash \Delta \text{ mctx} \quad i \in \mathcal{I}}{\vdash \Delta, \psi_i : G \text{ mctx}} \star$$

Fig. 10. Well-formed meta-contexts

names we choose are fresh. The noteworthy case arises when we extend Δ with a context variable ψ_i. Because all context variables ψ_j will describe parts of the same context, we require their schemas to be the same. This side condition ($\star$) can be formally stated as: $\forall j.\psi_j \in \mathsf{dom}(\Delta) \to \psi_j : G \in \Delta$. Moreover, to avoid manually ensuring that indices of context variables do not cross, we require that leaf context variables use elements of the carrier set $i \in \mathcal{I}$ (i.e. they are formed without using the $\bowtie$ operation).

Typing of meta-terms is straightforward and follows precisely the schema presented in previous work.

Because of the interdependencies when substituting for context variables, we diverge slightly from standard presentations of typing of meta-substitutions.

First, we do not at all consider single meta-substitutions, as they would be limited only to parameter and meta-variables. In the general case it is impossible to meaningfully substitute only one context variable, as this would break the invariant that all instantiations of context variables share variable names and the intuitionistic part of the context.

Second, the typing rules for the simultaneous meta-substitution (see Fig. 11) are specialized in the case of substituting for a context variable. When extending Θ with an instantiation Ψ_i for a context variable $\psi_i : G$, we first verify that context Ψ_i has the required schema G. We also have to check that Ψ_i can be joined with *any other* instantiation Ψ_j for context variable ψ_j already present in Θ (that is, $\Psi_i \perp_\psi \Theta$). This is enough to ensure the desired properties of meta-substitution for context variables.

We can now define the simultaneous meta-substitution. The operation itself is straightforward, as linearity does not complicate things on the meta-level. What is slightly more involved is the variable lookup function.

$$\boxed{\Psi \perp_\psi \Theta} \qquad \text{Context } \Psi \text{ is linearly disjoint from the range of } \Theta \text{ for } \psi_j$$

$$\frac{}{\Psi \perp_\psi (\cdot)} \qquad \frac{\Psi \perp_\psi \Theta \quad \Psi' = \Psi \bowtie \Psi_j}{\Psi \perp_\psi (\Theta, \Psi_j/\psi_j)} \qquad \frac{\Psi \perp_\psi \Theta \quad X \neq \psi_j}{\Psi \perp_\psi (\Theta, C/X)}$$

$$\boxed{\Delta \vdash \Theta \Leftarrow \Delta'} \qquad \Theta \text{ has domain } \Delta' \text{ and range } \Delta$$

$$\frac{}{\Delta \vdash \cdot \Leftarrow \cdot} \qquad \frac{\Delta \vdash \Theta \Leftarrow \Delta' \quad \Delta \vdash \Psi_i \Leftarrow G \quad \Psi_i \perp_\psi \Theta}{\Delta \vdash \Theta, \Psi_i/\psi_i \Leftarrow \Delta', \psi_i : G}$$

$$\frac{\Delta \vdash \Theta \Leftarrow \Delta' \quad \Delta \vdash C \Leftarrow [\![\Theta]\!]_{\Delta'} U}{\Delta \vdash \Theta, C/X \Leftarrow \Delta', X : U}$$

Fig. 11. Typing rules for meta-substitutions

$\boxed{\Theta_\Delta(X)}$ Contextual variable lookup

$(\Theta, \Psi/\psi_i)_{\Delta, \psi_i : G}(\psi_\epsilon) = \overline{\Psi}$

$(\Theta, \Psi/\psi_i)_{\Delta, \psi_i : G}(\psi_i) = \Psi$

$(\Theta, \Psi/\psi_i)_{\Delta, \psi_i : G}(\psi_m) = \Phi$ where $\Phi = \Psi \bowtie \Psi'$ and $m = i \bowtie n$
and $\Theta_\Delta(\psi_n) = \Psi'$

$(\Theta, \Psi/\psi_i)_{\Delta, \psi_i : G}(\psi_m) = \Theta_\Delta(\psi_m)$ where $i \perp_\psi m$

$(\Theta, C/X)_{\Delta, X : U}(X) = C : U$

$(\Theta, C/Y)_{\Delta, Y : \_}(X) = \Theta_\Delta(X)$ where $Y \neq X$

$\Theta_\Delta(X) = \perp$

On parameter and meta-variables it simply returns the correct meta-object, to which the simultaneous substitution from the corresponding closure is then applied. The lookup is a bit more complicated for context variables, since Θ only contains substitutions for leaf context variables ψ_i. For arbitrary ψ_m we must therefore deconstruct the index $m = i_1 \bowtie \cdots \bowtie i_k$ and return $\Theta_\Delta(\psi_{i_1}) \bowtie \cdots \bowtie \Theta_\Delta(\psi_{i_k})$. Finally, for ψ_ϵ we simply have to find any Ψ/ψ_i in Θ and return $\overline{\Psi}$ – the typing rules for Θ ensure that the choice of ψ_i is irrelevant, as the unrestricted part of the substituted context is shared.

Theorem 5 (Simultaneous meta-substitution property).
If $\Delta \vdash \Theta \Leftarrow \Delta'$ and $\Delta'; \Psi \vdash J$, then $\Delta; [\![\Theta]\!]_{\Delta'} \Psi \vdash [\![\Theta]\!]_{\Delta'} J$.

3.7   Writing Programs About Lincx Objects

We sketch here why Lincx is a suitable index language for writing programs and proofs. In [29], Thibodeau et al. describe several requirements for plugging in an index language into the (co)inductive foundation for writing programs and proofs about them. They fall into three different classes. We will briefly touch on each one.

First, it requires that the index domain satisfies meta-substitution properties that we also prove for Lincx. Second, comparing two objects should be decidable. We satisfy this criteria, since we only characterize $\beta\eta$-long canonical forms and equality reduces to syntactic equality. The third criterion is unification of index objects. While we do not describe a unification algorithm for Lincx objects, we believe it is a straightforward extension of Schack-Nielsen and Schürmann's work [27]. Finally, we require a notion of coverage of Lincx objects which is a straightforward extension of Pientka and Abel's approach [22].

4   Mechanization of Lincx

We have mechanized key properties of our underlying theory in the proof assistant Beluga. In particular, we encoded the syntax, typing rules of Lincx together with single and simultaneous hereditary substitution operations in the logical framework LF relying on HOAS encodings to model binding. Our encoding is similar to Martens and Crary's [15] of LF in LF, but we also handle meta-variables and simultaneous substitutions. Since BELUGA only intrinsically supports intuitionistic binding structures and contexts, linearity must be enforced separately. We do this through an explicit context of variable declarations, connecting each variable to a flag and a type. To model contexts with context variable indices we use a binary encoding. The implementation of LINCX in BELUGA was crucial to arrive at our understanding of modelling context variables using commutative monoids.

As mentioned in Sect. 3.2, the context variable indices take context splitting into account by describing elements from a countably infinite set $\mathcal{I}$, along with a neutral element and a join operation that is commutative and associative. We implement these indices using binary strings, where ϵ is the empty string, and a string with a single positive bit represents a leaf-level variable. In other words, through this abstraction, every context variable in Δ is a binary string with a single positive bit. Schack-Nielsen [26] uses a similar encoding for managing flags for linear, unrestricted, and unavailable assumptions in concrete contexts. Our encoding lifts these ideas to modelling context variables. We then implement the $\bowtie$ operation as a binary OR operation which fails when the two strings have a common positive (for instance a join between 001 and 011 would fail). The following describes the join of M and N, forming K.

```
LF bin_or : bin → bin → bin → type =
  | bin_or_nil_l : bin_or nil M M
  | bin_or_nil_r : bin_or M nil M
  | bin_or_l      : bin_or M N K → bin_or (cons one M) (cons zero N) (cons one K)
  | bin_or_r      : bin_or M N K → bin_or (cons zero M) (cons one N) (cons one K)
  | bin_or_zero   : bin_or M N K → bin_or (cons zero M) (cons zero N) (cons zero K)
;
```

We then proceed to prove commutativity, associativity and uniqueness of bin_or. Finally, we mechanized the proofs of the properties about our equational theory of context joins as total functions in BELUGA. In particular, we mechanized proofs of Lemmas 1 and 2. Here we take advantage of BELUGA's first-class contexts and in the base cases rely on the commutativity and associativity properties of the binary encoding of context variable indices. We note that context equality is entirely syntactic and can thus be defined simply in terms of reflection.

Although we had to model our mixed contexts of unrestricted and linear assumptions explicitly, BELUGA's support for encoding formal systems using higher-order abstract syntax still significantly simplified our definitions of typing rules and hereditary substitution operation. In particular, it allowed us to elegantly model variable bindings in abstractions and Π-types.

Inductive properties about typing and substitution are implemented as recursive functions in BELUGA. Many of the proofs in this paper become fairly tedious and complex on paper and mechanizing LINCX therefore helps us build trust in our foundation. Given the substantial amount of time and lines of code we devote to model contexts and context joins, our mechanization also demonstrate the value LINCX can bring to mechanizing linear systems or more generally systems that work with resources.[2]

5 Related Work

The idea of using logical framework methodology to build a specification language for linear logic dates back three decades, beginning with Cervesato's and Pfenning's linear logical framework LLF [9] providing $\multimap$, & and $\top$ operators from intuitionistic linear logic, the maximal set of connectives for which unique canonical forms exist. The idea was later expanded to the concurrent logical framework CLF [31], which uses a monad to encapsulate less well-behaved operators. The quest to design meta-logics that allow us to reason about linear logical frameworks has been marred with difficulties in the past.

In proof theory, McDowell and Miller [18,19] and later Gacek et al. [13] propose a two-level approach to reason about formal systems where we rely on a first-order sequent calculus together with inductive definitions and induction on natural numbers as a meta-reasoning language. We encode our fomal system in a specification logic that is then embedded in the first-order sequent calculus, the reasoning language. The design of the two-level approach is in principle modular and in fact McDowell's PhD thesis [18] describes a linear specification logic. However the context of assumptions is encoded as a list explicitly in this approach. As a consequence, we need to reason modulo the equational properties of context joins and we may need to prove properties about the uniqueness of assumptions. Such bureaucratic reasoning then still pollutes our main proof.

In type theory, McCreight and Schürmann [17] give a tailored meta-logic $\mathcal{L}_\omega^+$ for linear LF, which is an extension of the meta-logic for LF [28]. While $\mathcal{L}_\omega^+$ also characterize partial linear derivations using contextual objects that depend on a linear context, the approach does not define an equational theory on contexts and context variables. It also does not support reasoning about contextual objects modulo such an equational theory. In addition $\mathcal{L}_\omega^+$ does not cleanly separate the meta-theoretic (co)inductive reasoning about linear derivations from specifying and modelling the linear derivations themselves. We believe the modular design of BELUGA, i.e. the clean separation of representing and modelling specifications and derivations on one hand and reasoning about such derivations on the other, offers many advantages. In particular, it is more robust and also supports extensions to (co)inductive definitions [6,29].

The hybrid logical framework HLF by Reed [25] is in principle capable to support reasoning about linear specifications. In HLF, we reason about objects that are valid at a specific world, instead of objects that are valid within a context. However, contexts and worlds seem closely connected. Most recently Bock and Schürmann [4] propose a contextual logical framework XLF. Similarly to LINCX, it is also based on contextual modal type theory with first-class contexts. However, context variables have a strong nominal flavor in their system.

---

[2] Lincx   Mechanization: https://github.com/Beluga-lang/Beluga/tree/master/examples/lincx_mechanization.

In particular, Bock and Schürmann allow multiple context variables in the context and each context variable is associated with a list of variable names (and other context variable domains) from which it must be disjoint – otherwise the system is prone to repetition of linear variables upon instantiation.

On a more fundamental level the difference between HLF and XLF on the one hand and our approach on the other is how we think about encoding meta-theoretic proofs. HLF and XLF follow the philosophy of Twelf system and encoding proofs as relations. This makes it sometimes challenging to establish that a given relation constitutes an inductive proof and hence both systems have been rarely used to establish such meta-theoretic proofs. More importantly, the proof-theoretic strength of this approach is limited. For example, it is challenging to encode formal systems and proofs that rely on (co)inductive definitions such as proofs by logical relations and bisimulation proofs within the logical framework itself. We believe the modular design of separating cleanly between LINCX as a specification framework and embedding LINCX into the proof and programming language BELUGA provides a simpler foundation for representing the meta-theory of linear systems. Intuitively, meta-proofs about linear systems only rely on linearity to model the linear derivations – however the reasoning about these linear derivation trees is not linear, but remains intuitionistic.

6   Conclusion and Future Work

We have presented LINCX, a linear contextual modal logical framework with first-class contexts as a foundation to model linear systems and derivations. In particular, LINCX satisfies the necessary requirements to serve as a specification and index language for BELUGA and hence provides a suitable foundation for implementing proofs about (linear) derivation trees as recursive functions. We have also mechanized the key equational properties of context joins in BELUGA. This further increases our confidence in our development.

There is a number of research questions that naturally arise and we plan to pursue in the future. First, we plan to extend LINCX with additional linear connectives such as ⊤ and $A\&B$. These additional connectives are for example present in [9]. We omitted them here to concentrate on modelling context joins and their equational theory, but we believe it is straightforward to add them.

Dealing with first-class contexts in the presence of additive operators is more challenging, as they may break canonicity. We plan to follow the approach in CLF [31] enclosing them into a monad to control their behaviour. Having also additive operators would allow us to for example model the meta-theory of session type systems [5] and reason about concurrent computation. Further we plan to add first-class substitution variables [7] to LINCX. This woud allow us to abstractly describe relations between context. This seems particularly important as we allow richer schemas definitions that model structured sequences.

Last but not least, we would like to implement LINCX as a specification language for BELUGA to enable reasoning about linear specifications in practice.

References

1. Savary-Belanger, O., Monnier, S., Pientka, B.: Programming type-safe transformations using higher-order abstract syntax. In: Gonthier, G., Norrish, M. (eds.) CPP 2013. LNCS, vol. 8307, pp. 243–258. Springer, Cham (2013). doi:10.1007/978-3-319-03545-1_16
2. Bengtson, J., Jensen, J.B., Birkedal, L.: Charge! - A framework for higher-order separation logic in Coq. In: Beringer, L., Felty, A. (eds.) ITP 2012. LNCS, vol. 7406, pp. 315–331. Springer, Heidelberg (2012). doi:10.1007/978-3-642-32347-8_21
3. Berdine, J., O'Hearn, P.W., Reddy, U.S., Thielecke, H.: Linear continuation-passing. High.-Order Symbolic Comput. 15(2–3), 181–208 (2002)
4. Bock, P.B., Schürmann, C.: A contextual logical framework. In: Davis, M., Fehnker, A., McIver, A., Voronkov, A. (eds.) LPAR 2015. LNCS, vol. 9450, pp. 402–417. Springer, Heidelberg (2015). doi:10.1007/978-3-662-48899-7_28
5. Caires, L., Pfenning, F.: Session types as intuitionistic linear propositions. In: Gastin, P., Laroussinie, F. (eds.) CONCUR 2010. LNCS, vol. 6269, pp. 222–236. Springer, Heidelberg (2010). doi:10.1007/978-3-642-15375-4_16
6. Cave, A., Pientka, B.: Programming with binders and indexed data-types. In: 39th ACM SIGPLAN-SIGACT Symposium on Principles of Programming Languages (POPL 2012), pp. 413–424. ACM (2012)
7. Cave, A., Pientka, B.: First-class substitutions in contextual type theory. In: 8th ACM SIGPLAN International Workshop on Logical Frameworks and Meta-Languages: Theory and Practice (LFMTP 2013), pp. 15–24. ACM (2013)
8. Cave, A., Pientka, B.: A case study on logical relations using contextual types. In: Cervesato, I., Chaudhuri, K. (eds.) 10th International Workshop on Logical Frameworks and Meta-Languages: Theory and Practice (LFMTP 2015), pp. 18–33. Electronic Proceedings in Theoretical Computer Science (EPTCS) (2015)
9. Cervesato, I., Pfenning, F.: A linear logical framework. In: Clarke, E. (ed.) 11th Annual Symposium on Logic in Computer Science, pp. 264–275. IEEE Press, New Brunswick (1996)
10. Cervesato, I., Pfenning, F.: A linear spine calculus. J. Logic Comput. 13(5), 639–688 (2003)
11. Danvy, O., Filinski, A.: Representing control: a study of the CPS transformation. Math. Struct. Comput. Sci. 2(4), 361–391 (1992)
12. Fluet, M., Morrisett, G., Ahmed, A.: Linear regions are all you need. In: Sestoft, P. (ed.) ESOP 2006. LNCS, vol. 3924, pp. 7–21. Springer, Heidelberg (2006). doi:10.1007/11693024_2
13. Gacek, A., Miller, D., Nadathur, G.: A two-level logic approach to reasoning about computations. J. Autom. Reason. 49(2), 241–273 (2012)
14. Harper, R., Honsell, F., Plotkin, G.: A framework for defining logics. J. ACM 40(1), 143–184 (1993)
15. Martens, C., Crary, K.: LF in LF: mechanizing the metatheories of LF in Twelf. In: 7th International Workshop on Logical Frameworks and Meta-Languages: Theory and Practice (LFMTP 2012), pp. 23–32. ACM (2012)
16. McCreight, A.: Practical tactics for separation logic. In: Berghofer, S., Nipkow, T., Urban, C., Wenzel, M. (eds.) TPHOLs 2009. LNCS, vol. 5674, pp. 343–358. Springer, Heidelberg (2009). doi:10.1007/978-3-642-03359-9_24
17. McCreight, A., Schürmann, C.: A meta-linear logical framework. In: 4th International Workshop on Logical Frameworks and Meta-Languages (LFM 2004) (2004)

18. McDowell, R.: Reasoning in a logic with definitions and induction. Ph.D. thesis, University of Pennsylvania (1997)
19. McDowell, R.C., Miller, D.A.: Reasoning with higher-order abstract syntax in a logical framework. ACM Trans. Comput. Logic **3**(1), 80–136 (2002)
20. Nanevski, A., Pfenning, F., Pientka, B.: Contextual modal type theory. ACM Trans. Comput. Logic **9**(3), 1–49 (2008)
21. Pientka, B.: A type-theoretic foundation for programming with higher-order abstract syntax and first-class substitutions. In: 35th ACM SIGPLAN-SIGACT Symposium on Principles of Programming Languages (POPL 2008), pp. 371–382. ACM (2008)
22. Pientka, B., Abel, A.: Structural recursion over contextual objects. In: Altenkirch, T. (ed.) 13th International Conference on Typed Lambda Calculi and Applications (TLCA 2015), pp. 273–287. Leibniz International Proceedings in Informatics (LIPIcs) of Schloss Dagstuhl (2015)
23. Pientka, B., Cave, A.: Inductive beluga: programming proofs (system description). In: Felty, A.P., Middeldorp, A. (eds.) CADE 2015. LNCS (LNAI), vol. 9195, pp. 272–281. Springer, Cham (2015). doi:10.1007/978-3-319-21401-6_18
24. Pientka, B., Dunfield, J.: Beluga: a framework for programming and reasoning with deductive systems (system description). In: Giesl, J., Hähnle, R. (eds.) IJCAR 2010. LNCS (LNAI), vol. 6173, pp. 15–21. Springer, Heidelberg (2010). doi:10.1007/978-3-642-14203-1_2
25. Reed, J.: A hybrid logical framework. Ph.D. thesis, Carnegie Mellon (2009)
26. Schack-Nielsen, A.: Implementing substructural logical frameworks. Ph.D. thesis, IT University of Copenhagen (2011)
27. Schack-Nielsen, A., Schürmann, C.: Pattern unification for the lambda calculus with linear and affine types. In: Crary, K., Miculan, M. (eds.) International Workshop on Logical Frameworks and Meta-Languages: Theory and Practice (LFMTP 2010). Electronic Proceedings in Theoretical Computer Science (EPTCS), vol. 34, pp. 101–116, July 2010
28. Schürmann, C.: Automating the meta theory of deductive systems. Ph.D. thesis, Department of Computer Science, Carnegie Mellon University, CMU-CS-00-146 (2000)
29. Thibodeau, D., Cave, A., Pientka, B.: Indexed codata. In: Garrigue, J., Keller, G., Sumii, E. (eds.) 21st ACM SIGPLAN International Conference on Functional Programming (ICFP 2016), pp. 351–363. ACM (2016)
30. Walker, D., Watkins, K.: On regions and linear types. In: Pierce, B.C. (ed.) 6th ACM SIGPLAN International Conference on Functional Programming (ICFP 2001), pp. 181–192. ACM (2001)
31. Watkins, K., Cervesato, I., Pfenning, F., Walker, D.: A concurrent logical framework I: judgments and properties. Technical report CMU-CS-02-101, Department of Computer Science, Carnegie Mellon University (2002)

APLicative Programming with Naperian Functors

Jeremy Gibbons[✉]

University of Oxford, Oxford, UK
Jeremy.Gibbons@cs.ox.ac.uk

Abstract. Much of the expressive power of array-oriented languages such as Iverson's APL and J comes from their implicit lifting of scalar operations to act on higher-ranked data, for example to add a value to each element of a vector, or to add two compatible matrices pointwise. It is considered a shape error to attempt to combine arguments of incompatible shape, such as a 3-vector with a 4-vector. APL and J are dynamically typed, so such shape errors are caught only at run-time. Recent work by Slepak *et al.* develops a custom type system for an array-oriented language, statically ruling out such errors. We show here that such a custom language design is unnecessary: the requisite compatibility checks can already be captured in modern expressive type systems, as found for example in Haskell; moreover, generative type-driven programming can exploit that static type information constructively to automatically induce the appropriate liftings. We show also that the structure of multi-dimensional data is inherently a matter of *Naperian applicative functors*—lax monoidal functors, with strength, commutative up to isomorphism under composition—that also support *traversal*.

1 Introduction

Array-oriented programming languages such as APL [21] and J [23] pay special attention, not surprisingly, to manipulating *array structures*. These encompass not just rank-one vectors (sequences of values), but also rank-two matrices (which can be seen as rectangular sequences of sequences), rank-three cuboids (sequences of sequences of sequences), rank-zero scalars, and so on.

One appealing consequence of this unification is the prospect of *rank polymorphism* [34]—that a scalar function may be automatically lifted to act element-by-element on a higher-ranked array, a scalar binary operator to act pointwise on pairs of arrays, and so on. For example, numeric function *square* acts not only on scalars:

$$square \boxed{\ 3\ } = \boxed{\ 9\ }$$

but also pointwise on vectors:

$$square \boxed{\ 1\ 2\ 3\ } = \boxed{\ 1\ 4\ 9\ }$$

and on matrices and cuboids:

© Springer-Verlag GmbH Germany 2017
H. Yang (Ed.): ESOP 2017, LNCS 10201, pp. 556–583, 2017.
DOI: 10.1007/978-3-662-54434-1_21

$$square \begin{array}{|ccc|} \hline 1 & 2 & 3 \\ 4 & 5 & 6 \\ 7 & 8 & 9 \\ \hline \end{array} = \begin{array}{|ccc|} \hline 1 & 4 & 9 \\ 16 & 25 & 36 \\ 49 & 64 & 81 \\ \hline \end{array} \qquad square \begin{array}{|cc|} \hline 5 & 6 \\ \begin{array}{|cc} 1 & 2 \\ 3 & 4 \end{array} & 8 \\ \hline \end{array} = \begin{array}{|cc|} \hline 25 & 36 \\ \begin{array}{|cc} 1 & 4 \\ 9 & 16 \end{array} & 64 \\ \hline \end{array}$$

Similarly, binary operators act not only on scalars, but also on vectors:

$$\boxed{1\ 2\ 3} + \boxed{4\ 5\ 6} = \boxed{5\ 7\ 9}$$

and on matrices:

$$\begin{array}{|cc|} \hline 1 & 2 \\ 3 & 4 \\ \hline \end{array} + \begin{array}{|cc|} \hline 5 & 6 \\ 7 & 8 \\ \hline \end{array} = \begin{array}{|cc|} \hline 6 & 8 \\ 10 & 12 \\ \hline \end{array}$$

The same lifting can be applied to operations that do not simply act pointwise. For example, the *sum* and prefix *sums* functions on vectors can also be applied to matrices:

$$sum \boxed{1\ 2\ 3} = \boxed{6} \qquad sum \begin{array}{|ccc|} \hline 1 & 2 & 3 \\ 4 & 5 & 6 \\ \hline \end{array} = \begin{array}{|c|} \hline 6 \\ 15 \\ \hline \end{array}$$

$$sums \boxed{1\ 2\ 3} = \boxed{1\ 3\ 6} \qquad sums \begin{array}{|ccc|} \hline 1 & 2 & 3 \\ 4 & 5 & 6 \\ \hline \end{array} = \begin{array}{|ccc|} \hline 1 & 3 & 6 \\ 4 & 9 & 15 \\ \hline \end{array}$$

In the right-hand examples above, *sum* and *sums* have been lifted to act on the rows of the matrix. J also provides a *reranking* operator $"_1$, which will make them act instead on the columns—essentially a matter of matrix transposition:

$$sum\ "_1 \begin{array}{|ccc|} \hline 1 & 2 & 3 \\ 4 & 5 & 6 \\ \hline \end{array} = sum \left(transpose \begin{array}{|ccc|} \hline 1 & 2 & 3 \\ 4 & 5 & 6 \\ \hline \end{array} \right) = sum \begin{array}{|cc|} \hline 1 & 4 \\ 2 & 5 \\ 3 & 6 \\ \hline \end{array} = \boxed{5\ 7\ 9}$$

$$sums\ "_1 \begin{array}{|ccc|} \hline 1 & 2 & 3 \\ 4 & 5 & 6 \\ \hline \end{array} = transpose \left(sums \left(transpose \begin{array}{|ccc|} \hline 1 & 2 & 3 \\ 4 & 5 & 6 \\ \hline \end{array} \right) \right)$$

$$= transpose \left(sums \begin{array}{|cc|} \hline 1 & 4 \\ 2 & 5 \\ 3 & 6 \\ \hline \end{array} \right) = transpose \begin{array}{|cc|} \hline 1 & 5 \\ 2 & 7 \\ 3 & 9 \\ \hline \end{array} = \begin{array}{|ccc|} \hline 1 & 2 & 3 \\ 5 & 7 & 9 \\ \hline \end{array}$$

Furthermore, the arguments of binary operators need not have the same rank; the lower-ranked argument is implicitly lifted to align with the higher-ranked one. For example, one can add a scalar and a vector:

$$3 + \boxed{4\ 5\ 6} = \boxed{3\ 3\ 3} + \boxed{4\ 5\ 6} = \boxed{7\ 8\ 9}$$

or a vector and a matrix:

$$\boxed{1\ 2\ 3} + \begin{array}{|ccc|} \hline 4 & 5 & 6 \\ 7 & 8 & 9 \\ \hline \end{array} = \begin{array}{|ccc|} \hline 1 & 2 & 3 \\ 1 & 2 & 3 \\ \hline \end{array} + \begin{array}{|ccc|} \hline 4 & 5 & 6 \\ 7 & 8 & 9 \\ \hline \end{array} = \begin{array}{|ccc|} \hline 5 & 7 & 9 \\ 8 & 10 & 12 \\ \hline \end{array}$$

1.1 Static Types for Multi-dimensional Arrays

In recent work [34], Slepak *et al.* present static and dynamic semantics for a typed core language Remora. Their semantics clarifies the axes of variability illustrated above; in particular, it makes explicit the implicit control structures and data manipulations required for lifting operators to higher-ranked arguments and aligning arguments of different ranks. Moreover, Remora's type system makes it a static error if the *shapes* in a given dimension do not match—for example, when attempting to add a 2-vector to a 3-vector, or a 2×2-matrix to a 2×3-matrix. (Incidentally, we adopt Slepak *et al.*'s terminology: the *shape* of a multi-dimensional array is a sequence of numbers, specifying the extent in each dimension; the *rank* of the array is the length of that list, and hence the number of dimensions; and the *size* of the array is the product of that list, and hence the number of elements.)

Slepak *et al.* model the type and evaluation rules of Remora in PLT Redex [11], and use this model to prove important properties such as type safety. PLT Redex provides complete freedom to model whatever semantics the language designer chooses; but the *quid pro quo* for this freedom is that it does not directly lead to a full language implementation—with type inference, a compiler, libraries, efficient code generation, and so on. They write that "our hope [for future work] is that we can exploit this type information to compile programs written in the rank-polymorphic array computation model efficiently" and that "Remora is not intended as a language comfortable for human programmers to write array computations. It is, rather, an explicitly typed, 'essential' core language on which such a language could be based" [34, p. 29]. Moreover, "the transition from a core semantics modeled in PLT Redex to a complete programming system requires a more flexible surface language and a compiler [...] the added code is mostly type and index applications. Type inference would be necessary in order to make a surface language based on Remora practical" [34, p. 45].

1.2   Embedding Static Typing

This is the usual trade-off between standalone and embedded domain-specific languages. If the type rules of Remora had been embedded instead in a sufficiently expressive *typed* host language, then the surrounding ecosystem of that host language—type inference, the compiler, libraries, code generation—could be leveraged immediately to provide a practical programming vehicle. The challenge then becomes to find the right host language, and to work out how best to represent the rules of the DSL within the features available in that host language. Sometimes the representation comes entirely naturally; sometimes it takes some degree of encoding.

In this paper, we explore the embedded-DSL approach to capturing the type constraints and implicit lifting and alignment manipulations of rank-polymorphic array computation. We show how to capture these neatly in Haskell, a pure and strongly-typed functional programming language with growing abilities to express and exploit dependent types. To be more precise, we make use of a number of recent extensions to standard Haskell, which are supported in the primary implementation GHC [13]. We do not assume familiarity with fancy Haskell features, but explain them as we go along.

The point is not particularly to promote such fancy features; although the expressive power of modern type systems is quite impressive. Nor is the point to explain to aficionados of dependent types in Haskell how to perform rank-polymorphic array computation; most of our constructions are already folk-lore. Rather, the point is to demonstrate to a wider programming language audi-ence that it is often not necessary to invent a new special-purpose language in order to capture a sophisticated feature: we have sufficiently expressive general-purpose languages already.

1.3   The Main Idea

The main idea is that a rank-n array is essentially a data structure of type $D_1(D_2(\ldots(D_n\,a)))$, where each D_i is a *dimension*: a container type, categorically a functor; one might think in the first instance of lists. However, in order to be able to transpose arrays without losing information, each dimension should be represented by a functor of *fixed shape*; so perhaps vectors, of a fixed length in each dimension, but allowing different lengths in different dimensions.

The vector structure is sufficient to support all the necessary operations dis-cussed above: mapping (for pointwise operations), zipping (for lifting binary operations), replicating (for alignment), transposing (for reranking), folding (for example, for *sum*), and traversing (for *sums*). Moreover, these can also be han-dled crisply, with static types that both prevent incoherent combinations and explain the implicit lifting required for compatible ones. However, although suf-ficient, the vector structure is not necessary, and other functors (such as pairs, triples, block vectors, and even perfect binary trees) suffice; we show that the necessary structure is that of a *traversable, Naperian, applicative functor* (and we explain what that means). The richer type structure that this makes avail-able allows us to go beyond Remora, and in particular to explain the relationship between nested and flat representations of multi-dimensional data, leading the way towards higher-performance implementations of bulk operations, for exam-ple on multicore chips [24] and on GPUs [5].

Specifically, our novel contributions are as follows:

– formalizing the *lifting* required for rank polymorphism;
– doing so within an *existing type system*, rather than creating a new one;
– identifying *necessary and sufficient structure* for dimensions;
– *implementing* it all (in Haskell), and providing executable code;
– showing how to connect to *flat and sparse representations*.

Although our definitions are asymptotically efficient, or can easily be made so using standard techniques such as accumulating parameters, we do not make performance claims in comparison with serious array libraries such as Repa and Accelerate [5,24]. Rather, we see this work as providing a flexible but safe front-end, delegating performance-critical computations to such libraries.

1.4   Structure of This Paper

The remainder of this paper is structured as follows. Section 2 uses type-level nat-ural numbers for bounds checking of vectors; Sect. 3 explains the requirements on vectors to support maps, zips, and transposition; and Sect. 4 similarly for reduc-tions and scans; these are all fairly standard material, and together show how to generalize the dimensions of an array from concrete vectors to other suitable types. Our contribution starts in Sect. 5, where we show how to accommodate arrays of arbitrary rank. Section 6 shows how to automatically lift unary and binary operators to higher ranks. Section 7 shows how to avoid manifesting replication and transposition operations by representing them symbolically instead, and Sect. 8 shows a more efficient representation using flat built-in arrays, while still preserving the shape information in the type. Section 9 concludes.

This paper is a literate Haskell script, and the code in it is all type-checked and executable, albeit with tidier formatting in the PDF for publication purposes. The extracted code is available for experimentation [14]. We exploit a number of advanced type features, explained as we proceed; but we make no use of laziness or undefinedness, treating Haskell as a total programming language.

2   Vectors with Bounds Checking

Our approach makes essential use of lightweight dependent typing, which is now becoming standard practice in modern functional programming languages such as Haskell. We introduce these ideas gradually, starting with traditional algebraic datatypes, such as lists:

$$\textbf{data } List :: * \rightarrow * \textbf{ where}$$
$$Nil \quad :: \qquad\qquad List\ a$$
$$Cons :: a \rightarrow List\ a \rightarrow List\ a$$

This declaration defines a new datatype constructor $List$ of kind $* \rightarrow *$. Which is to say, kind $*$ includes all those types with actual values, such as Int and $List\ Int$ and $Int \rightarrow Int$; and $List$ is an operation on types, such that for any type A of kind $*$, there is another type $List\ A$ (also of kind $*$) of lists whose elements are drawn from A. The declaration also introduces two constructors Nil and $Cons$ of the declared types for the new datatype, polymorphic in the element type.

All lists with elements of a given type have the same type; for example, there is one type $List\ Int$ of lists of integers. This is convenient for operations that combine lists of different lengths; but it does not allow us to guarantee bounds safety by type checking. For example, the tail function

$$tail :: List\ a \rightarrow List\ a$$
$$tail\ (Cons\ x\ xs) = xs$$

and the list indexing operator

$$lookup :: List\ a \rightarrow Int \rightarrow a$$
$$lookup\ (Cons\ x\ xs)\ 0 \qquad\ = x$$
$$lookup\ (Cons\ x\ xs)\ (n+1) = lookup\ xs\ n$$

are partial functions, and there is no way statically to distinguish their safe from their unsafe uses through the types. The way to achieve that end is to partition the type $List\ A$ into chunks, so that each chunk contains only the lists of a given length, and to index these chunks by their common lengths. The index should be another type parameter, just like the element type is; so we need a type-level way of representing natural numbers. One recent Haskell extension [39] has made this very convenient, by implicitly promoting all suitable datatype constructors from the value to the type level, and the datatypes themselves from the type level to the kind level. For example, from the familiar datatype of Peano naturals

> **data** *Nat* :: * **where**
>   *Z* ::   *Nat*
>   *S* :: *Nat* → *Nat*

we get not only a new type *Nat* with value inhabitants $Z, S\ Z, ...$, but in addition a new kind, also called *Nat*, with type inhabitants $'Z, 'S\ 'Z, ...$ In Haskell, the inhabitants can be distinguished by the initial quote character (which is in fact almost always optional, but for clarity we will make explicit use of it throughout this paper). For convenience, we define synonyms for some small numbers at the type level:

> **type** *One*   = *'S 'Z*
> **type** *Two*   = *'S One*
> **type** *Three* = *'S Two*
> **type** *Four* = *'S Three*

We can now define a datatype of length-indexed vectors:

> **data** *Vector* :: *Nat* → * → * **where**
>   *VNil* ::   *Vector 'Z a*
>   *VCons* :: *a* → *Vector n a* → *Vector* (*'S n*) *a*

The length is encoded in the type: *VNil* yields a vector of length zero, and *VCons* prefixes an element onto an n-vector to yield an $(n + 1)$-vector. For example, *Vector Three Int* is the type of 3-vectors of integers, one of whose inhabitants is the vector $\langle 1, 2, 3 \rangle$:

> *v123* :: *Vector Three Int*
> *v123* = *VCons* 1 (*VCons* 2 (*VCons* 3 *VNil*))

The first type parameter of *Vector* is called a 'phantom type' [19] or 'type index' [38], because it is not related to the type of any elements: a value of type *Vector Three Int* has elements of type *Int*, but does not in any sense 'have elements of type *Three*'. The type index does not interfere with ordinary recursive definitions, such as the mapping operation that applies a given function to every element, witnessing to *Vector n* being a functor:

> *vmap* :: ($a → b$) → *Vector n a* → *Vector n b*
> *vmap f VNil*   = *VNil*
> *vmap f* (*VCons x xs*) = *VCons* (*f x*) (*vmap f xs*)

For example,

$v456 :: Vector\ Three\ Int$
$v456 = vmap\ (\lambda x \rightarrow 3 + x)\ v123$

More interestingly, we can now capture the fact that the 'tail' function should be applied only to non-empty vectors, and that it yields a result one element shorter than its argument:

$vtail :: Vector\ (S\ n)\ a \rightarrow Vector\ n\ a$
$vtail\ (VCons\ x\ xs) = xs$

Similarly, we can write a 'zip' function that combines two vectors element-by-element using a binary operator, and use the additional type information to restrict it to take vectors of a common length n and to produce a result of the same length:

$vzipWith :: (a \rightarrow b \rightarrow c) \rightarrow Vector\ n\ a \rightarrow Vector\ n\ b \rightarrow Vector\ n\ c$
$vzipWith\ f\ VNil\qquad\quad VNil\qquad\quad = VNil$
$vzipWith\ f\ (VCons\ a\ x)\ (VCons\ b\ y) = VCons\ (f\ a\ b)\ (vzipWith\ f\ x\ y)$

Because of the type constraints, the patterns on the left-hand side in both examples are exhaustive: it would be ill-typed to take the tail of an empty vector, or to zip two vectors of different lengths.

The functions $vtail$ and $vzipWith$ consume vectors; the length indices constrain the behaviour, but they are not needed at run-time because the value constructors provide sufficient information to drive the computation. The situation is different when producing vectors from scratch. Consider a function $vreplicate$ to construct a vector of a certain length by replicating a given value. The type $a \rightarrow Vector\ n\ a$ uniquely determines the implementation of such a function; however, it is the type of the result that contains the length information, and that isn't available for use at run-time. Nevertheless, for each n, there is an obvious implementation of $vreplicate$ on $Vector\ n$; it would be nice to be able to state that obvious fact formally. In Haskell, this sort of 'type-driven code inference' is modelled by type classes—it is the same mechanism that determines the appropriate definition of equality or printing for a given type. Similarly, there is an obvious implementation of $vlength :: Vector\ n\ a \rightarrow Int$, which in fact does not even need to inspect its vector argument—the length is statically determined. We introduce the class $Count$ of those types n (of kind Nat) that support these two 'obvious implementations':

class $Count\ (n :: Nat)$ **where**
$\quad vreplicate :: a \rightarrow Vector\ n\ a$
$\quad vlength\quad :: Vector\ n\ a \rightarrow Int$

Indeed, every type n of kind Nat is in the class $Count$, as we demonstrate by providing those two obvious implementations at each type n:

instance *Count 'Z* **where**
   vreplicate a = VNil
   vlength xs   = 0

instance *Count n ⇒ Count ('S n)* **where**
   vreplicate a = VCons a (vreplicate a)
   vlength xs   = 1 + vlength (vtail xs)

(One might see class *Count* as representing 'natural numbers specifically for vector purposes'; it is possible with some pain to represent 'natural numbers' in Haskell more generally [25].)

The operations *vmap*, *vzipWith*, and *vreplicate* are the essential ingredients for lifting and aligning operations to higher-ranked arguments (albeit not yet sufficient for the other operations). For example, to lift *square* to act on vectors, we can use *vmap square*; to lift (+) to act on two vectors of the same length, we can use *vzipWith* (+); and to align a scalar with a vector, we can use *vreplicate*:

$$v456 = vzipWith\ (+)\ (vreplicate\ 3)\ v123$$

(Note that the types of *vzipWith* and its second argument *v123* together determine which instance of *vreplicate* is required; so no explicit type annotation is needed.) But in order fully to achieve rank polymorphism, we want operators such as squaring and addition to implicitly determine the appropriate lifting and alignment, rather than having explicitly to specify the appropriate amount of replication. We see next how that can be done, without sacrificing static typing and type safety.

3   Applicative and Naperian Functors

We have seen that vectors show promise for representing the dimensions of an array, because they support at least three of the essential operations, namely mapping, zipping, and replicating. But vectors are not the only datatype to support such operations; if we can identify the actual requirements on dimensions, then there are other types that would serve just as well. In particular, one of the dimensions of an array might be 'pairs':

data *Pair a = P a a*

since these too support the three operations discussed above:

pmap   :: (a → b) → Pair a → Pair b
pzipWith :: (a → b → c) → Pair a → Pair b → Pair c
preplicate :: a → Pair a

Generalizing in this way would allow us to handle vectors of pairs, pairs of triples, and so on.

The first requirement for a type constructor *f* to be suitable as a dimension is to be a container type, that is, an instance of the type class *Functor* and so providing an *fmap* operator:

class *Functor f* **where**
    fmap :: $(a \rightarrow b) \rightarrow f\ a \rightarrow f\ b$

The other two operators arise from f being a fortiori an *applicative* functor [26]:

class *Functor f* $\Rightarrow$ *Applicative f* **where**
    pure :: $a \rightarrow f\ a$
    $(\circledast)$ :: $f\ (a \rightarrow b) \rightarrow f\ a \rightarrow f\ b$

Informally, *pure* should yield an f-structure of copies of its argument; this serves as the 'replicate' operation:

areplicate :: *Applicative f* $\Rightarrow a \rightarrow f\ a$
areplicate = *pure*

(Here, the context "*Applicative f* $\Rightarrow$" denotes that *areplicate* has type $a \rightarrow f\ a$ for any f in type class *Applicative*; in contrast, the type variable a is unconstrained.) The $(\circledast)$ method should combine an f-structure of functions with an f-structure of arguments to yield an f-structure of results. The two methods together give rise to the 'zip' operation:

azipWith :: *Applicative f* $\Rightarrow (a \rightarrow b \rightarrow c) \rightarrow f\ a \rightarrow f\ b \rightarrow f\ c$
azipWith h xs ys = $(pure\ h \circledast xs) \circledast ys$

Vectors, of course, are applicative functors:

instance *Functor* (*Vector n*) **where**
    fmap = *vmap*
instance *Count n* $\Rightarrow$ *Applicative* (*Vector n*) **where**
    pure = *vreplicate*
    $(\circledast)$ = *vzipWith* $(\lambda f\ x \rightarrow f\ x)$

Note that we make the assumption that the length index type n is in type class *Count*, so that we can infer the appropriate definition of *vreplicate*. This assumption is benign, because the length indices are of kind *Nat*, and we have provided a *Count* instance for every type of that kind.
    Pairs too are applicative functors:

instance *Functor Pair* **where**
    fmap f $(P\ x\ y) = P\ (f\ x)\ (f\ y)$
instance *Applicative Pair* **where**
    pure x   = $P\ x\ x$
    $P\ f\ g \circledast P\ x\ y = P\ (f\ x)\ (g\ y)$

However, being an applicative functor is not sufficient for serving as a dimension: that interface is not expressive enough to define transposition, which is needed in order to implement reranking. For that, we need to be able to commute the functors that represent dimensions: that is, to transform an $f\ (g\ a)$

into a $g\ (f\ a)$. The necessary additional structure is given by what Hancock [17] calls a *Naperian* functor, also known as a *representable* functor; that is, a container of fixed shape. Functor f is Naperian if there is a type p of 'positions' such that $f\ a \simeq p \to a$; then p behaves a little like a logarithm of f—in particular, if f and g are both Naperian, then $Log\ (f \times g) \simeq Log\ f + Log\ g$ and $Log\ (f \cdot g) \simeq Log\ f \times Log\ g$.

> **class** *Functor f* $\Rightarrow$ *Naperian f* **where**
>   **type** *Log f*
>   *lookup* $:: f\ a \to (Log\ f \to a)$
>   *tabulate* $:: (Log\ f \to a) \to f\ a$
>   *positions* $:: f\ (Log\ f)$
>
>   *tabulate h* = *fmap h positions*
>   *positions*   = *tabulate id*

Informally, *Log f* is the type of positions for f; *lookup xs i* looks up the element of *xs* at position i; *tabulate h* yields an f-structure where for each position i the element at that position is $h\ i$; and *positions* yields an f-structure where the element at each position i is i itself. The first two operations should be each other's inverses; they are witnesses to the isomorphism between $f\ a$ and $Log\ f \to a$. The latter two operations are interdefinable, so an instance need only provide one of them; it is often convenient to implement *positions*, but to use *tabulate*. For simplicity, we rule out empty data structures, insisting that the type *Log f* should always be inhabited. Naperian functors are necessarily applicative too:

> *pure a* = *tabulate* $(\lambda i \to a)$
> *fs* $\circledast$ *xs* = *tabulate* $(\lambda i \to (lookup\ fs\ i)\ (lookup\ xs\ i))$

Transposition in general consumes an f-structure of g-structures in which all the g-structures have the same shape, and produces a g-structure of f-structures in which all the f-structures have the same shape, namely the outer shape of the input. For general functors f and g, this is a partial function, or at best a lossy one. However, the essential point about Naperian functors is that all inhabitants of a datatype have a common shape. In particular, in an f-structure of g-structures where both f and g are Naperian, all the inner g-structures necessarily have the same (namely, the only possible) shape. Then transposition is total and invertible:

> *transpose* :: $(Naperian\ f, Naperian\ g) \Rightarrow f\ (g\ a) \to g\ (f\ a)$
> *transpose* = *tabulate* · *fmap tabulate* · *flip* · *fmap lookup* · *lookup*

Here, *flip* :: $(a \to b \to c) \to (b \to a \to c)$ is a standard function that swaps the argument order of a binary function. We use the *lookup* function for the outer and the inner structures of the input of type $f\ (g\ a)$, yielding a binary function of type $Log\ f \to Log\ g \to a$; we flip the arguments of this function, yielding one of type $Log\ g \to Log\ f \to a$; then we tabulate both structures again, yielding the result of type $g\ (f\ a)$ as required. For example, we have

$$VCons\ v123\ (VCons\ v456\ VNil)\ = \langle\langle 1, 2, 3\rangle, \langle 4, 5, 6\rangle\rangle$$
$$transpose\ (VCons\ v123\ (VCons\ v456\ VNil)) = \langle\langle 1, 4\rangle, \langle 2, 5\rangle, \langle 3, 6\rangle\rangle$$

As a consequence, composition of Naperian functors is commutative, up to iso-morphism; we will insist on our dimensions being at least Naperian functors.

Of course, pairs are Naperian, with two positions—the usual ordering on booleans in Haskell has $False \leq True$, so we use this ordering on the positions too:

> **instance** *Naperian Pair* **where**
>   **type** *Log Pair*   = *Bool*
>   *lookup* $(P\ x\ y)$ b = **if** b **then** y **else** x
>   *positions*   = *P False True*

And vectors are Naperian. An n-vector has n positions, so to represent the logarithm we need a type with precisely n inhabitants—the *bounded naturals*:

> **data** *Fin* :: *Nat* $\rightarrow$ * **where**
>   *FZ* ::   *Fin* ('S n)
>   *FS* :: *Fin* n $\rightarrow$ *Fin* ('S n)

Thus, *Fin* n has n inhabitants $FZ, FS\ FZ, ..., FS^{n-1}\ FZ$. Extracting an element from a vector is defined by structural induction simultaneously over the vector and the position—like with zipping, the type constraints make bounds violations a type error:

> *vlookup* :: *Vector* n a $\rightarrow$ *Fin* n $\rightarrow$ a
> *vlookup* $(VCons\ a\ x)$ FZ = a
> *vlookup* $(VCons\ a\ x)$ $(FS\ n)$ = *vlookup* x n

A vector of positions is obtained by what in APL is called the 'iota' function. As with replication, we need to provide the length as a run-time argument; but we can represent this argument as a vector of units, and then infer the appropriate value from the type:

> *viota* :: *Count* n $\Rightarrow$ *Vector* n (*Fin* n)
> *viota* = *viota'* (*vreplicate* ()) **where**
>   *viota'* :: *Vector* m () $\rightarrow$ *Vector* m (*Fin* m)
>   *viota'* *VNil*   = *VNil*
>   *viota'* $(VCons\ ()\ xs)$ = *VCons* FZ (*fmap* FS (*viota'* xs))

With these three components, we are justified in calling vectors Naperian:

> **instance** *Count* n $\Rightarrow$ *Naperian* (*Vector* n) **where**
>   **type** *Log* (*Vector* n) = *Fin* n
>   *lookup*   = *vlookup*
>   *positions*   = *viota*

4   Folding and Traversing

Another requirement on the dimensions of an array is to be able to reduce along one of them; for example, to sum. In recent versions of Haskell, that requirement is captured in the *Foldable* type class, the essence of which is as follows:

> **class** *Foldable t* **where**
> $foldr :: (a \to b \to b) \to b \to t\ a \to b$

Informally, *foldr* aggregates the elements of a collection one by one, from right to left, using the binary operator and initial value provided. Vectors are foldable in the same way that lists are:

> **instance** *Foldable* (*Vector n*) **where**
> $foldr\ f\ e\ VNil \qquad = e$
> $foldr\ f\ e\ (VCons\ x\ xs) = f\ x\ (foldr\ f\ e\ xs)$

and pairs are foldable by combining their two elements:

> **instance** *Foldable Pair* **where**
> $foldr\ f\ e\ (P\ x\ y) = f\ x\ (f\ y\ e)$

A foldable functor imposes a left-to-right ordering on its positions; so we can extract the elements as a list, in that order:

> $toList :: Foldable\ t \Rightarrow t\ a \to [a]$
> $toList = foldr\ (:)\ []$

Similarly, we can sum those elements, provided that they are of a numeric type:

> $sum :: (Num\ a, Foldable\ t) \Rightarrow t\ a \to a$
> $sum = foldr\ (+)\ 0$

An additional requirement for array dimensions is to be able to *transform* values along a dimension, for example to compute prefix sums. This is captured by the *Traversable* type class:

> **class** (*Functor t*, *Foldable t*) $\Rightarrow$ *Traversable t* **where**
> $traverse :: Applicative\ f \Rightarrow (a \to f\ b) \to t\ a \to f\ (t\ b)$

One way of thinking of *traverse* is as an effectful 'map' function [3], visiting each element in order, precisely once each, and collecting effects in some applicative functor f. For example, stateful computations can be modelled by state-transforming functions:

> **data** *State s a* = *State* { *runState* :: $s \to (a, s)$ }

(This construction declares *State s a* to be a record type, with a data constructor also called *State*, and a single field called *runState*; in this way, the function *runState* extracts the state-transformer from the record.) This datatype forms an applicative functor, in a standard way. Here is a little function to increase and return a numeric state—whatever the current state n, when applied to m, this yields the final state $m + n$, and returns as result the same value $m + n$:

$increase :: Num\ a \Rightarrow a \rightarrow State\ a\ a$
$increase\ m = State\ (\lambda n \rightarrow (m + n, m + n))$

Using this, one can compute prefix sums by traversing a data structure, starting with an initial state of 0, increasing the state by each element in turn, preserving the running totals and discarding the final state:

$sums :: (Num\ a, Traversable\ t) \Rightarrow t\ a \rightarrow t\ a$
$sums\ xs = fst\ (runState\ (traverse\ increase\ xs)\ 0)$

so in particular

$sums\ v123 = VCons\ 1\ (VCons\ 3\ (VCons\ 6\ VNil))$

Vectors and pairs are both traversable, with instances following a common pattern:

instance *Traversable Pair* **where**
   $traverse\ f\ (P\ x\ y) = (pure\ P \circledast f\ x) \circledast f\ y$
instance *Traversable* (*Vector n*) **where**
   $traverse\ f\ VNil\qquad\quad = pure\ VNil$
   $traverse\ f\ (VCons\ x\ xs) = (pure\ VCons \circledast f\ x) \circledast traverse\ f\ xs$

We take these various constraints as our definition of 'dimension':

class (*Applicative f*, *Naperian f*, *Traversable f*) $\Rightarrow$ *Dimension f* **where**
   $size :: f\ a \rightarrow Int$
   $size = length \cdot toList$

We have added a *size* method for convenience and with no loss of generality—it is in fact statically determined, so may admit better type-specific definitions:

instance   *Dimension Pair*   **where** $size = const\ 2$
instance *Count n* $\Rightarrow$ *Dimension* (*Vector n*) **where** $size = vlength$

But other less obvious datatypes, such as perfect binary trees of a given height, are suitable dimensions too:

data *Perfect* :: *Nat* $\rightarrow * \rightarrow *$ **where**
   $Leaf :: a \rightarrow\qquad\qquad\quad Perfect\ 'Z\ a$
   $Bin\ :: Pair\ (Perfect\ n\ a) \rightarrow Perfect\ ('S\ n)\ a$

For example, a *Perfect Three a* is essentially a *Pair (Pair (Pair a))*. Perhaps more usefully, rather than indexing vectors by a unary representation of the natural numbers, we can use a more compact binary representation:

data *Binary* :: ∗ **where**
   Unit   ::   *Binary*
   Twice   :: *Binary* → *Binary*
   Twice$_{+1}$ :: *Binary* → *Binary*

under the obvious interpretation

bin2int :: *Binary* → *Int*
bin2int Unit   = 1
bin2int (*Twice n*)   = 2 × *bin2int n*
bin2int (*Twice*$_{+1}$ *n*) = 2 × *bin2int n* + 1

Then we can define a datatype of (non-empty) vectors built up via balanced join rather than imbalanced cons:

data *BVector* :: *Binary* → ∗ → ∗ **where**
   VSingle :: *a* →   *BVector* '*Unit a*
   VJoin   ::   *BVector n a* → *BVector n a* → *BVector* ('*Twice n*) *a*
   VJoin$_{+1}$ :: *a* → *BVector n a* → *BVector n a* → *BVector* ('*Twice*$_{+1}$ *n*) *a*

When used as the dimensions of a matrix, this will allow a quad tree decomposition [12] for recursive functions. We leave the instance definitions as an exercise for the energetic reader.

In fact, one may start from any numeric representation and manufacture a corresponding datatype [18,29]. Sandberg Eriksson and Jansson [31] use a redundant binary representation of the positive natural numbers (with constructors 1 and +) as the type index in a formalization of block matrices. Each of these dimension types—pairs, triples, perfect binary trees of a given height, block vectors of a given structure—is equivalent to some vector type, so no additional expressivity is gained; but the alternatives may be more natural in given contexts.

As an example of a generic function, inner product involves summing pairwise products, and so works for any dimension type:

innerp :: (*Num a*, *Dimension f*) ⇒ *f a* → *f a* → *a*
innerp xs ys = *sum* (*azipWith* (∗) *xs ys*)

Multiplying an *f*×*g*-matrix by a *g*×*h*-matrix entails lifting both to *f*×*h*×*g*-matrices then performing pairwise inner product on the *g*-vectors:

matrixp :: (*Num a*, *Dimension f*, *Dimension g*, *Dimension h*) ⇒
        f (*g a*) → *g* (*h a*) → *f* (*h a*)
matrixp xss yss = *azipWith* (*azipWith innerp*) (*fmap areplicate xss*)
                                     (*areplicate* (*transpose yss*))

Again, this works for any dimension types *f*, *g*, *h*; the *same* definition works for vectors, pairs, block vectors, and any mixture of these.

5   Multidimensionality

Now that we can represent vectors with elements of an arbitrary type, we can of course represent matrices too, as vectors of vectors:

> $vv123456 :: Vector\ Two\ (Vector\ Three\ Int)$
> $vv123456 = VCons\ v123\ (VCons\ v456\ VNil)$

However, with this representation, integer vectors and integer matrices are of quite different types, and there is no immediate prospect of supporting rank polymorphism over them—for example, a single operation that can both add two matrices and add a vector to a matrix. In order to do that, we need one datatype that encompasses both vectors and matrices (and scalars, and arrays of higher rank).

One way to achieve this goal is with a *nested* [4] or *polymorphically recursive* [28] datatype:

> **data** $Hyper_0 :: * \rightarrow *$ **where**   -- to be refined later
> $Scalar_0 ::$ $a \rightarrow$ $Hyper_0\ a$
> $Prism_0 :: Count\ n \Rightarrow Hyper_0\ (Vector\ n\ a) \rightarrow Hyper_0\ a$

(we make a convention of subscripting definitions that will be refined later). This datatype corresponds to APL's multi-dimensional arrays. We use the name $Hyper_0$, for 'hypercuboid', so as not to clash with Haskell's $Array$ type that we will use later. Thus, $Scalar_0$ constructs a scalar hypercuboid from its sole element; and $Prism_0$ yields a hypercuboid of rank $r + 1$ from a hypercuboid of rank r whose elements are all n-vectors (for some n, but crucially, the same n for all elements at this rank). This definition makes essential use of polymorphic recursion, because a composite hypercuboid of as is constructed inductively not from smaller hypercuboids of as, but from a (single) hypercuboid of vectors of as.

This datatype satisfies the requirement of encompassing hypercuboids of arbitrary rank. However, it is somewhat unsatisfactory, precisely because it lumps together all hypercuboids of a given element type into a single type; for example, a vector and a matrix of integers both have the same type, namely $Hyper_0\ Int$. We have sacrificed any ability to catch rank errors through type checking. Perhaps worse, we have also sacrificed any chance to use the rank statically in order to automatically lift operators. We can solve this problem in much the same way as we did for bounds checking of vectors, by specifying the rank as a type index:

> **data** $Hyper_1 :: Nat \rightarrow * \rightarrow *$ **where**   -- to be refined later
> $Scalar_1 ::$ $a \rightarrow$ $Hyper_1\ 'Z\ a$
> $Prism_1 :: Count\ n \Rightarrow Hyper_1\ r\ (Vector\ n\ a) \rightarrow Hyper_1\ ('S\ r)\ a$

Now a vector of integers has type $Hyper_1\ One\ Int$, and a matrix of integers has type $Hyper_1\ Two\ Int$; it is a type error simply to try to add them pointwise, and the rank index can be used (we will see how in due course) to lift addition to act appropriately.

That is all well and good for rank, but we have a similar problem with size too: a 3-vector and a 4-vector of integers both have the same type when viewed as hypercuboids, namely $Hyper_1$ One Int; so we can no longer catch size mismatches by type checking. Apparently indexing by the rank alone is not enough; we should index by the size in each dimension—a list of natural numbers. Then the rank is the length of this list. Just as in Sect. 2 we promoted the datatype Nat to a kind and its inhabitants $Z, S\ Z, \ldots$ to types $'Z, 'S\ 'Z, \ldots$, we can also promote the datatype $[]$ of lists to the kind level, and its constructors $[]$ and $(:)$ to operators $'[]$ and $(':)$ at the type level:

> **data** $Hyper_2 :: [Nat] \rightarrow * \rightarrow *$ **where**   -- to be refined later
> $\quad Scalar_2 ::$ $\qquad\qquad\qquad a \rightarrow$ $\qquad\qquad\qquad\qquad Hyper_2\ '[]\ a$
> $\quad Prism_2 :: Count\ n \Rightarrow Hyper_2\ ns\ (Vector\ n\ a) \rightarrow Hyper_2\ (n ':\ ns)\ a$

Now a 3-vector of integers has type $Hyper_2\ '[Three]\ Int$, a 4-vector has type $Hyper_2\ '[Four]\ Int$, a 2×3-matrix has type $Hyper_2\ '[Three, Two]\ Int$, and so on. (Note that the latter is essentially a 2-vector of 3-vectors, rather than the other way round; it turns out to be most convenient for the first element of the list to represent the extent of the *innermost* dimension.) There is enough information at the type level to catch mismatches both of rank and of size; but still, the indexed types are all members of a common datatype, so can be made to support common operations.

That deals with multi-dimensional vectors. But as we discussed in Sect. 3, there is no a priori reason to restrict each dimension to be a vector; other datatypes work too, provided that they are instances of the type class *Dimension*. Then it is not enough for the datatype of hypercuboids to be indexed by a type-level list of lengths, because the lengths are no longer sufficient to characterize the dimensions—instead, we should use a type-level list of the dimension types themselves.

We call these type-level lists of dimension types *shapely* [22]. Following the example of vectors in Sect. 2, we introduce a type class of shapely types, which support replication and size:

> **class** $Shapely\ fs$ **where**
> $\quad hreplicate :: a \rightarrow Hyper\ fs\ a$
> $\quad hsize\qquad :: Hyper\ fs\ a \rightarrow Int$

We ensure that every possible type-level list of dimensions is an instance:

> **instance** $Shapely\ '[]$ **where**
> $\quad hreplicate\ a\qquad = Scalar\ a$
> $\quad hsize\qquad\qquad = const\ 1$
>
> **instance** $(Dimension\ f, Shapely\ fs) \Rightarrow Shapely\ (f ':\ fs)$ **where**
> $\quad hreplicate\ a\qquad = Prism\ (hreplicate\ (areplicate\ a))$
> $\quad hsize\ (Prism\ x) = size\ (first\ x) \times hsize\ x$

Here, *first* returns the first element of a hypercuboid, so *first x* is the first 'row' of *Prism x*:

$first :: Shapely\ fs \Rightarrow Hyper\ fs\ a \rightarrow a$
$first\ (Scalar\ a) = a$
$first\ (Prism\ x) = head\ (toList\ (first\ x))$

and the size of a hypercuboid is of course the product of the lengths of its dimensions.

Now, a hypercuboid of type $Hyper\ fs\ a$ has shape fs (a list of dimensions) and elements of type a. The rank zero hypercuboids are scalars; at higher ranks, one can think of them as geometrical 'right prisms'—congruent stacks of lower-rank hypercuboids.

data $Hyper :: [* \rightarrow *] \rightarrow * \rightarrow *$ **where**   -- final version
$\quad Scalar ::$ $a \rightarrow$ $Hyper\ '[]\ a$
$\quad Prism :: (Dimension\ f, Shapely\ fs) \Rightarrow Hyper\ fs\ (f\ a) \rightarrow Hyper\ (f\ ': fs)\ a$

For example, we can wrap up a vector of vectors as a rank-2 hypercuboid:

$h123456 :: Hyper\ '[Vector\ Three, Vector\ Two]\ Int$
$h123456 = Prism\ (Prism\ (Scalar\ vv123456))$

Hypercuboids are of course functorial:

instance $Functor\ (Hyper\ fs)$ **where**
$\quad fmap\ f\ (Scalar\ a) = Scalar\ (f\ a)$
$\quad fmap\ f\ (Prism\ x) = Prism\ (fmap\ (fmap\ f)\ x)$

Furthermore, they are applicative; the type class $Shapely$ handles replication, and zipping is simply a matter of matching structures:

$hzipWith :: (a \rightarrow b \rightarrow c) \rightarrow Hyper\ fs\ a \rightarrow Hyper\ fs\ b \rightarrow Hyper\ fs\ c$
$hzipWith\ f\ (Scalar\ a)\ (Scalar\ b) = Scalar\ (f\ a\ b)$
$hzipWith\ f\ (Prism\ x)\ (Prism\ y) = Prism\ (hzipWith\ (azipWith\ f)\ x\ y)$

With these two, we can install shapely hypercuboids as an applicative functor:

instance $Shapely\ fs \Rightarrow Applicative\ (Hyper\ fs)$ **where**
$\quad pure = hreplicate$
$\quad (\circledast) = hzipWith\ (\lambda f\ x \rightarrow f\ x)$

(In fact, hypercuboids are also Naperian, foldable, and traversable too, so they can themselves serve as dimensions; but we do not need that power in the rest of this paper.)

Now we can fold along the 'major' (that is, the innermost) axis of a hypercuboid, given a suitable binary operator and initial value:

$reduceBy :: (a \rightarrow a \rightarrow a, a) \rightarrow Hyper\ (f\ ': fs)\ a \rightarrow Hyper\ fs\ a$
$reduceBy\ (f, e)\ (Prism\ x) = fmap\ (foldr\ f\ e)\ x$

Moreover, we can transpose the hypercuboid in order to be able to fold along the 'minor' (that is, the next-to-innermost) axis:

$transposeHyper :: Hyper\ (f':(g':fs))\ a \rightarrow Hyper\ (g':(f':fs))\ a$
$transposeHyper\ (Prism\ (Prism\ x)) = Prism\ (Prism\ (fmap\ transpose\ x))$

Thus, given a hypercuboid of type $Hyper\ (f':(g':fs))\ a$, which by construction must be of the form $Prism\ (Prism\ x)$ with x of type $Hyper\ fs\ (g\ (f\ a))$, we *transpose* each of the inner hypercuboids from $g\ (f\ a)$ to $f\ (g\ a)$, then put the two *Prism* constructors back on to yield the result of type $Hyper\ (g':(f':fs))\ a$ as required. And with multiple transpositions, we can rearrange a hypercuboid to bring any axis into the 'major' position.

6   Alignment

We can easily lift a unary operator to act on a hypercuboid of elements:

$unary :: Shapely\ fs \Rightarrow (a \rightarrow b) \rightarrow (Hyper\ fs\ a \rightarrow Hyper\ fs\ b)$
$unary = fmap$

We can similarly lift a binary operator to act on hypercuboids of matching shapes, using *azipWith*. But what about when the shapes do not match? A shape *fs* is *alignable* with another shape *gs* if the type-level list of dimensions *fs* is a prefix of *gs*, so that they have innermost dimensions in common; in that case, we can replicate the *fs*-hypercuboid to yield a *gs*-hypercuboid.

class $(Shapely\ fs, Shapely\ gs) \Rightarrow Alignable\ fs\ gs$ **where**
    $align :: Hyper\ fs\ a \rightarrow Hyper\ gs\ a$

Scalar shapes are alignable with each other; alignment is the identity function:

instance $Alignable\ '[]\ '[]$ **where**
    $align = id$

Alignments can be extended along a common inner dimension:

instance $(Dimension\ f, Alignable\ fs\ gs) \Rightarrow Alignable\ (f':fs)\ (f':gs)$ **where**
    $align\ (Prism\ x) = Prism\ (align\ x)$

Finally, and most importantly, a scalar can be aligned with an arbitrary hypercuboid, via replication:

instance $(Dimension\ f, Shapely\ fs) \Rightarrow Alignable\ '[]\ (f':fs)$ **where**
    $align\ (Scalar\ a) = hreplicate\ a$

(Note that, ignoring the accompanying definitions of the *align* function, the heads of the three *Alignable* instance declarations can be read together as a logic program for when one sequence is a prefix of another.)

The *Alignable* relation on shapes is an ordering, and in particular asymmetric. In order to be able to lift a binary operator to act on two compatible hypercuboids, we should treat the two arguments symmetrically: we will align the two shapes with their least common extension, provided that this exists. We express that in terms of the *Max* of two shapes, a type-level function:

type family Max $(fs :: [* \rightarrow *])$ $(gs :: [* \rightarrow *]) :: [* \rightarrow *]$ **where**
$\quad Max\ '[]\qquad\ '[]\qquad\ = '[]$
$\quad Max\ '[]\qquad (f' : gs) = (f' : gs)$
$\quad Max\ (f' : fs)\ '[]\qquad = (f' : fs)$
$\quad Max\ (f' : fs)\ (f' : gs) = (f' : Max\ fs\ gs)$

For example, a 2×3-matrix can be aligned with a 3-vector:

$\quad Max\ '[Three, Two]\ '[Three] \sim\ '[Three, Two]$

Here, $\sim$ denotes type compatibility in Haskell. Provided that shapes fs and gs are compatible, we can align two hypercuboids of those shapes with their least common extension hs, and then apply a binary operator to them pointwise:

$binary_0 ::$ -- to be refined later
$\quad (Max\ fs\ gs \sim hs, Alignable\ fs\ hs, Alignable\ gs\ hs) \Rightarrow$
$\quad (a \rightarrow b \rightarrow c) \rightarrow (Hyper\ fs\ a \rightarrow Hyper\ gs\ b \rightarrow Hyper\ hs\ c)$
$binary_0\ f\ x\ y = hzipWith\ f\ (align\ x)\ (align\ y)$

For example,

$\quad binary_0\ (+)\ (Scalar\ 3)\ h123456 = \langle\langle 4, 5, 6\rangle, \langle 7, 8, 9\rangle\rangle$

Note that as a function on types, *Max* is partial: two shapes $f' : fs$ and $g' : gs$ are incompatible when $f \not\equiv g$, and then have no common extension. In that case, it is a type error to attempt to align two hypercuboids of those shapes. However, the type error can be a bit inscrutable. For example, when trying to align a 3-vector with a 4-vector, the compiler cannot simplify $Max\ '[Vector\ Three]\ '[Vector\ Four]$, and GHC (version 7.10.3) gives the following error:

```
No instance for
 (Alignable '[Vector Three] (Max '[Vector Three] '[Vector Four]))
 (maybe you haven't applied enough arguments to a function?)
```

We can use type-level functions to provide more helpful error messages too [33]. We define an additional type function as a predicate on types, to test whether the shapes are compatible:

type family $IsCompatible$ $(fs :: [* \rightarrow *])$ $(gs :: [* \rightarrow *]) :: IsDefined\ Symbol$ **where**
$\quad IsCompatible\ '[]\qquad\ '[]\qquad = Defined$
$\quad IsCompatible\ '[]\qquad (f' : gs) = Defined$
$\quad IsCompatible\ (f' : fs)\ '[]\qquad = Defined$
$\quad IsCompatible\ (f' : fs)\ (f' : gs) = IsCompatible\ fs\ gs$
$\quad IsCompatible\ (f' : fs)\ (g' : gs) = Undefined\ \texttt{"Mismatching dimensions"}$

Here, *Symbol* is the kind of type-level strings, and *IsDefined* is a type-level version of the booleans, but extended to incorporate also an explanation in the case that the predicate fails to hold:

data *IsDefined e = Defined | Undefined e*

If we now add this test as a constraint to the type of a lifted binary operator:

```
binary ::   -- final version
  (IsCompatible fs gs ~ Defined, Max fs gs ~ hs, Alignable fs hs, Alignable gs hs) ⇒
  (a → b → c) → (Hyper fs a → Hyper gs b → Hyper hs c)
binary f x y = binary₀ f x y
```

(note that the code is precisely the same, only the type has become more informative) then we get a slightly more helpful error message when things go wrong:

```
Couldn't match type 'Undefined "Mismatching dimensions"
                with 'Defined
Expected type: 'Defined
  Actual type: IsCompatible '[Vector Three] '[Vector Four]
```

7   Symbolic Transformations

Although alignment of arrays of compatible but different shapes morally entails replication, this is an inefficient way actually to implement it; instead, it is better simply to use each element of the smaller structure multiple times. One way to achieve this is perform the replication *symbolically*—that is, to indicate via the type index that an array is replicated along a given dimension, without manifestly performing the replication. This can be achieved by extending the datatype of hypercuboids to incorporate an additional constructor:

```
data HyperR :: [* → *] → * → * where
  ScalarR ::                                      a →              HyperR '[] a
  PrismR :: (Dimension f, Shapely fs) ⇒ HyperR fs (f a) → HyperR (f ': fs) a
  ReplR  :: (Dimension f, Shapely fs) ⇒ HyperR fs a →       HyperR (f ': fs) a
```

The idea is that *ReplR x* denotes the same array as *Prism (fmap areplicate x)*, but takes constant time and space to record the replication. It allows us to implement replication to multiple ranks in time and space proportional to the rank, rather than to the size. This would be of no benefit were it just to postpone the actual replication work until later. Fortunately, the work can often be avoided altogether. Mapping is straightforward, since it simply distributes through *ReplR*:

```
instance Functor (HyperR fs) where
  fmap f (ScalarR a) = ScalarR (f a)
  fmap f (PrismR x) = PrismR (fmap (fmap f) x)
  fmap f (ReplR x)   = ReplR (fmap f x)
```

Similarly for zipping two replicated dimensions. When zipping a replicated dimension (*ReplR*) with a manifest one (*PrismR*), we end up essentially with a map—that, after all, was the whole point of the exercise. The other cases are as before.

$rzipWith :: Shapely\ fs \Rightarrow (a \rightarrow b \rightarrow c) \rightarrow HyperR\ fs\ a \rightarrow HyperR\ fs\ b \rightarrow HyperR\ fs\ c$
$rzipWith\ f\ (ScalarR\ a)\ (ScalarR\ b) = ScalarR\ (f\ a\ b)$
$rzipWith\ f\ (PrismR\ x)\ (PrismR\ y) = PrismR\ (rzipWith\ (azipWith\ f)\ x\ y)$
$rzipWith\ f\ (PrismR\ x)\ (ReplR\ y)\ \ = PrismR\ (rzipWith\ (azipWithL\ f)\ x\ y)$
$rzipWith\ f\ (ReplR\ x)\ (PrismR\ y)\ \ = PrismR\ (rzipWith\ (azipWithR\ f)\ x\ y)$
$rzipWith\ f\ (ReplR\ x)\ (ReplR\ y)\ \ \ = ReplR\ (rzipWith\ f\ x\ y)$

Here, $azipWithL$ and $azipWithR$ are variants of $azipWith$ with one argument constant:

$azipWithL :: Functor\ f \Rightarrow (a \rightarrow b \rightarrow c) \rightarrow f\ a \rightarrow b \rightarrow f\ c$
$azipWithL\ f\ xs\ y = fmap\ (\lambda x \rightarrow f\ x\ y)\ xs$

$azipWithR :: Functor\ f \Rightarrow (a \rightarrow b \rightarrow c) \rightarrow a \rightarrow f\ b \rightarrow f\ c$
$azipWithR\ f\ x\ ys = fmap\ (\lambda y \rightarrow f\ x\ y)\ ys$

(note that they only need a *Functor* constraint rather than *Applicative*, since they only use *fmap* and not *pure* and ⊛).

Similarly for transposition; if either of the innermost two dimensions is symbolically replicated, it is just a matter of rearranging constructors, and only when they are both manifest do we have to resort to actual data movement:

$rtranspose :: (Shapely\ fs, Dimension\ f, Dimension\ g) \Rightarrow$
$\qquad HyperR\ (f\ ':\ g\ ':\ fs)\ a \rightarrow HyperR\ (g\ ':\ f\ ':\ fs)\ a$
$rtranspose\ (PrismR\ (PrismR\ x)) = PrismR\ (PrismR\ (fmap\ transpose\ x))$
$rtranspose\ (PrismR\ (ReplR\ x))\ \ = ReplR\ (PrismR\ x)$
$rtranspose\ (ReplR\ (PrismR\ x))\ \ = PrismR\ (ReplR\ x)$
$rtranspose\ (ReplR\ (ReplR\ x))\ \ \ = ReplR\ (ReplR\ x)$

It is only when it comes to folding or traversing a hypercuboid that a symbolic replication really has to be forced. This can be achieved by means of a function that expands a top-level *ReplR* constructor, if one is present, while leaving the hypercuboid abstractly the same:

$forceReplR :: Shapely\ fs \Rightarrow HyperR\ fs\ a \rightarrow HyperR\ fs\ a$
$forceReplR\ (ReplR\ x) = PrismR\ (fmap\ areplicate\ x)$
$forceReplR\ x\qquad\quad = x$

A similar technique can be used to represent transposition itself symbolically, via its own constructor:

data $HyperT :: [* \rightarrow *] \rightarrow * \rightarrow *$ **where**
$\quad ScalarT :: a \rightarrow \qquad\qquad\qquad HyperT\ '[]\ a$
$\quad PrismT :: (Dimension\ f, Shapely\ fs) \Rightarrow$
$\qquad\qquad HyperT\ fs\ (f\ a) \rightarrow \qquad HyperT\ (f\ ':\ fs)\ a$
$\quad TransT\ :: (Dimension\ f, Dimension\ g, Shapely\ fs) \Rightarrow$
$\qquad\qquad HyperT\ (f\ ':\ g\ ':\ fs)\ a \rightarrow HyperT\ (g\ ':\ f\ ':\ fs)\ a$

The idea is that $TransT\ x$ represents the transposition of x, without actually doing any work. We can maintain the invariant that there are never two adjacent

TransT constructors, by using the following 'smart constructor' in place of the real one, to remove a transposition if one is present and to add one otherwise:

$$trans\,T :: (Dimension\ f, Dimension\ g, Shapely\ fs) \Rightarrow$$
$$HyperT\ (f\,':g\,':fs)\ a \to HyperT\ (g\,':f\,':fs)\ a$$
$$trans\,T\ (Trans\,T\ x) = x$$
$$trans\,T\ x = Trans\,T\ x$$

Of course, with the help of this additional constructor, transposition is trivial, and replication is no more difficult than it was with plain *Hyper*; zipping is the only operation that requires any thought. Where the two structures match, zipping simply commutes with them—and in particular, symbolic transpositions may be preserved, as in the third equation for *tzipWith* below. Only when zipping a *TransT* with a *PrismT* does the symbolic transposition need to be forced, for which we provide a function that expands a top-most *TransT* constructor if one is present, while leaving the hypercuboid abstractly the same:

$$force\,Trans\,T :: (Dimension\ f, Dimension\ g, Shapely\ fs) \Rightarrow$$
$$HyperT\ (f\,':g\,':fs)\ a \to HyperT\ (f\,':g\,':fs)\ a$$
$$force\,Trans\,T\ (Trans\,T\ (Prism\,T\ (Prism\,T\ x)))$$
$$= Prism\,T\ (Prism\,T\ (fmap\ transpose\ x))$$
$$force\,Trans\,T\ (Trans\,T\ (Prism\,T\ x@(Trans\,T\ \_)))$$
$$= \mathbf{case}\ force\,Trans\,T\ x\ \mathbf{of}$$
$$Prism\,T\ x' \to Prism\,T\ (Prism\,T\ (fmap\ transpose\ x'))$$
$$force\,Trans\,T\ x = x$$

(Here, the 'as-pattern' $x@p$ binds x to the whole of an argument whilst simultaneously matching against the pattern p, and $\_$ is a wild card. On account of the type constraints, together with the invariant that there are no two adjacent *TransT* constructors, these three clauses are sufficient to guarantee that the outermost constructor is not a *TransT*.) Then we have:

$$tzip\,With :: Shapely\ fs \Rightarrow$$
$$(a \to b \to c) \to HyperT\ fs\ a \to HyperT\ fs\ b \to HyperT\ fs\ c$$
$$tzip\,With\ f\ (Scalar\,T\ a)\ (Scalar\,T\ b)\quad = Scalar\,T\ (f\ a\ b)$$
$$tzip\,With\ f\ (Prism\,T\ x)\ (Prism\,T\ y)\quad = Prism\,T\ (tzip\,With\ (azip\,With\ f)\ x\ y)$$
$$tzip\,With\ f\ (Trans\,T\ x)\ (Trans\,T\ y)\quad = Trans\,T\ (tzip\,With\ f\ x\ y)$$
$$tzip\,With\ f\ x@(Trans\,T\ \_)\ (Prism\,T\ y) = tzip\,With\ f\ (force\,Trans\,T\ x)\ (Prism\,T\ y)$$
$$tzip\,With\ f\ (Prism\,T\ x)\ y@(Trans\,T\ \_) = tzip\,With\ f\ (Prism\,T\ x)\ (force\,Trans\,T\ y)$$

Again, folding and traversing seem to require manifesting any symbolic transpositions.

We can even combine symbolic replication and transposition in the same datatype, providing trivial implementations of both operations. The only tricky part then is in zipping, while preserving as much of the symbolic representation as possible. We have all the cases of *rzipWith* for prisms interacting with replication, plus those of *tzipWith* for prisms interacting with transposition, plus some new cases for replication interacting with transposition. The details are not particularly surprising, so are left again to the energetic reader.

8   Flat Representation

The various nested representations above precisely capture the shape of a hyper-cuboid. This prevents dimension and size mismatches, by making them type errors; more constructively, it drives the mechanism for automatically aligning the arguments of heterogeneous binary operators. However, the nested representation is inefficient in time and space; high performance array libraries targetting GPUs arrange the data as a simple, flat, contiguous sequence of values, mediated via coordinate transformations between the nested index space and the flat one. In this section, we explore such flat representations.

Since each dimension of a hypercuboid is Naperian, with a fixed collection of positions, the total size of a hypercuboid is statically determined; so one can rather straightforwardly flatten the whole structure to an immutable linear array. To get the full benefits of the flat representation, that really should be an array of *unboxed* values [30]; for simplicity, we elide the unboxing here, but it should not be difficult to provide that too.

In order to flatten a hypercuboid into a linear array, we need the total size and a list of the elements. The former is provided as the *hsize* method of the type class *Shapely*; for the latter, we define

$$elements :: Shapely\ fs \Rightarrow Hyper\ fs\ a \rightarrow [\,a\,]$$
$$elements\ (Scalar\ a) = [\,a\,]$$
$$elements\ (Prism\ x) = concat\ (map\ toList\ (elements\ x))$$

As a representation of flattened hypercuboids, we introduce an indexed version of arrays, preserving the shape *fs* as a type index:

data *Flat fs a* **where**
    Flat :: *Shapely fs* ⇒ *Array Int a* → *Flat fs a*

to which we can transform a hypercuboid:

$$flatten :: Shapely\ fs \Rightarrow Hyper\ fs\ a \rightarrow Flat\ fs\ a$$
$$flatten\ x = Flat\ (listArray\ (0, hsize\ x - 1)\ (elements\ x))$$

Here, *listArray* is a standard Haskell function that constructs an array from a pair of bounds and an ordered list of elements. This representation is essentially the same as is used for high-performance array libraries such as Repa [24] for multicore architectures and Accelerate [5] for GPUs; so it should be straightforward to use the abstractions defined here as a front end to guarantee safety, with such a library as a back end for high performance.

The flat contiguous *Array* is one possible representation of the sequence of elements in a hypercuboid, but it is not the only possibility. In particular, we can accommodate *sparse* array representations too, recording the shape as a type index, and explicitly storing only the non-null elements together with their positions. When the elements are numeric, we could make the convention that the absent ones are zero; more generally, we could provide a single copy of the 'default' element:

data *Sparse fs a* **where**
    Sparse :: *Shapely fs* $\Rightarrow$ *a* $\rightarrow$ *Array Int* (*Int, a*) $\rightarrow$ *Sparse fs a*

so that *Sparse e xs* denotes a sparse array with default element *e* and list *xs* of proper elements paired with their positions. This can be expanded back to a traditional flat array as follows:

unsparse :: $\forall fs$ *a* . *Shapely fs* $\Rightarrow$ *Sparse fs a* $\rightarrow$ *Flat fs a*
unsparse *x*@(*Sparse e xs*) = *Flat* (*accumArray second e* (0, *l* − 1) (*elems xs*))
   where *l* = *hsize* (*hreplicate* () :: *Hyper fs* ())
        second b a = *a*

Here, *elems* yields the list of elements of an *Array*, which for us will be a list of pairs; and *accumArray f e* (*i, j*) *xs* constructs a *B*-array with bounds (*i, j*) from a list *xs* of *A*-elements paired with positions, accumulating the subsequence of elements labelled with the same position using the initial value *e* :: *B* and the binary operator *f* :: *B* $\rightarrow$ *A* $\rightarrow$ *B*. For us, the types *A, B* coincide, and *second* keeps the second of its two arguments. For simplicity, we compute the size *l* from a regular *Hyper* of the same shape; more sophisticated approaches are of course possible.

One could similarly provide a run-length-encoded representation, for arrays expected to have long constant sections of different values, and space-efficient representations of diagonal and triangular matrices.

Note that neither the *Flat* nor the *Sparse* representation as shown enforce the bounds constraints. The underlying array in both cases is merely assumed to have the appropriate length for the shape index *fs*. Moreover, for the sparse representation, the positions are additionally assumed to be within range; a more sophisticated representation using bounded naturals *Fin* could be used to enforce the constraints, should that be deemed important. One might also want to maintain the invariant that the elements in the sparse representation are listed in order of position, so that two arrays can easily be zipped via merging without first expanding out to a dense representation; it is straightforward to impose that ordering invariant on the position using dependent typing [27].

In order to provide efficient element access and manipulation, one could combine the array representation with an explicit *index transformation* [16]. Replication and transposition can then be represented by modifying the index transformation, without touching the array elements. We leave the pursuit of this possibility for future work.

9   Conclusions

We have shown how to express the rank and size constraints on multidimensional APL array operations statically, by embedding into a modern strongly typed functional programming language. This means that we benefit for free from all the infrastructure of the host language, such as the type checking, compilation, code optimizations, libraries, and development tools—all of which would have to be built from scratch for a standalone type system such as that of Remora [34].

The embedding makes use of lightweight dependently typed programming features, as exhibited in Haskell. What is quite remarkable is that there is no need for any sophisticated solver for size constraints; the existing traditional unification algorithm suffices (with admittedly many extensions since the days of Hindley and Milner, for example to encompass generalized algebraic datatypes, polymorphic recursion, type families, and so on). This is perhaps not surprising when all one does with sizes is to compare them, but it still applies for certain amounts of size arithmetic. For example, there is no difficulty at all in defining addition and multiplication of type-level numbers,

> **type family** *Add* (*m* :: *Nat*) (*n* :: *Nat*) :: *Nat* **where** ...
> **type family** *Mult* (*m* :: *Nat*) (*n* :: *Nat*) :: *Nat* **where** ...

and then writing functions to append and split vectors, and to concatenate and group vectors of vectors:

> *vappend* :: (*Vector m a*, *Vector n a*) → *Vector* (*Add m n*) *a*
> *vsplit*   :: *Count m* ⇒
>   *Vector* (*Add m n*) *a* → (*Vector m a*, *Vector n a*)
> *vconcat* :: *Vector m* (*Vector n a*) → *Vector* (*Mult m n*) *a*
> *vgroup* :: (*Count m*, *Count n*) ⇒
>   *Vector* (*Mult m n*) *a* → *Vector m* (*Vector n a*)

We have shown how the approach supports various important optimizations, such as avoiding unnecessary replication of data, and flat storage of multidimensional data. In future work, we plan to integrate this approach with existing libraries for high-performance GPU execution, notably Repa [24] and Accelerate [5].

9.1 Related Work

We are, of course, not the first to use a type system to guarantee size constraints on dimensions of array operations. The length-indexed vector example is the 'hello, world' of lightweight approaches to dependently typed programming, dating back at least to Xi's Dependent ML [38]. The particular case in which the shape is data-independent, as we address here, can also be traced back to Jay's work [22] on *shapely types*, in which data structures may be factored into 'shape' and 'contents', the latter a simple sequence of elements; then *shapely operations* are those for which the shape of the output depends only on the shape of the input, and not on its contents.

Jay already considered the example of two-dimensional matrices; many others have also used size information at the type level to statically constrain multidimensional array operations. Eaton [7] presented a demonstration of *statically typed linear algebra*, by which he meant "any tool which makes [static guarantees about matching dimensions] possible". Scholz's Single-Assignment C [32] represents the extents of multi-dimensional arrays in their types, and Trojahner and Grelck [36] discuss *shape-generic functional array programming* in SAC/Qube.

Abe and Sumii [1] present an array interface that enforces shape consistency through what they call *generative phantom types*, and conclude that "practical size checking for a linear algebra library can be constructed on the simple idea of verifying mostly the equality of sizes without significantly restructuring application programs".

Elsman and Dybdal's subset of APL [10] and Veldhuizen's Blitz++ [37] have array types indexed by rank but not size. Chakravarty *et al.*'s Haskell libraries Repa [24] and Accelerate [5] similarly express the rank of a multi-dimensional array in its type, but represent its shape only as part of the value, so that can only be checked at run-time (note that they use both "rank" and "shape" in their papers to refer to what we call rank). Thiemann and Chakravarty [35] explore the trade-offs in developing a front-end to Accelerate in the true dependently typed language Agda in order (among other things) to statically capture shape information; we have shown that it is not necessary to leave the more familiar world of Haskell to achieve that particular end.

None of these works cover full rank polymorphism as in APL and Remora and as in our work: although operations such as map may be applied at arbitrary shape, binary operations such as zip require both arguments to have the same shape—there is no lifting and alignment.

The representation of an array in terms of its *lookup* function, as in our *Naperian* class and our basis for transposition, also has quite a long history. The representation is known as *pull arrays* in the Chalmers work on the digital signal processing language Feldspar [2] and the GPU language Obsidian [6], and *delayed* arrays in Repa [24]. But it is also the essence of *functional reactive animation*, for example in Elliott's Pan [8] and his and Hudak's Fran [9], and in Hudak and Jones's earlier experiment on *geometric region servers* [20].

Acknowledgements. This paper has benefitted from helpful suggestions from Tim Zakian, Matthew Pickering, Sam Lindley, Andres Löh, Wouter Swierstra, Conor McBride, Simon Peyton Jones, the participants at IFIP WG2.1 Meeting #74 and WG2.11 Meeting #16, and the anonymous reviewers, to all of whom I am very grateful. The work was partially supported by EPSRC grant EP/K020919/1 on *A Theory of Least Change for Bidirectional Transformations*.

> O, my offence is rank, it smells to heaven;
> It hath the primal eldest curse upon 't.
> *Shakespeare, "Hamlet", Act III Scene 3*

References

1. Abe, A., Sumii, E.: A simple and practical linear algebra library interface with static size checking. In: Kiselyov, O., Garrigue, J. (eds.) ML Family Workshop. EPTCS, vol. 198, pp. 1–21 (2014)
2. Axelsson, E., Claessen, K., Sheeran, M., Svenningsson, J., Engdal, D., Persson, A.: The design and implementation of feldspar. In: Hage, J., Morazán, M.T. (eds.) IFL 2010. LNCS, vol. 6647, pp. 121–136. Springer, Heidelberg (2011). doi:10.1007/978-3-642-24276-2_8

3. Bird, R., Gibbons, J., Mehner, S., Voigtländer, J., Schrijvers, T.: Understanding idiomatic traversals backwards and forwards. In: Haskell Symposium. ACM (2013)
4. Bird, R., Meertens, L.: Nested datatypes. In: Jeuring, J. (ed.) MPC 1998. LNCS, vol. 1422, pp. 52–67. Springer, Heidelberg (1998). doi:10.1007/BFb0054285
5. Chakravarty, M.M.T., Keller, G., Lee, S., McDonell, T.L., Grover, V.: Accelerating Haskell array codes with multicore GPUs. In: Declarative Aspects of Multicore Programming, pp. 3–14. ACM (2011)
6. Claessen, K., Sheeran, M., Svensson, B.J.: Expressive array constructs in an embedded GPU kernel programming language. In: Declarative Aspects of Multicore Programming, pp. 21–30. ACM (2012)
7. Eaton, F.: Statically typed linear algebra in Haskell (demo). In: Haskell Workshop, pp. 120–121. ACM (2006)
8. Elliott, C.: Functional images. In: Gibbons, J., de Moor, O. (eds.) The Fun of Programming. Cornerstones in Computing, pp. 131–150. Palgrave, Basingstoke (2003)
9. Elliott, C., Hudak, P.: Functional reactive animation. In: International Conference on Functional Programming. ACM (1997)
10. Elsman, M., Dybdal, M.: Compiling a subset of APL into a typed intermediate language. In: Workshop on Libraries, Languages, and Compilers for Array Programming, pp. 101–106. ACM (2014)
11. Felleisen, M., Findler, R.B., Flatt, M.: Semantics Engineering with PLT Redex. MIT Press, Cambridge (2009)
12. Finkel, R.A., Bentley, J.L.: Quad trees: a data structure for retrieval on composite keys. Acta Informatica **4**(1), 1–9 (1974)
13. GHC Team: Glasgow Haskell Compiler. https://www.haskell.org/ghc/
14. Gibbons, J.: APLicative programming with Naperian functors: Haskell code, January 2017. http://www.cs.ox.ac.uk/jeremy.gibbons/publications/aplicative.hs
15. Gibbons, J., de Moor, O.: The Fun of Programming. Cornerstones in Computing. Palgrave, Basingstoke (2003)
16. Guibas, L.J., Wyatt, D.K.: Compilation and delayed evaluation in APL. In: Principles of Programming Languages, pp. 1–8. ACM (1978)
17. Peter Hancock. What is a Naperian container? June 2005. http://sneezy.cs.nott.ac.uk/containers/blog/?p=14
18. Hinze, R.: Manufacturing datatypes. J. Funct. Program. **11**(5), 493–524 (2001)
19. Hinze, R.: Fun with phantom types. In: Gibbons, J., de Moor, O. (eds.) The Fun of Programming. Cornerstones in Computing, pp. 245–262. Palgrave, Basingstoke (2003)
20. Hudak, P., Jones, M.P.: Haskell vs Ada vs C++ vs Awk vs ...: an experiment in software prototyping productivity. Department of Computer Science, Yale, July 1994
21. Iverson, K.E.: A Programming Language. Wiley, Hoboken (1962)
22. Jay, C.B., Cockett, J.R.B.: Shapely types and shape polymorphism. In: Sannella, D. (ed.) ESOP 1994. LNCS, vol. 788, pp. 302–316. Springer, Heidelberg (1994). doi:10.1007/3-540-57880-3_20
23. Jsoftware, Inc. Jsoftware: High performance development platform (2016). http://www.jsoftware.com
24. Keller, G., Chakravarty, M., Leschchinskiy, R., Jones, S.P., Lippmeier, B.: Regular, shape-polymorphic parallel arrays in Haskell. In: International Conference on Functional Programming, pp. 261–272. ACM (2010)
25. Lindley, S., McBride, C.: Hasochism: the pleasure and pain of dependently typed Haskell programming. In: Haskell Symposium, pp. 81–92. ACM (2013)

26. McBride, C., Paterson, R.: Applicative programming with effects. J. Funct. Program. **18**(1), 1–13 (2008)

27. McKinna, J.: Why dependent types matter. In: Principles of Programming Languages, p. 1. ACM (2006). http://www.cs.nott.ac.uk/psztxa/publ/ydtm.pdf

28. Mycroft, A.: Polymorphic type schemes and recursive definitions. In: Paul, M., Robinet, B. (eds.) Programming 1984. LNCS, vol. 167, pp. 217–228. Springer, Heidelberg (1984). doi:10.1007/3-540-12925-1_41

29. Okasaki, C.: Purely Functional Data Structures. CUP, Cambridge (1998)

30. Jones, S.P., Launchbury, J.: Unboxed values as first class citizens in a non-strict functional language. In: Functional Programming Languages and Computer Architecture, pp. 636–666. ACM (1991)

31. Eriksson, A.S., Jansson, P.: An Agda formalisation of the transitive closure of block matrices (extended abstract). In: Type-Driven Development, pp. 60–61. ACM (2016)

32. Scholz, S.-B.: Functional array programming in SAC. In: Horváth, Z. (ed.) CEFP 2005. LNCS, vol. 4164, pp. 62–99. Springer, Heidelberg (2006). doi:10.1007/11894100_3

33. Serrano, A., Hage, J., Bahr, P.: Type families with class, type classes with family. In: Haskell Symposium, pp. 129–140. ACM (2015)

34. Slepak, J., Shivers, O., Manolios, P.: An array-oriented language with static rank polymorphism. In: Shao, Z. (ed.) ESOP 2014. LNCS, vol. 8410, pp. 27–46. Springer, Heidelberg (2014). doi:10.1007/978-3-642-54833-8_3

35. Thiemann, P., Chakravarty, M.M.T.: Agda meets accelerate. In: Hinze, R. (ed.) IFL 2012. LNCS, vol. 8241, pp. 174–189. Springer, Heidelberg (2013). doi:10.1007/978-3-642-41582-1_11

36. Trojahner, K., Grelck, C.: Dependently typed array programs don't go wrong. J. Logic Algebraic Program. **78**(7), 643–664 (2009)

37. Veldhuizen, T.L.: Arrays in Blitz++. In: Caromel, D., Oldehoeft, R.R., Tholburn, M. (eds.) ISCOPE 1998. LNCS, vol. 1505, pp. 223–230. Springer, Heidelberg (1998). doi:10.1007/3-540-49372-7_24

38. Xi, H., Pfenning, F.: Eliminating array bound checking through dependent types. In: Programming Language Design and Implementation. ACM (1998)

39. Yorgey, B.A., Weirich, S., Cretin, J., Jones, S.P., Vytiniotis, D., Magalhães, J.P.: Giving Haskell a promotion. In: Types in Language Design and Implementation, pp. 53–66. ACM (2012)

Verified Characteristic Formulae for CakeML

Armaël Guéneau[1(✉)], Magnus O. Myreen[2], Ramana Kumar[3],
and Michael Norrish[4]

[1] ENS de Lyon and Inria, Paris, France
armael.gueneau@inria.fr
[2] CSE Department, Chalmers University of Technology, Gothenburg, Sweden
[3] Data61, CSIRO/UNSW, Sydney, Australia
[4] Data61, CSIRO/ANU, Canberra, Australia

Abstract. Characteristic Formulae (CF) offer a productive, principled approach to generating verification conditions for higher-order imperative programs, but so far the soundness of CF has only been considered with respect to an informal specification of a programming language (OCaml). This leaves a gap between what is established by the verification framework and the program that actually runs. We present a fully-fledged CF framework for the formally specified CakeML programming language. Our framework extends the existing CF approach to support exceptions and I/O, thereby covering the full feature set of CakeML, and comes with a formally verified soundness theorem. Furthermore, it integrates with existing proof techniques for verifying CakeML programs. This validates the CF approach, and allows users to prove end-to-end theorems for higher-order imperative programs, from specification to language semantics, within a single theorem prover.

1 Introduction

In previous work, Charguéraud introduced a framework for the verification of imperative higher-order programs, based on characteristic formulae (CF). Given a source-level program, the approach allows the user to state a specification for it, in the style of Separation Logic [22], and prove the specification using the full power of a proof assistant. It has proved successful in verifying robust and modular specifications for non-trivial programs [6], and even establishing complexity results [7].

The key component of such a framework is a function that produces, from a source-level program e, its characteristic formula cf e. Applying the logical predicate cf e to an environment env, a pre-condition H and a post-condition Q yields the proposition cf e env H Q, which implies program e admits H as a pre-condition and Q as a post-condition, in environment env. The user is left with the task of proving the goal cf e env H Q using specialised CF tactics alongside general-purpose tactics in an interactive theorem prover.

Charguéraud's work is realised in a tool named CFML, where (a subset of) OCaml is the language of the certified programs, and Coq is the proof assistant that hosts the characteristic formulae. Only part of the soundness theorem for CFML has been proved in Charguéraud's Coq formalisation.

© Springer-Verlag GmbH Germany 2017
H. Yang (Ed.): ESOP 2017, LNCS 10201, pp. 584–610, 2017.
DOI: 10.1007/978-3-662-54434-1_22

In this paper, we describe how a CF framework has been constructed and proved sound for the entire CakeML language [26], including its exception mechanism and I/O features. CakeML is a substantial subset of Standard ML, with the notable feature that its compiler has been verified (in the HOL4 proof assistant). In addition to capturing language features not modeled in CFML, we give this framework a fully verified soundness theorem. The entire development is formalised in HOL4, which also plays the role of the proof assistant hosting the characteristic formulae. Though tactic details are not the main topic of this paper, we also provide HOL4 tactic support for our CF framework, just as CFML provides Coq tactics to support the proof of cf *e* *H* *Q* theorems.

This paper's material goes beyond previous work on characteristic formulae and CFML in the following ways:

- We give a mechanised proof of soundness of characteristic formulae with respect to CakeML's formal semantics (Sect. 2). By way of contrast, CFML's soundness proof is mostly performed outside of Coq.
- We support additional language features, such as I/O (Sect. 3) and exceptions (Sect. 3.2). This makes our framework go beyond CFML, and thus able to handle all features of the CakeML programming language.
- We implement technology to make proofs using characteristic formulae interoperate with the existing synthesis tool for CakeML, namely the proof-producing translator from HOL functions to CakeML (Sect. 4).

As an appetiser, in Fig. 1 we show the code for a simple implementation of the Unix `cat` program, that we are able to verify using our framework. The

```
fun cat1 fname =
  let
    val fd = CharIO.openIn fname
    fun recurse () =
      case CharIO.read1 fd of
          NONE ⇒ ()
        | SOME c ⇒ (CharIO.write c; recurse ())
  in
    recurse () ;
    CharIO.close fd
  end

fun cat fnames =
  case fnames of
    [] ⇒ ()
  | f::fs ⇒ (cat1 f ; cat fs)
```

Fig. 1. Code implementing concatenation of files to standard out. The `CharIO` module is our verified implementation of an FFI interface to a rudimentary file-system model (see Sect. 5 for more details).

specification for cat, proven correct in our framework, and thus a HOL4 theorem, is given in Fig. 2. The main steps of the cat proof are described in Sect. 5.

$$\text{FILENAME } s \; sv \iff \text{STRING } s \; sv \wedge \text{noNullBytes } s \wedge \text{strlen } s < 256$$

$$\vdash \text{LIST FILENAME } fns \; fnsv \wedge \text{every } (\lambda \, fnm. \; \text{inFS\_fname } fnm \; fs) \; fns \wedge$$
$$\text{numOpenFDs } fs < 255 \Rightarrow$$
$$\{\!| \text{CATFS } fs * \text{STDOUT } out |\!\}$$
$$\text{cat\_v} \cdot [fnsv]$$
$$\{\!| \text{POSTv } u.$$
$$\langle \text{UNIT () } u \rangle * \text{CATFS } fs *$$
$$\text{STDOUT } (out @ \text{catfiles\_string } fs \; fns) |\!\}$$

Fig. 2. A CF specification of the cat function from Fig. 1. The app predicate underlies the $\{\!|H|\!\}$ $fv \cdot args$ $\{\!|Q|\!\}$ notation, giving a CF Hoare triple for a function, indicating that if fv is applied to $args$ in a state satisfying H, the result satisfies Q. The ($*$) operator (defined on page 14) corresponds to the separating conjunction of separation logic. Parts of specifications occurring within angle brackets (here, only in the post-condition) are conditions that do not depend on the state of the heap. Above, the implication's assumptions require that no file name contains a null byte or has 256 characters or more (enforced by the FILENAME predicate), that every file name corresponds to a real file in the system, and that fewer than 255 files are open. These various requirements naturally fall out of the way the interactions with the file-system are mediated by the FFI interface. The post-condition states that cat returns a unit value, that the CATFS component (the "cat file-system") of the state is unchanged, and that the standard output stream has been extended with the contents of all the files.

1.1 Background on CF

This subsection and the next one provide background on CF and CakeML. Readers familiar with these topics can skip ahead to Sect. 1.3.

Characteristic formulae, as introduced in Charguéraud's PhD thesis [4], are essentially total correctness Hoare triples for ML-style functional programs. The key component of any CF framework is a function cf that produces, from a source-level expression e, the expression's characteristic formula cf e. Applying cf e to an environment env, pre-condition H and post-condition Q yields a proposition cf e env H Q, which implies program expression e can have H as a pre-condition and Q as a post-condition, in environment env.

While the cf function is the main workhorse behind any CF framework, most user-proved specifications are stated in terms of a Hoare-triple-like judgement for functional applications, app, written with Hoare-triple notation. The intuition is that $\{\!|H|\!\}$ $f \cdot args$ $\{\!|Q|\!\}$ is true if the application of function-value f to curried arguments $args$ admits H as a pre-condition and Q as a post-condition. An example of a specification stated in terms of app is shown in Fig. 2.

Charguéraud's initial version of CF [5] only applied to pure ML programs. Charguéraud has since extended his approach to support reasoning about imperative stateful ML programs in a style inspired by separation logic and its frame rule [6]. More recently, Charguéraud and Pottier have verified amortized complexity results using CFML [7]. The version we have ported to CakeML is based on Charguéraud's framework for imperative stateful ML programs, but without support for proofs about complexity results.

In Charguéraud's implementation of CF, called CFML, the mechanism for generating characteristic formulae from OCaml programs, i.e., the cf function, is external to the proof assistant (Coq), and the translation from OCaml to Coq is not completely transparent, e.g., it translates the OCaml's fixed-size int type to the mathematical integers in Coq. The soundness theorem for CFML has been proved on paper using an idealised semantics for a subset of OCaml. In contrast, our CakeML formalisation of CF models all formal entities in the logic of the proof assistant (HOL4 in our case) and the key theorem, i.e., soundness, is proved as a theorem inside the proof assistant.

1.2 Background on CakeML

The original goal of the CakeML project, as outlined in the first CakeML paper [18], was to provide a fully proof-producing code generation tool (code extraction tool) that given ML-like functions in higher-order logic (HOL) automatically produces equivalent executable machine code. The CakeML *translator* [18] is a proof-producing tool which generates CakeML code from functions in HOL. The output of the translator can then be input into a verified compiler [15,26] that transforms CakeML programs to observationally compatible machine code. The verified CakeML compiler function was bootstrapped in logic using the fully proof-producing work-flow mentioned above [15].

As the compiler is maturing, the focus of CakeML project is shifting to the task of developing a general ecosystem of tools around the CakeML language. This is where CF technology comes into the picture. Our CF formalisation provides a verification framework that enables users to prove correctness theorems for imperative CakeML programs that use any of CakeML's language features, e.g., references, arrays, exceptions and I/O. One can, of course, prove correctness theorems directly over the CakeML semantics. However, such direct proofs would be incredibly tedious for anything but very simple programs.

The formal semantics of the CakeML language is central to its CF framework and the CF framework's soundness proof. Figures 3 and 5 provide some detail of CakeML's operational semantics, which we write in the functional bigstep style [20]. Figure 5 shows the definitions of the datatype for the deeply embedded CakeML values that the semantics operates over. Figure 3 shows a few cases of the expression evaluation function evaluate. The figure includes the case of function application App Opapp $[f;\ v]$, i.e., application of expression f to expression v, and shows the semantics, using the helper function do_opapp, of applying a non-recursive Closure value to an argument. For this application, the environment *env* from the Closure value is extended to map the variable

```
evaluate st env [Lit l] = (st,Rval [Litv l])
evaluate st env [Var n] =
  case lookup_var_id n env of
    None ⇒ (st,Rerr (Rabort Rtype_error))
  | Some v ⇒ (st,Rval [v])
evaluate st env [Fun x e] = (st,Rval [Closure env x e])
evaluate st env [App Opapp [f; v]] =
  case evaluate st env [v; f] of
    (st',Rval [v; f]) ⇒
      case do_opapp [f; v] of
        None ⇒ (st',Rerr (Rabort Rtype_error))
      | Some (env',e) ⇒
          if st'.clock = 0 then
            (st',Rerr (Rabort Rtimeout_error))
          else evaluate (dec_clock st') env' [e]
  | res ⇒ res
do_opapp vs =
  case vs of
    [Closure env n e; v] ⇒ Some ((n,v)::env,e)
  | [Recclosure env funs n; v] ⇒ ...
  | _ ⇒ None
```

Fig. 3. An extract of the CakeML semantics.

n to value v. Before evaluation enters the expression from the Closure a clock is checked and decremented, following the style of functional big-step semantics [20]. In the semantics, each function is only applied to one argument at a time.

1.3   A Tour of the Material

The remainder of this section provides a brief tour of the contributions of this paper: the soundness theorem, our extensions for I/O and exceptions, and our integration of the CakeML CF technology with our existing CakeML proof tools.

We formalise the theorem of soundness of CF with respect to the CakeML semantics. In CFML, the soundness proof is only captured on paper, using idealised semantics for a subset of ML, and the Coq library uses axioms in the places where it would relate to the language semantics. In contrast, we were able to implement an axiom-free CF library for the whole CakeML language, and perform a mechanical proof of soundness, using CakeML's pre-existing semantics.

This not only validates the CF approach introduced by Charguéraud, but also shows that it is flexible as well as extensible. Although CakeML's semantics were not designed with CF in mind, we could directly reuse the CakeML language without any modification, and we were able to carry out the proofs without any particular issue (although some technical details differ from the paper proof).

Moreover, as detailed in Sect. 3, we could extend the approach to handle new language features that are not supported by CFML.

The soundness theorem, which justifies proving properties about a characteristic formula to give equivalent properties about the program itself, is stated as follows. If the characteristic formula for the deeply embedded expression e (and environment env) holds for some shallowly embedded pre-condition H and shallowly embedded post-condition Q, i.e., cf e env H Q, then, starting from a state satisfying H, e is guaranteed to successfully evaluate in CakeML's functional big-step semantics [20], and reach a new state st' and value v satisfying Q. Here state_to_set converts a CakeML state into a representation to which one can apply separation logic connectives, and split asserts disjoint union: split s (s_1, s_2) $\iff$ $s_1 \cup s_2 = s \wedge s_1 \cap s_2 = \emptyset$.

$$\vdash \text{cf } e \text{ } env \text{ } H \text{ } Q \Rightarrow$$
$$\forall \text{ } st.$$
$$H \text{ (state\_to\_set } st) \Rightarrow$$
$$\exists \text{ } st' \text{ } h_f \text{ } h_g \text{ } v \text{ } ck.$$
$$\text{evaluate } (st \text{ with clock } := ck) \text{ } env \text{ } [e] = (st', \text{Rval } [v]) \wedge$$
$$\text{split (state\_to\_set } st') \text{ } (h_f, h_g) \wedge Q \text{ } v \text{ } h_f$$

This mechanised proof eliminates the last bits of paper proof that need to be trusted in CFML. Section 2 details the main steps leading to the proof.

We extend the CF framework introduced in CFML to handle two new language features: exceptions, and I/O through CakeML's foreign-function interface (FFI). These extensions are proved sound with respect to the CakeML semantics, and neatly make our framework able to handle all features of the CakeML programming language.[1]

The extension which adds support for I/O is implemented by carefully modifying the state_to_set function, shown in the soundness theorem above. We modified the state_to_set function so that it makes visible the state of the FFI in the pre- and post-conditions. There were numerous tricky details to get right in the definition of state_to_set because the design goal was to *make I/O reasoning local* in the style of separation logic. Our support for I/O is local in that the proof for a piece of code which only uses, say, the print-to-stdout FFI ports does not impose any assumptions on the behaviour, state, or even existence of other FFI ports, e.g., ports for reading-from-stdin. In the spirit of separation logic, our framework allows combining different assertions about the FFI using CF's equivalent to the separation logic frame rule. Section 3 provides details on how we modified state_to_set to make the FFI available in CF proofs.

Support for exceptions is implemented by making the post-conditions differentiate whether the result is a normal return with a value or a value raised as an exception. The new framework is able to reason about exception handling code.

---

[1] CakeML's module system is also supported in our CF framework, but supporting modules did not require extending the original ideas of CFML.

Section 3.2 explains how exceptions are supported and the effect their introduction had on the proofs.

With these extensions our framework covers all of CakeML's language features and makes it possible to develop a verified standard library for CakeML with complete specifications for library functions that perform I/O or must raise exceptions in certain circumstances. For example, our cat implementation has a routine for opening files, called openIn (whose specification is shown in Fig. 4). A call to the CakeML function for openIn raises an exception if the file could not be opened, e.g., if there is no file at the given path. More precisely, inFS_fname *fname fs* describes whether a file exists in *fs* with name *fname*, and the BadFileName exception is raised when no file could be found.

$$
\begin{aligned}
&\vdash \mathsf{FILENAME}\ s\ sv \wedge \mathsf{numOpenFDs}\ fs < 255 \Rightarrow \\
&\quad \{\!|\mathsf{CATFS}\ fs|\!\} \\
&\quad \mathsf{openIn\_v} \cdot [sv] \\
&\quad \{\!|\mathsf{POST} \\
&\qquad (\lambda\ wv. \\
&\qquad\quad \langle \mathsf{WORD}\ (\mathsf{n2w}\ (\mathsf{nextFD}\ fs))\ wv \wedge \mathsf{validFD}\ (\mathsf{nextFD}\ fs)\ (\mathsf{openFileFS}\ s\ fs) \wedge \\
&\qquad\quad \mathsf{inFS\_fname}\ s\ fs \rangle * \mathsf{CATFS}\ (\mathsf{openFileFS}\ s\ fs)) \\
&\qquad (\lambda\ e.\ \langle \mathsf{BadFileName\_exn}\ e \wedge \neg\mathsf{inFS\_fname}\ s\ fs \rangle * \mathsf{CATFS}\ fs)|\!\}
\end{aligned}
$$

Fig. 4. A specification of the openIn function.

In compiled CakeML code, the actual system call for opening a file is handled by a short stub of C code that is attached to the external side of CakeML's FFI. If an error occurs, the C code signals failure via the return value for the FFI call and, on the CakeML side, the library routine raises the relevant exception on receiving the error code from the C stub. At present, the external C code is unverified and we just make assumptions about its effect on the rest of the world. In the future, we aim to provide verified external assembly stubs that can replace the current unverified C code.

We integrate the CF framework into the CakeML ecosystem by making it interoperate with an existing synthesis tool, namely the automatic translation from HOL functions into CakeML. This tool [18] essentially implements a proof-producing extraction mechanism: given a function in higher-order logic (HOL), the tool generates CakeML code along with a proof that the produced code correctly implements the HOL function with respect to CakeML's semantics. As HOL functions are pure, the translator is essentially limited to producing purely functional CakeML code.[2]

---

[2] To be precise: Myreen and Owens [18] show that the tool can also be used for production of stateful CakeML code that maintains a hard-coded invariant over a hard-coded number of references. CF allows for much more flexibility.

At present, the most important use of this translation tool is in bootstrapping the verified CakeML compiler, where we now benefit from CF. The translation tool is used to generate CakeML code for the CakeML compiler's implementation. The compiler is defined as functions in HOL, so before we can run the compiler on itself, we need to transform the compiler definition into the source language of the compiler, i.e., CakeML abstract syntax. CF comes into the picture because the translation tool can only produce pure functions. Previously we had to manually verify low-level I/O code that reads the input and passes it to the compiler function, and separate code that prints the result of running the CakeML's compile function. By making the CF and translation tools able to build on each other's results, we have replaced the difficult manual I/O code proofs by understandable CF proofs about I/O.

The bootstrap has thus far benefited from automatic conversion of translator produced results to CF theorems. The bridge between them also works in the other direction: proved results from CF can be used in the translator. Since the translator essentially only deals in pure functions, the CF-verified programs have to implement a pure interface in order to fit the translator. Such programs are not necessarily pure themselves: they can allocate memory, and use imperative structures and algorithms. We plan to make use of the CF-to-translator direction in the future to provide more efficient drop-in replacements for parts of the bootstrapped compiler. These replacement parts would be verified using CF, and replace the code produced by the translator. The register allocator is a particular example that we believe would benefit from using an imperative-style implementation instead of the current automatically generated pure functional implementation.

Section 4 provides details on how we have connected the translation tool and the CakeML CF framework.

All our developments were carried out in the HOL4 theorem prover, and have been integrated into the main CakeML repository. They are available online at https://cakeml.org and https://code.cakeml.org under the `characteristic` sub-directory.

2   A Formal Proof of Soundness for Characteristic Formulae

In this section, we explain how CakeML CF differs from CFML, how we avoided axioms in our formalisation, and how we proved soundness of CF for CakeML.

2.1   Adapting CFML to CakeML

A first necessary step towards a proof of soundness was reimplementing the CFML definitions, lemmas and tactics in the CakeML setting. Most of them worked similarly to CFML – in particular the CF definitions and the various tactics (although they are implemented differently). There are however some technical differences worth noting.

CakeML's semantics uses environments, whereas CMFL assumes substitution semantics. As a consequence, CakeML environments (which map names to semantic values) are threaded through CakeML's characteristic formulae as a new parameter. Environments are accessed in the generated formulae, e.g., the CF for Var x, shown below, returns the value for x in the given environment. Here $\triangleright$ is the entailment relation on heap predicates, i.e., $H_1 \triangleright H_2$ is true if any heap satisfying H_1 also satisfies H_2, and defined by $p \triangleright q \iff \forall s.\, p\, s \Rightarrow q\, s$. The local predicate adds the frame rule of separation logic to the formula.

$$\text{cf (Var } name)\ env =$$
$$\text{local } (\lambda\, H\ Q.\ \exists v.\ \text{lookup\_var\_id } name\ env = \text{Some } v \wedge H \triangleright Q\, v)$$

In practice, environments are never manipulated explicitly by the user. The user states top-level specifications of the form "$\forall x_i.\ \{H\}\ f \cdot [x_1;\ \ldots;\ x_n]\ \{Q\}$", specifying the behavior of the application of the function value f to some arguments $x_1, \ldots, x_n$. The value f can be fetched given its name as a CakeML function, thanks to a small library that keeps track of top-level definitions.

As f is in fact a closure, the following lemma applies. This lemma, which is a consequence of the CF soundness theorem, turns the goal into proving the CF of the body of f, for the environment that was packed in the closure. Here naryClosure creates a Closure value that takes several curried arguments.

$$\vdash ns \neq [] \Rightarrow$$
$$\text{length } xvs = \text{length } ns \Rightarrow$$
$$\text{cf } body\ (\text{extend\_env } ns\ xvs\ env)\ H\ Q \Rightarrow$$
$$\{H\}\ \text{naryClosure } env\ ns\ body \cdot xvs\ \{Q\}$$

A custom pretty printer hides the contents of environments from the user. Sub-goals of the form "lookup_var_env x env = v" are always automatically proved by unfolding env.

CF for CakeML uses a deep embedding of CakeML values, while CFML translates ML values to corresponding Coq values. CakeML values are described by the HOL type v (shown in Fig. 5), which is defined as part of the semantics.

```
v =
    Litv lit
  | Conv ((string × tid_or_exn) option) (v list)
  | Closure (v environment) string exp
  | Recclosure (v environment) ((string × string × exp) list) string
  | Loc num
  | Vectorv (v list)
```

Fig. 5. The CakeML semantic value datatype.

To relate CakeML values of type v to logical values (such as int, bool, ...), we re-use the *refinement invariants* presented by Myreen and Owens [18] in the context of a proof-producing translation from HOL functions to CakeML programs. These refinement invariants are a collection of composable predicates that relate HOL types and data structures to the same concepts as deeply embedded CakeML values. The INT and BOOL refinement invariants are defined as follows:

$$\text{INT } i = (\lambda\, v.\ v = \text{Litv (IntLit } i))$$
$$\text{BOOL T} = (\lambda\, v.\ v = \text{Conv (Some (``true'', TypeId (Short ``bool''))) [])}$$
$$\text{BOOL F} = (\lambda\, v.\ v = \text{Conv (Some (``false'', TypeId (Short ``bool''))) [])}$$

A specification for the CakeML addition function can then be written as follows. Here the angle brackets turn a pure proposition into a heap predicate for heaps represented as sets: $\langle c \rangle = (\lambda\, s.\ s = \emptyset \wedge c)$; and emp is $\langle T \rangle$.

$$\vdash \text{INT } x_0\ v_0 \wedge \text{INT } x_1\ v_1 \Rightarrow$$
$$\{\!\text{[emp]}\!\}\ \text{plus\_v} \cdot [v_0;\ v_1]\ \{\!\{(\lambda\, v.\ \langle \text{INT } (x_0 + x_1)\ v\rangle)\}\!\}$$

This is somewhat heavier than CFML specifications, where Coq integers would simply be used in place of semantic values. We believe it is hardly an issue for more involved data structures, for which it is common to define such predicates anyway in CFML in order to keep track of additional invariants.

Normalisation of input programs and CF generation are performed in the logic, whereas in CFML they are performed by an external tool. Before being fed to the cf function, programs are normalised in a process similar to A-normalisation. The motivation is that it significantly simplifies formally reasoning about programs, while preserving their semantics. Figure 6 displays an example of the normalisation process. Due to the fact that cf is implemented as a total function in the logic, assumptions about the program being in normal form are made explicit in characteristic formulae. In CFML, the external CF generator simply fails on unhandled input programs.

```
if  x < 0 then
   print_int (~ x)
else
   print_int x
```

(a) Original program

```
let val _x1 = x < 0 in
if _x1 then
   (let val _x2 = ~ x in
       print_int _x2
    end)
else
   print_int x
end
```

(b) Normalised program

Fig. 6. An example of the normalisation pass.

The cf function assumes that the input program is in normal form. This assumption is reflected by the use of the exp_is_val predicate in characteristic formulae. This predicate, of type v environment → exp → v option, checks whether an expression is in fact a value or a name bound to a value. It is used in characteristic formulae to assert that some expression must be trivial, because of the normalisation pass. For example, the CF for If, below, uses exp_is_val to assert that evaluation of the condition must be dealt with beforehand, by introducing a let-binding, which the normalisation step does. If for some reason the program appears not to be in normal form, the corresponding CF reduces to F.

$$
\begin{aligned}
&\text{cf } p \ (\text{If } cond \ e_1 \ e_2) \ env = \\
&\quad \text{local} \\
&\quad (\lambda \, H \ Q. \\
&\qquad \exists \, condv \ b. \\
&\qquad \text{exp\_is\_val } env \ cond = \text{Some } condv \land \text{BOOL } b \ condv \land \\
&\qquad ((b \iff \text{T}) \Rightarrow \text{cf } p \ e_1 \ env \ H \ Q) \land \\
&\qquad ((b \iff \text{F}) \Rightarrow \text{cf } p \ e_2 \ env \ H \ Q))
\end{aligned}
$$

The sub-goals related to exp_is_val in characteristic formulae are always automatically proved by our CF tactics, and are thus kept hidden from the user.

2.2 Realising CFML Axioms

Using CakeML's semantics, we are able to give an implementation of the app predicate, which was axiomatised in CFML.

Let us first consider the semantics of a Hoare triple for an expression e in environment env, denoted $env \vdash \{\!|H|\!\} \ e \ \{\!|Q|\!\}$. We define validity for such a Hoare triple, which we then use to define app. The Hoare triple $env \vdash \{\!|H|\!\} \ e \ \{\!|Q|\!\}$ holds if and only if evaluation of the expression e, in a heap that satisfies the heap predicate H, terminates and produces a value v and a heap satisfying $Q \ v$.

$$
\begin{aligned}
&env \vdash \{\!|H|\!\} \ e \ \{\!|Q|\!\} \iff \\
&\quad \forall \, st \ h_i \ h_k. \\
&\qquad \text{split } (\text{state\_to\_set } st) \ (h_i, h_k) \Rightarrow \\
&\qquad H \ h_i \Rightarrow \\
&\qquad \exists \, v \ st' \ h_f \ h_g \ ck. \\
&\qquad\quad \text{split3 } (\text{state\_to\_set } st') \ (h_f, h_k, h_g) \land \\
&\qquad\quad \text{evaluate } (st \text{ with clock} := ck) \ env \ [e] = (st', \text{Rval } [v]) \land Q \ v \ h_f
\end{aligned}
$$

In this definition, split and split3 are used to split a state represented as a set of state elements into disjoint subsets: split $s \ (s_1, s_2) \iff s_1 \cup s_2 = s \land s_1 \cap s_2 = \emptyset$; similarly split3 $s \ (s_1, s_2, s_3)$ splits a set s into three disjoint subsets s_1, s_2, s_3. This state splitting is here in order to make the frame rule available, as explained further down.

We now define a simple version of app, called app_basic, which characterises the application of a closure to a single argument. When provided a valid function application, where do_opapp can extract the body of the closure and the extended environment, app_basic simply asserts the general Hoare triple defined above. When do_opapp fails, app_basic asserts that the pre-condition H cannot hold of any state (because otherwise the function application would need to succeed).

$$\{\!|H|\!\}\ f \cdot x\ \{\!|Q|\!\} \iff$$
$$\text{case do\_opapp } [f;\ x] \text{ of}$$
$$\text{None} \Rightarrow \forall st\ h_1\ h_2.\ \text{split (state\_to\_set } p\ st)\ (h_1, h_2) \Rightarrow \neg H\ h_1$$
$$|\ \text{Some } (env, exp) \Rightarrow env \vdash \{\!|H|\!\}\ exp\ \{\!|Q|\!\}$$

Finally we define the app predicate, which characterises the application of a closure to multiple arguments, by iterating app_basic.

$$\{\!|H|\!\}\ f \cdot [\,]\ \{\!|Q|\!\} \iff \mathsf{F}$$
$$\{\!|H|\!\}\ f \cdot [x]\ \{\!|Q|\!\} \iff \{\!|H|\!\}\ f \cdot x\ \{\!|Q|\!\}$$
$$\{\!|H|\!\}\ f \cdot x::x'::xs\ \{\!|Q|\!\} \iff$$
$$\{\!|H|\!\}\ f \cdot x\ \{\!|(\lambda g.\ \exists H'.\ H' * \langle\{\!|H'|\!\}\ g \cdot x'::xs\ \{\!|Q|\!\}\rangle)|\!\}$$

It is worth noting that our Hoare triple validity integrates the frame rule in its definition. The split predicate (respectively split3) expresses that some heap can be split into two (resp. three) disjoint parts. Therefore, the function application may involve only some subpart of the heap h_i, while the rest h_k is preserved. The function is also allowed to produce some garbage h_g, which is left unconstrained. This is necessary for top-level specifications to be modular, as they are formulated in terms of app.

The built-in frame rule also means that when carrying proofs using the framework, the definition of app is kept abstract and never unfolded. When faced with a "$\{\!|\dots|\!\}\ f \cdot \dots\ \{\!|\dots|\!\}$" goal, a specification for f, also of the form "$\{\!|\dots|\!\}\ f \cdot \dots\ \{\!|\dots|\!\}$" will be fetched and used to prove the goal, either directly or using the frame rule.

2.3   Proving CF Soundness

Soundness of characteristic formulae means that, for every expression e, if cf e env H Q holds, then the Hoare triple $env \vdash \{\!|H|\!\}\ e\ \{\!|Q|\!\}$ is valid. We define soundness for arbitrary formulae as follows.

$$\text{sound } e\ R \iff \forall env\ H\ Q.\ R\ env\ H\ Q \Rightarrow env \vdash \{\!|H|\!\}\ e\ \{\!|Q|\!\}$$

The main result of this section can now be stated. We prove soundness of cf as the following HOL theorem:

Theorem 1 (CF are sound wrt. CakeML semantics).

$$\vdash \text{sound } e\ (\text{cf } e)$$

Proof. By induction on the size of e.

This proof is most tricky for CakeML language constructs for which characteristic formulae differ significantly from the semantics. The reason is typically to abstract away from specifics of the semantics, and have proof-friendly characteristic formulae. Two instances of this are closures and pattern matching.

CakeML semantics has closure values. Functions evaluate to closures, and function application is defined in terms of applying a closure to values. The CF for function declaration introduces an abstract value fv, and a specification $\mathcal{H}$ for it. Our formulation differs from that in CFML [6] due to CakeML's use environment semantics instead of CFML's substitution semantics.

$$\mathsf{cf}\ (\mathsf{Let}\ (\mathsf{Some}\ f)\ (\mathsf{Fun}\ x\ e_1)\ e_2)\ env =$$
$$\mathsf{local}\ (\lambda\ H\ Q.\ \forall fv.\ \mathcal{H} \Rightarrow \mathsf{cf}\ e_2\ ((f,fv)::env)\ H\ Q)$$

where $\mathcal{H} \iff \forall xv\ H'\ Q'.\ \mathsf{cf}\ e_1\ ((x,xv)::env)\ H'\ Q' \Rightarrow \{\!|H'|\!\}\ fv \cdot [xv]\ \{\!|Q'|\!\}$

In the soundness proof, fv is instantiated by a function closure, and one has to prove that $\mathcal{H}$ characterises it.

Proving the soundness of CF for pattern-matching also requires some amount of proof engineering. CakeML semantics provides a logical function that implements a pattern-matching algorithm, and returns whether the match succeeded or not. Characteristic formulae for pattern-matching are instead formulated as nested ifs, which test the equality between the matched value and values produced from the successive patterns.

3   Sound Extensions of CF for I/O and Exceptions

This section explains how our CF framework has extended the original CFML framework to enable reasoning about I/O and exceptions.

3.1   Support for I/O

As mentioned earlier, the goal of our extension for I/O was to enable convenient *local reasoning* about I/O operations without unreasonable restrictions on the kind of I/O one can verify.

We start with a quick explanation of how I/O is supported in the CakeML language, then show how we made CF pre- and post-conditions able to make assertions about parts of the I/O state, what I/O looks like in the cf function's output, and finally how we have used these techniques in the bootstrapping of the latest CakeML compiler.

The CakeML language supports I/O through a byte-array-based foreign-function interface (FFI). The abstract syntax for CakeML includes an FFI expression. The semantics of executing an FFI expression is to update the state of the FFI which is threaded through the operational semantics together with the state of the CakeML references. The intuition is that CakeML's FFI state component models the state of the outside world and how the outside world will react to any calls made from the CakeML program to the external world.

The formal definition of the FFI state is shown in Fig. 7. When designing the CakeML semantics we wanted to make the FFI state as flexible as possible, so we left the type of the rest of the world as a type variable θ, and we only require that the user provide some oracle function s.oracle that describes how the outside world will react to any FFI call. The FFI state has a s.final_event field that indicates whether the outside world has stopped the process (e.g., due to a call to exit). The FFI state also keeps a list of all calls to the FFI (s.io_events): each event records the name of the FFI port[3] that was called, and a list of byte pairs, where map fst of that list is the input to the FFI call and map snd of the list is the state of the array on return from the FFI call.

θ ffi_state =
   <| oracle : (string $\rightarrow$ θ $\rightarrow$ byte list $\rightarrow$ θ oracle_result);
     ffi_state : θ;
     final_event : (final_event option);
     io_events : (io_event list) |>

final_event = Final_event string (byte list) ffi_outcome
ffi_outcome = FFI_diverged | FFI_failed
io_event = IO_event string ((byte $\times$ byte) list)
θ oracle_result = Oracle_return θ (byte list) | Oracle_diverge | Oracle_fail

Fig. 7. The type for an FFI state in the CakeML operational semantics.

We enable reasoning about I/O in CF by modifying the state_to_set function to expose an image of the FFI state as part of the set representation that the separation logic connectives operate over.

The role of the state_to_set function is to split the state into parts that can be separated using separating conjunction ($*$). For example, a CakeML state s_1 with references at locations 0, 1 and 2 becomes the following. Note that state_to_set can only produce one Mem l _ for each location l in the store.

$$\text{state\_to\_set } s_1 = \{ \text{ Mem 0 } val_0; \text{ Mem 1 } val_1; \text{ Mem 2 } val_2; \dots \}$$

We can use $p * q = (\lambda s. \exists u\ v. \text{ split } s\ (u,v) \wedge p\ u \wedge q\ v)$ to separate between assertions such as the following. Here Loc l is the value of a reference in the CakeML semantics (Fig. 5), and Refv, Varray, and W8array are constructors of the value type for store values.

$r \rightsquigarrow v = (\lambda s. \exists loc.\ r = \text{Loc } loc \wedge s = \{ \text{ Mem } loc\ (\text{Refv } v) \})$
array $r\ vs = (\lambda s. \exists loc.\ r = \text{Loc } loc \wedge s = \{ \text{ Mem } loc\ (\text{Varray } vs) \})$
byte_array $r\ bs = (\lambda s. \exists loc.\ r = \text{Loc } loc \wedge s = \{ \text{ Mem } loc\ (\text{W8array } bs) \})$

---

[3] We have recently switched to using strings for port names, while numbers were used previously [26] for FFI port names. Johannes Åman Pohjola made this improvement.

With these definitions it follows from $(r_1 \rightsquigarrow v_1 * r_2 \rightsquigarrow v_2 * \ldots)$ (state_to_set s) that $r_1 \neq r_2$ and that updates to reference r_1 do not affect $r_2 \rightsquigarrow v_2 * \ldots$.

The simplest way to make it possible to reason about FFI using CF would be to just make state_to_set produce sets that contain an element that contains the entire current state of the CakeML FFI, i.e., s.ffi_state. However, such a simplistic approach would mean that there can only be one assertion about the state of the FFI in any pre- or post-condition since the assertion could not be split by separating conjunction ($*$). We need to make state_to_set split the FFI state into multiple elements of the state component sets so that we can use the separating conjunction in reasoning about FFI states.

The splitting of the FFI state is non-trivial since we want to keep the FFI state as abstract as possible in the CakeML semantics. The FFI state is modelled by a type variable θ, and thus we know nothing about its structure. Our solution is to parametrise the state_to_set function with information on how to partition an FFI state. The information is a pair consisting of:

– *proj*: a projection function of type $\theta \rightarrow$ (string $\mapsto$ ffi), which given an FFI state of type θ returns a finite map from strings to a new type called ffi. Here ffi is a datatype that is meant to be convenient for modelling projected FFI states in general.[4]

$$
\begin{aligned}
\text{ffi} = &\\
&\text{Str string}\\
\mid\ &\text{Num num}\\
\mid\ &\text{Cons ffi ffi}\\
\mid\ &\text{List (ffi list)}\\
\mid\ &\text{Stream (num stream)}
\end{aligned}
$$

– *parts*: a list of partitions which are pairs: each pair contains a list of FFI port names (of type string list) and a behaviour modelling next-state function, i.e., a representation of part of the oracle function in CakeML's FFI state. The type of the behaviour modelling function is:

$$\text{string} \rightarrow \text{ffi} \rightarrow \text{byte list} \rightarrow (\text{byte list} \times \text{ffi})\,\text{option}$$

The partitioning information (*proj*,*parts*) is considered well-formed and applicable to an FFI state st if:

– the FFI state st has not hit a stopping state, i.e., st.final_event = None
– no partition has names that overlap with other partitions
– every I/O event has an index that belongs to one of the partitions

---

[4] We would have liked to use a type variable instead of ffi, but a type variable would have been shared between all partitions. Such sharing would need to be done across FFI partitions which goes against the design goal of local specifications and local reasoning. This is a restriction imposed by the HOL type system, which we could have avoided by using a variant of HOL with quantifiers for type variables [13].

– for each partition, *proj* maps all states to the same `ffi` value
– the update function *u* in each partition respects the FFI's oracle function[5]

The FFI-enabled definition of state_to_set maps CakeML states to the union of the parts of the state that describe the references and the partitioned parts of the FFI state. If the partition for the FFI state is well-defined, then the FFI state is split into a set of FFI_part elements, where each such element carries:

– *s*, the projected view of the state of this partition
– *u*, the update function for the partition
– *ns*, the FFI port names associated with the partition
– *ts*, a list of all previous I/O events for these names.

We can now make assertions about I/O in CF using state_to_set and separation logic connectives. We define a generic IO assertion as follows.

$$\text{IO } st\ u\ ns = (\lambda\, s.\ \exists\, ts.\ s = \{\ \text{FFI\_part } st\ u\ ns\ ts\ \})$$

With these we can make assertions about I/O. For example, the following asserts that the projected FFI state must have a part that is described by FFI_part $s_1\ u_1\ [n]$, and a disjoint part that is described by FFI_part $s_2\ u_2\ ns$.

$$(\text{IO } s_1\ u_1\ [n] * \text{IO } s_2\ u_2\ ns * \dots)\ (\text{state\_to\_set } pp\ st)$$

Using such statements in their pre- and post-conditions, the user may express strong specifications concisely.

The following proof obligation is generated every time the cf function is applied to the abstract syntax for an FFI expression. This proof obligation can be read as follows: pre-condition *H* must imply that there is a byte array and I/O partition in the state. The I/O partition must include the *name* of the called FFI entry point. Furthermore, the result of running the next-state function from the FFI partition, i.e., *u*, must successfully return a new state *s'* and this state and the updated byte array must imply the desired post-condition *Q*. FFI calls return unit_value.

$$
\begin{aligned}
&\text{cf } pp\ (\text{App } (\text{FFI } name)\ [array])\ env = \\
&\text{local} \\
&(\lambda\, H\ Q. \\
&\quad \exists\, rv. \\
&\quad\quad \text{exp\_is\_val } env\ array = \text{Some } rv\ \wedge \\
&\quad\quad \exists\, bs\ F\ bs'\ s\ s'\ u\ ns. \\
&\quad\quad\quad u\ name\ bs\ s = \text{Some } (bs',s')\ \wedge\ \text{mem } name\ ns\ \wedge \\
&\quad\quad\quad H \rhd F * \text{byte\_array } rv\ bs * \text{IO } s\ u\ ns\ \wedge \\
&\quad\quad\quad F * \text{byte\_array } rv\ bs' * \text{IO } s'\ u\ ns \rhd Q\ \text{unit\_value})
\end{aligned}
$$

---

[5] Our use of projection functions and updates at both a concrete and abstract view of the state bears some resemblance to lenses [21]. Note however that lenses must have *get* and *putback* functions. Our set up lacks the *putback* functions, i.e., we only project in one direction. Our initial formalisation had a *putback* function, but we decided to simplify the definitions and arrived at the current solution with only a *get* function, which we call *proj*.

The proof goal produced by cf mentions IO, which from the user's perspective is the primitive I/O assertion in CakeML CF. Users define their own specialisations of IO for each application, see Sect. 5.

This support for I/O has, together with the connection between CF and the CakeML translator (Sect. 4), been used to verify the I/O code required for giving input and producing output from the bootstrapped CakeML compiler. The I/O code is a little snippet of code that wraps around the translator-generated pure CakeML code which implements the logical CakeML compile function.

3.2   Support for Exceptions

We implement complete support for specifying CakeML programs that use exceptions. Up to this point, we required expressions to evaluate and reduce to a value: post-conditions were of type v $\rightarrow$ heap $\rightarrow$ bool, taking the returned value as an argument. We now allow expressions to raise an exception instead: we define a res datatype res = Val v | Exn v, and change the type of post-conditions to be res $\rightarrow$ heap $\rightarrow$ bool. We define some wrappers for writing post-conditions, in particular for the cases where the expression never (resp. always) raises an exception. POST handles both cases by taking one post-condition for each case.

$$(\text{POSTv})\ Q_v = (\lambda\, r.\ \text{case } r \text{ of Val } v \Rightarrow Q_v\, v\ |\ \text{Exn } e \Rightarrow \langle F \rangle)$$
$$(\text{POSTe})\ Q_e = (\lambda\, r.\ \text{case } r \text{ of Val } v \Rightarrow \langle F \rangle\ |\ \text{Exn } e \Rightarrow Q_e\, e)$$
$$\text{POST } Q_v\ Q_e = (\lambda\, r.\ \text{case } r \text{ of Val } v \Rightarrow Q_v\, v\ |\ \text{Exn } e \Rightarrow Q_e\, c)$$

We update the definitions that relate CF to CakeML semantics. For example, the definition of Hoare triple validity we presented earlier contains:

$$\dots \wedge \text{evaluate } (st \text{ with clock} := ck)\ env\ [exp] = (st', \text{Rval } [v])$$

The second component returned by evaluate, of which Rval is a constructor, is of type (v list, v) result, where:

$$(\alpha,\ \beta)\ \text{result} = \text{Rval } \alpha\ |\ \text{Rerr } (\beta\ \text{error\_result})$$
$$\alpha\ \text{error\_result} = \text{Rraise } \alpha\ |\ \text{Rabort abort}$$

This gives us two other cases: Rerr (Rraise *exn*) for expressions that raise an exception, and Rerr (Rabort *cause*) for expressions that fail to evaluate. We still rule out the latter, but add support for the former: the definition of Hoare triple validity becomes:

$env \vdash \{H\} \; e \; \{Q\} \iff$
$\forall \; st \; h_i \; h_k.$
  split (state_to_set p st) $(h_i, h_k) \Rightarrow$
   $H \; h_i \Rightarrow$
    $\exists \; r \; st' \; h_f \; h_g \; ck.$
     split3 (state_to_set p st') $(h_f, h_k, h_g) \land Q \; r \; h_f \land$
     case r of
      Val $v \Rightarrow$ evaluate (st with clock $:= \; ck$) $env \; [e] = (st', \mathsf{Rval} \; [v])$
      | Exn $v \Rightarrow$ evaluate (st with clock $:= \; ck$) $env \; [e] = (st', \mathsf{Rerr} \; (\mathsf{Rraise} \; v))$

We update the existing CF definitions as well. We add side-conditions to deal with exceptions; for example the CF for Let handles the case where an exception is raised by the first expression.

cf p (Let (Some x) e_1 e_2) $env =$
  local
   ($\lambda \, H \; Q.$
    $\exists \, Q'.$
     cf p e_1 env H $Q' \land Q' \blacktriangleright_e Q \land$
     $\forall \, xv.$ cf p e_2 $((x, xv) :: env)$ $(Q' \, (\mathsf{Val} \; xv))$ Q)

This uses the entailment relation on post-conditions for the exception case, written $Q_1 \blacktriangleright_e Q_2$, and defined as $\forall e. \; Q_1 \; (\mathsf{Exn} \; e) \rhd Q_2 \; (\mathsf{Exn} \; e)$. On exceptions, the post-condition for e_1 (Q') has to directly entail validity of the post-condition for the whole formula (Q), since e_2 does not get executed in case e_1 raises an exception.

Some other side-conditions are not needed for establishing the soundness theorem, but are added to enforce a "no garbage" property on post-conditions. For example, the CF for Var becomes as follows, where **F** is a post-condition false for any value and any heap:

cf p (Var *name*) $env =$
  local
   ($\lambda \, H \; Q.$
    $(\exists \, v.$ lookup_var_id *name* $env = \mathsf{Some} \; v \land H \rhd Q \; (\mathsf{Val} \; v)) \land$
    $Q \blacktriangleright_e \mathbf{F}$)

This requires Q to be false on exceptions, as evaluating a Var x always produces a value on well scoped code. We believe having such side-conditions make the following proposition true (and plan to prove it as future work): if the CF for e is true for pre-condition H and post-condition Q, then $Q \blacktriangleright_e \mathbf{F}$ if and only if e does not raise exceptions.

We update the existing tactics, so that easy side-conditions are automatically proved. We rely on the following lemma:

$$\vdash (\mathsf{POSTv}) \; Q_v \blacktriangleright_e Q$$

This is trivially true, as (POSTv) Q_v (Exn e) unfolds to $\langle F \rangle$. Thanks to this lemma, carrying out proofs about programs that do not involve exceptions requires no additional effort. The only modification necessary is changing the "$\lambda v. \ldots$" to "POSTv $v. \ldots$" in post-conditions.

Finally, we handle CakeML's primitives for exception handling, Raise and Handle, whose semantics match SML's. Here $(f \;\#\#\; g)\;(x,y) = (f\;x, g\;y)$.

cf p (Raise e) $env =$
  local ($\lambda H\; Q. \; \exists v.$ exp_is_val $env\; e =$ Some $v \wedge H \rhd Q$ (Exn v) $\wedge Q \blacktriangleright_v \mathbf{F}$)

cf p (Handle e $rows$) $env =$
  local
    ($\lambda H\; Q.$
      $\exists Q'.$
        cf $p\; e\; env\; H\; Q' \wedge Q' \blacktriangleright_v Q \wedge$
        $\forall ev.$
          cf_cases $ev\; ev$ (map (I $\#\#$ cf p) $rows$) $env\; (Q'$ (Exn ev)) Q)

The entailment relation on post-conditions for the value case, written $Q \blacktriangleright_v Q_2$, is without surprise defined as $\forall v.\; Q_1$ (Val v) $\rhd Q_2$ (Val v). The CFs for Raise and Handle resemble the CFs for Var and Let respectively, but with the respectives roles of exceptions and values swapped. The cf_cases auxiliary definition corresponds to the CF for pattern-matching.

Let us present an illustrative example. The cat program presented earlier in Fig. 1 doesn't do any exception handling, and for simplicity its specification (Fig. 2) requires that all input filenames represent existing files. In this way, our specification above only specifies the non-exceptional behaviour. Nonetheless, the various I/O primitives can be modeled so as to allow the possibility that they might raise various exceptions, and when they are, we can prove more detailed post-conditions capturing those behaviours.

We define a simple cat1exn program that handles invalid filenames. It is implemented as shown in Fig. 8, by calling cat1 and handling the CharIO.BadFileName exception that may be raised.

```
fun cat1exn fname =
    cat1 fname handle CharIO.BadFileName ⇒ ()
```

Fig. 8. Code displaying the contents of a single file.

Figure 9 shows the specification of cat1, and Fig. 10 shows the specification we prove for cat1exn. It relies on the catfile_string function, which corresponds to the text displayed by cat1exn, and is defined as:

catfile_string fs fnm = if inFS_fname fnm fs then file_contents fnm fs else []

$\vdash$ FILENAME fnm fnv $\wedge$ numOpenFDs $fs < 255 \Rightarrow$
    {|CATFS fs * STDOUT out|}
    cat1_v · [fnv]
    {|POST
      ($\lambda u.$
        $\exists content.$
          $\langle$UNIT () $u\rangle$ * $\langle$alist_lookup fs.files fnm = Some $content\rangle$ *
          CATFS fs * STDOUT (out @ $content$))
      ($\lambda e.$
        $\langle$BadFileName_exn $e\rangle$ * $\langle\neg$inFS_fname fnm $fs\rangle$ * CATFS fs *
        STDOUT out)|}

Fig. 9. A specification for cat1, which outputs the contents of a file on standard out, or raises an exception if the file could not be found.

$\vdash$ FILENAME fnm $fnmv$ $\wedge$ numOpenFDs $fs < 255 \Rightarrow$
    {|CATFS fs * STDOUT out|}
    cat1_v · [$fnmv$]
    {|POSTv $u.$
      $\langle$UNIT () $u\rangle$ * CATFS fs *
      STDOUT (out @ catfile_string fs fnm)|}

Fig. 10. A specification for cat1exn, which will not raise the BadFileName exception.

Proving the specification for cat1exn boils down to proving three subgoals, corresponding to the three conjunctions appearing in the Handle case of cf. The first one is trivially solved using the appropriate tactic. The second one requires proving that the post-condition of cat1 entails the post-condition of cat1exn, for the value case. This is true, using a lemma proving that inFS_fname fnm fs holds if the file could be found with some content in the file system. The last goal finally requires proving that the file system fs is unchanged in the exception case. Knowing $\neg$inFS_fname fnm fs, this is proved by unfolding catfile_string.

4   Interoperating with the CakeML Translator

We prove an equivalence result between the theorems produced by the translator, and a particular shape of CF specifications.

Called on a function succ of type int $\rightarrow$ int, the translator will produce a CakeML program succ_ml, and the following theorems. The theorems state that: running the succ_ml program results in an environment, succ_env, in which looking up the variable "succ" yields a value succ_v, and finally that this value implements the function succ.

$$\vdash \mathsf{run\_prog\ succ\_ml\ succ\_env}$$
$$\vdash \mathsf{lookup\_var\ \text{``succ''}\ succ\_env} = \mathsf{Some\ succ\_v}$$
$$\vdash (\mathsf{INT} \longrightarrow \mathsf{INT})\ \mathsf{succ\ succ\_v}$$

We are here mostly interested in the last theorem, expressed using the "arrow" predicate, "$(a \longrightarrow b)\ f\ fv$", which relates the HOL function f to the closure fv. It states that for any argument xv satisfying $a\ x$, evaluating the closure produces a value u satisfying $b\ (f\ x)$. Formally:

$$(a \longrightarrow b)\ f\ fv \iff$$
$$\forall x\ xv\ refs.$$
$$\quad a\ x\ xv \Rightarrow$$
$$\quad\quad \exists\ env\ exp\ refs'\ u\ c.$$
$$\quad\quad\quad \mathsf{do\_opapp}\ [fv;\ xv] = \mathsf{Some}\ (env, exp) \land$$
$$\quad\quad\quad \mathsf{evaluate\ (empty\_state\ with\ \langle | clock := }\ c;\ \mathsf{refs := }\ refs\ |\rangle)\ env\ [exp] =$$
$$\quad\quad\quad (\mathsf{empty\_state\ with\ \langle | clock := }\ 0;\ \mathsf{refs := }\ refs\ @\ refs'\ |\rangle, \mathsf{Rval}\ [u]) \land$$
$$\quad\quad\quad b\ (f\ x)\ u$$

This is reminiscent of the app_basic predicate used in CF, and indeed we prove that "arrow" is a special case of app_basic.

The CF specifications we prove equivalent to "arrow" are of the form $\{\!|\mathsf{emp}|\!\}\ f \cdot x\ \{\!|\mathsf{POSTv}\ v.\ \langle P\ v\rangle|\!\}$, where P is some logical predicate of type $\mathsf{v} \rightarrow \mathsf{bool}$. A pure function does not raise exceptions, hence the post-condition is false for exceptions. Both the pre- and post-condition assert emptiness of the heap.

A function f satisfying such a spec can still be called on any heap, thanks to the frame rule built into the CF framework. The specification simply means that the function cannot assume anything about the heap, or access it. Less obviously, this kind of specification allows the function to allocate heap objects (references, arrays, ...) for internal use. This becomes apparent after unfolding the definition of Hoare triple validity that underlies app_basic (which we recall below).

$$env \vdash \{\!|H|\!\}\ exp\ \{\!|Q|\!\} \iff$$
$$\forall st\ h_i\ h_k.$$
$$\quad \mathsf{split\ (state\_to\_set}\ p\ st)\ (h_i, h_k) \Rightarrow$$
$$\quad\quad H\ h_i \Rightarrow$$
$$\quad\quad\quad \exists r\ st'\ h_f\ h_g\ ck.$$
$$\quad\quad\quad\quad \mathsf{split3\ (state\_to\_set}\ p\ st')\ (h_f, h_k, h_g) \land Q\ r\ h_f \land \ldots$$

The final heap "state_to_set p st'" is split in three sub-heaps: h_f, h_k and h_g. The post-condition must be true on h_f, and h_k was present in the initial heap and is unchanged. There remains h_g, which represents heap objects that may have been allocated by the function and now need to be garbage collected. Consequently, even though such specifications require the function f to offer a pure interface, it is not necessarily pure itself: it can be implemented using imperative structures and algorithms.

The exact equivalence theorem we prove is as follows:

$$\vdash (a \longrightarrow b)\, f\, fv \iff \forall x\, xv.\ a\, x\, xv \Rightarrow \{|\mathsf{emp}|\}\, fv \cdot xv\, \{|\mathsf{POSTv}\, v.\ \langle b\, (f\, x)\, v \rangle|\}$$

The arrow-to-app_basic direction is the easiest to prove. With the right automation, it allows programs certified using CF to use programs produced by the translator, and automatically retrieve their specification. The app_basic-to-arrow direction is significantly trickier. It required changing the definition of "arrow" to allow heap allocation (represented by *refs'* earlier), and subsequent updating of the translator. Moreover, the proof itself involved careful reasoning about the state of the FFI. This direction makes it possible to provide programs certified using CF as drop-in replacements for translated functions.

5   Case Study: A Verified cat Implementation

Our case study builds a simple model coupling a read-only file-system with one standard output stream. The type of the read-only file-system is

$$
\begin{aligned}
&\mathsf{RO\_fs} =\\
&\quad \mathsf{<|\ files}:((\mathsf{mlstring}\ \times\ \mathsf{byte\ list})\ \mathsf{list});\\
&\quad\quad \mathsf{infds}:((\mathsf{num}\ \times\ \mathsf{mlstring}\ \times\ \mathsf{num})\ \mathsf{list})\ \mathsf{|>}
\end{aligned}
$$

The files and infds fields are association lists. The files field maps file names to file contents. The infds field maps file descriptors (numbers) to pairs of file names and offsets within that file. File names are of type mlstring; in CakeML, these map to vectors of characters occupying contiguous blocks of memory. This model supports multiple descriptors reading from a common file at different positions, and is also subject to realistic problems such as the possibility of file descriptors becoming stale.

The four file-system operations needed for our example are openFile, eof, read1, and closeFD. At this initial stage, we can define the type and its operations in a natural style, concerning ourselves only with the logical model, and not needing to worry about its realisation in the CF framework. (One exception is the use of association lists; it would be more natural to use finite maps, but we must ultimately encode our values into the ffi type presented on page 15.)

Making a model of this sort visible within the CF framework then requires us to cast the operations as messages being sent using single, fixed-size buffers (a mutable array of bytes, to be precise). For example, when accessed from CakeML, the read1 operation must begin by writing the file descriptor value into such a buffer. The same buffer is then used to store the return value. If the file descriptor passed to read1 is not valid, or if the file descriptor has come to the end of file, the error-condition must be returned using the same buffer.

We choose to use a one-byte buffer in the case of read1, partly because it is simple, but also because it naturally leads to realistic "misfeatures": bad inputs cause a −1 return code, which must be returned "in-band". To know whether or not this is genuine, the client has to call the eof test first.

The final part of the process requires us to write CakeML wrappers that make calls through the FFI. The wrapper code for read1, using the one-byte buffer onechar, is presented in Fig. 11.

```
fun read1 fd =
  let val eofp = eof fd in
    if eofp then NONE
    else
      let val _ = Word8Array.update onechar 0 fd
          val _ = FFI "read1" onechar
          val c = Word8Array.sub onechar 0
      in
          SOME c
      end
  end
```

Fig. 11. CakeML code implementing read1. For the purposes of simplicity this does not catch the error possible when the argument fd is not valid; rather the specification we use imposes "fd-validity" as a pre-condition. By using the eof function, the code *does* allow for the successful return of any character, including character 255 (−1).

We now have a piece of CakeML abstract syntax given the name read1, as well as a logical function of the same name operating over values of type RO_fs. We make the logical RO_fs values visible to the CF framework by lifting them into the language of assertions over I/O-extended heaps, using the IO function defined on page 16. The CATFS predicate is of type RO_fs → hprop. A proposition CATFS *fs* asserts that the state of the external file-system is as given by the logical value *fs*.

Our specification for read1 is given in Fig. 12. When this, and the specifications for the other entry-points have been proved, the verification of cat1 and then cat (see Figs. 1 and 2) proceeds quite straightforwardly. In particular, the low-level specifications ensure that the proofs are oblivious to the fact that I/O through the FFI is involved; instead, they proceed just as if the state of the file-system was a part of memory. The proof of cat1 is by induction on the length of the file still to be read; that of cat by induction on the list of arguments.

6   Discussion of Related Work

The CakeML projects aims to build an extensive ecosystem of verification tools around the CakeML programming language. By adapting CF techniques to the setting of CakeML, this paper has extended the toolset and, at the same time,

$\vdash$ WORD fdw fdv $\land$ validFD (w2n fdw) fs $\Rightarrow$
  {|CATFS fs|}
    read1_v · [fdv]
  {|POSTv $coptv$.
    ⟨OPTION WORD (FDchar (w2n fdw) fs) $coptv$⟩ *
    CATFS (bumpFD (w2n fdw) fs)|}

Fig. 12. The specification of read1. The read1_v value is the closure defined by the abstract-syntax for read1. The function FDchar returns the current character designated by the given file descriptor, if any; the function bumpFD increments the position of the file descriptor within its file. At the ML level, file descriptors are encoded as bytes, but the underlying model for file-system uses natural numbers. This is why the logic of the specification coerces from one to the other with w2n. This is also what causes the pre-condition in openFile's specification (Fig. 4) requiring that not too many files be open already.

validated some of the pen-and-paper proofs of prior word on CF. Prior work on CF and CakeML is discussed in Sects. 1.1 and 1.2.

In this section we discuss other verification projects that build ecosystems of verification tools around and within theorem provers such as HOL4, Isabelle/HOL, Coq, Nqthm and ACL2.

In the Isabelle/HOL theorem prover, a substantial ecosystem of verification technology has been developed around the Simpl framework by Schirmer [23], which is an extensible framework for Hoare logic over imperative programs. Simpl played a central role in the seL4 micro-kernel verification [14], where the C code was verified using Simpl. Later, a tool called AutoCorres by Greenaway [12] was developed for automatically lifting C programs written in Simpl into more-convenient-to-verify monadic functions in the logic. The AutoCorres tool and Simpl were subsequently used in the recent proof-producing Cogent compiler [19] for its translation validation step. The Cogent compiler compiles a by-design restrictive functional language to C and produces a correctness theorem in Isabelle/HOL for each compiler run.

The Isabelle Refinement Framework by Lammich [16,17] is a recent set of tools for producing verified code using the Isabelle/HOL prover. In this work, the Sepref tool can synthesise concrete code from high-level descriptions of imperative algorithms and data structures. Lammich's work takes a top-down path, in contrast to CF and AutoCorres, and the final translation from code in Isabelle/HOL to code running outside the prover is not proved correct w.r.t. any formal semantics of the target programming language.

In the context of Coq, the Bedrock project [9] lead by Chlipala has developed an impressive ecosystem around a separation-logic-inspired Hoare logic for low-level code. Bedrock connects to FIAT [11], which is a set of tools for performing refinement from high-level declarative specifications to concrete implementations. This technology has been applied to complicated examples such as a web server, database applications and even file systems [8].

The Verified Software Toolchain (VST) [2] from Princeton is another substantial verification framework in Coq. VST defines a C-like language, provides a separation logic on top of this C-like language and maps it into the CompCert C compiler, with proof in Coq relating properties proved at the top to the assembly that CompCert produces.

The CertiCoq project [1] also from Princeton aims to build a proof-producing code extraction mechanism for Coq, which will essentially do for Coq what CakeML's translator and CakeML compiler already does for HOL.

The Nqthm theorem prover hosted a project in this area that was two or three decades ahead of the field: the "CLI stack" project [3] developed a substantial verification toolchain with a verification-friendly programming language supported by a verified compiler, which targetted a machine language for which the project developed a verified hardware implementation. The logic of the Nqthm prover is a pure first-order functional language but the input language of the verified compiler is not functional.

The recent F* project [25] develops a new dependently-typed monadic language with refinement types. One can use F*'s expressive types to verify programs written in F*. Users can have extra confidence in the results since the typechecker for F* has been verified using Coq [24]. Programs developed in F* can be extracted to OCaml for compilation and execution.

There are many other functional languages with type-systems that allow verification using types. Ynot is one that has been re-implemented in Coq [10].

There are numerous verification ecosystem without connections to the above mentioned theorem provers. Most of these other ecosystems only consider imperative programs. HALO is one such system that applies to functional programs [28]. HALO enables verification of contracts for Haskell programs and uses first-order provers in its implementation.

7   Summary

In this paper, we have explained how to build a fully verified CF framework for the entirety of the CakeML language. We have shown how to add support for I/O and exceptions, as well as interoperability with the CakeML tool used for bootstrapping the verified CakeML compiler.

At a higher level, one can read this paper as a validation that Charguéraud's original work on CF is flexible as well as extensible.

Acknowledgements. We thank Arthur Charguéraud for advice on characteristic formulae. We thank Mike Gordon and Thomas Sewell for commenting on drafts of this paper. The second author was partially supported by the Swedish Research Council.

References

1. Anand, A., Appel, A., Morrisett, G., Paraskevopoulou, Z., Pollack, R., Belanger, O.S., Sozeau, M., Weaver, M.: CertiCoq: a verified compiler for Coq. In:

The Third International Workshop on Coq for Programming Languages (CoqPL) (2017).   http://conf.researchr.org/event/CoqPL-2017/main-certicoq-a-verified-compiler-for-coq

2. Appel, A.W.: Verified software toolchain. In: Barthe, G. (ed.) ESOP 2011. LNCS, vol. 6602, pp. 1–17. Springer, Heidelberg (2011). doi:10.1007/978-3-642-19718-5_1

3. Bevier, W.R., Hunt Jr., W.A., Moore, J.S., Young, W.D.: An approach to systems verification. J. Autom. Reason. **5**(4), 411–428 (1989). doi:10.1007/BF00243131

4. Charguéraud, A.: Characteristic formulae for mechanized program verification. Ph.D. thesis, Université Paris-Diderot (2010). http://arthur.chargueraud.org/research/2010/thesis/

5. Charguéraud, A.: Program verification through characteristic formulae. In: Hudak, P., Weirich, S. (eds.) International Conference on Functional programming (ICFP). ACM (2010)

6. Charguéraud, A.: Characteristic formulae for the verification of imperative programs. In: Chakravarty, M.M.T., Hu, Z., Danvy, O. (eds.) International Conference on Functional Programming (ICFP). ACM (2011). doi:10.1145/2034773.2034828

7. Charguéraud, A., Pottier, F.: Machine-checked verification of the correctness and amortized complexity of an efficient union-find implementation. In: Urban, C., Zhang, X. (eds.) ITP 2015. LNCS, vol. 9236, pp. 137–153. Springer, Heidelberg (2015). doi:10.1007/978-3-319-22102-1_9

8. Chen, H., Ziegler, D., Chajed, T., Chlipala, A., Kaashoek, M.F., Zeldovich, N.: Using crash hoare logic for certifying the FSCQ file system. In: Gulati, A., Weatherspoon, H. (eds.) USENIX Annual Technical Conference. USENIX Association (2016)

9. Chlipala, A.: The bedrock structured programming system: combining generative metaprogramming and hoare logic in an extensible program verifier. In: Morrisett, G., Uustalu, T. (eds.) International Conference on Functional Programming (ICFP). ACM (2013). http://doi.acm.org/10.1145/2500365.2500592, doi:10.1145/2500365.2500592

10. Chlipala, A., Malecha, J.G., Morrisett, G., Shinnar, A., Wisnesky, R.: Effective interactive proofs for higher-order imperative programs. In: Hutton, G., Tolmach, A.P. (eds.) International conference on Functional programming (ICFP). ACM (2009). http://doi.acm.org/10.1145/1596550.1596565, doi:10.1145/1596550.1596565

11. Delaware, B., Pit-Claudel, C., Gross, J., Chlipala, A.: Fiat: deductive synthesis of abstract data types in a proof assistant. In: Rajamani, S.K., Walker, D., (eds.) Principles of Programming Languages (POPL). ACM (2015). http://doi.acm.org/10.1145/2676726.2677006, doi:10.1145/2676726.2677006

12. Greenaway, D., Lim, J., Andronick, J., Klein, G.: Don't sweat the small stuff: formal verification of C code without the pain. In: ACM SIGPLAN Conference on Programming Language Design and Implementation, Edinburgh, UK, pp. 429–439. ACM, June 2014. doi:10.1145/2594291.2594296

13. Homeier, P.V.: The HOL-omega logic. In: Berghofer, S., Nipkow, T., Urban, C., Wenzel, M. (eds.) TPHOLs 2009. LNCS, vol. 5674, pp. 244–259. Springer, Heidelberg (2009). doi:10.1007/978-3-642-03359-9_18

14. Klein, G., Elphinstone, K., Heiser, G., Andronick, J., Cock, D., Derrin, P., Elkaduwe, D., Engelhardt, K., Kolanski, R., Norrish, M., Sewell, T., Tuch, H., Winwood, S.: seL4: formal verification of an OS kernel. In: ACM Symposium on Operating Systems Principles, Big Sky, MT, USA, pp. 207–220. ACM, October 2009

15. Kumar, R., Myreen, M.O., Norrish, M., Owens, S.: CakeML: a verified implementation of ML. In: Jagannathan, S., Sewell, P. (eds.) Principles of Programming Languages (POPL) (2014). doi:10.1145/2535838.2535841

16. Lammich, P.: Refinement to imperative/HOL. In: Urban, C., Zhang, X. (eds.) ITP 2015. LNCS, vol. 9236, pp. 253–269. Springer, Heidelberg (2015). doi:10.1007/978-3-319-22102-1_17

17. Lammich, P.: Refinement based verification of imperative data structures. In: Avigad, J., Chlipala, A. (eds.) Conference on Certified Programs (CPP). ACM (2016). http://dl.acm.org/citation.cfm?id=2854065, doi:10.1145/2854065.2854067

18. Myreen, M.O., Owens, S.: Proof-producing translation of higher-order logic into pure and stateful ML. J. Funct. Program. **24**(2-3) (2014). doi:10.1017/S0956796813000282

19. O'Connor, L., Chen, Z., Rizkallah, C., Amani, S., Lim, J., Murray, T.C., Nagashima, Y., Sewell, T., Klein, G.: Refinement through restraint: bringing down the cost of verification. In: Garrigue, J., Keller, G., Sumii, E. (eds.) International Conference on Functional Programming (ICFP). ACM (2016). http://doi.acm.org/10.1145/2951913.2951940, doi:10.1145/2951913.2951940

20. Owens, S., Myreen, M.O., Kumar, R., Tan, Y.K.: Functional big-step semantics. In: Thiemann, P. (ed.) ESOP 2016. LNCS, vol. 9632, pp. 589–615. Springer, Heidelberg (2016). doi:10.1007/978-3-662-49498-1_23

21. Pierce, B.C.: The weird world of bi-directional programming. ETAPS Invited Talk, March 2006

22. Reynolds, J.C.: Separation logic: a logic for shared mutable data structures. In: Logic in Computer Science (LICS). IEEE Computer Society (2002)

23. Schirmer, N.: Verification of sequential imperative programs in Isabelle/HOL. Ph.D. thesis, Technische Universitat Munchen (2006). http://arthur.chargueraud.org/research/2010/thesis/

24. Strub, P., Swamy, N., Fournet, C., Chen, J.: Self-certification: bootstrapping certified typecheckers in F* with Coq. In: Field, J., Hicks, M. (eds.) Principles of Programming Languages (POPL). ACM (2012). http://doi.acm.org/10.1145/2103656.2103723, doi:10.1145/2103656.2103723

25. Swamy, N., Hritcu, C., Keller, C., Rastogi, A., Delignat-Lavaud, A., Forest, S., Bhargavan, K., Fournet, C., Strub, P., Kohlweiss, M., Zinzindohoue, J.K., Béguelin, S.Z.: Dependent types and multi-monadic effects in F. In: Bodík, R., Majumdar, R. (eds.) Principles of Programming Languages (POPL). ACM (2016). http://doi.acm.org/10.1145/2837614.2837655, doi:10.1145/2837614.2837655

26. Tan, Y.K., Myreen, M.O., Kumar, R., Fox, A., Owens, S., Norrish, M.: A new verified compiler backend for CakeML. In: International Conference on Functional Programming (ICFP). ACM Press (2016)

27. Urban, C., Zhang, X. (eds.): ITP 2015. LNCS, vol. 9236. Springer, Heidelberg (2015)

28. Vytiniotis, D., Jones, S.L.P., Claessen, K., Rosén, D.: HALO: haskell to logic through denotational semantics. In: Giacobazzi, R., Cousot, R. (eds.) Principles of Programming Languages (POPL). ACM (2013). http://doi.acm.org/10.1145/2429069.2429121, doi:10.1145/2429069.2429121

Unified Reasoning About Robustness Properties of Symbolic-Heap Separation Logic

Christina Jansen[1], Jens Katelaan[2(✉)], Christoph Matheja[1(✉)],
Thomas Noll[1], and Florian Zuleger[2]

[1] Software Modeling and Verification Group,
RWTH Aachen University, Aachen, Germany
matheja@cs.rwth-aachen.de
[2] TU Wien, Vienna, Austria
jkatelaan@forsyte.at

Abstract. We introduce *heap automata*, a formalism for automatic reasoning about *robustness properties* of the symbolic heap fragment of separation logic with user-defined inductive predicates. Robustness properties, such as satisfiability, reachability, and acyclicity, are important for a wide range of reasoning tasks in automated program analysis and verification based on separation logic. Previously, such properties have appeared in many places in the separation logic literature, but have not been studied in a systematic manner. In this paper, we develop an algorithmic framework based on heap automata that allows us to derive asymptotically optimal decision procedures for a wide range of robustness properties in a uniform way.

We implemented a prototype of our framework and obtained promising results for all of the aforementioned robustness properties.

Further, we demonstrate the applicability of heap automata beyond robustness properties. We apply our algorithmic framework to the *model checking* and the *entailment problem* for symbolic-heap separation logic.

1 Introduction

Separation logic (SL) [38] is a popular formalism for Hoare-style verification of imperative, heap-manipulating programs. While its symbolic heap fragment originally emerged as an idiomatic form of assertions that occur naturally in hand-written proofs [4,5,34], a variety of program analyses based on symbolic-heap separation logic have been developed [2,5,9,16,22,30,35]. Consequently, it now serves as formal basis for a multitude of automated verification tools, such as [6,8,15,17,20,28,31,37], capable of proving complex properties of a program's heap, such as memory safety, for large code bases [15,16]. These tools typically

---

J. Katelaan—Supported by the Austrian Science Fund (FWF) under project W1255-N23.

J. Katelaan and F. Zuleger—Supported by the Austrian National Research Network S11403-N23 (RiSE).

C. Matheja—Supported by Deutsche Forschungsgemeinschaft (DFG) Grant NO. 401/2-1.

© Springer-Verlag GmbH Germany 2017
H. Yang (Ed.): ESOP 2017, LNCS 10201, pp. 611–638, 2017.
DOI: 10.1007/978-3-662-54434-1_23

rely on *systems of inductive predicate definitions (SID)* to specify the shape of data structures employed by a program, such as trees and linked lists. Originally, separation logic tools implemented highly-specialized procedures for such fixed SIDs. As this limits their applicability, there is an ongoing trend to support custom SIDs that are either defined manually [17,28] or even automatically generated. The latter may, for example, be obtained from the tool CABER [12].

Robustness Properties. Allowing for arbitrary SIDs, however, raises various questions about their *robustness*. A user-defined or auto-generated SID might, for example, be *inconsistent*, introduce *unallocated logical variables*, specify data structures that contain undesired *cycles*, or produce *garbage*, i.e., parts of the heap that are unreachable from any program variable. Accidentally introducing such properties into specifications can have a negative impact on performance, completeness, and even soundness of the employed verification algorithms:

- Brotherston et al. [11] point out that tools might waste time on inconsistent scenarios due to *unsatisfiability* of specifications.
- The absence of unallocated logical variables, also known as *establishment*, is required by the approach of Iosif et al. [26,27] to obtain a decidable fragment of symbolic heaps.
- Other verification approaches, such as the one by Habermehl et al. [23,24], assume that no garbage is introduced by data structure specifications.
- During program analysis and verification, questions such as *reachability*, *acyclicity* and *garbage-freedom* arise depending on the properties of interest. For example, as argued by Zanardini and Genaim [39], acyclicity of the heap is crucial in automated termination proofs.

Being able to check such *robustness properties* of custom SIDs is thus crucial (1) in debugging of separation-logic specifications prior to program analysis and (2) in the program analyses themselves. So far, however, all of the above properties have either been addressed individually or not systematically at all. For example, satisfiability is studied in detail by Brotherston et al. [11], whereas establishment is often addressed with ad-hoc solutions [23,26].

Several reasoning tasks arise in the context of robustness properties. As a motivation, consider the problem of acyclicity. If our program analysis requires acyclicity, we would like to decide whether all interpretations of a symbolic heap are acyclic; if not, to find out how cycles can be introduced into the heap (counterexample generation); and, finally, to be able to generate a new SID that does guarantee acyclicity (called *refinement* below). A systematic treatment of robustness properties should cover these reasoning tasks in general, not just for the problem of acyclicity.

Problem Statement. We would like to develop a framework that enables:

1. *Decision procedures for robustness properties.* In program analysis, we generally deal with symbolic heaps that reference SIDs specifying unbounded data structures and thus usually have infinitely many interpretations. We need to be able to decide whether all, or some, of these infinitely many interpretations are guaranteed to satisfy a given robustness property.

2. *Generation of counterexamples* that violate a desired property.
3. *Refinement* of SIDs to automatically generate a new SID that respects a given robustness property.
4. *Automatic combination of decision procedures* to derive decision procedures for complex robustness properties from simpler ingredients.

Motivating Example: Inductive Reasoning About Robustness Properties. The key insight underlying our solution to the above problems is that many properties of symbolic heaps can be decided iteratively by inductive reasoning. To motivate our approach, we illustrate this reasoning process with a concrete example. Consider an SID for acyclic singly-linked list segments with head x and tail y:

$$\mathtt{sll}(x,y) \; \Leftarrow \; \mathtt{emp} : \{x = y\} \qquad \mathtt{sll}(x,y) \; \Leftarrow \; \exists u . x \mapsto u * \mathtt{sll}(u,y) : \{x \neq y\}.$$

The two *rules* of the SID define a case distinction: A list is either empty or the first element has a successor u (specified by the *points-to assertion* $x \mapsto u$), which in turn is at the head of a (shorter) singly-linked list segment, $\mathtt{sll}(u,y)$. The inequality in the second rule guarantees that there is no cyclic model. Now, consider the following symbolic heap with *predicate calls* to $\mathtt{sll}$: $\varphi = \exists x,y,z \; . \; \mathtt{sll}(x,z) * z \mapsto y * \mathtt{sll}(y,x)$, which might appear as an assertion during program analysis. Say our program analysis depends on the acyclicity of φ, so we need to determine whether φ is acyclic. We can do so by *inductive reasoning* as follows.

- We analyze the call $\mathtt{sll}(x,z)$, the first list segment in the symbolic heap φ. If it is interpreted by the right-hand side of the first rule of the SID from above, then there is no cycle in $\mathtt{sll}(x,z)$ and z is reachable from x.
- If we already know for a call $\mathtt{sll}(u,z)$ that all of its models are acyclic structures and that z is reachable from u, then z is also reachable from x in the symbolic heap $\exists u . x \mapsto u * \mathtt{sll}(u,z) : \{x \neq z\}$ obtained by the second rule of the SID. Since our SID does not introduce dangling pointers, we also know that there is still no cycle.
- By induction, $\mathtt{sll}(x,z)$ is thus acyclic and z is reachable from x.
- Likewise, $\mathtt{sll}(y,x)$ is acyclic and x is reachable from y.
- Now, based on the information we discovered for $\mathtt{sll}(x,z)$ and $\mathtt{sll}(y,x)$, we examine φ and conclude that it is *cyclic*, as z is reachable from x, y is reachable from z, and x is reachable from y. Crucially, we reason inductively and thus do *not* re-examine the list segments to arrive at our conclusion.

In summary, we examine a symbolic heap and corresponding SID *bottom-up*, starting from the non-recursive base case. Moreover, at each stage of this analysis, we remember a fixed amount of information—namely what we discover about reachability between parameters and acyclicity of every symbolic heap we examine. Similar inductive constructions are defined explicitly for various robustness properties throughout the separation logic literature [11,13,26]. Our aim is to generalize such manual constructions following an *automata-theoretic approach*: We introduce automata that operate on symbolic heaps and store the relevant information of each symbolic heap they examine in their state space. Whenever such an automaton comes across a predicate that it has already analyzed, it can simply replace the predicate with the information that is encoded in the corresponding state. In other words, our automata *recognize* robustness properties *in a compositional way* by exploiting the *inductive structure* inherent in the SIDs.

Systematic Reasoning About Robustness Properties. Our novel automaton model, *heap automata*, works directly on the structure of symbolic heaps as outlined in the example, and can be applied to all the problems introduced before. In particular, heap automata enable *automatic refinement* of SIDs and enjoy a variety of closure properties through which we can derive counterexample generation as well as decision procedures for various robustness properties—including satisfiability, establishment, reachability, garbage-freedom, and acyclicity.

Our approach can thus be seen as an *algorithmic framework* for deciding a wide range of robustness properties of symbolic heaps. Furthermore, we show asymptotically optimal complexity of our automata-based decision procedures in a uniform way. By enabling this systematic approach to reasoning about robustness, our framework generalizes prior work that studied single robustness properties in isolation, such as the work by Brotherston et al. [11,13].

As a natural byproduct of our automata-based approach, we also derive decision procedures for the *model-checking problem*, which was recently studied, and proven to be EXPTIME–complete in general, by Brotherston et al. [13]. This makes it possible to apply our framework to *run-time verification*—a setting in which robustness properties are of particular importance [13,28,33].

Entailment Checking with Heap Automata. Finally, we also address the *entailment problem*. In Hoare-style program analysis, decision procedures for the *entailment problem* become essential to discharge implications between assertions, as required, for example, by the rule of consequence [25]. Because of this central role in verification, there is an extensive body of research on decision procedures for entailment; see, for example [3,10,14,21,26,27,32,36]. Antonopoulos et al. [1] study the complexity of the entailment problem and show that it is undecidable in general, and already EXPTIME–hard for SIDs specifying sets of trees.

We use heap automata to check entailment between *determined* symbolic heaps. Intuitively, determinedness is a strong form of the establishment property guaranteeing that two variables are either equal or unequal in every model. Unlike other decision procedures [3,26,27], our approach does not impose syntactic restrictions on the symbolic heap under consideration but merely requires that suitable heap automata for the predicates on the right-hand side of the entailment are provided. In particular, we show how to obtain EXPTIME decision procedures from such heap automata—which exist for highly non-trivial SIDs. If desired, additional syntactic restrictions can be integrated seamlessly into our approach to boost our algorithms' performance.

Contributions. Our main contributions can be summarized as follows.

- We introduce *heap automata*, a novel automaton model operating directly on symbolic heaps. We prove that heap automata enjoy various useful *closure properties*. Besides union, intersection and complement, they are closed under the conjunction with pure formulas, allowing the construction of complex heap automata from simple ones.
- We develop a powerful *algorithmic framework* for automated reasoning about and debugging of symbolic heaps with inductive predicate definitions based on heap automata.
- We show that key robustness properties, such as *satisfiability, establishment, reachability, garbage freedom* and *acyclicity*, can naturally be expressed as heap automata. Moreover, the upper bounds of decision procedures obtained from our framework are shown to be optimal—i.e., EXPTIME–complete—in each of these cases. Further, they enable automated *refinement* of SIDs to filter out (or expose) symbolic heaps with undesired properties.
- Additionally, we apply heap automata to tackle the *entailment* and the *model checking* problem for symbolic heaps. We show that if each predicate of an SID can be represented by a heap automaton, then the entailment problem for the corresponding fragment of symbolic heaps is decidable in 2-EXPTIME in general and EXPTIME-complete if the maximal arity of predicates and points-to assertions is bounded. For example, our framework yields an EXPTIME decision procedure for a symbolic heap fragment capable of representing trees with linked leaves—a fragment that is out of scope of most EXPTIME decision procedures known so far (cf. [3, 21, 27]).
- We implemented a prototype of our framework that yields promising results for all robustness properties considered in the paper.

Organization of the Paper. The fragment of symbolic heaps with inductive predicate definitions is briefly introduced in Sect. 2. Heap automata and derived decision procedures are studied in Sect. 3. Section 4 demonstrates that a variety of robustness properties can be checked by heap automata. We report on a prototypical implementation of our framework in Sect. 5. Special attention to the entailment problem is paid in Sect. 6. Finally, Sect. 7 concludes. Due to lack of space, most proofs as well as detailed constructions are provided in a full version of this paper that is available online [29].

2   Symbolic Heaps

This section briefly introduces the symbolic heap fragment of separation logic equipped with inductive predicate definitions.

Basic Notation. $\mathbb{N}$ is the set of natural numbers and 2^S is the powerset of a set S. $(co)\text{dom}(f)$ is the (co)domain of a (partial) function f. We abbreviate tuples $(u_1, \ldots, u_n)$, $n \geq 0$, by $\mathbf{u}$ and write $\mathbf{u}[i]$, $1 \leq i \leq \|\mathbf{u}\| = n$, to denote u_i, the i-th element of $\mathbf{u}$. By slight abuse of notation, the same symbol $\mathbf{u}$ is used for the set of all elements occurring in tuple $\mathbf{u}$. The empty tuple is ε and the set of all (non-empty) tuples [of length $n \geq 0$] over a finite set S is S^* (S^+ [S^n]). The concatenation of tuples $\mathbf{u}$ and $\mathbf{v}$ is $\mathbf{u}\mathbf{v}$.

Syntax. We usually denote *variables* taken from *Var* (including a dedicated variable **null**) by a, b, c, x, y, z, etc. Moreover, let Pred be a set of *predicate symbols* and ar : Pred $\rightarrow \mathbb{N}$ be a function assigning each symbol its *arity*. *Spatial formulas* Σ and *pure formulas* π are given by the following grammar:

$$\Sigma ::= \text{emp} \mid x \mapsto \mathbf{y} \mid \Sigma * \Sigma \qquad \pi ::= x = y \mid x \neq y,$$

where $\mathbf{y}$ is a non-empty tuple of variables. Here, emp stands for the *empty heap*, $x \mapsto \mathbf{y}$ is a *points-to assertion* and $*$ is the *separating conjunction*. Furthermore, for $P \in$ Pred and a tuple of variables $\mathbf{y}$ of length ar(P), $P\mathbf{y}$ is a *predicate call*. A *symbolic heap* $\varphi(\mathbf{x}_0)$ with variables $Var(\varphi)$ and free variables $\mathbf{x}_0 \subseteq Var(\varphi)$ is a formula of the form $\varphi(\mathbf{x}_0) = \exists \mathbf{z} . \Sigma * \Gamma : \Pi$, $\Gamma = P_1 \mathbf{x}_1 * \ldots * P_m \mathbf{x}_m$, where Σ is a spatial formula, Γ is a sequence of predicate calls and Π is a finite set of pure formulas, each with variables from $\mathbf{x}_0$ and $\mathbf{z}$. This normal form, in which predicate calls and points-to assertions are never mixed, is chosen to simplify formal constructions. If an element of a symbolic heap is empty, we usually omit it to improve readability. For the same reason, we fix the notation from above and write $\mathbf{z}^\varphi$, $\mathbf{x}_i^\varphi$, Σ^φ etc. to denote the respective component of symbolic heap φ in formal constructions. Hence, $\|\mathbf{x}_0^\varphi\|$ and $\|\Gamma^\varphi\|$ refer to the number of free variables and the number of predicate calls of φ, respectively. We omit the superscript whenever the symbolic heap under consideration is clear from the context. If a symbolic heap τ contains no predicate calls, i.e., $\|\Gamma^\tau\| = 0$, then τ is called *reduced*. Moreover, to simplify the technical development, we tacitly assume that **null** is a free variable that is passed to every predicate call. Thus, for each $i \in \mathbb{N}$, we write $\mathbf{x}_i[0]$ as a shortcut for **null** and treat $\mathbf{x}_i[0]$ as if $\mathbf{x}_i[0] \in \mathbf{x}_i$.[1]

Systems of Inductive Definitions. Every predicate symbol is associated with one or more symbolic heaps by a *system of inductive definitions* (SID). Formally, an SID is a finite set of rules of the form $P\mathbf{x}_0 \Leftarrow \varphi$, where φ is a symbolic heap with ar$(P) = \|\mathbf{x}_0^\varphi\|$. The set of all predicate symbols occurring in SID Φ and their maximal arity are denoted by Pred(Φ) and ar(Φ), respectively.

Example 1. An SID specifying doubly-linked list segments is defined by:

$$\text{dll}(x_1, x_2, x_3, x_4) \Leftarrow \text{emp} : \{x_1 = x_3, x_2 = x_4\}$$
$$\text{dll}(x_1, x_2, x_3, x_4) \Leftarrow \exists u . x_1 \mapsto (u, x_2) * \text{dll}(u, x_1, x_3, x_4),$$

where x_1 corresponds to the *head* of the list, x_2 and x_3 represent the *previous* and the *next* list element and x_4 represents the *tail* of the list. Further, the following rules specify binary trees with *root* x_1, *leftmost leaf* x_2 and *successor of the rightmost leaf* x_3 in which all leaves are connected by a singly-linked list from left to right.

$$\text{tll}(x_1, x_2, x_3) \Leftarrow x_1 \mapsto (\mathbf{null}, \mathbf{null}, x_3) : \{x_1 = x_2\}$$
$$\text{tll}(x_1, x_2, x_3) \Leftarrow \exists \ell\, r\, z . x_1 \mapsto (\ell, r, \mathbf{null}) * \text{tll}(\ell, x_2, z) * \text{tll}(r, z, x_3).$$

---

[1] Since $\mathbf{x}_i[0]$ is just a shortcut and not a proper variable, $\|\mathbf{x}_i\|$ refers to the number of variables in $\mathbf{x}_i$ *apart from* $\mathbf{x}_i[0]$.

$$s, h \models_\Phi x \sim y \qquad\qquad \Leftrightarrow\; s(x) \sim s(y), \text{ where } \sim \in \{=, \neq\}$$

$$s, h \models_\Phi \text{emp} \qquad\qquad \Leftrightarrow\; \text{dom}(h) = \emptyset$$

$$s, h \models_\Phi x \mapsto \mathbf{y} \qquad\qquad \Leftrightarrow\; \text{dom}(h) = \{s(x)\} \text{ and } h(s(x)) = s(\mathbf{y})$$

$$s, h \models_\Phi P\mathbf{y} \qquad\qquad \Leftrightarrow\; \exists \tau \in \mathbb{U}_\Phi(P\mathbf{y}) \, . \, s, h \models_\emptyset \tau$$

$$s, h \models_\Phi \varphi * \psi \qquad\qquad \Leftrightarrow\; \exists h_1, h_2 \, . \, h = h_1 \uplus h_2$$
$$\text{and } s, h_1 \models_\Phi \varphi \text{ and } s, h_2 \models_\Phi \psi$$

$$s, h \models_\Phi \exists \mathbf{z}.\varSigma * \varGamma : \varPi \qquad \Leftrightarrow\; \exists \mathbf{v} \in Val^{\|\mathbf{z}\|} \, . \, s \, [\mathbf{z} \mapsto \mathbf{v}], h \models_\Phi \varSigma * \varGamma$$
$$\text{and } \forall \pi \in \varPi \, . \, s \, [\mathbf{z} \mapsto \mathbf{v}], h \models_\Phi \pi$$

Fig. 1. Semantics of the symbolic heap fragment of separation logic with respect to an SID Φ and a state (s, h).

Definition 1. *We write* SH *for the set of all symbolic heaps and* SH^Φ *for the set of symbolic heaps restricted to predicate symbols taken from SID Φ. Moreover, given a computable function $\mathcal{C} : \text{SH} \to \{0, 1\}$, the set of symbolic heaps $\text{SH}_\mathcal{C}$ is given by* $\text{SH}_\mathcal{C} \triangleq \{\varphi \in \text{SH} \mid \mathcal{C}(\varphi) = 1\}$. *We collect all SIDs in which every right-hand side belongs to* $\text{SH}_\mathcal{C}$ *in* $\text{SID}_\mathcal{C}$. *To refer to the set of all reduced symbolic heaps (belonging to a set defined by $\mathcal{C}$), we write* RSH ($\text{RSH}_\mathcal{C}$).

Example 2. Let $\alpha \in \mathbb{N}$ and $\text{FV}^{\leq \alpha}(\varphi) \triangleq \begin{cases} 1, & \|\mathbf{x}_0^\varphi\| \leq \alpha \\ 0, & \text{otherwise} \end{cases}$.

Clearly, $\text{FV}^{\leq \alpha}$ is computable. Moreover, $\text{SH}_{\text{FV}^{\leq \alpha}}$ is the set of all symbolic heaps having at most α free variables.

Semantics. As in a typical RAM model, we assume heaps to consist of records with a finite number of fields. Let *Val* denote an infinite set of *values* and *Loc* $\subseteq$ *Val* an infinite set of addressable *locations*. Moreover, we assume the existence of a special non-addressable value **null** $\in$ *Val* \ *Loc*.

A *heap* is a finite partial function $h : Loc \rightharpoonup Val^+$ mapping locations to non-empty tuples of values. We write $h_1 \uplus h_2$ to denote the union of heaps h_1 and h_2 provided that $\text{dom}(h_1) \cap \text{dom}(h_2) = \emptyset$. Otherwise, $h_1 \uplus h_2$ is undefined. Variables are interpreted by a *stack*, i.e., a partial function $s : Var \rightharpoonup Val$ with $s(\mathbf{null}) = \mathbf{null}$. Furthermore, stacks are canonically extended to tuples of variables by componentwise application. We call a stack–heap pair (s, h) a *state*. The set of all states is *States*. The semantics of a symbolic heap with respect to an SID and a state is shown in Fig. 1. Note that the semantics of predicate calls is explained in detail next.

Unfoldings of Predicate Calls. The semantics of predicate calls is defined in terms of *unfolding trees*. Intuitively, an unfolding tree specifies how predicate calls are *replaced* by symbolic heaps according to a given SID. The resulting reduced symbolic heap obtained from an unfolding tree is consequently called an *unfolding*. Formally, let $\varphi = \exists \mathbf{z}.\varSigma * P_1\mathbf{x}_1 * \ldots * P_m\mathbf{x}_m : \varPi$. Then a predicate call $P_i \mathbf{x}_i$ may be *replaced* by a reduced symbolic heap τ if $\|\mathbf{x}_i\| = \|\mathbf{x}_0^\tau\|$ and $Var(\varphi) \cap Var(\tau) \subseteq \mathbf{x}_0^\tau$. The result of such a replacement is

$$\varphi[P_i/\tau] \triangleq \exists \mathbf{z}\, \mathbf{z}^\tau . \Sigma * \Sigma^{\tau[\mathbf{x}_0^\tau/\mathbf{x}_i]} *$$

$$P_1 \mathbf{x}_1 * \ldots * P_{i-1}\mathbf{x}_{i-1} * P_{i+1}\mathbf{x}_{i+1} * \ldots * P_m \mathbf{x}_m : \left(\Pi \cup \Pi^{\tau[\mathbf{x}_0^\tau/\mathbf{x}_i]} \right),$$

where $\tau[\mathbf{x}_0^\tau/\mathbf{x}_i]$ denotes the substitution of each free variable of τ by the corresponding parameter of P_i.

A *tree* over symbolic heaps SH^Φ is a finite partial function $t : \mathbb{N}^* \rightharpoonup SH^\Phi$ such that $\emptyset \neq dom(t) \subseteq \mathbb{N}^*$ is prefix-closed and for all $\mathbf{u} \in dom(t)$ with $t(\mathbf{u}) = \varphi$, we have $\{1, \ldots, \|\Gamma^\varphi\|\} = \{i \in \mathbb{N} \mid \mathbf{u}i \in dom(t)\}$. The element $\varepsilon \in dom(t)$ is called the *root* of tree t. Furthermore, the *subtree* $t|_\mathbf{u}$ of t with root $\mathbf{u}$ is $t|_\mathbf{u} : \{\mathbf{v} \mid \mathbf{u}\mathbf{v} \in dom(t)\} \to SH^\Phi$ with $t|_\mathbf{u}(\mathbf{v}) \triangleq t(\mathbf{u} \cdot \mathbf{v})$.

Definition 2. *Let $\Phi \in SID$ and $\varphi \in SH^\Phi$. Then the set of unfolding trees of φ w.r.t. Φ, written $\mathbb{T}_\Phi(\varphi)$, is the least set that contains all trees t that satisfy (1) $t(\varepsilon) = \varphi$ and (2) $t|_i \in \mathbb{T}_\Phi(\psi_i)$ for each $1 \leq i \leq \|\Gamma^\varphi\|$, where $P_i^\varphi \Leftarrow \psi_i \in \Phi$.*

Note that for every reduced symbolic heap τ, we have $\|\Gamma^\tau\| = 0$. Thus, $\mathbb{T}_\Phi(\tau) = \{t\}$, where $t : \{\varepsilon\} \to \{\tau\} : \varepsilon \mapsto \tau$, forms the base case in Definition 2. Every unfolding tree t specifies a reduced symbolic heap $[\![t]\!]$, which is obtained by recursively replacing predicate calls by reduced symbolic heaps:

Definition 3. *The unfolding of an unfolding tree $t \in \mathbb{T}_\Phi(\varphi)$ is*

$$[\![t]\!] \triangleq \begin{cases} t(\varepsilon) & , \|\Gamma^{t(\varepsilon)}\| = 0 \\ t(\varepsilon)[P_1/[\![t|_1]\!], \ldots, P_m/[\![t|_m]\!]] & , \|\Gamma^{t(\varepsilon)}\| = m > 0 \,, \end{cases}$$

where we tacitly assume that the variables $\mathbf{z}^{t(\varepsilon)}$, i.e., the existentially quantified variables in $t(\varepsilon)$, are substituted by fresh variables.

Example 3. Recall from Example 1 the two symbolic heaps τ (upper) and φ (lower) occurring on the right-hand side of the dll predicate. Then $t : \{\varepsilon, 1\} \to \{\varphi, \tau\} : \varepsilon \mapsto \varphi, 1 \mapsto \tau$ is an unfolding tree of φ. The corresponding unfolding is

$$[\![t]\!] = \varphi[P_1^\varphi/\tau] = \exists z . x_1 \mapsto (z, x_2) * \text{emp} : \{z = x_3, x_1 = x_4\}.$$

Definition 4. *The set of all unfoldings of a predicate call $P_i \mathbf{x}_i$ w.r.t. an SID Φ is denoted by $\mathbb{U}_\Phi(P_i \mathbf{x}_i)$. Analogously, the unfoldings of a symbolic heap φ are $\mathbb{U}_\Phi(\varphi) \triangleq \{[\![t]\!] \mid t \in \mathbb{T}_\Phi(\varphi)\}$.*

Then, as already depicted in Fig. 1, the semantics of predicate calls requires the existence of an unfolding satisfying a given state. This semantics corresponds to a particular iteration of the frequently used semantics of predicate calls based on least fixed points (cf. [11]). Further note that applying the SL semantics to a given symbolic heap coincides with applying them to a suitable unfolding.

Lemma 1. *Let $\varphi \in SH^\Phi$. Then, for every $(s, h) \in States$, we have*

$$s, h \models_\Phi \varphi \text{ iff } \exists \tau \in \mathbb{U}_\Phi(\varphi) . s, h \models_\emptyset \tau.$$

3 Heap Automata

In this section we develop a procedure to reason about robustness properties of symbolic heaps. This procedure relies on the notion of *heap automata*; a device that assigns one of finitely many states to any given symbolic heap.

Definition 5. *A* heap automaton *over* $\mathrm{SH}_\mathcal{C}$ *is a tuple* $\mathfrak{A} = (Q, \mathrm{SH}_\mathcal{C}, \Delta, F)$, *where* Q *is a finite set of* states *and* $F \subseteq Q$ *is a set of* final states, *respectively. Moreover,* $\Delta \subseteq Q^* \times \mathrm{SH}_\mathcal{C} \times Q$ *is a decidable* transition relation *such that* $(\mathbf{q}, \varphi, p) \in \Delta$ *implies that* $\|\mathbf{q}\| = \|\Gamma^\varphi\|$. *We often write* $\mathbf{q} \xrightarrow{\varphi}_\mathfrak{A} p$ *instead of* $(\mathbf{q}, \varphi, p) \in \Delta$.

A transition $\mathbf{q} \xrightarrow{\varphi}_\mathfrak{A} p$ takes a symbolic heap φ and an input state q_i for every predicate call P_i of φ—collected in the tuple $\mathbf{q}$—and assigns an output state p to φ. Thus, the intuition behind a transition is that φ has a property encoded by state p if every predicate call P_i of φ is replaced by a reduced symbolic heap τ_i that has a property encoded by state $\mathbf{q}[i]$.

Note that every heap automaton $\mathfrak{A}$ assigns a state p to a reduced symbolic heap τ within a single transition of the form $\varepsilon \xrightarrow{\tau}_\mathfrak{A} p$. Alternatively, $\mathfrak{A}$ may process a corresponding unfolding tree t with $[\![t]\!] = \tau$. In this case, $\mathfrak{A}$ proceeds similarly to the compositional construction of unfoldings (see Definition 3). However, instead of replacing every predicate call P_i of the symbolic heap $t(\varepsilon)$ at the root of t by an unfolding $[\![t|_i]\!]$ of a subtree of t, $\mathfrak{A}$ uses states to keep track of the properties of these unfolded subtrees. Consequently, $\mathfrak{A}$ assigns a state p to the symbolic heap $t(\varepsilon)$ if $(q_1, \ldots, q_m) \xrightarrow{t(\varepsilon)}_\mathfrak{A} p$ holds, where for each $1 \leq i \leq m$, q_i is the state assigned to the unfolding of subtree $t|_i$, i.e., there is a transition $\varepsilon \xrightarrow{[\![t|_i]\!]}_\mathfrak{A} q_i$. It is then natural to require that p should coincide with the state assigned directly to the unfolding $[\![t]\!]$, i.e., $\varepsilon \xrightarrow{[\![t]\!]}_\mathfrak{A} p$. Hence, we require all heap automata considered in this paper to satisfy a *compositionality property*.

Definition 6. *A heap automaton* $\mathfrak{A} = (Q, \mathrm{SH}_\mathcal{C}, \Delta, F)$ *is* compositional *if for every* $p \in Q$, *every* $\varphi \in \mathrm{SH}_\mathcal{C}$ *with* $m \geq 0$ *predicate calls* $\Gamma^\varphi = P_1\mathbf{x}_1 * \ldots * P_m\mathbf{x}_m$, *and all reduced symbolic heaps* $\tau_1, \ldots, \tau_m \in \mathrm{RSH}_\mathcal{C}$, *we have:*

$$\exists \mathbf{q} \in Q^m . (\mathbf{q}, \varphi, p) \in \Delta \text{ and } \bigwedge_{1 \leq i \leq m}(\varepsilon, \tau_i, \mathbf{q}[i]) \in \Delta$$
$$\textit{if and only if}$$
$$(\varepsilon, \varphi[P_1/\tau_1, \ldots, P_m/\tau_m], p) \in \Delta.$$

Due to the compositionality property, we can safely define the *language* $L(\mathfrak{A})$ *accepted* by a heap automaton $\mathfrak{A}$ as the set of all reduced symbolic heaps that are assigned a final state, i.e., $L(\mathfrak{A}) \triangleq \{\tau \in \mathrm{RSH}_\mathcal{C} \mid \exists q \in F . \varepsilon \xrightarrow{\tau}_\mathfrak{A} q\}$.

Example 4. Given a symbolic heap φ, let $|\Sigma^\varphi|$ denote the number of points-to assertions in φ. As a running example, we consider a heap automaton $\mathfrak{A} = (\{0,1\}, \mathrm{SH}, \Delta, \{1\})$, where Δ is given by

$$\mathbf{q} \xrightarrow{\varphi}_\mathfrak{A} p \text{ iff } p = \begin{cases} 1, & \text{if } |\Sigma^\varphi| + \sum_{i=1}^{\|\mathbf{q}\|} \mathbf{q}[i] > 0 \\ 0, & \text{otherwise.} \end{cases}$$

While $\mathfrak{A}$ is a toy example, it illustrates the compositionality property: Consider the reduced symbolic heap $\tau(x, y) = \exists z.\text{emp} * \text{emp} : \{x = z, z = y\}$. Since τ contains no points-to assertions, $\mathfrak{A}$ rejects τ in a single step, i.e., $\varepsilon \xrightarrow{\tau}_{\mathfrak{A}} 0 \notin \{1\}$. The compositionality property of $\mathfrak{A}$ ensures that $\mathfrak{A}$ yields the same result for every unfolding tree t whose unfolding $[\![t]\!]$ is equal to τ. For instance, τ is a possible unfolding of the symbolic heap $\varphi(x, y) = \exists z.\text{sll}(x, z) * \text{sll}(z, y)$, where sll is a predicate specifying singly-linked list segments as in Sect. 1. More precisely, if both predicate calls are replaced according to the rule $\text{sll}(x, y) \Leftarrow \text{emp} : \{x = y\}$, we obtain τ again (up to renaming of parameters as per Definition 3). In this case, $\mathfrak{A}$ rejects as before: We have $\varepsilon \xrightarrow{\text{emp}:\{x=y\}}_{\mathfrak{A}} 0$ for both base cases and $(0, 0) \xrightarrow{\varphi}_{\mathfrak{A}} 0$ for the symbolic heap φ. By the compositionality property, this is equivalent to $\varepsilon \xrightarrow{\tau}_{\mathfrak{A}} 0$. Analogously, if a predicate call, say the first, is replaced according to the rule $\text{sll}(x, y) \Leftarrow \psi$, where $\psi = \exists z.x \mapsto z * \text{sll}(z, y)$, then $0 \xrightarrow{\psi}_{\mathfrak{A}} 1$, $1 \xrightarrow{\psi}_{\mathfrak{A}} 1$ and $(1, 0) \xrightarrow{\varphi}_{\mathfrak{A}} 1$ holds, i.e., $\mathfrak{A}$ accepts. In general, $L(\mathfrak{A})$ is the set of all reduced symbolic heaps that contain at least one points-to assertion.

While heap automata can be applied to check whether a single reduced symbolic heap has a property of interest, i.e., belongs to the language of a heap automaton, our main application is directed towards reasoning about *infinite* sets of symbolic heaps, such as all unfoldings of a symbolic heap φ. Thus, given a heap automaton $\mathfrak{A}$, we would like to answer the following questions:

1. Does there *exist* an unfolding of φ that is accepted by $\mathfrak{A}$?
2. Are *all* unfoldings of φ accepted by $\mathfrak{A}$?

We start with a special case of the first question in which φ is a single predicate call. The key idea behind our corresponding decision procedure is to transform the SID Φ to *filter out* all unfoldings that are *not* accepted by $\mathfrak{A}$. One of our main results is that such a refinement is always possible.

Theorem 1 (Refinement Theorem). *Let $\mathfrak{A}$ be a heap automaton over SH_C and $\Phi \in \text{SID}_C$. Then one can effectively construct a refined $\Psi \in \text{SID}_C$ such that for each $P \in \text{Pred}(\Phi)$, we have $\mathbb{U}_\Psi(P\mathbf{x}_0) = \mathbb{U}_\Phi(P\mathbf{x}_0) \cap L(\mathfrak{A})$.*

Proof. We construct $\Psi \in \text{SID}_C$ over the predicate symbols $\text{Pred}(\Psi) = (\text{Pred}(\Phi) \times Q_\mathfrak{A}) \cup \text{Pred}(\Phi)$ as follows: If $P\mathbf{x}_0 \Leftarrow \varphi \in \Phi$ with $\Gamma^\varphi = P_1\mathbf{x}_1 * \ldots * P_m\mathbf{x}_m$, $m \geq 0$, and $(q_1, \ldots, q_m) \xrightarrow{\varphi}_{\mathfrak{A}} q_0$, we add a rule to Ψ in which P is substituted by $\langle P, q_0 \rangle$ and each predicate call $P_i\mathbf{x}_i$ is substituted by a call $\langle P_i, q_i \rangle\mathbf{x}_i$. Furthermore, for each $q \in F_\mathfrak{A}$, we add a rule $P\mathbf{x}_0 \Leftarrow \langle P, q \rangle\mathbf{x}_0$ to Ψ. See [29] for details. $\square$

Example 5. Applying the refinement theorem to the heap automaton from Example 4 and the SID from Example 1 yields a refined SID given by the rules:

$$\text{dll}\,\mathbf{x}_0 \Leftarrow \langle\text{dll}, 1\rangle\,\mathbf{x}_0 \qquad \langle\text{dll}, 0\rangle\mathbf{x}_0 \Leftarrow \text{emp} : \{x_1 = x_3, x_2 = x_4\}$$
$$\langle\text{dll}, 1\rangle\mathbf{x}_0 \Leftarrow \exists z . x_1 \mapsto (z, x_2) * \langle\text{dll}, 0\rangle(z, x_1, x_3, x_4)$$
$$\langle\text{dll}, 1\rangle\mathbf{x}_0 \Leftarrow \exists z . x_1 \mapsto (z, x_2) * \langle\text{dll}, 1\rangle(z, x_1, x_3, x_4)$$

Hence, the refined predicate $\text{dll}\,\mathbf{x}_0$ specifies all non-empty doubly-linked lists.

Input : SID Φ, $I \in \mathrm{Pred}(\Phi)$, $\mathfrak{A} = (Q, \mathrm{SH}_C, \Delta, F)$
Output: yes iff $\mathbb{U}_\Phi(I\mathbf{x}) \cap L(\mathfrak{A}) = \emptyset$

R $\leftarrow \emptyset$;
repeat
   | **if** R $\cap (\{I\} \times F) \neq \emptyset$ **then return** *no*;
   | pick a state q in Q; pick a rule $P \Leftarrow \varphi$ in Φ;
   | s $\leftarrow \varepsilon$; // list of states of $\mathfrak{A}$
   | **for** i *in* 1 *to* $\|\Gamma^\varphi\|$ **do**
   | | pick $(P_i^\varphi, p) \in$ R; append(s,p) // base case if $\|\Gamma^\varphi\| = 0$
   | **end**
   | **if** $(s, \varphi, q) \in \Delta$ **then** R $\leftarrow$ R $\cup \{(P, q)\}$;
until R *reaches a fixed point (w.r.t. all choices of rules)*;
return *yes*

Algorithm 1. On-the-fly construction of a refined SID with emptiness check.

To answer question (1) we then check whether the set of unfoldings of a refined SID is non-empty. This boils down to a simple reachability analysis.

Lemma 2. *Given an SID Φ and a predicate symbol $P \in \mathrm{Pred}(\Phi)$, it is decidable in linear time whether the set of unfoldings of P is empty, i.e., $\mathbb{U}_\Phi(P\mathbf{x}) = \emptyset$.*

Proof (sketch). It suffices to check whether the predicate P lies in the least set R such that (1) $I \in R$ if $I\mathbf{x}_0 \Leftarrow \tau \in \Phi$ for some $\tau \in \mathrm{RSH}$, and (2) $I \in R$ if $I\mathbf{x}_0 \Leftarrow \varphi \in \Phi$ and for each $P_i^\varphi \mathbf{x}_i^\varphi$, $1 \leq i \leq \|\Gamma^\varphi\|$, $P_i^\varphi \in R$. The set R is computable in linear time by a simple backward reachability analysis. $\square$

As outlined before, putting the Refinement Theorem and Lemma 2 together immediately yields a decision procedure for checking whether some unfolding of a predicate symbol P is accepted by a heap automaton: Construct the refined SID and subsequently check whether the set of unfoldings of P is non-empty.

To extend this result from unfoldings of single predicates to unfoldings of arbitrary symbolic heaps φ, we just add a rule $P \Leftarrow \varphi$, where P is a fresh predicate symbol, and proceed as before.

Corollary 1. *Let $\mathfrak{A}$ be a heap automaton over SH_C and $\Phi \in \mathrm{SID}_C$. Then, for each $\varphi \in \mathrm{SH}_C^\Phi$, it is decidable whether there exists $\tau \in \mathbb{U}_\Phi(\varphi)$ such that $\tau \in L(\mathfrak{A})$.*

The refinement and emptiness check can also be integrated: Algorithm 1 displays a simple procedure that constructs the refined SID Ψ from Theorem 1 on-the-fly while checking whether its set of unfoldings is empty for a given predicate symbol. Regarding complexity, the size of a refined SID[2] obtained from an SID Φ and a heap automaton $\mathfrak{A}$ is bounded by $\|\Phi\| \cdot \|Q_\mathfrak{A}\|^{M+1}$, where M

---

[2] We assume a reasonable function $\|.\|$ assigning a size to SIDs, symbolic heaps, unfolding trees, etc. For instance, the size $\|\Phi\|$ of an SID Φ is given by the product of its number of rules and the size of the largest symbolic heap contained in any rule.

is the maximal number of predicate calls occurring in any rule of Φ. Thus, the aforementioned algorithm runs in time $\mathcal{O}\left(\|\Phi\| \cdot \|Q_{\mathfrak{A}}\|^{M+1} \cdot \|\Delta_{\mathfrak{A}}\|\right)$, where $\|\Delta_{\mathfrak{A}}\|$ denotes the complexity of deciding whether the transition relation $\Delta_{\mathfrak{A}}$ holds for a given tuple of states and a symbolic heap occurring in a rule of Φ.

Example 6. Resuming our toy example, we check whether some unfolding of the doubly-linked list predicate $\mathtt{dll}\,\mathbf{x}_0$ (see Example 1) contains points-to assertions. Formally, we decide whether $\mathbb{U}_{\Phi}(\mathtt{dll}\,\mathbf{x}_0) \cap L(\mathfrak{A}) \neq \emptyset$, where $\mathfrak{A}$ is the heap automaton introduced in Example 4. Algorithm 1 first picks the rule that maps $\mathtt{dll}$ to the empty list segment and consequently adds $\langle \mathtt{dll}, 0 \rangle$ to the set R of reachable predicate–state pairs. In the next iteration, it picks the rule that maps to the non-empty list. Since $\langle \mathtt{dll}, 0 \rangle \in R$, s is set to 0 in the **do**-loop. Abbreviating the body of the rule to φ, we have $(0, \varphi, 1) \in \Delta$, so the algorithm adds $\langle \mathtt{dll}, 1 \rangle$ to R. After that, *no* is returned, because 1 is a final state of $\mathfrak{A}$. Hence, some unfolding of $\mathtt{dll}$ is accepted by $\mathfrak{A}$ and thus contains points-to assertions.

We now revisit question (2) from above–are all unfoldings accepted by a heap automaton?–and observe that heap automata enjoy several closure properties.

Theorem 2 [29]. *Let $\mathfrak{A}$ and $\mathfrak{B}$ be heap automata over SH_C. Then there exist heap automata $\mathfrak{C}_1, \mathfrak{C}_2, \mathfrak{C}_3$ over SH_C with $L(\mathfrak{C}_1) = L(\mathfrak{A}) \cup L(\mathfrak{B})$, $L(\mathfrak{C}_2) = L(\mathfrak{A}) \cap L(\mathfrak{B})$, and $L(\mathfrak{C}_3) = \mathrm{RSH}_C \setminus L(\mathfrak{A})$, respectively.*

Then, by the equivalence $X \subseteq Y \Leftrightarrow X \cap \overline{Y} = \emptyset$ and Theorem 2, it is also decidable whether every unfolding of a symbolic heap is accepted by a heap automaton.

Corollary 2. *Let $\mathfrak{A}$ be a heap automaton over SH_C and $\Phi \in \mathrm{SID}_C$. Then, for each $\varphi \in \mathrm{SH}_C$, it is decidable whether $\mathbb{U}_{\Phi}(\varphi) \subseteq L(\mathfrak{A})$ holds.*

Note that complementation of heap automata in general leads to an exponentially larger state space and exponentially higher complexity of evaluating Δ. Thus, $\mathbb{U}_{\Phi}(\varphi) \subseteq L(\mathfrak{A})$ is decidable in $\mathcal{O}\left((\|\varphi\| + \|\Phi\|) \cdot \|2^{Q_{\mathfrak{A}}}\|^{2(M+1)} \cdot \|\Delta_{\mathfrak{A}}\|\right)$. In many cases it is, however, possibly to construct smaller automata for the complement directly to obtain more efficient decision procedures. For example, this is the case for most heap automata considered in Sect. 4.

Apart from decision procedures, Theorem 1 enables systematic refinement of SIDs according to heap automata in order to establish desired properties. For instance, as shown in Sect. 4, an SID in which every unfolding is satisfiable can be constructed from any given SID. Another application of Theorem 1 is counterexample generation for systematic debugging of SIDs that are manually written as data structure specifications or even automatically generated. Such counterexamples are obtained by constructing the refined SID w.r.t. the complement of a given heap automaton. Then an unfolding of the SID that is rejected by the original heap automaton, i.e., a counterexample, can be reconstructed from a (failed) emptiness check. Further applications are examined in the following.

Remark 1. While we focus on the well-established symbolic heap fragment of separation logic, we remark that the general reasoning principle underlying heap automata is also applicable to check robustness properties of richer fragments. For example, permissions [7] are easily integrated within our framework.

4   A Zoo of Robustness Properties

This section demonstrates the wide applicability of heap automata to decide and establish robustness properties of SIDs. In particular, the sets of symbolic heaps informally presented in the introduction can be accepted by heap automata over the set $SH_{FV \leq \alpha}$ of symbolic heaps with at most $\alpha \geq 0$ free variables (cf. Example 2). Furthermore, we analyze the complexity of related decision problems. Towards a formal presentation, some terminology is needed.

Definition 7. *The set of* tight models *of a symbolic heap* $\varphi \in SH^{\Phi}$ *is defined as* $Models(\varphi) \triangleq \{(s, h) \in States \mid dom(s) = \mathbf{x}_0^{\varphi}, s, h \models_{\Phi} \varphi\}$.

We often consider relationships between variables that hold in every tight model of a reduced symbolic heap. Formally, let $\tau \triangleq \exists \mathbf{z}.\Sigma : \Pi \in RSH$. Moreover, let $strip(\tau)$ be defined as τ except that each of its variables is free, i.e., $strip(\tau) \triangleq \Sigma : \Pi$. Then two variables $x, y \in Var(\tau)$ are *definitely (un)equal* in τ, written $x =_\tau y$ $(x \neq_\tau y)$, if $s(x) = s(y)$ $(s(x) \neq s(y))$ holds for every $(s, h) \in Models(strip(\tau))$. Analogously, a variable is *definitely allocated* if it is definitely equal to a variable occurring on the left-hand side of a points-to assertion. Thus the set of definitely allocated variables in τ is given by

$$alloc(\tau) = \{x \in Var(\tau) \mid \forall (s, h) \in Models(strip(\tau)) . s(x) \in dom(h)\}.$$

Finally, a variable x *definitely points-to* variable y in τ, written $x \mapsto_\tau y$, if for every $(s, h) \in Models(strip(\tau))$, we have $s(y) \in h(s(x))$.

Example 7. Recall from Example 1 the symbolic heap τ in the first rule of $\mathtt{tll}\, \mathbf{x}_0$. Then $alloc(\tau) = \{x_1, x_2\}$ and neither $x_1 =_\tau x_3$ nor $x_1 \neq_\tau x_3$ holds. Further,

$x_1 =_\tau x_2$ is true,	$x_1 =_\tau x_3$ is false,	$x_1 \neq_\tau$ **null** is true,
$x_1 \neq_\tau x_3$ is false,	$x_1 \mapsto_\tau x_3$ is true,	$x_3 \mapsto_\tau x_1$ is false.

Remark 2. All definite relationships are decidable in polynomial time. In fact, each of these relationships boils down to first adding inequalities $x \neq$ **null** and $x \neq y$ for every pair x, y of distinct variables occurring on the left-hand side of points-to assertions to the set of pure formulas and then computing its (reflexive), symmetric (and transitive) closure with respect to $\neq$ (and $=$). Furthermore, if the closure contains a contradiction, e.g., **null** $\neq$ **null**, it is set to all pure formulas over the variables of a given reduced symbolic heap. After that, it is straightforward to decide in polynomial time whether variables are definitely allocated, (un)equal or pointing to each other.

4.1   Tracking Equalities and Allocation

Consider the symbolic heap $\varphi \triangleq \exists x, y, z. P_1(x, y) * P_2(y, z) : \{x = z\}$. Clearly, φ is unsatisfiable if $x = y$ holds for every unfolding of $P_1(x, y)$ and $y \neq z$ holds for every unfolding of $P_2(y, z)$. Analogously, φ is unsatisfiable if x is allocated in every unfolding of $P_1(x, y)$ and z is allocated in every unfolding of $P_2(y, z)$, because $x \mapsto \_ * z \mapsto \_$ implies $x \neq z$. This illustrates that robustness properties, such as satisfiability, require detailed knowledge about the relationships between parameters of predicate calls. Consequently, we construct a heap automaton $\mathfrak{A}_{\mathrm{TRACK}}$ that keeps track of this knowledge. More precisely, $\mathfrak{A}_{\mathrm{TRACK}}$ should accept those unfoldings in which it is guaranteed that

- given a set $A \subseteq \mathbf{x}_0$, exactly the variables in A are definitely allocated, and
- exactly the (in)equalities in a given set of pure formulas Π hold.

Towards a formal construction, we formalize the desired set of symbolic heaps.

Definition 8. *Let* $\alpha \in \mathbb{N}_{>0}$ *and* $\mathbf{x}_0$ *be a tuple of variables with* $\|\mathbf{x}_0\| = \alpha$. *Moreover, let* $A \subseteq \mathbf{x}_0$ *and* Π *be a finite set of pure formulas over* $\mathbf{x}_0$. *The tracking property* $\mathrm{TRACK}(\alpha, A, \Pi)$ *is the set*

$$\{\tau(\mathbf{x}_0) \in \mathrm{RSH}_{FV \leq \alpha} \mid \forall i, j \ . \ \mathbf{x}_0[i] \in A \ \textit{iff} \ \mathbf{x}_0[i] \in \mathit{alloc}(\tau)$$
$$\textit{and} \ \mathbf{x}_0[i] \sim \mathbf{x}_0[j] \in \Pi \ \textit{iff} \ \mathbf{x}_0^\tau[i] \sim_\tau \mathbf{x}_0^\tau[j]\}.$$

Intuitively, our heap automaton $\mathfrak{A}_{\mathrm{TRACK}}$ stores in its state space which free variables are definitely equal, unequal and allocated. Its transition relation then enforces that these stored information are correct, i.e., a transition $q \xrightarrow{\varphi}_{\mathfrak{A}_{\mathrm{TRACK}}} p$ is only possible if the information stored in p is consistent with φ and with the information stored in the states q for the predicate calls of φ.

Formally, let $\mathbf{x}_0$ be a tuple of variables with $\|\mathbf{x}_0\| = \alpha$ and $\mathrm{Pure}(\mathbf{x}_0) \triangleq 2^{\{\mathbf{x}_0[i] \sim \mathbf{x}_0[j] \mid 0 \leq i,j \leq \alpha, \sim \in \{=, \neq\}\}}$ be the powerset of all pure formulas over $\mathbf{x}_0$. The information stored by our automaton consists of a set of free variables $B \subseteq \mathbf{x}_0$ and a set of pure formulas $\Lambda \in \mathrm{Pure}(\mathbf{x}_0)$. Now, for some unfolding τ of a symbolic heap φ, assume that B is chosen as the set of all definitely allocated free variables of τ. Moreover, assume Λ is the set of all definite (in)equalities between free variables in τ. We can then construct a reduced symbolic heap $\mathit{kernel}(\varphi, (B, \Lambda))$ from B and Λ that precisely captures these relationships between free variables.

Definition 9. *Let* $\varphi \mathbf{x}_0$ *be a symbolic heap,* $B \subseteq \mathbf{x}_0$ *and* $\Lambda \in \mathrm{Pure}(\mathbf{x}_0)$. *Furthermore, let* $min(B, \Lambda) = \{\mathbf{x}_0^i \in B \mid \neg \exists \mathbf{x}_0^j \in B.j < i \ and \ \mathbf{x}_0^i =_\Lambda \mathbf{x}_0^j\}$ *be the set of minimal (w.r.t. to occurrence in* $\mathbf{x}_0$*) allocated free variables. Then*

$$\mathit{kernel}(\varphi, (B, \Lambda)) \triangleq \bigstar_{\mathbf{x}_0[i] \in min(B, \Lambda)} \mathbf{x}_0^\varphi[i] \mapsto \mathbf{null} : \Lambda,$$

where we write $\bigstar_{s \in S} s \mapsto \mathbf{null}$ *for* $s_1 \mapsto \mathbf{null} * \ldots * s_k \mapsto \mathbf{null}$, $S = \{s_1, \ldots, s_k\}$.

Consequently, the relationships between free variables remain unaffected if a predicate call of φ is replaced by $\mathit{kernel}(\varphi, (B, \Lambda))$ instead of τ. Thus, $\mathfrak{A}_{\mathrm{TRACK}}$ has one state per pair (B, Λ). In the transition relation of $\mathfrak{A}_{\mathrm{TRACK}}$ it suffices to replace each predicate call $P\mathbf{x}_0$ by the corresponding symbolic heap $\mathit{kernel}(P\mathbf{x}_0, (B, \Lambda))$. and check whether the current state is consistent with the resulting symbolic heap. Intuitively, a potentially large unfolding of a symbolic heap φ with m predicate calls is "compressed" into a small one that contains all necessary information about parameters of predicate calls. Here, $\mathbf{q}$ is a sequence of pairs (B, Λ) as explained above. Formally,

Definition 10. $\mathfrak{A}_{\text{TRACK}} = (Q, \text{SH}_{FV \leq \alpha}, \Delta, F)$ *is given by:*

$$Q \triangleq 2^{\mathbf{x}_0} \times \text{Pure}(\mathbf{x}_0), \qquad F \triangleq \{(A, \Pi)\},$$

$$\Delta \; : \; \mathbf{q} \xrightarrow{\varphi}_{\mathfrak{A}_{\text{TRACK}}} (A_0, \Pi_0) \text{ iff } \forall x, y \in \mathbf{x}_0 \; .$$
$$y \in A_0 \leftrightarrow y^\varphi \in alloc(compress(\varphi, \mathbf{q}))$$
$$\text{and } x \sim y \in \Pi_0 \; \leftrightarrow \; x^\varphi \sim_{compress(\varphi, \mathbf{q})} y^\varphi,$$

$$compress(\varphi, \mathbf{q}) \triangleq \varphi \left[P_1 / kernel(P_1 \mathbf{x}_1, \mathbf{q}[1]), \ldots, P_m / kernel(P_m \mathbf{x}_m, \mathbf{q}[m]) \right],$$

where $m = \|\Gamma^\varphi\| = \|\mathbf{q}\|$ *is the number of predicate calls in* φ *and* y^φ *denotes the free variable of* φ *corresponding to* $y \in \mathbf{x}_0$, *i.e., if* $y = \mathbf{x}_0[i]$ *then* $y^\varphi = \mathbf{x}_0^\varphi[i]$.

Since $compress(\tau, \varepsilon) = \tau$ holds for every reduced symbolic heap τ, it is straight-forward to show that $L(\mathfrak{A}_{\text{TRACK}}) = \text{TRACK}(\alpha, A, \Pi)$. Furthermore, $\mathfrak{A}_{\text{TRACK}}$ satisfies the compositionality property [29]. Hence,

Lemma 3. *For all* $\alpha \in \mathbb{N}_{>0}$ *and all sets* $A \subseteq \mathbf{x}_0$, $\Pi \in \text{Pure}(\mathbf{x}_0)$, *there is a heap automaton over* $\text{SH}_{FV < \alpha}$ *accepting* $\text{TRACK}(\alpha, A, \Pi)$.

4.2 Satisfiability

Tracking relationships between free variables of symbolic heaps is a useful aux-iliary construction that serves as a building block in automata for more natural properties. For instance, the heap automaton $\mathfrak{A}_{\text{TRACK}}$ constructed in Definition 10 can be reused to deal with the

Satisfiability Problem (SL-SAT)**:** Given $\Phi \in \text{SID}$, $\varphi \in \text{SH}^\Phi$, decide whether φ is satisfiable, i.e., there exists $(s, h) \in States$ such that $s, h \models_\Phi \varphi$.

Theorem 3. *For each* $\alpha \in \mathbb{N}_{>0}$, *there is a heap automaton over* $\text{SH}_{FV \leq \alpha}$ *accept-ing the set* $\text{SAT}(\alpha) \triangleq \{\tau \in \text{RSH}_{FV \leq \alpha} \mid \tau \text{ is satisfiable}\}$ *of all satisfiable reduced symbolic heaps with at most* α *free variables.*

Proof. A heap automaton accepting $\text{SAT}(\alpha)$ is constructed as in Definition 10 except for the set of final states $F \triangleq \{(A, \Pi) \mid \text{null} \neq \text{null} \notin \Pi\}$ (cf. [29]). $\square$

A heap automaton accepting the complement of $\text{SAT}(\alpha)$ is constructed analo-gously by choosing $F \triangleq \{(A, \Pi) \mid \text{null} \neq \text{null} \in \Pi\}$. Thus, together with Corollary 1, we obtain a decision procedure for the satisfiability problem sim-ilar to the one proposed in [11]. Regarding complexity, the heap automaton $\mathfrak{A}_{\text{SAT}}$ from Definition 10 has $2^{2\alpha^2 + \alpha}$ states. By Remark 2, membership in $\Delta_{\mathfrak{A}_{\text{SAT}}}$ is decidable in polynomial time. Thus, by Corollary 1, our construction yields an exponential-time decision procedure for SL-SAT. If the number of free vari-ables α is bounded, an algorithm in NP is easily obtained by guessing a suitable unfolding tree of height at most $\|Q_{\mathfrak{A}_{\text{SAT}}}\|$ and running $\mathfrak{A}_{\text{SAT}}$ on it to check whether its unfolding is decidable (cf. [29]. This is in line with the results of Brotherston et al. [11], where the satisfiability problem is shown to be EXPTIME–complete in general and NP–complete if the number of free variables is bounded. These complexity bounds even hold for the following special case [13]:

Restricted Satisfiability Problem (SL-RSAT): Given an SID Φ that contains no points-to assertions, and a predicate symbol P, decide whether $P\mathbf{x}$ is satisfiable w.r.t. Φ. The complement of this problem is denoted by $\overline{\text{SL-RSAT}}$.

4.3   Establishment

A symbolic heap φ is *established* if every existentially quantified variable of every unfolding of φ is definitely equal to a free variable or definitely allocated.[3] This property is natural for symbolic heaps that specify the shape of data structures; for example, the SIDs in Example 1 define sets of established symbolic heaps. Further, establishment is often required to ensure decidability of the entailment problem [26,27]. Establishment can also be checked by heap automata.

Theorem 4. *For all $\alpha \in \mathbb{N}_{>0}$, there is a heap automaton over $\mathrm{SH}_{FV \leq \alpha}$ accepting the set of all established reduced symbolic heaps with at most α free variables:*

$$\mathrm{EST}(\alpha) \triangleq \{\tau \in \mathrm{RSH}_{FV \leq \alpha} \mid \forall y \in \mathit{Var}(\tau) \,.\, y \in \mathit{alloc}(\tau) \text{ or } \exists x \in \mathbf{x}_0^\tau \,.\, x =_\tau y\}$$

Proof. The main idea in the construction of a heap automaton $\mathfrak{A}_{\mathrm{EST}}$ for $\mathrm{EST}(\alpha)$ is to verify that every variable is definitely allocated or equal to a free variable while running $\mathfrak{A}_{\mathrm{TRACK}}$ (see Definition 10) in parallel to keep track of the relationships between free variables. An additional flag $q \in \{0,1\}$ is attached to each state of $\mathfrak{A}_{\mathrm{TRACK}}$ to store whether the establishment condition is already violated ($q = 0$) or holds so far ($q = 1$). Formally, $\mathfrak{A}_{\mathrm{EST}} = (Q, \mathrm{SH}_{FV \leq \alpha}, \Delta, F)$, where

$$Q \triangleq Q_{\mathfrak{A}_{\mathrm{TRACK}}} \times \{0,1\}, \qquad F \triangleq Q_{\mathfrak{A}_{\mathrm{TRACK}}} \times \{1\},$$

$$\Delta \;:\; (p_1, q_1) \ldots (p_m, q_m) \xrightarrow{\varphi}_{\mathfrak{A}_{\mathrm{EST}}} (p_0, q_0)$$

iff $p_1 \ldots p_m \xrightarrow{\varphi}_{\mathfrak{A}_{\mathrm{TRACK}}} p_0$ and $q_0 = \min\{q_1, \ldots, q_m, \mathit{check}(\varphi, p_1 \ldots p_m)\}$.

Here, $\mathit{check} : \mathrm{SH}_{FV \leq \alpha} \times Q_{\mathfrak{A}_{\mathrm{TRACK}}}^* \to \{0,1\}$ is a predicate given by

$$\mathit{check}(\varphi, \mathbf{p}) \triangleq \begin{cases} 1, & \text{if } \forall y \in \mathit{Var}(\varphi) \,.\, y \in \mathit{alloc}(\mathit{compress}(\varphi, \mathbf{p})) \\ & \quad \text{or } \exists x \in \mathbf{x}_0^\varphi \,.\, x =_{\mathit{compress}(\varphi, \mathbf{p})} y \\ 0, & \text{otherwise,} \end{cases}$$

where $\mathit{compress}(\varphi, \mathbf{p})$ is the reduced symbolic heap obtained from the tracking property as in Definition 10. Moreover, unlike in the construction of $\mathfrak{A}_{\mathrm{TRACK}}$, we are not interested in a specific set of relationships between the pure formulas, so any state of $\mathfrak{A}_{\mathrm{TRACK}}$ is chosen as a final state provided that predicate *check* could be evaluated to 1. See [29] for a correctness proof.   □

Again, it suffices to swap the final- and non-final states of $\mathfrak{A}_{\mathrm{EST}}$ to obtain a heap automaton $\mathfrak{A}_{\overline{\mathrm{EST}}}$ accepting the complement of $\mathrm{EST}(\alpha)$. Thus, by Corollary 1 and Remark 2, we obtain an ExpTime decision procedure for the

Establishment Problem (SL-EST): Given an SID Φ and $\varphi \in \mathrm{SH}^\Phi$, decide whether every $\tau \in \mathbb{U}_\Phi(\varphi)$ is established.

---

[3] Sometimes this property is also defined by requiring that each existentially quantified variable is "eventually allocated" [26].

Lemma 4. $\overline{\text{SL-RSAT}}$ *is polynomial-time reducible to* SL-EST. *Hence, the establishment problem* SL-EST *is* ExpTime*–hard in general and* coNP*–hard if the maximal number of free variables is bounded.*

Proof. Let (Φ, P) be an instance of $\overline{\text{SL-RSAT}}$. Moreover, let $\varphi \mathbf{x_0} \triangleq \exists \mathbf{z} y \,.\, Pz :$ $\{\mathbf{x_0}[1] = \mathbf{null}, y \neq \mathbf{null}\}$. As y is neither allocated nor occurs in Pz, φ is established iff $\mathbf{x_0}[1] = y$ iff $\mathbf{null} \neq \mathbf{null}$ iff Px is unsatisfiable. Hence, $(\Phi, \varphi) \in$ SL-EST iff $(\Phi, P) \in \overline{\text{SL-RSAT}}$. A full proof is found in [29]. □

Lemma 5. SL-EST *is in* coNP *for a bounded number of free variables α.*

Proof. Let (Φ, φ) be an instance of SL-EST, $N = \|\Phi\| + \|\varphi\|$, and $M \leq N$ be the maximal number of predicate calls occurring in φ and any rule of Φ. Moreover, let $\mathfrak{A}_{\overline{\text{EST}}}$ be a heap automaton accepting $\overline{\text{EST}}(\alpha)$—the complement of $\text{EST}(\alpha)$ (cf. Theorem 4). Since α is bounded by a constant, so is the number of states of $\mathfrak{A}_{\overline{\text{EST}}}$, namely $\|Q_{\mathfrak{A}_{\overline{\text{EST}}}}\| \leq k = 2^{2\alpha^2 + \alpha + 1}$. Now, let $\mathbb{T}_\Phi(\varphi)^{\leq k}$ denote the set of all unfolding trees $t \in \mathbb{T}_\Phi(\varphi)$ of height at most k. Clearly, each of these trees is of size $\|t\| \leq M^k \leq N^k$, i.e., polynomial in N. Moreover, let $\omega : \text{dom}(t) \to Q_{\mathfrak{A}_{\overline{\text{EST}}}}$ be a function mapping each node of t to a state of $\mathfrak{A}_{\overline{\text{EST}}}$. Again, ω is of size polynomial in N; as such $\|\omega\| \leq k \cdot N^k$. Let Ω_t denote the set of all of these functions ω for a given unfolding tree t with $\omega(\varepsilon) \in F_{\mathfrak{A}_{\overline{\text{EST}}}}$. Given an unfolding tree $t \in \mathbb{T}_\Phi(\varphi)^{\leq k}$ and $\omega \in \Omega_t$, we can easily decide whether $\varepsilon \xrightarrow{\ \llbracket t \rrbracket\ }_{\mathfrak{A}_{\overline{\text{EST}}}} \omega(\varepsilon)$ holds: For each $u, u1, \ldots, un \in \text{dom}(t)$, $u(n+1) \notin \text{dom}(t)$, $n \geq 0$, it suffices to check whether $\omega(u1) \ldots \omega(un) \xrightarrow{\ t(u)\ }_{\mathfrak{A}_{\overline{\text{EST}}}} \omega(u)$. Since, by Remark 2, each of these checks can be performed in time polynomial in N the whole procedure is feasible in polynomial time. We now show that $(\Phi, \varphi) \in$ SL-EST if and only if

$$\forall t \in \mathbb{T}_\Phi(\varphi)^{\leq k} \,.\, \forall \omega \in \Omega_t \,.\, \text{not } \varepsilon \xrightarrow{\ \llbracket t \rrbracket\ }_{\mathfrak{A}_{\overline{\text{EST}}}} \omega(\varepsilon).$$

Since each $t \in \mathbb{T}_\Phi(\varphi)$ and each $\omega \in \Omega_t$ is of size polynomial in N, this is equivalent to SL-EST being in coNP. To complete the proof, note that $\mathbb{U}_\Phi(\varphi) \subseteq \text{EST}(\alpha)$ holds iff $\llbracket t \rrbracket \notin \overline{\text{EST}}(\alpha)$ for each $t \in \mathbb{T}_\Phi(\varphi)$. Furthermore, by a standard pumping argument, it suffices to consider trees in $\mathbb{T}_\Phi(\varphi)^{\leq k}$: If there exists a taller tree t with $\llbracket t \rrbracket \in \overline{\text{EST}}(\alpha)$ then there is some path of length greater k in t on which two nodes are assigned the same state by a function $\omega \in \Omega_t$ proving membership of t in $\overline{\text{EST}}(\alpha)$. This path can be shortened to obtain a tree of smaller height. □

Putting upper and lower bounds together, we conclude:

Theorem 5. SL-EST *is* ExpTime*–complete in general and* coNP*–complete if the number of free variables α is bounded.*

4.4   Reachability

Another family of robustness properties is based on reachability questions, e.g., "is every location of every model of a symbolic heap reachable from the location of a program variable?" or "is every model of a symbolic heap acyclic?". For established SIDs, heap automata accepting these properties are an extension of the tracking automaton introduced in Definition 10.

More precisely, a variable y is *definitely reachable* from x in $\tau \in \text{RSH}$, written $x \leadsto_\tau y$, if and only if $x \mapsto_\tau y$ or there exists a $z \in Var(\tau)$ such that $x \mapsto_\tau z$ and $z \leadsto_\tau y$.[4] Note that we define reachability to be transitive, but not reflexive. As for the other definite relationships between variables, definite reachability is computable in polynomial time for reduced symbolic heaps, e.g., by performing a depth-first search on the definite points-to relation $\mapsto_\tau$. Note that our notion of reachability does not take variables into account that are only reachable from one another in *some* models of a reduced symbolic heap. For example, consider the symbolic heap $\tau = x \mapsto y * z \mapsto \textbf{null}$. Then $x \leadsto_\tau z$ does *not* hold, but there exists a model (s, h) with $s(z) = s(y) \in h(s(x))$. Thus, reachability introduced by unallocated variables is not detected. However, the existence (or absence) of such variables can be checked first due to Theorem 4.

Theorem 6. *Let* $\alpha \in \mathbb{N}_{>0}$ *and* $R \subseteq \mathbf{x}_0 \times \mathbf{x}_0$ *be a binary relation over the variables* $\mathbf{x}_0$ *with* $\|\mathbf{x}_0\| = \alpha$. *Then the* reachability property $\text{REACH}(\alpha, R)$, *given by the set* $\{\tau \in \text{RSH}_{FV \leq \alpha} \mid \forall i, j \ . \ (\mathbf{x}_0[i], \mathbf{x}_0[j]) \in R \text{ iff } \mathbf{x}_0^\tau[i] \leadsto_\tau \mathbf{x}_0^\tau[j]\}$, *can be accepted by a heap automaton over* $\text{SH}_{FV \leq \alpha}$.

Proof (sketch). A heap automaton $\mathfrak{A}_{\text{REACH}}$ accepting $\text{REACH}(\alpha, R)$ is constructed similarly to the heap automaton $\mathfrak{A}_{\text{TRACK}}$ introduced in Definition 10. The main difference is that $\mathfrak{A}_{\text{REACH}}$ additionally stores a binary relation $S \subseteq \mathbf{x}_0 \times \mathbf{x}_0$ in its state space to remember which free variables are reachable from one another. Correspondingly, we adapt Definition 9 as follows:

$$kernel(\varphi, (B, \Lambda, S)) \triangleq \exists z \ . \ \bigstar_{\min(B, \Lambda)} \mathbf{x}_0^\varphi[i] \mapsto (\mathbf{v}_i) \ : \ \Lambda,$$

where z is a fresh variable and $\mathbf{v}_i[j] \triangleq \mathbf{x}_0^\varphi[j]$ if $(i, j) \in S$ and $\mathbf{v}_i[j] \triangleq z$, otherwise. The other parameters φ, B, Λ are the same as in Definition 10. Note that the additional variable z is needed to deal with allocated free variables that cannot reach any other free variable, including $\textbf{null}$. Moreover, the set of final states is $F_{\mathfrak{A}_{\text{REACH}}} = Q_{\mathfrak{A}_{\text{TRACK}}} \times \{R\}$. Correctness of this encoding is verified in the transition relation. Hence, the transition relation of $\mathfrak{A}_{\text{REACH}}$ extends the transition relation of $\mathfrak{A}_{\text{TRACK}}$ by the requirement $(x, y) \in S$ iff $x^\varphi \leadsto_{compress(\varphi, \mathbf{p})} y^\varphi$ for every pair of free variables $x, y \in \mathbf{x}_0$. Here, $compress(\varphi, \mathbf{p})$ is defined as in Definition 10 except that the new encoding $kernel(P_i \mathbf{x}_i, \mathbf{q}[i])$ from above is used. Since $compress(\tau, \varepsilon) = \tau$ holds for every reduced symbolic heap τ, it is straightforward to verify that $L(\mathfrak{A}_{\text{REACH}}) = \text{REACH}(\alpha)$. Further details are found in [29].   □

Furthermore, we consider the related

Reachability Problem (SL-REACH): Given an SID Φ, $\varphi \in \text{SH}^\Phi$ with $\alpha = \|\mathbf{x}_0^\varphi\|$ and variables $x, y \in \mathbf{x}_0^\varphi$, decide whether $x \leadsto_\tau y$ holds for all $\tau \in \mathbb{U}_\Phi(\varphi)$.

Theorem 7. *The decision problem* SL-REACH *is* ExpTime–*complete in general and* coNP–*complete if the number of free variables is bounded.*

---

[4] The definite points-to relation $\mapsto_\tau$ was defined at the beginning of Sect. 4.

Proof. Membership in EXPTIME follows from our upper bound derived for Algorithm 1, the size of the state space of $\mathfrak{A}_{\text{REACH}}$, which is exponential in α, and Remark 2. If α is bounded, membership in CONP is shown analogously to Lemma 5. Lower bounds are shown by reducing $\overline{\text{SL-RSAT}}$ to SL-REACH. Formally, let (Φ, P) be an instance of $\overline{\text{SL-RSAT}}$. Moreover, let $\varphi \mathbf{x}_0 \triangleq \exists \mathbf{z} . \mathbf{x}_0[1] \mapsto \mathbf{null} * Pz : \{\mathbf{x}_0[2] \neq \mathbf{null}\}$. As $\mathbf{x}_0[2]$ is neither allocated nor **null**, $\mathbf{x}_0[2]$ is *not* definitely reachable from $\mathbf{x}_0[1]$ in *any* model of φ. Hence $(\Phi, \varphi, \mathbf{x}_0[1], \mathbf{x}_0[2]) \in$ SL-REACH iff P is unsatisfiable. A detailed proof is found in [29]. □

4.5 Garbage-Freedom

Like the tracking automaton $\mathfrak{A}_{\text{TRACK}}$, the automaton $\mathfrak{A}_{\text{REACH}}$ is a useful ingredient in the construction of more complex heap automata.

For instance, such an automaton can easily be modified to check whether a symbolic heap is *garbage-free*, i.e., whether every existentially quantified variable in every unfolding is reachable from some program variable.[5]

Garbage-freedom is a natural requirement if SIDs represent data structure specifications. For example, the SIDs in Example 1 are garbage-free. Furthermore, this property is needed by the approach of Habermehl et al. [24].

Lemma 6. *For each* $\alpha \in \mathbb{N}_{>0}$, *the set* GFREE$(\alpha)$, *given by*

$$\{\tau \in \text{RSH}_{FV \leq \alpha} \mid \forall y \in Var(\tau) . \exists x \in \mathbf{x}_0^\tau . x =_\tau y \text{ or } x \rightsquigarrow_\tau y\},$$

of garbage-free symbolic heaps can be accepted by a heap automaton over $\text{SH}_{FV \leq \alpha}$.

Proof (sketch). A heap automaton $\mathfrak{A}_{\text{GFREE}}$ accepting GFREE(α) is constructed similarly to the heap automaton $\mathfrak{A}_{\text{EST}}$ introduced in the proof of Theorem 4. The main difference is that heap automaton $\mathfrak{A}_{\text{REACH}}$ is used instead of $\mathfrak{A}_{\text{TRACK}}$. Furthermore, the predicate $check : \text{SH}_{FV \leq \alpha} \times Q^*_{\mathfrak{A}_{\text{REACH}}} \to \{0, 1\}$ is redefined to verify that every variable of a symbolic heap φ is established in $compress(\varphi, \mathbf{p})$, where $compress(\varphi, \mathbf{p})$ is the same as in the construction of $\mathfrak{A}_{\text{REACH}}$ (see Theorem 6):

$$check(\varphi, \mathbf{p}) \triangleq \begin{cases} 1, & \text{if } \forall y \in Var(\varphi) . \exists x \in \mathbf{x}_0^\varphi . \\ & \qquad x =_{compress(\varphi, \mathbf{p})} y \text{ or } x \rightsquigarrow_{compress(\varphi, \mathbf{p})} y \\ 0, & \text{otherwise,} \end{cases}$$

Since $compress(\tau, \varepsilon) = \tau$ holds for every reduced symbolic heap τ, it is straightforward that $L(\mathfrak{A}_{\text{GFREE}}) = $ GFREE(α). A proof is found in [29]. □

To guarantee that symbolic heaps are garbage-free, we solve the

Garbage-Freedom Problem (SL-GF): Given an SID Φ and $\varphi \in \text{SH}^\Phi$, decide whether every $\tau \in \mathbb{U}_\Phi(\varphi)$ is garbage-free, i.e., $\tau \in$ GFREE(α) for some $\alpha \in \mathbb{N}$.

Theorem 8. SL-GF *is* EXPTIME*-complete in general and* CONP*-complete if the number of free variables* α *is bounded.*

---

[5] Note that a variable may be reachable from different program variables in different unfoldings as garbage-freedom is formally defined as a set of *reduced* symbolic heaps in which no form of disjunction exists (cf. Lemma 6).

4.6 Acyclicity

Automatic termination proofs of programs frequently rely on the acyclicity of employed data structures, i.e., they assume that no variable is reachable from itself (cf. [39]). Hence, we are interested in verifying that an SID is acyclic.

Lemma 7. *For each $\alpha \in \mathbb{N}_{>0}$, the set of all weakly acyclic symbolic heaps*

$$\texttt{ACYCLIC}(\alpha) \triangleq \{\tau \in \mathrm{RSH}_{FV \leq \alpha} \mid \textbf{null} \neq_\tau \textbf{null} \ or \ \forall x \in Var(\tau) \ . \ not \ x \leadsto_\tau x\}$$

can be accepted by a heap automaton over $\mathrm{SH}_{FV \leq \alpha}$.

Here, the condition $\textbf{null} \neq_\tau \textbf{null}$ ensures that an unsatisfiable reduced symbolic heap is considered weakly acyclic. Further, note that our notion of acyclicity is weak in the sense that dangling pointers may introduce cyclic models that are not considered. For example, $\exists z.x \mapsto z$ is weakly acyclic, but contains cyclic models if x and z are aliases. However, weak acyclicity coincides with the absence of cyclic models for established SIDs—a property considered in Sect. 4.3.

Proof (sketch). A heap automaton $\mathfrak{A}_{\text{ACYCLIC}}$ for the set of all weakly acyclic reduced symbolic heaps is constructed analogously to the heap automaton $\mathfrak{A}_{\text{GFREE}}$ in the proof of Lemma 6. The main difference is the predicate $check \ : \ \mathrm{SH}_{FV \leq \alpha} \times Q^*_{\mathfrak{A}_{\text{REACH}}} \to \{0,1\}$, which now checks whether a symbolic heap is weakly acyclic:

$$check(\varphi, \mathbf{p}) \triangleq \begin{cases} 1, & \text{if } \forall y \in Var(\varphi) \ . \ \text{not } x \leadsto_{compress(\varphi, \mathbf{p})} x \\ 0, & \text{otherwise.} \end{cases}$$

Moreover, the set of final states $F_{\mathfrak{A}_{\text{ACYCLIC}}}$ is chosen such that accepted symbolic heaps are unsatisfiable or $check(\varphi, \mathbf{p}) = 1$. See [29] for details. $\qquad\square$

For example, the symbolic heap $\texttt{sll} \, \mathbf{x}_0$ is weakly acyclic, but $\texttt{dll} \, \mathbf{x}_0$ (cf. Example 1) is not. In general, we are interested in the

Acyclicity Problem (SL-AC): Given an SID Φ and $\varphi \in \mathrm{SH}^\Phi$, decide whether every $\tau \in \mathbb{U}_\Phi(\varphi)$ is weakly acyclic, i.e., $\tau \in \texttt{ACYCLIC}(\alpha)$ for some $\alpha \in \mathbb{N}$.

Theorem 9. *SL-AC is* ExpTime*-complete in general and* coNP*-complete if the number of free variables α is bounded.*

Proof. Similar to the proof of Theorem 5. For lower bounds, we show that $\overline{\text{SL-RSAT}}$ is reducible to SL-AC. Let (Φ, P) be an instance of $\overline{\text{SL-RSAT}}$. Moreover, let $\varphi\mathbf{x}_0 = \exists \mathbf{z}.\mathbf{x}_0[1] \mapsto \mathbf{x}_0[1] * P\mathbf{z}$. Since $\mathbf{x}_0[1]$ is definitely reachable from itself, $\varphi\mathbf{x}_0$ is weakly acyclic iff $P\mathbf{x}_0$ is unsatisfiable. Thus, $(\Phi, \varphi) \in$ SL-AC iff $(\Phi, P) \in \overline{\text{SL-RSAT}}$. See [29] for details. $\qquad\square$

5 Implementation

We developed a prototype of our framework—called HARRSH[6]—that implements Algorithm 1 as well as all heap automata constructed in the previous sections.

---

[6] Heap Automata for Reasoning about Robustness of Symbolic Heaps.

In addition, our tool supports automatic refinement of SIDs. Algorithms for counterexample generation and automatic combination of decision procedures can be extracted from the (constructive) proof of Theorem 2, but have not yet been implemented. The code, the tool and our experiments are available online.[7]

For our experimental results, we first considered common SIDs from the literature, such as singly- and doubly-linked lists, trees, trees with linked-leaves etc. For each of these SIDs, we checked all robustness properties presented throughout this paper, i.e., the existence of points-to assertions (Example 4), the tracking property TRACK(B, Λ) (Sect. 4.1), satisfiability (Sect. 4.2), establishment (Sect. 4.3), the reachability property REACH(α, R) (Sect. 4.4), garbage-freedom (Sect. 4.5), and weak acyclicity (Sect. 4.6). All in all, our implementation of Algorithm 1 takes 300ms to successfully check these properties on all 45 problem instances. Since the SIDs under consideration are typically carefully handcrafted to be robust, the low runtime is to be expected. Moreover, we ran heap automata on benchmarks of the tool CYCLIST [11]. In particular, our results for the satisfiability problem—the only robustness property checked by both tools—were within the same order of magnitude.

Further details are found in [29].

6   Entailment Checking with Heap Automata

So far, we have constructed heap automata for reasoning about robustness properties, such as satisfiability, establishment and acyclicity. This section demonstrates that our approach can also be applied to discharge *entailments* for certain fragments of separation logic. Formally, we are concerned with the

Entailment Problem (SL-ENTAIL$_C^\Phi$): Given symbolic heaps $\varphi, \psi \in \mathrm{SH}_C^\Phi$, decide whether $\varphi \models_\Phi \psi$ holds, i.e., $\forall (s, h) \in States. \ s, h \models_\Phi \varphi$ implies $s, h \models_\Phi \psi$.

Note that the symbolic heap fragment of separation logic is *not* closed under conjunction and negation. Thus, a decision procedure for satisfiability (cf. Theorem 3) does *not* yield a decision procedure for the entailment problem. It is, however, essential to have a decision procedure for entailment, because this problem underlies the important rule of consequence in Hoare logic [25]. In the words of Brotherston et al. [10], "effective procedures for establishing entailments are at the foundation of automatic verification based on separation logic".

We show how our approach to decide robustness properties, is applicable to discharge entailments for certain fragments of symbolic heaps. This results in an algorithm deciding entailments between so-called *determined symbolic heaps* for SIDs whose predicates can be characterized by heap automata.

Definition 11. *A reduced symbolic heap τ is* determined *if all tight models of τ are isomorphic.*[8] *If τ is also satisfiable then we call τ* well-determined.

---

[7] https://bitbucket.org/jkatelaan/harrsh/.

[8] Two states $(s_1, h_1), (s_2, h_2)$ are *isomorphic* iff $\mathrm{dom}(s_1) = \mathrm{dom}(s_2)$ and there exists a bijective function $g : \mathrm{dom}(h_1) \to \mathrm{dom}(h_2)$ such that for all $x \in \mathrm{dom}(s_1)$ and all $\ell \in \mathrm{dom}(h_1)$, we have $g(s_1(x)) = s_2(x)$ and $g(h_1(\ell)) = h_2(g(\ell))$, where g is lifted to tuples by componentwise application.

Moreover, for some SID Φ, a symbolic heap $\varphi \in \mathrm{SH}^\Phi$ is (well-)determined if all of its unfoldings $\tau \in \mathbb{U}_\Phi(\varphi)$ are (well-)determined. Consequently, an SID Φ is (well-)determined if $P\mathbf{x}$ is (well-)determined for each predicate symbol P in Φ.

We present two sufficient conditions for determinedness of symbolic heaps. First, a reduced symbolic heap τ is determined if all equalities and inequalities between variables are explicit, i.e., $\forall x, y \in Var(\tau) . x = y \in \Pi^\tau$ or $x \neq y \in \Pi^\tau$ [29]. Furthermore, a reduced symbolic heap τ is determined if every variable is definitely allocated or definitely equal to **null**, i.e., $\forall x \in Var(\tau) . x \in alloc(\tau)$ or $x =_\tau$ **null**. These two notions can also be combined: A symbolic heap is determined if every variable x is definitely allocated or definitely equal to **null** or there is an explicit pure formula $x \sim y$ between x and each other variable y.

Example 8. By the previous remark, the SID generating acyclic singly-linked lists from Sect. 1 is well-determined. Furthermore, although the predicate $\mathtt{dll}\,\mathbf{x}_0$ from Example 1 is not determined, the following symbolic heap is well-determined: $\mathbf{x}_0[4] \mapsto$ **null** $* \mathtt{dll}\,\mathbf{x}_0 : \{\mathbf{x}_0[1] \neq \mathbf{x}_0[3]\}$.

6.1   Entailment Between Predicate Calls

We start by considering entailments between predicate calls of well-determined SIDs. By definition, an entailment $\varphi \models_\Phi \psi$ holds if for every stack–heap pair (s, h) that satisfies an unfolding of φ, there exists an unfolding of ψ that is satisfied by (s, h) as well. Our first observation is that, for well-determined unfoldings, two quantifiers can be switched: It suffices for each unfolding σ of φ to find *one* unfolding τ of ψ such that every model of σ is also a model of τ.

Lemma 8. *Let $\Phi \in$ SID and P_1, P_2 be predicate symbols with $ar(P_1) = ar(P_2)$. Moreover, let $\mathbb{U}_\Phi(P_1\mathbf{x})$ be well-determined. Then*

$$P_1\mathbf{x} \models_\Phi P_2\mathbf{x} \;\; iff \;\; \forall \sigma \in \mathbb{U}_\Phi(P_1\mathbf{x}) . \exists \tau \in \mathbb{U}_\Phi(P_2\mathbf{x}) . \sigma \models_\emptyset \tau.$$

Note that, even if only well-determined predicate calls are taken into account, it is undecidable in general whether an entailment $P_1\mathbf{x}_0 \models_\Phi P_2\mathbf{x}_0$ holds [1, Theorem 3]. To obtain decidability, we additionally require the set of reduced symbolic heaps entailing a given predicate call to be accepted by a heap automaton.

Definition 12. *Let $\Phi \in$ SID$_\mathcal{C}$ and $\varphi \in \mathrm{SH}_\mathcal{C}^\Phi$. Then*

$$H_{\varphi,\Phi}^\mathcal{C} \triangleq \{\sigma \in \mathrm{RSH}_\mathcal{C} \mid \|\mathbf{x}_0^\sigma\| = \|\mathbf{x}_0^\varphi\| \text{ and } \exists \tau \in \mathbb{U}_\Phi(\varphi) . \sigma \models_\emptyset \tau\}$$

is the set of all reduced symbolic heaps in $\mathrm{SH}_\mathcal{C}$ over the same free variables as φ that entail an unfolding of φ.

Example 9. Let $\varphi(\mathbf{x}_0) = \mathtt{tll}\,\mathbf{x}_0 : \{\mathbf{x}_0[1] \neq \mathbf{x}_0[2]\}$, where $\mathtt{tll}$ is a predicate of SID Φ introduced in Example 1. Then $H_{\varphi,\Phi}^{\mathrm{FV}^{\leq 3}}$ consists of all reduced symbolic heaps with three free variables representing non-empty trees with linked leaves. In particular, note that these symbolic heaps do not have to be derived using the SID Φ. For instance, they might contain additional pure formulas.

In particular, $H^{\mathcal{C}}_{P\mathbf{x},\Phi}$ can be accepted by a heap automaton for common predicates specifying data structures such as lists, trees, and trees with linked leaves. We are now in a position to decide entailments between predicate calls.

Lemma 9. *Let $\Phi \in \mathrm{SID}_{\mathcal{C}}$ and $P_1, P_2 \in \mathrm{Pred}(\Phi)$ be predicate symbols having the same arity. Moreover, let $\mathbb{U}_{\Phi}(P_1\mathbf{x})$ be well-determined and $H^{\mathcal{C}}_{P_2\mathbf{x},\Phi}$ be accepted by a heap automaton over $\mathrm{SH}_{\mathcal{C}}$. Then the entailment $P_1\mathbf{x} \models_{\Phi} P_2\mathbf{x}$ is decidable.*

Proof. Let $\mathfrak{A}_{P_2\mathbf{x}}$ be a heap automaton over $\mathrm{SH}_{\mathcal{C}}$ accepting $H^{\mathcal{C}}_{P_2\mathbf{x},\Phi}$. Then

$$\begin{aligned}
&P_1\mathbf{x} \models_{\Phi} P_2\mathbf{x} \\
\Leftrightarrow\ &\forall \sigma \in \mathbb{U}_{\Phi}(P_1\mathbf{x}) \,.\, \exists \tau \in \mathbb{U}_{\Phi}(P_2\mathbf{x}).\sigma \models_{\emptyset} \tau && \text{(Lemma 8)} \\
\Leftrightarrow\ &\forall \sigma \in \mathbb{U}_{\Phi}(P_1\mathbf{x}).\sigma \in H^{\mathcal{C}}_{P_2\mathbf{x},\Phi} && \text{(Definition 12)} \\
\Leftrightarrow\ &\mathbb{U}_{\Phi}(P_1\mathbf{x}) \subseteq L(\mathfrak{A}_{P_2\mathbf{x}}). && (L(\mathfrak{A}_{P_2\mathbf{x}}) = H^{\mathcal{C}}_{P_2\mathbf{x},\Phi})
\end{aligned}$$

where the last inclusion is decidable by Corollary 2. □

6.2   Entailment Between Symbolic Heaps

Our next step is to generalize Lemma 9 to arbitrary determined symbolic heaps φ instead of single predicate calls. This requires the construction of heap automata $\mathfrak{A}_{\varphi}$ accepting $H^{\mathcal{C}}_{\varphi,\Phi}$. W.l.o.g. we assume SIDs and symbolic heaps to be *well-determined* instead of determined only. Otherwise, we apply Theorem 1 with the heap automaton $\mathfrak{A}_{\mathsf{SAT}}$ (cf. Theorem 3) to obtain a *well*-determined SID. Thus, we restrict our attention to the following set.

Definition 13. *The set $\mathrm{SH}_{\langle \alpha \rangle}$ is given by $\langle \alpha \rangle : \mathrm{SH} \to \{0,1\}$, where $\langle \alpha \rangle(\varphi) = 1$ iff φ is well-determined and every predicate call of φ has $\leq \alpha \in \mathbb{N}$ parameters.*

Clearly, $\langle \alpha \rangle$ is decidable, because satisfiability is decidable (cf. Theorem 3) and verifying that a symbolic heap has at most α parameters amounts to a simple syntactic check. Note that, although the number of parameters in predicate calls is bounded by α, the number of free variables of a symbolic heap $\varphi \in \mathrm{SH}_{\langle \alpha \rangle}$ is not. We then construct heap automata for well-determined symbolic heaps.

Theorem 10 [29]. *Let $\alpha \in \mathbb{N}$ and $\Phi \in \mathrm{SID}_{FV \leq \alpha}$ be established. Moreover, for each predicate symbol $P \in \mathrm{Pred}(\Phi)$, let there be a heap automaton over $\mathrm{SH}_{\langle \alpha \rangle}$ accepting $H^{\langle \alpha \rangle}_{P\mathbf{x},\Phi}$. Then, for every well-determined symbolic heap $\varphi \in \mathrm{SH}^{\Phi}$, there is a heap automaton over $\mathrm{SH}_{\langle \alpha \rangle}$ accepting $H^{\langle \alpha \rangle}_{\varphi,\Phi}$.*

Remark 3. Brotherston et al. [13] studied the *model-checking problem* for symbolic heaps, i.e., the question whether $s, h \models_{\Phi} \varphi$ holds for a given stack–heap pair (s, h), an SID Φ, and a symbolic heap $\varphi \in \mathrm{SH}_{\Phi}$. They showed that this problem is ExpTime–complete in general and NP–complete if the number of free variables is bounded. We obtain these results for *determined* symbolic heaps in a natural way: Observe that every stack–heap pair (s, h) is characterized by an established, well-determined, reduced symbolic heap, say τ, that has exactly (s, h) as

---

Input : established SID Φ, $\varphi, \psi \in \mathrm{SH}^{\Phi}$ determined,
                  heap automaton $\mathfrak{A}_{P_i}$ for each $P_i \in \mathrm{Pred}(\Phi)$
Output: yes iff $\varphi \models_{\Phi} \psi$ holds

$\Omega \;\leftarrow\; \{P\mathbf{x}_0^{\varphi} \Leftarrow \varphi\} \cup \Phi$;   // P **fresh predicate symbol**
$\Psi \;\leftarrow\; \texttt{removeUnsat}(\Omega)$;   // **Theorem 3**
$\mathfrak{A}_{\psi} \;\leftarrow\; \texttt{automaton}(\psi, \mathfrak{A}_{P_1}, \mathfrak{A}_{P_2}, \ldots)$;   // **Theorem 10**
$\overline{\mathfrak{A}_{\psi}} \;\leftarrow\; \texttt{complement}(\mathfrak{A}_{\psi})$;   // **Lemma 2**
return *yes iff* $\mathbb{U}_{\Psi}(P\mathbf{x}) \cap L(\overline{\mathfrak{A}_{\psi}}) = \emptyset$;   // **Algorithm 1**

Algorithm 2. Decision procedure for $\varphi \models_{\Phi} \psi$.

a tight model up to isomorphism. Then Theorem 10 yields a heap automaton $\mathfrak{A}_{\tau}$ accepting $H_{\tau,\Phi}^{\langle \alpha \rangle}$, where α is the maximal arity of any predicate in Φ. Thus, $s, h \models_{\Phi} \varphi$ iff $L(\mathfrak{A}_{\tau}) \cap \mathbb{U}_{\Phi}(\varphi) \neq \emptyset$, which is decidable by Corollary 1. Further, note that the general model-checking problem is within the scope of heap automata. A suitable state space is the set of all subformulas of the symbolic heap τ.

Coming back to the entailment problem, it remains to put our results together. Algorithm 2 depicts a decision procedure for the entailment problem that, given an entailment $\varphi \models_{\Phi} \psi$, first removes all unsatisfiable unfoldings of φ, i.e. φ becomes well-determined. After that, our previous reasoning techniques for heap automata and SIDs from Sect. 3 are applied to decide whether $\varphi \models_{\Phi} \psi$ holds.

Theorem 11. *Let $\alpha \in \mathbb{N}$ and $\Phi \in \mathrm{SID}_{FV \leq \alpha}$ be established. Moreover, for every $P \in \mathrm{Pred}(\Phi)$, let $H_{P\mathbf{x},\Phi}^{\langle \alpha \rangle}$ be accepted by a heap automaton over $\mathrm{SH}_{\langle \alpha \rangle}$. Then $\varphi \models_{\Phi} \psi$ is decidable for determined $\varphi, \psi \in \mathrm{SH}^{\Phi}$ with $\mathbf{x}_0^{\varphi} = \mathbf{x}_0^{\psi}$.*

Proof. We define a new SID $\Omega \triangleq \Phi \cup \{P\mathbf{x} \Leftarrow \varphi\}$, where P is a fresh predicate symbol of arity $\|\mathbf{x}_0^{\varphi}\|$. Clearly, $\varphi \models_{\Phi} \psi$ iff $P\mathbf{x} \models_{\Omega} \psi$. Since φ and Φ are established, so is Ω. Then applying Theorem 1 to Ω and $\mathfrak{A}_{\mathsf{SAT}}$ (cf. Theorem 3), we obtain a well-determined SID $\Psi \in \mathrm{SID}_{\langle \alpha \rangle}$ where none of the remaining unfoldings of Ω is changed, i.e., for each $P \in \mathrm{Pred}(\Omega)$, we have $\mathbb{U}_{\Psi}(P\mathbf{x}) \subseteq \mathbb{U}_{\Omega}(P\mathbf{x})$. By Theorem 10, the set $H_{\psi,\Phi}^{\langle \alpha \rangle} = H_{\psi,\Psi}^{\langle \alpha \rangle}$ can be accepted by a heap automaton over $\mathrm{SH}_{\langle \alpha \rangle}$. Then, analogously to the proof of Lemma 9, $\varphi \models_{\Phi} \psi$ iff $P\mathbf{x} \models_{\Psi} \psi$ iff $\mathbb{U}_{\Psi}(P\mathbf{x}) \subseteq H_{\psi,\Psi}^{\langle \alpha \rangle}$, where the last inclusion is decidable by Corollary 2. $\qquad\square$

6.3 Complexity

Algorithm 2 may be fed with arbitrarily large heap automata. For a meaningful complexity analysis, we thus consider heap automata of bounded size only.

Definition 14. *An SID Φ is α–bounded if for each $P \in \mathrm{Pred}(\Phi)$ there exists a heap automaton $\mathfrak{A}_P$ over $\mathrm{SH}_{\langle \alpha \rangle}$ accepting $H_{P\mathbf{x},\Phi}^{\langle \alpha \rangle}$ such that $\Delta_{\mathfrak{A}_P}$ is decidable in $\mathcal{O}\left(2^{poly(\|\Phi\|)}\right)$ and $\|Q_{\mathfrak{A}_P}\| \leq 2^{poly(\alpha)}$.*

The bounds from above are natural for a large class of heap automata. In particular, all heap automata constructed in Sect. 4 stay within these bounds. Then a close analysis of Algorithm 2 for α–bounded SIDs yields the following complexity results. A detailed analysis is provided in [29].

Theorem 12. SL-ENTAIL$^{\Phi}_{\langle\alpha\rangle}$ *is decidable in* 2-ExpTime *for every α–bounded SID Φ. If $\alpha \geq 1$ is a constant then* SL-ENTAIL$^{\Phi}_{\langle\alpha\rangle}$ *is* ExpTime-*complete.*

Note that lower complexity bounds depend on the SIDs under consideration. Antonopoulos et al. [1, Theorem 6] showed that the entailment problem is already Π^P_2–complete (the second level of the polynomial hierarchy) for the base fragment, i.e., $\Phi = \emptyset$. Thus, under common complexity assumptions, the exponential time upper bound derived in Theorem 12 is asymptotically optimal for a deterministic algorithm. Since the entailment problem is already ExpTime–hard for points-to assertions of arity 3 and SIDs specifying regular sets of trees (cf. [1, Theorem 5] and [29]), exponential time is actually needed for certain SIDs.

6.4 Expressiveness

Most common data structures specified by SIDs, such as lists, trees, trees with linked leaves and combinations thereof can be encoded by heap automata [29]. However, SIDs are more expressive than heap automata. For example, consider two concatenated lists of the same length that use different fields. While such lists are outside the scope of heap automata, a suitable SID is given by:

$$P(x, y) \Leftarrow \exists z.x \mapsto (z, \mathbf{null}) * z \mapsto (\mathbf{null}, y)$$
$$P(x, y) \Leftarrow \exists u, v.x \mapsto (u, \mathbf{null}) * P(u, v) * v \mapsto (\mathbf{null}, y)$$

In general, the close relationship between established SIDs and context-free graph languages studied by Dodds [19, Theorem 1] and Courcelle's work on recognizable graph languages [18, Theorems 4.34 and 5.68], suggest that heap automata exist for every set of reduced symbolic heaps that can be specified in monadic second-order logic over graphs [18].

7 Conclusion

We developed an algorithmic framework for automatic reasoning about and debugging of the symbolic heap fragment of separation logic. Our approach is centered around a new automaton model, *heap automata*, that is specifically tailored to symbolic heaps. We show that many common robustness properties as well as certain types of entailments are naturally covered by our framework—often with optimal asymptotic complexity. There are several directions for future work including automated learning of heap automata accepting common data structures and applying heap automata to the abduction problem [16].

Acknowledgements. We thank Tomer Kotek, Georg Weissenbacher and the anonymous reviewers for their helpful comments.

References

1. Antonopoulos, T., Gorogiannis, N., Haase, C., Kanovich, M., Ouaknine, J.: Foundations for decision problems in separation logic with general inductive predicates. In: Muscholl, A. (ed.) FoSSaCS 2014. LNCS, vol. 8412, pp. 411–425. Springer, Heidelberg (2014). doi:10.1007/978-3-642-54830-7_27

2. Berdine, J., Calcagno, C., Cook, B., Distefano, D., O'Hearn, P.W., Wies, T., Yang, H.: Shape analysis for composite data structures. In: Damm, W., Hermanns, H. (eds.) CAV 2007. LNCS, vol. 4590, pp. 178–192. Springer, Heidelberg (2007). doi:10.1007/978-3-540-73368-3_22

3. Berdine, J., Calcagno, C., O'Hearn, P.W.: A decidable fragment of separation logic. In: Lodaya, K., Mahajan, M. (eds.) FSTTCS 2004. LNCS, vol. 3328, pp. 97–109. Springer, Heidelberg (2004). doi:10.1007/978-3-540-30538-5_9

4. Berdine, J., Calcagno, C., O'Hearn, P.W.: Smallfoot: modular automatic assertion checking with separation logic. In: de Boer, F.S., Bonsangue, M.M., Graf, S., de Roever, W.P. (eds.) FMCO 2005. LNCS, vol. 4111, pp. 115–137. Springer, Heidelberg (2006). doi:10.1007/11804192_6

5. Berdine, J., Calcagno, C., O'Hearn, P.W.: Symbolic execution with separation logic. In: Yi, K. (ed.) APLAS 2005. LNCS, vol. 3780, pp. 52–68. Springer, Heidelberg (2005). doi:10.1007/11575467_5

6. Berdine, J., Cook, B., Ishtiaq, S.: SLAYER: memory safety for systems-level code. In: Gopalakrishnan, G., Qadeer, S. (eds.) CAV 2011. LNCS, vol. 6806, pp. 178–183. Springer, Heidelberg (2011). doi:10.1007/978-3-642-22110-1_15

7. Bornat, R., Calcagno, C., O'Hearn, P.W., Parkinson, M.: Permission accounting in separation logic. In: ACM SIGPLAN Notices, vol. 40, pp. 259–270. ACM (2005)

8. Botincan, M., Distefano, D., Dodds, M., Grigore, R., Naudziuniene, D., Parkinson, M.J.: coreStar: the core of jStar. BOOGIE **2011**, 65–77 (2011)

9. Brookes, S.: A semantics for concurrent separation logic. Theoret. Comput. Sci. **375**(1), 227–270 (2007)

10. Brotherston, J., Distefano, D., Petersen, R.L.: Automated cyclic entailment proofs in separation logic. In: Bjørner, N., Sofronie-Stokkermans, V. (eds.) CADE 2011. LNCS (LNAI), vol. 6803, pp. 131–146. Springer, Heidelberg (2011). doi:10.1007/978-3-642-22438-6_12

11. Brotherston, J., Fuhs, C., Pérez, J.A.N., Gorogiannis, N.: A decision procedure for satisfiability in separation logic with inductive predicates. In: CSL-LICS 2014, pp. 25:1–25:10. ACM (2014)

12. Brotherston, J., Gorogiannis, N.: Cyclic abduction of inductively defined safety and termination preconditions. In: Müller-Olm, M., Seidl, H. (eds.) SAS 2014. LNCS, vol. 8723, pp. 68–84. Springer, Heidelberg (2014). doi:10.1007/978-3-319-10936-7_5

13. Brotherston, J., Gorogiannis, N., Kanovich, M.I., Rowe, R.: Model checking for symbolic-heap separation logic with inductive predicates. In: POPL 2016, pp. 84–96. ACM (2016)

14. Brotherston, J., Gorogiannis, N., Petersen, R.L.: A generic cyclic theorem prover. In: Jhala, R., Igarashi, A. (eds.) APLAS 2012. LNCS, vol. 7705, pp. 350–367. Springer, Heidelberg (2012). doi:10.1007/978-3-642-35182-2_25

15. Calcagno, C., Distefano, D.: Infer: an automatic program verifier for memory safety of C programs. In: Bobaru, M., Havelund, K., Holzmann, G.J., Joshi, R. (eds.) NFM 2011. LNCS, vol. 6617, pp. 459–465. Springer, Heidelberg (2011). doi:10.1007/978-3-642-20398-5_33

16. Calcagno, C., Distefano, D., O'Hearn, P., Yang, H.: Compositional shape analysis by means of bi-abduction. In: POPL 2009, pp. 289–300. ACM (2009)
17. Chin, W., David, C., Nguyen, H.H., Qin, S.: Automated verification of shape, size and bag properties via user-defined predicates in separation logic. Sci. Comput. Program. **77**(9), 1006–1036 (2012)
18. Courcelle, B., Engelfriet, J.: Graph Structure and Monadic Second-Order Logic: A Language-Theoretic Approach, vol. 138. Cambridge University Press, Cambridge (2012)
19. Dodds, M.: From separation logic to hyperedge replacement and back. In: Ehrig, H., Heckel, R., Rozenberg, G., Taentzer, G. (eds.) ICGT 2008. LNCS, vol. 5214, pp. 484–486. Springer, Heidelberg (2008). doi:10.1007/978-3-540-87405-8_40
20. Dudka, K., Peringer, P., Vojnar, T.: Predator: a practical tool for checking manipulation of dynamic data structures using separation logic. In: Gopalakrishnan, G., Qadeer, S. (eds.) CAV 2011. LNCS, vol. 6806, pp. 372–378. Springer, Heidelberg (2011). doi:10.1007/978-3-642-22110-1_29
21. Enea, C., Lengál, O., Sighireanu, M., Vojnar, T.: Compositional entailment checking for a fragment of separation logic. In: Garrigue, J. (ed.) APLAS 2014. LNCS, vol. 8858, pp. 314–333. Springer, Heidelberg (2014). doi:10.1007/978-3-319-12736-1_17
22. Gotsman, A., Berdine, J., Cook, B., Sagiv, M.: Thread-modular shape analysis. In: PLDI 2007, pp. 266–277. ACM (2007)
23. Habermehl, P., Holík, L., Rogalewicz, A., Šimáček, J., Vojnar, T.: Forest automata for verification of heap manipulation. In: Gopalakrishnan, G., Qadeer, S. (eds.) CAV 2011. LNCS, vol. 6806, pp. 424–440. Springer, Heidelberg (2011). doi:10.1007/978-3-642-22110-1_34
24. Habermehl, P., Holík, L., Rogalewicz, A., Šimáček, J., Vojnar, T.: Forest automata for verification of heap manipulation. Formal Methods Syst. Des. **41**(1), 83–106 (2012)
25. Hoare, C.A.R.: An axiomatic basis for computer programming. Commun. ACM **12**(10), 576–580 (1969)
26. Iosif, R., Rogalewicz, A., Simacek, J.: The tree width of separation logic with recursive definitions. In: Bonacina, M.P. (ed.) CADE 2013. LNCS (LNAI), vol. 7898, pp. 21–38. Springer, Heidelberg (2013). doi:10.1007/978-3-642-38574-2_2
27. Iosif, R., Rogalewicz, A., Vojnar, T.: Deciding entailments in inductive separation logic with tree automata. In: Cassez, F., Raskin, J.-F. (eds.) ATVA 2014. LNCS, vol. 8837, pp. 201–218. Springer, Heidelberg (2014). doi:10.1007/978-3-319-11936-6_15
28. Jacobs, B., Smans, J., Philippaerts, P., Vogels, F., Penninckx, W., Piessens, F.: VeriFast: a powerful, sound, predictable, fast verifier for C and Java. In: Bobaru, M., Havelund, K., Holzmann, G.J., Joshi, R. (eds.) NFM 2011. LNCS, vol. 6617, pp. 41–55. Springer, Heidelberg (2011). doi:10.1007/978-3-642-20398-5_4
29. Jansen, C., Katelaan, J., Matheja, C., Noll, T., Zuleger, F.: Unified reasoning about robustness properties of symbolic-heap separation logic. CoRR abs/1610.07041 (2016). http://arxiv.org/abs/1610.07041
30. Le, Q.L., Gherghina, C., Qin, S., Chin, W.-N.: Shape analysis via second-order bi-abduction. In: Biere, A., Bloem, R. (eds.) CAV 2014. LNCS, vol. 8559, pp. 52–68. Springer, Heidelberg (2014). doi:10.1007/978-3-319-08867-9_4
31. Magill, S., Tsai, M.-H., Lee, P., Tsay, Y.-K.: THOR: a tool for reasoning about shape and arithmetic. In: Gupta, A., Malik, S. (eds.) CAV 2008. LNCS, vol. 5123, pp. 428–432. Springer, Heidelberg (2008). doi:10.1007/978-3-540-70545-1_41

32. Navarro Pérez, J.A., Rybalchenko, A.: Separation logic modulo theories. In: Shan, C. (ed.) APLAS 2013. LNCS, vol. 8301, pp. 90–106. Springer, Heidelberg (2013). doi:10.1007/978-3-319-03542-0_7

33. Nguyen, H.H., Kuncak, V., Chin, W.-N.: Runtime checking for separation logic. In: Logozzo, F., Peled, D.A., Zuck, L.D. (eds.) VMCAI 2008. LNCS, vol. 4905, pp. 203–217. Springer, Heidelberg (2008). doi:10.1007/978-3-540-78163-9_19

34. O'Hearn, P., Reynolds, J., Yang, H.: Local reasoning about programs that alter data structures. In: Fribourg, L. (ed.) CSL 2001. LNCS, vol. 2142, pp. 1–19. Springer, Heidelberg (2001). doi:10.1007/3-540-44802-0_1

35. O'Hearn, P.W.: Resources, concurrency, and local reasoning. Theor. Comput. Sci. **375**(1–3), 271–307 (2007)

36. Piskac, R., Wies, T., Zufferey, D.: Automating separation logic with trees and data. In: Biere, A., Bloem, R. (eds.) CAV 2014. LNCS, vol. 8559, pp. 711–728. Springer, Heidelberg (2014). doi:10.1007/978-3-319-08867-9_47

37. Qiu, X., Garg, P., Ştefănescu, A., Madhusudan, P.: Natural proofs for structure, data, and separation. In: PLDI 2013, pp. 231–242. ACM (2013)

38. Reynolds, J.C.: Separation logic: a logic for shared mutable data structures. In: LICS 2002, pp. 55–74. IEEE (2002)

39. Zanardini, D., Genaim, S.: Inference of field-sensitive reachability and cyclicity. ACM Trans. Comput. Log. **15**(4), 33:1–33:41 (2014)

Proving Linearizability Using Partial Orders

Artem Khyzha[1](✉), Mike Dodds[2], Alexey Gotsman[1], and Matthew Parkinson[3]

[1] IMDEA Software Institute, Madrid, Spain
{artem.khyzha,alexey.gotsman}@imdea.org
[2] University of York, York, UK
mike.dodds@york.ac.uk
[3] Microsoft Research, Cambridge, UK
mattpark@microsoft.com

Abstract. Linearizability is the commonly accepted notion of correctness for concurrent data structures. It requires that any execution of the data structure is justified by a linearization—a linear order on operations satisfying the data structure's sequential specification. Proving linearizability is often challenging because an operation's position in the linearization order may depend on future operations. This makes it very difficult to incrementally construct the linearization in a proof.

We propose a new proof method that can handle data structures with such future-dependent linearizations. Our key idea is to incrementally construct not a single linear order of operations, but a partial order that describes multiple linearizations satisfying the sequential specification. This allows decisions about the ordering of operations to be delayed, mirroring the behaviour of data structure implementations. We formalise our method as a program logic based on rely-guarantee reasoning, and demonstrate its effectiveness by verifying several challenging data structures: the Herlihy-Wing queue, the TS queue and the Optimistic set.

1 Introduction

Linearizability is a commonly accepted notion of correctness of concurrent data structures. It matters for programmers using such data structures because it implies *contextual refinement*: any behaviour of a program using a concurrent data structure can be reproduced if the program uses its sequential implementation where all operations are executed atomically [4]. This allows the programmer to soundly reason about the behaviour of the program assuming a simple sequential specification of the data structure. Linearizability requires that for any execution of operations on the data structure there exists a linear order of these operations, called a *linearization*, such that: *(i)* the linearization respects the order of non-overlapping operations (the *real-time order*); and *(ii)* the behaviour of operations in the linearization matches the sequential specification of the data structure. To illustrate this, consider an execution in Fig. 1,

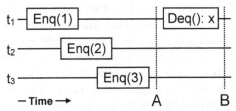

Fig. 1. Example execution.

© Springer-Verlag GmbH Germany 2017
H. Yang (Ed.): ESOP 2017, LNCS 10201, pp. 639–667, 2017.
DOI: 10.1007/978-3-662-54434-1_24

where three threads are accessing a queue. Linearizability determines which values x the dequeue operation is allowed to return by considering the possible linearizations of this execution. Given *(i)*, we know that in any linearization the enqueues must be ordered before the dequeue, and Enq(1) must be ordered before Enq(3). Given *(ii)*, a linearization must satisfy the sequential specification of a queue, so the dequeue must return the oldest enqueued value. Hence, the execution in Fig. 1 has three possible linearizations: [Enq(1); Enq(2); Enq(3); Deq():1], [Enq(1); Enq(3); Enq(2); Deq():1] and [Enq(2); Enq(1); Enq(3); Deq():2]. This means that the dequeue is allowed to return 1 or 2, but not 3.

For a large class of algorithms, linearizability can be proved by incrementally constructing a linearization as the program executes. Effectively, one shows that the program execution and its linearization stay in correspondence under each program step (this is formally known as a *forward simulation*). The point in the execution of an operation at which it is appended to the linearization is called its *linearization point*. This must occur somewhere between the start and end of the operation, to ensure that the linearization preserves the real-time order. For example, when applying the linearization point method to the execution in Fig. 1, by point (A) we must have decided if Enq(1) occurs before or after Enq(2) in the linearization. Thus, by this point, we know which of the three possible linearizations matches the execution. This method of establishing linearizability is very popular, to the extent that most papers proposing new concurrent data structures include a placement of linearization points. However, there are algorithms that cannot be proved linerizable using the linearization point method.

In this paper we consider several examples of such algorithms, including the *time-stamped (TS) queue* [2,7]—a recent high-performance data structure with an extremely subtle correctness argument. Its key idea is for enqueues to attach timestamps to values, and for these to determine the order in which values are dequeued. As illustrated by the above analysis of Fig. 1, linearizability allows concurrent operations, such as Enq(1) and Enq(2), to take effect in any order. The TS queue exploits this by allowing values from concurrent enqueues to receive incomparable timestamps; only pairs of timestamps for non-overlapping enqueue operations must be ordered. Hence, a dequeue can potentially have a choice of the "earliest" enqueue to take values from. This allows concurrent dequeues to go after different values, thus reducing contention and improving performance.

The linearization point method simply does not apply to the TS queue. In the execution in Fig. 1, values 1 and 2 could receive incomparable timestamps. Thus, at point (A) we do not know which of them will be dequeued first and, hence, in which order their enqueues should go in the linearization: this is only determined by the behaviour of dequeues later in the execution. Similar challenges exist for other queue algorithms such as the baskets queue [12], LCR queue [16] and Herlihy-Wing queue [11]. In all of these algorithms, when an enqueue operation returns, the precise linearization of earlier enqueue operations is not necessarily known. Similar challenges arise in the time-stamped stack [2] algorithm. We conjecture that our proof technique can be applied to prove the time-stamped stack linearizable, and we are currently working on a proof.

In this paper, we propose a new proof method that can handle algorithms where incremental construction of linearizations is not possible. We formalise it as a program logic, based on Rely-Guarantee [13], and apply it to give simple proofs to the TS queue [2], the Herlihy-Wing queue [11] and the Optimistic Set [17]. The key idea of our method is to incrementally construct not a single linearization of an algorithm execution, but an *abstract history*—a partially ordered history of operations such that it contains the real-time order of the original execution and *all* its linearizations satisfy the sequential specification. By embracing partiality, we enable decisions about order to be delayed, mirroring the behaviour of the algorithms. At the same time, we maintain the simple inductive style of the standard linearization-point method: the proof of linearizability of an algorithm establishes a simulation between its execution and a growing abstract history. By analogy with linearization points, we call the points in the execution where the abstract history is extended *commitment points*. The extension can be done in several ways: (1) committing to perform an operation; (2) committing to an order between previously unordered operatons; (3) completing an operation.

Consider again the TS queue execution in Fig. 1. By point (A) we construct the abstract history in Fig. 2(a). The edge in the figure is mandated by the real-time order in the original execution; Enq(1) and Enq(2) are left unordered, and so are Enq(2) and Enq(3). At the start of the execution of the dequeue, we update the history to the one in Fig. 2(b). A dashed ellipse represents an operation that is not yet completed, but we have committed to performing it (case 1 above). When the dequeue successfully removes a value, e.g., 2, we update the history to the one in Fig. 2(c). To this end, we complete the dequeue by recording its result (case 3). We also commit to an order between the Enq(1) and Enq(2) operations (case 2). This is needed to ensure that all linearizations of the resulting history satisfy the sequential queue specification, which requires a dequeue to remove the oldest value in the queue.

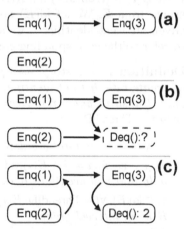

Fig. 2. Abstract histories constructed for prefixes of the execution in Fig. 1: (a) is at point (A); (b) is at the start of the dequeue operation; and (c) is at point (B). We omit the transitive consequences of the edges shown.

We demonstrate the simplicity of our method by giving proofs to challenging algorithms that match the intuition for why they work. Our method is also similar in spirit to the standard linearization point method. Thus, even though in this paper we formulate the method as a program logic, we believe that algorithm designers can also benefit from it in informal reasoning, using abstract histories and commitment points instead of single linearizations and linearization points.

2   Linearizability, Abstract Histories and Commitment Points

Preliminaries. We consider a data structure that can be accessed concurrently via operations op $\in$ Op in several threads, identified by $t \in$ ThreadID. Each operation takes one argument and returns one value, both from a set Val; we use a special value $\perp \in$ Val to model operations that take no argument or return no value. Linearizability relates the observable behaviour of an implementation of such a concurrent data structure to its sequential specification [11]. We formalise both of these by sets of *histories*, which are partially ordered sets of *events*, recording operations invoked on the data structure. Formally, an event is of the form $e = [i : (t, \text{op}, a, r)]$. It includes a unique identifier $i \in$ EventID and records an operation op $\in$ Op called by a thread $t \in$ ThreadID with an argument $a \in$ Val, which returns a value $r \in$ Val $\uplus$ {todo}. We use the special return value todo for events describing operations that have not yet terminated, and call such events *uncompleted*. We denote the set of all events by Event. Given a set $E \subseteq$ Event, we write $E(i) = (t, \text{op}, a, r)$ if $[i : (t, \text{op}, a, r)] \in E$ and let $\lfloor E \rfloor$ consist of all completed events from E. We let id(E) denote the set of all identifiers of events from E. Given an event identifier i, we also use $E(i)$.tid, $E(i)$.op, $E(i)$.arg and $E(i)$.rval to refer to the corresponding components of the tuple $E(i)$.

Definition 1. *A history[1] is a pair $H = (E, R)$, where $E \subseteq$ Event is a finite set of events with distinct identifiers and $R \subseteq$ id$(E) \times$ id(E) is a strict partial order (i.e., transitive and irreflexive), called the* real-time order. *We require that for each $t \in$ ThreadID:*

– *events in t are totally ordered by R:*

$\forall i, j \in$ id$(E). i \neq j \wedge E(i)$.tid $= E(j)$.tid $= t \implies (i \xrightarrow{R} j \vee j \xrightarrow{R} i)$;

– *only maximal events in R can be uncompleted:*

$\forall i \in$ id$(E). \forall t \in$ ThreadID. $E(i)$.rval $=$ todo $\implies \neg \exists j \in$ id$(E). i \xrightarrow{R} j$;

– *R is an interval order:*

$\forall i_1, i_2, i_3, i_4. i_1 \xrightarrow{R} i_2 \wedge i_3 \xrightarrow{R} i_4 \implies i_1 \xrightarrow{R} i_4 \vee i_2 \xrightarrow{R} i_3$.

We let History *be the set of all histories. A history (E, R) is* sequential, *written* seq(E, R), *if* id$(E) = \lfloor E \rfloor$ *and R is total on E.*

Informally, $i \xrightarrow{R} j$ means that the operation recorded by $E(i)$ completed before the one recorded by $E(j)$ started. The real-time order in histories produced by concurrent data structure implementations may be partial, since in this

---

[1] For technical convenience, our notion of a history is different from the one in the classical linearizability definition [11], which uses separate events to denote the start and the end of an operation. We require that R be an interval order, we ensure that our notion is consistent with an interpretation of events as segments of time during which the corresponding operations are executed, with R ordering i_1 before i_2 if i_1 finishes before i_2 starts [5].

case the execution of operations may overlap in time; in contrast, specifications are defined using sequential histories, where the real-time order is total.

Linearizability. Assume we are given a set of histories that can be produced by a given data structure implementation (we introduce a programming language for implementations and formally define the set of histories an implementation produces in Sect. 5). Linearizability requires all of these histories to be matched by a similar history of the data structure specification (its *linearization*) that, in particular, preserves the real-time order between events in the following sense: the real-time order of a history $H = (E, R)$ is *preserved* in a history $H' = (E', R')$, written $H \sqsubseteq H'$, if $E = E'$ and $R \subseteq R'$.

The full definition of linearizability is slightly more complicated due to the need to handle uncompleted events: since operations they denote have not terminated, we do not know whether they have made a change to the data structure or not. To account for this, the definition makes all events in the implementation history complete by discarding some uncompleted events and completing the remaining ones with an arbitrary return value. Formally, an event $e = [i : (t, \mathsf{op}, a, r)]$ *can be completed* to an event $e' = [i' : (t', \mathsf{op}', a', r')]$, written $e \trianglelefteq e'$, if $i = i'$, $t = t'$, $\mathsf{op} = \mathsf{op}'$, $a = a'$ and either $r = r' \neq \mathsf{todo}$ or $r' = \mathsf{todo}$. A history $H = (E, R)$ *can be completed* to a history $H' = (E', R')$, written $H \trianglelefteq H'$, if $\mathsf{id}(E') \subseteq \mathsf{id}(E)$, $\lfloor E \rfloor \subseteq \lfloor F' \rfloor$, $R \cap (\mathsf{id}(E') \times \mathsf{id}(E')) = R'$ and $\forall i \in \mathsf{id}(E'). [i : E(i)] \trianglelefteq [i : E''(i)]$.

Definition 2. *A set of histories $\mathcal{H}_1$ (defining the data structure implementation) is* linearized *by a set of sequential histories $\mathcal{H}_2$ (defining its specification), written $\mathcal{H}_1 \sqsubseteq \mathcal{H}_2$, if $\forall H_1 \in \mathcal{H}_1. \exists H_2 \in \mathcal{H}_2. \exists H_1'. H_1 \trianglelefteq H_1' \wedge H_1' \sqsubseteq \mathcal{H}_2$.*

Let $\mathcal{H}_{\mathsf{queue}}$ be the set of sequential histories defining the behaviour of a queue with $\mathsf{Op} = \{\mathsf{Enq}, \mathsf{Deq}\}$. Due to space constraints, we provide its formal definition in the extended version of this paper [14], but for example, [Enq(2); Enq(1); Enq(3); Deq():2] $\in \mathcal{H}_{\mathsf{queue}}$ and [Enq(1); Enq(2); Enq(3); Deq():2] $\notin \mathcal{H}_{\mathsf{queue}}$.

Proof Method. In general, a history of a data structure (H_1 in Definition 2) may have multiple linearizations (H_2) satisfying a given specification $\mathcal{H}$. In our proof method, we use this observation and construct a partially ordered history, an *abstract history*, all linearizations of which belong to $\mathcal{H}$.

Definition 3. *A history H is an* abstract history *of a specification given by the set of sequential histories $\mathcal{H}$ if $\{H' \mid \lfloor H \rfloor \sqsubseteq H' \wedge \mathsf{seq}(H')\} \subseteq \mathcal{H}$, where $\lfloor (E, R) \rfloor = (\lfloor E \rfloor, R \cap (\mathsf{id}(\lfloor E \rfloor) \times \mathsf{id}(\lfloor E \rfloor)))$. We denote this by $\mathsf{abs}(H, \mathcal{H})$.*

We define the construction of an abstract history $H = (E, R)$ by instrumenting the data structure operations with auxiliary code that updates the history at certain *commitment points* during operation execution. There are three kinds of commitment points:

```
PoolID insert(ThreadID t, Val v) {          (PoolID×TS) getOldest(ThreadID t) {
  p := new PoolID();                          if (∃p,τ.pools(t) = (p,_,τ)·_)
  pools(t) := pools(t)·(p,v,⊤);                 return (p,τ);
  return p;                                   else
}                                               return (NULL,NULL);
                                            }

Val remove(ThreadID t, PoolID p) {
  if (∃Σ,Σ',v,τ.                            setTimestamp(ThreadID t,
       pools(t) = Σ·(p,v,τ)·Σ') {                        PoolID p, TS τ) {
    pools(t) := Σ·Σ';                         if (∃Σ,Σ',v.
    return v;                                      pools(t) = Σ·(p,v,_)·Σ')
  } else return NULL;                           pools(t) := Σ·(p,v,τ)·Σ';
}                                           }
```

Fig. 3. Operations on abstract SP pools pools : ThreadID → Pool. All operations are atomic.

1. When an operation op with an argument a starts executing in a thread t, we extend E by a fresh event $[i : (t, \text{op}, a, \text{todo})]$, which we order in R after all events in $\lfloor E \rfloor$.
2. At any time, we can add more edges to R.
3. By the time an operation finishes, we have to assign its return value to its event in E.

Note that, unlike Definitions 2 and 3 uses a particular way of completing an abstract history H, which just discards all uncompleted events using $\lfloor - \rfloor$. This does not limit generality because, when constructing an abstract history, we can complete an event (item 3) right after the corresponding operation makes a change to the data structure, without waiting for the operation to finish.

In Sect. 6 we formalise our proof method as a program logic and show that it indeed establishes linearizability. Before this, we demonstrate informally how the obligations of our proof method are discharged on an example.

3   Running Example: The Time-Stamped Queue

We use the TS queue [7] as our running example. Values in the queue are stored in per-thread single-producer (SP) multi-consumer pools, and we begin by describing this auxiliary data structure.

SP Pools. SP pools have well-known linearizable implementations [7], so we simplify our presentation by using abstract pools with the atomic operations given in Fig. 3. This does not limit generality: since linerarizability implies contextual refinement (Sect. 1), properties proved using the abstract pools will stay valid for their linearizable implementations. In the figure and in the following we denote irrelevant expressions by _.

The SP pool of a thread contains a sequence of triples (p, v, τ), each consisting of a unique identifier $p \in \mathsf{PoolID}$, a value $v \in \mathsf{Val}$ enqueued into the TS queue by the thread and the associated timestamp $\tau \in \mathsf{TS}$. The set of timestamps TS is partially ordered by $<_{\mathsf{TS}}$, with a distinguished timestamp $\top$ that is greater than all others. We let pool be the set of states of an abstract SP pool. Initially all pools are empty. The operations on SP pools are as follows:

```
1  enqueue(Val v) {
2    atomic {
3      PoolID node := insert(myTid(), v);
4      Gts[myEid()] := ⊤;
5    }
6    TS timestamp := newTimestamp();
7    atomic {
8      setTimestamp(myTid(), node,
         timestamp);
9      Gts[myEid()] := timestamp;
10     E(myEid()).rval := ⊥;
11   }
12   return ⊥;
13 }
```

Fig. 4. The TS queue: enqueue. Shaded portions are auxiliary code used in the proof.

- `insert(t,v)` appends a value v to the back of the pool of thread t and associates it with the special timestamp $\top$; it returns an identifier for the added element.
- `setTimestamp(t,p,`τ`)` sets to τ the timestamp of the element identified by p in the pool of thread t.
- `getOldest(t)` returns the identifier and timestamp of the value from the front of the pool of thread t, or (NULL, NULL) if the pool is empty.
- `remove(t,p)` tries to remove a value identified by p from the pool of thread t. Note this can fail if some other thread removes the value first.

Separating `insert` from `setTimestamp` and `getOldest` from `remove` in the SP pool interface reduces the atomicity granularity, and permits more efficient implementations.

Core TS Queue Algorithm. Figures 4 and 5 give the code for our version of the TS queue. Shaded portions are auxiliary code needed in the linearizability proof to update the abstract history at commitment points; it can be ignored for now. In the overall TS queue, enqueuing means adding a value with a certain timestamp to the pool of the current thread, while dequeuing means searching for the value with the minimal timestamp across per-thread pools and removing it.

In more detail, the enqueue(v) operation first inserts the value v into the pool of the current thread, defined by `myTid` (line 3). At this point the value v has the default, maximal timestamp $\top$. The code then generates a new timestamp using `newTimestamp` and sets the timestamp of the new value to it (lines 6–8). We describe an implementation of `newTimestamp` later in this section. The key property that it ensures is that out of two non-overlapping calls to this function, the latter returns a higher timestamp than the former; only concurrent calls may generate incomparable timestamps. Hence, timestamps in each pool appear in the ascending order.

The dequeue operation first generates a timestamp start_ts at line 18, which it further uses to determine a consistent snapshot of the data structure. After

```
14  Val dequeue() {
15    Val ret := NULL;
16    EventID CAND;
17    do {
18      TS start_ts := newTimestamp();
19      PoolID pid, cand_pid := NULL;
20      TS ts, cand_ts := ⊤;
21      ThreadID cand_tid;
22      for each k in 1..NThreads do {
23        atomic {
24          (pid, ts) := getOldest(k);
25          R := (R ∪ {(e, myEid()) | e ∈ id(⌊E⌋) ∩ inQ(pools, E, G_ts)
26                                  ∧ ¬(start_ts <_TS G_ts(e))})⁺;
26        }
27        if (pid ≠ NULL && ts <_TS cand_ts && ¬(start_ts <_TS ts)) {
28          (cand_pid, cand_ts, cand_tid) := (pid, ts, k);
31          CAND := enqOf(E, G_ts, cand_tid, cand_ts);
32        }
33      }
34      if (cand_pid ≠ NULL)
35        atomic {
36          ret := remove(cand_tid, cand_pid);
37          if (ret ≠ NULL) {
38            E(myEid()).rval := ret;
39            R := (R ∪ {(CAND, e) | e ∈ inQ(pools, E, G_ts)}
40                     ∪ {(myEid(), d) | E(d).op = Deq ∧ d ∈ id(E \ ⌊E⌋)})⁺;
41          }
43        }
44    } while (ret = NULL);
45    return ret;
46  }
```

Fig. 5. The TS queue: dequeue. Shaded portions are auxiliary code used in the proof.

generating start_ts, the operation iterates through per-thread pools, searching for a value with a minimal timestamp (lines 22–33). The search starts from a random pool, to make different threads more likely to pick different elements for removal and thus reduce contention. The pool identifier of the current candidate for removal is stored in cand_pid, its timestamp in cand_ts and the thread that inserted it in cand_tid. On each iteration of the loop, the code fetches the earliest value enqueued by thread k (line 24) and checks whether its timestamp is smaller than the current candidate's cand_ts (line 27). If the timestamps are incomparable, the algorithm keeps the first one (either would be legitimate). Additionally, the algorithm never chooses a value as a candidate if its timestamp is greater than start_ts, because such values are not guaranteed to be read in a consistent manner.

If a candidate has been chosen once the iteration has completed, the code tries to remove it (line 35). This may fail if some other thread got there first, in which case the operation restarts. Likewise, the algorithm restarts if no candidate was identified (the full algorithm in [7] includes an emptiness check, which we omit for simplicity).

Timestamp Generation. The TS queue requires that sequential calls to newTimestamp generate ordered timestamps. This ensures that the two sequentially enqueued values cannot be dequeued out of order. However, concurrent calls to newTimestamp may generate incomparable timestamps. This is desirable because it increases flexibility in choosing which value to dequeue, reducing contention.

There are a number of implementations of newTimestamp satisfying the above requirements [2]. For concreteness, we consider the implementation given in Fig. 6. Here a timestamp is either $\top$ or a pair of integers (s, e), representing a time interval. In every timestamp (s, e), $s \leq e$. Two timestamps are considered ordered $(s_1, e_1) <_{\mathsf{TS}} (s_2, e_2)$ if $e_1 < s_2$, i.e., if the time intervals do not overlap. Intervals are generated with the help of a shared counter. The algorithm reads

```
37  int counter = 1;
38
39  TS newTimestamp() {
40    int ts = counter;
41    TS result;
42    if (CAS(counter, ts, ts+1))
43      result = (ts, ts);
44    else
45      result = (ts, counter-1);
46    return result;
47  }
```

Fig. 6. Timestamp generation algorithm.

the counter as the start of the interval and attempts to atomically increment it with a CAS (lines 40–42), which is a well-known atomic compare-and-swap operation. It atomically reads the counter and, if it still contains the previously read value ts, updates it with the new timestamp ts + 1 and returns true; otherwise, it does nothing and returns false. If CAS succeeds, then the algorithm takes the interval start and end values as equal (line 43). If not, some other thread(s) increased the counter. The algorithm reads the counter again and subtracts 1 to give the end of the interval (line 45). Thus, either the current call to newTimestamp increases the counter, or some other thread does so. In either case, subsequent calls will generate timestamps greater than the current one.

This timestamping algorithm allows concurrent enqueue operations in Fig. 1 to get incomparable timestamps. Then the dequeue may remove either 1 or 2 depending on where it starts traversing the pools[2] (line 22). As we explained in Sect. 1, this makes the standard method of linearization point inapplicable for verifying the TS queue.

4 The TS Queue: Informal Development

In this section we explain how the abstract history is updated at the commitment points of the TS Queue and justify informally why these updates preserve the key property of this history—that all its linearizations satisfy the sequential queue specification. We present the details of the proof of the TS queue in Sect. 7.

Ghost State and Auxiliary Definitions. To aid in constructing the abstract history (E, R), we instrument the code of the algorithm to maintain a piece

---

[2] Recall that the randomness is required to reduce contention.

of ghost state—a partial function G_{ts} : EventID $\rightharpoonup$ TS. Given the identifier i of an event $E(i)$ denoting an enqueue that has inserted its value into a pool, $G_{ts}(i)$ gives the timestamp currently associated with the value. The statements in lines 4 and 9 in Fig. 4 update G_{ts} accordingly. These statements use a special command myEid() that returns the identifier of the event associated with the current operation.

As explained in Sect. 3, the timestamps of values in each pool appear in strictly ascending order. As a consequence, all timestamps assigned by G_{ts} to events of a given thread t are distinct, which is formalised by the following property:

$$\forall i, j.\, i \neq j \wedge E(i).\text{tid} = E(j).\text{tid} \wedge i, j \in \text{dom}(G_{ts}) \implies G_{ts}(i) \neq G_{ts}(j)$$

Hence, for a given thread t and a timestamp τ, there is at most one enqueue event in E that inserted a value with the timestamp τ in the pool of a thread t. In the following, we denote the identifier of this event by $\text{enqOf}(E, G_{ts}, t, \tau)$ and let the set of the identifiers of such events for all values currently in the pools be $\text{inQ}(\text{pools}, E, G_{ts})$:

$$\text{inQ}(\text{pools}, E, G_{ts}) \triangleq \{\text{enqOf}(E, G_{ts}, t, \tau) \mid \exists p.\, \text{pools}(t) = \_ \cdot (p, \_, \tau) \cdot \_\}$$

Commitment Points and History Updates. We further instrument the code with statements that update the abstract history at commitment points, which we now explain. As a running example, we use the execution in Fig. 7, extending that in Fig. 1. As we noted in Sect. 2, when an operations starts, we automatically add a new uncompleted event to E to represent this operation and order it after all completed events in R. For example, before the start of Enq(3) in the execution of Fig. 7, the abstract history contains two events Enq(1) and Enq(2) and no edges in the real-time order. At the start of Enq(3) the history gets transformed to that in Fig. 8(a). The commitment point at line 8 in Fig. 4 completes the enqueue by giving it a return value $\perp$, which results in the abstract history in Fig. 8(b).

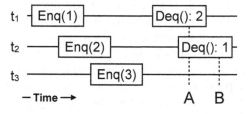

Fig. 7. Example execution extending Fig. 1. Dotted lines indicate commitment points at lines 35–43 of the dequeues.

Upon a dequeue's start, we similarly add an event representing it. Thus, by point (A) in Fig. 7, the abstract history is as shown in Fig. 8(c). At every iteration k of the loop, the dequeue performs a commitment point at lines 25–26, where we order enqueue events of values currently present in the pool of a thread k before the current dequeue event. Specifically, we add an edge $(e, \text{myEid}())$ for each identifier e of an enqueue event whose value is in the k's pool and whose timestamp is not greater than the dequeue's own timestamp start_ts. Such ordering ensures that in all linearizations of the abstract history, the values that

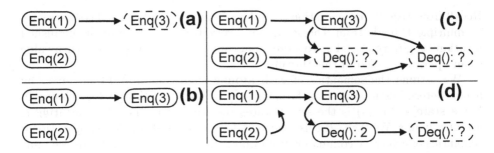

Fig. 8. Changes to the abstract history of the execution in Fig. 7.

the current dequeue observes in the pool according to the algorithm are also enqueued in the sequential queue prior to the dequeue. In particular, this also ensures that in all linearizations, the dequeue returns a value that has already been inserted.

The key commitment point in dequeue occurs in lines 35–43, where the abstract history is updated if the dequeue successfully removes a value from a pool. The ghost code at line 31 stores the event identifier for the enqueue that inserted this value in CAND. At the commitment point we first complete the current dequeue event by assigning the value removed from a pool as its return value. This ensures that the dequeue returns the same value in the concrete execution and the abstract history. Finally, we order events in the abstract history to ensure that all linearizations of the abstract history satisfy the sequential queue specification. To this end, we add the following edges to R and then transitively close it:

1. (CAND, e) for each identifier e of an enqueue event whose value is still in the pools. This ensures that the dequeue removes the oldest value in the queue.
2. (myEid(), d) for each identifier d of an uncompleted dequeue event. This ensures that dequeues occur in the same order as they remove values from the queue.

At the commitment point (A) in Fig. 7 the abstract history gets transformed from the one in Fig. 8(c) to the one in Fig. 8(d).

5   Programming Language

To formalise our proof method, we first introduce a programming language for data structure implementations. This defines such implementations by functions $D : \mathsf{Op} \to \mathsf{Com}$ mapping operations to *commands* from a set Com. The commands, ranged over by C, are written in a simple while-language, which includes *atomic* commands α from a set PCom (assignment, CAS, etc.) and standard control-flow constructs. To conserve space, we describe the precise syntax in the extended version of this paper [14].

Let $\mathsf{Loc} \subseteq \mathsf{Val}$ be the set of all memory locations. We let $\mathsf{State} = \mathsf{Loc} \to \mathsf{Val}$ be the set of all states of the data structure implementation, ranged over by s.

Recall from Sect. 2 that operations of a data structure can be called concurrently in multiple threads from ThreadID. For every thread t, we use distinguished locations $\text{arg}[t], \text{res}[t] \in \text{Loc}$ to store an argument, respectively, the return value of an operation called in this thread.

We assume the semantics of each atomic command $\alpha \in \text{PCom}$ given by a non-deterministic state transformers $[\![\alpha]\!]_t : \text{State} \to \mathcal{P}(\text{State}), t \in \text{ThreadID}$. For a state s, $[\![\alpha]\!]_t(s)$ is the set of states resulting from thread t executing α atomically in s. We then lift this semantics to a sequential small-step operational semantics of arbitrary commands from Com: $\langle C, s \rangle \longrightarrow_t \langle C', s' \rangle$. Again, we omit the standard rules of the semantics; see [14].

We now define the set of histories produced by a data structure implementation D, which is required by the definition of linearizability (Definition 2, Sect. 2). Informally, these are the histories produced by threads repeatedly invoking data structure operations in any order and with any possible arguments (this can be thought of as running the data structure implementation under its *most general client* [6]). We define this formally using a concurrent small-step semantics of the data structure D that also constructs corresponding histories: $\twoheadrightarrow_D \subseteq (\text{Cont} \times \text{State} \times \text{History})^2$, where $\text{Cont} = \text{ThreadID} \to (\text{Com} \uplus \{\text{idle}\})$. Here a function $c \in \text{Cont}$ characterises the progress of an operation execution in each thread t: $c(t)$ gives the continuation of the code of the operation executing in thread t, or idle if no operation is executing. The relation $\twoheadrightarrow_D$ defines how a step of an operation in some thread transforms the data structure state and the history:

$$\frac{i \notin \text{id}(E) \quad a \in \text{Val} \quad E' = E[i : (t, \text{op}, a, \text{todo})] \quad R' = R \cup \{(j, i) \mid j \in \lfloor E \rfloor\}}{\langle c[t : \text{idle}], s, (E, R) \rangle \twoheadrightarrow_D \langle c[t : D(\text{op})], s[\text{arg}[t] : a], (E', R') \rangle}$$

$$\frac{\langle C, s \rangle \longrightarrow_t \langle C', s' \rangle}{\langle c[t : C], s, (E, R) \rangle \twoheadrightarrow_D \langle c[t : C'], s', (E, R) \rangle}$$

$$\frac{i = \text{last}(t, (E, R)) \quad E(i) = (t, \text{op}, a, \text{todo}) \quad E' = E[i : (t, \text{op}, a, s(\text{res}[t]))]}{\langle c[t : \text{skip}], s, (E, R) \rangle \twoheadrightarrow_D \langle c[t : \text{idle}], s, (E', R) \rangle}$$

First, an idle thread t may call any operation $\text{op} \in \text{Op}$ with any argument a. This sets the continuation of thread t to $D(\text{op})$, stores a into $\text{arg}[t]$, adds a new event i to the history, ordered after all completed events. Second, a thread t executing an operation may do a transition allowed by the sequential semantics of the operation's implementation. Finally, when a thread t finishes executing an operation, as denoted by a continuation skip, the corresponding event is completed with the return value in $\text{res}[t]$. The identifier $\text{last}(t, (E, R))$ of this event is determined as the last one in E by thread t according to R: as per Definition 1, events by each thread are totally ordered in a history, ensuring that $\text{last}(t, H)$ is well-defined.

Now given an initial state $s_0 \in \text{State}$, we define the set of histories of a data structure D as $\mathcal{H}(D, s_0) = \{H \mid \langle (\lambda t. \text{idle}), s_0, (\emptyset, \emptyset) \rangle \twoheadrightarrow_D^* \langle \_, \_, H \rangle\}$. We say that a data structure (D, s_0) is *linearizable* with respect to a set of sequential histories $\mathcal{H}$ if $\mathcal{H}(D, s_0) \sqsubseteq \mathcal{H}$ (Definition 2).

6   Logic

We now formalise our proof method as a Hoare logic based on rely-guarantee [13]. We make this choice to keep presentation simple; our method is general and can be combined with more advanced methods for reasoning about concurrency [1,20,22].

Assertions $P, Q \in$ Assn in our logic denote sets of *configurations* $\kappa \in$ Config = State × History × Ghost, relating the data structure state, the abstract history and the ghost state from a set Ghost. The latter can be chosen separately for each proof; e.g., in the proof of the TS queue in Sect. 4 we used Ghost = EventID → TS. We do not prescribe a particular syntax for assertions, but assume that it includes at least the first-order logic, with a set LVars of special *logical variables* used in specifications and not in programs. We assume a function $[\![-]\!]_- :$ Assn × (LVars → Val) → $\mathcal{P}($Config$)$ such that $[\![P]\!]_\ell$ gives the denotation of an assertion P with respect to an interpretation $\ell :$ LVars → Val of logical variables.

Rely-guarantee is a *compositional* verification method: it allows reasoning about the code executing in each thread separately under some assumption on its environment, specified by a *rely*. In exchange, the thread has to ensure that its behaviour conforms to a *guarantee*. Accordingly, judgements of our logic take the form $\mathcal{R}, \mathcal{G} \vdash_t \{P\}\, C\, \{Q\}$, where C is a command executing in thread t, P and Q are Hoare pre- and post-conditions from Assn, and $\mathcal{R}, \mathcal{G} \subseteq$ Config^2 are relations defining the rely and the guarantee. Informally, the judgement states that C satisfies the Hoare specification $\{P\}_-\{Q\}$ and changes program configurations according to $\mathcal{G}$, assuming that concurrent threads change program configurations according to $\mathcal{R}$.

Our logic includes the standard Hoare proof rules for reasoning about sequential control-flow constructs, which we defer to [14] due to space constraints. We

$$\frac{\forall \ell.\, \mathcal{G} \vDash_t \{[\![P]\!]_\ell\}\ \alpha\ \{[\![Q]\!]_\ell\} \wedge \mathsf{stable}([\![P]\!]_\ell, \mathcal{R}) \wedge \mathsf{stable}([\![Q]\!]_\ell, \mathcal{R})}{\mathcal{R}, \mathcal{G} \vdash_t \{P\}\ \alpha\ \{Q\}}$$

where for $p, q \in \mathcal{P}($Config$)$:

$$\mathsf{stable}(p, \mathcal{R}) \triangleq \forall \kappa, \kappa'.\, \kappa \in p \wedge (\kappa, \kappa') \in \mathcal{R} \implies \kappa' \in p$$

$$\mathcal{G} \vDash_t \{p\}\ \alpha\ \{q\} \triangleq \forall s, s', H, G.\, (s, H, G) \in p \wedge s' \in [\![\alpha]\!]_t(s) \implies$$
$$\exists H', G'.\, (s', H', G') \in q \wedge H \rightsquigarrow^* H' \wedge ((s, H, G), (s', H', G')) \in \mathcal{G}$$

and for $(E, R), (E', R') \in$ History:

$$(E, R) \rightsquigarrow (E', R') \triangleq (E = E' \wedge R \subseteq R') \vee$$
$$(\exists i, t, \mathsf{op}, a, r.\, (\forall j.\, j \neq i \implies E(j) = E'(j)) \wedge$$
$$E(i) = (t, \mathsf{op}, a, \mathsf{todo}) \wedge E'(i) = (t, \mathsf{op}, a, r))$$

Fig. 9. Proof rule for primitive commands.

now explain the rule for atomic commands in Fig. 9, which plays a crucial role in formalising our proof method. The proof rule derives judgements of the form $\mathcal{R}, \mathcal{G} \vdash_t \{P\}\; \alpha\; \{Q\}$. The rule takes into account possible interference from concurrent threads by requiring the denotations of P and Q to be *stable* under the rely $\mathcal{R}$, meaning that they are preserved under transitions the latter allows. The rest of the requirements are expressed by the judgement $\mathcal{G} \vDash_t \{p\}\; \alpha\; \{q\}$. This requires that for any configuration (s, H, G) from the precondition denotation p and any data structure state s' resulting from thread t executing α in s, we can find a history H' and a ghost state G' such that the new configuration (s', H', G') belongs to the postcondition denotation q. This allows updating the history and the ghost state (almost) arbitrarily, since these are only part of the proof and not of the actual data structure implementation; the shaded code in Figs. 4 and 5 indicates how we perform these updates in the proof of the TS queue. Updates to the history, performed when α is a commitment point, are constrained by a relation $\rightsquigarrow \; \subseteq \mathsf{History}^2$, which only allows adding new edges to the real-time order or completing events with a return value. This corresponds to commitment points of kinds 2 and 3 from Sect. 2. Finally, as is usual in rely-guarantee, the judgement $\mathcal{G} \vDash_t \{p\}\; \alpha\; \{q\}$ requires that the change to the program configuration be allowed by the guarantee $\mathcal{G}$.

Note that $\rightsquigarrow$ does not allow adding new events into histories (commitment point of kind 1): this happens automatically when an operation is invoked. In the following, we use a relation $\dashrightarrow_t \; \subseteq \mathsf{Config}^2$ to constrain the change to the program configuration upon an operation invocation in thread t:

$$\langle s, (E, R), G \rangle \dashrightarrow_t \langle s', (E', R'), G' \rangle \iff (\forall l \in \mathsf{Loc}.\, l \neq \mathsf{arg}[t] \implies s(l) = s'(l))$$
$$\wedge \exists i \notin \mathsf{id}(E).\, E' = E \uplus \{[i : t, \_, \_, \mathsf{todo}]\}$$
$$\wedge R' = (R \cup \{(j, i) \mid j \in \lfloor E \rfloor\}) \wedge G = G'$$

Thus, when an operation is invoked in thread t, $\mathsf{arg}[t]$ is overwritten by the operation argument and an uncompleted event associated with thread t and a new identifier i is added to the history; this event is ordered after all completed events, as required by our proof method (Sect. 2).

The rule for primitive commands and the standard Hoare logic proof rules allow deriving judgements about the implementations $D(\mathsf{op})$ of every operation op in a data structure D. The following theorem formalises the requirements on these judgements sufficient to conclude the linearizability of D with respect to a given set of sequential histories $\mathcal{H}$. The theorem uses the following auxiliary assertions, describing the event corresponding to the current operation op in a thread t at the start and end of its execution (last is defined in Sect. 5):

$$[\![\mathsf{started}_{\mathcal{I}}(t, \mathsf{op})]\!]_\ell = \{(s, (E, R), G) \mid E(\mathsf{last}(t, (E, R))) = (t, \mathsf{op}, s(\mathsf{arg}[t]), \mathsf{todo})$$
$$\wedge\, \exists \kappa \in [\![\mathcal{I}]\!]_\ell.\, \langle \kappa \rangle \dashrightarrow_t \langle s, (E, R), G \rangle\};$$
$$[\![\mathsf{ended}(t, \mathsf{op})]\!]_\ell = \{(s, (E, R), G) \mid E(\mathsf{last}(t, (E, R))) = (t, \mathsf{op}, \_, s(\mathsf{res}[t]))\}.$$

The assertion $\mathsf{started}_{\mathcal{I}}(t, \mathsf{op})$ is parametrised by a global invariant $\mathcal{I}$ used in the proof. With the help of it, $\mathsf{started}_{\mathcal{I}}(t, \mathsf{op})$ requires that configurations in its denotation be results of adding a new event into histories satisfying $\mathcal{I}$.

Theorem 1. *Given a data structure D, its initial state $s_0 \in$ State and a set of sequential histories $\mathcal{H}$, we have (D, s_0) linearizable with respect to $\mathcal{H}$ if there exists an assertion $\mathcal{I}$ and relations $\mathcal{R}_t, \mathcal{G}_t \subseteq$ Config^2 for each $t \in$ ThreadID such that:*

1. $\exists G_0. \forall \ell. (s_0, (\emptyset, \emptyset), G_0) \in [\![\mathcal{I}]\!]_\ell$;
2. $\forall t, \ell.$ stable$([\![\mathcal{I}]\!]_\ell, \mathcal{R}_t)$;
3. $\forall H, \ell. (\_, H, \_) \in [\![\mathcal{I}]\!]_\ell \implies$ abs$(H, \mathcal{H})$;
4. $\forall t,$ op. $(\mathcal{R}_t, \mathcal{G}_t \vdash_t \{\mathcal{I} \wedge$ started$_\mathcal{I}(t, \mathsf{op})\} \ D(\mathsf{op}) \ \{\mathcal{I} \wedge$ ended$(t, \mathsf{op})\})$;
5. $\forall t, t'. t \neq t' \implies \mathcal{G}_t \cup {-}{-}{\rightarrow}_t \subseteq \mathcal{R}_{t'}$.

Here $\mathcal{I}$ is the invariant used in the proof, which item 1 requires to hold of the initial data structure state s_0, the empty history and some some initial ghost state G_0. Item 2 then ensures that the invariant holds at all times. Item 3 requires any history satisfying the invariant to be an abstract history of the given specification $\mathcal{H}$ (Definition 3, Sect. 2). Item 4 constraints the judgement about an operation op executed in a thread t: the operation is executed from a configuration satisfying the invariant and with a corresponding event added to the history; by the end of the operation's execution, we need to complete the event with the return value matching the one produced by the code. Finally, item 5 formalises a usual requirement in rely-guarantee reasoning: actions allowed by the guarantee of a thread t have to be included into the rely of any other thread t'. We also include the relation ${-}{-}{\rightarrow}_t$, describing the automatic creation of a new event upon an operation invocation in thread t.

7   The TS Queue: Proof Details

In this section, we present some of the details of the proof of the TS Queue. Due to space constraints, we provide the rest of them in the extended version of the paper [14].

Invariant. We satisfy the obligation 1 from Theorem 1 by proving the invariant INV defined in Fig. 10. The invariant is an assertion consisting of four parts: $\mathsf{INV_{LIN}}$, $\mathsf{INV_{ORD}}$, $\mathsf{INV_{ALG}}$ and $\mathsf{INV_{WF}}$. Each of them denotes a set of configurations satisfying the listed constraints for a given interpretation of logical variables ℓ. The first part of the invariant, $\mathsf{INV_{LIN}}$, ensures that every history satisfying the invariant is an abstract history of the queue, which discharges the obligation 1 from Theorem 1. In addition to that, $\mathsf{INV_{LIN}}$ requires that a relation same_data hold of a configuration (s, H, G_{ts}) and every linearization H'. In this way, we ensure that the pools and the final state of the sequential queue after H' contain values inserted by the same enqueue events (we formalise same_data in [14]). The second part, $\mathsf{INV_{ORD}}$, asserts ordering properties of events in the partial order that hold by construction. The third part, $\mathsf{INV_{ALG}}$, is a collection of properties relating the order on timestamps to the partial order in abstract history. Finally, $\mathsf{INV_{WF}}$ is a collection of well-formedness properties of the ghost state.

Loop Invariant. We now present the key verification condition that arises in the dequeue operation: demonstrating that the ordering enforced at the commitment points at lines 25–26 and 35–43 does not invalidate acyclicity of the

(INV$_{\text{LIN}}$) all linearizations of completed events of the abstract history satisfy the queue specification:

$$\forall H'. \lfloor H \rfloor \sqsubseteq H' \wedge \text{seq}(H') \implies H' \in \mathcal{H}_{\text{queue}} \wedge \text{same\_data}(s, H, G_{\text{ts}}, H')$$

(INV$_{\text{ORD}}$) properties of the partial order of the abstract history:
  (i) completed dequeues precede uncompleted ones:

$$\forall i \in \text{id}(\lfloor E \rfloor). \forall j \in \text{id}(E \setminus \lfloor E \rfloor). E(i).\text{op} = E(j).\text{op} = \text{Deq} \implies i \xrightarrow{R} j$$

  (ii) enqueues of already dequeued values precede enqueues of values in the pools:

$$\forall i \in \text{id}(\lfloor E \rfloor) \setminus \text{inQ}(s(\text{pools}), E, G_{\text{ts}}). \forall j \in \text{inQ}(s(\text{pools}), E, G_{\text{ts}}). i \xrightarrow{R} j$$

(INV$_{\text{ALG}}$) properties of the algorithm used to build the loop invariant:
  (i) enqueues of values in the pools are ordered only if so are their timestamps:

$$\forall i, j \in \text{inQ}(s(\text{pools}), E, G_{\text{ts}}). i \xrightarrow{R} j \implies G_{\text{ts}}(i) <_{\text{TS}} G_{\text{ts}}(j)$$

  (ii) values in each pool appear in the order of enqueues that inserted them:

$$\forall t, \tau_1, \tau_2. \text{pools}(t) = \_ \cdot (\_, \_, \tau_1) \cdot \_ \cdot (\_, \_, \tau_2) \cdot \_ \implies$$
$$\text{enqOf}(E, G_{\text{ts}}, t, \tau_1) \xrightarrow{R} \text{enqOf}(E, G_{\text{ts}}, t, \tau_2)$$

  (iii) the timestamps of values are smaller than the global counter:

$$\forall i, a, b. G_{\text{ts}}(i) = (a, b) \implies b < s(\text{counter})$$

(INV$_{\text{WF}}$) properties of ghost state:
  (i) G_{ts} associates timestamps with enqueue events:

$$\forall i. i \in \text{dom}(G_{\text{ts}}) \implies E(i).\text{op} = \text{Enq}$$

  (ii) each value in a pool has a matching event for the enqueue that inserted it:

$$\forall t, v, \tau. \text{pools}(t) = \_ \cdot (\_, v, \tau) \cdot \_ \implies \exists i. E(i) = (t, \text{Enq}, v, \_) \wedge G_{\text{ts}}(i) = \tau$$

  (iii) all timestamps assigned by G_{ts} to events of a given thread are distinct:

$$\forall i, j. i \neq j \wedge E(i).\text{tid} = E(j).\text{tid} \wedge i, j \in \text{dom}(G_{\text{ts}}) \implies G_{\text{ts}}(i) \neq G_{\text{ts}}(j)$$

  (iv) G_{ts} associates uncompleted enqueues events with the timestamp $\top$:

$$\forall i. E(i).\text{op} = \text{Enq} \implies (i \notin \text{id}(\lfloor E \rfloor) \iff i \notin \text{dom}(G_{\text{ts}}) \vee G_{\text{ts}}(i) = \top)$$

Fig. 10. The invariant INV = INV$_{\text{LIN}}$ $\wedge$ INV$_{\text{ORD}}$ $\wedge$ INV$_{\text{ALG}}$ $\wedge$ INV$_{\text{WF}}$

abstract history. To this end, for the `foreach` loop (lines 22–33) we build a loop invariant based on distinguishing certain values in the pools as *seen* by the `dequeue` operation. With the help of the loop invariant we establish that acyclicity is preserved at the commitment points.

Recall from Sect. 3, that the `foreach` loop starts iterating from a random pool. In the proof, we assume that the loop uses a thread-local variable A for storing a set of identifiers of threads that have been iterated over in the loop. We also assume that at the end of each iteration the set A is extended with the current loop index k.

(noCand): $\mathsf{seen}((s, H, G_{\mathsf{ts}}), \mathsf{myEid}()) = \emptyset \wedge s(\mathsf{cand\_pid}) = \mathrm{NULL}$

(minTS(e)): $\forall e' \in \mathsf{seen}((s, H, G_{\mathsf{ts}}), \mathsf{myEid}()). \neg(G_{\mathsf{ts}}(e') <_{\mathsf{TS}} G_{\mathsf{ts}}(e))$

(isCand): $\exists \mathsf{CAND}. \mathsf{CAND} = \mathsf{enqOf}(E, G_{\mathsf{ts}}, s(\mathsf{cand\_tid}), s(\mathsf{cand\_ts}))$

$\wedge \mathrm{minTS}(\mathsf{CAND}) \wedge (\mathsf{CAND} \in \mathsf{inQ}(s(\mathsf{pools}), E, G_{\mathsf{ts}}) \implies$

$\mathsf{CAND} \in \mathsf{seen}((s, H, G_{\mathsf{ts}}), \mathsf{myEid}()))) \wedge s(\mathsf{cand\_pid}) \neq \mathrm{NULL}$

Fig. 11. Auxiliary assertions for the loop invariant

Note also that for each thread k, the commitment point of a dequeue d at lines 25–26 ensures that enqueue events of values the operation sees in k's pool precede d in the abstract history. Based on that, during the foreach loop we can we distinguish enqueue events with values in the pools that a dequeue d has seen after looking into pools of threads from A. We define the set of all such enqueue events as follows:

$$\mathsf{seen}((s, (E, R), G_{\mathsf{ts}}), d) \triangleq \{e \mid e \in \mathsf{id}(\lfloor E \rfloor) \cap \mathsf{inQ}(s(\mathsf{pools}), E, G_{\mathsf{ts}})$$

$$\wedge\, e \xrightarrow{R} d \wedge \neg(s(\mathsf{start\_ts}) <_{\mathsf{TS}} G_{\mathsf{ts}}(e)) \wedge E(e).\mathsf{tid} \in \mathsf{A}\}$$

A loop invariant LI is simply a disjunction of two auxiliary assertions, isCand and noCand, which are defined in Fig. 11 (given an interpretation of logical variables ℓ, each of assertions denotes a set of configurations satisfying the listed constraints). The assertion noCand denotes a set of configurations $\kappa = (s, (E, R), G_{\mathsf{ts}})$, in which the dequeue operation has not chosen a candidate for removal after having iterated over the pools of threads from A. In this case, $s(\mathsf{cand\_pid}) = \mathrm{NULL}$, and the current dequeue has not seen any enqueue event in the pools of threads from A.

The assertion isCand denotes a set of configurations $\kappa = (s, (E, R), G_{\mathsf{ts}})$, in which an enqueue event $\mathsf{CAND} = \mathsf{enqOf}(E, G_{\mathsf{ts}}, \mathsf{cand\_tid}, \mathsf{cand\_ts})$ has been chosen as a candidate for removal out of the enqueues seen in the pools of threads from A. As CAND may be removed by a concurrent dequeue, isCand requires that CAND remain in the set $\mathsf{seen}(\kappa, \mathsf{myEid}())$ as long as CAND's value remains in the pools. Additionally, by requiring minTS(CAND), isCand asserts that the timestamp of CAND is minimal among other enqueues seen by $\mathsf{myEid}()$.

In the following lemma, we prove that the assertion isCand implies minimality of CAND in the abstract history among enqueue events with values in the pools of threads from A. The proof is based on the observation that enqueues of values seen in the pools by a dequeue are never preceded by unseen enqueues.

Lemma 1. *For every* $\ell : \mathsf{LVars} \to \mathsf{Val}$ *and configuration* $(s, (E, R), G_{\mathsf{ts}}) \in$ $[\![\mathsf{isCand}]\!]_\ell$, *if* $\mathsf{CAND} = \mathsf{enqOf}(E, G_{\mathsf{ts}}, \mathsf{cand\_tid}, \mathsf{cand\_ts})$ *and* $\mathsf{CAND} \in$ $\mathsf{inQ}(s(\mathsf{pools}), E, G_{\mathsf{ts}})$ *both hold, then the following is true:*

$$\forall e \in \mathsf{inQ}(s(\mathsf{pools}), \mathsf{E}, \mathsf{G_{ts}}). E(e).\mathsf{tid} \in \mathsf{A} \implies \neg(e \xrightarrow{R} \mathsf{CAND})$$

Acyclicity. At the commitment points extending the order of the abstract history, we need to show that the extended order is acyclic as required by

Definition 1 of the abstract history. To this end, we argue that the commitment points at lines 25–26 and lines 35–43 preserve acyclicity of the abstract history.

The commitment point at lines 25–26 orders certain completed enqueue events before the current uncompleted dequeue event myEid(). By Definition 1 of the abstract history, the partial order on its events is transitive, and uncompleted events do not precede other events. Since myEid() does not precede any other event, ordering any completed enqueue event before myEid() cannot create a cycle in the abstract history.

We now consider the commitment point at lines 35–43 in the current dequeue myEid(). Prior to the commitment point, the loop invariant LI has been established in all threads, and the check cand_pid $\neq$ NULL at line 34 has ruled out the case when noCand holds. Thus, the candidate for removal CAND has the properties described by isCand. If CAND's value has already been dequeued concurrently, the removal fails, and the abstract history remains intact (and acyclic). When the removal succeeds, we consider separately the two kind of edges added into the abstract history (E, R):

1. **The case of** (CAND, e) **for each** $e \in$ inQ(pools, E, G_{ts}). By Lemma 1, an edge (e, CAND) is not in the partial order R of the abstract history. There is also no sequence of edges $e \xrightarrow{R} \dots \xrightarrow{R} \text{CAND}$, since R is transitive by Definition 1. Hence, cycles do not arise from ordering CAND before e.

2. **The case of** (myEid(), d) **for each identifier** d **of an uncompleted dequeue event.** By Definition 1 of the abstract history, uncompleted events do not precede other events. Since d is uncompleted event, it does not precede myEid(). Hence, ordering myEid() in front of all such dequeue events does not create cycles.

Rely and Guarantee Relations. We now explain how we generate rely and guarantee relations for the proof. Instead of constructing the relations with the help of abstracted intermediate assertions of a proof outline for the enqueue and dequeue operations, we use the non-deterministic state transformers of primitive commands together with the ghost code in Figs. 4 and 5. To this end, the semantics of state transformers is extended to account for changes to abstract histories and ghost state. We found that generating rely and guarantee relations in such non-standard way results in cleaner stability proofs for the TS Queue, and makes them similar in style to checking non-interference in the Owicki-Gries method [18].

Let us refer to atomic blocks with corresponding ghost code at line 3, line 8, line 25 and line 35 as atomic steps insert, setTS, scan(k) (k $\in$ ThreadID) and remove respectively, and let us also refer to the CAS operation at line 42 as genTS. For each thread t and atomic step $\hat{\alpha}$, we assume a non-deterministic configuration transformer $[\![\hat{\alpha}]\!]_t$: Config $\rightarrow \mathcal{P}(\text{Config})$ that updates state according to the semantics of a corresponding primitive command, and history with ghost state as specified by ghost code.

Given an assertion P, an atomic step $\hat{\alpha}$ and a thread t, we associate them with the following relation $\mathcal{G}_{t,\hat{\alpha},P} \subseteq \mathsf{Config}^2$:

$$\mathcal{G}_{t,\hat{\alpha},P} \triangleq \{(\kappa, \kappa') \mid \exists \ell.\, \kappa \in [\![P]\!]_\ell \wedge \kappa' \in [\![\hat{\alpha}]\!]_t(\kappa)\}$$

Additionally, we assume a relation $\mathcal{G}_{t,\mathrm{local}}$, which describes arbitrary changes to certain program variables and no changes to the abstract history and the ghost state. That is, we say that pools and counter are *shared* program variables in the algorithm, and all others are *thread-local*, in the sense that every thread has its own copy of them. We let $\mathcal{G}_{t,\mathrm{local}}$ denote every possible change to thread-local variables of a thread t only.

For each thread t, relations $\mathcal{G}_t$ and $\mathcal{R}_t$ are defined as follows:

$$P_{\mathsf{op}} \triangleq \mathsf{INV} \wedge \mathrm{started}(t, \mathsf{op})$$
$$\mathcal{G}_t \triangleq (\textstyle\bigcup_{t' \in \mathsf{ThreadID}} \mathcal{G}_{t,\mathrm{scan}(t'),P_{\mathrm{Deq}}}) \cup \mathcal{G}_{t,\mathrm{remove},P_{\mathrm{Deq}}}$$
$$\qquad \cup\, \mathcal{G}_{t,\mathrm{insert},P_{\mathrm{Enq}}} \cup \mathcal{G}_{t,\mathrm{setTS},P_{\mathrm{Enq}}} \cup \mathcal{G}_{t,\mathrm{genTS},\mathsf{INV}} \cup \mathcal{G}_{t,\mathrm{local}},$$
$$\mathcal{R}_t \triangleq \textstyle\bigcup_{t' \in \mathsf{ThreadID}\setminus\{t\}} (\mathcal{G}_{t'} \cup \dashrightarrow_{t'})$$

As required by Theorem 1, the rely relation of a thread t accounts for addition of new events in every other thread t' by including $\dashrightarrow'_t$. Also, $\mathcal{R}_t$ takes into consideration every atomic step by the other threads. Thus, the rely and guarantee relations satisfy all the requirement 1 of the proof method from Theorem 1. It is easy to see that the requirement 1 is also fulfilled: the global invariant INV is simply preserved by each atomic step, so it is indeed stable under rely relations of each thread.

The key observation implying stability of the loop invariant in every thread t is presented in the following lemma, which states that environment transitions in the rely relation never extend the set of enqueues seen by a given dequeue.

Lemma 2. *If a dequeue event* DEQ *generated its timestamp* start_ts, *then:*

$$\forall \kappa, \kappa'.\, (\kappa, \kappa') \in \mathcal{R}_t \implies \mathsf{seen}(\kappa', \mathrm{DEQ}) \subseteq \mathsf{seen}(\kappa, \mathrm{DEQ})$$

8 The Optimistic Set: Informal Development

The Algorithm. We now present another example, the Optimistic Set [17], which is a variant of a classic algorithm by Heller et al. [8], rewritten to use atomic sections instead of locks. However, this is a highly-concurrent algorithm: every atomic section accesses a small bounded number of memory locations. In this section we only give an informal explanation of the proof and commitment points; the details are provided in [14].

The code in Fig. 12 implements the Optimistic Set as a sorted singly-linked list. Each node in the list has three fields: an integer val storing the key of the node, a pointer next to the subsequent node in the list, and a boolean flag marked that is set true when the node gets removed. The list also has sentinel nodes head and tail that store $-\infty$ and $+\infty$ as keys accordingly. The set defines

```
 1 struct Node {
 2   Node *next;
 3   Int val;
 4   Bool marked;
 5 }
 6
 7 Bool contains(v) {
 8   p, c := locate(v);
 9   return (c.val = v);
10 }
11
12 Bool insert(v) {
13   Node×Node p, c;
14   do {
15     p, c := locate(v);
16     atomic {
17       if (p.next = c
18         && !p.marked) {
18         commit_insert();
20         if (c.val ≠ v) {
21           Node *n := new Node;
22           n->next := c;
23           n->val := v;
24           n->marked := false;
25           p.next := n;
26           return true;
27         } else
28           return false;
29       }
30     }
31   } while (true);
32 }
```

```
33 Node×Node locate(v) {
34   Node prev := head;
35   Node curr := prev.next;
36   while (curr.val < v) {
37     prev := curr;
38     atomic {
39       curr := curr.next;
40       if (E(myEid()).op = contains
41         && (curr.val ≥ v))
42         commit_contains();
45       }
46   }
47   return prev, curr;
48 }
49
50 Bool remove(v) {
51   Node×Node p, c;
52   do {
53     p, c := locate(v);
54     atomic {
55       if (p.next = c
56         && !p.marked) {
55         commit_remove();
57         if (c.val = v) {
58           c.marked := true;
59           p.next := c.next;
60           return true;
61         } else
62           return false;
63       }
64     }
65   } while (true);
66 }
```

Fig. 12. The optimistic set. Shaded portions are auxiliary code used in the proof

three operations: insert, remove and contains. Each of them uses an internal operation locate to traverse the list. Given a value v, locate traverses the list nodes and returns a pair of nodes (p, c), out of which c has a key greater or equal to v, and p is the node preceding c.

The insert (remove) operation spins in a loop locating a place after which a new node should be inserted (after which a candidate for removal should be) and attempting to atomically modify the data structure. The attempt may fail if either p.next = c or !p.marked do not hold: the former condition ensures that concurrent operations have not removed or inserted new nodes immediately after p.next, and the latter checks that p has not been removed from the set. When either check fails, the operation restarts. Both conditions are necessary for preserving integrity of the data structure.

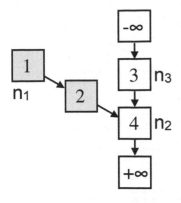

Fig. 13. Example state of the optimistic set. Shaded nodes have their "marked" field set.

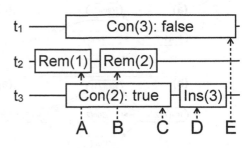

Fig. 14. Example execution of the set. "Ins" and "Rem" denote successful **insert** and **remove** operations accordingly, and "Con" denotes **contains** operations. A–E correspond to commitment points of operations.

When the elements are removed from the set, their corresponding nodes have the marked flag set and get unlinked from the list. However, the next field of the removed node is not altered, so marked and unmarked nodes of the list form a tree such that each node points towards the root, and only nodes reachable from the head of the list are unmarked. In Fig. 13, we have an example state of the data structure. The insert and remove operations determine the position of a node p in the tree by checking the flag p.marked. In remove, this check prevents removing the same node from the data structure twice. In insert, checking !p.marked ensures that the new node n is not inserted into a branch of removed nodes and is reachable from the head of the list.

In contrast to insert and remove, contains never modifies the shared state and never restarts. This leads to a subtle interaction that may happen due to interference by concurrent events: it may be correct for contains to return true even though the node may have been removed by the time contains finds it in the list.

In Fig. 13, we illustrate the subtleties with the help of a state of the set, which is a result of executing the trace from Fig. 14, assuming that values 1, 2 and 4 have been initially inserted in sequence by performing "Ins(1)", "Ins(2)" and "Ins(4)". We consider the following scenario. First, "Con(2)" and "Con(3)" start traversing through the list and get preempted when they reach the node containing 1, which we denote by n_1. Then the operations are finished in the order depicted in Fig. 14. Note that "Con(2)" returns true even though the node containing 2 is removed from the data structure by the time the contains operation locates it. This surprising behaviour occurs due to the values 1 and 2 being on the same branch of marked nodes in the list, which makes it possible for "Con(2)" to resume traversing from n_1 and find 2. On the other hand, "Con(3)" cannot find 3 by traversing the nodes from n_1: the contains operation will reach the node n_2 and return false, even though 3 has been concurrently inserted into the set by this time. Such behaviour is correct, since it can be

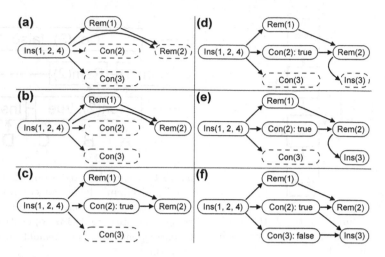

Fig. 15. Changes to the abstract history of the execution in Fig. 14. Edges implied by transitivity are omitted.

justified by a linearization ["Ins(1)", "Ins(2)", "Ins(4)", "Rem(1)", "Con(2): true", "Rem(2)", "Con(3): false", "Ins(3)"]. Intuitively, such linearization order is possible, because pairs of events ("Con(2): true", "Rem(2)") and ("Con(3): false", "Ins(3)") overlap in the execution.

Building a correct linearization order by identifying a linearization point of contains is complex, since it depends on presence of concurrent insert and remove operation as well as on current position in the traversal of the data structure. We demonstrate a different approach to the proof of the Optimistic Set based on the following insights. Firstly, we observe that only decisions about a relative order of operations with the same argument need to be committed into the abstract history, since linearizability w.r.t. the sequential specification of a set does not require enforcing any additional order on concurrent operations with different arguments. Secondly, we postpone decisions about ordering contains operations w.r.t. concurrent events till their return values are determined. Thus, in the abstract history for Fig. 14, "Con(2): true" and "Rem(2)" remain unordered until the former encounters the node removed by the latter, and the order between operations becomes clear. Intuitively, we construct a linear order on completed events with the same argument, and let contains operations be inserted in a certain place in that order rather than appended to it.

Preliminaries. We assume that a set NodeID is a set of pointers to nodes, and that the state of the linked list is represented by a partial map NodeID $\rightharpoonup$ NodeID $\times$ Int $\times$ Bool. To aid in constructing the abstract history (E, R), the code maintains a piece of ghost state—a partial function G_{node} : EventID $\rightharpoonup$ NodeID. Given the identifier i of an event $E(i)$ denoting an insert that has inserted its value into the set, $G_{node}(i)$ returns a node identifier (a pointer) of that value in the data structure. Similarly, for a successful remove event identifier i, $G_{node}(i)$ returns a node identifier that the corresponding operation removed from the data structure.

```
OrderInsRem() {
```

$$R := (R \cup \{(e, \text{myEid}()) \mid e \in \text{id}(\lfloor E \rfloor) \wedge E(e).\text{arg} = E(\text{myEid}()).\text{arg}\})^+;$$
$$R := (R \cup \{(\text{myEid}(), e) \mid e \in \text{id}(E \setminus \lfloor E \rfloor) \wedge E(e).\text{arg} = \text{myEid}().\text{arg}$$
$$\wedge\, E(e).\text{op} \neq \text{contains}\})^+;$$

```
}
```

```
commit_insert () {
```

$$E(\text{myEid}()).\text{rval} := (c.\text{val} \neq v);$$
```
    if (c.val ≠ v)
```
$$G_{\text{node}}[\text{myEid}()] := c;$$
```
    OrderInsRem();
}
```

```
commit_remove () {
```

$$E(\text{myEid}()).\text{rval} := (c.\text{val} = v);$$
```
    if (c.val = v)
```
$$G_{\text{node}}[\text{myEid}()] := c;$$
```
    OrderInsRem();
}
```

Fig. 16. The auxiliary code executed at the commitment points of `insert` and `remove`

Commitment Points. The commitment points in the `insert` and `remove` operations are denoted by ghost code in Fig. 16. They are similar in structure and update the order of events in the abstract history in the same way described by `OrderInsRem`. That is, these commitment points maintain a linear order on completed events of operations with the same argument: on the first line of `OrderInsRem`, the current `insert`/`remove` event identified by `myEid()` gets ordered after each operation e with the same argument as `myEid()`. On the second line of `OrderInsRem`, uncompleted `insert` and `remove` events with the same argument are ordered after `myEid()`. Note that uncompleted `contains` events remain unordered w.r.t. `myEid()`, so that later on at the commitment point of `contains` they could be ordered before the current `insert` or `remove` operation (depending on whether they return `false` or `true` accordingly), if it is necessary.

At the commitment point, the `remove` operation assigns a return value to the corresponding event. When the removal is successful, the commitment point associates the removed node with the event by updating G_{node}. Let us illustrate how `commit_remove` changes abstract histories on the example. For the execution in Fig. 14, after starting the operation "Rem(2)" we have the abstract history Fig. 15(a), and then at point (B) "Rem(2)" changes the history to Fig. 15(b). The uncompleted event "Con(2)" remains unordered w.r.t. "Rem(2)" until it determines its return value (`true`) later on in the execution, at which point it gets ordered before "Rem(2)".

At the commitment point, the `insert` operation assigns a return value to the event based on the check `c.val ≠ v` determining whether `v` is already in the set. In the execution Fig. 14, prior to the start of "Ins(3)" we have the abstract history Fig. 15(c). When the event starts, a new event is added into the history (commitment point of kind 1), which changes it to Fig. 15(d). At point (D) in the execution, `commit_insert` takes place, and the history is updated to Fig. 15(e). Note that "Ins(3)" and "Con(3)" remain unordered until the latter determines its return value (`false`) and orders itself before "Ins(3)" in the abstract history.

```
commit_contains() {
```

$E(\text{myEid}()).\text{rval} := (\text{curr.val} = \text{v});$
$\text{EventID obs} := \text{if } (\text{curr.val} = \text{v}) \text{ then } \text{insOf}(E, \text{curr})$
$\qquad\qquad\qquad\qquad\qquad\qquad \text{else } \text{lastRemOf}(E, R, \text{v});$
$\text{if } (\text{obs} \neq \bot)$
$\quad R := (R \cup \{(\text{obs}, \text{myEid}())\})^+;$
$R := (R \cup \{(\text{myEid}(), i) \mid \neg(i \xrightarrow{R} \text{myEid}()) \wedge E(i).\text{arg} = E(\text{myEid}()).\text{arg}\})^+;$

```
}
```

where for an abstract history (E, R), a node identifier n and a value v:

$$\text{insOf}(E, n) = \begin{cases} i, \text{if } G_{\text{node}}(i) = n, E(i).\text{op} = \text{insert and } E(i).\text{rval} = \text{true} \\ \text{undefined otherwise} \end{cases}$$

$$\text{lastRemOf}(E, R, v) = \begin{cases} i, & \text{if } E(i) = (\_, \text{remove}, v, \text{true}) \\ & \wedge (\forall i'. E(i).\text{op} = \text{remove} \wedge E(i').\text{arg} = v \implies \\ & \qquad\qquad\qquad\qquad\qquad\qquad\qquad i' \xrightarrow{R} i) \\ \bot, & \text{if } \neg\exists i. E(i) = (\_, \text{remove}, v, \text{true}) \end{cases}$$

Fig. 17. The auxiliary code executed at the commitment point of `contains`

The commitment point at lines 40–42 of the `contains` operation occurs at the last iteration of the sorted list traversal in the `locate` method. The last iteration takes place when `curr.val` $\geq v$ holds. In Fig. 17, we present the auxiliary code `commit_contains` executed at line 42 in this case. Depending on whether a requested value is found or not, the abstract history is updated differently, so we further explain the two cases separately. In both cases, the `contains` operation determines which event in the history it should immediately follow in all linearizations.

Case (i). If `curr.val = v`, the requested value `v` is found, so the current event `myEid()` receives `true` as its return value. In this case, `commit_contains` adds two kinds of edges in the abstract history.

– Firstly, $(\text{insOf}(E, \text{curr}), \text{myEid}())$ is added to ensure that `myEid()` occurs in all linearizations of the abstract history after the `insert` event of the node `curr`.
– Secondly, $(\text{myEid}(), i)$ is added for every other identifier i of an event that does not precede `myEid()` and has an argument v. The requirement not to precede `myEid()` is explained by the following. Even though at commitment points of `insert` and `remove` operations we never order events w.r.t. `contains` events, there still may be events preceding `myEid()` in real-time order. Consequently, it may be impossible to order `myEid()` immediately after $\text{insOf}(E, \text{curr})$.

At point (C) in the example from Fig. 14, commit$_{\text{contains}}$ in "Con(2)" changes the history from Fig. 15(b) to (c). To this end, "Con(2)" is completed with a return value true and gets ordered after "Ins(2)" (this edge happened to be already in the abstract history due to the real-time order), and also in front of events following "Ins(2)", but not preceding "Con(2)". This does not include "Ins(4)" due to the real-time ordering, but includes "Rem(2)", so the latter is ordered after the contains event, and all linearizations of the abstract history Fig. 15(c) meet the sequential specification in this example. In general case, we also need to show that successful remove events do not occur between insOf$(E, \text{curr}), \text{myEid}()$) and myEid() in the resulting abstract history, which we establish formally in [14]. Intuitively, when myEid() returns true, all successful removes after insOf(E, curr) are concurrent with myEid(): if they preceded myEid() in the real-time order, it would be impossible for the contains operation to reach the removed node by starting from the head of the list in order return true.

Case (ii). Prior to executing commit$_{\text{contains}}$, at line 40 we check that curr.val $\geq$ v. Thus, if curr.val = v does not hold in commit$_{\text{contains}}$, the requested value v is not found in the sorted list, and false becomes the return value of the current event myEid(). In this case, commit$_{\text{contains}}$ adds two kinds of edges in the abstract history.

– Firstly, (lastRemOf$(E, R, \text{v}), \text{myEid}())$ is added, when there are successful remove events of value v (note that they are linearly ordered by construction of the abstract history, so we can choose the last of them). This ensures that myEid() occurs after a successful remove event in all linearizations of the abstract history.
– Secondly, (myEid()$, i$) is added for every other identifier i of an event that does not precede myEid() and has an argument v, which is analogous to the case (i).

Intuitively, if v has never been removed from the set, myEid() needs to happen in the beginning of the abstract history and does not need to be ordered after any event.

For example, at point (D) in the execution from Fig. 14, commit$_{\text{contains}}$ changes the abstract history from Fig. 15(e) to (f). To this end, "Con(3)" is ordered in front of all events with argument 3 (specifically, "Ins(3)"), since there are no successful removes of 3 in the abstract history. Analogously to the case (i), in general to ensure that all linearizations of the resulting abstract history meet the sequential specification, we need to show that there cannot be any successful insert events of v between lastRemOf(E, R, v) (or the beginning of the abstract history, if it is undefined) and myEid(). We prove this formally in [14]. Intuitively, when myEid() returns false, all successful insert events after lastRemOf(E, R, v) (or the beginning of the history) are concurrent with myEid(): if they preceded myEid() in the real-time order, the inserted nodes would be possible to reach by starting from the head of the list, in which case the contains operation could not possibly return false.

9   Related Work

There has been a great deal of work on proving algorithms linearizable; see [3] for a broad survey. However, despite a large number of techniques, often supported by novel mathematical theory, it remains the case that all but the simplest algorithms are difficult to verify. Our aim is to verify the most complex kind of linearizable algorithms, those where the linearization of a set of operations cannot be determined solely by examining the prefix of the program execution consisting of these operations. Furthermore, we aim to do this while maintaining a relatively simple proof argument.

Much work on proving linearizability is based on different kinds of *simulation proofs*. Loosely speaking, in this approach the linearization of an execution is built incrementally by considering either its prefixes or suffixes (respectively known as *forward* and *backward* simulations). This supports inductive proofs of linearizability: the proof involves showing that the execution and its linearization stay in correspondence under forward or backward program steps. The linearization point method is an instance of forward simulation: a syntactic point in the code of an operation is used to determine when to add it to the linearization.

As we explained in Sect. 1, forward simulation alone is not sufficient in general to verify linearizability. However, Schellhorn et al. [19] prove that backward simulation alone *is* always sufficient. They also present a proof technique and use it to verify the Herlihy-Wing queue [11]. However, backwards simulation proofs are difficult to understand intuitively: programs execute forwards in time, and therefore it is much more natural to reason this way.

The queue originally proposed by Herlihy and Wing in their paper on linearizability [11] has proved very difficult to verify. Their proof sketch is based on reasoning about the possible linearizations arising from a given queue configuration. Our method could be seen as being midway between this approach and linearization points. We use partiality in the abstract history to represent sets of possible linearizations, which helps us simplify the proof by omitting irrelevant ordering (Sect. 2).

Another class of approach to proving linearizability is based on special-purpose program logics. These can be seen as a kind of forward simulation: assertions in the proof represent the connection between program execution and its linearization. To get around the incompleteness of forward simulation, several authors have introduced auxiliary notions that support limited reasoning about future behaviour in the execution, and thus allow the proof to decide the order of operations in the linearization [15,21,22]. However, these new constructs have subtle semantics, which results in proofs that are difficult to understand intuitively.

Our approach is based on program logic, and therefore is a kind of forward simulation. The difference between us and previous program logics is that we do not explicitly construct a linear order on operations, but only a partial order. This removes the need for special constructs for reasoning about future behaviour, but creates the obligation to show that the partially ordered abstract history can always be linearized.

One related approach to ours is that of Hemed et al. [9], who generalise linearizability to data structures with concurrent specifications (such as barriers) and propose a proof method for establishing it. To this end, they also consider histories where some events are partially ordered—such events are meant to happen concurrently. However, the goal of Hemed et al.'s work is different from ours: their abstract histories are never linearized, to allow concurrent specifications; in contrast, we guarantee the existence of a linearization consistent with a sequential specification. It is likely that the two approaches can be naturally combined.

Aspect proofs [10] are a non-simulation approach that is related to our work. An aspect proof imposes a set of forbidden shapes on the real-time order on methods; if an algorithm avoids these shapes, then it is necessarily linearizable. These shapes are specific to a particular data structure, and indeed the method as proposed in [10] is limited to queues (extended to stacks in [2]). In contrast, our proof method is generic, not tied to a particular kind of data structure. Furthermore, checking the absence of forbidden shapes in the aspect method requires global reasoning about the whole program execution, whereas our approach supports inductive proofs. The original proof of the TS stack used an extended version of the aspect approach [2]. However, without a way of reasoning inductively about programs, the proof of correctness reduced to a large case-split on possible executions. This made the proof involved and difficult. Our proof is based on an inductive argument, which makes it easier.

Another class of algorithms that are challenging to verify are those that use *helping*, where operations complete each others' work. In such algorithms, an operation's position in the linearization order may be fixed by a helper method. Our approach can also naturally reason about this pattern: the helper operation may modify the abstract history to mark the event of the operation being helped as completed.

The Optimistic set was also proven linearizable by O'Hearn et al. in [17]. The essence of the work is a collection of lemmas (including the Hindsight Lemma) proven outside of the logic to justify conclusions about properties of the past of executions based on the current state. Based on our case study of the Optimistic set algorithm, we conjecture that at commitment points we make a constructive decision about extending abstract history where the hindsight proof would use the Hindsight Lemma to non-constructively extend a linearization with the `contains` operation.

10   Conclusion and Future Work

The popular approach to proving linearizability is to construct a total linearization order by appending new operations as the program executes. This approach is straightforward, but is limited in the range of algorithms it can handle. In this paper, we present a new approach which lifts these limitations, while preserving the appealing incremental proof structure of traditional linearization points. As with linearization points, our fundamental idea can be explained simply:

at commitment points, operations impose order between themselves and other operations, and all linearizations of the order must satisfy the sequential specification. Nonetheless, our technique generalises to far more subtle algorithms than traditional linearization points.

We have applied our approach to two algorithms known to present particular problems for linearization points. Although, we have not presented it here, our approach scales naturally to *helping*, where an operation is completed by another thread. We can support this, by letting any thread complete the operation in an abstract history. In future work, we plan to apply our approach to the Time-Stamped stack [2], which poses verification challenges similar to the TS queue; a flat-combining style algorithm, which depends fundamentally on helping, as well as a range of other challenging algorithms. In this paper we have concentrated on simplifying manual proofs. However, our approach also seems like a promising candidate for automation, as it requires no special meta-theory, just reasoning about partial orders. We are hopeful that we can automate such arguments using off-the-shelf solvers such as Z3, and we plan to experiment with this in future.

References

1. Dinsdale-Young, T., Dodds, M., Gardner, P., Parkinson, M.J., Vafeiadis, V.: Concurrent abstract predicates. In: D'Hondt, T. (ed.) ECOOP 2010. LNCS, vol. 6183, pp. 504–528. Springer, Heidelberg (2010). doi:10.1007/978-3-642-14107-2_24
2. Dodds, M., Haas, A., Kirsch, C.M.: A scalable, correct time-stamped stack. In: POPL (2015)
3. Dongol, B., Derrick, J.: Verifying linearizability: a comparative survey. arXiv CoRR, 1410.6268 (2014)
4. Filipovic, I., O'Hearn, P.W., Rinetzky, N., Yang, H.: Abstraction for concurrent objects. Theor. Comput. Sci. **411**(51–52), 4379–4398 (2010)
5. Fishburn, P.C.: Intransitive indifference with unequal indifference intervals. J. Math. Psychol. **7**, 144–149 (1970)
6. Gotsman, A., Yang, H.: Linearizability with ownership transfer. In: Koutny, M., Ulidowski, I. (eds.) CONCUR 2012. LNCS, vol. 7454, pp. 256–271. Springer, Heidelberg (2012). doi:10.1007/978-3-642-32940-1_19
7. Haas, A.: Fast concurrent data structures through timestamping. Ph.D. thesis, University of Salzburg (2015)
8. Heller, S., Herlihy, M., Luchangco, V., Moir, M., Scherer, W.N., Shavit, N.: A lazy concurrent list-based set algorithm. In: Anderson, J.H., Prencipe, G., Wattenhofer, R. (eds.) OPODIS 2005. LNCS, vol. 3974, pp. 3–16. Springer, Heidelberg (2006). doi:10.1007/11795490_3
9. Hemed, N., Rinetzky, N., Vafeiadis, V.: Modular verification of concurrency-aware linearizability. In: Moses, Y. (ed.) DISC 2015. LNCS, vol. 9363, pp. 371–387. Springer, Heidelberg (2015). doi:10.1007/978-3-662-48653-5_25
10. Henzinger, T.A., Sezgin, A., Vafeiadis, V.: Aspect-oriented linearizability proofs. In: D'Argenio, P.R., Melgratti, H. (eds.) CONCUR 2013. LNCS, vol. 8052, pp. 242–256. Springer, Heidelberg (2013). doi:10.1007/978-3-642-40184-8_18
11. Herlihy, M., Wing, J.M.: Linearizability: a correctness condition for concurrent objects. In: ACM TOPLAS (1990)

12. Hoffman, M., Shalev, O., Shavit, N.: The baskets queue. In: Tovar, E., Tsigas, P., Fouchal, H. (eds.) OPODIS 2007. LNCS, vol. 4878, pp. 401–414. Springer, Heidelberg (2007). doi:10.1007/978-3-540-77096-1_29
13. Jones, C.B.: Specification and design of (parallel) programs. In: IFIP Congress (1983)
14. Khyzha, A., Dodds, M., Gotsman, A., Parkinson, M.: Proving linearizability using partial orders (extended version). arXiv CoRR, 1701.05463 (2017)
15. Liang, H., Feng, X.: Modular verification of linearizability with non-fixed linearization points. In: PLDI (2013)
16. Morrison, A., Afek, Y.: Fast concurrent queues for x86 processors. In: PPoPP (2013)
17. O'Hearn, P.W., Rinetzky, N., Vechev, M.T., Yahav, E., Yorsh, G.: Verifying linearizability with hindsight. In: PODC (2010)
18. Owicki, S.S., Gries, D.: An axiomatic proof technique for parallel programs I. Acta Informatica **6**, 319–340 (1976)
19. Schellhorn, G., Derrick, J., Wehrheim, H.: A sound and complete proof technique for linearizability of concurrent data structures. ACM TOCL **15**(4), 31 (2014)
20. Turon, A., Dreyer, D., Birkedal, L.: Unifying refinement and hoare-style reasoning in a logic for higher-order concurrency. In: ICFP (2013)
21. Turon, A.J., Thamsborg, J., Ahmed, A., Birkedal, L., Dreyer, D.: Logical relations for fine-grained concurrency. In: POPL (2013)
22. Vafeiadis, V.: Modular fine-grained concurrency verification. Ph.D. thesis, University of Cambridge, UK (2008). Technical report UCAM-CL-TR-726

The Power of Non-determinism in Higher-Order Implicit Complexity

Characterising Complexity Classes Using Non-deterministic Cons-Free Programming

Cynthia Kop[✉] and Jakob Grue Simonsen

Department of Computer Science,
University of Copenhagen (DIKU), Copenhagen, Denmark
{kop,simonsen}@di.ku.dk

Abstract. We investigate the power of non-determinism in purely functional programming languages with higher-order types. Specifically, we consider *cons-free* programs of varying data orders, equipped with explicit non-deterministic choice. Cons-freeness roughly means that data constructors cannot occur in function bodies and all manipulation of storage space thus has to happen indirectly using the call stack.

While cons-free programs have previously been used by several authors to characterise complexity classes, the work on *non-deterministic* programs has almost exclusively considered programs of data order 0. Previous work has shown that adding explicit non-determinism to cons-free programs taking data of order 0 does not increase expressivity; we prove that this—dramatically—is not the case for higher data orders: adding non-determinism to programs with data order at least 1 allows for a characterisation of the entire class of elementary-time decidable sets.

Finally we show how, even with non-deterministic choice, the original hierarchy of characterisations is restored by imposing different restrictions.

Keywords: Implicit computational complexity · Cons-free programming · EXPTIME hierarchy · Non-deterministic programming · Unitary variables

1 Introduction

Implicit complexity is, roughly, the study of how to create bespoke programming languages that allow the programmer to write programs which are guaranteed to (a) *only* solve problems within a certain complexity class (e.g., the class of polynomial-time decidable sets of binary strings), and (b) to be able to solve *all* problems in this class. When equipped with an efficient execution engine, the

The authors are supported by the Marie Skłodowska-Curie action "HORIP", program H2020-MSCA-IF-2014, 658162 and by the Danish Council for Independent Research Sapere Aude grant "Complexity via Logic and Algebra" (COLA).

© Springer-Verlag GmbH Germany 2017
H. Yang (Ed.): ESOP 2017, LNCS 10201, pp. 668–695, 2017.
DOI: 10.1007/978-3-662-54434-1_25

programs of such a language may themselves be guaranteed to run within the complexity bounds of the class (e.g., run in polynomial time), and the plethora of means available for analysing programs devised by the programming language community means that methods from outside traditional complexity theory can conceivably be brought to bear on open problems in computational complexity.

One successful approach to implicit complexity is to syntactically constrain the programmer's ability to create new data structures. In the seminal paper [12], Jones introduces *cons-free programming*. Working with a small functional programming language, cons-free programs are *read-only*: recursive data cannot be created or altered (beyond taking sub-expressions), only read from input. By imposing further restrictions on *data order* (i.e., order $0 =$ integers, strings; order $1 =$ functions on data of order 0; etc.) and recursion scheme (e.g., full/tail/primitive recursion), classes of cons-free programs turn out to characterise various deterministic classes in the time and space hierarchies of computational complexity.

However, Jones' language is deterministic and, perhaps as a result, his characterisations concern only deterministic complexity classes. It is tantalising to consider the method in a non-deterministic setting: could adding non-deterministic choice to Jones' language increase its expressivity; for example, from P to NP?

The immediate answer is *no*: following Bonfante [4], adding a non-deterministic choice operator to cons-free programs with data order 0 makes no difference in expressivity—deterministic or not, they characterise P. However, the details are subtle and depend heavily on other features of the language; when only primitive recursion is allowed, non-determinism *does* increase expressivity from L to NL [4].

While many authors consider the expressivity of higher types, the interplay of higher types and non-determinism is not fully understood. Jones obtains several hierarchies of deterministic complexity classes by increasing data orders [12], but these hierarchies have at most an exponential increase between levels. Given the expressivity added by non-determinism, it is *a priori* not evident that similarly "tame" hierarchies would arise in the non-deterministic setting.

The purpose of the present paper is to investigate the power of *higher-order* (cons-free) programming to characterise complexity classes. The main surprise is that while non-determinism does not add expressivity for first-order programs, the combination of second-order (or higher) programs and non-determinism characterises the full class of elementary-time decidable sets—and increasing the order beyond second-order programs does not further increase expressivity. However, we will also show that there are simple changes to the restrictions that allow us to obtain a hierarchy of characterisations as in the deterministic setting.

An extended version of this paper with full proofs is available online [15].

1.1   Overview and Contributions

We define a purely functional programming language with non-deterministic choice and, following Jones [12], consider the restriction to *cons-free* programs.

	data order 0	data order 1	data order 2	data order 3
cons-free deterministic	$P =$ EXP^0TIME	$\text{EXP} =$ EXP^1TIME	EXP^2TIME	EXP^3TIME
cons-free tail-recursive deterministic	L $=$ $\text{EXP}^{-1}\text{SPACE}$	PSPACE $=$ EXP^0SPACE	EXP^1SPACE	EXP^2SPACE
cons-free primitive recursive deterministic	L $=$ $\text{EXP}^{-1}\text{SPACE}$	P $=$ EXP^0TIME	PSPACE $=$ EXP^0SPACE	EXP $=$ EXP^1TIME

The characterisations obtained in [12], transposed to the more permissive language used here. The table should be imagined as extending infinitely to the right.

	data order 0	data order 1	data order 2	data order 3
cons-free	P	ELEMENTARY	ELEMENTARY	ELEMENTARY
cons-free unitary variables	$P =$ EXP^0TIME	$\text{EXP} =$ EXP^1TIME	EXP^2TIME	EXP^3TIME

The characterisations obtained by allowing non-deterministic choice.

	arrow depth 0	arrow depth 1	arrow depth 2	arrow depth 3
cons-free	P	ELEMENTARY	ELEMENTARY	ELEMENTARY

The characterisations obtained by allowing non-deterministic choice and considering *arrow depth* as the variable factor rather than data order

Fig. 1. Overview of the results discussed or obtained in this paper.

Our results are summarised in Fig. 1. For completeness, we have also included the results from [12]; although the language used there is slightly more syntactically restrictive than ours, the results easily generalise provided we limit interest to *deterministic* programs, where the **choose** operator is not used. As the technical machinations involved to procure the results for a language with full recursion are already intricate and lengthy, we have not yet considered the restriction to tail- or primitive recursion in the non-deterministic setting.

Essentially, our paper has two major contributions: (a) we show that previous observations about the increase in expressiveness when adding non-determinism change dramatically at higher types, and (b) we provide two characterisations of the EXPTIME hierarchy using a non-deterministic language—which may provide a basis for future characterisation of common non-deterministic classes as well.

Note that (a) is highly surprising: As evidenced by early work of Cook [6] merely adding full non-determinism to a restricted (i.e., non-Turing complete) computation model may result in it still characterising a *deterministic* class of problems. This also holds true for cons-free programs with non-determinism, as shown in different settings by Bonfante [4], by de Carvalho and Simonsen [7], and by Kop and Simonsen [14], all resulting only in characterisations of deterministic classes such as P. With the exception of [14], all of the above attempts at adding non-determinism consider data order at most 0, and one would expect few changes when passing to higher data orders. This turns out to be patently false as simply increasing to data order 1 already results in an explosion of expressive power.

1.2 Overview of the Ideas in the Paper

Cons-free programs (Definition 5) are, roughly, functional programs where function bodies are allowed to contain constant data and substructures of the function arguments, but *no data constructors*—e.g., clauses tl $(x::xs) = xs$ and tl $[] = []$ are both allowed, but append $(x::xs)$ $ys = x::($append xs $ys)$ is not.[1] This restriction severely limits expressivity, as it means no new data can be created.

A key idea in Jones' original work on cons-free programming is *counting*: expressions which represent numbers and functions to calculate with them. It is not in general possible to represent numbers in the usual unary way as 0, s 0, s (s 0), etc., or as lists of bits—since in a cons-free program these expressions cannot be built unless they already occur in the input—but counting up to limited bounds *can* be achieved by other tricks. By repeatedly simulating a single step of a Turing Machine up to such bounds, Jones shows that any decision problem in $\mathsf{EXP}^K\mathsf{TIME}$ can be decided using a cons-free program ([12] and Lemma 6).

The core insight in the present paper is that in the presence of non-determinism, an expression of type $\sigma \Rightarrow \tau$ represents a *relation* between expressions of type σ and expressions of type τ rather than a *function*. While the number of functions for a given type is exponential in the order of that type, the number of relations is exponential in the depth of arrows occurring in it. We exploit this (in Lemma 11) by counting up to arbitrarily high numbers using only first-order data. This observation also suggest that by limiting the *arrow depth* rather than the *order of types*, the increase in expressive power disappears (Theorem 3).

Conversely, we also provide an algorithm to compute the output of cons-free programs potentially much faster than the program's own running time, by using a tableaux to store results. Although similar to Jones' ideas, our proof style deviates to easily support both non-deterministic and deterministic programs.

1.3 Related Work

The creation of programming languages that characterise complexity classes has been a research area since Cobham's work in the 1960ies, but saw rapid development only after similar advances in the related area of *descriptive complexity* (see, e.g., [10]) in the 1980ies and Bellantoni and Cook's work on characterisations of P [2] using constraints on recursion in a purely functional language with programs reminiscent of classic recursion theoretic functions. Following Bellantoni and Cook, a number of authors obtained programming languages

---

[1] The formal definition is slightly more liberal to support easier implementations using pattern-matching, but the ideas remain the same.

by constraints on recursion, and under a plethora of names (e.g., *safe*, *tiered* or *ramified* recursion, see [5,19] for overviews), and this area continues to be active. The main difference with our work is that we consider full recursion in all variables, but place syntactic constraints on the function bodies (both cons-freeness and unitary variables). Also, as in traditional complexity theory we consider decision problems (i.e., what *sets* can be decided by programs), whereas much research in implicit complexity considers functional complexity (i.e., what *functions* can be computed).

Cons-free programs, combined with various limitations on recursion, were introduced by Jones [12], building on ground-breaking work by Goerdt [8,9], and have been studied by a number of authors (see, e.g., [3,4,17,18]). The main difference with our work is that we consider full recursion with full non-determinism, but impose constraints not present in the previous literature.

Characterisation of non-deterministic complexity classes via programming languages remains a largely unexplored area. Bellantoni obtained a characterisation of NP in his dissertation [1] using similar approaches as [2], but at the cost of having a minimisation operator (as in recursion theory), a restriction later removed by Oitavem [20]. A general framework for implicitly characterising a larger hierarchy of non-deterministic classes remains an open problem.

2   A Purely Functional, Non-deterministic, Call-by-Value Programming Language

We define a simple call-by-value programming language with explicit non-deterministic choice. This generalises Jones' toy language in [12] by supporting different types and pattern-matching as well as non-determinism. The more permissive language actually *simplifies* proofs and examples, since we do not need to encode all data as boolean lists, and have fewer special cases.

2.1   Syntax

We consider programs defined by the syntax in Fig. 2

$$
\begin{aligned}
\mathsf{p} \in \mathbf{Program} &::= \rho_1\ \rho_2\ \cdots\ \rho_N \\
\rho \in \mathbf{Clause} &::= \mathsf{f}\ \ell_1 \cdots \ell_k = s \\
\ell \in \mathbf{Pattern} &::= x \mid \mathsf{c}\ \ell_1 \cdots \ell_m \\
s,t \in \mathbf{Expr} &::= x \mid \mathsf{c} \mid \mathsf{f} \mid \mathsf{if}\ s_1\ \mathsf{then}\ s_2\ \mathsf{else}\ s_3 \mid \mathsf{choose}\ s_1 \cdots s_n \mid (s,t) \mid s\ t \\
x,y \in \mathcal{V} &::= \text{identifier} \\
\mathsf{c} \in \mathcal{C} &::= \text{identifier disjoint from } \mathcal{V} \quad (\text{we assume } \{\mathsf{true}, \mathsf{false}\} \subseteq \mathcal{C}) \\
\mathsf{f}, \mathsf{g} \in \mathcal{D} &::= \text{identifier disjoint from } \mathcal{V} \text{ and } \mathcal{C}
\end{aligned}
$$

Fig. 2. Syntax

We call elements of $\mathcal{V}$ *variables*, elements of $\mathcal{C}$ *data constructors* and elements of $\mathcal{D}$ *defined symbols*. The *root* of a clause $\mathsf{f}\ \ell_1 \cdots \ell_k = s$ is the defined symbol

f. The *main function* f_1 of the program is the root of ρ_1. We denote $Var(s)$ for the set of variables occurring in an expression s. An expression s is *ground* if $Var(s) = \emptyset$. Application is left-associative, i.e., $s\ t\ u$ should be read $(s\ t)\ u$.

Definition 1. *For expressions s, t, we say that t is a sub-expression of s, notation $s \trianglerighteq t$, if this can be derived using the clauses:*

$$s \trianglerighteq t \ if\ s = t\ or\ s \vartriangleright t$$
$$(s_1, s_2) \vartriangleright t\ if\ s_1 \trianglerighteq t\ or\ s_2 \trianglerighteq t \quad \textit{if } s_1 \textsf{ then } s_2 \textsf{ else } s_3 \vartriangleright t\ if\ s_i \trianglerighteq t\ for\ some\ i$$
$$s_1\ s_2 \vartriangleright t\ if\ s_1 \vartriangleright t\ or\ s_2 \trianglerighteq t \qquad \textsf{choose } s_1 \cdots s_n \vartriangleright t\ if\ s_i \trianglerighteq t\ for\ some\ i$$

Note: the head s of an application $s\ t$ is not considered a sub-expression of $s\ t$.

Note that the programs we consider have no pre-defined data structures like integers: these may be encoded using inductive data structures in the usual way.

Example 1. Integers can be encoded as bitstrings of unbounded length: $\mathcal{C} \supseteq \{\textsf{false}, \textsf{true}, ::, []\}$. Here, $::$ is considered infix and right-associative, and $[]$ denotes the end of the string. Using little endian, 6 is encoded by $\textsf{false}::\textsf{true}::\textsf{true}::[]$ as well as $\textsf{false}::\textsf{true}::\textsf{true}::\textsf{false}::\textsf{false}::[]$. We for instance have $\textsf{true}::(\textsf{succ } xs) \trianglerighteq xs$ (for $xs \in \mathcal{V}$). The program below imposes $\mathcal{D} = \{\textsf{succ}\}$:

$$\textsf{succ } [] = \textsf{true}::[] \quad \textsf{succ } (\textsf{false}::xs) = \textsf{true}::xs$$
$$\textsf{succ } (\textsf{true}::xs) = \textsf{false}::(\textsf{succ } xs)$$

2.2   Typing

Programs have explicit simple types without polymorphism, with the usual definition of type order $ord(\sigma)$; this is formally given in Fig. 3.

$\iota \in \mathcal{S} ::=$ sort identifier	$ord(\iota) = 0$ for $\iota \in \mathcal{S}$
$\sigma, \tau \in \textbf{Type} ::= \iota \mid \sigma \times \tau \mid \sigma \Rightarrow \tau$	$ord(\sigma \times \tau) = \max(ord(\sigma), ord(\tau))$
	$ord(\sigma \Rightarrow \tau) = \max(ord(\sigma) + 1, ord(\tau))$

Fig. 3. Types and type orders

The (finite) set $\mathcal{S}$ of sorts is used to type atomic data such as bits; we assume $\textsf{bool} \in \mathcal{S}$. The function arrow $\Rightarrow$ is considered right-associative. Writing κ for a sort or a pair type $\sigma \times \tau$, any type can be uniquely presented in the form $\sigma_1 \Rightarrow \ldots \Rightarrow \sigma_m \Rightarrow \kappa$. We will limit interest to *well-typed, well-formed* programs:

Definition 2. *A program p is well-typed if there is an assignment $\mathcal{F}$ from $\mathcal{C} \cup \mathcal{D}$ to the set of simple types such that:*

– *the main function f_1 is assigned a type $\kappa_1 \Rightarrow \ldots \Rightarrow \kappa_M \Rightarrow \kappa$, with $ord(\kappa_i) = 0$ for $1 \leq i \leq M$ and also $ord(\kappa) = 0$*

- *data constructors* $c \in \mathcal{C}$ *are assigned a type* $\kappa_1 \Rightarrow \ldots \Rightarrow \kappa_m \Rightarrow \iota$ *with* $\iota \in \mathcal{S}$ *and* $ord(\kappa_i) = 0$ *for* $1 \leq i \leq m$
- *for all clauses* $f\ \ell_1 \cdots \ell_k = s \in p$, *the following hold:*
  - $Var(s) \subseteq Var(f\ \ell_1 \cdots \ell_k)$ *and each variable occurs only once in* $f\ \ell_1 \cdots \ell_k$;
  - *there exist a type environment* Γ *mapping* $Var(f\ \ell_1 \cdots \ell_k)$ *to simple types, and a simple type* σ, *such that both* $f\ \ell_1 \cdots \ell_k : \sigma$ *and* $s : \sigma$ *using the rules in Fig. 4; we call* σ *the type of the clause.*

$$\frac{}{a : \sigma} \text{ if } a : \sigma \in \Gamma \cup \mathcal{F} \qquad \frac{s : \sigma \qquad t : \tau}{(s,t) : \sigma \times \tau} \qquad \frac{s : \sigma \Rightarrow \tau \qquad t : \sigma}{s\ t : \tau}$$

$$\frac{s_1 : \texttt{bool} \qquad s_2 : \sigma \qquad s_3 : \sigma}{\texttt{if } s_1 \texttt{ then } s_2 \texttt{ else } s_3 : \sigma} \qquad \frac{s_1 : \sigma \qquad \cdots \qquad s_n : \sigma}{\texttt{choose } s_1 \cdots s_n : \sigma}$$

Fig. 4. Typing (for fixed $\mathcal{F}$ and Γ, see Definition 2)

Note that this definition does not allow for polymorphism: there is a single type assignment $\mathcal{F}$ for the full program. The assignment $\mathcal{F}$ also forces a unique choice for the type environment Γ of variables in each clause. Thus, we may speak of *the* type of an expression in a clause without risk of confusion.

Example 2. The program of Example 1 is typed using $\mathcal{F} = \{\texttt{false} : \texttt{bool}, \texttt{true} : \texttt{bool}, [] : \texttt{list}, :: : \texttt{bool} \Rightarrow \texttt{list} \Rightarrow \texttt{list}, \texttt{succ} : \texttt{list} \Rightarrow \texttt{list}\}$. As all argument and output types have order 0, the variable restrictions are satisfied and all clauses can be typed using $\Gamma = \{xs : \texttt{list}\}$, the program is well-typed.

Definition 3. *A program* p *is* well-formed *if it is well-typed, and moreover:*

- *data constructors are always fully applied: for all* $c \in \mathcal{C}$ *with* $c : \kappa_1 \Rightarrow \ldots \Rightarrow \kappa_m \Rightarrow \iota \in \mathcal{F}$: *if a sub-expression* $c\ t_1 \cdots t_n$ *occurs in any clause, then* $n = m$;
- *the number of arguments to a given defined symbol is fixed: if* $f\ \ell_1 \cdots \ell_k = s$ *and* $f\ \ell'_1 \cdots \ell'_n = t$ *are both in* p, *then* $k = n$; *we let* $\texttt{arity}_p(f)$ *denote* k.

Example 3. The program of Example 1 is well-formed, and $\texttt{arity}_p(\texttt{succ}) = 1$.

However, the program would not be well-formed if the clauses below were added, as here the defined symbol or does not have a consistent arity.

$$\texttt{id } x = x \qquad \texttt{or true } x = \texttt{true} \qquad \texttt{or false} = \texttt{id}$$

Remark 1. Data constructors must (a) have a sort as output type (*not* a pair), and (b) occur only fully applied. This is consistent with typical functional programming languages, where sorts and constructors are declared with a grammar such as:

$$sdec \in \texttt{SortDec} ::= \texttt{data } \iota = cdec_1 \mid \cdots \mid cdec_n$$
$$cdec \in \texttt{ConstructorDec} ::= c\ \sigma_1 \cdots \sigma_m$$

In addition, we require that the arguments to data constructors have type order 0. This is not standard in functional programming, but is the case in [12]. We limit interest to such constructors because, practically, these are the only ones which can be used in a *cons-free* program (as we will discuss in Sect. 3).

Definition 4. *A program has* data order K *if all clauses can be typed using type environments* Γ *such that, for all* $x : \sigma \in \Gamma$: $ord(\sigma) \leq K$.

Example 4. We consider a higher-order program, operating on the same data constructors as Example 1; however, now we encode numbers using *functions*:

$$
\begin{aligned}
&\texttt{fsucc } F \; [] = \texttt{if } F \; [] \texttt{ then set } F \; [] \texttt{ false else set } F \; [] \texttt{ true} \\
&\texttt{fsucc } F \; xs = \texttt{if } F \; xs \texttt{ then fsucc (set } F \; xs \texttt{ false) (tl } xs) \\
&\qquad\qquad\qquad \texttt{else set } F \; xs \texttt{ true} \\
&\texttt{set } F \; val \; xs \; ys = \texttt{if eqlen } xs \; ys \texttt{ then } val \texttt{ else } F \; ys \\
&\texttt{tl } (x{::}xs) = xs \qquad\quad \texttt{eqlen } (x{::}xs) \; (y{::}ys) = \texttt{eqlen } xs \; ys \\
&\texttt{eqlen } [] \; [] = \texttt{true} \qquad\quad \texttt{eqlen } xs \; ys = \texttt{false}
\end{aligned}
$$

Only one typing is possible, with $\texttt{fsucc} : (\texttt{list} \Rightarrow \texttt{bool}) \Rightarrow \texttt{list} \Rightarrow \texttt{list} \Rightarrow \texttt{bool}$; therefore, F is always typed $\texttt{list} \Rightarrow \texttt{bool}$—which has type order 1—and all other variables with a type of order 0. Thus, this program has data order 1.

To explain the program: we use boolean lists as *unary* numbers of a limited size; assuming that (a) F represents a bitstring of length $N + 1$, and (b) *lst* has length N, the successor of F (modulo wrapping) is obtained by $\texttt{fsucc } F \; lst$.

2.3   Semantics

Like Jones, our language has a closure-based call-by-value semantics. We let data expressions, values and environments be defined by the grammar in Fig. 5.

$$
\begin{array}{ll}
d, b \in \textsf{Data} ::= c \; d_1 \cdots d_m \mid (d, b) & \textbf{Instantiation:} \\
v, w \in \textsf{Value} ::= d \mid (v, w) \mid f \; v_1 \cdots v_n & \qquad x\gamma := \gamma(x) \\
\qquad\qquad (n < \textsf{arity}_\textsf{p}(f)) & \quad (c \; \ell_1 \cdots \ell_n)\gamma := c \; (\ell_1\gamma) \cdots (\ell_n\gamma) \\
\gamma, \delta \in \textsf{Env} ::= \mathcal{V} \to \textsf{Value} &
\end{array}
$$

Fig. 5. Data expressions, values and environments

Let $\textsf{dom}(\gamma)$ denote the domain of an environment (partial function) γ. Note that values are ground expressions, and we only use well-typed values with fully applied data constructors. To every pattern ℓ and environment γ with $\textsf{dom}(\gamma) \supseteq Var(\ell)$, we associate a value $\ell\gamma$ by instantiation in the obvious way, see Fig. 5.

Note that, for every value v and pattern ℓ, there is at most one environment γ with $\ell\gamma = v$. We say that an expression $\texttt{f } s_1 \cdots s_n$ *instantiates* the left-hand side of a clause $\texttt{f } \ell_1 \cdots \ell_k$ if $n = k$ and there is an environment γ with each $s_i = \ell_i\gamma$.

Both input and output to the program are data expressions. If $\texttt{f}_1$ has type $\kappa_1 \Rightarrow \ldots \Rightarrow \kappa_M \Rightarrow \kappa$, we can think of the program as calculating a function $[\![\texttt{p}]\!](d_1, \ldots, d_M)$ from M input data arguments to an output data expression.

Expression and program evaluation are given by the rules in Fig. 6. Since, in [Call], there is at most one suitable γ, the only source of non-determinism is

Expression evaluation:

[Instance]: $$\frac{}{\mathsf{p}, \gamma \vdash x \to \gamma(x)}$$ [Function]: $$\frac{\mathsf{p} \vdash^{\mathtt{call}} \mathtt{f} \to w}{\mathsf{p}, \gamma \vdash \mathtt{f} \to w} \text{ for } \mathtt{f} \in \mathcal{D}$$

[Constructor]: $$\frac{\mathsf{p}, \gamma \vdash s_1 \to b_1 \quad \cdots \quad \mathsf{p}, \gamma \vdash s_m \to b_m}{\mathsf{p}, \gamma \vdash \mathsf{c}\, s_1 \cdots s_m \to \mathsf{c}\, b_1 \cdots b_m}$$

[Pair]: $$\frac{\mathsf{p}, \gamma \vdash s \to v \quad \mathsf{p}, \gamma \vdash t \to w}{\mathsf{p}, \gamma \vdash (s, t) \to (v, w)}$$

[Choice]: $$\frac{\mathsf{p}, \gamma \vdash s_i \to w}{\mathsf{p}, \gamma \vdash \mathtt{choose}\, s_1 \cdots s_n \to w} \text{ for } 1 \le i \le n$$

[Conditional]: $$\frac{\mathsf{p}, \gamma \vdash s_1 \to d \quad \mathsf{p}, \gamma \vdash^{\mathtt{if}} d, s_2, s_3 \to w}{\mathsf{p}, \gamma \vdash \mathtt{if}\, s_1\, \mathtt{then}\, s_2\, \mathtt{else}\, s_3 \to w}$$

[If-True]: $$\frac{\mathsf{p}, \gamma \vdash s_2 \to w}{\mathsf{p}, \gamma \vdash^{\mathtt{if}} \mathtt{true}, s_2, s_3 \to w}$$ [If-False]: $$\frac{\mathsf{p}, \gamma \vdash s_3 \to w}{\mathsf{p}, \gamma \vdash^{\mathtt{if}} \mathtt{false}, s_2, s_3 \to w}$$

[Appl]: $$\frac{\mathsf{p}, \gamma \vdash s \to \mathtt{f}\, v_1 \cdots v_n \quad \mathsf{p}, \gamma \vdash t \to v_{n+1} \quad \mathsf{p} \vdash^{\mathtt{call}} \mathtt{f}\, v_1 \cdots v_{n+1} \to w}{\mathsf{p}, \gamma \vdash s\, t \to w}$$

[Closure]: $$\frac{}{\mathsf{p} \vdash^{\mathtt{call}} \mathtt{f}\, v_1 \cdots v_n \to \mathtt{f}\, v_1 \cdots v_n} \text{ if } n < \mathtt{arity}_{\mathsf{p}}(\mathtt{f})$$

[Call]: $$\frac{\mathsf{p}, \gamma \vdash s \to w}{\mathsf{p} \vdash^{\mathtt{call}} \mathtt{f}\, v_1 \cdots v_k \to w}$$ if $\mathtt{f}\, \ell_1 \cdots \ell_k = s$ is the first clause in p such that $\mathtt{f}\, v_1 \cdots v_k$ instantiates $\mathtt{f}\, \ell_1 \cdots \ell_k$, and $dom(\gamma) = Var(\mathtt{f}\, \ell_1 \cdots \ell_k)$ and each $v_i = \ell_i \gamma$

Program execution:

$$\frac{\mathsf{p}, [x_1 := d_1, \ldots, x_M := d_M] \vdash \mathtt{f}_1\, x_1 \cdots x_M \to b}{[\![\mathsf{p}]\!](d_1, \ldots, d_M) \mapsto b}$$

Fig. 6. Call-by-value semantics

the `choose` operator. Programs without this operator are called *deterministic*. By contrast, we may refer to a *non-deterministic* program as one which is not explicitly required to be deterministic, so which may or may not contain `choose`.

Example 5. For the program from Example 1, $[\![\mathsf{p}]\!](\mathtt{true}{::}\mathtt{false}{::}\mathtt{true}{::}[]) \mapsto \mathtt{false}{::}\mathtt{true}{::}\mathtt{true}{::}[]$, giving $5 + 1 = 6$. In the program $\mathtt{f}_1\, x\, y = \mathtt{choose}\, x\, y$, we can both derive $[\![\mathsf{p}]\!](\mathtt{true}, \mathtt{false}) \mapsto \mathtt{true}$ and $[\![\mathsf{p}]\!](\mathtt{true}, \mathtt{false}) \mapsto \mathtt{false}$.

The language is easily seen to be Turing-complete unless further restrictions are imposed. In order to assuage any fears on whether the complexity-theoretic characterisations we obtain are due to brittle design choices, we add some remarks.

Remark 2. We have omitted some constructs common to even some toy pure functional languages, but these are in general simple syntactic sugar that can be readily expressed by the existing constructs in the language, even in the presence of non-determinism. For instance, a let-binding $\text{let } x = s_1 \text{ in } s_2$ can be straightforwardly encoded by a function call in a pure call-by-value setting (replacing $\text{let } x = s_1 \text{ in } s_2$ by $\text{helper } s_1$ and adding a clause $\text{helper } x = s_2$).

Remark 3. We do not require the clauses of a function definition to exhaust all possible patterns. For instance, it is possible to have a clause $\text{f true} = \cdots$ without a clause for f false. Thus, a program has zero or more values.

Data Order Versus Program Order. We have followed Jones in considering *data order* as the variable for increasing complexity. However, an alternative choice—which turns out to streamline our proofs—is *program order*, which considers the type order of the function symbols. Fortunately, these notions are closely related; barring unused symbols, $\langle\text{program order}\rangle = \langle\text{data order}\rangle + 1$.

More specifically, we have the following result:

Lemma 1. *For every well-formed program* p *with data order K, there is a well-formed program* p′ *such that* $[\![p]\!](d_1,\ldots,d_M) \mapsto b$ *iff* $[\![p']\!](d_1,\ldots,d_M) \mapsto b$ *for any* $b_1,\ldots,b_M, d$ *and: (a) all defined symbols in* p′ *have a type* $\sigma_1 \Rightarrow \ldots \Rightarrow \sigma_m \Rightarrow \kappa$ *such that both* $ord(\sigma_i) \leq K$ *for all i and* $ord(\kappa) \leq K$, *and (b) in all clauses, all sub-expressions of the right-hand side have a type of order $\leq K$ as well.*

Proof (Sketch). p′ is obtained from p through the following successive changes:

1. Replace any clause $\text{f } \ell_1 \cdots \ell_k = s$ where $s : \sigma \Rightarrow \tau$ with $ord(\sigma \Rightarrow \tau) = K+1$, by $\text{f } \ell_1 \cdots \ell_k \ x = s \ x$ for a fresh x. Repeat until no such clauses remain.
2. In any clause $\text{f } \ell_1 \cdots \ell_k = s$, replace all sub-expressions $(\text{choose } s_1 \cdots s_m) \, t_1 \cdots t_n$ or $(\text{if } s_1 \text{ then } s_2 \text{ else } s_3) \, t_1 \cdots t_n$ of s with $n > 0$ by $\text{choose } (s_1 \, t_1 \cdots t_n) \cdots (s_m \, t_1 \cdots t_n)$ or $\text{if } s_1 \text{ then } (s_2 \, t_1 \cdots t_n) \text{ else } (s_3 \, t_1 \cdots t_n)$ respectively.
3. In any clause $\text{f } \ell_1 \cdots \ell_k = s$, if s has a sub-expression $t = \text{g } s_1 \cdots s_n$ with $\text{g} : \sigma_1 \Rightarrow \ldots \Rightarrow \sigma_n \Rightarrow \tau$ such that $ord(\tau) \leq K$ but $ord(\sigma_i) > K$ for some i, then replace t by a fresh symbol $\bot_\tau$. Repeat until no such sub-expressions remain, then add clauses $\bot_\tau = \bot_\tau$ for the new symbols.
4. If there exists $\text{f} : \sigma_1 \Rightarrow \ldots \Rightarrow \sigma_m \Rightarrow \kappa \in \mathcal{F}$ with $ord(\kappa) > K$ or $ord(\sigma_i) > K$ for some i, then remove the symbol f and all clauses with root f.

The key observation is that if the derivation for $[\![p]\!](d_1,\ldots,d_M) \mapsto b$ uses some $\text{f } s_1 \cdots s_n : \sigma$ with $ord(\sigma) \leq K$ but $s_i : \tau$ with $ord(\tau) > K$, then there is a variable with type order $> K$. Thus, if a clause introduces such an expression, either the clause is never used, or the expression occurs beneath an if or choose and is never selected; it may be replaced with a symbol whose only rule is unusable. This also justifies step 1; for step 4, only unusable clauses are removed. □

Example 6. The following program has data order 0, but clauses of functional type; fst and snd have output type $\text{nat} \Rightarrow \text{nat}$ of order 1. The program is changed by replacing the last two clauses by $\texttt{fst } x\ y = \texttt{const } x\ y$ and $\texttt{snd } x\ y = \texttt{id } y$.

$$\texttt{start } xs\ ys = \texttt{choose } (\texttt{fst } xs\ ys)\ (\texttt{snd } xs\ ys)$$
$$\texttt{const } x\ y = x \qquad \texttt{fst } x = \texttt{const } x$$
$$\texttt{id } x = x \qquad\quad \texttt{snd } x = \texttt{id}$$

3   Cons-Free Programs

Jones defines a cons-free program as one where the list constructor :: does not occur in any clause. In our setting (where more constructors are in principle admitted), this translates to disallowing non-constant data constructors from being introduced in the right-hand side of a clause. We define:

Definition 5. *A program* p *is cons-free if all clauses in* p *are cons-free. A clause* $\texttt{f } \ell_1 \cdots \ell_k = s$ *is cons-free if for all* $s \trianglerighteq t$*: if* $t = \texttt{c } s_1 \cdots s_m$ *with* $\texttt{c} \in \mathcal{C}$*, then* t *is a data expression or* $\ell_i \trianglerighteq t$ *for some* i*.*

Example 7. Example 1 is not cons-free, due to the second and third clause (the first clause *is* cons-free). Examples 4 and 6 are both cons-free.

The key property of cons-free programming is that no *new* data structures can be created during program execution. Formally, in a derivation tree with root $[\![\mathsf{p}]\!](d_1, \ldots, d_M) \mapsto b$, all data values (including b) are in the set $\mathcal{B}^{\mathsf{p}}_{d_1,\ldots,d_M}$:

Definition 6. *Let* $\mathcal{B}^{\mathsf{p}}_{d_1,\ldots,d_M} := \{d \in \textit{Data} \mid \exists i[d_i \trianglerighteq d] \vee \exists (\texttt{f } \boldsymbol{\ell} = s) \in \mathsf{p}[s \trianglerighteq d]\}.$

$\mathcal{B}^{\mathsf{p}}_{d_1,\ldots,d_M}$ is a set of data expressions closed under $\triangleright$, with a linear number of elements in the size of $d_1, \ldots, d_M$ (for fixed p). The property that no new data is created during execution is formally expressed by the following lemma.

Lemma 2. *Let* p *be a cons-free program, and suppose that* $[\![\mathsf{p}]\!](d_1, \ldots, d_M) \mapsto b$ *is obtained by a derivation tree* T*. Then for all statements* $\mathsf{p}, \gamma \vdash s \to w$ *or* $\mathsf{p}, \gamma \vdash^{\texttt{if}} b', s_1, s_2 \to w$ *or* $\mathsf{p} \vdash^{\texttt{call}} \texttt{f } v_1 \cdots v_n \to w$ *in* T*, and all expressions* t *such that (a)* $w \trianglerighteq t$*, (b)* $b' \trianglerighteq t$*, (c)* $\gamma(x) \trianglerighteq t$ *for some* x *or (d)* $v_i \trianglerighteq t$ *for some* i*: if* t *has the form* $\texttt{c } b_1 \cdots b_m$ *with* $\texttt{c} \in \mathcal{C}$*, then* $t \in \mathcal{B}^{\mathsf{p}}_{d_1,\ldots,d_M}$*.*

That is, any data expression in the derivation tree of $[\![\mathsf{p}]\!](d_1, \ldots, d_M) \mapsto b$ (including occurrences as a sub-expression of other values) is also in $\mathcal{B}^{\mathsf{p}}_{d_1,\ldots,d_M}$.

Proof (Sketch). Induction on the form of T, assuming that for a statement under consideration, (1) the requirements on γ and the v_i are satisfied, and (2) γ maps expressions $t \trianglelefteq s, s_1, s_2$ to elements of $\mathcal{B}^{\mathsf{p}}_{d_1,\ldots,d_M}$ if $t = \texttt{c } t_1 \cdots t_m$ with $\texttt{c} \in \mathcal{C}$. $\square$

Note that Lemma 2 implies that the program result b is in $\mathcal{B}^{\mathsf{p}}_{d_1,\ldots,d_M}$. Recall also Remark 1: if we had admitted constructors with higher-order argument types, then Lemma 2 shows that they are never used, since any constructor appearing in a derivation for $[\![\mathsf{p}]\!](d_1, \ldots, d_M) \mapsto b$ must already occur in the (data!) input.

4   Turing Machines, Decision Problems and Complexity

We assume familiarity with the standard notions of Turing Machines and complexity classes (see, e.g., [11,21,22]); in this section, we fix the notation we use.

4.1   (Deterministic) Turing Machines

Turing Machines (TMs) are triples (A, S, T) where A is a finite set of tape symbols such that $A \supseteq \{0, 1, \lrcorner\}$, $S \supseteq \{\texttt{start}, \texttt{accept}, \texttt{reject}\}$ is a finite set of states, and T is a finite set of transitions (i, r, w, d, j) with $i \in S \backslash \{\texttt{accept}, \texttt{reject}\}$ (the *original state*), $r \in A$ (the *read symbol*), $w \in A$ (the *written symbol*), $d \in \{\texttt{L}, \texttt{R}\}$ (the *direction*), and $j \in S$ (the *result state*). We sometimes denote this transition as $i \xrightarrow{r/w\ d} j$. A *deterministic* TM is a TM such that every pair (i, r) with $i \in S \backslash \{\texttt{accept}, \texttt{reject}\}$ and $r \in A$ is associated with exactly one transition (i, r, w, d, j). Every TM in this paper has a single, right-infinite tape.

A *valid tape* is an element t of $A^{\mathbb{N}}$ with $t(p) \neq \lrcorner$ for only finitely many p. A *configuration* is a triple (t, p, s) with t a valid tape, $p \in \mathbb{N}$ and $s \in S$. The transitions T induce a relation $\Rightarrow$ between configurations in the obvious way.

4.2   Decision Problems

A *decision problem* is a set $X \subseteq \{0, 1\}^+$. A deterministic TM *decides* X if for any $x \in \{0, 1\}^+$: $x \in X$ iff $\lrcorner x_1 \ldots x_n \lrcorner\lrcorner \ldots, 0, \texttt{start}) \Rightarrow^* (t, i, \texttt{accept})$ for some t, i, and $(\lrcorner x_1 \ldots x_n \lrcorner\lrcorner \ldots, 0, \texttt{start}) \Rightarrow^* (t, i, \texttt{reject})$ iff $x \notin X$. Thus, the TM halts on all inputs, ending in $\texttt{accept}$ or $\texttt{reject}$ depending on whether $x \in X$.

If $h : \mathbb{N} \longrightarrow \mathbb{N}$ is a function, a deterministic TM *runs in time* $\lambda n.h(n)$ if for all $n \in \mathbb{N} \backslash \{0\}$ and $x \in \{0, 1\}^n$: any evaluation starting in $(\lrcorner x_1 \ldots x_n \lrcorner\lrcorner \ldots, 0, \texttt{start})$ ends in the $\texttt{accept}$ or $\texttt{reject}$ state in at most $h(n)$ transitions.

4.3   Complexity and the **EXPTIME** Hierarchy

We define classes of decision problem based on the *time* needed to accept them.

Definition 7. *Let* $h : \mathbb{N} \to \mathbb{N}$ *be a function. Then,* $TIME(h(n))$ *is the set of all* $X \subseteq \{0, 1\}^+$ *such that there exist a* > 0 *and a deterministic TM running in time* $\lambda n.a \cdot h(n)$ *that decides* X.

By design, $TIME(h(n))$ is closed under $\mathcal{O}$: $TIME(h(n)) = TIME(\mathcal{O}(h(n)))$.

Definition 8. *For* $K, n \geq 0$, *let* $\exp_2^0(n) = n$ *and* $\exp_2^{K+1}(n) = \exp_2^K(2^n) = 2^{\exp_2^K(n)}$. *For* $K \geq 0$, *define* $\mathsf{EXP}^K\mathsf{TIME} \triangleq \bigcup_{a,b \in \mathbb{N}} TIME(\exp_2^K(an^b))$.

Since for every polynomial h, there are $a, b \in \mathbb{N}$ such that $h(n) \leq a \cdot n^b$ for all $n > 0$, we have $\mathsf{EXP}^0\mathsf{TIME} = \mathsf{P}$ and $\mathsf{EXP}^1\mathsf{TIME} = \mathsf{EXP}$ (where EXP is the usual complexity class of this name, see e.g., [21, Ch. 20]). In the literature, EXP is sometimes called $\mathsf{EXPTIME}$ or $\mathsf{DEXPTIME}$ (e.g., in the celebrated proof that ML typability is complete for $\mathsf{DEXPTIME}$ [13]). Using the Time Hierarchy Theorem [22], it is easy to see that $\mathsf{P} = \mathsf{EXP}^0\mathsf{TIME} \subsetneq \mathsf{EXP}^1\mathsf{TIME} \subsetneq \mathsf{EXP}^2\mathsf{TIME} \subsetneq \cdots$.

Definition 9. *The set* ELEMENTARY *of elementary-time computable languages is* $\bigcup_{K \in \mathbb{N}} \mathsf{EXP}^K\mathsf{TIME}$.

4.4   Decision Problems and Programs

To solve decision problems by (cons-free) programs, we will consider programs with constructors true, false of type bool, [] of type list and :: of type bool $\Rightarrow$ list $\Rightarrow$ list, and whose main function f_1 has type list $\Rightarrow$ bool.

Definition 10. *We define:*

- *A* program p *accepts* $a_1 a_2 \ldots a_n \in \{0,1\}^*$ *if* $\llbracket p \rrbracket(\overline{a_1} :: \ldots :: \overline{a_n}) \mapsto$ true, *where* $\overline{a_i} =$ true *if* $a_i = 1$ *and* $\overline{a_i} =$ false *otherwise.*
- *The* set accepted by *program* p *is* $\{a \in \{0,1\}^* \mid$ p *accepts* a$\}$.

Although we focus on programs of this form, our proofs will allow for arbitrary input and output—with the limitation (as guaranteed by the rule for program execution) that both are data. This makes it possible to for instance consider decision problems on a larger input alphabet without needing encodings.

Example 8. The two-line program with clauses even [] = true and even $(x::xs) =$ if x then false else true accepts the problem $\{x \in \{0,1\}^* \mid x$ is a bitstring representing an even number (following Example 1)}.

We will sometimes speak of the input size, defined by:

Definition 11. *The* size *of a list of data expressions* $d_1, \ldots, d_M$ *is* $\sum_{i=1}^M size(d_i)$, *where* $size(c\ b_1 \cdots b_m)$ *is defined as* $1 + \sum_{i=1}^m size(b_i)$.

5   Deterministic Characterisations

As a basis, we transfer Jones' basic result on *time* classes to our more general language. That is, we obtain the first line of the first table in Fig. 1.

	data order 0	data order 1	data order 2	data order 3	...
cons-free deterministic	P = EXP^{0}TIME	EXP = EXP^{1}TIME	EXP^{2}TIME	EXP^{3}TIME	...

To show that deterministic cons-free programs of data order K characterise EXP^{K}TIME it is necessary to prove two things:

1. if $h(n) \leq \exp_2^K(a \cdot n^b)$ for all n, then for every deterministic Turing Machine M running in TIME $(h(n))$, there is a deterministic, cons-free program with data order at most K, which accepts $x \in \{0,1\}^+$ if and only if M does;
2. for every deterministic cons-free program p with data order K, there is a deterministic algorithm operating in TIME $\left(\exp_2^K(a \cdot n^b)\right)$ for some a, b which, given input expressions $d_1, \ldots, d_M$, determines b such that $\llbracket p \rrbracket(d_1, \ldots, d_M) \mapsto b$ (if such b exists). Like Jones [12], we assume our algorithms are implemented on a sufficiently expressive Turing-equivalent machine like the RAM.

We will show part (1) in Sect. 5.1, and part (2) in Sect. 5.2.

5.1 Simulating TMs Using Deterministic Cons-Free Programs

Let $M := (A, S, T)$ be a deterministic Turing Machine running in time $\lambda n.h(n)$. Like Jones, we start by assuming that we have a way to represent the numbers $0, \ldots, h(n)$ as expressions, along with successor and predecessor operators and checks for equality. Our simulation uses the data constructors true : bool, false : bool, [] : list and :: : bool $\Rightarrow$ list $\Rightarrow$ list as discussed in Sect. 4.4; a : symbol for $a \in A$ (writing B for the blank symbol), L, R : direc and s : state for $s \in S$; action : symbol $\Rightarrow$ direc $\Rightarrow$ state $\Rightarrow$ trans; and end : state $\Rightarrow$ trans. The rules to simulate the machine are given in Fig. 7.

run cs = test (state cs $[h(|cs|)]$)

test accept = true   transition i r = action w d j   for all $i \xrightarrow{r/w\ d} j \in T$
test reject = false   transition i x = end i   for $i \in \{\text{accept}, \text{reject}\}$

state cs $[n]$ = if $[n = 0]$ then start else get3 (transat cs $[n-1]$)
transat cs $[n]$ = transition (state cs $[n]$) (tapesymb cs $[n]$)

get1 (action x y z) = x get1 (end x) = B
get2 (action x y z) = y get2 (end x) = R
get3 (action x y z) = z get3 (end x) = x

tapesymb cs $[n]$ = tape cs $[n]$ (pos cs $[n]$)

tape cs $[n]$ $[p]$ = if $[n = 0]$ then inputtape cs $[p]$
                      else tapehelp cs $[n]$ $[p]$ (pos cs $[n-1]$)
tapehelp cs $[n]$ $[p]$ $[i]$ = if $[p = i]$ then get1 (transat cs $[n-1]$)
                            else tape cs $[n-1]$ $[p]$

pos cs $[n]$ = if $[n = 0]$ then $[0]$ else adjust cs (pos cs $[n-1]$) (get2 (transat cs $[n-1]$))
adjust cs $[p]$ L = $[p-1]$ adjust cs $[p]$ R = $[p+1]$

inputtape cs $[p]$ = if $[p = 0]$ then B else nth cs $[p-1]$
nth [] $[p]$ = B   bit true = 1
nth (x::xs) $[p]$ = if $[p = 0]$ then bit x else nth xs $[p-1]$ bit false = 0

Fig. 7. Simulating a deterministic Turing Machine (A, S, T)

Types of defined symbols are easily derived. The intended meaning is that state cs $[n]$, for cs the input list and $[n]$ a number in $\{0, \ldots, h(|cs|)\}$, returns the state of the machine at time $[n]$; pos cs $[n]$ returns the position of the reader at time $[n]$, and tape $cs[n]$ $[p]$ the symbol at time $[n]$ and position $[p]$.

Clearly, the program is highly exponential, even when $h(|cs|)$ is polynomial, since the same expressions are repeatedly evaluated. This apparent contradiction is not problematic: we do not claim that all cons-free programs with data order 0 (say) have a derivation tree of at most polynomial size. Rather, as we will see in Sect. 5.2, we can find their *result* in polynomial time by essentially using a caching mechanism to avoid reevaluating the same expression.

What remains is to simulate numbers and counting. For a machine running in TIME $(h(n))$, it suffices to find a value $[i]$ representing i for all $i \in \{0, \ldots, h(n)\}$ and cons-free clauses to calculate predecessor and successor functions and to perform zero and equality checks. This is given by a $(\lambda n. h(n) + 1)$-*counting module*. This defines, for a given input list cs of length n, a set of values $\mathcal{A}_\pi^n$ to represent numbers and functions seed_π, pred_π and zero_π such that (a) $\text{seed}_\pi\ cs$ evaluates to a value which represents $h(n)$, (b) if v represents a number k, then $\text{pred}_\pi\ cs\ v$ evaluates to a value which represents $k - 1$, and (c) $\text{zero}_\pi\ cs\ v$ evaluates to true or false depending on whether v represents 0. Formally:

Definition 12 (Adapted from [12]). *For $P : \mathbb{N} \to \mathbb{N} \setminus \{0\}$, a P-counting module is a tuple $C_\pi = (\alpha_\pi, \mathcal{D}_\pi, \mathcal{A}_\pi, \langle \cdot \rangle_\pi, \mathsf{p}_\pi)$ such that:*

- α_π *is a type (this will be the type of* numbers*);*
- $\mathcal{D}_\pi$ *is a set of defined symbols disjoint from $\mathcal{C}, \mathcal{D}, \mathcal{V}$, containing symbols* seed_π, pred_π *and* zero_π*, with types* $\text{seed}_\pi : \text{list} \Rightarrow \alpha_\pi$*,* $\text{pred}_\pi : \text{list} \Rightarrow \alpha_\pi \Rightarrow \alpha_\pi$ *and* $\text{zero}_\pi : \text{list} \Rightarrow \alpha_\pi \Rightarrow \text{bool}$*;*
- *for $n \in \mathbb{N}$, $\mathcal{A}_\pi^n$ is a set of values of type α_π, all built over $\mathcal{C} \cup \mathcal{D}_\pi$ (this is the set of values used to represent numbers);*
- *for $n \in \mathbb{N}$, $\langle \cdot \rangle_\pi^n$ is a total function from A_π^n to $\mathbb{N}$;*
- p_π *is a list of cons-free clauses on the symbols in $\mathcal{D}_\pi$, such that, for all lists $cs : \text{list} \in Data$ with length n:*
  - *there is a unique value v such that $\mathsf{p}_\pi \vdash^{\text{call}} \text{seed}_\pi\ cs \to v$;*
  - *if $\mathsf{p}_\pi \vdash^{\text{call}} \text{seed}_\pi\ cs \to v$, then $v \in \mathcal{A}_\pi^n$ and $\langle v \rangle_\pi^n = P(n) - 1$;*
  - *if $v \in \mathcal{A}_\pi$ and $\langle v \rangle_\pi^n = i > 0$, then there is a unique value w such that $\mathsf{p}_\pi \vdash^{\text{call}} \text{pred}_\pi\ cs\ v \to w$; we have $w \in \mathcal{A}_\pi^n$ and $\langle w \rangle_\pi^n = i - 1$;*
  - *for $v \in \mathcal{A}_\pi^n$ with $\langle v \rangle_\pi^n = i$: $\mathsf{p}_\pi \vdash^{\text{call}} \text{zero}_\pi\ cs\ v \to \text{true}$ if and only if $i = 0$, and $\mathsf{p}_\pi \vdash^{\text{call}} \text{zero}_\pi\ cs\ v \to \text{false}$ if and only if $i > 0$.*

It is easy to see how a P-counting module can be plugged into the program of Fig. 7. We only lack successor and equality functions, which are easily defined:

$$\text{succ}_\pi\ cs\ i = \text{sc}_\pi\ cs\ (\text{seed}_\pi\ cs)\ i$$
$$\text{sc}_\pi\ cs\ j\ i = \text{if } \text{equal}_\pi\ cs\ (\text{pred}_\pi\ cs\ j)\ i \text{ then } j \text{ else sc } cs\ (\text{pred}_\pi\ cs\ j)\ i$$
$$\text{equal}_\pi\ cs\ i\ j = \text{if } \text{zero}_\pi\ cs\ i \text{ then } \text{zero}_\pi\ cs\ j$$
$$\qquad\qquad \text{else if } \text{zero}_\pi\ cs\ j \text{ then false}$$
$$\qquad\qquad \text{else } \text{equal}_\pi\ cs\ (\text{pred}_\pi\ cs\ i)\ (\text{pred}_\pi\ cs\ j)$$

Since the clauses in Fig. 7 are cons-free and have data order 0, we obtain:

Lemma 3. *Let x be a decision problem which can be decided by a deterministic TM running in TIME $(h(n))$. If there is a cons-free $(\lambda n. h(n) + 1)$-counting module C_π with data order K, then x is accepted by a cons-free program with data order K; the program is deterministic if the counting module is.*

Proof. By the argument given above. □

The obvious difficulty is the restriction to cons-free clauses: we cannot simply construct a new number type, but will have to represent numbers using only subexpressions of the input list cs, and constant data expressions.

Example 9. We consider a P-counting module C_x where $P(n) = 3 \cdot (n+1)^2$. Let $\alpha_x := \texttt{list} \times \texttt{list} \times \texttt{list}$ and for given n, let $\mathcal{A}_\pi^n := \{(d_0, d_1, d_2) \mid d_0$ is a list of length ≤ 2 and d_1, d_2 are lists of length $\leq n\}$. Writing $\mid x_1 {::} \ldots {::} x_k {::} [] \mid = k$, let $\langle (d_0, d_1, d_2) \rangle_x^n := |d_0| \cdot (n+1)^2 + |d_1| \cdot (n+1) + |d_2|$. Essentially, we consider 3-digit numbers $i_0 i_1 i_2$ in base $n+1$, with each i_j represented by a list. p_x is:

$$\texttt{seed}_x \; cs = (\texttt{false}{::}\texttt{false}{::}[], \; cs, \; cs)$$

$$\begin{array}{ll}
\texttt{pred}_x \; cs \; (x_0, x_1, y{::}ys) = (x_0, x_1, ys) & \texttt{zero}_x \; cs \; (x_0, x_1, y{::}ys) = \texttt{false} \\
\texttt{pred}_x \; cs \; (x_0, y{::}ys, []) = (x_0, ys, cs) & \texttt{zero}_x \; cs \; (x_0, y{::}ys, []) = \texttt{false} \\
\texttt{pred}_x \; cs \; (y{::}ys, [], []) = (ys, cs, cs) & \texttt{zero}_x \; cs \; (y{::}ys, [], []) = \texttt{false} \\
\texttt{pred}_x \; cs \; ([], [], []) = ([], [], []) & \texttt{zero}_x \; cs \; ([], [], []) = \texttt{true}
\end{array}$$

If $cs = \texttt{true}{::}\texttt{false}{::}\texttt{true}{::}[]$, one value in $\mathcal{A}_x^3$ is $v = (\texttt{false}{::}[], \texttt{false}{::}\texttt{true}{::}[], [])$, which is mapped to the number $1 \cdot 4^2 + 2 \cdot 4 + 0 = 24$. Then $\mathsf{p}_x \vdash^{\texttt{call}} \texttt{pred}_x \; cs \; v \to w := (\texttt{false}{::}[], \texttt{true}{::}[], cs)$, which is mapped to $1{\cdot}4^2+1{\cdot}4+3 = 23$ as desired.

Example 9 suggests a systematic way to create polynomial counting modules.

Lemma 4. *For any $a, b \in \mathbb{N} \setminus \{0\}$, there is a $(\lambda n. a \cdot (n+1)^b)$-counting module $C_{\langle a,b \rangle}$ with data order 0.*

Proof (Sketch). A straightforward generalisation of Example 9. □

By increasing type orders, we can obtain an exponential increase of magnitude.

Lemma 5. *If there is a P-counting module C_π of data order K, then there is a $(\lambda n. 2^{P(n)})$-counting module $C_{e[\pi]}$ of data order $K + 1$.*

Proof (Sketch). Let $\alpha_{e[\pi]} := \alpha_\pi \Rightarrow \texttt{bool}$; then $ord(\alpha_{e[\pi]}) \leq K + 1$. A number i with bit representation $b_0 \ldots b_{P(n)-1}$ (with b_0 the most significant digit) is represented by a value v such that, for w with $\langle w \rangle_\pi = i$: $\mathsf{p}_{e[\pi]} \vdash^{\texttt{call}} v \; w \to \texttt{true}$ iff $b_i = 1$, and $\mathsf{p}_{e[\pi]} \vdash^{\texttt{call}} v \; w \to \texttt{false}$ iff $b_i = 0$. We use the clauses of Fig. 8.

$$
\begin{array}{l}
\texttt{seed}_{e[\pi]} \; cs \; x = \texttt{true} \\
\texttt{zero}_{e[\pi]} \; cs \; F = \texttt{zhelp}_{e[\pi]} \; cs \; F \; (\texttt{seed}_\pi \; cs) \\
\texttt{zhelp}_{e[\pi]} \; cs \; F \; k = \texttt{if} \; F \; k \; \texttt{then false} \\
\qquad\qquad\qquad\qquad\quad \texttt{else if} \; \texttt{zero}_\pi \; cs \; k \; \texttt{then true} \\
\qquad\qquad\qquad\qquad\quad \texttt{else} \; \texttt{zhelp}_{e[\pi]} \; cs \; F \; (\texttt{pred}_\pi \; cs \; k) \\
\texttt{pred}_{e[\pi]} \; cs \; F = \texttt{phelp}_{e[\pi]} \; cs \; F \; (\texttt{seed}_\pi \; cs) \\
\texttt{phelp}_{e[\pi]} \; cs \; F \; k = \texttt{if} \; F \; k \; \texttt{then} \; \texttt{flip}_{e[\pi]} \; cs \; F \; k \\
\qquad\qquad\qquad\qquad\quad \texttt{else if} \; \texttt{zero}_\pi \; cs \; k \; \texttt{then} \; \texttt{seed}_{e[\pi]} \; cs \\
\qquad\qquad\qquad\qquad\quad \texttt{else} \; \texttt{phelp}_{e[\pi]} \; cs \; (\texttt{flip}_{e[\pi]} \; cs \; F \; k) \; (\texttt{pred}_\pi \; cs \; k) \\
\texttt{flip}_{e[\pi]} \; cs \; F \; k \; i = \texttt{if} \; \texttt{equal}_\pi \; cs \; k \; i \; \texttt{then not} \; (F \; i) \; \texttt{else} \; F \; i \\
\texttt{not} \; b = \texttt{if} \; b \; \texttt{then false else true}
\end{array}
$$

Fig. 8. The clauses used in $\mathsf{p}_{e[\pi]}$, extending p_π with an exponential step.

We also include all clauses in p_π. Here, note that a bitstring $b_0 \ldots b_m$ represents 0 if each $b_i = 0$, and that the predecessor of $b_0 \ldots b_i 10 \ldots 0$ is $b_0 \ldots b_i 01 \ldots 1$. $\qquad\square$

Combining these results, we obtain:

Lemma 6. *Every decision problem in* $\mathsf{EXP}^K\mathsf{TIME}$ *is accepted by a deterministic cons-free program with data order* K.

Proof. A decision problem is in $\mathsf{EXP}^K\mathsf{TIME}$ if it is decided by a deterministic TM operating in time $\exp_2^K(a \cdot n^b))$ for some a, b. By Lemma 3, it therefore suffices if there is a Q-counting module for some $Q \geq \lambda n.\exp_2^K(a \cdot n^b) + 1$, with data order K. Certainly $Q(n) := \exp_2^K(a \cdot (n+1)^b)$ is large enough. By Lemma 4, there is a $(\lambda n.a \cdot (n+1)^b)$-counting module $C_{\langle a,b \rangle}$ with data order 0. Applying Lemma 5 K times, we obtain the required Q-counting module $C_{\mathbf{e}[\ldots[\mathbf{e}[\langle a,b \rangle]]]}$. $\qquad\square$

Remark 4. Our definition of a counting module significantly differs from the one in [12], for example by representing numbers as *values* rather than *expressions*, introducing the sets $\mathcal{A}_\pi^n$ and imposing evaluation restrictions. The changes enable an easy formulation of the non-deterministic counting module in Sect. 6.

5.2   Simulating Deterministic Cons-Free Programs Using an Algorithm

We now turn to the second part of characterisation: that every decision problem solved by a deterministic cons-free program of data order K is in $\mathsf{EXP}^K\mathsf{TIME}$. We give an algorithm which determines the result of a fixed program (if any) on a given input in $\mathrm{TIME}\left(\exp_2^K(a \cdot n^b)\right)$ for some a, b. The algorithm is designed to extend easily to the non-deterministic characterisations in subsequent settings.

Key Idea. The principle of our algorithm is easy to explain when variables have data order 0. Using Lemma 2, all such variables must be instantiated by (tuples of) elements of $\mathcal{B}_{d_1,\ldots,d_M}^{\mathsf{p}}$, of which there are only polynomially many in the input size. Thus, we can make a comprehensive list of all expressions that might occur as the left-hand side of a [Call] in the derivation tree. Now we can go over the list repeatedly, filling in reductions to trace a top-down derivation of the tree.

In the higher-order setting, there are infinitely many possible values; for example, if $\mathtt{id} : \mathtt{bool} \Rightarrow \mathtt{bool}$ has arity 1 and $\mathtt{g} : (\mathtt{bool} \Rightarrow \mathtt{bool}) \Rightarrow \mathtt{bool} \Rightarrow \mathtt{bool}$ has arity 2, then $\mathtt{id}$, $\mathtt{g}\ \mathtt{id}$, $\mathtt{g}\ (\mathtt{g}\ \mathtt{id})$ and so on are all values. Therefore, instead of looking directly at values we consider an extensional replacement.

Definition 13. *Let $\mathcal{B}$ be a set of data expressions closed under $\rhd$. For $\iota \in \mathcal{S}$, let $\langle\!\langle \iota \rangle\!\rangle_{\mathcal{B}} = \{d \in \mathcal{B} \mid\ \vdash d : \iota\}$. Inductively, let $\langle\!\langle \sigma \times \tau \rangle\!\rangle_{\mathcal{B}} = \langle\!\langle \sigma \rangle\!\rangle_{\mathcal{B}} \times \langle\!\langle \tau \rangle\!\rangle_{\mathcal{B}}$ and $\langle\!\langle \sigma \Rightarrow \tau \rangle\!\rangle_{\mathcal{B}} = \{A_{\sigma \Rightarrow \tau} \mid A \subseteq \langle\!\langle \sigma \rangle\!\rangle_{\mathcal{B}} \times \langle\!\langle \tau \rangle\!\rangle_{\mathcal{B}} \wedge \forall e \in \langle\!\langle \sigma \rangle\!\rangle_{\mathcal{B}}$ there is at most one u with $(e, u) \in A_{\sigma \Rightarrow \tau}\}_{\sigma \Rightarrow \tau}$. We call the elements of any $\langle\!\langle \sigma \rangle\!\rangle_{\mathcal{B}}$ deterministic extensional values.*

Note that deterministic extensional values are data expressions in $\mathcal{B}$ if σ is a sort, *pairs* if σ is a pair type, and sets of pairs labelled with a type otherwise; these sets are exactly partial functions, and can be used as such:

Definition 14. *For* $e \in \langle\!\langle \sigma_1 \Rightarrow \ldots \Rightarrow \sigma_n \Rightarrow \tau \rangle\!\rangle_{\mathcal{B}}$ *and* $u_1 \in \langle\!\langle \sigma_1 \rangle\!\rangle_{\mathcal{B}}, \ldots, u_n \in$ $\langle\!\langle \sigma_n \rangle\!\rangle_{\mathcal{B}}$, *let* $e(u_1, \ldots, u_n)$ *be* $\{e\}$ *if* $n = 0$ *and* $\bigcup_{A_{\sigma_n \Rightarrow \tau} \in e(u_1, \ldots, u_{n-1})} \{o \in \langle\!\langle \tau \rangle\!\rangle_{\mathcal{B}} \mid$ $(u_n, o) \in A\}$ *if* $n > 0$.

By induction on n, each $e(u_1, \ldots, u_n)$ has at most one element as would be expected of a partial function. We also consider a form of matching.

Definition 15. *Fix a set $\mathcal{B}$ of data expressions. An* extensional expression *has the form* $\mathbf{f}\ e_1 \cdots e_n$ *where* $\mathbf{f} : \sigma_1 \Rightarrow \ldots \Rightarrow \sigma_n \Rightarrow \tau \in \mathcal{D}$ *and each* $e_i \in \langle\!\langle \sigma_i \rangle\!\rangle_{\mathcal{B}}$. *Given a clause* ρ: $\mathbf{f}\ \ell_1 \cdots \ell_k = r$ *with* $\mathbf{f} : \sigma_1 \Rightarrow \ldots \Rightarrow \sigma_k \Rightarrow \tau \in \mathcal{F}$ *and variable environment* Γ, *an* ext-environment *for* ρ *is a partial function* η *mapping each* $x : \tau \in \Gamma$ *to an element of* $\langle\!\langle \tau \rangle\!\rangle_{\mathcal{B}}$, *such that* $\ell_j \eta \in \langle\!\langle \sigma_j \rangle\!\rangle_{\mathcal{B}}$ *for* $1 \leq j \leq n$. *Here,*

– $\ell\eta = \eta(\ell)$ *if* ℓ *is a variable and* $\ell\eta = (\ell^{(1)}\eta, \ell^{(2)}\eta)$ *if* $\ell = (\ell^{(1)}, \ell^{(2)})$;
– $\ell\eta = \ell[x := \eta(x) \mid x \in Var(\ell)]$ *otherwise (in this case, ℓ is a pattern with data order 0, so all its variables have data order 0, so each* $\eta(x) \in \mathbf{Data}$).

Then $\ell\eta$ *is a deterministic extensional value for* ℓ *a pattern. We say* ρ matches *an extensional expression* $\mathbf{f}\ e_1 \cdots e_k$ *if there is an ext-environment* η *for* ρ *such that* $\ell_i \eta = e_i$ *for all* $1 \leq i \leq k$. *We call* η *the* matching ext-environment.

Finally, for technical reasons we will need an ordering on extensional values:

Definition 16. *We define a relation* $\sqsupseteq$ *on extensional values of the same type:*

– *For* $d, b \in \langle\!\langle \iota \rangle\!\rangle_{\mathcal{B}}$ *with* $\iota \in \mathcal{S}$: $d \sqsupseteq b$ *if* $d = b$.
– *For* $(e_1, e_2), (u_1, u_2) \in \langle\!\langle \sigma \times \tau \rangle\!\rangle_{\mathcal{B}}$: $(e_1, e_2) \sqsupseteq (u_1, u_2)$ *if each* $e_i \sqsupseteq u_i$.
– *For* $A_\sigma, B_\sigma \in \langle\!\langle \sigma \rangle\!\rangle_{\mathcal{B}}$ *with* σ *functional:* $A_\sigma \sqsupseteq B_\sigma$ *if for all* $(e, u) \in B$ *there is* $u' \sqsupseteq u$ *such that* $(e, u') \in A$.

The Algorithm. Let us now define our algorithm. We will present it in a general form—including a case 2d which does not apply to deterministic programs—so we can reuse the algorithm in the non-deterministic settings to follow.

Algorithm 7. Let $\mathbf{p}$ be a fixed, deterministic cons-free program, and suppose $\mathbf{f}_1$ has a type $\kappa_1 \Rightarrow \ldots \Rightarrow \kappa_M \Rightarrow \kappa \in \mathcal{F}$.
    Input: data expressions $d_1 : \kappa_1, \ldots, d_M : \kappa_M$.
    Output: The set of values b with $[\![\mathbf{p}]\!](d_1, \ldots, d_M) \mapsto b$.

1. Preparation.
    (a) Let $\mathbf{p}'$ be obtained from $\mathbf{p}$ by the transformations of Lemma 1, and by adding a clause $\mathbf{start}\ x_1 \cdots x_M = \mathbf{f}_1\ x_1 \cdots x_M$ for a fresh symbol $\mathbf{start}$ (so that $[\![\mathbf{p}]\!](d_1, \ldots, d_M) \mapsto b$ iff $\mathbf{p}' \vdash^{\mathtt{call}} \mathbf{start}\ d_1 \cdots d_M \to b$).

(b) Denote $\mathcal{B} := \mathcal{B}^{\mathsf{p}}_{d_1,\dots,d_M}$ and let $\mathcal{X}$ be the set of all "statements":

   i. $\vdash \mathsf{f}\ e_1 \cdots e_n \rightsquigarrow o$ for (a) $\mathsf{f} \in \mathcal{D}$ with $\mathsf{f} : \sigma_1 \Rightarrow \dots \Rightarrow \sigma_m \Rightarrow \kappa' \in \mathcal{F}$,
      (b) $0 \le n \le \mathtt{arity}_\mathsf{p}(\mathsf{f})$ such that $ord(\sigma_{n+1} \Rightarrow \dots \Rightarrow \sigma_m \Rightarrow \kappa') \le K$,
      (c) $e_i \in \langle\!\langle \sigma_i \rangle\!\rangle_\mathcal{B}$ for $1 \le i \le n$ and (d) $o \in \langle\!\langle \sigma_{n+1} \Rightarrow \dots \Rightarrow \sigma_m \Rightarrow \kappa' \rangle\!\rangle_\mathcal{B}$;

   ii. $\eta \vdash t \rightsquigarrow o$ for (a) $\rho\colon \mathsf{f}\ \ell_1 \cdots \ell_k = s$ a clause in p', (b) $s \trianglerighteq t : \tau$, (c) $o \in \langle\!\langle \tau \rangle\!\rangle_\mathcal{B}$ and (d) η an ext-environment for ρ.

(c) Mark statements of the form $\eta \vdash t \rightsquigarrow o$ in $\mathcal{X}$ as confirmed if either $t \in \mathcal{V}$ and $\eta(t) \sqsupseteq o$, or if $t = \mathsf{c}\ t_1 \cdots t_m$ with $\mathsf{c} \in \mathcal{C}$ and $t\eta = o$. All statements not of either form are marked unconfirmed.

2. Iteration: repeat the following steps, until no further changes are made.

  (a) For all unconfirmed statements $\vdash \mathsf{f}\ e_1 \cdots e_n \rightsquigarrow o$ in $\mathcal{X}$ with $n < \mathtt{arity}_\mathsf{p}(\mathsf{f})$: write $o = O_\sigma$ and mark the statement as confirmed if for all $(e_{n+1}, u) \in O$ there exists $u' \sqsupseteq u$ such that $\vdash \mathsf{f}\ e_1 \cdots e_{n+1} \rightsquigarrow u'$ is marked confirmed.

  (b) For all unconfirmed statements $\vdash \mathsf{f}\ e_1 \cdots e_k \rightsquigarrow o$ in $\mathcal{X}$ with $k = \mathtt{arity}_\mathsf{p}(\mathsf{f})$:

    i. find the first clause $\rho\colon \mathsf{f}\ \ell_1 \cdots \ell_k = s$ in p' that matches $\mathsf{f}\ e_1 \cdots e_k$ and let η be the matching ext-environment (if any);

    ii. determine whether $\eta \vdash s \rightsquigarrow o$ is confirmed and if so, mark the statement $\mathsf{f}\ e_1 \cdots e_k \rightsquigarrow o$ as confirmed.

  (c) For all unconfirmed statements of the form $\eta \vdash \mathtt{if}\ s_1\ \mathtt{then}\ s_2\ \mathtt{else}\ s_3 \rightsquigarrow o$ in $\mathcal{X}$, mark the statement confirmed if both $\eta \vdash s_1 \rightsquigarrow \mathtt{true}$ and $\eta \vdash s_2 \rightsquigarrow o$ are confirmed, or both $\eta \vdash s_1 \rightsquigarrow \mathtt{false}$ and $\eta \vdash s_3 \rightsquigarrow o$ are confirmed.

  (d) For all unconfirmed statements $\eta \vdash \mathtt{choose}\ s_1 \cdots s_n \rightsquigarrow o$ in $\mathcal{X}$, mark the statement as confirmed if $\eta \vdash s_i \rightsquigarrow o$ for any $i \in \{1, \dots, n\}$.

  (e) For all unconfirmed statements $\eta \vdash (s_1, s_2) \rightsquigarrow (o_1, o_2)$ in $\mathcal{X}$, mark the statement confirmed if both $\eta \vdash s_1 \rightsquigarrow o_1$ and $\eta \vdash s_2 \rightsquigarrow o_2$ are confirmed.

  (f) For all unconfirmed statements $\eta \vdash x\ s_1 \cdots s_n \rightsquigarrow o$ in $\mathcal{X}$ with $x \in \mathcal{V}$, mark the statement as confirmed if there are $e_1 \in \langle\!\langle \sigma_1 \rangle\!\rangle_\mathcal{B}, \dots, e_n \in \langle\!\langle \sigma_n \rangle\!\rangle_\mathcal{B}$ such that each $\eta \vdash s_i \rightsquigarrow e_i$ is marked confirmed, and there exists $o' \in \eta(x)(e_1, \dots, e_n)$ such that $o' \sqsupseteq o$.

  (g) For all unconfirmed statements $\eta \vdash \mathsf{f}\ s_1 \cdots s_n \rightsquigarrow o$ in $\mathcal{X}$ with $\mathsf{f} \in \mathcal{D}$, mark the statement as confirmed if there are $e_1 \in \langle\!\langle \sigma_1 \rangle\!\rangle_\mathcal{B}, \dots, e_n \in \langle\!\langle \sigma_n \rangle\!\rangle_\mathcal{B}$ such that each $\eta \vdash s_i \rightsquigarrow e_i$ is marked confirmed, and:

    i. $n \le \mathtt{arity}_\mathsf{p}(\mathsf{f})$ and $\vdash \mathsf{f}\ e_1 \cdots e_n \rightsquigarrow o$ is marked confirmed, *or*

    ii. $n > k := \mathtt{arity}_\mathsf{p}(\mathsf{f})$ and there are u, o' such that $\vdash \mathsf{f}\ e_1 \cdots e_k \rightsquigarrow u$ is marked confirmed and $u(e_{k+1}, \dots, e_n) \ni o' \sqsupseteq o$.

3. Completion: return $\{b \mid b \in \mathcal{B} \wedge\ \vdash \mathtt{start}\ d_1 \cdots d_M \rightsquigarrow b$ is marked confirmed$\}$.

Note that, for programs of data order 0, this algorithm closely follows the earlier sketch. Values of a higher type are abstracted to deterministic extensional values. The use of $\sqsupseteq$ is needed because a value of higher type is associated to many extensional values; e.g., to confirm a statement $\vdash \mathtt{plus}\ 3 \rightsquigarrow \{(1,4),(0,3)\}_{\mathtt{nat}\Rightarrow\mathtt{nat}}$ in some program, it may be necessary to first confirm $\vdash \mathtt{plus}\ 3 \rightsquigarrow \{(0,3)\}_{\mathtt{nat}\Rightarrow\mathtt{nat}}$.

The complexity of the algorithm relies on the following key observation:

Lemma 8. *Let* p *be a cons-free program of data order K. Let Σ be the set of all types σ with $ord(\sigma) \leq K$ which occur as part of an argument type, or as an output type of some* f $\in \mathcal{D}$. *Suppose that, given input of total size n, $\langle\!\langle\sigma\rangle\!\rangle_{\mathcal{B}}$ has cardinality at most $F(n)$ for all $\sigma \in \Sigma$, and testing whether $e_1 \sqsupseteq e_2$ for $e_1, e_2 \in [\![\sigma]\!]_{\mathcal{B}}$ takes at most $F(n)$ steps. Then Algorithm 7 runs in $TIME\left(a \cdot F(n)^b\right)$ for some a, b.*

Here, the cardinality $\mathsf{Card}(A)$ of a set A is just the number of elements of A.

Proof (Sketch). Due to the use of p$'$, all intensional values occurring in Algorithm 7 are in $\bigcup_{\sigma \in \Sigma} \langle\!\langle\sigma\rangle\!\rangle_{\mathcal{B}}$. Writing a for the greatest number of arguments any defined symbol f or variable x in p$'$ may take and r for the greatest number of sub-expressions of any right-hand side in p$'$ (which is independent of the input!), $\mathcal{X}$ contains at most $a \cdot |\mathcal{D}| \cdot F(n)^{a+1} + |p'| \cdot r \cdot F(n)^{a+1}$ statements. Since in all but the last step of the iteration at least one statement is flipped from unconfirmed to confirmed, there are at most $|\mathcal{X}| + 1$ iterations, each considering $|\mathcal{X}|$ statements. It is easy to see that the individual steps in both the preparation and iteration are all polynomial in $|\mathcal{X}|$ and $F(n)$, resulting in a polynomial overall complexity. $\quad\square$

The result follows as $\mathsf{Card}(\langle\!\langle\sigma\rangle\!\rangle_{\mathcal{B}})$ is given by a tower of exponentials in $ord(\sigma)$:

Lemma 9. *If $1 \leq \mathsf{Card}(\mathcal{B}) < N$, then for each σ of length L (where the length of a type is the number of sorts occurring in it, including repetitions), with $ord(\sigma) \leq K$: $\mathsf{Card}(\langle\!\langle\sigma\rangle\!\rangle_{\mathcal{B}}) < \exp_2^K(N^L)$. Testing $e \sqsupseteq u$ for $e, u \in \langle\!\langle\sigma\rangle\!\rangle_{\mathcal{B}}$ takes at most $\exp_2^K(N^{(L+1)^3})$ comparisons between elements of $\mathcal{B}$.*

Proof (Sketch). An easy induction on the form of σ, using that $\exp_2^K(X) \cdot \exp_2^K(Y) \leq \exp_2^K(X \cdot Y)$ for $X \geq 2$, and that for $A_{\sigma_1 \Rightarrow \sigma_2}$, each key $e \in \langle\!\langle\sigma_1\rangle\!\rangle_{\mathcal{B}}$ is assigned one of $\mathsf{Card}(\langle\!\langle\sigma_2\rangle\!\rangle_{\mathcal{B}}) + 1$ choices: an element u of $\langle\!\langle\sigma_2\rangle\!\rangle_{\mathcal{B}}$ such that $(e, u) \in A$, or non-membership. The second part (regarding $\sqsupseteq$) uses the first. $\quad\square$

We will postpone showing correctness of the algorithm until Sect. 6.3, where we can show the result together with the one for non-deterministic programs. Assuming correctness for now, we may conclude:

Lemma 10. *Every decision problem accepted by a deterministic cons-free program* p *with data order K is in* $\mathsf{EXP}^K\mathsf{TIME}$.

Proof. We will see in Lemma 20 in Sect. 6.3 that $[\![p]\!](d_1, \ldots, d_M) \mapsto b$ if and only if Algorithm 7 returns the set $\{b\}$. For a program of data order K, Lemmas 8 and 9 together give that Algorithm 7 operates in $\mathrm{TIME}\left(\exp_2^K(n)\right)$. $\quad\square$

Theorem 1. *The class of deterministic cons-free programs with data order K characterises* $\mathsf{EXP}^K\mathsf{TIME}$ *for all $K \in \mathbb{N}$.*

Proof. A combination of Lemmas 6 and 10. $\quad\square$

6 Non-deterministic Characterisations

A natural question is what happens if we do not limit interest to deterministic programs. For data order 0, Bonfante [4] shows that adding the choice operator to Jones' language does not increase expressivity. We will recover this result for our generalised language in Sect. 7. However, in the higher-order setting, non-deterministic choice *does* increase expressivity—dramatically so. We have:

	data order 0	data order 1	data order 2	data order 3	...
cons-free	P	ELEMENTARY	ELEMENTARY	ELEMENTARY	...

As before, we will show the result—for data orders 1 and above—in two parts: in Sect. 6.1 we see that cons-free programs of data order 1 suffice to accept all problems in ELEMENTARY; in Sect. 6.2 we see that they cannot go beyond.

6.1 Simulating TMs Using (Non-deterministic) Cons-Free Programs

We start by showing how Turing Machines in ELEMENTARY can be simulated by non-deterministic cons-free programs. For this, we reuse the core simulation from Fig. 7. The reason for the jump in expressivity lies in Lemma 3: by taking advantage of non-determinism, we can count up to arbitrarily high numbers.

Lemma 11. *If there is a P-counting module C_π with data order $K \leq 1$, there is a (non-deterministic) $(\lambda n.2^{P(n)-1})$-counting module $C_{\psi[\pi]}$ with data order 1.*

Proof. We let $\alpha_{\psi[\pi]} := \mathtt{bool} \Rightarrow \alpha_\pi$ (which has type order $\max(1, ord(\alpha_\pi))$), and:

- $\mathcal{A}^n_{\psi[\pi]} :=$ the set of those values $v : \alpha_{\psi[\pi]}$ such that:
  - there is $w \in \mathcal{A}_\pi$ with $\langle w \rangle^n_\pi = 0$ such that $\mathsf{p}_{\psi[\pi]} \vdash^{\mathtt{call}} v\ \mathtt{true} \to w$;
  - there is $w \in \mathcal{A}_\pi$ with $\langle w \rangle^n_\pi = 0$ such that $\mathsf{p}_{\psi[\pi]} \vdash^{\mathtt{call}} v\ \mathtt{false} \to w$;
  and for all $1 \leq i < P(n)$ exactly one of the following holds:
  - there is $w \in \mathcal{A}^n_\pi$ with $\langle w \rangle^n_\pi = i$ such that $\mathsf{p}_{\psi[\pi]} \vdash^{\mathtt{call}} v\ \mathtt{true} \to w$;
  - there is $w \in \mathcal{A}^n_\pi$ with $\langle w \rangle^n_\pi = i$ such that $\mathsf{p}_{\psi[\pi]} \vdash^{\mathtt{call}} v\ \mathtt{false} \to w$;
  We will say that $v\ \mathtt{true} \mapsto i$ or $v\ \mathtt{false} \mapsto i$ respectively.
- $\langle v \rangle^n_{\psi[\pi]} := \sum_{i=1}^{P(n)-1} \{ 2^{P(n)-1-i} \mid v\ \mathtt{true} \mapsto i \}$;
- $\mathsf{p}_{\psi[\pi]}$ be given by Fig. 9 appended to p_π, and $\mathcal{D}_{\psi[\pi]}$ by the symbols in $\mathsf{p}_{\psi[\pi]}$.

So, we interpret a value v as the number given by the bitstring $b_1 \ldots b_{P(n)-1}$ (most significant digit first), where b_i is 1 if $v\ \mathtt{true}$ evaluates to a value representing i in C_π, and b_i is 0 otherwise—so exactly if $v\ \mathtt{false}$ evaluates to such a value. □

To understand the counting program, consider 4, with bit representation 100. If $0, 1, 2, 3$ are represented in C_π by values O, w_1, w_2, w_3 respectively, then in $C_{\psi[\pi]}$, the number 4 corresponds to $Q := \mathtt{st1}\ w_1\ (\mathtt{st0}\ w_2\ (\mathtt{st0}\ w_3\ (\mathtt{base}_{\psi[\pi]}\ O)))$.

– core elements; $\mathtt{st}i\ n\ F$ sets bit n in F to the value i

$\mathtt{base}_{\psi[\pi]}\ x\ b = x$

$\mathtt{st1}_{\psi[\pi]}\ n\ F\ \mathtt{true} = \mathtt{choose}\ n\ (F\ \mathtt{true})$ $\mathtt{st0}_{\psi[\pi]}\ n\ F\ \mathtt{true} = F\ \mathtt{true}$

$\mathtt{st1}_{\psi[\pi]}\ n\ F\ \mathtt{false} = F\ \mathtt{false}$ $\mathtt{st0}_{\psi[\pi]}\ n\ F\ \mathtt{false} = \mathtt{choose}\ n\ (F\ \mathtt{false})$

– testing bit values (using non-determinism and non-termination)

$\mathtt{bitset}_{\psi[\pi]}\ cs\ F\ i = \mathtt{if}\ \mathtt{equal}_{\pi}\ cs\ (F\ \mathtt{true})\ i\ \mathtt{then}\ \mathtt{true}$
$\phantom{\mathtt{bitset}_{\psi[\pi]}\ cs\ F\ i = }\mathtt{else\,if}\ \mathtt{equal}_{\pi}\ cs\ (F\ \mathtt{false})\ i\ \mathtt{then}\ \mathtt{false}$
$\phantom{\mathtt{bitset}_{\psi[\pi]}\ cs\ F\ i = }\mathtt{else}\ \mathtt{bitset}_{\psi[\pi]}\ cs\ F\ i$

– the seed function

$\mathtt{nul}_{\pi}\ cs = \mathtt{nul'}_{\pi}\ cs\ (\mathtt{seed}_{\pi}\ cs)$

$\mathtt{nul'}_{\pi}\ cs\ n = \mathtt{if}\ \mathtt{zero}_{\pi}\ cs\ n\ \mathtt{then}\ n\ \mathtt{else}\ \mathtt{nul'}_{\pi}\ cs\ (\mathtt{pred}_{\pi}\ cs\ n)$

$\mathtt{seed}_{\psi[\pi]}\ cs = \mathtt{seed'}_{\psi[\pi]}\ cs\ (\mathtt{seed}_{\pi}\ cs)\ (\mathtt{base}_{\psi[\pi]}\ (\mathtt{nul}_{\pi}\ cs))$

$\mathtt{seed'}_{\psi[\pi]}\ cs\ i\ F = \mathtt{if}\ \mathtt{zero}_{\pi}\ cs\ i\ \mathtt{then}\ F\ \mathtt{else}\ \mathtt{seed'}_{\psi[\pi]}\ cs\ (\mathtt{pred}_{\pi}\ cs\ i)\ (\mathtt{st1}_{\psi[\pi]}\ i\ F)$

– the zero test

$\mathtt{zero}_{\psi[\pi]}\ cs\ F = \mathtt{zero'}_{\psi[\pi]}\ cs\ F\ (\mathtt{seed}_{\pi}\ cs)$

$\mathtt{zero'}_{\psi[\pi]}\ cs\ F\ i = \mathtt{if}\ \mathtt{zero}_{\pi}\ i\ \mathtt{then}\ \mathtt{true}$
$\phantom{\mathtt{zero'}_{\psi[\pi]}\ cs\ F\ i = }\mathtt{else\,if}\ \mathtt{bitset}_{\psi[\pi]}\ cs\ F\ i\ \mathtt{then}\ \mathtt{false}$
$\phantom{\mathtt{zero'}_{\psi[\pi]}\ cs\ F\ i = }\mathtt{else}\ \mathtt{zero'}_{\psi[\pi]}\ cs\ F\ (\mathtt{pred}_{\pi}\ cs\ i)$

– the predecessor

$\mathtt{pred}_{\psi[\pi]}\ cs\ F = \mathtt{pr}_{\psi[\pi]}\ cs\ F\ (\mathtt{seed}_{\pi}\ cs)\ (\mathtt{base}_{\psi[\pi]}\ (\mathtt{nul}_{\pi}\ cs))$

$\mathtt{pr}_{\psi[\pi]}\ cs\ F\ i\ G = \mathtt{if}\ \mathtt{bitset}_{\psi[\pi]}\ cs\ F\ i\ \mathtt{then}\ \mathtt{cp}_{\psi[\pi]}\ cs\ F\ (\mathtt{pred}_{\pi}\ cs\ i)\ (\mathtt{st0}_{\psi[\pi]}\ i\ G)$
$\phantom{\mathtt{pr}_{\psi[\pi]}\ cs\ F\ i\ G = }\mathtt{else}\ \mathtt{pr}_{\psi[\pi]}\ cs\ F\ (\mathtt{pred}_{\pi}\ cs\ i)\ (\mathtt{st1}_{\psi[\pi]}\ i\ G)$

$\mathtt{cp}\ cs\ F\ i\ G = \mathtt{if}\ \mathtt{zero}_{\pi}\ cs\ i\ \mathtt{then}\ G$
$\phantom{\mathtt{cp}\ cs\ F\ i\ G = }\mathtt{else\,if}\ \mathtt{bitset}_{\psi[\pi]}\ cs\ F\ i\ \mathtt{then}\ \mathtt{cp}_{\psi[\pi]}\ cs\ F\ (\mathtt{pred}_{\pi}\ cs\ i)\ (\mathtt{st1}_{\psi[\pi]}\ i\ G)$
$\phantom{\mathtt{cp}\ cs\ F\ i\ G = }\mathtt{else}\ \mathtt{cp}_{\psi[\pi]}\ cs\ F\ (\mathtt{pred}_{\pi}\ cs\ i)\ (\mathtt{st0}_{\psi[\pi]}\ i\ G)$

Fig. 9. Clauses for the counting module $C_{\psi[\pi]}$.

The null-value O functions as a default, and is a possible value of both $Q\ \mathtt{true}$ and $Q\ \mathtt{false}$ for any function Q representing a bitstring.

The non-determinism comes into play when determining whether $Q\ \mathtt{true} \mapsto i$ or not: we can evaluate $F\ \mathtt{true}$ to *some* value, but this may not be the value we need. Therefore, we find some value of both $F\ \mathtt{true}$ and $F\ \mathtt{false}$; if either represents i in C_{π}, then we have confirmed or rejected that $b_i = 1$. If both evaluations give a different value, we repeat the test. This gives a non-terminating program, but there is always exactly one value b such that $\mathsf{P}_{\psi[\pi]} \vdash^{\mathtt{call}} \mathtt{bitset}_{\psi[\pi]}\ cs\ F\ i \to b$.

The $\mathtt{seed}_{\psi[\pi]}$ function generates the bit string $1 \ldots 1$, so the function F with $F\ \mathtt{true} \mapsto i$ for all $i \in \{0, \ldots, P(n) - 1\}$ and $F\ \mathtt{false} \mapsto i$ for only $i = 0$. The $\mathtt{zero}_{\psi[\pi]}$ function iterates through $b_{P(n)-1}, b_{P(n)-2}, \ldots, b_1$ and tests whether all bits are set to 0. The clauses for $\mathtt{pred}_{\psi[\pi]}$ assume given a bitstring $b_1 \ldots b_{i-1} 1 0 \ldots 0$, and recursively build $b_1 \ldots b_{i-1} 0 1 \cdots 1$ in the parameter G.

Example 10. Consider an input string of length 3, say $\mathtt{false::false::true::[]}$. Recall from Lemma 4 that there is a $(\lambda n.n{+}1)$-counting module $C_{\langle 1,1 \rangle}$ representing $i \in \{0, \ldots, 3\}$ as suffixes of length i from the input string. Therefore, there is also a second-order $(\lambda n.2^n)$-counting module $C_{\psi[\langle 1,1 \rangle]}$ representing $i \in \{0, \ldots, 7\}$. The number 6—with bitstring 110—is represented by the value w_6:

$$w_6 = \mathtt{st1}_{\psi[\langle 1,1\rangle]} \ (\mathtt{true}::[]) \ (\ \mathtt{st1}_{\psi[\langle 1,1\rangle]} \ (\mathtt{false}::\mathtt{true}::[]) \ ($$
$$\mathtt{st0}_{\psi[\langle 1,1\rangle]} \ (\mathtt{false}::\mathtt{false}::\mathtt{true}::[]) \ (\ \mathtt{cons}_{\psi[\langle 1,1\rangle]} \ [] \ ) \ ) \ ) : \mathtt{bool} \Rightarrow \mathtt{list}$$

But then there is also a $(\lambda n.2^{2^n-1})$-counting module $C_{\psi[\psi[\langle 1,1\rangle]]}$, representing $i \in \{0, \ldots, 2^7 - 1\}$. For example 97—with bit vector 1100001—is represented by:

$$S = \mathtt{st1}_{\psi[\psi[\langle 1,1\rangle]]} \ w_1 \ (\ \mathtt{st1}_{\psi[\psi[\langle 1,1\rangle]]} \ w_2 \ (\ \mathtt{st0}_{\psi[\psi[\langle 1,1\rangle]]} \ w_3 \ (\ $$
$$\mathtt{st0}_{\psi[\psi[\langle 1,1\rangle]]} \ w_4 \ (\ \mathtt{st0}_{\psi[\psi[\langle 1,1\rangle]]} \ w_5 \ (\ \mathtt{st0}_{\psi[\psi[\langle 1,1\rangle]]} \ w_6 \ (\ $$
$$\mathtt{st1}_{\psi[\psi[\langle 1,1\rangle]]} \ w_7 \ (\ \mathtt{cons}_{\psi[\psi[\langle 1,1\rangle]]} \ w_7 \ ) \ ) \ ) \ ) \ ) \ ) \ )$$

Here $\mathtt{st1}_{\psi[\psi[\langle 1,1\rangle]]}$ and $\mathtt{st0}_{\psi[\psi[\langle 1,1\rangle]]}$ have the type $(\mathtt{bool} \Rightarrow \mathtt{list}) \Rightarrow (\mathtt{bool} \Rightarrow \mathtt{bool} \Rightarrow \mathtt{list}) \Rightarrow \mathtt{bool} \Rightarrow \mathtt{bool} \Rightarrow \mathtt{list}$ and each w_i represents i in $C_{\psi[\langle 1,1\rangle]}$, as shown for w_6 above. Note: $S \ \mathtt{true} \mapsto w_1, w_2, w_7$ and $S \ \mathtt{false} \mapsto w_3, w_4, w_5, w_6$.

Since $2^{2^m-1} - 1 \geq 2^m$ for all $m \geq 2$, we can count up to arbitrarily high bounds using this module. Thus, already with data order 1, we can simulate Turing Machines operating in TIME $\left(\exp_2^K(n)\right)$ for any K.

Lemma 12. *Every decision problem in* ELEMENTARY *is accepted by a non-deterministic cons-free program with data order 1.*

Proof. A decision problem is in ELEMENTARY if it is in some $\mathsf{EXP}^K\mathsf{TIME}$ which, by Lemma 3, is certainly the case if for any a, b there is a Q-counting module with $Q \geq \lambda n. \exp_2^K(a \cdot n^b)$. Such a module exists for data order 1 by Lemma 11. $\qquad\square$

6.2 Simulating Cons-Free Programs Using an Algorithm

Towards a characterisation, we must also see that every decision problem accepted by a cons-free program is in ELEMENTARY—so that the result of every such program can be found by an algorithm operating in TIME $\left(\exp_2^K(a \cdot n^b)\right)$ for some a, b, K. We can reuse Algorithm 7 by altering the definition of $\langle\!\langle \sigma \rangle\!\rangle_{\mathcal{B}}$.

Definition 17. *Let $\mathcal{B}$ be a set of data expressions closed under $\rhd$. For $\iota \in \mathcal{S}$, let $[\![\iota]\!]_{\mathcal{B}} = \{d \in \mathcal{B} \mid \vdash d : \iota\}$. Inductively, define $[\![\sigma \times \tau]\!]_{\mathcal{B}} = [\![\sigma]\!]_{\mathcal{B}} \times [\![\tau]\!]_{\mathcal{B}}$ and $[\![\sigma \Rightarrow \tau]\!]_{\mathcal{B}} = \{A_{\sigma \Rightarrow \tau} \mid A \subseteq [\![\sigma]\!]_{\mathcal{B}} \times [\![\tau]\!]_{\mathcal{B}}\}$. We call the elements of any $[\![\sigma]\!]_{\mathcal{B}}$ non-deterministic extensional values.*

Where the elements of $\langle\!\langle \sigma \Rightarrow \tau \rangle\!\rangle_{\mathcal{B}}$ are partial functions, $[\![\sigma \Rightarrow \tau]\!]_{\mathcal{B}}$ contains arbitrary relations: a value v is associated to a set of pairs (e, u) such that $v \ e$ *might* evaluate to u. The notions of extensional expression, $e(u_1, \ldots, u_n)$ and $\sqsupseteq$ immediately extend to non-deterministic extensional values. Thus we can define:

Algorithm 13. *Let p be a fixed, non-deterministic cons-free program, with $\mathtt{f}_1 : \kappa_1 \Rightarrow \ldots \Rightarrow \kappa_M \Rightarrow \kappa \in \mathcal{F}$.*

Input: *data expressions $d_1 : \kappa_1, \ldots, d_M : \kappa_M$.*

Output: *The set of values b with $[\![\mathsf{p}]\!](d_1, \ldots, d_M) \mapsto b$.*

Execute Algorithm 7, but using $[\![\sigma]\!]_{\mathcal{B}}$ in place of $\langle\!\langle \sigma \rangle\!\rangle_{\mathcal{B}}$.

In Sect. 6.3, we will see that indeed $[\![\mathsf{p}]\!](d_1, \ldots, d_M) \mapsto b$ if and only if Algorithm 13 returns a set containing b. But as before, we first consider complexity. To properly analyse this, we introduce the new notion of *arrow depth*.

Definition 18. *A type's* arrow depth *is given by: $depth(\iota) = 0$, $depth(\sigma \times \tau) = \max(depth(\sigma), depth(\tau))$ and $depth(\sigma \Rightarrow \tau) = 1 + \max(depth(\sigma), depth(\tau))$.*

Now the cardinality of each $[\![\sigma]\!]_\mathcal{B}$ can be expressed using its arrow depth:

Lemma 14. *If $1 \leq \mathsf{Card}(\mathcal{B}) < N$, then for each σ of length L, with $depth(\sigma) \leq K$: $\mathsf{Card}([\![\sigma]\!]_\mathcal{B}) < \exp_2^K(N^L)$. Testing $e \sqsupseteq u$ for $e, u \in [\![\sigma]\!]_\mathcal{B}$ takes at most $\exp_2^K(N^{(L+1)^3})$ comparisons.*

Proof (Sketch). A straightforward induction on the form of σ, like Lemma 9. $\square$

Thus, once more assuming correctness for now, we may conclude:

Lemma 15. *Every decision problem accepted by a non-deterministic cons-free program p is in* ELEMENTARY.

Proof. We will see in Lemma 18 in Sect. 6.3 that $[\![\mathsf{p}]\!](d_1, \ldots, d_M) \mapsto b$ if and only if Algorithm 13 returns a set containing b. Since all types have an arrow depth and the set Σ in Lemma 8 is finite, Algorithm 13 operates in some $\mathsf{TIME}\left(\exp_2^K(n)\right)$. Thus, the problem is in $\mathsf{EXP}^K\mathsf{TIME} \subseteq$ ELEMENTARY. $\square$

Theorem 2. *The class of non-deterministic cons-free programs with data order K characterises* ELEMENTARY *for all $K \in \mathbb{N} \setminus \{0\}$.*

Proof. A combination of Lemmas 12 and 15. $\square$

6.3   Correctness proofs of Algorithms 7 and 13

Algorithms 7 and 13 are the same—merely parametrised with a different set of extensional values to be used in step 1b. Due to this similarity, and because $(\!(\sigma)\!)_\mathcal{B} \subseteq [\![\sigma]\!]_\mathcal{B}$, we can largely combine their correctness proofs. The proofs are somewhat intricate, however; details are provided in [15, Appendix E].

We begin with *soundness*:

Lemma 16. *If Algorithm 7 or 13 returns a set $A \cup \{b\}$, then $[\![\mathsf{p}]\!](d_1, \ldots, d_M) \mapsto b$.*

Proof (Sketch). We define for every value $v : \sigma$ and $e \in [\![\sigma]\!]_\mathcal{B}$: $v \Downarrow e$ iff: (a) $\sigma \in \mathcal{S}$ and $v = e$; or (b) $\sigma = \sigma_1 \times \sigma_2$ and $v = (v_1, v_2)$ and $e = (e_1, e_2)$ with $v_1 \Downarrow e_1$ and $v_2 \Downarrow e_2$; or (c) $\sigma = \sigma_1 \Rightarrow \sigma_2$ and $e = A_\sigma$ with $A \subseteq \{(u_1, u_2) \mid u_1 \in [\![\sigma_1]\!]_\mathcal{B} \wedge u_2 \in [\![\sigma_2]\!]_\mathcal{B} \wedge$ for all values $w_1 : \sigma_1$ with $w_1 \Downarrow u_1$ there is some value $w_2 : \sigma_2$ with $w_2 \Downarrow u_2$ such that $\mathsf{p}' \vdash^{\mathtt{call}} v \; w_1 \to w_2\}$.

We now prove two statements together by induction on the *confirmation time* in Algorithm 7, which we consider equipped with *unspecified* subsets $[\sigma]$ of $[\![\sigma]\!]_\mathcal{B}$:

1. Let: (a) $\mathbf{f} : \sigma_1 \Rightarrow \ldots \Rightarrow \sigma_m \Rightarrow \kappa \in \mathcal{F}$ be a defined symbol; (b) $v_1 : \sigma_1, \ldots, v_n : \sigma_n$ be values, for $1 \leq n \leq \mathtt{arity}_{\mathsf{p}}(\mathbf{f})$; (c) $e_1 \in [\![\sigma_1]\!]_{\mathcal{B}}, \ldots, e_n \in [\![\sigma_n]\!]_{\mathcal{B}}$ be such that each $v_i \Downarrow e_i$; (d) $o \in [\![\sigma_{n+1} \Rightarrow \ldots \Rightarrow \sigma_m \Rightarrow \kappa]\!]_{\mathcal{B}}$. If $\vdash \mathbf{f}\ e_1 \cdots e_n \rightsquigarrow o$ is eventually confirmed, then $\mathsf{p}' \vdash^{\mathtt{call}} \mathbf{f}\ v_1 \cdots v_n \rightarrow w$ for some w with $w \Downarrow o$.
2. Let: (a) $\rho \colon \mathbf{f}\ \ell = s$ be a clause in p'; (b) $t : \tau$ be a sub-expression of s; (c) η be an ext-environment for ρ; (d) γ be an environment such that $\gamma(x) \Downarrow \eta(x)$ for all $x \in \mathit{Var}(\mathbf{f}\ \ell)$; (e) $o \in [\![\tau]\!]_{\mathcal{B}}$. If the statement $\eta \vdash t \rightsquigarrow o$ is eventually confirmed, then $\mathsf{p}', \gamma \vdash t \rightarrow w$ for some w with $w \Downarrow o$.

Given the way p' is defined from p, the lemma follows from the first statement. The induction is easy, but requires minor sub-steps such as transitivity of $\sqsupseteq$. $\square$

The harder part, where the algorithms diverge, is *completeness*:

Lemma 17. *If* $[\![\mathsf{p}]\!](d_1, \ldots, d_M) \mapsto b$, *then Algorithm 13 returns a set* $A \cup \{b\}$.

Proof (Sketch). If $[\![\mathsf{p}]\!](d_1, \ldots, d_M) \mapsto b$, then $\mathsf{p}' \vdash^{\mathtt{call}} \mathtt{start}\ d_1 \cdots d_M \rightarrow b$. We label the nodes in the derivation trees with strings of numbers (a node with label l has immediate subtrees of the form $l \cdot i$), and let $>$ denote lexicographic comparison of these strings, and $\succ$ lexicographic comparison without prefixes (e.g., $1 \cdot 2 > 1$ but not $1 \cdot 2 \succ 1$). We define the following function:

- $\psi(v, l) = v$ if $v \in \mathcal{B}$, and $\psi((v_1, v_2), l) = (\psi(v_1, l), \psi(v_2, l))$;
- for $\mathbf{f}\ v_1 \cdots v_n : \tau = \sigma_{n+1} \Rightarrow \ldots \Rightarrow \sigma_m \Rightarrow \kappa$ with $m > n$, let $\psi(\mathbf{f}\ v_1 \cdots v_n, l) = \{(e_{n+1}, u) \mid \exists q \succ p > l$ [the subtree with index p has a root $\mathsf{p}' \vdash^{\mathtt{call}} \mathbf{f}\ v_1 \cdots v_{n+1} \rightarrow w$ with $\psi(w, q) = u$ and $e_{n+1} \sqsupseteq' \psi(v_{n+1}, p)]\}_\tau$.

Here, $\sqsupseteq'$ is defined the same as $\sqsupseteq$, except that $A_\sigma \sqsupseteq' B_\sigma$ iff $A \supseteq B$. Note that clearly $A \sqsupseteq' B$ implies $A \sqsupseteq B$, and that $\sqsupseteq'$ is transitive by transitivity of $\supseteq$. Then, using induction on the labels of the tree in reverse lexicographical order (so going through the tree right-to-left, top-to-bottom), we can prove:

1. If the subtree labelled l has root $\mathsf{p}' \vdash^{\mathtt{call}} \mathbf{f}\ v_1 \cdots v_n \rightarrow w$, then for all $e_1, \ldots, e_n$ such that each $e_i \sqsupseteq' \psi(v_i, l)$, and for all $p \succ l$ there exists $o \sqsupseteq' \psi(w, p)$ such that $\vdash \mathbf{f}\ e_1 \cdots e_n \rightsquigarrow o$ is eventually confirmed.
2. If the subtree labelled l has root $\mathsf{p}', \gamma \vdash t \rightarrow w$ and $\eta(x) \sqsupseteq' \psi(\gamma(x), l)$ for all $x \in \mathit{Var}(t)$, then for all $p \succ l$ there exists $o \sqsupseteq' \psi(w, p)$ such that $\eta \Vdash t \rightsquigarrow o$ is eventually confirmed.

Assigning the main tree a label 0 (to secure that $p \succ 0$ exists), we obtain that $\vdash \mathtt{start}\ d_1 \cdots d_M \rightsquigarrow b$ is eventually confirmed, so b is indeed returned. $\square$

By Lemmas 16 and 17 together we may immediately conclude:

Lemma 18. $[\![\mathsf{p}]\!](d_1, \ldots, d_M) \mapsto b$ *iff Algorithm 13 returns a set containing* b.

The proof of the general case provides a basis for the deterministic case:

Lemma 19. *If* $[\![\mathsf{p}]\!](d_1, \ldots, d_M) \mapsto b$ *and* p *is deterministic, then Algorithm 13 returns a set* $A \cup \{b\}$.

Proof (Sketch). We define a consistency measure $\wr$ on non-deterministic extensional values: $e \wr u$ iff $e = u \in \mathcal{B}$, or $e = (e_1, e_2)$, $u = (u_1, u_2)$, $e_1 \wr u_1$ and $e_2 \wr u_2$, or $e = A_\sigma$, $u = B_\sigma$ and for all $(e_1, u_1) \in A$ and $(e_2, u_2) \in B$: $e_1 \wr e_2$ implies $u_1 \wr u_2$.

In the proof of Lemma 17, we trace a derivation in the algorithm. In a deterministic program, we can see that if both $\vdash f\ e_1 \cdots e_n \to o$ and $\vdash f\ e_1' \cdots e_n' \to o'$ are confirmed, and each $e_i \wr e_n'$, then $o \wr o'$—and similar for statements $\eta \vdash s \Rightarrow o$. We use this to remove statements which are not necessary, ultimately leaving only those which use deterministic extensional values as used in Algorithm 7. $\square$

Lemma 20. $[\![p]\!](d_1, \ldots, d_M) \mapsto b$ *iff Algorithm 7 returns a set containing b.*

Proof. This is a combination of Lemmas 16 and 19. $\square$

Note that it is a priori not clear that Algorithm 7 returns only one value; however, this is obtained as a consequence of Lemma 20.

7   Recovering the **EXPTIME** hierarchy

While interesting, Lemma 12 exposes a problem: non-determinism is unexpectedly powerful in the higher-order setting. If we still want to use non-deterministic programs towards characterising non-deterministic complexity classes, we must surely start by considering restrictions which avoid this explosion of expressivity.

One direction is to consider *arrow depth* instead of data order. Using Lemma 14, we easily recover the original hierarchy—and obtain the last line of Fig. 1.

	arrow depth 0	arrow depth 1	arrow depth 2	...
cons-free	$P = EXP^0TIME$	$EXP = EXP^1TIME$	EXP^2TIME	...

Theorem 3. *The class of non-deterministic cons-free programs where all variables are typed with a type of arrow depth K characterises $EXP^K TIME$.*

Proof (Sketch). Both in the base program in Fig. 7, and in the counting modules of Lemmas 4 and 5, type order and arrow depth coincide. Thus every decision problem in $EXP^K TIME$ is accepted by a cons-free program with "data arrow depth" K. For the other direction, the proof of Lemma 1 is trivially adapted to use arrow depth rather than type order. Thus, altering the preparation step in Algorithm 13 gives an algorithm which determines the possible outputs of a program with data arrow depth K, with the desired complexity by Lemma 14.

$\square$

A downside is that, by moving away from data order, this result is hard to compare with other characterisations using cons-free programs. An alternative is to impose a restriction alongside cons-freeness: *unitary variables*. This gives no restrictions in the setting with data order 0—thus providing the first column in the table from Sect. 6—and brings us the second-last line in Fig. 1:

	data order 0	data order 1	data order 2	data order 3
cons-free unitary variables	$P = EXP^0 TIME$	$EXP = EXP^1 TIME$	$EXP^2 TIME$	$EXP^3 TIME$

Definition 19. *A program* p *has* unitary variables *if clauses are typed with an assignment mapping each variable* x *to a type* κ *or* $\sigma \Rightarrow \kappa$, *with* $ord(\kappa) = 0$.

Thus, in a program with unitary variables, a variable of a type (list × list × list) ⇒ list is admitted, but list ⇒ list ⇒ list ⇒ list is not. The crucial difference is that the former must be applied to all its arguments at the same time, while the latter may be partially applied. This avoids the problem of Lemma 11.

Theorem 4. *The class of (deterministic or non-deterministic) cons-free programs with unitary variables of data order* K *characterises* $EXP^K TIME$.

Proof (Sketch). Both the base program in Fig. 7 and the counting modules of Lemmas 4 and 5 have unitary variables, and are deterministic—this gives one direction. For the other, let a recursively unitary type be κ or $\sigma \Rightarrow \kappa$ with $ord(\kappa) = 0$ and σ recursively unitary. The transformations of Lemma 1 are easily extended to transform a program with unitary variables of type order $\leq K$ to one where all sub-expressions have a recursively unitary type. Since here data order and arrow depth are the same in this case, we complete with Theorem 3. □

8   Conclusion and Future Work

We have studied the effect of combining higher types and non-determinism for cons-free programs. This has resulted in the—highly surprising—conclusion that naively adding non-deterministic choice to a language that characterises the $EXP^K TIME$ hierarchy for increasing data orders immediately increases the expressivity of the language to ELEMENTARY. Recovering a more fine-grained complexity hierarchy can be done, but at the cost of further syntactical restrictions.

The primary goal that we will pursue in future work is to use non-deterministic cons-free programs to characterise hierarchies of *non*-deterministic complexity classes such as $NEXP^K TIME$ for $K \in \mathbb{N}$. In addition, it would be worthwhile to make a full study of the ramifications of imposing restrictions on recursion, such as tail-recursion or primitive recursion, in combination with non-determinism and higher types (akin to the study of primitive recursion in a successor-free language done in [16]). We also intend to study characterisations of classes more restrictive than P, such as LOGTIME and LOGSPACE.

Finally, given the surprising nature of our results, we urge readers to investigate the effect of adding non-determinism to other programming languages used in implicit complexity that manipulate higher-order data. We conjecture that the effect on expressivity there will essentially be the same as what we have observed.

References

1. Bellantoni, S.: Ph.D. thesis, University of Toronto (1993)
2. Bellantoni, S., Cook, S.: A new recursion-theoretic characterization of the polytime functions. Comput. Complex. **2**, 97–110 (1992)
3. Ben-Amram, A.M., Petersen, H.: CONS-free programs with tree input. In: Larsen, K.G., Skyum, S., Winskel, G. (eds.) ICALP 1998. LNCS, vol. 1443, pp. 271–282. Springer, Heidelberg (1998). doi:10.1007/BFb0055060
4. Bonfante, G.: Some programming languages for LOGSPACE and PTIME. In: Johnson, M., Vene, V. (eds.) AMAST 2006. LNCS, vol. 4019, pp. 66–80. Springer, Heidelberg (2006). doi:10.1007/11784180_8
5. Clote, P.: Computation models and function algebras. In: Handbook of Computability Theory, pp. 589–681. Elsevier (1999)
6. Cook, S.A.: Characterizations of pushdown machines in terms of time-bounded computers. J. ACM **18**(1), 4–18 (1971)
7. de Carvalho, D., Simonsen, J.G.: An implicit characterization of the polynomial-time decidable sets by cons-free rewriting. In: Dowek, G. (ed.) RTA 2014. LNCS, vol. 8560, pp. 179–193. Springer, Cham (2014). doi:10.1007/978-3-319-08918-8_13
8. Goerdt, A.: Characterizing complexity classes by general recursive definitions in higher types. Inf. Comput. **101**(2), 202–218 (1992)
9. Goerdt, A.: Characterizing complexity classes by higher type primitive recursive definitions. Theor. Comput. Sci. **100**(1), 45–66 (1992)
10. Immerman, N.: Descriptive Complexity. Springer, New York (1999)
11. Jones, N.: Computability and Complexity from a Programming Perspective. MIT Press, Cambridge (1997)
12. Jones, N.: The expressive power of higher-order types or, life without CONS. J. Funct. Program. **11**(1), 55–94 (2001)
13. Kfoury, A.J., Tiuryn, J., Urzyczyn, P.: An analysis of ML typability. J. ACM **41**(2), 368–398 (1994)
14. Kop, C., Simonsen, J.: Complexity hierarchies and higher-order cons-free rewriting. In: Kesner, D., Pientka, B. (eds.) FSCD. LIPIcs, vol. 52, pp. 23:1–23:18 (2016). 10.4230/LIPIcs.FSCD.2016.23
15. Kop, C., Simonsen, J.: The power of non-determinism in higher-order implicit complexity (extended version). Technical report, University of Copenhagen (2017). https://arxiv.org/pdf/1701.05382.pdf
16. Kristiansen, L., Mender, B.M.W.: Non-determinism in Gödel's system T. Theory Comput. Syst. **51**(1), 85–105 (2012)
17. Kristiansen, L., Niggl, K.-H.: Implicit computational complexity on the computational complexity of imperative programming languages. Theor. Comput. Sci. **318**(1), 139–161 (2004)
18. Kristiansen, L., Voda, P.J.: Programming languages capturing complexity classes. Nord. J. Comput. **12**(2), 89–115 (2005)
19. Dal Lago, U.: A short introduction to implicit computational complexity. In: Bezhanishvili, N., Goranko, V. (eds.) ESSLLI 2010-2011. LNCS, vol. 7388, pp. 89–109. Springer, Heidelberg (2012). doi:10.1007/978-3-642-31485-8_3
20. Oitavem, I.: A recursion-theoretic approach to NP. Ann. Pure Appl. Log. **162**(8), 661–666 (2011)
21. Papadimitriou, C.: Computational Complexity. Addison-Wesley, Reading (1994)
22. Sipser, M.: Introduction to the Theory of Computation. Thomson Course Technology, Boston (2006)

The Essence of Higher-Order Concurrent Separation Logic

Robbert Krebbers[1]([✉]), Ralf Jung[2], Aleš Bizjak[3], Jacques-Henri Jourdan[2],
Derek Dreyer[2], and Lars Birkedal[3]

[1] Delft University of Technology, Delft, The Netherlands
mail@robbertkrebbers.nl
[2] MPI-SWS, Saarland Informatics Campus, Saarbrücken, Germany
{jung,jjourdan,dreyer}@mpi-sws.org
[3] Aarhus University, Aarhus, Denmark
{abizjak,birkedal}@cs.au.dk

Abstract. Concurrent separation logics (CSLs) have come of age, and
with age they have accumulated a great deal of complexity. Previous
work on the Iris logic attempted to reduce the complex logical mechanisms of modern CSLs to two orthogonal concepts: partial commutative
monoids (PCMs) and invariants. However, the realization of these concepts in Iris still bakes in several complex mechanisms—such as weakest
preconditions and mask-changing view shifts—as primitive notions.

In this paper, we take the Iris story to its (so to speak) logical conclusion, applying the reductionist methodology of Iris to Iris itself. Specifically, we define a small, resourceful *base logic*, which distills the essence
of Iris: it comprises only the assertion layer of vanilla separation logic,
plus a handful of simple modalities. We then show how the much fancier
logical mechanisms of Iris—in particular, its entire program specification
layer—can be understood as merely derived forms in our base logic. This
approach helps to explain the *meaning* of Iris's program specifications
at a much higher level of abstraction than was previously possible. We
also show that the step-indexed "later" modality of Iris is an *essential*
source of complexity, in that removing it leads to a logical inconsistency.
All our results are fully formalized in the Coq proof assistant.

1 Introduction

In his paper *The Next 700 Separation Logics*, Parkinson [26] observed that "separation logic has brought great advances in the world of verification. However,
there is a disturbing trend for each new library or concurrency primitive to
require a new separation logic." He argued that what is needed is a general
logic for concurrent reasoning, into which a variety of useful specifications can
be encoded via the abstraction facilities of the logic. "By finding the right core
logic," he wrote, "we can concentrate on the difficult problems."

The logic he suggested as a potential candidate for such a core concurrency
logic was *deny-guarantee* [12]. Deny-guarantee was indeed groundbreaking in its
support for "fictional separation"—the idea that even if threads are concurrently
manipulating the same *shared* piece of physical state, one can view them as operating on *logically disjoint* pieces of it and use separation logic to reason modularly

© Springer-Verlag GmbH Germany 2017
H. Yang (Ed.): ESOP 2017, LNCS 10201, pp. 696–723, 2017.
DOI: 10.1007/978-3-662-54434-1_26

about those pieces. It was, however, far from the last word on the subject. Rather, it spawned a new breed of logics with ever more powerful fictional-separation mechanisms for reasoning modularly about interference [9,11,16,27,29,30]. Several of these also incorporated support for *impredicative invariants* [4,17,18,28], which are needed if one aims to verify code in languages with semantically cyclic features (such as ML or Rust, which support higher-order state).

Although exciting, the progress in this area has come at a cost: as these new separation logics become ever more expressive, each one accumulates increasingly baroque and bespoke proof rules, which are *primitive* in the sense that their soundness is established by direct appeal to the also baroque and bespoke model of the logic. As a result, it is difficult to understand what program specifications in these logics really mean, how they relate to one another, or whether they can be soundly combined in one reasoning framework. In short, we feel, it is high time to renew Parkinson's quest for "the right core logic" of concurrency.

Toward this end, Jung *et al.* [17,18] recently developed **Iris**, a higher-order concurrent separation logic with the goal of simplification and consolidation. The key idea of Iris is that even the fanciest of the interference-control mechanisms in recent concurrency logics can be expressed by a combination of two orthogonal ingredients: *partial commutative monoids* (PCMs) and *invariants*. PCMs enable the user of the logic to roll their own type of fictional (or "logical" or "ghost") state, and invariants serve to tie that fictional state to the underlying physical state of the program. Using just these two mechanisms, Jung *et al.* showed how to take complex primitive proof rules from prior logics and *derive them within* Iris, leading to the slogan: "Monoids and invariants are all you need."

Unfortunately, that slogan does not tell the whole story. Although monoids and invariants do indeed constitute the two main conceptual elements of Iris— and they are arguably "canonical" in their simplicity and universality—the realization of these concepts in Iris involves a number of interacting logical mechanisms, some of which are simple and canonical, others not so much:

- Ownership assertions, $\lceil\underline{a}\rceil^\gamma$, for logical (ghost) state.
- Named invariant assertions, $\boxed{P}^\iota$, asserting that ι is the name of an invariant that enforces that P holds of some piece of the shared state. Invariants in Iris are *impredicative*, which means that $\boxed{P}^\iota$ can be used anywhere where normal assertions can be used, *e.g.*, in invariants themselves.
- A necessity modality, $\Box P$, which asserts that P holds *persistently*, as opposed to an assertion describing exclusive ownership of some resource.
- A "later" modality, $\triangleright P$. To support impredicative higher-order quantification and recursively defined assertions, the model of Iris employs the technique of *step-indexing* [2]. This is reflected in the logic in the form of $\triangleright P$, which roughly asserts that P will be true after the next step of computation.
- Invariant masks, $\mathcal{E}$, which are sets of invariant names, ι. Masks are used to track which invariants are enabled (*i.e.*, currently satisfied by some piece of shared state) at a given point in a program proof.

- Mask-changing view shifts, $P \overset{\mathcal{E}_1}{\Rrightarrow}{}^{\mathcal{E}_2} Q$. These describe a kind of logical update operation, asserting (roughly) that, if the invariants in $\mathcal{E}_1$ hold, P can be transformed to Q, after which point the invariants in $\mathcal{E}_2$ hold. These view shifts are useful for expressing the temporary disabling and re-enabling of invariants within the verification of an atomic step of computation.
- Weakest preconditions, $\mathsf{wp}_{\mathcal{E}} e \{\Phi\}$, which establish that e is safe to execute assuming the invariants in $\mathcal{E}$ hold, and that if e computes to a value v, then $\Phi(v)$ holds. Hoare triples are encodable in terms of weakest preconditions.

Associated with each of these logical mechanisms are a significant number of primitive proof rules. For certain features, such as the $\square P$ modality, the rules are mostly standard, and the model is very simple. In contrast, the primitive proof rules for weakest preconditions and view shifts are non-standard, and the model of these features is extremely involved, making the justification of the primitive rules—not to mention the very *meaning* of Iris's Hoare-style program specifications—painfully difficult to understand or explain. Indeed, the previous Iris papers [17, 18] have avoided even attempting to present the formal model of program specifications in any detail at all.

In the present paper, we rectify this situation by taking the Iris story to its (so to speak) logical conclusion—that is, by applying the reductionist Iris methodology to Iris itself! Specifically, we present a small, resourceful *base logic*, which distills the essence—the minimal, primitive core—of Iris: it comprises only the assertion layer of vanilla separation logic (*i.e.*, including $P * Q$ but not Hoare triples) extended with $\square P, \rhd P$, and a simple, novel, monadic *update* modality, $\Rrightarrow P$. Using these basic mechanisms, the fancier mechanisms of mask-changing view shifts and weakest preconditions—and their associated proof rules—*can all be derived within the logic*. And by expressing the fancier mechanisms as derived forms, we can now explain the meaning of Iris's program specifications at a much higher level of abstraction than was previously possible.

In Sect. 2, we begin by presenting from first principles the reduced base logic that constitutes the primitive core of our new version of Iris (version 3.0). Then, in Sect. 3, we explain step-by-step how to encode weakest preconditions in the Iris 3.0 base logic. Next, in Sect. 4, we show how our base logic is sufficient to derive the remaining mechanisms and proof rules of full Iris, including named invariants and mask-changing view shifts.

On the negative side, there is one point of unfortunate complexity that Iris 3.0 inherits from earlier versions without simplification: the aforementioned "later" modality, $\rhd P$. The Iris rule for accessing an invariant $\boxed{P}^{\iota}$ says that when we gain control of the resource satisfying the invariant, we only learn $\rhd P$, not P. It has proven very difficult to explain to users of Iris the role of $\rhd$ here because it boils down to "the model made me do it": the $\rhd$ reflects a corresponding place in the existing step-indexed model of Iris where the step-index is decreased to ensure a well-founded construction. Moreover, $\rhd P$ is in general strictly weaker than P, and experience working with Iris has shown that in certain cases this weakness forces the user of the logic into painful workarounds. In Sect. 5, we show that in the proof rule for accessing an invariant, the use of $\triangleright$ (or something like it) is in fact *essential*, because if $\triangleright$ is removed from the rule, Iris becomes inconsistent. This provides evidence that $\triangleright$ is a kind of necessary evil.

Finally, in Sect. 6, we discuss related work, and in Sect. 7, we conclude.

All results in this paper have been formalized in the Coq proof assistant [1].

2   The Iris 3.0 Base Logic

The goal of this section is to introduce the *Iris 3.0 base logic*, which is the core logic that all of Iris rests on: all its program-logic mechanisms will be defined in terms of just the primitive assertions of our base logic.

The Iris base logic is a higher-order logic with a couple of extensions, most of which are standard. We will discuss each of these extensions in turn. The primitive logical assertions are defined by the following grammar:

$$P, Q, R \in \mathsf{Prop} ::= \mathsf{True} \mid \mathsf{False} \mid t = u \mid P \wedge Q \mid P \vee Q \mid P \Rightarrow Q \mid \forall x.\, P \mid \exists x.\, P$$
$$\mid P * Q \mid P \mathbin{-\!\!*} Q \mid \mathsf{Own}(a) \mid \mathcal{V}(a) \mid \Box P \mid \mathrel{\Rrightarrow} P \mid \mu x.\, P \mid \triangleright P$$

Since the logic is higher-order, the full grammar of (multi-sorted) terms also involves the usual connectives of the simply-typed lambda calculus. This is common practice; the full details are spelled out in the technical appendix [1].

The rules for the logical entailment[1] $P \vdash Q$ are displayed in Fig. 1. Note that $P \dashv\vdash Q$ is shorthand for having both $P \vdash Q$ and $Q \vdash P$.

We omit the ordinary rules for intuitionistic higher-order logic with equality, which are standard and displayed in the appendix [1]. The remaining connectives and proof principles fall into two broad categories: those dealing with ownership of resources (Sects. 2.1–2.5) and those related to step-indexing (Sects. 2.6–2.7).

2.1   Separation Logic

The connectives $*$ and $-\!\!*$ of bunched implications [25] make our base logic a *separation logic*: they let us reason about *ownership of resources*. The key point is that $P * Q$ describes ownership of a resource that can be *separated* into two disjoint pieces, one satisfying P and one satisfying Q. This is in contrast to $P \wedge Q$, which describes ownership of a resource satisfying both P and Q.

For example, consider the resources owned by different threads in a concurrent program. Because these threads operate concurrently, it is crucial that their ownership is *disjoint*. As a consequence, separating conjunction is the natural operator to combine the ownership of concurrent threads.

Together with separating conjunction, we have a second form of implication: the *magic wand* $P \mathbin{-\!\!*} Q$. It describes ownership of "Q minus P", *i.e.*, it describes resources such that, if you (disjointly) add resources satisfying P, you obtain resources satisfying Q.

---

[1] The full judgment is of the shape $\Gamma \mid P \vdash Q$, where Γ assigns types to free variables. However, since Γ only plays a role in the rules for quantifiers, we omit it.

Laws of (affine) bunched implications.

$\text{True} * P \dashv\vdash P$

$P * Q \vdash Q * P$

$(P * Q) * R \vdash P * (Q * R)$

$\dfrac{*\text{-MONO}}{\dfrac{P_1 \vdash Q_1 \quad P_2 \vdash Q_2}{P_1 * P_2 \vdash Q_1 * Q_2}}$

$\dfrac{-\!*\text{-INTRO}}{\dfrac{P * Q \vdash R}{P \vdash Q -\!* R}}$

$\dfrac{-\!*\text{-ELIM}}{\dfrac{P \vdash Q -\!* R}{P * Q \vdash R}}$

Laws for resources and validity.

OWN-OP
$\text{Own}(a) * \text{Own}(b) \dashv\vdash \text{Own}(a \cdot b)$

OWN-UNIT
$\text{True} \vdash \text{Own}(\varepsilon)$

OWN-CORE
$\text{Own}(a) \vdash \square\,\text{Own}(|a|)$

OWN-VALID
$\text{Own}(a) \vdash \mathcal{V}(a)$

VALID-OP
$\mathcal{V}(a \cdot b) \vdash \mathcal{V}(a)$

VALID-ALWAYS
$\mathcal{V}(a) \vdash \square\,\mathcal{V}(a)$

Laws for the basic update modality.

$\dfrac{\text{UPD-MONO}}{\dfrac{P \vdash Q}{\Rrightarrow P \vdash \Rrightarrow Q}}$

UPD-INTRO
$P \vdash \Rrightarrow P$

UPD-TRANS
$\Rrightarrow \Rrightarrow P \vdash \Rrightarrow P$

UPD-FRAME
$Q * \Rrightarrow P \vdash \Rrightarrow (Q * P)$

$\dfrac{\text{UPD-UPDATE}}{\dfrac{a \rightsquigarrow B}{\text{Own}(a) \vdash \Rrightarrow \exists b \in B.\, \text{Own}(b)}}$

Laws for the always modality.

$\dfrac{\square\text{-MONO}}{\dfrac{P \vdash Q}{\square P \vdash \square Q}}$

$\dfrac{\square\text{-ELIM}}{\square P \vdash P}$

$\text{True} \vdash \square\,\text{True}$

$\square(P \wedge Q) \vdash \square(P * Q)$

$\square P \wedge Q \vdash \square P * Q$

$\square P \vdash \square\square P$

$\forall x.\, \square P \vdash \square \forall x.\, P$

$\square \exists x.\, P \vdash \exists x.\, \square P$

Laws for the later modality.

$\dfrac{\triangleright\text{-MONO}}{\dfrac{P \vdash Q}{\triangleright P \vdash \triangleright Q}}$

$\dfrac{\text{LÖB}}{(\triangleright P \Rightarrow P) \vdash P}$

$\forall x.\, \triangleright P \vdash \triangleright \forall x.\, P$

$\triangleright \exists x.\, P \vdash \triangleright\,\text{False} \vee \exists x.\, \triangleright P$

$\triangleright(P * Q) \dashv\vdash \triangleright P * \triangleright Q$

$\square \triangleright P \dashv\vdash \triangleright \square P$

Laws for timeless assertions.

$\triangleright\text{-TIMELESS}$
$\triangleright P \vdash \triangleright\,\text{False} \vee (\triangleright\,\text{False} \Rightarrow P)$

$\triangleright\text{-OWN}$
$\triangleright\,\text{Own}(a) \vdash \exists b.\, \text{Own}(b) \wedge \triangleright(a = b)$

Fig. 1. Proof rules of the Iris 3.0 base logic.

2.2   Resource Algebras

The purpose of the $\text{Own}(a)$ connective is to assert ownership of the resource a. Before we go on introducing this connective, we need to answer the following question: *what is a resource?*

The Iris base logic does not answer this question by fixing a particular set of resources. Instead, the set of resources is kept general, and it is up to the user of the logic to make a suitable choice. All the logic demands is that the set of resources forms a *unital resource algebra* (uRA), as defined in Fig. 2.

A *resource algebra* (RA) is a tuple $(M, \mathcal{V} \subseteq M, |-| : M \to M^?, (\cdot) : M \times M \to M)$ satisfying:

$$\forall a, b, c. (a \cdot b) \cdot c = a \cdot (b \cdot c) \qquad \forall a, b. a \cdot b = b \cdot a$$
$$\forall a, b. (a \cdot b) \in \mathcal{V} \Rightarrow a \in \mathcal{V} \qquad \forall a. |a| \in M \Rightarrow |a| \cdot a = a$$
$$\forall a. |a| \in M \Rightarrow ||a|| = |a| \qquad \forall a, b. |a| \in M \wedge a \preccurlyeq b \Rightarrow |b| \in M \wedge |a| \preccurlyeq |b|$$

where $M^? \triangleq M \uplus \{\bot\}$ with $a^? \cdot \bot \triangleq \bot \cdot a^? \triangleq a^?$

$$a \preccurlyeq b \triangleq \exists c \in M. b = a \cdot c$$
$$a \rightsquigarrow B \triangleq \forall c^? \in M^?. a \cdot c^? \in \mathcal{V} \Rightarrow \exists b \in B. b \cdot c^? \in \mathcal{V}$$
$$a \rightsquigarrow b \triangleq a \rightsquigarrow \{b\}$$

A *unital resource algebra* (uRA) is a resource algebra M with an element ε satisfying:

$$\varepsilon \in \mathcal{V} \qquad \forall a \in M. \varepsilon \cdot a = a \qquad |\varepsilon| = \varepsilon$$

Fig. 2. Resource algebras.

Resource algebras are similar to *partial commutative monoids* (PCMs), which are often used to describe ownership in concurrent separation logics because:

- Ownership of different threads can be *composed* using the $\cdot$ operator.
- Composition of ownership is *associative and commutative*, reflecting the associative and commutative semantics of parallel composition.
- Combinations of ownership that do not make sense are ruled out by *partiality*, e.g., multiple threads claiming to have ownership of an exclusive resource.

However, there are some differences between RAs and PCMs:

1. Instead of partiality, RAs use *validity* to rule out invalid combinations of ownership. Specifically, there is a subset $\mathcal{V}$ of *valid* elements. As shown previously [17], this take on partiality is necessary when defining *higher-order* ghost state, which we will need for modeling invariants in Sect. 4.3.
2. Instead of having one "unit" that acts as the identity for *every* element, RAs have a partial function $|-|$ assigning the *(duplicable) core* $|a|$ to each element a. The core of an RA is a strict generalization of the unit of a PCM: the core can be *different* for different elements, and since the core is *partial*, there can actually be elements of the RA for which there is no identity element.

Although the Iris base logic is parameterized by a uRA (that is, an RA with a single, global unit), we do not demand that every RA have a unit because we typically compose RAs from smaller parts. Requiring all of these "intermediate" RAs to be unital would render many of our compositions impossible [17].

Let us now give some examples of RAs; more appear in Sects. 3.3 and 4.2.

Exclusive. Given a set X, the task of the *exclusive RA* $\text{Ex}(X)$ is to make sure that one party *exclusively* owns a value $x \in X$. (We are using a datatype-like notation to declare the possible elements of $\text{Ex}(X)$.)

$$\text{Ex}(X) \triangleq \text{ex}(x : X) \mid \frac{1}{2} \qquad \mathcal{V} \triangleq \{\text{ex}(x) \mid x \in X\} \qquad |\text{ex}(x)| \triangleq \perp$$

Composition is always undefined (using the invalid dummy element $\frac{1}{2}$) to ensure that ownership is *exclusive*, *i.e.*, exactly one party has full control over the resource. This RA does not have a unit.

Finite Partial Function. Given a set of keys K and an RA M, the *finite partial function* uRA $K \xrightarrow{\text{fin}} M$ is defined by lifting the core and the composition operator pointwise, and by defining validity as the conjunction of pointwise validities. The unit ε is defined to be the empty partial function $\emptyset$.

2.3   Resource Ownership

Having completed the discussion of RAs, we now come back to the base logic and its connective $\text{Own}(a)$, which describes ownership of the RA element a. It forms the "primitive" form of ownership in our logic, which can then be composed into more interesting assertions using the previously described connectives. The most important fact about ownership is that separating conjunction "reflects" the composition operator of RAs into the logic (OWN-OP).

Besides the $\text{Own}(a)$ connective, we have the primitive connective $\mathcal{V}(a)$, which reflects validity of RA elements into the logic. Note that ownership is connected to validity: the rule OWN-VALID says that only valid elements can be owned.

2.4   Resource Updates

So far, resources have been *static*: the logic provides assertions to reason about resources you own, the consequences of that ownership, and how ownership can be disjointly separated. The *(basic) update modality* $\Rrightarrow P$, however, lets you talk about what you *could own* after performing an update to what you do own.

Updates to resources are called *frame-preserving updates* and can be performed using the rule UPD-UPDATE. We can perform a frame-preserving update $a \rightsquigarrow B$ if for any resource (called a *frame*) a_{f} such that $a \cdot a_{\text{f}} \in \mathcal{V}$, there exists a resource $b \in B$ such that $b \cdot a_{\text{f}} \in \mathcal{V}$. If we think of those frames as being the resources owned by other threads, then a frame-preserving update is guaranteed not to invalidate the resources of concurrently-running threads. By doing only frame-preserving updates, we know we will never "step on anybody else's toes".

Before discussing how frame-preserving updates are reflected into the logic, we give some examples of frame-preserving updates. Since ownership in the exclusive RA is exclusive, there is nobody whose assumptions could be invalidated by changing the value of the resource. To that end, we have $\text{ex}(x) \rightsquigarrow \text{ex}(y)$ for any x and y. The updates for the finite partial functions $K \xrightarrow{\text{fin}} M$ are as follows:

FPFN-UPDATE

$$\frac{a \rightsquigarrow_M B}{f[i := a] \rightsquigarrow \{f[i := b] \mid b \in B\}}$$

FPFN-ALLOC

$$\frac{a \in \mathcal{V} \qquad K \text{ infinite}}{\emptyset \rightsquigarrow \{[i := a] \mid i \in K\}}$$

The first rule witnesses pointwise lifting of updates on M. The second rule is more interesting: it allows us to *allocate* a fresh slot in the finite partial function. This is always possible because only finitely many indices $i \in K$ will be used at any given point in time.

The update modality reflects frame-preserving updates into the logic, in the sense that $\Rrightarrow P$ asserts ownership of resources *that can be updated to* resources satisfying P. The rule UPD-UPDATE witnesses this relationship, while the remaining proof rules essentially say that $\Rrightarrow$ is a *strong monad* with respect to separating conjunction [19,20].

This gives rise to an alternative interpretation of the basic update modality: we can think of $\Rrightarrow P$ as a *thunk* that captures some resources in its environment and that, when executed, will "return" resources satisfying P. The various proof rules then let us perform additional reasoning on the result of the thunk (UPD-MONO), create a thunk that does nothing (UPD-INTRO), compose two thunks into one (UPD-TRANS), and add resources to those captured by the thunk (UPD-FRAME).

2.5 The Always Modality

The intuition for the *always modality* $\Box P$ is that P holds *without asserting any exclusive ownership*. This is useful because an assumption $\Box P$ can be used arbitrarily often, *i.e.*, it cannot be "used up". In particular, while $P \twoheadrightarrow Q$ is a "linear implication" and can only be applied once, $\Box(P \twoheadrightarrow Q)$ can be applied arbitrarily often. We use this in the encoding of Hoare triples in Sect. 3.2.

We call an assertion P *persistent* if proofs of P can never assert exclusive ownership, which formally means it enjoys $P \vdash \Box P$. As soon as either P or Q is persistent, their separating conjunction $(P * Q)$ and normal conjunction $(P \land Q)$ coincide, thus enabling one to use "normal" intuitionistic reasoning.

Under which circumstances is $\mathsf{Own}(a)$ persistent? RAs provide a flexible answer to this: the core $|a|$ defines the *duplicable* part of a, and hence $\mathsf{Own}(|a|)$ does not assert any exclusive ownership, which is reflected into the logic using the rule OWN-CORE. In Sect. 4.2, we will consider an example of an RA with a non-trivial core, and we will make use of the fact that $\mathsf{Own}(|a|)$ is persistent.

2.6 The Later Modality and Guarded Fixed-Points

Although RAs provide a powerful way to instantiate our logic with the user's custom type of resources, they have an inherent limitation: the user-chosen RA must be defined *a priori*. But what if the user wants to define their resources *in terms of* the assertions of the logic? In prior work [17], we called this phenomenon *higher-order ghost state*, and showed how to incorporate it into the Iris 2.0 logic. Iris 3.0 inherits higher-order ghost state from Iris 2.0 without change.

The challenge of supporting higher-order ghost state is that the user-chosen RA depends on the type of propositions of our logic, which in turn depends on the user-chosen RA. In Iris 2.0, we showed how to cut this circularity using a novel algebraic structure called a *CMRA* ("camera"), which synthesizes the features of an RA together with a *step-indexed* structure [2]. Since a proper understanding of CMRAs is not needed in order to appreciate the contribution of the present paper, we refer the reader to the Iris 2.0 paper [17] for details, and instead focus briefly here on how the presence of higher-order ghost state affects our base logic. (We will see a concrete instance of higher-order ghost state in Sect. 4.2, where we use it to encode impredicative invariants.)

The step-indexing aspect of CMRAs is internalized into the logic by adding a new modality: the *later modality*, $\triangleright P$ [3,23]. Intuitively, $\triangleright P$ asserts that P holds "at the next step-index" (or "one step later"). In the definition of weakest preconditions in Sect. 3.3, we connect $\triangleright$ to computation steps, allowing one to think of $\triangleright P$ as saying that P holds at the next step of computation.

Beyond higher-order ghost state, step-indexing allows us to include a fixed-point operator $\mu x. P$ into the logic, which can be used to define recursive predicates *without any restriction on the variance* of the recursive occurrences of x in P. Instead, all recursive occurrences must be *guarded*: they have to appear below a later modality $\triangleright$. In Sect. 3, we will show how guarded recursion is used for defining weakest preconditions. Moreover, as shown in [28], guarded recursion is useful to define specifications for higher-order concurrent data structures.

A crucial proof rule for $\triangleright$ is Löb, which facilitates proving properties about fixed-points: we can essentially assume that the recursive occurrences are already proven correct (as they are under a later). Note that many of the usual rules for later, such as introduction $P \vdash \triangleright P$) and commutativity with other operators ($\triangleright(P \wedge Q) \dashv\vdash \triangleright P \wedge \triangleright Q$) are derivable from the rules in Fig. 1.

2.7 Timeless Assertions

There are some occasions where we inevitably end up with hypotheses below a later. An example is the Iris rule for accessing invariants (WP-INV in Sect. 4). Although one can always introduce a later, one cannot just eliminate a later, so the later may make certain reasoning steps impossible. However, as we will prove in Sect. 5, it is crucial for logical consistency that the later is present in WP-INV.

Still, for many assertions, their semantics is independent of step-indexing, so adding a $\triangleright$ in front of them does not really "change" anything. When accessing an invariant containing such an assertion, we thus do not want the later to be in the way. Ideally, for such assertions, we would like to have $\triangleright P \vdash P$. However, that does not work: indeed, *at step-index* 0, $\triangleright P$ trivially holds and, consequently, does not imply P. Instead, we say that an assertion P is *timeless* when $\triangleright P \vdash \diamond P$, where the modality $\diamond$ is defined by $\diamond P \triangleq P \vee \triangleright \mathsf{False}$. We call this new $\diamond$ modality "except 0": it states that the given assertion holds at all step-indices greater than 0. Under this modality, we can strip away a later from a timeless assertion, *i.e.*, given a timeless P, to prove $\triangleright P \vdash \diamond Q$, it is sufficient to prove $P \vdash \diamond Q$.

Using the rules for timeless assertions in Fig. 1, we can prove that some frequently occurring assertions are timeless. In particular, if a CMRA is *discrete*— *i.e.*, if it degenerates to a plain RA that ignores the step-indexing structure, as is the case for many types of resources—then equality, ownership and validity of such resources are timeless. Furthermore, most of the connectives of our logic (not including ▷) preserve timelessness.

2.8 Consistency

Logical consistency is usually stated as True $\nvdash$ False, *i.e.*, from a closed context one cannot prove a contradiction. However, when building a program logic within our base logic, we wish to prove that the postconditions of our Hoare triples actually represent program behavior (Sect. 4.6), so we need a stronger statement:

Theorem 2.1 (Soundness of first-order interpretation). *Given a first-order proposition ϕ (not involving ownership, higher-order quantification, nor any of the modalities) and* True $\vdash$ $(\Rrightarrow\triangleright)^n \phi$, *then the "standard" (meta-logic) interpretation of ϕ holds. Here, $(\Rrightarrow\triangleright)^n$ is notation for nesting $\Rrightarrow\triangleright$ n times.*

The proposition ϕ should be a first-order predicate to ensure it can be used both inside our logic and at the meta-level. Furthermore, the theorem makes sure that even when reasoning below any combination of modalities, we cannot prove a contradiction. Consistency, *i.e.*, True $\nvdash$ False, is a trivial consequence of this theorem: just pick $\phi = $ False and $n = 0$.

Theorem 2.1 is proven by defining a suitable semantic domain of assertions, interpreting all connectives into that domain, and proving soundness of all proof rules. For further details, we refer the reader to [1,17].

3 Weakest Preconditions

This section shows how to encode a program logic in the Iris base logic. Usually, program logics are centered around Hoare triples, but instead of directly defining Hoare triples in the base logic, we first define the notion of a *weakest precondition*. There are two reasons for defining Hoare triples in terms of the weakest precondition connective: First, weakest preconditions are more primitive and, as such, more natural to encode. Second, weakest preconditions are more convenient for performing interactive proofs with Iris [21].

We will first give some intuition about weakest preconditions and how to work with them. After that, we present the encoding of weakest preconditions in three stages, gradually adding support for reasoning about state and concurrency. For simplicity, we use a concrete programming language in this section. The version including all features of Iris for an arbitrary language is given in Sect. 4.

3.1   Programming Language

For the purpose of this example, we use a call-by-value λ-calculus with references and fork. The syntax and semantics are given in Fig. 3.

Head-reduction $(e, \sigma) \rightarrow_h (e', \sigma', \vec{e}_f)$ is defined on pairs (e, σ) consisting of an expression e and a shared heap σ (a finite partial map from locations to values). Moreover, $\vec{e}_f$ is a list of forked off expressions, which is used to define the semantics of $\mathtt{fork}\ \{e\}$. The head-reduction is lifted to a per-thread reduction $(e, \sigma) \rightarrow (e', \sigma', \vec{e}_f)$ using evaluation contexts. We define an expression e to be reducible in a shared heap σ, and we note $\mathrm{red}(e, \sigma)$, if it can make a thread-local step. The thread-pool reduction $(T, \sigma) \rightarrow_{\mathsf{tp}} (T', \sigma')$ is an interleaving semantics where the *thread-pool* T denotes the existing threads as a list of expressions.

Syntax:

$$v \in \mathit{Val} ::= () \mid \ell \mid \lambda x.e$$
$$e \in \mathit{Expr} ::= v \mid x \mid e_1(e_2) \mid \mathtt{fork}\ \{e\} \mid \mathtt{ref}(e) \mid\ !e \mid e_1 \leftarrow e_2$$
$$K \in \mathit{Ctx} ::= \bullet \mid K(e) \mid v(K) \mid \mathtt{ref}(K) \mid\ !K \mid K \leftarrow e \mid v \leftarrow K$$

Head reduction:

$$((\lambda x.e)v, \sigma) \rightarrow_h (e[v/x], \sigma, \epsilon)$$
$$(!\ell, \sigma) \rightarrow_h (v, \sigma, \epsilon) \qquad\qquad \text{if } \sigma(\ell) = v$$
$$(\ell \leftarrow w, \sigma) \rightarrow_h ((), \sigma[\ell := w], \epsilon) \quad \text{if } \sigma(\ell) = v$$
$$(\mathtt{ref}(v), \sigma) \rightarrow_h (\ell, \sigma[\ell := v], \epsilon) \quad\ \text{if } \sigma(\ell) = \bot$$
$$(\mathtt{fork}\ \{e\}, \sigma) \rightarrow_h ((), \sigma, e)$$

Thread-local reduction:

$$\frac{(e, \sigma) \rightarrow_h (e', \sigma', \vec{e}_f)}{(K[e], \sigma) \rightarrow (K[e'], \sigma', \vec{e}_f)}$$

Thread-pool semantics:

$$\frac{(e, \sigma) \rightarrow (e', \sigma', \vec{e}_f)}{(T_1; e; T_2, \sigma) \rightarrow_{\mathsf{tp}} (T_1; e'; T_2; \vec{e}_f, \sigma')}$$

Fig. 3. Lambda calculus with references and fork.

3.2   Proof Rules

Before coming to the actual contribution of this section—which is the encoding of weakest preconditions using our base logic in Sect. 3.3—we give some idea of how to reason using weakest preconditions by discussing its proof rules. These proof rules are inspired by [15], but presented in weakest precondition style.

Given a predicate $\Phi : \mathit{Val} \rightarrow \mathsf{Prop}$, called the postcondition, the connective $\mathsf{wp}\ e\ \{\Phi\}$ gives the *weakest precondition* under which all executions of e are *safe*, and all return values v of e satisfy the postcondition $\Phi(v)$. For an execution to be safe, we demand that it *does not get stuck*, which in the case of our language means the program must never access invalid locations.

Figure 4 shows some rules of the $\mathsf{wp}\ e\ \{\Phi\}$ connective. To reason about state, we use the well-known *points-to assertion* $\ell \mapsto v$, which states that we *exclusively own* the location ℓ, and that it currently stores value v. As part of defining weakest preconditions, we will also have to define the points-to assertion.

As usual in a weakest precondition style system [10], the postcondition of the conclusion of each rule involves an arbitrary predicate Φ. For example, imagine we want to prove $\ell \mapsto v * P \vdash \mathsf{wp}\,(\ell \leftarrow w)\,\{\Phi\}$. The rule WP-STORE tells us what we have to show about Φ for this to hold:

$$\cfrac{\cfrac{\cfrac{P * \ell \mapsto w \vdash \Phi()}{P \vdash \ell \mapsto w \mathbin{-\!\!*} \Phi()}\;\text{WAND-INTRO}}{\ell \mapsto v * P \vdash \ell \mapsto v * \triangleright(\ell \mapsto w \mathbin{-\!\!*} \Phi())}\;\text{SEP-MONO},\;\triangleright\text{-INTRO}}{\ell \mapsto v * P \vdash \mathsf{wp}\,(\ell \leftarrow w)\,\{\Phi\}}\;\text{WP-STORE}$$

Here, we use $-\!\!*$ MONO to show that we own the location ℓ – this should not be surprising; in a separation logic, we have to demonstrate ownership of a location to access it. Furthermore, using our remaining resources P we have to prove $\ell \mapsto w \mathbin{-\!\!*} \Phi()$. It does not matter what Φ says for values other than (), which corresponds to the fact that the store expression terminates with ().

Notice the end-to-end effect of applying this little derivation: we had to show that we own $\ell \mapsto v$, and it got replaced in our context with $\ell \mapsto w$. However, this was all expressed in the *premise* of WP-STORE (and similarly for the other rules), with the conclusion applying to an *arbitrary* postcondition Φ. We could have equivalently written the rule as $\ell \mapsto v \mathbin{-\!\!*} \mathsf{wp}\,(\ell \leftarrow w)\,\{\ell \mapsto w\}$, but applying rules in such a style requires using the rules of framing (WP-FRAME) and monotonicity (WP-MONO) for every instruction. We thus prefer the style of rules in Fig. 4.

WP-MONO
$$\frac{\forall v.\,\Phi(v) \vdash \Psi(v)}{\mathsf{wp}\,e\,\{\Phi\} \vdash \mathsf{wp}\,e\,\{\Psi\}}$$

WP-FRAME
$$\frac{P * \mathsf{wp}\,e\,\{\Phi\}}{\mathsf{wp}\,e\,\{P * \Phi\}}$$

WP-VAL
$$\frac{\Phi(v)}{\mathsf{wp}\,v\,\{\Phi\}}$$

WP-BIND
$$\frac{\mathsf{wp}\,e\,\{v.\,\mathsf{wp}\,K[\,v\,]\,\{\Phi\}\}}{\mathsf{wp}\,K[e]\,\{\Phi\}}$$

WP-FORK
$$\frac{\triangleright\Phi() * \triangleright \mathsf{wp}\,e\,\{v.\,\mathsf{True}\}}{\mathsf{wp}\,\mathsf{fork}\,\{e\}\,\{\Phi\}}$$

WP-λ
$$\frac{\triangleright \mathsf{wp}\,e[v/x]\,\{\Phi\}}{\mathsf{wp}\,(\lambda x.e)v\,\{\Phi\}}$$

WP-LOAD
$$\frac{\ell \mapsto v * \triangleright(\ell \mapsto v \mathbin{-\!\!*} \Phi(v))}{\mathsf{wp}\,!\,\ell\,\{\Phi\}}$$

WP-STORE
$$\frac{\ell \mapsto v * \triangleright(\ell \mapsto w \mathbin{-\!\!*} \Phi())}{\mathsf{wp}\,(\ell \leftarrow w)\,\{\Phi\}}$$

WP-ALLOC
$$\frac{\triangleright(\forall \ell.\,\ell \mapsto v \mathbin{-\!\!*} \Phi(\ell))}{\mathsf{wp}\,\mathsf{ref}(v)\,\{\Phi\}}$$

Fig. 4. Rules for weakest preconditions.

Hoare Triples. Traditional Hoare triples can be defined in terms of weakest preconditions as $\{P\}\,e\,\{\Phi\} \triangleq \Box(P \mathbin{-\!\!*} \mathsf{wp}\,e\,\{\Phi\})$. The $\Box$ modality ensures that the triple asserts no exclusive ownership, and as such, can be used multiple times.

3.3   Definition of Weakest Preconditions

We now discuss how to *define* weakest preconditions using the Iris base logic, proceeding in three stages of increasing complexity.

First Stage. To get started, let us assume the program we want to verify makes no use of fork or shared heap access. The idea of wp e $\{\Phi\}$ is to ensure that given any reduction $(e, \sigma) \to \cdots \to (e_n, \sigma_n)$, either (e_n, σ_n) is reducible, or the program terminated, *i.e.*, e_n is a value v for which we have $\Phi(v)$. The natural candidate for encoding this is using the fixed-point operator $\mu x. P$ of our logic. Consider the following:

$$
\begin{aligned}
\mathsf{wp}\, e\, \{\Phi\} \triangleq\ & (e \in \mathit{Val} \land \Phi(e)) && (\mathit{return\, value}) \\
& \lor (e \notin \mathit{Val} \land \forall \sigma.\ \mathsf{red}(e, \sigma) && (\mathit{safety}) \\
& \quad \land \rhd (\forall e_2, \sigma_2.\ (e, \sigma) \to (e_2, \sigma_2, \epsilon)\ \twoheadrightarrow\ \mathsf{wp}\, e_2\, \{\Phi\}) && (\mathit{preservation})\quad)
\end{aligned}
$$

Weakest precondition is defined by case-distinction: either the program has already terminated (e is a value), in which case the postcondition should hold. Alternatively, the program is *not* a value, in which case there are two requirements. First, for any possible heap σ, the program should be reducible (called *program safety*). Second, *if* the program makes a step, then the weakest precondition of the reduced program e_2 must hold (called *preservation*).

Note that the recursive occurrence wp e_2 $\{\Phi\}$ appears under a $\rhd$-modality, so the above can indeed be defined using the fixed-point operator μ. In some sense, this "ties" the steps of the program to the step-indices implicit in the logic, by adding another $\rhd$ for every program step.

So, how useful is this definition? The rules WP-VAL and WP-λ are almost trivial, and using LÖB induction we can prove WP-MONO, WP-FRAME and WP-BIND. We can thus reason about programs that do not fork or make use of the heap.

But unfortunately, this definition cannot be used to verify programs involving heap accesses: the states σ and σ_2 are universally quantified and not related to anything. The program must always be able to proceed under *any* heap, so we cannot possibly prove the rules of the load, store and allocation constructs.

The usual way to proceed in constructing a separation logic is to define the pre- and post-conditions as *predicates* over states, but that is not the direction we take. After all, our base logic *already* has a notion of "resources that can be updated"—*i.e.*, a notion of state—built in to its model of assertions. Of course we want to make use of this power in building our program logic.

Second Stage: Adding State. We now consider programs that access the shared heap but still do not fork. To use the resources provided by the Iris base logic, we have to start by thinking about the right RA. An obvious candidate would be to use $\mathit{Loc} \xrightarrow{\text{fin}} \mathsf{Ex}(\mathit{Val})$ (which is isomorphic to finite partial functions with composition being disjoint union) and define $\ell \mapsto v$ as $\mathsf{Own}([\ell := \mathsf{ex}(v)])$. However, that leaves us with a problem: how do we tie those resources to the actual heap that the program executes on? We have to make sure that from *owning* $\ell \mapsto v$, we can actually deduce that ℓ is allocated in σ.

To this end, we will actually have *two* heaps in our resources, *both* elements of $Loc \xrightarrow{\text{fin}} Ex(Val)$. The *authoritative heap* $\bullet\, \sigma$ is managed by the weakest precondition, and tied to the physical state occurring in the program reduction. There will only ever be one authoritative heap resource, *i.e.*, we want $\bullet\, \sigma \cdot \bullet\, \sigma'$ to be invalid. At the same time, the *heap fragments* $\circ\, \sigma$ will be owned by the program itself and used to give meaning to $\ell \mapsto v$. These fragments can be composed the usual way $(\circ\, \sigma \cdot \circ\, \sigma' = \circ\, (\sigma \uplus \sigma'))$. Finally, we need to tie these two pieces together, making sure that the fragments are always a "part" of the authoritative state: if $\bullet\, \sigma \cdot \circ\, \sigma'$ is valid, then $\sigma' \preccurlyeq \sigma$ should hold.

This is called the *authoritative RA*, $\text{AUTH}(Loc \xrightarrow{\text{fin}} Ex(Val))$ [18]. Before we explain how to define the authoritative RA, let us see why it is useful in the definition of weakest preconditions. The new definition is (changes are in red):

$$\text{wp}\, e\, \{\varPhi\} \triangleq (e \in Val \land \Rrightarrow \varPhi(e))$$
$$\vee (e \notin Val \land \forall \sigma.\, \text{Own}(\bullet\, \sigma) \twoheadrightarrow \Rrightarrow \text{red}(e, \sigma)$$
$$\land \, \triangleright (\forall e_2, \sigma_2.\, (e, \sigma) \to (e_2, \sigma_2, \epsilon) \twoheadrightarrow \Rrightarrow \text{Own}(\bullet\, \sigma_2) * \text{wp}\, e_2\, \{\varPhi\}))$$
$$\ell \mapsto v \triangleq \text{Own}(\circ\, [\ell := v])$$

The difference from the first definition is that the second disjunct (the one covering the case of a program that can still reduce) requires proving safety and preservation under the assumption that the authoritative heap $\bullet\, \sigma$ *matches the physical one*. Moreover, when the program makes a step to some new state σ_2, the proof must be able to *produce* a matching authoritative heap. Finally, the basic update modality permits the proof to perform frame-preserving updates.

To see why this is useful, consider proving WP-LOAD, the weakest precondition of $!\, \ell$. After picking the right disjunct and introducing all assumptions, we can combine the assumptions made by the rule, $\ell \mapsto v$, with the assumptions provided by the definition of weakest preconditions to obtain $\text{Own}(\bullet\, \sigma \cdot \circ\, [\ell := v])$. By OWN-VALID, we learn that this RA element is valid, which (as discussed above) implies $[\ell := v] \preccurlyeq \sigma$, so $\sigma(\ell) = v$. In other words, because the RA ties the authoritative heap and the heap fragments together, and because weakest precondition ties the authoritative heap and the physical heap used in program reduction together, we can make a connection between $\ell \mapsto v$ and the physical heap.

Completing the proof of safety and progress now is straightforward. Since all possible reductions of $!\, \ell$ do not change the heap, we can produce the authoritative heap $\bullet\, \sigma_2$ by just "forwarding" the one we got earlier in the proof. In this case, we did not even make use of the fact that we are allowed to perform frame-preserving updates. This is, however, necessary to prove weakest preconditions of operations that actually *change* the state (like allocation or storing), because in these cases, the authoritative heap needs to be changed likewise.

Authoritative RA. To complete the definition, we need to define the *authoritative RA* [18]. We can do so in general (*i.e.*, the definition is not specific to heaps), so assume we are given some uRA M and let:

$$\text{AUTH}(M) \triangleq \text{Ex}(M)^? \times M$$

$$\mathcal{V} \triangleq \{(\bot, b) \mid b \in \mathcal{V}\} \cup \left\{(\text{ex}(a), b) \,\middle|\, a \in \mathcal{V} \wedge b \preccurlyeq a\right\}$$

$$(x_1, b_1) \cdot (x_2, b_2) \triangleq (x_1 \cdot x_2, b_2 \cdot b_2)$$

$$|(x, b)| \triangleq (\bot, |b|)$$

With $a \in M$, we write $\bullet\, a$ for $(\text{ex}(a), \varepsilon)$ to denote *authoritative* ownership of a and $\circ\, a$ for $(\bot, a)$ to denote *fragmentary* ownership of a.

It can be easily verified that this RA has the three key properties discussed above: ownership of $\bullet\, a$ is exclusive, ownership of $\circ\, a$ composes like that of a, and the two are tied together in the sense that validity of $\bullet\, a \cdot \circ b$ implies $b \preccurlyeq a$. Beyond this, it turns out that we can show the following frame-preserving updates that are needed for WP-STORE and WP-ALLOC:

$$\bullet\, \sigma \cdot \circ\, [\ell := v] \rightsquigarrow \bullet\, \sigma[\ell := w] \cdot \circ\, [\ell := w]$$

$$\bullet\, \sigma \rightsquigarrow \bullet\, \sigma[\ell := w] \cdot \circ\, [\ell := w] \qquad \text{if } \ell \notin \text{dom}(\sigma)$$

Third Stage: Adding Fork. Our previous definition of $\text{wp}\, e\, \{\Phi\}$ only talked about reductions $(e, \sigma) \to (e_2, \sigma_2, \epsilon)$ which do *not* fork off threads, and hence one could not prove WP-FORK. This new definition lifts this limitation:

$$\text{wp}\, e\, \{\Phi\} \triangleq (e \in \mathit{Val} \wedge \mathbin{\Rrightarrow} \Phi(e))$$

$$\vee \big(e \notin \mathit{Val} \wedge \forall \sigma.\, \text{Own}(\bullet\, \sigma) \mathbin{-\!\!*} \mathbin{\Rrightarrow} \text{red}(e, \sigma)$$

$$\wedge \triangleright (\forall e_2, \sigma_2, \vec{e}_f.\, (e, \sigma) \to (e_2, \sigma_2, \vec{e}_f) \mathbin{-\!\!*} \mathbin{\Rrightarrow}$$

$$\text{Own}(\bullet\, \sigma_2) * \text{wp}\, e_2\, \{\Phi\} * \mathbin{\text{\Large$*$}}_{e' \in \vec{e}_f} \text{wp}\, e'\, \{v.\text{True}\}))$$

$$\ell \mapsto v \triangleq \text{Own}(\circ\, [\ell := v])$$

Instead of just demanding a proof of the weakest precondition of the thread e under consideration, we also demand proofs that all the forked-off threads $\vec{e}_f$ are safe. We do not care about their return values, so the postcondition is trivial.

This encoding shows how much mileage we get out of building on top of the Iris base logic. Because said logic supports ownership and step-indexing, we can get around explicitly managing resources and step-indices in the weakest precondition definition. We do not have to explicitly account for the way resources are subdivided between the current thread and the forked-off thread. Instead, all we have to do is surgically place some update modalities, a single $\triangleright$, and some standard separation logic connectives. This keeps the definition of, and the reasoning about, weakest preconditions nice and compact.

4   Recovering the Iris Program Logic

In this section, we show how to encode the reasoning principles of *full Iris* [17,18] within our base logic. The main remaining challenge is to encode *invariants*, which are the key feature for reasoning about *sharing* in concurrent programs [5].

An invariant is simply a property that holds at all times: each thread accessing the state may assume the invariant holds before each step of its computation, but it must also ensure that it continues to hold after each step. Since we work in a separation logic, the invariant does not just "hold"; it expresses ownership of some resources, and threads accessing the invariant get access to those resources. The rule that realizes this idea looks as follows:

WP-INV
$$\frac{\rhd P \vdash \mathsf{wp}_{\mathcal{E}\backslash\{\iota\}}\, e\,\{v.\, \rhd P * \Phi(v)\} \qquad \mathsf{atomic}(e) \qquad \iota \in \mathcal{E}}{\boxed{P}^{\iota} \vdash \mathsf{wp}_{\mathcal{E}}\, e\,\{\Phi\}}$$

This rule is quite a mouthful, so we will go over it carefully. First of all, there is a new assertion $\boxed{P}^{\iota}$, which states that P (an arbitrary assertion) is maintained as an invariant. The rule says that having this assertion in the context permits us to access the invariant, which involves acquiring ownership of $\rhd P$ *before* the verification of e and giving back ownership of $\rhd P$ *after* said verification. Crucially, we require that e is *atomic*, meaning that computation is guaranteed to complete in a single step. This is essential for soundness: the rule allows us to temporarily use and even break the invariant, but after a single atomic step (*i.e.,* before any other thread could take a turn), we have to establish it again.

The $\rhd$ modality arises because of the inherently cyclic nature (*i.e., impredicativity*) of our invariants: P can be *any* assertion, including assertions about invariants. We will show in Sect. 5 that removing the $\rhd$ leads to an unsound logic.

Finally, we come to the *mask* $\mathcal{E}$ and *invariant name* ι: they avoid the issue of *reentrancy*. We have to make sure that the same invariant is not accessed twice at the same time, as that would incorrectly duplicate the underlying resource. To this end, each invariant has a *name* ι identifying it. Furthermore, weakest preconditions are annotated with a *mask* to keep track of which invariants are still enabled. Accessing an invariant removes its name from the mask, ensuring that it cannot be accessed again in a nested fashion.

In order to recover the full power of the Iris program logic (including WP-INV), we start this section by lifting a limitation of the base logic, namely, that it is restricted to a *single* uRA of resources (Sect. 4.1). Then we explain how resources are used to keep track of invariants (Sect. 4.2), and define *world satisfaction*, a protocol enforcing how invariants are maintained (Sect. 4.3). We follow on by defining the *fancy update modality*, which supports accessing invariants (Sect. 4.4), before finally giving an enriched version of weakest preconditions that validates WP-INV (Sect. 4.5).

4.1   Dynamic Composable Resources

The base logic as described in Sect. 2 is limited to resources formed by a *single* RA. However, for the construction in this section, we will need multiple RAs, so we need to find a way to lift this limitation. Furthermore, we frequently need to use not just a single instance of an RA, but multiple, entirely independent instances (*e.g.*, one instance of the RA per instance of a data structure).

As prior work already observed [17,18], it turns out that RAs themselves are already flexible enough to solve this, we just have to pick the right RA. Concretely, assume we are given a *family* of RAs $(M_i)_{i \in \mathcal{I}}$ indexed by some finite index set $\mathcal{I}$. Then, we instantiate our base logic with the following global resource algebra:

$$M \triangleq \prod_{i \in \mathcal{I}} \mathbb{N} \xrightarrow{\text{fin}} M_i$$

First of all, we use a finite partial function to obtain an arbitrary number of instances of any of the given RAs. Furthermore, we take the product over the entire family to make all the chosen RAs available inside the logic.

Typically, we will only own some resource a in one particular instance named $\gamma \in \mathbb{N}$ of a given RA M_i. To express that, we introduce the following notation:

$$\boxed{a : M_i}^\gamma \triangleq \mathsf{Own}((\ldots, \emptyset, i : [\gamma := a], \emptyset, \ldots))$$

Often, we will even leave away the M_i because it is clear from context.

All the rules about $\mathsf{Own}(\cdot)$ can now also be derived for $\boxed{\cdot}$. In addition, we obtain a rule to create new instances of RAs with an arbitrary valid initial state:

$$a \in \mathcal{V}_{M_i} \vdash \Rrightarrow \exists \gamma. \boxed{a : M_i}^\gamma$$

Obtaining Modular Proofs. Even with multiple RAs at our disposal, it may still seem like we have a modularity problem: every proof is done in an instantiation of Iris with some particular family of RAs. As a result, if two proofs make different choices about the RAs, they are carried out in entirely different logics and hence cannot be composed.

To solve this problem, we *generalize* our proofs over the family of RAs that Iris is instantiated with. So in the following, all proofs are carried out in Iris instantiated with some unknown $(M_i)_{i \in \mathcal{I}}$. If the proof needs a particular RA, it further assumes that there exists some j *s.t.* M_j is the desired RA. Composing two proofs is thus easily possible; the resulting proof works in any family of RAs that contains all the particular RAs needed by either proof. Finally, if we want to obtain a "closed form" of some particular proof in a concrete instance of Iris, we simply construct a family of RAs that contains everything the proof needs.

4.2   A Registry of Invariants

Since we wish to be able to share the $\boxed{P}^\iota$ assertion among threads, we will need a central "invariant registry" that keeps track of all invariants and witnesses the fact that P has been registered as invariant.

In Sect. 3.3, we already saw the authoritative resource algebra. This RA allowed us to have an "authoritative" registry with fragments shared by various parties. However, for the case of invariants, we are not interested in expressing exclusive ownership of invariants, like we did for heap locations. Instead, the entire point of invariants is *sharing*, so we need that everybody *agrees* on what the invariant with a given name is. An RA for *agreement* on a set X is defined by:

$$\mathrm{AG}(X) \triangleq \mathsf{ag}(x : X) \mid \frac{4}{2} \qquad\qquad \mathcal{V} \triangleq \{\mathsf{ag}(x) \mid x \in X\}$$

$$\mathsf{ag}(x) \cdot \mathsf{ag}(y) \triangleq \begin{cases} \mathsf{ag}(x) & \text{if } x = y \\ \frac{4}{2} & \text{otherwise} \end{cases} \qquad |\mathsf{ag}(x)| \triangleq \mathsf{ag}(x)$$

The key property of this RA is that from $\mathsf{ag}(x) \cdot \mathsf{ag}(y) \in \mathcal{V}$, we can deduce $x = y$. We can then compose our RAs as follows to obtain an "invariant registry":

$$\mathrm{INV} \triangleq \mathrm{AUTH}(\mathbb{N} \xrightarrow{\text{fin}} \mathrm{AG}(\blacktriangleright\mathsf{Prop}))$$

This construction is an example of *higher-order ghost state*, which we already mentioned in Sect. 2.6. The Prop here is actually a recursive occurrence of logical assertions within resources, which has to be *guarded* by a "type-level later" $\blacktriangleright$. Furthermore, to make this really work, the agreement RA must be generalized to a proper CMRA (Sect. 2.6), so the actual definition is more involved. See the Iris 2.0 paper for details [17].

For present purposes, the only relevant outcome is the following assertions:

- $\boxed{\circ\,[\iota := P]}^{\gamma}$, stating that P is registered as an invariant with name ι; and
- $\boxed{\bullet\,I}^{\gamma}$, stating that $I \in \mathbb{N} \xrightarrow{\text{fin}} \mathsf{Prop}$ is the full map of all registered invariants.

These assertions enjoy the following three rules:

$$\boxed{\circ\,[\iota := P]}^{\gamma_{\mathrm{INV}}} \vdash \square\,\boxed{\circ\,[\iota := P]}^{\gamma_{\mathrm{INV}}} \qquad\qquad (\textsc{invreg-persist})$$

$$\boxed{\bullet\,I}^{\gamma_{\mathrm{INV}}} * \boxed{\circ\,[\iota := P]}^{\gamma_{\mathrm{INV}}} \vdash \triangleright I(\iota) \Leftrightarrow \triangleright P \qquad\qquad (\textsc{invreg-agree})$$

$$\iota \notin \mathrm{dom}(I) \wedge \boxed{\bullet\,I}^{\gamma_{\mathrm{INV}}} \vdash \Rrightarrow \boxed{\bullet\,I[\iota := P]}^{\gamma_{\mathrm{INV}}} * \boxed{\circ\,[\iota := P]}^{\gamma_{\mathrm{INV}}} \qquad (\textsc{invreg-alloc})$$

Intuitively, INVREG-PERSIST states that the non-authoritative fragment is persistent, *i.e.*, that it can be freely moved below the $\square$ modality and shared. INVREG-AGREE witnesses that the registry and the fragments *agree* on the proposition managed at a particular name. Note that we only get the equivalence with a $\triangleright$ because the definition of the RA (INV) contains a $\blacktriangleright$. Finally, INVREG-ALLOC lets one create a new invariant, provided the new name is not already used.

4.3 World Satisfaction

To recover the invariant mechanism of Iris, we need to attach a meaning to the invariant registry from Sect. 4.2, in the sense that we must make sure that the invariants actually *hold*! We do this by defining a single global invariant called *world satisfaction*, which enforces the meaning of the invariant registry. World satisfaction itself will be enforced by threading it through the weakest preconditions.

Naively, we may think that world satisfaction always requires all invariants to hold. However, this does not work: after all, threads are allowed to *temporarily break* invariants for an atomic "instant" during program execution. To support this, world satisfaction keeps invariants in one of two states: either they are *enabled* (currently enforced), or they are *disabled* (currently broken by some thread). The definition of the weakest precondition connective will then ensure that invariants are never disabled for more than an atomic period of time. That is, no invariant is left disabled between physical computation steps.

The protocol for opening (*i.e.*, disabling) and closing (*i.e.*, re-enabling) an invariant employs two *exclusive tokens*: an *enabled* token, which witnesses that the invariant is currently enabled and giving the right to disable it; and dually, a *disabled* token. These tokens are controlled by the following two simple RAs:

$$\text{EN} \triangleq \wp(\mathbb{N}) \qquad\qquad \text{DIS} \triangleq \wp^{\text{fin}}(\mathbb{N})$$

The composition for both RAs is disjoint union.[2]

We can now give the actual definition of world satisfaction, W. To this end, we need instances of INV, EN and DIS, which we assume to have names γ_{INV}, γ_{EN} and γ_{DIS}, respectively:

$$W \triangleq \exists I. \; \boxed{\bullet I}^{\gamma_{\text{INV}}} * \text{\Large$*$}_{\iota \in \text{dom}(I)} \left((\triangleright I(\iota) * \boxed{\{\iota\}}^{\gamma_{\text{DIS}}}) \vee \boxed{\{\iota\}}^{\gamma_{\text{EN}}} \right)$$

$$\boxed{P}^{\iota} \triangleq \boxed{\circ [\iota := P]}^{\gamma_{\text{INV}}}$$

World satisfaction controls the authoritative registry I of *all* existing invariants. This allows it to maintain an additional assertion for every single one of them, namely: either the invariant is enabled and maintained—in which case world satisfaction actually *owns* $\triangleright I(\iota)$—or the invariant is disabled. Unsurprisingly, $\boxed{P}^{\iota}$ just means that the registry maps ι to P—but ι may or may not be enabled.

With this encoding, we can prove the following key properties modeling the allocation, opening, and closing of invariants:

WSAT-ALLOC
$$\frac{\mathcal{E} \text{ is infinite}}{W * \triangleright P \twoheadrightarrow \Rrightarrow (W * \exists \iota \in \mathcal{E}. \boxed{P}^{\iota})}$$

WSAT-OPENCLOSE
$$\boxed{P}^{\iota} \vdash W * \boxed{\{\iota\}}^{\gamma_{\text{EN}}} \Leftrightarrow W * \triangleright P * \boxed{\{\iota\}}^{\gamma_{\text{DIS}}}$$

Let us look at the proof of the direction $\boxed{P}^{\iota} \vdash W * \boxed{\{\iota\}}^{\gamma_{\text{EN}}} \Rightarrow W * \triangleright P * \boxed{\{\iota\}}^{\gamma_{\text{DIS}}}$ of WSAT-OPENCLOSE in slightly more detail. We start by using INVREG-AGREE to learn that the authoritative registry I maintained by world satisfaction contains our invariant P at index ι. We thus obtain from the big separating conjunction that $\triangleright P * \boxed{\{\iota\}}^{\gamma_{\text{DIS}}} \vee \boxed{\{\iota\}}^{\gamma_{\text{EN}}}$. Since we moreover own the enabled token $\boxed{\{\iota\}}^{\gamma_{\text{EN}}}$, we can exclude the right disjunct and deduce that the invariant is currently

---

[2] Implicitly, they also have an *invalid* element $\frac{4}{7}$, for composition of overlapping sets.

enabled. So we take out the $\triangleright P$ and the disabled token, and instead put the enabled token into W, disabling the invariant. This concludes the proof.

The proof of WSAT-ALLOC is slightly more subtle. In particular, we have to be careful in picking the new invariant name such that: (a) it is in $\mathcal{E}$, (b) it is not used in I yet, and (c) we can create a disabled token for that name and put it into W alongside $\triangleright P$. Since disabled tokens are modeled by *finite* sets, only finitely many of them can ever be allocated, so it is always possible to pick an appropriate fresh name.

4.4 Fancy Update Modality

Before we will prove the rules for invariants, there is actually one other piece of the original Iris logic we should cover: *view shifts*. View shifts serve three roles:

1. They permit frame-preserving updates (like the basic update modality does).
2. They allow one to access invariants. The *mask* $\mathcal{E}$ defines which invariants are available.
3. They allow one to strip away the $\triangleright$ modality from timeless assertions (like the $\diamond$ modality does, see Sect. 2.7).

The view shifts of the original Iris were of the form $P \; ^{\mathcal{E}_1}\!\Rrightarrow^{\mathcal{E}_2} Q$ where P is the precondition, Q the postcondition, and $\mathcal{E}_1$ and $\mathcal{E}_2$ are invariant masks. For the same reason that we prefer weakest preconditions over Hoare triples (Sect. 3), we will present view shifts as a modality instead of a binary connective. The modality, called the *fancy update modality* $^{\mathcal{E}_1}\!\Rrightarrow^{\mathcal{E}_2}$, is defined as follows:

$$^{\mathcal{E}_1}\!\!\Rrightarrow^{\mathcal{E}_2} P \triangleq W * \lceil \mathcal{E}_1 \rceil^{\gamma_{\mathrm{EN}}} \;{-\!\!*}\; \Rrightarrow \diamond (W * \lceil \mathcal{E}_2 \rceil^{\gamma_{\mathrm{EN}}} * P) \qquad\qquad \Rrightarrow_{\mathcal{E}} P \triangleq {}^{\mathcal{E}}\!\!\Rrightarrow^{\mathcal{E}} P$$

In the same way that Hoare triples are defined in terms of weakest preconditions, the binary view shift can be defined in terms of the modality.

The intuition behind $^{\mathcal{E}_1}\!\Rrightarrow^{\mathcal{E}_2} P$ is to express ownership of resources such that, if we further assume that the invariants in $\mathcal{E}_1$ are enabled, we can perform a *frame-preserving update* to the resources and the invariants, and we end up owning P and the invariants in $\mathcal{E}_2$ are enabled. By looking at the definition, we can see how it supports all the fancy features formerly handled by view shifts:

1. At the heart of the fancy update modality is a basic update modality, which permits doing frame-preserving updates (see the rule FUP-UPD in Fig. 5).
2. The modality "threads through" world satisfaction, in the sense that a proof of $^{\mathcal{E}_1}\!\Rrightarrow^{\mathcal{E}_2} P$ can use W, but also has to prove it again. Furthermore, controlled by the two masks $\mathcal{E}_1$ and $\mathcal{E}_2$, the modality provides and takes away enabled tokens. The first mask controls which invariants are available to the modality, while the second mask controls which invariants remain available after (see INV-OPEN). Furthermore, it is possible to allocate new invariants (INV-ALLOC).
3. Finally, the modality is able to remove laters from timeless assertions by incorporating the "except 0" modality $\diamond$ (see Sect. 2.7 and FUP-TIMELESS).

FUP-MONO
$$\dfrac{P \vdash Q}{{}^{\mathcal{E}_1}\!\Rrightarrow^{\mathcal{E}_2} P \vdash {}^{\mathcal{E}_1}\!\Rrightarrow^{\mathcal{E}_2} Q}$$

FUP-INTRO-MASK
$$\dfrac{\mathcal{E}_2 \subseteq \mathcal{E}_1}{P \vdash {}^{\mathcal{E}_1}\!\Rrightarrow^{\mathcal{E}_2}\, {}^{\mathcal{E}_2}\!\Rrightarrow^{\mathcal{E}_1} P}$$

FUP-TRANS
$${}^{\mathcal{E}_1}\!\Rrightarrow^{\mathcal{E}_2}\, {}^{\mathcal{E}_2}\!\Rrightarrow^{\mathcal{E}_3} P \vdash {}^{\mathcal{E}_1}\!\Rrightarrow^{\mathcal{E}_3} P$$

FUP-FRAME
$$Q * {}^{\mathcal{E}_1}\!\Rrightarrow^{\mathcal{E}_2} P \vdash {}^{\mathcal{E}_1 \uplus \mathcal{E}_f}\!\Rrightarrow^{\mathcal{E}_2 \uplus \mathcal{E}_f} Q * P$$

FUP-UPD
$$\Rrightarrow P \vdash \Rrightarrow_{\mathcal{E}} P$$

FUP-TIMELESS
$$\dfrac{\mathsf{timeless}(P)}{\rhd P \vdash \Rrightarrow_{\mathcal{E}} P}$$

INV-PERSIST
$$\boxed{P}^{\iota} \vdash \Box \boxed{P}^{\iota}$$

INV-ALLOC
$$\dfrac{\mathcal{E}\ \text{is infinite}}{\rhd P \vdash \Rrightarrow_{\mathcal{E}},\ \exists \iota \in \mathcal{E}.\,\boxed{P}^{\iota}}$$

INV-OPEN
$$\dfrac{\iota \in \mathcal{E}}{\boxed{P}^{\iota} \vdash {}^{\mathcal{E}}\!\Rrightarrow^{\mathcal{E}\setminus\{\iota\}}\, \rhd P * (\rhd P \rightarrow\!\!* \ {}^{\mathcal{E}\setminus\{\iota\}}\!\Rrightarrow^{\mathcal{E}}\mathsf{True})}$$

Fig. 5. Rules for the fancy update modality and invariants.

Ignoring the style of presentation as a modality, there are some differences here from view shifts in previous versions of Iris. Firstly, in previous versions, the rule FUP-TRANS had a side condition restricting the masks it could be instantiated with, whereas now it does not. Secondly, in previous versions, instead of FUP-INTRO-MASK, only mask-invariant view shifts could be introduced ($P \vdash \Rrightarrow_{\mathcal{E}} P$). The reason we can now support FUP-INTRO-MASK is that masks are actually just sugar for owning or providing particular *resources* (namely, the enabled tokens). This is in contrast to previous versions of Iris, where masks were entirely separate from resources and treated in a rather ad-hoc manner. Our more principled treatment of masks significantly simplifies building abstractions involving invariants; however, for lack of space, we cannot further discuss these abstractions.

The rules FUP-MONO, FUP-TRANS, and FUP-FRAME correspond to the related rules of the basic update modality in Fig. 1. The rule INV-OPEN may look fairly cryptic; we will see in the next section how it can be used to derive WP-INV.

4.5 Weakest Preconditions

We will now define weakest preconditions that support not only the rules in Fig. 4, but also the ones in Fig. 6. We will also show how, from WP-ATOMIC and INV-OPEN, we can derive the rule motivating this entire section, WP-INV.

WP-VUP
$$\Rrightarrow_{\mathcal{E}} \mathsf{wp}_{\mathcal{E}}\, e\, \{v.\, \Rrightarrow_{\mathcal{E}} \Phi(v)\} \vdash \mathsf{wp}_{\mathcal{E}}\, e\, \{\Phi\}$$

WP-ATOMIC
$$\dfrac{\mathsf{atomic}(e)}{{}^{\mathcal{E}_1}\!\Rrightarrow^{\mathcal{E}_2} \mathsf{wp}_{\mathcal{E}_2}\, e\, \{v.\, {}^{\mathcal{E}_2}\!\Rrightarrow^{\mathcal{E}_1} \Phi(v)\} \vdash \mathsf{wp}_{\mathcal{E}_1}\, e\, \{\Phi\}}$$

Fig. 6. New rules for weakest precondition with invariants.

Compared to the definition developed in Sect. 3, there are two key differences: first of all, we use the fancy update modality instead of the basic update modality. Secondly, we do not want to tie the definition of weakest preconditions to a particular language, and instead operate generically over any notion of expressions and state, and any reduction relation.

As a consequence of this generality, we can no longer assume that our physical state is a heap of values with disjoint union as composition. Therefore, instead of using the authoritative heap defined in Sect. 3.3, we parameterize weakest preconditions by a predicate $I : State \to iProp$ called the *state interpretation*. In case $State = Loc \xrightarrow{\text{fin}} Val$, we can recover the definition and rules from Sect. 3.3 by taking:

$$I(\sigma) \triangleq \boxed{\bullet\, \sigma : Loc \xrightarrow{\text{fin}} Ex(Val)}^{\gamma}$$

More sophisticated forms of separation like fractional permissions [7,8] can be encoded by using an appropriate RA and defining I accordingly.

Given an $I : State \to iProp$, our definition of weakest precondition looks as follows (changes from Sect. 3 are colored red):

$$\mathsf{wp}_{\mathcal{E}}\, e\, \{\Phi\} \triangleq (e \in Val \wedge \Rrightarrow_{\mathcal{E}} \Phi(e))$$
$$\vee \big(e \notin Val \wedge \forall \sigma.\, I(\sigma) \mathrel{-\!\!*} {}^{\mathcal{E}}\!\!\Rrightarrow^{\emptyset} red(e, \sigma)$$
$$\wedge \triangleright (\forall e_2\, \sigma_2\, \vec{e}_f.\, (e, \sigma) \to (e_2, \sigma_2, \vec{e}_f) \mathrel{-\!\!*} {}^{\emptyset}\!\!\Rrightarrow^{\mathcal{E}}$$
$$I(\sigma_2) * \mathsf{wp}_{\mathcal{E}}\, e_2\, \{\Phi\} * {\Large*}_{e' \in \vec{e}_f} \mathsf{wp}_{\top}\, e'\, \{v.\mathsf{True}\}\big))$$

The mask $\mathcal{E}$ of $\mathsf{wp}_{\mathcal{E}}\, e\, \{\Phi\}$ is used for the "outside" of the fancy update modalities, providing them with access to these invariants. The "inner" masks are $\emptyset$, indicating that the reasoning about safety and progress can temporarily open *all* invariants (and none have to be left enabled). The forked-off threads $\vec{e}_f$ have access to the full mask $\top$ as they will only start running in the *next* instruction, so they are not constrained by whatever invariants are available right now. Note that the definition requires all invariants in $\mathcal{E}$ to be enabled again after every physical step: this corresponds to the fact that an invariant can only be opened atomically.

In addition to the rules already presented in Sect. 3, this version of the weakest precondition connective lets us prove (among others) the new rules in Fig. 6. WP-VUP witnesses that the entire connective as well as its postcondition are living below the fancy update modality, so we can freely add/remove that modality.

Finally, we come to WP-ATOMIC to open an invariant around an atomic expression. The rule is similar to WP-VUP, with the key difference being that it can *change the mask*. On the left hand side of the turnstile, we are allowed to first open some invariants, then reason about e, and then close invariants again. This is sound because e is atomic. WP-ATOMIC is the rule we need to derive WP-INV:

$$\dfrac{\rhd P \vdash \mathsf{wp}_{\mathcal{E}\backslash\{\iota\}}\, e\, \{v.\, \rhd P * \varPhi(v)\}}{\begin{array}{c}\rhd P * (\rhd P \mathbin{-\!\!*} {}^{\mathcal{E}\backslash\{\iota\}}\!\!\Rrightarrow^{\mathcal{E}} \mathsf{True}) \vdash \\[2pt] \mathsf{wp}_{\mathcal{E}\backslash\{\iota\}}\, e\, \left\{v.\, \rhd P * \varPhi(v) * (\rhd P \mathbin{-\!\!*} {}^{\mathcal{E}\backslash\{\iota\}}\!\!\Rrightarrow^{\mathcal{E}_1} \mathsf{True})\right\}\end{array}}\ \text{WP-FRAME}$$

$$\dfrac{}{\rhd P * (\rhd P \mathbin{-\!\!*} {}^{\mathcal{E}\backslash\{\iota\}}\!\!\Rrightarrow^{\mathcal{E}} \mathsf{True}) \vdash \mathsf{wp}_{\mathcal{E}\backslash\{\iota\}}\, e\, \left\{v.\, {}^{\mathcal{E}\backslash\{\iota\}}\!\!\Rrightarrow^{\mathcal{E}} \varPhi(v)\right\}}\ \text{WP-MONO}$$

$$\dfrac{}{\boxed{P}^{\iota} \vdash {}^{\mathcal{E}}\!\!\Rrightarrow^{\mathcal{E}\backslash\{\iota\}} \mathsf{wp}_{\mathcal{E}\backslash\{\iota\}}\, e\, \left\{x.\, {}^{\mathcal{E}\backslash\{\iota\}}\!\!\Rrightarrow^{\mathcal{E}} \varPhi(v)\right\}}\ \text{INV-OPEN}$$

$$\dfrac{}{\boxed{P}^{\iota} \vdash \mathsf{wp}_{\mathcal{E}}\, e\, \{\varPhi\}}\ \text{WP-ATOMIC}$$

4.6   Adequacy

To demonstrate that $\mathsf{wp}\, e\, \{\phi\}$ actually makes the expected statements about program executions, we prove the following *adequacy theorem*.

Theorem 4.1 (Adequacy of weakest preconditions). *Let ϕ be a first-order predicate. If* $\mathsf{True} \vdash \Rrightarrow_{\top} I(\sigma) * \mathsf{wp}_{\top}\, e\, \{\phi\}$ *and* $(e, \sigma) \rightarrow^{*}_{\mathsf{tp}} (e'_1 \ldots e'_n, \sigma')$, *then:*

1. *For any e'_i we have that either e'_i is a value, or* $\mathrm{red}(e'_i, \sigma')$;
2. *If e'_1 (the main thread) is a value v, then $\phi(v)$.*

The proof of this theorem relies on Theorem 2.1 (in Sect. 2.8). We also impose the same restrictions on ϕ as we have done there: ϕ has to be a *first-order* predicate. This ensures we can use ϕ both *inside* our logic and at the meta level.

5   Paradoxes Involving the "later" Modality

A recurring element of concurrent separation logics with impredicative invariants [17,18,28] is the later modality $\rhd$, which is used to guard resources when opening invariants. The use of $\rhd$ has heretofore been forced by the models which were used to show soundness of these logics. It has been an open question, however, whether the need for the later modality is a mere artifact of the model, or whether it is in some sense required. In this section, we show that at the very least it plays an *essential* role: if we omit the later modality from the invariant opening rule, then we can derive a contradiction *in the logic*.

Theorem 5.1. *Assume we add the following proof rule to Iris:*

$$\dfrac{\iota \in \mathcal{E}}{\boxed{P}^{\iota} \vdash {}^{\mathcal{E}}\!\!\Rrightarrow^{\mathcal{E}\backslash\{\iota\}} P * (P \mathbin{-\!\!*} {}^{\mathcal{E}\backslash\{\iota\}}\!\!\Rrightarrow^{\mathcal{E}} \mathsf{True})}$$

Then, if we pick an appropriate RA, $\mathsf{True} \vdash \Rrightarrow_{\top} \mathsf{False}$.

Notice that the above rule is the same as INV-OPEN in Fig. 5, *except that it does not add a $\rhd$ in front of P.*

Of course, this does not prove that we absolutely must have a $\rhd$ modality, but it *does* show that the stronger rule one would prefer to have for invariants is unsound. Step-indexing is but one way to navigate around this unsoundness. However, we are not aware of another technique that would yield a logic with comparably powerful impredicative invariants.

The proof of this theorem does not use the fact that fancy updates are defined in a particular way in terms of basic updates, but just uses the proof rules for this modality. The proof also makes no use of higher-order ghost state. In fact, the result holds for all versions of Iris [17, 18], as is shown by the following theorem:

Theorem 5.2. *Assume a higher-order separation logic with $\Box$ and an update modality with a binary mask $\Rrightarrow_{\{0,1\}}$ (think: empty mask and full mask) satisfying strong monad rules with respect to separating conjunction and such that:*

$$\text{WEAKEN-MASK}$$
$$\Rrightarrow_0 P \vdash \Rrightarrow_1 P$$

Assume a type $\mathcal{I}$ and an assertion $\boxed{\cdot}^\cdot : \mathcal{I} \to \text{Prop} \to \text{Prop}$ satisfying:

$$\text{INV-ALLOC}$$
$$P \vdash \Rrightarrow_1 \exists \iota. \boxed{P}^\iota$$

$$\text{INV-PERSIST}$$
$$\boxed{P}^\iota \vdash \Box \boxed{P}^\iota$$

$$\text{INV-OPEN-NOLATER}$$
$$\frac{P * Q \vdash \Rrightarrow_0 (P * R)}{\boxed{P}^\iota * Q \vdash \Rrightarrow_1 R}$$

Finally, assume the existence of a type $\mathcal{G}$ and two tokens $\boxed{S}^\cdot : \mathcal{G} \to \text{Prop}$ and $\boxed{F}^\cdot : \mathcal{G} \to \text{Prop}$ parameterized by $\mathcal{G}$ and satisfying the following properties:

$$\text{START-ALLOC}$$
$$\vdash \Rrightarrow_0 \exists \gamma. \boxed{S}^\gamma$$

$$\text{START-FINISH}$$
$$\boxed{S}^\gamma \vdash \Rrightarrow_0 \boxed{F}^\gamma$$

$$\text{START-NOT-FINISHED}$$
$$\boxed{S}^\gamma * \boxed{F}^\gamma \vdash \textit{False}$$

$$\text{FINISHED-DUP}$$
$$\boxed{F}^\gamma \vdash \boxed{F}^\gamma * \boxed{F}^\gamma$$

Then $\textit{True} \vdash \Rrightarrow_1 \textit{False}$.

In other words, the theorem requires three ingredients to be present in the logic in order to derive a contradiction:

- An update modality that satisfies the laws of Iris's basic update modality (Fig. 1). The modality needs a mask for the same reason that Iris's fancy update modality has a mask: to prevent opening the same invariant twice.
- Invariants that can be opened around the update modality, and that can be opened without a later.
- A two-state protocol whose only transition is from the first to the last state. This is what $\boxed{S}^\cdot$ and $\boxed{F}^\cdot$ encode. The proof does not actually depend on how that protocol is made available to the logic. For example, to apply this proof to iCAP [28], one could use iCAP's built-in support for state-transition systems

to achieve the same result. However, for the purpose of the theorem, we had to pick *some* way of expressing protocols. We picked the token-based approach common in Iris.

All versions of Iris easily satisfy the first and third of these requirements, by using fancy updates (Iris 3) or primitive view shifts (Iris 1 and 2) for the update modality, and by constructing an appropriate RA (Iris 2 and 3) or PCM (Iris 1) for the two-state protocol. Of course, INV-OPEN-NOLATER is the one assumption of the theorem that no version of Iris satisfies, which is the entire point.

Unsurprisingly, the proof works by constructing an assertion that is equivalent (in some rather loose sense) to its own negation. The full details of this construction are spelled out in the appendix [1].

6   Related Work

Since O'Hearn introduced the original concurrent separation logic (CSL) [24], many more CSLs have been developed [9,11,12,14,16–18,27–30]. Though these logics have explored different techniques for reasoning about concurrency, they have one thing in common: their proof rules and models are complicated.

There have been attempts at mitigating the difficulty of the models of these logics. Most notably, Svendsen and Birkedal [28] defined the model of the iCAP logic in the internal logic of the topos of trees, which includes a *later* connective to reason about step-indexing abstractly. However, their model of Hoare triples still involves explicit resource management, which ours does not.

On the other end of the spectrum, there has been work on encoding binary logical relations in a concurrent separation logic [13,21,22,30]. These encodings are relying on a base logic that already includes a plethora of high-level concepts, such as weakest preconditions and view shifts. Our goal, in contrast, is precisely to *define* these concepts in simpler terms.

FCSL [27] takes an opposite approach to our work. To ease reasoning about programs in a proof assistant, they avoid reasoning in separation logic as much as possible, and reason mostly in the model of their logic. This requires the model to stay as simple as possible; in particular, FCSL does not make use of step-indexing. As a consequence, they do not support impredicative invariants, which we believe are an important feature of Iris. For example, they are needed to model impredicative type systems [21] or to model a reentrant event loop library [28]. Furthermore, as we have shown in recent work [21], one *can* actually reason conveniently in a separation logic in Coq, so the additional complexity of our model is hardly visible to users of our logic.

Additionally, there is a difference in expressiveness w.r.t. "hiding" of invariants. FCSL supports a certain kind of hiding, namely the ability to transfer some local state into an invariant (actually a "concurroid"), which is enforced during the execution of a single expression e, but after which the state governed by the invariant is returned to local control. Iris can support such hiding as well, via an encoding of what we call "cancelable invariants" [1]. Additionally, we allow a different kind of hiding, namely the ability to hide invariants used by (nested)

Hoare-triple specifications. For example, a higher-order function f may return another function g, whose Hoare-triple specification is only correct under some invariant I (which was established during execution of f). Since invariants in Iris are persistent assertions, I can be hidden, *i.e.*, it need not infect the specification of f or g. To our knowledge, FCSL does not support hiding of this form.

The Verified Software Toolchain (VST) [4] is a framework that provides machinery for constructing sophisticated higher-order separation logics with support for impredicative invariants in Coq. However, VST is not a logic and, as such, does not abstract over step-indices and resources the way working in a logic like Iris 3.0 does. Defining a program logic in VST thus still requires significant manual management of such details, which are abstracted away when defining a program logic in the Iris base logic. Furthermore, VST has so far only been demonstrated in the context of sequential reasoning and coarse-grained (lock-based) concurrency [6], whereas the focus of Iris is on fine-grained concurrency.

7   Conclusion

We have presented a minimal *base logic* in which we can define concurrent separation logics in a concise and abstract way. This has the benefit of making higher-level concepts (like weakest preconditions) easier to define, easier to understand, and easier to reason about.

Definitions become simpler as they can be performed at a much higher level of abstraction. In particular, the definitions of logical connectives such as the fancy update modality and weakest preconditions do not have to deal with any details about disjointness of resources or step-indexing—this is all abstractly handled by the base logic. Proofs become simpler since only the rules of the primitive connectives of the base logic have to be verified w.r.t. the model. The proofs about fancier connectives are carried out *inside* the logic, again abstracting over details that have to be managed manually when working in the model.

Thanks to these simplifications, we are able now, for the first time, to explain what the program logic connectives in Iris actually *mean*. Furthermore, we have ported the Coq formalization of Iris [1], including a rich body of examples, over to the new connectives defined in the base logic. The interactive proof mode (IPM) [21] provided crucial tactic support for reasoning with interesting combinations of separation-logic assertions and our modalities (as they arise, *e.g.*, in weakest preconditions). In performing the port, the definitions and proofs related to weakest preconditions, view shifts, and invariants shrank in size significantly, indicating that proofs and definitions can now be carried out with considerably greater ease.

Acknowledgments. This research was supported in part by a European Research Council (ERC) Consolidator Grant for the project "RustBelt", funded under the European Union's Horizon 2020 Framework Programme (grant agreement no. 683289); and by the ModuRes Sapere Aude Advanced Grant from The Danish Council for Independent Research for the Natural Sciences (FNU).

References

1. The Iris 3.0 documentation and Coq development. Available on the Iris project website at: http://iris-project.org
2. Appel, A., McAllester, D.: An indexed model of recursive types for foundational proof-carrying code. TOPLAS **23**(5), 657–683 (2001)
3. Appel, A., Melliès, P.-A., Richards, C., Vouillon, J.: A very modal model of a modern, major, general type system. In: POPL (2007)
4. Appel, A.W. (ed.): Program Logics for Certified Compilers. Cambridge University Press, Cambridge (2014)
5. Ashcroft, E.A.: Proving assertions about parallel programs. JCSS **10**(1), 110–135 (1975)
6. Beringer, L., Stewart, G., Dockins, R., Appel, A.W.: Verified compilation for shared-memory C. In: Shao, Z. (ed.) ESOP 2014. LNCS, vol. 8410, pp. 107–127. Springer, Heidelberg (2014). doi:10.1007/978-3-642-54833-8_7
7. Bornat, R., Calcagno, C., O'Hearn, P.W., Parkinson, M.J.: Permission accounting in separation logic. In: POPL, pp. 259–270 (2005)
8. Boyland, J.: Checking interference with fractional permissions. In: Cousot, R. (ed.) SAS 2003. LNCS, vol. 2694, pp. 55–72. Springer, Heidelberg (2003). doi:10.1007/3-540-44898-5_4
9. Rocha Pinto, P., Dinsdale-Young, T., Gardner, P.: TaDA: a logic for time and data abstraction. In: Jones, R. (ed.) ECOOP 2014. LNCS, vol. 8586, pp. 207–231. Springer, Heidelberg (2014). doi:10.1007/978-3-662-44202-9_9
10. Dijkstra, E.W.: Guarded commands, nondeterminacy and formal derivation of programs. CACM **18**(8), 453–457 (1975)
11. Dinsdale-Young, T., Dodds, M., Gardner, P., Parkinson, M.J., Vafeiadis, V.: Concurrent abstract predicates. In: D'Hondt, T. (ed.) ECOOP 2010. LNCS, vol. 6183, pp. 504–528. Springer, Heidelberg (2010). doi:10.1007/978-3-642-14107-2_24
12. Dodds, M., Feng, X., Parkinson, M., Vafeiadis, V.: Deny-guarantee reasoning. In: Castagna, G. (ed.) ESOP 2009. LNCS, vol. 5502, pp. 363–377. Springer, Heidelberg (2009). doi:10.1007/978-3-642-00590-9_26
13. Dreyer, D., Neis, G., Rossberg, A., Birkedal, L.: A relational modal logic for higher-order stateful ADTs. In: POPL (2010)
14. Hobor, A., Appel, A.W., Nardelli, F.Z.: Oracle semantics for concurrent separation logic. In: Drossopoulou, S. (ed.) ESOP 2008. LNCS, vol. 4960, pp. 353–367. Springer, Heidelberg (2008). doi:10.1007/978-3-540-78739-6_27
15. Ishtiaq, S.S., O'Hearn, P.W.: BI as an assertion language for mutable data structures. In: POPL, pp. 14–26 (2001)
16. Jacobs, B., Piessens, F.: Expressive modular fine-grained concurrency specification. In: POPL (2011)
17. Jung, R., Krebbers, R., Birkedal, L., Dreyer, D.: Higher-order ghost state. In: ICFP, pp. 256–269 (2016)
18. Jung, R., Swasey, D., Sieczkowski, F., Svendsen, K., Turon, A., Birkedal, L., Dreyer, D.: Iris: Monoids and invariants as an orthogonal basis for concurrent reasoning. In: POPL, pp. 637–650 (2015)
19. Kock, A.: Monads on symmetric monoidal closed categories. Arch. Math. **21**(1), 1–10 (1970)
20. Kock, A.: Strong functors and monoidal monads. Arch. Math. **23**(1), 113–120 (1972)

21. Krebbers, R., Timany, A., Birkedal, L.: Interactive proofs in higher-order concurrent separation logic. In: POPL, pp. 205–217 (2017)
22. Krogh-Jespersen, M., Svendsen, K., Birkedal, L.: A relational model of types-and-effects in higher-order concurrent separation logic. In: POPL (2017)
23. Nakano, H.: A modality for recursion. In: LICS (2000)
24. O'Hearn, P.: Resources, concurrency, and local reasoning. TCS **375**(1), 271–307 (2007)
25. O'Hearn, P.W., Pym, D.J.: The logic of bunched implications. Bull. Symb. Logic **5**(2), 215–244 (1999)
26. Parkinson, M.: The next 700 separation logics. In: Leavens, G.T., O'Hearn, P., Rajamani, S.K. (eds.) VSTTE 2010. LNCS, vol. 6217, pp. 169–182. Springer, Heidelberg (2010). doi:10.1007/978-3-642-15057-9_12
27. Sergey, I., Nanevski, A., Banerjee, A.: Mechanized verification of fine-grained concurrent programs. In: PLDI, pp. 77–87 (2015)
28. Svendsen, K., Birkedal, L.: Impredicative concurrent abstract predicates. In: Shao, Z. (ed.) ESOP 2014. LNCS, vol. 8410, pp. 149–168. Springer, Heidelberg (2014). doi:10.1007/978-3-642-54833-8_9
29. Svendsen, K., Birkedal, L., Parkinson, M.: Modular reasoning about separation of concurrent data structures. In: Felleisen, M., Gardner, P. (eds.) ESOP 2013. LNCS, vol. 7792, pp. 169–188. Springer, Heidelberg (2013). doi:10.1007/978-3-642-37036-6_11
30. Turon, A., Dreyer, D., Birkedal, L.: Unifying refinement and Hoare-style reasoning in a logic for higher-order concurrency. In: ICFP, pp. 377–390 (2013)

Comprehending Isabelle/HOL's Consistency

Ondřej Kunčar[1](✉) and Andrei Popescu[2,3]

[1] Fakultät für Informatik, Technische Universität München, München, Germany
kuncar@in.tum.de
[2] Department of Computer Science, Middlesex University London, London, UK
[3] Institute of Mathematics Simion Stoilow of the Romanian Academy,
Bucharest, Romania

Abstract. The proof assistant Isabelle/HOL is based on an extension of Higher-Order Logic (HOL) with ad hoc overloading of constants. It turns out that the interaction between the standard HOL type definitions and the Isabelle-specific ad hoc overloading is problematic for the logical consistency. In previous work, we have argued that standard HOL semantics is no longer appropriate for capturing this interaction, and have proved consistency using a nonstandard semantics. The use of an exotic semantics makes that proof hard to digest by the community. In this paper, we prove consistency by proof-theoretic means—following the healthy intuition of definitions as abbreviations, realized in HOLC, a logic that augments HOL with comprehension types. We hope that our new proof settles the Isabelle/HOL consistency problem once and for all. In addition, HOLC offers a framework for justifying the consistency of new deduction schemas that address practical user needs.

1 Introduction

Isabelle/HOL [35,36] is a popular proof assistant, with hundreds of users worldwide in both academia and industry. It is being used in major verification projects, such as the seL4 operating system kernel [24]. In addition, Isabelle/HOL is a framework for certified programming: functional programming (including lazy (co)programming [9]) is supported natively and imperative programming is supported via a monadic extension [10]. Programs can be written and verified in Isabelle/HOL, and efficient code for them (in Haskell, Standard ML, OCaml and Scala) can be produced using a code generator [19]. This certified programming methodology has yielded a wide range of verified software systems, from a Java compiler [32] to an LTL model checker [14] to a conference management system [23]. The formal guarantees of all such systems, as well as those considered by some formal certification agencies [21], are based on one major assumption: the *correctness/consistency of Isabelle/HOL's inference engine.*

Keeping the underlying logic simple, hence manifestly consistent, along with reducing all the user developments to the logic kernel, has been a major tenet of the LCF/HOL approach to formal verification, originating from Robin Milner and Mike Gordon [17]. Yet, Isabelle/HOL, one of the most successful incarnations

© Springer-Verlag GmbH Germany 2017
H. Yang (Ed.): ESOP 2017, LNCS 10201, pp. 724–749, 2017.
DOI: 10.1007/978-3-662-54434-1_27

of this approach, takes some liberties beyond the well-understood higher-order logic kernel. Namely, its definitional mechanism allows *delayed ad hoc overloading of constant definitions*—in turn, this enables Haskell-style type classes [46] on top of HOL [37].

In standard HOL, a polymorphic constant should either be *only declared* (and forever left uninterpreted), or *fully defined* at its most general type.[1] By contrast, Isabelle/HOL allows first declaring a constant, and at later times overloading it by defining some of its instances, as in the following example:[2]

consts 0 : α

. . .

definition 0 : real $\equiv$ real_zero

. . .

definition 0 : α list $\equiv$ []

Recursive overloading is also supported, as in:

definition 0 : α list $\equiv$ [0:α]

In between the declaration and the instance definitions, arbitrary commands may occur, including type definitions ("typedef") and (co)datatype definitions (which are derived from typedef [7, 45]). For example, the following definition introduces a type of polynomials over an arbitrary domain α, where $\forall_\infty$ is the "for all but finitely many" quantifier:

typedef α poly $\equiv$ {f : nat $\to$ α | $\forall_\infty$ n. f n = 0}

When 0 is defined for concrete types, such as real and α list, the library theorems about arbitrary-domain polynomials are enabled for polynomials over these concrete types.[3]

To avoid inconsistency, this overloading mechanism is regulated by syntactic checks for *orthogonality* and *termination*. Examples like the above should be allowed, whereas examples like the following encoding of Russell's paradox [29, Sect. 1] should be forbidden:

---

[1] There are other specification schemes supported by some HOL provers, allowing for more abstract (under)specification of constants—but these schemes are known to be captured or over-approximated by the standard (equational) definition scheme [5].

[2] To improve readability, in the examples we use a simplified Isabelle syntax. To run these examples in Isabelle, one must enclose in **overloading** blocks the overloaded definitions of constants and add the **overloaded** attribute to type definitions that depend on overloaded constants; in addition, one must provide nonemptiness proofs for type definitions [47, Sect. 11(3,7)]. Note also that Isabelle uses $\Rightarrow$ instead of $\to$ for function types and :: instead of : for typing.

[3] Isabelle/HOL implements a type-class infrastructure allowing fine control over such instantiations. In this case, α is assumed to be of type class zero; then real, α list etc. are registered as members of zero as soon as 0 is defined for them. Polymorphic properties can also be associated to type classes, and need to be verified upon instantiation. Type classes do not require any logical extension, but are representable as predicates inside the logic—[48, Sect. 5] explains the mechanism in detail.

consts c : α
typedef T $\equiv$ {True, c}
definition c : bool $\equiv \neg (\forall(x{:}T)\ y.\ x = y)$

The above would lead to a proof of false taking advantage of the circularity $T \rightsquigarrow c_{\mathsf{bool}} \rightsquigarrow T$ in the dependency relation introduced by the definitions: one first defines the type T to contain precisely one element just in case c_{bool} is True, and then defines c_{bool} to be True just in case T contains more than one element.

Because Isabelle/HOL has a large user base and is heavily relied upon, it is important that the consistency of its logic be established with a high degree of *clarity* and a high degree of *rigor*. In 2014, we started an investigation into the foundations of this logic, which has revealed a few consistency problems (including the above "paradox"). These issues have generated quite a lot of discussion in the Isabelle community, during which some philosophical disagreements and misunderstandings among the users and the developers have surfaced [1]. The technical issues have been addressed [27, 29] and are no longer exhibited in Isabelle2016.[4]

In addition to taking care of these issues, one of course needs some guarantees that similar issues are not still present in the logic. To address this, in previous work [29] we have proved that the logic is now consistent, employing a *semantic argument* in terms of a nonstandard semantics for HOL. Our original proof was somewhat sketchy and lacking in rigor—full (pen-and-paper) proofs are now included in an extended report [28]. Of course, a machine-checked proof, perhaps building on a recent formalization of HOL [15, 25], would make further valuable progress on the rigor aspect.

In this paper, we hope to improve on the *clarity* aspect and provide deeper insight into why Isabelle/HOL's logic is consistent. As mentioned, Isabelle/HOL is richer than HOL not in the rules of deduction, but in the definitional mechanism. A natural reluctance that comes to mind concerning our semantic proof of consistency is best expressed by Isabelle's creator's initial reaction to our proof idea [40]:

> It's a bit puzzling, not to say worrying, to want a set-theoretic semantics for plain definitions. The point of definitions (and the origin of the idea that they preserve consistency) is that they are abbreviations.

This paper's first contribution is a new proof of consistency for Isabelle/HOL's logic, easy to digest by the large community of "syntacticists" who (quite legitimately) wish to regard definitions as a form of abbreviations. The problem is that type definitions cannot simply be unfolded (and inlined)— a type definition is an axiom that postulates a new type and an embedding-projection pair between the new type and the original type (from where the

---

[4] The philosophical dispute about foundations is far from having come to an end [4], and unfortunately tends to obscure what should be a well-defined mathematical problem: the consistency of the Isabelle/HOL *logical system* (which is of course not the same as the overall reliability of the Isabelle/HOL *implementation*).

new type is carved out by a nonempty predicate). But the syntactic intuition persists: what if we *were* allowed to unfold type definitions? As it turns out, this can be achieved in a gentle extension of HOL featuring comprehension types. This extended logic, called HOL with Comprehension (HOLC), is a syntacticist's paradise, allowing for a consistency proof along their intuition. This proof is systematically developed in Sect. 3. First, HOLC is introduced (Sect. 3.1) and shown consistent by a standard argument (Sect. 3.2). Then, a translation is defined from well-formed Isabelle/HOL definitions to HOLC, which is proved sound, i.e., deduction-preserving (Sect. 3.3). The key to establishing soundness is the use of a modified deduction system for HOL where type instantiation is restricted—this tames the inherent lack of uniformity brought about by ad hoc overloading. Finally, soundness of the translation together with consistency of HOLC ensures consistency of Isabelle/HOL.

As a second contribution, we use HOLC to justify some recently proposed extensions of Isabelle/HOL—namely, two new deduction schemas [30]. One enables local type definitions inside proof contexts; the other allows replacing undefined instances of overloaded constants with universally quantified variables. As we argue in [30], both extensions are useful for simplifying proof development by enabling the transition from light type-based theorems to heavier but more flexible set-based theorems. However, proving that these extensions do not introduce inconsistency is surprisingly difficult. In particular, our previously defined (consistency-justifying) semantics [29] has a blind spot on the second extension—it is only from the viewpoint of HOLC that the consistency of both extensions is manifest (Sect. 4).

More details on our constructions and proofs can be found in a technical report made available online [31].

2   The Isabelle/HOL Logic Recalled

The *logic of Isabelle/HOL* consists of:

- HOL, that is, classical higher-order logic with rank 1 polymorphism, Hilbert choice and the Infinity axiom (recalled in Sect. 2.1)
- A definitional mechanism for introducing new types and constants *in an overloaded fashion* (recalled in Sect. 2.2)

2.1   HOL Syntax and Deduction

The syntax and deduction system we present here are minor variations of the standard ones for HOL (as in, e.g., [3,18,20]). What we call *HOL axioms* correspond to the theory INIT from [3].

Syntax. Throughout this section, we fix the following:

- an infinite set TVar, of *type variables*, ranged by α, β
- an infinite set VarN, of *(term) variable names*, ranged by x, y, z

– a set K of symbols, ranged by k, called *type constructors*, containing three special symbols: bool, ind and $\rightarrow$ (aimed at representing the type of booleans, an infinite type and the function type constructor, respectively)

We fix a function $\mathsf{arOf} : K \rightarrow \mathbb{N}$ giving arities to type constructors, such that $\mathsf{arOf}(\mathsf{bool}) = \mathsf{arOf}(\mathsf{ind}) = 0$ and $\mathsf{arOf}(\rightarrow) = 2$. Types, ranged by σ, τ, are defined as follows:

$$\sigma = \alpha \mid (\sigma_1, \ldots, \sigma_{\mathsf{arOf}(k)}) \, k$$

Thus, a type is either a type variable or an n-ary type constructor k postfix-applied to a number of types corresponding to its arity. If $n = 1$, instead of $(\sigma) \, k$ we write $\sigma \, k$. We write Type for the set of types.

Finally, we fix the following:

– a set Const, ranged over by c, of symbols called *constants*, containing five special symbols: $\longrightarrow$, $=$, ε, zero and suc (aimed at representing logical implication, equality, Hilbert choice of some element from a type, zero and successor, respectively)
– a function $\mathsf{tpOf} :$ Const $\rightarrow$ Type associating a type to every constant, such that:

$$\begin{aligned} \mathsf{tpOf}(\longrightarrow) &= \mathsf{bool} \rightarrow \mathsf{bool} \rightarrow \mathsf{bool} & \mathsf{tpOf}(\mathsf{zero}) &= \mathsf{ind} \\ \mathsf{tpOf}(=) &= \alpha \rightarrow \alpha \rightarrow \mathsf{bool} & \mathsf{tpOf}(\mathsf{suc}) &= \mathsf{ind} \rightarrow \mathsf{ind} \\ \mathsf{tpOf}(\varepsilon) &= (\alpha \rightarrow \mathsf{bool}) \rightarrow \alpha \end{aligned}$$

$\mathsf{TV}(\sigma)$ is the set of variables of a type σ. Given a function $\rho : \mathsf{TVar} \rightarrow \mathsf{Type}$, its *support* is the set of type variables where ρ is not the identity: $\mathsf{supp}(\rho) = \{\alpha \mid \rho(\alpha) \neq \alpha\}$. A *type substitution* is a function $\rho : \mathsf{TVar} \rightarrow \mathsf{Type}$ with finite support. We let TSubst denote the set of type substitutions. Each $\rho \in \mathsf{TSubst}$ extends to a function $\overline{\rho} : \mathsf{Type} \rightarrow \mathsf{Type}$ by defining $\overline{\rho}(\alpha) = \rho(\alpha)$ and $\overline{\rho}((\sigma_1, \ldots, \sigma_n) \, k) = (\overline{\rho}(\sigma_1), \ldots, \overline{\rho}(\sigma_n)) \, k$. We write $\sigma[\tau/\alpha]$ for $\overline{\rho}(\sigma)$, where ρ is the type substitution that sends α to τ and each $\beta \neq \alpha$ to β. Thus, $\sigma[\tau/\alpha]$ is obtained from σ by substituting τ for all occurrences of α.

We say that σ is an *instance* of τ *via a substitution* of $\rho \in \mathsf{TSubst}$, written $\sigma \leq_\rho \tau$, if $\overline{\rho}(\tau) = \sigma$. We say that σ is an *instance* of τ, written $\sigma \leq \tau$, if there exists $\rho \in \mathsf{TSubst}$ such that $\sigma \leq_\rho \tau$. Two types σ_1 and σ_2 are called *orthogonal*, written $\sigma_1 \# \sigma_2$, if they have no common instance; i.e., for all τ it holds that $\tau \not\leq \sigma_1$ or $\tau \not\leq \sigma_2$.

A *(typed) variable* is a pair of a variable name x and a type σ, written x_σ. Let Var denote the set of all variables. A *constant instance* is a pair of a constant and a type, written c_σ, such that $\sigma \leq \mathsf{tpOf}(c)$. We let CInst denote the set of constant instances. We extend the notions of being an instance ($\leq$) and being orthogonal ($\#$) from types to constant instances:

$$c_\tau \leq d_\sigma \text{ iff } c = d \text{ and } \tau \leq \sigma \qquad\qquad c_\tau \# d_\sigma \text{ iff } c \neq d \text{ or } \tau \# \sigma$$

The tuple $(K, \mathsf{arOf}, \mathsf{Const}, \mathsf{tpOf})$, which will be fixed in what follows, is called a *signature*. This signature's *terms*, ranged over by s, t, are defined by the grammar:

$$t = x_\sigma \mid c_\sigma \mid t_1 \, t_2 \mid \lambda x_\sigma . t$$

Thus, a term is either a typed variable, or a constant instance, or an application, or an abstraction. As usual, we identify terms modulo alpha-equivalence. Typing is defined as a binary relation between terms and types, written $t : \sigma$, inductively as follows:

$$\frac{x \in \mathsf{VarN}}{x_\sigma : \sigma} \qquad \frac{c \in \mathsf{Const} \quad \tau \leq \mathsf{tpOf}(c)}{c_\tau : \tau} \qquad \frac{t_1 : \sigma \to \tau \quad t_2 : \sigma}{t_1 \, t_2 : \tau} \qquad \frac{t : \tau}{\lambda x_\sigma . t : \sigma \to \tau}$$

A term is a well-typed term if there exists a (necessarily unique) type τ such that $t : \tau$. We write $\mathsf{tpOf}(t)$ for this unique τ. We let Term_w be the set of well-typed terms. We can apply a type substitution ρ to a term t, written $\overline{\rho}(t)$, by applying $\overline{\rho}$ to the types of all variables and constant instances occurring in t. $\mathsf{FV}(t)$ is the set of t's free variables. The term t is called *closed* if it has no free variables: $\mathsf{FV}(t) = \emptyset$. We write $t[s/x_\sigma]$ for the term obtained from t by capture-free substituting s for all free occurrences of x_σ.

A *formula* is a term of type bool. The formula connectives and quantifiers are defined in a standard way, starting from the implication and equality primitives. When writing terms, we sometimes omit the types of variables if they can be inferred.

Deduction. A *theory* is a set of closed formulas. The HOL axioms, forming a set denoted by Ax, are the standard ones, containing axioms for equality, infinity, choice, and excluded middle. (The technical report [31] gives more details.) A *context* Γ is a finite set of formulas. The notation $\alpha \notin \Gamma$ (or $x_\sigma \notin \Gamma$) means that the variable α (or x_σ) is not free in any of the formulas in Γ. We define *deduction* as a ternary relation $\vdash$ between theories D, contexts Γ and formulas φ, written $D; \Gamma \vdash \varphi$.

$$\frac{}{D; \Gamma \vdash \varphi} \, [\varphi \in \mathsf{Ax} \cup D] \; (\textsc{Fact}) \qquad\qquad \frac{}{D; \Gamma \vdash \varphi} \, [\varphi \in \Gamma] \; (\textsc{Assum})$$

$$\frac{D; \Gamma \vdash \varphi}{D; \Gamma \vdash \varphi[\sigma/\alpha]} \, [\alpha \notin \Gamma] \; (\textsc{T-Inst}) \qquad \frac{D; \Gamma \vdash \varphi}{D; \Gamma \vdash \varphi[t/x_\sigma]} \, [x_\sigma \notin \Gamma] \; (\textsc{Inst})$$

$$\frac{}{D; \Gamma \vdash (\lambda x_\sigma . t) \, s = t[s/x_\sigma]} \; (\textsc{Beta}) \qquad \frac{D; \Gamma \vdash \varphi \longrightarrow \chi \quad D; \Gamma \vdash \varphi}{D; \Gamma \vdash \chi} \; (\textsc{MP})$$

$$\frac{D; \Gamma \cup \{\varphi\} \vdash \chi}{D; \Gamma \vdash \varphi \longrightarrow \chi} \; (\textsc{ImpI}) \qquad \frac{D; \Gamma \vdash f \, x_\sigma = g \, x_\sigma}{D; \Gamma \vdash f = g} \, [x_\sigma \notin \Gamma] \; (\textsc{Ext})$$

A theory D is called *consistent* if $D; \emptyset \not\vdash \mathsf{False}$.

Built-Ins and Non-built-Ins. A *built-in type* is any type of the form bool, ind, or $\sigma \to \tau$ for $\sigma, \tau \in$ Type. We let Type$^\bullet$ denote the set of types that are *not* built-in. Note that a non-built-in type can have a built-in type as a subexpression, and vice versa; e.g., if list is a type constructor, then bool list and $(\alpha \to \beta)$ list are non-built-in types, whereas $\alpha \to \beta$ list is a built-in type.

Given a type σ, we define types$^\bullet(\sigma)$, the *set of non-built-in types* of σ, as follows:

$$\text{types}^\bullet(\alpha) = \text{types}^\bullet(\text{bool}) = \text{types}^\bullet(\text{ind}) = \emptyset$$
$$\text{types}^\bullet((\sigma_1, \ldots, \sigma_n)\, k) = \{(\sigma_1, \ldots, \sigma_n)\, k\}, \text{ if } k \text{ is different from } \to$$
$$\text{types}^\bullet(\sigma_1 \to \sigma_2) = \text{types}^\bullet(\sigma_1) \cup \text{types}^\bullet(\sigma_2)$$

Thus, types$^\bullet(\sigma)$ is the smallest set of non-built-in types that can produce σ by repeated application of the built-in type constructors. E.g., if the type constructors real (nullary) and list (unary) are in the signature and if σ is (bool $\to \alpha$ list) $\to$ real $\to$ (bool $\to$ ind) list, then types$^\bullet(\sigma)$ has three elements: α list, real and (bool $\to$ ind) list.

A built-in constant is a constant of the form $\longrightarrow$, $=$, ε, zero or suc. We let Clnst$^\bullet$ be the set of constant instances that are *not* instances of built-in constants.

As a general notation rule, the superscript $\bullet$ indicates non-built-in items, where an item can be either a type or a constant instance.

Given a term t, we let consts$^\bullet(t) \subseteq$ Clnst$^\bullet$ be the set of all non-built-in constant instances occurring in t and types$^\bullet(t) \subseteq$ Type$^\bullet$ be the set of all non-built-in types that compose the types of non-built-in constants and (free or bound) variables occurring in t. Note that the types$^\bullet$ operator is overloaded for types and terms.

$$\text{consts}^\bullet(x_\sigma) = \emptyset \qquad\qquad\qquad \text{types}^\bullet(x_\sigma) = \text{types}^\bullet(\sigma)$$
$$\text{consts}^\bullet(c_\sigma) = \begin{cases} \{c_\sigma\} & \text{if } c_\sigma \in \text{Clnst}^\bullet \\ \emptyset & \text{otherwise} \end{cases} \qquad \text{types}^\bullet(c_\sigma) = \text{types}^\bullet(\sigma)$$
$$\text{consts}^\bullet(t_1\, t_2) = \text{consts}^\bullet(t_1) \cup \text{consts}^\bullet(t_2) \qquad \text{types}^\bullet(t_1\, t_2) = \text{types}^\bullet(t_1) \cup \text{types}^\bullet(t_2)$$
$$\text{consts}^\bullet(\lambda x_\sigma.\, t) = \text{consts}^\bullet(t) \qquad\qquad \text{types}^\bullet(\lambda x_\sigma.\, t) = \text{types}^\bullet(\sigma) \cup \text{types}^\bullet(t)$$

2.2   The Isabelle/HOL Definitional Mechanisms

Constant(-Instance) Definitions. Given $c_\sigma \in$ Clnst$^\bullet$ and a closed term $t : \sigma$, we let $c_\sigma \equiv t$ denote the formula $c_\sigma = t$. We call $c_\sigma \equiv t$ a *constant-instance definition* provided $\text{TV}(t) \subseteq \text{TV}(c_\sigma)$ (i.e., $\text{TV}(t) \subseteq \text{TV}(\sigma)$).

Type Definitions. Given the types $\tau \in$ Type$^\bullet$ and $\sigma \in$ Type and the closed term t whose type is $\sigma \to$ bool, we let $\tau \equiv t$ denote the formula

$$(\exists x_\sigma.\, t\, x) \longrightarrow \exists rep_{\tau \to \sigma}.\, \exists abs_{\sigma \to \tau}.\, (\tau \approx t)^{abs}_{rep} \tag{1}$$

where $(\tau \approx t)^{abs}_{rep}$ is the formula $(\forall x_\tau.\, t\, (rep\, x)) \land (\forall x_\tau.\, abs\, (rep\, x) = x) \land (\forall y_\sigma.\, t\, y \longrightarrow rep\, (abs\, y) = y)$. We call $\tau \equiv t$ a *type definition*, provided τ has the form $(\alpha_1, \ldots, \alpha_n)\,k$ such that α_i are all distinct type variables and $\mathsf{TV}(t) \subseteq \{\alpha_1, \ldots, \alpha_n\}$. (Hence, we have $\mathsf{TV}(t) \subseteq \mathsf{TV}(\tau)$, which also implies $\mathsf{TV}(\sigma) \subseteq \mathsf{TV}(\tau)$.)

Thus, $\tau \equiv t$ means: provided t represents a nonempty subset of σ, the new type τ is isomorphic to this subset via abs and rep. Note that this is a *conditional* type definition, which distinguishes Isabelle/HOL from other HOL-based provers where an *unconditional* version is postulated (but only after the user proves nonemptiness). We shall see that this conditional approach, known among the Isabelle developers as the Makarius Wenzel trick, is useful in the overall scheme of proving consistency.

However, as far as user interaction is concerned, Isabelle/HOL proceeds like the other HOL provers, in particular, it requires nonemptiness proofs. When the user issues a command to define τ via $t : \sigma \to \mathsf{bool}$, the system asks the user to prove $\exists x_\sigma.\ t\ x$, after which the new type τ and the morphisms abs and rep are produced and $(\tau \approx t)_{rep}^{abs}$ is proved by applying Modus Ponens.

An Isabelle/HOL development proceeds by declaring types and constants, issuing constant-instance and type definitions, and proving theorems about them via HOL deduction.[5] Therefore, at any point in the development, there is a finite set D of registered constant-instance and type definitions (over a HOL signature Σ)—we call such a set a *definitional theory*. We are interested in proving the consistency of definitional theories, under the syntactic well-formedness restrictions imposed by the system.

Well-Formed Definitional Theories. Given any binary relation R on $\mathsf{Type}^\bullet \cup \mathsf{CInst}^\bullet$, we write $R^\downarrow$ for its (type-)substitutive closure, defined as follows: $p\,R^\downarrow\,q$ iff there exist p', q' and a type substitution ρ such that $p = \overline{\rho}(p')$, $q = \overline{\rho}(q')$ and $p'\,R\,q'$. We say that a relation R is *terminating* if there exists no sequence $(p_i)_{i \in \mathbb{N}}$ such that $p_i\,R\,p_{i+1}$ for all i. We shall write R^+ and R^* for the transitive and the reflexive-transitive closure of R.

Let us fix a definitional theory D. We say D is *orthogonal* if the following hold for any two distinct definitions $def_1, def_2 \in D$:

- either one of them is a type definition and the other is a constant-instance definition
- or both are type definitions with orthogonal left-hand sides, i.e., def_1 has the form $\tau_1 \equiv \ldots$, def_2 has the form $\tau_2 \equiv \ldots$, and $\tau_1 \# \tau_2$.
- or both are constant-instance definitions with orthogonal left-hand sides, i.e., def_1 has the form $c_{\tau_1} \equiv \ldots$, def_2 has the form $d_{\tau_2} \equiv \ldots$, and $c_{\tau_1} \# d_{\tau_2}$.

We define the binary relation $\rightsquigarrow$ on $\mathsf{Type}^\bullet \cup \mathsf{CInst}^\bullet$ by setting $u \rightsquigarrow v$ iff one of the following holds:

---

[5] Isabelle/HOL is a complex software system, allowing interaction at multiple levels, including by the insertion of ML code. What we care about here is of course an abstract notion of an Isabelle/HOL development—employing the logical mechanisms alone.

1. there exists in D a definition of the form $u \equiv t$ such that $v \in \text{consts}^\bullet(t) \cup \text{types}^\bullet(t)$.
2. $u \in \text{CInst}^\bullet$ such that u has the form $c_{\text{tpOf}(c)}$, and $v \in \text{types}^\bullet(\text{tpOf}(c))$.

We call $\leadsto$ the *dependency relation* associated to D: it shows how the types and constant instances depend on each other through definitions in D. The fact that built-in items do not participate at this relation (as shown by the bullets which restrict to non-built-in items) is justified by the built-in items having a pre-determined interpretation, which prevents them from both "depending" and "being depended upon" [29].

We call the definitional theory D *well-formed* if it is orthogonal and the substitutive closure of its dependency relation, $\leadsto^\downarrow$, is terminating. Orthogonality prevents inconsistency arising from overlapping left-hand sides of definitions: defining $c_{\alpha \times \text{ind} \to \text{bool}}$ to be $\lambda x_{\alpha \times \text{ind}}.\text{False}$ and $c_{\text{ind} \times \alpha \to \text{bool}}$ to be $\lambda x_{\text{ind} \times \alpha}.\text{True}$ yields $\lambda x_{\text{ind} \times \text{ind}}.\text{False} = c_{\text{ind} \times \text{ind} \to \text{bool}} = \lambda x_{\text{ind} \times \text{ind}}.\text{True}$ and hence $\text{False} = \text{True}$. Termination prevents inconsistency arising from circularity, as in the encoding of Russel's paradox in the introduction.

In previous work [29], we proved that these prevention measures are sufficient:

Theorem 1. If D is well-formed, then D is consistent.

Let us briefly recall the difficulties arising in proving the consistency theorem. A main problem problem rests in the fact that (recursive) overloading does not interact well with set-theoretic semantics. This makes it difficult to give a meaning to the overloaded definitions, in spite of the fact that their syntactic dependency terminates.

Example 2. consts $c : \alpha \to \text{bool}$ consts $d : \alpha$
typedef $(\alpha, \beta)\ k \equiv \{(x,y) : \alpha \times \beta \mid c\ x \wedge c\ y \vee (x,y) = (d,d)\}$
consts $l : (\alpha, \beta)\ k \to \alpha$ consts $r : (\alpha, \beta)\ k \to \beta$
definition $c : \text{bool} \to \text{bool} \equiv \lambda\ x.\ \text{True}$
definition $c : \text{nat} \to \text{bool} \equiv \lambda\ x.\ \text{False}$
definition $c : (\alpha, \beta)\ k \to \text{bool} \equiv \lambda\ x.\ c\ (l\ x) \wedge \neg\ c\ (r\ x)$

Here, c and k are mutually dependent. Hence, since c is overloaded, both c and k behave differently depending on the types they are instantiated with or applied to. Here are some examples. Because $c_{\text{bool} \to \text{bool}}$ is (vacuously) true, $(\text{bool}, \text{bool})\ k$ contains four elements (corresponding to all elements of $\text{bool} \times \text{bool}$). On the other hand, because $c_{\text{nat} \to \text{bool}}$ is (vacuously) false, $(\alpha, \text{nat})\ k$ and $(\text{nat}, \alpha)\ k$ each contain one single element (corresponding to (d,d)). Moreover, $(\text{bool}, (\text{bool}, \text{nat})\ k)\ k$ contains two elements, for the following reason: both $c_{\text{bool} \to \text{bool}}$ and $c_{(\text{bool},\text{nat})\ k \to \text{bool}}$ are true, the latter since $c_{\text{bool} \to \text{bool}}$ is true and $c_{\text{nat} \to \text{bool}}$ is false (as required in the definition of $c_{(\alpha,\beta)\ k \to \text{bool}}$); so $(\text{bool}, (\text{bool}, \text{nat})\ k)\ k$ has as many elements as its host type, $\text{bool} \times (\text{bool}, \text{nat})\ k$; and $(\text{bool}, \text{nat})\ k$ has only one element (corresponding to (d,d)). Finally, $(\text{bool}, (\text{nat}, \text{bool})\ k)\ k$ contains only one element, because $c_{(\text{nat},\text{bool})\ k \to \text{bool}}$ is false (by the definitions of $c_{(\alpha,\beta)\ k \to \text{bool}}$ and $c_{\text{nat} \to \text{bool}}$).

In the standard HOL semantics [41], a type constructor such as k is interpreted compositionally, as an operator $[k]$ on sets (from a suitable universe) obtained from k's type definition—here, as a binary operator taking the sets A and B to the set $\{(a, b) \in A \times B \mid [c]_A(a) \wedge [c]_B(b) \vee (a, b) = ([d]_A, [d]_B)\}$, where $([c]_A)_A$ and $([d]_A)_A$ would be the interpretations of c and d as families of sets, with each $[c]_A$ a predicate on A and each $[d]_A$ an element of A. But defining $[k]$ in one go for any sets A and B is impossible here, since the needed instances of $[c]$ are not yet known, and in fact are mutually dependent with $[k]$. This means that, when defining $[k]$ and $[c]$, the inputs A and B would need to be analyzed in an ad hoc fashion, for the (syntactic!) occurrences of $[k]$ itself. The orthogonality and termination of such semantic definitions would be problematic (and, as far as we see, could only be worked out by a heavy machinery that would constrain semantics to behave like syntax—adding syntactic annotations to the interpreting sets). Using John Reynolds's famous wording [42], we conclude that *ad hoc* polymorphism is not set-theoretic.[6]

In [29], we proposed a workaround based on acknowledging that ad hoc overloading regards different instances of the same non-built-in polymorphic type as *completely unrelated types*. Instead of interpreting type constructors as operators on sets, we interpret each non-built-in ground type and constant instance separately, in the order prescribed by the terminating dependency relation. Here, for example, $c_{\mathsf{bool} \to \mathsf{bool}}$ and $c_{\mathsf{nat} \to \mathsf{bool}}$ are interpreted before $(\mathsf{bool}, \mathsf{nat})\, k$, which is interpreted before $c_{(\mathsf{bool},\mathsf{nat})\, k \to \mathsf{bool}}$, which is interpreted before $((\mathsf{bool}, \mathsf{nat})\, k, \mathsf{bool})\, k$, etc. (But note that termination does not necessarily come from structural descent on types: definitions such as $e_{\mathsf{nat}} \equiv \mathsf{head}(e_{\mathsf{nat}\ \mathsf{list}})$ are also acceptable.) Finally, polymorphic formulas are interpreted as the infinite conjunction of the interpretation of all their ground instances: for example, $c_{\alpha \to \mathsf{bool}}\, d_\alpha$ is true iff $c_{\sigma \to \mathsf{bool}}\, d_\sigma$ is true for all ground types σ. This way, we were able to construct a ground model for the definitional theory. And after showing that the deduction rules for (polymorphic) HOL are sound for ground models, we inferred consistency. Thus, our solution was based on a mixture of syntax and semantics: interpret type variables by universally quantifying over all ground instances, and interpret non-built-in ground types disregarding their structure.

Such a hybrid approach, involving a nonstandard semantics, may seem excessive. There is a more common-sense alternative for accommodating the observation that standard semantics cannot be married with ad hoc overloading: view overloaded definitions as mere textual abbreviations. The "semantics" of an overloaded constant will then be the result of unfolding the definitions—but, as we have seen, types must also be involved in this process. This is the alternative taken by our new proof.

3   New Proof of Consistency

The HOL logical infrastructure allows unfolding constant definitions, but not type definitions. To amend this limitation, we take an approach common in mathematics. The reals were introduced by closing the rationals under Cauchy

---

[6] Reynolds's result of course refers to (higher-rank) *parametric* polymorphism.

convergence, the complex numbers were introduced by closing the reals under roots of polynomials. Similarly, we introduce a logic, HOL with Comprehension (HOLC), by closing HOL under type comprehension—that is, adding to HOL comprehension types to express subsets of the form $\{x : \sigma \mid t\,x\}$ (Sect. 3.1). While there is some tension between these subsets being possibly empty and the HOLC types having to be nonempty due to the Hilbert choice operator, this is resolved thanks to the HOLC comprehension axioms being conditioned by nonemptiness. With this proviso, HOLC admits standard set-theoretical models, making it manifestly consistent (Sect. 3.2). In turn, Isabelle/HOL-style overloaded constants and types can be normalized in HOLC by unfolding their definitions (Sect. 3.3). The normalization process provides an intuition and a justification for the syntactic checks involving non-built-in types and constants. Finally, consistency of Isabelle/HOL is inferable from consistency of HOLC.

3.1   HOL with Comprehension (HOLC)

Syntax. Just like for HOL, we fix the sets TVar (of type variables) and VarN (of term variable names), as well as the following:

- a set K of type constructors including the built-in ones bool, ind, $\rightarrow$.
- a function arOf : $K \rightarrow \mathbb{N}$ assigning an arity to each type constructor.
- a set Const of constants, including the built-in ones $\longrightarrow$, $=$, ε, zero and suc.

The HOLC types and terms, which we call *ctypes* and *cterms*, are defined as follows:

$$\sigma = \alpha \mid (\sigma_1, \ldots, \sigma_{\mathsf{arOf}(k)})\,k \mid \{\!|t|\!\} \qquad\qquad t = x_\sigma \mid c_\sigma \mid t_1\,t_2 \mid \lambda x_\sigma.t$$

Above, we highlight the only difference from the HOL types and terms: the comprehension types, whose presence makes the ctypes and cterms mutually recursive. Indeed, $\{\!|t|\!\}$ contains the term t, whereas a typed variable x_σ and a constant instance c_σ contain the type σ. We think of a comprehension type $\{\!|t|\!\}$ with $t : \sigma \rightarrow$ bool as representing a set of elements which in standard mathematical notation would be written $\{x : \sigma \mid t\,x\}$, that is, the set of all elements of σ satisfying t. Var denotes the set of (typed) variables, x_σ. CType and CTerm denotes the sets of ctypes and cterms.

We also fix a function tpOf : Const $\rightarrow$ CType, assigning ctypes to constants. Similarly to the case of HOL, we call the tuple $(K, \mathsf{arOf}, \mathsf{Const}, \mathsf{tpOf})$, which shall be fixed in what follows, a *HOLC signature*. Since ctypes contain cterms, we define typing mutually inductively together with the notion of a ctype being well-formed (i.e., only containing well-typed terms):

$$\frac{\alpha \in \mathsf{TVar}}{\mathsf{wf}(\alpha)}\ (\mathrm{W_1}) \qquad \frac{\mathsf{wf}(\sigma_1)\ \ldots\ \mathsf{wf}(\sigma_{\mathsf{arOf}(k)})}{\mathsf{wf}((\sigma_1, \ldots, \sigma_{\mathsf{arOf}(k)})\,k)}\ (\mathrm{W_2}) \qquad \frac{t :: \sigma \rightarrow \mathsf{bool}}{\mathsf{wf}(\{\!|t|\!\})}\ (\mathrm{W_3}) \qquad \frac{t :: \tau\ \ \mathsf{wf}(\sigma)}{\lambda x_\sigma.t :: \sigma \rightarrow \tau}\ (\mathrm{Abs})$$

$$\frac{x \in \mathsf{VarN}\ \ \mathsf{wf}(\sigma)}{x_\sigma :: \sigma}\ (\mathrm{Var}) \qquad \frac{c \in \mathsf{Const}\ \ \mathsf{wf}(\tau)\ \ \tau \leq \mathsf{tpOf}(c)}{c_\tau :: \tau}\ (\mathrm{Const}) \qquad \frac{t_1 :: \sigma \rightarrow \tau\ \ t_2 :: \sigma}{t_1\,t_2 :: \tau}\ (\mathrm{App})$$

We let CType_w and CTerm_w be the sets of well-formed ctypes and well-typed cterms. Also, we let Var_w be the set of variables x_σ that are well-typed as cterms, i.e., have their ctype σ well-formed.

The notions of type substitution, a type or a constant instance being an instance of ($\leq$) or being orthogonal with ($\#$) another type or constant instance, are defined similarly to those for HOL. Note that a type $\{|t|\}$ is unrelated to another type $\{|t'|\}$ even when the extent of the predicate t' includes that of t. This is because HOLC, like HOL (and unlike, e.g., PVS [39]), has no subtyping—instead, traveling between smaller and larger types is achieved via embedding-projection pairs.

Since in HOLC types may contain terms, we naturally lift term concepts to types. Thus, the free (cterm) variables of a ctype σ, written $\mathsf{FV}(\sigma)$, are all the free variables occurring in the cterms contained in σ. A type is called closed if it has no free variables.

A Note on Declaration Circularity. In HOLC we allow tpOf to produce declaration cycles—for example, the type of a constant may contain instances of that constant, as in $\mathsf{tpOf}(c) = \{|c_{\mathsf{bool}}|\}$. However, the typing system will ensure that no such cyclic entity will be well-typed. For example, to type an instance c_σ, we need to apply the rule (CONST), requiring that $\{|c_{\mathsf{bool}}|\}$ be well-formed. For the latter, we need the rule (W_3), requiring that c_{bool} be well-typed. Finally, to type c_{bool}, we again need the rule (CONST), requiring that $\{|c_{\mathsf{bool}}|\}$ be well-formed. So c_σ can never be typed. It may seem strange to allow constant declarations whose instances cannot be typed (hence cannot belong to well-typed terms and well-formed types)—however, this is harmless, since HOLC deduction only deals with well-typed and well-formed items. Moreover, all the constants translated from HOL will be shown to be well-typed.

Deduction. The notion of formulas and all the related notions are defined similarly to HOL, so that HOL formulas are particular cases of HOLC formulas. In addition to the axioms of HOL (the set Ax), HOLC shall include the following type comprehension axiom type_comp:

$$\forall t_{\alpha\to\mathsf{bool}}.\,(\exists x_\alpha.\,t\,x) \longrightarrow \exists rep_{\{|t|\}\to\alpha}.\,\exists abs_{\alpha\to\{|t|\}}.\,(\{|t|\} \approx t)_{rep}^{abs}$$

This axiom is nothing but a generalization of the HOL type definition $\tau \equiv t$, taking advantage of the fact that in HOLC we have a way to write the expression defining τ as the type $\{|t|\}$. Note that α is a type variable standing for an arbitrary type, previously denoted by σ. Thus, HOLC allows us to express what in HOL used to be a schema (i.e., an infinite set of formulas, one for each type σ) by a single axiom.

HOLC's deduction $\Vdash$ is defined by the same rules as HOL's deduction $\vdash$, but applied to ctypes and cterms instead of types and terms and using the additional axiom type_comp. Another difference from HOL is that HOLC deduction does not factor in a theory D—this is because we do not include any definitional principles in HOLC.

$$\frac{}{\Gamma \Vdash \varphi} \; [\varphi \in \mathsf{Ax} \cup \{\mathsf{type\_comp}\} \,] \; (\text{Fact}) \qquad\qquad \frac{}{\Gamma \Vdash \varphi} \; [\varphi \in \Gamma] \; (\text{Assum})$$

$$\frac{\Gamma \Vdash \varphi}{\Gamma \Vdash \varphi[\sigma/\alpha]} \; [\alpha \notin \Gamma] \; (\text{T-Inst}) \qquad\qquad \frac{\Gamma \Vdash \varphi}{\Gamma \Vdash \varphi[t/x_\sigma]} \; [x_\sigma \notin \Gamma] \; (\text{Inst})$$

$$\frac{}{\Gamma \Vdash (\lambda x_\sigma.\, t)\, s = t[s/x_\sigma]} \; (\text{Beta}) \qquad\qquad \frac{\Gamma \Vdash \varphi \longrightarrow \chi \qquad \Gamma \Vdash \varphi}{\Gamma \Vdash \chi} \; (\text{MP})$$

$$\frac{\Gamma \cup \{\varphi\} \Vdash \chi}{\Gamma \Vdash \varphi \longrightarrow \chi} \; (\text{ImpI}) \qquad\qquad \frac{\Gamma \Vdash f\, x_\sigma = g\, x_\sigma}{\Gamma \Vdash f = g} \; [x \notin \Gamma] \; (\text{Ext})$$

3.2   Consistency of HOLC

In a nutshell, HOLC is consistent for a similar reason that HOL (without definitions) is consistent: the types have a straightforward set-theoretic interpretation and the deduction rules are manifestly sound w.r.t. this interpretation. Similar logics, employing mutual dependency between types and terms, have been shown to be consistent for the foundations of Coq [6] and PVS [39].

Compared to these logics, the only twist of HOLC is that all types have to be nonempty. Indeed, HOLC inherits from HOL the polymorphic Hilbert choice operator, $\varepsilon : (\alpha \to \mathsf{bool}) \to \alpha$, which immediately forces all types to be inhabited, e.g., by $\varepsilon\,(\lambda x_\sigma.\, \mathsf{True})$.

From a technical point of view, this nonemptiness requirement is easy to satisfy. The only types that are threatened by emptiness are the comprehension types $\{\!|t|\!\}$. We will interpret them according to their expected semantics, namely, as the subset of σ for which t holds, *only if this subset turns out to be nonempty*; otherwise we will interpret them as a fixed singleton set $\{*\}$. This is consistent with the HOLC comprehension axiom, $\mathsf{type\_comp}$, which only requires that $\{\!|t|\!\}$ have the expected semantics if $\exists x_\alpha.\, t\, x$ holds. Notice how the Makarius Wenzel trick of introducing type definitions as conditional statements in Isabelle/HOL (recalled on page 7), which has inspired a similar condition for $\mathsf{type\_comp}$, turns out to be very useful in our journey. Of all the HOL-based provers, this "trick" is only used by Isabelle/HOL, as if anticipating the need for a more involved argument for consistency.

A Full-Frame Model for HOLC. We fix a Grothendieck universe $\mathcal{V}$ and let $\mathcal{U} = \mathcal{V} \setminus \{\emptyset\}$ (since all types will have nonempty interpretations). We fix the following items in $\mathcal{U}$ and operators on $\mathcal{U}$:

- a two-element set $\mathbb{B} = \{\mathsf{false}, \mathsf{true}\} \in \mathcal{U}$
- a singleton set $\{*\} \in \mathcal{U}$
- for each $k \in K$, a function $\boxed{k} : \mathcal{U}^{\mathsf{arOf}(k)} \to \mathcal{U}$
- a global choice function, choice, that assigns to each nonempty set $A \in \mathcal{U}$ an element $\mathsf{choice}(A) \in A$.

We wish to interpret well-formed ctypes and well-typed cterms, u, as items $[u]$ in $\mathcal{U}$. Since ctypes and cterms are mutually dependent, not only the interpretations, but also their domains need to be defined recursively. Namely, we define the following notions together, by structural recursion on $u \in \mathsf{CType}_w \cup \mathsf{CTerm}_w$:

– the set $\mathsf{Compat}(u)$, of *compatible valuation functions* $\xi : \mathsf{TV}(u) \cup \mathsf{FV}(u) \to \mathcal{U}$
– the interpretation $[u] : \mathsf{Compat}(u) \to \mathcal{U}$

For each u, assuming $[v]$ has been defined for all structurally smaller $v \in \mathsf{CType}_w \cup \mathsf{CTerm}_w$, we take $\mathsf{Compat}(u)$ to consist of all functions $\xi : \mathsf{TV}(u) \cup \mathsf{FV}(u) \to \mathcal{U}$ such that $\xi(x_\sigma) \in [\sigma](\xi \restriction_{\mathsf{TV}(\sigma) \cup \mathsf{FV}(\sigma)})$ for all $x_\sigma \in \mathsf{FV}(u)$. (Here, $\xi \restriction_{\mathsf{TV}(\sigma) \cup \mathsf{FV}(\sigma)}$ denotes the restriction of ξ to the indicated set, which is clearly included in ξ's domain, since $\mathsf{TV}(\sigma) \subseteq \mathsf{TV}(u)$ and $\mathsf{FV}(\sigma) \subseteq \mathsf{FV}(u)$.)

In turn, $[u]$ is defined as shown below. First, the equations for type interpretations:

$$[\alpha](\xi) = \xi(\alpha) \tag{2}$$

$$[\mathsf{bool}](\xi) = \mathbb{B} \tag{3}$$

$$[\mathsf{ind}](\xi) = \mathbb{N} \quad \text{(the set of natural numbers)} \tag{4}$$

$$\begin{aligned}&[\sigma_1 \to \sigma_2](\xi) = [\sigma_1](\xi_1) \to [\sigma_2](\xi_2)\\&\text{(the set of functions from } [\sigma_1](\xi_1) \text{ to } [\sigma_2](\xi_2))\\&\text{where } \xi_i \text{ is the restriction of } \xi \text{ to } \mathsf{Compat}(\sigma_i)\end{aligned} \tag{5}$$

$$\begin{aligned}&[(\sigma_1, \ldots, \sigma_n)\, k](\xi) = \boxed{k}([\sigma_1](\xi_1), \ldots, [\sigma_n](\xi_n)) \text{ for } \overline{\sigma}\, k \in \mathsf{Type}^\bullet\\&\text{where } \xi_i \text{ is the restriction of } \xi \text{ to } \mathsf{Compat}(\sigma_i)\end{aligned} \tag{6}$$

$$[\{t\}](\xi) = \begin{cases} \{x \in [\sigma](\xi) \mid [t](\xi)\, x = \mathsf{true}\} & \text{if set nonempty and } t : \sigma \to \mathsf{bool}\\ \{*\} & \text{otherwise} \end{cases} \tag{7}$$

The Eq. (7) shows how we interpret comprehension types with no inhabitants (e.g., $\{\lambda x_{\mathsf{ind}}.\, \mathsf{False}\}$)—we chose the singleton set $\{*\}$ (in fact, any nonempty set would do the job). As previously discussed, this conforms to the type_comp axiom, which only prescribes the meaning of inhabited comprehension types.

Next, the equations for term interpretations:

$$[\longrightarrow_{\mathsf{bool} \to \mathsf{bool} \to \mathsf{bool}}](\xi) \text{ as the logical implication on } \mathbb{B} \tag{8}$$

$$[=_{\tau \to \tau \to \mathsf{bool}}](\xi) \text{ as the equality predicate in } [\tau](\xi) \to [\tau](\xi) \to \mathbb{B} \tag{9}$$

$$\begin{aligned}&[\varepsilon_{(\tau \to \mathsf{bool}) \to \tau}](\xi)(f) = \begin{cases} \mathsf{choice}(A_f) & \text{if } A_f \text{ is nonempty}\\ \mathsf{choice}([\tau](\xi)) & \text{otherwise,} \end{cases}\\&\text{where } A_f = \{a \in [\tau](\xi) \mid f(a) = \mathsf{true}\} \text{ for each } f : [\tau](\xi) \to \mathbb{B}\end{aligned} \tag{10}$$

$$[\mathsf{zero_{ind}}](\xi) = 0 \text{ and } [\mathsf{suc_{ind\to ind}}](\xi) \text{ as the successor function for } \mathbb{N} \qquad (11)$$

$$[c_\sigma](\xi) = \mathsf{choice}\,([\sigma](\xi)) \qquad (12)$$

$$[x_\sigma](\xi) = \begin{cases} \xi(x_\sigma) & \text{if } \xi(x_\sigma) \in [\sigma](\xi') \\ \mathsf{choice}\,([\sigma](\xi')) & \text{otherwise,} \end{cases} \qquad (13)$$
where ξ' is the restriction of ξ to $\mathsf{Compat}(\sigma)$

$$[t_1\,t_2](\xi) = [t_1](\xi_1)\,[t_2](\xi_2) \text{ where } \xi_i \text{ is the restriction of } \xi \text{ to } \mathsf{Compat}(t_i) \quad (14)$$

$$[\lambda x_\sigma.\,t](\xi) = \Lambda_{a\in[\sigma](\xi')}[t](\xi[x_\sigma \leftarrow a]) \qquad (15)$$
where ξ' is the restriction of ξ to $\mathsf{Compat}(\sigma)$

Since the logic has no definitions, we are free to choose any interpretation for non-built-in constant instances—as seen in (12), we do this using the global choice operator choice. In (15), we use Λ for meta-level lambda-abstraction.

We say that a formula φ *is true under the valuation* $\xi \in \mathsf{Compat}(\varphi)$ if $[\varphi](\xi) = \mathsf{true}$. We say that φ *is (unconditionally) true* if it is true under all $\xi \in \mathsf{Compat}(\varphi)$. Given a context Γ and a formula φ, we write $\Gamma \models \varphi$ to mean that $\bigwedge \Gamma \longrightarrow \varphi$ is true, where $\bigwedge \Gamma$ is the conjunction of all formulas in Γ.

Theorem 3. HOLC is consistent, in that $\emptyset \not\Vdash \mathsf{False}$.

Proof. It is routine to verify that HOLC's deduction is sound w.r.t. to its semantics: for every HOLC deduction rule of the form

$$\frac{\Gamma_1 \Vdash \varphi_1 \qquad \cdots \qquad \Gamma_n \Vdash \varphi_n}{\Gamma \Vdash \varphi}$$

it holds that $\Gamma \models \varphi$ if $\Gamma_i \models \varphi_i$ for all $i \le n$. Then $\emptyset \not\Vdash \mathsf{False}$ follows from $\emptyset \not\models \mathsf{False}$.   □

3.3   Translation of Isabelle/HOL to HOLC

We fix a HOL signature $\Sigma = (K, \mathsf{arOf}, \mathsf{Const}, \mathsf{tpOf})$ and an Isabelle/HOL well-formed definitional theory D over Σ. We will produce a translation of the types and well-typed terms of Σ into well-formed ctypes and well-typed cterms of the HOLC signature $\Sigma_D = (K, \mathsf{arOf}, \mathsf{Const}, \mathsf{tpOf}_D)$ (having the same type constructors and constants as Σ). The typing function $\mathsf{tpOf}_D : \mathsf{Const} \to \mathsf{CType}$ will be defined later. For Σ_D, we use all the notations from Sect. 3.1—we write CType and CTerm for the sets of cterms and ctypes, etc.

The translation will consist of two homonymous "normal form" functions $\mathsf{NF} : \mathsf{Type} \to \mathsf{CType}_w$ and $\mathsf{NF} : \mathsf{Term}_w \to \mathsf{CTerm}_w$. However, since we have not yet defined tpOf_D, the sets CType_w and CTerm_w (of well-formed ctypes and well-typed cterms) are not yet defined either. To bootstrap the definitions, we first define $\mathsf{NF} : \mathsf{Type} \to \mathsf{CType}$ and $\mathsf{NF} : \mathsf{Term}_w \to \mathsf{CTerm}$, then define tpOf_D, and finally show that the images of the NF functions are included in CType_w and CTerm_w.

The NF functions are defined mutually recursively by two kinds of equations. First, there are equations for recursive descent in the structure of terms and types:

$$\mathsf{NF}(t_1\,t_2) = \mathsf{NF}(t_1)\,\mathsf{NF}(t_2) \qquad (16)$$
$$\mathsf{NF}(\lambda x_\sigma.\,t) = \lambda x_{\mathsf{NF}(\sigma)}.\,\mathsf{NF}(t) \qquad (17)$$
$$\mathsf{NF}(x_\sigma) = x_{\mathsf{NF}(\sigma)} \qquad (18)$$
$$\mathsf{NF}(c_\sigma) = c_{\mathsf{NF}(\sigma)} \text{ if } c_\sigma \notin \mathsf{CInst}^\bullet \qquad (19)$$

$$\mathsf{NF}(\sigma \to \tau) = \mathsf{NF}(\sigma) \to \mathsf{NF}(\tau) \qquad (20)$$
$$\mathsf{NF}(\mathsf{bool}) = \mathsf{bool} \qquad (21)$$
$$\mathsf{NF}(\mathsf{ind}) = \mathsf{ind} \qquad (22)$$
$$\mathsf{NF}(\alpha) = \alpha \qquad (23)$$

Second, there are equations for unfolding the definitions in D. But before listing these, we need some notation. Given $u, v \in \mathsf{Type} \cup \mathsf{Term}_w$, we write $u \equiv^\downarrow v$ to mean that there exists a definition $u' \equiv v'$ in D and a type substitution ρ such that $u = \rho(u')$ and $v = \rho(v')$. This notation is intuitively consistent (although slightly abusively so) with the notation for the substitutive closure of a relation, where we would pretend that $\equiv$ is a relation on $\mathsf{Type} \cup \mathsf{Term}_w$, with $u' \equiv v'$ meaning $(u' \equiv v') \in D$. By Orthogonality, we have that, for all $u \in \mathsf{Type}^\bullet \cup \mathsf{CInst}^\bullet$, there exists at most one $v \in \mathsf{Type} \cup \mathsf{Term}_w$ such that $u \equiv^\downarrow v$. Here are the equations for unfolding:

$$\mathsf{NF}(c_\sigma) = \begin{cases} c_{\mathsf{NF}(\sigma)} & \text{if there is no matching definition for } c_\sigma \text{ in } D \\ \mathsf{NF}(t) & \text{if there exists } t \text{ such that } c_\sigma \equiv^\downarrow t \end{cases} \qquad (24)$$

$$\mathsf{NF}(\sigma) = \begin{cases} \sigma & \text{if there is no matching definition for } \sigma \text{ in } D \\ \{\!|\mathsf{NF}(t)|\!\} & \text{if there exists } t : \tau \to \mathsf{bool} \text{ such that } \sigma \equiv^\downarrow t \end{cases} \qquad (25)$$

Thus, the functions NF first traverse the terms and types "vertically," delving into the built-in structure (function types, λ-abstractions, applications, etc.). When a non-built-in item is being reached that is matched by a definition in D, NF proceed "horizontally" by unfolding this definition. Since the right-hand side of the definition can be any term, NF switch again to vertical mode. Hence, NF repeatedly unfold the definitions when a definitional match in a subexpression is found, following a topmost-first strategy (with the exception that proper subexpressions of non-built-in types are not investigated). For example, if a constant c_σ is matched by a definition, as in $c_\sigma \equiv^\downarrow t$, then c_σ is eagerly unfolded to t, as opposed to unfolding the items occurring in σ. This seems to be a reasonable strategy, given that after unfolding c_σ the possibility to process σ is not lost: since $t : \sigma$, we have that σ occurs in t.

Example 4. consts c : $\alpha \to$ bool   consts d : α
typedef α k $\equiv \{$x : α | c d$\}$
definition c : α k $\to$ bool $\equiv \lambda$ x : α k. (c : $\alpha \to$ bool) d

Let us show the results of applying NF on some of the constant instances and types in the above example.

$$\mathsf{NF}(\alpha\,k) = \{\!|\lambda x_\alpha.\,c_{\alpha \to \mathsf{bool}}\,d_\alpha|\!\}$$
$$\mathsf{NF}(c_{\mathsf{bool}\,k \to \mathsf{bool}}) = \lambda x_{\{\!|\lambda x_{\mathsf{bool}}.\,c_{\mathsf{bool} \to \mathsf{bool}}\,d_{\mathsf{bool}}|\!\}}.\,c_{\mathsf{bool} \to \mathsf{bool}}\,d_{\mathsf{bool}}$$
$$\mathsf{NF}(\mathsf{bool}\,k^2) = \{\!|\lambda x_{\{\!|\lambda x_{\mathsf{bool}}.\,c_{\mathsf{bool} \to \mathsf{bool}}\,d_{\mathsf{bool}}|\!\}}.$$
$$(\lambda x_{\{\!|\lambda x_{\mathsf{bool}}.\,c_{\mathsf{bool} \to \mathsf{bool}}\,d_{\mathsf{bool}}|\!\}}.\,c_{\mathsf{bool} \to \mathsf{bool}}\,d_{\mathsf{bool}})\,d_{\{\!|\lambda x_{\mathsf{bool}}.\,c_{\mathsf{bool} \to \mathsf{bool}}\,d_{\mathsf{bool}}|\!\}}|\!\}$$

The evaluation of NF on bool k^n terminates in a number of steps depending on n, and the result contains n levels of comprehension-type nesting.

The first fact that we need to show is that NF is well-defined, i.e., its recursive calls terminate. For this, we take the relation $\blacktriangleright$ to be $\equiv^{\downarrow} \cup \rhd$, where $\equiv^{\downarrow}$ was defined above and $\rhd$ simply contains the structural recursive calls of NF:

$$t_1 t_2 \rhd t_1 \qquad\qquad \lambda x_\sigma . t \rhd \sigma \qquad\qquad x_\sigma \rhd \sigma \qquad\qquad \sigma_1 \to \sigma_2 \rhd \sigma_1$$

$$t_1 t_2 \rhd t_2 \qquad\qquad \lambda x_\sigma . t \rhd t \qquad\qquad c_\sigma \rhd \sigma \qquad\qquad \sigma_1 \to \sigma_2 \rhd \sigma_2$$

It is immediate to see that $\blacktriangleright$ captures the recursive calls of NF: the structural calls via $\rhd$ and the unfolding calls via $\equiv^{\downarrow}$. So the well-definedness of NF is reduced to the termination of $\blacktriangleright$.

Lemma 5. The relation $\blacktriangleright$ is terminating (hence the functions NF are well-defined).

Proof. We shall use the following crucial fact, which follows by induction using the definitions of $\rhd$ and $\rightsquigarrow^{\downarrow}$: If $u, v \in \mathsf{Type}^{\bullet} \cup \mathsf{CInst}^{\bullet}$ and $u \equiv^{\downarrow} t \rhd^* v$, then $u \rightsquigarrow^{\downarrow} v$. (*)

Let us assume, for a contradiction, that $\blacktriangleright$ does not terminate. Then there exists an infinite sequence $(w_i)_{i \in \mathbb{N}}$ such that $w_i \blacktriangleright w_{i+1}$ for all i. Since $\blacktriangleright$ is defined as $\equiv^{\downarrow} \cup \rhd$ and $\rhd$ clearly terminates, there must exist an infinite subsequence $(w_{i_j})_{j \in \mathbb{N}}$ such that $w_{i_j} \equiv^{\downarrow} w_{i_j + 1} \rhd^* w_{i_{j+1}}$ for all j. Since from the definition of $\equiv$ we have $w_{i_j} \in \mathsf{Type}^{\bullet} \cup \mathsf{CInst}^{\bullet}$, we obtain from (*) that $w_{i_j} \rightsquigarrow^{\downarrow} w_{i_{j+1}}$ for all j. This contradicts the termination of $\rightsquigarrow^{\downarrow}$. □

With NF in place, we can define the missing piece of the target HOLC signature: we take tpOf_D to be the normalized version of tpOf, i.e. $\mathsf{tpOf}_D(c) = \mathsf{NF}(\mathsf{tpOf}(c))$.

Lemma 6. NF preserves typing, in the following sense:

- $\mathsf{NF}(\sigma)$ is well-formed in HOLC.
- If $t : \tau$, then $\mathsf{NF}(t) :: \mathsf{NF}(\tau)$.

Our main theorem about the translation will be its soundness:

Theorem 7. If $D; \emptyset \vdash \varphi$ in HOL, then $\emptyset \Vdash \mathsf{NF}(\varphi)$ in HOLC.

Let us focus on proving this theorem. If we define $\mathsf{NF}(\Gamma)$ as $\{\mathsf{NF}(\varphi) \mid \varphi \in \Gamma\}$, the proof that $D; \Gamma \vdash \varphi$ implies $\mathsf{NF}(\Gamma) \Vdash \mathsf{NF}(\varphi)$ should proceed by induction on the definition of $D; \Gamma \vdash \varphi$. Due to the similarity of $\vdash$ and $\Vdash$, most of the cases go smoothly.

For the HOL rule (BETA), we need to prove $\mathsf{NF}(\Gamma) \Vdash \mathsf{NF}((\lambda x_\sigma . t) s = t[s/x_\sigma])$, that is, $\mathsf{NF}(\Gamma) \Vdash (\lambda x_{\mathsf{NF}(\sigma)} . \mathsf{NF}(t)) \mathsf{NF}(s) = \mathsf{NF}(t[s/x_\sigma])$. Hence, in order to conclude the proof for this case using the HOLC rule (BETA), we need that NF commutes with term substitution—this is not hard to show, since substituting terms for variables does not influence the matching of definitions, i.e., the behavior of NF:

Lemma 8. $\mathsf{NF}(t[s/x_\sigma]) = \mathsf{NF}(t)\,[\mathsf{NF}(s)/x_{\mathsf{NF}(\sigma)}]$.

However, our proof (of Theorem 7) gets stuck when handling the (T-Inst) case. It is worth looking at this difficulty, since it is revealing about the nature of our encoding. We assume that in HOL we inferred $D; \Gamma \vdash \varphi[\sigma/\alpha]$ from $D; \Gamma \vdash \varphi$, where $\alpha \notin \Gamma$. By the induction hypothesis, we have $\mathsf{NF}(\Gamma) \Vdash \mathsf{NF}(\varphi)$. Hence, by applying (T-Inst) in HOLC, we obtain $\mathsf{NF}(\Gamma) \Vdash \mathsf{NF}(\varphi)[\mathsf{NF}(\sigma)/\mathsf{NF}(\alpha)]$. Therefore, to prove the desired fact, we would need that the NF functions commute with type substitutions in formulas, and therefore also in arbitrary terms (which may be contained in formulas):

$$\mathsf{NF}(t[\sigma/\alpha]) = \mathsf{NF}(t)[\mathsf{NF}(\sigma)/\alpha]$$

But this is not true, as seen, e.g., when $\mathsf{tpOf}(c) = \alpha$ and $c_{\mathsf{bool}} \equiv \mathsf{True}$ is in D:

$$\mathsf{NF}(c_\alpha[\mathsf{bool}/\alpha]) = \mathsf{NF}(c_{\mathsf{bool}}) = \mathsf{True} \neq c_{\mathsf{bool}} = c_\alpha[\mathsf{bool}/\alpha] = \mathsf{NF}(c_\alpha)\,[\mathsf{NF}(\mathsf{bool})/\alpha]$$

The problem resides at the very essence of overloading: a constant c is declared at a type σ (α in the above example) and defined at a less general type τ (bool in the example). Our translation reflects this: it leaves c_σ as it is, whereas it compiles away c_τ by unfolding its definition. So then how can such a translation be sound? Essentially, it is sound because in HOL nothing interesting can be deduced about the undefined c_σ that may affect what is being deduced about c_τ—hence it is OK to decouple the two when moving to HOLC.

To capture this notion, of an undefined c_σ not affecting a defined instance c_τ in HOL, we introduce a variant of HOL deduction that restricts type instantiation—in particular, it will not allow arbitrary statements about c_σ to be instantiated to statements about c_τ. Concretely, we define $\vdash'$ by modifying $\vdash$ as follows. We remove (T-Inst) and strengthen (Fact) to a rule that combines the use of axioms with type instantiation:

$$\frac{}{D; \Gamma \vdash' \overline{\rho}(\varphi)} \;\; [\varphi \in \mathsf{Ax} \cup D \text{ and } \forall \alpha \in \mathsf{supp}(\rho).\ \alpha \notin \Gamma]\;\; (\textsc{Fact-T-Inst})$$

(where ρ is a type substitution). Note the difference between (Fact-T-Inst) and the combination of (Fact) and (T-Inst): in the former, only axioms and elements of D are allowed to be type-instantiated, whereas in the latter instantiation can occur at any moment in the proof. It is immediate to see that $\vdash$ is at least as powerful as $\vdash'$, since (Fact-T-Inst) can be simulated by (Fact) and (T-Inst). Conversely, it is routine to show that $\vdash'$ is closed under type substitution, and a fortiori under (T-Inst); and (Fact-T-Inst) is stronger than (Fact).

Using $\vdash'$ instead of $\vdash$, we can prove Theorem 7. All the cases that were easy with $\vdash$ are also easy with $\vdash'$. In addition, for the case (Fact-T-Inst) where one infers $D; \Gamma \vdash \rho(\varphi)$ with $\varphi \in \mathsf{Ax}$, we need a less general lemma than commutation of NF in an arbitrary term. Namely, *noticing that the HOL axioms do not contain non-built-in constants or types*, we need the following lemma, which can be proved by routine induction over t:

Lemma 9. $\mathsf{NF}(\overline{\rho}(t)) = \overline{\mathsf{NF} \circ \rho}(t)$ whenever $\mathsf{types}^\bullet(t) \cup \mathsf{consts}^\bullet(t) = \emptyset$.

Now, assume (FACT-T-INST) is being used to derive $D; \Gamma \vdash' \overline{\rho}(\varphi)$ for $\varphi \in \mathsf{Ax}$. We need to prove $\Gamma \Vdash \mathsf{NF}(\overline{\rho}(\varphi))$, that is, $\Gamma \Vdash \overline{\mathsf{NF} \circ \rho}(\varphi)$. But this follows from n applications of the (T-INST) rule (in HOLC), where n is the size of $\overline{\mathsf{NF} \circ \rho}$'s support (as any finite-support simultaneous substitution can be reduced to a sequence of unary substitutions).

It remains to handle the case when (FACT-T-INST) is being used to derive $D; \Gamma \vdash' \overline{\rho}(\varphi)$ for $\varphi \in D$. Here, Lemma 9 does not apply, since of course the definitions in D contain non-built-in items. However, we can take advantage of the particular shape of the definitions. The formula φ necessarily has the form $u \equiv t$. By Orthogonality, it follows that $\overline{\rho}(t)$ is the unique term such that $\overline{\rho}(u) \equiv^\downarrow \overline{\rho}(t)$. We have two cases:

- If u is a constant instance c_σ, then by the definition of NF we have $\mathsf{NF}(\overline{\rho}(u)) = \mathsf{NF}(\overline{\rho}(t))$. But then $\Gamma \Vdash \mathsf{NF}(\rho(\varphi))$, that is, $\Gamma \Vdash \mathsf{NF}(\overline{\rho}(u)) = \mathsf{NF}(\overline{\rho}(t))$, follows from (FACT) applied with the reflexivity axiom.
- If u is a type σ and $t : \tau \to \mathsf{bool}$, then $\overline{\rho}(\varphi)$ is $\overline{\rho}(\sigma) \equiv^\downarrow \overline{\rho(t)}$. In other words, $\overline{\rho}(\varphi)$ has the format of a HOL type definition, just like φ. Hence, $\mathsf{NF}(\overline{\rho}(\varphi))$ is seen to be an instance of $\mathsf{type\_comp}$, namely, $\mathsf{type\_comp}[\mathsf{NF}(\overline{\rho}(\sigma))/\alpha]$ together with $\mathsf{NF}(\overline{\rho}(t))$ substituted for the first quantifier. Hence $\Gamma \Vdash \mathsf{NF}(\overline{\rho}(\varphi))$ follows from (FACT) applied with $\mathsf{type\_comp}$, followed by $\forall$-instantiation (the latter being the standardly derived rule for $\forall$).

In summary, our HOLC translation of overloading emulates overloading itself in that it treats the defined constant instances c_τ as being disconnected from their "mother" instances $c_{\mathsf{tpOf}(c)}$. The translation is sound thanks to the fact that the considered theory has no axioms about these constants besides the overloaded definitions. This sound translation immediately allows us to reach our overall goal:

Proof of Theorem 1 (Consistency of Isabelle/HOL). By contradiction. Let $D; \emptyset \vdash \mathsf{False}$. Then by Theorem 7, we obtain $\emptyset \Vdash \mathsf{NF}(\mathsf{False})$ and since $\mathsf{NF}(\mathsf{False}) = \mathsf{False}$, we derive contradiction with Theorem 3.   □

4   Application: Logical Extensions

We introduced HOLC as an auxiliary for proving the consistency of Isabelle/HOL's logic. However, a natural question that arises is whether HOLC would be itself a practically useful extension. We cannot answer this question yet, beyond noting that it would be a significant implementation effort due to the need to reorganize types as mutually dependent with terms. Over the years, some other proposals to go beyond HOL arose. For example, an interesting early proposal by Melham to extend the terms with explicit type quantifiers [34] was never implemented. Homeier's HOL_ω [22], an implemented and currently maintained extension of HOL with first-class type constructors, is another example.

A strong argument for using HOL in theorem proving is that it constitutes a sweet spot between expressiveness and simplicity. The expressiveness part of the claim is debatable—and has been challenged, as shown by the above examples, as well as by Isabelle/HOL itself which extends HOL in a nontrivial way. In our recent work we joined the debate club and advocated a new sweet spot for HOL (and for Isabelle/HOL, respectively) [30] by introducing local type definitions and an unoverloading rule expressing parametricity. HOLC plays a special role in this proposal because we use it to prove the extensions' consistency.

In the following, we first introduce and motivate the extensions (Sect. 4.1), and then discuss how we applied HOLC to justify their consistency and why our previous ground semantic [29] is not suitable for this job (Sect. 4.2).

4.1   Two Extensions for Traveling from Types to Sets

We start with a theorem stating that all compact sets are closed in T2 spaces (a topological space), whose definition uses an overloaded constant open : α set $\rightarrow$ bool:

$$\forall \alpha_{\text{T2-space}}. \ \forall S_{\alpha \, \text{set}}. \, \text{compact } S \longrightarrow \text{closed } S \tag{26}$$

Since we quantify over spaces defined on α here, the theorem is not applicable to spaces defined on a proper subset A of α. Let us recall that types and sets are different syntactic categories in HOL. Defining a new ad hoc type isomorphic to A is undesirable or not even allowed since A can be an open term. Thus a more flexible theorem quantifying over all nonempty carriers A and unary predicates *open* forming a T2 space is needed:

$$\forall \alpha. \ \forall A_{\alpha \, \text{set}}. \, A \neq \emptyset \longrightarrow \forall open_{\alpha \, \text{set} \rightarrow \text{bool}}. \, \text{T2-space}^{\text{on}}_{\text{with}} \, A \ open \longrightarrow$$
$$\forall S_{\alpha \, \text{set}} \subseteq A. \, \text{compact}^{\text{on}}_{\text{with}} \, A \ open \ S \longrightarrow \text{closed}^{\text{on}}_{\text{with}} \, A \ open \ S \tag{27}$$

As the proof automation works better with types, ideally one should only prove type-based theorems such as (26) and automatically obtain set-based theorems such as (27). Unfortunately, this is not possible in HOL, which is frustrating given that (26) and (27) are semantically equivalent (in the standard interpretation of HOL types).

To address the discrepancy and achieve the automatic translation, we extended the logic of Isabelle/HOL by two new rules: Local Typedef (LT) and Unoverloading (UO).

$$\frac{\Gamma \vdash A \neq \emptyset \qquad \Gamma \vdash (\exists abs \ rep. \, (\beta \approx A)^{abs}_{rep}) \longrightarrow \varphi}{\Gamma \vdash \varphi} \ [\beta \text{ fresh}] \ (\text{LT})$$

where $(\beta \approx A)^{abs}_{rep}$ means that β is isomorphic to A via morphisms *abs* and *rep*; basically the core of the formula (1) from Sect. 2.2, where for notation convenience we identify the set A with its characteristic predicate $\lambda x. \, x \in A$. The rule allows us to assume the existence of a type isomorphic to a nonempty set A (which syntactically is a possibly *open* term) inside of a proof.

To formulate (UO), let us recall that $\leadsto^{\downarrow}$ is the substitutive closure of the constant–type dependency relation $\leadsto$ from Sect. 2.2 on page 8 and let us define Δ_c to be the set of all types for which the constant c was overloaded. The notation $\sigma \not\leq S$ means that σ is not an instance of any type in S. We write $\leadsto^{\downarrow+}$ for the transitive closure of $\leadsto^{\downarrow}$.

$$\frac{\varphi[c_\sigma/x_\sigma]}{\forall x_\sigma.\,\varphi} \; [\sigma \not\leq \Delta_c; \text{ and } u \leadsto^{\downarrow+} c_\sigma \text{ does not hold for any type or constant } u \text{ in } \varphi] \;(\text{UO})$$

Thus, (UO) tells us that if a constant c was not overloaded for σ (or a more general type), the meaning of the constant instance c_σ is unrestricted, i.e., it behaves as a free term variable of the same type. That is to say, the truth of a theorem φ containing c_σ *cannot* depend on the definition of c_τ for some $\tau < \sigma$. In summary, (UO) imposes a certain notion of parametricity, which is willing to cohabitate with ad hoc overloading.

We use the two rules in the translation as follows: the (UO) rule allows us to compile out the overloaded constants from (26) (by a dictionary construction) and thus obtain

$$\forall \alpha.\, \forall open_{\alpha\,\text{set}\to\text{bool}}.\, \text{T2-space}_{\text{with}}\; open \longrightarrow \ldots . \tag{28}$$

Then we fix a nonempty set A, locally "define" a type β isomorphic to A by (LT) and obtain (27) from the β-instance of (28) along the isomorphism between β and A.

The extensions have already been picked up by Isabelle/HOL power users for translating between different representations of matrices [12,13], for implementing a certified and efficient algorithm for factorization [11], and for tightly integrating invariants in proof rules for a probabilistic programming language [33].

4.2   Consistency of the Extensions

We will fist show that HOL + (LT) is consistent by showing (LT) to be admissible in HOLC (as a straightforward consequence of type_comp).

Theorem 10. The inference system consisting of the deduction rules of Isabelle/HOL and the (LT) rule is consistent (in that it cannot prove False).

Proof sketch. It is enough if we show that for every step

$$\frac{\Gamma \vdash A \neq \emptyset \qquad \Gamma \vdash (\exists abs\; rep.\,(\beta \approx A)^{abs}_{rep}) \longrightarrow \varphi}{\Gamma \vdash \varphi}\;[\beta \text{ is fresh}]$$

in a HOL proof, we can construct a step in a HOLC proof of $\mathsf{NF}(\Gamma) \Vdash \mathsf{NF}(\varphi)$ given

$$\mathsf{NF}(\Gamma) \Vdash \mathsf{NF}(A) \neq \mathsf{NF}(\emptyset) \tag{29}$$

$$\mathsf{NF}(\Gamma) \Vdash (\exists abs \; rep. \, (\beta \approx \mathsf{NF}(A))_{rep}^{abs}) \longrightarrow \mathsf{NF}(\varphi). \tag{30}$$

The side-condition of the (LT) (freshness of β) transfers into HOLC: if β is fresh for some $u \in \mathsf{Type} \cup \mathsf{Term}$, it must also be fresh for $\mathsf{NF}(u)$. This follows from the fact that unfolding a (type or constant) definition $u \equiv t$ cannot introduce new type variables since we require $\mathsf{TV}(t) \subseteq \mathsf{TV}(u)$. Thus we obtain

$$\mathsf{NF}(\Gamma) \Vdash (\exists abs \; rep. \, (\{\!|\mathsf{NF}(A)|\!\} \approx \mathsf{NF}(A))_{rep}^{abs}) \longrightarrow \mathsf{NF}(\varphi), \tag{31}$$

an instance of (30) where we substituted the witness $\{\!|\mathsf{NF}(A)|\!\}$ for β. As a last step, we discharge the antecedent of (31) by using type_comp (with the help of (29)) and obtain the desired $\mathsf{NF}(\Gamma) \Vdash \mathsf{NF}(\varphi)$. $\qquad\square$

We were also able to prove Theorem 10 by using our previous ground semantics, as discussed in Kunčar's thesis [26, Sect. 7.2]. The proof is more technically elaborate and the main idea is to prove that the following principle holds in the semantic world of HOL:

$$\forall \alpha. \, \forall A_{\alpha \, \mathsf{set}}. \, A \neq \emptyset \longrightarrow \exists \beta. \, \exists abs_{\alpha \to \beta} \; rep_{\beta \to \alpha}. \, (\beta \approx A)_{rep}^{abs} \tag{$\star$}$$

Working in HOLC gives us the advantage to get closer to ($\star$) in the following sense: for every nonempty set $A : \sigma \, \mathsf{set}$, not only we can postulate that there always exists a type isomorphic to A, but we can even directly express such a type in HOLC as the comprehension $\{\!|A|\!\}$. That is basically what the axiom type_comp tells us. Thus, informally speaking, the property ($\star$) is more first-class in HOLC than in HOL.

In contrast to (LT), we could not use the ground semantics for the consistency of (UO) and this is where HOLC shows its power.

Theorem 11. The inference system consisting of the deduction rules of Isabelle/HOL, the (LT) rule and the (UO) rule is consistent.

Proof sketch. We will first argue that HOLC + (UO) (without its side-conditions, since they do not make sense in HOLC) is still a consistent logic. This means, from $\varphi[c_\sigma/x_\sigma]$ we can derive $\forall x_\sigma. \, \varphi$ in HOLC + (UO). W.l.o.g. let us assume that the interpretation of type constructors in the semantics of HOLC from Sect. 3.2 is nonoverlapping. Since HOLC does not contain any definitions, we interpret c_σ arbitrarily (as long as the value belongs to the interpretation of σ) in the model construction for HOLC. That is to say, the proof of consistency does not rely on the actual value of c_σ's interpretation, hence we can replace c_σ by a term variable x_σ. Therefore the formula φ must be fulfilled for every evaluation of x_σ.

The second step is to show that NF is a sound embedding of Isabelle/HOL + (LT) + (UO) into HOLC + (UO). Since we have shown that the translation of (LT) is admissible in HOLC, we only need to focus on (UO). The first side condition of (UO) guarantees that unfolding by NF does not introduce any new c_σ and the second one guarantees that NF does not unfold any c_σ. Therefore the substitution $[c_\sigma/x_\sigma]$ commutes with NF, i.e., $\mathsf{NF}(\varphi[c_\sigma/x_\sigma])$ $= (\mathsf{NF}(\varphi))[c_{\mathsf{NF}(\sigma)}/x_{\mathsf{NF}(\sigma)}]$.   □

The reason we could not use the ground semantics to prove Theorem 11 is because the semantics is too coarse to align with the meaning of (UO): that the truth of a theorem φ stating a property of c_σ cannot depend on the fact that a proper instance of c_σ, say, c_τ for $\tau < \sigma$, was already overloaded, say, by a definition $c_\tau \equiv t$. In semantic terms, this means that the interpretation of c_σ cannot depend on the interpretation of c_τ. Recall that in the ground semantics we considered a polymorphic HOL formula φ to be true just in case all its ground type instances are true. (See also the discussion on page 9.) This definition of truth cannot validate (UO). To see this, let us assume that φ is polymorphic only in α and τ is ground. We want to assume the truth of $\varphi[\sigma/\alpha][c_\sigma/x_\sigma]$ and infer the truth of $\forall x_\sigma.\, \varphi[\sigma/\alpha]$. In particular, since $\forall x_\tau.\, \varphi[\tau/\alpha]$ is a ground instance of the latter, we would need to infer that $\forall x_\tau.\, \varphi[\tau/\alpha]$ is true, and in particular that $\varphi[\tau/\alpha][c_\tau/x_\tau]$ is true. But this is impossible, since the interpretation of c_τ in $\varphi[\tau/\alpha][c_\tau/x_\tau]$ is fixed and dictated by the definitional theorem $c_\tau \equiv t$.

5   Conclusions and Related Work

It took the Isabelle/HOL community almost twenty years to reach a definitional mechanism that is consistent by construction, w.r.t. both types and constants.[7] This paper, which presents a clean syntactic argument for consistency, is a culmination of previous efforts by Wenzel [48], Obua [38], ourselves [27, 29], and many other Isabelle designers and developers.

The key ingredients of our proof are a type-instantiation restricted version of HOL deduction and HOLC, an extension of HOL with comprehension types. HOLC is similar to a restriction of Coq's Calculus of Inductive Constructions (CiC) [8], where: (a) proof irrelevance and excluded middle axioms are enabled; (b) polymorphism is restricted to rank 1; (c) the formation of (truly) dependent product types is suppressed. However, unlike CiC, HOLC stays faithful to the HOL tradition of avoiding empty types. HOLC also bears some similarities to HOL with predicate subtyping [43] as featured by PVS [44]. Yet, HOLC does not have real subtyping: from $t : \sigma \to \mathsf{bool}$ and $s :: \{|t|\}$ we cannot infer $s :: \sigma$. Instead, HOLC retains HOL's separation between a type defined by comprehension and the original type: the former is not included, but merely embedded in the latter. Comprehension types are also known in the programming language literature as refinement types [16].

Wiedijk defines *stateless HOL* [49], a version of HOL where types and terms carry definitions *in their syntax*. Kumar et al. [25] define a translation from standard (stateful) HOL with definitions to stateless HOL, on the way of proving the consistency of both. Their translation is similar to our HOL to HOLC translation, in that it internalizes HOL definitions as part of "stateless" formulas in a richer logic.

---

[7] Isabelle is by no means the only prover with longstanding foundational issues [29, Sect. 1].

Although a crucial property, consistency is nevertheless rather weak. One should legitimately expect definitions to enjoy a much stronger property: that they can be compiled away without affecting provability *not in a richer logic (like HOLC), but in HOL itself.* Wenzel calls this property "meta-safety" and proves it for Isabelle/HOL *constant* definitions [48]. In particular, meta-safety yields *proof-theoretic conservativity*, itself stronger than consistency: if a formula that contains no defined item is deducible from a definitional theory, then it is deducible in the core (definition-free) logic. Meta-safety and conservativity for arbitrary definitional theories (factoring in not only constant, but also type definitions) are important meta-theoretic problems, which seem to be open not only for Isabelle/HOL, but also for standard HOL [2]. We leave them as future work.

Acknowledgments. We thank Tobias Nipkow, Larry Paulson, Makarius Wenzel, and the members of the Isabelle mailing list for inspiring and occasionally intriguing opinions and suggestions concerning the foundations of Isabelle/HOL. We also thank the reviewers for suggestions on how to improve the presentation and for indicating related work. Kunčar is supported by the German Research Foundation (DFG) grant "Security Type Systems and Deduction" (Ni 491/13-3) in the priority program "$\mathcal{R}S^3$ – Reliably Secure Software Systems" (SPP 1496). Popescu is supported by the UK Engineering and Physical Sciences Research Council (EPSRC) starting grant "VOWS – Verification of Web-based Systems" (EP/N019547/1).

References

1. Isabelle Foundation & Certification (2015). https://lists.cam.ac.uk/pipermail/cl-isabelle-users/2015-September/thread.html
2. Conservativity of HOL constant and type definitions (2016). https://sourceforge.net/p/hol/mailman/message/35448054/
3. The HOL system logic (2016). https://sourceforge.net/projects/hol/files/hol/kananaskis-10/kananaskis-10-logic.pdf
4. Type definitions in Isabelle; article "A Consistent Foundation for Isabelle/HOL" by Kunčar/Popescu (2016). https://lists.cam.ac.uk/pipermail/cl-isabelle-users/2016-August/thread.html
5. Arthan, R.: On definitions of constants and types in HOL. J. Autom. Reason. **56**(3), 205–219 (2016)
6. Barras, B.: Sets in Coq, Coq in sets. J. Formal. Reason. **3**(1), 29–48 (2010)
7. Berghofer, S., Wenzel, M.: Inductive datatypes in HOL – lessons learned in formal-logic engineering. In: Bertot, Y., Dowek, G., Théry, L., Hirschowitz, A., Paulin, C. (eds.) TPHOLs 1999. LNCS, vol. 1690, pp. 19–36. Springer, Heidelberg (1999). doi:10.1007/3-540-48256-3_3
8. Bertot, Y., Casteran, P.: Interactive Theorem Proving and Program Development. Coq'Art: The Calculus of Inductive Constructions. Springer, Heidelberg (2004)
9. Blanchette, J.C., Popescu, A., Traytel, D.: Foundational extensible corecursion. In: ICFP 2015. ACM (2015)
10. Bulwahn, L., Krauss, A., Haftmann, F., Erkök, L., Matthews, J.: Imperative functional programming with Isabelle/HOL. In: Mohamed, O.A., Muñoz, C., Tahar, S. (eds.) TPHOLs 2008. LNCS, vol. 5170, pp. 134–149. Springer, Heidelberg (2008). doi:10.1007/978-3-540-71067-7_14

11. Divasón, J., Joosten, S., Thiemann, R., Yamada, A.: A formalization of the Berlekamp-Zassenhaus factorization algorithm. In: CPP, pp. 17–29 (2017)
12. Divasón, J., Kunčar, O., Thiemann, R., Yamada, A.: Certifying exact complexity bounds for matrix interpretations. In: LCC (2016)
13. Divasón, J., Kunčar, O., Thiemann, R., Yamada, A.: Perron-Frobenius theorem for spectral radius analysis. Archive of Formal Proofs (2016). https://www.isa-afp. org/entries/Perron_Frobenius.shtml
14. Esparza, J., Lammich, P., Neumann, R., Nipkow, T., Schimpf, A., Smaus, J.-G.: A fully verified executable LTL model checker. In: Sharygina, N., Veith, H. (eds.) CAV 2013. LNCS, vol. 8044, pp. 463–478. Springer, Heidelberg (2013). doi:10.1007/ 978-3-642-39799-8_31
15. Fallenstein, B., Kumar, R.: Proof-producing reflection for HOL - with an application to model polymorphism. In: ITP, pp. 170–186 (2015)
16. Freeman, T., Pfenning, F.: Refinement types for ML. In: PLDI, pp. 268–277 (1991)
17. Geuvers, H.: Proof assistants: history, ideas and future. Sadhana 34(1), 3–25 (2009)
18. Gordon, M.J.C., Melham, T.F. (eds.): Introduction to HOL: A Theorem Proving Environment for Higher Order Logic. Cambridge University Press, Cambridge (1993)
19. Haftmann, F., Nipkow, T.: Code generation via higher-order rewrite systems. In: Blume, M., Kobayashi, N., Vidal, G. (eds.) FLOPS 2010. LNCS, vol. 6009, pp. 103–117. Springer, Heidelberg (2010). doi:10.1007/978-3-642-12251-4_9
20. Harrison, J.: HOL Light: an overview. In: Berghofer, S., Nipkow, T., Urban, C., Wenzel, M. (eds.) TPHOLs 2009. LNCS, vol. 5674, pp. 60–66. Springer, Heidelberg (2009). doi:10.1007/978-3-642-03359-9_4
21. Holger Blasum, O.H., Tverdyshev, S.: Euro-mils: secure European virtualisation for trustworthy applications in critical domains - formal methods used. www.euromils.eu/downloads/Deliverables/Y2/ 2015-EM-UsedFormalMethods-WhitePaper-October2015.pdf
22. Homeier, P.V.: The HOL-Omega logic. In: Berghofer, S., Nipkow, T., Urban, C., Wenzel, M. (eds.) TPHOLs 2009. LNCS, vol. 5674, pp. 244–259. Springer, Heidelberg (2009). doi:10.1007/978-3-642-03359-9_18
23. Kanav, S., Lammich, P., Popescu, A.: A conference management system with verified document confidentiality. In: Biere, A., Bloem, R. (eds.) CAV 2014. LNCS, vol. 8559, pp. 167–183. Springer, Heidelberg (2014). doi:10.1007/978-3-319-08867-9_11
24. Klein, G., Andronick, J., Elphinstone, K., Heiser, G., Cock, D., Derrin, P., Elkaduwe, D., Engelhardt, K., Kolanski, R., Norrish, M., Sewell, T., Tuch, H., Winwood, S.: seL4: formal verification of an operating-system kernel. Commun. ACM 53(6), 107–115 (2010)
25. Kumar, R., Arthan, R., Myreen, M.O., Owens, S.: HOL with definitions: semantics, soundness, and a verified implementation. In: Klein, G., Gamboa, R. (eds.) ITP 2014. LNCS, vol. 8558, pp. 308–324. Springer, Heidelberg (2014). doi:10.1007/ 978-3-319-08970-6_20
26. Kunčar, O.: Types, abstraction and parametric polymorphism in higher-order logic. Ph.D. thesis, Fakultät für Informatik, Technische Universität München (2016). http://www21.in.tum.de/~kuncar/documents/kuncar-phdthesis.pdf
27. Kunčar, O.: Correctness of Isabelle's cyclicity checker: implementability of overloading in proof assistants. In: CPP, pp. 85–94 (2015)
28. Kunčar, O., Popescu, A.: A Consistent Foundation for Isabelle/HOL - Extended Version. http://www21.in.tum.de/~kuncar/kuncar-popescu-isacons2016.pdf

29. Kunčar, O., Popescu, A.: A consistent foundation for Isabelle/HOL. In: Urban, C., Zhang, X. (eds.) ITP 2015. LNCS, vol. 9236, pp. 234–252. Springer, Heidelberg (2015). doi:10.1007/978-3-319-22102-1_16

30. Kunčar, O., Popescu, A.: From types to sets by local type definitions in higher-order logic. In: Blanchette, J.C., Merz, S. (eds.) ITP 2016. LNCS, vol. 9807, pp. 200–218. Springer, Heidelberg (2016). doi:10.1007/978-3-319-43144-4_13

31. Kunčar, O., Popescu, A.: Comprehending Isabelle/HOL's consistency. Technical report (2017). http://andreipopescu.uk/pdf/compr_IsabelleHOL_cons_TR.pdf

32. Lochbihler, A.: Verifying a compiler for Java threads. In: Gordon, A.D. (ed.) ESOP 2010. LNCS, vol. 6012, pp. 427–447. Springer, Heidelberg (2010). doi:10.1007/978-3-642-11957-6_23

33. Lochbihler, A.: Probabilistic functions and cryptographic oracles in higher order logic. In: Thiemann, P. (ed.) ESOP 2016. LNCS, vol. 9632, pp. 503–531. Springer, Heidelberg (2016). doi:10.1007/978-3-662-49498-1_20

34. Melham, T.F.: The HOL logic extended with quantification over type variables. In: TPHOLs, pp. 3–17 (1992)

35. Nipkow, T., Paulson, L., Wenzel, M.: Isabelle/HOL - A Proof Assistant for Higher-Order Logic. LNCS, vol. 2283. Springer, Heidelberg (2002)

36. Nipkow, T., Klein, G.: Concrete Semantics - With Isabelle/HOL. Springer, Heidelberg (2014)

37. Nipkow, T., Snelting, G.: Type classes and overloading resolution via order-sorted unification. In: Hughes, J. (ed.) FPCA 1991. LNCS, vol. 523, pp. 1–14. Springer, Heidelberg (1991). doi:10.1007/3540543961_1

38. Obua, S.: Checking conservativity of overloaded definitions in higher-order logic. In: Pfenning, F. (ed.) RTA 2006. LNCS, vol. 4098, pp. 212–226. Springer, Heidelberg (2006). doi:10.1007/11805618_16

39. Owre, S., Shankar, N.: The formal semantics of PVS, SRI Technical report, March 1999. http://www.csl.sri.com/papers/csl-97-2/

40. Paulson, L.: Personal communication (2014)

41. Pitts, A.: The HOL logic. In: Introduction to HOL: A Theorem Proving Environment for Higher Order Logic, pp. 191–232 (1993). Gordon and Melham [18]

42. Reynolds, J.C.: Polymorphism is not set-theoretic. In: Kahn, G., MacQueen, D.B., Plotkin, G. (eds.) SDT 1984. LNCS, vol. 173, pp. 145–156. Springer, Heidelberg (1984). doi:10.1007/3-540-13346-1_7

43. Rushby, J.M., Owre, S., Shankar, N.: Subtypes for specifications: predicate subtyping in PVS. IEEE Trans. Softw. Eng. 24(9), 709–720 (1998)

44. Shankar, N., Owre, S., Rushby, J.M.: PVS Tutorial. Computer Science Laboratory, SRI International, Menlo Park (1993)

45. Traytel, D., Popescu, A., Blanchette, J.C.: Foundational, compositional (co)datatypes for higher-order logic: category theory applied to theorem proving. In: LICS, pp. 596–605 (2012)

46. Wadler, P., Blott, S.: How to make ad-hoc polymorphism less ad-hoc. In: POPL (1989)

47. Wenzel, M.: The Isabelle/Isar reference manual (2016). http://isabelle.in.tum.de/doc/isar-ref.pdf

48. Wenzel, M.: Type classes and overloading in higher-order logic. In: Gunter, E.L., Felty, A. (eds.) TPHOLs 1997. LNCS, vol. 1275, pp. 307–322. Springer, Heidelberg (1997). doi:10.1007/BFb0028402

49. Wiedijk, F.: Stateless HOL. In: TYPES, pp. 47–61 (2009)

The Essence of Functional Programming on Semantic Data

Martin Leinberger[1]([⊠]), Ralf Lämmel[2], and Steffen Staab[1,3]

[1] Institute for Web Science and Technologies, University of Koblenz-Landau,
Koblenz, Germany
mleinberger@uni-koblenz.de
[2] The Software Languages Team, University of Koblenz-Landau,
Koblenz, Germany
[3] Web and Internet Science Research Group,
University of Southampton, Southampton, England

Abstract. Semantic data fuels many different applications, but is still lacking proper integration into programming languages. Untyped access is error-prone. Mapping approaches cannot fully capture the conceptualization of semantic data. In this paper, we present λ_{DL}, a typed λ-calculus with constructs for operating on semantic data. This is achieved by the integration of description logics into the λ-calculus for both typing and data access or querying. The language is centered around several key design principles, in particular: (1) the usage of semantic conceptualizations as types, (2) subtype inference for these types, and (3) type-checked query access to the data by both ensuring the satisfiability of queries as well as typing query results precisely. The paper motivates the use of a designated type system for semantic data and it provides the theoretic foundation for the integration of description logics as well as the core formal definition of λ_{DL} including a proof of type safety.

1 Introduction

Semantic data allows for capturing knowledge in a natural manner. Its characteristics include the representation of conceptualizations inside the data and an entity-relation or graph-like description of data. Both, on their own and together, they allow for precisely specifying the knowledge represented within semantic data. A knowledge system manages semantic data and may infer new facts by logic inference. Different use cases are fueled by the semantic-data approach. The knowledge graphs of Google and Microsoft enhance Internet search. Wikidata [38] is an open source knowledge graph that stores structured data for Wikipedia. It consists of one billion statements and contains 1,148,230 different concepts and 2515 relations. The ontology defined by Schema.org[1] provides structure for data. This data is then used in search as well as personal assistants such as Google Now and Cortana. Google stores more than 3 trillion semantic

---

[1] https://schema.org/.

© Springer-Verlag GmbH Germany 2017
H. Yang (Ed.): ESOP 2017, LNCS 10201, pp. 750–776, 2017.
DOI: 10.1007/978-3-662-54434-1_28

statements crawled from the web. In the field of Life Sciences, semantic data was applied in the form of Bio2RDF[2], providing 11 billion triples. Semantic data has also interlinked large, varied data sources, such as provided by Fokus[3] containing more than 200,000 different data sets. These examples demonstrate that semantic data models (e.g., RDF or OWL) are important for representing knowledge in complex use cases. In order to fully exploit the advantages of these data models, it is also necessary to facilitate programmatic access and operating over such data in programs.

As the running example, consider semantic data about music artists formalized in the description logic $ALCOI(D)$. Listing 1 shows that everyone, or rather every object, for which a `recorded` relation that connects the object to another entity of type `Song`, exists is considered to be a `MusicArtist` (Line 2). The object `beatles` is of type `MusicArtist` (Line 4) and `machineGun` is a `Song` (Line 5). The object `hendrix` has recorded the song `machineGun` (Line 6) and was influenced by the object `beatles` (Line 7).

```
1  // Conceptualization
2  ∃recorded.Song ⊑ MusicArtist
3  // Graph data
4  beatles : MusicArtist
5  machineGun : Song
6  (hendrix, machineGun) : recorded
7  (hendrix,beatles) : influencedBy
```

Listing 1. Initial example of semantic data.

The example shows several challenges we need to deal with when working with semantic data in a programming language. (1) Conceptualizations rely on a mixture of nominal (`MusicArtist`) and structural typing ($\exists$`recorded.Song`). (2) It is also not uncommon to have a very general or no conceptualization at all, as exemplified by the `influencedBy` role that expresses that `hendrix` has been influenced by the `beatles`. (3) Additional, implicit statements may be derived by logical reasoning, e.g., in our running example `hendrix : MusicArtist` can be inferred. Another challenge is not illustrated: (4) In real data sources, the sheer size of potential types may become a problem. It is practically infeasible to explicitly convert all 1,148,230 different concepts of Wikidata into types of a programming language.

Integration of data models into programming languages can be achieved in different ways. The three most important are (1) via generic types, (2) via a mapping to the type system of a programming language, or (3) by using a custom type system. A generic approach (1) can represent semantic data using types such as `GraphNode` or `Axiom` (cf. [20]). While this approach can represent anything the data can model, it does not leverage static typing: such generic representations are not error-checked. Mapping approaches (2) such as [22] aim at mapping the data model to the type system of the programming language so

---
[2] http://bio2rdf.org/.
[3] https://www.fokus.fraunhofer.de/en.

that static typing is leveraged. However, the mixing of structural and nominal typing, inferred statements, and a high number of concepts worth mapping are problematic. We therefore propose a third, a novel approach: A type system designed for semantic data (3).

In this paper, we present λ_{DL}, a functional language for working with knowledge systems. λ_{DL} uses concept expressions such as ∃recorded.Song as types. This ensures that every conceptualization can be represented in the language and allows for typing values precisely. It avoids pitfalls of other approaches by forwarding typing and subtyping judgments to the knowledge system, thereby allowing facts to be considered only if required. Lastly, the language contains a simple querying mechanism based on description logics. The querying mechanism allows for checking of satisfiability of queries as well as for typing the query results in the programming language. As a result, λ_{DL} provides a type-safe method of working with semantic data.

To highlight a simple kind of error that type checking can catch, consider a function f that takes ∃influencedBy.⊤ as input. In other words, the functions accepts all entities for which an **influencedBy** relation exists. Using a query-operator that searches for entities in the data, a developer might simply query for music artists because he has seen that **hendrix** has an influence. Applying any value of the result set to the function f can cause runtime errors, as not all music artists have a known influence. Typing in λ_{DL} is precise enough to detect such errors (see Listing 2).

```
1  let f = λ(x:∃influencedBy.⊤) . x.influencedBy in
2      f (head (query MusicArtist))
```

Listing 2. Rejected code—music artist is not a subtype of ∃influencedBy.⊤.

In summary, the main contributions of the paper are as follows:

1. We motivate and describe λ_{DL}, a language containing constructs for working with semantic data. In particular, we provide typing, querying constructs and a typecase. Semantics of these constructs rely on description logics, the theoretical foundations of semantic data.
2. We present a formal proof of type safety for λ_{DL}. We highlight how design decisions in λ_{DL} solve many of the problems that occur when dealing with semantic data and allow for a straightforward proof.

As we extend a standard λ-calculus, large parts of the semantics and proof of type safety are routine. We therefore focus on cases particular to our language. The full rules and complete proof can be found in the technical report[4]. Along with the technical report, we also provide a prototypical implementation to show the feasibility of the presented theories in practice.

Road-Map of the Paper. The remaining paper is organized as follows. In Sect. 2, we introduce description logics as the theoretic foundation of semantic data. In Sect. 3, we illustrate λ_{DL} with an extension of the running example and an

---

[4] https://west.uni-koblenz.de/lambda-dl.

informal view on the calculus. In Sect. 4, we describe the core language and its evaluation rules. In Sect. 5, we describe the type system. In Sect. 6, we provide a proof of type soundness. In Sect. 7, we examine related work. In Sect. 8, we conclude the paper including a discussion of future work.

2   Description Logics

Semantic data is often formalized in the RDF data model or in the more expressive Web Ontology Language (OWL[5]). Formal theories about the latter are grounded in research on description logics. Description logics is a family of logical languages for describing conceptual knowledge and graph data. All description logic languages are sub-languages of first-order predicate logic. They are defined to allow for decidable or even PTIME decision procedures. Their usefulness for modeling semantic data has been shown with such diverse use cases as reasoning on UML class diagrams [6], semantic query optimization on object-oriented database systems [4], or improving database access through abstraction [10].

Syntax and Semantics. Semantic data, also called a knowledge base, comprises of a set of description logics axioms that are composed using a signature $Sig(\mathcal{K})$ and a set of logical and concept operators and comparisons. A signature Sig of a knowledge base $\mathcal{K}$ is a triple $Sig(\mathcal{K}) = (\mathcal{A}, \mathcal{Q}, \mathcal{O})$ where $\mathcal{A}$ is a set of concept names, $\mathcal{Q}$ is a set of role names, and $\mathcal{O}$ is a set of object names. As common in DL research, we use a intuitive interpretation-based semantics. An interpretation $\mathcal{I}$ is a pair consisting of a non-empty universe $\Delta^{\mathcal{I}}$ and an interpretation function $\cdot^{\mathcal{I}}$ that maps each object $a, b \in \mathcal{O}$ to an element of the universe. Furthermore, it assigns each concept name $A \in \mathcal{A}$ a set $A^{\mathcal{I}} \subseteq \Delta^{\mathcal{I}}$ and each role name $Q \in \mathcal{Q}$ to a binary relation $Q^{\mathcal{I}} \subseteq \Delta^{\mathcal{I}} \times \Delta^{\mathcal{I}}$. In our running example, the signature of Listing 1 contains the concepts[6] MusicArtist and Song, the roles recorded and influencedBy as well as the objects beatles, hendrix, and machineGun. An interpretation $\mathcal{I}$ could map objects like hendrix to their real-life counterparts, e.g., the artist Jimi Hendrix. Furthermore, the interpretation of concept MusicArtist might be MusicArtist$^{\mathcal{I}}$ = {hendrix, beatles}, and the interpretation of Song might be Song$^{\mathcal{I}}$ = {machineGun}. The interpretation of the recorded role might be recorded$^{\mathcal{I}}$ = {(hendrix, machineGun)} and influencedBy$^{\mathcal{I}}$ = {(hendrix, beatles)}.

Given these element names, complex expressions, e.g. as highlighted by Listing 1, can be built. For the course of the paper, the specific description logics dialect needed to cover all necessary constructs is *ALCOI*, consisting of the most commonly used *Attributive Language with Complements* plus the addition of nominal concept expressions and inverse role expressions. Table 1 summarizes

---

[5] https://www.w3.org/OWL/.

[6] As common in description logics research, we use "concept C" to refer to both the concept name C and the interpretation of this concept name C^I, unless the distinction between the two is explicitly required. Likewise, we do for role names and object names.

Table 1. Role expressions and associated semantics.

Role expression	Syntax	Semantics
Atomic role	Q	$Q^{\mathcal{I}} \subseteq \Delta^{\mathcal{I}} \times \Delta^{\mathcal{I}}$
Inverse	R^-	$\{(b,a) \in \Delta^{\mathcal{I}} \times \Delta^{\mathcal{I}} | (a,b) \in R^{\mathcal{I}}\}$

Table 2. Concept expressions and associated semantics.

Concept expression	Syntax	Semantics
Nominal concept	$\{a\}$	$\{a^{\mathcal{I}}\}$
Atomic concept	A	$A^{\mathcal{I}} \subseteq \Delta^{\mathcal{I}}$
Top	$\top$	$\Delta^{\mathcal{I}}$
Bottom	$\bot$	$\emptyset$
Negation	$\neg C$	$\Delta^{\mathcal{I}} \setminus C$
Intersection	$C \sqcap D$	$C^{\mathcal{I}} \cap D^{\mathcal{I}}$
Union	$C \sqcup D$	$C^{\mathcal{I}} \cup D^{\mathcal{I}}$
Existential quantification	$\exists R.C$	$\{a^{\mathcal{I}} \in \Delta^{\mathcal{I}} | \exists b^{\mathcal{I}} : (a^{\mathcal{I}}, b^{\mathcal{I}}) \in R^{\mathcal{I}} \wedge b^{\mathcal{I}} \in C^{\mathcal{I}}\}$
Universal quantification	$\forall R.C$	$\{a^{\mathcal{I}} \in \Delta^{\mathcal{I}} | \forall b^{\mathcal{I}} : (a^{\mathcal{I}}, b^{\mathcal{I}}) \in R^{\mathcal{I}} \wedge b^{\mathcal{I}} \in C^{\mathcal{I}}\}$

syntax and semantics of role expressions represented through the metavariable R. A role expression is either an atomic role or the inverse of a role expression.

Concept expressions are composed from other concept expressions and may also include role expressions. Concept expressions, represented through the metavariables C and D, are either atomic concepts, $\top$, $\bot$ or the negation of a concept. Concept expressions can also be composed from intersection or through existential and universal quantification on a role expression. An example of such a concept expression from Listing 1 is the concept ∃recorded.Song that describes the set of objects, which have recorded at least one song. Lastly, it is also possible to define a concept by enumerating its objects. This constitutes a nominal type in description logics and allows the description of sets such as the one only containing hendrix and the beatles through the expression {hendrix} ⊔ {beatles}. Table 2 summarizes the syntax and semantics of concept expressions.

Furthermore, in the context of programming with semantic data, it makes sense to add additional data types such as string or integer. We then arrive at the language *ALCIO(D)*, the language *ALCIO* plus the addition of data types for constructing knowledge bases. In the OWL standard, the use of XSD[7] data types is common. We therefore also include XSD data types wherever it is appropriate. As an example, consider the concept expression ∃artistName.xsd : string describing the set of all objects having an artist name that is a string. As the integration of such smaller, closed set of data types can be achieved via mappings to appropriate types in the programming language, we do not go into details about them in the remainder of the paper.

---

[7] https://www.w3.org/TR/xmlschema-2/.

Table 3. Terminological and assertional axioms.

Name	Syntax	Semantics
Concept inclusion	$C \sqsubseteq D$	$C^{\mathcal{I}} \subseteq D^{\mathcal{I}}$
Concept equality	$C \equiv D$	$C^{\mathcal{I}} = D^{\mathcal{I}}$
Concept assertion	$a : C$	$a^{\mathcal{I}} \in C^{\mathcal{I}}$
Role assertion	$(a, b) : R$	$(a^{\mathcal{I}}, b^{\mathcal{I}}) \in R^{\mathcal{I}}$
Object equivalence	$a \equiv b$	$a^{\mathcal{I}} = b^{\mathcal{I}}$

$$\text{Domain}(R, C) \stackrel{\text{def}}{=} \exists R.\top \sqsubseteq C$$

$$\text{Range(R,C)} \stackrel{\text{def}}{=} \top \sqsubseteq \forall R.C$$

Fig. 1. Syntactical abbreviations for DL.

Given such concept (and datatype) expressions, we may now define semantic statements, also called a knowledge base, as pointed out before. A knowledge base $\mathcal{K}$ is a pair $\mathcal{K} = (\mathcal{T}, \mathcal{A})$ consisting of the set of terminological axioms $\mathcal{T}$, the conceptualization of the data and the set of assertional axioms $\mathcal{A}$, the actual data. Schematically, a knowledge base can express that two concepts are either equivalent or that two concepts are in a subsumptive relationship. In terms of actual data, objects can either express that belong to a certain concept or that they are related to another object via a role. Furthermore, it is possible to axiomatize that two objects are equivalent. Table 3 summarizes syntax and semantics of possible axioms in the knowledge base.

Even weak axiomatizations such as RDFS[8] allow for the definition of domains and ranges of roles used in the ontology. As shown in Fig. 1, Domain and Range definition can be defined as abbreviations of axioms built according to Table 3.

Using our running example, we can now define a more sophisticated knowledge base (Listing 3). We assume everyone who has recorded a song to be a music artist, but not all music artists have recorded one (Line 2). Music artists who have been played at a radio station however must have recorded a song (Lines 3–4). Music groups are a special kind of music artists (Line 5). Every music artist has an artist name, which is always of type xsd:string (Lines 6 and 7). As might happen when semantic data is crawled from the Web, a role like `influenceBy` might not be defined in the schema. Thus, it remains a role that is not restricted by any terminological axiom. The actual data includes descriptions of the `beatles` which are a music group (Line 9), `machineGun` which is a song (Line 10) `coolFm` which is a radio station (Line 11). `machineGun` has been recorded by `hendrix` (Line 12), who has been `influencedBy` the `beatles` (Line 13). Lastly, we know that both, `hendrix` and `beatles` have been played by `coolFm` (Line 14–15). It is not explicitly stated that `hendrix` is a music artist. Furthermore, even though we know that the music group `beatles` has been played at `coolFm`, we do not know any song that they recorded.

---

[8] RDF Schema, one of the weakest forms of terminological axioms.

```
1   // Conceptualization
2   ∃recorded.Song ⊑ MusicArtist
3   MusicArtist ⊓ ∃playedAt.RadioStation ⊑
4       ∃recorded.Song
5   MusicGroup ⊑ MusicArtist
6   MusicArtist ⊑ ∃artistName.⊤
7   Range(artistName, xsd:String)
8   // Graph data
9   beatles : MusicGroup
10  machineGun : Song
11  coolFm : RadioStation
12  (hendrix, machineGun) : recorded
13  (hendrix, beatles) : influencedBy
14  (hendrix, coolFm) : playedAt
15  (beatles, coolFm) : playedAt
16  (hendrix,"Jimmy Hendrix") : artistName
17  (beatles,"The Beatles") : artistName
```

Listing 3. Advanced example of semantic data.

As illustrated by the example, ALCIO(D) is a description logics language which is already rather expressive to describe complex concept and object relationships. As we want to focus on the "essence of programming with semantic data", we refrain from using more powerful languages, such as OWL2DL, as this would distract from the core contributions of this paper without significantly changing its methods.

Inference. In terms of inference, interpretations have to be reconsidered. Axioms built according to Table 3 may or may not be true in a given interpretation. An interpretation I is said to satisfy an axiom F, if its considered to be true in the interpretation. The notation $I \models F$ is used to indicate this. An interpretation I satisfies a set of axioms $\mathcal{F}$, if $\forall F \in \mathcal{F} : I \models F$. An interpretation that satisfies a knowledge base $\mathcal{K} = (\mathcal{T}, \mathcal{A})$, written $I \models \mathcal{K}$ if $I \models \mathcal{T}$ and $I \models \mathcal{A}$, is also called a model. For an axiom to be inferred from the given facts, the axiom needs to be true in all models of the knowledge base (see Definition 1).

Definition 1 (Inference). *Let $\mathcal{K} = (\mathcal{T}, \mathcal{A})$ be a knowledge base, F an axiom and $\mathcal{I}$ the set of all interpretations. F is inferred, written $\mathcal{K} \models F$, if $\forall I \in \mathcal{I} : I \models \mathcal{K}$ then $I \models F$.*

An example of this is the axiom hendrix : MusicArtist. hendrix has recorded a song and must therefore be element of ∃recorded.Song. As ∃recorded.Song ⊑ MusicArtist must be true in all models, hendrix must also be element of MusicArtist. A knowledge system might introduce anonymous objects to fulfill the explicitly given axioms. Take the object beatles as an example. The object is a music artist and has been played in the radio. Therefore, according to lines 3–4 in the example, they must have recorded a song. However, the knowledge system does not know any song recorded by them. It will therefore introduce at least one anonymous object representing this song in order to satisfy the axioms.

Queries. Interaction between the programming language and the knowledge system can be realized via querying. Two basic forms of queries can be distinguished. Queries that check whether an axiom is true have already been introduced in the previous paragraph ($\mathcal{K} \models F$). A more expressive form of querying introduces variables, to which the knowledge system responds with unifications for which the axiom is true. Querying introduces variables, to which the knowledge system responds with unifications for which the axiom is known to be true (see Definition 2).

Definition 2 (Querying with variables). *Let $\mathcal{K}$ be a knowledge base and C a concept expression. The set of all objects a such that $a : C$ is true is then $\{?X | \mathcal{K} \models ?X : C\}$, where $?X$ represents a variable being unified with said objects.*

As an example, consider the query $\mathcal{K} \models ?X : \texttt{MusicArtist}$, the variable $?X$ is unified with all objects that belong to the concept $\texttt{MusicArtist}$. However, this form of query can be problematic as, depending on the knowledge system, an infinite number of unifications might exist. Consider the knowledge base in Listing 4. A person is someone who has a father who is again a person (Line 1). An object $\texttt{someone}$ is defined to be a person (Line 2).

```
1  Person ⊑ ∃hasFather.Person
2  someone : Person
```

Listing 4. Infinitely large knowledge system.

If $\texttt{someone}$ is a person, then he or she must have an father which is a anonymous object and a person himself, again implying that this anonymous object has a father. A query $\mathcal{K} \models ?X : \texttt{Person}$ therefore yields an infinite number of unifications. We therefore use a simple form of so called DL-safe queries (cf. [28]), which restrict unifications to objects defined in the signature (see Definition 3).

Definition 3 (DL-safe queries). *Let $\mathcal{K}$ be a knowledge base, $Sig(\mathcal{K}) = (\mathcal{A}, \mathcal{Q}, \mathcal{O})$ its signature and C a concept expression. The set of all objects for which $a : C$ is true and that are not anonymous can be queried by $\{?X | \mathcal{K} \models ?X : C \wedge ?X \in \mathcal{O}\}$.*

In case of the example shown in Listing 4, only the object $\texttt{someone}$ would be returned, even though anonymous objects are considered for inferencing.

Open World and No Unique Name Assumption. Semantic data employs an open world semantics. Axioms are *true* if they are true in all models of the knowledge base. Likewise, an axiom is *false* if they are false in all models of the knowledge. Contrary to a closed world, axioms that are true in some models, but false in others are not false but rather *unknown*. This allows the modeling of incomplete data without inconsistencies. Furthermore, there is no unique name assumption. Two syntactically different objects might be equivalent. As an example, consider the two objects $\texttt{prince}$ and $\texttt{theArtistFormerlyKnownAsPrince}$. While they are syntactically different, they might be semantically equivalent.

3 λ_{DL} in a Nutshell

Developing applications for knowledge systems, as introduced in the previous section, is difficult and error-prone. λ_{DL} has been created to achieve a type-safe way of programming with such data sources.

3.1   Key Design Principles

Concepts as Types. Type safety can only be achieved if terms are typed precisely. This is only possible if the conceptualizations of semantic data are usable in the programming language. Therefore, concept expressions must be seen as types in the language.

Subtype Inferences. The facts about subsumptive relationships between concepts must be added to the system during the type checking process by forwarding these checks to the knowledge system. This allows for taking inferred statements into account and avoids problems with large number of conceptualizations.

Typing of Queries. To avoid runtime errors, queries must be properly type-checked. Queries can be checked in two ways: First, unsatisfiable queries must be rejected. This means that queries for which no possible A-Box instance can produce a result are detected and treated as an error. Second, usage of queries must be type-safe, meaning that the query result must be properly typed. Queries always return lists in λ_{DL}.

DL-Safe Queries. A knowledge system might introduce anonymous objects to satisfy axioms. In the worst case, this can lead to infinitely large query results. However, very little information can be gained of such objects aside from their existence. As shown in Definition 3, λ_{DL} relies on a simplified form of DL-safe queries. Queries are enforced to be finite by only allowing unifications with known objects, even though this might lead to empty result sets in some cases.

Open-World Querying. When looking at inferencing, axioms may be *true*, *false* or *unknown*. For simplicity, λ_{DL} considers axioms to be true only if the axiom is *true* in all models. In other cases, the axiom is considered false. While this view is close to a developers expectation, it also introduces the side effect that union of two queries such as **query** C and **query** $\neg C$ does not yield all objects. For some objects, it is simply unknown whether they belong to either C or $\neg C$.

3.2   Example Use Case

Consider an application that works on the knowledge system defined in Listing 3. Four necessary functions should be implemented: First, the application should query for all music artists that have recorded a song. Second, the application should provide a mapping from a music artist to the list of their songs. Third, a mapping from a music artist to his artist name must be created. Fourth, the application should display all influences of an artist—therefore a mapping from a music artist to his influences is needed. However, these influences should also be human-readable, meaning that they should also be mapped to their name.

The first requirement is implemented by the querying mechanism in λ_{DL}. The necessary list of music artists that have recorded at least one song can be queried using MusicArtist ⊓ ∃recorded.Song (see Listing 5). Applied to a knowledge system working on the facts in Listing 3, this yields a list containing both hendrix and beatles. This expression is typed by the concept expression used in the querying, assigning a type of (MusicArtist ⊓ ∃recorded.Song) list to the evaluation result.

```
1  query MusicArtist ⊓ ∃recorded.Song
```

Listing 5. Querying for music artists that have recorded a song.

Mapping a member of this list to his or her recorded songs can be done using role projections. The input type for such a mapping function is ∃recorded.Song which is a super type of MusicArtist ⊓ ∃recorded.Song. Listing 6 shows the code for the mapping function. As mentioned before, for the object beatles, the semantic data does not contain any recorded songs, even though such a song must exist. The anonymous object introduced by the knowledge system is removed and an empty list is returned. Yet, the developer knows that an anonymous object must exist and that the knowledge system might know this song at some point in the future—otherwise typing would have rejected the function application.

```
1  let getRecordings = λ(a:∃recorded.Song).
2      a.recorded
```

Listing 6. Mapping to the recordings.

A function mapping a music artist to his name is again built by role projections. As our knowledge systems claims that every music artist has an artist name (Listing 3, line 5), the input type for this function can be the music artist concept. Additionally, the knowledge system states that the returned list of values are all of type string. We can therefore simply take the head of the returned list. Listing 7 shows the code of the mapping function. However, this code also shows a problem λ_{DL} still faces—if the knowledge system would not know the name of an artist, the resulting list would be empty and the code would still produce a runtime error.

```
1  let getArtistName = λ(a:∃artistName.xsd:string).
2      head (a.artistName)
```

Listing 7. Mapping a artist to his name.

The last requirement, mapping a music artist to his influences introduces casting, as music artists are not in a direct subtype relation to influencedBy.⊤. This casting is important, as simply allowing the projection could cause runtime errors if, e.g., used on the object beatles. λ_{DL} provides a typecase for this use case. Listing 8 shows the code for such a mapping from a `MusicArtist` to an influence. In case that the argument of the function is of type `influencedBy.⊤`, the actual mapping function is applied to the value—otherwise, an empty list is returned.

```
1  let getArtistInfluences = λ(artist:MusicArtist).
2    case artist of
3        type ∃influencedBy.⊤ as x -> getInfluences x
4        default nil[∃influencedBy⁻.MusicArtist]
```

Listing 8. Casting a music artist to `influencedBy.⊤`.

The function computing the actual influences can use a projection and then apply a function that converts influences to their human-readable name However, this getting the name of an influence is problematic due to the weak schematic restrictions of the `influencedBy` role. The code must therefore proceed on a case by case basis. If the influence is a music artist, the projection to the human-readable string is known. Otherwise, the influence cannot be converted. Listing 9 shows the complete code for the function.

```
1  let getInfluences = λ(obj:∃influencedBy.⊤).
2    let toName = λ(x:∃influencedBy⁻.⊤).
3      case x of
4        type MusicArtist as y -> getName y
5        default"cannot convert to name"
6    in letrec getNames:(∃influencedBy⁻.⊤ list -> string list) =
7        λ(source:∃influencedBy⁻.⊤ list) .
8          if (null source)
9            then nil[string]
10           else cons (toName (head source)) (getNames (tail source))
11   in
12       getNames obj.influencedBy
```

Listing 9. Mapping influences to their human-readable representations.

4   Core Language

Syntax. Our core language λ_{DL} (Fig. 2) is a simply typed call-by-value λ-calculus. Terms of the language include let-statements, a fixed point operator for recursion, function application and if-then-else expressions. Constructs for lists are included in the language: **cons**, **nil** including a type parameter, **null**, **head** and **tail**. Specific to our language is the querying construct for selecting data in the knowledge system based on a concept expression and projections from an object to a set of objects using role expressions. We use a typecase constructs that provides branch control based on types. It contains an arbitrary number of cases plus a default case. If a branch matches, the object is considered to be of the matched type inside the case itself. It therefore acts as a type-safe casting construct.

$t ::=$ *(terms)*

    let $x = t$ **in** t (let binding)

    | **fix** t (fixed point of t)

    | $t\ t$ (application)

    | **if** t **then** t **else** t (if-then-else)

    | **cons** $t\ t$ (list constructor)

    | **null** t (test for empty list)

    | **head** t (head of a list)

    | **tail** t (tail of a list)

    | **query** C (query)

    | $t.R$ (projection)

    | **case** t **of**   (typecase)

      $\overline{case}$ (typecases)

      default t (default case)

    | $t = t$ (equivalence)

    | x (identifier)

    | v (value)

$v ::=$ *(values)*

    a (object)

    | **nil**$[T]$ (empty list)

    | **cons** $v\ v$ (list constructor)

    | $\lambda(x : T).t$ (abstraction)

    | p (primitive value)

$p ::=$ *(primitive values)*

    true   (true)

    | false   (false)

$case ::= $ **type** C **as** x -> t *(typecase)*

$T ::=$ *(types)*

    C (concept type)

    | $T \to T$ (function type)

    | T list   (list type)

    | Π (primitive types)

$\Pi ::=$ *(primitive types)*

    bool   (boolean)

$\Gamma ::=$ *(context)*

    $\emptyset$ (empty context)

    | $\Gamma, x : T$ (type binding)

Fig. 2. Syntax (terms, values, types) of λ^{DL}.

$$\textbf{letrec } x : T_1 = t_1 \textbf{ in } t_2 \overset{\text{def}}{=} \textbf{let } x = \textbf{ fix } (\lambda x : T_1.t_1) \textbf{ in } t_2$$

Fig. 3. Syntactical abbreviations of λ^{DL}.

We use an overbar notation to represent sequences of syntactical elements. That is, $\overline{a}$ stands for $a_1, a_2, \ldots, a_n$. As DL has no unique name assumption, objects can be syntactically different but semantically equivalent. Therefore, we also included the equality operator in our representation. Values (v) include objects defined in the knowledge base, nil and cons to represent lists, λ-abstractions and primitive values. λ-abstractions indicate the type of their variable. In terms of primitive values, we assume data types such as integers and strings, but omit routine details. To illustrate them, we usually just include booleans in our syntax. Types (T) consist of concept expressions built according to Table 3, type constructors for function and list types and primitive types. Additionally, we use a typing context to store type bindings for λ-abstractions. To simplify recursion, we also define a letrec as an abbreviation of the fixpoint operator (see Fig. 3).

Semantics. The operational semantics is defined using a reduction relation, which extends the standard ones. Reduction of lists and terms not related to

$$\textbf{query } C \rightarrow \sigma(\{?X \mid ?X \in \mathcal{O} \wedge \mathcal{K} \models ?X : C\}) \qquad \text{[E-QUERY]}$$

$$a.R \rightarrow \sigma(\{?X \mid ?X \in \mathcal{O} \wedge \mathcal{K} \models (a, ?X) : R\}) \qquad \text{[E-PROJV]}$$

$$\frac{t_1 \rightarrow t_1'}{t_1.R \rightarrow t_1'.R} \qquad \text{[E-PROJ]}$$

$$\frac{\mathcal{K} \models a \equiv b}{a{=}b \rightarrow \textbf{true}} \qquad \text{[EQ-NOMINAL-TRUE]}$$

$$\frac{\mathcal{K} \not\models a \equiv b}{a{=}b \rightarrow \textbf{false}} \qquad \text{[EQ-NOMINAL-FALSE]}$$

$$p_1{=}p_1 \rightarrow \textbf{true} \qquad \text{[EQ-PRIM-TRUE]}$$

$$\frac{p_1 \neq p_2}{p_1{=}p_2 \rightarrow \textbf{false}} \qquad \text{[EQ-PRIM-FALSE]}$$

$$\frac{t_1 \rightarrow t_1'}{t_1 = t_2 \rightarrow t_1' = t_2} \qquad \text{[E-EQ1]}$$

$$\frac{t_2 \rightarrow t_2'}{v_1 = t_2 \rightarrow v_1 = t_2'} \qquad \text{[E-EQ2]}$$

Fig. 4. Reduction rules related to KB.

the knowledge bears no significant difference from rules as, e.g., defined in [34]. We therefore omit these rules and focus on the constructs specific to λ_{DL} (see Figs. 4 and 5). The full semantics can be found in the technical report.

A term representing a query can be directly evaluated to a list of objects (E-QUERY). Even though lists create an implicit ordering, we chose them over sets as they are the more basic programming language constructs and subsequent processing of query result introduces a ordering anyways. The query reduction rule queries the knowledge system for all $?X$ for which the axiom $\mathcal{K} \models ?X : C$ is true. As λ_{DL} relies on DL-safe queries, only objects actually defined in the signature are allowed. For simplicity's sake, we consider the result to be a list and introduce a σ-operator that takes care of communication between the knowledge system and λ_{DL}. As queries yield sets of objects, this operator essentially works by concatenating every object of the query result into a list. Projections (E-PROJ and E-PROJV) behave similarly. Once the term has been reduced to a object a, the knowledge system is queried for all $?X$ for which $\mathcal{K} \models (a, ?X) : R$. Again, anonymous objects are not considered and the result is converted into a list by the σ-operator.

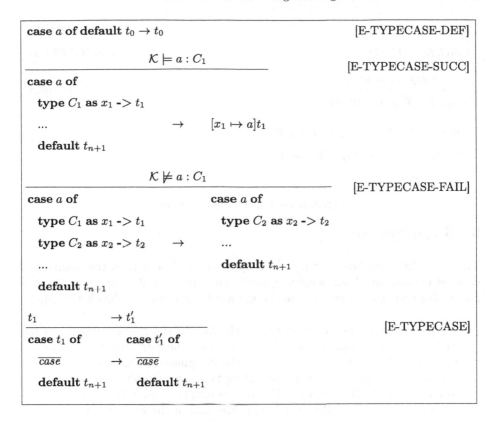

Fig. 5. Reduction rules for typecase terms.

In case of equivalence, both terms must first be reduced to values (E-EQ1 and E-EQ2). Once both terms are values, equivalence can be computed. Equivalence is distinguished into equivalence for objects (EQ-NOMINAL-TRUE and EQ-NOMINAL-FALSE) and equivalence for primitive values (EQ-PRIM-TRUE and EQ-PRIM-FALSE). λ_{DL} considers two primitive values only equivalent if they are syntactically equal. In case of objects, the knowledge base is queried. If the knowledge system can unambiguously prove that a is equivalent to b, the two objects are considered to be equal. Due to the open-world querying, objects are considered to be different if the knowledge system is unsure or if it can actually prove that the two objects are not equivalent. We do not consider equivalence for lists or λ-abstractions.

Evaluation of typecase terms (see Fig. 5) is somewhat special. The terms are first reduced to an object (E-TYPECASE). The semantics can then test the object, case by case, until one of them matches (E-TYPECASE-SUCC and E-TYPECASE-FAIL). For each case the knowledge system is queried whether the axiom $\mathcal{K} \models a : C$ is true. Due to the open-world querying, it might happen that the knowledge system cannot compute such a membership. In this case, the typecase is reduced to its default.

$$lub(\pi_1, \pi_1) \Rightarrow \pi_1 \hspace{4cm} \text{[LUB-PRIMITIVE]}$$

$$lub(C, D) \Rightarrow C \sqcup D \hspace{3.5cm} \text{[LUB-CONCEPT]}$$

$$\frac{lub(S, T) \Rightarrow W}{lub(S \text{ list}, T \text{ list}) \Rightarrow W \text{ list}} \hspace{2cm} \text{[LUB-LIST]}$$

$$\frac{glb(S_1, T_1) \Rightarrow W_1 \hspace{1cm} lub(S_2, T_2) \Rightarrow W_2}{lub(S_1 \rightarrow S_2, T_1 \rightarrow T_2) \Rightarrow W_1 \rightarrow W_2} \hspace{1cm} \text{[LUB-FUNC]}$$

Fig. 6. Least upper bound of types.

5   Type System

The most distinguishing feature of the type system for λ_{DL} is the addition of concept expressions, built according to the rules of Table 2, as types in the language. For constructs unrelated to the knowledge system, this has little impact.

Least Upper Bound and Greatest Lower Bound. In the typing rules for a few constructs, e.g., for typing if-then-else expressions, the least upper bound of two types S and T has to be determined; see the designated judgment *lub* in Fig. 6. In case of a least upper bound for primitive types, we simply assume the types to be equal (LUB-PRIMITIVE). For two concepts C and D, a new concept $C \sqcup D$ is constructed (LUB-CONCEPT). For lists of the form S list and T list, we compute the least upper bound of S and T as a new element type for the list. For two functions, $S_1 \rightarrow S_2$ and $T_1 \rightarrow T_2$, the greatest-lower bound of the argument types S_1 and T_1 ('contra-variance') as well as the least upper bound of S_2 and T_2 ('co-variance') are computed.

The greatest-lower bound of two types S and T is defined analogously. For instance, the greatest lower bound of two concepts C and D is the concept $C \sqcap D$. The complete definition of the designated judgment *glb* can be found in the technical report.

Typing Knowledge-Base Unrelated Constructs. The typing rules for constructs unrelated to the knowledge base are mainly the standard ones as in common simple (applied) lambda calculi. We only include rules here for constructs that need special attention due to λ_{DL}.

The typing rule for if-then-else expressions needs to be adjusted in a manner similar to type systems with subtyping; see the use of the *lub*-judgment in Fig. 7.

$$\frac{\Gamma \vdash t_1 : \text{bool} \hspace{1cm} \Gamma \vdash t_2 : S \hspace{1cm} \Gamma \vdash t_3 : T \hspace{1cm} lub(S, T) \Rightarrow W}{\Gamma \vdash \textbf{if } t_1 \textbf{ then } t_2 \textbf{ else } t_3 : W} \hspace{1cm} \text{[T-IF]}$$

Fig. 7. Typing rules for constructs unrelated to the KB.

$$\Gamma \vdash \textbf{nil}[T_1] \; : T_1 \text{ list} \qquad\qquad\qquad \text{[T-NIL]}$$

$$\frac{\Gamma \vdash t_1 : T_1 \qquad \Gamma \vdash t_2 : T_2 \text{ list} \qquad lub(T_1, T_2) \Rightarrow T_3}{\Gamma \vdash \textbf{cons}\; t_1\; t_2 : T_3 \text{ list}} \qquad \text{[T-CONS]}$$

$$\frac{\Gamma \vdash t_1 : T \text{ list}}{\Gamma \vdash \textbf{null}\; t_1 : \text{Bool}} \qquad \text{[T-NULL]}$$

$$\frac{\Gamma \vdash t_1 : T \text{ list}}{\Gamma \vdash \textbf{head}\; t_1 : T} \qquad \text{[T-HEAD]}$$

$$\frac{\Gamma \vdash t_1 : T \text{ list}}{\Gamma \vdash \textbf{tail}\; t_1 : T \text{ list}} \qquad \text{[T-TAIL]}$$

Fig. 8. Typing rules for lists

$$\frac{\mathcal{K} \not\models C \equiv \bot}{\Gamma \vdash \textbf{query}\; C : C \text{ list}} \qquad \text{[T-QUERY]}$$

$$\frac{\Gamma \vdash t_1 : C}{\Gamma \vdash t_1.R : (\exists R^-.C) \text{ list}} \qquad \text{[T-PROJ]}$$

$$\frac{\Gamma \vdash t_1 : C \qquad \Gamma \vdash t_2 : D \qquad \mathcal{K} \not\models C \sqcap D \equiv \bot}{\Gamma \vdash t_1 = t_2 : \text{bool}} \qquad \text{[T-EQN]}$$

$$\frac{\Gamma \vdash t_1 : \Pi_1 \qquad \Gamma \vdash t_2 : \Pi_1}{\Gamma \vdash t_1 = t_2 : \text{bool}} \qquad \text{[T-EQP]}$$

$$\Gamma \vdash a : \{\, a \,\} \qquad\qquad\qquad \text{[T-OBJECT]}$$

Fig. 9. Typing rules for constructs related to the KB.

Figure 8 shows the typing rules for list-related forms of terms. The empty list constructor has a type parameter (T-NIL). A cons function (T-CONS) is typed using the least upper bound judgment. The remaining typing rules for functions on lists are the standard ones. For instance, a null function takes a well-typed list and returns a boolean value.

Typing of Knowledge-Base Related Constructs. Typing of terms related to the knowledge base is summarized in Fig. 9. Queries (T-QUERY) have a concept C; thus, the result is of type C list. Unsatisfiable queries are rejected by the type system on the grounds of querying the knowledge system on whether C

$$\frac{\begin{array}{ll} \Gamma \vdash t_0 : D & \Gamma, x_i : C_i \vdash t_i : T_i \text{ for } i=1,..n \\ \mathcal{K} \not\models C_i \sqsubseteq C_j \text{ for } i < j & \mathcal{K} \not\models C_i \sqcap D \equiv \bot \text{ for } i = 1,..,n \\ \Gamma \vdash t_{n+1} : T_{n+1} & \overline{lub}(T_1, ..., T_{n+1}) \Rightarrow W \end{array}}{\begin{array}{l} \Gamma \vdash \textbf{case } t_0 \textbf{ of} \\ \quad \textbf{type } C_1 \textbf{ as } x_1 \text{ -> } t_1 \\ \quad ... \qquad\qquad\qquad : \qquad\qquad W \\ \quad \textbf{type } C_n \textbf{ as } x_n \text{ -> } t_n \\ \quad \textbf{default } t_{n+1} \end{array}} \quad \text{[T-TYPECASE]}$$

Fig. 10. Typing rule for typecase

is equivalent to $\bot$. Projections (T-PROJ) require a term of type C and can then be typed by the inverse of the relation used for the projection. This may seem suprising at first sight, but it is actually the most precise type that can be assigned to this term. Range-definitions of roles may be very general (e.g., the range definition for influencedBy in the running example). Equivalence requires two well-typed operands with either a non-empty intersection of the associated concepts (T-EQN) or the same primitive type (T-EQ-P); the result is of type bool. Lastly, single objects can be typed using a nominal concept—a concept expression created through enumerating its members.

Consider the typing rule for typecase in Fig. 10. The term to be dispatched on, t_0, is of type D, i.e., a concept. The types of the non-default cases are determined in a context where the variable x_i for each case is bound to the type C_i of the case. The idea is here that t_0 is casted to C_i type-safely and to be accessed as x_i within t_i. The result type of typecase is the least upper bound of the types of all cases including the default case. (We use $\overline{lub}$ as a shortcut for the repeated application of the lub-judgment.) There are additional premises to ensure meaningful cases. That is, the intersection between all the C_i and D should not be equivalent to $\bot$, as it would then be impossible for a case to ever match. Also, a case should never be subsumed by a preceding case, as cases are tried sequentially.

Subtyping. Subtyping rules are summarized in Fig. 11. We rely on a standard subtyping relation. A term t of type S is also of type T, if $S <: T$ is true (T-SUB). Any type is always a subtype of itself (S-RELF). Subtyping for concepts is handled by the knowledge system. A concept C is a subtype of concept D if the knowledge base can infer that $\mathcal{K} \models C \sqsubseteq D$ (S-CONCEPT). The forwarding of this decision to the knowledge system is important because the knowledge system can take inferred facts into account before making the conclusion. Subtyping for list and function types is reduced to subtyping checks for their associated types. A list S list is a subtype of T list if $S <: T$ is true (S-LIST). Function types are in a subtyping relationship (S-FUNC) if their domains are in

$$\frac{\Gamma \vdash t : S \quad S <: T}{\Gamma \vdash t : T} \qquad \text{[T-SUB]}$$

$$S <: S \qquad \text{[S – RELF]}$$

$$\frac{\mathcal{K} \models C \sqsubseteq D}{C <: D} \qquad \text{[S – CONCEPT]}$$

$$\frac{S <: T}{S \text{ list} <: T \text{ list}} \qquad \text{[S – LIST]}$$

$$\frac{T_1 <: S_1 \quad S_2 <: T_2}{S_1 \to S_2 <: T_1 \to T_2} \qquad \text{[S – FUNC]}$$

Fig. 11. Subtyping rules.

a flipped subtyping relationship ('contra-variance') and their co-domains are in a subtyping relationship ('co-variance').

Algorithmic Type Checking. We mention in passing that the type system is more or less directly suited for algorithmic type checking. That is, the rules are completely syntax driven with the routine exception of the rule for adding subtyping for terms (T-SUB). There is no problematic rule like transitivity of subtyping, as concept subtyping is taken care of by the knowledge systems.

6   Type Soundness

We show the soundness of λ_{DL} by proving that, given the design choices of λ_{DL}, well-typed programs do not get stuck. As with many other languages, there are exceptions to this rule, e.g., down-casting in object-oriented languages, cf. [2]. One may expect that typecases of λ_{DL} may constitute an exception, but the default case avoids this problem. Thus, the only exception concerns lists.

We show that if a program is well-typed, then the only way it can get stuck is by reaching a point where it tries to compute **head nil** or **tail nil**. We proceed in two steps, by showing that a well-typed term is either a value or it can take a step (progress) and by showing that if that term takes a step, the result is also well-typed (preservation). We start by providing some forms about the possible well-typed values (canonical forms) for each type.

Lemma 1 (Canonical Forms Lemma). *Let v be a well-typed value. Then the following observations can be made:*

1. *If v is a value of type C, then v is of the form a.*
2. *If v is a value of type $T_1 \to T_2$, then v is of the form $\lambda(x : S_1).t_2$ with $T_1 <: S_1$.*

3. If v is a value of type C list, then v is either of the form ($\boldsymbol{cons}\ v_1...$) or $\boldsymbol{nil}$.
4. If v is a value of type bool, then either v is either true or false.

Proof. Immediate from the typing relation.

Given Lemma 1, we can show that a well-typed term is either a value or it can take a step. Given the design decisions of λ_{DL}, this is straightforward. In particular, we rely on the interpretation of *unknown* facts as false (open-world querying). We also foresee that no case of typecase fits to the runtime value and thus insist on default case. Further, progress for querying relies on the restriction to DL-safe queries, as this leads to finite query results that can be transformed into lists of objects in one step.

Theorem 1 (Progress). *Let t be a well-typed closed term. If t is not a value, then there exists a term t' such that $t \rightarrow t'$. If $\Gamma \vdash t : T$, then t is either a value, a term containing the forms $\boldsymbol{head\ nil}$ and $\boldsymbol{tail\ nil}$, or there is some t' with $t \rightarrow t'$.*

Proof. By induction on the derivation of $\Gamma \vdash t : T$. As large parts of the proof are standard cases, we focus on the part specific to our language. The remaining standard cases can be found in the technical report.

(**T-QUERY**) $t = $ **query** C, $\Gamma \vdash t : C$ list. Immediate since rule E-QUERY applies (see Fig. 4).

(**T-PROJ**) $t = t_1.R$, $\Gamma \vdash t_1 : C$, $\Gamma \vdash t : (\exists R^-.C)$. By hypothesis, either t_1 is a value or it can take a step. If it can take a step, rule E-PROJ applies. If its a value, then by Lemma 1 $t_1 = a$, therefore rule E-PROJV applies.

(**T-TYPECASE**)
$t = $ **case** t_0 **of**
$\overline{case}$
default t_{n+1}
$\Gamma \vdash t_0 : D$, $\Gamma \vdash t : W$
By hypothesis, t_0 is either a value or it can take a step. If it can take a step, rule E-TYPECASE applies. If its a value, by Lemma 1, $t_0 = a$. If $\overline{case}$ is non-empty, either rules E-TYPECASE-SUCC or E-TYPECASE-FAIL apply. Otherwise, rule E-TYPECASE-DEF applies (see Fig. 5).

(**T-EQN**) $t_1 = t_2$, $\Gamma \vdash t_1 : C$, $\Gamma \vdash t_2 : D$. Either t_1 and t_2 are values or they can take a step. If they can take a step, rules E-EQ1 and E-EQ2 apply. If both are values, by Lemma 1, $t_1 = a$, $t_2 = b$. Therefore, either rule EQ-NOMINAL-TRUE or EQ-NOMINAL-FALSE applies.

(**T-EQP**) $t_1 = t_2$, $\Gamma \vdash t_1 : \Pi_1$, $\Gamma \vdash t_2 : \Pi_1$. Either t_1 and t_2 are values or they can take a step. If they can take a step, rules E-EQ1 and E-EQ2 apply. If both are values, them they are either syntactically equal or not. Therefore either EQ-PRIM-TRUE or EQ-PRIM-FALSE applies.

(**T-OBJ**) Immediate, since $t = a$ is a value.

For proving preservation, two additional Lemmas are required. One, that substitution preserves the type and two, that the least upper bound judgment computes a type that is really a supertype of its two input types.

Lemma 2 (Substitution). *If* $\Gamma, x : S \vdash t : T$ *and* $\Gamma \vdash s : S$, *then* $\Gamma \vdash [x \mapsto s]t : T$.

Proof. Substitution in λ_{DL} does not differ from standard approaches, e.g., as described in [34]. Therefore, the proof is omitted.

Lemma 3 (Least Upper Bound). *Let* S, T *and* W *be types. If* $lub(S, T) \Rightarrow W$, *then* $S <: W$ *and* $T <: W$.

Proof. Four cases must be considered: S and T are either primitives, concepts, lists or functions.

Primitives: Result is immediate since $S = T = W$. By subtyping rule S-REFL, $S <: W$ and $T <: W$ holds.

Concepts: $S = C$, $T = D$, $W = C \sqcup D$. Since $\mathcal{K} \models C \sqsubseteq C \sqcup D$ and $\mathcal{K} \models D \sqsubseteq C \sqcup D$, $S <: W$ and $T <: W$ hold via subtyping rule S-CONCEPT.

Lists: Immediate through the induction hypothesis and subtyping rules for lists.

Functions: Immediate through induction hypothesis and subtyping rules for functions.

Given these lemmas, we can now continue to show that if a term takes a step by the evaluation rules, its type is preserved. A problematic case for preservation are projections. Existing approaches have problems assigning the most specific type to such terms (e.g., projections involving `influencedBy`). They resolve this by using assigning rather general types, which is ultimately not very helpful. The usage of concept expressions as types on the other hand allows for assigning the most specific type.

Theorem 2 (Preservation). *Let* t *be a term and* T *a type. If* $\Gamma \vdash t : T$ *and* $t \to t'$, *then* $\Gamma \vdash t' : T$.

Proof. By induction on the derivation of $\Gamma \vdash t : T$. Again, we examine only the specific cases while the full proof can be found in the technical report.

(T-QUERY) $t = $ **query** C, $\Gamma \vdash t : C$ list. By applying rule E-QUERY, $t' = $ **cons** a_1 .... However, for each a, it is known that $\mathcal{K} \models a : C$, therefore $\{ a \} <: C$ holds for each a and $\{ a_1 \} \sqcup$ ... $<: C$ list.

(T-PROJ) $t = t_1.R$, $\Gamma \vdash t_1 : C$, $\Gamma \vdash t : (\exists R^-.C)$. There are two rules by which t' can be computed: E-PROJ and E-PROJV:

   (1) $t' = t_1'.R$. By induction hypothesis, typing is preserved for t_1. Therefore, by T-PROJ, $t' : (\exists R^-.C)$ list.

   (2) $t' = \sigma(\{?X \mid ?X \in \mathcal{O} \wedge \mathcal{K} \models (a, ?X) : R\}) = $ **cons** b_1 .... For a, it is known that $\mathcal{K} \models a : C$ and for each b is known that $\mathcal{K} \models (a, b) : R$ holds. Therefore, $\mathcal{K} \models b : (\exists R^-.C)$ must hold for each b. Thereby, $\{ b_1 \} \sqcup$ ... $<: (\exists R^-.C)$ and by S-LIST $(\{ b_1 \} \sqcup$ ...$)$ list $<: (\exists R^-.C)$ list

(T-TYPECASE)

$t = \mathbf{case}\ t_0\ \mathbf{of}$
  $\mathbf{type}\ C_1\ \mathbf{as}\ x_1 \mathrel{-}> t_1$
  ...
  $\mathbf{type}\ C_n\ \mathbf{as}\ x_n \mathrel{-}> t_n$
  $\mathbf{default}\ t_{n+1}$
$\Gamma \vdash t_0 : D,\ \Gamma \vdash t_1 : T_1,\ ...,\ \Gamma \vdash t_n : T_n,\ \Gamma \vdash t_{n+1} : T_{n+1},$
$\overline{lub}(T_1, ..., T_{n+1}) \Rightarrow W,\ \Gamma \vdash t : W$
There are four rules by which t' can be computed: E-TYPECASE, E-TYPECASE-SUCC, E-TYPECASE-FAIL and E-TYPECASE-DEF.

(1)
  $t' = \mathbf{case}\ t_0'\ \mathbf{of}$
    $\mathbf{type}\ C_1\ \mathbf{as}\ x_1 \mathrel{-}> t_1$
    ...
    $\mathbf{type}\ C_n\ \mathbf{as}\ x_n \mathrel{-}> t_n$
    $\mathbf{default}\ t_{n+1}$
  By induction hypothesis, $t_1 \to t_1'$ preserves the type. Therefore, by T-TYPECASE, $t' : W$.

(2) $t' = [x_1 \mapsto a]t_1$, $\Gamma \vdash t_1 : T_1$. By Lemma 2, substitution does not change the type of t_1. By Lemma 3, $T_1 <: W$ and therefore by rule T-SUB $t_1 : W$.

(3)
  $t' = \mathbf{case}\ a\ \mathbf{of}$
    $\mathbf{type}\ C_2\ \mathbf{as} x_2 \mathrel{-}> t_2$
    ...
    $\mathbf{type}\ C_n\ \mathbf{as} x_n \mathrel{-}> t_n$
    $\mathbf{default}\ t_{n+1}$
  $\Gamma \vdash t_2 : T_1,\ ...,\ \Gamma \vdash t_n : T_n,\ \Gamma \vdash t_{n+1} : T_{n+1},$
  $\overline{lub}(T_2, ..., T_{n+1}) \Rightarrow W',\ \Gamma \vdash t' : W'$
  The removal of the first case causes T-TYPECASE to assign type $t' : W'$. Removal of T_1 makes W' more specific then W, but $W' <: W$ holds. Therefore by, T-SUB $t' : W$.

(4) $t' = t_{n+1}$ $\Gamma \vdash t_{n+1} : T_{n+1}$. By Lemma 3, $T_{n+1} <: W$, therefore by T-SUB $t' : W$.

(**T-EQN**) $t_1 = t_2$, $\Gamma \vdash t_1 : C$, $\Gamma \vdash t_2 : D$, $\Gamma \vdash t : \mathrm{bool}$. There are 6 different rules by which t' can be computed: E-NOMINAL-TRUE, E-NOMINAL-FALSE, E-PRIM-TRUE, E-PRIM-FALSE, E-EQ1 and E-EQ2.

(1) $t' = \mathrm{true}$. Immediate by rule T-TRUE.
(2) $t' = \mathrm{false}$. Immediate by rule T-FALSE.
(3) $t' = \mathrm{true}$. Immediate by rule T-TRUE.
(4) $t' = \mathrm{false}$. Immediate by rule T-FALSE.
(5) $t' = t_1' = t_2$. By induction hypothesis, $t_1 \to t_1'$. preserves the type. Therefore, by rule T-EQN, $t' : \mathrm{bool}$.
(6) $t' = v_1 = t_2'$. By induction hypothesis, $t_2 \to t_2'$. preserves the type. Therefore, by rule T-EQN, $t' : \mathrm{bool}$.

(**T-EQP**) $t_1 = t_2$, $\Gamma \vdash t_1 : \Pi_1$, $\Gamma \vdash t_2 : \Pi_1$. Same as T-EQN.

(**T-OBJ**) Vacuously fulfilled since $t = a$ is a value.

As a direct consequence of Theorems 1 and 2, a well-typed closed term does not get stuck during evaluation. The only exception concerns the handling of lists, which can get stuck if **head** or **tail** is applied to an empty list. Empty lists might be produced by queries with empty result sets.

To a certain degree, type safety holds even when the knowledge system is evolving. Additional axioms are unproblematic, as DL is a monotonous logic— they do not invalidate existing inferences. Deletion and modification of the actual data (A-Box) is unproblematic unless the program contains statements explicitly referencing the objects under modification. Of course, type safety cannot be guaranteed if schematic parts (T-Box) of the knowledge system are altered.

7   Related Work

λ_{DL} is generally related to the integration of data models into programming languages. We consider four different ways of integrating a data model: by using generic representations, by mappings into the target language, through a pre-processing step before compilation, or through language extensions or custom languages.

Generic Representations. Generic representations offer easy integration into programming languages and have the advantage that they can represent anything the data can model, e.g., generic representations (such as DOM[9]) for XML [39]. This approach has also been applied to semantic data. Representations can vary, however the most popular ones include axiom-based approaches (e.g., [20]), graph-based ones (e.g., [11]) or statement-based ones (e.g., RDF4J[10]). All these approaches are error-prone in so far that code on the generic representations is not type-checked in terms of the involved conceptualizations.

Mappings. Mapping approaches on the other hand use schematic information of the data model to create types in the target language. Type checking can be used thus to check the valid use of the derived types in programs. This approach has been successfully used for SQL [30], XML [3, 26, 39], and more generally [25, 37]. Naturally, mappings have been studied in a semantic data context, too. The focus is on transforming conceptual statements into types of the programming language. Frameworks include ActiveRDF [31], Alibaba[11], Owl2Java [22], Jastor[12], RDFReactor[13], OntologyBeanGenerator[14], Àgogo [33] and LITEQ [27]. However, mapping approaches are problematic for semantic data. For one, the transformation of statements such as those shown in line 1 of Listing 3 is not trivial due to the mixture of nominal and structural typing. Extremely general

---

[9] https://www.w3.org/DOM/.
[10] http://rdf4j.org/.
[11] https://bitbucket.org/openrdf/alibaba.
[12] http://jastor.sourceforge.net/.
[13] http://semanticweb.org/wiki/RDFReactor.
[14] http://protege.cim3.net/cgi-bin/wiki.pl?OntologyBeanGenerator.

information on domains and ranges of roles such as `influencedBy` occurs frequently. The question arises what types support such a role. Frameworks usually resolve the situation by assigning the role to every type they create. In terms of the range of the role, they usually assign the most general available type and leave it to the developer to cast the values to their correct types—this is an error-prone approach. Lastly, all mapping frameworks have problems with the large number of potential types in semantic data sources.

Precompilation. A separate precompilation step, where the source code is statically analyzed and then transformed is another way to solve the problem of integrating data models into programming languages. Especially queries embedded in programming languages can be verified in this manner. This approach has been applied to, for example, SQL queries [40]. The approach has been applied to semantic data in a limited manner [17]—for queries that can be typed with primitive types such as integer.

Language Extensions and Custom Type Systems. The most powerful approaches extend existing languages or create new type systems to accommodate the specific requirements of the data model. Examples for such extensions are concerned with relationships between objects [7] and easy data access to relational and XML data [8]. Another example concerns programming language support for the XML data model specifically in terms of regular expression type, as in the languages CDuce [5] and XDuce [21]. While semantic data can be seen as somewhat semi-structured and is often serialized in XML, the XML-focused approaches do not address the logics-based challenges regarding semantic data. Similarly, polymorphic record types in object oriented database system [29] are oriented towards structural typing. For semantic data, a mixture between nominal and structural typing as combined in DL is required. Refinement types, e.g., as provided by F* [12], are somewhat closer to λ_{DL}. They allow for capturing pre- and postconditions of functions at the type level and to verify correctness statically. By contrast, DL expressions are logic formulae over nominal and structural type properties. They define new types which are subject to DL-based reasoning for type checking. Another related approach is the idea of functional logic programming [18]. However, λ_{DL} emphasizes type-checking on data axiomatized in logic over the integration of the logic programming paradigm into a language.

The typecase construct of λ_{DL} is inspired by other forms of typecase such as those in the context of dynamic typing [1], intensional polymorphism [14], and generic functional programming [24]. None of these forms are concerned with semantic data or description logics.

Language extensions and custom approaches have also been implemented for semantic data. In one approach [32], the C# compiler was extended to allow for OWL and XSD types in C#. The main technical difference to λ_{DL} is that λ_{DL} makes use of the knowledge system for typing and subtyping judgments. λ_{DL} can therefore make use of inferred data and has a strong typing mechanism. There is also work on custom languages that use static type-checking for querying and light scripting in order to avoid runtime errors [13,15]. However, the types are again limited in these cases, as they only consider explicitly given statements. Furthermore, they face the same difficulties as mapping approaches when it comes to schema information—they rely on domain and range specifications for predicates to assign types.

8   Summary and Future Work

In this paper, we have motivated, introduced, and studied λ_{DL}: a typed λ-calculus for semantic data that is built around concept expressions as types as well as queries. We have shown that by using conceptualizations as they are defined in the knowledge system itself, type safety can be achieved. This helps in writing less error-prone programs, even when facing knowledge systems that evolve or lack role definitions. There are these directions for future work.

Fixed-Domain Reasoning. While description logics usually employs an open-world assumption that allows for the modeling of unknown facts, in some cases, a closed-world assumption might be preferable. The semantics as presented in Sect. 2 could be replaced by a fixed-domain semantics, e.g., as described by [16]. Future work aims to examine how expressiveness and the type safety property of λ_{DL} are affected by such a semantics.

Contracts. Type-safety has been achieved in λ_{DL} by some rather harsh restrictions, e.g., by requiring a default case in typecase constructs. Additionally, it is still possible to get stuck, e.g., when taking the head of an empty query response. A possible improvement could be the introduction of contracts, as they are applicable to functional programming [19]. Contracts have been applied already to semantic data [23] while focusing on constraints regarding existence and cardinality. We envision a form of contracts that also covers anonymous objects.

$\lambda_{\mathbf{DL}}$ *and System F.* The presented calculus essentially combines 'simple' types and concepts with subtyping. Parametric polymorphism à la *System F* would be needed to arrive at a sufficiently expressive language for purposes of actual programming. Further, the subtyping aspects of $\lambda_{\mathbf{DL}}$ may also call for a comprehensive integration of description logics and polymorphism with subtyping à la *System $F_{<:}$* [36]. Such an integration is not straightforward.

Modification of the Semantic Data. It is clearly desirable that semantic data can also be modified. A corresponding extension of λ_{DL} is non-trivial because of the aspect that facts are inferred by the knowledge system. Consider the facts about music artists in Listing 3 and let us assume that we want to remove the (implicit) fact that the `beatles` have made a song. The fact cannot be removed directly. Instead, either the fact that the `beatles` are of type `MusicArtist` or the fact that they have been played by `coolFm` must be removed. In order to integrate modification of knowledge systems into λ_{DL}, the theory of knowledge revision based on the AGM theory [35] can be considered and integrated into the language.

Enhanced Querying. Queries, as they are currently implemented, are limited in their expressive power. A simple extension are queries for roles, such as `influencedBy` that result in sets of pairs. Typing such queries is possible via the addition of tuples to λ_{DL}. The addition of query languages closer to the power of SQL is also possible. The biggest challenge in this regard is query subsumption. When such queries are typed in the programming language, subsumption checks are necessary to determine whether a function can be applied to query results. Therefore only query languages with decidable query subsumption are to be considered, e.g., [9].

References

1. Abadi, M., Cardelli, L., Pierce, B.C., Rémy, D.: Dynamic typing in polymorphic languages. J. Funct. Program. **5**(1), 111–130 (1995)
2. Igarashi, A., Pierce, B.C., Wadler, P.: Featherweight Java: a minimal core calculus for Java and GJ. ACM Trans. Program. Lang. Syst. **23**(3), 396–450 (2001)
3. Alagić, S., Bernstein, P.A.: Mapping XSD to OO schemas. In: Norrie, M.C., Grossniklaus, M. (eds.) ICOODB 2009. LNCS, vol. 5936, pp. 149–166. Springer, Heidelberg (2010). doi:10.1007/978-3-642-14681-7_9
4. Beneventano, D., Bergamaschi, S., Sartori, C.: Description logics for semantic query optimization in object-oriented database systems. Trans. Database Syst. **28**(1), 1–50 (2003)
5. Benzaken, V., Castagna, G., Frisch, A.: Cduce: an XML-centric general-purpose language. SIGPLAN Not. **38**(9), 51–63 (2003)
6. Berardi, D., Calvanese, D., De Giacomo, G.: Reasoning on UML class diagrams. Artif. Intell. **168**(1–2), 70–118 (2005)
7. Bierman, G., Wren, A.: First-class relationships in an object-oriented language. In: Black, A.P. (ed.) ECOOP 2005. LNCS, vol. 3586, pp. 262–286. Springer, Heidelberg (2005). doi:10.1007/11531142_12
8. Bierman, G., Meijer, E., Schulte, W.: The essence of data access in Cω. In: Black, A.P. (ed.) ECOOP 2005. LNCS, vol. 3586, pp. 287–311. Springer, Heidelberg (2005). doi:10.1007/11531142_13
9. Bourhis, P., Krötzsch, M., Rudolph, S.: Reasonable highly expressive query languages. In: Proceedings of International Joint Conference on Artificial Intelligence, pp. 2826–2832. AAAI Press (2015)
10. Calvanese, D., De Giacomo, G., Lembo, D., Lenzerini, M., Poggi, A., Rosati, R.: Ontology-based database access. In: Proceedings of Advanced Database Systems, pp. 324–331 (2007)
11. Carroll, J.J., Dickinson, I., Dollin, C., Reynolds, D., Seaborne, A., Wilkinson, K.: Jena: implementing the semantic web recommendations. In: Proceedings of WWW - Alternate Track Papers and Posters, pp. 74–83. ACM (2004)
12. Chen, J., Bharagavan, K., Yang, J., Strub, P.-Y., Nikhil Swamy, C.F.: Secure distributed programming with value-dependent types. Technical report, March 2011
13. Ciobanu, G., Horne, R., Sassone, V.: Descriptive types for linked data resources. In: Voronkov, A., Virbitskaite, I. (eds.) PSI 2014. LNCS, vol. 8974, pp. 1–25. Springer, Heidelberg (2015). doi:10.1007/978-3-662-46823-4_1
14. Crary, K., Weirich, S., Morrisett, J.G.: Intensional polymorphism in type-erasure semantics. J. Funct. Program. **12**(6), 567–600 (2002)

15. Ciobanu, G., Horne, R., Sassone, V.: Minimal type inference for linked data consumers. J. Log. Algebr. Meth. Program. **84**(4), 485–504 (2015)
16. Gaggl, S.A., Rudolph, S., Schweizer, L.: Fixed-domain reasoning for description logics. In: ECAI 2016. Frontiers in Artificial Intelligence and Applications, vol. 285, pp. 819–827. IOS Press (2016)
17. Groppe, S., Neumann, J., Linnemann, V.: SWOBE - embedding the semantic web languages RDF, SPARQL and SPARUL into Java for guaranteeing type safety, for checking the satisfiability of queries and for the determination of query result types. In: Proceedings of Symposium on Applied Computing, pp. 1239–1246. ACM (2009)
18. Hanus, M.: The integration of functions into logic programming: from theory to practice. J. Log. Program. **19** & **20**, 583–628 (1994)
19. Hinze, R., Jeuring, J., Löh, A.: Typed contracts for functional programming. In: Hagiya, M., Wadler, P. (eds.) FLOPS 2006. LNCS, vol. 3945, pp. 208–225. Springer, Heidelberg (2006). doi:10.1007/11737414_15
20. Horridge, M., Bechhofer, S.: The OWL API: a Java API for OWL ontologies. Semant. Web **2**(1), 11–21 (2011)
21. Hosoya, H., Pierce, B.C.: Xduce: a statically typed XML processing language. ACM Trans. Internet Technol. **3**(2), 117–148 (2003)
22. Kalyanpur, A., Pastor, D.J., Battle, S., Padget, J.A.: Automatic mapping of OWL ontologies into Java. In: Proceedings of International Conference on Software Engineering and Knowledge Engineering, pp. 98–103 (2004)
23. Kremen, P., Kouba, Z.: Ontology-driven information system design. IEEE Trans. Syst. Man Cybern. Part C **42**(3), 334–344 (2012)
24. Lämmel, R., Peyton Jones, S.L.: Scrap your boilerplate: a practical design pattern for generic programming. In: Proceedings of TLDI 2003, pp. 26–37. ACM (2003)
25. Lämmel, R., Meijer, E.: Mappings make data processing go 'round. In: Lämmel, R., Saraiva, J., Visser, J. (eds.) GTTSE 2005. LNCS, vol. 4143, pp. 169–218. Springer, Heidelberg (2006). doi:10.1007/11877028_6
26. Lämmel, R., Meijer, E.: Revealing the X/O impedance mismatch. In: Backhouse, R., Gibbons, J., Hinze, R., Jeuring, J. (eds.) SSDGP 2006. LNCS, vol. 4719, pp. 285–367. Springer, Heidelberg (2007). doi:10.1007/978-3-540-76786-2_6
27. Leinberger, M., Scheglmann, S., Lämmel, R., Staab, S., Thimm, M., Viegas, E.: Semantic web application development with LITEQ. In: Mika, P., et al. (eds.) ISWC 2014. LNCS, vol. 8797, pp. 212–227. Springer, Cham (2014). doi:10.1007/978-3-319-11915-1_14
28. Motik, B., Sattler, U., Studer, R.: Query answering for OWL-DL with rules. J. Web Sem. **3**(1), 41–60 (2005)
29. Ohori, A., Buneman, P., Breazu-Tannen, V.: Database programming in machiavelli—a polymorphic language with static type inference. In: Proceedings of International Conference on Management of Data, (SIGMOD 1989), SIGMOD 1989, pp. 46–57. ACM (1989)
30. O'Neil, E.J.: Object/relational mapping 2008: hibernate and the entity data model (EDM). In Proceedings of International Conference on Management of Data, pp. 1351–1356. ACM (2008)
31. Oren, E., Heitmann, B., Decker, S.: Activerdf: embedding semantic web data into object-oriented languages. Web Semant. **6**(3), 191–202 (2008)
32. Paar, A., Vrandečić, D.: Zhi# – OWL aware compilation. In: Antoniou, G., Grobelnik, M., Simperl, E., Parsia, B., Plexousakis, D., Leenheer, P., Pan, J. (eds.) ESWC 2011. LNCS, vol. 6644, pp. 315–329. Springer, Heidelberg (2011). doi:10.1007/978-3-642-21064-8_22

33. Parreiras, F.S., Saathoff, C., Walter, T., Franz, T., Staab, S.: A gogo: automatic generation of ontology APIs. In: ICSC 2009. IEEE (2009)
34. Pierce, B.C.: Types and Programming Languages. The MIT Press, Cambridge (2002)
35. Qi, G., Liu, W., Bell, D.A.: Knowledge base revision in description logics. In: Fisher, M., Hoek, W., Konev, B., Lisitsa, A. (eds.) JELIA 2006. LNCS (LNAI), vol. 4160, pp. 386–398. Springer, Heidelberg (2006). doi:10.1007/11853886_32
36. Reynolds, J.C.: Types, abstraction and parametric polymorphism. In: IFIP Congress, pp. 513–523 (1983)
37. Syme, D., Battocchi, K., Takeda, K., Malayeri, D., Petricek, T.: Themes in information-rich functional programming for internet-scale data sources. In: Proceedings of the DDFP, pp. 1–4. ACM (2013)
38. Vrandecic, D., Krötzsch, M.: Wikidata: a free collaborative knowledgebase. Commun. ACM **57**(10), 78–85 (2014)
39. Wallace, M., Runciman, C.: Haskell and XML: Generic combinators or type-based translation? In: Proceedings of the International Conference on Functional Programming, pp. 148–159. ACM (1999)
40. Wassermann, G., Gould, C., Su, Z., Devanbu, P.T.: Static checking of dynamically generated queries in database applications. ACM Trans. Softw. Eng. Methodol. **16**(4), 14 (2007)

A Classical Sequent Calculus with Dependent Types

Étienne Miquey[1,2]([⊠])

[1] PI.R2 (INRIA), IRIF, Université Paris-Diderot, Paris, France
emiquey@irif.fr
[2] IMERL, Facultad de Ingeniería, Universidad de la República, Montevideo, Uruguay

Abstract. Dependent types are a key feature of type systems, typically used in the context of both richly-typed programming languages and proof assistants. Control operators, which are connected with classical logic along the proof-as-program correspondence, are known to misbehave in the presence of dependent types, unless dependencies are restricted to values. We place ourselves in the context of the sequent calculus which has the ability to smoothly provide control under the form of the μ operator dual to the common `let` operator, as well as to smoothly support abstract machine and continuation-passing style interpretations.

We start from the call-by-value version of the $\lambda\mu\tilde{\mu}$ language and design a minimal language with a value restriction and a type system that includes a list of explicit dependencies and maintains type safety. We then show how to relax the value restriction and introduce delimited continuations to directly prove the consistency by means of a continuation-passing-style translation. Finally, we relate our calculus to a similar system by Lepigre [19], and present a methodology to transfer properties from this system to our own.

Keywords: Dependent types · Sequent calculus · Classical logic · Control operators · Call-by-value · Delimited continuations · Continuation-passing style translation · Value restriction

1 Introduction

1.1 Control Operators and Dependent Types

Originally created to deepen the connection between programming and logic, dependent types are now a key feature of numerous functional programing languages. On the programming side, they allow for the expression of very precise specifications, while on the logical side, they permit definitions of proof terms for axioms like the full axiom of choice. This is the case in Coq or Agda, two of the most actively developed proof assistants, which both provide dependent types. However, both of them rely on a constructive type theory (Coquand and Huet's calculus of constructions for Coq [6], and Martin-Löf's type theory [20] for Agda), and lack classical logic.

© Springer-Verlag GmbH Germany 2017
H. Yang (Ed.): ESOP 2017, LNCS 10201, pp. 777–803, 2017.
DOI: 10.1007/978-3-662-54434-1_29

In 1990, Griffin discovered [12] that the control operator `call/cc` (short for *call with current continuation*) of the Scheme programming language could be typed by Peirce's $((A \to B) \to A) \to A)$, thus extending the formulæ-as-types interpretation [17]. As Peirce's law is known to imply, in an intuitionistic framework, all the other forms of classical reasoning (excluded middle, *reductio ad absurdum*, double negation elimination, etc.), this discovery opened the way for a direct computational interpretation of classical proofs, using control operators and their ability to *backtrack*. Several calculi were born from this idea, such as Parigot's $\lambda\mu$-calculus [22], Barbanera and Berardi's symmetric λ-calculus [3], Krivine's λ_c-calculus [18] or Curien and Herbelin's $\bar\lambda\mu\tilde\mu$-calculus [7].

Nevertheless, dependent types are known to misbehave in the presence of control operators, causing a degeneracy of the domain of discourse [14]. Some restrictions on the dependent types are thus necessary to make them compatible with classical logic. Although dependent types and classical logic have been deeply studied separately, the question to know how to design a system compatible with both features does not have yet a general and definitive answer. Recent works from Herbelin [15] and Lepigre [19] proposed some restrictions on the dependent types to tackle the issue in the case of a proof system in natural deduction, while Blot [5] designed a hybrid realizability model where dependent types are restricted to an intuitionistic fragment. Other works by Ahman et al. [1] or Vákár [23] also studied the interplay of dependent types and different computational effects (*e.g.* divergence, I/O, local references, exceptions).

1.2   Call-By-Value and Value Restriction

In languages enjoying the Church-Rosser property (like the λ-calculus or Coq), the order of evaluation is irrelevant, and any reduction path will ultimately lead to the same value. In particular, the call-by-name and call-by-value evaluation strategies will always give the same result. However, this is no longer the case in presence of side-effects. Indeed, consider the simple case of a function applied to a term producing some side-effects (for instance increasing a reference). In call-by-name, the computation of the argument is delayed to the time of its effective use, while in call-by-value the argument is reduced to a value before performing the application. If, for instance, the function never uses its argument, the call-by-name evaluation will not generate any side-effect, and if it uses it twice, the side-effect will occurs twice (and the reference will have its value increased by two). On the contrary, in both cases the call-by-value evaluation generates the side-effect exactly once (and the reference has its value increased by one).

In this paper, we present a language following the call-by-value reduction strategy, which is as much a design choice as a goal in itself. Indeed, when considering a language with control operators (or other kind of side-effects), soundness often turns out to be subtle to preserve in call-by-value. The first issues in call-by-value in the presence of side-effects were related to references [25] and polymorphism [13]. In both cases, a simple and elegant solution (but way too restrictive in practice [11,19]) to solve the inconsistencies consists in a restriction to values for the problematic cases, restoring then a sound type system. Recently,

Lepigre presented a proof system providing dependent types and a control operator [19], whose consistency is preserved by means of a semantical value restriction defined for terms that behave as values up to observational equivalence. In the present work, we will rather use a syntactic restriction to a fragment of proofs that allows slightly more than values. This restriction is inspired by the negative-elimination-free fragment of Herbelin's dPAω system [15].

1.3 A Sequent Calculus Presentation

The main achievement of this paper is to give a sequent calculus presentation of a call-by-value language with a control operator and dependent types, and to justify its soundness through a continuation-passing style translation. Our calculus is an extension of the $\lambda\mu\tilde{\mu}$-calculus [7] to dependent types. Amongst other motivations, such a calculus is close to an abstract machine, which makes it particularly suitable to define CPS translations or to be an intermediate language for compilation [8]. In particular, the system we develop might be a first step to allow the adaption of the well-understood continuation-passing style translations for ML in order to design a typed compilation of a system with dependent types such as Coq.

However, in addition to the simultaneous presence of control and dependent types, the sequent calculus presentation itself is responsible for another difficulty. As we will see in Sect. 2.5, the usual call-by-value strategy of the $\lambda\mu\tilde{\mu}$-calculus causes subject reduction to fail. The problem can be understood as a desynchronization of the type system with the reduction. It can be solved by the addition of an explicit list of dependencies in the type derivations.

1.4 Delimited Continuations and CPS Translation

Yet, we will show that the compensation within the typing derivations does not completely fix the problem, and in particular that we are unable to derive a continuation-passing style translation. We present a way to solve this issue by introducing delimited continuations, which are used to force the purity needed for dependent types in an otherwise impure language. It also justifies the relaxation of the value restriction and leads to the definition of the negative-elimination-free fragment (Sect. 3). Finally, it permits the design in Sect. 4 of a continuation-passing style translation that preserves dependent types and allows for proving the soundness of our system.

1.5 Contributions of the Paper

Our main contributions in this paper are:

- we soundly combine dependent types and control operators by mean of a syntactic restriction to the negative-elimination-free fragment;
- we give a sequent calculus presentation and solve the type-soundness issues it raises in two different ways;

- our second solution uses delimited continuations to ensure consistency with dependent types and provides us with a CPS translation (carrying dependent types) to a calculus without control operator;
- we relate our system to Lepigre's calculus, which offers an additional way of proving the consistency of our system.

For economy of space, most of our statements only comes with sketches of their proofs, full proofs are given in the appendices of a longer version available at:

https://hal.inria.fr/hal-01375977.

2   A Minimal Classical Language

2.1   A Brief Recap on the $\lambda\mu\tilde{\mu}$-Calculus

We recall here the spirit of the $\lambda\mu\tilde{\mu}$-calculus, for further details and references please refer to the original article [7]. The syntax and reduction rules (parameterized over a sets of proofs $\mathcal{V}$ and a set of contexts $\mathcal{E}$) are given by:

$$
\begin{array}{lll}
\text{Proofs} & p ::= V \mid \mu\alpha.c \\
\text{Values} & V ::= a \mid \lambda a.p & \langle t \| \tilde{\mu}x.c \rangle & \rightarrow & c[x := t] & v \in \mathcal{V} \\
\text{Contexts} & e ::= E \mid \tilde{\mu}a.c & \langle \mu\alpha.c \| e \rangle & \rightarrow & c[\alpha := e] & e \in \mathcal{E} \\
\text{Co-values} & E ::= \alpha \mid p \cdot e & \langle \lambda x.t \| u \cdot e \rangle & \rightarrow & \langle u \| \tilde{\mu}x.\langle t \| e \rangle \rangle \\
\text{Commands} & c ::= \langle p \| e \rangle
\end{array}
$$

where $\tilde{\mu}a.c$ can be read as a context **let** $a = [\ ]$ **in** c. A command can be understood as a state of an abstract machine, representing the evaluation of a proof (the program) against a context (the stack). The μ operator comes from Parigot's $\lambda\mu$-calculus [22], $\mu\alpha$ binds an evaluation context to a context variable α in the same way $\tilde{\mu}a$ binds a proof to some proof variable a.

The $\lambda\mu\tilde{\mu}$-calculus can be seen as a proof-as-program correspondence between sequent calculus and abstract machines. Right introduction rules correspond to typing rules for proofs, while left introduction are seen as typing rules for evaluation contexts. For example, the left introduction rule of implication can be seen as a typing rule for pushing an element q on a stack e leading to the new stack $q \cdot e$:

$$
\frac{\Gamma \vdash q : A \mid \Delta \quad \Gamma \mid e : B \vdash \Delta}{\Gamma \mid q \cdot e : A \rightarrow B \vdash \Delta} \rightarrow_l
$$

Note that this presentation of sequent calculus involves three kinds of judgments one with a focus on the right for programs, one with a focus on the left for contexts and one with no focus for states, as reflected on the CUT typing rule:

$$
\frac{\Gamma \vdash p : A \mid \Delta \quad \Gamma \mid e : A \vdash \Delta}{\langle p \| e \rangle : \Gamma \vdash \Delta} \text{ CUT}
$$

As for the reduction rules, we can see that there is a critical pair if $\mathcal{V}$ and $\mathcal{E}$ are not restricted:

$$c[\alpha := \tilde{\mu}x.c'] \quad \longleftarrow \quad \langle \mu\alpha.c \| \tilde{\mu}x.c' \rangle \quad \longrightarrow \quad c'[x := \mu\alpha.c].$$

The difference between call-by-name and call-by-value can be characterized by how this critical pair is solved, by defining $\mathcal{V}$ and $\mathcal{E}$ such that the two rules do not overlap. The call-by-name evaluation strategy amounts to the case where $\mathcal{V} \triangleq$ *Proofs* and $\mathcal{E} \triangleq$ *Co-values*, while call-by-value corresponds to $\mathcal{V} \triangleq$ *Values* and $\mathcal{E} \triangleq$ *Contexts*. Both strategies can also been characterized through different CPS translations [7, Sect. 8].

2.2   The Language

As shown by Herbelin [14], it is possible to derive inconsistencies from a minimal classical language with dependent types. Intuitively, the incoherence comes from the fact that if p is a classical proof of the form

$$\mathtt{call/cc}_k \, (0, \mathtt{throw} \, k \, (1, \mathtt{refl})) : \Sigma x.x = 1,$$

the seek of a witness by a term wit p is likely to reduce to 0, while the reduction of prf p would have backtracked before giving 1 as a witness and the corresponding certificate. The easiest and usual approach to prevent this is to impose a restriction to values for proofs appearing inside dependent types and operators. In this section we will focus on this solution in the similar minimal framework, and show how it permits to keep the proof system coherent. We shall see further in Sect. 3 how to relax this constraint.

We give here a stratified presentation of dependent types, by syntactically distinguishing *terms*—that represent mathematical objects—from *proof terms*—that represent mathematical proofs[1]. We place ourselves in the framework of the $\lambda\mu\tilde{\mu}$-calculus to which we add:

- a category of *terms* which contain an encoding[2] of the natural numbers,
- proof terms (t, p) to inhabit the strong existential $\exists x^{\mathbb{N}} A$ together with the corresponding projections wit and prf ,
- a proof term refl for the equality of terms and a proof term subst for the convertibility of types over equal terms.

For simplicity reasons, we will only consider terms of type $\mathbb{N}$ throughout this paper. We address the question of extending the domain of terms in Sect. 6.2.

---

[1] This design choice is usually a matter of taste and might seem unusual for some readers. However, it has the advantage of clearly enlighten the different treatments for term and proofs through the CPS in the next sections.

[2] The nature of the representation is irrelevant here as we will not compute over it. We can for instance add one constant for each natural number.

The syntax of the corresponding system, that we call dL, is given by:

$$
\begin{array}{lll}
\text{Terms} & t ::= x \mid n \in \mathbb{N} \mid \mathsf{wit}\, p \\
\text{Proofs} & p ::= V \mid \mu\alpha.c \mid (t,p) \mid \mathsf{prf}\, p \mid \mathsf{subst}\, p\, q \\
\text{Values} & V ::= a \mid \lambda a.p \mid \lambda x.p \mid (t,V) \mid \mathsf{refl} \\
\text{Contexts} & e ::= \alpha \mid p \cdot e \mid t \cdot e \mid \tilde{\mu}a.c \\
\text{Commands} & c ::= \langle p \| e \rangle
\end{array}
$$

The formulas are defined by:

$$
A, B \quad ::= \quad \top \mid \bot \mid t = u \mid \forall x^{\mathbb{N}}.A \mid \exists x^{\mathbb{N}}.A \mid \Pi_{a:A}B.
$$

Note that we included a dependent product $\Pi_{a:A}B$ at the level of proof terms, but that in the case where $a \notin FV(B)$ this amounts to the usual implication $A \to B$.

2.3   Reduction Rules

As explained in the introduction of this section, a backtracking proof might give place to different witnesses and proofs according to the context of reduction, leading to incoherences [14]. On the contrary, the call-by-value evaluation strategy forces a proof to reduce first to a value (thus furnishing a witness) and to share this value amongst all the commands. In particular, this maintains the value restriction along reduction, since only values are substituted.

The reduction rules, defined below (where $t \to t'$ denotes the reduction of terms and $c \rightsquigarrow c'$ the reduction of commands), follow the call-by-value evaluation principle:

$$
\begin{array}{ll}
\langle \mu\alpha.c \| e \rangle \rightsquigarrow c[e/\alpha] & \langle (t,p) \| e \rangle \rightsquigarrow \langle p \| \tilde{\mu}a.\langle (t,a) \| e \rangle \rangle \quad (p \notin V) \\
\langle V \| \tilde{\mu}a.c \rangle \rightsquigarrow c[V/a] & \langle \mathsf{prf}\, (t,V) \| e \rangle \rightsquigarrow \langle V \| e \rangle \\
\langle \lambda a.p \| q \cdot e \rangle \rightsquigarrow \langle q \| \tilde{\mu}a.\langle p \| e \rangle \rangle & \langle \mathsf{subst}\, p\, q \| e \rangle \rightsquigarrow \langle p \| \tilde{\mu}a.\langle \mathsf{subst}\, a\, q \| e \rangle \rangle \quad (p \notin V) \\
\langle \lambda x.p \| t \cdot e \rangle \rightsquigarrow \langle p[t/x] \| e \rangle & \langle \mathsf{subst}\, \mathsf{refl}\, q \| e \rangle \rightsquigarrow \langle q \| e \rangle
\end{array}
$$

$$
\mathsf{wit}\, (t,V) \to t \qquad\qquad t \to t' \Rightarrow c[t] \rightsquigarrow c[t']
$$

In particular one can see that whenever the command is of the shape $\langle C[p] \| e \rangle$ where $C[p]$ is a proof built on top of p which is not a value, it reduces to $\langle p \| \tilde{\mu}a.\langle C[a] \| e \rangle \rangle$, opening the construction to evaluate p[3].

Additionally, we denote by $A \equiv B$ the transitive-symmetric closure of the relation $A \rhd B$, defined as a congruence over term reduction (*i.e.* if $t \to t'$ then $A[t] \rhd A[t']$) and by the rules:

$$
\begin{array}{ll}
0 = 0 \;\rhd\; \top & 0 = S(u) \;\rhd\; \bot \\
S(t) = 0 \;\rhd\; \bot & S(t) = S(u) \;\rhd\; t = u
\end{array}
$$

2.4   Typing Rules

As we previously explained, in this section we will limit ourselves to the simple case where dependent types are restricted to values, to make them compatible

---

[3] The reader might recognize the rule (ς) of Wadler's sequent calculus [24].

with classical logic. But even with this restriction, defining the type system in the most naive way leads to a system in which subject reduction will fail. Having a look at the β-reduction rule gives us an insight of what happens. Let us consider a proof $\lambda a.p : \Pi_{a:A}B$ and a context $q \cdot e : \Pi_{a:A}B$ (with q a value). A typing derivation of the corresponding command is of the form:

$$\dfrac{\dfrac{\Pi_p}{\Gamma, a : A \vdash p : B \mid \Delta} \qquad \dfrac{\Pi_q \qquad \Pi_e}{\Gamma \vdash q : A \mid \Delta \quad \Gamma \mid e : B[q/a] \vdash \Delta}}{\dfrac{\Gamma \vdash \lambda a.p : \Pi_{a:A}B \mid \Delta \qquad \qquad \Gamma \mid q \cdot e : \Pi_{a:A}B \vdash \Delta}{\langle \lambda a.p \| q \cdot e \rangle : \Gamma \vdash \Delta}}$$

while the command will reduce as follows:

$$\langle \lambda a.p \| q \cdot e \rangle \rightsquigarrow \langle q \| \tilde{\mu}a.\langle p \| e \rangle \rangle.$$

On the right side, we see that p, whose type is $B[a]$, is now cut with e which type is $B[q]$. Consequently we are not able to derive a typing judgment for this command any more.

The intuition is that in the full command, a has been linked to q at a previous level of the typing judgment. However, the command is still safe, since the head-reduction imposes that the command $\langle p \| e \rangle$ will not be executed until the substitution of a by q[4] and by then the problem would have been solved. Somehow, this phenomenon can be seen as a desynchronization of the typing process with respect to the computation. The synchronization can be re-established by making explicit a *dependencies list* in the typing rules, allowing this typing derivation:

$$\dfrac{\dfrac{\Pi_q}{\Gamma \vdash q : A \mid \Delta} \quad \dfrac{\dfrac{\Pi_p}{\Gamma, a : A \vdash p : B[a] \mid \Delta} \quad \dfrac{\Pi_e}{\Gamma, a : A \mid e : B[q] \vdash \Delta; \{a|q\}}}{\dfrac{\langle p \| e \rangle : \Gamma, a : A \vdash \Delta; \{a|q\}}{\Gamma \mid \tilde{\mu}a.\langle p \| e \rangle : A \vdash \Delta; \{.|q\}}}}{\langle q \| \tilde{\mu}a.\langle p \| e \rangle \rangle : \Gamma \vdash \Delta; \varepsilon}$$

Formally, we denote by $\mathcal{D}$ the set of proofs we authorize in dependent types, and define it for the moment as the set of values:

$$\mathcal{D} \triangleq V.$$

We define a dependencies list σ as a list binding pairs of proof terms[5]:

$$\sigma ::= \varepsilon \mid \sigma\{p|q\},$$

---

[4] Note that even if we were not restricting ourselves to values, this would still hold: if at some point the command $\langle p \| e \rangle$ is executed, it is necessarily after that q has produced a value to substitute for a.

[5] In practice we will only bind a variable with a proof term, but it is convenient for proofs to consider this slightly more general definition.

$$\dfrac{\Gamma \vdash p : A \mid \Delta;\sigma \quad \Gamma \mid e : A' \vdash \Delta;\sigma\{\cdot|p\} \quad A' \in A_\sigma}{\langle p \| e \rangle : \Gamma \vdash \Delta;\sigma}\ \textsc{Cut}$$

$$\dfrac{(a : A) \in \Gamma}{\Gamma \vdash a : A \mid \Delta;\sigma}\ \text{Ax}_r \qquad \dfrac{(\alpha : A) \in \Delta}{\Gamma \mid \alpha : A \vdash \Delta;\sigma\{\cdot|p\}}\ \text{Ax}_l \qquad \dfrac{c : (\Gamma \vdash \Delta, \alpha : A;\sigma)}{\Gamma \vdash \mu\alpha.c : A \mid \Delta;\sigma}\ \mu$$

$$\dfrac{c : (\Gamma, a : A \vdash \Delta;\sigma\{a|p\})}{\Gamma \mid \tilde{\mu}a.c : A \vdash \Delta;\sigma\{\cdot|p\}}\ \tilde{\mu} \qquad \dfrac{\Gamma, a : A \vdash p : B \mid \Delta;\sigma}{\Gamma \vdash \lambda a.p : \Pi_{a:A}B \mid \Delta;\sigma}\ \to_r$$

$$\dfrac{\Gamma \vdash q : A \mid \Delta;\sigma \quad \Gamma \mid e : B[q/a] \vdash \Delta;\sigma\{\cdot|\dagger\} \quad q \notin \mathcal{D} \to a \notin FV(B)}{\Gamma \mid q \cdot e : \Pi_{a:A}B \vdash \Delta;\sigma\{\cdot|p\}}\ \to_l$$

$$\dfrac{\Gamma, x : \mathbb{N} \vdash p : A \mid \Delta;\sigma}{\Gamma \vdash \lambda x.p : \forall x^{\mathbb{N}}A \mid \Delta;\sigma}\ \forall_l \qquad \dfrac{\Gamma \vdash t : \mathbb{N} \vdash \Delta;\sigma \quad \Gamma \mid e : A[t/x] \vdash \Delta;\sigma\{\cdot|\dagger\}}{\Gamma \mid t \cdot e : \forall x^{\mathbb{N}}A \vdash \Delta;\sigma\{\cdot|p\}}\ \forall_r$$

$$\dfrac{\Gamma \vdash t : \mathbb{N} \mid \Delta;\sigma \quad \Gamma \vdash p : A(t) \mid \Delta;\sigma}{\Gamma \vdash (t,p) : \exists x^{\mathbb{N}}A(x) \mid \Delta;\sigma}\ \exists \qquad \dfrac{\Gamma \vdash p : \exists x^{\mathbb{N}}A(x) \mid \Delta;\sigma \quad p \in \mathcal{D}}{\Gamma \vdash \text{prf}\,p : A(\text{wit}\,p) \mid \Delta;\sigma}\ \text{prf}$$

$$\dfrac{\Gamma \vdash p : A \mid \Delta;\sigma \quad A \equiv B}{\Gamma \vdash p : B \mid \Delta;\sigma}\ \equiv_r \qquad \dfrac{\Gamma \mid e : A \vdash \Delta;\sigma \quad A \equiv B}{\Gamma \mid e : B \vdash \Delta;\sigma}\ \equiv_l$$

$$\dfrac{\Gamma \vdash p : t = u \mid \Delta;\sigma \quad \Gamma \vdash q : B[t/x] \mid \Delta;\sigma}{\Gamma \vdash \text{subst}\,p\,q : B[u/x] \mid \Delta;\sigma}\ \text{subst} \qquad \dfrac{\Gamma \vdash t : T \mid \Delta;\sigma}{\Gamma \vdash \text{refl} : t = t \mid \Delta;\sigma}\ \text{refl}$$

$$\dfrac{}{\Gamma, x : \mathbb{N} \vdash x : \mathbb{N} \mid \Delta;\sigma} \qquad \dfrac{n \in \mathbb{N}}{\Gamma \vdash n : \mathbb{N} \mid \Delta;\sigma} \qquad \dfrac{\Gamma \vdash p : \exists x A(x) \mid \Delta;\sigma \quad p \in \mathcal{D}}{\Gamma \vdash \text{wit}\,p : \mathbb{N} \mid \Delta;\sigma}\ \text{wit}$$

Fig. 1. Typing rules

and we define A_σ as the set of types that can be obtained from A by replacing none or all occurrences of p by q for each binding $\{p|q\}$ in σ such that $q \in \mathcal{D}$:

$$A_\varepsilon \triangleq \{A\} \qquad A_{\sigma\{p|q\}} \triangleq \begin{cases} A_\sigma \cup (A[q/p])_\sigma & \text{if } q \in \mathcal{D} \\ A_\sigma & \text{otherwise.} \end{cases}$$

Furthermore, we introduce the notation $\Gamma \mid e : A \vdash \Delta;\sigma\{\cdot|\dagger\}$ to avoid the definition of a second type of sequent $\Gamma \mid e : A \vdash \Delta;\sigma$ to type contexts when dropping the (open) binding $\{\cdot|p\}$. Alternatively, one can think of $\dagger$ as any proof term not in $\mathcal{D}$, which is the same with respect to the dependencies list. The resulting set of typing rules is given in Fig. 1, where we assume that every variable bound in the typing context is bound only once (proofs and contexts are considered up to α-conversion).

Note that we work with two-sided sequents here to stay as close as possible to the original presentation of the $\lambda\mu\tilde{\mu}$-calculus [7]. In particular it means that a type in Δ might depend on a variable previously introduced in Γ and reciprocally, so that the split into two contexts makes us lose track of the order of introduction of the hypothesis. In the sequel, to be able to properly define a typed CPS translation, we consider that we can unify both contexts into a single one that is coherent with respect to the order in which the hypothesis have been introduced. We denote by $\Gamma \cup \Delta$ this context, where the assumptions of Γ remain unchanged, while the former assumptions $(\alpha : A)$ in Δ are denoted by $(\alpha : A^{\perp\perp})$.

2.5 Subject Reduction

We start by proving a few technical lemmas we will use to prove the subject reduction property. First, we prove that typing derivations allow weakening on the dependencies list. For this purpose, we introduce the notation $\sigma \Rightarrow \sigma'$ to denote that whenever a judgment is derivable with σ as dependencies list, then it is derivable using σ':

$$\sigma \Rightarrow \sigma' \triangleq \forall c \forall \Gamma \forall \Delta (c : (\Gamma \vdash \Delta; \sigma) \Rightarrow c : (\Gamma \vdash \Delta; \sigma')).$$

This clearly implies that the same property holds when typing contexts, *i.e.* if $\sigma \Rightarrow \sigma'$ then σ can be replaced by σ' in any derivation for typing a context.

Lemma 1 (Dependencies weakening). *For any dependencies list σ we have:*

$$1.\ \forall V(\sigma\{V|V\} \Rightarrow \sigma) \qquad\qquad 2.\ \forall \sigma'(\sigma \Rightarrow \sigma\sigma').$$

Proof. The first statement is obvious. The proof of the second is straightforward from the fact that for any p and q, by definition $A_\sigma \subset A_{\sigma\{a|q\}}$. □

As a corollary, we get that † can indeed be replaced by any proof term when typing a context.

Corollary 2. *If $\sigma \Rightarrow \sigma'$, then for any p, e, Γ, Δ:*

$$\Gamma \mid e : A \vdash \Delta; \sigma\{\cdot|\dagger\} \ \Rightarrow\ \Gamma \mid e : A \vdash \Delta; \sigma'\{\cdot|p\}.$$

We can now prove the safety of reduction, using the previous lemmas for rules performing a substitution and the dependencies lists to resolve local inconsistencies for dependent types.

Theorem 3 (Subject reduction). *If c, c' are two commands of dL such that $c : (\Gamma \vdash \Delta)$ and $c \rightsquigarrow c'$, then $c' : (\Gamma \vdash \Delta)$.*

Proof. The proof is done by induction on the typing rules, assuming that for each typing proof, the CONV rules are always pushed down and right as much as possible. To save some space, we sometimes omit the dependencies list when empty, noting $c : \Gamma \vdash \Delta$ instead of $c : \Gamma \vdash \Delta; \varepsilon$, and denote the CONV-rules by

$$\frac{\Gamma \mid e : B \vdash \Delta; \sigma}{\Gamma \mid e : A \vdash \Delta; \sigma} \equiv$$

where the hypothesis $A \equiv B$ is implicit. We only give the key case of β-reduction.

Case $\langle \lambda a.p \| q \cdot e \rangle \rightsquigarrow \langle q \| \tilde{\mu}a.\langle p \| e \rangle \rangle$:

A typing proof for the command on the left is of the form:

$$
\cfrac{
\cfrac{\Pi_p}{\Gamma, a : A \vdash p : B \mid \Delta}
\qquad
\cfrac{\cfrac{\Pi_q \qquad \cfrac{\Pi_e}{\Gamma \mid e : B'[q/a] \vdash \Delta; \{\cdot|\dagger\}}}{\Gamma \mid q \cdot e : \Pi_{a:A'}B' \vdash \Delta; \{\cdot|\lambda a.p\}}}{\Gamma \mid q \cdot e : \Pi_{a:A}B \vdash \Delta; \{\cdot|\lambda a.p\}}
}{\langle \lambda a.p \| q \cdot e \rangle : \Gamma \vdash \Delta} \equiv
$$

If $q \notin \mathcal{D}$, we define $B'_q \triangleq B'$ which is the only type in $B'_{\{a|q\}}$. Otherwise, we define $B'_q \triangleq B'[q/a]$ which is a type in $B'_{\{a|q\}}$. In both cases, we can build the following derivation:

$$
\cfrac{
\cfrac{\Pi_q}{\cfrac{\Gamma \vdash q : A' \mid \Delta}{\Gamma \vdash q : A \mid \Delta} \equiv}
\qquad
\cfrac{
\cfrac{\cfrac{\Pi_p}{\Gamma, a : A \vdash p : B \mid \Delta} \equiv \cfrac{\Pi_e}{\Gamma, a : A \mid e : B'_q \vdash \Delta; \{a|q\}\{\cdot|p\}}}{\Gamma, a : A \vdash p : B' \mid \Delta}
}{
\cfrac{\langle p \| e \rangle : \Gamma, a : A \vdash \Delta; \{a|q\}}{\Gamma \mid \tilde{\mu}a.\langle p \| e \rangle : A \vdash \Delta; \{.|q\}}
}
}{\langle q \| \tilde{\mu}a.\langle p \| e \rangle \rangle : \Gamma \vdash \Delta; \varepsilon}
$$

using Corollary 2 to weaken the dependencies in Π_e. $\qquad\qquad\square$

2.6 Soundness

We sketch here a proof of the soundness of dL with a value restriction. A more interesting proof through a continuation-passing translation is presented in Sect. 4. We first show that typed commands of dL normalize by translation to the simply-typed $\lambda\mu\tilde{\mu}$-calculus with pairs (*i.e.* extended with proofs of the form (p_1, p_2) and contexts of the form $\tilde{\mu}(a_1, a_2).c$). The translation essentially consists of erasing the dependencies in types, turning the dependent products into arrows and the dependent sum into a pair. The erasure procedure is defined by:

$$
\begin{array}{llll}
(\forall x^{\mathbb{N}} A)^* & \triangleq & \mathbb{N}^* \to A^* & \quad \top^* & \triangleq & \mathbb{N}^* \to \mathbb{N}^* \\
(\exists x^{\mathbb{N}} A)^* & \triangleq & \mathbb{N}^* \wedge A^* & \quad \bot^* & \triangleq & \mathbb{N}^* \to \mathbb{N}^* \\
(\Pi_{a:A}B)^* & \triangleq & A^* \to B^* & \quad (t = u)^* & \triangleq & \mathbb{N}^* \to \mathbb{N}^*
\end{array}
$$

and the translation for proofs, terms, contexts and commands is defined by:

$$
\begin{array}{lll}
\langle p \| e \rangle^* \triangleq \langle p^* \| e^* \rangle & x^* \triangleq x & (\lambda a.p)^* \triangleq \lambda a.p^* \\
\alpha^* \triangleq \alpha & n^* \triangleq \bar{n} & (\lambda x.p)^* \triangleq \lambda x.p^* \\
(t \cdot e)^* \triangleq t^* \cdot e^* & (\text{wit }p)^* \triangleq \pi_1(p^*) & (\mu\alpha.c)^* \triangleq \mu\alpha.c^* \\
(q \cdot e)^* \triangleq q^* \cdot e^* & a^* \triangleq a & (\text{prf }p)^* \triangleq \pi_2(p^*) \\
(\tilde{\mu}a.c)^* \triangleq \tilde{\mu}a.c^* & \text{refl}^* \triangleq \lambda x.x & (t, p)^* \triangleq \mu\alpha.\langle p^* \| \tilde{\mu}a.\langle (t^*, a) \| \alpha \rangle \rangle
\end{array}
$$

$$
\begin{array}{l}
(\text{subst } V \, q)^* \triangleq \mu\alpha.\langle q^* \| \alpha \rangle \\
(\text{subst } p \, q)^* \triangleq \mu\alpha.\langle p^* \| \tilde{\mu}_-.\langle \mu\alpha.\langle q^* \| \alpha \rangle \| \alpha \rangle \rangle \qquad\qquad (p \notin V)
\end{array}
$$

where $\pi_i(p) \triangleq \mu\alpha.\langle p \| \tilde{\mu}(a_1, a_2).\langle a_1 \| \alpha \rangle \rangle$. We define $\bar{n}$ as any encoding of the natural numbers with its type $\mathbb{N}^*$, the encoding being irrelevant here.

We can extend the erasure procedure to contexts, and show that it is adequate with respect to the translation of proofs.

Proposition 4. *If $c : \Gamma \vdash \Delta; \sigma$, then $c^* : \Gamma^* \vdash \Delta^*$. The same holds for proofs and contexts.*

We can then deduce the normalization of dL from the normalization of the $\lambda\mu\tilde{\mu}$-calculus, by showing that the translation preserves the normalization in the sense that if c does not normalize, neither does c^*.

Proposition 5. *If $c : (\Gamma \vdash \Delta; \varepsilon)$, then c normalizes.*

Using the normalization, we can finally prove the soundness of the system.

Theorem 6 *(Soundness). For any $p \in dL$, we have $\nvdash p : \bot$.*

Proof. (Sketch) Proof by contradiction, assuming that there is a proof p such that $\vdash p : \bot$, we can form the well-typed command $\langle p \| \star \rangle : (\vdash \star : \bot)$ where $\star$ is any fresh α-variable, and use the normalization to reduce to a command $\langle V \| \star \rangle$. By subject reduction, V would be a value of type $\bot$, which is absurd. $\square$

2.7 Toward a Continuation-Passing Style Translation

The difficulty we encountered while defining our system mostly came from the simultaneous presence of a control operator and dependent types. Removing one of these two ingredients leaves us with a sound system in both cases: without the part necessary for dependent types, our calculus amounts to the usual $\lambda\mu\tilde{\mu}$-calculus. Without control operator, we would obtain an intuitionistic dependent type theory that would be easy to prove sound.

To demonstrate the correctness of our system, we might be tempted to define a translation to a subsystem without dependent types or control operator. We will discuss later in Sect. 5 a solution to handle the dependencies. We will focus here on the possibility of removing the classical part from dL, that is to define a translation that gets rid of the control operator. The use of continuation-passing style translations to address this issue is very common, and it was already studied for the simply-typed $\lambda\mu\tilde{\mu}$-calculus [7]. However, as it is defined to this point, dL is not suitable for the design of a CPS translation.

Indeed, in order to fix the problem of desynchronization of typing with respect to the execution, we have added an explicit dependencies list to the type system of dL. Interestingly, if this solved the problem inside the type system, the very same phenomenon happens when trying to define a CPS-translation carrying the type dependencies.

Let us consider the same case of a command $\langle q \| \tilde{\mu}a.\langle p \| e \rangle \rangle$ with $p : B[a]$ and $e : B[q]$. Its translation is very likely to look like:

$$[\![q]\!]\,[\![\tilde{\mu}a.\langle p \| e \rangle]\!] = [\![q]\!]\,(\lambda a.([\![p]\!])[\![e]\!]),$$

where $\llbracket p \rrbracket$ has type $(B[a] \to \bot) \to \bot$ and $\llbracket e \rrbracket$ type $B[q] \to \bot$, hence the sub-term $\llbracket p \rrbracket \llbracket e \rrbracket$ will be ill-typed. Therefore the fix at the level of typing rules is not satisfactory, and we need to tackle the problem already within the reduction rules.

We follow the idea that the correctness is guaranteed by the head-reduction strategy, preventing $\langle p \| e \rangle$ from reducing before the substitution of a was made. We would like to ensure the same thing happens in the target language (that will also be equipped with a head-reduction strategy), namely that $\llbracket p \rrbracket$ cannot be applied to $\llbracket e \rrbracket$ before $\llbracket q \rrbracket$ has furnished a value to substitute for a. This would correspond informally to the term[6]:

$$(\llbracket q \rrbracket (\lambda a.\llbracket p \rrbracket)) \llbracket e \rrbracket.$$

The first observation is that if q was a classical proof throwing the current continuation away instead of a value (for instance $\mu\alpha.c$ where $\alpha \notin FV(c)$), this would lead to an incorrect term $\llbracket c \rrbracket \llbracket e \rrbracket$. We thus need to restrict at least to proof terms that could not throw the current continuation.

The second observation is that such a term suggests the use of delimited continuations[7] to temporarily encapsulate the evaluation of q when reducing such a command:

$$\langle \lambda a.p \| q \cdot e \rangle \rightsquigarrow \langle \mu\hat{\mathsf{tp}}.\langle q \| \tilde{\mu}a.\langle p \| \hat{\mathsf{tp}} \rangle \rangle \| e \rangle.$$

This command is safe under the guarantee that q will not throw away the continuation $\tilde{\mu}a.\langle p \| \hat{\mathsf{tp}} \rangle$. This will also allow us to restrict the use of the dependencies list to the derivation of judgments involving a delimited continuation, and to fully absorb the potential inconsistency in the type of $\hat{\mathsf{tp}}$.

In Sect. 3, we will extend the language according to this intuition, and see how to design a continuation-passing style translation in Sect. 4.

3   Extension of the system

3.1   Limits of the Value Restriction

In the previous section, we strictly restricted the use of dependent types to proof terms that are values. In particular, even though a proof-term might be computationally equivalent to some value (say $\mu\alpha.\langle V \| \alpha \rangle$ and V for instance), we cannot use it to eliminate a dependent product, which is unsatisfying. We shall then relax this restriction to allow more proof terms within dependent types.

---

[6] We will see in Sect. 4.3 that such a term could be typed by turning the type $A \to \bot$ of the continuation that $\llbracket q \rrbracket$ is waiting for into a (dependent) type $\Pi_{a:A}R[a]$ parameterized by R. This way we could have $\llbracket q \rrbracket : \forall R(\Pi_{a:A}R[a] \to R[q])$ instead of $\llbracket q \rrbracket : ((A \to \bot) \to \bot)$. For $R[a] := (B(a) \to \bot) \to \bot$, the whole term is well-typed. Readers familiar with realizability will also note that such a term is realizable, since it eventually terminates on a correct position $\llbracket p[q/a] \rrbracket \llbracket e \rrbracket$.

[7] We stick here to the presentations of delimited continuations in [2,16], where $\hat{\mathsf{tp}}$ is used to denote the top-level delimiter.

We can follow several intuitions. First, we saw in the previous section that we could actually allow any proof terms as long as its CPS translation uses its continuation and uses it only once. We do not have such a translation yet, but syntactically, these are the proof terms that can be expressed (up to α-conversion) in the $\lambda\mu\tilde{\mu}$-calculus with only one continuation variable $\star$ (see Fig. 2), and which do not contain application[8]. Interestingly, this corresponds exactly to the so-called *negative-elimination-free* (NEF) proofs of Herbelin [15]. To interpret the axiom of dependent choice, he designed a classical proof system with dependent types in natural deduction, in which the dependent types allow the use of NEF proofs.

Second, Lepigre defined in a recent work [19] a classical proof system with dependent types, where the dependencies are restricted to values. However, the type system allows derivations of judgments up to an observational equivalence, and thus any proof computationally equivalent to a value can be used. In particular, any proof in the NEF fragment is observationally equivalent to a value, hence is compatible with the dependencies of Lepigre's calculus.

From now on, we consider $dL_{\hat{\mathfrak{tp}}}$ the system dL of Sect. 2 extended with delimited continuations, and define the fragment of *negative-elimination-free* proof terms (NEF). The syntax of both categories is given by Fig. 2, the proofs in the NEF fragment are considered up to α-conversion for the context variables[9]. The reduction rules, given below, are slightly different from the rules in Sect. 2:

$$\langle \mu\alpha.c \| e \rangle \rightsquigarrow c[e/\alpha]$$

$$\langle \lambda a.p \| q \cdot e \rangle \overset{q \in \text{NEF}}{\rightsquigarrow} \langle \mu\hat{\mathfrak{tp}}.\langle q \| \tilde{\mu}a.\langle p \| \hat{\mathfrak{tp}} \rangle\rangle \| e \rangle$$

$$\langle \lambda a.p \| q \cdot e \rangle \rightsquigarrow \langle q \| \tilde{\mu}a.\langle p \| e \rangle\rangle$$

$$\langle \lambda x.p \| V_t \cdot e \rangle \rightsquigarrow \langle p[V_t/x] \| e \rangle$$

$$\langle V_p \| \tilde{\mu}a.c \rangle \rightsquigarrow c[V_p/a]$$

$$\langle (V_t, p) \| e \rangle \overset{p \notin V}{\rightsquigarrow} \langle p \| \tilde{\mu}a.\langle (V_t, a) \| e \rangle\rangle$$

$$\langle \text{prf}\,(V_t, V_p) \| e \rangle \rightsquigarrow \langle V \| e \rangle$$

$$\langle \text{prf}\,p \| e \rangle \rightsquigarrow \langle \mu\hat{\mathfrak{tp}}.\langle p \| \tilde{\mu}a.\langle \text{prf}\,a \| \hat{\mathfrak{tp}} \rangle\rangle \| e \rangle$$

$$\langle \text{subst}\,p\,q \| e \rangle \overset{p \notin V}{\rightsquigarrow} \langle p \| \tilde{\mu}a.\langle \text{subst}\,a\,q \| e \rangle\rangle$$

$$\langle \text{subst refl}\,q \| e \rangle \rightsquigarrow \langle q \| e \rangle$$

$$\langle \mu\hat{\mathfrak{tp}}.\langle p \| \hat{\mathfrak{tp}} \rangle \| e \rangle \rightsquigarrow \langle p \| e \rangle$$

$$c \rightarrow c' \Rightarrow \langle \mu\hat{\mathfrak{tp}}.c \| e \rangle \rightsquigarrow \langle \mu\hat{\mathfrak{tp}}.c' \| e \rangle$$

$$\text{wit}\,p \rightarrow t \Leftarrow \forall\alpha, \langle p \| \alpha \rangle \rightsquigarrow \langle (t, p') \| \alpha \rangle$$

$$t \rightarrow t' \Rightarrow c[t] \rightsquigarrow c[t']$$

where:

$$V_t ::= x \mid n \qquad V_p ::= a \mid \lambda a.p \mid \lambda x.p \mid (V_t, V_p) \mid \text{refl}.$$

In the case $\langle \lambda a.p \| q \cdot e \rangle$ with $q \in \text{NEF}$ (resp. $\langle \text{prf}\,p \| e \rangle$), a delimited continuation is now produced during the reduction of the proof term q (resp. p) that is involved in dependencies. As terms can now contain proofs which are not values, we enforce the call-by-value reduction by asking proof values to only contain term values. We elude the problem of reducing terms, by defining meta-rules for them[10]. We add standard rules for delimited continuations [2, 16], expressing

---

[8] Indeed, $\lambda a.p$ is a value for any p, hence proofs like $\mu\alpha.\langle \lambda a.p \| q \cdot \alpha \rangle$ can drop the continuation in the end once p becomes the proof in active position.

[9] We actually even consider α-conversion for delimited continuations $\hat{\mathfrak{tp}}$, to be able to insert such terms inside a type, even though it might seem strange it will make sense when proving subject reduction.

[10] Everything works as if when reaching a state where the reduction of a term is needed, we had an extra abstract machine to reduce it. Note that this abstract machine could possibly need another machine itself, etc. We could actually solve this by making

$$
\begin{array}{ll}
\text{Proofs} & p \quad ::= \quad \cdots \mid \mu\hat{\mathrm{tp}}.c_{\hat{\mathrm{tp}}} \\
\text{Delimited} & c_{\hat{\mathrm{tp}}} \quad ::= \quad \langle p_N \| e_{\hat{\mathrm{tp}}} \rangle \mid \langle p \| \hat{\mathrm{tp}} \rangle \\
\text{continuations} & e_{\hat{\mathrm{tp}}} \quad ::= \quad \tilde{\mu}a.c_{\hat{\mathrm{tp}}}
\end{array}
$$

$$
\begin{array}{ll}
\text{NEF} & p_N \quad ::= \quad V \mid (t, p_N) \mid \mu\star.c_N \\
& \qquad \mid \mathsf{prf}\, p_N \mid \mathsf{subst}\, p_N\, q_N \\
& c_N \quad ::= \quad \langle p_N \| e_N \rangle \\
& e_N \quad ::= \quad \star \mid \tilde{\mu}a.c_N
\end{array}
$$

(a) Language

$$
\frac{c : (\Gamma \vdash_d \Delta, \hat{\mathrm{tp}} : A; \varepsilon)}{\Gamma \vdash \mu\hat{\mathrm{tp}}.c : A \mid \Delta} \;\; \hat{\mathrm{tp}}_I
\qquad
\frac{\Gamma \vdash p : A \mid \Delta \quad \Gamma \mid e : A \vdash_d \Delta, \hat{\mathrm{tp}} : B; \sigma\{\cdot | p\}}{\langle p \| e \rangle : \Gamma \vdash_d \Delta, \hat{\mathrm{tp}} : B; \sigma}
$$

$$
\frac{B \in A_\sigma}{\Gamma \mid \hat{\mathrm{tp}} : A \vdash_d \Delta, \hat{\mathrm{tp}} : B; \sigma\{\cdot | p\}} \;\; \hat{\mathrm{tp}}_E
\qquad
\frac{c : (\Gamma, a : A \vdash_d \Delta, \hat{\mathrm{tp}} : B; \sigma\{a | p\})}{\Gamma \mid \tilde{\mu}a.c : A \vdash_d \Delta, \hat{\mathrm{tp}} : B; \sigma\{\cdot | p\}}
$$

(b) Typing rules

Fig. 2. dL$_{\hat{\mathrm{tp}}}$: extension of dL with delimited continuations

the fact that when a proof $\mu\hat{\mathrm{tp}}.c$ is in active position, the current context is temporarily frozen until c is fully reduced.

3.2 Delimiting the Scope of Dependencies

For the typing rules, we can extend the set $\mathcal{D}$ to be the NEF fragment:

$$
\mathcal{D} \triangleq \text{NEF}
$$

and we now distinguish two modes. The regular mode corresponds to a derivation without dependency issues whose typing rules are the same as in Fig. 1 without the dependencies list (we do not recall them to save some space); plus the new rule of introduction of a delimited continuation $\hat{\mathrm{tp}}_I$. The dependent mode is used to type commands and contexts involving $\hat{\mathrm{tp}}$, and we use the sign $\vdash_d$ to denote the sequents. There are three rules: one to type $\hat{\mathrm{tp}}$, which is the only one where we use the dependencies to unify dependencies; one to type context of the form $\tilde{\mu}a.c$ (the rule is the same as the former rule for $\tilde{\mu}a.c$ in Sect. 2); and a last one to type commands $\langle p \| e \rangle$, where we observe that the premise for p is typed in regular mode.

Additionally, we need to extend the congruence to make it compatible with the reduction of NEF proof terms (that can now appear in types), thus we add the rules:

$$
\begin{array}{lll}
A[p] & \rhd \quad A[q] & \text{if } \forall\alpha\,(\langle p \| \alpha \rangle \rightsquigarrow \langle q \| \alpha \rangle) \\
A[\langle q \| \tilde{\mu}a.\langle p \| \star \rangle \rangle] & \rhd \quad A[\langle p[q/a] \| \star \rangle] & \text{with } p, q \in \text{NEF}
\end{array}
$$

the reduction of terms explicit, introducing for instance commands and contexts for terms with the appropriate typing rules. However, this is not necessary from a logical point of view and it would significantly increase the complexity of the proofs, therefore we rather chose to stick to the actual presentation.

Due to the presence of NEF proof terms (which contain a delimited form of control) within types and dependencies lists, we need the following technical lemma to prove subject reduction.

Lemma 7. *For any context Γ, Δ, any type A and any $e, \mu\star.c$:*

$$\langle \mu\star.c\|e\rangle : \Gamma \vdash_d \Delta, \hat{\mathtt{tp}} : B; \varepsilon \quad \Rightarrow \quad c[e/\star] : \Gamma \vdash_d \Delta; \varepsilon.$$

Proof. By definition of the NEF proof terms, $\mu\star.c$ is of the general form $\mu\star.c = \mu\star.\langle p_1\|\tilde\mu a_1.\langle p_2\|\tilde\mu a_2.\langle\ldots\|\tilde\mu a_n.\langle p_n\|\star\rangle\rangle\rangle\rangle$. In the case $n = 2$, proving the lemma essentially amounts to showing that for any variable a and any σ:

$$\{a|\mu\star.c\}\sigma \Rightarrow \{a_1|p_1\}\{a|p_2\}\sigma.$$

$\square$

We can now prove subject reduction for $\mathrm{dL}_{\hat{\mathtt{tp}}}$.

Theorem 8 (Subject reduction). *If c, c' are two commands of $\mathrm{dL}_{\hat{\mathtt{tp}}}$ such that $c : (\Gamma \vdash \Delta)$ and $c \rightsquigarrow c'$, then $c' : (\Gamma \vdash \Delta)$.*

Proof. Actually, the proof is slightly easier than for Theorem 3, because most of the rules do not involve dependencies. We only present one case here, other key cases are proved in the appendix.

Case $\langle \lambda a.p\|q \cdot e\rangle \rightsquigarrow \langle \mu\hat{\mathtt{tp}}.\langle q\|\tilde\mu a.\langle p\|\hat{\mathtt{tp}}\rangle\rangle\|e\rangle$ with $q \in$ NEF:
A typing derivation for the command on the left is of the form:

$$\frac{\dfrac{\Pi_p}{\dfrac{\Gamma, a : A \vdash p : B \mid \Delta}{\Gamma \vdash \lambda a.p : \Pi_{a:A}B \mid \Delta}} \quad \dfrac{\Pi_q \quad \Pi_e}{\dfrac{\Gamma \vdash q : A \mid \Delta \quad \Gamma \mid e : B[q/a] \vdash \Delta}{\Gamma \mid q \cdot e : \Pi_{a:A}B \vdash \Delta}}}{\langle \lambda a.p\|q \cdot e\rangle : \Gamma \vdash \Delta}$$

We can thus build the following derivation for the command on the right:

$$\frac{\dfrac{\Pi_q}{\Gamma \vdash q : A \mid \Delta} \quad \dfrac{\dfrac{\dfrac{\Pi_p}{\Gamma, a : A \vdash p : B[a] \mid \Delta} \quad \dfrac{B[q] \in (B[a])_{\{a|q\}}}{\Gamma \mid \hat{\mathtt{tp}} : B[a] \vdash_d \Delta, \hat{\mathtt{tp}} : B[q]; \{a|q\}\{\cdot|\dagger\}}}{\dfrac{\langle p\|\hat{\mathtt{tp}}\rangle : \Gamma, a : A \vdash_d \Delta, \hat{\mathtt{tp}} : B[q]; \{a|q\}}{\dfrac{\Gamma \mid \tilde\mu a.\langle p\|\hat{\mathtt{tp}}\rangle : A \vdash_d \Delta, \hat{\mathtt{tp}} : B[q]; \{\cdot|q\}}{\langle q\|\tilde\mu a.\langle p\|\hat{\mathtt{tp}}\rangle\rangle : \Gamma \vdash_d \Delta, \hat{\mathtt{tp}} : B[q]; \varepsilon}}}}{\Gamma \vdash \mu\hat{\mathtt{tp}}.\langle q\|\tilde\mu a.\langle p\|\hat{\mathtt{tp}}\rangle\rangle \mid \Delta} \quad \dfrac{\Pi_e}{\Gamma \mid e : B[q/a] \vdash \Delta}}{\langle \mu\hat{\mathtt{tp}}.\langle q\|\tilde\mu a.\langle p\|\hat{\mathtt{tp}}\rangle\rangle\|e\rangle : \Gamma \vdash \Delta}$$

$\square$

We invite the reader to check that interestingly, we could have already taken $\mathcal{D} \triangleq$ NEF in dL and still be able to prove the subject reduction. This shows that the relaxation to the NEF fragment is valid even without delimited continuations.

4   A Continuation-Passing Style Translation

We shall now see how to define a continuation-passing style translation from $dL_{\hat{tp}}$ to an intuitionistic type theory, and use this translation to prove the soundness of $dL_{\hat{tp}}$. Continuation-passing style translations are indeed very useful to embed languages with control operators into purely functional ones [7,12]. From a logical point of view, they generally amount to negative translations that allow to embed classical logic into intuitionistic logic [9]. Yet, we know that removing the control operator (*i.e.* classical logic) of our language leaves us with a sound intuitionistic type theory. We will now see how to design a CPS translation for our language which will allow us to prove its soundness.

4.1   Target Language

We choose the target language an intuitionistic theory in natural deduction that has exactly the same elements as $dL_{\hat{tp}}$ but the control operator: the language makes the difference between terms (of type $\mathbb{N}$) and proofs, it also includes dependent sums and products for type referring to term as well as a dependent product at the level of proofs. As it is common for CPS translations, the evaluation follows a head-reduction strategy. The syntax of the language and its reduction rules are given by Fig. 3.

The type system, presented in Fig. 3, is defined as expected, with the addition of a second-order quantification that we will use in the sequel to refine the type of translations of terms and NEF proofs. As for $dL_{\hat{tp}}$ the type system has a conversion rule, where the relation $A \equiv B$ is the symmetric-transitive closure of $A \triangleright B$, defined once again as the congruence over the reduction $\longrightarrow$ and by the rules:

$$0 = 0 \; \triangleright \; \top \qquad\qquad 0 = S(u) \; \triangleright \; \bot$$
$$S(t) = 0 \; \triangleright \; \bot \qquad\qquad S(t) = S(u) \; \triangleright \; t = u.$$

4.2   Translation of the Terms

We can now define the translation of terms, proofs, contexts and commands. The translation for delimited continuation follows the intuition we presented in Sect. 2.7, and the definition for stacks $t \cdot e$ and $q \cdot e$ (with q NEF) inline the reduction producing a command with a delimited continuation. All the other rules are natural, except for the translation of pairs (t, p) in the NEF case:

$$[\![(t, p)]\!]_p \triangleq \lambda k.([\![t]\!]_t \, (\lambda ur.r \, (\lambda q.k \, (u, q)))) [\![p]\!]_p$$

The natural definition is the one given in the non NEF case, but as we observe in the proof of Lemma 11, this definition is incompatible with the expected type for the translation of NEF proofs. This somehow strange definition corresponds to the intuition that we reduce $[\![t]\!]_t$ within a delimited continuation, in order to guarantee that we will not reduce $[\![p]\!]_p$ before $[\![t]\!]_t$ has returned a value to substitute for u. Indeed, the type of $[\![p]\!]_p$ depends on t, while the continuation

$$t \quad ::= x \mid \bar{n} \mid \mathsf{wit}\, p \qquad (n \in \mathbb{N})$$
$$p \quad ::= a \mid \lambda a.p \mid \lambda x.p \mid p\,q \mid p\,t$$
$$\quad \mid (t,p) \mid \mathsf{prf}\, p \mid \mathsf{refl} \mid \mathsf{subst}\, p\, q$$

$$A, B ::= \top \mid \bot \mid t = u \mid \Pi_{a:A}B$$
$$\quad \mid \forall x^{\mathbb{N}} A \mid \exists x^{\mathbb{N}} A \mid \forall X.A$$

(a) Language and formulas

$$(\lambda x.p)\, t \quad \longrightarrow \quad p[t/x]$$
$$(\lambda a.p)\, q \quad \longrightarrow \quad p[q/a]$$
$$p\, q \quad \longrightarrow \quad p'\, q \qquad (\text{if } p \longrightarrow p')$$
$$k(\mathsf{wit}\,(t,p)) \quad \longrightarrow \quad k\, t$$
$$\mathsf{prf}\,(t,p) \quad \longrightarrow \quad p$$
$$\mathsf{subst}\,\mathsf{refl}\, q \quad \longrightarrow \quad q$$

(b) Reduction rules

$$\frac{}{\Gamma \vdash \bar{n} : \mathbb{N}}\ \mathrm{Ax}_n \qquad \frac{(x : \mathbb{N}) \in \Gamma}{\Gamma \vdash x : \mathbb{N}}\ \mathrm{Ax}_t \qquad \frac{(a : A) \in \Gamma}{\Gamma \vdash a : A}\ \mathrm{Ax}_p$$

$$\frac{\Gamma, a : A \vdash p : B}{\Gamma \vdash \lambda a.p : \Pi_{a:A}B}\ \rightarrow_i \qquad \frac{\Gamma \vdash p : \Pi_{a:A}B \quad \Gamma \vdash q : A}{\Gamma \vdash p\, q : B[q/a]}\ \rightarrow_E \qquad \frac{\Gamma, x : \mathbb{N} \vdash p : A}{\Gamma \vdash \lambda x.p : \forall x^{\mathbb{N}} A}\ \forall_i$$

$$\frac{\Gamma \vdash p : \forall x^{\mathbb{N}} A \quad \Gamma \vdash t : \mathbb{N}}{\Gamma \vdash p\, t : A[t/x]}\ \forall_e \qquad \frac{\Gamma \vdash p : A \quad X \notin FV(\Gamma)}{\Gamma \vdash p : \forall X.A}\ \forall_I \qquad \frac{\Gamma \vdash p : \forall X.A}{\Gamma \vdash p : A[P/X]}\ \forall_E$$

$$\frac{\Gamma \vdash t : \mathbb{N} \quad \Gamma \vdash p : A[u/x]}{\Gamma \vdash (t,p) : \exists x^{\mathbb{N}} A}\ \exists_i \qquad \frac{\Gamma \vdash p : \exists x^{\mathbb{N}} A}{\Gamma \vdash \mathsf{prf}\, p : A(\mathsf{wit}\, p)}\ \mathrm{prf} \qquad \frac{\Gamma \vdash p : \exists x^{\mathbb{N}} A}{\Gamma \vdash \mathsf{wit}\, p : \mathbb{N}}\ \mathrm{wit}$$

$$\frac{}{\Gamma \vdash \mathsf{refl} : x = x}\ \mathrm{refl} \qquad \frac{\Gamma \vdash q : t = u \quad \Gamma \vdash q : A[t]}{\Gamma \vdash \mathsf{subst}\, p\, q : A[u]}\ \mathrm{subst} \qquad \frac{\Gamma \vdash p : A \quad A \equiv B}{\Gamma \vdash p : B}\ \equiv$$

(c) Type system

Fig. 3. Target language

$$[\![x]\!]_t \quad \triangleq \lambda k.k\, x \qquad\qquad\qquad\qquad [\![n]\!]_t \quad \triangleq \lambda k.k\, \bar{n}$$
$$[\![\mathsf{wit}\, p]\!]_t \quad \triangleq \lambda k.[\![p]\!]_p\, (\lambda q.k\,(\mathsf{wit}\, q))$$

$$[\![a]\!]_p \quad \triangleq \lambda k.k\, a \qquad\qquad\qquad\qquad [\![\mathsf{refl}]\!]_p \quad \triangleq \lambda k.k\, \mathsf{refl}$$
$$[\![\lambda a.p]\!]_p \quad \triangleq \lambda k.k\,(\lambda a.[\![p]\!]_p) \qquad\qquad\qquad [\![\lambda a.p]\!]_p \quad \triangleq \lambda k.k\,(\lambda a.[\![p]\!]_p)$$
$$[\![\mu \alpha.c]\!]_p \quad \triangleq \lambda k.[\![c]\!]_c[k/\alpha] \qquad\qquad\qquad [\![\mu \hat{\mathsf{tp}}.c]\!]_p \quad \triangleq \lambda k.[\![c]\!]_{\hat{\mathsf{tp}}} k$$
$$[\![\mathsf{prf}\, p]\!]_p \quad \triangleq \lambda k.([\![p]\!]_p\,(\lambda q k'.k'\,(\mathsf{prf}\, q)))\, k$$
$$[\![(t,p)]\!]_p \quad \triangleq \lambda k.([\![t]\!]_t\,(\lambda u r.r\,(\lambda q.k\,(u,q))))\,[\![p]\!]_p \qquad\qquad (p \in \mathrm{NEF})$$
$$[\![(t,p)]\!]_p \quad \triangleq \lambda k.[\![t]\!]_t\,(\lambda u.[\![p]\!]_p\,\lambda q.k\,(u,q)) \qquad\qquad\qquad (p \notin \mathrm{NEF})$$
$$[\![\mathsf{subst}\, p\, q]\!]_p \quad \triangleq \lambda k.[\![p]\!]_p\,(\lambda p'.[\![q]\!]_p(\lambda q'.k\,(\mathsf{subst}\, p'\, q')))$$

$$[\![\alpha]\!]_e \quad \triangleq \lambda p.\alpha\, p \qquad\qquad\qquad\qquad [\![\tilde{\mu} a.c]\!]_e \quad \triangleq \lambda a.[\![c]\!]_c$$
$$[\![t \cdot e]\!]_e \quad \triangleq \lambda p.([\![t]\!]_t\,(\lambda v.p\, v))\,[\![e]\!]_e$$
$$[\![q_N \cdot e]\!]_e \quad \triangleq \lambda p.([\![q_N]\!]_p\,(\lambda v.p\, v))\,[\![e]\!]_e \qquad\qquad\qquad (q_N \in \mathrm{NEF})$$
$$[\![q \cdot e]\!]_e \quad \triangleq \lambda p.[\![q]\!]_p\,(\lambda v.p\, v\,[\![e]\!]_e) \qquad\qquad\qquad (q \notin \mathrm{NEF})$$

$$[\![\langle p \| e \rangle]\!]_c \quad \triangleq [\![e]\!]_e\,[\![p]\!]_p \qquad\qquad\qquad\qquad [\![\langle p \| \hat{\mathsf{tp}} \rangle]\!]_{\hat{\mathsf{tp}}} \quad \triangleq [\![p]\!]_p$$
$$[\![\langle p \| e \rangle]\!]_{\hat{\mathsf{tp}}} \quad \triangleq [\![p]\!]_p\,[\![e]\!]_{e_{\hat{\mathsf{tp}}}} \qquad (e \neq \hat{\mathsf{tp}}) \qquad\qquad [\![\tilde{\mu} a.c]\!]_{e_{\hat{\mathsf{tp}}}} \quad \triangleq \lambda a.[\![c]\!]_{\hat{\mathsf{tp}}}$$

Fig. 4. Continuation-passing style translation

$(\lambda q.k\,(u,q))$ depends on u, but both become compatible once u is substituted by the value return by $[\![t]\!]_t$. The complete translation is given in Fig. 4.

Before defining the translation of types, we first state a lemma expressing the fact that the translations of terms and NEF proof terms use the continuation they are given once and only once. In particular, it makes them compatible with delimited continuations and a parametric return type. This will allow us to refine the type of their translation.

Lemma 9. *The translation satisfies the following properties:*

1. *For any term t in $dL_{\hat{\mathbb{p}}}$, there exists a term t^+ such that for any k we have $[\![t]\!]_t\,k =_\beta k\,t^+$.*
2. *For any NEF proof term p, there exists a proof p^+ such that for any k we have $[\![p]\!]_p\,k =_\beta k\,p^+$.*

Proof. Straightforward mutual induction on the translation, adding similar induction hypothesis for NEF contexts and commands. The terms t^+ and proofs p^+ are given in Fig. 5. We detail the case (t, p) with $p \in$ NEF to give an insight of the proof.

$$
\begin{aligned}
[\![(t,p)]\!]_p\,k &=_\beta ([\![t]\!]_t\,(\lambda u r.r\,(\lambda q.k\,(u,q))))\,[\![p]\!]_p &&\text{(by def.)}\\
&=_\beta ((\lambda u r.r\,(\lambda q.k\,(u,q)))\,t^+)\,[\![p]\!]_p &&\text{(by induction)}\\
&=_\beta [\![p]\!]_p\,(\lambda q.k\,(t^+,q))\\
&=_\beta (\lambda q.k\,(t^+,q))\,p^+ &&\text{(by induction)}\\
&=_\beta k\,(t^+,p^+)
\end{aligned}
$$

$\square$

$$
\begin{array}{lll}
x^+ \triangleq x & (\lambda a.p)^+ \triangleq \lambda a.[\![p]\!]_p & (\mu\star.c)^+ \triangleq c^+\\
n^+ \triangleq \bar{n} & (\lambda x.p)^+ \triangleq \lambda x.[\![p]\!]_p & (\mu\hat{\mathbb{p}}.c)^+ \triangleq c^+\\
(\text{wit}\,p)^+ \triangleq \text{wit}\,p^+ & (t,p)^+ \triangleq (t^+,p^+) & (\langle p\|\star\rangle)^+ \triangleq p^+\\
a^+ \triangleq a & (\text{prf}\,p)^+ \triangleq \text{prf}\,p^+ & (\langle p\|\hat{\mathbb{p}}\rangle)^+ \triangleq p^+\\
\text{refl}^+ \triangleq \text{refl} & (\text{subst}\,p\,q)^+ \triangleq \text{subst}\,p^+\,q^+ & (\langle p\|\tilde{\mu}a.c_{\hat{\mathbb{p}}}\rangle)^+ \triangleq c^+[p^+/a]
\end{array}
$$

Fig. 5. Linearity of the translation for NEF proofs

Moreover, we easily verify by induction on the reduction rules for $\rightsquigarrow$ that the translation preserves the reduction:

Proposition 10 (Preservation of reduction). *Let c, c' be two commands of $dL_{\hat{\mathbb{p}}}$. If $c \rightsquigarrow c'$, then $[\![c]\!]_c =_\beta [\![c']\!]_c$*

We could actually prove a finer result to show that any reduction step in $dL_{\hat{\mathbb{p}}}$ is responsible for at least one step of reduction through the translation, and use the preservation of typing (Proposition 12) together with the normalization of the target language to prove the normalization of $dL_{\hat{\mathbb{p}}}$ for typed proof terms.

Claim 1 *If $c : \Gamma \vdash \Delta$, then c normalizes.*

4.3 Translation of Types

We can now define the translation of types, in order to show further that the translation $[\![p]\!]_p$ of a proof p of type A is of type $[\![A]\!]^*$, where $[\![A]\!]^*$ is the double-negation of a type $[\![A]\!]^+$ that depends on the structure of A. Thanks to the restriction of dependent types to NEF proof terms, we can interpret a dependency in p (resp. t) in $dL_{\hat{\mathfrak{tp}}}$ by a dependency in p^+ (resp. t^+) in the target language. Lemma 9 indeed guarantees that the translation of a NEF proof p will eventually return p^+ to the continuation it is applied to. The translation is defined by:

$$
\begin{aligned}
[\![A]\!]^* &\triangleq ([\![A]\!]^+ \to \bot) \to \bot & \qquad [\![t = u]\!]^+ &\triangleq t^+ = u^+ \\
[\![\forall x^{\mathbb{N}}.A]\!]^+ &\triangleq \forall x^{T^+}.[\![A]\!]^* & \qquad [\![\top]\!]^+ &\triangleq \top \\
[\![\exists x^{\mathbb{N}}.A]\!]^+ &\triangleq \exists x^{T^+}.[\![A]\!]^+ & \qquad [\![\bot]\!]^+ &\triangleq \bot \\
[\![\Pi_{a:A}B]\!]^+ &\triangleq \Pi_{a:[\![A]\!]^+}[\![B]\!]^* & \qquad \mathbb{N}^+ &\triangleq \mathbb{N}
\end{aligned}
$$

Observe that types depending on a term of type T are translated to types depending on a term of the same type T, because terms can only be of type $\mathbb{N}$. As we shall discuss in Sect. 6.2, this will no longer be the case when extending the domain of terms. We naturally extend the translation for types to the translation of contexts, where we consider unified contexts of the form $\Gamma \cup \Delta$:

$$
\begin{aligned}
[\![\Gamma, a : A]\!]^+ &\triangleq [\![\Gamma]\!]^+, a : [\![A]\!]^+ \\
[\![\Gamma, x : \mathbb{N}]\!]^+ &\triangleq [\![\Gamma]\!]^+, x : T^+ \\
[\![\Gamma, \alpha : A^{\perp\!\perp}]\!]^+ &\triangleq [\![\Gamma]\!]^+, \alpha : [\![A]\!]^+ \to \bot.
\end{aligned}
$$

As explained informally in Sect. 2.7 and stated by Lemma 9, the translation of a NEF proof term p of type A uses its continuation linearly. In particular, this allows us to refine its type to make it parametric in the return type of the continuation. From a logical point of view, it amounts to replace the double-negation $(A \to \bot) \to \bot$ by Friedman's translation [10]: $\forall R.(A \to R) \to R$. Moreover, we can even make the return type of the continuation dependent on its argument $\Pi_{a:A} \to R(a)$, so that the type of $[\![p]\!]_p$ will correspond to the elimination rule:

$$
\forall R.(\Pi_{a:A} \to R(a)) \to R(p^+).
$$

This refinement will make the translation of NEF proofs compatible with the translation of delimited continuations.

Lemma 11. *The following holds:*

1. $\Gamma \vdash t : \mathbb{N} \mid \Delta \; \Rightarrow \; [\![\Gamma \cup \Delta]\!] \vdash [\![t]\!]_t : \forall X (\forall x^{T^+} X(x) \to X(t^+))$.
2. $\forall p \in \text{NEF}, (\Gamma \vdash p : A \mid \Delta \; \Rightarrow \; [\![\Gamma \cup \Delta]\!] \vdash [\![p]\!]_p : \forall X.(\Pi_{a:[\![A]\!]^+} X(a) \to X(p^+)))$.
3. $\forall c \in \text{NEF}, (c : \Gamma \vdash \Delta, \star : B \; \Rightarrow \; [\![\Gamma \cup \Delta]\!], \star : \Pi_{b:B^+} X(b) \vdash [\![c]\!]_c : X(c^+))$.

Proof. The proof is done by mutual induction on the typing rule of $dL_{\hat{\mathfrak{tp}}}$ for terms and NEF proofs. We only give one case here to give an insight of the proof.

Case (t, p): in $dL_{\hat{\mathfrak{p}}}$ the typing rule for (t, p) is the following:

$$\frac{\Gamma \vdash t : \mathbb{N} \mid \Delta \quad \Gamma \vdash p : A(t) \mid \Delta}{\Gamma \vdash (t, p) : \exists x^{\mathbb{N}} A(x) \mid \Delta} \exists_i$$

Hence we obtain by induction, using the same notation Γ' for $[\![\Gamma \cup \Delta]\!]$:

$$\Gamma' \vdash [\![t]\!]_t : \forall X.(\forall x^{T^+} X(x) \to X(t^+))$$
$$\Gamma' \vdash [\![p]\!]_p : \forall Y.(\Pi_{a:A(t^+)} Y(a) \to Y(p^+))$$

and we want to show that for any Z:

$$\Gamma' \vdash [\![(t, p)]\!]_p : \Pi_{a:\exists x^{T^+} A} Z(a) \to Z(t^+, p^+).$$

By definition, we have:

$$[\![(t, p)]\!]_p = \lambda k.([\![t]\!]_t \, (\lambda ur.r \, (\lambda q.k \, (u, q)))) [\![p]\!]_p,$$

so we need to prove that:

$$\Gamma_k \vdash ([\![t]\!]_t \, (\lambda ur.r \, (\lambda q.k \, (u, q)))) [\![p]\!]_p : Z(t^+, p^+)$$

where $\Gamma_k = \Gamma', k : \Pi_{a:\exists x^{T^+} A} Z(a)$. We let the reader check that such a type is derivable by using $X(x) \triangleq P(x) \to Z(x, a)$ in the type of $[\![t]\!]_p$ where $P(t^+)$ is the type of $[\![p]\!]_p$, and using $Y(a) \triangleq Z(t^+, a)$ in the type of $[\![p]\!]_p$. The crucial point is to see that the bounded variable r is abstracted with type $P(x)$ in the derivation, which would not have been possible in the definition of $[\![(t, p)]\!]_p$ with $p \notin \text{NEF}$. $\square$

Using the previous Lemma, we can now prove that the CPS translation is well-typed in the general case.

Proposition 12 (Preservation of typing). *The translation is well-typed, i.e. the following holds:*

1. *if $\Gamma \vdash p : A \mid \Delta$ then $[\![\Gamma \cup \Delta]\!] \vdash [\![p]\!]_p : [\![A]\!]^*$,*
2. *if $\Gamma \mid e : A \vdash \Delta$ then $[\![\Gamma \cup \Delta]\!] \vdash [\![e]\!]_e : [\![A]\!]^+ \to \bot$,*
3. *if $c : \Gamma \vdash \Delta$ then $[\![\Gamma \cup \Delta]\!] \vdash [\![c]\!]_c : \bot$.*

Proof. The proof is done by induction on the typing rules of $dL_{\hat{\mathfrak{p}}}$. It is clear that for the NEF cases, Lemma 11 implies the result by taking $X(a) = \bot$. The rest of the cases are straightforward, except for the delimited continuations that we detail hereafter. We consider a command $\langle \mu\hat{\mathfrak{p}}.\langle q \| \tilde{\mu}a.\langle p \| \hat{\mathfrak{p}} \rangle \rangle \| e \rangle$ produced by the reduction of the command $\langle \lambda a.p \| q \cdot e \rangle$ with $q \in \text{NEF}$. Both commands are translated by a proof reducing to $([\![q]\!]_p \, (\lambda a.[\![p]\!]_p)) [\![e]\!]_e$. The corresponding typing derivation in $dL_{\hat{\mathfrak{p}}}$ is of the form:

$$\frac{\dfrac{\Pi_p}{\Gamma, a : A \vdash p : B \mid \Delta} \quad \dfrac{\dfrac{\Pi_q}{\Gamma \vdash q : A \mid \Delta} \quad \dfrac{\Pi_e}{\Gamma \mid e : B[q/a] \vdash \Delta}}{\Gamma \mid q \cdot e : \Pi_{a:A} B \vdash \Delta}}{\dfrac{\Gamma \vdash \lambda a.p : \Pi_{a:A} B \mid \Delta \qquad \Gamma \mid q \cdot e : \Pi_{a:A} B \vdash \Delta}{\langle \lambda a.p \| q \cdot e \rangle : \Gamma \vdash \Delta}}$$

By induction hypothesis for e and p we obtain:

$$\Gamma' \vdash \llbracket e \rrbracket_e : \llbracket B[q^+] \rrbracket^+ \to \bot$$
$$\Gamma', a : A^+ \vdash \llbracket p \rrbracket_p : \llbracket B[a] \rrbracket^*$$
$$\Gamma' \vdash \lambda a.\llbracket p \rrbracket_p : \Pi_{a:A^+} \llbracket B[a] \rrbracket^*,$$

where $\Gamma' = \llbracket \Gamma \cup \Delta \rrbracket$. Applying Lemma 11 for $q \in$ NEF we can derive:

$$\frac{\Gamma' \vdash \llbracket q \rrbracket_p : \forall X.(\Pi_{a:A^+} X(a) \to X(q^+))}{\Gamma' \vdash \llbracket q \rrbracket_p : (\Pi_{a:A^+} \llbracket B[a] \rrbracket^* \to \llbracket B[q^+] \rrbracket^*} \; \forall_E$$

We can thus derive that:

$$\Gamma' \vdash \llbracket q \rrbracket_p (\lambda a.\llbracket p \rrbracket_p) : \llbracket B[q^+] \rrbracket^*,$$

and finally conclude that:

$$\Gamma' \vdash (\llbracket q \rrbracket_p (\lambda a.\llbracket p \rrbracket_p)) \, \llbracket e \rrbracket_e : \bot.$$

□

We can finally deduce the correctness of dL$_{\hat{tp}}$ through the translation, since a closed proof term of type $\bot$ would be translated in a closed proof of $(\bot \to \bot) \to \bot$. The correctness of the target language guarantees that such proof cannot exist.

Theorem 13 (Soundness). *For any $p \in dL_{\hat{tp}}$, we have:* $\nvdash p : \bot$.

5 Embedding in Lepigre's Calculus

In a recent paper [19], Lepigre presented a classical system allowing the use of dependent types with a semantic value restriction. In practice, the type system of his calculus does not contain a dependent product $\Pi_{a:A}B$ strictly speaking, but it contains a predicate $a \in A$ allowing the decomposition of the dependent product into

$$\forall a((a \in A) \to B)$$

as it is usual in Krivine's classical realizability [18]. In his system, the relativization $a \in A$ is restricted to values, so that we can only type $V : V \in A$, but the typing judgments are defined up to observational equivalence, so that if t is observationally equivalent to V, one can derive the judgment $t : V \in A$.

Interestingly, as highlighted through the CPS translation by Lemma 9, any NEF proof $p : A$ is observationally equivalent to some value p^+, so that we could derive $p : (p \in A)$ from $p^+ : (p^+ \in A)$. The NEF fragment is thus compatible with the semantical value restriction. The converse is obviously false, observational equivalence allowing us to type realizers that would otherwise be untyped[11].

---

[11] In particular, Lepigre's semantical restriction is so permissive that it is not decidable, while it is easy to decide wheter a proof term of dL$_{\hat{tp}}$ is in NEF.

We sketch here an embedding of $dL_{\hat{tp}}$ into Lepigre's calculus, and explain how to transfer normalization and correctness properties along this translation. Actually, his language is more expressive than ours, since it contains records and pattern-matching (we will only use pairs, *i.e.* records with two fields), but it is not stratified: no distinction is made between a language of terms and a language of proofs. We only recall here the syntax for the fragment of Lepigre's calculus we use, for the reduction rules and the type system the reader should refer to [19]:

$$
\begin{aligned}
v, w &::= x \mid \lambda x.t \mid \{l_1 = v_1, l_2 = v_2\} \\
t, u &::= a \mid v \mid t\,u \mid \mu\alpha.t \mid p \mid v.l_i \\
\pi, \rho &::= \alpha \mid v \cdot \pi \mid [t]\pi \\
p, q &::= t * \pi \\
A, B &::= X_n(t_1, \ldots, t_n) \mid A \to B \mid \forall a.A \mid \exists a.A \\
&\quad \mid \forall X_n.A \mid \{l_1 : A_1, l_2 : A_2\} \mid t \in A
\end{aligned}
$$

Even though records are only defined for values, we can define pairs and projections as syntactic sugar:

$$
\begin{aligned}
(p_1, p_2) &\triangleq (\lambda v_1 v_2.\{l_1 = v_1, l_2 = v_2\})\,p_1\,p_2 \\
\pi_i(p) &\triangleq (\lambda x.(x.l_i))\,p \\
A_1 \wedge A_2 &\triangleq \{l_1 : A_1, l_2 : A_2\}
\end{aligned}
$$

We first define the translation for types (extended for typing contexts) where the predicate $\mathsf{Nat}(x)$ is defined as usual in second-order logic:

$$
\mathsf{Nat}(x) \triangleq \forall X(X(0) \to \forall y(X(y) \to X(S(y))) \to X(x))
$$

and $[\![t]\!]_t$ is the translation of the term t given in Fig. 6:

$$
\begin{aligned}
(\forall x^{\mathbb{N}}.A)^* &\triangleq \forall x(\mathsf{Nat}(x) \to A^*) & (\Pi_{a:A}B)^* &\triangleq \forall a((a \in A^*) \to B^*) \\
(\exists x^{\mathbb{N}}.A)^* &\triangleq \exists x(\mathsf{Nat}(x) \wedge A^*) & (\Gamma, x : \mathbb{N})^* &\triangleq \Gamma^*, x : \mathsf{Nat}(x) \\
(t = u)^* &\triangleq \forall X(X[\![t]\!]_t \to X[\![u]\!]_t) & (\Gamma, a : A)^* &\triangleq \Gamma^*, a : A^* \\
\top^* &\triangleq \forall X(X \to X) & (\Gamma, \alpha : A^{\perp\!\!\!\perp})^* &\triangleq \Gamma^*, \alpha : \neg A^* \\
\perp^* &\triangleq \forall XY(X \to Y) &
\end{aligned}
$$

Note that the equality is mapped to Leibniz equality, and that the definitions of $\perp^*$ and $\top^*$ are completely ad hoc, in order to make the conversion rule admissible through the translation.

The translation for terms, proofs, contexts and commands of $dL_{\hat{tp}}$, given in Fig. 6 is almost straightforward. We only want to draw the reader's attention on a few points:

- the equality being translated as Leibniz equality, refl is translated as the identity $\lambda a.a$, which also matches with $\top^*$,
- the strong existential is encoded as a pair, hence wit (resp. prf) is mapped to the projection π_1 (resp. π_2).

$$[\![x]\!]_t \triangleq x \qquad\qquad [\![(t,p)]\!]_p \triangleq ([\![t]\!]_t, [\![p]\!]_p) \qquad [\![q \cdot e]\!]_e \triangleq [\![q]\!]_p \cdot [\![e]\!]_e$$

$$[\![n]\!]_t \triangleq \lambda zs.s^n(z) \qquad [\![\mu\alpha.c]\!]_p \triangleq \mu\alpha.[\![c]\!]_c \qquad [\![t \cdot e]\!]_e \triangleq [\![t]\!]_t \cdot [\![e]\!]_e$$

$$[\![\text{wit } p]\!]_t \triangleq \pi_1([\![p]\!]_p) \qquad [\![\text{prf } p]\!]_p \triangleq \pi_2([\![p]\!]_p) \qquad [\![\tilde{\mu}a.c]\!]_e \triangleq [\lambda a.[\![c]\!]_c]\star$$

$$[\![a]\!]_p \triangleq a \qquad\qquad [\![\text{refl}]\!]_p \triangleq \lambda a.a \qquad [\![\langle p \| e \rangle]\!]_c \triangleq [\![p]\!]_p * [\![e]\!]_e$$

$$[\![\lambda a.p]\!]_p \triangleq \lambda a.[\![p]\!]_p \qquad [\![\text{subst } p\,q]\!]_p \triangleq [\![p]\!]_p\,[\![q]\!]_p \qquad [\![\mu\hat{\mathfrak{tp}}.c]\!]_p \triangleq \mu\alpha.[\![c]\!]_{\hat{\mathfrak{tp}}}$$

$$[\![\lambda x.p]\!]_p \triangleq \lambda x.[\![p]\!]_p \qquad [\![\alpha]\!]_e \triangleq \alpha \qquad\qquad [\![\langle p \| \hat{\mathfrak{tp}} \rangle]\!]_{\hat{\mathfrak{tp}}} \triangleq [\![p]\!]_p$$

$$[\![\langle p \| \tilde{\mu}a.c \rangle]\!]_{\hat{\mathfrak{tp}}} \triangleq (\mu\alpha.[\![p]\!]_p * [\lambda a.[\![c]\!]_{\hat{\mathfrak{tp}}}]\alpha) * \alpha$$

Fig. 6. Translation of proof terms to Lepigre's calculus

In [19], the coherence of the system is justified by a realizability model, and the type system does not allow us to type stacks. Thus we cannot formally prove that the translation preserves the typing, unless we extend the type system in which case this would imply the adequacy. We might also directly prove the adequacy of the realizability model (through the translation) with respect to the typing rules of $dL_{\hat{\mathfrak{tp}}}$. We detail a proof of adequacy using the former method in the appendix.

Proposition 14 (Adequacy). *If $\Gamma \vdash p : A \mid \Delta$ and σ is a substitution realizing $(\Gamma \cup \Delta)^*$, then $[\![p]\!]_p\sigma \in [\![A^*]\!]_\sigma^{\perp\perp}$.*

This immediately implies the soundness of $dL_{\hat{\mathfrak{tp}}}$, since a closed proof p of type $\perp$ would be translated as a realizer of $\top \to \perp$, so that $[\![p]\!]_p\,\lambda x.x$ would be a realizer of $\perp$, which is impossible. Furthermore, the translation clearly preserves normalization (that is that for any c, if c does not normalize then neither does $[\![c]\!]_c$), and thus the normalization of $dL_{\hat{\mathfrak{tp}}}$ is a consequence of adequacy.

It is worth noting that without delimited continuations, we would not have been able to define an adequate translation, since we would have encountered the same problem as for the CPS translation (see Sect. 2.7).

6   Further Extensions

As we explained in the preamble of Sect. 2, we defined dL and $dL_{\hat{\mathfrak{tp}}}$ as minimal languages containing all the potential sources of inconsistency we wanted to mix: a control operator, dependent types, and a sequent calculus presentation. It had the benefit to focus our attention on the difficulties inherent to the issue, but on the other hand, the language we obtain is far from being as expressive as other usual proof systems. We claimed our system to be extensible, thus we shall now discuss this matter.

6.1   Adding Expressiveness

From the point of view of the proof language (that is of the tools we have to build proofs), $dL_{\hat{\mathfrak{tp}}}$ only enjoys the presence of a dependent sum and a dependent product over terms, as well as a dependent product at the level of proofs (which

subsume the non-dependent implication). If this is obviously enough to encode
the usual constructors for pairs (p_1, p_2) (of type $A_1 \wedge A_2$), injections $\iota_i(p)$ (of
type $A_1 \vee A_2$), etc., it seems reasonable to wonder whether such constructors
can be directly defined in the language of proofs. Actually this is a case, and we
claim that is possible to define the constructors for proofs (for instance (p_1, p_2))
together with their destructors in the contexts (in that case $\tilde{\mu}(a_1, a_2).c$), with
the appropriate typing rules. In practice, it is enough to:

- extend the definitions of the NEF fragment according to the chosen extension,
- extend the call-by-value reduction system, opening if needed the constructors
  to reduce it to a value,
- in the dependent typing mode, make some pattern-matching within the
  dependencies list for the destructors. For instance, for the case of the pairs,
  the corresponding rule would be:

$$\frac{c : \Gamma, a_1 : A_1, a_2 : A_2 \vdash_d \Delta, \hat{\mathrm{t}}\mathrm{p} : B; \sigma\{(a_1, a_2)|p\}}{\Gamma \mid \tilde{\mu}(a_1, a_2).c : (A_1 \wedge A_2) \vdash_d \Delta, \hat{\mathrm{t}}\mathrm{p} : B; \sigma\{\cdot|p\}} \wedge_E$$

The soundness of such extensions can be justified either by extending the CPS
translation, or by defining a translation to Lepigre's calculus (which already
allows records and pattern-matching over general constructors) and proving the
adequacy of the translation with respect to the realizability model.

6.2   Extending the Domain of Terms

Throughout the article, we only worked with terms of a unique type $\mathbb{N}$, hence it is
natural to wonder whether it is possible to extend the domain of terms in $\mathrm{dL}_{\hat{\mathrm{t}}\mathrm{p}}$, for
instance with terms in the simply-typed λ-calculus. A good way to understand
the situation is to observe what happens through the CPS translation. We see
that a *term* of type $T = \mathbb{N}$ is translated into a *proof* of type $\neg\neg T^+ = \neg\neg\mathbb{N}$,
from which we can extract a *term* of type $\mathbb{N}$. However, if T was for instance
the function type $\mathbb{N} \to \mathbb{N}$, we would only be able to extract a *proof* of type
$T^+ = \mathbb{N} \to \neg\neg\mathbb{N}$. In particular, such a proof would be of the form $\lambda x.p$, where p
might backtrack to a former position, for instance before it was extracted, and
furnish another proof. This accounts for a well-know phenomenon in classical
logic, where witness extraction is limited to formulas in the Σ_0^1-fragment [21].
It also corresponds to the type we obtain for the image of a dependent product
$\Pi_{a:A}B$, that is translated to a type $\neg\neg\Pi_{a:A+}B^*$ where the dependence is in a
proof of type A^+. This phenomenon is not surprising and was already observed
for other CPS translations for type theories with dependent types [4].

In other words, there is no hope to define a correct translation of (t_f, p) :
$\exists f^{\mathbb{N}\to\mathbb{N}}A$ that would allow the extraction of a strong pair $(\llbracket t_f \rrbracket, \llbracket p \rrbracket) : \exists f^{\mathbb{N}\to\mathbb{N}}A^*$.
More precisely, the proof $\llbracket t_f \rrbracket$ is no longer a witness in the usual sense, but a
realizer of $f \in \mathbb{N} \to \mathbb{N}$ in the sense of Krivine classical realizability.

This does not mean that we cannot extend the domain of terms in $\mathrm{dL}_{\hat{\mathrm{t}}\mathrm{p}}$ (in
particular, it should affect neither the subject reduction nor the soundness), but

it rather means that the stratification between terms and proofs is to be lost through a CPS translation. However, it should still be possible to express the fact that the image of a function through the CPS is a realizer corresponding to this function, by cleverly adapting the predicate $f \in \mathbb{N} \to \mathbb{N}$ to make it stick to the intuition of a realizer.

6.3 A Fully Sequent-Style Dependent Calculus

While the aim of this paper was to design a sequent-style calculus embedding dependent types, we only present the Π-type in sequent-style. Indeed, we wanted to ensure ourselves in a first time that we were able of having the key ingredients of dependent types in our language, even presented in a natural deduction spirit. Rather than having left-rules, we presented the existential type and the equality type with the following elimination rules:

$$\frac{\Gamma \vdash p : \exists x^{\mathbb{N}} A(x) \mid \Delta; \sigma \quad p \in \mathcal{D}}{\Gamma \vdash \mathsf{prf}\, p : A(\mathsf{wit}\, p) \mid \Delta; \sigma}\ \mathsf{prf} \qquad \frac{\Gamma \vdash p : t = u \mid \Delta; \sigma \quad \Gamma \vdash q : B[t/x] \mid \Delta; \sigma}{\Gamma \vdash \mathsf{subst}\, p\, q : B[u/x] \mid \Delta; \sigma}\ \mathsf{subst}$$

However, it is now easy to have both rules in a sequent calculus fashion, for instance we could rather have contexts of the shape $\tilde{\mu}(x,a).c$ (to be dual to proofs (t,p)) and $\tilde{\mu}=.c$ (dual to refl). We could then define the following typing rules (where we extend the dependencies list to terms, to compensate the conversion from $A[t]$ to $A[u]$ in the former (subst)-rule):

$$\frac{c : \Gamma, x : \mathbb{N}, a : A(x) \vdash \Delta; \sigma\{(x,a)|p\}}{\Gamma \mid \tilde{\mu}(x,a).c \vdash \Delta; \sigma\{\cdot|p\}}\ \exists \qquad \frac{c : \Gamma \vdash \Delta; \sigma\{t|u\}}{\Gamma \mid \tilde{\mu}=.c : t = u \vdash \Delta; \sigma\{\cdot|p\}}\ =_l$$

and define $\mathsf{prf}\, p$ and $\mathsf{subst}\, p\, q$ as syntactic sugar:

$$\mathsf{prf}\, p \triangleq \mu\alpha.\langle p \| \tilde{\mu}(x,a).\langle a \| \alpha \rangle \rangle \qquad \mathsf{subst}\, p\, q \triangleq \mu\alpha.\langle p \| \tilde{\mu}=.\langle q \| \alpha \rangle \rangle.$$

For any $p \in \mathrm{NEF}$ and any variables a, α, $A(\mathsf{wit}\, p)$ is in $A(\mathsf{wit}\,(x,a))_{\{(x,a)|p\}}$ which allows us to derive (using this in the (cut)-rule) the admissibility of the former (prf)-rule (we let the reader check the case of the (subst)-rule):

$$\cfrac{\Gamma \vdash p : \exists x^{\mathbb{N}}.A \mid \Delta; \sigma \quad \cfrac{\cfrac{\cfrac{a : A(x) \vdash a : A(x)}{a : A(x) \vdash a : A(\mathsf{wit}\,(x,a))} \equiv \quad \Gamma \mid \alpha : A(\mathsf{wit}\, p) \vdash \alpha : A(\mathsf{wit}\, p) \mid \Delta}{\langle a \| \alpha \rangle : \Gamma, x : \mathbb{N}, a : A(x) \vdash \Delta, \alpha : A(\mathsf{wit}\, p); \sigma\{(x,a)|p\}}\ \mathrm{cut}}{\Gamma \mid \tilde{\mu}(x,a).\langle a \| \alpha \rangle : \exists x^{\mathbb{N}} A \vdash \Delta, \alpha : A(\mathsf{wit}\, p); \sigma\{\cdot|p\}}}{\cfrac{\langle p \| \tilde{\mu}(x,a).\langle a \| \alpha \rangle \rangle : \Gamma \vdash \Delta, \alpha : A(\mathsf{wit}\, p); \sigma\{\cdot|p\}}{\Gamma \vdash \mu\alpha.\langle p \| \tilde{\mu}(x,a).\langle a \| \alpha \rangle \rangle : A(\mathsf{wit}\, p) \mid \Delta; \sigma}}$$

As for the reduction rules, we can define the following (call-by-value) reductions:

$$\langle (V_t, V) \| \tilde{\mu}(x,a).c \rangle \rightsquigarrow c[V_t/x][V/a] \qquad \langle \mathsf{refl} \| \tilde{\mu}=.c \rangle \rightsquigarrow c$$

and check that they advantageously simulate the previous rules (the expansion rules become useless):

$$\langle \mathsf{subst\ refl}\ q \| e \rangle \rightsquigarrow \langle q \| e \rangle \qquad\qquad \langle \mathsf{subst}\ p\ q \| e \rangle \overset{p \notin V}{\rightsquigarrow} \langle p \| \tilde{\mu}a.\langle \mathsf{subst}\ a\ q \| e \rangle \rangle$$

$$\langle \mathsf{prf}\ (V_t, V_p) \| e \rangle \rightsquigarrow \langle V \| e \rangle \qquad\qquad \langle \mathsf{prf}\ p \| e \rangle \rightsquigarrow \langle \mu \hat{\mathsf{tp}}.\langle p \| \tilde{\mu}a.\langle \mathsf{prf}\ a \| \hat{\mathsf{tp}} \rangle \rangle \| e \rangle.$$

Acknowledgments. The author wish to thanks Pierre-Marie Pédrot for a discussion that led to the idea of using delimited continuations, Gabriel Scherer for his accurate observations and the constant interest he showed for this work, as well as the anonymous referees of an earlier version of this paper for their remarks.

References

1. Ahman, D., Ghani, N., Plotkin, G.D.: Dependent types and fibred computational effects. In: Jacobs, B., Löding, C. (eds.) FoSSaCS 2016. LNCS, vol. 9634, pp. 36–54. Springer, Heidelberg (2016). doi:10.1007/978-3-662-49630-5_3
2. Ariola, Z.M., Herbelin, H., Sabry, A.: A type-theoretic foundation of delimited continuations. High.-Order Symbolic Comput. **22**(3), 233–273 (2009)
3. Barbanera, F., Berardi, S.: A symmetric lambda calculus for classical program extraction. Inf. Comput. **125**(2), 103–117 (1996)
4. Barthe, G., Hatcliff, J., Sørensen, M.H.B.: CPS translations and applications: the cube and beyond. High.-Order Symbolic Comput. **12**(2), 125–170 (1999)
5. Blot, V.: Hybrid realizability for intuitionistic and classical choice. In: LICS 2016, New York, USA, 5–8 July 2016
6. Coquand, T., Huet, G.: The calculus of constructions. Inf. Comput. **76**(2), 95–120 (1988)
7. Curien, P.-L., Herbelin, H.: The duality of computation. In: Proceedings of ICFP 2000, SIGPLAN Notices, vol. 35, no. 9, pp. 233–243. ACM (2000)
8. Downen, P., Maurer, L., Ariola, Z.M., Jones, S.P.: Sequent calculus as a compiler intermediate language. In: ICFP 2016 (2016)
9. Ferreira, G., Oliva, P.: On various negative translations. In: van Bakel, S., Berardi, S., Berger, U. (eds.) Proceedings Third International Workshop on Classical Logic and Computation, CL&C 2010. EPTCS, Brno, Czech Republic, 21–22 August 2010, vol. 47, pp. 21–33 (2010)
10. Friedman, H.: Classically and intuitionistically provably recursive functions. In: Müller, G.H., Scott, D.S. (eds.) Higher Set Theory. LNM, vol. 669, pp. 21–27. Springer, Heidelberg (1978). doi:10.1007/BFb0103100
11. Garrigue, J.: Relaxing the value restriction. In: Kameyama, Y., Stuckey, P.J. (eds.) FLOPS 2004. LNCS, vol. 2998, pp. 196–213. Springer, Heidelberg (2004). doi:10.1007/978-3-540-24754-8_15
12. Griffin, T.G.: A formulae-as-type notion of control. In: Proceedings of the 17th ACM SIGPLAN-SIGACT Symposium on Principles of Programming Languages, POPL 1990, pp. 47–58. ACM, New York (1990)
13. Harper, R., Lillibridge, M.: Polymorphic type assignment and CPS conversion. LISP Symbolic Comput. **6**(3), 361–379 (1993)
14. Herbelin, H.: On the degeneracy of Σ-types in presence of computational classical logic. In: Urzyczyn, P. (ed.) TLCA 2005. LNCS, vol. 3461, pp. 209–220. Springer, Heidelberg (2005). doi:10.1007/11417170_16

15. Herbelin, H.: A constructive proof of dependent choice, compatible with classical logic. In: Proceedings of the 27th Annual IEEE Symposium on Logic in Computer Science, LICS 2012, Dubrovnik, Croatia, 25–28 June 2012, pp. 365–374. IEEE Computer Society (2012)

16. Herbelin, H., Ghilezan, S.: An approach to call-by-name delimited continuations. In: Necula, G.C.,. Wadler, P. (eds.) Proceedings of the 35th ACM SIGPLAN-SIGACT Symposium on Principles of Programming Languages, POPL 2008, San Francisco, California, USA, 7–12 January 2008, pp. 383–394. ACM, January 2008

17. Howard, W.A.: The formulae-as-types notion of construction. Privately circulated notes (1969)

18. Krivine, J.-L.: Realizability in classical logic. Panoramas et synthèses **27**, 197–229 (2009). In: Interactive Models of Computation and Program Behaviour

19. Lepigre, R.: A classical realizability model for a semantical value restriction. In: Thiemann, P. (ed.) ESOP 2016. LNCS, vol. 9632, pp. 476–502. Springer, Heidelberg (2016). doi:10.1007/978-3-662-49498-1_19

20. Martin-Löf, P.: Constructive mathematics and computer programming. In: Proceedings of a Discussion Meeting of the Royal Society of London on Mathematical Logic and Programming Languages, pp. 167–184. Prentice-Hall, Inc., Upper Saddle River (1985)

21. Miquel, A.: Existential witness extraction in classical realizability and via a negative translation. Log. Methods Comput. Sci. **7**(2), 1–47 (2011)

22. Parigot, M.: Proofs of strong normalisation for second order classical natural deduction. J. Symb. Log. **62**(4), 1461–1479 (1997)

23. Vákár, M.: A framework for dependent types and effects. CoRR, abs/1512.08009 (2015)

24. Wadler, P.: Call-by-value is dual to call-by-name. In: Runciman, C., Shivers, C. (eds.) Proceedings of the Eighth ACM SIGPLAN International Conference on Functional Programming, ICFP 2003, Uppsala, Sweden, 25–29 August 2003, pp. 189–201. ACM (2003)

25. Wright, A.: Simple imperative polymorphism. LISP Symbolic Comput. **8**(4), 343–356 (1995)

Context-Free Session Type Inference

Luca Padovani[✉]

Dipartimento di Informatica, Università di Torino, Torino, Italy
luca.padovani@di.unito.it

Abstract. Some interesting communication protocols can be precisely
described only by context-free session types, an extension of conventional
session types with a general form of sequential composition. The complex metatheory of context-free session types, however, hinders the definition of corresponding checking and inference algorithms. In this work
we address and solve these problems introducing a new type system for
context-free session types of which we provide two OCaml embeddings.

1 Introduction

Session types [9,10,12] are an established formalism for the enforcement of communication protocols through static analysis. Recently, Thiemann and Vasconcelos [25] have proposed *context-free session types* to enhance the expressiveness of
conventional session types. Protocols that benefit from such enhancement include
the serialization of tree-like data structures and XML documents [25], interactions
with non-uniform objects such as stacks and reentrant locks [6,19], and recursive
protocols for trust management [24]. Thiemann and Vasconcelos [25] study the
metatheory of context-free session types, leaving the definition of a type checking algorithm for future work. In this paper we point out additional issues that
specifically afflict context-free session type inference and we describe a practical
solution to its implementation.

Let us consider the OCaml code
on the right to illustrate the problem concretely. The code models a
stack, a non-uniform object [19,22]
offering different interfaces through a
session endpoint u depending on its
internal state. An empty stack (lines
2–7) accepts either a Push or an End
operation. In the first case, the stack
receives the element x to be pushed
and moves into the non-empty state
with the recursive application some x
u. In the second case, it just returns

```
let stack =                          1
  let rec none u =                   2
    match branch u with              3
    | `Push u →                      4
        let x, u = receive u         5
        in none (some x u)           6
    | `End u → u                     7
  and some y u =                     8
    match branch u with              9
    | `Push u →                      10
        let x, u = receive u         11
        in some y (some x u)         12
    | `Pop u → send y u              13
  in none                           14
```

L. Padovani—Partly supported by European project HyVar (grant agreement H2020-
644298).

H. Yang (Ed.): ESOP 2017, LNCS 10201, pp. 804–830, 2017.
DOI: 10.1007/978-3-662-54434-1_30

the endpoint u. A non-empty stack (lines 8–13) with y on top accepts either a Push operation, as in the empty case, or a Pop operation, in which case it sends y back to the client. When an application some x u terminates, meaning that x has been popped, the stack returns to its previous state, whatever it was (lines 6 and 12). Note that, according to established conventions [8], all session primitives including send return the endpoint u possibly paired with the received message (receive) or injected through a tag that represents an operation (branch). Using the FuSe implementation of binary sessions [21], OCaml infers for stack the type $S_{reg} \to \beta$ where S_{reg} is the (equi-recursive) session type that satisfies the equation

$$S_{reg} = \& \, [\text{Push} : ?\alpha; S_{reg}] \tag{1.1}$$

according to which the client can only push elements of type α. To understand the reason why the End and Pop operations are not allowed by S_{reg}, we have to consider that conventional session types can only describe protocols whose set of (finite) traces is regular, whereas the set of (finite) traces that describe legal interactions with stack is isomorphic to the language of balanced parentheses, a typical example of context-free language that is not regular. The session type S_{reg} above corresponds to the best ω-regular and safe approximation of this context-free language that OCaml manages to infer from the code of stack. When OCaml figures that the session type cannot precisely track whether the stack is empty or not, it computes the "intersection" of the interfaces of these two states, which results in S_{reg} (along with warnings informing that lines 7 and 13 are dead code).

Driven by similar considerations, Thiemann and Vasconcelos [25] propose *context-free session types* as a more expressive protocol description language. The key idea is to enforce the order of interactions in a protocol using a general form of sequential composition _;_ instead of the usual prefix operator. For example, the context-free session types S_{none} and S_{some} that satisfy the equations

$$S_{none} = \& \, [\text{Push} : ?\alpha; S_{some}; S_{none}, \ \text{End} : 1]$$
$$S_{some} = \& \, [\text{Push} : ?\alpha; S_{some}; S_{some}, \ \text{Pop} : !\alpha] \tag{1.2}$$

provide accurate descriptions of the legal interactions with stack: all finite, maximal traces described by S_{none} have each Push eventually followed by a matching Pop. The "empty" protocol 1 marks the end of a legal interaction. Using Thiemann and Vasconcelos' type system, it is then possible to work out a typing derivation showing that stack has type $S_{none}; A \to A$, where A is a session type variable that can be instantiated with any session type.

In the present work we address the problem of *inferring* a type as precise as $S_{none}; A \to A$ from the code of a function like stack. There are two major obstacles that make the type system in [25] unfit as the basis for a type inference algorithm: (1) a structural rule that rearranges session types according to the monoidal and distributive laws of sequential composition and (2) the need to support polymorphic recursion which, as explained in [25], ultimately arises as a consequence of (1). Type inference in presence of polymorphic recursion is known to be undecidable in general [13], a problem which often requires programmers to explicitly annotate polymorphic-recursive functions with their type. In addition, the liberal handling of sequential compositions means that functions like `stack` admit very different types (such as $S_{\text{reg}} \to \beta$ and $S_{\text{none}} ; A \to A$) which do not appear to be instances of a unique, more general type scheme. It is therefore unclear which notion of principal type should guide the type inference algorithm.

These observations lead us to reconsider the way sequential compositions are handled by the type system. More specifically, we propose to eliminate sequential compositions through an explicit, higher-order combinator `@>` called *resumption* that is akin to functional application but has the following signature:

$$\texttt{@>} : (T \to \mathbf{1}) \to T ; S \to S \tag{1.3}$$

Suppose $f : T \to \mathbf{1}$ is a function that, applied to a session endpoint of type T, carries out the communication over the endpoint and returns the depleted endpoint, of type $\mathbf{1}$. Using `@>` we can supply to f an endpoint u of type $T ; S$ knowing that f will take care of the prefix T of $T ; S$ leaving us with an endpoint of type S. In other words, `@>` allows us to modularize the enforcement of a sequential protocol $T ; S$ by partitioning the program into a part – the function f – that carries out the prefix T of the protocol and another part – the evaluation context in which $f\texttt{@>}u$ occurs – that carries out the continuation S.

This informal presentation of `@>` uncovers a potential flaw of our approach. The type $T \to \mathbf{1}$ describes a function that takes an endpoint of type T and returns an endpoint of type $\mathbf{1}$, but does not guarantee that the returned endpoint is *the same endpoint* supplied to the function. Only in this case the endpoint can be safely resumed. What we need is a type-level mechanism to reason about the *identity* of endpoints. Similar requirements have already arisen in different contexts, to identify regions [2,30] and to associate resources with capabilities [1,26,28]. Reframing the techniques used in these works to our setting, the idea is to refine endpoint types to a form $[T]_\rho$ where ρ is a variable that represents the abstract identity of the endpoint at the type level. The signature of `@>` becomes

$$\texttt{@>} : ([T]_\rho \to [\mathbf{1}]_\rho) \to [T ; S]_\rho \to [S]_\rho \tag{1.4}$$

where the fact that the *same* ρ decorates both $[T]_\rho$ and $[\mathbf{1}]_\rho$ means that `@>` can only be used on functions that accept and return the *same* endpoint. In turn, the fact that the *same* ρ decorates both $[T ; S]_\rho$ and $[S]_\rho$ guarantees that $f\texttt{@>}u$ evaluates to the *same* endpoint u that was supplied to f, but with type S.

Going back to `stack`, how should we patch its code so that the (inferred) session type of the endpoint accepted by `stack` is S_{none} instead of S_{reg}? We are guided by an easy rule of thumb: place resumptions in the code anywhere a `_;_` is expected in the corresponding point of the protocol. In this specific case, looking at the protocols (1.2), we turn the recursive applications (`some x u`) on lines 6 and 12 to (`some x @> u`). Thus, using the type system we present in this paper, we obtain a typing derivation proving that the revised `stack` has type $[S_{\text{none}}]_\rho \to [\mathbf{1}]_\rho$. Most importantly, the type system makes no use of structural rules or polymorphic recursion and there is no ambiguity as to which protocol `stack` is supposed to carry out, for occurrences of `_;_` in a protocol are tied to the occurrences of `@>` in code that complies with such protocol.

As we will see, these properties make our type system easy to embed in any host programming language supporting parametric polymorphism and (optionally) existential types. This way, we can benefit from an off-the-shelf solution to context-free session type checking and inference instead of developing specific checking/inference algorithms. In the remainder of the paper:

- We formalize a core functional programming language called $\mathrm{FuSe}^{\{\}}$ featuring threads, session-based communication primitives and a distinctive low-level construct for resuming session endpoints (Sect. 2). The semantics of resumption combinators (including `@>`) will be explained using this construct.
- We equip $\mathrm{FuSe}^{\{\}}$ with an original sub-structural type system that features context-free session types and abstract endpoint identities (Sect. 3). We prove fundamental properties of well-typed programs emphasizing the implications of these properties in presence of resumptions.
- We detail two implementations of $\mathrm{FuSe}^{\{\}}$ primitives as `OCaml` modules which embed $\mathrm{FuSe}^{\{\}}$ type discipline into `OCaml`'s type system (Sect. 4). The two modules solve the problems of context-free session type checking [25] and inference, striking different balances between static safety and portability.

We defer a more technical discussion of related work to the end of the paper (Sect. 5). Proofs and additional technical material can be found in the associated technical report [20]. All the code in shaded background can be type checked, compiled and run using `OCaml` and both implementations of $\mathrm{FuSe}^{\{\}}$ [21].

2   A Calculus of Functions, Sessions and Resumptions

The syntax of $\mathrm{FuSe}^{\{\}}$ is given in Table 1 and is based on infinite sets of *variables*, *identity variables*, and of *session channels*. We use an involution $\bar{\cdot}$ that turns an identity variable or channel into the (distinct) corresponding identity co-variable or co-channel. Each session channel a has two *endpoints*, one denoted by the channel a itself, the other by the corresponding co-channel $\bar{a}$. We say that a is the *peer endpoint* of $\bar{a}$ and vice versa. Given an endpoint ε, we write $\bar{\varepsilon}$ for its peer. A *name* is either an endpoint or a variable. An *identity* is either an endpoint or an identity (co-)variable. We write $\bar{\iota}$ for the co-identity of ι, which is defined in such a way that $\bar{\bar{\rho}} = \rho$.

The syntax of expressions is mostly standard and comprises constants, variables, abstractions, applications, and two forms for splitting pairs and matching tagged values. Constants, ranged over by c, comprise the unitary value 0, the pair constructor `pair`, an arbitrary set of tags C for tagged unions, the fixpoint operator `fix`, a primitive `fork` for creating new threads, and a standard set of session primitives [8] whose semantics will be detailed shortly. To improve readability, we write (e_1, e_2) in place of the saturated application `pair` $e_1 e_2$. In addition, the calculus provides abstraction, application, packing and unpacking of identities. These respectively correspond to introduction and elimination

Table 1. FuSe$^{\{\}}$: syntax (‡ marks the runtime syntax not used in source programs).

Notation	x, y	$\in$	Var	variables
	ρ	$\in$	$IdVar$	identity variables
	a, b	$\in$	$Channel$	session channels
	ε	$\in$	$Channel \cup \overline{Channel}$	endpoints
	u	$\in$	$Channel \cup \overline{Channel} \cup Var$	names
	ι	$\in$	$Channel \cup \overline{Channel} \cup IdVar \cup \overline{IdVar}$	identities
Process	P, Q	$::=$	$\langle e \rangle$	thread
		$\mid$	$P \mid Q$	parallel composition‡
		$\mid$	$(\nu a)P$	session‡
Expression	e	$::=$	v	value
		$\mid$	x	variable
		$\mid$	$e\,e'$	value application
		$\mid$	$e\,[\iota]$	identity application
		$\mid$	$\texttt{let } x, y = e_1 \texttt{ in } e_2$	pair splitting
		$\mid$	$\texttt{match } e \texttt{ with } \{C_i \Rightarrow e_i\}_{i \in I}$	pattern matching
		$\mid$	$\lceil \iota, e \rceil$	packing
		$\mid$	$\texttt{let } \lceil \rho, x \rceil = e_1 \texttt{ in } e_2$	unpacking
		$\mid$	$\{e\}_u$	resumption
Value	v, w	$::=$	$\texttt{c} \mid (v, w) \mid \texttt{C } v$	data
		$\mid$	$\texttt{pair } v \mid \texttt{fork } v \mid \texttt{send } v \mid \texttt{select } v$	partial application
		$\mid$	$\lambda x.e \mid \Lambda\rho.v \mid \texttt{fix } v$	abstraction
		$\mid$	ε	endpoint‡
		$\mid$	$\lceil \varepsilon, v \rceil$	package‡
Constant	$\texttt{c}$	$::=$	$() \mid \texttt{pair} \mid \texttt{C} \mid \texttt{fix} \mid \texttt{fork}$	
		$\mid$	$\texttt{create} \mid \texttt{send} \mid \texttt{receive} \mid \texttt{select} \mid \texttt{branch}$	

constructs for universal and existential types, which are limited to identities in the formal development of FuSe$^{\{\}}$. The distinguishing feature of FuSe$^{\{\}}$ is the resumption construct $\{e\}_u$ indicating that e uses the endpoint u for completing some prefix of a sequentially composed protocol. As we will see in Example 1, resumptions are key to define operators such as @> introduced in Sect. 1. Values are fairly standard except for two details that are easy to overlook. First, $\texttt{fix } v$ is a value and reduces only when applied to a further argument. This approach, already used by Tov [26], simplifies the operational semantics (and the formal proofs) sparing us the need to η-expand $\texttt{fix}$ each time it is unfolded [31]. Second, the body of an identity abstraction $\Lambda\rho.v$ is a value and not an arbitrary expression. This restriction, inspired by [26,28], simplifies the type system without affecting expressiveness since the body of an identity abstraction is usually another (identity or value) abstraction. In this respect, the fact that $\texttt{fix } v$ is a value allows us to write identity-monomorphic, recursive functions of the form $\Lambda\rho.\texttt{fix } \lambda f.\cdots$ which are both common and useful in practice. Processes are parallel compositions of threads possibly connected by sessions. Note that the restriction $(\nu a)P$ binds the two endpoints a and $\bar{a}$ in P. The definition of free and bound names for both expressions and processes is the obvious one. We identify terms modulo alpha-renaming of bound names.

Table 2. FuSe$^{\{\}}$: operational semantics.

Reduction of expressions $\boxed{e \to e'}$

[R1] $(\lambda x.e)\ v \to e\{v/x\}$

[R2] $(\Lambda \rho.v)\ [\varepsilon] \to v\{\varepsilon/\rho\}$

[R3] $\text{fix}\ v\ w \to v\ (\text{fix}\ v)\ w$

[R4] $\text{let}\ x,y = (v,w)\ \text{in}\ e \to e\{v,w/x,y\}$

[R5] $\text{match}\ (\mathtt{C}_k\ v)\ \text{with}\ \{\mathtt{C}_i \Rightarrow e_i\}_{i \in I} \to e_k\ v$ $k \in I$

[R6] $\text{let}\ \lceil \rho, x \rceil = \lceil \varepsilon, v \rceil\ \text{in}\ e \to e\{\varepsilon/\rho\}\{v/x\}$

[R7] $\{(v,\varepsilon)\}_\varepsilon \to (v,\varepsilon)$

Reduction of processes $\boxed{P \to Q}$

[R8] $\langle \mathscr{E}[\text{fork}\ v\ w] \rangle \to \langle \mathscr{E}[()] \rangle\ |\ \langle v\ w \rangle$

[R9] $\langle \mathscr{E}[\text{create}\ ()] \rangle \to (\nu a)\langle \mathscr{E}[[a,(a,\bar{a})]] \rangle$ a fresh

[R10] $\langle \mathscr{E}[\text{send}\ v\ \varepsilon] \rangle\ |\ \langle \mathscr{E}'[\text{receive}\ \bar{\varepsilon}] \rangle \to \langle \mathscr{E}[\varepsilon] \rangle\ |\ \langle \mathscr{E}'[(v,\bar{\varepsilon})] \rangle$

[R11] $\langle \mathscr{E}[\text{select}\ v\ \varepsilon] \rangle\ |\ \langle \mathscr{E}'[\text{branch}\ \bar{\varepsilon}] \rangle \to \langle \mathscr{E}[\varepsilon] \rangle\ |\ \langle \mathscr{E}'[v\ \bar{\varepsilon}] \rangle$

[R12] $\langle \mathscr{E}[e] \rangle \to \langle \mathscr{E}[e'] \rangle$ if $e \to e'$

[R13] $P\ |\ R \to Q\ |\ R$ if $P \to Q$

[R14] $(\nu a)P \to (\nu a)Q$ if $P \to Q$

[R15] $P \to Q$ if $P \equiv P' \to Q' \equiv Q$

Table 2 defines the (call-by-value) operational semantics of FuSe$^{\{\}}$, where we write $e\{v/x\}$ and $e\{\iota/\rho\}$ for the (capture-avoiding) substitutions of values and identities in place of variables and identity variables, respectively. Evaluation contexts are essentially standard, with the obvious addition of $\{\mathcal{E}\}_u$:

Context $\mathcal{E} ::= [\ ]\ |\ \mathcal{E}\ e\ |\ v\ \mathcal{E}\ |\ \lceil \iota, \mathcal{E} \rceil\ |\ \text{let}\ \lceil \rho, x \rceil = \mathcal{E}\ \text{in}\ e\ |\ \{\mathcal{E}\}_u$
                 $|\ \text{let}\ x,y = \mathcal{E}\ \text{in}\ e\ |\ \text{match}\ \mathcal{E}\ \text{with}\ \{\mathtt{C}_i \Rightarrow e_i\}_{i \in I}$

Reduction of expressions is mostly conventional. The reduction rule [R7] erases the resumption $\{\ \cdot\ \}_\varepsilon$ around a pair (v, ε), provided that the endpoint in the right component of the pair matches the annotation of the resumption. The type system for FuSe$^{\{\}}$ that we are going to define enforces this condition statically. However, the rule also suggests an implementation of resumptions based on a simple runtime check: $\{(v, \varepsilon)\}_{\varepsilon'}$ reduces to (v, ε) if ε and ε' are the same endpoint and fails (*e.g.* raising an exception) otherwise. This alternative semantics may be useful if the type system of the host language is not expressive enough to enforce the typing discipline described in Sect. 3. We will consider this alternative semantics for one of the two implementations of FuSe$^{\{\}}$ (Sect. 4.2).

Reduction of processes is essentially the same appearing in [8,25]. Rule [R8] describes the spawning of a new thread, whose body is the application of fork's arguments. We have chosen this semantics of fork so that it matches OCaml's. Rule [R9] models session initiation, whereby create reduces a pair with the two endpoints of the newly created session. Compared to [8], we have one primitive that returns both endpoints of a new session instead of a pair of primitives that synchronize over shared/public channels. This choice is mostly a matter of simplicity: session initiation based on shared/public channels can be programmed on top of this mechanism. Also, the pair returned by `create` is packed to account for the fact that the caller of `create` does not know the identities of the endpoints therein. Note that, in the residual process, the leftmost occurrence of a represents an identity, hence it does not count as an actual usage of the endpoint a. Rules [R10] and [R11] model the exchange of messages. The first one moves the message from the sender to the receiver, pairing the message with the continuation endpoint on the receiver side. The second one applies the first argument of `select` to the receiver's continuation endpoint. Typically, the first argument of `select` will be a tag C which is effectively the message being exchanged in this case. We adopt this slightly unusual semantics of `select` because it models accurately the implementation and, at the same time, it calls for specific features of the type system concerning the type-level identification of endpoints. Rule [R12] lifts reductions from expressions to processes and rules [R13–R15] close reductions under parallel compositions, restrictions, and structural congruence, which is basically the same of the π-calculus and is therefore omitted.

3   Type System

In this section we define the typing discipline for $\mathtt{FuSe}^{\{\}}$. To keep the formal development as simple as possible, we work with a minimal type system and limit polymorphism to identity variables. These limitations do not have interesting effects on resumptions and will be lifted in the actual implementation.

The (finite) syntax of kinds, types, and session types is given below:

$$
\begin{array}{rl}
\textbf{Kind} & \kappa ::= \mathsf{U} \mid \mathsf{L} \\
\textbf{Type} & t, s ::= \mathtt{unit} \mid t \times s \mid \{\mathtt{C}_i \text{ of } t_i\}_{i \in I} \mid t \to^\kappa s \mid [T]_\iota \mid \exists \rho.t \mid \forall \rho.t \\
\textbf{Session type} & T, S ::= 0 \mid 1 \mid ?t \mid !t \mid \&[\mathtt{C}_i : T_i]_{i \in I} \mid \oplus[\mathtt{C}_i : T_i]_{i \in I} \mid T\,;S
\end{array}
$$

Instead of introducing concrete syntax for recursive (session) types, we let t, s and T, S range over the possibly infinite, regular trees generated by the above constructors for types and session types, respectively. We introduce recursive (session) types as solutions of finite systems of (session) type equations, such as (1.1). The shape of the equation, with the metavariable $S_{\mathbf{reg}}$ occurring unguarded on the lhs and guarded by at least one constructor on the rhs, guarantees that the equation has exactly one solution [3]. Type equality corresponds to regular tree equality.

The kinds U and L are used to classify types as unlimited and linear, respectively. Types of kind U denote values that can be used any number of times. Types of kind L denote values that must be used exactly once. We have to introduce a few more notions before seeing how kinds are assigned to types.

Types include a number of *base types* (such as `unit`, `int` and possibly others used in the examples), *products* $t \times s$, and *tagged unions* $\{\mathtt{C}_i \text{ of } t_i\}_{i \in I}$. The *function type* $t \to^\kappa s$ has a kind annotation κ indicating whether the function can be applied any number of times ($\kappa = \mathsf{U}$) or must be applied exactly once ($\kappa = \mathsf{L}$). This latter constraint typically arises when the function contains linear values in its closure. We omit the annotation κ when it is U. An *endpoint type*

$[T]_\iota$ consists of a session type T, describing the protocol according to which the endpoint must be used, and an identity ι of the endpoint. Finally, we have *existential and universal quantifiers* $\exists \rho.t$ and $\forall \rho.t$ over identity variables. These are the only binders in types. We write fid(t) for the set of identities occurring free in t and we identify (session) types modulo renaming of bound identities.

A session type describes the sequence of actions to be peformed on an endpoint. The basic actions $?t$ and $!t$ respectively denote the input and the output of a message of type t. As in [25] and unlike most presentations of session types, these forms do not specify a continuation, which can be attached using sequential composition. External choices $\&\,[C_i : T_i]_{i \in I}$ and internal choices $\oplus[C_i : T_i]_{i \in I}$ describe protocols that can proceed according to different continuations T_i each associated with a tag C_i. When the choice is internal, the process using the endpoint selects the continuation. When the choice is external, the process accepts the selection performed on the peer endpoint. Therefore, an external choice corresponds to an input (of a tag C_i) and an internal choice to an output. Sequential composition $T;S$ combines two sub-protocols T and S into a protocol where all the actions in T are supposed to be performed before any action in S. We have two terminal protocols: $\mathbf{0}$ indicates that no further action is to be performed on the endpoint; $\mathbf{1}$ indicates that the endpoint is meant to be resumed. As we will see, this distinction affects also the kinding of endpoint types: an endpoint whose protocol is $\mathbf{0}$ can be discarded for it serves no purpose; an endpoint whose protocol is $\mathbf{1}$ must be resumed exactly once.

We proceed defining a *labeled transition system* that formalizes the (observable) actions allowed by a protocol. This notion is instrumental in defining protocol equivalence which, in turn, is key in various parts of the type system.

Definition 1 (protocol LTS). *Let* done($\cdot$) *be the least predicate on protocols inductively defined by the following axiom and rule:*

$$\text{done}(\mathbf{1}) \qquad \frac{\text{done}(T) \qquad \text{done}(S)}{\text{done}(T;S)}$$

Let $\xrightarrow{\mu}$ *be the least family of relations on protocols inductively defined by the following axioms and rules, where μ ranges over labels* $?t;, !t;, ?C;, !C;:$

$$?t \xrightarrow{?t} \mathbf{1} \qquad !t \xrightarrow{!t} \mathbf{1} \qquad \frac{k \in I}{\&\,[C_i : T_i]_{i \in I} \xrightarrow{?C_k} T_k} \qquad \frac{k \in I}{\oplus[C_i : T_i]_{i \in I} \xrightarrow{!C_k} T_k}$$

$$\frac{T \xrightarrow{\mu} T'}{T;S \xrightarrow{\mu} T';S} \qquad \frac{\text{done}(T) \qquad S \xrightarrow{\mu} S'}{T;S \xrightarrow{\mu} S'}$$

Protocol equivalence is defined in terms of a bisimulation relation:

Definition 2 (equivalent protocols). *We write $\sim$ for the largest binary relation on protocols such that $T \sim S$ implies:*

- $\mathsf{done}(T)$ *if and only if* $\mathsf{done}(S)$;
- $T \xrightarrow{\mu} T'$ *implies* $S \xrightarrow{\mu} S'$ *and* $T' \sim S'$;
- $S \xrightarrow{\mu} S'$ *implies* $T \xrightarrow{\mu} T'$ *and* $T' \sim S'$.

We say that T and S are equivalent *if* $T \sim S$ holds.

Note that $\mathbf{0}$ is equivalent to all non-resumable session types that cannot make any progress. For example, $T_1 = T_1; S$ and $T_2 = 1; T_2$ are all equivalent to $\mathbf{0}$.

Proposition 1 (properties of $\sim$). *The following properties hold:*

1. *(equivalence)* $\sim$ *is reflexive and transitive;*
2. *(associativity)* $T;(S;R) \sim (T;S);R$;
3. *(unit)* $\mathbf{1};T \sim T; \mathbf{1} \sim T$.
4. *(congruence)* $T \sim T'$ *and* $S \sim S'$ *imply* $T;S \sim T';S'$.

The congruence property of $\sim$ is particularly important in our setting since we use sequential composition as a modular construct for structuring programs. We do *not* identify equivalent session types and assume that sequential composition associates to the right: $T;S;R$ means $T;(S;R)$. Although equivalence is decidable, this fact has little importance in our setting compared to [25] since $\sim$ is never used in the typing rules concerning user syntax.

We are now ready to classify types according to their kind. We resort to a coinductive definition to cope with possibly infinite types.

Definition 3 (kinding). *Let* $::$ *be the largest relation between types and kinds such that* $t :: \kappa$ *implies either* $\kappa = \mathsf{L}$ *or*

- $t = \mathsf{unit}$ *or* $t = t_1 \to t_2$ *or* $t = [T]_\iota$ *and* $T \sim \mathbf{0}$, *or*
- $t = \exists \rho.s$ *or* $t = \forall \rho.s$ *and* $s :: \kappa$, *or*
- $t = t_1 \times t_2$ *and* $t_i :: \kappa$ *for every* $i = 1, 2$, *or*
- $t = \{\mathsf{C}_i \text{ of } t_i\}_{i \in I}$ *and* $t_i :: \kappa$ *for every* $i \in I$.

We say that t is *unlimited* if $t :: \mathsf{U}$ and that t is *linear* if its only kind is L, namely if $t :: \kappa$ implies $\kappa = \mathsf{L}$. Endpoint types with a non-terminated session type and function types with kind annotation L are linear since they denote values that must be used exactly once. Base types and function types with kind annotation U are unlimited since they denote values that can be used (or discarded) without restrictions. Note that the kind of a function type $t \to^\kappa s$ solely depends on κ, but not on the kind of t or s. For example, $[?\mathsf{int}]_\iota \to \mathsf{int}$ is unlimited even if $[?\mathsf{int}]_\iota$ is not. Endpoint types $[T]_\iota$ are unlimited if $T \sim \mathbf{0}$: non-resumable endpoints on which no further actions can be performed can be discarded. On the contrary, $[\mathbf{1}]_\iota$ is linear, since it denotes an endpoint that must be resumed once. The kind of existential and universal types, products and tagged unions is determined by that of the component types. For example, the type $t = \{\mathsf{Nil} \text{ of } \mathsf{unit}, \mathsf{Cons} \text{ of } \mathsf{int} \times t\}$ of integer lists is unlimited, whereas the type $\mathsf{int} \times [\mathbf{1}]_\iota$ is linear. Finally, note that Definition 3 accounts for a form of *subkinding*: $t :: \mathsf{U}$ implies $t :: \mathsf{L}$. This is motivated by the observation that it is safe to use a value of an unlimited type exactly once.

As usual, the session types associated with peer endpoints must be dual to each other to guarantee communication safety. Duality expresses the fact that every input action performed on an endpoint is matched by a corresponding output performed on its peer and is defined thus:

Definition 4 (session type duality). *Session type duality is the function* $\overline{\cdot}$ *coinductively defined by the following equations:*

$$\overline{0} = 0 \qquad \overline{?t} = !t \qquad \overline{\&\,[C_i : T_i]_{i \in I}} = \oplus [C_i : \overline{T_i}]_{i \in I}$$
$$\overline{1} = 1 \qquad \overline{!t} = ?t \qquad \overline{\oplus\,[C_i : T_i]_{i \in I}} = \&\,[C_i : \overline{T_i}]_{i \in I} \qquad \overline{T;S} = \overline{T};\overline{S}$$

It is easy to verify that duality is an involution, that is $\overline{\overline{T}} = T$.

The type system makes use of two environments: identity environments Δ are sets of identities written $\iota_1, \ldots, \iota_n$, representing the endpoints statically known to a program fragment; type environments Γ are finite maps from names to types written $u_1 : t_1, \ldots, u_n : t_n$ associating a type with every (free) name occurring in an expression. We write Δ, Δ' for $\Delta \cup \Delta'$ when $\Delta \cap \Delta' = \emptyset$. We write $\Gamma(u)$ for the type associated with u in Γ, $\mathrm{dom}(\Gamma)$ for the domain of Γ, and Γ_1, Γ_2 for the union of Γ_1 and Γ_2 when $\mathrm{dom}(\Gamma_1) \cap \mathrm{dom}(\Gamma_2) = \emptyset$. We extend kinding to type environments in the obvious way, writing $\Gamma :: \kappa$ if $\Gamma(u) :: \kappa$ for all $u \in \mathrm{dom}(\Gamma)$. We also need a more flexible way of combining type environments that allows names with unlimited types to be used any number of times.

Definition 5 (environment combination [15]). *We write* $+$ *for the partial operation on type environments such that:*

$$\Gamma + \Gamma' \stackrel{\mathrm{def}}{=} \Gamma, \Gamma' \qquad\qquad \textit{if}\,\mathrm{dom}(\Gamma) \cap \mathrm{dom}(\Gamma') = \emptyset$$
$$(\Gamma, u : t) + (\Gamma', u : t) \stackrel{\mathrm{def}}{=} (\Gamma + \Gamma'), u : t \qquad \textit{if}\, t :: \mathsf{U}$$

Note that $\Gamma + \Gamma'$ is undefined if Γ and Γ' contain associations for the same name with different or linear types. When $\Gamma :: \mathsf{U}$, we have that $\Gamma + \Gamma$ is always defined and equal to Γ itself.

The type schemes of $\mathtt{FuSe}^{\{\}}$ constants are given in Table 3 as associations $\mathtt{c} : t$. Note that, in general, each constant has infinitely many types. Although most associations are as expected, it is worth commenting on a few details. First, observe that the kind annotation κ in the types of $\mathtt{pair}, \mathtt{send}$ and $\mathtt{select}$ coincides with the kind of the first argument of these constants. In particular, when t is linear and $\mathtt{pair/send/select}$ is supplied one argument v of type t, the resulting partial application is also linear. Second, in accordance with their operational semantics (Table 2) all the primitives for session communications ($\mathtt{send}, \mathtt{receive}, \mathtt{select}$, and $\mathtt{branch}$) return the very same endpoint they take as input as indicated by the identity ι that annotates the endpoint types in both the domain and range of these constants. Finally, in an application $\mathtt{select}\ v\varepsilon$ the function v is meant to be applied to the *peer* of ε. This constraint is indicated by the use of the co-identity $\bar{\iota}$ and is key for the soundness of the type system. Note

Table 3. Type schemes of $\mathtt{FuSe}^{\{\}}$ constants.

$\mathtt{()}$	:	$\mathtt{unit}$	
$\mathtt{pair}$	:	$t \to s \to^\kappa t \times s$	$t :: \kappa$
$\mathtt{C}_j$	:	$t_j \to \{\mathtt{C}_i \text{ of } t_i\}_{i \in I}$	$j \in I$
$\mathtt{fix}$	:	$((t \to s) \to t \to s) \to t \to s$	
$\mathtt{fork}$	:	$(t \to \mathtt{unit}) \to t \to \mathtt{unit}$	
$\mathtt{create}$	:	$\mathtt{unit} \to \exists \rho.([T]_\rho \times [\overline{T}]_{\overline{\rho}})$	
$\mathtt{send}$	:	$t \to [!t;T]_\iota \to^\kappa [T]_\iota$	$t :: \kappa$
$\mathtt{receive}$	:	$[?t;T]_\iota \to t \times [T]_\iota$	
$\mathtt{select}$	:	$([\overline{T_j}]_{\overline{\iota}} \to^\kappa \{\mathtt{C}_i \text{ of } [\overline{T_i}]_{\overline{\iota}}\}_{i \in I}) \to [\oplus[\mathtt{C}_i : T_i]_{i \in I}]_\iota \to^\kappa [T_j]_\iota$	$j \in I$
$\mathtt{branch}$	:	$[\&[\mathtt{C}_i : T_i]_{i \in I}]_\iota \to \{\mathtt{C}_i \text{ of } [T_i]_\iota\}_{i \in I}$	

also that the codomain of v matches the return type of **branch**, following the fact that v is applied to the peer of ε *after* the communication has occurred (Table 2). Finally, **create** returns a packaged pair of endpoints with dual session types. The package must be opened before the endpoints can be used for communication.

The typing rules for $\mathtt{FuSe}^{\{\}}$ are given in Table 4 and derive judgments $\Delta; \Gamma \vdash e : t$ for expressions and $\Delta; \Gamma \vdash P$ for processes. When present, side conditions are written to the right of the rule to which they apply. A judgment is well formed if all the identities occurring free in Γ and t are included in Δ. From now on we make the implicit assumption that all judgments are well formed.

We now discuss the most important aspects of the typing rules. In [T-CONST], the implict well-formedness constraint on typing judgments restricts the set of types that we can give to a constant to those whose free identities occur in Δ. In [T-CONST] and [T-NAME], the unused part of the type environment must be unlimited, to make sure that no linear name is left unused. The elimination rules for products and tagged unions are standard. Note the use of $+$ for combining type environments so that the same linear resource is not used multiple times in different parts of an expression. Rules [T-FUN] and [T-APP] deal with function types. In [T-FUN], the kind annotation on the arrow must be consistent with the kind of the environment in which the function is typed. If any name in the environment has a linear type, then the function must be linear itself to avoid repeated use of such name. By contrast, the kind annotation plays no role in [T-APP]. Abstraction and application of identities are standard. The side condition in [T-ID-APP] makes sure that the supplied identity is in scope. This condition is not necessarily captured by the well formedness of judgments in case ρ does not occur in t. Packing and unpacking are also standard. The identity variable ρ introduced in [T-UNPACK] is different from any other identity known to e_2. This prevents e_2 from using ρ in any context where a specific identity is required. Also, well formedness of judgments requires $\mathsf{fid}(s) \subseteq \Delta$, meaning that ρ is not allowed to escape its scope. The most interesting and distinguishing typing rule of $\mathtt{FuSe}^{\{\}}$ is [T-RESUME]. Let us discuss the rule clockwise, starting from $\{e\}_u$ and recalling that the purpose of this expression is to resume u once

Table 4. FuSe$^{\{\}}$: static semantics.

Typing rules for expressions $\boxed{\Delta; \Gamma \vdash e : t}$

[T-CONST]
$$\frac{}{\Delta; \Gamma \vdash c : t} \ c : t \qquad \Gamma :: \mathsf{U}$$

[T-SPLIT]
$$\frac{\Delta; \Gamma_1 \vdash e_1 : t_1 \times t_2 \qquad \Delta; \Gamma_2, x : t_1, y : t_2 \vdash e_2 : t}{\Delta; \Gamma_1 + \Gamma_2 \vdash \mathtt{let}\ x, y = e_1\ \mathtt{in}\ e_2 : t}$$

[T-NAME]
$$\frac{}{\Delta; \Gamma, u : t \vdash u : t} \ \Gamma :: \mathsf{U}$$

[T-CASE]
$$\frac{\Delta; \Gamma_1 \vdash e : \{\mathsf{C}_i\ \mathsf{of}\ t_i\}_{i \in I} \qquad \Delta; \Gamma_2 \vdash e_i : t_i \to^{\kappa_i} t \ ^{(i \in I)}}{\Delta; \Gamma_1 + \Gamma_2 \vdash \mathtt{match}\ e\ \mathtt{with}\ \{\mathsf{C}_i \Rightarrow e_i\}_{i \in I} : t}$$

[T-FUN]
$$\frac{\Delta; \Gamma, x : t \vdash e : s}{\Delta; \Gamma \vdash \lambda x.e : t \to^{\kappa} s} \ \Gamma :: \kappa$$

[T-APP]
$$\frac{\Delta; \Gamma_1 \vdash e_1 : t \to^{\kappa} s \qquad \Delta; \Gamma_2 \vdash e_2 : t}{\Delta; \Gamma_1 + \Gamma_2 \vdash e_1\ e_2 : s}$$

[T-ID-FUN]
$$\frac{\Delta, \rho; \Gamma \vdash v : t}{\Delta; \Gamma \vdash \Lambda \rho.v : \forall \rho.t}$$

[T-ID-APP]
$$\frac{\Delta; \Gamma \vdash e : \forall \rho.t}{\Delta; \Gamma \vdash e\,[\iota] : t\{\iota/\rho\}} \ \iota \in \Delta$$

[T-RESUME]
$$\frac{\Delta; \Gamma, u : [T]_\iota \vdash e : t \times [1]_\iota}{\Delta; \Gamma, u : [T; S]_\iota \vdash \{e\}_u : t \times [S]_\iota}$$

[T-PACK]
$$\frac{\Delta; \Gamma \vdash e : t\{\iota/\rho\}}{\Delta; \Gamma \vdash \lceil \iota, e \rceil : \exists \rho.t} \ \iota \in \Delta$$

[T-UNPACK]
$$\frac{\Delta; \Gamma_1 \vdash e_1 : \exists \rho.t \qquad \Delta, \rho; \Gamma_2, x : t \vdash e_2 : s}{\Delta; \Gamma_1 + \Gamma_2 \vdash \mathtt{let}\ \lceil \rho, x \rceil = e_1\ \mathtt{in}\ e_2 : s}$$

Typing rules for processes $\boxed{\Delta; \Gamma \vdash P}$

[T-THREAD]
$$\frac{\Delta; \Gamma \vdash e : \mathtt{unit}}{\Delta; \Gamma \vdash \langle e \rangle}$$

[T-PAR]
$$\frac{\Delta; \Gamma_i \vdash P_i \ ^{(i=1,2)}}{\Delta; \Gamma_1 + \Gamma_2 \vdash P_1 \mid P_2}$$

[T-SESSION]
$$\frac{\Delta, a, \bar{a}; \Gamma, a : [T]_a, \bar{a} : [S]_{\bar{a}} \vdash P}{\Delta; \Gamma \vdash (\nu a)P} \ T \sim \overline{S}$$

---

the evaluation of e is completed. The rule requires u to have a type of the form $[T; S]_\iota$, which specifies the identity ι of the endpoint and the protocols T and S to be completed in this order. Within e the type of u is changed to $[T]_\iota$ and the evaluation of e must yield a pair whose first component, of type t, is the result of the computation and whose second component, of type $[1]_\iota$, witnesses the fact that the prefix protocol T has been entirely carried out on u. Once the evaluation of e is completed, the type of the endpoint in the pair is reset to the suffix S. The same identity ι relates all the occurrences of the endpoint both in the type environments and in the expressions. Note that the annotation u in $\{\cdot\}_u$ does not count as a proper "use" of u. Its purpose is solely to identify the endpoint being resumed.

The typing rules for processes are mostly unremarkable. In [T-SESSION] the two peers of a session are introduced both in the type environment and in the identity environment. The protocols T and S of peer endpoints are required to be dual to each other modulo protocol equivalence. The use of $\sim$ accounts for the possibility that sequential compositions may be arranged differently in the threads using the two peers. For instance, one thread might be using an endpoint with protocol T, and its peer could have type $\mathbf{1};\overline{T}$ in a thread that has not resumed it yet. Still, $T \sim \mathbf{1};\overline{T} = \mathbf{1};T$.

We state a few basic properties of the typing discipline focusing on those more closely related to resumptions. To begin with, we characterize the type environments in which expressions and processes without free variables reduce.

Definition 6. *We say that Γ is* ground *if* $\mathrm{dom}(\Gamma)$ *contains endpoints only; that it is* well formed *if* $\varepsilon \in \mathrm{dom}(\Gamma)$ *implies* $\Gamma(\varepsilon) = [T]_\varepsilon$; *that it is* balanced *if* $\varepsilon, \overline{\varepsilon} \in \mathrm{dom}(\Gamma)$ *implies* $\Gamma(\varepsilon) = [T]_\varepsilon$ *and* $\Gamma(\overline{\varepsilon}) = [S]_{\overline{\varepsilon}}$ *and* $T \sim \overline{S}$.

Note that in a well-formed environment the type associated with endpoint ε is annotated with the correct identity of ε, that is ε itself.

As usual for session type systems, we must take into account the possibility that the type associated with session endpoints changes over time. Normally this only happens when processes use endpoints for communications. In our case, however, also expressions may change endpoint types because of resumptions. In order to track these changes, we introduce two relations that characterize the evolution of type environments alongside expressions and processes. The first relation is the obvious extension of equivalence $\sim$ to type environments:

Definition 7 (equivalent type environments). *Let $\Gamma = \{\varepsilon_i : [T_i]_{\varepsilon_i}\}_{i \in I}$ and $\Gamma' = \{\varepsilon_i : [S_i]_{\varepsilon_i}\}_{i \in I}$. We write $\Gamma \sim \Gamma'$ if $T_i \sim S_i$ for every $i \in I$.*

The second relation includes $\sim$ and mimics communications at the type level:

Definition 8. *Let $\rightsquigarrow$ be the least relation between type environments such that:*

$$\Gamma \rightsquigarrow \Gamma' \qquad\qquad\qquad \text{if } \Gamma \sim \Gamma'$$
$$\Gamma, \varepsilon : [!t;T]_\varepsilon, \overline{\varepsilon} : [?t;S]_{\overline{\varepsilon}} \rightsquigarrow \Gamma, \varepsilon : [T]_\varepsilon, \overline{\varepsilon} : [S]_{\overline{\varepsilon}}$$
$$\Gamma, \varepsilon : [\oplus[\mathtt{C}_i : T_i]_{i \in I}]_\varepsilon, \overline{\varepsilon} : [\& [\mathtt{C}_i : S_i]_{i \in I}]_{\overline{\varepsilon}} \rightsquigarrow \Gamma, \varepsilon : [T_k]_\varepsilon, \overline{\varepsilon} : [S_k]_{\overline{\varepsilon}} \qquad \text{if } k \in I$$

Concerning subject reduction for expressions, we have:

Theorem 1 (SR for expressions). *Let $\Delta; \Gamma \vdash e : t$ where Γ is ground and well formed. If $e \rightarrow e'$, then $\Delta; \Gamma' \vdash e' : t$ for some Γ' such that $\Gamma \sim \Gamma'$.*

Theorem 1 guarantees that resumptions in well-typed programs do not change arbitrarily the session types of endpoints. The only permitted changes are those allowed by session type equivalence. Concerning progress, we have:

Theorem 2 (progress for expressions). *If Γ is ground and well formed and $\Delta; \Gamma \vdash e : t$ and $e \nrightarrow$, then either e is a value or $e = \mathcal{E}[K\ v]$ for some $\mathcal{E}$, v, w, and $K \in \{\mathtt{fork}\ w, \mathtt{create}, \mathtt{send}\ w, \mathtt{receive}, \mathtt{select}\ w, \mathtt{branch}\}$.*

That is, an irreducible expression that is not a value is a term that is meant to reduce at the level of processes. Note that a resumption $\{(v, \varepsilon)\}_{\varepsilon'}$ is *not* a value and is meant to reduce at the level of expressions via [R7]. Hence, Theorem 2 guarantees that in a well-typed program all such resumptions are such that $\varepsilon = \varepsilon'$. An alternative reading for this observation is that each endpoint is guaranteed to have a unique identity in every well-typed program.

Theorem 3 (SR for processes). *Let* $\Delta; \Gamma \vdash P$ *where* Γ *is ground, well formed and balanced. If* $P \to Q$, *then* $\Delta; \Gamma' \vdash Q$ *for some* Γ' *such that* $\Gamma \rightsquigarrow^* \Gamma'$.

Apart from being a fundamental sanity check for the type system, Theorem 3 states that the communications occurring in processes are precisely those permitted by the session types in the type environments. Therefore, Theorem 3 gives us a guarantee of protocol fidelity. A particular instance of protocol fidelity concerns sequential composition: a well-typed process using an endpoint with type $T;S$ is guaranteed to perform the actions described by T first, and then those described by S. Other standard properties including communication safety and (partial) progress for processes can also be proved [21].

Example 1 (resumption combinators). In prospect of devising a library implementation of FuSe$^{\{\}}$, the resumption expression $\{\cdot\}_u$ is challenging to deal with, for its typing rule involves an non-trivial manipulation of the type environment whereby the type of u changes as u flows into and out of the expression. In practice, it is convenient to encapsulate $\{\cdot\}_u$ expressions in two combinators that can be easily implemented as higher-order functions (Sects. 4.2 and 4.3):

$$@= \stackrel{\text{def}}{=} \lambda f.\lambda x.\{f\ x\}_x$$
$$@> \stackrel{\text{def}}{=} \lambda f.\lambda x.\texttt{let}\ \_, x = \{((),f\ x)\}_x\ \texttt{in}\ x$$

The combinator $@=$ is a general version of $@>$ that applies to functions returning an actual result in addition to the endpoint to be resumed. We derive

$$\cfrac{\cfrac{\cfrac{\Delta; f : [T]_\iota \to^\kappa t \times [1]_\iota \vdash f : [T]_\iota \to^\kappa t \times [1]_\iota \quad \Delta; x : [T]_\iota \vdash x : [T]_\iota}{\Delta; f : [T]_\iota \to^\kappa t \times [1]_\iota, x : [T]_\iota \vdash f\ x : t \times [1]_\iota}}{\cfrac{\Delta; f : [T]_\iota \to^\kappa t \times [1]_\iota, x : [T;S]_\iota \vdash \{f\ x\}_x : t \times [S]_\iota}{\cfrac{\Delta; f : [T]_\iota \to^\kappa t \times [1]_\iota \vdash \lambda x.\{f\ x\}_x : [T;S]_\iota \to^\kappa t \times [S]_\iota}{\Delta; \emptyset \vdash \lambda f.\lambda x.\{f\ x\}_x : ([T]_\iota \to^\kappa t \times [1]_\iota) \to [T;S]_\iota \to^\kappa t \times [S]_\iota}}}$$

for every T, ι, t and S such that $\mathsf{fid}(T) \cup \mathsf{fid}(t) \cup \mathsf{fid}(S) \cup \{\iota\} \subseteq \Delta$. A similar derivation allows us to derive

$$\Delta; \emptyset \vdash @> : ([T]_\iota \to^\kappa [1]_\iota) \to [T;S]_\iota \to^\kappa [S]_\iota$$

In the implementation we will give $@=$ and $@>$ their most general type by leveraging OCaml's support for parametric polymorphism. Other combinators for resuming two or more endpoints can be defined similarly. For example,

$$@@> \stackrel{\text{def}}{=} \lambda f.\lambda x.\lambda y.\texttt{let}\ y, x = \{\texttt{let}\ x, y = \{f\ x\ y\}_y\ \texttt{in}\ (y,x)\}_x\ \texttt{in}\ (x,y)$$

is analogous to $@>$, but resumes two endpoints at once. ∎

Example 2 (alternative communication API). It could be argued that the communication primitives `send` and `receive` are not really "primitive" because their types make use of *both* I/O actions *and* sequential composition. Alternatively, we could equip $\mathsf{FuSe}^{\{\}}$ with two primitives `send'` and `receive'` having the same operational semantics as `send` and `receive` but the following types:

$$\mathtt{send'} : t \to [!t]_\iota \to^\kappa [\mathbf{1}]_\iota \qquad t :: \kappa$$
$$\mathtt{receive'} : [?t]_\iota \to t \times [\mathbf{1}]_\iota$$

Starting from `send'` and `receive'`, `send` and `receive` could then be derived with the help of `@=` and `@>`, used below in infix notation:

$$\mathtt{send} \overset{\text{def}}{=} \lambda z.\lambda x.\mathtt{send'}\ z\ \mathtt{@>}\ x$$
$$\mathtt{receive} \overset{\text{def}}{=} \lambda x.\mathtt{receive'}\ \mathtt{@=}\ x$$

We find a communication API based on `send'` and `receive'` appealing for its cleaner correspondence between primitives and session type constructors. In particular, with this API the resumption combinators account for *all* occurrences of $\_;\_$ in protocols. In the formal model of $\mathsf{FuSe}^{\{\}}$, we have decided to stick to the conventional typing of `send` and `receive` for continuity with other presentations of similar calculi [8,25,29]. ∎

Example 3. This example illustrates the sort of havoc that could be caused if two endpoints had the same identity. As a particular instance, we see the importance of distinguishing the identity of peer endpoints. The derivation

$$\vdots$$

$$\cfrac{\cfrac{x : [\mathbf{1}]_\iota, y : [\mathbf{1}]_\iota \vdash (y,x) : [\mathbf{1}]_\iota \times [\mathbf{1}]_\iota}{\cfrac{x : [\mathbf{1}]_\iota, y : [\mathbf{1};S]_\iota \vdash \{(y,x)\}_y : [\mathbf{1}]_\iota \times [S]_\iota \qquad \hat{x} : [S]_\iota, \hat{y} : [\mathbf{1}]_\iota \vdash (\hat{x},\hat{y}) : [S]_\iota \times [\mathbf{1}]_\iota}{\cfrac{x : [\mathbf{1}]_\iota, y : [\mathbf{1};S]_\iota \vdash \mathtt{let}\ \hat{y},\hat{x} = \{(y,x)\}_y\ \mathtt{in}\ (\hat{x},\hat{y}) : [S]_\iota \times [\mathbf{1}]_\iota}{\cfrac{x : [\mathbf{1};T]_\iota, y : [\mathbf{1};S]_\iota \vdash \{\mathtt{let}\ \hat{y},\hat{x} = \{(y,x)\}_y\ \mathtt{in}\ (\hat{x},\hat{y})\}_x : [S]_\iota \times [T]_\iota}{\cfrac{x : [\mathbf{1};T]_\iota \vdash \lambda y.\{\mathtt{let}\ \hat{y},\hat{x} = \{(y,x)\}_y\ \mathtt{in}\ (\hat{x},\hat{y})\}_x : [\mathbf{1};S]_\iota \to^\mathsf{L} [S]_\iota \times [T]_\iota}{\vdash \lambda x.\lambda y.\{\mathtt{let}\ \hat{y},\hat{x} = \{(y,x)\}_y\ \mathtt{in}\ (\hat{x},\hat{y})\}_x : [\mathbf{1};T]_\iota \to [\mathbf{1};S]_\iota \to^\mathsf{L} [S]_\iota \times [T]_\iota}}}}}$$

can be used to type check a function that, applied to two endpoints x and y whose types are $[\mathbf{1};T]_\iota$ and $[\mathbf{1};S]_\iota$ respectively, returns a pair containing the same two endpoints, but with their types changed to $[S]_\iota$ and $[T]_\iota$. If there existed two endpoints ε_1 and ε_2 with the same identity ι from two different sessions, the function could be used to exchange their protocols, almost certainly causing communication errors in the rest of the computation. If ε_1 and ε_2 were the peers of the same session, then communication safety would still be guaranteed by the condition $T \sim \overline{S}$, but protocol fidelity would be violated nonetheless. ∎

4   Context-Free Session Types in `OCaml`

In this section we detail two different implementations of $\mathsf{FuSe}^{\{\}}$ communication and resumption primitives as `OCaml` functions. We start defining a few basic data structures and a convenient OCaml representation of session types (Sect. 4.1) before describing the actual implementations. The first one (Sect. 4.2) is easily portable to any programming language supporting parametric polymorphism, but relies on lightweight runtime checks to verify when an endpoint can be safely resumed. The second implementation (Sect. 4.3) closely follows the typing discipline of FuSe$^{\{\}}$ presented in Sect. 3, but relies on more advanced features (existential types) of the host language. The particular implementation we describe is based on OCaml's first-class modules [7,32]. We conclude the section revisiting and extending the running example of [25] (Sect. 4.4).

4.1 Basic Setup

To begin with, we define a simple module Channel that implements *unsafe* communication channels. In turn, Channel is based on OCaml's Event module, which implements communication primitives in the style of Concurrent ML [23].

```
module Channel : sig
  type t
  val create  : unit → t        (* create a new unsafe channel *)
  val send    : α → t → unit    (* send a message of type α    *)
  val receive : t → α           (* receive a message of type α *)
end = struct
  type t        = unit Event.channel
  let create    = Event.new_channel
  let send x u  = Event.sync (Event.send u (Obj.magic x))
  let receive u = Obj.magic (Event.sync (Event.receive u))
end
```

An unsafe channel is just an Event.channel for exchanging messages of type unit. The unit type parameter is just a placeholder, for communication primitives perform unsafe casts (with Obj.magic) on every exchanged message. Note that Event.send and Event.receive only create synchronization events, and communication only happens when these events are passed to Event.sync. Using Event channels is convenient but not mandatory: the rest of our implementation is essentially independent of the underlying communication framework.

The second ingredient of our library is an implementation of *atomic boolean flags*. Since OCaml's type system is not substructural we are unable to distinguish between linear and unlimited types and, in particular, we are unable to prevent multiple endpoint usages solely using the type system. Following ideas of Tov and Pucella [27] and Hu and Yoshida [11] and the design of FuSe [21], the idea is to associate each endpoint with a boolean flag indicating whether the endpoint can be safely used or not. The flag is initially set to true, indicating that the endpoint can be used, and is tested by every operation that uses the endpoint. If the flag is still true, then the endpoint can be used and the flag is reset to false. If the flag is false, then the endpoint has already been used in the past and the operation aborts raising an exception. Atomicity is needed to make sure

that the flag is tested and updated in a consistent way in case multiple threads
try to use the same endpoint simultaneously.

```
module Flag : sig
  type t
  val create : unit → t (* create a new atomic boolean flag *)
  val use    : t → unit (* mark as used or raise exception  *)
end = struct
  type t     = Mutex.t
  let create = Mutex.create
  let use f  = if not (Mutex.try_lock f) then raise Error
end
```

We represent an atomic boolean flag as a `Mutex.t`, that is a lock in `OCaml`'s
standard library. The value of the flag is the state of the mutex: when the mutex
is unlocked, the flag is `true`. Using the flag means attempting to acquire the
lock with the non-blocking function `Mutex.try_lock`. As for `Event` channels, the
mutex is a choice of convenience more than necessity. Alternative realizations,
possibly based on lightweight compare-and-swap operations, can be considered.

We conclude the setup phase by defining a bunch of `OCaml` singleton types
in correspondence with the session type constructors:

```
type 0          = End
type 1          = Resume
type φ msg      = Message  (* either ?φ or !φ     *)
type φ tag      = Tag      (* either &[φ] or ⊕[φ] *)
type (α,β) seq  = Sequence (* α;β                 *)
```

The type parameter φ is the type of the exchanged message in `msg` and a
polymorphic variant type representing the available choices in `tag`. The type
parameteres α and β in `seq` stand for the prefix and suffix protocols of a sequential composition $\alpha \, ; \, \beta$. The data constructors of these types are never used and
are given only because `OCaml` is more liberal in the construction of recursive
types when these are concrete rather than abstract. Hereafter, we use $\tau_1, \tau_2, \ldots$
to range over `OCaml` types and $\alpha, \beta, \ldots, \varphi$ to range over `OCaml` type variables.
Considering that `OCaml` supports equi-recursive types, we ignore once again the
concrete syntax for expressing infinite session types and work with infinite trees
instead. `OCaml` uses the notation τ `as` α for denoting a type τ in which occurrences of α stand for the type as a whole.

4.2 A Dynamically Checked, Portable Implementation

The first implementation of the library that we present ignores identities in types
and verifies the soundness of resumptions by means of a runtime check. In this
case, an endpoint type $[T]_\iota$ is encoded as the `OCaml` type $(\tau_1 \, , \, \tau_2)$ `t` where τ_1
and τ_2 are roughly determined as follows:

– when T is a self-dual session type constructor (either $\mathbf{0}$, $\mathbf{1}$, or $\_;\_$), then both
  τ_1 and τ_2 are the corresponding `OCaml` type ($\mathtt{0}$, $\mathtt{1}$, or `seq`, respectively);

– when T is an input (either $?t$ or $\&\,[C_i : T_i]_{i \in I}$), then τ_1 is the encoding the received message/choice and τ_2 is 0; dually when T is an output.

More precisely, types and session types are encoded thus:

Definition 9 (encoding of types and session types). *Let $[\![\cdot]\!]$ and $\langle\!\langle\cdot\rangle\!\rangle$ be the encoding functions coinductively defined by the following equations:*

$$[\![0]\!] = (0,0)\ \mathsf{t} \qquad\qquad [\![\&\,[C_i : T_i]_{i \in I}]\!] = (\{C_i\ \mathsf{of}\ [\![T_i]\!]\}_{i \in I}\ \mathsf{tag}, 0)\ \mathsf{t}$$

$$[\![1]\!] = (1,1)\ \mathsf{t} \qquad\qquad [\![\oplus\,[C_i : T_i]_{i \in I}]\!] = (0, \{C_i\ \mathsf{of}\ [\![\overline{T_i}]\!]\}_{i \in I}\ \mathsf{tag})\ \mathsf{t}$$

$$[\![?t]\!] = (\langle\!\langle t \rangle\!\rangle\ \mathsf{msg}, 0)\ \mathsf{t} \qquad\qquad [\![T;S]\!] = (([\![T]\!], [\![S]\!]\ \mathsf{seq}, ([\![\overline{T}]\!], [\![\overline{S}]\!]\ \mathsf{seq})\ \mathsf{t}$$

$$[\![!t]\!] = (0, \langle\!\langle t \rangle\!\rangle\ \mathsf{msg})\ \mathsf{t} \qquad\qquad \langle\!\langle [T]_\iota \rangle\!\rangle = [\![T]\!]$$

where $\langle\!\langle\cdot\rangle\!\rangle$ is extended homomorphically to all the remaining type constructors erasing kind annotations on arrows and existential and universal quantifiers.

Note that identities ι in endpoint types are simply erased; we will revise this choice in the second implementation (Sect. 4.3). The encoding is semantically grounded through the relationship between sessions and linear channels [4,5, 14,21] and is extended here to sequential composition for the first time. The distinguishing feature of this encoding is that is makes it easy to express session type duality constraints solely in terms of type equality:

Theorem 4. *If $[\![T]\!] = (\tau_1, \tau_2)\ \mathsf{t}$, then $[\![\overline{T}]\!] = (\tau_2, \tau_1)\ \mathsf{t}$.*

That is, we pass from a session type to its dual by flipping the type parameters of the t type. This also works for unknown or partially known session types: the dual of $(\alpha, \beta)\ \mathsf{t}$ is $(\beta, \alpha)\ \mathsf{t}$.

We can now look at the concrete representation of the type $(\alpha, \beta)\ \mathsf{t}$:

```
type (α,β) t = { chan : Channel.t; pol : int; once : Flag.t }
```

An endpoint is a record with three fields, a reference `chan` to the unsafe channel used for the actual communications, an integer number $\mathsf{pol} \in \{+1, -1\}$ representing the endpoint's polarity, and an atomic boolean flag `once` indicating whether the endpoint can be safely used or not. Of course, this representation is hidden from the user of the library and any direct access to these fields occurs via one of the public functions that we are going to discuss.

The $\mathsf{FuSe}^{\{\}}$ primitives for session communication are implemented by corresponding OCaml functions with the following signatures, which are directly related to the type schemes in Table 3 through the encoding in Definition 9:

```
val create   : unit → (α,β) t × (β,α) t
val send'    : φ → (0,φ msg) t → (1,1) t
val receive' : (φ msg,0) t → φ × (1,1) t
val select   : ((β,α) t → φ) → (0,φ tag) t → (α,β) t
val branch   : (φ tag,0) t → φ
val (@=)     : ((α,β) t → φ × (1,1) t) →
               (((α,β) t,(γ,δ) t) seq,((β,α) t,(δ,γ) t) seq) t →
               φ × (γ,δ) t
```

We take advantage of parametric polymorphism to give these functions their most general types. We implement the alternative communication API with the primitives `send'` and `receive'` because their type signatures are simpler. From these functions, `send` and `receive` can be easily derived as shown in Example 2. We also omit `@>` which is just a particular instance of `@=` (Example 1). The types for `select` and `branch` are slightly more general than those in Table 3, but the tossing of tags between choices and unions cannot be expressed as accurately in OCaml without fixing the set of tags. The given typing is still sound though.

Since this version of the library ignores endpoint identities, the endpoints returned by `create` are already unpackaged. The implementation of `create` is

```
let create () = let ch = Channel.create () in
                { chan = ch; pol = +1; once = Flag.create () },
                { chan = ch; pol = -1; once = Flag.create () }
```

and consists of the creation of a new unsafe channel `ch` and two records referring to it with opposite polarities and each with its own validity flag.

The communication primitives are defined in terms of corresponding operations on the underlying unsafe channel and make use of an auxiliary function

```
let fresh u = { u with once = Flag.create () }
```

that returns a copy of `u` with `once` overwritten by a fresh flag. We have:

```
let send' x u  = Flag.use u.once; Channel.send x u.chan; fresh u
let receive' u = Flag.use u.once; (Channel.receive u.chan, fresh u)
let select f u = Flag.use u.once; Channel.send f u.chan; fresh u
let branch u   = Flag.use u.once; Channel.receive u.chan (fresh u)
```

The flag associated with the endpoint `u` is used before communication takes place and refreshed just before the endpoint is returned to the user. It is not possible to refresh the flag by just releasing the lock in it, for any existing alias to the endpoint must be permanently marked as invalid [21].

We complete the module with the implementation of `@=`, shown below:

```
let (@=) scope u =
  let res, v = scope (Obj.magic u) in
  if u.chan == v.chan && u.pol = v.pol then (res, Obj.magic v)
  else raise Error
```

The endpoint `u` is passed to `scope`, which evaluates to a pair made of the result `res` of the computation and the endpoint `v` to be resumed. The cast `Obj.magic u` is necessary to turn the type of `u` from $T;S$ to T, as required by `scope`. The second line in the body of `@=` checks that the endpoint `v` resulting from the evaluation of `scope` is indeed the same endpoint `u` that was fed in it. Note the key role of the polarity in checking that `u` and `v` are the same endpoint and the use of the physical equality operator `==`, which compares only the *references* to the involved unsafe channels. An exception is raised if `v` is not the same endpoint as `u`. Otherwise, the result of the computation and `v` are returned. The cast `Obj.magic v` effectively resumes the endpoint turning its type from 1 to S. The two casts roughly delimit the region of code that we would write within $\{ \cdot \}_u$ in the formal model.

4.3   A Statically Checked Implementation

The second implementation we present reflects more accurately the typing information in endpoint types, which includes the identity of endpoints. In this case, we represent an endpoint type $[T]_\rho$ as an OCaml type $(\tau_1 , \tau_2 , \rho , \bar{\rho})$ t where τ_1 and τ_2 are determined from T in a similar way as before. In addition, the phantom type parameter ρ is the (abstract) identity of the endpoint and $\bar{\rho}$ that of its peer (we represent identity variables as OCaml type variables and assume that $\bar{\rho}$ is another OCaml type variable distinct from ρ). More formally, the revised encoding of (session) types into OCaml types is given below:

Definition 10 (revised encoding of types and session types). *Let $[\![\cdot]\!]_\iota$ and $\langle\!\langle\cdot\rangle\!\rangle$ be the encoding functions coinductively defined by the following equations:*

$$[\![0]\!]_\iota = (0,0,\iota,\bar{\iota}) \text{ t} \qquad [\![\& [C_i : T_i]_{i\in I}]\!]_\iota = (\{C_i \text{ of } [\![T_i]\!]_\iota\}_{i\in I} \text{ tag},0,\iota,\bar{\iota}) \text{ t}$$
$$[\![1]\!]_\iota = (1,1,\iota,\bar{\iota}) \text{ t} \qquad [\![\oplus [C_i : T_i]_{i\in I}]\!]_\iota = (0,\{C_i \text{ of } [\![\overline{T_i}]\!]_{\overline{\iota}}\}_{i\in I} \text{ tag},\iota,\bar{\iota}) \text{ t}$$
$$[\![?t]\!]_\iota = (\langle\!\langle t\rangle\!\rangle \text{ msg},0,\iota,\bar{\iota}) \text{ t} [\![T;S]\!]_\iota = ((\![T]\!]_\iota,[\![S]\!]_\iota) \text{ seq},([\![\overline{T}]\!]_{\overline{\iota}},[\![\overline{S}]\!]_{\overline{\iota}}) \text{ seq},\iota,\bar{\iota}) \text{ t}$$
$$[\![!t]\!]_\iota = (0,\langle\!\langle t\rangle\!\rangle \text{ msg},\iota,\bar{\iota}) \text{ t} \qquad \langle\!\langle [T]_\iota\rangle\!\rangle = [\![T]\!]_\iota$$

where $\langle\!\langle\cdot\rangle\!\rangle$ is extended homomorphically to all the remaining type constructors erasing kind annotations on arrows and existential and universal quantifiers.

In Definition 10, ι is always an identity (co-)variable for we apply the encoding to user types in which these variables are never instantiated. Once again, the relation between the encoding of a session type and that of its dual can be expressed in terms of type equality:

Theorem 5. *If $[\![T]\!]_\iota = (\tau_1 , \tau_2 , \iota, \bar{\iota})$ t, then $[\![\overline{T}]\!]_{\overline{\iota}} = (\tau_2 , \tau_1 , \overline{\iota}, \iota)$ t.*

The concrete representation of $(\alpha , \beta , \iota, \bar{\iota})$ t is the same that we have given in Sect. 4.2. As an optimization, the pol field of that representation could be omitted since there it is only necessary to verify an endpoint equality condition which is statically guaranteed by the implementation we are discussing now.

The easiest way of representing an existential type in OCaml is by means of its built-in module system [17]. In our case, we have to make sure that create returns a packaged pair of peer endpoints, each with its own identity. The OCaml representation of this type can be given by the following module signature

```
module type Package = sig
   type i and j
   val unpack : unit → (α,β,i,j) t × (β,α,j,i) t
end
```

which contains two abstract type declarations i and j, corresponding to the identities of the two endpoints, and a function unpack to retrieve the endpoints once the module with this signature has been opened. Concerning the implementation of `Package`, there are two technical issues we have to address, both related to the fact that there cannot be two different endpoints with the same identity. First, we have to make sure that each session has its own implementation of the `Package` module signature. To this aim, we take advantage of `OCaml`'s support for *first-class modules* [7,32], allowing us to write a function (`create` in the specific case) that returns a module implementation. The second issue is that we cannot store the two endpoints directly in the module, for the types of the endpoints contain type variables (α and β in the above signature) which are not allowed to occur free in a module. For this reason, we delay the actual creation of the endpoints at the time `unpack` is applied. This means, however, that the same implementation of `Package` could in principle be unpacked several times, instantiating different sessions whose endpoints would share the same identities. To make sure that `unpack` is applied at most once for each implementation of `Package` we resort once again to an atomic boolean flag.

The signatures of the functions implementing the communication primitives are essentially the same that we have already seen in Sect. 4.2, except for the presence of identity variables ρ and σ and the type of `create`, which now returns a packaged pair of endpoints:

```
val create   : unit → (module Package)
val send'    : φ → (0,φ msg,ρ,σ) t → (1,1,ρ,σ) t
val receive' : (φ msg,0,ρ,σ) t → φ × (1,1,ρ,σ) t
val select   : ((β,α,σ,ρ) t → φ) → (0,φ tag,ρ,σ) t → (α,β,ρ,σ) t
val branch   : (φ tag,0,ρ,σ) t → φ
val (@=)     : ((α,β,ρ,σ) t → φ × (1,1,ρ,σ) t) →
                 (((α,β,ρ,σ) t,(γ,δ,ρ,σ) t) seq,
                  ((β,α,σ,ρ) t,(δ,γ,σ,ρ) t) seq,ρ,σ) t →
                 φ × (γ,δ,ρ,σ) t
```

Note in particular the type of `select`, where we refer to both an endpoint and its peer by flipping the type parameters corresponding to session types (α and β) and those corresponding to identity variables (ρ and σ) as well.

The implementation of `create` is shown below, in which `Previous.create` refers to the version of `create` detailed in Sect. 4.2:

```
let create () =
  let once = Flag.create () in
  (module struct
     type i and j
     let unpack () = Flag.use once; Previous.create ()
   end : Package)
```

The implementation of the I/O primitives is the same as in Sect. 4.2 and need not be repeated here. The resumption combinator shrinks to a simple cast

```
let (@=) = Obj.magic
```

since the equality condition on endpoints that is necessary for its soundness is now statically guaranteed by the type system. The cast is necessary because @= coerces its first argument to a function with a different type. With this implementation of FuSe$^{\{\}}$, a session is typically created thus

```
let module A = (val create ()) in (* create session  *)
let a, b = A.unpack () in          (* unpack endpoints *)
fork server a;                     (* fork server      *)
client b                           (* run client       *)
```

where client and server are suitable functions that use the two endpoints of the session without making any assumption on their identities. Otherwise, the abstract types A.i and A.j would escape their scope, resulting in a type error.

4.4   Extended Example: Trees over Sessions

In this section we revisit and expand an example taken from [25] to show how context-free session types help improving the precision of (inferred) protocols and the robustness of code. We start from the declaration

```
type α tree = Leaf | Node of α × α tree × α tree
```

defining an algebraic representation of binary trees, and we consider the following function, which sends a binary tree over a session endpoint. Note that, for the sake of readability, in this section we assume that OCaml polymorphic variant tags are curried as in the formal model and write for example `Node instead of its $\eta$-expansion fun x → `Node x.

```
1    let send_tree t u =
2      let rec send_tree_aux t u =
3        match t with
4        | Leaf → select `Leaf u
5        | Node (x, l, r) → let u = select `Node u in
6                           let u = send x u in
7                           let u = send_tree_aux l u in
8                           let u = send_tree_aux r u in u
9      in select `Done (send_tree_aux t u)
```

The auxiliary function send_tree_aux serializes a (sub)tree t on the endpoint u, whereas send_tree invokes send_tree_aux once and finally sends a sentinel label `Done that signals the end of the stream of messages. FuSe infers for send_tree the type α tree → T_{reg} → A where T_{reg} is the session type

$$T_{\text{reg}} = \oplus[\,`\text{Leaf} : T_{\text{reg}}, `\text{Node} : !\alpha; T_{\text{reg}}, `\text{Done} : A] \qquad (4.1)$$

and A is a session type variable (the code in send_tree does not specify in any way how u will be used when send_tree returns). Without the sentinel `Done, the protocol T_{reg} inferred by OCaml would never terminate (like S_{reg} in (1.1)) making it hardly useful. Even with the sentinel, though, T_{reg} is very imprecise.

For example, it allows the labels `Node, `Leaf, and `Done to be selected in this order, even though send_tree never generates such a sequence.[1]

To illustrate the sort of issues that this lack of precision may cause, it helps to look at a consumer process that receives a tree sent with send_tree:

```
1   let receive_tree u =
2     let rec receive_tree_aux u =
3       match branch u with
4       | `Leaf u → Leaf, u
5       | `Node u → let x, u = receive u in
6                   let l, u = receive_tree_aux u in
7                   let r, u = receive_tree_aux u in
8                   Node (x, l, r), u
9       | _ → assert false (* impossible *)
10    in let t, u = receive_tree_aux u in
11      match branch u with
12      | `Done u → (t, u)
13      | _ → assert false (* impossible *)
```

This function consists of a main body (lines 2–9) responsible for building up a (sub)tree received from u, the bootstrap of the reception phase (line 10), and a final reception that awaits for the sentinel (lines 11–13). For receive_tree, OCaml infers the type $\overline{T_{\mathrm{reg}}} \to \alpha$ tree $\times \overline{A}$. The fact that send_tree and receive_tree use endpoints with dual session types should be enough to reassure us that the two functions communicate safely within the same session. Unfortunately, our confidence is spoiled by two suspicious catch-all cases (lines 9 and 13) without which receive_tree would be ill typed. In particular, omitting line 9 would result in a non-exhaustive pattern matching (lines 3–8) because label `Done can in principle be received along with `Leaf and `Node. A similar issue would arise omitting line 13. Omitting both lines 9 and 13 would also be a problem. In search of a typing derivation for receive_tree, OCaml would try to compute the intersection of the labels handled by the two pattern matching constructs, only to find out that such intersection is empty.

We clean up and simplify send_tree and receive_tree using resumptions:

```
1   let rec send_tree t u =
2     match t with
3     | Leaf → select `Leaf u
4     | Node (x, l, r) → let u = select `Node u in
5                        let u = send x u in
6                        let u = send_tree l @> u in (*resumption*)
7                        let u = send_tree r u in u
8   let rec receive_tree u =
9     match branch u with
```

---

[1] The claim made in [25] that send_tree_aux is ill typed is incorrect. There exist typing derivations for send_tree_aux proving that it has type α tree $\to T \to T$ for every T that satisfies the equation $T = \oplus[\text{`Leaf} : T, \text{`Node} : !\alpha;T,\dots]$.

```
10        | `Leaf u  →  Leaf, u
11        | `Node u  →  let x, u = receive u in
12                       let l, u = receive_tree @= u in     (*resumption*)
13                       let r, u = receive_tree u in Node (x, l, r), u
```

In send_tree we use the simple resumption @> since the function only returns the endpoint u. In receive_tree we use @= since the function returns the received tree in addition to the continuation endpoint. Note that we no longer need an explicit sentinel message `Done that marks the end of the message stream because the protocol now specifies exactly the number of messages needed to serialize a tree. For the same reason, the catch-all cases in receive_tree are no longer necessary. For these functions, OCaml respectively infers the types α tree $\to [T_{cf}]_\rho \to [1]_\rho$ and $[\overline{T_{cf}}]_\rho \to \alpha$ tree $\times [1]_\rho$ where T_{cf} is the session type such that

$$T_{cf} = \oplus[`\text{Leaf} : 1, `\text{Node} : !\alpha; T_{cf}; T_{cf}]$$

The leftmost occurrence of _;_ in $!\alpha; T_{cf}; T_{cf}$ is due to the communication primitive (either send or receive) and the rightmost one to the resumption.

Note that the only difference between the revised send_tree and the homonymous function presented in [25] is the occurrence of @>. All the other examples in [25] can be patched similarly by resuming endpoints at the appropriate places.

5   Related Work

The work most closely related to ours is [25] in which Thiemann and Vasconcelos introduce context-free session types, develop their metatheory, and prove that session type equivalence is decidable. In [25], the only typing rules that can eliminate sequential compositions are those concerning send and receive. This choice calls for a type system with (1) a structural rule that rearranges sequential compositions in session types and (2) support for polymorphic recursion. As a consequence, context-free session type checking, left as an open problem in [25], appears to rely crucially on type annotations provided by the programmer. In contrast, our approach relies on the use of resumptions inserted in the code. As we have seen in Sect. 4, this approach makes it easy to embed the resulting typing discipline in a host programming language and to take advantage of its type inference engine. Overall, we think that our approach strikes a good balance between expressiveness and flexibility: resumptions are unobtrusive and typically sparse, their location is easy to spot in the code, and they give the programmer complete control over the occurrences of sequential compositions in session types, resolving the ambiguities that arise with context-free session type inference (Sects. 1 and 4.4).

A potential limitation of our approach compared to [25] is that we require processes operating on peer endpoints of a session to mirror each other as far as the placement of resumptions is concerned. For example, a process using an endpoint with type (!int;1);?bool may interact with another process that uses an endpoint with type $(?\texttt{int};\mathbf{1});!\texttt{bool}$, but not with a process using an endpoint with type $?\texttt{int};!\texttt{bool}$ even though $(?\texttt{int};\mathbf{1});!\texttt{bool} \sim ?\texttt{int};!\texttt{bool}$. Both processes must resume the endpoints they use after the exchange of the first message. Understanding the practical impact of this limitation requires an extensive analysis of code that deals with context-free protocols. We have not pursued such investigation, but we can make two observations nonetheless. First, resumptions are often used in combination with recursion and interacting recursive processes already tend to mirror each other by their own recursive nature. We can see this by comparing send_tree and receive_tree (Sect. 4.4) and also by looking at the examples in [25]. Second, it is easy to provide *explicit coercions* corresponding to laws of $\sim$. Such coercions, whose soundness is already accounted for by Theorem 1, can be used to rearrange sequential compositions in session types. For example, a coercion $(A;\mathbf{1});B \rightarrow A;B$ composed with a function $?\texttt{int};!\texttt{bool} \rightarrow \alpha$ would turn it into a function $(?\texttt{int};\mathbf{1});!\texttt{bool} \rightarrow \alpha$. The use of coercions augments the direct involvement of the programmer, but is a low-cost solution to broaden the cases already addressed by plain resumptions.

FuSe [21] is an OCaml implementation of binary sessions that combines static protocol enforcement with runtime checks for endpoint linearity [11,27] and resumption safety (Sect. 4.2). Support for sequential composition of session types based on resumptions was originally introduced in FuSe to describe *iterative protocols*, showing that a class of unbounded protocols could be described without resorting to (equi-)recursive types. The work of Thiemann and Vasconcelos [25] prompted us to formalize resumptions and to study their implications to the precision of protocol descriptions. This led to the discovery of a bug in early versions of FuSe where peer endpoints were given the same identity (*cf.* the discussion at the end of Example 3) and then to the development of a fully static typing discipline to enforce resumption safety (Sects. 3 and 4.3).

The use of type variables abstracting over the identity of endpoints has been inspired by works on regions and linear types [2,30], by L^3 [1], a language with locations supporting strong updates, and Alms [26,28], an experimental general-purpose programming language with affine types. In these works, abstract identities are used to associate an object with the region it belongs to [2,30], or to link the (non-linear) reference to a mutable object with the (linear or affine) capability for accessing it. Interestingly, in these works separating the reference from the capability (hence the use of abstract identities) is not really a necessity, but rather a technique that results in increased flexibility: the reference can be aliased without restrictions to create cyclic graphs [1] or to support "dirty" operations on shared data structures [28]. In our case, endpoint identities are crucial for checking the safety of resumptions. As one of the anonymous reviewers pointed out, the technique of using type variables abstracting over regions can be traced back to the implementation of stateful computations in Haskell [16], which was further elaborated and proven safe in [18].

Acknowledgments. The author is grateful to the anonymous ESOP reviewers for their detailed and valuable feedback and to Hernán Melgratti for reading and commenting on an early draft of the paper.

References

1. Ahmed, A., Fluet, M., Morrisett, G.: L^3: a linear language with locations. Fundam. Informaticae **77**(4), 397–449 (2007)
2. Charguéraud, A., Pottier, F.: Functional translation of a calculus of capabilities. In: Proceedings of ICFP 2008, pp. 213–224. ACM (2008)
3. Courcelle, B.: Fundamental properties of infinite trees. Theor. Comput. Sci. **25**, 95–169 (1983)
4. Dardha, O., Giachino, E., Sangiorgi, D.: Session types revisited. In: Proceedings of PPDP 2012, pp. 139–150. ACM (2012)
5. Demangeon, R., Honda, K.: Full abstraction in a subtyped pi-calculus with linear types. In: Katoen, J.-P., König, B. (eds.) CONCUR 2011. LNCS, vol. 6901, pp. 280–296. Springer, Heidelberg (2011). doi:10.1007/978-3-642-23217-6_19
6. Florijn, G.: Object protocols as functional parsers. In: Tokoro, M., Pareschi, R. (eds.) ECOOP 1995. LNCS, vol. 952, pp. 351–373. Springer, Heidelberg (1995). doi:10.1007/3-540-49538-X_17
7. Frisch, A., Garrigue, J.: First-class modules and composable signatures in Objective Caml 3.12. In: ACM SIGPLAN Workshop on ML (2010)
8. Gay, S.J., Vasconcelos, V.T.: Linear type theory for asynchronous session types. J. Funct. Program. **20**(1), 19–50 (2010)
9. Honda, K.: Types for dyadic interaction. In: Best, E. (ed.) CONCUR 1993. LNCS, vol. 715, pp. 509–523. Springer, Heidelberg (1993). doi:10.1007/3-540-57208-2_35
10. Honda, K., Vasconcelos, V.T., Kubo, M.: Language primitives and type discipline for structured communication-based programming. In: Hankin, C. (ed.) ESOP 1998. LNCS, vol. 1381, pp. 122–138. Springer, Heidelberg (1998). doi:10.1007/BFb0053567
11. Hu, R., Yoshida, N.: Hybrid session verification through endpoint API generation. In: Stevens, P., Wąsowski, A. (eds.) FASE 2016. LNCS, vol. 9633, pp. 401–418. Springer, Heidelberg (2016). doi:10.1007/978-3-662-49665-7_24
12. Hüttel, H., Lanese, I., Vasconcelos, V.T., Caires, L., Carbone, M., Deniélou, P.-M., Mostrous, D., Padovani, L., Ravara, A., Tuosto, E., Vieira, H.T., Zavattaro, G.: Foundations of session types and behavioural contracts. ACM Comput. Surv. **49**(1), 3 (2016)
13. Kfoury, A.J., Tiuryn, J., Urzyczyn, P.: Type reconstruction in the presence of polymorphic recursion. ACM Trans. Program. Lang. Syst. **15**(2), 290–311 (1993)
14. Kobayashi, N.: Type systems for concurrent programs. In: Aichernig, B.K., Maibaum, T. (eds.) Formal Methods at the Crossroads. From Panacea to Foundational Support. LNCS, vol. 2757, pp. 439–453. Springer, Heidelberg (2003). doi:10.1007/978-3-540-40007-3_26. http://www.kb.ecei.tohoku.ac.jp/koba/papers/tutorial-type-extended.pdf
15. Kobayashi, N., Pierce, B.C., Turner, D.N.: Linearity and the pi-calculus. ACM Trans. Program. Lang. Syst. **21**(5), 914–947 (1999)
16. Launchbury, J., Jones, S.L.P.: State in Haskell. Lisp Symbolic Comput. **8**(4), 293–341 (1995)
17. Mitchell, J.C., Plotkin, G.D.: Abstract types have existential type. ACM Trans. Program. Lang. Syst. **10**(3), 470–502 (1988)
18. Moggi, E., Sabry, A.: Monadic encapsulation of effects: a revised approach (extended version). J. Funct. Program. **11**(6), 591–627 (2001)
19. Nierstrasz, O.: Regular types for active objects. In: Proceedings of OOPSLA 1993, pp. 1–15. ACM (1993)

20. Padovani, L.: Context-free session type inference. Technical report, Università di Torino (2016). https://hal.archives-ouvertes.fr/hal-01385258/document. Accessed 04 Jan 2017
21. Padovani, L.: A simple library implementation of binary sessions. J. Funct. Program. **27** (2017). https://doi.org/10.1017/S0956796816000289
22. Ravara, A., Vasconcelos, V.T.: Typing non-uniform concurrent objects. In: Palamidessi, C. (ed.) CONCUR 2000. LNCS, vol. 1877, pp. 474–489. Springer, Heidelberg (2000). doi:10.1007/3-540-44618-4_34
23. Reppy, J.H.: Concurrent Programming in ML. Cambridge University Press, Cambridge (1999)
24. Südholt, M.: A model of components with non-regular protocols. In: Gschwind, T., Aßmann, U., Nierstrasz, O. (eds.) SC 2005. LNCS, vol. 3628, pp. 99–113. Springer, Heidelberg (2005). doi:10.1007/11550679_8
25. Thiemann, P., Vasconcelos, V.T.: Context-free session types. In: Proceedings of ICFP 2016, pp. 462–475. ACM (2016)
26. Tov, J.A.: Practical programming with substructural types. Ph.D. thesis, Northeastern University (2012)
27. Tov, J.A., Pucella, R.: Stateful contracts for affine types. In: Gordon, A.D. (ed.) ESOP 2010. LNCS, vol. 6012, pp. 550–569. Springer, Heidelberg (2010). doi:10.1007/978-3-642-11957-6_29
28. Tov, J.A., Pucella, R.: Practical affine types. In: Proceedings of POPL 2011, pp. 447–458. ACM (2011)
29. Wadler, P.: Propositions as sessions. J. Funct. Program. **24**(2–3), 384–418 (2014)
30. Walker, D., Watkins, K.: On regions and linear types. In: Proceedings of ICFP 2001, pp. 181–192. ACM (2001)
31. Wright, A.K., Felleisen, M.: A syntactic approach to type soundness. Inf. Comput. **115**(1), 38–94 (1994)
32. Yallop, J., Kiselyov, O.: First-class modules: hidden power and tantalizing promises. In: ACM SIGPLAN Workshop on ML (2010)

Modular Verification of Higher-Order Functional Programs

Ryosuke Sato$^{(\boxtimes)}$ and Naoki Kobayashi

The University of Tokyo, Tokyo, Japan
{ryosuke,koba}@kb.is.s.u-tokyo.ac.jp

Abstract. Fully automated verification methods for higher-order functional programs have recently been proposed based on higher-order model checking and/or refinement type inference. Most of those methods are, however, whole program analyses, suffering from the scalability problem. To address the problem, we propose a modular method for fully automated verification of higher-order programs. Our method takes a program consisting of multiple top-level functions as an input, and repeatedly applies procedures for (i) guessing refinement intersection types of each function in a counterexample-guided manner, and (ii) checking that each function indeed has the guessed refinement intersection types, until the whole program is proved/disproved to be safe. To avoid the whole program analysis, we introduce the notion of *modular counterexamples*, and utilize them in (i), and employ Sato et al.'s technique of reducing refinement type checking to assertion checking in (ii). We have implemented the proposed method as an extension to MoCHi, and confirmed its effectiveness through experiments.

1 Introduction

Thanks to the recent advance in higher-order model checking and refinement type inference, various methods and tools for automated verification of functional programs have been proposed recently [9,12,15,20,21]. For example, MoCHi [9, 18], a software model checker for functional programs, statically checks whether a given program may fail due to run-time errors such as assertion failures, uncaught exceptions, and pattern match failures, in a fully automatic manner. It outputs refinement (intersection) types as certificates of the safety if the program does not fail, and outputs a concrete execution path that causes a run-time error otherwise. Most of the *fully* automated verification methods proposed so far are whole program analyses, suffering from the scalability problem. (On the other hand, *semi*-automated methods that rely on users' annotations on invariants usually work in a compositional manner [6,11,16,19,28].)

To address the scalability problem, we propose a modular verification method for higher-order functional programs, which utilizes an existing software model checker for functional programs as a backend. An input for the verification method is a pair consisting of (i) a program P of the form:

$$\textbf{let rec } f_1 \ \widetilde{x}_1 = t_1 \textbf{ in } \cdots \textbf{ let rec } f_n \ \widetilde{x}_n = t_n \textbf{ in } f_n$$

© Springer-Verlag GmbH Germany 2017
H. Yang (Ed.): ESOP 2017, LNCS 10201, pp. 831–854, 2017.
DOI: 10.1007/978-3-662-54434-1_31

(which is abbreviated as $\langle f_1 \, \widetilde{x} = t_1, \ldots, f_n \, \widetilde{x} = t_n \rangle$) and (ii) a refinement type specification τ. Here, $f_1, \ldots, f_i$ may occur in t_i.[1] Each function definition $f_i \, \widetilde{x}_i = t_i$, which may contain local function definitions, is treated as a "module", i.e., the unit of verification in our modular verification method. The goal is to check whether $\models P : \tau$, i.e., whether P has (semantically) type τ (which entails that P does not fail; for example, P has type $\mathbf{int} \to \mathbf{int}$ only if, for every integer n, $P \, n$ does not fail, and either returns an integer or diverges).

Our method infers refinement types of each function by using the following two components:

- **typeSynthesizer**, which generates a candidate refinement type environment $f_1 : \sigma_1, \ldots, f_n : \sigma_n$ (which maps each f_i to the *set* σ_i of types) such that $\tau \in \sigma_n$ from the type checking problem $\models^? \langle f_1 \, \widetilde{x}_1 = t_1, \ldots, f_n \, \widetilde{x}_n = t_n \rangle : \tau$ and *modular counterexamples* (which will be explained later).
- **typeChecker**, which checks whether

$$f_1 : \sigma_1, \ldots, f_{k-1} : \sigma_{k-1} \models \mathbf{fix}(f_k, \lambda \widetilde{x}_k. t_k) : \tau_k$$

holds (where $\mathbf{fix}(f_k, \lambda \widetilde{x}_k. t_k)$ denotes the recursive function defined by $f_k \, \widetilde{x}_k = t_k$), given a refinement type environment $f_1 : \sigma_1, \ldots, f_{k-1} : \sigma_{k-1}$, a candidate τ_k of refinement type of f_k, and a function definition $f_k \, \widetilde{x}_k = t_k$ for some $k \in \{1, \ldots, n\}$, and outputs a modular counterexample if $f_1 : \sigma_1, \ldots, f_{k-1} : \sigma_{k-1} \models \mathbf{fix}(f_k, \lambda \widetilde{x}_k. t_k) : \tau_k$ does not hold

Figure 1 describes the overall procedure of our method, utilizing the two components mentioned above. Given a program P and a refinement type specification τ, the main function first sets (i) the type environment Γ (which keeps the set of types that have already been proved to be valid) to the empty type environment (line 2), (ii) the candidate type environment $\Gamma_{\mathtt{cand}}$ to one containing only $f_n : \{\tau\}$ (line 3), and (iii) the set of (modular) counterexamples to the empty set (line 4). The main function then calls **validateTE** (line 5). Given the current type environment Γ and the current candidate type environment $\Gamma_{\mathtt{cand}}$, the function **validateTE** checks whether each $\tau' \in \Gamma(f_i)$ is a valid type for f_i for each $i \in \{1, \ldots, n\}$, by repeatedly calling **typeChecker** (line 10). Here, $P(f_i)$ denotes $\mathbf{fix}(f_i, \lambda \widetilde{x}_i. t_i)$, the function defined by $f_i \, \widetilde{x}_i = t_i$. If τ' is a valid type, then it is added to the set $\Gamma(f_i)$ of valid types of f_i (line 11); otherwise the counterexample returned by **typeChecker** is added to Π (line 12). If the type τ of the whole program has been proved correct, then the verification succeeds (line 13). Otherwise, **typeSynthesizer** is called to obtain a refined candidate type environment (line 15), and **validateTE** is called again (line 16). If there is no way to refine the candidate, we can conclude that the program is untypable, i.e., does not meet the specification (line 17).

---

[1] Mutual recursion can be realized by passing $f_{i+1}, \ldots, f_n$ as arguments of f_i. For example, **let rec** $f_1 \, x = C_1[f_1, f_2]$ **and** $f_2 \, x = C_2[f_1, f_2]$ **in** f_2 can be expressed as **let rec** $f_1 \, f_2 \, x = C_1[f_1 \, f_2, f_2]$ **in let rec** $f_2' \, x = C_2[f_1 \, f_2', f_2']$ **in** f_2'.

```
1: main(P, τ) =
2:   let Γ = {f₁ : ∅,..., fₙ : ∅} in (* types that have been validated so far *)
3:   let Γ_cand = {f₁ : ∅,..., f_{n-1} : ∅, fₙ : {τ}} in (* initial type candidates *)
4:   let Π = ∅ in (* the set of counterexamples found so far *)
5:     validateTE(P, τ, Γ, Γ_cand, Π)
6:
7: validateTE(P, τ, Γ, Γ_cand, Π) =
8:   for i=1 to n do (* Check each type candidate *)
9:     {for each τ' in Γ_cand(fᵢ) do
10:        match typeChecker(Γ, P(fᵢ), τ') with
11:          OK -> add τ' to Γ(fᵢ)
12:          | NG(π) -> add π to Π };
13:   if τ ∈ Γ(fₙ) then return "yes"
14:   else
15:     match typeSynthesizer(P, τ, Π) with
16:       Some(Γ'_cand) -> validateTE(P, τ, Γ, Γ'_cand, Π)
17:       | None -> return "no"
```

Fig. 1. The overall procedure

Our verification method is modular in that the (semantic) typability of each function definition is checked separately by using `typeChecker`. The component `typeSynthesizer` takes the whole program as an input, but as we describe later, it looks at only part of the program that is relevant to the set Π of modular counterexamples found so far. Thus, our new method is expected to scale to larger programs than the previous whole program analysis approach [9,18], as confirmed by experiments.

The description above explains how to verify a single whole program in a modular manner. There is a further benefit when our modular verification method is applied to verification of multiple programs that share the same library. Suppose we have a library function $f\,x = t_1$ and two client functions $g\,y = t_2$ and $h\,z = t_3$, whose refinement type specifications are τ_2 and τ_3. In that case, we run the procedure in Fig. 1 first for $\models^? \langle f\,x = t_1, g\,y = t_2 \rangle : \tau_2$. If the verification is successful, we obtain a witness type environment $f : \sigma_1, g : \sigma_2$. The information that f has types σ_1 can then be used in the verification of the other client program. For that purpose, when the procedure in Fig. 1 is called for the query $\models^? \langle f\,x = t_1, h\,z = t_3 \rangle : \tau_3$, we just need to set $\Gamma(f)$ to σ_1 (instead of $\emptyset$) on the second line. If the type information $f : \sigma_1$ is sufficient, then the verification of h will succeed without re-analyzing the definition of f. Otherwise, additional types for f may be inferred by reanalyzing the definition of f, and can later be used for analyzing other client programs.

The rest of this paper is structured as follows. Section 2 introduces the target language of our verification method. Section 3 overviews our method through an example. Section 4 describes the two components. Section 5 reports an implementation and experimental results. Section 6 discusses related work, and Sect. 7 concludes the paper.

2 Language

In this section, we introduce the target language of our verification method.

2.1 Syntax and Semantics

The target of our method is a simply-typed, call-by-value, higher-order functional language with recursion. Its syntax is summarized in Fig. 2.

$$P \text{ (programs)} ::= \langle f_1 \; \widetilde{x_1} = t_1, \ldots, f_n \; \widetilde{x_n} = t_n \rangle$$

$$t \text{ (terms)} ::= n \mid x \mid *_{\mathsf{int}} \mid \mathsf{op}(\widetilde{t}) \mid \mathbf{fix}(f, \lambda x. t) \mid t_1 \, t_2$$

$$\mid \mathbf{if}^\ell \; t_1 \; \mathbf{then} \; t_2 \; \mathbf{else} \; t_3 \mid \mathbf{fail}$$

$$\kappa \text{ (simple types)} ::= \mathsf{int} \mid \kappa_1 \to \kappa_2$$

Fig. 2. Syntax

We use the meta-variables x, y, z, f, g, $\ldots$ for variables. We write $\widetilde{\cdot}$ for a sequence; for example, $\widetilde{x}$ stands for a sequence of variables. For the sake of simplicity, we consider only integers as base type values. We represent Booleans using integers, and sometimes write **true** for 1 and **false** for 0. The meta-variables n and op range over the sets of integers, and primitive operations on integers, respectively.

A program P is a sequence of recursive function definitions $\langle f_1 \; \widetilde{x_1} = t_1, \ldots, f_n \; \widetilde{x_n} = t_n \rangle$. Here, we require that $\widetilde{x_i}$ may not be an empty sequence and f_i may occur only in $t_i, \ldots, t_n$. When $P = \langle f_1 \; \widetilde{x_1} = t_1, \ldots, f_n \; \widetilde{x_n} = t_n \rangle$, we write $dom(P)$ for $\{f_1, \ldots, f_n\}$, and $P(f_i)$ for $\mathbf{fix}(f_i, \lambda \widetilde{x_i}. t_i)$.

The term $*_{\mathsf{int}}$ evaluates to some integer in a non-deterministic manner. We write $*_{\mathsf{bool}}$ for $*_{\mathsf{int}} \geq 0$, which represents a non-deterministic Boolean. The term $\mathsf{op}(t_1, \ldots, t_k)$ applies the operation op to the values of $t_1, \ldots, t_k$. We sometimes use the infix notation for a binary operation and write $x \, \mathsf{op} \, y$ for $\mathsf{op}(x, y)$. The term $\mathbf{fix}(f, \lambda x. t)$ denotes the recursive function defined by $f \; x = t$.[2] We write $\lambda x. t$ for $\mathbf{fix}(f, \lambda x. t)$ if f does not occur in t. The term $t_1 \, t_2$ applies t_1 to t_2. We write **let** $x = t_1$ **in** t_2 for $(\lambda x. t_2) \, t_1$, and also write $t_1; t_2$ if x does not occur in t_2. The conditional expression $\mathbf{if}^\ell \; t_1 \; \mathbf{then} \; t_2 \; \mathbf{else} \; t_3$ evaluates t_2 if the value of t_1 is non-zero and t_3 otherwise; ℓ is a label used only during verification. We assume that a unique label is assigned to each conditional expression. We omit labels when they are not important. The term **fail** aborts the execution. We write $\mathbf{assert}^\ell(t)$ for $\mathbf{if}^\ell \; t \; \mathbf{then} \; 1 \; \mathbf{else} \; \mathbf{fail}$, which aborts the program if the value of t is **false** (i.e., 0). We also write $\mathbf{assume}^\ell(t)$ for $\mathbf{if}^\ell \; t \; \mathbf{then} \; 1 \; \mathbf{else} \; \mathbf{fix}(f, \lambda x. f \, x) \, 0$.

---

[2] Thus, whether a recursive function is introduced by a top-level function definition or by $\mathbf{fix}(f, \lambda x. t)$ does not matter for an execution of a program; it matters only for the modular verification method, which treats each top-level function definition as the unit of modular verification.

We consider only programs that are well-typed in the standard simple type system; the typing rules are omitted. We write $\mathcal{K} \vdash_{ST} t : \kappa$ if t has simple type κ under simple type environment $\mathcal{K}$.

$$E[*_{\mathbf{int}}] \longrightarrow_P E[n]$$

$$E[\mathbf{op}(v_1, \ldots, v_k)] \longrightarrow_P E[\llbracket \mathbf{op} \rrbracket(v_1, \ldots, v_k)]$$

$$E[\mathbf{fix}(f, \lambda x.\, t)\, v] \longrightarrow_P E[[v/x][\mathbf{fix}(f, \lambda x.\, t)/f]t]$$

$$\frac{v \neq 0}{E[\mathbf{if}^\ell \ v \ \mathbf{then} \ t_1 \ \mathbf{else} \ t_2] \longrightarrow_P E[t_1]}$$

$$\frac{v = 0}{E[\mathbf{if}^\ell \ v \ \mathbf{then} \ t_1 \ \mathbf{else} \ t_2] \longrightarrow_P E[t_2]}$$

$$\frac{(f\, \widetilde{x} = t) \in P}{E[f] \longrightarrow_P E[\mathbf{fix}(f, \lambda \widetilde{x}.\, t)]} \qquad\qquad \frac{E \neq [\,]}{E[\mathbf{fail}] \longrightarrow_P \mathbf{fail}}$$

E (evaluation contexts) $::= [\,] \mid \mathbf{op}(\widetilde{v}, E, \widetilde{t}) \mid E\, t \mid v\, E \mid \mathbf{if}^\ell \ E \ \mathbf{then} \ t_1 \ \mathbf{else} \ t_2$
v (values) $::= n \mid \mathbf{fix}(f, \lambda x.\, t)$

Fig. 3. Operational semantics of the language

The (small-step) operational semantics of the language is defined in Fig. 3. In the figure, $\llbracket \mathbf{op} \rrbracket$ is the semantic integer function denoted by op. We write $\longrightarrow_P^*$ for the reflexive and transitive closure of $\longrightarrow_P$. We omit the subscript P when it is clear from the context.

2.2 Refinement Intersection Types

We use refinement intersection types for describing properties of programs or terms. The syntax of (refinement intersection) types is defined by:

$$\tau \ (\text{refinement types}) ::= \{x : \mathbf{int} \mid \phi\} \mid (x : \sigma) \to \tau$$
$$\sigma \ (\text{intersection types}) ::= \{\tau_1, \ldots, \tau_k\}_\kappa$$
$$\phi \ (\text{refinement predicates}) ::= n \mid x \mid \mathbf{op}(\phi_1, \phi_2).$$

The refinement type $\{x : \mathbf{int} \mid \phi\}$ denotes the set of integers x that satisfy the refinement predicate ϕ. For example, $\{x : \mathbf{int} \mid x \geq 0\}$ is the type of non-negative integers. We often abbreviate $\{x : \mathbf{int} \mid \mathbf{true}\}$ to $\mathbf{int}$. The intersection type $\{\tau_1, \ldots, \tau_k\}_\kappa$ describes values that have type τ_i whose simple type is κ for every $i \in \{1, \ldots, k\}$. We often omit the subscript κ when they are not important, and treat $\{\tau_1, \ldots, \tau_k\}_\kappa$ as a set of refinement types. The type $(x : \sigma) \to \tau$ denotes the set of functions that take an argument v of (intersection) type σ and return a value of type $[v/x]\tau$. For example, $(x : \{y : \mathbf{int} \mid \mathbf{true}\}) \to \{r : \mathbf{int} \mid r \geq x\}$ is the type of functions that take any integer as an argument and return an integer no less than the argument. In $(x : \sigma) \to \tau$, we allow x to occur in τ only if σ is of the form $\{y : \mathbf{int} \mid \phi\}$. In other words, we do not allow dependencies on function variables. We write $\sigma \to \tau$ for $(x : \sigma) \to \tau$ if x does not occur in τ.

We say that τ is a *refinement* of a simple type κ if $\tau :: \kappa$ is derivable from the following rules:

$$\{x : \mathbf{int} \mid \phi\} :: \mathbf{int} \qquad \frac{\sigma :: \kappa_1 \quad \tau :: \kappa_2}{((x : \sigma) \to \tau) :: (\kappa_1 \to \kappa_2)} \qquad \frac{\tau_i :: \kappa \quad \text{for each } i \in \{1, \ldots, n\}}{\{\tau_1, \ldots, \tau_n\}_\kappa :: \kappa}$$

Henceforth, we consider only refinement types and intersection types that are refinements of some simple types. For such a refinement type τ (an intersection type σ, resp.), the simple type κ such that $\tau :: \kappa$ ($\sigma :: \kappa$, resp.) is uniquely determined. We write $ST(\tau)$ ($ST(\sigma)$, resp.) for it. We also write $ST(\Gamma)$ for $f_1 : ST(\sigma_1), \ldots, f_k : ST(\sigma_k)$ when $\Gamma = f_1 : \sigma_1, \ldots, f_k : \sigma_k$.

$f_1 : \sigma_1, \ldots, f_n : \sigma_n \models^P t : \tau \quad \overset{\text{def}}{\equiv}$

$\qquad f_1 : ST(\sigma_1), \ldots, f_n : ST(\sigma_n) \vdash_{\mathrm{ST}} t : ST(\tau) \quad \text{and}$

$\qquad \models^P [v_1/f_1, \ldots, v_n/f_n] t : \tau \text{ for any } v_1, \ldots, v_n \text{ s.t. } \models^P_{\mathrm{v},\wedge} v_i : \sigma_i \text{ for all } i \in \{1, \ldots, n\}$

$\models^P t : \tau \quad \overset{\text{def}}{\equiv}$

$\qquad \vdash_{\mathrm{ST}} t : ST(\tau), \ t \not\longrightarrow^*_P \mathbf{fail}, \text{ and } \models^P_{\mathrm{v}} v : \tau \text{ for every } v \text{ such that } t \longrightarrow^*_P v$

$\models^P_{\mathrm{v}} n : \{x : \mathbf{int} \mid \phi\} \quad \overset{\text{def}}{\equiv} \quad \models^P_{\mathrm{p}} [n/x]\phi$

$\models^P_{\mathrm{v}} \mathbf{fix}(f, \lambda x.\, t) : (y : \sigma) \to \tau \quad \overset{\text{def}}{\equiv}$

$\qquad \models^P \mathbf{fix}(f, \lambda x.\, t)\, v' : [v'/y]\tau \text{ for every } v' \text{ s.t. } \models^P_{\mathrm{v},\wedge} v' : \sigma$

$\models^P_{\mathrm{v},\wedge} v : \{\tau_1, \ldots, \tau_n\}_\kappa \quad \overset{\text{def}}{\equiv} \quad \vdash_{\mathrm{ST}} v : \kappa \quad \text{and} \quad \models^P_{\mathrm{v}} v : \tau_i \text{ for all } i \in \{1, \ldots, n\}$

$\models^P_{\mathrm{p}} \phi \quad \overset{\text{def}}{\equiv} \quad v = \mathbf{true} \text{ for any } v \text{ s.t. } \phi \longrightarrow^*_P v$

Fig. 4. Semantics of types

The semantics of types is defined in Fig. 4 using logical relations. The relation $\models^P_{\mathrm{v}} v : \tau$ means that the value v has type τ, and $\models^P t : \tau$ means that reduction of the closed (where the top-level functions $f_1, \ldots, f_n$ are considered bound variables) term t never fails, and that every value v (if there is any) of t has type τ. The relation $\Gamma \models^P t : \tau$ (where Γ is a type environment of the form $f_1 : \sigma_1, \ldots, f_n : \sigma_n$) means that for any values $v_1, \ldots, v_n$ that have types $\sigma_1, \ldots, \sigma_n$, $[v_1/f_1, \ldots, v_n/f_n] t$ have type τ. We often omit the superscript P when it is clear from the context.

For a program $P = \langle f_1\, \widetilde{x_1} = t_1, \ldots, f_n\, \widetilde{x_n} = t_n \rangle$ and a type τ as a specification, we write $\models P : \tau$ if there exists $\Gamma = f_1 : \sigma_1, \ldots, f_{n-1} : \sigma_{n-1}$ such that $\Gamma \models P(f_n) : \tau$ and $\Gamma \models P(f_i) : \tau_{ij}$ for each $i \in \{1, \ldots, n-1\}$ and $\tau_{ij} \in \sigma_i$. We call such Γ a *witness* for $\models P : \tau$. The goal of our verification is to check whether $\models P : \tau$ holds for a given program P and a refinement type specification τ.

2.3   Examples

In this section, we introduce two examples. Using the first example, we will explain how our method works in Sect. 3.

Example 1. Consider the following program P_{sum}:

$$\langle \ \mathsf{add}\ x\ y = \mathbf{if}^{\ell_1}\ y \leq 0\ \mathbf{then}\ x\ \mathbf{else}\ 1 + (\mathsf{add}\ x\ (y - 1)),$$
$$\mathsf{sum}\ x = \mathbf{if}^{\ell_2}\ x \leq 0\ \mathbf{then}\ 0\ \mathbf{else}\ \mathsf{add}\ x\ (\mathsf{sum}\ (x - 1)),$$
$$\mathsf{main}\ n = \mathbf{assert}^{\ell_3}\,(0 \leq \mathsf{sum}\ n)\ \rangle.$$

The function main takes an integer n as an argument, computes the sum of integers up to n, and asserts that the sum is no less than 0. The relation $\models P_{\mathsf{sum}} : \mathbf{int} \rightarrow \mathbf{int}$ means that $\mathsf{main}\ n$ never fails for any integer n. It is witnessed by the following type environment Γ_{sum}:

$$\mathsf{add} : \{\{x : \mathbf{int} \mid x \geq 0\} \rightarrow \mathbf{int} \rightarrow \{r : \mathbf{int} \mid r \geq 0\}\},$$
$$\mathsf{sum} : \{\mathbf{int} \rightarrow \{r : \mathbf{int} \mid r \geq 0\}\},$$
$$\mathsf{main} : \{\mathbf{int} \rightarrow \mathbf{int}\}.$$

$\square$

Example 2. Consider the following program P_{twice}:

$$\langle \ \mathsf{mult}\ x\ y = \mathbf{if}^{\ell_1}\ y = 0\ \mathbf{then}\ 0$$
$$\mathbf{else}\ \mathbf{if}^{\ell_2}\ y < 0\ \mathbf{then}\ -x + \mathsf{mult}\ x\ (y + 1)$$
$$\mathbf{else}\ x + \mathsf{mult}\ x\ (y - 1),$$
$$\mathsf{twice}\ f\ x = f\ (f\ x),$$
$$\mathsf{main}\ n = \mathbf{if}^{\ell_3}\ n < 0\ \mathbf{then}\ \mathbf{assert}^{\ell_4}(\mathsf{twice}\ (\mathsf{mult}\ n)\ 1 > 0)\ \mathbf{else}\ 0\ \rangle.$$

The function main takes an integer n as an argument. If n is negative, then it computes the square of n, and asserts that the square is greater than 0. The relation $\models P_{\mathsf{twice}} : \mathbf{int} \rightarrow \mathbf{int}$ is witnessed by the following type environment Γ_{twice}:

$$\mathsf{mult} : \{\mathbf{neg} \rightarrow \mathbf{neg} \rightarrow \mathbf{pos},\ \mathbf{neg} \rightarrow \mathbf{pos} \rightarrow \mathbf{neg}\},$$
$$\mathsf{twice} : \{\{\mathbf{neg} \rightarrow \mathbf{pos},\ \mathbf{pos} \rightarrow \mathbf{neg}\} \rightarrow \mathbf{pos} \rightarrow \mathbf{pos}\},$$
$$\mathsf{main} : \{\mathbf{int} \rightarrow \mathbf{int}\}.$$

Here, $\mathbf{pos}$ and $\mathbf{neg}$ are the types of positive and negative integers, which are defined as $\{n : \mathbf{int} \mid n > 0\}$ and $\{n : \mathbf{int} \mid n < 0\}$, respectively. Note here that intersection types are required to make the analysis context-sensitive; in the argument type of twice, $\mathbf{neg} \rightarrow \mathbf{pos}$ and $\mathbf{pos} \rightarrow \mathbf{neg}$ represent the types of the first and second occurrences of f in the body of twice, respectively. $\square$

3 An Overview of the Method Through an Example

We explain how our method works using the program P_{sum} in Example 1. Suppose we wish to verify that $\models P_{\text{sum}} : \text{int} \to \text{int}$.

On lines 2–4 of the overall procedure in Fig. 1, Γ (a type environment that records the types that have been proved valid), Γ_{cand} (a candidate type environment), and Π (a set of modular counterexamples) are initialized as follows:

$$\Gamma = \text{add} : \emptyset, \text{ sum} : \emptyset, \text{ main} : \emptyset$$
$$\Gamma_{\text{cand}} = \text{add} : \emptyset, \text{ sum} : \emptyset, \text{ main} : \{\text{int} \to \text{int}\}$$
$$\Pi = \emptyset$$

The main procedure then calls validateTE, to check the validity of the type of main, i.e., whether $\Gamma \models \lambda n.\,\text{assert}(0 \leq \text{sum } n) : \text{int} \to \text{int}$, by invoking typeChecker. To check $\Gamma \models t : \tau$ in general, typeChecker uses the technique of Sato et al. [17]: we prepare a context $C_{\Gamma,\tau}$ that is most general in the sense that $C_{\Gamma,\tau}[t]$ fails if and only if $\Gamma \models t : \tau$, and uses a software model checker [9,18] to check whether $C_{\Gamma,\tau}[t]$ fails. In the case of $\Gamma \models \lambda n.\text{assert}(0 \leq \text{sum } n) : \text{int} \to \text{int}$, the context $C_{\Gamma,\text{int}\to\text{int}}$ is:

$$\text{let add} = \lambda x.\lambda y.\text{fail in let sum} = \lambda x.\text{fail in } [\,] \, *_{\text{int}} \,.$$

An important point to notice here is that instead of using the original definitions of add and sum, functions synthesized from their types are used. This enables modular verification of each top-level function. In the present case, since $\Gamma(\text{sum})$ is empty, the *weakest* term (in the sense that it is most likely to fail) is chosen as the code of sum. A model checker can output the following error path (i.e., a reduction sequence that leads to **fail**):[3]

$$C_{\Gamma,\text{int}\to\text{int}}[\lambda n.\text{assert}(0 \leq \text{sum } n)]$$
$$\longrightarrow_P \text{let add} = \cdots \text{ in let sum} = \cdots \text{ in } (\lambda n.\text{assert}(0 \leq \text{sum } n))m$$
$$\longrightarrow_P \text{let add} = \cdots \text{ in let sum} = \cdots \text{ in assert}(0 \leq \text{sum } m)$$
$$\longrightarrow_P \text{let add} = \cdots \text{ in let sum} = \cdots \text{ in assert}(0 \leq (\lambda x.\text{fail})m)$$
$$\longrightarrow_P \text{let add} = \cdots \text{ in let sum} = \cdots \text{ in assert}(0 \leq \text{fail})$$

as a counterexample (where m is some integer). Thus, typeChecker can conclude that $\Gamma \models \lambda n.\text{assert}(0 \leq \text{sum } n) : \text{int} \to \text{int}$ does not hold. The counterexample is useful for refining the candidate type environment, but since it is redundant (it contains information about how the part $C_{\Gamma,\text{int}\to\text{int}}$ is reduced, which is irrelevant to the original program), we keep only information about which branches have been taken inside the term being checked. In the present case, since no branch has been taken, typeChecker returns (main, ϵ) (which means that main may fail before encountering any conditional branch) as a *modular* counterexample. Since the only candidate type main : $\text{int} \to \text{int}$ has been rejected, Γ remains to be empty: add : $\emptyset$, sum : $\emptyset$, main : $\emptyset$.

---

[3] Here, for the readability of the reduction sequence, we treat let-expressions as primitives and extend the evaluation contexts with $E ::= \cdots \mid \text{let } x = v \text{ in } E$.

Now, `typeSynthesizer` is called to construct a new candidate type environment (line 15), using the modular counterexamples collected so far. The component `typeSynthesizer` prepares a kind of program slice[4] of the original program, which covers all the modular counterexamples. Since $(\mathtt{main}, \epsilon)$ is the only counterexample found so far, the following program slice is prepared.

$$\langle\; \mathtt{add}\; x\; y = \mathbf{assume}\,(\mathbf{false})\,,$$
$$\mathtt{sum}\; x = \mathbf{assume}\,(\mathbf{false})\,,$$
$$\mathtt{main}\; n = \mathbf{let}\; \_ = 0 \le \mathtt{sum}\; n\; \mathbf{in}\; \mathbf{assume}\,(\mathbf{false})\; \rangle.$$

The program above contains only the part of the original program that runs the main function up to the first branch; the rest of the code has been replaced by the dummy code $\mathbf{assume}\,(\mathbf{false})$, which just diverges and never fails. We then apply to the above program slice the technique of refinement intersection type inference [21], which is complete for recursion-free programs (modulo a certain assumption on the underlying logic). For the above program, we may obtain the following candidate type environment (note that the type of `sum` has changed):

$$\mathtt{add} : \emptyset, \quad \mathtt{sum} : \{\mathbf{int} \to \mathbf{int}\}\,, \quad \mathtt{main} : \{\mathbf{int} \to \mathbf{int}\}\,.$$

We then recheck whether the new candidate types are valid (line 16). This time, `typeChecker` would fail for `sum`; it tries to prove that $C[\mathbf{fix}(\mathtt{sum}, \lambda x. \cdots)]$ does not fail for

$$C \equiv \mathbf{let}\; \mathtt{add} = \lambda x.\lambda y.\mathbf{fail}\; \mathbf{in}\; [\,]\; *_{\mathbf{int}},$$

but finds that the term actually fails when `add` is called. The new modular counterexample $(\mathtt{sum}, (\ell_2, \mathbf{else}))$ (which means that the else-branch has been taken at ℓ_2) is then added. Since Γ has not changed, the type checking for `main` also fails again, and `typeSynthesizer` is called with $\Pi = \{(\mathtt{sum}, (\ell_2, \mathbf{else})), (\mathtt{main}, \epsilon)\}$.

Suppose that the candidate type environment has been further updated, for example, to:

$$\mathtt{add} : \{\mathbf{int} \to \mathbf{int} \to \mathbf{int}\}\,, \quad \mathtt{sum} : \{\mathbf{int} \to \mathbf{int}\}\,, \quad \mathtt{main} : \{\mathbf{int} \to \mathbf{int}\}\,.$$

This time, `typeChecker` succeeds for `add` and `sum`, and $\mathtt{add} : \{\mathbf{int} \to \mathbf{int} \to \mathbf{int}\}$, $\mathtt{sum} : \{\mathbf{int} \to \mathbf{int}\}$ are added to Γ. The type check for `main` fails, however. To check the type of `main`, `typeChecker` tries to prove that $C'[\lambda n.\mathbf{assert}(0 \le \mathtt{sum}\; n)]$ does not fail for

$$C' = \mathbf{let}\; \mathtt{add} = \cdots\; \mathbf{in}\; \mathbf{let}\; \mathtt{sum} = \lambda x.*_{\mathbf{int}}\; \mathbf{in}\; [\,]\; *_{\mathbf{int}},$$

but the term actually fails when $\mathtt{sum} = \lambda x.*_{\mathbf{int}}$ returns a negative integer. From the error reduction sequence, the new modular counterexample $(\mathtt{main}, (\ell_3, \mathbf{else}))$ is extracted and added to Π. (Recall that $\mathbf{assert}^{\ell}(b)$ is treated as a shorthand form of $\mathbf{if}^{\ell}\; b\; \mathbf{then}\; 1\; \mathbf{else}\; \mathbf{fail}$; thus, the else-branch is taken at ℓ_3 in the error

---

[4] It is actually an extension of straightline programs [9], and deviates from the standard notion of program slices; see Sect. 4.

reduction sequence.) The component `typeSynthesizer` then discovers that the return type of `sum` should be $\{r : \text{int} \mid r \geq 0\}$.

By repeating these steps, we may end up with the following set of modular counterexamples (we only keep those that are maximal with respect to the prefix relation):

$$\{(\text{add}, (\ell_1, \text{then})), (\text{add}, (\ell_1, \text{else})(\ell_1, \text{then})),$$
$$(\text{sum}, (\ell_2, \text{else})(\ell_2, \text{then})), (\text{main}, (\ell_3, \text{else}))\}.$$

The element $(\text{sum}, (\ell_2, \text{else})(\ell_2, \text{then}))$ means that, inside the function `sum`, the else-branch is taken on the first visit of ℓ_2, and then the then-branch is taken on the next visit. The component `typeSynthesizer` constructs the following program slice:

$$\langle \text{ add}' \; x \; y = \textbf{if} \; y \leq 0 \; \textbf{then} \; x \; \textbf{else assume}\,(\textbf{false}),$$
$$\text{add} \; x \; y = \textbf{if} \; y \leq 0 \; \textbf{then} \; x \; \textbf{else} \; 1 + (\text{add}' \; x \; (y - 1)),$$
$$\text{sum}' \; x = \textbf{if} \; x \leq 0 \; \textbf{then} \; 0 \; \textbf{else assume}\,(\textbf{false}),$$
$$\text{sum} \; x = \textbf{if} \; x \leq 0 \; \textbf{then assume}\,(\textbf{false}) \; \textbf{else add} \; x \; (\text{sum}' \; (x - 1)),$$
$$\text{main} \; n = \textbf{let} \; b = 0 \leq \text{sum} \; n \; \textbf{in if} \; b \; \textbf{then assume}\,(\textbf{false}) \; \textbf{else fail} \; \rangle.$$

Here, the functions `add` and `sum` have been duplicated (i) to avoid recursion and (ii) to exclude out the part irrelevant to the modular counterexamples. The refinement (intersection) type inference [21, 23] is applied to the above program slice, and the candidate type environment is updated accordingly to:

$$\text{add} : \{\{x : \text{int} \mid x \geq 0\} \rightarrow \text{int} \rightarrow \{r : \text{int} \mid r \geq 0\}\},$$
$$\text{sum} : \{\text{int} \rightarrow \{r : \text{int} \mid r \geq 0\}\}, \quad \text{main} : \{\text{int} \rightarrow \text{int}\}.$$

The component `typeChecker` can now successfully verify that all the above types are valid, and add them to Γ. Since Γ now contains $\text{int} \rightarrow \text{int}$ as a type of `main`, the verification succeeds (on line 13 of Fig. 1). The final type environment that has been proved valid is:

$$\text{add} : \{\text{int} \rightarrow \text{int} \rightarrow \text{int}, \{x : \text{int} \mid x \geq 0\} \rightarrow \text{int} \rightarrow \{r : \text{int} \mid r \geq 0\}\},$$
$$\text{sum} : \{\text{int} \rightarrow \text{int}, \text{int} \rightarrow \{r : \text{int} \mid r \geq 0\}\},$$
$$\text{main} : \{\text{int} \rightarrow \text{int}\}.$$

The example above is oversimplified in that neither higher-order functions nor local function definitions occur, and that intersection types are not used. We present our method more formally in the next section.

4   Verification Method

This section describes our verification method in detail. As mentioned in Sect. 1, our method consists of the two components `typeChecker` and `typeSynthesizer`, which are described in Sects. 4.1 and 4.2, respectively.

4.1   typeChecker: Checking type candidate

The method typeChecker verifies whether

$$f_1 : \sigma_1, \dots, f_{k-1} : \sigma_{k-1} \models \mathbf{fix}(f_k, \lambda \widetilde{x}_k. t_k) : \tau_k$$

holds for each $k \in \{1, \dots, n\}$, given the program $\langle f_1 \, \widetilde{x}_1 = t_1, \dots, f_n \, \widetilde{x}_n = t_n \rangle$, the current type environment $f_1 : \sigma_1, \dots, f_n : \sigma_n$, and the current refinement type candidate τ_n of f_n.

We reduce a type judgment $\Gamma \overset{?}{\models} t : \tau$ to a safety checking problem by using an extension of Sato et al.'s method [17]. For example, the type checking problem

$$f : (\{x : \mathbf{int} \mid x > 0\} \to \{r : \mathbf{int} \mid r \geq x\}) \overset{?}{\models}$$
$$t : \{y : \mathbf{int} \mid y \neq 0\} \to \{s : \mathbf{int} \mid s > y\}$$

is reduced to the safety checking problem for the following program:

$$\mathbf{let}\, f = \lambda x.\, \mathbf{if}\ x > 0\ \mathbf{then}\ \mathbf{let}\ r = *_{\mathsf{int}}\ \mathbf{in}\ \mathbf{assume}\,(r \geq x);\ r$$
$$\mathbf{else}\ \mathbf{fail}\ \mathbf{in}$$
$$\mathbf{let}\ y = \mathbf{let}\ y' = *_{\mathsf{int}}\ \mathbf{in}\ \mathbf{assume}\,(y' \neq 0);\ y'\ \mathbf{in}$$
$$\mathbf{let}\ s = t\, y\ \mathbf{in}\ \mathbf{assert}(s > y)$$

Here, the bodies of f and y are "universal" terms of types $\{x : \mathbf{int} \mid x > 0\} \to \{r : \mathbf{int} \mid r \geq x\}$ and $\{y : \mathbf{int} \mid y \neq 0\}$, respectively. A universal term t of type τ can simulate all the values of type τ, in the sense that, for any context C, term t' of type τ, and integer n, $C[t'] \longrightarrow^* n$ implies $C[t] \longrightarrow^* n$, and $C[t'] \longrightarrow^* \mathbf{fail}$ implies $C[t] \longrightarrow^* \mathbf{fail}$.

As seen above, by using universal terms, we can reduce a type judgment problem to a safety problem. In general, there exists a most general context $C_{\Gamma,\tau}$ with respect to a type environment Γ and a refinement type τ such that

$$C_{\Gamma,\tau}[t] \not\longrightarrow^* \mathbf{fail} \quad \text{if and only if} \quad \Gamma \models t : \tau$$

for any t such that $ST(\Gamma) \vdash_{\mathrm{ST}} t : ST(\tau)$. Hence, we can check $\Gamma \models t : \tau$ by checking the safety of term $C_{\Gamma,\tau}[t]$. If the term is safe, then t has type τ, and otherwise, t does not have type τ for some $f_1, \dots, f_n$ that have types $\Gamma(f_1), \dots, \Gamma(f_n)$, respectively.

Note that, even if the term $C_{\Gamma,\tau}[t]$ is unsafe, we cannot conclude that t does not have type τ in the original program P. The unsafety of $C_{\Gamma,\tau}[t]$ just indicates the untypability of t under the given type environment Γ, i.e., the type environment is too weak to prove the typability of t.

Sato et al. [17] formalized the construction of $C_{\Gamma,\tau}$ for refinement types *without* intersection types. Below we extend their method to deal with refinement intersection types. We define the most general context $C_{\Gamma,\tau}$ with respect to Γ and τ by using universal terms. The universal term synthesizer $\alpha_\wedge (-)$ is defined in Fig. 5. The function $\alpha_\wedge (\sigma)$ ($\alpha (\tau)$, resp.) synthesizes a universal term of type σ

$$\alpha\left(\{x : \mathbf{int} \mid P\}\right) = \mathbf{let}\ x = *_{\mathbf{int}}\ \mathbf{in\ assume}\,(P);\ x$$

$$\alpha\left((x : \sigma) \to \tau\right) = \lambda x.\,\mathbf{if}\ *_{\mathbf{bool}} \vee \beta_\wedge\,(x : \sigma)\ \mathbf{then}\ \alpha\,(\tau)\ \mathbf{else\ fail}$$

$$\alpha_\wedge\left(\{\{x : \mathbf{int} \mid P_1\}, \ldots, \{x : \mathbf{int} \mid P_n\}\}_{\mathbf{int}}\right) = \alpha\left(\{x : \mathbf{int} \mid P_1 \wedge \cdots \wedge P_n\}\right)$$

$$\alpha_\wedge\left(\{(x : \sigma_1) \to \tau_1, \ldots, (x : \sigma_n) \to \tau_n\}_{\kappa_1 \to \kappa_2}\right) =$$
$$\qquad wrap((x : \sigma_1) \to \tau_1, wrap(\cdots, wrap((x : \sigma_n) \to \tau_n, \lambda x.\,\mathbf{fail})\cdots))$$

$$\mathbf{where}\ wrap((x : \sigma) \to \tau, v) =$$
$$\qquad \lambda x.\,\mathbf{let}\ f = v\ \mathbf{in}$$
$$\qquad\qquad \mathbf{if}\ *_{\mathbf{bool}} \vee \beta_\wedge\,(x : \sigma)\ \mathbf{then}$$
$$\qquad\qquad\qquad \mathbf{try\ let}\ r = f\,x\ \mathbf{in}\ wrap(\tau, r)\ \mathbf{with\ fail} \to \alpha\,(\tau)$$
$$\qquad\qquad \mathbf{else}\ f\,x$$
$$\qquad wrap(\{x : \mathbf{int} \mid P\}, v) = \mathbf{assume}\,([v/x]P);\ v$$

$$\beta\left(v : \{x : \mathbf{int} \mid P\}\right) = [v/x]P$$

$$\beta\left(v : (x : \sigma) \to \tau\right) = \mathbf{let}\ x = \alpha_\wedge\,(\sigma)\ \mathbf{in\ let}\ r = v\,x\ \mathbf{in}\ \beta\,(r : \tau)$$

$$\beta_\wedge\left(v : \{\tau_1, \ldots, \tau_n\}_\kappa\right) = \beta\,(v : \tau_1) \wedge \cdots \wedge \beta\,(v : \tau_n)$$

Fig. 5. Synthesis of universal terms

(τ, resp.). The function $\beta_\wedge\,(v : \sigma)$ ($\beta\,(v : \tau)$, resp.) checks whether v has type σ (τ, resp.). If $\beta_\wedge\,(v : \sigma)$ returns **false** or aborts with **fail**, then v does not have type σ. In the case of an intersection of function types, we use exceptions and treat **fail** as an exception, which can be removed by CPS transformation. The function $wrap(\tau, v)$, intuitively, forces v to have type τ by inserting assume expressions into v. For integer types, $wrap(\{x : \mathbf{int} \mid P\}, v)$ just assumes $[v/x]P$ and returns v. For functions types, $wrap((x : \sigma) \to \tau, v)$ returns a new function that is an eta-expansion of v and in which assume expressions are inserted. In the body of the new function, if the then-branch is taken (which indicates that the argument x may have type σ), the return value must have type τ. If $f\,x$ is evaluated to some value r, then the new function returns $wrap(\tau, r)$, which is forced to have type τ. If the evaluation of $f\,x$ fails, then the new function returns the universal term of τ. If the else-branch is taken (which indicates that the argument x does not have type σ), since the return value of the new function need not have type τ, $wrap((x : \sigma) \to \tau, v)$ returns the original result $f\,x$. Note that we can remove "$*_{\mathbf{bool}} \vee$" in the definitions of $\alpha\left((x : \sigma) \to \tau\right)$ and $wrap((x : \sigma) \to \tau, v)$, if we know that $\beta_\wedge\,(x : \sigma)$ terminates. Especially, we can remove "$*_{\mathbf{bool}} \vee$" when σ is an integer type like the example above.

By using $\alpha_\wedge\,(-)$ and $\beta\,(- : -)$, the most general context $C_{\Gamma, \tau}$ can be defined as follows:

$$C_{(f_1 : \sigma_1, \ldots, f_n : \sigma_n), \tau} = \mathbf{let}\ f_1 = \alpha_\wedge\,(\sigma_1)\ \mathbf{in}\ \ldots\ \mathbf{let}\ f_n = \alpha_\wedge\,(\sigma_n)\ \mathbf{in}$$
$$\qquad\qquad \mathbf{let}\ f = [\,]\ \mathbf{in\ assert}(\beta\,(f : \tau))$$

The following lemma states the correctness of the construction of $C_{\Gamma,\tau}$, which can be proved in a manner similar to the original construction of Sato et al. [17] for refinement types without intersections.

Lemma 1. *Suppose $ST(\Gamma) \vdash_{\mathrm{ST}} t : ST(\tau)$.*

$$\Gamma \models^P t : \tau \quad \text{if and only if} \quad C_{\Gamma,\tau}[t] \not\longrightarrow^*_P \textbf{fail}.$$

The reduced problem can be checked by an existing safety checker (e.g., MoCHi [9,18]) that satisfies the following properties:

- It can check the safety of a given program t, i.e., whether $t \not\longrightarrow^*_P \textbf{fail}$.
- It can generate a counterexample, i.e., a concrete reduction sequence of the form $t \longrightarrow^*_P \textbf{fail}$, given an unsafe program.

We use counterexamples obtained by the checker to find type candidates of top-level functions. Instead of using the counterexamples themselves, we use their subsequence related to the target function. We call them *modular counterexamples*. A modular counterexample π of top-level function f is a sequence of pairs of labels and branching information $\{\textbf{then}, \textbf{else}\}$, i.e., $\pi : (L \times \{\textbf{then}, \textbf{else}\})^*$ where L is the set of labels.

A modular counterexample of f is obtained from an ordinary counterexample π as follows. We write $L(t)$ for the set of the labels occurred in t, and write L_f for $L(t)$ where $(f \, \tilde{x} = t) \in P$. Suppose the given counterexample π is of the following form

$$C_{\Gamma,\tau}[t] \longrightarrow^* E_1[\textbf{if}^{\ell_1} \, v_1 \textbf{ then } t_{12} \textbf{ else } t_{13}]$$
$$\longrightarrow^* E_2[\textbf{if}^{\ell_2} \, v_2 \textbf{ then } t_{22} \textbf{ else } t_{23}]$$
$$\vdots$$
$$\longrightarrow^* E_n[\textbf{if}^{\ell_n} \, v_n \textbf{ then } t_{n2} \textbf{ else } t_{n3}]$$
$$\longrightarrow^* \textbf{fail}.$$

Then, a modular counterexample of function f is

$$(\ell_{j_1}, b_{j_1}) \ldots (\ell_{j_k}, b_{j_k}) \quad \text{where } 1 \leq j_1 < \cdots < j_k \leq n,$$
$$\{j_1, \ldots, j_k\} = \{j \mid \ell_j \in L_f\}, \text{ and}$$
$$b_j = \begin{cases} \textbf{then} & v_j \neq 0 \\ \textbf{else} & v_j = 0 \end{cases} \quad \text{for each } j \in \{j_1, \ldots, j_k\}.$$

Example 3. Recall the program P_{sum} in Example 1. Suppose that $\tau = \textbf{int} \rightarrow \{r : \textbf{int} \mid r = 0\}$ is given as a type candidate of sum and the following type environment is given:

$$\Gamma = \textbf{add} : \{\textbf{int} \rightarrow \textbf{int} \rightarrow \textbf{int}\}.$$

Then, the most general context $C_{\Gamma,\tau}$ is

$$C_{\Gamma,\tau} = \textbf{let add} = \lambda x. \, \lambda y. \, *_{\textbf{int}} \textbf{ in}$$
$$\textbf{let } x = *_{\textbf{int}} \textbf{ in let } r = [\,] \, x \textbf{ in assert}(r = 0).$$

Since sum does not have type τ under the type environment, we have the following counterexample for some $m \neq 0$:

$$C_{\Gamma,\tau}[t_{\mathsf{sum}}]$$
$$\longrightarrow^* \mathbf{let}\ r = t'_{\mathsf{sum}}\,1\ \mathbf{in}\ \mathbf{assert}(r = 0)$$
$$\longrightarrow^* \mathbf{let}\ r = \mathbf{if}^{\ell_2}\,1 \leq 0\ \mathbf{then}\ 0\ \mathbf{else}\ t_{\mathsf{add}}\,1\,(t'_{\mathsf{sum}}\,(1-1))\ \mathbf{in}\ \mathbf{assert}(r = 0)$$
$$\longrightarrow^* \mathbf{let}\ r = t_{\mathsf{add}}\,1\,(\mathbf{if}^{\ell_2}\,0 \leq 0\ \mathbf{then}\ 0\ \mathbf{else}\ \ldots)\ \mathbf{in}\ \mathbf{assert}(r = 0)$$
$$\longrightarrow^* \mathbf{let}\ r = t_{\mathsf{add}}\,1\,0\ \mathbf{in}\ \mathbf{assert}(r = 0)$$
$$\longrightarrow^* \mathbf{let}\ r = m\ \mathbf{in}\ \mathbf{assert}(r = 0)$$
$$\longrightarrow^* \mathbf{fail}$$

where

$$t_{\mathsf{sum}} = P(\mathsf{sum}) = \mathbf{fix}(\mathsf{sum}, \lambda x.\,\mathbf{if}^{\ell_2}\,x \leq 0\ \mathbf{then}\ 0\ \mathbf{else}\ \mathsf{add}\,x\,(\mathsf{sum}\,(x-1)))$$
$$t'_{\mathsf{sum}} = [t_{\mathsf{add}}/\mathsf{add}]t_{\mathsf{sum}}$$
$$t_{\mathsf{add}} = \lambda x.\,\lambda y.\,*_{\mathsf{int}}\,.$$

There are two branches labeled with ℓ_2, which occurs in the body of sum. The else-branch is taken on the first visit of ℓ_2, and the then-branch is taken on the next visit. We then obtain the following modular counterexample:

$$(\mathsf{sum}, (\ell_2, \mathbf{else})(\ell_2, \mathbf{then})).$$

□

4.2   typeSynthesizer: Synthesizing new refinement types

The function typeSynthesizer finds type candidates by using the modular counterexamples found so far. It first generates a program slice of the original program corresponding to modular counterexamples, and infers a refinement type of the program slice. The inferred refinement type can be used as a type candidate of the original program.

Given a set of modular counterexamples

$$\Pi \subseteq \mathcal{P}\left(dom(P) \times (L \times \{\mathbf{then}, \mathbf{else}\})^*\right),$$

we generate a program slice of $P(f_i)$ that corresponds to Π, for which we write D_{P,Π,f_i}. We first construct a computation tree whose path corresponds to a execution trace that follows the modular counterexamples. The corresponding program D_{P,Π,f_i} is obtained by (i) making a copy of each function for each call in the computation tree, and (ii) for each copy, removing the branches not taken in the corresponding execution trace.

Example 4. Recall the program P_{sum} in Example 3. Suppose the target function and the type are main and $\text{int} \to \text{int}$, and the following set Π of modular counterexamples is given:

$$\begin{aligned}
\{ &(\text{add}, (\ell_1, \textbf{then})), \\
&(\text{add}, (\ell_1, \textbf{else})(\ell_1, \textbf{then})), \\
&(\text{sum}, (\ell_2, \textbf{else})(\ell_2, \textbf{else})(\ell_2, \textbf{then})), \\
&(\text{main}, (\ell_3, \textbf{else})) \ \}.
\end{aligned}$$

Then the program $D_{P_{\text{sum}}, \Pi, \text{main}}$ corresponding to the modular counterexamples is

$$\begin{aligned}
\langle \ \text{add}_1 \ x \ y &= \textbf{if } y \leq 0 \textbf{ then } x \textbf{ else assume} (\text{false}), \\
\text{add}_2' \ x \ y &= \textbf{if } y \leq 0 \textbf{ then } x \textbf{ else assume} (\text{false}), \\
\text{add}_2 \ x \ y &= \textbf{if } y \leq 0 \textbf{ then assume} (\text{false}) \textbf{ else } 1 + \text{add}_2' \ x \ (y - 1), \\
\text{add} \ x \ y &= \text{add}_1 \ x \ y \ \square \ \text{add}_2 \ x \ y, \\
\text{sum}_1'' \ x &= \textbf{if } x \leq 0 \textbf{ then } 0 \textbf{ else assume} (\text{false}), \\
\text{sum}_1' \ x &= \textbf{if } x \leq 0 \textbf{ then assume} (\text{false}) \textbf{ else add } x \ (\text{sum}_1'' \ (x - 1)), \\
\text{sum}_1 \ x &= \textbf{if } x \leq 0 \textbf{ then assume} (\text{false}) \textbf{ else add } x \ (\text{sum}_1' \ (x - 1)), \\
\text{sum} \ x &= \text{sum}_1 \ x, \\
\text{main}_1 \ n &= \textbf{if } 0 \leq \text{sum} \ n \ 0 \textbf{ then assume} (\text{false}) \textbf{ else fail}, \\
\text{main} \ n &= \text{main}_1 \ n \ \rangle.
\end{aligned}$$

A function corresponding to each modular counterexample is generated: add_1 from $(\text{add}, (\ell_1, \textbf{then}))$, add_2 from $(\text{add}, (\ell_1, \textbf{else})(\ell_1, \textbf{then}))$, sum_1 from $(\text{sum}, (\ell_2, \textbf{else})(\ell_2, \textbf{else})(\ell_2, \textbf{then}))$, and main_1 from $(\text{main}, (\ell_3, \textbf{else}))$. The function typeSynthesizer then infers a refinement type of $C_{\emptyset, \text{int} \to \text{int}}[D_{P_{\text{sum}}, \Pi, \text{main}}]$, and obtains the following types:

$$\begin{aligned}
\text{add} &: \{\{x : \text{int} \mid x \geq 0\} \to \text{int} \to \{r : \text{int} \mid r \geq 0\}\}, \\
\text{sum} &: \{\text{int} \to \{r : \text{int} \mid r \geq 0\}\}.
\end{aligned}$$

We use the above types as type candidates of add and sum. $\qquad\square$

If the constructed program is not typable, so is the original program. Then, the function typeSynthesizer answers "There are no candidates" and our method returns "no". In this case, we can obtain an untypable execution trace, and output the trace as an ordinary counterexample.

The concrete definition of typeSynthesizer is shown in Appendix A. The construction is similar to that of straightline programs used in MoCHi [9].

The following lemma guarantees that the modular counterexample π is indeed a counterexample in that a slice of $P(f_i)$ containing a path corresponding to π is indeed (semantically) untypable.

Lemma 2. *Let P be a program, and π be a modular counterexample against $\Gamma \models P(f_i) : \tau_i$. If $\pi \in \Pi$ and D_{P, Π, f_i} is the slice of $P(f_i)$ corresponding to Π, then $\Gamma \not\models D_{P, \Pi, f_i} : \tau_i$.*

4.3 Properties of the Method

We now discuss properties of our method. The method is sound (under the assumption that the underlying verifier is sound), in the sense that, if the method returns "yes" ("no", resp.), then the given program has (does not have, resp.) the given type. This is an easy consequence of the soundness of typeChecker, i.e., the soundness of the reduction from refinement type checking to assertion checking.

Our method also satisfies a progress property, in that the set of modular counterexamples monotonically increases until the method terminates. More precisely, in the overall procedure in Fig. 1, either Γ or Π strictly increases upon each recursive call of validateTE. We can prove the progress as follows. Suppose that validateTE is called with a non-empty candidate type environment Γ_{cand}, that Γ does not change in the for-loop, and that $\tau \in \Gamma(f_n)$ does not hold on line 13. Let i be the least i such that $\Gamma_{\text{cand}}(f_i) \neq \emptyset$, and there exists $\tau' \in \Gamma_{\text{cand}}(f_i)$ such that $\Gamma \not\models P(f_i) : \tau'$; note that there always exists such i by the assumption that $\tau \in \Gamma(f_n)$ does not hold on line 13. Since $\Gamma_{\text{cand}}(f_i) \neq \emptyset$, typeChecker($\Gamma, P(f_i), \tau'$) returns NG($\pi$) for some π. We show $\pi \notin \Pi$ by contradiction. Suppose $\pi \in \Pi$. By Lemma 2, $\Gamma \not\models D_{P,\Pi,f_i} : \tau'$, where D_{P,Π,f_i} is the slice of $P(f_i)$ corresponding to Π. This contradicts $\tau' \in \Gamma_{\text{cand}}(f_i)$, since in the previous call of validateTE, Γ_{cand} has been constructed from Π (so, τ' has been chosen so that $\Gamma \models D_{P,\Pi,f_i} : \tau'$ holds). Thus, we have $\pi \notin \Pi$, which implies that Π strictly increases on line 12.

With a certain assumption on the underlying reachability checker used in typeChecker, we can also guarantee the completeness for finding a counterexample. Suppose that, for the problem $C_{\Gamma,\tau}[P(f_i)] \stackrel{?}{\longrightarrow^*_P}$ **fail** obtained from a type checking problem $\Gamma \stackrel{?}{\models} P(f_i) : \tau$, if there is a counterexample, the reachability checker returns the one corresponding to the *least* (with respect to a certain total order on modular counterexamples) modular counterexample that does not belong to Π (if there is any). Then, by the progress property, every counterexample is eventually enumerated, so that a counterexample to the original verification problem is eventually found if there is any.

In order to guarantee the relative completeness for verification in the sense of [24] (i.e., if $\models P : \tau$, then the method is eventually able to prove it, modulo a certain assumption on the underlying logic), we need to extend the method to automatically infer implicit parameters (as in [24]) for each function module, which is left for future work.

5 Experiments

We have implemented an automated verification tool for a subset of OCaml, based on the proposed method. We use MoCHi [9] as the backend safety checker used in typeChecker. We have tested our tool for programs taken from the benchmark for MoCHi and Caml Examples [27]. We have conducted the experiments on a machine with Intel Core i7-3930K (3.20 GHz, 16 GB of memory), with timeout of 600 s. All the programs are available on the web http://www-kb. is.s.u-tokyo.ac.jp/~ryosuke/modular/.

Table 1 summarizes the experimental results. The column "program" shows the names of the programs. The column "LOC" shows the number of lines of code excluding comments and blank lines. The column "#module" shows the number of modules, i.e., top-level functions. The columns "MoCHI" and "modular" show the running time in seconds of the original MoCHI and our new verifier respectively. The column "#typeChecker" shows the number of calls to typeChecker.

All the benchmark programs are safe except various-e and queen_simple-e, i.e., they are free from assertion failures, pattern matching failures, uncaught exceptions, and array bound errors. We explain each benchmark program below. The program sum_add is P_{sum} in Example 1. The programs harmonic, fold_div, and risers have been taken from the benchmark of MoCHI [18]. We have chosen the programs which are no less than 18 lines and have no less than 3 modules. The program various is a composition of small programs taken from the benchmark of MoCHI, namely sum, mult, and mc91.

The other programs colwheel–doctor have been taken from Caml Examples [27]. The program colwheel displays a color chart, which uses exceptions and variants defined in Graphics module. The program queen solves the eight queen problem, which uses arrays. We encode arrays as functions, and insert assertions on array bounds. We insert assertions that the index used in an operation on array is no less than 0. The program queen_simple is a simplified version of queen, but the assertions on array bounds are more strict than queen. We also insert assertions that the index used in an operation is less than the size of the

Table 1. Results of experiments

Program	LOC	#module	MoCHI (sec)	Modular (sec)	#typeChecker
sum_add	3	3	0.57	1.64	11
harmonic	18	4	0.88	5.48	17
fold_div	19	4	0.86	5.71	18
risers	21	3	8.93	2.66	4
various	23	3	TIMEOUT	0.04	5
colwheel	69	5	TIMEOUT	25.06	7
queen	45	4	5.69	9.70	8
queen_simple	20	2	TIMEOUT	14.86	7
soli	93	5	TIMEOUT	17.84	8
spir	75	11	5.06	48.94	21
doctor	568	12	TIMEOUT	543.93	45
various-e	23	3	0.34	2.24	5
queen_simple-e	19	2	0.74	4.02	5

array. The program `soli` solves a Peg solitaire game, which also uses exceptions, variants, and arrays. The program `spir` shows an animation of a colorful spiral, which uses an array. The program `doctor` is a chatterbot, which uses exceptions. A program of name "xxx-e" is a buggy version of the program "xxx".

As seen in Table 1, our new tool successfully verifies all the benchmark programs, whereas MoCHi failed to verify `various`, `colwheel`, `queen_simple`, `soli`, and `doctor` in 600 s. For the other programs (that MoCHi could also verify) except `risers`, our new tool is actually slower than MoCHi. For those programs, `typeChecker` was called many times before appropriate refinement types were discovered. There is an obvious trade-off between the modular and whole program verification; in reasoning about each function, the latter can use more precise information about the other functions. We expect that the advantage of the modular verification is clearer for larger programs.

6   Related Work

As mentioned in Sect. 1, most of the fully-automated verification methods for higher-order functional programs [9,10,13–15,18,26] are whole program analyses. The exceptions are those based on refinement type inference [21,30,31], which have similarities to our method in that they consist of two components: one to infer candidate refinement types of functions, and the other to check the validity of the candidate refinement types; the latter can be carried out in a compositional manner, based on a refinement type system. Each component is, however, significantly different from ours. For the first component, Terauchi [21] applies the technique of refinement type inference [23] to the recursion-free programs obtained by finitely unfolding recursive functions, whereas Zhu et al. [30] apply a machine learning technique. Our `typeSynthesizer` component is closer to Terauchi's one [21], but only looks at a part of the program relevant to modular counterexamples found so far. It would be interesting to integrate Zhu et al.'s machine learning technique [30,31] into our `typeSynthesizer` component, which is left for future work. For the second component, both Terauchi [21] and Zhu et al. [30] use a specific set of syntactic typing rules for refinement types, which is not complete with respect to the semantic refinement type judgment. Our `typeChecker` component reduces the semantic type judgment to a reachability checking problem and delegates the latter to a software model checker [9,24], so that the component is relatively complete in the sense of [24]. As a result, our modular verification tool is as powerful as MoCHi, and can generate a concrete error path as a counterexample if a given program does not satisfy a specification, unlike Terauchi and Zhu et al.'s methods [21,30]. For the `typeChecker` component, we have extended Sato et al.'s technique [17] to deal with intersection types. Voirol et al. [26] and Unno et al. [23] reduce the verification of higher-order programs to the satisfiability checking of quantifier-free formulas and Horn clauses, respectively, and then use constraint solvers; thus, the scalability of the methods depends on those of the underlying solvers. We are not aware of a good modular method for checking the satisfiability.

In contrast with fully-automated verification methods, semi-automated verification methods for functional programs [6,11,16,28,29] usually work in a compositional manner. Those methods, however, rely on annotations of invariants (or predicates used in invariants [16]). Among them, liquid types [16,25] require less annotations. Since the liquid types also rely on syntactic refinement typing rules, the comment above on Zhu et al. and Terauchi's methods [21,30] applies.

For finite state systems, a lot of techniques have been proposed for compositional verification [1–5,7,8,22]. Some of them infer the interfaces of components based on lazy parallel composition [3,22] and assume-guarantee reasoning [5,7]. It is not clear how to extend those methods to deal with higher-order functional programs.

7   Conclusion

We have proposed an automated modular verification method for higher-order functional programs. We have introduced the notion of modular counterexamples to infer candidate refinement intersection types of each function module, and extended Sato et al.'s method [17] to check the validity of the inferred candidate types in a modular manner. We have implemented the proposed method and confirmed its effectiveness through experiments.

Further optimizations are required to make our verification tool more scalable for larger programs. Future work also includes a relatively complete modular verification method (recall the discussion at the end of Sect. 4.3), and extensions of the modular method for proving liveness properties.

Acknowledgment. We would like to thank anonymous referees for useful comments. This work was supported by JSPS KAKENHI Grant Number JP15H05706.

A   Definition of typeSynthesizer

This section gives the definition of the component `typeSynthesizer`. For the simplicity, we use the intermediate language defined as follows:

$$D ::= \left\{ f_1\, \widetilde{x}_1 = e_{10}\, \square^\ell\, e_{11}, \ldots, f_m\, \widetilde{x}_m = e_{m0}\, \square\, e_{m1} \right\}$$
$$e ::= a \mid \mathbf{assume}\,(v)\, ;\, e \mid \mathbf{let}\ x = *_{\mathsf{int}}\ \mathbf{in}\ e$$
$$a ::= \langle\rangle \mid x\,\widetilde{v} \mid f\,\widetilde{v} \mid \mathbf{fail}$$
$$v ::= c \mid x\,\widetilde{v} \mid f\,\widetilde{v} \mid \mathsf{op}(\widetilde{v}).$$

The semantics of the intermediate language is given in Fig. 6. When transforming the original program, we keep information on the function definition dependencies as relation $R \subseteq dom(P) \times F$ where F denote the set of functions (including local functions). $R(f, g)$ means that f is a top-level function and function g is defined in the body of f in the original program. We write F_{top} for the top-level function of the original program P, i.e., $dom(P)$. We assume that the translated program contains a distinguished function symbol main $\in \{f_1, \ldots, f_n\}$ whose simple type is $\mathbf{int} \to \mathbf{int}$, and main does not use its argument. The transformation from the target language to the intermediate language can be defined as a combination of CPS transformation and λ-lifting.

$$\frac{f \notin F_{\mathsf{top}} \qquad (f\,\widetilde{x} = e_1 \,\square^\ell\, e_2) \in D}{(D, f\,\widetilde{v}) \longrightarrow (D, [\widetilde{v}/\widetilde{x}](e_1 \,\square^\ell\, e_2))}$$

$$(D, e_1 \,\square^\ell\, e_2) \longrightarrow (D, e_b)$$

$$(D, \mathbf{assume}\,(\mathbf{true})\,;e) \longrightarrow (D, e)$$

$$(D, \mathbf{let}\ x = *_{\mathsf{int}}\ \mathbf{in}\ a) \longrightarrow (D, [n/x]a)$$

Fig. 6. Operational semantics of the intermediate language

The operational semantics is given by Fig. 7. This semantics is used just for collecting information on which branch is taken, and which function is called in each application. The reduction is labeled with

$$\rho \in \{\varepsilon\} \cup \{(\mathbf{br}, b) \mid b \in \{\mathbf{then}, \mathbf{else}\}\} \cup \{(\mathbf{sp}, \pi) \mid \pi : (L \times \{\mathbf{then}, \mathbf{else}\})^*\}$$

for recording which branch has been taken and which modular counterexample has been used. The label $(\mathbf{br}, \mathbf{then})$ $((\mathbf{br}, \mathbf{else})$, resp.) represents that the then-branch (else-branch, resp.) is taken. The label $(\mathbf{sp}, \pi)$ represents that the modular counterexample π is used for the top-level function f on the application of f. The evaluation ignores base values, as $\mathbf{assume}\,(v)\,;e$ and $\mathbf{let}\ x = *_{\mathsf{int}}\ \mathbf{in}\ e$ are reduced to e. In the application of top-level function f, the function is duplicated by the function $\mathbf{Spawn}(D, R, f, \pi)$ with respect to modular counterexample π. We write $(D, B, t) \overset{\rho_1 \cdots \rho_n}{\Longrightarrow}_{R,\Pi} (D', B', t')$ if

$$(D, B, t)\,(\overset{\varepsilon}{\longrightarrow}_{R,\Pi})^*\,\overset{\rho_1}{\longrightarrow}_{R,\Pi}\,(\overset{\varepsilon}{\longrightarrow}_{R,\Pi})^* \cdots$$
$$(\overset{\varepsilon}{\longrightarrow}_{R,\Pi})^*\,\overset{\rho_n}{\longrightarrow}_{R,\Pi}\,(\overset{\varepsilon}{\longrightarrow}_{R,\Pi})^*(D', B', t').$$

To construct a program corresponding to modular counterexamples, we first extract the set of sequences of labels, which can be viewed as a set of ordinary counterexamples. We define the set $\mathfrak{B}$ of sequence of labels from reduction sequences according to Π by

$$\mathfrak{B} = \left\{ \widetilde{\rho} \ \middle|\ (D, \emptyset, \mathtt{main}\,\langle\rangle) \overset{\widetilde{\rho}}{\Longrightarrow}_{R,\Pi} (D', B', t')\ \text{for some } D', B',\ \text{and } t' \right\}.$$

We then construct a program from $\mathfrak{B}$ by using function $\mathbf{Construct}(-, -)$, which is defined in Fig. 8. In the figure, $t_{\rho_1 \ldots \rho_n}$ is a term satisfying

$$(D, \emptyset, \mathtt{main}\,\langle\rangle) \overset{\rho_1 \cdots \rho_n}{\Longrightarrow}_{R,\Pi} (D', B', t_{\rho_1 \ldots \rho_n})$$

$$\frac{f \notin F_{\text{top}} \qquad (f\,\widetilde{x} = e_1 \,\square^l\, e_2) \in D}{(D, B, f\,\widetilde{v}) \xrightarrow{\varepsilon}_{R,\Pi} (D, B, [\widetilde{v}/\widetilde{x}](e_1 \,\square^l\, e_2))}$$

$$\frac{f \in F_{\text{top}} \quad (f\,\widetilde{x} = t) \in D \quad |\widetilde{x}| = |\widetilde{v}| \quad (D', \pi', f') = \mathbf{Spawn}(D, R, f, \pi) \quad (f, \pi) \in \Pi}{(D, B, f\,\widetilde{v}) \xrightarrow{(\mathbf{sp},\pi)}_{R,\Pi} (D' \cup D, \{\pi'\} \cup B, f'\widetilde{v})}$$

$$\frac{\pi = (\ell_1, b_1) \ldots (\ell_i, b_i) \ldots (\ell_n, b_n) \qquad \ell_i = \ell \qquad \ell_j \neq \ell \quad \text{for } j \in \{1, \ldots, i-1\}}{\pi' = (\ell_1, b_1) \ldots (\ell_{i-1}, b_{i-1})(\ell_{i+1}, b_{i+1}) \ldots (\ell_n, b_n)}$$
$$(D, \{\pi\} \uplus B, e_1 \,\square^l\, e_2) \xrightarrow{(\mathbf{br},b)}_{R,\Pi} (D, \{\pi'\} \uplus B, e_b)$$

$$(D, B, \mathbf{assume}\,(v)\,; e) \xrightarrow{\varepsilon}_{R,\Pi} (D, B, e)$$

$$(D, B, \mathbf{let}\ x = *_{\mathbf{int}}\ \mathbf{in}\ a) \xrightarrow{\varepsilon}_{R,\Pi} (D, B, e)$$

$\mathbf{Spawn}(D, R, f, \pi) \stackrel{\text{def}}{=} (D', \pi', f')$

$\quad$ where $\{g_1, \ldots, g_n\} = \{g \mid R(f, g)\}$

$\qquad \{l_f\} = \left\{ l \mid (f\,\widetilde{x} = e_1 \,\square^\ell\, e_2) \in D \right\}$

$\qquad \{l_i\} = \left\{ l \mid (g_i\,\widetilde{x} = e_1 \,\square^\ell\, e_2) \in D \right\} \quad$ for each $i \in \{1, \ldots, n\}$

$\qquad f', g'_1, \ldots, g'_n, l'_f, l'_1, \ldots, l'_n$ are fresh

$\qquad \sigma = [f'/f, g'_0/g_0, \ldots, g'_n/g_n]$

$\qquad D' = \left\{ f\,\widetilde{x} = \sigma e_1 \,\square^\ell\, \sigma e_2 \mid (f\,\widetilde{x} = e_1 \,\square^\ell\, e_2) \in D \right\}$

$\qquad\qquad \cup \left\{ g_i\,\widetilde{x} = \sigma e_1 \,\square^{l'_i}\, \sigma e_2 \mid i \in \{1, \ldots, n\}, (g_i\,\widetilde{x} = e_1 \,\square\, e_2) \in D \right\}$

$\qquad \pi = (l_{j_1}, b_1) \ldots (l_{j_k}, b_k)$

$\qquad \pi' = (l'_{j_1}, b_1) \ldots (l'_{j_k}, b_k)$

Fig. 7. Operational semantics of the intermediate language with respect to modular counterexamples

for some D' and B'. We assign an index to each element of $\mathfrak{B}$, and write $I(\widetilde{\rho})$ for the index of $\widetilde{\rho}$. We assume $I(\widetilde{\rho}) \leq I(\widetilde{\rho'})$ if $\widetilde{\rho}$ is a prefix of $\widetilde{\rho'}$. We write $\widetilde{\rho}_j$ for the element of $\mathfrak{B}$ whose index is j.

$\quad$ Finally, by using the refinement (intersection) type inference [21,23], we infer a refinement type of the constructed program in the context $C_{\emptyset, \tau}$ where τ is the target type, and return the inferred types as type candidates.

$\mathbf{Construct}(\{f_1\,\widetilde{x}_1 = e_{10}\,\square\,e_{11}, \ldots, f_m\,\widetilde{x}_m = e_{m0}\,\square\,e_{m1}\}, \mathfrak{B}) \overset{\mathrm{def}}{=}$

$\quad\{f_i^{(\widetilde{\rho}(\mathbf{br},k))}\,\widetilde{x}_i = [e_{ik}]_{\widetilde{\rho}(\mathbf{br},k)\rho'} \mid i \in \{1, \ldots, m\},\, j \in \{1, \ldots, |\mathfrak{B}|\},\, f_i \notin F,$

$\qquad\widetilde{\rho}(\mathbf{br}, k)\rho' \in \mathfrak{B},\, t_{\widetilde{\rho}(\mathbf{br},k)}$ is an application of $f_i\}$

$\cup\{f_i^{(\widetilde{\rho})}\,\widetilde{x}_i = \langle\rangle \mid i \in \{1, \ldots, m\},\, j \in \{1, \ldots, |\mathfrak{B}|\},\, f_i \notin F,$

$\qquad t_{\widetilde{\rho}}$ is not an application of $f_i\}$

$\cup\{f_i^{(\widetilde{\rho})}\,\widetilde{x}_i = f_i^{(\widetilde{\rho}(\mathbf{sp},\Pi_1))}\,\widetilde{x}_i\,\square\cdots\square\,f_i^{(\widetilde{\rho}(\mathbf{sp},\Pi_k))}\,\widetilde{x}_i \mid i \in \{1, \ldots, m\},\, j \in \{1, \ldots, |\mathfrak{B}|\},$

$\qquad f_i \in F, \{c_1, \ldots, c_k\} = \{c \mid (f_i, c) \in \Pi\},\, t_{\widetilde{\rho}}$ is an application of $f_i\}$

$\cup\{f_i^{(\widetilde{\rho})}\,\widetilde{x}_i = \langle\rangle \mid i \in \{1, \ldots, m\},\, j \in \{1, \ldots, |\mathfrak{B}|\},$

$\qquad f_i \in F, \{c_1, \ldots, c_k\} = \{c \mid (f_i, c) \in \Pi\},\, t_{\widetilde{\rho}}$ is not an application of $f_i\}$

$\cup\left\{\mathbf{main}\langle\rangle = \mathbf{main}^{(\varepsilon)}\langle\rangle\right\}$

$[\mathbf{assume}\,(v)\,a]_j = \mathbf{assume}\,(v)\,[a]_j$

$[\mathbf{let}\,x = \mathbf{op}(\widetilde{v})\,\mathbf{in}\,a]_j = \mathbf{let}\,x = \mathbf{op}(\widetilde{v})\,\mathbf{in}\,[a]_j$

$[\langle\rangle]_j = \langle\rangle$

$[\mathbf{fail}]_j = \mathbf{fail}$

$[x]_j = x$

$[x\,v_1\cdots v_k]_j = \natural_j(x)\,v_1^{\diamond_{j+1}}\cdots v_k^{\diamond_{j+1}} \qquad (k \geq 1)$

$[f\,v_1\cdots v_k]_j = f^{(\widetilde{\rho}j)}\,v_1^{\diamond_{j+1}}\cdots v_k^{\diamond_{j+1}}$

$c^{\diamond_j} = c$

$x^{\diamond_j} = x \quad$ (if x is a variable of a base type)

$(x\,\widetilde{v})^{\diamond_j} = \langle\underbrace{\lambda\widetilde{y}.\langle\rangle, \ldots, \lambda\widetilde{y}.\langle\rangle}_{j-1}, \natural_j(x)(\widetilde{v}^{\diamond_j}), \ldots, \natural_{|\mathfrak{B}|}(x)(\widetilde{v}^{\diamond_j})\rangle$

(if x is a function variable)

$(f\,\widetilde{v})^{\diamond_j} = \langle\underbrace{\lambda\widetilde{y}.\langle\rangle, \ldots, \lambda\widetilde{y}.\langle\rangle}_{j-1}, f^{(\rho_j)}(\widetilde{v}^{\diamond_j}), \ldots, f^{(\rho_{|\mathfrak{B}|})}(\widetilde{v}^{\diamond_j})\rangle$

Fig. 8. The definition of $\mathbf{Construct}(D, \mathfrak{B})$

References

1. Berezin, S., Campos, S., Clarke, E.M.: Compositional reasoning in model checking. In: Roever, W.-P., Langmaack, H., Pnueli, A. (eds.) COMPOS 1997. LNCS, vol. 1536, pp. 81–102. Springer, Heidelberg (1998). doi:10.1007/3-540-49213-5_4
2. Burch, J., Clarke, E.M., Long, D.: Symbolic model checking with partitioned transition relations. In: Proceedings of the IFIP TC10/WG 10.5 International Conference on Very Large Scale Integration (VLSI 1991), pp. 49–58 (1991)

3. Campos, S.V.A.: A quantitative approach to the formal verification of real-time systems. Ph.D. thesis, Carnegie Mellon University (1996)
4. Chaki, S., Gurfinkel, A.: Automated assume-guarantee reasoning for omega-regular systems and specifications. Innov. Syst. Softw. Eng. **7**(2), 131–139 (2011)
5. Cobleigh, J.M., Giannakopoulou, D., PǍsǍreanu, C.S.: Learning assumptions for compositional verification. In: Garavel, H., Hatcliff, J. (eds.) TACAS 2003. LNCS, vol. 2619, pp. 331–346. Springer, Heidelberg (2003). doi:10.1007/3-540-36577-X_24
6. Filliâtre, J.C., Paskevich, A.: Why3 - where programs meet provers. In: Proceedings of the 22nd European Conference on Programming Languages and Systems (ESOP 2013), pp. 125–128 (2013)
7. Gheorghiu Bobaru, M., Pǎsǎreanu, C.S., Giannakopoulou, D.: Automated assume-guarantee reasoning by abstraction refinement. In: Gupta, A., Malik, S. (eds.) CAV 2008. LNCS, vol. 5123, pp. 135–148. Springer, Heidelberg (2008). doi:10.1007/978-3-540-70545-1_14
8. Grumberg, O., Long, D.E.: Model checking and modular verification. ACM Trans. Program. Lang. Syst. **16**(3), 843–871 (1994)
9. Kobayashi, N., Sato, R., Unno, H.: Predicate abstraction and CEGAR for higher-order model checking. In: Proceedings of the 32nd ACM SIGPLAN Conference on Programming Language Design and Implementation (PLDI 2011), pp. 222–233 (2011)
10. Kobayashi, N., Tabuchi, N., Unno, H.: Higher-order multi-parameter tree transducers and recursion schemes for program verification. In: Proceedings of the 37th ACM SIGACT-SIGPLAN Symposium on Principles of Programming Languages (POPL 2010), pp. 495–508 (2010)
11. Leino, K.R.M.: Dafny: an automatic program verifier for functional correctness. In: Clarke, E.M., Voronkov, A. (eds.) LPAR 2010. LNCS (LNAI), vol. 6355, pp. 348–370. Springer, Heidelberg (2010). doi:10.1007/978-3-642-17511-4_20
12. Matsumoto, Y., Kobayashi, N., Unno, H.: Automata-based abstraction for automated verification of higher-order tree-processing programs. In: Feng, X., Park, S. (eds.) APLAS 2015. LNCS, vol. 9458, pp. 295–312. Springer, Cham (2015). doi:10.1007/978-3-319-26529-2_16
13. Nguyen, P.C., Horn, D.V.: Relatively complete counterexamples for higher-order programs. In: Proceedings of the 36th ACM SIGPLAN Conference on Programming Language Design and Implementation (PLDI 2015), pp. 446–456. ACM (2015)
14. Nguyen, P.C., Tobin-Hochstadt, S., Horn, D.V.: Soft contract verification. In: Proceedings of the 19th ACM SIGPLAN International Conference on Functional Programming (ICFP 2014), pp. 139–152 (2014)
15. Ong, C.H.L., Ramsay, S.J.: Verifying higher-order functional programs with pattern-matching algebraic data types. In: Proceedings of the 38th annual ACM SIGPLAN-SIGACT Symposium on Principles of Programming Languages (POPL 2011), pp. 587–598 (2011)
16. Rondon, P.M., Kawaguchi, M., Jhala, R.: Liquid types. In: Proceedings of the 2008 ACM SIGPLAN Conference on Programming Language Design and Implementation (PLDI 2008), pp. 159–169 (2008)
17. Sato, R., Asada, K., Kobayashi, N.: Refinement type checking via assertion checking. J. Inf. Process. **23**(6), 827–834 (2015)
18. Sato, R., Unno, H., Kobayashi, N.: Towards a scalable software model checker for higher-order programs. In: Proceedings of the ACM SIGPLAN 2013 Workshop on Partial Evaluation and Program Manipulation (PEPM 2013), pp. 53–62. ACM Press (2013)

19. Swamy, N., Kohlweiss, M., Zinzindohoue, J.K., Zanella-Béguelin, S., HriÅ£cu, C., Keller, C., Rastogi, A., Delignat-Lavaud, A., Forest, S., Bhargavan, K., Fournet, C., Strub, P.Y., Swamy, N., HriÅ£cu, C., Keller, C., Rastogi, A., Delignat-Lavaud, A., Forest, S., Bhargavan, K., Fournet, C., Strub, P.Y., Kohlweiss, M., Zinzindohoue, J.K., Zanella-Béguelin, S.: Dependent types and multi-monadic effects in F*. In: Proceedings of the 43rd Annual ACM SIGPLAN-SIGACT Symposium on Principles of Programming Languages (POPL 2016), pp. 256–270 (2016)

20. Terao, T., Tsukada, T., Kobayashi, N.: Higher-order model checking in direct style. In: Igarashi, A. (ed.) APLAS 2016. LNCS, vol. 10017, pp. 295–313. Springer, Cham (2016). doi:10.1007/978-3-319-47958-3_16

21. Terauchi, T.: Dependent types from counterexamples. In: Proceedings of the 37th ACM SIGACT-SIGPLAN Symposium on Principles of Programming Languages (POPL 2010), pp. 119–130 (2010)

22. Touati, H., Savoj, H., Lin, B., Brayton, R., Sangiovanni-Vincentelli, A.: Implicit state enumeration of finite state machines using BDD's. In: 1990 IEEE International Conference on Computer-Aided Design (ICCAD 1990), pp. 130–133 (1990)

23. Unno, H., Kobayashi, N.: Dependent type inference with interpolants. In: Proceedings of the 11th International ACM SIGPLAN Conference on Principles and Practice of Declarative Programming (PPDP 2009), pp. 277–288 (2009)

24. Unno, H., Terauchi, T., Kobayashi, N.: Automating relatively complete verification of higher-order functional programs. In: Proceedings of the 40th Annual ACM SIGPLAN-SIGACT Symposium on Principles of Programming Languages (POPL 2013), pp. 75–86 (2013)

25. Vazou, N., Seidel, E.L., Jhala, R., Vytiniotis, D., Jones, S.L.P.: Refinement types for haskell. In: Proceedings of the 19th ACM SIGPLAN International Conference on Functional Programming, pp. 269–282 (2014)

26. Voirol, N., Kneuss, E., Kuncak, V.: Counter-example complete verification for higher-order functions. In: Proceedings of the 6th ACM SIGPLAN Symposium on Scala (Scala 2015), pp. 18–29 (2015)

27. Weis, P.: Caml examples (2001). http://caml.inria.fr/pub/old_caml_site/Examples/

28. Xi, H., Pfenning, F.: Dependent types in practical programming. In: Proceedings of the 26th ACM SIGPLAN-SIGACT Symposium on Principles of Programming Languages (POPL 1999), pp. 214–227 (1999)

29. Zhu, H., Jagannathan, S.: Compositional and lightweight dependent type inference for ML. In: Giacobazzi, R., Berdine, J., Mastroeni, I. (eds.) VMCAI 2013. LNCS, vol. 7737, pp. 295–314. Springer, Heidelberg (2013). doi:10.1007/978-3-642-35873-9_19

30. Zhu, H., Nori, A.V., Jagannathan, S.: Learning refinement types. In: Proceedings of the 20th ACM SIGPLAN International Conference on Functional Programming (ICFP 2015), pp. 400–411 (2015)

31. Zhu, H., Petri, G., Jagannathan, S.: Automatically learning shape specifications. In: Proceedings of the 37th ACM SIGPLAN Conference on Programming Language Design and Implementation, (PLDI 2016), pp. 491–507 (2016)

Commutative Semantics for Probabilistic Programming

Sam Staton[✉]

University of Oxford, Oxford, UK
sam.staton@cs.ox.ac.uk

Abstract. We show that a measure-based denotational semantics for probabilistic programming is commutative.

The idea underlying probabilistic programming languages (Anglican, Church, Hakaru, etc.) is that programs express statistical models as a combination of prior distributions and likelihood of observations. The product of prior and likelihood is an unnormalized posterior distribution, and the inference problem is to find the normalizing constant. One common semantic perspective is thus that a probabilistic program is understood as an unnormalized posterior measure, in the sense of measure theory, and the normalizing constant is the measure of the entire semantic domain.

A programming language is said to be commutative if only data flow is meaningful; control flow is irrelevant, and expressions can be re-ordered. It has been unclear whether probabilistic programs are commutative because it is well-known that Fubini-Tonelli theorems for reordering integration fail in general. We show that probabilistic programs are in fact commutative, by characterizing the measures/kernels that arise from programs as 's-finite', i.e. sums of finite measures/kernels.

The result is of theoretical interest, but also of practical interest, because program transformations based on commutativity help with symbolic inference and can improve the efficiency of simulation.

1 Introduction

The key idea of probabilistic programming is that programs describe statistical models. Programming language theory can give us tools to build and analyze the models. Recall Bayes' law: the posterior probability is proportional to the product of the likelihood of observed data and the prior probability.

$$\text{Posterior} \propto \text{Likelihood} \times \text{Prior} \tag{1}$$

One way to understand a probabilistic program is that it describes the measure that is the product of the likelihood and the prior. This product is typically not a probability measure, it does not sum to one. The inference problem is to find the normalizing constant so that we can find (or approximate) the posterior probability measure.

A probabilistic programming language is an ML-like programming language with three special constructs, corresponding to the three terms in Bayes' law:

© Springer-Verlag GmbH Germany 2017
H. Yang (Ed.): ESOP 2017, LNCS 10201, pp. 855–879, 2017.
DOI: 10.1007/978-3-662-54434-1_32

- *sample*, which draws from a prior distribution, which may be discrete (like a Bernoulli distribution) or continuous (like a Gaussian distribution);
- *score*, or *observe*, which records the likelihood of a particular observed data point, sometimes called 'soft conditioning';
- *normalize*, which finds the normalization constant and the posterior probability distribution.

The implementation of normalize typically involves simulation. One hope is that we can use program transformations to improve the efficiency of this simulation, or even to symbolically calculate the normalizing constant. We turn to some transformations of this kind in Sect. 4.1. But a very first program transformation is to reorder the lines of a program, as long as the data dependencies are preserved, e.g.

$$
\begin{array}{ccc}
\boxed{\begin{array}{l} \mathsf{let}\, x = t\, \mathsf{in} \\ \mathsf{let}\, y = u\, \mathsf{in} \\ v \end{array}} & = & \boxed{\begin{array}{l} \mathsf{let}\, y = u\, \mathsf{in} \\ \mathsf{let}\, x = t\, \mathsf{in} \\ v \end{array}}
\end{array}
\tag{2}
$$

where x not free in u, y not free in t. This is known as *commutativity*. For example, in a traditional programming language with memory, this transformation is valid provided t and u reference different locations. In probabilistic programming, a fundamental intuition is that programs are stateless. From a practical perspective, it is essential to be able to reorder lines and so access more sophisticated program transformations (e.g. Sect. 4.1); reordering lines can also affect the efficiency of simulation. The main contribution of this paper is the result:

Theorem 4 (Sect. 4.2). *The commutativity Eq. (2) is always valid in probabilistic programs.*

1.1   A First Introduction to Probabilistic Programming

To illustrate the key ideas of probabilistic programming, consider the following simple problem, which we explain in English and then specify as a probabilistic program.

1. A telephone operator has forgotten what day it is.
2. He receives on average ten calls per hour in the week and three calls per hour at the weekend.
3. He observes four calls in a given hour.
4. What is the probability that it is a week day?

We describe this as a probabilistic program as follows:

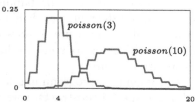

```
1.   normalize(
2.       let x = sample(bern(5/7)) in
3.       let r = if x then 10 else 3 in
4.       observe 4 from poisson(r);
5.       return(x))
```

Lines 2–5 describe the combination of the likelihood and the prior. First, on line 2, we sample from the prior: the chance that it is a week day is $\frac{5}{7}$. On line 3, we set the rate of calls, depending on whether it is a week day. On line 4 we record the observation that six calls were received when the rate was r, using the Poisson distribution. For a discrete distribution, the likelihood is the probability of the observation point, which for the Poisson distribution with rate r is $r^4 e^{-r}/4!$.

We thus find a semantics for lines 2–5, an unnormalized posterior measure on {true, false}, by considering the only two paths through the program, depending on the outcome of the Bernoulli trial.

- The Bernoulli trial (line 2) produces true with prior probability $\frac{5}{7}$ (it is a week day), and then the rate is 10 (line 3) and so the likelihood of the data is $10^4 e^{-10}/4! \approx 0.019$ (line 4). So the unnormalized posterior probability of true is $\frac{5}{7} \times 0.019 \approx 0.014$ (prior×likelihood).
- The Bernoulli trial produces false with prior probability $\frac{2}{7}$ (it is the weekend), and then the likelihood of the observed data is $3^4 e^{-3}/4! \approx 0.168$; so the unnormalized posterior measure of false is $\frac{2}{7} \times 0.168 \approx 0.048$.

The measure (true $\mapsto 0.014$, false $\mapsto 0.048$) is not a probability measure because it doesn't sum to 1. To build a probability measure we divide by $0.014 + 0.048 = 0.062$, to get a posterior probability measure (true $\mapsto 0.22$, false $\mapsto 0.78$). The normalizing constant, 0.062, is sometimes called model evidence; it is an indication of how well the data fits the model.

Next we consider a slightly different problem. Rather than observing four calls in a given hour, suppose the telephone operator merely observes that the time between two given calls is 15 min. We describe this as a probabilistic program as follows:

```
1.  normalize(
2.      let x = sample(bern(5/7)) in
3.      let r = if x then 10 else 3 in
4.      observe (15/60) from exp(r);
5.      return(x))
```

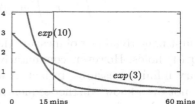

The difference here is that the observation is from the exponential distribution ($exp(r)$), which is a continuous distribution. In Bayesian statistics, the likelihood of a continuous distribution is taken to be the value of the probability density function at the observation point. The density function of the exponential distribution $exp(r)$ with rate r is $(x \mapsto re^{-rx})$. So if the decay rate is 10, the likelihood of time $\frac{15}{60}$ is $10e^{-2.5} \approx 0.82$, and if the decay rate is 3, the likelihood is $3e^{-0.75} \approx 1.42$. We thus find that the unnormalized posterior measure of true is $\frac{5}{7} \times 0.82 \approx 0.586$ (prior×likelihood), and the unnormalized posterior measure of false is $\frac{2}{7} \times 1.42 \approx 0.405$. In this example, the model evidence is $0.586 + 0.405 \approx 0.991$. We divide by this to find the normalized posterior, which is (true $\mapsto 0.592$, false $\mapsto 0.408$).

In these simple examples, there are only two paths through the program. In general the prior may be a continuous distribution over an uncountable set, such as the uniform distribution on an interval, in which case a simulation can only find an approximate normalizing constant. Suppose that the telephone operator does not know what time it is, but knows a function $f : [0, 24) \to (0, \infty)$ mapping each time of day to the average call rate. Then by solving the following problem, he can ascertain a posterior probability distribution for the current time.

$$\mathsf{normalize}\big(\mathsf{let}\, t = \mathsf{sample}(\mathit{uniform}([0, 24)))\, \mathsf{in}\, \mathsf{observe}\, (\tfrac{15}{60})\, \mathsf{from}\, \mathit{exp}(f(t)); \mathsf{return}(t)\big). \tag{3}$$

Although simulation might only be approximate, we can give a precise semantics to the language using measure theory. In brief,

- programs of type $\mathbb{A}$ are interpreted as measures on $\mathbb{A}$, and more generally expressions of type $\mathbb{A}$ with free variables in Γ are measure kernels $\Gamma \rightsquigarrow \mathbb{A}$;
- sampling from a prior describes a probability measure;
- observations are interpreted by multiplying the measure of a path by the likelihood of the data;
- sequencing is Lebesgue integration: $\mathsf{let}\, x = t\, \mathsf{in}\, u \approx \int t(\mathrm{d}x)\, u$;
- normalization finds the measure of the whole space, the normalizing constant.

To put it another way, the programming language is a language for building measures. For full details, see Sect. 3.2.

1.2 Commutativity and Infinite Measures

If, informally, sequencing is integration, then commutativity laws such as (2) amount to changing the order of integration, e.g.

$$\int t(\mathrm{d}x) \int u(\mathrm{d}y)\, v \;=\; \int u(\mathrm{d}y) \int t(\mathrm{d}x)\, v \tag{4}$$

A first non-trivial fact of measure theory is Fubini's theorem: for finite measures, Eq. (4) holds. However, commutativity theorems like this do not hold for arbitrary infinite measures. In fact, if we deal with arbitrary infinite measures, we do not even know whether sequencing $\int t(\mathrm{d}x)\, v$ is a genuine measure kernel. As we will show, for the measures that are definable in our language, sequencing *is* well defined, and commutativity *does* hold. But let us first emphasize that infinite measures appear to be unavoidable because

- there is no known useful syntactic restriction that enforces finite measures;
- a program with finite measure may have a subexpression with infinite measure, and this can be useful.

To illustrate these points, consider the following program, a variation on (3).

$$\mathsf{let}\, x = \mathsf{sample}(\mathit{gauss}(0,1))\, \mathsf{in}\, \mathsf{observe}\, d\, \mathsf{from}\, \mathit{exp}(1/f(x)); \mathsf{return}(x) \quad : \mathbb{R} \tag{5}$$

Here $gauss(0,1)$ is the standard Gaussian distribution with mean 0 and standard deviation 1; recall that its density f is $f(x) = \frac{1}{\sqrt{2\pi}}e^{-\frac{x^2}{2}}$. The illustration on the right shows the unnormalized posterior for (5) as the observed data goes from $d = 0.1$ (blue dotted line) to $d = 0$ (red straight line). Notice that at $d = 0$, the resulting unnormalized posterior mea-

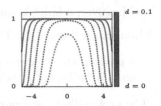

sure on $\mathbb{R}$ is the flat Lebesgue measure on $\mathbb{R}$, which assigns to each interval (m, n) its size, $(n - m)$. The Lebesgue measure of the entire real line, the would-be normalizing constant, is ∞, so we cannot find a posterior probability measure. A statistician would probably not be very bothered about this, because a tiny change in the observed data yields a finite normalizing constant. But that is not good enough for a semanticist, who must give a meaning to *every* program.

It is difficult to see how a simple syntactic restriction could eliminate program (5) while keeping other useful programs such as (3). Another similar program is

$$\text{let } x = \mathsf{sample}(gauss(0,1)) \text{ in score}(g(x)/f(x)); \mathsf{return}(x) \quad : \mathbb{R} \qquad (6)$$

where $g(x) = \frac{1}{\pi(1+x^2)}$ is the density function of the standard Cauchy distribution and $\mathsf{score}(r)$ is shorthand for (observe 0 from $exp(r)$)—recall that the density of the exponential distribution $exp(r)$ at 0 is $r = re^{-r\times 0}$. Program (6) is the importance sampling algorithm for simulating a Cauchy distribution from a Gaussian. To see why this algorithm is correct, i.e. $(6) = \mathsf{sample}(cauchy(0,1))$, it is helpful to rewrite it:

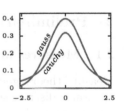

$$\text{let } x = \mathsf{sample}(gauss(0,1)) \text{ in } \underline{\mathsf{score}(1/f(x))} ; \mathsf{score}(g(x)) ; \mathsf{return}(x) \quad : \mathbb{R}.$$

Notice that the underlined subexpression is the Lebesgue measure, as in (5), and recall that sequencing is integration. So program (6) is correct because it is integrating the density g over the Lebesgue measure; this is equal to the Cauchy probability measure, by definition of density.

1.3   Commutativity Through s-Finite Kernels

It is known that commutativity holds not just for finite measures but also for s-finite measures, which are formed from a countable sum of finite measures. The key contribution of this paper is that all closed probabilistic programs define s-finite measures. To show this compositionally, we must also give a semantics to open programs, which we interpret using a notion of s-finite kernel (Definition 2), which is a countable sum of finite, bounded kernels; these support sequential composition (Lemma 3). Iterated integrals and interchange (4) are no problem for s-finite measures (Proposition 5). We conclude (Theorem 4) that the commutativity Eq. (2) is always valid in probabilistic programs.

Moreover, s-finite kernels are exactly what is needed, because:

Theorem 6 (Sect. 5.1). *The following are equivalent:*

- *a probabilistic program expression of type* $\mathbb{A}$ *and free variables in* Γ;
- *an s-finite kernel* $\Gamma \rightsquigarrow \mathbb{A}$.

(The probabilistic programming language here is an idealized one that includes countable sum types, all measurable functions, and all probability distributions.)

Summary of Contribution. We use s-finite kernels to provide the first semantic model (Sect. 3.2) of a probabilistic programming language that

- interprets programs such as those in Sect. 1.1;
- supports basic program transformations such as commutativity (Theorem 4);
- justifies program transformations based on statistical ideas such as conjugate priors, importance sampling and resampling, in a compositional way (Sect. 4.1).

In Sect. 6 we relate our contributions with earlier attempts at this problem.

2   Preliminaries

2.1   Measures and Kernels

Measure theory generalizes the ideas of size and probability distribution from countable discrete sets to uncountable sets. To motivate, recall that if we sample a real number from a standard Gaussian distribution then it is impossible that we should sample the precise value 0, even though that is the expected value. We resolve this apparent paradox by recording the probability that the sample drawn lies within an interval, or more generally, a measurable set. For example, a sample drawn from a standard Gaussian distribution will lie in the interval $(-1, 1)$ with probability 0.68. We now recall some rudiments of measure theory; see e.g. [32] for a full introduction.

A *σ-algebra* on a set X is a collection of subsets of X that contains $\emptyset$ and is closed under complements and countable unions. A *measurable space* is a pair (X, Σ_X) of a set X and a σ-algebra Σ_X on it. The sets in Σ_X are called *measurable sets*.

For example, the Borel sets are the smallest σ-algebra on $\mathbb{R}$ that contains the intervals. We will always consider $\mathbb{R}$ with this σ-algebra. Similarly the Borel sets on $[0, \infty]$ are the smallest σ-algebra containing the intervals. For any countable set (e.g. $\mathbb{N}$, $\{0, 1\}$) we will consider the discrete σ-algebra, where all sets are measurable.

A *measure* on a measurable space (X, Σ_X) is a function $\mu : \Sigma_X \to [0, \infty]$ into the set $[0, \infty]$ of extended non-negative reals that takes countable disjoint unions to sums, i.e. $\mu(\emptyset) = 0$ and $\mu(\biguplus_{n \in \mathbb{N}} U_n) = \sum_{n \in \mathbb{N}} \mu(U_n)$ for any $\mathbb{N}$-indexed sequence of disjoint measurable sets U. A *probability measure* is a measure μ such that $\mu(X) = 1$.

For example, the Lebesgue measure λ on $\mathbb{R}$ is generated by $\lambda(a, b) = b - a$. For any $x \in X$, the Dirac measure δ_x has $\delta_x(U) = [x \in U]$. (Here and elsewhere we regard a property, e.g. $[x \in U]$, as its characteristic function $X \rightarrow \{0, 1\}$.) To give a measure on a countable discrete measurable space X it is sufficient to assign an element of $[0, \infty]$ to each element of X. For example, the counting measure γ is determined by $\gamma(\{x\}) = 1$ for all $x \in X$.

A function $f : X \rightarrow Y$ between measurable spaces is *measurable* if $f^{-1}(U) \in \Sigma_X$ for all $U \in \Sigma_Y$. This ensures that we can form a *pushforward* measure $f_* \mu$ on Y out of any measure μ on X, with $(f_* \mu)(U) = \mu(f^{-1}(U))$.

For example, the arithmetic operations on $\mathbb{R}$ are all measurable. If $U \in \Sigma_X$ then the characteristic function $[- \in U] : X \rightarrow \{0, 1\}$ is measurable.

We can integrate a measurable function $f : X \rightarrow [0, \infty]$ over a measure μ on X to get number $\int_X \mu(dx) f(x) \in [0, \infty]$. (Some authors use different notation, e.g. $\int f \, d\mu$.) Integration satisfies the following properties (e.g. [32, Theorem 12]): $\int_X \mu(dx) [x \in U] = \mu(U)$, $\int_X \mu(dx) r f(x) = r \int_X \mu(dx) f(x)$, $\int_X \mu(dx) 0 = 0$, $\int_X \mu(dx) (f(x) + g(x)) = (\int_X \mu(dx) f(x)) + (\int_X \mu(dx) g(x))$, and

$$\lim_i \int_X \mu(dx) f_i(x) = \int_X \mu(dx) (\lim_i f_i(x)) \tag{7}$$

for any monotone sequence $f_1 \leq f_2 \leq \ldots$ of measurable functions $f : X \rightarrow [0, \infty]$. These properties entirely determine integration, since every measurable function is a limit of a monotone sequence of simple functions [32, Lemma 11]. It follows that countable sums commute with integration:

$$\int_X \mu(dx) \left(\sum_{i \in \mathbb{N}} f_i(x) \right) = \sum_{i \in \mathbb{N}} \int_X \mu(dx) f_i(x). \tag{8}$$

For example, integration over the Lebesgue measure on $\mathbb{R}$ is Lebesgue integration, generalizing the idea of the area under a curve. Integration with respect to the counting measure on a countable discrete space is just summation, e.g. $\int_{\mathbb{N}} \gamma(di) f(i) = \sum_{i \in \mathbb{N}} f(i)$.

We can use integration to build new measures. If μ is a measure on X and $f : X \rightarrow [0, \infty]$ is measurable then we define a measure μ_f on X by putting $\mu_f(U) \stackrel{\text{def}}{=} \int_U \mu(dx) f(x)$. We say f is the *density function* for μ_f. For example, the function $x \mapsto \frac{1}{\sqrt{2\pi}} e^{-\frac{1}{2}x^2}$ is the density function for the standard Gaussian probability measure on $\mathbb{R}$ with respect to the Lebesgue measure.

A *kernel* k from X to Y is a function $k : X \times \Sigma_Y \rightarrow [0, \infty]$ such that each $k(x, -) : \Sigma_Y \rightarrow [0, \infty]$ is a measure and each $k(-, U) : X \rightarrow [0, \infty]$ is measurable. Because each $k(x, -)$ is a measure, we can integrate any measurable function $f : Y \rightarrow [0, \infty]$ to get $\int_Y k(x, dy) f(y) \in [0, \infty]$. We write $k : X \rightsquigarrow Y$ if k is a kernel. We say that k is a *probability kernel* if $k(x, Y) = 1$ for all $x \in X$.

2.2   s-Finite Measures and Kernels

We begin with a lemma about sums of kernels.

Proposition 1. *Let* X, Y *be measurable spaces. If* $k_1 \dots k_n \cdots : X \rightsquigarrow Y$ *are kernels then the function* $(\sum_{i=1}^{\infty} k_i) : X \times \Sigma_Y \to [0, \infty]$ *given by*

$$(\textstyle\sum_{i=1}^{\infty} k_i)(x, U) \stackrel{\text{def}}{=} \sum_{i=1}^{\infty} (k_i(x, U))$$

is a kernel $X \rightsquigarrow Y$. *Moreover, for any measurable function* $f : Y \to [0, \infty]$,

$$\int_Y (\textstyle\sum_{i=1}^{\infty} k_i)(x, dy) \, f(y) = \sum_{i=1}^{\infty} \int_Y k_i(x, dy) \, f(y).$$

Proof. That $\sum_{i \in \mathbb{N}} k_i : X \times \Sigma_Y \to [0, \infty]$ is a kernel is quite straightforward: it is measurable in X because a countable sum of measurable functions is measurable (e.g. [32, Sect. 2.2]); it is a measure in Y because countable positive sums commute:

$$\textstyle\sum_{i=1}^{\infty} (k_i(x, \biguplus_{j=1}^{\infty} U_j)) = \sum_{i=1}^{\infty} (\sum_{j=1}^{\infty} k_i(x, U_j)) = \sum_{j=1}^{\infty} (\sum_{i=1}^{\infty} k_i(x, U_j))$$

The second part of the proposition follows once we understand that every measurable function $f : Y \to [0, \infty]$ is a limit of simple functions and apply the monotone convergence theorem (7). □

Definition 2. *Let* X, Y *be measurable spaces. A kernel* $k : X \rightsquigarrow Y$ *is* finite *if there is finite* $r \in [0, \infty)$ *such that, for all* x, $k(x, Y) < r$.

A kernel $k : X \rightsquigarrow Y$ *is* s-finite *if there is a sequence* $k_1 \dots k_n \dots$ *of finite kernels and* $\sum_{i=1}^{\infty} k_i = k$.

Note that the bound in the finiteness condition, and the choice of sequence in the s-finiteness condition, are uniform, across all arguments to the kernel.

The definition of s-finite kernel also appears in recent work by Kallenberg [20] and Last and Penrose [23, Appendix A]. The idea of s-finite measures is perhaps more established ([9, Lemma 8.6], [39, Sect. A.0]).

3   Semantics of a Probabilistic Programming Language

We give a typed first order probabilistic programming language in Sect. 3.1, and its semantics in Sect. 3.2. The semantics is new: we interpret programs as s-finite kernels. The idea of interpreting programs as kernels is old (e.g. [21]), but the novelty here is that we can treat infinite measures. It is not a priori obvious that a compositional denotational semantics based on kernels makes sense for infinite measures; the trick is to use s-finite kernels as an invariant, via Lemma 3.

3.1   A Typed First Order Probabilistic Programming Language

Our language syntax is not novel: it is the same language as in [43], and as such an idealized, typed, first order version of Anglican [46], Church [11], Hakaru [30], Venture [26] and so on.

Types. The language has types

$$\mathbb{A}, \mathbb{B} :: = \mathbb{R} \mid \mathsf{P}(\mathbb{A}) \mid 1 \mid \mathbb{A} \times \mathbb{B} \mid \sum_{i \in I} \mathbb{A}_i$$

where I ranges over countable, non-empty sets. Alongside the usual sum and product types, we have a special type $\mathbb{R}$ of real numbers and types $\mathsf{P}(\mathbb{A})$ of probability distributions. For example, $(1+1)$ is a type of booleans, and $\mathsf{P}(1+1)$ is a type of distributions over booleans, and $\sum_{i \in \mathbb{N}} 1$ is a type of natural numbers. This is not a genuine programming language because we include countably infinite sums rather than recursion schemes; this is primarily because countably infinite disjoint unions play such a crucial role in classical measure theory, and constructive measure theory is an orthogonal issue (but see e.g. [1]).

Types $\mathbb{A}$ are interpreted as measurable spaces $[\![\mathbb{A}]\!]$.

- $[\![\mathbb{R}]\!]$ is the measurable space of reals, with its Borel sets.
- $[\![\mathsf{P}(\mathbb{A})]\!]$ is the set $P([\![\mathbb{A}]\!])$ of probability measures on $[\![\mathbb{A}]\!]$ together with the σ-algebra generated by the sets $\{\mu \mid \mu(U) < r\}$ for each $U \in \Sigma_X$ and $r \in [0,1]$ (the 'Giry monad' [10]).
- $[\![1]\!]$ is the discrete measurable space with one point.
- $[\![\mathbb{A} \times \mathbb{B}]\!]$ is the product space $[\![\mathbb{A}]\!] \times [\![\mathbb{B}]\!]$. The σ-algebra $\Sigma_{[\![\mathbb{A} \times \mathbb{B}]\!]}$ is generated by rectangles $(U \times V)$ with $U \in \Sigma_{[\![\mathbb{A}]\!]}$ and $V \in \Sigma_{[\![\mathbb{B}]\!]}$ (e.g. [32, Definition 16]).
- $[\![\sum_{i \in I} \mathbb{A}_i]\!]$ is the coproduct space $\biguplus_{i \in I}[\![\mathbb{A}_i]\!]$. The σ-algebra $\Sigma_{[\![\sum_{i \in I} \mathbb{A}_i]\!]}$ is generated by sets $\{(i,a) \mid a \in U\}$ for $U \in \Sigma_{[\![\mathbb{A}_i]\!]}$.

Terms. We distinguish typing judgements: $\Gamma \vdash_{\mathsf{d}} t : \mathbb{A}$ for deterministic terms, and $\Gamma \vdash_{\mathsf{p}} t : \mathbb{A}$ for probabilistic terms. Formally, a context $\Gamma = (x_1 : \mathbb{A}_1, \ldots, x_n : \mathbb{A}_n)$ means a measurable space $[\![\Gamma]\!] \stackrel{\text{def}}{=} \prod_{i=1}^{n}[\![\mathbb{A}_i]\!]$. Deterministic terms $\Gamma \vdash_{\mathsf{d}} t : \mathbb{A}$ denote measurable functions from $[\![\Gamma]\!] \to [\![\mathbb{A}]\!]$, and probabilistic terms $\Gamma \vdash_{\mathsf{p}} t' : \mathbb{A}$ denote kernels $[\![\Gamma]\!] \rightsquigarrow [\![\mathbb{A}]\!]$. We give a syntax and type system here, and a semantics in Sect. 3.2.

Sums and Products. The language includes variables, and standard constructors and destructors for sum and product types.

$$\frac{}{\Gamma, x : \mathbb{A}, \Gamma' \vdash_{\mathsf{d}} x : \mathbb{A}} \qquad \frac{\Gamma \vdash_{\mathsf{d}} t : \mathbb{A}_i}{\Gamma \vdash_{\mathsf{d}} (i,t) : \sum_{i \in I} \mathbb{A}_i}$$

$$\frac{\Gamma \vdash_{\mathsf{d}} t : \sum_{i \in I} \mathbb{A}_i \quad (\Gamma, x : \mathbb{A}_i \vdash_{\mathsf{z}} u_i : \mathbb{B})_{i \in I}}{\Gamma \vdash_{\mathsf{z}} \mathsf{case}\ t\ \mathsf{of}\ \{(i,x) \Rightarrow u_i\}_{i \in I} : \mathbb{B}} \quad (\mathsf{z} \in \{\mathsf{d}, \mathsf{p}\})$$

$$\frac{}{\Gamma \vdash_{\mathsf{d}} () : 1} \qquad \frac{\Gamma \vdash_{\mathsf{d}} t_0 : \mathbb{A}_0 \quad \Gamma \vdash_{\mathsf{d}} t_1 : \mathbb{A}_1}{\Gamma \vdash_{\mathsf{d}} (t_0, t_1) : \mathbb{A}_0 \times \mathbb{A}_1} \qquad \frac{\Gamma \vdash_{\mathsf{d}} t : \mathbb{A}_0 \times \mathbb{A}_1}{\Gamma \vdash_{\mathsf{d}} \pi_j(t) : \mathbb{A}_j}$$

In the rules for sums, I may be infinite. In the last rule, j is 0 or 1. We use some standard syntactic sugar, such as false and true for the injections in the type bool $= 1 + 1$, and if for case in that instance.

Sequencing. We include the standard constructs for sequencing (e.g. [25,29]).

$$\frac{\Gamma \vdash_{\mathsf{d}} t\colon \mathbb{A}}{\Gamma \vdash_{\mathsf{p}} \mathsf{return}(t)\colon \mathbb{A}} \qquad\qquad \frac{\Gamma \vdash_{\mathsf{p}} t\colon \mathbb{A} \quad \Gamma, x\colon \mathbb{A} \vdash_{\mathsf{p}} u\colon \mathbb{B}}{\Gamma \vdash_{\mathsf{p}} \mathsf{let}\ x = t\ \mathsf{in}\ u\colon \mathbb{B}}$$

Language-Specific Constructs. So far the language is very standard. We also include constant terms for all measurable functions.

$$\frac{\Gamma \vdash_{\mathsf{d}} t\colon \mathbb{A}}{\Gamma \vdash_{\mathsf{d}} f(t)\colon \mathbb{B}} \quad (f\colon [\![\mathbb{A}]\!] \to [\![\mathbb{B}]\!]\ \text{measurable}) \tag{9}$$

Thus the language contains all the arithmetic operations (e.g. $+\colon \mathbb{R} \times \mathbb{R} \to \mathbb{R}$) and predicates (e.g. $(=)\colon \mathbb{R} \times \mathbb{R} \to$ bool). Moreover, all the families of probability measures are in the language. For example, the Gaussian distributions *gauss* : $\mathbb{R} \times \mathbb{R} \to P(\mathbb{R})$ are parameterized by mean and standard deviation, so that we have a judgement $\mu\colon \mathbb{R}, \sigma\colon \mathbb{R} \vdash_{\mathsf{d}} gauss(\mu,\sigma)\colon P(\mathbb{R})$. (Some families are not defined for all parameters, e.g. the standard deviation should be positive, but we make ad-hoc safe choices throughout rather than using exceptions or subtyping.)

The core of the language is the constructs corresponding to the terms in Bayes' law (1): sampling from prior distributions, recording likelihood scores,

$$\frac{\Gamma \vdash_{\mathsf{d}} t\colon P(\mathbb{A})}{\Gamma \vdash_{\mathsf{p}} \mathsf{sample}(t)\colon \mathbb{A}} \qquad\qquad \frac{\Gamma \vdash_{\mathsf{d}} t\colon \mathbb{R}}{\Gamma \vdash_{\mathsf{p}} \mathsf{score}(t)\colon 1}$$

and calculating the normalizing constant and a normalized posterior.

$$\frac{\Gamma \vdash_{\mathsf{p}} t\colon \mathbb{A}}{\Gamma \vdash_{\mathsf{d}} \mathsf{normalize}(t)\colon \mathbb{R} \times P(\mathbb{A}) + 1 + 1}$$

Normalization will fail if the normalizing constant is zero or infinity. Notice that normalization produces a probability distribution; in a complex model this could then be used as a prior and sampled from. This is sometimes called a 'nested query'.

Note About Observations. Often a probability distribution d has a widely understood density function f with respect to some base measure. For example, the exponential distribution with rate r is usually defined in terms of the density function $x \mapsto re^{-rx}$ with respect to the Lebesgue measure on $\mathbb{R}$. The score construct is typically called with a density. In this circumstance, we use the informal notation observe t from d for $\mathsf{score}(f(t))$. For example, observe t from $exp(r)$ is informal notation for $\mathsf{score}(re^{-r \times t})$. In a more realistic programming language, this informality is avoided by defining a 'distribution object' to be a pair of a probability measure and a density function for it. There is no difference in expressivity between an observe construction and a score construct. For example, $\mathsf{score}(r)$ can be understood as observe 0 from $exp(r)$, since $re^{-r0} = r$.

(Technical point: although density functions can be understood as Radon-Nikodym derivatives, these are not uniquely determined on measure-zero sets, and so a distribution object does need to come with a given density function. Typically the density is continuous with respect to some metric so that the likelihood is not vulnerable to small inaccuracies in observations. See e.g. [43, Sect. 9] for more details.)

3.2 Denotational Semantics

Recall that types A are interpreted as measurable spaces $[\![A]\!]$. We now explain how to interpret a deterministic term in context, $\Gamma \vdash_\mathsf{d} t \colon A$ as a measurable function $[\![t]\!] : [\![\Gamma]\!] \to [\![A]\!]$, and how to interpret a probabilistic term in context, $\Gamma \vdash_\mathsf{p} t \colon A$, as an s-finite kernel $[\![t]\!] : [\![\Gamma]\!] \rightsquigarrow [\![A]\!]$.

The semantics is given by induction on the structure of terms. Before we begin we need a lemma.

Lemma 3. *Let X, Y, Z be measurable spaces, and let $k : X \times Y \rightsquigarrow Z$ and $l : X \rightsquigarrow Y$ be s-finite kernels (Definition 2). Then we can define a s-finite kernel $(k \star l) : X \rightsquigarrow Z$ by*

$$(k \star l)(x, U) \overset{\mathrm{def}}{=} \int_Y l(x, \mathrm{d}y)\, k(x, y, U)$$

so that

$$\int_Z (k \star l)(x, \mathrm{d}z)\, f(z) \;=\; \int_Y l(x, \mathrm{d}y) \int_Z k(x, y, \mathrm{d}z)\, f(z)$$

Proof. Suppose $k = \sum_{i=1}^{\infty} k_i$ and $l = \sum_{j=1}^{\infty} l_j$ are s-finite kernels, and that the k_i's and l_j's are finite kernels. We need to show that $k \star l$ is a kernel and moreover s-finite. We first show that each $k_i \star l_j$ is a finite kernel. Each $(k_i \star l_j)(x, -) : \Sigma_Z \to [0, \infty]$ is a measure:

$$
\begin{aligned}
(k_i \star l_j)(x, \biguplus_{a=1}^{\infty} U_a) &= \int_Y l_j(x, \mathrm{d}y)\, k_i(x, y, \biguplus_{a=1}^{\infty} U_a) \\
&= \int_Y l_j(x, \mathrm{d}y) \sum_{a=1}^{\infty} k_i(x, y, U_a) &\text{k is a kernel} \\
&= \sum_{a=1}^{\infty} \int_Y l_j(x, \mathrm{d}y)\, k_i(x, y, U_a) &\text{Eq. (8)}
\end{aligned}
$$

The measurability of each $(k_i \star l_j)(-, U) : X \to [0, \infty]$ follows from the general fact that for any measurable function $f : X \times Y \to [0, \infty]$, the function $\int_Y l_j(-, \mathrm{d}y)\, f(-, y) : X \to [0, \infty]$ is measurable (e.g. [32, Theorem 20(ii)]). Thus $(k_i \star l_j)$ is a kernel. This step crucially uses the fact that each measure $l_j(x, -)$ is finite.

To show that $(k_i \star l_j)$ is a *finite* kernel, we exhibit a bound. Since k_i and l_j are finite, we have $r, s \in (0, \infty)$ such that $k_i(x, y, Z) < r$ and $l_j(x, Y) < s$ for all x, y. Now rs is a bound on $(k_i \star l_j)$ since

$$(k_i \star l_j)(x, Z) = \int_Y l_j(x, \mathrm{d}y)\, k(x, y, Z) < \int_Y l_j(x, \mathrm{d}y)\, r = r l_j(x, Y) < rs.$$

So each $(k_i \star l_j)$ is a finite kernel. Note that here we used the uniformity in the definition of finite kernel.

We conclude that $(k \star l)$ is an s-finite kernel by showing that it is a countable sum of finite kernels:

$$
\begin{aligned}
(k \star l)(x, U) &= ((\textstyle\sum_i k_i) \star (\textstyle\sum_j l_j))(x, U) \\
&= \textstyle\int_Y \sum_j (l_j(x, \mathrm{d}y)) \sum_i (k_i(x, y, U)) \\
&= \textstyle\sum_i \int_Y \sum_j (l_j(x, \mathrm{d}y)) \, k_i(x, y, U) && \text{Eq. (8)} \\
&= \textstyle\sum_i \sum_j \int_Y l_j(x, \mathrm{d}y) \, k_i(x, y, U) && \text{Proposition 1} \\
&= \textstyle\sum_i \sum_j (k_i \star l_j)(x, U)
\end{aligned}
$$

The final part of the statement follows by writing f as a limit of a sequence of simple functions and using the monotone convergence property (7).

Remark. It seems unlikely that we can drop the assumption of s-finiteness in Lemma 3. The difficulty is in showing that $(k \star l) : X \times \Sigma_Z \to [0, \infty]$ is measurable in its first argument without some extra assumption. (I do not have a counterexample, but then examples of non-measurable functions are hard to find.)

Semantics. We now explain the semantics of the language, beginning with variables, sums and products, which is essentially the same as a set-theoretic semantics.

$$
[\![x]\!]_{\gamma, d, \gamma'} \stackrel{\mathrm{def}}{=} d \qquad\qquad [\![(i, t)]\!]_\gamma \stackrel{\mathrm{def}}{=} (i, [\![t]\!]_\gamma)
$$

$$
[\![\mathsf{case}\ t\ \mathsf{of}\ \{(i, x) \Rightarrow u_i\}_{i \in I}]\!]_\gamma \stackrel{\mathrm{def}}{=} [\![u_i]\!]_{\gamma, d} \quad \text{if } [\![t]\!]_\gamma = (i, d)
$$

$$
[\![()]\!]_\gamma \stackrel{\mathrm{def}}{=} () \qquad [\![(t_0, t_1)]\!]_\gamma \stackrel{\mathrm{def}}{=} ([\![t_0]\!]_\gamma, [\![t_1]\!]_\gamma) \qquad [\![\pi_j(t)]\!]_\gamma \stackrel{\mathrm{def}}{=} d_i \quad \text{if } [\![t]\!]_\gamma = (d_0, d_1)
$$

Here we have only treated the **case** expressions when the continuation is deterministic; we return to the probabilistic case later.

The semantics of sequencing are perhaps the most interesting: **return** is the Dirac delta measure, and **let** is integration.

$$
[\![\mathsf{return}(t)]\!]_{\gamma, U} \stackrel{\mathrm{def}}{=} \begin{cases} 1 & \text{if } [\![t]\!]_\gamma \in U \\ 0 & \text{otherwise} \end{cases} \qquad [\![\mathsf{let}\ x = t\ \mathsf{in}\ u]\!]_{\gamma, U} \stackrel{\mathrm{def}}{=} \int_A [\![t]\!]_{\gamma, \mathrm{d}x}\ [\![u]\!]_{\gamma, x, U}
$$

The interpretation $[\![\mathsf{return}(t)]\!]$ is finite, hence s-finite. The fact that $[\![\mathsf{let}\ x = t\ \mathsf{in}\ u]\!]$ is an s-finite kernel is Lemma 3: this is the most intricate part of the semantics.

We return to the case expression where the continuation is probabilistic:

$$
[\![\mathsf{case}\ t\ \mathsf{of}\ \{(i, x) \Rightarrow u_i\}_{i \in I}]\!]_{\gamma, U} \stackrel{\mathrm{def}}{=} [\![u_i]\!]_{\gamma, d, U} \quad \text{if } [\![t]\!]_\gamma = (i, d).
$$

We must show that this is an s-finite kernel. Recall that $[\![u_i]\!] : [\![\Gamma \times A_i]\!] \rightsquigarrow [\![B]\!]$, s-finite. We can also form $\overline{[\![u_i]\!]} : [\![\Gamma]\!] \times \biguplus_j [\![A_j]\!] \rightsquigarrow [\![B]\!]$ with

$$
\overline{[\![u_i]\!]}_{\gamma, (j, a), U} \stackrel{\mathrm{def}}{=} \begin{cases} [\![u_i]\!]_{\gamma, a, U} & i = j \\ 0 & \text{otherwise} \end{cases}
$$

and it is easy to show that $\overline{[\![u_i]\!]}$ is an s-finite kernel. Another easy fact is that a countable sum of s-finite kernels is again an s-finite kernel, so we can build an s-finite kernel $(\sum_i \overline{[\![u_i]\!]}) : [\![\Gamma]\!] \times \biguplus_j [\![A_j]\!] \rightsquigarrow [\![\mathbb{B}]\!]$. Finally, we use a simple instance of Lemma 3 to compose $(\sum_i \overline{[\![u_i]\!]})$ with $[\![t]\!] : [\![\Gamma]\!] \to \biguplus_j [\![A_j]\!]$ and conclude that $[\![\text{case } t \text{ of } \{(i, x) \Rightarrow u_i\}_{i \in I}]\!]$ is an s-finite kernel.

The language specific constructions are straightforward.

$$[\![\text{sample}(t)]\!]_{\gamma, U} \overset{\text{def}}{=} [\![t]\!]_\gamma(U) \qquad [\![\text{score}(t)]\!]_{\gamma, U} \overset{\text{def}}{=} \begin{cases} |[\![t]\!]_\gamma| & \text{if } U = \{()\} \\ 0 & \text{if } U = \emptyset. \end{cases}$$

In the semantics of sample, we are merely using the fact that to give a measurable function $X \to P(Y)$ is to give a probability kernel $X \rightsquigarrow Y$. Probability kernels are finite, hence s-finite.

The semantics of score is a one point space whose measure is the argument. (We take the absolute value of $[\![t]\!]_\gamma$ because measures should be non-negative. An alternative would be to somehow enforce this in the type system.) We need to show that $[\![\text{score}(t)]\!]$ is an s-finite kernel. Although $[\![\text{score}(t)]\!]_{\gamma, 1}$ is always finite, $[\![\text{score}(t)]\!]$ is not necessarily a *finite kernel* because we cannot find a uniform bound. To show that it is *s-finite*, for each $i \in \mathbb{N}_0$, define a kernel $k_i : [\![\Gamma]\!] \rightsquigarrow 1$

$$k_i(\gamma, U) \overset{\text{def}}{=} \begin{cases} [\![\text{score}(t)]\!]_{\gamma, U} & \text{if } [\![\text{score}(t)]\!]_{\gamma, U} \subset [i, i+1) \\ 0 & \text{otherwise} \end{cases}$$

So each k_i is a finite kernel, bounded by $(i+1)$, and $[\![\text{score}(t)]\!] = \sum_{i=0}^{\infty} k_i$, so it is s-finite.

We give a semantics to normalization by finding the normalizing constant and dividing by it, as follows. Consider $\Gamma \vdash_{\mathsf{p}} t \colon A$ and let $\text{evidence}_t \overset{\text{def}}{=} [\![t]\!]_{\gamma, [\![A]\!]}$.

$$[\![\text{normalize}(t)]\!]_\gamma \overset{\text{def}}{=} \begin{cases} (0, (\text{evidence}_t, \frac{[\![t]\!]_{\gamma, (-)}}{\text{evidence}_t})) & \text{evidence}_t \in (0, \infty) \\ (1, ()) & \text{evidence}_t = 0 \\ (2, ()) & \text{evidence}_t = \infty \end{cases}$$

(In practice, the normalization will only be approximate. We leave it for future work to develop semantic notions of approximation in this setting, e.g. [27].)

4   Properties and Examples

4.1   Examples of Statistical Reasoning

Lebesgue Measure, Densities and Importance Sampling. The Lebesgue measure on $\mathbb{R}$ is not a primitive in our language, because it is not a probability measure, but it is definable. For example, we can score the standard Gaussian by the inverse of its density function, $f(x) = \frac{1}{\sqrt{2\pi}} e^{-\frac{1}{2}x^2}$.

$$\llbracket \vdash_{\overline{p}} \text{ let } x = \text{sample}(gauss(0,1)) \text{ in score}(\tfrac{1}{f(x)}); \text{return}(x) \; : \; \mathbb{R} \rrbracket_{-,U} \tag{10}$$

$$= \int_U gauss(0,1)(\mathrm{d}x)\,(\tfrac{1}{f(x)})$$

$$= \int_U lebesgue(\mathrm{d}x)\,(f(x))(\tfrac{1}{f(x)}) \qquad \text{since } gauss(0,1)(V) = \int_V lebesgue(\mathrm{d}x)\,f(x)$$

$$= lebesgue(U)$$

(On the third line, we use the definition of density function.)

Some languages (such as Stan [40], also Core Hakaru [38]) encourage the use of the Lebesgue measure as an 'improper prior'. We return to the example of importance sampling, proposed in the introduction. Consider a probability measure p with density g. Then

$$\llbracket \text{sample}(p) \rrbracket \;=\; \llbracket \text{let } x = lebesgue \text{ in observe } x \text{ from } p; \text{return}(x) \rrbracket \tag{11}$$

— a simple example of how an improper prior can lead to a proper posterior. We can derive the importance sampling algorithm for p by combining (11) with (10):

$$\llbracket \text{sample}(p) \rrbracket = \llbracket \text{let } x = lebesgue \text{ in observe } x \text{ from } p; \text{return}(x) \rrbracket$$

$$= \llbracket \text{let } x = gauss(0,1) \text{ in score}(\tfrac{1}{f(x)}); \text{score}(g(x)); \text{return}(x) \rrbracket$$

$$= \llbracket \text{let } x = gauss(0,1) \text{ in score}(\tfrac{g(x)}{f(x)}); \text{return}(x) \rrbracket.$$

Conjugate Prior Relationships and Symbolic Bayesian Update. A key technique for Bayesian inference involves conjugate prior relationships. In general, inference problems are solved by simulation, but sometimes we can work symbolically, when there is a closed form for updating the parameters of a prior according to an observation. In a probabilistic programming language, this symbolic translation can be done semi-automatically as a program transformation (see e.g. [5]).

Recall that $beta(\alpha, \beta)$ is a probability measure on $[0,1]$ describing the distribution of a bias of a coin from which we have observed $(\alpha - 1)$ heads and $(\beta - 1)$ tails. This has a conjugate prior relationship with the Bernoulli distribution. For instance,

$\llbracket \text{let } x = \text{sample}(beta(2,2)) \text{ in observe } 1 \text{ from } bern(x); x \rrbracket$
$=$
$\llbracket \text{observe } 1 \text{ from } bern(\tfrac{2}{2+2}); \text{sample}(beta(2+1,2)) \rrbracket$

In the graph, notice that $beta(3,2)$ depicts the updated posterior belief of the bias of the coin after an additional observation: it is more probable that the coin is biassed to heads.

Resampling. In many situations, particularly in Sequential Monte Carlo simulations, it is helpful to freeze a simulation and resample from a histogram that has been built (e.g. [31]). In practical terms, this avoids having too many threads of low weight. Resampling in this way is justified by the following program equation:

$$\llbracket t \rrbracket \;=\; \llbracket \mathsf{case\,normalize}(t)\ \mathsf{of}\ (1,(e,d)) \Rightarrow \mathsf{score}(e); \mathsf{sample}(d)$$
$$\mid (2,()) \Rightarrow \mathsf{score}(0); t$$
$$\mid (3,()) \Rightarrow t \qquad \rrbracket$$

Notice that we cannot resample if the model evidence is ∞. For example, we cannot resample from the expression above computing the Lebesgue measure (10), although of course this doesn't prevent us from resampling from programs that contain it (e.g. (11)).

Hard Constraints. A hard constraint is a score of 0; a non-zero score is a soft constraint. In our language, every type is inhabited, so for each type $\mathbb{A}$ we can define a term

$$\mathsf{fail}_{\mathbb{A}} \stackrel{\mathrm{def}}{=} \mathsf{score}(0); f() : \mathbb{A} \tag{12}$$

picking arbitrary $f : 1 \to \llbracket \mathbb{A} \rrbracket$ at each type $\mathbb{A}$. The semantics is $\llbracket \mathsf{fail}_{\mathbb{A}} \rrbracket_{\gamma,U} = 0$.

Hard constraints suffice for scores below 1, because then

$$\llbracket \mathsf{score}(r) \rrbracket = \llbracket \mathsf{if\,sample}(bern(r))\ \mathsf{then}\ ()\ \mathsf{else\,fail}_1 \rrbracket.$$

Hard constraints cannot express scores above 1, which can arise from continuous likelihoods — for instance, in the example in the introduction, the likelihoods were 0.82 and 1.42. Inference algorithms often perform better when soft constraints are used.

4.2   Basic Semantic Properties

Standard β/η laws and associativity of let. The standard β/η laws for sums and products hold. These are easy to verify. For instance,

$$\llbracket \mathsf{case}\ (i,t)\ \mathsf{of}\ \{(j,x) \Rightarrow u_j\}_{j \in I} \rrbracket \;=\; \llbracket u_i[t/x] \rrbracket.$$

We also have the standard associativity and identity laws for let:

$$\llbracket \mathsf{let}\ x = \mathsf{return}(t)\ \mathsf{in}\ u \rrbracket = \llbracket u[t/x] \rrbracket \qquad\qquad \llbracket \mathsf{let}\ x = u\ \mathsf{in\,return}(x) \rrbracket = \llbracket u \rrbracket$$

$$\llbracket \mathsf{let}\ y = (\mathsf{let}\ x = t\ \mathsf{in}\ u)\ \mathsf{in}\ v \rrbracket \;=\; \llbracket \mathsf{let}\ x = t\ \mathsf{in\,let}\ y = u\ \mathsf{in}\ v \rrbracket$$

For instance, the associativity law follows from Lemma 3.

Commutativity.

Theorem 4. *For any terms* $\Gamma \vdash_{\mathsf{p}} t\colon \mathbb{A}$, $\Gamma \vdash_{\mathsf{p}} u\colon \mathbb{B}$, $\Gamma, x\colon \mathbb{A}, y\colon \mathbb{B} \vdash_{\mathsf{p}} v\colon \mathbb{C}$, *we have*

$$[\![\mathsf{let}\, x = t\, \mathsf{in}\, \mathsf{let}\, y = u\, \mathsf{in}\, v]\!] \;=\; [\![\mathsf{let}\, y = u\, \mathsf{in}\, \mathsf{let}\, x = t\, \mathsf{in}\, v]\!].$$

This theorem is an immediate consequence of Proposition 5:

Proposition 5. *Let* μ *and* λ *be s-finite measures on* X *and* Y *respectively, and let* $f\colon X \times Y \to [0, \infty]$ *be measurable. Then*

$$\int_X \mu(\mathrm{d}x) \int_Y \lambda(\mathrm{d}y)\, f(x,y) = \int_Y \lambda(\mathrm{d}y) \int_X \mu(\mathrm{d}x)\, f(x,y)$$

Proof. This result is known (e.g. [39]) and it is easy to prove. Since μ and λ are s-finite, we have $\mu = \sum_{i=1}^{\infty} \mu_i$ and $\lambda = \sum_{j=1}^{\infty} \lambda_j$, with the μ_i's and λ_j's all finite. Now,

$\int_X (\sum_i \mu_i)(\mathrm{d}x) \int_Y (\sum_j \lambda_j)(\mathrm{d}y)\, f(x,y)$

$= \sum_i \int_X \mu_i(\mathrm{d}x) \sum_j \int_Y \lambda_j(\mathrm{d}y)\, f(x,y)$ using Proposition 2

$= \sum_i \sum_j \int_X \mu_i(\mathrm{d}x) \int_Y \lambda_j(\mathrm{d}y)\, f(x,y)$ using (8)

$= \sum_i \sum_j \int_Y \lambda_j(\mathrm{d}y) \int_X \mu_i(\mathrm{d}x)\, f(x,y)$ finite measures commute, [32, Theorem 25]

$= \sum_i \int_Y (\sum_j \lambda_j)(\mathrm{d}y) \int_X \mu_i(\mathrm{d}x)\, f(x,y)$ using Proposition 2

$= \int_Y (\sum_j \lambda_j)(\mathrm{d}y) \sum_i \int_X \mu_i(\mathrm{d}x)\, f(x,y)$ using (8)

$= \int_Y (\sum_j \lambda_j)(\mathrm{d}y) \int_X (\sum_i \mu_i)(\mathrm{d}x)\, f(x,y)$ using Proposition 2.

(The commutativity for finite measures is often called Fubini's theorem.)

Iteration. We did not include iteration in our language but in fact it is definable. In brief, we can use the probabilistic constructs to guess how many iterations are needed for termination. (We do not envisage this as a good implementation strategy, we merely want to show that the language and semantic model can accommodate reasoning about iteration.)

In detail, we define a construction $\mathsf{iterate}\, t\, \mathsf{from}\, x{=}u$, that keeps calling t, starting from $x{=}u$; if t returns $u'\colon \mathbb{A}$, then we repeat with $x{=}u'$, if t finally returns in $\mathbb{B}$, then we stop. This has the following derived typing rule:

$$\frac{\Gamma, x\colon \mathbb{A} \vdash_{\mathsf{p}} t\colon (\mathbb{A} + \mathbb{B}) \qquad \Gamma \vdash_{\mathsf{d}} u\colon \mathbb{A}}{\Gamma \vdash_{\mathsf{p}} \mathsf{iterate}\, t\, \mathsf{from}\, x{=}u\colon \mathbb{B}}$$

We begin by defining the counting measure on $\mathbb{N}$, which assigns to each set its size. This is not a primitive, because it isn't a probability measure, but we can define it in a similar way to the Lebesgue measure:

$$counting_{\mathbb{N}} = [\![\vdash_{\mathsf{p}} \mathsf{let}\, x = \mathsf{sample}(poisson(1))\, \mathsf{in}\, \mathsf{score}(x!e); \mathsf{return}(x)\colon \mathbb{N}]\!] \qquad (13)$$

(Recall that the Poisson distribution has $poisson(1)(\{x\}) = \frac{1}{x!e}$.)

Now we can define

$$\text{iterate}\, t \,\text{from}\, x = u \overset{\text{def}}{=} \text{case } counting_\mathbb{N} \text{ of } (n, ()) \Rightarrow \text{iterate}^n\, t \,\text{from}\, x = u$$

where $\Gamma \vdash_{\bar{p}} \text{iterate}^n\, t \,\text{from}\, x{=}u \colon \mathbb{B}$ is the program that returns $v : \mathbb{B}$ if t returns v after exactly n iterations and fails otherwise:

$$
\begin{aligned}
\text{iterate}^1\, t \,\text{from}\, x = u &\overset{\text{def}}{=} \text{case } t[u/x] \text{ of}(1, u') \Rightarrow \text{fail} \\
&\qquad\qquad\qquad\quad | (2, v) \Rightarrow \text{return}(v) \\
\text{iterate}^{n+1}\, t \,\text{from}\, x = u &\overset{\text{def}}{=} \text{case } t[u/x] \text{ of}(1, u') \Rightarrow \text{iterate}^n\, t \,\text{from}\, x = u' \\
&\qquad\qquad\qquad\quad | (2, v) \Rightarrow \text{fail}
\end{aligned}
$$

For a simple illustration, von Neumann's trick for simulating a fair coin from a biassed one d can be written $d : \mathsf{P}(\mathsf{bool}) \vdash_{\bar{p}} \text{iterate}\, t \,\text{from}\, x{=}() \colon \mathsf{bool}$ where

$$
\begin{aligned}
t \overset{\text{def}}{=}\ &(\text{let } y = \text{sample}(d) \text{ in} \\
&\text{let } z = \text{sample}(d) \text{ in if } y \neq z \text{ then return}(2, y) \text{ else return}(1, ())) \quad : 1 + \mathsf{bool}
\end{aligned}
$$

We leave for future work the relation between this iteration and other axiomatizations of iteration (e.g. [12, Chap. 3]).

5 Remarks About s-Finite Kernels

5.1 Full Definability

Theorem 6. *If $k : [\![\Gamma]\!] \rightsquigarrow [\![A]\!]$ is s-finite then there is a term $\Gamma \vdash_{\bar{p}} t \colon A$ such that $k = [\![t]\!]$.*

Proof. We show that probability kernels are definable. Consider a probability kernel $k : [\![\Gamma]\!] \rightsquigarrow [\![A]\!]$ with $\Gamma = (x_1 : \mathbb{B}_1 \ldots x_n : \mathbb{B}_n)$. This corresponds to a measurable function $f : [\![\prod_{i=1}^n \mathbb{B}]\!] \rightarrow P([\![A]\!])$, with $f(b_1, \ldots, b_n)(U) = k(b_1, \ldots, b_n, U)$, and $k = [\![\Gamma \vdash_{\bar{p}} \text{sample}(f(x_1, \ldots, x_n)) \colon A]\!]$.

We move on to subprobability kernels, which are kernels $k : [\![\Gamma]\!] \rightsquigarrow [\![A]\!]$ such that $k(\gamma, [\![A]\!]) \leq 1$ for all γ. We show that they are all definable. Recall that to give a subprobability kernel $k : [\![\Gamma]\!] \rightsquigarrow [\![A]\!]$ is to give a probability kernel $\bar{k} : [\![\Gamma]\!] \rightsquigarrow [\![A + 1]\!]$. Define

$$
\bar{k}(\gamma, U) = \begin{cases} k(\gamma, \{a \mid (1, a) \in U\}) + (1 - k(\gamma, [\![A]\!])) & (2, ()) \in U \\ k(\gamma, \{a \mid (1, a) \in U\}) & \text{otherwise} \end{cases}
$$

This probability kernel $\bar{k}$ is definable, with $\bar{k} = [\![t]\!]$, say, and this has the property that

$$k = [\![\text{case } t \text{ of } (1, x) \Rightarrow \text{return}(x) \mid (2, ()) \Rightarrow \text{fail}]\!].$$

where fail is the zero kernel defined in (12). So the subprobability kernel k is definable.

Next, we show that all finite kernels $k : \llbracket \Gamma \rrbracket \rightsquigarrow \llbracket A \rrbracket$ are definable. If k is finite then there is a bound $r \in (0, \infty)$ such that $k(\gamma, \llbracket A \rrbracket) < r$ for all γ. Then $\frac{1}{r}k$ is a subprobability kernel, hence definable, so we have t such that $\frac{1}{r}k = \llbracket t \rrbracket$. So $k = r\llbracket t \rrbracket = \llbracket \mathsf{score}(r); t \rrbracket$.

Finally, if k is s-finite then there are finite kernels $k_i : \llbracket \Gamma \rrbracket \rightsquigarrow \llbracket A \rrbracket$ such that $k = \sum_{i=1}^{\infty} k_i$. Since the k_i's are finite, we have terms t_i with $k_i = \llbracket t_i \rrbracket$. Recall that a countable sum is merely integration over the counting measure on $\mathbb{N}$, which we showed to be definable in (13). So we have $k = \llbracket \mathsf{case}\ counting_{\mathbb{N}}\ \mathsf{of}\ i \Rightarrow t_i \rrbracket$.

5.2 Failure of Commutativity in General

The standard example of the failure of Tonelli's theorem (e.g. [32, Chap. 4., Example 12] can be used to explain why the commutativity program Eq. (2) fails if we allow arbitrary measures as programs.

Let *lebesgue* be the Lebesgue measure on $\mathbb{R}$, and let $counting_{\mathbb{R}}$ be the counting measure on $\mathbb{R}$. Recall that $counting_{\mathbb{R}}(U)$ is the cardinality of U if U is finite, and ∞ if U is infinite. Then

$$\int_{\mathbb{R}} lebesgue(\mathrm{d}r) \int_{\mathbb{R}} counting_{\mathbb{R}}(\mathrm{d}s)\, [r = s] \;=\; \int_{\mathbb{R}} lebesgue(\mathrm{d}r)\, 1 \;=\; \infty$$

$$\int_{\mathbb{R}} counting_{\mathbb{R}}(\mathrm{d}s) \int_{\mathbb{R}} lebesgue(\mathrm{d}r)\, [r = s] \;=\; \int_{\mathbb{R}} counting_{\mathbb{R}}(\mathrm{d}s)\, 0 \;=\; 0$$

So, by Proposition 5, the counting measure on $\mathbb{R}$ is not s-finite, and hence it is not definable in our language. (This is in contrast to the counting measure on $\mathbb{N}$, see (13).)

Just for this subsection, we suppose that we can add the counting measure on $\mathbb{R}$ to our language as a term constructor $\vdash_{\bar{\mathsf{p}}} counting_{\mathbb{R}} : \mathbb{R}$ and that we can extend the semantics to accommodate it. (This would require some extension of Lemma 3.) The Lebesgue measure is already definable in our language (10). In this extended language we would have

$$\llbracket \vdash_{\bar{\mathsf{p}}} \mathsf{let}\, r = lebesgue\ \mathsf{in}\ \mathsf{let}\, s = counting_{\mathbb{R}}\ \mathsf{in}\ [r = s] : \mathsf{bool} \rrbracket_{(),\{\mathsf{true}\}} \;=\; \infty$$

$$\llbracket \vdash_{\bar{\mathsf{p}}} \mathsf{let}\, s = counting_{\mathbb{R}}\ \mathsf{in}\ \mathsf{let}\, r = lebesgue\ \mathsf{in}\ [r = s] : \mathsf{bool} \rrbracket_{(),\{\mathsf{true}\}} \;=\; 0.$$

So if such as language extension was possible, we would not have commutativity.

5.3 Variations on s-Finiteness

Infinite versions of Fubini/Tonelli theorems are often stated for σ-finite measures. Recall that a measure μ on X is $\sigma - finite$ if $X = \biguplus_{i=1}^{\infty} U_i$ with each $U_i \in \Sigma_X$ and each $\mu(U_i)$ finite. The restriction to σ-finite measures is too strong for our purposes. For example, although the Lebesgue measure (*lebesgue*) is σ-finite, and definable (10), the measure $\llbracket \vdash_{\bar{\mathsf{p}}} \mathsf{let}\, x = lebesgue\ \mathsf{in}\ () : 1 \rrbracket$ is the infinite measure on the one-point space, which is not σ-finite. This illustrates the difference between σ-finite and s-finite measures:

Proposition 7. *A measure is s-finite if and only if it is a pushforward of a σ-finite measure.*

Proof. From left to right, let $\mu = \sum_{i=1}^{\infty} \mu_i$ be a measure on X with each μ_i finite. Then we can form a σ-finite measure ν on $\mathbb{N} \times X$ with $\nu(U) = \sum_{i=1}^{\infty} \mu_i(\{x \mid (i, x) \in U\})$. The original measure μ is the pushforward of ν along the projection $\mathbb{N} \times X \to X$.

From right to left, let ν be a σ-finite measure on $X = \biguplus_{i=1}^{\infty} U_i$ with each restricted measure $\nu(U_i)$ finite. Let $f : X \to Y$ be measurable. For $i \in \mathbb{N}$, let $\mu_i(V) = \nu(\{x \in U_i \mid f(x) \in V\})$. Then each μ_i is a finite measure on Y and $\sum_{i=1}^{\infty} \mu_i$ is the pushforward of ν along f, as required. (See also [9, Lemma 8.6].)

However, this does not mean that s-finite kernels (Definition 2) are 'just' kernels whose images are pushforwards of σ-finite measures. In the proof of commutativity, we did only need kernels $k : X \rightsquigarrow Y$ such that $k(x)$ is an s-finite measure for all $x \in X$. This condition is implied by the definition of s-finite kernel (Definition 2) but the definition of s-finite kernel seems to be strictly stronger because of the uniformity in the definition. (This is not known for sure; see also the discussion about σ-finite kernels in [32, Sect. 4.10].) The reason we use the notion of s-finite kernel, rather than this apparently weaker notion, is that Lemma 3 (and hence the well-defined semantics of let) appears to require the uniformity in the definition of finite and s-finite kernels. In brief, the stronger notion of s-finite kernel provides a compositional semantics giving s-finite measures.

6   Concluding Remarks

6.1   Related Work on Commutativity for Probabilistic Programs

Work Using Finite Kernels. Several other authors have given a semantics for probabilistic programs using kernels. Subprobability kernels and finite measures already appear in Kozen's work on probabilistic programming [21]. Ramsey and Pfeffer [34] focus on a language like ours but without score or normalize; they give a semantics in terms of probability kernels. The measure-transformer-semantics of Börgstrom et al. [3] incorporates observations by moving to finite kernels; their semantics is similar to ours (Sect. 3.2), but they are able to make do with finite kernels by considering a very limited language. In the more recent operational semantics by Börgstrom et al. [4], problems of commutativity are avoided by requiring scores to be less than 1, so that all the measures are subprobability measures. Jacobs and Zanasi [18] also impose this restriction to make a connection with an elegant mathematical construction. With discrete countable distributions, this is fine because density functions and likelihoods lie below 1. But when dealing with continuous distributions, it is artificial to restrict to scores below 1, since the likelihood of a continuous distribution may just as well lie above 1 as below it. For example, the subprobability semantics could not handle the example in Sect. 1.1. This is not merely a matter of scaling, because density functions are sometimes unbounded, as shown in $beta(0.5, 0.5)$ on the right. Our results here show that, by using s-finite kernels, one can consider arbitrary likelihoods without penalty.

Verification Conditions for Commutativity. Shan and Ramsey [38] use a similar semantics to ours to justify their disintegration program transformation. They interpret a term $\Gamma \vdash_{\overline{p}} t \colon \mathbb{A}$ as a measurable function into a monad $\mathbb{M}$ of measures, $[t]_{SR} \colon [\Gamma] \to \mathbb{M}(\mathbb{A})$, which actually amounts to the same thing as a kernel. However, there is a problem with the seman-tics in this style: we do not know a proof for Lemma 3

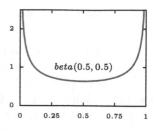

without the s-finiteness restriction. In other words, we do not know whether the monad of all measures $\mathbb{M}$ is a strong monad. A strength is needed to give a semantics for the let construction. So it is not clear whether the semantics is well-defined. Even if $\mathbb{M}$ is strong, it is certainly not commutative, as we have discussed in Sect. 5.2, a point also emphasized by Ramsey [35]. Shan and Ramsey [38] regain commutativity by imposing additional verification condi-tions. Our results here show that these conditions are always satisfied because all definable programs are s-finite kernels and hence commutative.

Contextual Equivalence. Very recently, Culpepper and Cobb [6] have proposed an operational notion of contextual equivalence for a language with arbitrary like-lihoods, and shown that this supports commutativity. The relationship between their argument and s-finite kernels remains to be investigated.

Sampling Semantics. An alternative approach to denotational semantics for probabilistic programs is based on interpreting an expression $\Gamma \vdash_{\overline{p}} t \colon \mathbb{A}$ as a probability kernel $[t]' \colon [\Gamma] \rightsquigarrow ([0, \infty) \times [\mathbb{A}])$, so that $[t]'(\gamma)$ is a probability measure on pairs (r, x) of a result x and a weight r. In brief, the probability mea-sure comes from sampling priors, and the weight comes from scoring likelihoods of observations. Börgstrom et al. [4] call this a *sampling* semantics by contrast with the *distribution* semantics that we have considered here. This sampling semantics, which has a more intensional flavour and is closer to an operational intuition, is also considered by Ścibor et al. [37] and Staton et al. [43], as well as Doberkat [7]. The two methods are related because every probability kernel $k \colon X \rightsquigarrow ([0, \infty) \times Y)$ induces a measure kernel $\bar{k} \colon X \rightsquigarrow Y$ by summing over the possible scores:

$$\bar{k}(x, U) \stackrel{\text{def}}{=} \int_{[0,\infty) \times U} k(x, \mathrm{d}(r, y))\, r \tag{14}$$

An advantage to the sampling semantics is that it is clearly commutative, because it is based on a commutative monad $(P([0, \infty) \times (-)))$, built by combin-ing the commutative Giry monad P and the commutative monoid monad trans-former. However, the sampling semantics does not validate many of the semantic equations in Sect. 4.1: importance sampling, conjugate priors, and resampling are only sound in the sampling semantics if we wrap the programs in normalize(...). (See e.g. [43].) This makes it difficult to justify applying program transformations compositionally. The point of this paper is that we can verify the semantic equa-tions in Sect. 4.1 directly, while retaining commutativity, by using the measure based (distributional) semantics.

As an aside we note that the probability kernels $X \rightsquigarrow ([0, \infty) \times Y)$ used in the sampling semantics are closely related to the s-finite kernels advocated in this paper:

Proposition 8. *A kernel* $l : X \rightsquigarrow Y$ *is s-finite if and only if there exists a probability kernel* $k : X \rightsquigarrow ([0, \infty) \times Y)$ *and* $l(x, U) = \int_{[0,\infty) \times U} k(x, \mathrm{d}(r, y)) \, r$.

Proof (notes). We focus on the case where $X = \llbracket A \rrbracket$ and $Y = \llbracket B \rrbracket$. From left to right: build a probability kernel from an s-finite kernel by first understanding it as a probabilistic program (via Theorem 6) and then using the denotational semantics in [43]. From right to left: given a probability kernel $k : \llbracket A \rrbracket \rightsquigarrow ([0, \infty) \times \llbracket B \rrbracket)$, we build an s-finite kernel

$$\llbracket x : A \vdash_{\bar{p}} \text{let } (r, y) = \text{sample}(k(x)) \text{ in score}(r); \text{return}(y) : B \rrbracket : \llbracket A \rrbracket \rightsquigarrow \llbracket B \rrbracket.$$

Valuations Versus Measures. Some authors advocate using valuations on topological spaces instead of measures on measurable spaces. This appears to rule out the problematic examples, such as the counting measure on $\mathbb{R}$. Indeed, Vickers [45] has shown that a monad of valuations on locales is commutative. This suggests a constructive or topological model of probabilistic programming (see [8,15]) but a potential obstacle is that conditioning is not always computable [1].

6.2   Related Work on Commutativity More Generally

Multicategories and Data Flow Graphs. An early discussion of commutativity is in Lambek's work on deductive systems and categories [22]. A judgement $x_1 : A_1, \ldots, x_n : A_n \vdash t : B$ is interpreted as a multimorphism $(A_1 \ldots A_n) \to B$. These could be drawn as triangles:

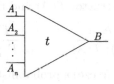

(This hints at a link with the graphical ideas underlying several probabilistic programming languages e.g. Stan [40].) Alongside requiring associativity of composition, Lambek requires commutativity:

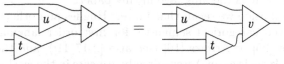

which matches with our commutativity condition (2). (See also [42].) In this diagrammatic notation, commutativity says that the semantics is preserved under topological transformations. Without commutativity, one would need extra control flow wires to give a topological description of what rewritings are acceptable (e.g. [19,28]). Our main technical results (Lemma 3 and Proposition 5) can be phrased as follows:

Measurable spaces and s-finite kernels $X_1 \times \cdots \times X_n \rightsquigarrow Y$ form a multi-category.

Monoidal Categories, Monads and Arrows. There is a tight connection between multicategories and monoidal categories [13,24,42]. Our main technical results (Lemma 3 and Proposition 5) together with the basic facts in Sect. 4.2 can be phrased as follows:

Consider the category whose objects are measurable spaces and morphisms are s-finite kernels. The cartesian product of spaces extends to a monoidal structure which distributes over the coproduct structure.

From this point of view, the key step is that given s-finite kernels $k : X_1 \rightsquigarrow Y_1$ and $k_2 : X_2 \rightsquigarrow Y_2$, we can form $(k_1 \otimes k_2) : X_1 \times X_2 \rightsquigarrow Y_1 \times Y_2$, with

$$(k_1 \otimes k_2)((x_1, x_2), U) = \int_{X_1} k_1(x_1, dy_1) \int_{X_2} k_2(x_2, dy_2)[(y_1, y_2) \in U]$$

and the interchange law holds, in particular, $(k_1 \otimes \mathrm{id}) \circ (\mathrm{id} \otimes k_2) = (\mathrm{id} \otimes k_2) \circ (k_1 \otimes \mathrm{id})$.

One way of building monoidal categories is as Kleisli categories for commutative monads. For example, the monoidal category of probability kernels is the Kleisli category for the Giry monad [10]. However, we conjecture that s-finite kernels do *not* form a Kleisli category for a commutative monad on the category of measurable spaces. One could form a space $M_{\mathsf{sfin}}(Y)$ of s-finite measures on a given space Y, but, as discussed in Sect. 5.3, it is unlikely that every measurable function $X \rightarrow M_{\mathsf{sfin}}(Y)$ is an s-finite kernel in general, because of the uniformity in the definition (Definition 2). This makes it difficult to ascertain whether M_{sfin} is a strong commutative monad. Having a monad would give us a slightly-higher-order type constructor $T(A)$ and the rules

$$\frac{\Gamma \vdash_{\mathsf{p}} t : \mathbb{A}}{\Gamma \vdash_{\mathsf{d}} \mathsf{thunk}(t) : T(\mathbb{A})} \qquad\qquad \frac{\Gamma \vdash_{\mathsf{d}} t : T(\mathbb{A})}{\Gamma \vdash_{\mathsf{p}} \mathsf{force}(t) : \mathbb{A}}$$

allowing us to thunk (suspend, freeze) a probabilistic computation and then force (resume, run) it again [25,29]. The rules are reminiscent of, but not the same as, the rules for normalize and sample. Although monads are a convenient way of building a semantics for programming languages, they are not essential for first order languages such as the language in this paper.

As a technical aside we recall that Power, Hughes and others have eschewed monads and given categorical semantics for first order languages in terms of Freyd categories [25] or Arrows [16] (see also [2,17,41]), and the idea of structuring the finite kernels as an Arrow already appears in the work of Börgstrom et al. [3] (see also [36,44]). Our semantics based on s-finite kernels forms a 'countably distributive commutative Freyd category', which is to say that the identity-on-objects functor

$$\left(\begin{array}{c} \text{measurable spaces} \\ \text{\& measurable functions} \end{array} \right) \longrightarrow \left(\begin{array}{c} \text{measurable spaces} \\ \text{\& s-finite kernels} \end{array} \right)$$

preserves countable sums and is monoidal. In fact every countably distributive commutative Freyd category $\mathcal{C} \to \mathcal{D}$ corresponds to a commutative monad, not on the category $\mathcal{C}$ but on the category of countable-product-preserving functors $\mathcal{C}^{\mathrm{op}} \to \mathbf{Set}$ (e.g. [33,43]). This functor category is cartesian closed, and so it is also a fairly canonical semantics for higher order programs. (For a more concrete variant, see also [14].)

6.3 Summary

We have given a denotational semantics for a probabilistic programming language using s-finite kernels (Sect. 3.2). Compositionality relied on a technical lemma (Lemma 3). This semantic model supports reasoning based on statistical techniques (Sect. 4.1), such as conjugate priors, as well as basic equational reasoning (Sect. 4.2), such as commutativity (Theorem 4). The model is actually completely described by the syntax, according to our full definability theorem (Theorem 6).

Acknowledgements. I am profoundly grateful to my coauthors on [43] for many discussions about the problems and examples in this subject (C. Heunen, O. Kammar, F. Wood, H. Yang). The MFPS 2016 special session on Probabilistic Programming was also illuminating and it was helpful to discuss these issues with the participants (J Börgstrom, D Roy, CC Shan and others). Thanks too to Adam Ścibior and the ESOP reviewers.

Research supported by a Royal Society University Research Fellowship.

References

1. Ackerman, N.L., Freer, C.E., Roy, D.M.: Noncomputable conditional distributions. In: Proceedings of the LICS 2011 (2011)
2. Atkey, R.: What is a categorical model of arrows? In: Proceedings of the MSFP 2008 (2008)
3. Borgström, J., Gordon, A.D., Greenberg, M., Margetson, J., van Gael, J.: Measure transformer semantics for Bayesian machine learning. LMCS **9**(3), 11 (2013)
4. Borgström, J., Lago, U.D., Gordon, A.D., Szymczak, M.: A lambda-calculus foundation for universal probabilistic programming. In: Proceedings of the ICFP (2016)
5. Carette, J., Shan, C.-C.: Simplifying probabilistic programs using computer algebra. In: Gavanelli, M., Reppy, J. (eds.) PADL 2016. LNCS, vol. 9585, pp. 135–152. Springer, Cham (2016). doi:10.1007/978-3-319-28228-2_9
6. Culpepper, R., Cobb, A.: Contextual equivalence for probabilistic programs with continuous random variables and scoring. In: Proceedings of the ESOP 2017 (2017, to appear)
7. Doberkat, E.E.: Stochastic Relations: Foundations for Markov Transition Systems. Chapman & Hall, London (2007)
8. Faissole, F., Spitters, B.: Synthetic topology in homotopy type theory for probabilistic programming. In: Proceedings of the PPS 2017 (2017)
9. Getoor, R.K.: Excessive Measures. Birkhäuser (1990)
10. Giry, M.: A categorical approach to probability theory. Categorical Aspects Topology Anal. **915**, 68–85 (1982)

11. Goodman, N., Mansinghka, V., Roy, D.M., Bonawitz, K., Tenenbaum, J.B.: Church: a language for generative models. In: UAI (2008)

12. Haghverdi, E.: A categorical approach to linear logic, geometry of proofs and full completeness. Ph.D. thesis, Ottawa (2000)

13. Hermida, C.: Representable multicategories. Adv. Math. **151**, 164–225 (2000)

14. Heunen, C., Kammar, O., Staton, S., Yang, H.: A convenient category for higher-order probability theory (2017). arXiv:1701.02547

15. Huang, D., Morrisett, G.: An application of computable distributions to the semantics of probabilistic programs: part 2. In: Proceedings of the PPS 2017 (2017)

16. Hughes, J.: Generalising monads to arrows. Sci. Comput. Program. **37**(1–3), 67–111 (2000)

17. Jacobs, B., Heunen, C., Hasuo, I.: Categorical semantics for arrows. J. Funct. Program. **19**(3–4), 403–438 (2009)

18. Jacobs, B., Zanasi, F.: A predicate/state transformer semantics for Bayesian learning. In: Proceedings of the MFPS 2016 (2016)

19. Jeffrey, A.: Premonoidal categories and a graphical view of programs. Unpublished (1997)

20. Kallenberg, O.: Stationary and invariant densities and disintegration kernels. Probab. Theory Relat. Fields **160**, 567–592 (2014)

21. Kozen, D.: Semantics of probablistic programs. J. Comput. Syst. Sci. **22**, 328–350 (1981)

22. Lambek, J.: Deductive systems and categories II. In: Hilton, P.J. (ed.) Category Theory, Homology Theory and Their Applications. LNM, vol. 86, pp. 76–122. Springer, Heidelberg (1969)

23. Last, G., Penrose, M.: Lectures on the Poisson process. CUP (2016)

24. Leinster, T.: Higher operads, higher categories. CUP (2004)

25. Levy, P.B., Power, J., Thielecke, H.: Modelling environments in call-by-value programming languages. Inf. Comput. **185**(2), 182–210 (2003)

26. Mansinghka, V.K., Selsam, D., Perov, Y.N.: Venture: a higher-order probabilistic programming platform with programmable inference (2014). http://arxiv.org/abs/1404.0099

27. Mardare, R., Panangaden, P., Plotkin, G.: Quantitative algebraic reasoning. In: Proceedings of the LICS 2016 (2016)

28. Møgelberg, R.E., Staton, S.: Linear usage of state. Logical Methods Comput. Sci. **10** (2014)

29. Moggi, E.: Notions of computation and monads. Inf. Comput. **93**(1), 55–92 (1991)

30. Narayanan, P., Carette, J., Romano, W., Shan, C., Zinkov, R.: Probabilistic inference by program transformation in Hakaru (system description). In: Kiselyov, O., King, A. (eds.) FLOPS 2016. LNCS, vol. 9613, pp. 62–79. Springer, Cham (2016). doi:10.1007/978-3-319-29604-3_5

31. Paige, B., Wood, F.: A compilation target for probabilistic programming languages. In: ICML (2014)

32. Pollard, D.: A user's guide to measure theoretic probability. CUP (2002)

33. Power, J.: Generic models for computational effects. TCS **364**(2), 254–269 (2006)

34. Ramsey, N., Pfeffer, A.: Stochastic lambda calculus and monads of probability distributions. In: POPL (2002)

35. Ramsey, N.: All you need is the monad.. what monad was that again? In: PPS Workshop (2016)

36. Scherrer, C.: An exponential family basis for probabilistic programming. In: Proceedings of the PPS 2017 (2017)

37. Ścibor, A., Ghahramani, Z., Gordon, A.D.: Practical probabilistic programming with monads. In: Proceedings of the Haskell Symposium. ACM (2015)
38. Shan, C.C., Ramsey, N.: Symbolic Bayesian inference by symbolic disintegration (2016)
39. Sharpe, M.: General Theory of Markov Processes. Academic Press, Cambridge (1988)
40. Stan Development Team: Stan: A C++ library for probability and sampling, version 2.5.0 (2014). http://mc-stan.org/
41. Staton, S.: Freyd categories are enriched Lawvere theories. In: Algebra, Coalgebra and Topology, ENTCS, vol. 303 (2013)
42. Staton, S., Levy, P.: Universal properties for impure programming languages. In: Proceedings of the POPL 2013 (2013)
43. Staton, S., Yang, H., Heunen, C., Kammar, O., Wood, F.: Semantics for probabilistic programming: higher-order functions, continuous distributions, and soft constraints. In: Proceedings of the LICS 2016 (2016)
44. Toronto, N., McCarthy, J., Van Horn, D.: Running probabilistic programs backwards. In: Vitek, J. (ed.) ESOP 2015. LNCS, vol. 9032, pp. 53–79. Springer, Heidelberg (2015). doi:10.1007/978-3-662-46669-8_3
45. Vickers, S.: A monad of valuation locales available from the author's website (2011)
46. Wood, F., van de Meent, J.W., Mansinghka, V.: A new approach to probabilistic programming inference. In: AISTATS (2014)

Conditional Dyck-CFL Reachability Analysis for Complete and Efficient Library Summarization

Hao Tang[1], Di Wang[1], Yingfei Xiong[1]([✉]), Lingming Zhang[2], Xiaoyin Wang[3], and Lu Zhang[1]

[1] Key Laboratory of High Confidence Software Technologies,
Ministry of Education, Peking University, Beijing, China
{tanghaoth90,wayne.wangdi,xiongyf,zhanglucs}@pku.edu.cn
[2] Department of Computer Science, University of Texas at Dallas,
Richardson, TX, USA
lingming.zhang@utdallas.edu
[3] Department of Computer Science, University of Texas at San Antonio,
San Antonio, TX, USA
xiaoyin.wang@utsa.edu

Abstract. Library summarization is an effective way to accelerate the analysis of client code. However, information about the client is unknown at the library summarization, preventing complete summarization of the library. An existing approach utilizes tree-adjoining languages (TALs) to provide conditional summaries, enabling the summarization of a library under certain premises. However, the use of TAL imposes several problems, preventing a complete summarization of a library and reducing the efficiency of the analysis.

In this paper we propose a new conditional summarization technique based on the context-free language (CFL) reachability analysis. Our technique overcomes the above two limitations of TAL, and is more accessible since CFL reachability is much more efficient and widely-used than TAL reachability. Furthermore, to overcome the high cost from premise combination, we also provide a technique to confine the number of premises while maintaining full summarization of the library.

We empirically compared our approach with the state-of-art TAL conditional summarization technique on 12 Java benchmark subjects from the SPECjvm2008 benchmark suite. The results demonstrate that our approach is able to significantly outperform TAL on both efficiency and precision.

1 Introduction

Building a summary for a library is a key technique for scaling static analysis of the library's client programs [3,7,17]. Such a summary can significantly boost client analysis, since client analysis can directly utilize the summary without further analyzing the library. However, in most analysis, it is not possible to treat library code as a complete program during the summarization, because

© Springer-Verlag GmbH Germany 2017
H. Yang (Ed.): ESOP 2017, LNCS 10201, pp. 880–908, 2017.
DOI: 10.1007/978-3-662-54434-1_33

many components required for the analysis are unknown without the presence of the client. For example, when a library calls a virtual method, the actual callee may depend on the client code. Furthermore, if the callee is a call-back method, the body of the callee also depends on the client code.

Typical techniques (e.g., Rountev et al. [31,33], Lattner et al. [13], Madhavan et al. [17], and Arzt et al. [1]) for dealing with unknown in library summarization are based on distinguishing the known part from the unknown part, and building summaries only for the known part. These techniques are based on the principle of component level analysis (CLA) [31,33]. However, since the unknown components are often required in critical steps of the analysis, the summaries we can build for libraries are significantly limited. For example, in Java, any method that is not declared as final or private can be overridden by a sub class, and thus we cannot statically determine the target of most calls. As a result, in a major portion of a library, we can build summaries for only intra-procedural analysis, and postpone the more expensive inter-procedure analysis to the client analysis. We refer to these techniques as *unconditional summarization*, in contrast to the conditional summarization techniques discussed below.

To overcome the limitation in unconditional summarization, a recent approach by Tang et al. [39] provides *conditional summaries* for data dependency analysis, based on the tree-adjoining language (TAL) reachability analysis. We shall refer to this technique as TALCRA (TAL Conditional Reachability Analysis). The basic idea is to assume all possibilities of each unknown component, where each possibility is called a *premise*, and pre-compute a conditional summary for all possible clients. When the client code is available, TALCRA obtains the previously unknown component and instantiate the conditional summary into an unconditional summary. In this way, TALCRA can obtain a more complete summary than unconditional summarization techniques can.

However, TALCRA has several limitations. First, by nature, TAL reachability analysis may assume premises that would not exist, and thus is computationally more expensive than other analysis techniques such as context-free language (CFL) reachability [27]. Second, due to the expressiveness of TAL reachability, there can be only one premise for each conditional relation, and the premise cannot cross method boundaries. Thus, in the cases where there are more than one components, or the unknown component crosses multiple methods, TALCRA cannot build a complete summary for the library.

To understand these problems concretely, let us consider an example program in Fig. 1a. A dependency graph for this program is shown in Fig. 1b. In this figure, nodes are variables and edges are flows-to relations between the variables, i.e., the inverse of dependency relations. The solid nodes and edges can be deduced from the library alone, while the hollow nodes and dashed edges require client code. Using unconditional summarization techniques, we are able to infer only the following relations:

$$a_{pub} \text{ flows to } b_{pub}; \tag{1}$$

$$c_{pub} \text{ flows to } d_{pub}. \tag{2}$$

```
 1 package library;                        15    return x3; }
 2 public abstract class                   16    private final int m4(int x4){
     LibraryClass {                        17       int x5 = 100; return x5; }
 3   public final int pub(int a){          18 }
 4     int b = m1(a);                       19
 5     int c = m2(b);                       20 package client;
 6     int d = c;                           21 class ClientClass extends
 7     int e;                                   library.LibraryClass {
 8     if (...) e = m3(d);                  22   protected int m2(int x2){
 9     else e = m4(d);                      23     return x2; }
10     return e; }                          24   public static void main(){
11   private final int m1(int x1){         25     ClientClass client = new
12     return x1; }                                ClientClass();
13   abstract protected int                26     int z = 255;
       m2(int x2);                         27     int z1 = client.pub(z); }
14   protected int m3(int x3){             28 }
```

(a) Example Program

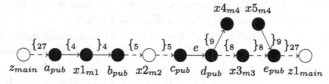

(b) Data-Dependency Graph

Fig. 1. A data dependency example

Using TALCRA, we can further infer the following conditional relations:

$$a_{pub} \text{ flows to } c_{pub} \text{ if } b_{pub} \text{ flows to } c_{pub}; \tag{3}$$

$$c_{pub} \text{ flows to } e_{pub} \text{ if } d_{pub} \text{ flows to } e_{pub}. \tag{4}$$

However, TALCRA cannot infer the following two relations, both needed to fully summarize the library.

$$a_{pub} \text{ flows to } e_{pub} \text{ if } b_{pub} \text{ flows to } c_{pub} \text{ and } d_{pub} \text{ flows to } e_{pub}, \text{ because TAL summarization does not support more than one premises.} \tag{5}$$

$$c_{pub} \text{ flows to } e_{pub} \text{ if line 8 calls the method defined at line 14, because TAL summarization does not allow premises to cross method boundaries, and these premises are in fact two edges between nodes in different methods } (d_{pub} \xrightarrow{\{8} x3_{m3} \text{ and } x3_{m3} \xrightarrow{\}8} e_{pub}); \tag{6}$$

As a result, to build a complete summary of the library, TALCRA has to make the most conservative assumption, possibly reducing the precision of the analysis. For example, to build a summary for the library, we can use class hierarchy analysis (CHA) [5] to generate unconditional virtual call edges. The result from CHA is guaranteed to cover any client, but is not precise for the analysis of one client, where we can use more precise control flow analysis.

Also, TALCRA infers unnecessary conditional relations during library summarization, such as the following one. This relation is useless because its premise can never be satisfied, but TAL cannot utilize this fact and may further deduce more useless relations based on this. This is because TAL reachability analysis views a conditional reachability relation from the known component by nature, and would treat any two separated paths as potentially connectable.

$$d_{pub} \text{ flows to } e_{pub} \text{ if } x4_{m4} \text{ flows to } x5_{m4}; \tag{7}$$

In this paper, we propose a novel approach to overcoming the limitations in TALCRA, called *ConCRA* (Conditional Dyck-CFL Reachability Analysis). Unlike TALCRA that relies on expensive TAL reachability analysis, our approach is built upon the well-known Dyck-context-free-language (Dyck-CFL) reachability analysis. CFL reachability analysis [27] is known to be applicable to a large class of program analysis problems, and the Dyck-CFL reachability problem is known to be able to express "almost all the applications of CFL reachability" [10]. Therefore, our approach is applicable to a large class of program analysis problems besides data dependency analysis.

The key idea of our approach is to attach premises to standard edges, and analyze using standard CFL rules by assuming the existence of premises. In this way, we can overcome the limitations in TALCRA. First, as we start from the unknown component, in contrast to TALCRA that starts from the known component, we can enumerate only the premises that may exist in some clients, avoiding the high computation cost of producing unnecessary conditional reachability relations. Second, as the premises are basically an attachment, there is no particular constraint over the premises and multiple premises per one relation is also supported. In the above example, our approach can produce the following conditional relations, which completely summarize the flows-to behavior in the library.

$$a_{pub} \text{ flows to } e_{pub} \text{ if } b_{pub} \text{ flows to } c_{pub} \text{ and } d_{pub} \text{ flows to } e_{pub}. \tag{8}$$

$$a_{pub} \text{ flows to } c_{pub} \text{ if } b_{pub} \text{ flows to } c_{pub} \text{ and line 8 calls the method defined}$$
$$\text{at line 14 (i.e., edges } d_{pub} \xrightarrow{(8} x3_{m3} \text{ and } x3_{m3} \xrightarrow{)8} e_{pub} \text{ exist}). \tag{9}$$

However, allowing too many premises in one conditional relation may lead to too many conditional relations due to the combinatorial effect of the premises. We further propose to confine the number of premises in a reachability relation by introducing *bridging edges*. In this way, our approach can still achieve complete summaries with at most k premises in a relation. We denote the approach with at most k premises as ConCRA-k and the approach with any number of premises as ConCRA-f.

To evaluate the effectiveness and efficiency of ConCRA, we implemented a context-sensitive, SSA-based, and field-insensitive data dependency analysis tool based on ConCRA. In particular, our approach was empirically compared with TALCRA technique on 12 Java benchmark subjects from the SPECjvm2008 benchmark suite. Because of the configurable nature of our approach, we also compare ConCRA-f and ConCRA-k with $k \in \{1, 5\}$.

The evaluation has several findings. (1) ConCRA is able to significantly outperform TALCRA, with up to 1.93X speedup for the library analysis and 5.04X speedup for the client analysis (46.45X if compared to standard CFL technique). (2) When computing complete summaries, ConCRA is up to 24.7% (100% vs. 80.2%) more precise than TALCRA, where the latter relies on CHA to compute control flow analysis on library when the client information is not available. (3) By balancing the library summarization time and the client analysis time, ConCRA-1 seems to be the overall best configuration for the dependency analysis used in our evaluation.

To sum up, the paper makes the following main contributions:

- A general extension to the well-known Dyck-CFL reachability analysis for conditional reachability analysis, providing better efficiency and more complete library summarization than the state-of-the-art TALCRA approach.
- An efficient technique for confining the number of premises to avoid combinatorial explosion of premises.
- An empirical evaluation demonstrating the superiority of our techniques over the state-of-the-art TALCRA approach.

We organize the rest of this paper as follows. Section 2 presents the technical background. Section 3 presents our approach to conditional reachability analysis. Section 4 presents an experimental evaluation of the proposed approach. Section 5 discusses deeper issues of our research. Section 6 discusses existing research related to ours. Section 7 concludes this paper.

2   Background

Our approach is designed for the Dyck-CFL reachability problem. CFL reachability is a generalization of a large class of program analysis problems. CFL reachability concerns about the reachability between nodes on a graph. The nodes of the graph are usually the values under analysis at different program points, and the edges usually show possible reachability or dependencies between values. To increase the precision of the analysis, a CFL is used to confine the reachability. The edges are labelled with members of an alphabet Σ, and a node is considered to be CFL reachable to another node if and only if the labels on a path between the two nodes form a word in this language.

A frequently used CFL is the Dyck language, which is defined by the following grammars.

$$S \rightarrow \{_i\ S\ \}_i\ |\ S\ S\ |\ e\ |\ \epsilon$$
$$L \rightarrow L\ L\ |\ S\ |\ \{_i$$
$$R \rightarrow R\ R\ |\ S\ |\ \}_i$$
$$D \rightarrow R\ D\ |\ D\ L\ |\ S$$

Basically, the Dyck language consists of a family of parentheses, which must be matched when paired. In the above definition, $\{_i$ and $\}_i$ are a family of parenthesis, and e is a terminal to be put on edges that are not parentheses. According to the nature of the problem, the start symbol could be one of S, L, R or D, which allows no unpaired parentheses, only unpaired left parentheses, only unpaired right parentheses, or both.

The Dyck language captures the call-return relationship between procedures. When a procedure is called, the edges from the caller to the callee are labelled with $\{_i$, where i is the identifier of this call site. When the callee returns, the edges from the callee to the caller are labelled with $\}_i$. An example of Dyck-CFL reachability analysis is the data dependency analysis that we have seen in Sect. 1.

The CFL reachability problem can be solved by a dynamic programming algorithm that adds edges of nonterminals to the graph. The context free grammar is first normalized so that the right hand side of each production has at most two symbols. For example, $S \rightarrow \{_i\ S\ \}_i$ is normalized into $S \rightarrow \{_i\ P_i$ and $P_i \rightarrow S\ \}_i$. Then the three rules in Fig. 2 are applied on the graph to add new edges on the graph. The solid lines are existing edges and the dotted lines are the added edges. The three rules can be exhaustively applied with a proper worklist algorithm to achieve a complexity of $O(l^3 n^3)$ where l is the number of nonterminal symbols and n is the number of nodes in the graph. When all rules have been thoroughly applied, the reachability between two nodes is equal to the existence of a direct edge with the start symbol between the two nodes.

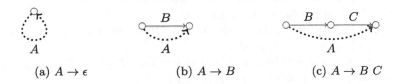

(a) $A \rightarrow \epsilon$ (b) $A \rightarrow B$ (c) $A \rightarrow B\ C$

Fig. 2. Rules for solving a CFL reachability problem

3   Approach

As mentioned in the introduction, our approach is based on conditional reachability. The core concept to implement conditional reachability is the *conditional edge*, which is a special edge whose existence depends on the existence of a set of other edges (known as *premises*). As a result, our summary for a library is a set of conditional edges, where the premises capture the potential reachability built by client code, and the conditional edges themselves capture the reachability between the boundary nodes of the library. When the client code is available, we can instantiate the conditional edges by analyzing the client code, which directly gives us the reachability between the boundary nodes of the library without analyzing the library code.

In the following sub-sections, we first present the basic definitions, then show how we analyze the client with the conditional edges, and finally show our two algorithms, i.e., ConCRA-f and ConCRA-k. The data-dependency graph in Fig. 1b will be used to make our description more clearly.

3.1 Definitions

Suppose an alphabet Σ containing all symbols in a Dyck language. We start by defining general program graphs.

Definition 1 (Program Graph). *A program graph G is a pair (V, E) where V is a set of nodes, E is a set of directed edges between the nodes in V, labelled with the symbols in Σ. We use $G.V$ and $G.E$ to denote the nodes and edges of G, respectively. We use $s \xrightarrow{A} t$ to denote an edge e from s to t with label A, and use $e.src$, $e.tgt$ and $e.tag$ to denote s, t, A.*

Since our approach summarizes library code for client analysis, we need to define library graphs. The difference between a library graph and a program graph is that a library graph has a set of boundary nodes for interacting with the clients, and there are a set of premises that may be instantiated by a client.

Definition 2 (Library Graph). *A **library graph** G is a program graph (V, E) with the following additional components.*
- *V_{input} (Input to library code): The nodes in $G.V$ that can be connected from a client node via a $\{_i$-edge (e.g., a_{pub}).*
- *V_{output} (Output from library code): The nodes in $G.V$ that can connect to a client node via a $\}_i$-edge (e.g., e_{pub}).*
- *V_{call} (Input to call-backs). The nodes in $G.V$ that can be connected to a client node via a $\{_i$-edge (e.g., b_{pub}, d_{pub}).*
- *V_{return} (Output from call-backs). The nodes in $G.V$ that can be connected from a client node via a $\}_i$-edge (e.g., c_{pub}, e_{pub}).*
- ***P** (Premises). Premises are edges that can potentially be created using the information from a client, $P \cap G.E = \emptyset$.*

We call the set of nodes $V_{input} \cup V_{output} \cup V_{call} \cup V_{return}$ boundary nodes. Correspondingly, the rest of the nodes are called *inner nodes*. We further use $V_{entries} = V_{input} \cup V_{return}$ to denote all incoming boundary nodes and use $V_{exits} = V_{output} \cup V_{call}$ to denote all outgoing boundary nodes.

When the client code is available, the part of the graph representing the client code is added to the library graph, forming an *application graph*.

Definition 3 (Application Graph). *Let G be a library graph. Program graph G' is an **application graph** using G if and only if G' satisfies the following constraints:*

*1. $G.V \subset G'.V \wedge G.E \subseteq G'.E$. We call $G.V$ **library nodes**, denoted as $G'.V_{lib}$, and the nodes in $G'.V - G.V$ as **client nodes**, denoted as $G'.V_{clt}$.*

2. Any edge $s \xrightarrow{A} t$ in $G'.E - G.E$ satisfies one of the following conditions.

*(1) **Edges between client nodes.** $s \in G'.V_{clt} \wedge t \in G'.V_{clt}$.*

(2) **Edges between library nodes.** $s \in G.V$, $t \in G.V$, and $s \xrightarrow{A} t \in G.P$.

(3) **Input edges to the library.** $s \in G'.V_{clt}$, $t \in G.V_{input}$, A is $\{_i$ for some i, and any edge labelled with $\}_i$ is an output edge from the library (e.g.,

$$z_{main} \xrightarrow{\{27} a_{pub}).$$

(4) **Output edges from the library.** $s \in G.V_{output}$, $t \in G'.V_{clt}$, A is $\}_i$ for some i, and any edge labelled with $\{_i$ is an input edge to the library (e.g.,

$$e_{pub} \xrightarrow{\}27} z1_{main}).$$

(5) **Input edges to call-backs.** $s \in G.V_{call}$, $t \in G'.V_{clt}$, A is $\{_i$ for some i, and any edge labelled with $\}_i$ is an output edge from call-backs (e.g., $b_{pub} \xrightarrow{\{5} x2_{m2}$).

(6) **Output edges from call-backs.** $s \in G'.V_{clt}$, $t \in G.V_{return}$, A is $\}_i$ for some i, and any edge labelled with $\{_i$ is an input edge to call-backs (e.g.,

$$x2_{m2} \xrightarrow{\}5} c_{pub}).$$

3. For an input edge $s_1 \xrightarrow{\{_i} t_1$ to call-backs and an output edge $s_2 \xrightarrow{\}_i} t_2$ from call-backs, there is a premise $s_1 \xrightarrow{S} t_2 \in G.P$.

The premises P should satisfy constraints 2(2) and 3. Let us consider data-dependency library graphs. We notice that only values on virtual call sites (e.g., b_{pub}, c_{pub}, d_{pub}, e_{pub}) are related to these constraints. For each parameter and the return value of a virtual call site, we create a premise with label S between them (e.g., $b_{pub} \xrightarrow{S} c_{pub}$, $d_{pub} \xrightarrow{S} e_{pub}$) to satisfy constraint 3. For each virtual call site and any of its potential targets, we create premises between their parameters and return values (e.g., $d_{pub} \xrightarrow{\{8} x3_{m3}$, $x3_{m3} \xrightarrow{\}8} e_{pub}$) to satisfy constraint 2(2). We refer to these premises as *call-back premises* and *virtual-call premises*.

Since we are only concerned with the reachability between client nodes, we only need to summarize the reachability between the boundary nodes. As a result, the conditional reachability is defined as the reachability between two boundary nodes under the condition that some pairs of boundary nodes are reachable. The conditional edge is the key concept to implement conditional reachability.

Definition 4 (Conditional Edge). *A conditional edge e is a four-tuple, (A, X, s, t), denoted as $s \xrightarrow{A|X} t$, where A is a nonterminal, X is a subset of the premises P.*

Given a conditional edge $s \xrightarrow{A|X} t$, when all edges in X are present on the graph, we consider the premises of this conditional edge as satisfied, and instantiate this conditional edge by putting a normal edge $s \xrightarrow{A} t$ on the graph (e.g., $a_{pub} \xrightarrow{S|X} e_{pub}$ $(X=\{b_{pub} \xrightarrow{S} c_{pub}, d_{pub} \xrightarrow{\{8} x3_{m3}, x3_{m3} \xrightarrow{\}8} e_{pub}\})$). Note that the premises of a conditional edge can also be an empty set, e.g., $s \xrightarrow{A|\emptyset} t$. In such cases a conditional edge is the same as a normal unconditional edge. In this paper, we do not distinguish a normal edge and a conditional edge with zero premise, and refer to them both as *unconditional edges* (e.g., $a_{pub} \xrightarrow{S|\emptyset} b_{pub}$ and $a_{pub} \xrightarrow{S} b_{pub}$ are the same unconditional edge).

With conditional edges, we can summarize a library as a set of conditional edges, where the premises of these edges represent the potential reachability relationships between the boundary nodes.

In some cases, two conditional edges may have the subsumption relationship.

Definition 5 (Edge Subsumption). $(s_1 \xrightarrow{A|X} t_1) \sqsupseteq (s_2 \xrightarrow{B|Y} t_2)$ *if and only if $A = B$, $X \subseteq Y$, $s_1 = s_2$ and $t_1 = t_2$.*

This represents that the latter edge requires additional premises compared with the former edge, and thus is completely subsumed by the former edge and can be removed from the graph.

3.2 Analyzing Libraries with ConCRA-f

We summarize the library by adding conditional edges to the graph in a way similar to the standard CFL reachability analysis. Figure 3 depicts the rules for generating conditional edges. Initially, the algorithm properly handles $G.E$ and $G.P$ as initial conditional edges. The algorithm regards each original edge $s \xrightarrow{A} t$ in $G.E$ as $s \xrightarrow{A|\emptyset} t$. The additional rule (d) handles each edge $s \xrightarrow{A} t$ in $G.P$ by adding $s \xrightarrow{A|_{\{s \xrightarrow{A} t\}}} t$ (a conditional edge that depends on exactly the same edge) to the graph. These initial conditional edges with zero or one premise are served as the starting points to generate conditional edges with more premises. Rules (a), (b), and (c) correspond to the three standard rules in Fig. 2 to generate a conditional edge $s \xrightarrow{A|X} t$. The algorithm handles A, s, and t by the standard rules. The only difference is that the algorithm sets X as the union of the premises of the concatenated conditional edges. Rules (a), (b), and (c) are the cases for zero, one, and two concatenated conditional edges, respectively. Note that the algorithm does not limit the number of premises in a conditional edge. Therefore, we denote the algorithm as ConCRA-f (The "f" means "full").

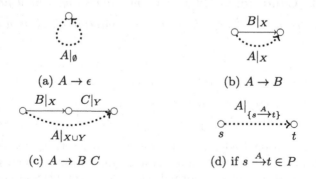

(a) $A \to \epsilon$ (b) $A \to B$

(c) $A \to B\ C$ (d) if $s \xrightarrow{A} t \in P$

Fig. 3. Rules for building conditional edges in ConCRA-f

We exhaustively apply these rules until no more edges can be added. Then we locate each (un)conditional edge connecting two boundary nodes, i.e., $e.src$ and $e.tgt$ are both in $V_{entries} \cup V_{exits}$. The set of such edges is the summary of the library. In this way we capture all reachability relationships between boundary nodes under all possible premises.

While this basic approach works, we can further optimize it in the following ways:

- In complex situations, two conditional edges e_1 and e_2, where e_1 subsumes e_2, may both be added to the graph. In such cases, we can safely remove e_2 from the graph.
- We can sort the edges in the worklist by the number of premises, so that the edges with fewer premises are created first. In this way we can ensure the subsumed edges are removed once created.

These optimizations lead to Algorithm 1. Algorithm 1 is a worklist algorithm that implements the four rules in Fig. 3 with the optimizations mentioned above. This algorithm maintains a worklist of edges W, iteratively adds each edge in W to the graph (by storing to $G.E$), and checks whether any new edge can be generated based on the current edge. Finally, the algorithm returns a set of conditional edges between boundary nodes. The first optimization is applied in line 11, where we process an edge only when there is no subsuming edge on the graph. Furthermore, the worklist W is also a priority queue on the number of the premises, ensuring that the edges with smaller number of premises are added first, implementing the second optimization.

Complexity. Let us denote the total number of premises as m, the number of symbols as l, and the number of nodes as n. Since each edge may be labelled with one of the $O(l)$ symbols and one of the $O(2^m)$ possible premises, the number of edges in a graph is $O(2^m n^2 l)$. In each iteration, we need to check the applicability of rules (a), (b), (c) for one edge and each production rule. Checking applicability of rules (a) and (b) on one edge has $O(1)$ complexity, and for rule (c), we may need to look at $O(2^m nl)$ other edges. As a result, we have a complexity of $O(2^{2m} n^3 l^3)$, exponential to the number of premises m.

3.3 Analyzing Clients

Client analysis is performed on the basis of the set of conditional edges computed by library summarization. When the client code is present, we build an application graph for the client. In the building process, we do not have to include all nodes and edges for the library graph, but include only the boundary nodes, the conditional edges between boundary nodes, and needed bridging edges. The last one is needed for the ConCRA-k analysis as explained later.

When the application graph is built, a further filtering can be performed. We remove those boundary nodes that do not connect to any client node by a direct edge. All conditional edges that connect to these nodes are also removed.

ALGORITHM 1. Analyzing libraries with ConCRA-f

Input: Γ, a context free grammar
Input: G, an library graph
Output: R, a set of conditional edges
Data: W, a priority queue of edges, where edges with smaller number of premises has higher priority

```
1  for each n in G.V do
2      for each A → ε do
3          │   W ← W ∪ {n ──A|∅──→ n} ;                        /* rule (a) */
4  for each s ──A──→ t in G.P do
5      x ← s ──A──→ t
6      W ← W ∪ {s ──A|{x}──→ t} ;                              /* rule (d) */
7  W ← W ∪ G.E
8  G.E ← ∅
9  while W is not empty do
10     (e : s ──A|X──→ t) ← the first edge in W
11     if ∀e' ∈ G.E : ¬(e' ⊒ e) then
12         G.E ← G.E ∪ {e}
13         for any B → A ∈ Γ do
14             │   W ← W ∪ {s ──B|X──→ t} ;                    /* rule (b) */
15         for any B → A C ∈ Γ ∧ t ──C|Y──→ t' ∈ G.E do
16             │   W ← W ∪ {s ──B|X∪Y──→ t'} ;                 /* rule (c) */
17         for any B → C A ∈ Γ ∧ s' ──C|Y──→ s ∈ G.E do
18             │   W ← W ∪ {s' ──B|X∪Y──→ t} ;                 /* rule (c) */
19     W ← W − {e}
20 for each e in G.E do
21     if e.src and e.tgt are both boundary nodes then
22         │   R ← R ∪ {e}
```

Client analysis with conditional edges is the same as the standard CFL reachability analysis using rules in Fig. 2, with one additional rule described in Fig. 4. This rule captures the instantiation of a conditional edge. When all premises for a conditional edge are present in the graph, we instantiate this conditional edge by adding an unconditional edge to the graph. The worklist algorithm implementing these rules is depicted in Algorithm 2.

3.4 Soundness

Theorem 1 (Soundness of ConCRA-f). *Let G be an arbitrary application graph using library G', analyzing G via the ConCRA-f summary of G' produces exactly the same set of edges between client nodes as analyzing G directly.*

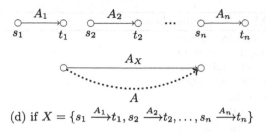

$$(d) \text{ if } X = \{s_1 \xrightarrow{A_1} t_1, s_2 \xrightarrow{A_2} t_2, \ldots, s_n \xrightarrow{A_n} t_n\}$$

Fig. 4. Additional rule for client analysis

Proof. To prove this theorem, first, we need to show that any path between two client nodes recognized by our ConCRA-f summary together with client analysis will be recognized by the Dyck-CFL. This is easy to prove as our summarization rules in Fig. 3 is a direct extension to CFL rules in Fig. 2.

Second, we need to show that any path between two client nodes recognized by the Dyck-CFL will be recognized by our ConCRA-f summary together with client analysis. This part is more difficult. Due to space limit, we shall show only how to prove this theorem for edges labelled with S. The other labels L, R, and D can be similarly proved.

The proof is an induction over the length n of the path to show the following two propositions hold, where the first one directly responds to our theorem: (1) any path with length equal or less than n between two client nodes recognized by Dyck-CFL will be recognized by client analysis; (2) any path with length equal or less than n between two library nodes recognized by Dyck-CFL will be recognized as a conditional edge in library summarization, and its premises will be produced by client analysis.

When $n = 0$, the path can only be produced by rule $S \rightarrow \epsilon$, and the two propositions trivially hold.

When $n = 1$, the path can only be produced by rule $S \rightarrow e$, or rule $S \rightarrow S\ S$ where one S on the righthand side is ϵ, and the two propositions trivially hold.

Suppose the two propositions hold for any length up to k. When length is $k + 1$, the edge can be recognized by either $S \rightarrow \{_i\ S_1\ \}_i$ or $S \rightarrow S_1\ S_2$. Let us consider $S \rightarrow \{_i\ S_1\ \}_i$ first. In the case where S is between two client nodes, S_1 can be a path between two client nodes or two library boundary nodes, but cannot be a path between one client node and a library node because of the pairing of parentheses in Definition 3. Thus, S_1 will be recognized because of induction hypothesis, and then S will be recognized.

In the case where S is between two library nodes, similarly S_1 can be a path between two client nodes or two library nodes. In the former case, S is a path between V_{call} and V_{return}, and thus is a premise itself. Also, S_1 will be recognized by client analysis because of the induction hypothesis, and thus S will be recognized. In the latter case, S_1 will be produced as a conditional edge with all its premises recognizable because of the induction hypothesis, and thus S will be recognized with all its premises recognized.

ALGORITHM 2. Analyzing clients

Input: Γ, a context free grammar
Input: G, an application graph
Input: M, a set of conditional edges
Data: W, a worklist of edges

```
1  for each n in G.V do
2  |   for each A → ε do
3  |   |   W ← W ∪ {n --A--> n} ;                        /* rule (a) */
4  W ← W ∪ G.E
5  G.E ← ∅
6  while W is not empty do
7  |   (e : s --A--> t) ← an edge in W
8  |   if e ∉ G.E then
9  |   |   G.E ← G.E ∪ {e}
10 |   |   for any B → A ∈ Γ do
11 |   |   |   W ← W ∪ {s --B--> t} ;                     /* rule (b) */
12 |   |   for any B → A C ∈ Γ ∧ t --C--> t' ∈ G.E do
13 |   |   |   W ← W ∪ {s --B--> t'} ;                    /* rule (c) */
14 |   |   for any B → C A ∈ Γ ∧ s' --C--> s ∈ G.E do
15 |   |   |   W ← W ∪ {s' --B--> t} ;                    /* rule (c) */
16 |   |   for any s' --B|X--> t' ∈ M ∧ X ⊆ G.E do
17 |   |   |   W ← W ∪ {s' --B--> t'} ;                   /* rule (d) */
18 |   |   |   M ← M − {s' --B|X--> t'}
19 |   W ← W − {e}
```

Then let us consider $S \rightarrow S_1\ S_2$. In the case where S is between two client nodes, S_1 and S_2 are also between two client nodes, otherwise the parentheses cannot be balanced. Thus, S_1 and S_2 will both be recognized by induction hypothesis, and then S will be recognized. The case where S is between two library nodes is similar.

Based on the above analysis, the two propositions hold for paths of any length, and thus the theorem holds.

3.5   Analyzing Libraries with ConCRA-k

As analyzed before, the time complexity of ConCRA-f is exponential to the number of premises, making it difficult to scale up. This time complexity is caused by the massive number of edges with different premises between two nodes. To avoid this, we can set an upper bound k on the number of the premises of each conditional edge. We denote this technique as ConCRA-k.

Now the problem is how to represent all conditional edges with only k premises. Our idea is to introduce bridging edges to represent conditional edges with more premises using conditional edges with less premises.

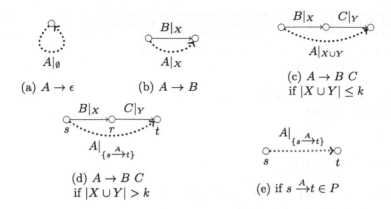

Fig. 5. Rules for building conditional edges in ConCRA-k

This idea leads to the rules in Fig. 5. The only difference from the rules in Fig. 3 is that the original rule (c) is separated into two rules (c) and (d) in Fig. 5. If the generated edge has less than or equal to k premises, the rule is the same as before (rule (c)). If the generated edge requires more than k premises, we reset its premises to one premise by introducing a new premise containing only the edge itself (rule (d)). The edges $s \xrightarrow{B|x} r$ and $r \xrightarrow{C|Y} t$ are the bridging edges of $A|_{\{s \xrightarrow{A} t\}}$.

The concrete algorithm is listed in Algorithm 3. This algorithm is mostly the same as Algorithm 1, and we only show the changed lines. The number at the left of each line in Algorithm 3 indicates the corresponding line number in the original algorithm. First, when the premises of rules (c) or (d) are satisfied (line 15 and line 17), we also record any potential dependencies in M if the generated edge has more than k premises. When we add the edge with more than k premises to the graph (line 12), we reset its premise to one. Note that we only reset premise when the edge is about to be added to the graph. In this way we can ensure that line 12 could still filter some subsumed edges. Finally, when the conditional edges between boundary nodes are selected, we perform a backtracking to add back all needed intermediate conditional edges (line 22).

Theorem 2 (Soundness of ConCRA-k). *Let G be an arbitrary application graph using library G', analyzing G via the ConCRA-k summary of G' produces exactly the same set of edges between client nodes as analyzing G directly.*

Proof. The proof of this theorem is similar to Theorem 1. The only difference is that this time we need to reason that the chain of conditional edges produced by rule 5d is complete, and this can be easily seen by examining all rules that introduce new premises.

Complexity. Let us denote the number of premises as m, the number of production rules as l, and the number of nodes as n. There are two differences

---

ALGORITHM 3. Analyzing libraries with ConCRA-k

$\cdots$

Output: M, a dictionary from intermediate conditional edges to their dependencies

$\cdots$

11 **if** $\forall e' \in G.E : \neg(e' \sqsupseteq e)$ **then**

12   **if** $|X| > k$ **then**

      $x \leftarrow (s \xrightarrow{A} t)$

      $e \leftarrow (s \xrightarrow{A|_{\{x\}}} t)$

   $G.E \leftarrow G.E \cup \{e\}$

   $\cdots$

15   **for** *any* $B \to A$ $C \in \Gamma \wedge t \xrightarrow{C|_Y} t' \in G.E$ **do**

16       $W \leftarrow W \cup \{s \xrightarrow{B|_{X \cup Y}} t'\}$;   /* rule (c), (d) */

      if $|X \cup Y| > k$ **then**

         /* *append*(k, v) **adds** v **to key** k */

         $M.append(s \xrightarrow{B} t', \{e, t \xrightarrow{C|_Y} t'\})$

17   **for** *any* $B \to C$ $A \in \Gamma \wedge s' \xrightarrow{C|_Y} s \in G.E$ **do**

18       $W \leftarrow W \cup \{s' \xrightarrow{B|_{X \cup Y}} t\}$;   /* rule (c), (d) */

      if $|X \cup Y| > k$ **then**

         $M.append(s' \xrightarrow{B} t, \{s' \xrightarrow{C|_Y} s, e\})$

   $\cdots$

22 $R \leftarrow$ AddDependencies(R)

---

from ConCRA-f. First, since any newly added edges may have its premises reset, we need to consider $m + n^2 l$ rather than just m. Second, there is only $C^k_{m+n^2 l}$ possible sets of premises. As a result, we have a complexity of $O((C^k_{m+n^2 l})^2 n^3 l^3)$. This complexity is much smaller than ConCRA-f with a small k. For example, we have a polynomial complexity when $k = 1$.

4 Empirical Evaluation

This section empirically evaluates the proposed techniques.

4.1 Evaluated Analyses

Our evaluation is based on the same context-sensitive, SSA-based, and field-insensitive dependency analysis used in evaluating TALCRA [39] so that we can compare with TALCRA. More concretely, we track the flows-to relations (the inverse of dependency relations) between stack variables; we treat each variable as a node and an assignment x=y as an edge from y to x; a method call z=x.f(y) corresponds to a left-parenthesis edge from y to the argument of x.f() and a right-parenthesis edge from the return value to z (The call site determines the index of the parenthesis). We refer to a parenthesis edge as a call edge.

Procedure AddDependencies(E)

```
1  for each s  --A|X-->  t ∈ E do
2  |   W ← W ∪ X
3  end
4  while W is not empty do
5  |   e ← an edge in W
6  |   if M contains e then
   |       /* lookup(e) returns the dependencies of e          */
7  |       for each e' = s'  --A'|X'-->  t' ∈ M.lookup(e) do
8  |       |   E ← E ∪ {e'}
9  |       |   W ← W ∪ X'
10 |       end
11 |   end
12 |   W ← W − {e}
13 end
14 return E
```

A virtual-call edge is a call edge belonging to a virtual call site. Our example in Fig. 1 demonstrates the graph used in this analysis.

To summarize a library for this analysis, we need to provide the set of premises $G.P$. $G.P$ obtains *call-back premises* and *virtual-call premises* as we mentioned in Sect. 3. Note that TALCRA does not support the latter type of premises, so we also evaluate our techniques on the configuration where each virtual-call edge in the library is treated as a normal edge. Therefore, the evaluation contains two configurations: (1) *VC-config*: virtual-call edges are reserved as premises in the library graph; (2) *CHA-config*: virtual-call edges are treated as normal edges in the library graph. *CHA-config* library summaries are imprecise because the virtual-call edges generated by imprecise library call graph construction approaches (e.g., class hierarchy analysis) are treated as normal edges.

4.2   Implementation

Our implementation has two parts. The first part, implemented in Java using the SOOT framework[1], generates the dependency graphs and exports the graphs to files. The virtual call sites are resolved by CHA [5] in the library analysis, and are resolved by Spark [14] in the client analysis. The virtual-call premises are those produced by CHA. The second part, implemented in C++, reads the files and performs the library summarization and client analysis of ConCRA, TAL-CRA, as well as CLA [31]. We obtained the newest TALCRA implementation from TALCRA web site[2]. We reimplemented CLA to use CFL reachability as summary representation, rather than the original functional approach. Bascially,

---

[1] http://sable.github.io/soot/.

[2] http://www.utdallas.edu/%7elxz144130/tal.html, accessed 2016-01-29.

there are two differences with CLA and ConCRA: (1) CLA does not use premises and only summarizes unconditional edges between boundary nodes; (2) Boundary nodes used by CLA include not only boundary nodes used by ConCRA, but also the call-site nodes to procedures that may (transitively) call a virtual call.

We adopt several efficient data structures in library summarization and client analysis. The worklist W for ConCRA-k and ConCRA-f is segregated into several sets $W_1, W_2, \cdots$. All newly-generated conditional edges with i premises are put into W_i. The first edge returned by W is thus always an edge in the non-empty W_i with the smallest i. Each conditional edge $s \xrightarrow{A|x} t$ added into $G.E$ is indexed by $\langle A, s \rangle$, $\langle A, t \rangle$ using 2-dimensional arrays, and $\langle A, s, t \rangle$ using a 2-dimensional array of hash tables. The two arrays are used for efficiently acquiring the edges with specific labels and common source or target nodes. The array of hash tables is used to check whether an edge e is subsumed (Definition 5) by other edge e'.

We also implemented a standard whole-program CFL reachability analysis as a control technique.

4.3 Setup

Benchmark. Our benchmark includes all 12 subjects in the SPECjvm2008[3] benchmark. The SPECjvm benchmark was widely used in evaluating the state-of-art library-summarization work [39] as well as many related approaches in the program analysis area [36,37,41,42].

In our evaluation, we treat JDK as library and build summaries for a major portion of JDK. More specifically, we build summaries for two JAR files, rt.jar and jce.jar, which include most commonly used Java packages, such as java.util, java.io, java.lang, etc. Summarizing a popular portion of the library instead of the whole library is a common practice used in existing evaluation on summarization techniques [1,17,32] to reduce the summarization time.

Table 1 shows the statistics. Columns 1 lists all the benchmark subjects. Columns 2–4 show the numbers of client nodes, the library nodes accessed by the client, and all nodes in each subject's data dependency graph[4]. Similarly, Columns 5–7 present the Jimple code lines of the client, the library methods called by the client, and the whole application for each subject. Here the library nodes and library code refer to only the part of JDK in our summary.

Table 2 shows the information about summarized part of JDK including the Jimple code lines, the size of the dependency graph, and the two types of premises. Jimple is the fundamental intermediate representation of Java in Soot. We use the lines of Jimple code instead of Java source code because we do not have full Java source code for the benchmark. Based on our experience with

---

[3] http://www.spec.org/jvm2008/.

[4] Please note the statistics are different from the TALCRA paper [39] because that evaluation was performed on an early version of the TALCRA tool that built the graph differently.

Table 1. Benchmark statistics

Bench.	# Nodes			# Jimple code lines		
	Clt	Lib	Total	Clt	Lib	Total
check	1701	10838	12539	7752	160078	167830
compiler	917	10699	11616	4184	160042	164226
compress	1428	10576	12004	5025	160042	165067
crypto	2515	19002	21517	11547	229158	240705
derby	1380	16722	18102	10189	210054	220243
hello	598	10881	11479	847	160042	160889
mpeg	17588	37980	55568	243007	402569	645576
scimark	1557	10709	12266	7034	160042	167076
serial	11509	38419	49928	187517	407990	595507
startup	1083	16512	17595	2472	200060	202532
sunflow	19021	26606	45627	139362	283016	422378
xml	11749	23444	35193	122631	268431	391062
Total	71046	232388	303434	741567	2801524	3543091

JDK, the Jimple code lines are about 4 times as many as the original source code, excluding comments and empty lines.

Table 2. Library statistics

Jimple code lines	526648
Dependency graph nodes	66736
Dependency graph edges	161239
Virtual call premises	64777
Call-back premises	10236

Compared Techniques. On both *CHA-config* and *VC-config*, we evaluated ConCRA-f and ConCRA-k (with k values between 1 and 5) techniques, as well as a standard CFL-reachability analysis and the CLA technique [31]. Moreover, on the *CHA-config*, we evaluated the state-of-art TALCRA technique [39].

To evaluate the effectiveness of each studied technique, we measured the time cost for each technique in both library summarization and client analysis. Furthermore, we evaluated the precision of client analysis by measuring the produced dependency edges.

Evaluation Platform. Our evaluation was performed on a Dell PowerEdge R730 Server with 8-core 16-thread Intel(R) Xeon(R) CPU E5-2640 v2 @ 2.00 GHz and 256 Gigabyte RAM running OpenJDK 1.7.0_79 on Ubuntu 14.10.

4.4 ConCRA-f/ConCRA-k vs. TALCRA

On the *CHA-config*, we compare our techniques against TALCRA.

The results of library summarization are shown in Table 3. Columns 1 to 5 list the library summarization statistics of CLA, TALCRA, ConCRA-1, ConCRA-2, and ConCRA-f, respectively. Row 2 shows the summarization time. Row 2 also lists the speedup information compared with the CLA technique in Columns 2 to 5. Row 3 shows the maximal memory usage during the summarization. We omit the results of ConCRA-k ($k = 3, 4, 5$) because they are almost identical to the result of ConCRA-f.

Table 3. Library summarization (*CHA-config*)

CLA	TALCRA	ConCRA-1	ConCRA-2	ConCRA-f
72.50s	87.78s 0.83X	45.33s 1.60X	63.30s 1.15X	71.79s 1.01X
1.45G	3.66G	5.15G	6.81G	7.39G

The experimental results of client analysis are shown in Table 4. In the table, Column 1 lists all the benchmark subjects. Column 2 presents the time cost for the standard CFL reachability analysis on the entire application graph (including all the client and library nodes) as the control technique. Column 3 presents the client analysis time for the CLA approach. Column 4 presents the client analysis time for the TALCRA approach. Columns 5 to 7 present the corresponding client analysis time for our ConCRA-k ($k = 1, 2$) and ConCRA-f techniques. Columns 4 to 7 also contains the speedup information compared with the standard CFL reachability analysis. The last row presents the arithmetic mean of speedups on all subjects achieved by these techniques. Again, we omit the results of ConCRA-k ($k = 3, 4, 5$) because the results are very close to ConCRA-f's (less than 8% variation).

Library Summarization. To summarize the JDK library, ConCRA-f and ConCRA-k are both faster than TALCRA. Compared with the TALCRA approach, ConCRA-1, ConCRA-2, and ConCRA-f have 1.93X, 1.39X, and 1.22X speed-up, respectively. We can observe that the library summarization time grows when k increases, and the time is close to ConCRA-f when $k > 2$. The reason is that the conditional edges with more than 2 premises in the summary of ConCRA-f only account for 26.4% (9,070,850 out of 34,363,200) of the summary. This finding also explains why our techniques are practical despite the high theoretical complexity upper bound analyzed in Sect. 3. The overall amount of conditional edges (34,363,200) is reasonable in practice.

Client Analysis. Compared to standard CFL technique, all the ConCRA implementations significantly reduce the client analysis time. Across all subjects, ConCRA-1 speeds up the client analysis time by 3.34X to 46.45X, with an arithmetic mean of 14.10X. Our ConCRA implementations also outperform TALCRA with speedups up to 5.04X.

Table 4. Client analysis for *CHA-config* (run times in milliseconds)

Benchmark	CFL	CLA		TALCRA		ConCRA-1		ConCRA-2		ConCRA-f	
check	433	397	1.09X	303	1.43X	82	5.29X	84	5.14X	85	5.09X
compiler	401	380	1.06X	274	1.46X	80	5.01X	80	5.00X	80	5.03X
compress	412	399	1.03X	290	1.42X	98	4.21X	94	4.37X	94	4.40X
crypto	4058	1820	2.23X	468	8.68X	101	40.18X	105	38.70X	102	39.63X
derby	4121	1486	2.77X	430	9.59X	96	42.97X	96	43.11X	94	43.94X
helloworld	400	390	1.02X	270	1.48X	75	5.32X	76	5.27X	76	5.26X
mpegaudio	623527	518671	1.20X	253623	2.46X	154986	4.02X	154384	4.04X	154580	4.03X
scimark	444	417	1.06X	306	1.45X	104	4.26X	106	4.18X	105	4.24X
serial	619523	518384	1.20X	247012	2.51X	151562	4.09X	151937	4.08X	151478	4.09X
startup	3745	1523	2.46X	406	9.21X	81	46.45X	84	44.62X	84	44.39X
sunflow	21675	33741	0.64X	12843	1.69X	5292	4.10X	5290	4.10X	5265	4.12X
xml	9361	7291	1.28X	3566	2.62X	2799	3.34X	2835	3.30X	2801	3.34X
			1.42X		3.67X		14.10X		13.83X		13.96X

Interestingly, ConCRA-f and ConCRA-k with a large k do not exhibit superiority over ConCRA-1. We suspect that there are two possible reasons: (1) larger k leads to larger summaries, and the memory management time increases significantly; (2) there is only a few number of instantiated conditional edges that has many premises, so the performance boost from larger k is not significant.

4.5 ConCRA-f/ConCRA-k vs. CLA

On the *VC-config*, we compare our techniques against CLA.

The results of library summarization are shown in Table 5, in the same format as Table 3. Columns 1 to 4 list the library summarization statistics of CLA, ConCRA-1, ConCRA-2, and ConCRA-f, respectively. All of ConCRA-k with $k = 3, 4, 5$ and ConCRA-f fail to build summaries on the *VC-config* within the 2-hour time limit.

Table 5. Library summarization (*VC-config*)

CLA	ConCRA-1	ConCRA-2	ConCRA-f
0.40s	34.74s 0.01X	1059.61s 0.00X	TimeOut
0.26G	5.34G	32.71G	-

The results of client analysis are shown in Table 6. The meaning of Column 1 to 2 are same as in Table 4. Column 3 presents the client analysis time for the CLA approach. Columns 4 to 5 present the corresponding client analysis time for our ConCRA-k ($k = 1, 2$) techniques.

Library Summarization. ConCRA-1 and ConCRA-2 spends more time than CLA, since ConCRA calculates a more complete summary than CLA does.

Table 6. Client analysis for *VC-config* (run times in milliseconds)

Benchmark	CFL	CLA		ConCRA-1		ConCRA-2	
check	433	142	3.05X	137	3.16X	770	0.56X
compiler	401	139	2.88X	157	2.55X	728	0.55X
compress	412	149	2.77X	225	1.83X	954	0.43X
crypto	4058	1079	3.76X	151	26.94X	356	11.40X
derby	4121	1040	3.96X	120	34.23X	153	26.93X
helloworld	400	137	2.91X	77	5.21X	83	4.80X
mpegaudio	623527	340015	1.83X	167021	3.73X	169673	3.67X
scimark	444	167	2.66X	246	1.81X	986	0.45X
serial	619523	334689	1.85X	165408	3.75X	166616	3.72X
startup	3745	988	3.79X	239	15.70X	2978	1.26X
sunflow	21675	10844	2.00X	4755	4.56X	8183	2.65X
xml	9361	4724	1.98X	3164	2.96X	6496	1.44X
		2.79X		8.87X		4.82X	

ConCRA-1 can finish summarization in less than 1 min. ConCRA-2 spends much more time than ConCRA-1, since the introduction of virtual call premises significantly enlarges the set of premises, causing ConCRA-2 to consider much more potential combinations of premises than ConCRA-1.

Client Analysis. Compared to standard CFL technique, ConCRA-1 speeds up the client analysis time significantly with an arithmetic mean of 8.87X. ConCRA-1 also achieves an average speedup about 3 times as high as CLA does. ConCRA-1 is slightly slower than CLA on a few subjects (compiler, compress, and scimark). We can observe these subjects are relatively small, which caused the memory management became bottleneck in the analysis.

ConCRA-2 does not perform as well as ConCRA-1, and on some subjects, it is even slower than the whole-program CFL technique. The summary ConCRA-2 calculates is so large that the overhead of memory management time becomes prominent in client analysis. This finding indicates that ConCRA-1 has the overall best performance on the data dependency analysis in our evaluation.

4.6   Precision

As we analyzed before, techniques on the *VC-config* should be as precise as the standard CFL reachability analysis while techniques on the *CHA-config* may be imprecise due to the missing client information. In our evaluation, we count the number of dependency edges produced by each algorithm, and we also compare the analysis results against each other algorithm.

Table 7 shows client results about precision. Column 2 presents the number of dependencies found by standard CFL reachability analysis on the entire application graph. Column 3 presents the number of dependencies found on the *CHA-config* and its precision compared to CFL results. Column 4 stands for the *VC-config*. The precision is calculated by dividing the number from CFL analysis with the number from the respective analysis.

There are two major findings. First, the dependency relations produced by techniques on the *VC-config* are the same as those produced by the standard CFL analysis, and both are a subset of the dependency relations produced by techniques on the *CHA-config*. This serves as a side evidence that our implementation is correct. Second, the results by techniques on the *CHA-config* are imprecise. On some subjects, the precision can be as low as 80.20%.

Table 7. Analysis precision

Benchmark	CFL	*CHA-config* (CLA, TALCRA, ConCRA)	*VC-config* (CLA, ConCRA)
check	2012	2012(100.00%)	2012(100.00%)
compiler	764	836(91.39%)	764(100.00%)
compress	9729	9801(99.27%)	9729(100.00%)
crypto	4593	5197(88.38%)	4593(100.00%)
derby	7166	7180(99.81%)	7166(100.00%)
helloworld	329	337(97.63%)	329(100.00%)
mpegaudio	2713173	2793994(97.11%)	2713173(100.00%)
scimark	16028	16100(99.55%)	16028(100.00%)
serial	2479497	2551066(97.19%)	2479497(100.00%)
startup	840	841(99.88%)	840(100.00%)
sunflow	407547	508150(80.20%)	407547(100.00%)
xml	554780	555576(99.86%)	554780(100.00%)

In conclusion, both ConCRA-f and ConCRA-k are able to achieve speedups over the state-of-art TALCRA technique on the *CHA-config*. They significantly outperform traditional CFL technique for client analysis (e.g. ConCRA-1 and ConCRA-f can achieve speedups of up to 46.45X and 44.39X, respectively). They also achieve speedups up to 5.04X compared to TALCRA. In case of the *VC-config*, ConCRA-1 achieves significant speedups over the standard CFL technique for client analysis up to 34.23X, without precision loss. ConCRA-1 also generally outperforms the CLA technique.

5   Discussion

Multiple Library Summaries. For the simplicity of the evaluation, we treat the JDK implementation as the library code and all the other code and third-party libraries of each subject as the client code. However, our approach supports the client code analysis with multiple library summaries. For example, for client code c using two external libraries (l_1 and l_2). The client code analysis of c can be directly built on top of the two separate library summaries by simply collecting all conditional edges. We can even combine the two summaries into a large summary by assuming virtual-call premises between them and apply the library summarization rules.

Field Sensitivity. Following existing work for conditional reachability analysis [39], we also evaluate our approach based on the context-sensitive, flow-sensitive, and field-insensitive data-dependency analysis. Field-sensitivity can also be encoded as a CFL reachability problem. However, achieving both context-sensitive and field-sensitive analysis has been shown to be undecidable [26]. To maintain both sensitivity to some extent, researchers have proposed to use regular language to approximate one CFL and keep the other one complete [37]. Our conditional reachability analysis based on CFL provides a natural way to adapt existing technique to further obtain field sensitivity to some extent. For example, we can regularize the CFL for field sensitivity (i.e., RL_f) and keep the CFL for context sensitivity (i.e., CFL_c). Therefore, data-dependency analysis considering both sensitivity can be approximated as the CFL-reachability problem using $RL_f \cap CFL_c$. Then, we may still use our conditional reachability analysis based on CFL to obtain library summary information to speed up client analysis. Furthermore, in parallel with our work, Zhang and Su [45] recently proposed an efficient algorithm based on linear-conjunctive-language reachability for solving context-sensitive and field-sensitive data dependence analysis. The idea of conditional reachability may also be applied to their approach, which is a future work remaining to be explored.

Heap Objects and Global Variables. A standard way to handle heap objects in dependence graphs is to promote them to the input and output of respective methods by interprocedural mod-ref analysis. Existing tools such as WALA can directly generate such graphs (system dependence graph with heap paramters). However, this kind of graphs cannot be directly summarized by our approach because heap objects and global variables defined in the clients may need to promote to the library side. A possible solution is to assume the promoted nodes and edges are part of the client graph. First we analyze library without the promoted nodes and edges from the clients. Then when a client is available, we analyze the precise boundary between the library and the client, and turn the library analysis result into a summary. The concrete algorithm is a future work to be explored.

6   Related Work

Our work is mainly related to existing research efforts on conditional analysis, CFL reachability, and software library summarization.

6.1   Conditional Analysis

Our analysis differs from normal reachability analysis because our analysis further takes into account the conditions under which a code element can reach another code element. In this sense, our research is related to existing research efforts on conditional data dependency and information flow. Snelting et al. [35] proposed a technique to extract conditions defined on program input variables that must hold for certain data dependency in the program under analysis. Komondoor and Ramalingam [11] proposed to identify conditional data dependency for recovery of data models in programs written with weakly-typed languages. Sukumaran et al. [38] proposed to extend the program dependency graph with conditions on the edges to specify the corresponding condition of a certain dependency edge. Tschantz and Wing [40] developed a technique that detects not only active but also passive conditional information flows to extract confidentiality policies from software programs. Lochbihler and Snelting [15] further considered data dependency controlled by temporal path conditions. Recently, Jaffar et al. [9] proposed path-sensitive backward slicing that considers path conditions when locating code elements that may affect certain program outputs. The conditions considered in the above research efforts are all path conditions in branch predicates. In contrast, the conditions considered in our approach are reachability relationships between code elements.

Conditional must-not-alias analysis [19] calculates whether a pair of variables must not refer to a same memory location when another pair of variables do not refer to a same memory location. This analysis is first used to detect race conditions [19], and later in accelerating CFL-reachability-based points-to analysis [42]. Similar to conditional must-not-alias analysis, our approach also considers the reachability relationship between variables as conditions. However, since the purpose of our approach is different (i.e., summarizing library code with unknown components), we use as conditions the reachability relationships at the library-client interface that are not available at the time of summarization, and we further consider conditional reachability with multiple premises, neither of which are covered in conditional must-not-alias analysis.

6.2   CFL Reachability

CFL reachability is a general framework developed in the area of database by Yannakakis [43], and Reps et al. [28] first applied the framework to inter-procedural slicing. Later, the framework is applied to a series of program analysis tasks, including inter-procedural dataflow analysis [20,23,27], points-to analysis [37,42], alias analysis [44,47], shape analysis [8,24,30], constant propagation [34], label-flow analysis [20], information flow analysis [16,18], race detection [21], and specification inference [2]. In 1998, Reps [25] wrote a survey on the application of CFL reachability on various program analysis tasks.

Similar to us, the IDE framework [34] also attaches additional information to the graph. This framework is designed to problems such as constant propagation, where the "environment information", such as the values of variables, is attached to each node. Later, Reps et al. [29] proposed a novel data flow analysis framework based on reachability analysis of pushdown automata which allows adding weights to the edges of pushdown automata. Compared to these approaches, our approach attaches conditional information to the edges, and solves the library summarization problem with the conditional edges.

6.3 Library Summarization

The main purpose of our proposed technique is to summarize libraries with consideration of unknown components from client side, which is one of the emerging but not well-solved problem in static analysis. In literature, we notice several existing research efforts that try to address unknown components (e.g., callbacks) when summarizing library code.

Rountev et al. [31,33] proposed a technique to accelerate dataflow analysis by summarizing library code. Madhaven et al. [17] developed a general framework to deal with unknown components in library summarization. Arzt et al. [1] applies Rountev et al.'s technique [33] to taint analysis on Android applications. These approaches identify the part of the library code that is not affected by the unknown components, and build a partial summary for this part of library code. Compared to these approaches, ConCRA is able to generate summaries (i.e., in the form of conditional reachability) for the code affected by unknown components. Lattner et al. [13] proposed a heap-cloning-based approach to context-sensitive summarization of libraries with call-backs for pointer analysis. This approach is in principle similar to Rountev et al. [31,33] and Madhaven et al. [17], but is specifically tuned for pointer analysis. Furthermore, their approach is tightly coupled with the problem of pointer analysis, and cannot be easily migrated to other problems, whereas ConCRA is able to be applied on a large class of problem using Dyck-CFL reachability analysis.

Other research efforts eliminate unknown components by make the most conservative assumptions on them. Ravitch et al. [22] developed a technique to automatically generate bindings for inter-programming language function calls. Bastani et al. [2] deals with a related but different problem. Instead of building library summaries for client analysis, they deal with the case where the library code is missing, and try to infer a specification of the library code for manual revision. Das et al. [4] proposed angelic verification to handle unknown external function calls in program verification.

The work most closely related to our approach is by Tang et al. [39]. As mentioned before, they proposed the TAL (Tree Adjoining Language) reachability, and a summarization technique based on TAL reachability. TAL is a class of languages that can be generated by production rules over two strings, rather than CFL whose production rules are over one string, and the two strings can be viewed as two separated paths that can be connected by a premise. Because the types of premises are confined by TAL, it is not easy to extend this approach to support multiple premises and more types of premises. Furthermore, in the TALCRA, a technique called chaining nodes is used, whose effect is similar to our ConCRA-1 analysis. However, they require a separate algorithm to identify chaining nodes, in contrast that our approach generates the bridging edges naturally within one pass. Because of this separation, TALCRA may generate more "bridging edges" than necessary and can remove them only after the identification of chaining nodes, on the other hand our approach would not generate extra bridging edges and is thus more efficient. Moreover, our approach also allows to be adapted to ConCRA-k with any k, which is not supported by TALCRA.

There have been some other recent advancements on library code summarization. Dillig et al. [6] proposed a flow-sensitive memory-safety analysis, in which they used library summarization, and considered strong updates in the summary building process. Kulkarni et al. [12] proposed to learn summaries from a training corpus to accelerate the analysis of other programs that share code with the corpus. In constract to our approach, they require the developers to write a check function for each analysis to determine the soundness of the summary with respect to the current analysis task. Zhu et al. [48] proposed to infer information-flow specifications of library code by analyzing the client code. However, these specifications need to be manually verified against library documents to ensure correctness. Zhang et al. [46] proposed a general framework to hybrid top-down and bottom-up analysis. In their analysis, bottom-up analysis and top-down analysis can complement each other to achieve better performance. None of the above four approaches support automatic summarization of library code with unknown components.

7   Conclusion

In this paper, we demonstrate that by directly extending CFL-reachability analysis rules with premises, we can turn a standard CFL-reachability analysis into a conditional summarization approach with client analysis, and this approach is more efficient and more general than existing summarization techniques based on the dedicated TAL-reachability analysis. We believe that this approach indicates the potential existence of a more generic method to extend existing analysis techniques into a library summarization technique. This is a future direction to be explored.

Acknowledgement. This work is supported by the National Key Research and Development Program under Grant No. 2016YFB1000105, and the National Natural Science Foundation of China under Grant Nos. 61421091, 61225007, 61672045.

References

1. Arzt, S., Bodden, E.: Stubdroid: automatic inference of precise data-flow summaries for the android framework. In: Proceedings of ICSE, pp. 725–735 (2016)
2. Bastani, O., Anand, S., Aiken, A.: Specification inference using context-free language reachability. In: Proceedings of POPL, pp. 553–566 (2015)
3. Cousot, P., Cousot, R.: Modular static program analysis. In: Horspool, R.N. (ed.) CC 2002. LNCS, vol. 2304, pp. 159–179. Springer, Heidelberg (2002). doi:10.1007/3-540-45937-5_13

4. Das, A., Lahiri, S.K., Lal, A., Li, Y.: Angelic verification: precise verification modulo unknowns. In: Kroening, D., Păsăreanu, C.S. (eds.) CAV 2015. LNCS, vol. 9206, pp. 324–342. Springer, Heidelberg (2015). doi:10.1007/978-3-319-21690-4_19

5. Dean, J., Grove, D., Chambers, C.: Optimization of object-oriented programs using static class hierarchy analysis. In: Tokoro, M., Pareschi, R. (eds.) ECOOP 1995. LNCS, vol. 952, pp. 77–101. Springer, Heidelberg (1995). doi:10.1007/3-540-49538-X_5

6. Dillig, I., Dillig, T., Aiken, A., Sagiv, M.: Precise and compact modular procedure summaries for heap manipulating programs. In: Proceedings of PLDI, pp. 567–577 (2011)

7. Hind, M.: Pointer analysis: haven't we solved this problem yet? In: Proceedings of PASTE, pp. 54–61 (2001)

8. Itzhaky, S., Bjørner, N., Reps, T., Sagiv, M., Thakur, A.: Property-directed shape analysis. In: Biere, A., Bloem, R. (eds.) CAV 2014. LNCS, vol. 8559, pp. 35–51. Springer, Heidelberg (2014). doi:10.1007/978-3-319-08867-9_3

9. Jaffar, J., Murali, V., Navas, J.A., Santosa, A.E.: Path-sensitive backward slicing. In: Miné, A., Schmidt, D. (eds.) SAS 2012. LNCS, vol. 7460, pp. 231–247. Springer, Heidelberg (2012). doi:10.1007/978-3-642-33125-1_17

10. Kodumal, J., Aiken, A.: The set constraint/CFL reachability connection in practice. In: Proceedings of PLDI, pp. 207–218 (2004)

11. Komondoor, R., Ramalingam, G.: Recovering data models via guarded dependences. In: Proceedings of WCRE, pp. 110–119 (2007)

12. Kulkarni, S., Mangal, R., Zhang, X., Naik, M.: Accelerating program analyses by cross-program training. In: Proceedings of OOPSLA, pp. 359–377 (2016)

13. Lattner, C., Lenharth, A., Adve, V.: Making context-sensitive points-to analysis with heap cloning practical for the real world. In: Proceedings of PLDI, pp. 278–289 (2007)

14. Lhoták, O., Hendren, L.: Scaling Java points-to analysis using spark. In: Hedin, G. (ed.) CC 2003. LNCS, vol. 2622, pp. 153–169. Springer, Heidelberg (2003). doi:10.1007/3-540-36579-6_12

15. Lochbihler, A., Snelting, G.: On temporal path conditions in dependence graphs. ASE 16(2), 263–290 (2009)

16. Macedo, H.D., Touili, T.: Mining malware specifications through static reachability analysis. In: Crampton, J., Jajodia, S., Mayes, K. (eds.) ESORICS 2013. LNCS, vol. 8134, pp. 517–535. Springer, Heidelberg (2013). doi:10.1007/978-3-642-40203-6_29

17. Madhavan, R., Ramalingam, G., Vaswani, K.: Modular heap analysis for higher-order programs. In: Miné, A., Schmidt, D. (eds.) SAS 2012. LNCS, vol. 7460, pp. 370–387. Springer, Heidelberg (2012). doi:10.1007/978-3-642-33125-1_25

18. Milanova, A., Huang, W., Dong, Y.: CFL-reachability and context-sensitive integrity types. In: Proceedings of PPPJ, pp. 99–109 (2014)

19. Naik, M., Aiken, A.: Conditional must not aliasing for static race detection. In: Proceedings of POPL, pp. 327–338 (2007)

20. Pratikakis, P., Foster, J.S., Hicks, M.: Existential label flow inference via CFL reachability. In: Yi, K. (ed.) SAS 2006. LNCS, vol. 4134, pp. 88–106. Springer, Heidelberg (2006). doi:10.1007/11823230_7

21. Pratikakis, P., Foster, J.S., Hicks, M.W.: LOCKSMITH: context-sensitive correlation analysis for race detection. In: Proceedings of PLDI, pp. 320–331 (2006)

22. Ravitch, T., Jackson, S., Aderhold, E., Liblit, B.: Automatic generation of library bindings using static analysis. In: Proceedings of PLDI, pp. 352–362 (2009)

23. Rehof, J., Fähndrich, M.: Type-based flow analysis: from polymorphic subtyping to CFL-reachability. In: Proceedings of POPL, pp. 54–66 (2001)

24. Reps, T.: Shape analysis as a generalized path problem. In: Proceedings of PEPM, pp. 1–11 (1995)
25. Reps, T.: Program analysis via graph reachability. Inf. Softw. Technol. **40**(11–12), 701–726 (1998)
26. Reps, T.: Undecidability of context-sensitive data-dependence analysis. TOPLAS **22**(1), 162–186 (2000)
27. Reps, T., Horwitz, S., Sagiv, M.: Precise interprocedural dataflow analysis via graph reachability. In: Proceedings of POPL, pp. 49–61 (1995)
28. Reps, T., Horwitz, S., Sagiv, M., Rosay, G.: Speeding up slicing. In: Proceedings of FSE, pp. 11–20 (1994)
29. Reps, T., Schwoon, S., Jha, S.: Weighted pushdown systems and their application to interprocedural dataflow analysis. In: Cousot, R. (ed.) SAS 2003. LNCS, vol. 2694, pp. 189–213. Springer, Heidelberg (2003). doi:10.1007/3-540-44898-5_11
30. Rinetzky, N., Poetzsch-Heffter, A., Ramalingam, G., Sagiv, M., Yahav, E.: Modular shape analysis for dynamically encapsulated programs. In: Nicola, R. (ed.) ESOP 2007. LNCS, vol. 4421, pp. 220–236. Springer, Heidelberg (2007). doi:10.1007/978-3-540-71316-6_16
31. Rountev, A., Kagan, S., Marlowe, T.: Interprocedural dataflow analysis in the presence of large libraries. In: Mycroft, A., Zeller, A. (eds.) CC 2006. LNCS, vol. 3923, pp. 2–16. Springer, Heidelberg (2006). doi:10.1007/11688839_2
32. Rountev, A., Ryder, B.G.: Points-to and side-effect analyses for programs built with precompiled libraries. In: Wilhelm, R. (ed.) CC 2001. LNCS, vol. 2027, pp. 20–36. Springer, Heidelberg (2001). doi:10.1007/3-540-45306-7_3
33. Rountev, A., Sharp, M., Xu, G.: IDE dataflow analysis in the presence of large object-oriented libraries. In: Hendren, L. (ed.) CC 2008. LNCS, vol. 4959, pp. 53–68. Springer, Heidelberg (2008). doi:10.1007/978-3-540-78791-4_4
34. Sagiv, M., Reps, T., Horwitz, S.: Precise interprocedural dataflow analysis with applications to constant propagation. Theor. Comput. Sci. **167**(1–2), 131–170 (1996)
35. Snelting, G., Robschink, T., Krinke, J.: Efficient path conditions in dependence graphs for software safety analysis. TOSEM **15**(4), 410–457 (2006)
36. Sridharan, M., Gopan, D., Shan, L., Bodík, R.: Demand-driven points-to analysis for Java. In: Proceedings of OOPSLA, pp. 57–76 (2005)
37. Sridharan, M., Bodík, R.: Refinement-based context-sensitive points-to analysis for Java. In: Proceedings of PLDI, pp. 387–400 (2006)
38. Sukumaran, S., Sreenivas, A., Metta, R.: The dependence condition graph: precise conditions for dependence between program points. Comput. Lang. Syst. Struct. **36**(1), 96–121 (2010)
39. Tang, H., Wang, X., Zhang, L., Xie, B., Zhang, L., Mei, H.: Summary-based context-sensitive data-dependence analysis in presence of callbacks. In: Proceedings of POPL, pp. 83–95 (2015)
40. Tschantz, M.C., Wing, J.M.: Extracting conditional confidentiality policies. In: Proceedings of SEFM, pp. 107–116 (2008)
41. Xu, G., Rountev, A.: Merging equivalent contexts for scalable heap-cloning-based context-sensitive points-to analysis. In: Proceedings of ISSTA, pp. 225–235 (2008)
42. Xu, G., Rountev, A., Sridharan, M.: Scaling CFL-reachability-based points-to analysis using context-sensitive must-not-alias analysis. In: Drossopoulou, S. (ed.) ECOOP 2009. LNCS, vol. 5653, pp. 98–122. Springer, Heidelberg (2009). doi:10.1007/978-3-642-03013-0_6
43. Yannakakis, M.: Graph-theoretic methods in database theory. In: Proceedings of PODS, pp. 230–242 (1990)

44. Zhang, Q., Lyu, M.R., Yuan, H., Su, Z.: Fast algorithms for Dyck-CFL reachability with applications to alias analysis. In: Proceedings of PLDI, pp. 435–446 (2013)
45. Zhang, Q., Su, Z.: Context-sensitive data-dependence analysis via linear conjunctive language reachability. In: Proceedings of POPL, pp. 344–358 (2017)
46. Zhang, X., Mangal, R., Naik, M., Yang, H.: Hybrid top-down and bottom-up interprocedural analysis. In: Proceedings of PLDI, pp. 249–258 (2014)
47. Zheng, X., Rugina, R.: Demand-driven alias analysis for C. In: Proceedings of POPL, pp. 351–363 (2008)
48. Zhu, H., Dillig, T., Dillig, I.: Automated inference of library specifications for source-sink property verification. In: Shan, C. (ed.) APLAS 2013. LNCS, vol. 8301, pp. 290–306. Springer, Heidelberg (2013). doi:10.1007/978-3-319-03542-0_21

A Higher-Order Logic for Concurrent Termination-Preserving Refinement

Joseph Tassarotti[1(✉)], Ralf Jung[2(✉)], and Robert Harper[1(✉)]

[1] Carnegie Mellon University, Pittsburgh, USA
jtassaro@andrew.cmu.edu, rwh@cs.cmu.edu
[2] MPI-SWS, Saarland Informatics Campus, Saarbrücken, Germany
rwh@cs.cmu.edu

Abstract. Compiler correctness proofs for higher-order concurrent languages are difficult: they involve establishing a termination-preserving refinement between a *concurrent* high-level source language and an implementation that uses low-level shared memory primitives. However, existing logics for proving concurrent refinement either neglect properties such as termination, or only handle first-order state. In this paper, we address these limitations by extending Iris, a recent higher-order concurrent separation logic, with support for reasoning about termination-preserving refinements. To demonstrate the power of these extensions, we prove the correctness of an efficient implementation of a higher-order, session-typed language. To our knowledge, this is the first program logic capable of giving a compiler correctness proof for such a language. The soundness of our extensions and our compiler correctness proof have been mechanized in Coq.

1 Introduction

Parallelism and concurrency impose great challenges on both programmers and compilers. In order to make compiled code more efficient and help programmers avoid errors, languages can provide type systems or other features to constrain the structure of programs and provide useful guarantees. The design of these kinds of concurrent languages is an active area of research. However, it is frequently difficult to prove that efficient compilers for these languages are correct, and that important properties of the source-level language are preserved under compilation.

For example, in work on session types [8,14,16,38,41], processes communicate by sending messages over channels. These channels are given a type which describes the kind of data sent over the channel, as well as the order in which each process sends and receives messages. Often, the type system in these languages ensures the absence of undesired behaviors like races and deadlocks; for instance, two threads cannot both be trying to send a message on the same channel simultaneously.

Besides preventing errors, the invariants enforced by session types also permit these language to be compiled efficiently to a shared-memory target language [39]. For example, because only one thread can be sending a message

© Springer-Verlag GmbH Germany 2017
H. Yang (Ed.): ESOP 2017, LNCS 10201, pp. 909–936, 2017.
DOI: 10.1007/978-3-662-54434-1_34

on a given channel at a time, channels can be implemented without performing locking to send and receive messages. It is particularly important to prove that such an implementation does not *introduce* races or deadlocks, since this would destroy the very properties that make certain session-typed languages so interesting.

In this paper, we develop a higher-order program logic for proving the correctness of such concurrent language implementations, in a way that ensures that termination is preserved. We have used this program logic to give a machine-checked proof of correctness for a lock-free implementation of a *higher-order* session-typed language, *i.e.*, a language in which closures and channels can be sent over channels. To our knowledge, this is the *first such proof* of its kind.

As we describe below, previously developed program logics cannot be used to obtain these kinds of correctness results due to various limitations. In the remainder of the introduction, we will explain why it is so hard to prove refinements between higher-order, concurrent languages. To this end, we first have to provide some background.

Refinement for concurrent languages. To show that a compiler is correct, one typically proves that if a source expression E is well-typed, its translation $\widehat{E}$ *refines* E. In the sequential setting, this notion of refinement is easy to define[1]: (1) if the target program $\widehat{E}$ terminates in some value v, we expect E to also have an execution that terminates with value v, and (2) if $\widehat{E}$ diverges, then E should also have a diverging execution.

In the concurrent setting, however, we need to change this definition. In particular, the condition (2) concerning diverging executions is too weak. To see why, consider the following program, where x initially contains 0:

```
while (*x == 0)   {}    ||    *x = 1;
```

Here, || represents parallel composition of two threads. In every execution where the thread on the right eventually gets to run, this program will terminate. However, the program does have a diverging execution in which only the left thread runs: because x remains 0, the left thread continues to loop. Such executions are "unrealistic" in the sense that generally, we rely on schedulers to be *fair* and not let a thread starve. As a consequence, for purposes of compiler correctness, we do not want to consider these "unrealistic" executions which only diverge because the scheduler never lets a thread run.

Formally, an infinite execution is said to be *fair* [23] if every thread which does not terminate in a value takes infinitely many steps.[2] In the definition of refinement above, we change (2) to demand that if $\widehat{E}$ has a *fair* diverging execution, then E also has a *fair* diverging execution. We impose no such requirement about unfair diverging executions. This leads us to *fair termination-preserving refinement.*

---

[1] Setting aside issues of IO behavior.

[2] This definition is simpler than the version found in Lehmann et al. [23], because there threads can be temporarily *disabled, i.e.,* blocked and unable to take a step. In the languages we consider, threads can always take a step unless they have finished executing or have "gone wrong".

Logics for proving refinement. To prove our compiler correct, we need to reason about the concurrent execution and (non)termination of the source and target programs. Rather than reason directly about all possible executions of these programs, we prefer to use a concurrent program logic in order to re-use ideas found in rely-guarantee reasoning [18] and concurrent separation logic [29]. However, although a number of concurrency logics have recently been developed for reasoning about termination and refinements, they cannot be used to prove our compiler correctness result because they either:

- are restricted to first-order state [15,24–26,31],
- only deal with termination, not refinement [15,31], or
- handle a weaker form of refinement that is not fair termination-preserving [25,26,36].

Although the limitations are different in each of the above papers, let us focus on the approach by Turon et al. [36] since we will build on it. That paper establishes a termination-*insensitive* form of refinement, *i.e.,* a diverging program refines every program. Refinement is proven in a higher-order concurrent separation logic which, in addition to the usual points-to assertions $l \hookrightarrow v$, also provides assertions *about the source language's state*. For instance, the assertion[3] source(i, E) says thread i in the source language's execution is running expression E. A thread which "owns" this resource is allowed to modify the state of the source program by simulating steps of the execution of E. Then, we can prove that e refines E by showing:

$$\{\mathsf{source}(i, E)\}\ e\ \{v.\,\mathsf{source}(i, v)\}$$

As usual, the triple enforces that the post-condition holds on termination of e. Concretely for the triple above, the soundness theorem for the logic implies that if target expression e terminates with a value v, then there is an execution of source expression E that also terminates with value v. However, the Hoare triple above only expresses *partial correctness*. That means if e does not terminate, then the triple above is trivial, and so these triples can only be used to prove termination-insensitive refinements.

Ideally, one would like to overcome this limitation by adapting ideas from logics that deal with termination for first-order state. Notably, Liang *et al.* [24] have recently developed a logic for establishing *fair* refinements (as defined above).

However, there is a serious difficulty in trying to adapt these ideas. Semantic models of concurrency logics for higher-order state usually involve *step-indexing* [2,5]. In step-indexed logics, the validity of Hoare triples is restricted to program executions of arbitrary *but finite* length. How can we use these to reason about fairness, a property which is inherently about *infinite* executions?

In this paper, we show how to overcome this difficulty: the key insight is that when the source language has only *bounded non-determinism*, step-indexed Hoare triples are actually sufficient to establish properties of infinite program

---

[3] The notation in Turon et al. [36] is different.

executions. Using this observation, we extend Iris [19,20], a recent higher-order concurrent separation logic, to support reasoning about fair termination-preserving refinement. The soundness of our extensions to Iris and our case studies have been verified in Coq.

Overview. We start by introducing the case study that we will focus on in this paper: a session-typed source language, a compiler into an ML-like language, and the compiler's correctness property – fair, termination-preserving refinement (Sect. 2). Then we present our higher-order concurrent separation logic for establishing said refinement (Sect. 3). We follow on by explaining the key changes to Iris that were necessary to perform this kind of reasoning (Sect. 4). We then use the extended logic to prove the correctness of the compiler for our session-typed language (Sect. 5). Finally, we conclude by describing connections to related work and limitations of our approach that we hope to address in future work (Sect. 6).

2   Session-Typed Language and Compiler

This section describes the case study that we chose to demonstrate our logic: a concurrent message-passing language and a type system establishing safety and race-freedom for this language. On top of that, we explain how to implement the message-passing primitives in terms of shared-memory concurrency, *i.e.*, we define a compiler translating the source language into an ML-like target language. Finally, we discuss the desired correctness statement for this compiler.

2.1   Source Language

The source language for our compiler is a simplified version of the language described in Gay and Vasconcelos [14]. The syntax and semantics are given in Fig. 1. It is a functional language extended with primitives for message passing and a command $\mathsf{fork}\{E\}$ for creating threads. The semantics is defined by specifying a reduction relation for a single thread, which is then lifted to a concurrent semantics on thread-pools in which at each step a thread is selected non-deterministically to take the next step.

Threads can communicate asynchronously with each other by sending messages over *channels*. For example, consider the following program (which will be a running example of the paper):

$$\mathsf{let}\ (x, y) = \mathsf{newch}\ \mathsf{in}\ \big(\mathsf{fork}\{\mathsf{send}(x, 42)\};\ \mathsf{let}\ (\_, v) = \mathsf{recv}(y)\ \mathsf{in}\ v\big) \qquad (1)$$

The command newch creates a new channel and returns two *end-points* (bound to x and y in the example). An end-point consists of a channel id c and a side s (either left or right), and is written as c_s. Each channel is a pair of buffers $(b_\rightarrow, b_\leftarrow)$, which are lists of messages. Buffer $b_\rightarrow$ stores messages traveling left-to-right (from x to y, in the example above), and $b_\leftarrow$ is for right-to-left messages, as shown in the visualization in Fig. 1.

Syntax:

Side	s ::= left | right	
Val	V ::= c_s | $\lambda x.\, E_1$ | (V_1, V_2) | $()$ | n	where $c \in \mathbb{N}$
Expr	E ::= x | V | $E_1\, E_2$ | (E_1, E_2) | fork$\{E\}$ | newch | recv(E)	
	$\quad$ | send(E_1, E_2) | let $(x,y) = E_1$ in E_2 | ...	
Eval Ctx	K ::= $[]$ | $K\,E$ | $V\,K$ | (K, E) | (V, K) | recv(K) | send(K, E)	
	$\quad$ | send(V, K) | let $(x, y) = K$ in E | ...	
State	$\Sigma \in \mathbb{N} \to$ *List Val* $\times$ *List Val*	
Config	ρ ::= $[E_1, ..., E_n]; \Sigma$	
Type	τ ::= Int | Unit | $\tau_1 \otimes \tau_2$ | $\tau_1 \multimap \tau_2$ | S	
Session Type	S ::= $!\tau.\,S$ | $?\tau.\,S$ | end $\quad$ (co-inductive)	
Dual Type	$\overline{?\tau.\,S} \triangleq\, !\tau.\,\overline{S}$ $\quad$ $\overline{!\tau.\,S} \triangleq\, ?\tau.\,\overline{S}$ $\quad$ $\overline{\text{end}} \triangleq$ end	

Per-Thread Reduction $E; \Sigma \to E'; \Sigma'$: $\qquad$ (Pure and symmetric rules ommitted.)

NEWCH
$$\frac{c = \min\{c' \mid c' \notin \mathrm{dom}(\Sigma)\}}{\text{newch}; \Sigma \to (c_{\text{left}}, c_{\text{right}}); [c \hookrightarrow ([], [])]\Sigma}$$

SENDLEFT
$$\frac{\Sigma(c) = (b_\to, b_\leftarrow)}{\text{send}(c_{\text{left}}, V); \Sigma \;\rightarrow\; c_{\text{left}}; [c \hookrightarrow (b_\to V, b_\leftarrow)]\Sigma}$$

RECVRIGHTIDLE
$$\frac{\Sigma(c) = ([], b_\leftarrow)}{\text{recv}(c_{\text{right}}); \Sigma \to \text{recv}(c_{\text{right}}); \Sigma}$$

RECVRIGHT
$$\frac{\Sigma(c) = (V\,b_\to, b_\leftarrow)}{\text{recv}(c_{\text{right}}); \Sigma \to (c_{\text{right}}, V); [c \hookrightarrow (b_\to, b_\leftarrow)]\Sigma}$$

Concurrent Semantics $\rho \to \rho'$:

$$\frac{E_i; \Sigma \to E_i'; \Sigma'}{[..., K[E_i], ...]; \Sigma \to [..., K[E_i'], ...]; \Sigma'} \qquad [..., K[\text{fork}\{E_f\}], ...]; \Sigma \to [..., K[()], ..., E_f]; \Sigma$$

Type system: $\qquad$ (Standard rules for variables, integers and lambda omitted.)

FUN-ELIM
$$\frac{\Gamma \vdash E : \tau_1 \multimap \tau_2 \qquad \Gamma' \vdash E' : \tau_1}{\Gamma \uplus \Gamma' \vdash E\,E' : \tau_2}$$

PAIR-INTRO
$$\frac{\Gamma_1 \vdash E_1 : \tau_1 \qquad \Gamma_2 \vdash E_2 : \tau_2}{\Gamma_1 \uplus \Gamma_2 \vdash (E_1, E_2) : \tau_1 \otimes \tau_2}$$

PAIR-ELIM
$$\frac{\Gamma \vdash E : \tau_1 \otimes \tau_2 \qquad \Gamma', x : \tau_1, y : \tau_2 \vdash E' : \tau'}{\Gamma \uplus \Gamma' \vdash \text{let } (x, y) = E \text{ in } E' : \tau'}$$

FORK
$$\frac{\Gamma_1 \vdash E_f : \tau' \qquad \Gamma_2 \vdash E : \tau}{\Gamma_1 \uplus \Gamma_2 \vdash \text{fork}\{E_f\}; E : \tau}$$

NEWCHTYP
$$\Gamma \vdash \text{newch} : S \otimes \overline{S}$$

SEND
$$\frac{\Gamma_1 \vdash E_1 :\, !\tau.\,S \qquad \Gamma_2 \vdash E_2 : \tau}{\Gamma_1 \uplus \Gamma_2 \vdash \text{send}(E_1, E_2) : S}$$

RECV
$$\frac{\Gamma \vdash E :\, ?\tau.\,S}{\Gamma \vdash \text{recv}(E) : S \otimes \tau}$$

Buffer visualization: Message V has been sent from the left end-point to the right.

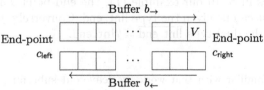

Fig. 1. Syntax, semantics, and session type system of message-passing source language

A thread can then use $\mathsf{send}(c_s, V)$ to send a value V along the channel c, with the side s specifying which buffer is used to store the message. For instance, when s is left, it inserts the value at the end of the first buffer (SENDLEFT). This value will then later be taken by a thread receiving on the *right* side (RECVRIGHT). Alternatively, if the buffer is empty when receiving, recv takes an "idle" step and tries again (RECVRIGHTIDLE). (The reason send and recv return the end-point again will become clear when we explain the type system.)

In the example above, after creating a new channel, the initial thread forks off a child which will send 42 from the left end-point, x. Meanwhile, the parent thread tries to receive from the right end-point y, and returns the message it gets. If the parent thread does this recv *before* the child has done its send, there will be no message and the parent thread will take an idle step. Otherwise, the receiver will see the message and the program will evaluate to 42.

2.2   Session Type System

A type system for this language is shown in Fig. 1. This is a simplified version of the type system given in Gay and Vasconcelos [14].[4] In addition to base types Int and Unit, we have pair types $\tau_1 \otimes \tau_2$, function types $\tau_1 \multimap \tau_2$, and *session types* S. Session types are used to type the end-points of a channel. These types describe a kind of *protocol* specifying what types of data will flow over the channel, and in what order messages are sent. Notice that this type system is *higher-order* in the sense that both closures and channel end-points are first-class values and can, in particular, be sent over channels.

Session types. The possible session types are specified by the grammar in Fig. 1. If an end-point has the session type $!\tau. S$, this means that the next use of this end-point must be to send a value of type τ (SEND). Afterward, the end-point that is returned by the send will have type S. Dually, $?\tau. S$ says that the end-point can be used in a receive (RECV), in which case the message read will have type τ, and the returned end-point will have type S. Notice that this is the same end-point that was passed to the command, but *at a different type*. The type of the end-point *evolves* as messages are sent and received, always representing the current state of the protocol. Finally, end is a session type for an end-point on which no further messages will be sent or received.

When calling newch to create a new channel, it is important that the types of the two end-points match: whenever one side sends a message of type τ, the other side should be expecting to receive a message of the same type. This relation is called *duality*. Given a session type S, its *dual* $\overline{S}$ is the result of swapping sends and receives in S. In our example (1), the end-point x is used to send a single integer, so it can be given the type $!\mathsf{Int. end}$. Conversely, y receives a single integer, so it has the dual type $\overline{!\mathsf{Int. end}} = ?\mathsf{Int. end}$.

---

[4] For the reader familiar with that work: we leave out subtyping and choice types. Also, we present an affine type system instead of a linear one.

Affinity. The type system of the source language is *affine*, which means that a variable in the context can be used at most once. This can be seen, *e.g.,* in the rule FORK: the forked-off thread E_f and the local continuation E are typed using the two disjoint contexts Γ_1 and Γ_2, respectively.

One consequence of affinity is that after using an end-point to send or receive, the variable passed to send/recv has been "used up" and cannot be used anymore. Instead, the program has to use the channel returned from send/recv, which has the new "evolved" type for the end-point.

The type system given here ensures safety and race-freedom. However, it does not guarantee termination. We discuss alternative type systems guaranteeing different properties in the conclusion.

2.3   Compilation

We now describe a simple translation from this session-typed source language to a MiniML language with references and a forking primitive like the one in the source language. We omit the details of the MiniML syntax and semantics as they are standard.

Our translation needs to handle essentially one feature: the implementation of channel communication in terms of shared memory references.

The code for the implementation of the channel primitives is shown in Fig. 2. We write $\widehat{E}$ for the translation in which we replace the primitives of the source language with the corresponding implementations. Concretely, applying the translation to our running example program we get:

$$
\begin{array}{lcl}
\text{let } (x,y) = \text{newch in} & & \text{let } (x,y) = \text{heapNewch in} \\
\text{fork}\{\text{send}(x,42)\}; & \Rightarrow & \text{fork}\{\text{heapSend } x\ 42\}; \\
\text{let } (\_,v) = \text{recv}(y) \text{ in } v & & \text{let } (\_,v) = \text{heapRecv } y \text{ in } v
\end{array}
$$

Each channel is implemented as a linked list which represents *both* buffers. Nodes in this list are pairs (l,v), where l is a reference to the (optional) next node, and v is the message that was sent. Why is it safe to use just one list? Duality in the session types guarantees that if a thread is sending from one end-point, no thread can at the same time be sending a message on the other end-point. This ensures that at least one of the two buffers in a channel is always empty. Hence we just need one list to represent both buffers.

$$
\begin{array}{lll}
\text{heapNewch} \triangleq & \text{heapSend } l\ v \triangleq & \text{heapRecv} \triangleq \text{rec } f\ l. \\
\quad \text{let } l = \text{ref none in } (l,l) & \quad \text{let } (l',v') = (l,v) \text{ in} & \quad \text{match } !l \text{ with} \\
& \quad \text{let } l_{new} = \text{ref none in} & \quad \mid \text{none} \Rightarrow f\ l \\
& \quad l' := \text{some } (l_{new}, v'); & \quad \mid \text{some } (l',v) \Rightarrow (l',v) \\
& \quad l_{new} & \quad \text{end}
\end{array}
$$

Fig. 2. Implementation of message passing primitives.

The implementation of newch, given by heapNewch, creates a new empty linked list by allocating a new reference l which initially contains none. The function heapSend implements send by appending a node to the end (l') of the list, and returning the new end. Meanwhile, for recv, heapRecv takes an end-point l and waits in a loop until it finds that the end-point contains a node.

2.4   Refinement

Having given the implementation, let us now clarify what it means for the compiler to be correct. Intuitively, we want to show that if we take a well-typed source expression E, all the *behaviors* of its translation $\widehat{E}$ are also *possible* behaviors of E. We say that $\widehat{E}$ *refines* E.

Before we come to the formal definition of refinement, we need to answer the question: which behaviors do we consider equivalent? In our case, the only observation that can be made about a whole program is its return value, so classifying "behaviors" amounts to relating return values. Formally speaking:

$$ n \approx n \qquad () \approx () \qquad l \approx c_s \qquad \lambda x.e \approx \lambda x.E \qquad \frac{v_1 \approx V_1 \qquad v_2 \approx V_2}{(v_1, v_2) \approx (V_1, V_2)} $$

For integer and unit values, we expect them to be exactly equal; similarly, pairs are the same if their components are. Coming to locations/end-points and closures, we do not consider them to be interpretable by the user looking at the result of a closed program. So, we just consider all closures to be equivalent, and all heap locations to relate to all channel end-points. Of course, the *proof* of compiler correctness will use a more fine-grained logical relation between source and target values.

Based on this notion of equivalent observations, we define what it means for a MiniML program e to *refine* a source program E, written $e \sqsubseteq E$. When executing from an initial "empty" state $\emptyset$, the following conditions must hold:

1. If $([e], \emptyset) \to^* ([e_1, \dots, e_n], \sigma)$ then no e_i is stuck in state σ.
   In other words: the target program does not reach a stuck state.
2. If $([e], \emptyset) \to^* ([v_1, \dots, v_n], \sigma)$ then either:
   (a) $([E], \emptyset) \to^* ([V_1, \dots, V_m], \Sigma)$ and $v_1 \approx V_1$, or
   (b) there is an execution of $([E], \emptyset)$ in which some thread gets stuck.
   That is, if *all threads* of the target program terminate with a value, then either *all threads* of the source program terminate in some execution *and* the return values of the first (main) source thread and target thread are equivalent; or the source program can get stuck.
3. If $([e], \emptyset)$ has a fair diverging execution, then $([E], \emptyset)$ also has a fair diverging execution. Recall that an infinite execution is *fair* if every non-terminating thread takes infinitely many steps. This last condition makes the refinement a *fair, termination-preserving* refinement.

To understand why we have emphasized the importance of fair termination-preservation, suppose we had miscompiled our running example as:

$$\mathsf{let}\ (x, y) = \mathsf{heapNewch}\ \mathsf{in}\ \mathsf{let}\ (\_, v) = \mathsf{heapRecv}\ y\ \mathsf{in}\ v$$

That is, we removed the sender thread. We consider this to be an incorrect compilation; *i.e.*, this program should *not* be considered a refinement of the source program. But imagine that we removed the word "fair" from condition (3) above: then this bad target program would be considered a refinement of the source. How is that? The program does not get stuck, so it satisfies condition (1). Condition (2) holds vacuously since the target program will never terminate; it will loop in $\mathsf{heapRecv}\ y$, forever waiting for a message. Finally, to satisfy condition (3), we have to exhibit a diverging execution in the source program. Without the fairness constraint, we can pick the (unfair) execution in which the sender source thread never gets to run.

Notice that this unfair execution is very much like the example we gave in the introduction, where a thread waited forever for another one to perform a change in the shared state.

We consider such unfair executions to be unrealistic [23]; they should not give license to a compiler to entirely remove a thread from the compiled program. That's why our notion of refinement restricts condition (3) to *fair* executions, *i.e.*, executions in which all non-terminating threads take infinitely many steps.

Compiler correctness. We are now equipped to formally express the correctness statement of our compiler:

Theorem 1. *For every* well-typed *source program E, we have that:*

$$\widehat{E} \sqsubseteq E$$

We prove this theorem in Sect. 5. In the intervening sections, we first develop and explain a logic to help carry out this proof.

3   A Logic for Proving Refinement

Proving Theorem 1 is a challenging exercise. Both the source and the target program are written in a concurrent language with higher-order state, which is always a difficult combination to reason about. Moreover, the invariant relating the channels and buffers to their implementation as linked lists is non-trivial and relies on well-typedness of the source program.

The contribution of this paper is to provide a logic powerful enough to prove theorems like Theorem 1. In this section, we will give the reader an impression of both the logic and the proof by working through a proof of one concrete instance of our general result: we will prove that the translation of our running example is in fact a refinement of its source.

3.1   Refinement as a Hoare Logic

Our logic is an extension of *Iris* [19, 20], a concurrent higher-order separation logic. We use the ideas presented by Turon et al. [36] to extend this (unary) Hoare logic with reasoning principles for refinement. Finally, we add some further extensions which become necessary due to the *termination-preserving* nature of our refinement. We will highlight these extensions as we go.

The following grammar covers the assertions from our logic that we will need:[5]

$$P ::= \mathsf{False} \mid \mathsf{True} \mid P \vee P \mid P * P \mid \mathcal{A}(P) \mid \exists x.\, P \mid \forall x.\, P \mid l \hookrightarrow v \mid \mathsf{source}(i, E, d) \mid$$
$$\mathsf{Stopped} \mid c \hookrightarrow_{\mathsf{s}} (b_\rightarrow, b_\leftarrow) \mid \mathsf{StsSt}(s, T) \mid \{P\}\, e\, \{x.\, Q\} \mid P \Rrightarrow Q \mid P \Rrightarrow Q \mid \ldots$$

Many of these assertions are standard in separation logics, and our example proof will illustrate the non-standard ones.

Recalling the example and its translation, we want to prove:

let $(x, y) = \mathsf{heapNewch}$ in
fork$\{\mathsf{heapSend}\, x\, 42\}$;
let $(\_, v) = \mathsf{heapRecv}\, y$ in v

$\sqsubseteq$

let $(x, y) = \mathsf{newch}$ in
fork$\{\mathsf{send}(x, 42)\}$;
let $(\_, v) = \mathsf{recv}(y)$ in v

or, for short, $e_{\mathsf{ex}} \sqsubseteq E_{\mathsf{ex}}$. Following HT-REFINE (Fig. 3), it is enough to prove

$$\{\mathsf{source}(i, E_{\mathsf{ex}}, d)\}\, e_{\mathsf{ex}}\, \{v.\, \exists V.\, \mathsf{source}(i, V, 0) * v \approx V\} \tag{2}$$

In other words, we "just" prove a Hoare triple for e_{ex} (the MiniML program). In order to obtain a refinement from a Hoare proof, we equip our logic with assertions talking about the source program E. The assertion $\mathsf{source}(i, E, d)$ states that source-level thread i is about to execute E, and we have *delay* d left. (We will come back to delays shortly.) The assertion $c \hookrightarrow_{\mathsf{s}} (b_\rightarrow, b_\leftarrow)$ says that source-level channel c currently has buffer contents $(b_\rightarrow, b_\leftarrow)$. As usual in separation logic, both of these assertions furthermore assert *exclusive ownership* of their thread or channel. For example, in the case of $c \hookrightarrow_{\mathsf{s}} (b_\rightarrow, b_\leftarrow)$, this means that no other thread can access the channel and we are free to mutate it (*i.e.*, send or receive messages) – we will see later how the logic allows threads to share these resources. Put together, these two assertions let us control the complete state of the source program's execution.

So far, we have not described anything new. However, to establish *termination-preserving* refinement, we have to add two features to this logic: *step shifts* and *linear assertions*.

---

[5] Note that many of these assertions are not primitive to the logic, but are themselves defined using more basic assertions provided by the logic. For instance, the Hoare triple is actually defined in terms of a *weakest precondition* assertion. See Jung et al. [19, 20] for further details.

Step shifts. The rules given in Fig. 3 let us manipulate the state of the source program's execution by *taking steps in the source program.* Such steps are expressed using *step shifts* $\Rrightarrow$. Every step shift corresponds to one rule in the operational semantics (Fig. 1). For example, SRC-NEWCH expresses that if we have source$(i, K[\mathsf{newch}], d)$ (which means that the source is about to create a new channel), we can "execute" that newch and obtain some fresh channel c and ownership of the channel ($c \hookrightarrow_s ([], [])$). We also obtain source$(i, K[c], d')$, so we can go on executing the source thread.

Crucially, having $P \Rrightarrow Q$ shows that in going from P to Q, the source *has* taken a step. We need to force the source to take steps because the refinement we show is *termination-preserving.* If a proof could just decide not to ever step the source program, we could end up with a MiniML program e diverging, while the corresponding source program E cannot actually diverge. That would make HT-REFINE unsound. So, to avoid this, all rules that take a step in the MiniML program (Fig. 3) force us to also take a step shift.

A strict implementation of this idea requires a lock-step execution of source and target program. This is too restrictive. For that reason, the source assertion does not just record the state of the source thread, but also a *delay d.* Decrementing the delay counts as taking a step in the source (SRC-DELAY). When we take an actual source step, we get to reset the delay to some new d' – so long as d' is less than or equal to some fixed upper bound D that we use throughout the proof. There are also rules that allow executing *multiple* source steps when taking just a single step in the target program; we omit these rules for brevity. For the remainder of this proof, we will also gloss over the bookkeeping for the delay and just write source(i, e).

The assertion Stopped expresses that a source thread can no longer take steps. As expected, this happens when the source thread reaches a value (SRC-STOPPED).

Linearity. There is one last ingredient we have to explain before we start the actual verification: *linearity.* Assertions in our logic are generally *linear,* which means they cannot be "thrown away", *i.e.,* $P * Q \vdash P$ does not hold generically in P and Q. As a consequence, assertions represent not only the *right* to perform certain actions (like modifying memory), but also the *obligation* to keep performing steps in the source program. This ensures that we do not "lose track" of a source thread and stop performing step shifts justifying its continued execution.

The modality $\mathcal{A}(P)$ says that we have a proof of P, and that this is an *affine* proof – so there are no obligations encoded in this assertion, and we can throw it away. Some rules are restricted to affine assertions, *e.g.,* rules for framing around a Hoare triple or a step shift (HT-FRAME and STEP-FRAME). Again, this affine requirement ensures that we do not "smuggle" a source thread around the obligation to perform steps in the source. All the base assertions, with the exception of source(i, e), are affine.

Coming back to the Hoare triple (2) above that we have to prove, the precondition source(i, E_{ex}) expresses that we start out with a source program executing E_{ex} (and not owning any channels), and we somehow have to take steps

Step Shift Rules: (all d and d' must be $\leq$ some fixed upper-bound D)

SRC-NEWCH
$$\mathsf{source}(i, K[\mathsf{newch}], d) \Rrightarrow \exists c.\, \mathsf{source}(i, K[(c_{\mathsf{left}}, c_{\mathsf{right}})], d') * c \hookrightarrow_{\mathsf{s}} ([], [])$$

SRC-RECV-RIGHT-MISS
$$\mathsf{source}(i, K[\mathsf{recv}(c_{\mathsf{right}})], d) * c \hookrightarrow_{\mathsf{s}} ([], b_{\leftarrow}) \Rrightarrow \mathsf{source}(i, K[\mathsf{recv}(c_{\mathsf{right}})], d') * c \hookrightarrow_{\mathsf{s}} ([], b_{\leftarrow})$$

SRC-RECV-RIGHT-HIT
$$\mathsf{source}(i, K[\mathsf{recv}(c_{\mathsf{right}})], d) * c \hookrightarrow_{\mathsf{s}} (v\, b_{\rightarrow}, b_{\leftarrow}) \Rrightarrow \mathsf{source}(i, K[(c_{\mathsf{right}}, v)], d') * c \hookrightarrow_{\mathsf{s}} (b_{\rightarrow}, b_{\leftarrow})$$

SRC-SEND-LEFT
$$\mathsf{source}(i, K[\mathsf{send}(c_{\mathsf{left}}, v)], d) * c \hookrightarrow_{\mathsf{s}} (b_{\rightarrow}, b_{\leftarrow}) \Rrightarrow \mathsf{source}(i, K[c_{\mathsf{left}}], d') * c \hookrightarrow_{\mathsf{s}} (b_{\rightarrow} v, b_{\leftarrow})$$

SRC-FORK
$$\mathsf{source}(i, K[\mathsf{fork}\{E\}], d) \Rrightarrow \exists j.\, \mathsf{source}(i, K[()], d') * \mathsf{source}(j, E, d_{\mathsf{f}})$$

SRC-DELAY
$$d' < d \vdash \mathsf{source}(i, K[E], d) \Rrightarrow \mathsf{source}(i, K[E], d')$$

SRC-PURE-STEP
$$\frac{e_1 \rightarrow e_2}{\mathsf{source}(i, e_1, d) \Rrightarrow \mathsf{source}(i, e_2, d')}$$

SRC-STOPPED
$$\mathsf{source}(i, V, 0) \vdash \mathsf{Stopped}$$

(Symmetric rules and side-condition on d' omitted.)

Basic Hoare Triples:

ML-ALLOC
$$\frac{\forall x.\, P \Rrightarrow Q}{\{P\}\ \mathsf{ref}\ v\ \{x.\, Q * x \hookrightarrow v\}}$$

ML-LOAD
$$\frac{P \Rrightarrow [v/y]Q}{\{P * x \hookrightarrow v\}\ !x\ \{y.\, Q * x \hookrightarrow v\}}$$

ML-STORE
$$\frac{P \Rrightarrow Q}{\{P * x \hookrightarrow v\}\ x := w\ \{Q * x \hookrightarrow w\}}$$

ML-FORK
$$\frac{P \Rrightarrow Q_0 * Q_1 \qquad \{Q_0\}\ e\ \{\mathsf{Stopped}\} \qquad \{Q_1\}\ e'\ \{R\}}{\{P\}\ \mathsf{fork}\{e\}; e'\ \{R\}}$$

ML-REC
$$\frac{P \Rrightarrow P' \qquad (\forall v.\, \{P\}\ (\mathsf{rec}\, f\, x.\, e)\, v\ \{w.\, Q\}) \Rightarrow \forall v.\, \{P'\}\ [\mathsf{rec}\, f\, x.\, e/f, v/x]e\ \{w.\, Q\}}{\forall v.\, \{P\}\ (\mathsf{rec}\, f\, x.\, e)\, v\ \{w.\, Q\}}$$

HT-FRAME
$$\frac{\{P\}\ e\ \{v.\, Q\}}{\{P * \mathcal{A}(R)\}\ e\ \{v.\, Q * \mathcal{A}(R)\}}$$

STEP-FRAME
$$\frac{P \Rrightarrow Q}{P * \mathcal{A}(R) \Rrightarrow Q * \mathcal{A}(R)}$$

HT-CSQ
$$\frac{P \Rrightarrow P' \qquad \{P'\}\ e\ \{v.\, Q'\} \qquad \forall v.\, Q' \Rrightarrow Q}{\{P\}\ e\ \{v.\, Q\}}$$

Refinement Rule:

HT-REFINE
$$\frac{\{\mathsf{source}(i, E, d)\}\ e\ \{v.\, \exists V.\, \mathsf{source}(i, V, 0) * v \approx V\}}{e \sqsubseteq E}$$

Fig. 3. Selection of rules for step shifts and Hoare triples

in the source program to end up with $\mathsf{source}(i, V)$ such that V is "equivalent" (in the sense defined in Sect. 2.4) to the return value of the target program. Intuitively, because we can only manipulate source by taking steps in the source program, and because we end up stepping from $\mathsf{source}(i, E_{\mathsf{ex}})$ to "the same" return value as the one obtained from e, proving the Hoare triple actually establishes a refinement between the two programs. Furthermore, since source is linear and we perform a step shift at every step of the MiniML program, the refinement holds even for diverging executions.

3.2   Proof of the Example

The rest of this section will present in great detail the proof of our example (2). The rough structure of this proof goes as follows: after a small introduction covering the allocation of the channel, we will motivate the need for *state-transition systems* (STS), a structured way of controlling the interaction between cooperating threads. We will define the STS used for the example and decompose the remainder of the proof into two pieces: one covering the sending thread and one for the receiving thread.

Getting started. The first statement in both source and target program is the allocation of a channel. The following Hoare triple that's easily derived from ML-ALLOC summarizes the action of heapNewch: It allocates a channel in *both* programs.

$$\{\mathsf{source}(i, K[\mathsf{newch}])\}\ \mathsf{heapNewch}$$
$$\{x.\ \exists l, c.\ x = (l, l) * l \hookrightarrow \mathsf{none} * c \hookrightarrow_\mathsf{s} ([], []) * \mathsf{source}(i, K[(c_{\mathsf{left}}, c_{\mathsf{right}})])\} \tag{3}$$

Let us pause a moment to expand on that post-condition. On the source side, we have a channel c with both buffers being empty; on the target side we have a location l representing the empty buffer with none. The return value x is a pair with both components being l. Finally, the source thread changed from $K[\mathsf{newch}]$ in the pre-condition to $K[(c_{\mathsf{left}}, c_{\mathsf{right}})]$, meaning that the newch has been executed and the context can now go on with its evaluation based on the pair $(c_{\mathsf{left}}, c_{\mathsf{right}})$.

We apply this triple for heapNewch with the appropriate evaluation context K for the source program, and the post-condition of (3) becomes our new context of current assertions. Next, we reduce the let on both sides, so we end up with

$$l \hookrightarrow \mathsf{none} * c \hookrightarrow_\mathsf{s} ([], []) * \mathsf{source}(i, e_{\mathsf{comm}}(c)) \tag{4}$$

where

$$e_{\mathsf{comm}}(c) \triangleq \mathsf{fork}\{\mathsf{send}(c_{\mathsf{left}}, 42)\}; \mathsf{let}\ (\_, v) = \mathsf{recv}(c_{\mathsf{right}})\ \mathsf{in}\ v$$

and the remaining MiniML code is

$$\mathsf{fork}\{\mathsf{heapSend}\ l\ 42\}; \mathsf{let}\ (\_, v) = \mathsf{heapRecv}\ l\ \mathsf{in}\ v$$

(In the following, we will perform these pure reduction steps and the substitutions implicitly.)

As we can see, both programs are doing a fork to concurrently send and receive messages on the same channel. Usually, this would be ruled out by the exclusive nature of ownership in separation logic. To enable sharing, the logic provides a notion of *protocols* coordinating the interaction of multiple threads on the same shared state. The protocol governs ownership of both l (in the target) and c (in the source), and describes which thread can perform which actions on this shared state.

State-transition systems. A structured way to describe protocols is the use of state-transition systems (STS), following the ideas of Turon et al. [36]. An STS $\mathcal{S}$ consists of a directed graph with the nodes denoting *states* and the arrows denoting *transitions*.

The STS for our example is given in Fig. 4. It describes the interaction of our two threads over the shared buffer happening in three phases. In the beginning, the buffer is empty (INIT). Then the message is sent by the forked-off sending thread (SENT). Finally, the message is received by the main thread (RECEIVED).

The STS also contains two *tokens*. Tokens are used to represent actions that only particular threads can perform. In our example, the state SENT requires the token [S]. The STS enforces that, in order to step from INIT to SENT, a thread must *provide* (and give up) ownership of [S]. This is called the *law of token preservation* [36]: Because SENT contains more tokens than INIT, the missing tokens have to be provided by the thread performing the transition. Similarly, [R] is needed to transition to the final state RECEIVED.

To tie the abstract state of the STS to the rest of the verification, every STS comes with an *interpretation* φ. For every state, it defines an affine assertion that has to hold at that state. In our case, we require the buffer to be initially empty, and to contain 42 in state SENT. Once we reach the final state, the programs no longer perform any action on their respective buffers, so we stop keeping track.

We need a way to track the state of the STS in our proof. To this end, the assertion $\mathsf{StsSt}(s, T)$ states that the STS is *at least* in state s, and that we own tokens T. We cannot know the *exact* current state of the STS because other threads may have performed further transitions in the mean time. The proof rules for STSs can be found in the appendix [34]; in the following, we will keep the reasoning about the STS on an intuitive level to smooth the exposition.

Plan for finishing the proof. Let us now come back to our example program. We already described the STS we are going to use for the verification (Fig. 4). The next step in the proof is thus to initialize said STS.

Remember our current context is (4). When allocating an STS, we get to pick its initial state – that would be INIT, of course. We have to provide $\varphi(\text{INIT})$ to initialize the STS, so we give up ownership of l and c. In exchange, we obtain StsSt and the tokens. Our context is now

$$\mathsf{StsSt}(\text{INIT}, \{[\mathsf{S}], [\mathsf{R}]\}) * \mathsf{source}(i, e_{\mathrm{comm}}(c)) \tag{5}$$

The next command executed in both programs is fork. We are thus going to apply ML-FORK and prove the step shift using SRC-FORK. The two remaining premises of ML-FORK are the following two Hoare triples:

$$\{\mathsf{StsSt}(\text{INIT}, [\mathsf{S}]) * \mathsf{source}(j, \mathsf{send}(c_{\mathsf{left}}, 42))\}\ \mathsf{heapSend}\ l\ 42\ \{\mathsf{Stopped}\} \tag{6}$$

$$\{\mathsf{StsSt}(\text{INIT}, [\mathsf{R}]) * \mathsf{source}(j, \mathsf{let}\ (\_, v) = \mathsf{recv}(c_{\mathsf{right}})\ \mathsf{in}\ v)\}$$
$$\mathsf{let}\ (\_, v) = \mathsf{heapRecv}\ l\ \mathsf{in}\ v \tag{7}$$
$$\{n.\, n = 42 * \mathsf{source}(j, 42)\}$$

Showing these will complete the proof. The post-condition Stopped of (6) is mandated by ML-FORK; we will discuss it when verifying that Hoare triple. Note that we are splitting the StsSt to hand the two tokens that we own to two different threads.

Verifying the sender. To prove the sending Hoare triple (6), the context we have available is $\mathsf{StsSt}(\text{INIT}, [\mathsf{S}]) * \mathsf{source}(j, \mathsf{send}(c_{\mathsf{left}}, 42))$, and the code we wish to verify is (unfolding the definition of heapSend, and performing some pure reductions):

$$\mathsf{let}\ l_{new} = \mathsf{ref\ none}\ \mathsf{in}\ l := \mathsf{some}\ (l_{new}, 42); l_{new}$$

The allocation is easily handled with ML-ALLOC, and it turns out we don't even need to remember anything about the returned l_{new}.

The next step is the core of this proof: showing that we can change the value stored in l. Notice that we do not own $l \hookrightarrow \_$; the STS "owns" l as part of its interpretation. So we will *open* the STS to get access to l.

Looking at Fig. 4, we can see that doing the transition from INIT to SENT requires the token [S], *which we own* – as a consequence, nobody else could perform this transition. It follows that the STS is currently in state INIT. We obtain $\varphi(\text{INIT})$, so that we can apply ML-STORE with SRC-SEND-LEFT, yielding

$$l \hookrightarrow \mathsf{some}\ (l', 42) * c \hookrightarrow_{\mathsf{s}} ([], []) * \mathsf{source}(j, c_{\mathsf{left}}) \tag{8}$$

To finish up accessing the STS, we have to pick a new state and show that we actually possess the tokens to move to said state. In our case, we *cannot* pick RECEIVED, since we do not own the token [R] necessary for that step. Instead, we will pick SENT and give up our token. This means we have to establish $\varphi(\text{SENT})$. Doing so consumes most of our context (8), leaving only $\mathsf{source}(j, c_{\mathsf{left}})$. What remains to be done? We have to establish the post-condition of our triple (6),

$$\varphi(\text{INIT}) \triangleq l \hookrightarrow \mathsf{none} * c \hookrightarrow_{\mathsf{s}} ([], [])$$
$$\varphi(\text{SENT}) \triangleq l \hookrightarrow \mathsf{some}\ (\_, 42) * c \hookrightarrow_{\mathsf{s}} ([42], [])$$
$$\varphi(\text{RECEIVED}) \triangleq \mathsf{True}$$

Fig. 4. STS for the example

which is Stopped. By SRC-STOPPED, this immediately follows from the fact that we reduced the source thread to c_{left}, which is a value.

Notice that this last step was important: We showed that when the MiniML thread terminates, so does the source thread. The original fork rule for Iris allows picking *any* post-condition for the forked-off thread, because nothing happens any more with this thread once it terminates. However, we wish to establish that if all MiniML threads terminate, then so do all source threads – and for this reason, ML-FORK forces us to prove Stopped, which asserts that all the threads we keep track of have reduced to a value. This finishes the proof of the sender.

Verifying the receiver. The next (and last) step in establishing the refinement (2) is to prove the Hoare triple for the receiving thread (7). This is the target code to verify:

$$\mathsf{let}\ (\_, v) = \mathsf{heapRecv}\ l\ \mathsf{in}\ v$$

Since heapRecv is a recursive function, we use ML-REC, which says that we can assume that recursive occurrences of heapRecv have already been proven correct. It may be surprising to see this rule – after all, rules like ML-REC are usually justified by saying that all we do is partial correctness. Notice, however, that we are *not* showing that E_{ex} terminates. All we show is that, *if* E_{ex} diverges, then so does e_{ex}. That is, we are establishing termination-*preservation*, not termination.

In continuing the proof, we thus get to assume correctness of the recursive call. Our current context is

$$\mathsf{StsSt}(\text{INIT}, [\mathsf{R}]) * \mathsf{source}(j, \mathsf{let}\ (\_, v) = \mathsf{recv}(c_{\text{right}})\ \mathsf{in}\ v) \tag{9}$$

and the code we are verifying is

$$\mathsf{match}\ !l\ \mathsf{with}\ \mathsf{none} \Rightarrow \mathsf{heapRecv}\ l\ |\ \mathsf{some}\ (l', v) \Rightarrow (l', v)\ \mathsf{end}$$

with post-condition $(\_, n).\, n = 42 * \mathsf{source}(j, 42)$.

The first command of this program is $!l$. To access l, we have to again open the STS. Since we own $[\mathsf{R}]$, we can rule out being in state RECEIVED. We perform a case distinction over the remaining two states.

- If we are in INIT, we get $l \hookrightarrow \mathsf{none} * c \hookrightarrow_{\mathsf{s}} ([], [])$ from the STS's $\varphi(\text{RECEIVED})$. We use ML-LOAD with SRC-RECV-RIGHT-MISS. Notice how we use $c \hookrightarrow_{\mathsf{s}} ([], [])$ to justify performing an "idle" step in the source. This is crucial – after all, we are potentially looping indefinitely in the target, reading l over and over; we have to exhibit a corresponding diverging execution in the source.

  Since we did not change any state, we close the invariant again in the INIT state. Next, the program executes the none arm of the match: heapRecv l. Here, we use our assumption that the recursive call is correct to finish the proof.
- Otherwise, the current state is SENT, and we obtain $l \hookrightarrow \mathsf{some}\ (\_, 42) * c \hookrightarrow_{\mathsf{s}} ([42], [])$. We use ML-LOAD with SRC-RECV-RIGHT-HIT; this time we know that the recv in the source will succeed. We also know that we are loading $(\_, 42)$

from l. We pick RECEIVED as the next state (giving up our STS token), and trivially establish $\varphi(\text{RECEIVED})$. We can now throw away ownership of l and c as well as $\text{StsSt}(\text{RECEIVED})$ since we no longer need them – we can do this because all these assertions are affine.

All that remains is the source thread:

$$\text{source}(j, \text{let } (\_, v) = (c_{\text{right}}, 42) \text{ in } v)$$

Next, the target program will execute the some branch of the match. To finish, we need to justify the post-condition: $(\_, n).\, n = 42 * \text{source}(j, 42)$. We already established that the second component of the value loaded from l is 42, and the source thread is easily reduced to 42 as well.

This finishes the proof of (7) and therefore of (2): we proved that $e_{\text{ex}} \sqsubseteq E_{\text{ex}}$.

4   Soundness of the Logic

We have seen how to use our logic to establish a refinement for a particular simple instance of our translation. We now need to show that this logic is sound.

As already mentioned, our logic is an extension of Iris, so we need to adapt the soundness proof of Iris [19]. The two extensions that were described in Sect. 3.1 are:

1. We add a notion of a *step shift*, which is used to simulate source program threads.
2. We move from an affine logic to a linear logic. This is needed to capture the idea that some resources (like source) represent *obligations* that cannot be thrown away.

In this section we describe how we adapt the semantic model of Iris to handle these changes. Although our extensions sound simple, the modification of the model requires some care. Many of the features we used in Sect. 3, such as STSs [20] and reasoning about the source language, are *derived* constructions that are not "baked-in" to the logic. As we change the model, we need to ensure that all of these features can still be encoded. We also strive to keep our extensions as general as possible so as to not unnecessarily restrict the flexibility of Iris.

Brief review of the Iris model. We start by recalling some aspects of the Iris model [19] that we modify in our extensions. A key concept is the notion of a *resource*. Resources describe the physical state of the program as well as additional *ghost state* that is added for the purpose of verification and used, *e.g.,* to interpret STSs or the assertions talking about source programs. Resources are instances of a partial commutative monoid-like algebraic structure; in particular, two resources a, b can be *composed* to $a \cdot b$. This operation is used to combine resources held by different threads. When the composition $a \cdot b$ is defined, the elements a and b are said to be *compatible*. Iris always ensures that the resources held by different threads are compatible. This guarantees that, *e.g.,* different threads cannot own the same channel or the same STS token. The operation also gives rise to a pre-order on resources, defined as $a_1 \preccurlyeq a_2 \triangleq \exists a_3. a_1 \cdot a_3 = a_2$, *i.e.*, a_1 is included in a_2 if the former can be *extended* to the latter by adding some additional resource a_3.

Ideally, we would just interpret an assertion P as a set of resources. For technical reasons (that we will mostly gloss over), Iris needs an additional component: the *step-index* n. An assertion is thus interpreted as a set of pairs (n, a) of step-indices and resources. We write $n, a \models P$ to indicate that $(n, a) \in P$, and read this as saying that a satisfies P for n steps of the target program's execution.

Iris furthermore demands that assertions (interpreted as sets) satisfy two *closure properties*: They must be closed under larger resources and smaller step-indices. Formally:

1. If $n, a \models P$ and $a \preccurlyeq a'$, then $n, a' \models P$.
2. If $n, a \models P$ and $n' \leq n$, then $n', a \models P$.

The first point above makes Iris an *affine* as opposed to a linear logic: we can always "add-on" more resources and continue to satisfy an assertion. Put differently, there is no way to state an *upper bound* on our resources. The second point says that if P holds for n steps, then it also holds for fewer than n steps.

To give a model to assertions like $l \hookrightarrow v$, we need a function $\mathsf{HeapRes}(l, v)$ describing, as a resource, a heap which maps location l to v. We then define:

$$n, a \models l \hookrightarrow v \quad \text{iff} \quad \mathsf{HeapRes}(l, v) \preccurlyeq a$$

Notice the use of $\preccurlyeq$, ensuring that the closure property (1) holds.

Equipping Iris with linear assertions. In order to move to a linear setting with minimal disruption to the existing features of Iris, we replace the judgment $n, a \models P$ with $n, a, b \models P$. That is, assertions are now sets of triples: a step-index and *two* resources. The downward closure condition on n and the upward closure condition on a still apply, but we do not impose such a condition on b: this second resource will represent the "linear piece" of an assertion. Crucially, whereas affine assertions like $l \hookrightarrow v$ continue to "live" in the a piece, the linear source resides in b:

$$n, a, b \models l \hookrightarrow v \qquad \text{iff} \quad \mathsf{HeapRes}(l, v) \preccurlyeq a \wedge b = \varepsilon$$
$$n, a, b \models \mathsf{source}(i, E, d) \quad \text{iff} \quad \mathsf{SourceRes}(i, E, d) = b$$

where ε is the unit of the monoid. We assume $\mathsf{SourceRes}(i, E, d)$ to define, as a resource, a source thread i executing E with d delay steps left.

As we can see, source describes the *exact* linear resources b that we own, whereas $\hookrightarrow$ merely states a *lower bound* on the affine resources a (due to the upwards closure on a). Notice that a and b are both elements of the same set of resources; it is just their treatment in the closure properties of assertions which makes one affine and the other linear. Because there is no upward closure condition on the second monoid element, the resulting logic is not affine: if $n, a, b \models P * Q$, then it is not necessarily the case that $n, a, b \models P$.

We define the affine modality by:

$$n, a, b \models \mathcal{A}(P) \quad \text{iff} \quad n, a, b \models P \wedge b = \varepsilon$$

This says that in addition to satisfying P, b should equal the unit of the monoid. That is, the linear part is "empty"; there are no obligations encoded in P. That makes it sound to throw away P or to frame it.

The advantage of this "two world" model is that it does not require us to change many of the encodings already present in Iris, like STSs.

Step Shifts. We are now ready to explain the ideas behind the *step shift*. Remember the goal here is to account for the steps taken in the source program, in a way that we can prove refinements by proving Hoare triples (HT-REFINE). This is subtle because by the definition of refinement (Sect. 2.4), we need to make statements even about infinite executions, *i.e.*, executions that never have to satisfy the post-condition.

The key idea is to equip the resources of Iris with a relation that represents a notion of *taking a (resource) step*. We write $a \curvearrowright b$, and say that a *steps to* b. We will then pick the resources in such a way as to represent the status of a source program,[6] and we define the resource step to be taking a step in the source program. All the other components of the resource, like STSs, will not be changed by resource steps.

Recall that the resources owned by different threads always need to be compatible. To ensure this, we define a relation that performs a step while maintaining compatibility with the resources owned by other threads. Formally, a *frame-preserving step-update* $a, b \rightsquigarrow a', b'$ holds if $b \curvearrowright b'$ and for all c such that $a \cdot b \cdot c$ is defined, so is $a' \cdot b' \cdot c$. The intuition is that, if a thread owns some resources a and b, that restricts the ownership of other threads to *frames* c that are compatible with a and b. Since a' and b' are also compatible with the frame, the step is guaranteed not to interfere with resources owned by other threads.

These frame-preserving step-updates are reflected into the logic through the *step shift* assertions: $P \Rrightarrow Q$ holds if, whenever some resources satisfy P, it is possible to perform a frame-preserving step-update to resources satisfying Q.

We then connect Hoare triples to these resource steps. To this end, we change the definition of Hoare triples so that whenever a target thread takes a step, we have to also take a step on our resources. This gives rise to the proof rules in Fig. 3, which force the user of the logic to perform a step shift alongside every step of the MiniML program. We also enforce that forked-off threads must have a post-condition of Stopped, ensuring that target language threads cannot stop executing while source language threads are still running.

---

[6] Iris is designed to be parametric in the choice of resources, so we can pick a particular resource for this source language and still use most of the general Iris machinery.

Soundness of the refinement. Having extended the definition of Hoare triples in this way, we can prove our refinement theorem. Recall that the definition of refinement had three parts. For each of these parts, we proved an adequacy theorem for our extensions relating Hoare triples to properties of program executions. These theorems are parameterized by the kind of resource picked by the user, and in particular the kind of resource *step*. Below, we show these theorems specialized to the case where resource steps correspond to source language steps.

The first refinement condition, which says that the target program must not get stuck, follows from a "safety" theorem that was already present in the original Iris:

Lemma 2. *If* $\{source(i, E, d)\}$ e $\{v.\,source(i, V, 0) * \mathcal{A}(v \approx V)\}$ *holds and we have* $([e], \emptyset) \to^* ([e_1, \ldots, e_n], \sigma)$, *then each* e_i *is either a value or it can take a step in state* σ.

The second refinement condition says that if the execution of e terminates, then there should be a related terminating execution in the source. Remember that the definition of the Hoare triple requires us to take a step in the source whenever the target steps (modulo a finite number of delays). Hence a proof of such a triple must have "built-up" the desired source execution:

Lemma 3. *If* $\{source(i, E, d)\}$ e $\{v.\,source(i, V, 0) * \mathcal{A}(v \approx V)\}$ *holds and we have* $([e], \emptyset) \to^* ([v_1, \ldots, v_n], \sigma)$, *then there exists* V_1, E_2, $\ldots$, E_m, Σ *s.t.* $([E], \emptyset) \to^* ([V_1, E_2, \ldots, E_m], \Sigma)$. *Moreover, each* E_i *is either stuck or a value, and* $v_1 \approx V_1$.

Here, we are already making crucial use of both linearity of source and the fact that forked-off threads must have post-condition Stopped: if it were not for these requirements, even when all target threads terminated with a value v_i, we could not rule out the existence of source threads that can go on executing.

Finally, we come to the third condition, which says fair diverging executions of the target should correspond to fair diverging executions of the source:

Lemma 4. *If* $\{source(i, E, d)\}$ e $\{v.\,source(i, V, 0) * \mathcal{A}(v \approx V)\}$ *holds and* $([e], \emptyset)$ *has a diverging execution, then* $([E], \emptyset)$ *has a diverging execution as well. Moreover, if the diverging target execution is fair, then the source execution is too.*

This is the hardest part of the soundness proof. We would like to start by arguing that, just as for the finite case, if the target program took an infinite number of steps, then the proof of the refinement triple must give a corresponding infinite number of steps in the source program. Unfortunately, this argument is not so simple because of step-indexing.

In Iris, Hoare triples are themselves step-indexed sets. We write $n \models \{P\}\, e\, \{Q\}$ to say that the triple holds at step-index n. Then, when we say we have proved a Hoare triple, we mean the triple holds for all step-indices n and all resources satisfying the precondition. As is usual with step-indexing, when a triple $\{P\}\, e\, \{Q\}$ holds for step-index n, that means when the precondition is satisfied, execution of e is safe for up-to n steps, and if it terminates within those n steps, the post-condition holds. In our case, it also means that each step of the target program gives a step of the source program, for up to n target steps.

This restriction to only hold "up to n steps" arises due to the way Hoare triples are defined in the model: when proving the Hoare triple at step-index n, if e steps to e', we are only required to show $(n-1) \models \{P'\}\, e'\, \{Q\}$ for some P'.

The restriction to a finite number of steps did not bother us for Lemmas 2 and 3. Since they only deal with finite executions, and the Hoare triple holds for *all* starting indices n, we can simply pick n to be greater than the finite execution we are considering. But we cannot do this when we want to prove something about a diverging execution of the target. Whatever n we start with, it is not big enough to get the infinite source execution we need.

Bounded non-determinism, infinite executions, and step-indexing. Our insight is that when the source language has only *bounded non-determinism*, we can set up a more careful inductive argument. By bounded non-determinism, we mean that each configuration $([E, \ldots], \Sigma)$ only has *finitely many* possible successor configurations. The key result is the following quantifier inversion lemma:

Lemma 5. *Let R be a step-indexed predicate on a finite set X. Then:*

$$(\forall n.\, \exists x.\, n \models R(x)) \Rightarrow (\exists x.\, \forall n.\, n \models R(x))$$

Proof. By assumption, for each n, there exists $x_n \in X$ such that $n \models R(x_n)$. Since X is finite, by the pigeon-hole principle, there must be some $x \in X$ such that $m \models R(x)$ for infinitely many values of m. Now, given arbitrary n, this means there exists $m > n$ such that $m \models R(x)$. Since step-indexed predicates are downward-closed, $n \models R(x)$. Hence $\forall n.\, n \models R(x)$. ∎

Ignoring delay steps for the moment, we apply this lemma to our setting to get:

Lemma 6. *Suppose e steps to e' and $\forall n.\, \exists P_n.\, n \models \{source(i, E) * P_n\}\, e\, \{Q\}$. Then, $\exists E'$ such that E steps to E' and $\forall n.\, \exists P'_n.\, n \models \{source(i, E') * P'_n\}\, e'\, \{Q\}$.*

Proof. Let X by the set of E' that E can step to, which we know to be finite.[7] Consider the step-indexed predicate R on X defined by $n \models R(E') \triangleq (E \to E' \wedge \exists P'_n.\, n \models \{source(i, E') * P'_n\}\, e'\, \{Q\})$. By assumption, for each $n > 0$, $n \models \{source(i, E) * P_n\}\, e\, \{Q\}$ for some P_n. The definition of Hoare triples implies that there exists some E' such that $(n-1) \models R(E')$. Thus, $\forall n.\, \exists E'.\, n \models R(E')$, so we can apply Lemma 5 to get the desired result. ∎

Notice that in the conclusion of Lemma 6, if e' takes another step, we can apply Lemma 6 again to the triples for e'. So, given some initial triple $\{source(i, E)\}\, e\, \{Q\}$ and a diverging execution of e, by induction we can repeatedly apply Lemma 6 to construct an infinite execution of the source program.

---

[7] To be precise we ought to mention the initial states σ and Σ that e and E run in and assume they satisfy the precondition of the triple.

Finally, we prove that if the execution of e was fair, this source execution will be fair as well, giving us Lemma 4. Of course, for the full mechanized proof we have to take into account the delay steps and consider the case where the target thread owns multiple source threads. But all of these are *finite* additional possibilities, they do not fundamentally change the argument sketched above.

5   Proof of Compiler Correctness

We now give a brief overview of our proof of Theorem 1. Recall that we want to show that if E is a well-typed source expression, then $\widehat{E} \sqsubseteq E$.

Our proof is a binary logical relations argument. We interpret each type τ as a relation on values from the target and source language, writing $v \simeq^{\mathcal{V}} V : \tau$ to say that v and V are related at type τ. However, following the example of [21,22], these are relations *in our refinement logic*, which means we can use all of the constructs of the logic to describe the meaning of types. We then prove a fundamental lemma showing that well-typed expressions are logically related to their translation. Next, we show that our logical relation implies the triple used in HT-REFINE. Theorem 1 is then a direct consequence of these two lemmas.

Details of these proofs can be found in the appendix [34]; here we focus on the definition of the logical relation itself. For most types, the interpretation is straight-forward and fairly standard. For instance, $v \simeq^{\mathcal{V}} V : \mathsf{Int}$ holds exactly when $v = V = n$, for some integer n. The important exception, of course, is the interpretation of session types, in which we need to relate the encoding of channels as linked-lists to the source language's primitive buffers.

Sessions as an STS. To interpret session types, we generalize the state transition system from the example in Sect. 3 to handle the more complicated "protocols" that session types represent.

What should the states of this STS be? In the STS used in Sect. 3, we had three states: INIT, in which the message had not been sent; SENT, where a message had been sent from the left end-point, but not received; and RECEIVED, where the message had now been received at the right end-point. In the general case, we will have more than one message, so our states need to track how many messages have been sent/received on each end-point. We also need to know the "current" type of the end-points, but notice that if we know the starting type of an end-point, and how many messages have been sent/received on it, we can always recover these current types. We write S^n for the type after n messages have been sent/received starting from S.

We also need to know which heap locations l_{l} and l_{r} currently represent the end-points of the channel. All together then, the states will be tuples $(n_{\mathsf{l}}, n_{\mathsf{r}}, l_{\mathsf{l}}, l_{\mathsf{r}})$ describing how many messages have been sent/received on each end-point, and the corresponding heap locations.

Remember that we also need to define the tokens and transitions associated with each state of our STS. The transitions are simple: we can either advance the left end-point, incrementing n_{l} and updating l_{l}, and similarly for the right end-point. For the tokens, recall that in our example proof, we had [S] and [R] tokens used by each thread to advance the state when they had interacted with their respective end-points. In general, the threads will now use the end-points multiple times, so we need a token for each of these uses on both sides. Concretely, we will have two kinds of tokens, [Left n] and [Right n], which are used when advancing the left and right end-point counter to n, respectively.

To complete the description of the STS, we have to talk about the interpretation of the states. This interpretation has to relate the messages in the source channel's current buffers to the nodes in the linked list on the target heap. The individual messages should, of course, be related by our logical relation $(\simeq^{\mathcal{V}})$. We lift this relation to lists of messages $(\simeq^{\mathcal{L}})$ as follows:

$$
[] \simeq^{\mathcal{L}} [] : S
\qquad
\frac{\vartriangleright(v \simeq^{\mathcal{V}} V : \tau) * (L_h \simeq^{\mathcal{L}} L_c : S)}{vL_h \simeq^{\mathcal{L}} VL_c : ?\tau.\,S} \; \text{L-CONS}
$$

For now, ignore the $\vartriangleright$ symbol. The left rule says that two empty lists are equivalent at any session type. The right rule says two lists are related *at a receive type* $?\tau.\,S$, if their heads are related under τ, and the remainders of each list are related at S. It is important that this is a receive type: if the current type of the end-point is a send type, then there should not be any messages in its receive buffer, so the rule for empty lists is the only one that applies.

We can now give our state interpretation, φ, which is parameterized by (a) the starting type S of the left end-point (the right end-point's starting type is by necessity dual so there is no need to track it), and (b) the name c of the channel:

$$
\varphi_{S,c}(n_l, n_r, l_l, l_r) \triangleq \exists L_c, L_h. \quad \Big(c \hookrightarrow_s (L_c, []) * \text{linklist}(L_h, l_l, l_r) * \tag{10}
$$

$$
(L_h \simeq^{\mathcal{L}} L_c : S^{n_l}) * n_l + |L_c| = n_r\Big) \vee \ldots \tag{11}
$$

Let us explain this piece by piece. To start, we have that there exists a list of *source* values L_c and a list of *target* values L_h, representing the messages that are stored in the buffer right now. We then distinguish between two cases: either the first buffer is empty or the second buffer is empty. We omit the second case (corresponding to the second disjunct) because it is symmetric. In the first case, the channel's first buffer contains L_c and the second buffer is empty (10, left). On the target side, the buffer is represented as a linked list from l_l to l_r containing the values L_h (10, right). Of course, the lists of values need to be related according to the end-point's current type S^{n_l} (11, left). Finally, the number of messages sent/received through the left end-point, plus the number of messages still in the buffer, should equal the total number of messages sent/received through the right end-point (11, right). Therefore, when these remaining messages are received by the left end-point, the two types will again be dual.

Informally then, the value relation at session types $l \simeq^{\mathcal{V}} c_s : S$ says that there exists an appropriate STS and tokens for the session S which relates l and c_s.

We can then prove Hoare triples for the message-passing primitives that manipulate this STS. For instance, for heapRecv we have (omitting delay steps):

$$\{\mathsf{source}(i, K[\mathsf{recv}(c_s)]) * l \simeq^{\mathcal{V}} c_s : \, ?\tau. \, S\} \qquad \mathsf{heapRecv} \, l$$
$$\{(l', v). \, \exists V. \, \mathsf{source}(i, K[(c_s, V)]) * (v \simeq^{\mathcal{V}} V : \tau) * l' \simeq^{\mathcal{V}} c_s : S\}$$

This triple closely corresponds to the typing rule RECV (Fig. 1): typing judgments in the premise become value relations in the pre-condition, and the conclusion is analogously transformed into the postcondition. Indeed, the proof of the fundamental lemma for the logical relation essentially just appeals to these triples.

There is something we have glossed over: when we defined the logical relation, we used the STS, but the STS interpretation used the logical relation! This circularity is the reason for the $\triangleright$ symbol guarding the recursive occurrence of $(\simeq^{\mathcal{V}})$ in L-CONS. The details are spelled out in the appendix.

6   Conclusion and Related Work

We have presented a logic for establishing *fair, termination-preserving* refinement of higher-order, concurrent languages. To our knowledge, this is the first logic combining higher-order reasoning (and in particular, step-indexing) with reasoning for termination-sensitive concurrent refinement. Moreover, we applied this logic to verify the correctness of a compiler that translates a session-typed source language with channels into an ML-like language with a shared heap.

All of these results have been fully mechanized in Coq. Our mechanization builds on the Coq development described in Jung et al. [19] and the proof-mode from Krebbers et al. [21]. The proofs use the axioms of excluded middle and indefinite description. The proof scripts can be found online [1].

Second Case Study. Our logic is not tied to this source language and translation: we have used it to mechanize a proof that the Craig-Landin-Hagersten queue lock [9, 27] refines a ticket lock. Further details can be found in the appendix [34].

Linearity. Linearity has been used in separation logics to verify the absence of memory leaks: if heap assertions like $l \hookrightarrow v$ are linear, and the only way to "dispose" of them is by freeing the location l, then post conditions must mention all memory that persists after a command completes [17]. Our treatment of linearity has limitations that make it unsuitable for tracking resources like the heap. First, in our logic, only affine assertions can be framed (see HT-FRAME), because framing could hide the obligation to perform steps on source threads. Of course, for resources like the heap this would be irrelevant, and this rule could be generalized. Second, linear resources cannot be put in STS interpretations, so they cannot be shared between threads. Since STSs are implemented in terms of a more primitive feature in Iris called *invariants*, which are affine, allowing linear resources to be put inside would circumvent the precise accounting that motivates linearity in the first place. Thus, we would need to extend Iris with a useful form of "linear" shared invariants, which we leave to future work.

Session Types. Starting from the seminal work of Honda [16], a number of session-type systems have been presented with different features [8,14,35,38,41] (among many others). The language presented here is a simplified version of the one in Gay and Vasconcelos [14]. Wadler [38] has shown that a restricted subset of the language in [14] does enjoy a deadlock freedom property. This property holds only when the type system is *linear*, like the original in [14]. Pérez et al. [30] and Caires et al. [7] give logical relations for session-typed languages, which they use to prove strong normalization and contextual equivalence results. Their logical relation is defined "directly", instead of translating into an intermediary logic. Early versions of another session-typed system [39] used a ring-buffer to represent channels instead of linked lists, which would be interesting to verify.

Logics for Concurrency, Termination, and Refinement. There is a vast literature on program logics for concurrency [6,10–13,15,19,20,24–26,28,29,31,32,36,37]. Indeed, the reason for constructing a logical relation on top of a program logic, as in Krogh-Jespersen et al. [22], is so that we can take advantage of the many ideas that have proliferated in this community.

Focusing on logics for refinement and termination properties: Benton [3] pioneered the use of a *relational* Hoare logic for showing the correctness of compiler transformations in the sequential setting. Yang [40] generalized this to relational separation logic. We have already described [36], which developed a higher-order concurrent separation logic for termination-insensitive refinement. Liang et al. [25] also allow non-terminating programs to refine terminating ones. This was extended in [26] for a termination-preserving refinement, but this deals with termination-preservation *without* fairness. Most recently Liang and Feng [24] addressed fair termination-preserving refinement. In their logic, threads can explicitly reason about how their actions may or may not further delay other threads, which is more general than our approach and may be needed for verifying some of the examples they consider. It would be interesting to adapt this more explicit fairness reasoning to the higher-order setting.

Hoffmann et al. [15] features a concurrent separation logic for total correctness. Threads own resources called "tokens", which must be "used up" every time a thread repeats a while loop. This "using up" of tokens inspired our step shifts. Later, da Rocha Pinto et al. [31] generalized this by using ordinals instead of tokens: threads decrease the ordinal they own as they repeat a loop. This is useful for languages with unbounded non-determinism. Our technique for coping with step-indexing in Sect. 4 relied on bounded non-determinism. It may be possible to remove this limitation by using *transfinite* step-indexing [4,33] instead.

Acknowledgments. The authors thank Robbert Krebbers, Jeehoon Kang, Max Willsey, Frank Pfenning, Derek Dreyer, Lars Birkedal, and Jan Hoffmann for helpful discussions and feedback. This research was conducted with U.S. Government support under and awarded by DoD, Air Force Office of Scientific Research, National Defense Science and Engineering Graduate (NDSEG) Fellowship, 32 CFR 168a; and with support by a European Research Council (ERC) Consolidator Grant for the project "RustBelt", funded under the European Union's Horizon 2020 Framework Programme (grant agreement no. 683289). Any opinions, findings and conclusions or recommendations expressed in this material are those of the authors and do not necessarily reflect the views of these funding agencies.

References

1. Website with Coq development (2016). http://www.cs.cmu.edu/~jtassaro/papers/iris-refinement
2. Appel, A., McAllester, D.: An indexed model of recursive types for foundational proof-carrying code. TOPLAS **23**(5), 657–683 (2001)
3. Benton, N.: Simple relational correctness proofs for static analyses and program transformations. In: POPL (2004)
4. Birkedal, L., Bizjak, A., Schwinghammer, J.: Step-indexed relational reasoning for countable nondeterminism. Logical Methods Comput. Sci. **9**(4), 1–22 (2013)
5. Birkedal, L., Støvring, K., Thamsborg, J.: The category-theoretic solution of recursive metric-space equations. Theor. Comput. Sci. **411**(47), 4102–4122 (2010)
6. Brookes, S.D.: Variables as resource for shared-memory programs: semantics and soundness. Electr. Notes Theor. Comput. Sci. **158**, 123–150 (2006)
7. Caires, L., Pérez, J.A., Pfenning, F., Toninho, B.: Behavioral polymorphism and parametricity in session-based communication. In: Felleisen, M., Gardner, P. (eds.) ESOP 2013. LNCS, vol. 7792, pp. 330–349. Springer, Heidelberg (2013). doi:10.1007/978-3-642-37036-6_19
8. Caires, L., Pfenning, F.: Session types as intuitionistic linear propositions. In: Gastin, P., Laroussinie, F. (eds.) CONCUR 2010. LNCS, vol. 6269, pp. 222–236. Springer, Heidelberg (2010). doi:10.1007/978-3-642-15375-4_16
9. Craig, T.S.: Building fifo and priority-queueing spin locks from atomic swap. Technical report 93-02-02, Computer Science Department, University of Washington (1993)
10. da Rocha Pinto, P., Dinsdale-Young, T., Gardner, P.: TaDA: a logic for time and data abstraction. In: Jones, R. (ed.) ECOOP 2014. LNCS, vol. 8586, pp. 207–231. Springer, Heidelberg (2014). doi:10.1007/978-3-662-44202-9_9
11. Dinsdale-Young, T., Dodds, M., Gardner, P., Parkinson, M.J., Vafeiadis, V.: Concurrent abstract predicates. In: D'Hondt, T. (ed.) ECOOP 2010. LNCS, vol. 6183, pp. 504–528. Springer, Heidelberg (2010). doi:10.1007/978-3-642-14107-2_24
12. Dinsdale-Young, T., Birkedal, L., Gardner, P., Parkinson, M.J., Yang, H.: Views: compositional reasoning for concurrent programs. In: POPL (2013)
13. Feng, X.: Local rely-guarantee reasoning. In: POPL, pp. 315–327 (2009)
14. Gay, S.J., Vasconcelos, V.T.: Linear type theory for asynchronous session types. J. Funct. Program. **20**(1), 19–50 (2010)
15. Hoffmann, J., Marmar, M., Shao, Z.: Quantitative reasoning for proving lock-freedom. In: LICS, pp. 124–133 (2013)
16. Honda, K.: Types for dyadic interaction. In: Best, E. (ed.) CONCUR 1993. LNCS, vol. 715, pp. 509–523. Springer, Heidelberg (1993). doi:10.1007/3-540-57208-2_35
17. Ishtiaq, S.S., O'Hearn, P.W.: BI as an assertion language for mutable data structures. In: POPL, pp. 14–26 (2001)
18. Jones, C.B.: Tentative steps toward a development method for interfering programs. TOPLAS **5**(4), 596–619 (1983)
19. Jung, R., Krebbers, R., Birkedal, L., Dreyer, D.: Higher-order ghost state. In: ICFP, pp. 256–269 (2016, to appear)

20. Jung, R., Swasey, D., Sieczkowski, F., Svendsen, K., Turon, A., Birkedal, L., Dreyer, D.: Iris: monoids and invariants as an orthogonal basis for concurrent reasoning. In: POPL, pp. 637–650 (2015)
21. Krebbers, R., Timany, A., Birkedal, L.: Interactive proofs in higher-order concurrent separation logic. In: POPL, pp. 205–217 (2017, to appear)
22. Krogh-Jespersen, M., Svendsen, K., Birkedal, L.: A relational model of types-and-effects in higher-order concurrent separation logic. In: POPL, pp. 218–231 (2017, to appear)
23. Lehmann, D., Pnueli, A., Stavi, J.: Impartiality, justice and fairness: the ethics of concurrent termination. In: Even, S., Kariv, O. (eds.) ICALP 1981. LNCS, vol. 115, pp. 264–277. Springer, Heidelberg (1981). doi:10.1007/3-540-10843-2_22
24. Liang, H., Feng, X.: A program logic for concurrent objects under fair scheduling. In: POPL, pp. 385–399 (2016)
25. Liang, H., Feng, X., Fu, M.: Rely-guarantee-based simulation for compositional verification of concurrent program transformations. ACM Trans. Program. Lang. Syst. **36**(1), 3 (2014)
26. Liang, H., Feng, X., Shao, Z.: Compositional verification of termination-preserving refinement of concurrent programs. In: CSL-LICS, pp. 65:1–65:10 (2014)
27. Magnusson, P.S., Landin, A., Hagersten, E.: Queue locks on cache coherent multi-processors. In: International Symposium on Parallel Processing, pp. 165–171 (1994)
28. Nanevski, A., Ley-Wild, R., Sergey, I., Delbianco, G.A.: Communicating state transition systems for fine-grained concurrent resources. In: Shao, Z. (ed.) ESOP 2014. LNCS, vol. 8410, pp. 290–310. Springer, Heidelberg (2014). doi:10.1007/978-3-642-54833-8_16
29. O'Hearn, P.: Resources, concurrency, and local reasoning. TCS **375**(1), 271–307 (2007)
30. Pérez, J.A., Caires, L., Pfenning, F., Toninho, B.: Linear logical relations for session-based concurrency. In: Seidl, H. (ed.) ESOP 2012. LNCS, vol. 7211, pp. 539–558. Springer, Heidelberg (2012). doi:10.1007/978-3-642-28869-2_27
31. da Rocha Pinto, P., Dinsdale-Young, T., Gardner, P., Sutherland, J.: Modular termination verification for non-blocking concurrency. In: Thiemann, P. (ed.) ESOP 2016. LNCS, vol. 9632, pp. 176–201. Springer, Heidelberg (2016). doi:10.1007/978-3-662-49498-1_8
32. Svendsen, K., Birkedal, L.: Impredicative concurrent abstract predicates. In: Shao, Z. (ed.) ESOP 2014. LNCS, vol. 8410, pp. 149–168. Springer, Heidelberg (2014). doi:10.1007/978-3-642-54833-8_9
33. Svendsen, K., Sieczkowski, F., Birkedal, L.: Transfinite step-indexing: decoupling concrete and logical steps. In: Thiemann, P. (ed.) ESOP 2016. LNCS, vol. 9632, pp. 727–751. Springer, Heidelberg (2016). doi:10.1007/978-3-662-49498-1_28
34. Tassarotti, J., Jung, R., Harper, R.: A higher-order logic for concurrent termination-preserving refinement. Available as arXiv:1701.05888 [cs.PL] (2017). http://iris-project.org/pdfs/2017-esop-refinement-final.pdf. Extended version with appendices
35. Toninho, B., Caires, L., Pfenning, F.: Higher-order processes, functions, and sessions: a monadic integration. In: Felleisen, M., Gardner, P. (eds.) ESOP 2013. LNCS, vol. 7792, pp. 350–369. Springer, Heidelberg (2013). doi:10.1007/978-3-642-37036-6_20
36. Turon, A., Dreyer, D., Birkedal, L.: Unifying refinement and Hoare-style reasoning in a logic for higher-order concurrency. In: ICFP, pp. 377–390 (2013)

37. Vafeiadis, V., Parkinson, M.: A marriage of rely/guarantee and separation logic. In: Caires, L., Vasconcelos, V.T. (eds.) CONCUR 2007. LNCS, vol. 4703, pp. 256–271. Springer, Heidelberg (2007). doi:10.1007/978-3-540-74407-8_18
38. Wadler, P.: Propositions as sessions. J. Funct. Program. **24**(2–3), 384–418 (2014)
39. Willsey, M., Prabhu, R., Pfenning, F.: Design and implementation of concurrent C0. In: Linearity (2016)
40. Yang, H.: Relational separation logic. TCS **375**(1–3), 308–334 (2007)
41. Yoshida, N., Vasconcelos, V.T.: Language primitives and type discipline for structured communication-based programming revisited: Two systems for higher-order session communication. Electr. Notes Theor. Comput. Sci. **171**(4), 73–93 (2007)

Modular Verification of Procedure Equivalence in the Presence of Memory Allocation

Tim Wood[1]([✉]), Sophia Drossopoulou[1], Shuvendu K. Lahiri[2],
and Susan Eisenbach[1]

[1] Imperial College London, London, UK
tw00@doc.ic.ac.uk, {S.Drossopoulou,S.Eisenbach}@imperial.ac.uk
[2] Microsoft Research, Redmond, USA
Shuvendu.Lahiri@microsoft.com

Abstract. For most high level languages, two procedures are equivalent if they transform a pair of isomorphic stores to isomorphic stores. However, tools for modular checking of such equivalence impose a stronger check where isomorphism is strengthened to equality of stores. This results in the inability to prove many interesting program pairs with recursion and dynamic memory allocation.

In this work, we present RIE, a methodology to modularly establish equivalence of procedures in the presence of memory allocation, cyclic data structures and recursion. Our technique addresses the need for finding witnesses to isomorphism with angelic allocation, supports reasoning about equivalent procedures calls when the stores are only locally isomorphic, and reasoning about changes in the order of procedure calls. We have implemented RIE by encoding it in the Boogie program verifier. We describe the encoding and prove its soundness.

Keywords: Program equivalence · Program verification · Version-aware verification

1 Introduction

Program maintenance dominates the program lifecycle. A study of application bugs that took more than one attempt to fix [35] found that 22–33% of fixes required a supplementary fix, and found a diverse range of errors including incomplete refactorings. A study of refactorings [8] found that across 12,922 refactorings from three software projects, 15% of refactorings induced a bug. *Automatic program equivalence verification* [19,21,29,36] offers the potential to reduce problems by allowing a programmer to automatically (without programmer annotations) verify that the new version is behaviourally equivalent to the old.

The goal of these verification tools is to make the benefits of program equivalence verification available to programmers who are not verification experts. An automatic equivalence verification tool *takes a pair of programs as input and then*

© Springer-Verlag GmbH Germany 2017
H. Yang (Ed.): ESOP 2017, LNCS 10201, pp. 937–963, 2017.
DOI: 10.1007/978-3-662-54434-1_35

outputs whether the programs are equivalent or not (or perhaps times-out). Program equivalence is undecidable in the general case, however, some success has been achieved on programs with substantially similar structure. Since software is frequently modified in small incremental steps, versions tend to be structurally similar.

We know of two tools designed for fully-automatic program equivalence verification of programs with heaps: Symdiff [29] and RVT [21]. Symdiff [22,26,29,30] is built on top of the Boogie [3] intermediate verification language which, in turn, uses the Z3 [16] satisfiability modulo theories (SMT) solver to discharge proof obligations. RVT uses a designed-for-purpose verification algorithm, which passes program fragments to the CBMC [14] bounded model checker.

Symdiff relates heaps using equality (of arrays modelling the heaps), which we will call *e-equivalence*, so programs that differ in the order or amount of dynamic memory allocation or garbage cannot be verified as equivalent by Symdiff. RVT does support differences in allocation, but assumes that all heap data structures are tree-like.[1]

E-equivalence is too restrictive for programmers, who expect to be able to replace one procedure with another if the two have identical observable behaviour. A more intuitive notion of procedure equivalence for programs with dynamic memory allocation can be constructed using isomorphism between memory locations. Definitions of program equivalence based on a notion of isomorphism have been used in several formal systems [11,37]. Our definition of equivalence is:

> *Two procedures are* equivalent, *if they terminate for the same set of initial stores, and if both procedures run to completion from isomorphic initial stores, they result in isomorphic final stores.*

Our definition of equivalence matches intuition: it allows for differences in the order or amount of memory allocation and garbage and is not restricted to tree-like structures. Achieving automatic and modular verification presents several challenges:

Challenge 1 What kind of input do we need to give to an SMT solver so that it can even do the verification? We need to establish an isomorphism between unbounded heaps of arbitrary shape, which is computationally infeasible in general. Furthermore, a direct axiomatisation of isomorphism involves existentially quantifying the mapping between memory locations that characterises the isomorphism. SMT based verification systems are not very good at producing witnesses to such existentials and so a direct axiomatisation of isomorphism is ineffective.

Sometimes calls to equivalent procedures occur from stores that are not fully isomorphic, rather the stores are isomorphic in the footprint of the called procedures. This leads to the next two challenges:

---

[1] For details, see *Definition 2* (and the paragraph following) on page 5 of the 2009 paper by Godlin and Strichman [21].

Challenge 2 How can our tool determine when stores correspond in the footprint of a called procedure?

Challenge 3 What should we do about equivalent calls from non-isomorphic stores since they do not necessarily result in isomorphic stores?

Challenge 4 How do we decide which calls are equivalent when there may be many possible candidates? Equivalent calls may occur in different orders in each procedure, and moreover the procedure calls which correspond may differ from execution to execution depending on the initial state (i.e. program inputs).

1.1 Example

Consider the pair of equivalent procedures in Fig. 1 that differ in the order of memory allocation.

```
 1  lcopy(t,r) modifies {r} {        14  rcopy(t,r) modifies {r} {
 2    if(t ≠ null  ∧  r ≠ null) {     15    if(t ≠ null  ∧  r ≠ null) {
 3      rl := new;                    16      rl := new;
 4      rr := new;                    17      rr := new;
 5      n := new;                     18
 6                                    19        rcopy(t.r, rr);
 7      lcopy(t.l, rl);               20        rcopy(t.l, rl);
 8      lcopy(t.r, rr);               21
 9                                    22      n := new;
10      n.l := rl.v;                  23      n.l := rl.v;
11      n.r := rr.v;                  24      n.r := rr.v;
12      r.v := n;                     25      r.v := n;
13  } }                              26  } }
```

Fig. 1. Both procedures copy a binary tree.

Both procedures are intended to copy the passed structure t. The procedures are equivalent on *any* input, whether the input is tree shaped or not. Our methodology RIE (**R**eplace **I**somorphism with **E**quality) and tool APE (**A**utomatic **P**rogram **E**quivalence tool) can verify that. The procedures differ in two ways: Firstly, the allocation of the copied node has been moved from before the recursive calls on line 5 to after the recursive calls on line 22. Secondly, the order of the recursive calls on lines 7 and 8 has been reversed on lines 19 and 20. The procedures are written in a simple language we call $\mathcal{L}$, formalised in Sect. 3.

The procedures are equivalent. An intuition as to why is: when t or r are null both procedures leave the heap unchanged. Otherwise, both procedures recursively copy all the nodes to the left, and all the nodes to the right, and return a newly allocated root node via the parameter r. The only pre-existing object modified by the procedures is the one pointed to by r. It is possible that r aliases a node reachable from t, but even so only the v field of r is written to, and only after the nodes have been copied. The objects allocated to rl and rr do not alias anything, so the recursive calls cannot modify the tree, and hence swapping the order of the recursive calls does not affect the result. The postcondition `modifies` {r} asserts that no existing object, other than r, is modified. For this example, our tool APE requires this framing assertion. Our approach can take advantage of any contracts that are available.

The procedures are not e-equivalent (so would fail to match in Symdiff) when the stores are related with equality. With non-deterministic allocation a procedure is not even equivalent to itself! It is straightforward to resolve with a deterministic allocator, e.g. one that starts at 0 and allocates the next address. Under this deterministic approach [29] a procedure is e-equivalent with itself, but `lcopy` and `rcopy` are still not e-equivalent as the allocations on Line 5 and Line 22 are allocated different addresses.

The example illustrates the challenges in the following ways. **Challenge 1**: equivalence requires that the final stores are isomorphic, but the recursive calls are unbounded so a tool has to check isomorphism of a graph of arbitrary shape and unbounded size. **Challenge 2**: the stores are not equivalent prior to the recursive calls. For instance, in `lcopy` three allocations (Lines 3 to 5) have occurred before the recursive calls, but in `rcopy` only two allocations have occurred (Lines 16 to 17). **Challenge 3**: the stores after the related calls on Line 7 and Line 20 are not generally isomorphic, since the store after Line 20 contains the effects of two recursive calls but the store after Line 7 contains the effect of only one recursive call. **Challenge 4**: we do not know in advance which recursive call in `lcopy` (Lines 7 and 8) corresponds to which recursive call in `rcopy` (Lines 19 and 20).

1.2   Contributions

We propose a sound methodology, RIE, for establishing isomorphic procedure equivalence which is effective in an SMT solver. RIE enables our tool APE to tackle **challenge 1** by automatically establishing isomorphism using under-approximation and heap equality! RIE works by proving equivalence under the *angelic allocation* assumption; the memory locations are, as far as possible, assumed to be allocated in such a way as to make isomorphic heaps also equal.

We describe a simple language $\mathcal{L}$ for which isomorphism implies equivalence of observable behaviours, and give a formal definition of what it means for $\mathcal{L}$ to be closed under isomorphism.

RIE also simplifies challenges two, three and four. RIE allows us to use equality in place of isomorphism, so **challenge 2** is addressed by extending the notion of heap equality to support partial heap equality, which we then apply to an over-approximation of the footprint of the procedures. Furthermore RIE rescues us from the need to produce a witness (from **challenge 1**) to the correspondence between procedure behaviour, instead we address **challenge 3** by equating the write effects of equivalent procedures (soundly ignoring unobservable behavioural differences). We combine our technique with mutual summaries to address **challenge 4**.

In Sect. 2 we describe how RIE can be implemented to verify program equivalence. In Sect. 3 we formalise equivalence and isomorphism and outline RIE's soundness proof. In Sect. 4 we discuss the effectiveness and limitations of RIE. Finally in Sect. 5 we discuss some related work and conclude.

2 Encoding in a Verifier

Our tool APE takes as input an L program and produces as output 'success', 'failure', or times out. It does this by translating the input program into Boogie code, which is fed into the Z3 SMT solver. The source code is available at https://github.com/lexicalscope/ape.

In this section we illustrate RIE by showing how APE encodes the example from Sect. 1.1 and how that encoding helps overcome the challenges detailed in the introduction. In particular, we show how verification under the assumption of "angelic allocation" proceeds. Previous work typically takes the approach of abstracting or overapproximating programs with dynamic allocation [11, 27, 40, 43], *storeless semantics* [13] go as far as abstracting away the observable store entirely. We make the surprising observation that under-approximating memory allocation is also a useful approach, and our formal system proves it sound. RIE establishes procedure equivalence by checking equivalence for only one pair of execution traces for each initial store. Specifically:

> *All* pairs of executions from isomorphic initial stores result in *isomorphic* final stores if at least *one* pair of executions from each initial store results in *equal* final stores.

In particular, it is not necessary to consider all pairs of isomorphic initial stores. We prove this in Sect. 3.

RIE combines our ideas about establishing isomorphism using SMT technology with the prior work on product programs and mutual summaries to produce an automatic program equivalence tool that can verify our example. Standard single program verification tools can be applied to the problem of procedure equivalence using *product programs* [5, 7, 21, 29, 41], which encode the bodies of a pair of procedures into a single procedure such that verifying a safety property of the product procedure is equivalent to verifying a relational property of the procedure pair [5]. Furthermore, a technique called *mutual summaries* [22] can be applied to induce an SMT solver to search for interesting relations between procedure calls.

2.1 Angelic Allocation

APE checks equivalence for one pair of executions for each initial store. It does so by searching amongst the possible pairs of executions for a pair that result in equal stores (modulo garbage). Of interest, then, are pairs of executions where particular allocation sites (new) in each procedure are allocated the same addresses. In Fig. 1 there are three allocation sites in each procedure. This gives six possible correspondences between allocation sites (the variables on the left of the equality are from lcopy, and the variables on the right are from rcopy):

```
27 procedure lcopy_rcopy(..., h:Heap, t,r:Ref) {
28 // make twelve copies of the initial heap, h
29 h_a0,h_a1,h_b0,h_b1,h_c0,h_c1,h_d0,h_d1,h_e0,h_e1,h_f0,h_f1
30    := h,h,h,h,h,h,h,h,h,h,h,h;
31
32 // inline each procedure once with variables renamed with the given suffix
33 inline lcopy with variable suffix _a0 and heap h_a0
34 inline rcopy with variable suffix _a1 and heap h_a1
35 assume rl_a0 = rl_a1 ∧ rr_a0 = rr_a1 ∧ n_a0 = n_a1;
36
37 // and again for correspondence b
38 inline lcopy with var suffix _b0 and heap h_b0
39 inline rcopy with var suffix _b1 and heap h_b1
40 assume rl_b0 = rl_b1 ∧ rr_b0 = n_b1 ∧ n_b0 = rr_b1;
41
42 // and so on for c,d,e,f
43
44 assert equal#heaps(...,h_a0,h_a1)
45    ∨ equal#heaps(...,h_b0,h_b1)
46    ∨ ... /* and so on for c,d,e,f */ }
```

Fig. 2. A product procedure encoding of equivalence verification under angelic memory allocation for procedures lcopy and rcopy.

$$a) \quad rl = rl, rr = rr, n = n \qquad b) \quad rl = rl, rr = n, n = rr$$
$$c) \quad rl = rr, rr = rl, n = n \qquad d) \quad rl = rr, rr = n, n = rl$$
$$e) \quad rl = n, rr = rl, n = rr \qquad f) \quad rl = n, rr = rr, n = rl$$

We do not know in advance which correspondence will be useful for verification[2]. In our example, it happens that correspondence (a) is the useful one. Pairs of (terminating) executions from the same initial store that have allocations in this correspondence will result in equal final stores. Hence, no *direct* checks for isomorphism are required. We will detail how procedure calls are handled shortly.

We induce the solver to search for the useful correspondence by constructing a pair of executions for each correspondence and using a disjunction to assert that at least one of them results in equivalent final stores. The Boogie-like pseudo code in Fig. 2 shows how APE encodes lcopy and rcopy into a single (Symdiff-style) product procedure. The **inline** commands (e.g. line 33) are not actual Boogie syntax but should be taken to mean that the statements from the body of the relevant procedure are copied into the product procedure at that point. When the procedures are inlined, they are rewritten to work on their own private copy of the heap with fresh variable names. After each inlined pair a different correspondence between allocation sites is assumed (lines 35 and 40). Finally a disjunction is asserted to challenge the verifier to prove that the final heaps are equal for at least one of the inlined pairs (line 44).

Thus, RIE allows us to establish isomorphism using only heap equality!

---

[2] It is interesting to note that in this example the variable names suggest which correspondence is important, perhaps indicating that there may be useful heuristics that could improve performance—such as trying correspondence (a) first.

2.2 Heap Equality

Here we described how APE establishes heap equality, and discuss why our approach is powerful. Tools can relate programs in an intensional or extensional way [10]. Intensionally equal heaps are defined in the same way, whereas extensionally equal heaps have the same observable properties. For example, the heaps[3] $h_1 = h_0[(5, \mathtt{f}) \mapsto 7][(5, \mathtt{g}) \mapsto 8]$ and $h_2 = h_0[(5, \mathtt{g}) \mapsto 8][(5, \mathtt{f}) \mapsto 7]$ are not intensionally equal, but they are extensionally equal. Extensional relationships provide a powerful means to reason about reordering of store updates.

```
47 function $Heap#ReachableEqual($h_1, $h_2:Heap, $roots:Roots) : bool {
48   $Heap#ReachableEqual'($h_1, $h_2, $roots) ∧
49   $Heap#ReachableEqual'($h_2, $h_1, $roots) }
50
51 function $Heap#ReachableEqual'($h_1, $h_2:Heap, $roots:Roots) : bool {
52   (∀$a:Ref :: {...} (∀<alpha> $f:Field alpha ::
53     $Reachable($h_1, $roots, $a)⟹$Read($h_1, $a, $f)=$Read($h_2, $a, $f)))}
54
55 function $Reachable($h:Heap, $roots:Roots, $a:Ref) : bool {
56   (∃$r:Ref :: {...} $Root($roots, $r) ∧ $Reach($h, $r, $a)) }
```

Fig. 3. Extensional equality of the reachable heap region. Written in Boogie.

APE uses the extensional axiomatisation of heap equality shown in Fig. 3. The axiomatisation allows procedures to create different garbage by only requiring equality of the reachable heap. The parameter $roots is a set of references, and it overapproximates the references that are on the stack. The predicate $Reachable is an axiomatisation of heap reachability (something is unreachable when in a disjoint part of the heap) and is discussed in Sect. 4.3.

We define equality between heaps using a pair of implications that say that if an object is reachable in either heap, its fields must be equal in both heaps. An alternative, and perhaps more obvious, definition would be that the reachable sets are equal, and that each object in the reachable set has equal fields in both the heaps. The definitions are equivalent—since heaps that are equal in their reachable parts have the same reachability relation. On several examples the solver was unable to prove that the reachable sets are equal, but it is able to prove our definition.

2.3 Procedure Call

Challenges two, three and four in the introduction relate to the need to reason modularly about the behaviour of nested procedure calls, such as the recursive calls in the example Fig. 1. In this section we describe how our encoding in Fig. 4 leverages RIE to address these challenges.

Equivalent procedure calls do not always occur from isomorphic stores (**challenge 2**). This is overcome by considering only the region of the heap

---

[3] $h_0[(5, \mathtt{f}) \mapsto 7]$ is the heap made by copying h_0 and setting field $\mathtt{f}$ of object 5 to 7.

```
57 function $abs_lcopy($strat:int, $h_pre:Heap, t:Ref,r:Ref, $h_post:Heap):bool;
58 function $abs_rcopy($strat:int, $h_pre:Heap, t:Ref,r:Ref, $h_post:Heap):bool;
59
60 procedure lcopy($strat:int, $h_pre:Heap, t:Ref,r:Ref) returns ($h_post:Heap)
61  free ensures $abs_lcopy($strat, $h_pre, t, r, $h_post);
62  ...
63  free ensures (∀<alpha> $a:Ref,$f:Field alpha ::
64    $a ≠ $Null ∧ $Allocated($h_pre,$a) ∧ $Read($h_pre,$a,$f)!=$Read($h_post,$a,$f)
65    ⟹ $ReachableFromParams($h_pre, t, r, $a));
66 procedure rcopy($strat:int, $h_pre:Heap, t:Ref,r:Ref) returns ($h_post:Heap)
67  free ensures $abs_rcopy($strat, $h_pre, t, r, $h_post);
68  ...
69  free ensures (∀<alpha> $a:Ref,$f:Field alpha ::
70    $a ≠ $Null ∧ $Allocated($h_pre,$a) ∧ $Read($h_pre,$a,$f)!=$Read($h_post,$a,$f)
71    ⟹ $ReachableFromParams($h_pre, t, r, $a));
72
73 axiom (∀$strat:int,$h_pre_0,$h_post_0,$h_pre_1,$h_post_1:Heap,
74         t_0,r_0,t_1,r_1:Ref ::
75   {$abs_lcopy($strat,$h_pre_0, t_0, r_0, $h_post_0),
76    $abs_rcopy($strat,$h_pre_1, t_1, r_1, $h_post_1)}
77   $abs_lcopy($strat,$h_pre_0, t_0, r_0, $h_post_0) ∧
78   $abs_rcopy($strat,$h_pre_1, t_1, r_1, $h_post_1)
79   ∧ $Heap#EqualFromParams($h_pre_0, t_0, r_0, $h_pre_1, t_1, r_1)
80    ⟹ $SameDiff($h_pre_0, $h_post_0, $h_pre_1, $h_post_1));
81 function $SameDiff($h_pre_0, $h_post_0, $h_pre_1, $h_post_1:Heap) : bool {
82   (∀<alpha> $a:Ref,$f:Field alpha ::
83    ($Read($h_pre_0, $a, $f) ≠ $Read($h_post_0, $a, $f)
84    ⟹ $Read($h_post_0, $a, $f)==$Read($h_post_1, $a, $f)) ∧
85    ($Read($h_pre_1, $a, $f) ≠ $Read($h_post_1, $a, $f)
86    ⟹ $Read($h_post_0, $a, $f)==$Read($h_post_0, $a, $f))) }
```

Fig. 4. Mutual summary of the lcopy and rcopy procedures. Written in Boogie.

reachable from the procedure parameters when trying to establish equivalence of procedure calls. This corresponds to the predicate $Heap#EqualFromParams on line 79, detailed in Sect. 3.6.

Equivalent procedure calls do not necessarily result in isomorphic stores (**challenge 3**). This is overcome through our choice of procedure summary (line 80) and a frame axiom. The write effects of a pair of equivalent procedure calls are related by the predicate $SameDiff (line 81). The frame axiom appears as a free postcondition[4] of every procedure (lines 63 and 69). Both are described below.

Equivalent procedure calls are summarised by the predicate $SameDiff that relates the pre and post stores of both calls. $SameDiff approximates the actual behaviour of the procedures a surprising way, although equivalent procedures can vary in the amount and shape of garbage, $SameDiff states that equivalent procedure calls will always have equal effects, we justify this in Sect. 3.

The framing axioms (lines 63 and 69) restrict the write effects of the procedures to the part of the heap that was reachable from the procedure parameters. The axiom follows from the semantics of $\mathcal{L}$. It is not known in advance which

---

[4] A free postcondition may be assumed after a call, but is not checked.

procedure calls might be equivalent (**challenge 4**). This is overcome by how the summary of the behaviour of equivalent procedures is encoded. Specifically, the encoding of mutual summaries presented by Hawblitzel et al. [22] is used to induce the SMT solver to search for related pairs of procedure calls. We detailed this encoding below.

Figure 4 shows how APE encodes the mutual summary for the procedures `lcopy` and `rcopy`. The encoding consists of several parts. Encountered calls to the procedures are abstracted by a pair of uninterpreted predicates (lines 57 and 58) which we call *abstraction predicates*. The predicates are uninterpreted so we precisely control their instantiation. They are given as free postconditions of the procedures `lcopy` (line 61) and `rcopy` (line 67). Encountering calls to these procedures causes the abstraction predicates to be instantiated in the solver's E-graph. We set *triggers* (lines 75 and 76) so that the solver will instantiate the mutual summary axiom's quantifiers (line 74) for each pair of instantiations of the abstraction predicates. Non-vacuous instantiations of the axiom occur when the solver is able to establish that the heaps reachable from the call parameters are equal, and hence the antecedent is satisfied.

During a Simplify [17] style SMT solver proof search the quantifiers that appear in an axiom are instantiated with ground terms from the solver's E-graph that match *triggers* associated with the quantifier. In-turn, the axiom is applied to those instantiations to introduce new terms into the E-graph and so on. Thus, APE controls the proof search by a combination of the logical meaning of the axioms and the quantifier triggers.

The synthetic parameter `$strat` of `lcopy` (line 60) and `rcopy` (line 66) is introduced to prevent the proof search from trying to establish equivalence between procedure calls occurring under different allocation correspondences. For example, in Fig. 2, the inlining of `lcopy` on line 33 and line 39 will contain recursive calls to `lcopy` and `rcopy` respectively—but it is not useful to find relations between these calls as they pertain to different allocations correspondences. Specifically, the disjunction on line 44 asserts nothing about the relationship between those heaps. The parameter `$strat` represents the allocation correspondence in effect for that call, and the mutual summary trigger (lines 75 and 76 of Fig. 4) restricts instantiation of the quantifiers to calls which occurred under the same allocation correspondence.

We have completed our illustration of how the RIE methodology is implemented in a modular program equivalence tool. Discussion about the effectiveness and limitations of our approach is in Sect. 4.

3   Soundness of RIE

We now give a model of RIE and summarise a proof of its soundness. The semantics of $\mathcal{L}$ come in two flavours: the $\mathcal{V}$ semantics is the ordinary semantics of $\mathcal{L}$. The $\mathcal{A}$ semantics models our Boogie encoding, which includes the various approximations detailed in Sect. 2. We establish soundness of RIE by showing that equivalence under $\mathcal{A}$ implies equivalence under $\mathcal{V}$.

We expect a mapping between procedures names, $\mathcal{E}$, which pairs procedures that are suspected to be equivalent. RIE takes the program and $\mathcal{E}$ as input and tries to prove that indeed all pairs in $\mathcal{E}$ are equivalent.

We start with an overview of the semantics of $\mathcal{L}$, then define isomorphism and procedure equivalence. Then we detail how the various approximations are modelled in the $\mathcal{A}$ semantics. Finally we give RIE's soundness theorem[5].

3.1   Semantics of $\mathcal{L}$

$\mathcal{L}$ is a simple imperative language. Figure 5 describes the standard aspects of $\mathcal{L}$, while Fig. 6 describes the non-standard aspects. The following points are interesting about our semantics:

- We distinguish between execution under $\mathcal{V}$ and $\mathcal{A}$ with a subscript, writing $\leadsto_{\mathcal{L}}$ where $\mathcal{L} \in \{\mathcal{V}, \mathcal{A}\}$.
- We split procedure call into two: a "call" rule and a "body" rule, similar to Godlin and Strichman [21], to treat procedure call concretely in $\mathcal{V}$ but abstractly in $\mathcal{A}$. The latter is a first ingredient in reflecting mutual summaries.
- Execution of pairs of procedures is included in the operational semantics, modelled by the rules COMV and COMA:

$$\sigma_1, s_1 \parallel \sigma_2, s_2 \overset{tr_1, tr_2}{\underset{\mathcal{L}}{\leadsto}} \sigma_3 \parallel \sigma_4$$

meaning statement s_1 executed on store σ_1 results in store σ_3 producing trace tr_1, and similarly for statement s_2. These rules reflect product programs [1, 5, 29].
- We require the program adhere to a specification given by Con[6].
- The semantics are instrumented to produce a trace of the states reached during execution which we use to distinguish particular executions.
- although our semantics is a big step semantics, we keep the whole calling context as part of the runtime configuration to allow us to give useful meaning to isomorphism of stores.
- We assume loops have been encoded as recursive procedures.

We only discuss some of the rules of the operational semantics. NEW allocates a new object.[7] The address of the object must be fresh, and the object has all fields set to null. ASSIGN updates a stack variable x with the result of evaluating an expression e in the store σ.

BOD executes the body of a procedure p by looking up and executing p's statements. Our assumption that procedure contracts have already been verified, is

---

[5] Full details of the proof can be found in the first author's PhD thesis [44].

[6] We expect single program contracts to have been verified; programs with no contracts are also acceptable.

[7] In a concrete implementation we do not require that there is no garbage collection, just that the programmer cannot manipulate addresses.

$$s_a \in AtomicStmt := x := e \mid x := \mathbf{new}() \mid \mathbf{assume}\ b \mid \mathbf{assert}\ b \mid \mathbf{call}\ \mathbf{p}(x,\ldots,x) \mid$$
$$e.f := e$$
$$s \in Stmt \qquad := s_a \mid \mathbf{if}(b)\{s_a\} \mid s; s$$
$$e \in ScalarExpr := \mathbf{null} \mid x \mid e.f \mid b$$
$$b \in BoolExpr \qquad := x = y \mid !b \mid b \wedge b \mid \mathbf{true} \mid \mathbf{false}$$

Sets $a \in Addr$, $x \in Lid$, $f \in Fid$, $p \in Pid$, $v \in Val \stackrel{\text{def}}{=} Addr \cup \{\mathbf{true}, \mathbf{false}\}$.
Set $Addr$ has one reserved element $\mathbf{null}$.

$$h \in Heap \qquad \stackrel{\text{def}}{=} (Addr \times Fid) \rightharpoonup Val \text{ where } \forall h, f : h(\mathbf{null}, f) = \mathbf{null}.$$
$$\phi \in StackF \qquad \stackrel{\text{def}}{=} Lid \rightharpoonup Val$$
$$\tilde{\phi} \in Stack \qquad \stackrel{\text{def}}{=} StackF^*$$
$$\sigma \in Store \qquad \stackrel{\text{def}}{=} Stack \times Heap, \text{ where } \sigma(x) \text{ means } \phi(x) \text{ when } \sigma = (\tilde{\phi} \cdot \phi, h)$$
$$tr \in Trace \qquad \stackrel{\text{def}}{=} (Stmt \times Store \times Store)^*$$
$$mkframe(\sigma, x_1 \ldots x_n) \stackrel{\text{def}}{=} (\sigma^{\text{stack}} \cdot [x_1 \mapsto \sigma(x_1), \ldots, x_n \mapsto \sigma(x_n)], \sigma^{\text{heap}})$$
$$\mathcal{B} : Pid \rightarrow Stmt \qquad \text{looks up procedure bodies from procedure names.}$$

$$\sigma^{\text{heap}} \stackrel{\text{def}}{=} h \text{ and } \sigma^{\text{stack}} \stackrel{\text{def}}{=} \tilde{\phi} \cdot \phi \text{ and } \sigma^{\text{pop}} \stackrel{\text{def}}{=} (\tilde{\phi}, h) \text{ and } \sigma^{\text{top}} \stackrel{\text{def}}{=} \phi \text{ when } \sigma = (\tilde{\phi} \cdot \phi, h)$$

$$\frac{}{\sigma, e_1.f := e_2 \hookrightarrow (\sigma^{\text{stack}}, \sigma^{\text{heap}}[([\![e_1]\!]_\sigma, f) \mapsto [\![e_2]\!]_\sigma])} \text{ STORE}$$

$$\frac{a \notin dom(h) \quad \{f_1, \ldots, f_n\} = Fid \quad a \neq \mathbf{null}}{(\tilde{\phi} \cdot \phi, h), x := \mathbf{new}() \hookrightarrow (\tilde{\phi} \cdot \phi[x \mapsto a], h[(a, f_1) \mapsto \mathbf{null}, \ldots, (a, f_n) \mapsto \mathbf{null}]))} \text{ NEW}$$

$$\frac{\sigma \vDash b}{\sigma, \mathbf{assert}\ b \hookrightarrow \sigma} \text{ ASSERTT} \qquad\qquad \frac{\sigma_1, s \hookrightarrow \sigma_2}{\sigma_1, s \leadsto_{\mathcal{L}}^{s, \sigma_1, \sigma_2} \sigma_2} \text{ ATOM}$$

$$\frac{\sigma \vDash b}{\sigma, \mathbf{assume}\ b \hookrightarrow \sigma} \text{ ASSUME} \qquad\qquad \frac{\neg(\sigma \vDash b)}{\sigma, \mathbf{assert}\ b \hookrightarrow \mathbf{error}} \text{ ASSERTF}$$

$$\frac{}{\sigma, x := e \hookrightarrow (\sigma^{\text{stack}}[x \mapsto [\![e]\!]_\sigma], \sigma^{\text{heap}})} \text{ ASSIGN} \qquad \frac{\sigma_1 \vDash b \quad \sigma_1, s_a \leadsto_{\mathcal{L}}^{tr} \sigma_2}{\sigma_1, \mathbf{if}(b)\{s_a\} \leadsto_{\mathcal{L}}^{tr} \sigma_2} \text{ CONDT}$$

$$\frac{\neg(\sigma \vDash b)}{\sigma, \mathbf{if}(b)\{s_a\} \leadsto_{\mathcal{L}}^{\mathbf{if}(b)\{s_a\}, \sigma, \sigma} \sigma} \text{ CONDF} \qquad \frac{\sigma_1, s_1 \leadsto_{\mathcal{L}}^{tr_1} \sigma_2 \quad \sigma_2, s_2 \leadsto_{\mathcal{L}}^{tr_2} \sigma_3}{\sigma_1, s_1; s_2 \leadsto_{\mathcal{L}}^{tr_1 \cdot tr_2} \sigma_3} \text{ TRANS}$$

$$\frac{}{[\![\mathbf{null}]\!]_\sigma = \mathbf{null}} \qquad \frac{}{[\![x]\!]_\sigma = \sigma(x)} \qquad \frac{\neg(\sigma \vDash b)}{\sigma \vDash !b} \qquad \frac{\sigma \vDash b}{[\![b]\!]_\sigma = \mathbf{true}} \qquad \frac{\neg(\sigma \vDash b)}{[\![b]\!]_\sigma = \mathbf{false}}$$

$$\frac{}{[\![e.f]\!]_\sigma = \sigma^{\text{heap}}([\![e]\!]_\sigma, f)} \qquad \frac{\sigma(x) = \sigma(y)}{\sigma \vDash x = y} \qquad \frac{\sigma(x) = \mathbf{true}}{\sigma \vDash x} \qquad \frac{\sigma \vDash b_1 \quad \sigma \vDash b_2}{\sigma \vDash b_1 \wedge b_2}$$

Fig. 5. Grammar and operations of $\mathcal{L}$

$$\frac{(\sigma_1, \sigma_3) \in Con(\mathrm{p}) \quad \sigma_1, \mathcal{B}(\mathrm{p}) \rightsquigarrow_{\mathcal{L}}^{tr} \sigma_3}{\sigma_1, \mathtt{body\ p} \rightsquigarrow_{\mathcal{L}}^{tr \cdot (\mathtt{ret}, \sigma_3, \sigma_3^{\mathtt{pop}})} \sigma_3^{\mathtt{pop}}} \ \mathrm{BOD}$$

$$\frac{mkframe(\sigma_1, x_1 \ldots x_n), \mathtt{body\ p} \rightsquigarrow_{\mathcal{V}}^{tr} \sigma_3}{(\sigma_1, \mathtt{call\ p}(x_1 \ldots x_n)) \rightsquigarrow_{\mathcal{V}}^{(\mathtt{call\ p}(x_1 \ldots x_n), \sigma_1, \sigma_3)} \sigma_3} \ \mathrm{CALLV}$$

$$\frac{\begin{array}{c} dom(h_2) \supseteq dom(h_1) \\ ((mkframe(\sigma_1, x_1 \ldots x_n), h_1)(\tilde{\phi}_1 \cdot \phi, h_2)) \in Con(\mathrm{p}) \end{array}}{(\tilde{\phi}_1, h_1), \mathtt{call\ p}(x_1 \ldots x_n) \rightsquigarrow_{\mathcal{A}}^{(\mathtt{call\ p}(x_1 \ldots x_n), (\tilde{\phi}_1, h_1), (\tilde{\phi}_1, h_2))} (\tilde{\phi}_1, h_2)} \ \mathrm{CALLA}$$

$$\frac{\sigma_1, s_1 \rightsquigarrow_{\mathcal{V}}^{tr_1} \sigma_2 \quad \sigma_2, s_2 \rightsquigarrow_{\mathcal{V}}^{tr_2} \sigma_4}{(\sigma_1, s_1) \parallel (\sigma_2, s_2) \rightsquigarrow_{\mathcal{V}}^{tr_1, tr_2} (\sigma_3, \sigma_4)} \ \mathrm{COMV}$$

$$\frac{\mathcal{I}(tr_1, tr_2) \quad \mathcal{M}(tr_1, tr_2) \quad \sigma_1, s_1 \rightsquigarrow_{\mathcal{A}}^{tr_1} \sigma_2 \quad \sigma_2, s_2 \rightsquigarrow_{\mathcal{A}}^{tr_2} \sigma_4}{(\sigma_1, s_1) \parallel (\sigma_2, s_2) \rightsquigarrow_{\mathcal{A}}^{tr_1, tr_2} (\sigma_3, \sigma_4)} \ \mathrm{COMA}$$

Fig. 6. Procedure call and composition rules of $\mathcal{L}$

modelled by the requirement $(\sigma_1, \sigma_3) \in Con(\mathrm{p})$. Note that BOD pops the top of the final stack, while CALLA and CALLV push new frames (using the function *mkframe*).

CALLA models abstraction of procedure calls. The behaviour of the abstracted call is restricted by the procedure's contract $Con(\mathrm{p})$, and the call may not free any allocated address (All that RIE actually requires is that the language not have concrete addresses so any language with garbage collection which does not support pointer arithmetic can be handled).

Angelic allocation in the rule COMA is modelled by the predicate over trace pairs $\mathcal{I}$. The behaviour of called procedures in the $\mathcal{A}$ semantics is modelled by the predicate over trace pairs $\mathcal{M}$. We define $\mathcal{I}$ and $\mathcal{M}$, as the paper progresses.

3.2 Isomorphism

Stores are isomorphic if they differ only in the actual values of heap addresses or in garbage. An isomorphism is characterised by a bijection between values, π. Definition 1 says that σ_1 is isomorphic to σ_2 with relation π iff the stacks of σ_1 and σ_2 are the same height; for each corresponding stack frame the same variables are defined; and π is an injection. Where π is the uniquely defined relation that maps the stack variables of σ_1 to σ_2, commutes with field dereference, and preserves the meaning of null, true, and false.

Definition 1 (Isomorphism).

$$\sigma_1 \approx_\pi \sigma_2 \overset{def}{\Longleftrightarrow}$$

$- |\sigma_1| = |\sigma_2| \wedge \forall i \leq |\sigma_1| : dom(\sigma_1[i]) = dom(\sigma_2[i])$
$- \pi$ *is an injection*[8]*, written* $in(\pi)$

Where π *is the smallest relation that satisfies:*

$$\pi = \pi_v \cup \{\sigma_1[i](x) \mapsto \sigma_2[i](x) \mid x \in dom(\sigma_1[i]) \wedge i \leq |\sigma_1|\} \cup$$
$$\{\sigma_1(a, f) \mapsto \sigma_2(\pi(a), f) \mid a \in dom(\pi)\}$$

And $\pi_v \stackrel{def}{=} [\texttt{null} \mapsto \texttt{null}, \texttt{true} \mapsto \texttt{true}, \texttt{false} \mapsto \texttt{false}]$

In our notation: The number of stack frames in store σ is $|\sigma|$. The value of variable x in the ith stack frame is $\sigma[i](x)$. The domain of the mapping π is $dom(\pi)$, and $dom(\sigma[i])$ is the set of variables defined in the ith stack frame.

We also require that any contracts in the program are not sensitive to address values or garbage. We write $\sigma_{i...j}$ to mean $\sigma_i, \ldots, \sigma_j$.

Definition 2 (Contracts in $\mathcal{L}$). *The contracts* $Con : Pid \rightarrow \mathcal{P}(Store \times Store)$, *are sets of pairs of Store representing the set of acceptable pre and post stores of each procedure. We require that:*

$$\forall p, \sigma_{1...4}, \pi_{1,2} : \sigma_1 \approx_{\pi_1} \sigma_2 \wedge \sigma_3 \approx_{\pi_2} \sigma_4 \wedge (\sigma_1, \sigma_3) \in Con(p) \wedge in(\pi_1 \cup \pi_2)$$
$$\implies (\sigma_2, \sigma_4) \in Con(p)$$

Lemma 1 (Isomorphism is an equivalence relation). *The relation* $\approx$ *is an equivalence relation (reflexive, symmetric, transitive).*

The crucial property of $\approx$ is that it is closed under execution. Namely, executing a statement from isomorphic stores results in isomorphic executions. Executions are isomorphic iff the elements of their traces are pairwise isomorphic (written $tr_1 \approx tr_2$), and have isomorphic write effects.

Lemma 2 ($\mathcal{L}$ closed under isomorphism).
For every execution $\sigma_1, s \rightsquigarrow_{\mathcal{L}}^{tr_1} \sigma_3$, *store* σ_2, *and injection* π_1 *if* $\sigma_1 \approx_{\pi_1} \sigma_2$ *then*

- *there exists an execution* $\sigma_2, s \rightsquigarrow_{\mathcal{L}}^{tr_2} \sigma_4$
- *if* $\mathcal{L} = \mathcal{V}$, *every execution* $\sigma_2, s \rightsquigarrow_{\mathcal{V}}^{tr_2} \sigma_4$ *is isomorphic to* $\sigma_1, s \rightsquigarrow_{\mathcal{V}}^{tr_1} \sigma_3$

Executions $\sigma_1, s \rightsquigarrow_{\mathcal{L}}^{tr_1} \sigma_3$ *and* $\sigma_2, s \rightsquigarrow_{\mathcal{L}}^{tr_2} \sigma_4$ *are isomorphic iff* $\exists \pi_{1,2}$:

$$\sigma_1 \approx_{\pi_1} \sigma_2 \wedge tr_1 \approx tr_2 \wedge in(\pi_1 \cup \pi_2) \wedge effect(\sigma_1, \sigma_3) \approx_{\pi_2} effect(\sigma_2, \sigma_4)$$

Where trace isomorphism is:

$$tr_1 \approx tr_2 \stackrel{def}{\Longleftrightarrow} tr_1 \approx_\emptyset tr_2$$
$$tr_1 \approx_\pi tr_2 \stackrel{def}{\Longleftrightarrow} \exists n : |tr_1| = |tr_2| = n \wedge \exists \pi_1 \ldots \pi_{2n} :$$
$$(\forall i \leq n : tr_1[i]\downarrow_2 \approx_{\pi_{2i-1}} tr_2[i]\downarrow_2) \wedge$$
$$(\forall i \leq n : tr_1[i]\downarrow_3 \approx_{\pi_{2i}} tr_2[i]\downarrow_3) \wedge$$
$$(\forall i, j \leq 2n : in(\pi \cup \pi_i \cup \pi_j))$$

---

[8] $in(\pi) \stackrel{def}{\Longleftrightarrow} \forall (a, b), (c, d) \in \pi : (a = c \Longleftrightarrow b = d)$.

And where effect$(\sigma_1, \sigma_3) \overset{def}{=} \sigma_3{}^{\text{heap}} \setminus \sigma_1{}^{\text{heap}}$

Proof. By induction on the derivation of $\sigma_1, s \leadsto_{\mathcal{L}}^{tr_1} \sigma_3$. Most cases are straightforward since no instruction is sensitive to the actual value of addresses. Note that every instruction makes the set of reachable addresses smaller, apart from **new** which expands it by exactly one fresh address—this corresponds to the fact that addresses are never synthesised and garbage is never resurrected.   □

A way to think of closure under isomorphism is that $\mathcal{L}$ is not sensitive to the actual values of addresses nor garbage. Many industrial languages (such as C, Java, Python, C$^\sharp$, etc.) contain features that are sensitive to the actual values of heap addresses or order of allocation. Such sensitivity is typically not central to the language and it is often not necessary to use such features.

3.3   Regional Isomorphism

As discussed in Sect. 2, APE works by establishing isomorphisms between the heap regions reachable from procedure parameters (Line 79 of Fig. 4), so we introduce a notion of isomorphism between heap regions. The heap regions reachable from two sequences of parameter names W and X are isomorphic iff the sequences have the same length, and the relation (π) constructed by following all paths from the parameters is an injection:

Definition 3 (Regional Isomorphism).

$$\sigma_1 \approx_\pi^{W,X} \sigma_2 \overset{def}{\Longleftrightarrow}$$
$$|W| = |X| \wedge W \subseteq dom(\sigma_1{}^{\text{top}}) \wedge X \subseteq dom(\sigma_2{}^{\text{top}}) \wedge in(\pi)$$

Where π is the smallest relation which satisfies:

$$\pi = \pi_v \cup \{\sigma_1(W[i]) \mapsto \sigma_2(X[i]) \mid i \leq |X|\} \cup \{\sigma_1(a, f) \mapsto \sigma_2(\pi(a), f) \mid a \in dom(\pi)\}$$

3.4   Procedure Equivalence

Procedures are equivalent if executing their bodies from isomorphic stores results in isomorphic stores. Executing **body p** means looking up and executing the statements that form the body of procedure p. Note that rule BOD pops the top stack frame before completing, so stores σ_3, σ_4 in Definition 4 are as observed by a caller. This means that equivalence relates to the observable behaviour of the procedure body, and that differences in local variables, etc., are ignored. The same definition of procedure equivalence applies to both the $\mathcal{A}$ and the $\mathcal{V}$ semantics.

Definition 4 (Procedure equivalence).

$$p_1 \lessapprox p_2 \overset{def}{\Longleftrightarrow}$$
$$\forall \sigma_{1...4} : \sigma_1 \approx \sigma_2 \wedge \sigma_1, \textbf{body } p_1 \parallel \sigma_2, \textbf{body } p_2 \leadsto_{\mathcal{L}} \sigma_3 \parallel \sigma_4 \implies \sigma_3 \approx \sigma_4$$

3.5   Angelic Allocation

We describe how angelic allocation is modelled by the predicate $\mathcal{I}$ in the $\mathcal{A}$ semantics rule COMA. The predicate selects the pairs of execution traces that exhibit desirable allocation patterns.

Predicate $\mathcal{I}$ (Definition 6) retains only traces with heap regions that are equal at particular isomorphic points (Definition 5) in the traces. In APE, these points correspond to procedure entry, equivalent procedure calls and allocation sites. APE only verifies procedures from equal (rather than isomorphic) initial stores, discards execution pairs which don't have interesting correspondences between allocations, and assumes procedures have equal effects. Because we are only trying to prove soundness of RIE, it is not necessary to fully specify how APE chooses which stores to equate. Rather, we prove that *any* assumption of store equality that the tool makes is sound, subject to the caveats in Definition 5.

Definition 5 (Isomorphic Points).
Any tool using RIE must define a function

$$pts : (Trace \times Trace) \rightarrow \mathcal{P}(\mathbb{N} \times \mathbb{N} \times Lid^* \times Lid^*)$$

with the following properties:

1. *The same set of points is produced for isomorphic traces:*

$$\forall tr_{3,4} : tr_1 \approx tr_3 \wedge tr_2 \approx tr_4 \implies pts(tr_1, tr_2) = pts(tr_3, tr_4)$$

2. *The traces are isomorphic at each of the points:*

$$\forall (i, j, W, X) \in pts(tr_1, tr_2) : \exists \pi_1 : tr_1[i] \approx_{\pi_1}^{W,X} tr_2[j]$$

3. *If the initial stores of tr_1, tr_2 are isomorphic, then the isomorphism is injective with all the other isomorphisms. Otherwise the isomorphisms are empty.*
   - $in(\pi \cup \Pi(tr_1, tr_2))$
   - $\nexists \pi : fst(tr_1) \approx_\pi fst(tr_2) \implies \Pi(tr_1, tr_2) = \emptyset$

Where

$$\Pi(tr_1, tr_2) = \bigcup \left\{ \pi \mid \exists (i, j, X, Y) \in pts(tr_1, tr_2) \wedge tr_1[i] \approx_\pi^{X,Y} tr_2[j] \right\}$$

Definition 6 (Angelic Allocation).

$$\mathcal{I}(tr_1, tr_2) \overset{def}{\iff} \Pi(tr_1, tr_2) \subseteq id$$

Definition 5 requires that the points are selected symmetrically for isomorphic traces. This symmetry is critical for the soundness of RIE, which must verify at least one pair of execution traces for each initial state. Furthermore, the definition requires that the union of the isomorphisms between the selected heap regions is an injection. This corresponds to the fact that RIE is implemented by equating allocation sites, and will be discussed further in later sections, particularly Sect. 4.

3.6   Mutual Summaries of Equivalent Procedures

APE uses mutual summaries, lines 73 and 80 in Fig. 4, to allow the verifier to use facts about the behaviour of equivalent procedure calls in its proofs. It is needed in order for procedure equivalence to be a transitive relation.

APE's use of mutual summaries is modelled by the rule CALLA, which over-approximates the behaviour of concrete procedure call. And the predicate $\mathcal{M}$ in the rule COMA, which restricts the traces to those where the procedure pairs in $\mathcal{E}$ behave equivalently.

The antecedent $\sigma_1 \approx_{\pi_1}^{\{x_1 \ldots x_n\}, \{y_1 \ldots y_n\}} \sigma_2$ expresses that the regions reachable from the parameters are isomorphic (as needed for challenge 2), while the conclusion $\mathit{effect}(\sigma_1, \sigma_3) \approx_{\pi_2} \mathit{effect}(\sigma_2, \sigma_4)$ expresses that the procedures have isomorphic write effects (as needed for challenge 3). In our example, the encoding of the antecedent is $Heap\#EqualFromParams on line 79 of Fig. 4, while the encoding of the conclusion is $SameDiff on line 80 of Fig. 4.

Definition 7 (Mutual Summaries of Equivalent Procedures).

$$\mathcal{M}(tr_1, tr_2) \overset{def}{\iff} \forall \pi_1, \sigma_{1\ldots 4}, (p_1, p_2) \in \mathcal{E} :$$
$$(\texttt{call } p_1(x_1 \ldots x_n), \sigma_1, \sigma_3) \in tr_1 \ \wedge$$
$$(\texttt{call } p_2(y_1 \ldots y_n), \sigma_2, \sigma_4) \in tr_2 \ \wedge$$
$$\sigma_1 \approx_{\pi_1}^{\{x_1 \ldots x_n\}, \{y_1 \ldots y_n\}} \sigma_2$$
$$\implies \exists \pi_2 : in(\pi_1 \cup \pi_2) \ \wedge \ \mathit{effect}(\sigma_1, \sigma_3) \approx_{\pi_2} \mathit{effect}(\sigma_2, \sigma_4)$$

3.7   Soundness of RIE

We now give the theorem which guarantees soundness of RIE, and describe some keys points in its proof. Theorem 1 states that if all pairs in $\mathcal{E}$ are mutually terminating and equivalent under the $\mathcal{A}$ semantics, then they are also equivalent under the $\mathcal{V}$ semantics. Mutual termination (mt) means that both procedures terminate for the same set of initial stores[9].

Theorem 1 (RIE is sound).

$$\textit{If } \forall (p_3, p_4) \in \mathcal{E} : mt_\mathcal{V}(p_3, p_4) \ \wedge \ p_3 \not\approx p_4$$
$$\textit{Then } \forall (p_1, p_2) \in \mathcal{E} : p_1 \not\approx p_2$$

$$\textit{Where } mt_\mathcal{L}(p_3, p_4) \overset{def}{\iff} \forall \sigma_{1\ldots 3} : \sigma_1 \approx \sigma_2 \implies$$
$$\left(\sigma_1, \texttt{body } p_3 \rightsquigarrow_\mathcal{L} \sigma_3 \implies \exists \sigma_4 : \sigma_2, \texttt{body } p_4 \rightsquigarrow_\mathcal{L} \sigma_4 \right) \ \wedge$$
$$\left(\sigma_1, \texttt{body } p_4 \rightsquigarrow_\mathcal{L} \sigma_3 \implies \exists \sigma_4 : \sigma_2, \texttt{body } p_3 \rightsquigarrow_\mathcal{L} \sigma_4 \right)$$

---

[9] We could produce a total definition of procedure equivalence by including a notion of mutual termination [18,22] in Definition 4. However, APE does not yet reason about the termination behaviour of the procedures. A total notion of procedure equivalence is important, particularly where a transitive procedure equivalence relation is needed. Since our tool takes the same basic approach as Symdiff, it should be straightforward to incorporate existing mutual termination checking techniques [18,20,22].

Proof. The proof proceeds by showing that for any pair of executions (tr_1, tr_2) from isomorphic initial stores in the $\mathcal{V}$ semantics there exist an isomorphic execution $(tr_5$ with $tr_1 \approx tr_5)$ such that that $\mathcal{I}$ and $\mathcal{M}$ hold for (tr_1, tr_5) and thus the tr_5 and tr_2 executions compose by $\parallel$ in the $\mathcal{A}$ semantics. Then by the assumptions and transitivity of $\approx$ we know that tr_1, tr_2 end in isomorphic stores. The proof goes by an inner induction nested within an outer induction. We now write the proof in some more detail:

Assume $\forall (\mathrm{p}_3, \mathrm{p}_4) \in \mathcal{E} : mt_\mathcal{V}(\mathrm{p}_3, \mathrm{p}_4) \wedge \mathrm{p}_3 \not\approx \mathrm{p}_4$.
To show:

$$\forall (\mathrm{p}_1, \mathrm{p}_2) \in \mathcal{E}, \sigma_{1...4}, tr_{1,2} :$$

$$\sigma_1 \approx \sigma_2 \wedge \sigma_1, \mathbf{body}\ \mathrm{p}_1 \parallel \sigma_2, \mathbf{body}\ \mathrm{p}_2 \overset{tr_1, tr_2}{\leadsto_\mathcal{V}} \sigma_3 \parallel \sigma_4 \implies \sigma_3 \approx \sigma_4$$

First Part: From Definition 5 we see that there is a $\pi_2 = \Pi(tr_1, tr_2)$ (1). By Lemma 3 (below) there exists a third execution $\sigma_2, \mathbf{body}\ \mathrm{p}_1 \leadsto_\mathcal{V}^{tr_3} \sigma_5$ such that tr_1 is isomorphic to tr_3 with π_2, i.e. $tr_1 \approx_{\pi_2} tr_3$, which means by Lemma 1 (symmetry) we get $tr_3 \approx_{\pi_2^{-1}} tr_1$ (2). Take any point $(i, j, X, Y) \in pts(tr_1, tr_2)$. To show: $tr_3[i] \approx_{id}^{X,Y} tr_2[j]$. By (1) exists π_4 such that $tr_1[i] \approx_{\pi_4}^{X,Y} lr_2[j]$ and $\pi_4 \subseteq \pi_2$ (4). By (2) there exists π_3 such that $tr_3[i] \approx_{\pi_3} tr_1[i]$ and $\pi_3 \subseteq \pi_2^{-1}$ (3). Hence, by Lemma 1 (transitivity), we have that $tr_3[i] \approx_{\pi_3 \circ \pi_4}^{X,Y} tr_2[j]$, we know π_3 composed with π_4 is large enough because X is a subset of the stack variables defined in $tr_1[i]$, and $dom(\pi_3)$ includes the values of all stack variables. By (3), (4), we know that π_3 composed with π_4 is a subset of the identity relation. So $tr_3[i] \approx_{id}^{X,Y} tr_2[j]$. Because $tr_1 \approx tr_3$ we have by definition $pts(tr_1, tr_2) = pts(tr_3, tr_2)$. Then we get $\forall (i, j, X, Y) \in pts(tr_3, tr_2) : tr_3[i] \approx_{id}^{X,Y} tr_2[j]$. And thus we have $\Pi(tr_3, tr_2) \subseteq id$, which in turn gives us $\mathcal{I}(tr_3, tr_2)$ (5).

Second Part: We now proceed by induction on the size of the derivation of $\sigma_2, \mathbf{body}\ \mathrm{p}_1 \leadsto_\mathcal{V}^{tr_3} \sigma_5$.

It remains to show that, tr_2 is also a trace under $\mathcal{A}$ and that there is an $\mathcal{A}$ trace tr_5 isomorphic to tr_3 such that $\mathcal{M}(tr_5, tr_2)$ holds. Note that it is trivial to prove that apart from $\parallel$ all the rules of $\mathcal{A}$ semantics overapproximate the $\mathcal{V}$ semantics (11). By (11) and induction on the derivation of $\sigma_2, \mathbf{body}\ \mathrm{p}_2 \leadsto_\mathcal{V}^{tr_2} \sigma_4$ we get $\sigma_2, \mathbf{body}\ \mathrm{p}_2 \leadsto_\mathcal{A}^{tr_2} \sigma_4$.

Base Case: there are no procedure calls in $\sigma_1, \mathbf{body}\ \mathrm{p}_1 \leadsto_\mathcal{V}^{tr_1} \sigma_3$. By Lemma 2 then $\sigma_2, \mathbf{body}\ \mathrm{p}_1 \leadsto_\mathcal{V}^{tr_3} \sigma_5$ also has no procedure calls. By (11) and induction on the derivation of $\sigma_2, \mathbf{body}\ \mathrm{p}_1 \leadsto_\mathcal{V}^{tr_3} \sigma_5$ we get $\sigma_2, \mathbf{body}\ \mathrm{p}_1 \leadsto_\mathcal{A}^{tr_3} \sigma_5$. Since there are no procedure calls, trivially $\mathcal{M}(tr_3, tr_2)$ and $\sigma_2, \mathbf{body}\ \mathrm{p}_1 \parallel \sigma_2, \mathbf{body}\ \mathrm{p}_2 \leadsto_\mathcal{A}^{tr_3, tr_2} \sigma_5 \parallel \sigma_4$. From the antecedent we know that $lst(tr_3) \approx lst(tr_2)$, and since $tr_1 \approx tr_3$ then by transitivity of $\approx$ we have $lst(tr_1) \approx lst(tr_2)$. And since $lst(tr_1) = \sigma_3$ and $lst(tr_2) = \sigma_4$ base case is done.

Inductive Step: there are procedure calls in $\sigma_1, \mathbf{body}\ \mathrm{p}_1 \leadsto_\mathcal{V}^{tr_1} \sigma_3$.

To show: there exists an execution $\sigma_2, \mathbf{body}\ \mathrm{p}_1 \leadsto_\mathcal{A}^{tr_5} \sigma_7$ such that $\mathcal{M}(tr_5, tr_2)$ and $tr_5 \approx_{id} tr_3$ (6). Proceed by an inner induction over the derivation of

$\sigma_2, \text{body } p_1 \leadsto_{\mathcal{V}}^{tr_3} \sigma_5$. Most cases are trivial. The interesting cases are CALLV where the called procedure is in $\mathcal{E}$, and the inductive case TRANS.

Inner Case: CALLV where the called procedure is in $\mathcal{E}$. By case there is $\sigma_2, \text{call } p_3(x_1 \ldots x_n) \leadsto_{\mathcal{V}} \sigma_5$ and $(p_3, p_4) \in \mathcal{E}$. Rule CALLV can only be applied if a shallower tree is derivable for the body of the called procedure. Therefore we apply the outer induction hypothesis, the antecedent $mt_{\mathcal{V}}(p_3, p_4)$, and Lemma 3, to deduce that there exists σ_7 such that $\sigma_2, \text{call } p_4(x_1 \ldots x_n) \leadsto_{\mathcal{V}}^{tr_5} \sigma_7$ and $\sigma_5 \approx_{id} \sigma_7$. From CALLA we see that $\sigma_2, \text{call } p_3(x_1 \ldots x_n) \leadsto_{\mathcal{A}}^{(\text{call } p_3(x_1 \ldots x_n), \sigma_2, \sigma_7)} \sigma_7$ (intuition: we swap the behaviour of p_3 for the behaviour of p_4). Take $tr_5 = (\text{call } p_3(x_1 \ldots x_n), \sigma_2, \sigma_7)$ and we have $tr_3 \approx_{id} tr_5$. To show: $\mathcal{M}(tr_5, tr_2)$. Take arbitrary $(\text{call } p_4(y_1 \ldots y_n), \sigma_8, \sigma_{10}) \in tr_2$ such that $\sigma_2 \approx_{\pi_5}^{\{x_1 \ldots x_n\}, \{y_1 \ldots y_n\}} \sigma_8$. To show: $\exists \pi_6 : in(\pi_5 \cup \pi_6) \wedge effect(\sigma_2, \sigma_5) \approx_{\pi_6} effect(\sigma_8, \sigma_{10})$. This follows straightforwardly from Lemma 2 and the fact that the same procedure p_4 was executed to obtain σ_5 as to obtain σ_{10}. Inner case **done.**

Inner Case: TRANS By case there is $\sigma_2, s_1; s_2 \leadsto_{\mathcal{V}}^{tr_3} \sigma_5$ and hence exists $\sigma_9, tr_{7,9}$ such that $\sigma_2, s_1 \leadsto_{\mathcal{V}}^{tr_7} \sigma_9, s_2 \leadsto_{\mathcal{V}}^{tr_9} \sigma_5$. The proof goes as expected, by applying the inner induction hypothesis twice with one slight complexity. The first application constructs another execution of s_1 with the desired properties; but that execution's final store is not σ_9! Rather it is some other store (say σ_{11}) that is isomorphic to σ_9. Before we apply the inner induction hypothesis a second time, we use Lemma 3 to construct an execution isomorphic to $\sigma_9, s_2 \leadsto_{\mathcal{V}}^{tr_9} \sigma_5$ but with initial store σ_{11}. $\mathcal{M}$ holds for the resultant traces by the same argument as the CALLV case. Inner case **done.**

Hence $\mathcal{M}(tr_5, tr_2)$. From (5) and (6) we also have $\mathcal{I}(tr_5, tr_2)$. So we get that $\sigma_2, \text{body } p_1 \parallel \sigma_2, \text{body } p_2 \leadsto_{\mathcal{A}}^{tr_5, tr_2} \sigma_7 \parallel \sigma_4$ is an execution under the $\mathcal{A}$ semantics. Finally, from the antecedent we know that $lst(tr_3) \approx lst(tr_4)$, and since $tr_1 \approx tr_3 \approx tr_5$ and $tr_2 \approx tr_4$ then by transitivity of $\approx$ we have $lst(tr_1) \approx lst(tr_2)$. And since $lst(tr_1) = \sigma_3$ and $lst(tr_2) = \sigma_4$ we are done.

$\square$

The soundness proof of Theorem 1 relies on constructing alternative executions that are isomorphic using the identity bijection, Lemma 3 states that all such alternative executions are derivable in $\mathcal{L}$.

Lemma 3 (Sufficent non-determinism). *Given statement s, stores $\sigma_{1 \ldots 3}$, mapping π_1, and alternative allocation strategy π_2, such that:*

- *σ_1 and σ_2 are isomorphic with mapping π_1: $\sigma_1 \approx_{\pi_1} \sigma_2$*
- *s can execute to completion from σ_1: $\sigma_1 : \sigma_1, s \leadsto_{\mathcal{L}}^{tr_1} \sigma_3$*
- *π_1 and π_2 map common addresses in the same way in $(\pi_1 \cup \pi_2)$*
- *$\forall (a_1, a_2) \in \pi_2 : (a_1 \in \sigma_1^{\text{heap}} \iff a_2 \in \sigma_2^{\text{heap}})$*

Then there exists an isomorphic execution $\sigma_2, s \leadsto_{\mathcal{L}}^{tr_2} \sigma_4$ such that:

$$tr_1 \approx_{\pi_2} tr_2 \wedge \forall (a_1, a_2) \in \pi_2 : (a_1 \in \sigma_3^{\text{heap}} \iff a_2 \in \sigma_4^{\text{heap}})$$

Proof. By induction on the derivation of $\sigma_1, s \leadsto_{\mathcal{L}}^{tr_1} \sigma_3$ the alternative execution is constructed. In particular note that because π_2 does not map between allocated and unallocated addresses, the appropriate alternative address is always unallocated when an allocation statement is reached. And that, since $in(\pi_1 \cup \pi_2)$ then all addresses that were already allocated at the start of the execution do not need to be allocated alternatives. The proof goes through for both $\mathcal{V}$ and $\mathcal{A}$.   □

4   Discussion

The number of correspondences between allocations (Sect. 2) is factorial in the maximum number of allocation sites in either procedure. Hence RIE is only practical for relatively small numbers of allocation sites. However, this is not as restrictive as it may seem because our approach is modular. In practice, when loops are encoded as procedure calls, then many interesting procedures contain only small numbers of allocations. In some cases it is also possible to split a procedure into chunks or abstract common parts. It is also likely that the applicability of this technique can be significantly extended by using additional static analysis to eliminate some of the permutations in advance. For example, the types of the objects being allocated could be used to eliminate permutations that aligned objects of different types.

Framing of procedure calls is important in verifying equivalence for many examples. APE has a fairly naive approach to framing and disjointness of heap regions, which restricts the class of examples it can currently deal with. However, our techniques, and choice of Dafny [32] style heap encoding, should be amenable to a more powerful framing methodology. Improving APE's framing support is likely to significantly improve its completeness.

We considered many alternative approaches to establishing isomorphism. The natural approach using existentials does not work very well. We investigated several approaches using universal quantification. We tried defining heaps to be isomorphic if all pairs of paths that lead to related addresses in one heap also lead to related addresses in the other. We tried several approaches for limiting which, and what depth of paths should be considered by the solver. But the underlying doubly exponential complexity of comparing all pairs of paths impedes the applicability of that approach. The requirement that disjoint heap effects of procedure calls commute was an important design force: many alternative approaches required extensive additional axioms to handle the various cases, whereas our current approach of enumerating allocators seems to handle many cases naturally.

4.1   Examples

There are a collection of programs available from https://github.com/lexical scope/ape\#automatic-procedure-equivalence-tool that show the capabilities of

Description	Allocations	Timing
Empty program	0	1.5s
Making the same procedures calls	0	1.5s
Change amount of garbage allocated	1	1.5s
Allocations moved past calls	1	1.5s
Change order of allocation	2	1.5s
Isomorphism of heap reachable from call parameters	2	1.8s
Recursive calls reordered	2	8s
Copying a cyclic data structure	2	4s
Inserting a row into a table	2	31s
Copying a list	2	7s
Copying a tree with calls same order	3	84s
Copying a tree with calls reordered	3	130s

Fig. 7. Examples with the maximum number of allocations per procedure and timings

APE. Several of them have been listed in Fig. 7 with timings performed on an Intel Core i5-3210M@2.5 GHz processor with 8 GB memory.

We surmise that the amount of time APE takes to verify an example is related to the number of allocations, the number of paths through the procedure, the number of procedure calls, the complexity of any framing reachability that needs to be solved, and the order that Z3 happens to apply the axioms (i.e. how far into the search space the solution lies—for example, reordering procedure calls usually slows the verification down).

RIE's approach of using equality to establish isomorphism does prevent APE from establishing isomorphism in some cases where it would be helpful to do so. The example in Fig. 8 is from a refactoring of some code which manipulates a doubly linked list. Both procedures add an element to a list, but first remove it if it is already present. The left procedure has a redundant check that the item is in the list, in the right procedure this redundancy is removed.

The isomorphism between lines 88 and 105 relates the addresses in rf0 and rf. The isomorphism between lines 91 and 105 relates the addresses in rf1 and rf. If we were to assume equality for both of these isomorphisms then we would have rf = rf0 = rf1. However, rf0 is allocated by the new statement on line 87 whereas rf1 is allocated by the subsequent new statement on line 90. The semantics of new require that each allocation gives an address which was not previously allocated—i.e. that rf0 ≠ rf1.

RIE, therefore, restricts the selected points in Definition 6 to prevent contradictory isomorphisms being selected. Due to this restriction a verifier using RIE alone may fail to produce a proof for some procedures that are in fact equivalent according to our definitions. Any tool using RIE in practice may choose to equate one pair of calls to find, but it must find some other way to deal with the other pair of calls (such as manually adding an additional specification of find).

```
87  new rf0;                                  104  new rf;
88  find(1,x,rf0); _ _ _ _ _ _ _ _ _ _ _ _ _ 105  find(1,x,rf);
89  if(!rf0.v.sentinel) {            _ _ - - 106
90     new rf1;                       _ _    107
91     find(1,x,rf1); _ - - ˊ               108
92     node := rf1.v;                        109  node := rf.v;
93     if (!node.sentinel) {                 110  if(!node.sentinel){
94        node.prev.next := node.next;       111     node.prev.next := node.next;
95        node.next.prev := node.prev;       112     node.next.prev := node.prev;
96     }                                     113  }
97     add(1,x);                             114  add(1,x);
98  } else {                                 115
99     add(1,x);                             116
100 }                                        117
101                                          118
102 find(1,x,r) modifies {r} ...             119  find(1,x,r) modifies {r} ...
103 add(1,x) ...                             120  add(1,x) ...
```

Fig. 8. A difficult example where two stores in one execution are isomorphic with the same store in the other execution.

4.2 Definitions of Isomorphism and Procedure Equivalence

Our definition of procedure equivalence is useful because it is a contextual equivalence [34] for $\mathcal{L}$. This means that given equivalent procedures p_1, p_2 and a program that calls p_1, one can always change the program to call p_2 instead without affecting the observable behaviour of the program. Of particular interest to programmers is Corollary 1: the relation $\approx$ preserves the meaning of all assertions.

Corollary 1 (Isomorphism is assertion preserving).

$$\forall \sigma_1, \sigma_2, b : \sigma_1 \approx \sigma_2 \implies (\sigma_1 \vDash b \iff \sigma_2 \vDash b)$$

Proof. Follows from Lemma 2. □

Interestingly, it is possible to define isomorphism almost equivalently as the least-fixed-point interpretation of the relation:

$$\sigma_1 \approx' \sigma_2 \overset{\text{def}}{\iff}$$

$$\sigma_1 = \sigma_2 = \sigma_\emptyset \vee \left(\exists s_a, \sigma_{3,4} : \sigma_3 \approx' \sigma_4 \wedge \sigma_3, s_a \overset{\rightarrow}{\curvearrowright} \sigma_1 \wedge \sigma_4, s_a \overset{\rightarrow}{\curvearrowright} \sigma_2 \right)$$

where $\sigma_\emptyset$ is the empty store. That is, it could be defined as a smallest relation closed under the atomic operations of the semantics. However, even though the semantics is naturally closed under $\approx'$, the definition is not as helpful when trying to decide if a particular pair of stores are isomorphic. Regardless, a definition in this least-fixed-point style would allow us to construct a notion of isomorphism even for a semantics where we did not know an appropriate direct definition. Perhaps it is interesting to consider what assertion language would be preserved for any particular semantics given such a definition.

4.3 Reachability

Establishing reachability enables APE to prove interesting examples, but is ancillary to the focus of this paper RIE and angelic allocation. Still, our definition of equivalence allows differences in garbage (which is unreachable memory), and APE use reachability to reason about read and write effect framing as described in Sect. 2.3—so an useful axiomatisation of reachability is needed.

```
121  // Reachability is uninterpreted but axiomatised
122  function $Reach($h:Heap, $a:Ref, $b:Ref) : bool;
123
124  axiom (∀$h:Heap, $a:Ref :: $Reach($h, $a, $a));
125  axiom (∀$h:Heap, $a,$b:Ref :: {...}
126    $Reach($h, $a, $b) ∧ $NoInboundEdges($h,$b)⟹$a = $b);
127  axiom (∀$h:Heap, $a,$b:Ref :: {...} $Reach($h,$a,$b)⟹
128    $a = $b ∨
129    (∃$c:Ref,$f:Field Ref :: $Reach($h, $a, $c)∧$Edge($h, $c, $f, $b)));
130  axiom (∀$h:Heap, $a,$b:Ref :: {...} $Reach($h,$a,$b)⟹
131    $a = $b ∨
132    (∃$c:Ref,$f:Field Ref :: $Edge($h, $a, $f, $c)∧$Reach($h, $c, $b)));
133
134  function $NoInboundEdges($h:Heap, $a:Ref) : bool
135  { (∀$b:Ref, $f:Field Ref :: !$Edge($h,$b,$f,$a)) }
```

Fig. 9. The partial axiomatisation of reachability used by APE, written in Boogie. The triggers are elided {...}. The function $Read(h,a,f) is the value of field f of object a in heap h, the predicate $Allocated($h,$a) holds if object $a is allocated in heap $h. The predicate $Edge($h, $a, $f, $c) holds if the field $f of object $a has the value $c in heap $h.

Figure 9 shows our Boogie encoding of reachability. We give several axioms for the predicate $Reach, which the tool instantiates in different circumstances controlled by various triggers (controlled programatically, users cannot write them). Rather than precisely deciding the reachability set, often it is necessary to prove disjointness of certain heap regions. For example, garbage objects are disjoint from the reachable region, and a property of a region is preserved over a procedure call if the region is disjoint from the call effects. Our choice of axioms enable the tool to establish a lack of reachability by showing either that there are no outgoing (line 130) or no incoming (line 127) edges to a particular heap region. Although the axioms line 127 and line 130 are logically equivalent, we use triggers to unroll them in different situations.

5 Related Work and Conclusions

The study of program equivalence arguably pre-dates the study of functional correctness. In his 1969 paper [23], Hoare identified that "Many [previous] axiomatic treatments of computer programming [2,24,46] tackle the problem of proving the equivalence, rather than the correctness, of algorithms". To date, practical approaches to program equivalence rely on structural similarity of the programs. Many works focus on methods to account for some structural differences. The importance of program structure in proving program equivalence was observed by Dijkstra in 1972 [15], where he also observes that programmers are often called upon to modify existing programs.

Key developments in program equivalence have come from research into *non-interference* in *secure information flow* and compiler *translation validation*. Non-interference is the property that the values of secret inputs do not influence public outputs. Translation validation provides assurances that the program output by a compiler is correct with respect to the input program. Translation validation concerns itself with correctness of particular compiler runs, and does prove the compiler implementation correct. Non-interference can be formalised in terms of program equivalence [25], or more generally as a safety property over pairs of program traces [7,41]. Methods for reducing safety properties over trace pairs to safety properties over single traces have been explored [9,33] and generalised, particularly via product programs [4,6] and similar [38,42,47]. *Product programs* combine a pair of programs into one, such that useful invariants can be formulated at interesting points in the product, and can generalise to relations between programs [5]. Compiler translation validation [28,31,38,42,47] is inherently a program equivalence question. Many techniques have been applied, several variations of product programs [47], constructing bisimulations between control flow graphs [28], iteratively applying equality axioms [38], or normalising [42] graph representations of the programs.

Relational Hoare Logic [5,10–12,45] (RHL) was proposed by Benton, in 2004 [10], in the course of proving the correctness of various compiler optimisations. The Hoare triple $\{P\}S\{Q\}$ is extended to a Hoare quadruple by inclusion of two statements, rather than one, $\{P\}C_1 \sim C_2\{Q\}$. The pre and post conditions are lifted to relations over stores. RHL has been extended by various rules to account for differences in structure between the programs [5,10]. Barthe, Crespo, and Kunz [5] pointed out that RHL is closely related to the idea of product programs. Several formal works tackle the problem of proving program equivalence in the presence of dynamic memory allocation. Pitts uses a simulation between memory locations when defining a semantic approach to program equivalence [37], the memory model is flat not a heap. Benton et al. uses isomorphism between heap regions when proposing an RHL that supports dynamic allocation [11]. Yang constructs a relational separation logic with support for dynamic allocation [45]. Sumner and Zhang propose a different approach, canonical memory addresses are constructed based on program control flow and syntactic elements. Banerjee, Schmidt, and Nikouei [1] propose a logic for weaving programs with structural differences so that relational properties of programs can be expressed. They extend this with a region logic to support reasoning about encapsulation in dynamically allocating programs; catering for equivalence between programs which vary the representation of objects.

5.1 Fully Automatic Equivalence Verification Tools

To our knowledge there are four other tools with the objective of fully automated verification of procedure equivalence for imperative programs: Symdiff [29], RVT [21], SCORE [36], and Rêve [19]. Symdiff [29] uses program verification to prove or provide counter examples of equivalence. It uses mutual
summaries, and can infer intermediate summaries to establish equivalence. Conditional equivalence [22] can show partial equivalence over a subset of procedure inputs and construct summaries of interprocedural behavioural differences.
Symdiff is built on Boogie [3]. Symdiff has no built-in support for procedures
that differ in memory allocation. RVT [21] proves equivalence of some C programs. RVT generates loop and recursion free program fragments, which are
verified by the CBMC [14] bounded model checker. Loops are encoded as recursive functions. Recursive calls are replaced by uninterpreted functions. Recently
support for unbalanced recursive functions has been added [39]. RVT is extended
to dynamic data structures involving pointers by generating (symbolic) bounded
tree-like data structures as inputs for procedures. These initial tree-like structures are isomorphic up to some bound. RVT then verifies (up to the same
bound) that those data structures remain isomorphic, at procedure calls and
procedure return. The bound is determined by a syntactic overapproximation
of the maximum depth of modification. No rigorous proof is presented for this
extension to pointers. Rêve [19] and SCORE [36] support numerical programs
without heaps. Rêve uses Horn constraints to verify equivalence of deterministic
imperative programs with unbounded integer variables. Rêve infers inductive
coupling predicates and as such can deal with loops and recursion where, for
example, the number and meaning of procedure parameters has changed. The
authors of Rêve propose in the future to extend their tool with an RVT-like
approach to the heap. SCORE uses abstract interpretation over an interleaving of the programs. A good interleaving is found by searching. SCORE deals
with numerical programs. For non-equivalent programs SCORE can compute an
overapproximation of the semantic difference. The precision of this overapproximation is related to the size of the syntactic difference.

5.2 Conclusion

We defined procedure equivalence, and a sound methodology RIE, for automatically proving equivalence of programs which vary in dynamic memory allocation. We described our RIE encoding APE for equivalence verification (available
at https://github.com/lexicalscope/ape). Our approach is fully automatic, and
applicable to programs which manipulate heap data structures of any shape.

References

1. Banerjee, A., Schmidt, D.A., Nikouei, M.: Relational logic with framing and
   hypotheses. In: FSTTCS (2016)
2. de Barker, J.W.: Axiomatics of simple assignment statements. In: MR 94 (1968)

3. Barnett, M., Chang, B.-Y.E., DeLine, R., Jacobs, B., Leino, K.R.M.: Boogie: a modular reusable verifier for object-oriented programs. In: Boer, F.S., Bonsangue, M.M., Graf, S., Roever, W.-P. (eds.) FMCO 2005. LNCS, vol. 4111, pp. 364–387. Springer, Heidelberg (2006). doi:10.1007/11804192_17

4. Barthe, G., Crespo, J.M., Kunz, C.: Beyond 2-safety: asymmetric product programs for relational program verification. In: Artemov, S., Nerode, A. (eds.) LFCS 2013. LNCS, vol. 7734, pp. 29–43. Springer, Heidelberg (2013). doi:10.1007/978-3-642-35722-0_3

5. Barthe, G., Crespo, J.M., Kunz, C.: Product programs and relational program logics. J. Logical Algebraic Methods Program. 85(5), 847–859 (2016)

6. Barthe, G., Crespo, J.M., Kunz, C.: Relational verification using product programs. In: Butler, M., Schulte, W. (eds.) FM 2011. LNCS, vol. 6664, pp. 200–214. Springer, Heidelberg (2011). doi:10.1007/978-3-642-21437-0_17

7. Barthe, G., D'Argenio, P.R., Rezk, T.: Secure information flow by self-composition. In: Proceedings of the 17th IEEE Workshop on Computer Security Foundations. IEEE Computer Society (2004)

8. Bavota, G., et al.: When does a refactoring induce bugs? An empirical study. In: 2012 IEEE 12th International Working Conference on Source Code Analysis and Manipulation (SCAM). IEEE (2012)

9. Benton, N.: Abstracting allocation. In: Ésik, Z. (ed.) CSL 2006. LNCS, vol. 4207, pp. 182–196. Springer, Heidelberg (2006). doi:10.1007/11874683_12

10. Benton, N.: Simple relational correctness proofs for static analyses and program transformations. In: Proceedings of the 31st ACM SIGPLAN-SIGACT Symposium on Principles of Programming Languages. ACM (2004)

11. Benton, N., et al.: Relational semantics for effect-based program transformations with dynamic allocation. In: Proceedings of the 9th ACM SIGPLAN International Conference on Principles and Practice of Declarative Programming. ACM (2007)

12. Beringer, L.: Relational decomposition. In: Eekelen, M., Geuvers, H., Schmaltz, J., Wiedijk, F. (eds.) ITP 2011. LNCS, vol. 6898, pp. 39–54. Springer, Heidelberg (2011). doi:10.1007/978-3-642-22863-6_6

13. Bozga, M., Iosif, R., Laknech, Y.: Storeless semantics and alias logic. In: Proceedings of the 2003 ACM SIGPLAN Workshop on Partial Evaluation and Semantics-based Program Manipulation, PEPM 2003, San Diego, California, USA. ACM (2003)

14. Clarke, E., Kroening, D., Yorav, K.: Behavioral consistency of C and verilog programs using bounded model checking. In: 2003 Proceedings of the Design Automation Conference. IEEE (2003)

15. Dahl, O.J., Dijkstra, E.W., Hoare, C.A.R.: Structured Programming. Academic Press Ltd., Cambridge (1972)

16. Moura, L., Bjørner, N.: Z3: an efficient SMT solver. In: Ramakrishnan, C.R., Rehof, J. (eds.) TACAS 2008. LNCS, vol. 4963, pp. 337–340. Springer, Heidelberg (2008). doi:10.1007/978-3-540-78800-3_24

17. Detlefs, D., Nelson, G., Saxe, J.B.: Simplify: a theorem prover for program checking. J. ACM 52(3), 365–473 (2005)

18. Elenbogen, D., Katz, S., Strichman, O.: Proving mutual termination. Form. Methods Syst. Des. 47(2), 204–229 (2015)

19. Felsing, D., et al.: Automating regression verification. In: Proceedings of the 29th ACM/IEEE International Conference on Automated Software Engineering, ASE 2014. ACM (2014)

20. Godlin, B., Strichman, O.: Inference rules for proving the equivalence of recursive procedures. Acta Informatica 45(6), 403–439 (2008)

21. Godlin, B., Strichman, O.: Regression verification. In: Proceedings of the 46th Annual Design Automation Conference. ACM (2009)
22. Hawblitzel, C., Kawaguchi, M., Lahiri, S.K., Rebêlo, H.: Towards modularly comparing programs using automated theorem provers. In: Bonacina, M.P. (ed.) CADE 2013. LNCS (LNAI), vol. 7898, pp. 282–299. Springer, Heidelberg (2013). doi:10. 1007/978-3-642-38574-2_20
23. Hoare, C.A.R.: An axiomatic basis for computer programming. Commun. ACM **12**(10), 576–580 (1969)
24. Igarishi, S.: An axiomatic approach to equivalence problems of algorithms with applications. Ph.D. thesis (1964)
25. Joshi, R., Leino, K.R.M.: A semantic approach to secure information flow. Sci. Comput. Program. **37**, 1–3 (2000)
26. Kawaguchi, M., Lahiri, S.K., Rebêlo, H.: Conditional equivalence. Technical report MSR-TR-2010-119. Microsoft, October 2010
27. Koutavas, V., Wand, M.: Small bisimulations for reasoning about higher-order imperative programs. In: Conference Record of the 33rd ACM SIGPLAN-SIGACT Symposium on Principles of Programming Languages. ACM (2006)
28. Kundu, S., Tatlock, Z., Lerner, S.: Proving optimizations correct using parameterized program equivalence. In: Proceedings of the 30th ACM SIGPLAN Conference on Programming Language Design and Implementation. ACM (2009)
29. Lahiri, S.K., Hawblitzel, C., Kawaguchi, M., Rebêlo, H.: SYMDIFF: a language-agnostic semantic diff tool for imperative programs. In: Madhusudan, P., Seshia, S.A. (eds.) CAV 2012. LNCS, vol. 7358, pp. 712–717. Springer, Heidelberg (2012). doi:10.1007/978-3-642-31424-7_54
30. Lahiri, S., et al.: Differential assertion checking. In: Foundations of Software Engineering. ACM (2013)
31. Le, V., Afshari, M., Su, Z.: Compiler validation via equivalence modulo inputs'. In: Proceedings of the 35th ACM SIGPLAN Conference on Programming Language Design and Implementation, PLDI 2014. ACM (2014)
32. Leino, K.R.M.: Dafny: an automatic program verifier for functional correctness. In: Clarke, E.M., Voronkov, A. (eds.) LPAR 2010. LNCS (LNAI), vol. 6355, pp. 348–370. Springer, Heidelberg (2010). doi:10.1007/978-3-642-17511-4_20
33. Leino, K.R.M., Müller, P.: Verification of equivalent-results methods. In: Drossopoulou, S. (ed.) ESOP 2008. LNCS, vol. 4960, pp. 307–321. Springer, Heidelberg (2008). doi:10.1007/978-3-540-78739-6_24
34. Milner, R.: Fully abstract models of typed λ-calculi. Theor. Comput. Sci. **4**(1), 1–22 (1977)
35. Park, J., et al.: An empirical study of supplementary bug fixes. In: 2012 9th IEEE Working Conference on Mining Software Repositories (MSR) (2012)
36. Partush, N., Yahav, E.: Abstract semantic differencing via speculative correlation. In: Proceedings of the 2014 ACM International Conference on Object Oriented Programming Systems Languages & Applications. ACM (2014)
37. Pitts, A.M.: Operational semantics and program equivalence. In: Barthe, G., Dybjer, P., Pinto, L., Saraiva, J. (eds.) APPSEM 2000. LNCS, vol. 2395, pp. 378–412. Springer, Heidelberg (2002). doi:10.1007/3-540-45699-6_8
38. Stepp, M., Tate, R., Lerner, S.: Equality-based translation validator for LLVM. In: Gopalakrishnan, G., Qadeer, S. (eds.) CAV 2011. LNCS, vol. 6806, pp. 737–742. Springer, Heidelberg (2011). doi:10.1007/978-3-642-22110-1_59

39. Strichman, O., Veitsman, M.: Regression verification for unbalanced recursive functions. In: Fitzgerald, J., Heitmeyer, C., Gnesi, S., Philippou, A. (eds.) FM 2016. LNCS, vol. 9995, pp. 645–658. Springer, Heidelberg (2016). doi:10.1007/978-3-319-48989-6_39
40. Tennent, R.D., Ghica, D.R.: Abstract models of storage. High.-Order Symbolic Comput. **13**(1), 119–129 (2000)
41. Terauchi, T., Aiken, A.: Secure information flow as a safety problem. In: Hankin, C., Siveroni, I. (eds.) SAS 2005. LNCS, vol. 3672, pp. 352–367. Springer, Heidelberg (2005). doi:10.1007/11547662_24
42. Tristan, J.-B., Govereau, P., Morrisett, G.: Evaluating value-graph translation validation for LLVM. In: Proceedings of the 32nd ACM SIGPLAN Conference on Programming Language Design and Implementation. ACM (2011)
43. Tzevelekos, N.: Program equivalence in a simple language with state. Comput. Lang. Syst. Struct. **38**(2), 181–198 (2012)
44. Wood, T.: Equivalence verification for memory allocating procedures. Ph.D. thesis, Imperial College London, Under Submission
45. Yang, H.: Relational separation logic. Theor. Comput. Sci. **375**, 1–3 (2007)
46. Yanov, Y.: Logical operator schemes. In: Kybernetilca I (1958)
47. Zaks, A., Pnueli, A.: CoVaC: compiler validation by program analysis of the crossproduct. In: Cuellar, J., Maibaum, T., Sere, K. (eds.) FM 2008. LNCS, vol. 5014, pp. 35 51. Springer, Heidelberg (2008). doi:10.1007/978-3-540-68237-0_5

Abstract Specifications for Concurrent Maps

Shale Xiong[(✉)], Pedro da Rocha Pinto, Gian Ntzik, and Philippa Gardner

Imperial College London, London, UK
{sx14,pmd09,gn408,pg}@ic.ac.uk

Abstract. Despite recent advances in reasoning about concurrent data structure libraries, the largest implementations in `java.util.concurrent` have yet to be verified. The key issue lies in the development of modular specifications, which provide clear logical boundaries between clients and implementations. A solution is to use recent advances in fine-grained concurrency reasoning, in particular the introduction of *abstract atomicity* to concurrent separation logic reasoning. We present two specifications of concurrent maps, both providing the clear boundaries we seek. We show that these specifications are equivalent, in that they can be built from each other. We show how we can verify client programs, such as a concurrent set and a producer-consumer client. We also give a substantial first proof that the main operations of `ConcurrentSkipListMap` in `java.util.concurrent` satisfy the map specification. This work demonstrates that we now have the technology to verify the largest implementations in `java.util.concurrent`.

1 Introduction

We study reasoning about fine-grained concurrent data-structure libraries, with the aim of developing modular specifications which provide a clear logical boundary between client programs and implementations. We refer to a specification as modular if it enables us to verify client programs without exposing the details of the underlying implementation. Implementations should be provably correct with respect to such specifications. Specifications should be general enough to allow for the verification of strong functional properties of arbitrary clients. Such a balance has been difficult to achieve.

There has been substantial recent work on the modular specification of concurrent libraries and the verification of their clients and implementations using concurrent separation logics: see for example [7]. However, we have only just reached a stage where specifications are fully modular. In particular, an important step has been the introduction of *abstract atomicity* to concurrent separation-logic reasoning [6,16,17,20,26,27]. We revisit the concurrent map example, a pivotal example in the original development of concurrent abstract predicates [5,10]. We demonstrate significant improvement with this work, by presenting two specifications of concurrent maps: one based on the whole map data structure; and the other on key-value pairs. These specifications are more general, yielding better functional properties of client programs

© Springer-Verlag GmbH Germany 2017
H. Yang (Ed.): ESOP 2017, LNCS 10201, pp. 964–990, 2017.
DOI: 10.1007/978-3-662-54434-1_36

and simpler proofs that implementations meet the specifications. In particular, we are able to give a substantial first proof that the main operations of `ConcurrentSkipListMap` in `java.util.concurrent` satisfy the map specification. This work demonstrates that we now have the reasoning techniques required to verify the largest implementations in `java.util.concurrent`.

The specification and verification of concurrent maps has been fundamental to the development of abstract fine-grained concurrent reasoning. At one point, it was known how to verify Sagiv's B^{Link} tree algorithm [24] in RGSep [28], but it was not known how that reasoning could be lifted to an abstract specification. In an effort to answer this question, concurrent abstract predicates and the associated CAP reasoning were introduced [10], and a specification of concurrent maps using key-value pairs presented [5]. At the time, it was quite an achievement that such a complex algorithm could be proven correct with respect to a simple abstract specification. However, it was also known that the specification had substantial limitations. It was not general enough, in that it had specific protocol tags embedded in the specification to manage interaction between threads. This meant that, although CAP reasoning was sufficiently expressive to demonstrate the memory safety of all clients, it could only verify functional correctness properties for some. It also meant that, although implementations such as Sagiv's B^{Link} tree were indeed proven correct with respect to the specification, the proofs were complex due to the explosion of cases caused by the protocol tags. The key point is that CAP reasoning was not able to establish the correct specification boundary.

In this paper, we present two modular specifications for concurrent maps, which we believe provide clear logical boundaries for verifying implementations and clients. First, we present an abstract concurrent map specification where the focus is on the entire map data structure; such a specification is particularly suitable for verifying implementations. Using this map specification we verify an implementation of an abstract concurrent set specification, similar to `ConcurrentSkipListSet` from `java.util.concurrent`. Second, we present an alternate concurrent map specification, in which the focus is on key-value pairs, rather than on the entire map data structure. This type of specification is more appropriate for clients who only require access to some of the key-value pairs of the map. These two specifications are equivalent in the sense that the key-value specification can be built as a client of the map specification, and vice versa; they present two different views of the same data structure.

We demonstrate how to build the CAP specification from our more general key-value specification in the technical report [29], immediately inheriting all of the client examples given in [5]. We verify a functional correctness property of a simple producer-consumer client using the key-value specification, which cannot be verified using the CAP specification. We also verify that the main operations of `ConcurrentSkipListMap` from `java.util.concurrent` satisfy the map specification. As far as we are aware, this is the largest verified example of an algorithm of `java.util.concurrent` in the literature. Despite this, the proof is comparatively simpler than the CAP-style proof Sagiv's B^{Link} tree algorithm.

This is because the verification of our specification is decoupled from how the map is used by concurrent clients.

The strength of our results is due to advances in fine-grained concurrent reasoning, in particular the introduction of *abstract atomicity* made popular with the work on linearisability [15] and recently integrated into the reasoning of concurrent separation logics [6,16,17,20,26,27]. Atomicity is a common and useful abstraction for operations of concurrent data structures. Intuitively, an operation is abstractly atomic if it appears to take effect at a single instant during its execution. The implementation of the operation may take multiple steps to complete, updating the underlying representation of the data structure several times. However, only one of these updates should effect the abstract change in the data structure corresponding to the abstract atomic operation. The benefit of abstract atomicity is that a programmer can use such a data structure in a concurrent setting while only being concerned with the abstract effects of its operations. We use TaDA [6], a program logic which captures abstract atomicity by introducing the notion of an *atomic triple*. These triples generalise the concept of linearisability, in the sense that they specify operations to be atomic with respect to interference restrictions on the data abstraction, in contrast to unrestricted interference on the module boundary given by linearisability. The outcome is the clear specification boundary that we seek. In fact, whilst studying the concurrent map example, we realised that we could extend TaDA with additional proof rules to provide more modular specifications than before.

The results in this paper demonstrate that choosing the right abstraction for the specification is essential for scalable reasoning about concurrent data structures in general, and concurrent maps in particular. For concurrent maps, we have demonstrated that the right abstraction is feasible using the TaDA program logic. With TaDA, we have introduced two general specifications of concurrent maps, which do not impose unnecessary constraints on the client reasoning. We have verified the main operations of `ConcurrentSkipListMap`, a large real-world concurrent data structure algorithm given in `java.util.concurrent`.

2   Abstract Map Specification

Our goal is to specify formally a fragment of the `ConcurrentMap` module from `java.util.concurrent`. The map module consists of a constructor `makeMap` which creates an empty map, a `get` operation which returns the value currently mapped to a given key, a `put` operation which changes the mapping associated with a given key, and a `remove` operation which removes the mapping for a given key. None of these operations allows zero to be either a key or a value.

Figure 1 shows our abstract specification for the main operations of the `ConcurrentMap` module. This specification is abstract in the sense that it does not contain any references to the underlying implementation. To represent the map as a resource, we introduce an abstract predicate $\mathsf{Map}(s, x, \mathcal{M})$. The first parameter of the predicate, $s \in \mathbb{T}_1$, ranges over an abstract type $\mathbb{T}_1$. It captures invariant implementation-specific information about the map, which does

$$\vdash \{\mathsf{True}\}\ \mathtt{makeMap}()\ \{\exists s \in \mathbb{T}_1.\, \mathsf{Map}(s, \mathsf{ret}, \emptyset)\}$$

$$\vdash \mathbb{W}\mathcal{M}.\left\langle \begin{array}{c} \mathsf{Map}(s, \mathbf{x}, \mathcal{M}) \\ \wedge\, \mathbf{k} \neq 0 \end{array} \right\rangle \mathtt{get}(\mathbf{x}, \mathbf{k}) \left\langle \begin{array}{c} \mathsf{Map}(s, \mathbf{x}, \mathcal{M}) \wedge \underline{\mathbf{if}}\ \mathbf{k} \in \mathrm{dom}(\mathcal{M}) \\ \underline{\mathbf{then}}\ \mathsf{ret} = \mathcal{M}(\mathbf{k})\ \underline{\mathbf{else}}\ \mathsf{ret} = 0 \end{array} \right\rangle$$

$$\vdash \mathbb{W}\mathcal{M}.\left\langle \begin{array}{c} \mathsf{Map}(s, \mathbf{x}, \mathcal{M}) \\ \wedge\, \mathbf{k} \neq 0 \wedge \mathbf{v} \neq 0 \end{array} \right\rangle \mathtt{put}(\mathbf{x}, \mathbf{k}, \mathbf{v}) \left\langle \begin{array}{c} \mathsf{Map}(s, \mathbf{x}, \mathcal{M}[\mathbf{k} \mapsto \mathbf{v}]) \wedge \underline{\mathbf{if}}\ \mathbf{k} \in \mathrm{dom}(\mathcal{M}) \\ \underline{\mathbf{then}}\ \mathsf{ret} = \mathcal{M}(\mathbf{k})\ \underline{\mathbf{else}}\ \mathsf{ret} = 0 \end{array} \right\rangle$$

$$\vdash \mathbb{W}\mathcal{M}.\left\langle \begin{array}{c} \mathsf{Map}(s, \mathbf{x}, \mathcal{M}) \\ \wedge\, \mathbf{k} \neq 0 \end{array} \right\rangle \mathtt{remove}(\mathbf{x}, \mathbf{k}) \left\langle \begin{array}{c} \underline{\mathbf{if}}\ \mathbf{k} \notin \mathrm{dom}(\mathcal{M})\ \underline{\mathbf{then}}\ \mathsf{Map}(s, \mathbf{x}, \mathcal{M}) \wedge \mathsf{ret} = 0 \\ \underline{\mathbf{else}}\ \mathsf{Map}(s, \mathbf{x}, \mathcal{M} \backslash \{(\mathbf{k}, \mathcal{M}(\mathbf{k}))\}) \wedge \mathsf{ret} = \mathcal{M}(\mathbf{k}) \end{array} \right\rangle$$

Fig. 1. Specification for a concurrent map.

not change during the execution of the operation. To the client, the type is opaque; the implementation realises the type appropriately. The second parameter, $x \in \mathsf{Loc}$, represents the physical address of the map object. The last parameter, $\mathcal{M}$, contains a set of mappings that represent the abstract state of the map.

The $\mathtt{makeMap}$ operation is specified with a standard Hoare triple that asserts that it will return a freshly allocated map object with no mappings. We should note here that, since TaDA is an intuitionistic logic, the precondition True has the same behaviour as the emp of classical separation logic. Also, ret is a special variable that holds the return value of an operation.

The $\mathtt{get}$, $\mathtt{put}$ and $\mathtt{remove}$ operations are specified with an *atomic triple*, with the intended meaning that these operations appear to take place atomically, at a distinct point in time. TaDA is designed so that shared resources can only be accessed by atomic operations; a non-atomic operation could potentially violate any invariant that the shared resources are expected to have.

The atomic triple, introduced by TaDA [6], specifies an atomic operation:

$$\vdash \mathbb{W}x \in X.\langle P(x) \rangle\ \mathbb{C}\ \langle Q(x) \rangle$$

the intuitive meaning of which we will explain shortly. Prior to that, we need to introduce the notion of a *linearisation point*: a linearisation point of an operation is the instant at which that operation appears to take effect [15]. The precondition $P(x)$ and postcondition $Q(x)$ specify the program state before and after the linearisation point of the program $\mathbb{C}$. The pseudo-quantification $\mathbb{W}x \in X$ specifies that the environment is allowed to freely change the value of x before the linearisation point of $\mathbb{C}$, as long as $x \in X$ and $P(x)$ continues to hold. At and only at the linearisation point, current program $\mathbb{C}$ changes the program state from $P(x)$ to $Q(x)$. Afterwards there are no guarantees as to the truthfulness of $Q(x)$ because the environment can interfere with no constraint[1]. For example, the specification for $\mathtt{get}$ in Fig. 1 means that immediately after the linearisation point, $\mathtt{get}$ preserves the state of the mappings and returns the current value associated with the key $\mathbf{k}$, or 0 if the mapping does not exist. Before the linearisation point, the environment can change the value of the mappings, but cannot deallocate the structure because the precondition mandates its existence; after

---

[1] For a detailed exposition of the atomic triples, readers should refer to [6,7].

the linearisation point, the environment can interfere fully and even deallocate the structure.

The put operation is similar to get, except that it inserts or replaces the mapping for the key k with the value v ($\mathcal{M}[k \mapsto v]$ denotes the update of the existing key k with value v, or the addition of a new (k, v) pair, depending on the mapping previously existed). The operation returns the previous mapping associated with the key, or 0 if that mapping did not exist. Finally, the remove operation removes an existing mapping associated with the key k and returns its previous contents, similarly to the put operation.

We show that our specification is strong enough to reason about arbitrary clients, e.g. a concurrent set and producer-consumer, in Sect. 3, and verify that a complex skiplist implementation satisfies it in Sect. 4. Moreover, we derive an alternative key-value specification which provides a fiction of disjointness and can also be used for client reasoning.

3   Client Reasoning

We illustrate the advantages of our specification by showing three different ways of using it. The first example is an implementation of a concurrent set module, similar to the ConcurrentSkipListSet found in java.util.concurrent, that makes use of a map internally and illustrates the modularity of our specification. The second example is a new key-value specification that incorporates atomicity and allows dynamic control of the number of abstract key-value predicates being used. It is motivated by the fact that some clients find it preferable to work with individual key-value pairs rather than the whole map and is inspired by the original key-value specification for concurrent maps presented in Concurrent Abstract Predicates (CAP) [5,10]. The third example is a simplified producer-consumer scenario that makes use of the key-value specification. We use it to show how abstract atomicity can be used to improve client reasoning, allowing us to prove stronger properties about functional correctness than previous approaches [1,2,5].

In this section, when necessary, we will elaborate on certain important notions of TaDA. The reader can refer to the full set of TaDA rules in [4], which also includes the two additional rules with which we have extended TaDA.

3.1   Concurrent Set

We consider a concurrent set module, with the specification given in Fig. 2. This module consists of two methods: setPut, which inserts an element in the set and returns true if the element did not previously exist and false if it did; and setRemove, which removes an element from the set and returns true if the element previously existed in the set and false otherwise. The implementation internally uses a concurrent map to keep track of the elements that are in the set. If an element e is in the set, then there exists a corresponding mapping with the key e in the underlying map.

$$\vdash \mathbb{W}\mathcal{S}.\langle \mathsf{Set}(s, \mathbf{x}, \mathcal{S})\rangle \; \texttt{setPut}(\mathbf{x}, \mathbf{e}) \; \langle \mathsf{Set}(s, \mathbf{x}, \mathcal{S} \cup \{\mathbf{e}\}) \wedge \mathsf{ret} = (\mathbf{e} \notin \mathcal{S})\rangle$$

$$\vdash \mathbb{W}\mathcal{S}.\langle \mathsf{Set}(s, \mathbf{x}, \mathcal{S})\rangle \; \texttt{setRemove}(\mathbf{x}, \mathbf{e}) \; \langle \mathsf{Set}(s, \mathbf{x}, \mathcal{S} \setminus \{\mathbf{e}\}) \wedge \mathsf{ret} = (\mathbf{e} \in \mathcal{S})\rangle$$

Fig. 2. Specification for a concurrent set.

Shared Regions, Transition Systems and Guards. In order to verify the specification using TaDA [6], we must provide an interpretation for the abstract predicate $\mathsf{Set}(s, \mathbf{x}, \mathcal{S})$. For this, we will introduce the *shared regions, transition systems* and *guards* of TaDA.

A *shared region* encapsulates resources that may be shared by multiple threads, with the proviso that they can only be accessed by atomic operations. It has an abstract state with a concrete interpretation denoted by $I(-)$. Each region is identified by a unique region identifier and adheres to a region type.

For the concurrent set module, we introduce a region type **SLSet**. A region of this type is parameterised by the physical address x of the underlying map and an additional physical address y, which corresponds to the address of the set. It also carries the parameter s, which captures the invariant information of the underlying map implementation. Lastly, the abstract state $\mathcal{S}$ corresponds to the contents of the set. The interpretation of **SLSet** is as follows:

$$I(\mathbf{SLSet}_r(s, x, y, \mathcal{S})) \stackrel{\text{def}}{=} \exists \mathcal{M}. \, x \mapsto y * \mathsf{Map}(s, y, \mathcal{M}) \wedge \mathcal{S} = \mathrm{dom}(\mathcal{M})$$

Therefore, we have that **SLSet** encapsulates a heap cell that contains the address of the underlying map as well as the underlying map itself, and also relates the abstract state of the region to the domain of the mappings. The subscript r is the unique region identifier.

A shared region is associated with abstract resources, called guards, and a labelled transition system, where labels are guards, that defines how the region can be updated. In TaDA, the assertion $[\mathsf{G}]_r$ denotes a guard named G for the region r. The guards for a region form a partial commutative monoid (PCM), to which we refer to as a *guard algebra*, with a composition operation $\bullet$, which is lifted to $*$ in TaDA assertions. For the **SLSet** region, we introduce two types of guards, G and **0**. The guard algebra for the set module is as follows:

$$\mathsf{G} \bullet \mathbf{0} = \mathbf{0} \bullet \mathsf{G} = \mathsf{G} \qquad \mathbf{0} \bullet \mathbf{0} = \mathbf{0} \qquad \mathsf{G} \bullet \mathsf{G} \text{ is undefined}$$

where the guard **0** is the unit of this PCM. This guard algebra ensures that the guard G is unique. The type of the region, t, defines the transition system and the guard algebra associated with the region.

The labelled transition system associates certain actions with certain guards; these actions determine how a thread that holds this guard can update the shared state of the region. An action is a pair consisting of a pre- and a post-condition. The labelled transition system for the set region is as follows:

$$\mathsf{G} : \forall \mathcal{S}, e. \, \mathcal{S} \rightsquigarrow \mathcal{S} \cup \{e\} \qquad \mathsf{G} : \forall \mathcal{S}, e. \, \mathcal{S} \rightsquigarrow \mathcal{S} \setminus \{e\}$$

The guard G allows a thread to change its abstract state $\mathcal{S}$, effectively changing the contents of the set by either adding or removing an element e. The **0** guard has no bound action. Note that in the following discussion, if there is no ambiguity, each region implicitly has a unit guard **0** with no bound action.

Given the region and its guards, we are now ready to give the interpretation of the abstract type and our abstract predicate:

$$\mathbb{T}_2 \stackrel{\text{def}}{=} \mathsf{RId} \times \mathbb{T}_1 \times \mathsf{Loc} \qquad \mathsf{Set}((r, s', y), x, \mathcal{S}) \stackrel{\text{def}}{=} \mathbf{SLSet}_r(s', x, y, \mathcal{S}) * [\mathrm{G}]_r$$

where RId is the set of region identifiers, $\mathbb{T}_1$ is the abstract type of the concurrent map specification and Loc is the set of physical addresses. For the first parameter of Set, s, we have that $s \in \mathbb{T}_2$. Recall that abstract types $\mathbb{T}_1$ and $\mathbb{T}_2$ encapsulate invariant, implementation-specific information and are opaque for clients.

Given this interpretation of the set module, it remains to prove that the implementations of the operations, which use a concurrent map, satisfy the set specifications. We present the proof of the `setPut` in Fig. 3, whereas we omit the proof for `setRemove` due to its similarity and it can be found in technical report [29]. The proof begins by substituting the abstract predicate $\mathsf{Set}(s, \mathtt{x}, \mathcal{S})$ with its interpretation, where we also substitute the logical parameter $s \in \mathbb{T}_2$ with its interpretation as the triple (r, s', y), where r is the identifier of the **SLSet** region, s' is the abstract logical parameter of the underlying Map predicate, and y is the physical address of the underlying Map predicate.

The remaining proof rules used will be explained shortly. We also show a further example of how to use the set specification in the technical report [29], by proving a parallel sieve of Eratosthenes.

Proof Rules. There are four key rules that are used in Fig. 3: *make atomic*, *update region*, and *atomicity weakening*. The first rule that we will describe is

abstract; substitute $s = (r, s', y)$
make atomic
atomic exists and atomicity weakening
update region
atomic exists

$$\mathbb{V}\mathcal{S}.\langle \mathsf{Set}(s, \mathtt{x}, \mathcal{S}) \rangle$$
$$\mathbb{V}\mathcal{S}.\langle \mathbf{SLSet}_r(s', \mathtt{x}, y, \mathcal{S}) * [\mathrm{G}]_r \rangle$$
$$r : \mathcal{S} \rightsquigarrow \mathcal{S} \cup \{\mathtt{e}\} \vdash \{\exists \mathcal{S}.\, \mathbf{SLSet}_r(s', \mathtt{x}, y, \mathcal{S}) * r \Rrightarrow \blacklozenge\}$$
$$\mathtt{y} := [\mathtt{x}];$$
$$\{\exists \mathcal{S}.\, \mathbf{SLSet}_r(s', \mathtt{x}, \mathtt{y}, \mathcal{S}) * r \Rrightarrow \blacklozenge\}$$
$$\mathbb{V}\mathcal{S}.\langle \mathbf{SLSet}_r(s', \mathtt{x}, \mathtt{y}, \mathcal{S}) * r \Rrightarrow \blacklozenge \rangle$$
$$\mathbb{V}\mathcal{S}.\langle \exists \mathcal{M}.\, \mathtt{x} \mapsto \mathtt{y} * \mathsf{Map}(s', \mathtt{y}, \mathcal{M}) \land \mathcal{S} = \mathrm{dom}(\mathcal{M}) \rangle$$
$$\mathbb{V}\mathcal{M}.\langle \mathsf{Map}(s', \mathtt{y}, \mathcal{M}) \rangle$$
$$\mathtt{r} := \mathtt{put}(\mathtt{y}, \mathtt{e}, 1)$$
$$\langle \mathsf{Map}(s', \mathtt{y}, \mathcal{M}[\mathtt{e} \mapsto 1]) \land \underline{\mathbf{if}}\ \mathtt{e} \in \mathrm{dom}(\mathcal{M})\ \underline{\mathbf{then}}\ \mathtt{r} \neq 0\ \underline{\mathbf{else}}\ \mathtt{r} = 0 \rangle$$
$$\left\langle \begin{array}{l} \exists \mathcal{M}.\, \mathtt{x} \mapsto \mathtt{y} * \mathsf{Map}(s', \mathtt{y}, \mathcal{M}[\mathtt{e} \mapsto 1]) \land \mathcal{S} = \mathrm{dom}(\mathcal{M}[\mathtt{e} \mapsto 1]) \land \\ \underline{\mathbf{if}}\ \mathtt{v} \in \mathrm{dom}(\mathcal{M})\ \underline{\mathbf{then}}\ \mathtt{r} \neq 0\ \underline{\mathbf{else}}\ \mathtt{r} = 0 \end{array} \right\rangle$$
$$\langle r \Rrightarrow (\mathcal{S}, \mathcal{S} \cup \{\mathtt{e}\}) * \mathbf{SLSet}_r(s', \mathtt{x}, \mathtt{y}, \mathcal{S} \cup \{\mathtt{e}\}) \land \underline{\mathbf{if}}\ \mathtt{e} \in \mathcal{S}\ \underline{\mathbf{then}}\ \mathtt{r} \neq 0\ \underline{\mathbf{else}}\ \mathtt{r} = 0 \rangle$$
$$\{\exists \mathcal{S}.\, r \Rrightarrow (\mathcal{S}, \mathcal{S} \cup \{\mathtt{e}\}) \land \underline{\mathbf{if}}\ \mathtt{e} \in \mathcal{S}\ \underline{\mathbf{then}}\ \mathtt{r} \neq 0\ \underline{\mathbf{else}}\ \mathtt{r} = 0\}$$
$$\mathtt{return}\ (\mathtt{r} = 0);$$
$$\langle \mathbf{SLSet}_r(s', \mathtt{x}, y, \mathcal{S} \cup \{\mathtt{e}\}) * [\mathrm{G}]_r \land \mathsf{ret} = (\mathtt{e} \notin \mathcal{S}) \rangle$$
$$\langle \mathsf{Set}(s, \mathtt{x}, \mathcal{S} \cup \{\mathtt{e}\}) \land \mathsf{ret} = (\mathtt{e} \notin \mathcal{S}) \rangle$$

Fig. 3. Proof of correctness of the `setPut` operation.

make atomic, which allows us to prove that program $\mathbb{C}$ can be seen as abstractly atomic. A simplified version of this rule is as follows:

$$\frac{\{(x,y) \mid x \in X, y \in f(x)\} \subseteq \mathcal{T}_t(G)^* \qquad r : x \in X \rightsquigarrow f(x) \vdash \{\exists x \in X.\, \mathbf{t}_r(\vec{z}, x) * r \Mapsto \blacklozenge\}\ \mathbb{C}\ \{\exists x \in X, y \in f(x).\, r \Mapsto (x, y)\}}{\vdash \mathbb{W}x \in X.\langle \mathbf{t}_r(\vec{z}, x) * [G]_r \rangle\ \mathbb{C}\ \langle \exists y \in f(x).\, \mathbf{t}_r(\vec{z}, y) * [G]_r \rangle}$$

This rule establishes that $\mathbb{C}$ atomically updates the region r, from a state $x \in X$ to a state $y \in Q(x)$. To do so, it requires the guard G for the region, which must permit the update according to the appropriate transition system $\mathcal{T}_t(G)^*$, where t is the region type; this is established by the first premiss. Here, the region type t is **SLSet**, the guard G is our guard G, and the transition system is $\mathcal{T}_t(G) = \{\mathcal{S}, \mathcal{S} \cup \{e\}\} \cup \{\mathcal{S}, \mathcal{S} \setminus \{e\}\}$. The * denotes reflexive-transitive closure.

We use $\mathbf{t}_a(\vec{z}, x)$ to represent a region with region type t, identifier a, parameters $\vec{z}$ and abstract state x. In our example, the **SLSet** region is parametrised with the physical address of the underlying map, the physical address of the set, the invariant implementation-specific information, and the abstract state, which corresponds to the contents of the set. The second premiss introduces two notations. The first, $r : x \in X \rightsquigarrow f(x)$, is called the *atomicity context*. The atomicity context records the abstract atomic action that is to be performed. The second, $r \Mapsto -$, is the *atomic tracking resource*. The atomic tracking resource indicates whether or not the atomic update has occurred (the $r \Mapsto \blacklozenge$ indicates it has not) and, if so, the state of the shared region immediately before and after (the $r \Mapsto (x, y)$). The resource $r \Mapsto \blacklozenge$ also plays two special roles that are normally filled by guards. Firstly, it limits the interference on region r: the environment may only update the state so long as it remains in the set X, as specified by the atomicity context. Secondly, it confers permission for the thread to update the region from state $x \in X$ to any state $y \in f(x)$; in doing so, the thread also updates $r \Mapsto \blacklozenge$ to $r \Mapsto (x, y)$. This permission is expressed by the *update region* rule (see below), and ensures that the atomic update happens only once.

In essence, the second premiss is capturing the notion of atomicity (with respect to the abstraction in the conclusion) and expressing it as a proof obligation. Specifically, the region must be in the state x for some $x \in X$, which may be changed by the environment, until at some point the thread updates it to some $y \in f(x)$. The atomic tracking resource bears witness to this.

In the proof shown in Fig. 3, we apply the *make atomic* rule to declare an atomic update. The local variable y holds the address of the underlying map. Then, at the linearisation point, i.e. the put operation, we apply the update region rule to update the tracking resource from $r \Mapsto \blacklozenge$ to $r \Mapsto (\mathcal{S}, \mathcal{S} \cup \{e\})$. The slightly simplified version of the *update region* rule is as follows:

$$\frac{\vdash \mathbb{W}x \in X.\left\langle I(\mathbf{t}_r()\vec{z}, x) * P(x) \right\rangle\ \mathbb{C}\ \left\langle \begin{array}{c} \exists y \in f(x) I(\mathbf{t}_r()\vec{z}, y) * Q_1(x, y) \\ \vee\, I(\mathbf{t}_r(\vec{z}, x)) * Q_2(x) \end{array} \right\rangle}{r : x \in X \rightsquigarrow f(x) \vdash \mathbb{W}x \in X.\left\langle \begin{array}{c} \mathbf{t}_r(\vec{z}, x) * P(x) \\ * r \Mapsto \blacklozenge \end{array} \right\rangle\ \mathbb{C}\ \left\langle \begin{array}{c} \exists y \in f(x).\, \mathbf{t}_r(\vec{z}, y) * Q_1(x, y) * \\ r \Mapsto (x, y) \vee \mathbf{t}_r(\vec{z}, x) * Q_2(x) * r \Mapsto \blacklozenge \end{array} \right\rangle}$$

In the conclusion, the first disjunct of the postcondition specifies that an atomic update has occurred, and that $\mathbb{C}$ updates the abstract state of the region r (of type $\mathbf{t}$ and parameters $\vec{z}$) from x to y and also $P(x)$ to $Q_1(x, y)$, and in doing so consumes the tracking resource. As the atomic update might affect resources contained in $P(x)$, the postcondition $Q_1(x, y)$ is parametrised by y. By having $y = x$, we can also allow for the abstract state of the region to remain unchanged and not perform the atomic update, which is useful when reasoning about an atomic read. The second disjunct of the postcondition specifies that $\mathbb{C}$ only change the local resource to $Q_2(x)$ and that the atomic action has not taken place. Note that the tracking resource is only allowed to change only once from $\blacklozenge$ to (x, y), at the instant in which the atomic update takes effect.

TaDA allows eliminating existential quantification only for Hoare triples. However, a rule of following form would not be sound:

$$\frac{\vdash \langle P(x) \rangle \; \mathbb{C} \; \langle Q(x) \rangle}{\vdash \langle \exists x.\, P(x) \rangle \; \mathbb{C} \; \langle \exists x.\, Q(x) \rangle}$$

The conclusion allows the environment to change the value of x because of the quantification, while in the premiss the value cannot be changed by the environment. This means that anything that could be potentially existentially quantified has to be exposed as a parameter and bounded by the pseudo-quantification $\mathbb{A}$. We overcome this problem by extending the logic with the *atomic exists* proof rule that allows the elimination of existential quantification, as follows:

$$\frac{\vdash \mathbb{A}x \in X.\langle P(x) \rangle \; \mathbb{C} \; \langle Q(x) \rangle}{\vdash \langle \exists x \in X.\, P(x) \rangle \; \mathbb{C} \; \langle \exists x \in X.\, Q(x) \rangle}$$

In this rule, $\mathbb{C}$ tolerates changes of the value of x as long as they are contained in X by lifting the existential quantification to pseudo-quantification. This proof rule allows us to hide the underlying states from the abstract specification of a module, while maintaining the soundness of TaDA. We apply this rule both before and after the update region rule in Fig. 3.

We now show how standard Hoare triples are derived from atomic Hoare triples. In fact, the proof in Fig. 3 implicitly performs this step when applying the *update region* rule. In TaDA, this is captured by the *atomicity weakening* rule, a simplified form of which is given below:

$$\frac{\vdash \mathbb{A}x \in X.\langle P(x) \rangle \; \mathbb{C} \; \langle Q(x) \rangle}{\forall x \in X \vdash \{P(x)\} \; \mathbb{C} \; \{Q(x)\}}$$

The Hoare triple in the conclusion states that the program $\mathbb{C}$ updates the state from $P(x)$ to $Q(x)$ without any interference from the environment on x, since $\forall x \in X$ in the context fixes the value of x during execution. Note that in TaDA, assertions are implicitly required to be stable, which means that the assertions must hold with respect to a protocol. Recall the atomic specification of put in Fig. 1: at that level, no protocol for how the concurrent map is used is defined, and therefore the precondition and postcondition assertions are trivially stable. However, when applying the *update region* rule in Fig. 3, we are using the concurrent map as part of the protocol defined for the **SLSet** region, so we must keep assertions stable with respect to that protocol. For example, at the point of the *update region*, we implicitly weaken the atomic postcondition before transitioning to the non-atomic postcondition, to keep the postcondition stable.

3.2   Key-Value Specification

The concurrent map specification in Fig. 1 is given in terms of all the key-value mappings present in the map and we have used this specification to verify a concurrent set implementation. However, for some clients it may be preferable to work with individual key-value pairs rather than the whole map. Inspired by the key-value specification using Concurrent Abstract Predicates (CAP) [5,10], we introduce a new key-value specification. This new specification is atomic, in contrast to the CAP-stype specification. We show how to build a key-value specification from the map specification and vice versa, meaning that these two specifications are, in fact, equivalent and simply represent two different ways of thinking about a concurrent map.

CAP-Style Approach. Concurrent map specifications in terms of individual key-value pairs were first introduced using CAP [5,10]. To allow sharing between threads, concurrent abstract predicates associate key-value pairs with fractional permissions [3] and special tags $\{\mathtt{def}, \mathtt{ins}, \mathtt{rem}, \mathtt{unk}\}$ that define the protocol via which multiple threads access shared key-value pairs. Each operation is specified for all protocol tags. For example, consider the following CAP-style specification of `remove` (the specifications for `get` and `put` are in the technical report [29]):

$$\{\mathsf{CAPKey}_{\mathtt{def}}(x, k, v)_1\}\ \mathtt{remove}(x, k)\ \{\mathsf{CAPKey}_{\mathtt{def}}(x, k, 0)_1 \wedge \mathsf{ret} = v\}$$
$$\{\mathsf{CAPKey}_{\mathtt{rem}}(x, k, v)_\pi\}\ \mathtt{remove}(x, k)\ \{\mathsf{CAPKey}_{\mathtt{rem}}(x, k, 0)_\pi \wedge \mathsf{ret} \in \{v, 0\}\}$$
$$\{\mathsf{CAPKey}_{\mathtt{unk}}(x, k)_\pi\}\ \mathtt{remove}(x, k)\ \{\mathsf{CAPKey}_{\mathtt{unk}}(x, k)_\pi\}$$

The concurrent abstract predicate CAPKey is used as a key-value pair resource for the map with address x. The tag determines what the current thread and the environment can do with this resource in accordance to Table 1. The subscript π is a fractional permission, in the range $(0, 1]$, controlling how the resource is shared between threads: when $\pi = 1$, the current thread fully owns the key-value pair resource, whereas when $\pi < 1$, the resource is shared. In the `def` case, if $v \neq 0$, $\mathsf{CAPKey}_{\mathtt{def}}(x, k, v)_1$ asserts the existence of the key-value pair (k, v); otherwise, if $v = 0$ the key `key` is not mapped to a value. In this case, only the current thread is manipulating this key-value pair with full permission $\pi = 1$. In the `ins` case, $\mathsf{CAPKey}_{\mathtt{ins}}(x, k, v)_\pi$ asserts that the current thread and the environment are allowed to insert the value v for key `key`. Consequently, the specification prohibits threads from performing a `remove` in this case. In the `rem` case, $\mathsf{CAPKey}_{\mathtt{rem}}(x, k, v)_\pi$ asserts that the both the current thread and the environment are allowed to remove the key `key` from the map. Consequently, in the precondition of the specification, the key may or may not exist in the map. However, it certainly does not exist in the postcondition. Finally, in the unk case, $\mathsf{CAPKey_{unk}(x,k)_\pi}$ asserts that both the thread and the environment are arbitrarily manipulating the key **key**. This case allows arbitrary interference and thus we know nothing about the existence of the key or its value. Specifications with unk are overly weak and only allow memory-safety proofs.

Table 1. Sharing protocols for key-value pairs of a concurrent map in CAP.

	Thread		Environment			Thread		Environment	
	put	remove	put	remove		put	remove	put	remove
def	✓	✓	✗	✗	ins	✓	✗	✓	✗
unk	✓	✓	✓	✓	rem	✗	✓	✗	✓

There are two significant drawbacks in the CAP approach. First, the specification hard-codes specific protocols by which threads access the shared resource, i.e. the tag and the fractional permission. This limits the verification of functional correctness properties to only those clients that fit the hard-coded protocols; the producer-consumer example in Sect. 3.3 does not. Second, each operation has to be separately verified per each protocol tag, drastically increasing the proof effort.

Atomic Key-Value Specification. We introduce our key-value based specification in Fig. 4. This specification allows us to provide a functional correctness proof of the producer-consumer example shown in Sect. 3.3. It can derive the CAP-style specification, which is in the technical report [29].

$$\{\mathsf{True}\}\ \mathtt{makeMap}()\ \{\exists s.\ \mathsf{Collect}(s,\mathsf{ret},\emptyset)\}$$
$$\vdash \mathbb{W}v \in \mathbb{N}.\langle \mathsf{Key}(s,\mathbf{x},\mathbf{k},v) \wedge \mathbf{k} \neq 0\rangle\ \mathtt{get}(\mathbf{x},\mathbf{k})\ \langle \mathsf{Key}(s,\mathbf{x},\mathbf{k},v) \wedge \mathsf{ret} = v\rangle$$
$$\vdash \mathbb{W}v \in \mathbb{N}.\langle \mathsf{Key}(s,\mathbf{x},\mathbf{k},v) \wedge \mathbf{k} \neq 0 \wedge \mathbf{v} \neq 0\rangle\ \mathtt{put}(\mathbf{x},\mathbf{k},\mathbf{v})\ \langle \mathsf{Key}(s,\mathbf{x},\mathbf{k},\mathbf{v}) \wedge \mathsf{ret} = v\rangle$$
$$\vdash \mathbb{W}v \in \mathbb{N}.\langle \mathsf{Key}(s,\mathbf{x},\mathbf{k},v) \wedge \mathbf{k} \neq 0\rangle\ \mathtt{remove}(\mathbf{x},\mathbf{k})\ \langle \mathsf{Key}(s,\mathbf{x},\mathbf{k},0) \wedge \mathsf{ret} = v\rangle$$
$$\mathsf{Collect}(s,x,\mathcal{S}) \iff \mathsf{Collect}(s,x,\mathcal{S} \uplus \{k\}) * \mathsf{Key}(s,x,k,0),\ \text{if } k > 0$$

Fig. 4. Key-value specification for a concurrent map.

The specification uses two abstract predicates: Key and Collect. Both predicates are parametrised with s and x. The former abstracts implementation-defined invariant information, and the latter is the physical address identifying the map. When v is not 0, the predicate $\mathsf{Key}(s,x,k,v)$ represents a mapping from key k to value v in the map. When $v = 0$, it states that the key k is not in the map. The predicate $\mathsf{Collect}(s,x,\mathcal{S})$ keeps track of how many Key predicates are in use: one for each element of $\mathcal{S}$. Initially, the set $\mathcal{S}$ is empty. The axiom at the bottom of Fig. 4 allows constructing new Key predicates by increasing the size of the set tracked by Collect.

In order to verify the specification with respect to the map specification in Fig. 1, we introduce a shared region with type **KVMap**. The interpretation of the region is defined to be a façade of the concurrent map predicate as follows:

$$I(\mathbf{KVMap}_r(s', x, \mathcal{M})) \overset{\text{def}}{=} \mathsf{Map}(s', x, \mathcal{M})$$

We associate the region with guards $\mathrm{K}(k)$ and $\mathrm{COLLECT}(\mathcal{S})$. The guard $\mathrm{K}(k)$ grants the capability to insert and remove mappings with the key k according to the following transition system defined for the region:

$$\mathrm{K}(k) : \forall \mathcal{M}, v.\, \mathcal{M} \rightsquigarrow \mathcal{M}[k \mapsto v] \qquad \mathrm{K}(k) : \forall \mathcal{M}.\, \mathcal{M} \rightsquigarrow \mathcal{M} \setminus \{(k, \mathcal{M}(k))\}$$

The guard $\mathrm{COLLECT}(\mathcal{S})$ is used to track how many guards K are in use. We impose the following guard algebra:

$$\mathrm{COLLECT}(\mathcal{S}) = \mathrm{COLLECT}(\mathcal{S} \uplus \{k\}) \bullet \mathrm{K}(k)$$

where $k > 0$. This equivalence enforces that the number of K guards matches the set in $\mathrm{COLLECT}$.

Now we define the interpretation of the abstract predicates as follows:

$$\mathbb{T}_3 \overset{\text{def}}{=} \mathsf{RId} \times \mathbb{T}_1$$
$$\mathsf{Collect}((r, s'), x, \mathcal{S}) \overset{\text{def}}{=} \exists \mathcal{M}.\, \mathbf{KVMap}_r(s', x, \mathcal{M}) * [\mathrm{COLLECT}(\mathcal{S})]_r \wedge \mathrm{dom}(\mathcal{M}) \subseteq \mathcal{S}$$
$$\mathsf{Key}((r, s'), x, k, v) \overset{\text{def}}{=} \exists \mathcal{M}.\, \mathbf{KVMap}_r(s', x, \mathcal{M}) * [\mathrm{K}(k)]_r$$
$$\wedge \underline{\mathbf{if}}\ v = 0\ \underline{\mathbf{then}}\ k \notin \mathrm{dom}(\mathcal{M})\ \underline{\mathbf{else}}\ (k, v) \in \mathcal{M}$$

The abstract predicate $\mathsf{Collect}((r, s'), x, \mathcal{S})$ is defined so that the **KVMap** region contains a map $\mathcal{M}$, the keys of which are a subset of $\mathcal{S}$. Through the guard $\mathrm{COLLECT}(\mathcal{S})$, the set $\mathcal{S}$ tracks the keys that are currently in use. The abstract predicate $\mathsf{Key}((r, s'), x, k, v)$ is defined such that the **KVMap** region contains a map $\mathcal{M}$, in which a mapping for key k either exists or not, depending on the value of v, with the guard $\mathrm{K}(k)$, granting the capability to modify the mapping. The client axiom shown in Fig. 4 follows directly from the guard equivalence and the interpretation of the abstract predicates.

In Fig. 5 we prove that the **get** operation satisfies its key-value specification given in Fig. 4. The proof in Fig. 5 begins by substituting the abstract predicate $\mathsf{Key}(s, x, k, v)$ with its interpretation, where we also substitute the logical parameter $s \in \mathbb{T}_3$ with its interpretation as the pair (r, s'), where r is the identifier of the **KVMap** region, and s' is the abstract logical parameter of the underlying Map predicate. From there we use the atomic exists rule to eliminate the existential quantification of the abstract map $\mathcal{M}$ to a pseudo-quantification which allows $\mathcal{M}$ to be changed by the environment up to the point where **get** atomically takes effect. To justify the atomic read on the **KVMap** region, we make use of the *use atomic* TaDA proof rule discussed below.

$\mathbb{W}v.\langle \mathsf{Key}(s, \mathbf{x}, \mathbf{k}, v) \wedge \mathbf{k} \neq 0\rangle$

$$
\begin{array}{l}
\left|\mathbb{W}v.\langle \exists \mathcal{M}. \mathbf{KVMap}_r(s', \mathbf{x}, \mathcal{M}) * [K(\mathbf{k})]_r \wedge \underline{\mathbf{if}}\ v = 0\ \underline{\mathbf{then}}\ k \notin \mathrm{dom}(\mathcal{M})\ \underline{\mathbf{else}}\ (\mathbf{k}, v) \in \mathcal{M}\rangle \right. \\
\left|\mathbb{W}\mathcal{M}.\langle \mathbf{KVMap}_r(s', \mathbf{x}, \mathcal{M}) * [K(\mathbf{k})]_r \wedge \underline{\mathbf{if}}\ v = 0\ \underline{\mathbf{then}}\ k \notin \mathrm{dom}(\mathcal{M})\ \underline{\mathbf{else}}\ (\mathbf{k}, v) \in \mathcal{M}\rangle \right. \\
\left|\mathbb{W}\mathcal{M}.\langle \mathsf{Map}(s', \mathbf{x}, \mathcal{M}) * [K(\mathbf{k})]_r \wedge \underline{\mathbf{if}}\ v = 0\ \underline{\mathbf{then}}\ k \notin \mathrm{dom}(\mathcal{M})\ \underline{\mathbf{else}}\ (\mathbf{k}, v) \in \mathcal{M}\rangle \right. \\
\left|\mathsf{get}(\mathbf{x}, \mathbf{k}) \right. \\
\left|\langle \mathsf{Map}(s', \mathbf{x}, \mathcal{M}) * [K(\mathbf{k})]_r \wedge \underline{\mathbf{if}}\ v = 0\ \underline{\mathbf{then}}\ k \notin \mathrm{dom}(\mathcal{M})\ \underline{\mathbf{else}}\ (\mathbf{k}, v) \in \mathcal{M} \wedge \mathsf{ret} = v\rangle \right. \\
\left|\langle \mathbf{KVMap}_r(s', \mathbf{x}, \mathcal{M}) * [K(\mathbf{k})]_r \wedge \underline{\mathbf{if}}\ v = 0\ \underline{\mathbf{then}}\ k \notin \mathrm{dom}(\mathcal{M})\ \underline{\mathbf{else}}\ (\mathbf{k}, v) \in \mathcal{M} \wedge \mathsf{ret} = v\rangle \right. \\
\left|\langle \exists \mathcal{M}. \mathbf{KVMap}_r(s', \mathbf{x}, \mathcal{M}) * [K(\mathbf{k})]_r \wedge \right. \\
\left.\ \underline{\mathbf{if}}\ v = 0\ \underline{\mathbf{then}}\ k \notin \mathrm{dom}(\mathcal{M})\ \underline{\mathbf{else}}\ (\mathbf{k}, v) \in \mathcal{M} \wedge \mathsf{ret} = v\rangle \right.
\end{array}
$$

(marginal labels: abstract; substitute $s = (r, s')$ | atomic exists | use atomic)

$\langle \mathsf{Key}(s, \mathbf{x}, \mathbf{k}, v) \wedge \mathsf{ret} = v\rangle$

Fig. 5. Proof of correctness of the `get` operation.

Proof Rule. The *use atomic* proof rule of TaDA allows us to justify an atomic update on the abstract state of a shared region by an atomic update on the region's interpretation. A simplified form of this rule is as follows:

$$
\frac{\{(x, y) \mid x \in X, y \in f(x)\} \subseteq \mathcal{T}_t(G)^* \qquad \vdash \mathbb{W}x \in X.\langle I(\mathbf{t}_r(\vec{z}, x)) * [G]_r\rangle\ \mathbb{C}\ \langle \exists y \in f(x).\, I(\mathbf{t}_r(\vec{z}, y)) * [G]_r\rangle}{\vdash \mathbb{W}x \in X.\langle \mathbf{t}_r(\vec{z}, x) * [G]_r\rangle\ \mathbb{C}\ \langle \exists y \in f(x).\, \mathbf{t}_r(\vec{z}, y) * [G]_r\rangle}
$$

Similarly to the *make atomic* rule, in order to justify the atomic update on region r of type $\mathbf{t}$ from abstract state x to abstract state $y \in f(x)$, the precondition is required to include a guard G for which this update is allowed by the region's transition system according to the first premiss.

We use the *use atomic* rule in the last step in the proof in Fig. 5 to justify the atomic read of the key $\mathbf{k}$ by the atomic map specification of the `get` operation in Fig. 1. The key-value based specifications for the rest of the concurrent map operations are proven similarly.

Rebuilding the Atomic Map Specification. So far, we have started with a concurrent map specification in terms of the entire map, from which we then justified a key-value based specification. We now show that the opposite direction, of starting from a key-value based specification and then deriving a whole-map specification, is also possible. First, we introduce a region type **NewMap**. We interpret this region as all the key-values pairs in use:

$$
I(\mathbf{NewMap}_r(s, x, \mathcal{M})) \overset{\text{def}}{=} \exists \mathcal{K}.\ \mathsf{Collect}(s, x, \mathcal{K}) \wedge \mathrm{dom}(\mathcal{M}) \subseteq \mathcal{K}* \\
\underset{k \in \mathcal{K}}{\circledast} \left(\begin{array}{l} \exists v.\, \mathsf{Key}(s, x, k, v) \wedge \\ \underline{\mathbf{if}}\ v \neq 0\ \underline{\mathbf{then}}\ (k, v) \in \mathcal{M}\ \underline{\mathbf{else}}\ k \notin \mathrm{dom}(\mathcal{M}) \end{array} \right)
$$

where $\circledast$ denotes the iteration of $*$. The abstract state $\mathcal{M}$ includes all key-value mappings that exist in the concurrent map, as well as keys that do not exist but are in use in the form of Key predicates. Recall that if the fourth parameter of the Key predicate is 0, the corresponding key does not exist in the concurrent map. Also, those Key are allocated through Collect, their key fields are in the set $\mathcal{K}$, which is the reason of $\mathrm{dom}(\mathcal{M}) \subseteq \mathcal{K}$.

The labelled transition system for this region is defined as follows:

$$\mathrm{NMAP} : \forall \mathcal{M}, k, v. \, \mathcal{M} \rightsquigarrow \mathcal{M}[k \mapsto v]$$
$$\mathrm{NMAP} : \forall \mathcal{M}, k. \, \mathcal{M} \rightsquigarrow \mathcal{M} \setminus \{(k, \mathcal{M}(k))\}$$

where the guard algebra is defined so that the composition $\mathrm{NMAP} \bullet \mathrm{NMAP}$ is undefined. This guarantees the uniqueness of the NMAP guard.

We can now give an alternative implementation of the abstract predicate Map in terms of the **NewMap** region and the NMAP guard:

$$\mathsf{Map}((r, s'), x, \mathcal{M}) \stackrel{\mathrm{def}}{=} \mathbf{NewMap}_r(s', x, \mathcal{M}) * [\mathrm{NMAP}]_r$$

By starting from the key-value based concurrent map specification in Fig. 4 we can justify the whole-map specification in Fig. 1, similarly to the proof in Fig. 5.

We have shown that the whole-map specification and key-value based specification are equivalent in the sense that they specify the same structure in two different ways. Clients are free to pick the specification that suits them best.

3.3   Producer-Consumer

We now consider a simplified producer-consumer example that uses the key-value specification. Sergey *et al.* [25] proved a producer-consumer example, but here we only mean to use the producer-consumer to explain the improvement of our specification for concurrent map. The example, shown in Fig. 6, consists of a program that creates two threads, one that inserts ten elements into a map, and another that removes those elements from the map. By using TaDA's guards and shared regions, we can prove that, at the end, the map is empty. We contrast this with the CAP-style approach from [5], where we cannot know anything about the state of the map after both threads finish processing. Note that our programming language and TaDA support dynamic creation of threads. We use the parallel composition ($\|$) in this example to simplify the presentation.

Shared Region, Transition System and Guards. In order to verify the program, we introduce a region type **PC** that encapsulates the shared key-value mappings ranging from l to u. This region is parametrised by the address of the map x and mappings $\mathcal{M}$. Moreover, we introduce a distinguished abstract state $\circ$ to represent the state where the region is no longer required. This is the state we reach after both threads return. Before showing the interpretation of the region, we define the transition system for the **PC** region, as follows:

$$\mathrm{PUT}(\{k\}) : \forall v, \mathcal{M}. \, \mathcal{M} \rightsquigarrow \mathcal{M} \uplus \{(k, v)\}$$
$$\mathrm{REM}(\mathbb{N}_l^u) : \forall k \in \mathbb{N}_l^u, v, \mathcal{M}. \, \mathcal{M} \uplus \{(k, v)\} \rightsquigarrow \mathcal{M}$$
$$\mathrm{PUT}(\mathbb{N}_l^u) \bullet \mathrm{REM}(\mathbb{N}_l^u) : \forall \mathcal{M}. \, \mathcal{M} \rightsquigarrow \circ$$

where $\mathbb{N}_l^u$ denotes $\{k \mid k \in \mathbb{N} \wedge l \leq k \leq u\}$. The guard $\mathrm{PUT}(\mathcal{S})$ allows a thread to insert any element whose key is in $\mathcal{S}$ to the map, while $\mathrm{REM}(\mathbb{N}_l^u)$ allows

$$\{\mathsf{True}\}$$
$$\mathtt{x} := \mathtt{makeMap}();$$
$$\{\exists s.\, \mathsf{Collect}(s, \mathtt{x}, \emptyset)\}$$
$$\left\{\exists s.\, \mathsf{Collect}(s, \mathtt{x}, \mathbb{N}_1^{10}) * \underset{k \in \mathbb{N}_1^{10}}{\circledast} \mathsf{Key}(s, \mathtt{x}, k, 0))\right\}$$
$$\left\{\exists r, s.\, \mathbf{PC}_r(s, \mathtt{x}, 1, 10, \emptyset) * [\mathrm{PUT}(\mathbb{N}_1^{10})]_r * [\mathrm{REM}(\mathbb{N}_1^{10})]_r\right\}$$

`i := 1;`	`j := 1;`
$\left\{\begin{array}{l}\exists r, s.\, \mathbf{PC}_r(s, \mathtt{x}, 1, 10, \emptyset) \\ * [\mathrm{PUT}(\mathbb{N}_i^{10})]_r\end{array}\right\}$	$\left\{\begin{array}{l}\exists r, s, \mathcal{M}.\, \mathbf{PC}_r(s, \mathtt{x}, 1, 10, \mathcal{M}) * [\mathrm{REM}(\mathbb{N}_1^{10})]_r * \\ [\mathrm{PUT}(\mathbb{N}_1^{j-1})]_r \wedge \mathrm{dom}(\mathcal{M}) \cap \mathbb{N}_1^{j-1} = \emptyset\end{array}\right\}$
`while (i ≤ 10) {`	`while (j ≤ 10) {`
$\left\{\begin{array}{l}\exists r, s, \mathcal{M}.\, \mathbf{PC}_r(s, \mathtt{x}, 1, 10, \mathcal{M}) \\ * [\mathrm{PUT}(\mathbb{N}_i^{10})]_r\end{array}\right\}$	$\left\{\begin{array}{l}\exists r, s, \mathcal{M}.\, \mathbf{PC}_r(s, \mathtt{x}, 1, 10, \mathcal{M}) * [\mathrm{REM}(\mathbb{N}_1^{10})]_r * \\ [\mathrm{PUT}(\mathbb{N}_1^{j-1})]_r \wedge \mathrm{dom}(\mathcal{M}) \cap \mathbb{N}_1^{j-1} = \emptyset\end{array}\right\}$
`v := random();` `put(x, i, v);`	`b := remove(x, j);`
$\left\{\begin{array}{l}\exists r, s, \mathcal{M}.\, \mathbf{PC}_r(s, \mathtt{x}, 1, 10, \mathcal{M}) \\ * [\mathrm{PUT}(\mathbb{N}_{i+1}^{10})]_r\end{array}\right\}$	$\left\{\begin{array}{l}\exists r, s, \mathcal{M}.\, \mathbf{PC}_r(s, \mathtt{x}, 1, 10, \mathcal{M}) * [\mathrm{REM}(\mathbb{N}_1^{10})]_r * \\ \underline{\mathbf{if}}\ b \neq 0\ \underline{\mathbf{then}}\ [\mathrm{PUT}(\mathbb{N}_1^{j})]_r \wedge \mathrm{dom}(\mathcal{M}) \cap \mathbb{N}_1^{j} = \emptyset \\ \quad\underline{\mathbf{else}}\ [\mathrm{PUT}(\mathbb{N}_1^{j-1})]_r \wedge \mathrm{dom}(\mathcal{M}) \cap \mathbb{N}_1^{j-1} = \emptyset\end{array}\right\}$
`i := i + 1;`	`if (b ≠ 0) { j := j + 1; }`
$\left\{\begin{array}{l}\exists r, s, \mathcal{M}.\, \mathbf{PC}_r(s, \mathtt{x}, 1, 10, \mathcal{M}) \\ * [\mathrm{PUT}(\mathbb{N}_i^{10})]_r\end{array}\right\}$	$\left\{\begin{array}{l}\exists r, s, \mathcal{M}.\, \mathbf{PC}_r(s, \mathtt{x}, 1, 10, \mathcal{M}) * [\mathrm{REM}(\mathbb{N}_1^{10})]_r * \\ [\mathrm{PUT}(\mathbb{N}_1^{j-1})]_r \wedge \mathrm{dom}(\mathcal{M}) \cap \mathbb{N}_1^{j-1} = \emptyset\end{array}\right\}$
`}`	`}`
$\{\mathsf{True}\}$	$\left\{\exists r, s.\, \mathbf{PC}_r(s, \mathtt{x}, 1, 10, \emptyset) * [\mathrm{REM}(\mathbb{N}_1^{10})]_r * [\mathrm{PUT}(\mathbb{N}_1^{10})]_r\right\}$

$$\left\{\exists r, s.\, \mathbf{PC}_r(s, \mathtt{x}, 1, 10, \circ) * [\mathrm{REM}(\mathbb{N}_1^{10})]_r * [\mathrm{PUT}(\mathbb{N}_1^{10})]_r\right\}$$
$$\left\{\exists s.\, \mathsf{Collect}(s, \mathtt{x}, \mathbb{N}_1^{10}) * \underset{k \in \mathbb{N}_1^{10}}{\circledast} \mathsf{Key}(s, \mathtt{x}, k, 0))\right\}$$
$$\{\exists s.\, \mathsf{Collect}(s, \mathtt{x}, \emptyset)\}$$

Fig. 6. Producer-consumer proof.

the removal of a key-value mapping from the map. The composition $\mathrm{PUT}(\mathbb{N}_l^u) \bullet \mathrm{REM}(\mathbb{N}_l^u)$ allows the map to transition from a state $\mathcal{M}$ to $\circ$, where the region is no longer needed.

The guard algebra allows PUT guards to be combined according to the following equivalence:

$$\mathrm{PUT}(\mathcal{S}) \bullet \mathrm{PUT}(\mathcal{S}') = \mathrm{PUT}(\mathcal{S} \uplus \mathcal{S}')$$

Additionally, the $\bullet$ operator does not allow the following compositions:

$$\mathrm{REM}(-) \bullet \mathrm{REM}(-) \qquad \mathrm{PUT}(\mathcal{S}) \bullet \mathrm{PUT}(\mathcal{S}')\ \text{if}\ \mathcal{S} \cap \mathcal{S}' \neq \emptyset$$

This guarantees that there is only one $\mathrm{REM}(-)$ guard and one guard of type PUT for each key.

We can now define the interpretation of the region states:

$$I(\mathbf{PC}_r(s, x, l, u, \mathcal{M})) \overset{\mathrm{def}}{=} ([\mathrm{PUT}(\mathrm{dom}(\mathcal{M}))]_r \wedge \mathrm{dom}(\mathcal{M}) \subseteq \mathbb{N}_l^u) *$$
$$\underset{k \in \mathbb{N}_l^u}{\circledast} (\mathsf{Key}(s, x, k, v) \wedge \underline{\mathbf{if}}\ k \in \mathrm{dom}(\mathcal{M})\ \underline{\mathbf{then}}\ v \neq 0\ \underline{\mathbf{else}}\ v = 0)$$
$$I(\mathbf{PC}_r(s, x, l, u, \circ)) \overset{\mathrm{def}}{=} \mathsf{True}$$

where l and u are immutable parameters and indicate the range of keys. The **PC** region requires that after a thread inserts an element into the map, it must also leave the corresponding PUT guard that allowed it inside the region. This ensures that when a thread removes the element, it can guarantee that other threads do not insert it back by owning the guard that allows the insertion. Additionally, by interpreting the state ∘ as True, we allow a thread transitioning into the state ∘ to acquire the map that previously belonged to that region.

After the constructing the map with `makeMap`, the main thread owns the keys in the range 1 to 10 used subsequently by the producer and consumer threads. To allow for the keys to be shared, we create an instance of the **PC** region encapsulating those keys, which is done by the *create region* rule. Given that the producer and consumer work on key range from 1 to 10, the **PC** region is parametrised by 1 and 10.

Proof Rule. In the original TaDA, the allocation of shared regions was deferred to the semantic model. In contrast, we introduce a new proof rule that enables the creation of a shared region in the logic, using view shifts [9]. The rule to create a new shared region, of type $\mathbf{t}$ at state x, is as follows:

$$\frac{G \in \mathcal{G}_{\mathbf{t}} \quad \forall r.\, P * [G]_r \preceq I(\mathbf{t}_r(z, x)) * Q(r)}{P \preceq \exists r.\, \mathbf{t}_r(z, x) * Q(r)}$$

The first premiss ensures that the guard G must be part of the guard algebra of the region type $\mathbf{t}$. The second premiss states that if the guard G is compatible with P for a region identifier r, then we must be able to satisfy the interpretation of the region at state x and some frame $Q(r)$. The guard G may be split to satisfy the interpretation of the region at state x and $Q(r)$. All the other resources, such as heap resources or guards from other regions, required to satisfy the interpretation must be already in P. Note that the premiss must hold for any fresh region identifier r, as we do not decide which particular identifier will be used to create the region. The conclusion of the rule specifies that we can allocate a new region and the required guard G, where r is a fresh region identifier. Note that forgetting a region can be done by logical implication, because TaDA is an intuitionistic logic. We can see the use of creating a region and forgetting a region at the beginning and the end of the proof shown in Fig. 6.

In the proof shown in Fig. 6, after creating the region, we split the $[\text{PUT}]_r$ and $[\text{REM}]_r$ guards between the producer and consumer threads, respectively, using the standard parallel composition rule of concurrent separation logic [21]. We implicitly use the *use atomic* rule for the `put` and `remove` operations in each thread. The left thread, after performing the `put` operation, must release the corresponding guard $[\text{PUT}(\{\mathtt{i}\})]_r$ back into the region, so that the invariant of the region is maintained. The right thread, if the `remove` operation has successfully removed the key j from the map, takes the corresponding $[\text{PUT}(\{\mathtt{j}\})]_r$ from the region. This describes the ownership transfer of key-value pairs from the left thread to the right. At the end, we transfer the state of **PC** from $\emptyset$ to ∘ and forget this region. Therefore, the Key predicates for the keys in the example range have value 0, meaning that they do not exist in the map.

Contrast the producer-consumer proof with one which uses the CAP-style approach previously summarised in Sect. 3.2. According to Table 1, the only protocol tag that allows threads to both insert and remove keys from the map is unk. However, the specifications of the map operations for this protocol in the CAP-approach are too weak, losing all information about the value associated with the key or even its existence in the map:

$$\{\mathsf{CAPKey}_{\mathrm{unk}}(\mathsf{x},\mathsf{k})_\pi\} \ \ \mathsf{put}(\mathsf{x},\mathsf{k},\mathsf{v}) \ \ \{\mathsf{CAPKey}_{\mathrm{unk}}(\mathsf{x},\mathsf{k})_\pi\}$$
$$\{\mathsf{CAPKey}_{\mathrm{unk}}(\mathsf{x},\mathsf{k})_\pi\} \ \ \mathsf{remove}(\mathsf{x},\mathsf{k}) \ \ \{\mathsf{CAPKey}_{\mathrm{unk}}(\mathsf{x},\mathsf{k})_\pi\}$$

Thus, the postcondition derived can only establish memory safety.

By hard-coding predetermined protocols according to which multiple threads can access a data structure, CAP-style specifications restrict how clients can concurrently access the data structure whilst retaining strong information about the shared state. It is possible to amend the original specification with a protocol that fits a particular client, such as the producer-consumer example. However, this would break modularity as it requires the same implementation to be reproved with respect to each additional protocol. In effect, if we want to reason about strong functional properties of arbitrary clients with the CAP-style approach, we are unable to completely forget the implementation details by using a general abstract specification for the data structure.

In contrast, atomic specifications, such as those in Fig. 4, are decoupled from the clients' use cases. Clients are free to define the protocols according to which the data structure is accessed, by selecting the guards, guard algebras and state transition systems. Therefore, atomic triples in the style of TaDA lead to general specifications and modular reasoning.

4   Implementation: Concurrent Skiplist

In Sect. 2, we have introduced the abstract specification for the ConcurrentMap. One of its implementations is the ConcurrentSkipListMap of java.util.concurrent. We extract the main structure of the ConcurrentSkipListMap implementation (OpenJDK 8) and prove that its operations satisfy the atomic specification previously shown in Fig. 1. This is one of the largest examples available in the java.util.concurrent library and highlights the scalability of modern concurrent separation logics.

Data Structure. A skiplist is built from layers of linked lists. The bottom layer is a linked list of key-value pairs, stored in key order. Each higher layer is a linked list that acts as an index to the layer below it, with approximately half the number of nodes of the lower layer. This results in obtaining a fast search performance, comparable to that of B-trees [23].

Figure 7a depicts a snapshot of the Java concurrent skiplist. The linked list at the bottom layer is the *node-list*. The first node of the node-list is always the *sentinel node*; for example, the node m in Fig. 7a. Nodes after the sentinel node store key-value pairs of the map in key order, where keys are immutable. A *dead node* is a node whose value is 0 and a *marker node*, or a *marker*, is a node whose value is a pointer to itself.[2] Markers are used to ensure the correct removal of dead nodes from the node-list, as we will explain shortly.

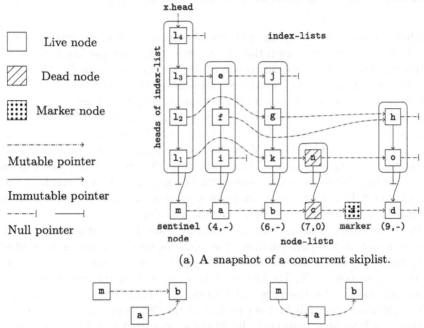

(a) A snapshot of a concurrent skiplist.

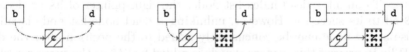

(b) Link a new node a: set the next pointer of new node a to b and then link it into the node-list by CAS, and similarly for linking a new index-list node.

(c) Unlink node c: append a marker z after node c by CAS, then unlink the dead node and the marker also by CAS. The links between c and z, and z and d are immutable.

Fig. 7. Concurrent skiplist.

Each layer above the node-list is an *index-list*. An index-list node stores three pointers as its value: (a) a right-pointer to the next index-list node, (b) an immutable down-pointer to a node in the lower layer (the down-pointers from the lowest layer point to `null`) and (c) an immutable node-pointer to a node from the node-list. The key of each index-list node is the key of the node-list

---

[2] In Java, the value of a non-marker node is a pointer to its concrete value. For simplicity, here we assume that non-marker nodes directly store concrete values and there is no clash between concrete values and pointers.

node to which it points, and is also immutable. All index-list nodes connected by their down-pointers should point to the same node-list node. For instance, in Fig. 7a, the index-list nodes e, f, and i are grouped vertically because they all point to the node-list node a. The first node of an index-list, also called the *head node*, additionally stores the level of the index-list, which is an immutable field. All head nodes point to the sentinel node, as shown in Fig. 7a.

Algorithm. A search for a key, the `get` operation, proceeds from the top index-list and from its left to right, until the current key is the greatest key lower than or equal to the target key. If the key is equal, the key has been found. Otherwise, the search moves down to the lower layer through the down-pointer. The search stops if the key has been found or if all layers have been traversed.

The `put` operation searches for the given key first. If the key is found, it replaces the associated value with the new value by performing an atomic *compare-and-set* (CAS). Otherwise, if the key is not found, a new node is added to the node-list as the successor of the node with the greatest key lower than the new node key. To do so, a new node with the key-value pair is created, and its next-pointer field is set to its predecessor's successor. Then, this new node is linked into the node-list by a CAS. This is shown in Fig. 7b.

Adding a node-list node also involves adding some index-list nodes as well, in order to maintain the performance. A column of index-list nodes is created first, and then they are linked into the corresponding layer from top to bottom by the process shown in Fig. 7b. Due to interference from the environment, a situation such as that for the f, g and h nodes in Fig. 7a may appear. In this case, the right-pointer of f is first set to g, and the CAS is performed again.

To delete a key-value mapping, the `remove` operation CAS the value to 0, turning the node, and all index-list nodes pointing to it, into dead nodes. Dead nodes are unlinked by subsequent key searches, and then left for the garbage collector. To unlink a dead index-list node, the right-pointer of its predecessor is CASsed to its successor. However, unlinking a dead node-list node is subtle, because a new node may be concurrently added to the position after the dead node [13]. To prevent this, a marker node is added by CAS as the successor to the dead node first, which stops other threads from modifying the structure between the marker and its successor. Then, the marker and the dead node are unlinked by doing another CAS. Figure 7c illustrates unlinking the node-list node c.

Shared Region, Transition System and Guards. In Table 2, we introduce predicates for the various skiplist node types and two reachability predicates. They are formally defined in the technical report [29].

To prove that the skiplist satisfies the map specification, we introduce a new region type **SLMap**. The region is parametrised by the physical address x, a list of key-value pairs $\mathcal{L}$, a set of live node-list nodes $\mathcal{N}$, a set of dead node-list nodes $\mathcal{B}$ and an immutable sentinel node m, for example in Fig. 7a, $x = \mathtt{x}$, $\mathcal{L} = [(4, -), (6, -), (9, -)]$, $\mathcal{N} = \{\mathtt{a}, \mathtt{b}, \mathtt{d}\}$, $\mathtt{c} \in \mathcal{B}$ and $m = \mathtt{m}$. The interpretation of the **SLMap** region is defined in terms of the index-lists described by the

Table 2. Auxiliary predicates.

Predicate	Meaning	Example in Fig. 7a
$\mathsf{node}(x, k, v, n)$	A node-list node at the address x with a key-value pair (k, v) and its next node n	$\mathsf{node}(\mathsf{a}, 4, \_, \mathsf{b})$
$\mathsf{index}(x, p, d, r)$	An index-list node at the address x with three pointers, a node-pointer p, a down-pointer d and a right-pointer r	$\mathsf{index}(\mathsf{f}, \mathsf{a}, \mathsf{i}, \mathsf{h})$
$\mathsf{head}(x, l, p, d, r)$	A head node at level l at the address x with p, d and r having the same meaning as in index	$\mathsf{head}(\mathsf{l}_2, 2, \mathsf{m}, \mathsf{l}_1, \mathsf{g})$
$\mathsf{marker}(x, n)$	A marker node at the address x and its next node n	$\mathsf{marker}(\mathsf{z}, \mathsf{d})$
$x \rightsquigarrow^* y$	The node x reaches y in the same layer	$\mathsf{a} \rightsquigarrow^* \mathsf{c}$
$x \rightsquigarrow^* \mathcal{N}$	The node x reaches one node in the set $\mathcal{N}$	$\mathsf{m} \rightsquigarrow \{\mathsf{a}, \mathsf{b}\}$

predicate iLists and the node-list described by the predicate nList:

$$I(\mathbf{SLMap}_r(x, \mathcal{M}, \mathcal{N}, \mathcal{B}, m)) \overset{\text{def}}{=} \exists h.\, x.\mathbf{head} \mapsto h * \mathsf{iLists}(h, m, \mathcal{N}, \mathcal{B}) * \mathsf{nList}(m, \mathcal{M}, \mathcal{N}, \mathcal{B})$$

where the `.head` denotes the offset 0.

The predicate iLists describes the index-lists and it is defined as follows:

$$\mathcal{P} \in (\mathsf{Loc} \times \mathsf{Loc}^*)^*$$
$$\mathsf{iLists}(h, m, \mathcal{N}, \mathcal{B}) \overset{\text{def}}{=} \exists \mathcal{P}, \mathcal{H}.\, \mathcal{P} \downarrow_1 \subseteq \mathcal{N} \uplus \mathcal{B} \wedge \mathsf{wellForm}(\mathcal{P}) \wedge \mathsf{rows}(m, \mathcal{H} +\!\!+ [h], \mathcal{P}, l)$$

where $\downarrow_i$ denotes the i-th projection and $+\!\!+$ denotes list concatenation. The $\mathcal{P}$ is a list of tuples. For each tuple, the first element is an address of a node-list node and the second element is a list of addresses of index-list nodes. The predicate $\mathsf{wellForm}(\mathcal{P})$ asserts that each tuple in $\mathcal{P}$ is a grouped column and the node it points to in Fig. 7a. It is also asserts that all tuples are in key order. In the end, this gives us $\mathcal{P} = [(\mathsf{a}, [\mathsf{i}, \mathsf{f}, \mathsf{e}]), (\mathsf{b}, [\mathsf{k}, \mathsf{g}, \mathsf{j}]), (\mathsf{c}, [\mathsf{n}]), (\mathsf{d}, [\mathsf{o}, \mathsf{h}])]$ in Fig. 7a. The predicate rows describes the concrete heap structure of all index-lists. Note that TaDA is intuitionistic logic, so $P \wedge Q$ can assert overlapping resources.

The predicate wellForm and an auxiliary predicate chain are defined as follows:

$$\mathsf{wellForm}(\mathcal{P}) \overset{\text{def}}{=} \mathcal{P} = [] \vee \exists p, k, \mathcal{I}, i, \mathcal{I}', \mathcal{P}'.$$
$$\begin{pmatrix} \mathcal{P} = [(p, \mathcal{D})] +\!\!+ \mathcal{P}' \wedge \mathsf{wellForm}(\mathcal{P}') \wedge \mathsf{node}(p, k, \_, \_) \wedge \mathsf{chain}(p, d, \mathcal{D}') \wedge \\ \bigwedge_{p' \in \mathcal{P}' \downarrow_1} (\exists k'.\, \mathsf{node}(p', k', \_, \_) \wedge k < k') \wedge \mathcal{D} = \mathcal{D}' +\!\!+ [d] \end{pmatrix}$$
$$\mathsf{chain}(p, d, \mathcal{D}) \overset{\text{def}}{=} (\mathcal{D} = [] \wedge d = 0) \vee$$
$$(\exists d', \mathcal{D}'.\, \mathcal{D} = \mathcal{D}' +\!\!+ [d'] \wedge \mathsf{index}(d, p, d', \_) * \mathsf{chain}(p, d', \mathcal{D}'))$$

where $\bigwedge$ denotes iteration of conjunct. The predicate wellForm describes that the order of the tuples in the list $\mathcal{P}$ is the order of the first elements, by asserting that the key of the node p smaller than others in $\mathcal{P}'$ (the first conjunct in the third line). The predicate chain asserts that the second element of each tuple in $\mathcal{P}$, denoted by $\mathcal{D}$, represents a linked list of index-list nodes that point to the same node-list node p.

The predicate rows describes the index-list at level l and all below:

$$\text{rows}(m, \mathcal{H}, \mathcal{P}, l) \stackrel{\text{def}}{=} (l = 0 \wedge \mathcal{H}(0) = 0) \vee$$
$$\left(\begin{array}{l} \exists i, \mathcal{I}.\, \text{head}(\mathcal{H}(l), l, m, \mathcal{H}(l-1), i) * \\ \mathcal{P} \downarrow_2 \downarrow_l = [i] +\!\!+ \mathcal{I} \wedge \text{iTail}(i, \mathcal{I}) * \text{rows}(m, \mathcal{H}, \mathcal{P}, l-1) \end{array} \right)$$
$$\text{iTail}(i, \mathcal{I}) \stackrel{\text{def}}{=} (\mathcal{I} = \emptyset \wedge i = 0) \vee \exists i', i'', \mathcal{I}'.$$
$$(\mathcal{I} = [i'] +\!\!+ \mathcal{I}' \wedge i'' \in \mathcal{I} \uplus \{0\} \wedge \text{index}(i, \_, \_, i'') * \text{iTail}(i', \mathcal{I}'))$$

where $\mathcal{H}$ represents a list of head nodes, and $\mathcal{H}(l)$ denotes the l-th element of the list. An index-list is a linked list that starts with a head node followed by the rest index-list nodes. Note that the head node, described by the predicate head, must point to the sentinel node m. The notation $\mathcal{P} \downarrow_2$ denotes the second projection of $\mathcal{P}$ that is a list in which each element is a list of index-list nodes. Therefore, $\mathcal{P} \downarrow_2 \downarrow_l$ denotes a list of index-nodes at level l, e.g. in Fig. 7a, $\mathcal{P} \downarrow_2 \downarrow_2 = [\mathbf{f}, \mathbf{g}, \mathbf{h}]$. Due to the situation shown in Fig. 7a, the predicate iTail asserts a quasi list starting with i, where each node points to an index-list note with larger key, but this quasi list is not strictly ordered.

The predicate nList describes the node-list of the skiplist:

$$\text{nList}(m, \mathcal{M}, \mathcal{N}, \mathcal{B}) \stackrel{\text{def}}{=} \exists n, \mathcal{L}.\, \text{node}(m, \_, \_, n) * toList(\mathcal{M}) = [n] +\!\!+ \mathcal{L} \wedge$$
$$\text{nTail}(n, \mathcal{L}, \mathcal{N}, \mathcal{B}) \wedge \bigwedge_{n \in \mathcal{B}} (n \rightsquigarrow^* \mathcal{N} \uplus \{0\})$$

$$toList(\mathcal{M}) \stackrel{\text{def}}{=} \begin{cases} [] & \mathcal{M} = \emptyset \\ [(k, \mathcal{M}(k))] +\!\!+ toList(\mathcal{M} \setminus \{(k, \mathcal{M}(k))\}) & otherwise \\ \quad \text{where } k = \min(\text{dom}(\mathcal{M})) & \end{cases}$$

The node-list starts with the sentinel node m, followed by the rest described by the predicate nTail. Note that the tail also includes some dead nodes and markers pending unlinking. The function $toList$ converts the partial function from keys to values, to a list of key-value pairs in the order of ascending keys. The last conjunct of the predicate nList asserts that all dead nodes must eventually reach a live node or null. The predicate nTail is defined as follows:

$$\text{nTail}(n, \mathcal{L}, \mathcal{N}, \mathcal{B}) \stackrel{\text{def}}{=} (\mathcal{N} = \emptyset \wedge \mathcal{L} = [] \wedge n = 0) \vee$$
$$\left(\begin{array}{l} \exists n' \in \mathcal{N} \uplus \mathcal{B}, k, v, \mathcal{L}'.\, n \in \mathcal{N} \wedge \mathcal{L} = [k, v] +\!\!+ \mathcal{L}' \wedge \\ \text{node}(n, k, v, n') * \text{nTail}(n', \mathcal{L}', \mathcal{N} \setminus \{n\}, \mathcal{B}) \end{array} \right) \vee$$
$$\left(\begin{array}{l} \exists n' \in \mathcal{N} \uplus \mathcal{B}, .\, n \in \mathcal{B} \wedge \text{nTail}(n', \mathcal{L}, \mathcal{N}, \mathcal{B} \setminus \{n\}) * \\ (\exists n''.\, \text{node}(n, \_, 0, n') \vee (\text{node}(n, \_, 0, n'') * \text{marker}(n'', n'))) \end{array} \right)$$

where the second disjunct asserts a live node and the third disjunct asserts a dead node and a potentially marker.

Finally, The predicate $\text{node}(x, k, v, n)$ asserts a node-list node at the address x that stores the key-value pair (k, v) and the next-pointer n. The predicate $\text{marker}(x, n)$ asserts a marker. They are interpreted as concrete heap cells:

$$\text{node}(x, k, v, n) \stackrel{\text{def}}{=} x.\mathbf{key} \mapsto k * x.\mathbf{value} \mapsto v * x.\mathbf{next} \mapsto n$$
$$\text{marker}(x, n) \stackrel{\text{def}}{=} \text{node}(x, \_, x, n)$$

where the field notation $E.\texttt{field}$ is shorthand for $E + \textsf{offset}(\texttt{field})$. Here, $\textsf{offset}(\texttt{key}) = 0$, $\textsf{offset}(\texttt{value}) = 1$, and $\textsf{offset}(\texttt{next}) = 2$.

We associate the **SLMap** region with a single guard L, with $\text{L} \bullet \text{L}$ being undefined. The labelled transition system of the region comprises three transitions:

$$\text{L} : \forall \mathcal{L}, \mathcal{N}, \mathcal{B}, k, v, v'. \, (\mathcal{M}[k \mapsto v], \mathcal{N}, \mathcal{B}) \rightsquigarrow (\mathcal{M}[k \mapsto v'], \mathcal{N}, \mathcal{B})$$
$$\text{L} : \forall \mathcal{L}, \mathcal{N}, \mathcal{B}, k, v, n. \, (\mathcal{M}, \mathcal{N}, \mathcal{B}) \rightsquigarrow (\mathcal{M} \uplus \{(k, v)\}, \mathcal{N} \uplus \{n\}, \mathcal{B})$$
$$\text{L} : \forall \mathcal{L}, \mathcal{N}, \mathcal{B}, k, v, n. \, (\mathcal{M} \uplus \{(k, v)\}, \mathcal{N} \uplus \{n\}, \mathcal{B}) \rightsquigarrow (\mathcal{M}, \mathcal{N}, \mathcal{B} \uplus \{n\})$$

The first allows to replace an old value v with a new value v'; the second inserts a new key-value pair (k, v) and the corresponding new node n; and the third deletes a key k with the associated value and moves the node n to the dead nodes set.

Given the new region, guards and transition system, we instantiate the abstract map predicate and the abstract type:

$$\mathbb{T}_1 \overset{\text{def}}{=} \textsf{RId} \times \textsf{Loc} \qquad \textsf{Map}((r, m), x, \mathcal{M}) \overset{\text{def}}{=} \exists \mathcal{N}, \mathcal{B}. \, \mathbf{SLMap}_r(x, \mathcal{M}, \mathcal{N}, \mathcal{B}, m) * [\text{L}]_r$$

Code of the put Operation. The implementation, shown in Fig. 8, is given in a simple imperative programming language, following the structure of the `ConcurrentSkiplistMap` implementation found in `java.util.concurrent` (OpenJDK 8). In the Java implementation, shared fields are declared as either `final` field, i.e. immutable field, or `volatile` field, i.e. no caching or reordering, so that there is no weak memory behaviour[3]. In the language we use, the semantics of single heap cell read and write are equivalent to those of `volatile` fields in Java. We use the `outer`, `inner` and `continue` variables to emulate the control flow commands `break` and `continue`. We introduce variables to record intermediate values to eliminate the side-effects of boolean expressions. This algorithm assumes a garbage-collector as it only unlinks dead nodes.

The `put` operation has two layer of loops. The inner loop traverses the node-list until finding a node with the target key `k`, or the processor where a new node will be added. If it observes any unexpected state due to the interference from the environment, for example dead nodes, the inner loop stops and jumps to the beginning of the outer loop. If a new node has been successfully added, it jumps to the end outer loop and then adds index-list nodes to preserve the performance. The code and proofs of `buildIndexChain` and `insertIndexChain` are present in the technical report [29]. These operations, which are opaque to clients, preserve the invariant of the skiplist.

Proof of the put Operation. We present the sketch proof that `put` satisfies the map specification in Fig. 1. A detail version is in the technical report [29]. For brevity, we use $\top$ and $\bot$ to denote the boolean value `true` and `false` respectively. We use the predicate `flow` to describe the control flow within the outer loop.

$$\top \equiv \texttt{true} \quad \bot \equiv \texttt{false} \qquad \textsf{flow}(c, i) \equiv \texttt{continue} = c \land \texttt{inner} = i$$

---

[3] More detail in JSR 133 (Java Memory Model).

$\mathbb{W}\mathcal{M}.\ \langle \mathrm{Map}(s,\mathbf{x},\mathcal{M})\rangle$

$\quad|\mathbb{W}\mathcal{M},\mathcal{N},\mathcal{B}.\langle \mathbf{SLMap}_r(\mathbf{x},\mathcal{M},\mathcal{N},\mathcal{B},m)*[\mathrm{L}]_r\rangle$

$\quad\left|\ r:(\mathcal{M},\mathcal{N},\mathcal{B})\rightsquigarrow\begin{array}{l}\underline{\mathbf{if}}\ \mathbf{k}\in\mathrm{dom}(\mathcal{M})\ \underline{\mathbf{then}}\ (\mathcal{M}[\mathbf{k}\mapsto\mathbf{v}],\mathcal{N},\mathcal{B})\\ \underline{\mathbf{else}}\ \exists n.\,(\mathcal{M}[\mathbf{k}\mapsto\mathbf{v}],\mathcal{N}\uplus\{n\},\mathcal{B})\end{array}\vdash\right.$

$\quad\ \{\exists\mathcal{M},\mathcal{N},\mathcal{B}.\,r\mapsto\blacklozenge*\mathbf{SLMap}_r(\mathbf{x},\mathcal{M},\mathcal{N},\mathcal{B},m)\}\quad\mathrm{outer}:=\mathrm{true};$

$\quad\ \left\{\begin{array}{l}\exists\mathcal{M},\mathcal{N},\mathcal{B}.\,\mathbf{SLMap}_r(\mathbf{x},\mathcal{M},\mathcal{N},\mathcal{B},m)\wedge\mathrm{outer}=\top*\\ \underline{\mathbf{if}}\ \mathrm{outer}=\top\ \underline{\mathbf{then}}\ a\mapsto\blacklozenge\ \underline{\mathbf{else}}\ r\mapsto((\mathcal{M},\mathcal{N},\mathcal{B}),(\mathcal{M}\uplus[(\mathbf{k},\mathbf{v})],\mathcal{N}\uplus\{\mathbf{z}\},\mathcal{B}))\end{array}\right\}$

$\quad\ \mathbf{while}\ (\mathrm{outer}=\mathrm{true})\ \{$

$\qquad\ \mathrm{inner}:=\mathrm{true};\ \mathbf{b}:=\mathrm{findPredecessor}(\mathbf{x},\mathbf{k});\ \mathbf{n}:=[\mathbf{b}.\mathrm{next}];$

$\qquad\ \left\{\begin{array}{l}\left(\begin{array}{l}\underline{\mathbf{if}}\ \mathrm{outer}=\top\ \underline{\mathbf{then}}\ r\mapsto\blacklozenge\\ \underline{\mathbf{else}}\ r\mapsto((\mathcal{M},\mathcal{N},\mathcal{B}),(\mathcal{M}[\mathbf{k}\mapsto\mathbf{v}],\mathcal{N}\uplus\{\mathbf{z}\},\mathcal{B}))\end{array}\right)*\mathrm{wkNdReach}(\mathbf{b},\mathbf{n})\wedge\\ (\mathbf{b}.\mathrm{key}<\mathbf{k}\vee\mathbf{b}=m)\wedge\mathrm{inner}=\mathrm{outer}=\top\wedge\mathrm{inter}=\bot\implies\mathrm{restart}\end{array}\right\}$

$\qquad\ \mathbf{while}\ (\mathrm{inner}=\mathrm{true})\ \{\quad\mathrm{continue}:=\mathrm{true};$

$\qquad\qquad\ \mathbf{if}\ (\mathbf{n}\neq0)\ \{\ \ \mathbf{f}:=[\mathbf{n}.\mathrm{next}];\ \mathbf{tv}:=[\mathbf{n}.\mathrm{value}];\ \mathrm{marker}:=\mathrm{isMarker}(\mathbf{n});$

$\qquad\qquad\qquad\ \mathbf{n2}:=[\mathbf{b}.\mathrm{next}]\ \mathbf{vb}:=[\mathbf{b}.\mathrm{value}];\quad\{r\mapsto\blacklozenge*\mathrm{bnf}\wedge\mathrm{flow}(\top,\top)\}$

$\qquad\qquad\qquad\ \mathbf{if}\ (\mathbf{n}\neq\mathbf{n2})\ \{\ \ \mathrm{inner}:=\mathrm{false};\quad\{r\mapsto\blacklozenge*\mathrm{bnf}\wedge\mathbf{n}\neq\mathbf{n2}\wedge\mathrm{flow}(\top,\bot)\}$

$\qquad\qquad\ \}\ \mathbf{else\ if}\ (\mathbf{tv}=0)\{\ \ \mathrm{helpDelete}(\mathbf{b},\mathbf{n},\mathbf{f});\ \ \mathrm{inner}:=\mathrm{false};$

$\qquad\qquad\qquad\ \{r\mapsto\blacklozenge*\mathrm{bnf}\wedge\mathbf{tv}=\mathbf{n}.\mathrm{value}=0\wedge\mathrm{flow}(\top,\bot)\}$

$\qquad\qquad\ \}\ \mathbf{else\ if}\ (\mathbf{vb}=0\ ||\ \mathrm{marker}=\mathrm{true})\{\ \mathrm{inner}:=\mathrm{false};$

$\qquad\qquad\qquad\ \{r\mapsto\blacklozenge*\mathrm{bnf}\wedge(\mathbf{b}.\mathrm{value}=0\vee\mathrm{marker}(\mathbf{n},\_))\wedge\mathrm{flow}(\top,\bot)\}$

$\qquad\qquad\ \}\ \mathbf{else}\ \{\ \mathbf{tk}:=[\mathbf{n}.\mathrm{key}];\ \mathbf{c}:=\mathrm{compare}(\mathbf{k},\mathbf{tk});$

$\qquad\qquad\qquad\ \mathbf{if}\ (\mathbf{c}>0)\ \{\ \mathbf{b}:=\mathbf{n};\ \mathbf{n}:=\mathbf{f};\ \mathrm{continue}:=\mathrm{false};$

$\qquad\qquad\qquad\qquad\ \{r\mapsto\blacklozenge*\mathrm{wkNdReach}(\mathbf{b},\mathbf{n})\wedge\mathbf{b}.\mathrm{key}<\mathbf{k}\wedge\mathrm{flow}(\bot,\top)\}$

$\qquad\qquad\qquad\ \}\ \mathbf{else\ if}\ (\mathbf{c}=0)\ \{\quad\{r\mapsto\blacklozenge*\mathrm{bnf}\wedge\mathbf{n}.\mathrm{key}=\mathbf{k}\wedge\mathrm{flow}(\top,\top)\}$

$\qquad\qquad\qquad\qquad\ \left|\begin{array}{l}\mathbb{W}v.\ \langle\mathrm{node}(\mathbf{n},\mathbf{k},v,\_)\rangle\\ \mathrm{cas}:=\mathrm{CASValue}(\mathbf{n},\mathbf{tv},\mathbf{v});\\ \langle\mathrm{cas}=\top\implies\mathrm{node}(\mathbf{n},\mathbf{k},v,\_)\wedge\mathbf{tv}=v\rangle\end{array}\right.$

$\qquad\qquad\qquad\ \left\{\begin{array}{l}\mathrm{flow}(\top,\top)\wedge\underline{\mathbf{if}}\ \mathrm{cas}=\bot\ \underline{\mathbf{then}}\ r\mapsto\blacklozenge\\ \underline{\mathbf{else}}\ (r\mapsto((\mathcal{M},\mathcal{N},\mathcal{B}),(\mathcal{M}[\mathbf{k}\mapsto\mathbf{v}],\mathcal{N},\mathcal{B})))\end{array}\right\}$

$\qquad\qquad\qquad\ \mathbf{if}\ (\mathrm{cas}=\mathrm{true})\ \{\ \ \mathbf{return}\ \mathbf{tv};\ \ \}\ \mathbf{else}\ \{\ \ \mathrm{inner}:=\mathrm{false};\ \ \}$

$\qquad\ \}\ \}\ \}\quad\left\{\begin{array}{l}r\mapsto\blacklozenge*\mathrm{wkNdReach}(\mathbf{b},\mathbf{n})\wedge(\mathbf{b}.\mathrm{key}<\mathbf{k}\vee\mathbf{b}=m)\wedge\\ \underline{\mathbf{if}}\ \mathrm{inter}=\bot\ \underline{\mathbf{then}}\ \mathrm{restart}\ \underline{\mathbf{else}}\ (\mathrm{continue}=\top\implies\mathbf{k}<\mathbf{n}.\mathrm{key})\end{array}\right\}$

$\qquad\ \mathbf{if}\ (\mathrm{inner}=\mathrm{true}\ \&\&\ \mathrm{continue}=\mathrm{true})\ \{\ \ \mathbf{z}:=\mathrm{makeNode}(\mathbf{k},\mathbf{v},\mathbf{n});$

$\qquad\qquad\ \{r\mapsto\blacklozenge*\mathrm{wkNdReach}(\mathbf{b},\mathbf{n})\wedge(\mathbf{b}.\mathrm{key}<\mathbf{k}\vee\mathbf{b}=m)\wedge\mathbf{k}<\mathbf{n}.\mathrm{key}\wedge\mathbf{z}.\mathrm{key}=\mathbf{k}\}$

$\qquad\qquad\ \left|\begin{array}{l}\mathbb{W}n.\\ \langle\mathrm{node}(\mathbf{b},\mathbf{k},\mathbf{v},n)\rangle\\ \mathrm{cas}:=\mathrm{CASNext}(\mathbf{b},\mathbf{n},\mathbf{z});\\ \langle\mathrm{cas}=\top\implies\mathrm{node}(\mathbf{b},\mathbf{k},\mathbf{v},\mathbf{z})\wedge n=\mathbf{n}\rangle\end{array}\right.$

$\qquad\qquad\ \{\underline{\mathbf{if}}\ \mathrm{cas}=\bot\ \underline{\mathbf{then}}\ r\mapsto\blacklozenge\ \underline{\mathbf{else}}\ r\mapsto((\mathcal{M},\mathcal{N},\mathcal{B}),(\mathcal{M}[\mathbf{k}\mapsto\mathbf{v}],\mathcal{N}\uplus\{\mathbf{z}\},\mathcal{B}))\}$

$\qquad\qquad\ \mathbf{if}\ (\mathrm{cas}=\bot)\ \{\mathrm{inner}:=\bot;\}\ \mathbf{else}\ \{\mathrm{inner}:=\bot;\mathrm{outer}:=\bot;\}$

$\quad\ \}\ \}\ \}\quad\{r\mapsto((\mathcal{M},\mathcal{N},\mathcal{B}),(\mathcal{M}[\mathbf{k}\mapsto\mathbf{v}],\mathcal{N}\uplus\{\mathbf{z}\},\mathcal{B}))\}$

$\quad\ \mathrm{level}:=\mathrm{getRandomMevel}();$

$\quad\ \mathbf{if}\ (\mathrm{level}>0)\ \{\mathrm{buildIndexChain};\ \ \mathrm{insertIndexChain};\}$

$\quad\ \mathbf{return}\ 0;\quad\{r\mapsto((\mathcal{M},\mathcal{N},\mathcal{B}),(\mathcal{M}[\mathbf{k}\mapsto\mathbf{v}],\mathcal{N}\uplus\{\mathbf{z}\},\mathcal{B}))\wedge\mathrm{ret}=0\}$

$\quad\left\langle\begin{array}{l}\exists\mathcal{N}'.\,\mathbf{SLMap}_r(\mathbf{x},\mathcal{M}[\mathbf{k}\mapsto\mathbf{v}],\mathcal{N}',\mathcal{B},m)*[\mathrm{L}]_r\wedge\\ \underline{\mathbf{if}}\ \mathbf{k}\in\mathrm{dom}(\mathcal{M})\ \underline{\mathbf{then}}\ \mathcal{N}=\mathcal{N}'\wedge\mathrm{ret}=\mathcal{M}(\mathbf{k})\ \underline{\mathbf{else}}\ \mathcal{N}=\mathcal{N}\uplus\{\mathbf{z}\}\wedge\mathrm{ret}=0\end{array}\right\rangle$

$\langle\mathrm{Map}(s,\mathbf{x},\mathcal{M}[\mathbf{k}\mapsto\mathbf{v}])\wedge\underline{\mathbf{if}}\ \mathbf{k}\in\mathcal{M}\ \underline{\mathbf{then}}\ \mathrm{ret}=\mathcal{M}(\mathbf{k})\ \underline{\mathbf{else}}\ \mathrm{ret}=0\rangle$

Fig. 8. Skiplist's put proof.

The predicate wkNdReach used in the sketch proof asserts that either x reaches y, or y is a dead node. Since the algorithm works on three nodes b, n and f, we use the predicate bnf to describe their reachability relations.

$$\text{wkNdReach}(x, y) \stackrel{\text{def}}{=} x \rightsquigarrow^* y \vee ((y \rightsquigarrow^* \mathcal{N} \uplus \{0\}) \wedge y \in \mathcal{B})$$
$$\text{bnf} \equiv \text{wkNdReach}(b, n) * \text{wkNdReach}(n, f) \wedge (b.\text{key} < k \vee b = m)$$

The node b is the sentinel node m, or its key is smaller than the target key k.

The predicate restart describes the cases when the algorithm needs to restart: (a) CAS fails; (b) node n is dead or a marker; (c) node b is dead; (d) n2, which is the second read of the successor of node b, is inconsistent with n.

$$\text{restart} \equiv \text{cas} = \bot \vee n.\text{value} = 0 \vee \text{marker}(n, \_) \vee b.\text{value} = 0 \vee n \neq n2$$

Additional specifications and proofs of auxiliary operations used in the proof of put, such as CASValue and findPredecessor, are given in the technical report [29]. We also prove that the skiplist implementation of the remove operation satisfies the specification of Fig. 1 in the same report.

5   Related Work

There is much recent work on modular specification of concurrent libraries using concurrent separation logic [6,16,17,20,26,27]. Here we focus on related work which uses separation logic to either reason about concurrent Java programs and java.util.concurrent, or reason about concurrent sets and maps.

Amighi et al. [1] used concurrent separation logic with permissions to reason about several lock modules in java.util.concurrent and their clients. Their approach is modular, but is not general enough to prove strong functional properties about arbitrary clients.

Blom et al. [2] reason about concurrent sets in a Java-like language, using a proof theory based on concurrent separation logic extended with histories and permissions. They specify and prove a coarse-grained concurrent set implementation using a specification that exposes histories to the client. The histories allow them to prove properties about client in a modular way. However, the concurrent set specification abstracts the values in the set, losing information about the exact state of the set, which limits its applicability to the clients. There has been some work on lock-coupling list implementations of concurrent sets, such as the original work on Concurrent Abstract Predicates reasoning [10,12]. Liang and Feng [19] and separately O'Hearn et al. [22] have reasoned about Heller's lazy set [14], and the latter is not able to reason about clients. Jacobs et al. [16] has given an atomic specification of a concurrent set using higher-order reasoning and proved that a simple course-grained linked-list satisfies the specification. None of this work is aimed at java.util.concurrent.

In this paper, using TaDA [6], we have specified concurrent maps, have given modular proofs of functional properties of clients, and have verified the main operations of the ConcurrentSkiplistMap from java.util.concurrent. The most challenging part was the verification of the skiplist algorithm, due to its size and complexity. As far as we know, this is the first formal proof of this algorithm.

In fact, there has been little reasoning with separation logic about concurrent maps. Da Rocha Pinto *et. al.* use CAP [10] to develop map specifications that allow thread-local reasoning combined with races over elements of the data structure [5]. They prove several map implementations, including Sagiv's B^{Link} Tree algorithm [24]. They cannot prove strong functional properties about a client using the map, e.g. when two threads perform concurrent insert and remove operations over the same key, they can only conclude the set of possibilities at the end of the execution. The closest specification to our work is a map specification using Total-TaDA [8], which was used to verify an implementation of a map based on a linked list in a total-correctness setting. We improve upon this specification by moving to a more abstract specification, which was possible due to the way in which we extended TaDA.

6   Conclusions

We have given an abstract map specification that captures the atomicity intended in the `java.util.concurrent` English specification [18]. We have used it to specify a concurrent set module that makes use of the map internally. We have shown how to build a key-value specification on top of the map specification, to present clients with an alternative view of the data structure, and demonstrated that these two specifications are equivalent. We have verified a functional correctness property for a simple producer-consumer client. Lastly, we have given the first formal proof of the `ConcurrentSkipListMap` and shown that it satisfies the atomic map specification.

These results are substantially stronger than related results found in previous work [1,2,5]. They are possible due to the abstract atomicity given by the TaDA atomic triples. So far, all of the proofs using TaDA [6] have been done by hand, but despite this, our examples are comparatively substantial. Indeed, the verification of the `ConcurrentSkipListMap` is one of the most complex examples studied in the literature. This example, we believe, is at the limit of what is possible to be done with hand-written proofs.

6.1   Future Work

Tool support. We recognise the need for mechanisation and automation in order to increase the level of confidence in our proofs. We are currently working on extending CAPER [11] for a fragment of TaDA. This will allow us to provide machine-checked proofs and tackle more modules of the `java.util.concurrent` package.

Object-Oriented languages. Another avenue for future work is to adapt TaDA to handle object-oriented features from Java, such as monitors, inheritance and interfaces. Our logical abstractions seem particularly well suited to reason about such programming language features.

Acknowledgements. We thank Andrea Cerone, Petar Maksimović, Julian Sutherland and the anonymous reviewers for useful feedback. This research was supported by the EPSRC Programme Grants EP/H008373/1 and EP/K008528/1, and the Department of Computing in Imperial College London.

References

1. Amighi, A., Blom, S., Huisman, M., Mostowski, W., Zaharieva-Stojanovski, M.: Formal specifications for java's synchronisation classes. In: Proceedings of PDP 2014, pp. 725–733 (2014)
2. Blom, S., Huisman, M., Zaharieva-Stojanovski, M.: History-based verification of functional behaviour of concurrent programs. In: Calinescu, R., Rumpe, B. (eds.) SEFM 2015. LNCS, vol. 9276, pp. 84–98. Springer, Cham (2015). doi:10.1007/978-3-319-22969-0_6
3. Bornat, R., Calcagno, C., O'Hearn, P., Parkinson, M.: Permission accounting in separation logic. In: Proceedings of POPL 2005, pp. 259–270 (2005)
4. da Rocha Pinto, P.: Reasoning with time and data abstractions. Ph.D. thesis, Imperial College London (2017)
5. da Rocha Pinto, P., Dinsdale-Young, T., Dodds, M., Gardner, P., Wheelhouse, M.J.: A simple abstraction for complex concurrent indexes. In: Proceedings of OOPSLA 2011, pp. 845–864 (2011)
6. Rocha Pinto, P., Dinsdale-Young, T., Gardner, P.: TaDA: a logic for time and data abstraction. In: Jones, R. (ed.) ECOOP 2014. LNCS, vol. 8586, pp. 207–231. Springer, Heidelberg (2014). doi:10.1007/978-3-662-44202-9_9
7. da Rocha Pinto, P., Dinsdale-Young, T., Gardner, P.: Steps in modular specifications for concurrent modules (invited tutorial paper). Electr. Notes. Theor. Comput. Sci. **319**, 3–18 (2015)
8. Rocha Pinto, P., Dinsdale-Young, T., Gardner, P., Sutherland, J.: Modular termination verification for non-blocking concurrency. In: Thiemann, P. (ed.) ESOP 2016. LNCS, vol. 9632, pp. 176–201. Springer, Heidelberg (2016). doi:10.1007/978-3-662-49498-1_8
9. Dinsdale-Young, T., Birkedal, L., Gardner, P., Parkinson, M., Yang, H.: Views: compositional reasoning for concurrent programs. In: POPL, pp. 287–300 (2013)
10. Dinsdale-Young, T., Dodds, M., Gardner, P., Parkinson, M.J., Vafeiadis, V.: Concurrent abstract predicates. In: D'Hondt, T. (ed.) ECOOP 2010. LNCS, vol. 6183, pp. 504–528. Springer, Heidelberg (2010). doi:10.1007/978-3-642-14107-2_24
11. Dinsdale-Young, T., da Rocha Pinto, P., Andersen, K.J., Birkedal, L.: Caper: automatic verification for fine-grained concurrency. In: Proceedings of ESOP 2017 (2017)
12. Dodds, M., Feng, X., Parkinson, M., Vafeiadis, V.: Deny-guarantee reasoning. In: Castagna, G. (ed.) ESOP 2009. LNCS, vol. 5502, pp. 363–377. Springer, Heidelberg (2009). doi:10.1007/978-3-642-00590-9_26
13. Harris, T.L.: A pragmatic implementation of non-blocking linked-lists. In: Welch, J. (ed.) DISC 2001. LNCS, vol. 2180, pp. 300–314. Springer, Heidelberg (2001). doi:10.1007/3-540-45414-4_21
14. Heller, S., Herlihy, M., Luchangco, V., Moir, M., Scherer, W.N., Shavit, N.: A lazy concurrent list-based set algorithm. In: Anderson, J.H., Prencipe, G., Wattenhofer, R. (eds.) OPODIS 2005. LNCS, vol. 3974, pp. 3–16. Springer, Heidelberg (2006). doi:10.1007/11795490_3

15. Herlihy, M.P., Wing, J.M.: Linearizability: a correctness condition for concurrent objects. ACM Trans. Program. Lang. Syst. **12**(3), 463–492 (1990)
16. Jacobs, B., Piessens, F.: Expressive modular fine-grained concurrency specification. In: Proceedings of POPL 2011, pp. 271–282 (2011)
17. Jung, R., Swasey, D., Sieczkowski, F., Svendsen, K., Turon, A., Birkedal, L., Dreyer, D.: Iris: monoids and invariants as an orthogonal basis for concurrent reasoning. In: Proceedings of POPL 2015, pp. 637–650 (2015)
18. Lea, D., et al.: Java specification request 166: Concurrency utilities (2004)
19. Liang, H., Feng, X.: Modular verification of linearizability with non-fixed linearization points. SIGPLAN Not. **48**(6), 459–470 (2013)
20. Nanevski, A., Ley-Wild, R., Sergey, I., Delbianco, G.A.: Communicating state transition systems for fine-grained concurrent resources. In: Shao, Z. (ed.) ESOP 2014. LNCS, vol. 8410, pp. 290–310. Springer, Heidelberg (2014). doi:10.1007/978-3-642-54833-8_16
21. O'Hearn, P.W.: Resources, concurrency, and local reasoning. Theor. Comput. Sci. **375**(1-3), 271–307 (2007)
22. O'Hearn, P.W., Rinetzky, N., Vechev, M.T., Yahav, E., Yorsh, G.: Verifying linearizability with hindsight. In: Proceedings of PODC 2010, pp. 85–94 (2010)
23. Pugh, W.: Skip lists: a probabilistic alternative to balanced trees. Commun. ACM **33**(6), 668–676 (1990)
24. Sagiv, Y.: Concurrent operations on b-trees with overtaking. In: Proceedings of PODS 1985, pp. 28–37 (1985)
25. Sergey, I., Nanevski, A., Banerjee, A.: Specifying and verifying concurrent algorithms with histories and subjectivity. In: Vitek, J. (ed.) ESOP 2015. LNCS, vol. 9032, pp. 333–358. Springer, Heidelberg (2015). doi:10.1007/978-3-662-46669-8_14
26. Svendsen, K., Birkedal, L.: Impredicative concurrent abstract predicates. In: Shao, Z. (ed.) ESOP 2014. LNCS, vol. 8410, pp. 149–168. Springer, Heidelberg (2014). doi:10.1007/978-3-642-54833-8_9
27. Turon, A., Dreyer, D., Birkedal, L.: Unifying refinement and Hoare-style reasoning in a logic for higher-order concurrency. In: Proceedings of ICFP 2013, pp. 377–390 (2013)
28. Vafeiadis, V., Parkinson, M.: A marriage of rely/guarantee and separation logic. In: Caires, L., Vasconcelos, V.T. (eds.) CONCUR 2007. LNCS, vol. 4703, pp. 256–271. Springer, Heidelberg (2007). doi:10.1007/978-3-540-74407-8_18
29. Xiong, S., da Rocha Pinto, P., Ntzik, G., Gardner, P.: Abstract specifications for concurrent maps (extended version). Technical Report 2017/1, Department of Computing, Imperial College London (2017). https://www.doc.ic.ac.uk/research/technicalreports/2017/#1

Author Index

Printed in the United States
by Baker & Taylor Publisher Services